GUINNESS ROCKOPEDIA®

As Rock and Pop tighten their grip on the universe, there's never been a better time for a full-colour encyclopedia of the 20th century's most thrilling art form.

To bring you the facts behind 40 years of Rock and Pop, we've consulted record companies, fanzines, managers and the stars themselves. We've selected hundreds of dazzling pictures, from the heavenly Kylie Minogue to the bizarre Marilyn Manson. For more than 700 acts – from Abba to ZZ Top, Van Halen to Armand Van Helden – you'll find bands and biographies, dates and discographies, recommended books and web sites. You'll also find entries for legendary record labels, music pioneers and festivals, plus guides to different styles of music, from Glam to Grunge, Heavy Metal to House, and Rock 'n' Roll to Reggae.

Guinness Rockopedia® is also full of the trivia that makes the music world go round. We've taken an in-depth look at modern movers and shakers – Spice Girls, Wu-Tang Clan, Radiohead – along with mega-selling veterans like Madonna, Eric Clapton and The Beatles. Which member of Suede had a lizard named after him? Who tried to copyright the term Rock 'n' Roll? Who's Jon Bon Jovi's favourite Spice Girl? How did The Simpsons give James Taylor his finest hour? You'll find the answers here.

The world of Rock and Pop is littered with triumphs, tragedies, fortunes and failures. But every act included in this book, for different reasons and different lengths of time, contributed something significant. They mattered. Guinness Rockopedia® celebrates all the artists who make Rock and Pop exciting, exasperating, delicate, dumb, colourful, crude, weird and wonderful.

How to use Rockopedia...

WHO Includes the most recent line-up, unless there is a 'classic' line-up (one which either lasted the longest or produced the most influential or successful music). Listed in order of instruments played, artist's name and pseudonym (and original name if different), date and place of birth (and death where applicable)

WHEN Year started – and finished

WHERE Location of band's formation

WHAT Brief definition of character of music and, in some cases, personality of act

Music style entry – describes WHAT it sounds like, WHERE it began, WHEN it began and WHO exemplifies that style of music with a list of recommended releases. Album and movie titles are underlined

Albums, movies, TV programmes, books and plays are indicated by italics

Singles, EPs or album tracks are indicated by single quotation marks

The date following refers to year of release

Record label entry (colour-coded red) – album titles are underlined

ALBUM SALES
'Platinum' indicates sales of 300,000 in the UK and 1 million in the USA
'Gold' indicates sales of 100,000 in the UK and 500,000 in the USA

SINGLE SALES
'Platinum' indicates sales of 600,000 in the UK and 1 million in the USA
'Gold' indicates sales of 400,000 in the UK and 500,000 in the USA

CHART POSITIONS
All chart positions are as recorded in *The Guinness Book Of British Hit Singles* and *The Guinness Book Of British Hit Albums* for the UK and *The Billboard Book Of Top 40 Albums* and *The Billboard Book Of Top 40 Hits* and *Billboard* magazine for the USA

GUINNESS ROCKOPEDIA®

GUINNESS PUBLISHING

Managing Editor David Roberts

Designer/Picture Researcher Jo Brewer

Editor Sally McFall

Editor Mark Bennett

Editor Bruno MacDonald

Picture Researcher/Data Manager Emma Brown

Researcher Georgina Lowin

Proofreader Mary Novakovich

Index Emma Brown & Jo Brewer

Design Concept John Mitchell & Peter Jackson

Cover Daniel Jackson (Avco), Ron Callow (Design 23)

Publishing Director Ian Castello-Cortes

Writers

Mark Bennett, Bruno MacDonald, Chris Shade, Andy Gill, Ian McCann, Sylvie Simmons, Fred Tomsett, Phil Sutcliffe, Paul Du Noyer, Dave Jennings, Neil Nixon, Mary Novakovich, Brian Southall, Colin Shearman, Dave McAleer, Chris Ovenden, Peter Lewry, Jamie Sellers, Rob Jovanovic, David Rowley, Neil Crossley, Emma Brown, Sally McFall, David Roberts, Trevor Hodgett, Colin Harper, Elizabeth Sears, Malcolm Dome, Andy Mabbett, Stuart Bailie, Mark Turner, Graeme Kay, John Van der Kiste, Nicholas Warburton, Steven Rosen, Matt Hill, Tim Farthing, Mary Richards, Chris Whippet

Thanks to Andy Seal @ Retna, Marianne Lassen @ SIN, Helen Ledger & Darren Hendry @ Idols, John Halsall @ London Features International, Derek Ferguson & Dann @ Corbis, Dede Millar @ Redferns, Emma Murray @ EMI, Francesca Cotton @ Warner, Tim Wilde @ East West, Gerald Orakwusi @ Sony, Imogen Hollingsworth @ Virgin, Helter Skelter, Rachel @ Warp, Stewart Newport, Keith Jackson, Karen O'Brien, Adam Kelsey, Nicky King, Sam Skivington, Sampath Karunaratne, Charlie Soyka, Rupert Farthing, Stuart & Neil Barnes, Katie Bennett, Ben Keith, Shirley Brooks, Lady Christine Cobbold, Kathryn Courtney-O'Neill, Gus Dudgeon, Barbara Edwards, Joe Geesin, Rob Johnstone, Greg King, Andy Langran, Phillip Littlemore, Anne Marshall, Gary Numan, Chrissie Oakes, Ian Overgage, Sanjiv Sachdev, Helen Weller, Paul Wilkinson, Mark Young, Margaret Bennett, Julie Mundy, Cathryn Harker

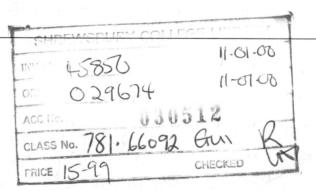

Cover pictures
Liam Gallagher : Heidie Lee Locke : Idols
Goldie : Steve Double : Retna
Madonna : Steve Granitz : Retna
Jarvis Cocker : Steve Double : Retna
Mick Jagger: Pierre Terrasson : Idols
Ice-T : Andrew Catlin : London Features International
Björk : Gavin Evans : Retna

p. 104   Crowded House *Recurring Dream…The Very Best Of Crowded House* © 1996 Capitol Records Inc
p. 130   Dubstar *Disgraceful* © 1996 Capitol Records Inc
p. 260   Mansun *Attack Of The Grey Lantern* © 1997 EMI Records Ltd
p. 351   Radiohead *OK Computer* © 1997 EMI Records Ltd
p. 433   Supergrass *In It For The Money* © 1995 EMI Records Ltd

Music pioneer or major music event entry (colour-coded purple) – album, movie and book titles are underlined

 R O C K **L** P E D I A

LIVING COLOUR

WHO Vocals **Corey Glover** (b. 6 Nov 1964, Brooklyn, New York, USA), guitar **Vernon Reid** (b. 22 Aug 1958, London, England), bass **Muzz Skillings** (b. Manuel Skillings, 6 Jan 1960, Queens, New York), drums **William Calhoun** (b. 22 Jul 1964, Brooklyn)

WHEN 1983–1995

WHERE Brooklyn, New York, USA

WHAT Politically aware Metal

Named after an NBC TV introduction ("The following programme is brought to you in living colour"), Living Colour spearheaded 'The Black Rock Coalition' – promoting awareness of African American artists' importance to Rock. They backed Mick Jagger on his *Primitive Cool* (1986) and Vernon Reid guested with Public Enemy. A Jagger-produced demo clinched a deal with Epic and *Vivid* (1988) began a slow climb up the US chart, aided by the hit 'Cult Of Personality'. After more Stonesy shenanigans (support slots, Reid's appearance on Keith Richards' 1988 *Talk Is Cheap*), *Time's Up* (1990) spawned the UK hit 'Love Rears Its Ugly Head'.

However, by 1991's 'Biscuits' EP, Living Colour's Funk Metal was overtaken by Grunge and internal rifts prompted Skillings' replacement with session bassist Doug Wimbish for 1993's swan song, *Stain*. Reid released his debut *Mistaken Identity* (1996).

surf www.geocities.com/Hollywood/Hills/9892/

LL COOL J

WHO b. James Todd Smith, 16 Aug 1968, Queens, New York, USA

WHAT Rap's smooth-talking superstar

Rap's endurance champion, 'Ladies Love Cool James' exploded with classics like 'I Need A Beat' from *Radio* (1985). His good-humoured arrogance and gold chains epitomized pre-Gangsta Rap – hence *Bigger And Deffer* (1987). The latter's hit ballad 'I Need Love' was a first for the genre, but weakened his credibility – a decline accelerated when *Walking With A Panther* (1989) emerged post-Gangsta and LL participated in First Lady Nancy Reagan's anti-drug campaign.

Mama Said Knock You Out (1990) was a spectacular comeback and *14 Shots To The Dome* (1993) became a sixth platinum chartbuster. After false starts in the movies *The Hard Way* (1991) and *Toys* (1992), his acting took off with the US TV series In *The House*.

Mr. Smith (1995) spawned a clutch of hits, of which 'I Shot Ya' launched Rap rude-girl Foxy Brown, who returned the favour by revamping his 'Rock The Bells' on her platinum *All Na Na* (1997).

He crowned the resurrection with the hits set *All World* (1996) and UK No.1 'Ain't Nobody'. With Puff Daddy covering his 'Big Ol' Butt' on *In Tha Beginning... There Was Rap* (1997) and upstarts like Method Man and Redman paying respect on the phenomenal *Phenomenon* (1997), 'LL' clearly stands now for 'longer lasting'.

read Make My Own Rules (1997), LL Cool J & Karen Hunter

surf www.geocities.com/Hollywood/Hills/1569/allworld.html

Lollapalooza

Inspired by Britain's Reading Festival, Jane's Addiction visionary Perry Farrell created Lollapalooza – the USA's top 'alternative' outdoor extravaganza. Lollapalooza's touring format brings diverse bills to audiences who might never witness conventional tours. Line-ups have included Jane's Addiction, Body Count, Siouxsie & The Banshees, Henry Rollins, Butthole Surfers and Nine Inch Nails (1991), Red Hot Chili Peppers, Ice Cube, Pearl Jam, Lush, The Jesus & Mary Chain, Soundgarden and Ministry (1992), Babes In Toyland, Dinosaur Jr, Arrested Development, Primus and Rage Against The Machine (1993), A Tribe Called Quest, The Breeders, Nick Cave, L7, George Clinton, Green Day, Stereolab, Luscious Jackson, The Beastie Boys and Smashing Pumpkins (1994), Hole, Sonic Youth, Pavement, Beck, Sinead O'Connor and Cypress Hill (1995), Metallica, The Ramones, Rancid, Screaming Trees, Wu-Tang Clan, Devo and Cocteau Twins (1996) and Orbital, Prodigy, Snoop Doggy Dogg, Korn and eels (1997). One dollar of each ticket sale is donated to homeless, environmental, AIDS and education charities.

Lollapalooza's future looked shaky when Farrell declined to headline the 1998 bill with Jane's Addiction, and its thunder was stolen by two other festivals: Sarah McLachlan's Lilith Fair and Ozzy Osbourne's Ozz-Fest. However, the event had already passed into legend when it was immortalized by *The Simpsons'* spoof 'Homerpalooza', a 1996 show featuring Cypress Hill and Smashing Pumpkins. "Wow, it's like Woodstock," said Lisa Simpson. "only with advertisements and tons of security guards."

LOUISE

WHO b. Louise Elizabeth Nurding, 4 Nov 1974, Lewisham, London, England

WHAT Singer, dancer, glamorous girl-next-door

Pop was rocked twice in July 1995: Robbie Williams left Take That and Louise Nurding exited Eternal. While Robbie played drug-crazed rogue, Louise went wide-eyed innocent – simultaneously whiter-than-white (a factor thought to have inhibited Eternal's R&B credibility in the USA) and red-hot (poll-topping pin-up status quickly ensued). Meanwhile, the Madonna-esque *Naked* (1996) blended ballads like first hit 'Light Of My Life' with the groovy 'In Walked Love' and steamy title tune.

Woman In Me (1997) ignited with 'Arms Around the World' and flamed on with The Average White Band's 'Let's Go Round Again'. Canoodling with footballer Jamie Redknapp, a somewhat premature autobiography and hints of rivalry with Eternal (intriguingly, she performed none of their hits on her first solo tour in 1997) kept the Pop pot bubbling.

read Louise – My Story (1997), Kate Thornton & Jane Preston

fan The Official Louise Fan Club, PO Box 888, High Wycombe, HP11 2NY, UK

surf www.profound.demon.co.uk/Music/louise/index.htm

R O C K **L** P E D I A

LOVE

WHO Vocals/guitar **Arthur Lee** (b. 7 Mar 1944, Memphis, Tennessee, USA), guitar/vocals **Bryan Maclean** (b. 1947, Los Angeles, California, USA), guitar **John Echols** (b. 1944, Memphis), bass **Ken Forssi** (b. 1943, Cleveland, Ohio, USA), drums/keyboards **Alban 'Snoopy' Pfisterer** (b. 1947, Switzerland)

WHEN 1965–1971

WHERE Los Angeles, California, USA

WHAT Acid Rock with Punk attitude

Led by Arthur Lee, Love's groundbreaking, self-titled debut (1966) combined Garage Rock with Folk. Included was 'My Little Red Book', a Bacharach-David song previously performed by Manfred Mann, which became a small American hit for Love.

The more psychedelic *Da Capo* (1967), featuring drummer Michael Stuart and flautist/saxophonist Tjay Cantrelli, included '7&7 Is' – Love's biggest US single, reaching No.33. Pfisterer and Cantrelli left before their masterpiece *Forever Changes* (1968): a dazzling blend of acoustic and electric instruments, exotic strings, Mariachi-style brass, Psychedelia and Latin and Broadway musical influences.

Although the music was beautiful and certainly acid-inspired, Love was not a flower-power band, for the songs were mostly dark and unsettling. 'Alone Again Or' – one of two Bryan Maclean-composed tracks – was later covered by The Damned and UFO.

Four Sail (1969) featured a changed line-up, with Lee now accompanied by Jay Donnellan (guitar), Frank Fayad (bass) and George Suranovich.

> "I used to drive my parents crazy, especially on car journeys, because I'd be singing constantly. My dad used to open the windows so the traffic noise would drown me out"

247

Fantastic photos and insightful quotes

Recommended:

READ further reading

FAN fanzine or fan club devoted to the act or type of music

SURF web site for updated further information

Each symbol represents a UK or US No.1 album (up to and including 6 June 1998)

⦿ = UK

★ = US

R O C K **W** P E D I A

WU-TANG CLAN ⦿ ★

WU'S WHO Producer **The RZA** aka Bobby Steels aka Rakeem Allah aka The Rzarector aka Chief Abbot aka Prince Rakeem (b. Robert F. Diggs), **Method Man** aka Johnny Blaze aka Meth Tical aka Shakwon aka The MZA aka Ticallion Stallion (b. Clifford Smith, 1 Apr 1971), **Ol' Dirty Bastard** aka Osirus aka Unique Ason aka Dirt McGirt/Joe Bananas aka Big Baby Jesus (b. Russell Jones, 15 Nov 1968), **Ghostface Killah** aka Ironman aka Tony Starks aka Sun God (b. Dennis Coles, 9 May 1970), **The GZA** aka Genius aka Maximillion aka Justice (b. Gary Grice), **Raekwon The Chef** aka Shallah Raekwon aka Lex Diamonds (Louis Rich Diamonds) (b. Corey Woods), **Inspectah Deck** aka Rebel INS aka Rollie Fingers (b. Jason Hunter), **U God** aka Baby-U aka Golden Arms aka 4-Bar Killer aka Lucky Hands (b. Lamont Hawkins), **Masta Killa** aka Noodles (b. Elgin Turner)

WU'S WHEN 1990–

WU'S WHERE Staten Island, New York, USA

WU'S WHAT The Spice Girls of Rap

"KA-BOOM! GUESS WHO STEPPED IN THE ROOM? THE CLAN! COMIN' FROM THE SHAOLIN ISLE!"

This cheery hello is from SWV's 'Anything': the most swaggeringly superb Rap 'n' Swing cut ever and an example of the phenomenon whereby no 90s Hip Hop record is complete without a link to the wacky world of the Wu-Tang Clan.

In the decade before the Wu landed on Earth, Rap had become as much about image as music (not that pre-1983 pioneers like Grandmaster Flash & The Furious Five didn't have an image, but you wouldn't find many Hip Hop fans wearing glittery shoulder pads and cowboy boots with the jeans tucked into the tops). From Run DMC through NWA and Public Enemy to Snoop Doggy Dogg, the biggest Hip Hop stars were those who not only made great records, but also offered the opportunity to buy into a visual image, a lyrical philosophy and a warped world view.

The Wu offer all that and more. For a start, there are nine core members, out-numbering even Public Enemy's massed military ranks. There are so many solo albums, affiliated acts and cameos with other artists that even determined discographies give up in despair. There's a barely believable belief system. Most tellingly, there's a ubiquitous Batman-esque "W" logo that adorns all their records and the grossly overpriced Wu Wear line of clothing *and* their branded cosmetics. Blimey, they're the Spice Girls of Rap!

Wordwheel for at-a-glance access to key elements of the entry

Their myth-making has been so meticulous that it's almost a shame to admit the Wu came about because solo efforts by Clan mainstays Genius (1991's *Words From The Genius*) and his cousin RZA (1992's 'Ooh We Love You Rakeem', as Prince Rakeem) had mounted no threat to Rap's then biggest noise, Ice Cube. "I'm still proud of it, though," Genius told *Select* magazine of his album. "The beats ain't all that but, lyrically, shit was bangin'. So it wasn't all peaches an' cream, but I was determined to break through."

With Ol' Dirty Bastard, they conceived Wu-Tang Clan, drawing inspiration from martial arts movies. The original Wu-Tang were rebels from China's Shaolin temple, skilled in the art of 'Wu-Tang Sword', whereby victims are despatched via blows to any one of 36 death points on the body. The new Clan were Staten Island (or 'Shaolin' as it became in WuWorld) low-lifes: RZA had been tried for attempted murder and, as *Select* reported, "Inspectah Deck and Dirty have done time, while Raekwon, Method Man and RZA have all either dealt or spent time ingesting a chemical panoply that includes crack, weed, angel dust and mescaline."

The Clan debuted on their own Wu-Tang Records label with 1992's 'Protect Ya Neck' single. Its flip, 'Method Man', showcased their secret weapon: the six-foot-plus Clifford Smith, aka Method Man.

Although Ol' Dirty Bastard – a manic mix of Public Enemy's court jester Flavor Flav and a rottweiler – is the Wu's obvious focal point, Meth is their star. While his bandmates hector, the raspy, laconic Meth is the cool voice of authority.

The other key element was RZA's production. Rap was then graduating from the multi-layered cacophony of Public Enemy to the G-Funk of Dr Dre. But RZA stripped the Wu's backing to starkly minimal beats, punctuated by scratchy snatches of violin and piano – the cinematic flavour of which grew into the 'horrorcore' of his sideline Gravediggaz' *Niggamortis* (1994) and *The Pick, The Sickle And The Shovel* (1997). Having created a buzz on the Rap underground, the Wu were signed by Loud Records for 1993's *Enter The Wu-Tang (36 Chambers)*, its title a reference to the levels, or 'chambers' of attainment in Wu-Tang Sword. As students progressed through the 36 chambers, they replaced their teeth with gold incisors, then platinum at the final chamber, adding authenticity to RZA and Dirty's decorative dentistry.

36 Chambers had everything: the ear-catching cuts 'Protect Ya Neck' and 'Method Man', the soon-to-be anthems 'C.R.E.A.M.' (or 'Cash Rules Everything Around Me') and 'Bring Da Ruckus', the myth making 'Wu-Tang 7th Chamber' and 'Da Mystery Of Chess-boxin'. But, crucially, it also had 'Can It Be All So Simple', whose mournful title phrase was sampled from Gladys Knight's 1975 hit 'The Way We Were'. The beautiful result was an unlikely radio hit and sped the album to platinum sales. Suddenly, there was an alternative for Hip Hop heads who viewed with distaste the MTV-ization of Rap by the likes of Snoop Doggy Dogg.

484

D'You Know What I Mean?

AMA *n.* American Music Association: gives out awards.

American Bandstand *n.* Late 50s/60s US TV show spotlighting Pop acts.

AOR *n.* Adult Oriented Rock or Album Oriented Rock. Like Led Zeppelin with rough bits sanded off (e.g. Foreigner, Journey, Mr Mister).

B-Boy *n.* Person who admires or performs Hip Hop, hence Beastie Boys.

Baggy *n., adj.* Musical movement from late 80s Manchester, England, distinguished by bands' and fans' fondness for drugs, dance and capacious clothing (hence the name).

Beavis & Butt-Head *n.* "Uh hur... they said 'Baggy'." Snickering, socially challenged Metal lovers (especially AC/DC and Metallica) – the voice of the MTV generation.

Be-Bop *n.* Crazy Jazz wig-outs (improvisations) à la Charlie Parker.

Bluegrass *n.* Yee-hawing variety of Country.

BPI *n.* British Phonographic Institute: people in suits who give out BRIT awards (*see* BRIT).

Bratpack *n.* Group of young actors – including pre-superstar Demi Moore, Emilio Estevez and the beautiful Ally Sheedy – who made epochal mid-80s movies like *The Breakfast Club*, *St Elmo's Fire* and *Pretty In Pink*.

Breakbeat *n.* What put the hop in Hip Hop. Hence Roni Size's protégés Breakbeat Era.

Brill Building *n.* New York City's 60s hit factory.

BRIT *n.* British music award given at annual televised ceremony: Annie Lennox receives one almost every year. Challenged by *NME*'s (*see* NME) BRAT awards.

Brummie *n.* Person from Birmingham, England, oft found in early 70s bands like Black Sabbath.

Bubblegum *n., adj.* Bright, breezy, cheery, chirpy, disposable Pop. Yum!

Burroughs, William *n.* Drug-fuelled US author of *The Naked Lunch*, etc.

C86 *n.* Cassette given away with *NME* (*see* NME) which became synonymous with pale-faced, duffel-coat-wearing, Indie Rock of post-Smiths Britain.

Crusty *n., adj.* Anti-establishment, tree-hugging, soap-dodging, dog-on-a-string-dragging Levellers fan.

Devil, The *n.* Inventor of Rock 'n' Roll; scared Robert Johnson to death; favourite golfing partner of Jimmy Page and Marilyn Manson.

Dis *v.* To express disapproval.

DIY *n., adj.* Do-It-Yourself.

Dizbuster *n.* Exciting thing (from Blüe Öyster Cult's 'Seven Screaming Dizbusters').

Doo Wop *n.* The bridge from barbershop quartets to Soul.

Ed Sullivan Show, The *n.* 50s/60s US TV vehicle for Richard Nixon lookalike who reluctantly showcased Pop's finest new acts.

Electronica *n.* American term for Techno.

EP *n.* 7" single with more than the traditional two songs.

Fairlight *n.* Prohibitively expensive synthesizer/sampler; impossible to use, hence four-year gaps between Kate Bush and Peter Gabriel albums.

Feedback *n.* Noise which Neil Young produces as guitar solos and Sonic Youth produce as albums.

Fleadh *n.* Guinness-sponsored, annual early summer festival showcasing mostly Irish artists in New York and London.

Frazzled *adj.* Descriptive of music influenced by something stronger than wine.

Gabba *n.* Insanely fast Techno (from the equally brain-bashing Ramones' catchphrase 'Gabba gabba hey').

Garage *n.* 1) Raw and simplistic 60s Rock, e.g. The Seeds. 2) Slick House.

Geordie *n.* 1) Person from Newcastle, England. 2) Band in which Bon Scott (first AC/DC singer) saw Brian Johnson (second AC/DC singer).

Girl Power *n.* Brand of feminism invented by Spice Girls: "Strength and courage in a Wonderbra".

Gizmo *n.* Electronic device – not to be confused with cute hero of *Gremlins*.

Gospel *n.* Church music. Adopted by R&B in late 50s, became much less Praise The Lord! and much more Woah Baby! Still influential in modern R&B: e.g. Sounds Of Blackness, Kirk Franklin, En Vogue.

Grammy *n.* American music award given at annual televised ceremony: Mariah Carey receives one almost every year.

Grand Ole Opry, The *n.* "Let her go, boys" – legendary Country music variety show from Nashville, started in 1927.

Greaser *n.* Slick-haired, leather-jacket-wearing, motorcyle-loving figure like The Fonz. Also appears in movie *Grease*, played by John Travolta.

Grebo *n.* Leather-clad, cough-mixture-swigging blend of Glam, Punk and Metal. Practised by Gaye Bykers On Acid and Zodiac Mindwarp.

Hammond *n.* Organ used by psychedelic and proggy 60s bands and pretend-psychedelic and proggy 90s bands.

Hardcore *n.* 1) Brutal Techno. 2) Brutal Punk.

Hillsborough Justice Concert *n.* Benefit concert in May 1997, in Liverpool, England, which raised money for appeal fund, support group and families of those killed in 1989 Hillsborough football ground disaster.

Hit Factory *n.* Studio of hit songwriter/producers Stock, Aitken & Waterman (*see* Stock, Aitken & Waterman).

Jugband *n.* Players of unsophisticated Folk or Jazz, often using home-made instruments.

Juno *n.* Canadian award given to Blue Rodeo on more or less annual basis.

Lo-fi *n.* Closest America has got to C86 (*see* C86).

Madchester *n.* Happy Mondays' term for Baggy, hence 'Madchester Rave On' EP.

Mariachi *n.* Traditional Mexican street music, best represented in Pop by Herb Alpert.

Mellotron *n.* Tape-driven strings, choir and flute synthesizer ('Strawberry Fields Forever', 'Nights In White Satin', 'Blue Monday'). Broke down a lot.

Melody Maker n.	British music paper established in 1926.
Mercury Prize, The *n.*	Album award instigated in 1992, won by Primal Scream, Suede, M People, Portishead, Pulp and Roni Size.
Minneapolis Sound *n.*	Slick Soul, big on electronic drums, sweeping synths and sexist lyrics. Sort of invented by Prince and perfected by producers Jimmy Jam & Terry Lewis.
Mod *n.*	R&B-loving 60s youth without whom The Who would be "Who?"
Moonwalk *n., v.*	Shuffly dance manoeuvre invented by Michael Jackson.
MOR *n.*	Middle Of The Road. Inoffensive music, e.g. Carpenters.
Mosh *v.*	To throw oneself about enthusiastically at a concert.
Moshpit *n.*	Area in which concert-goers congregate to mosh.
MTV *n.*	24-hour music video channel: world's ultimate arbiter of musical taste.
Mullet *n.*	Phrase coined by Beastie Boys to describe short-on-top, long-at-back haircut once famously favoured by Michael Bolton.
New Age *n.*	Tranquil electronic music, associated more with relaxation than entertainment.
New Jill Swing *n.*	Feminine equivalent of Swing, e.g. En Vogue. Derived from New Jack Swing.
New Wave *n.*	Catch-all term for everything Punk-influenced that wasn't Punk.
New Wave of New Wave *n.*	Short-lived 'movement' invented by British music press for New Wavey 90s acts like Elastica and Echobelly.
NME n.	Market-leading British music paper.
No Wave *n.*	Post post-Punk Art Rock, e.g. Arto Lindsay's DNA, Lydia Lunch's Teenage Jesus & The Jerks and Mars, who influenced bands such as Ut and Sonic Youth.
Noodling *v.*	*See* Widdling.
Peel, John *n.*	British DJ considered instrumental in many an Alternative Rock act's career.
Radio 1 *n.*	BBC's national Pop station.
Raga Rock *n.*	Droning, Indian-influenced Rock.
Ragga *n.*	Rap-flavoured variety of Reggae, e.g. Shaggy.
Ready Steady Go! n.	Seminal British TV Pop programme. Dave Clark liked it so much he bought the rights to it. Invariably starred The Rolling Stones. Presented by Cathy McGowan. "Fab", "gear", "the sound of Swinging England", etc.
RIAA *n.*	Recording Industry Association of America: compile album/single sales; hand out Gold/Platinum awards.
Riot Grrrl *n.*	Name of short-lived movement populated by shouty women like Huggy Bear and Bikini Kill. Made famous by Courtney Love's contempt ("Riot Grrrls, think you can stop me…?") and latterly eclipsed by Girl Power.
Rolling Stone n.	Market-leading US music magazine.
Ronnie Scott's *n.*	UK club associated with Jazz, Blues and R&B, owned by late British Jazz saxophonist Ronnie Scott.
Sampling *v.*	Stealing bits of other people's songs (usually George Clinton's thumping 'Atomic Dog') to make better ones.
Scratching *v.*	Making excitingly graunchy sounds on Hip Hop records by using styli/turntables/vinyl in ways not recommended by manufacturers.
Shoegazing *v.*	Staring at floor while playing feedback-drenched Indie Rock, as invented by My Bloody Valentine and copied by Ride.
Simpsons, The *n.*	Archetypal American family with impeccable Rock credentials.
Skiffle *n.*	British, plucky, home-made, watered-down Rock 'n' Roll and R&B.
Soul Train n.	70s/80s US TV's first-class ticket to Soul heaven.
Stiltskinesque *adj.*	Descriptive of fleetingly successful association with an advertisement. From 'Inside' by Stiltskin, cod-Grunge cut used on 1994 Levi's ad.
Stock, Aitken & Waterman *n.*	British Pop producers. Dominated UK charts at tail-end of 80s, thanks to Kylie Minogue and lesser others.
Summer Of Love *n.*	1) 1967, year of hippie heaven. 2) 1987, year in which white people started taking Ecstasy and listening to Dance music.
Sunset Sound *n.*	Poppier version of Minneapolis Sound invented by producers LA & Babyface.
Superduperdom *n.*	Galaxy-gobbling level of fame; e.g. that achieved by Whitney Houston.
Supergroup *n.*	Usually short-lived agglomeration of musicians with egos too big to stay in bands with whom they became famous, e.g. Blind Faith. Not to be confused with groups who are super, e.g. Clock.
Surf Rock *n.*	Briefly popular form of twangy guitar Rock 'n' Roll. Only Keith Moon listened to it after early 60s, but whole world pretended to have always loved it after Dick Dale appeared on *Pulp Fiction* soundtrack.
Theremin *n.*	Hard to play, spacey instrument. Staple of 50s B-movie soundtracks, made famous in Pop by 'Whole Lotta Love', 'Good Vibrations' and Jon Spencer Blues Explosion.
Top Of The Pops n.	Enduring weekly British TV Pop programme.
Transatlantic adj.	Most over-used word in *Rockopedia*. Descriptive of something that is successful in both UK and USA.
Transit-core *n.*	Indie Rock played by bands who can't afford proper tour buses, e.g. Ned's Atomic Dustbin.
12″ *n.*	Big brother to traditional 7″ vinyl single. Gained popularity in 80s owing to their convenience for Dance club DJs. Source of many a DJ's ribald remark: "Have you seen my 12″?", etc. Another variety, the 10″, began as a norm for Blues records (hence Aerosmith's 'Big Ten Inch Record') but descended into marketing novelty.
Unleash *v.*	To issue work that is exciting. Oasis unleashed *Definitely Maybe*, but only released *Be Here Now*.
Wah wah *n.*	Funky guitar effect, made famous by Hendrix and Starsky & Hutch.
Widdling *v.*	1) Playing music to impress rather than entertain. 2) Playing music with no apparent beginning, middle or end.
World Music *n.*	Generic term for any non-Anglo American music that can't be traced to Chuck Berry.

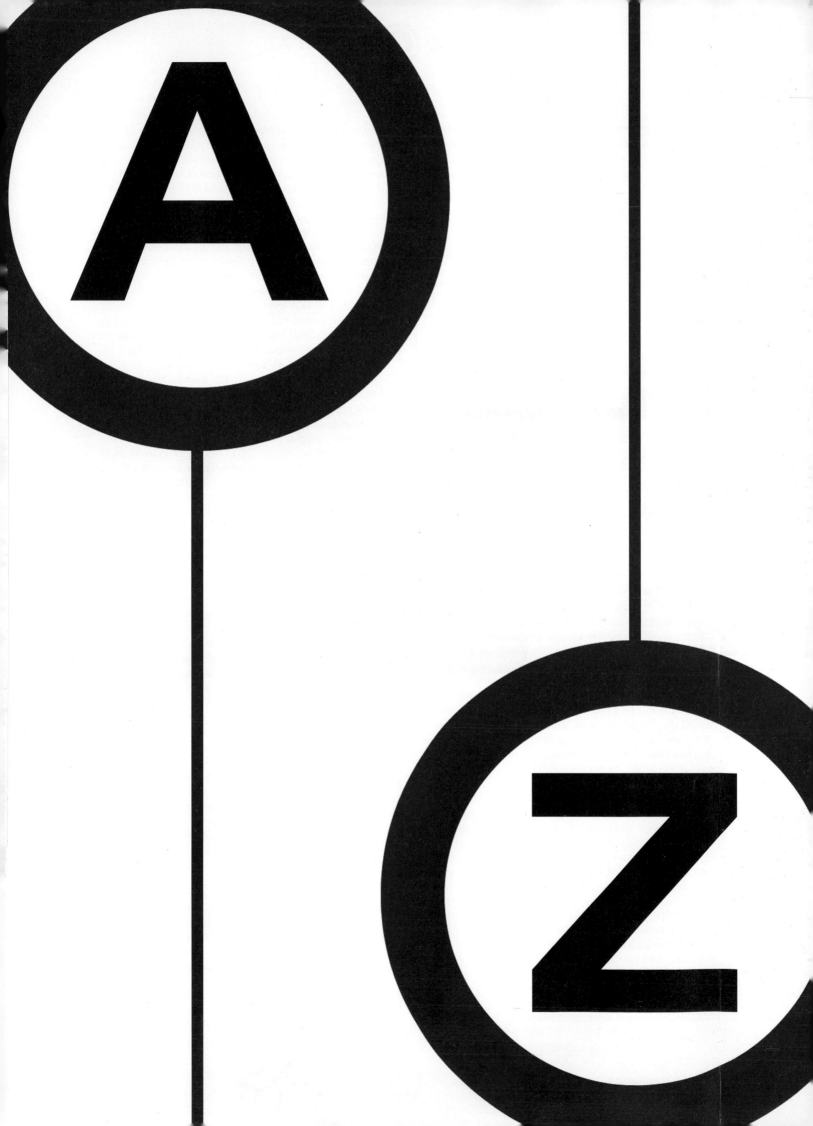

A&M Records

Trumpeter/producer Herb Alpert and producer/promoter Jerry Moss used the initials from their surnames to create A&M Records in 1962. The LA-based label's earliest releases featured Alpert, The Sandpipers and Sergio Mendes, but their first international hit was Alpert's 'This Guy's In Love With You' in 1968.

A distribution deal with Ode Records linked A&M with Carole King, and success with The Carpenters and Supertramp established the label internationally in the 70s. The signing of such major acts as The Police, Janet Jackson, Bryan Adams, Dina Carroll, Sting and Sheryl Crow furthered their fortunes. In 1989, Alpert and Moss sold the company to Polygram for a reported $500 million, but remained involved with the label until 1994 when they formed a new company, Almo Sounds.

ABBA ⊙⊙⊙⊙⊙⊙⊙⊙⊙

WHO Vocals/guitar **Björn Ulvaeus** (b. 25 Apr 1945, Gothenburg, Sweden), vocals/keyboards **Benny Andersson** (b. Goran Bror Benny Andersson, 16 Dec 1946, Vallingby, Stockholm, Sweden), vocals **Agnetha Fältskog** (b. Agnetha Åse Fältskog, 5 Apr 1950, Jönköping, Sweden), vocals **Frida Lyngstad** (b. Anni-Frid Lyngstad-Ruess, 15 Nov 1945, Björkasen, Narvik, Norway)

WHEN 1972–1983

WHERE Stockholm, Sweden

WHAT Scandinavian Pop perfection

Björn Ulvaeus and Benny Andersson were no strangers to Pop stardom when they formed a songwriting partnership in 1966. Björn was part of Folk/Skiffle group The Hootenanny Singers, while Benny's group The Hep Stars outsold The Beatles in 60s Sweden. Agnetha Fältskog and Frida Lyngstad were solo stars. Frida began her singing career at 13, joined a Jazz band led by Bengt Sandlund, then formed her own group, Anni-Frid Four. In 1967 she won a talent show, appeared on TV show *Hylands Corner* and signed with EMI. Agnetha's career began at 15 when she joined Bengt Enghardt's Orchestra as a vocalist. By 17, she was signed to CBS Sweden, and her 1968 debut, 'I Was So In Love', topped the national chart.

By 1969 Benny and Frida, and Agnetha and Björn were engaged couples. In 1970, Frida and Agnetha sang on their future husbands' *Lycka* and, later that year, the four appeared as Festfolket (Engaged Couples) at a Gothenburg restaurant – by all accounts a disaster. By their next performance in November 1971, Björn and Agnetha were married and he and Benny had become producers at the Polar Music label, founded by Swedish impresario and future manager Stig Anderson. 'She's My Kind Of Girl' – featuring Agnetha and Frida on background vocals – was a smash in Japan, selling over 250,000 copies. They also wrote 'Better To Have Loved', Sweden's 1972 Eurovision Song Contest entry and, that year, formed the group Björn & Benny, Agnetha & Anni-Frid – their debut single 'People Need Love' reaching No.1 in Sweden. Invited to write another Eurovision entry in 1973, Björn, Benny and Stig Anderson contributed 'Ring Ring'. It came third, but was a massive domestic hit. At one point, the

English and Swedish versions of 'Ring Ring', and their album of the same name, occupied the Top 3 of the combined Swedish chart. In a bid for more widespread success, Anderson streamlined the group's awkward name to ABBA (Agnetha, Björn, Benny, Anni-Frid), also the name of Sweden's biggest canned fish company. Oddly, the latter responded not with a lawsuit but the goodwill gift of a box of tuna!

Despite enormous success in Sweden, the group were eager to gain international recognition and the Eurovision Song Contest appeared the most promising route. Their third Eurovision attempt – 1974's Glam Rock singalong 'Waterloo' – won the contest and realized their international aspirations, becoming a UK No.1 and US No.6. 'Ring Ring' was re-released with similar success, but 'So Long' and 'I Do I Do I Do I Do I Do' failed to dent the UK Top 30. In 1975, however, 'SOS', 'Mamma Mia' and *ABBA* all climbed the UK chart. Meanwhile, Agnetha and Frida had continued solo success in Sweden.

ABBA's golden age began in 1976. 'Mamma Mia', 'Fernando', 'Dancing Queen' and *Greatest Hits* were all UK No.1s. ABBA mania swept Australia: the *ABBA In Australia* TV special attracted more viewers than the Moon landings and 'Fernando' became the country's biggest-selling single. *Arrival* (1976) yielded the hits 'Money Money Money' (1976) and 'Knowing Me Knowing You' (1977) and a sell-out tour of Europe and Australia in 1977 was filmed for *ABBA The Movie* (1978). Another UK chart-topper, 'The Name Of The Game', rounded off 1977.

Following completion of their ultra-modern Polar Music studio in Stockholm (first clients included Led Zeppelin) and No.1 hits with the discofied 'Take A Chance On Me' (1978) and *ABBA – The Album* (1978), May 1978 was declared 'ABBA Month' in the USA. Despite the collapse of Agnetha and Björn's marriage, their status as the most successful group of the 70s was well intact: 1979 saw a world tour, hits with 'Chiquitita' (donated to UNICEF for the International Year Of The Child), 'Does Your Mother Know', the double A-side 'Angel Eyes'/'Voulez Vous', 'Gimme! Gimme! Gimme! (A Man After Midnight)', 'I Have A Dream', two UK No.1 albums – *Voulez Vous* and *Greatest Hits Volume 2* – and worldwide TV special *ABBA In Switzerland,* a film of one of the concerts during their tour of the USA, Canada and Europe, which ended in Japan in 1980.

Their juggernaut rolled on into the dawning decade. *Super Trouper* (1980), 'The Winner Takes It All' and 'Super Trouper' were all UK No.1s and 'Lay All Your Love On Me' (1981) was a pioneering 12" single hit. Other successes included 1981's 'One Of Us' and *The Visitors* (UK No.1), but the break-up of Benny and Frida's marriage renewed rumours of a split. In 1982, three hits – 'Head Over Heels', 'The Day Before You Came' and 'Under Attack', along with *ABBA The Singles – The First Ten Years*, celebrated the group's tenth anniversary. However, with solo albums from Frida and Agnetha in 1982 and 1983 and the launch of the latter's film career, *Thank You For The Music – A Collection of Love Songs* (1983) was effectively an epitaph.

Benny and Björn collaborated with lyricist Tim Rice on the successful musical *Chess* (1984), which subsequently toured the UK, USA and Australia. ABBA contributed to a 1984 Swedish TV tribute to Stig Anderson, but subsequently resisted calls for a reunion – even during a 90s revival that threatened to repeat their earlier success. U2 performed 'Dancing Queen' on their 1992 Zoo TV tour, for which Benny and Björn guested on stage in Stockholm. The same year, *ABBA Gold – Greatest Hits* topped the UK chart, as did Synth-Poppers Erasure with their covers EP

"I can get lost in Abba. . . just being silly and happy and stupid, but it's pure, as pure as pure can get. You just want to dance on the table"

Björk

'ABBA-esque'. Successful Australian tribute band Björn Again responded with the ABBA-styled 'Erasure-ish'. The use of ABBA songs in Australian films *Muriel's Wedding* (1995) and *The Adventures Of Priscilla Queen Of The Desert* (1994) confirmed their impact on the country.

Benny and Björn continue to write together, with hits for Swedish artists Gemini and Jaregin Nilsson and another musical, *Kristina Från Duvemala* (1995), which premiered in Sweden to critical acclaim. Frida released *Djupa Andelag* (Deep Breath) in 1996, which reached No.1 in Sweden, while Agnetha released a Scandinavian greatest hits compilation, *My Love My Life* (1996). Her autobiography, *Som Jag Är*, was published in English as *As I Am – ABBA Before And Beyond* in 1997. Former ABBA manager Stig Anderson died in 1997, but ABBA's legacy lives on, their albums continuing to sell millions worldwide.

READ *Abba Gold – The Complete Story* (1993), John Tobler

FAN ABBA News Service, PO Box 21, Avonmouth, Bristol, BS11 9AZ, UK

SURF abbanews.netgutes.co.uk

Abbey Road Studios

Abbey Road houses the world's most famous recording studios, since The Beatles named their 1969 album after the place in north London where they recorded it. Owned by EMI Music and opened in 1931 by composer Sir Edward Elgar, it hosted many of the world's leading Classical and Popular recording artists – Yehudi Menuhin, Noel Coward, Johnnie Ray, Ruby Murray, Eddie Calvert and Alma Cogan – over the next three decades. In the late 50s, with EMI striving to compete with emerging American performers, new Pop talent, such as Cliff Richard, The Shadows, Adam Faith and Helen Shapiro, recorded British No.1s at Abbey Road, which then recorded only EMI artists. The arrival of The Beatles in 1962, followed by Cilla Black, Gerry & The Pacemakers and The Hollies, turned Abbey Road into a shrine for both fans and other artists. The wall surrounding the studio became a repository of fan graffiti. In the 70s and 80s, Pink Floyd led a new wave of artists, followed by Steve Harley, Kate Bush and Sky, while Paul McCartney continued to work there.

Abbey Road remains at the forefront of recording technology. Recent visitors have included Michael Jackson, Oasis, Radiohead and Page & Plant. Former Abbey Road engineer and founder of the Project group, Alan Parsons, was appointed Vice President of EMI Studios in 1997.

ABBEY ROAD NW8
CITY OF WESTMINSTER

ABC ◉

WHO Vocals **Martin Fry** (b. 9 Mar 1958, Manchester, England), saxophone **Stephen Singleton** (b. 16 Apr 1959, Sheffield, England), guitar/keyboards **Mark White** (b. 1 Apr 1961, Sheffield), bass **Mark Lickley**, drums **David Robinson**

WHEN 1980–

WHERE Sheffield, Yorkshire, England

WHAT Glittering, Soul-influenced Pop

After their group Vice Versa retired in 1980, Singleton, Fry and White began rehearsing with Robinson (replaced by David Palmer) and Lickley as ABC, signing to Phonogram in 1981. Their debut 'Tears Are Not Enough' (1981) abandoned Vice Versa's rough electronic experiments for a modern interpretation of classic Motown Pop. Producer Trevor Horn drenched the first album, *The Lexicon Of Love* (1982), in sweeping strings, creating some of the first fully formed Pop sounds of the 80s. Phenomenally successful over a short period of time – 'Poison Arrow', 'The Look Of Love' and 'All Of My Heart' were massive hits – their image, a kind of updated Temptations with gold lamé suits, quickly faded with *Beauty Stab* (1983). Now without Palmer and Lickley, ABC changed direction and became a Rock group.

The relative failure of *Beauty Stab* led to Singleton's departure in 1984. Fry and White, now in the USA, recruited models Eden and David Yarritu as non-performing members for the Dance-oriented *How To Be A Zillionaire* (1985). While not a huge commercial success, the album and singles '(How To Be A) Millionaire' and 'Vanity Kills' sold respectably, with 'Be Near Me' becoming ABC's first US Top 10 hit.

After recovering from Hodgkin's disease in 1986, Fry worked with White on ABC's comeback, *Alphabet City* (1987) – a return to their golden Pop origins – yielding the hits 'When Smokey Sings' and 'The Night You Murdered Love' (both produced by Bernard Edwards of Chic). Signed to EMI in 1989, the group released a final studio album for Phonogram, the heavily House-influenced *Up* (1989), and the compilation *Absolutely* (1990), promoted by an ill-received remix of 'The Look Of Love'. After their unsuccessful EMI debut *Abracadabra* (1991) and White's

departure in 1992, ABC were dropped by EMI and small reissue labels such as Connoisseur and Pickwick released some compilations, including *The Remix Collection* and *Tears Are Not Enough* (both 1993).

Fry collaborated with Heaven 17's Glenn Gregory on 'Seven Day Weekend' for the movie *When Saturday Comes* (1996). Joined by guitarist Keith Lowndes, the trio recorded Techno instrumentals as The Magic Skulls before releasing a new ABC album, *Skyscraping* (1997), and three singles – the title track, 'Stranger Things' and 'Rolling Sevens', which were accompanied by two sell-out UK tours. Fry contributed 'Thunderball' to an album of Bond themes, *Shaken Not Stirred*, by David Arnold in October 1997.

surf www.path.unimelb.edu.au/~new_wave/abc.html

PAULA ABDUL ✪ ✪

WHO b. 19 Jun 1963, Los Angeles, California, USA

WHAT Hi-energy Pop

Abdul was born into showbusiness: her mother worked with legendary Hollywood director Billy Wilder. Abdul's early dance training paid off when she became choreographer for the LA Lakers' cheerleaders. Headhunted by the MTV generation, she choreographed videos for Debbie Gibson, ZZ Top, George Michael, INXS and, notably, Janet Jackson. She embarked on solo stardom with the seven-million-selling *Forever Your Girl* (1988) and four US No.1s – the title track, 'Cold Hearted', 'Straight Up' and 'Opposites Attract' (with its clever integration of live-action film and animated cartoon character MC Skat Kat). All, not surprisingly, benefited from striking videos featuring Paula's dancing talents. After the remix collection *Shut Up And Dance* (1990), *Spellbound* (1991) – featuring collaborations with The Family Stand, Prince and John Hiatt – yielded another US chart-topper, 'Rush, Rush'. A brief marriage to actor Emilio Estevez put music on hold until she returned with 1995's *Head Over Heels*. In 1996, she concentrated on acting with appearances on TV sitcoms such as *Single Guy* and *Cybill* and in the TV movie *Touched By Evil*. In 1997, Abdul began work on a new album and started her own line of clothing called Groove Girl, which is due to hit the shops in 1998.

read *Paula Abdul – Straight Up* (1992), M. Thomas Ford

surf www.fortunecity.com/tinpan/mercury/24/paula.html

AC/DC ◉ ✪

WHO Vocals **Bon Scott** (b. Ronald Belford, 9 Jul 1946, Kirriemuir, Scotland, d. 20 Feb 1980, London, England), guitar **Angus Young** (b. 31 Mar 1959, Glasgow, Scotland), guitar **Malcolm Young** (b. 6 Jan 1953, Glasgow), bass **Cliff Williams** (b. 14 Dec 1949, Romford, Essex, England), drums **Phil Rudd** (b. 19 May 1954, Melbourne, Australia)

WHEN 1973–

WHERE Sydney, New South Wales, Australia

WHAT Purveyors of platinum Metal

AC/DC – Heavy Metal's answer to The Rolling Stones – are as timeless as it is possible for a Rock band to be. Their basic sound, a Blues-based crunch with hoarse, powerful vocals and a backline solid enough to rattle bedroom windows with the stereo on half volume, was established by *High Voltage* (1976) and *Let There Be Rock* (1977). It's stayed more or less the same, although Young's solos have added rounder and more Bluesy tones as the band developed. Lyrically, they've kept it close to bad boys, willing girls and sweaty tales of Rock living. They've also written their share of Rock anthems. If they gave Grammys for sheer consistency, AC/DC would be up there with ZZ Top.

By 1975, with a sound that used their limited musical armoury to perfection, they relocated to England and signed with Atlantic Records. Their ceaseless gigging got attention, as did the schoolboy outfit worn by the diminutive Young, who would gradually undress as a gig progressed, throwing off his satchel, blazer, etc as he stomped around the stage dripping sweat. Young could also knock off a short solo perched on Scott's shoulders as the pair ventured out into the crowd. By *Powerage* (1978), the band had a hard, solid album worthy of their live work and some respectable chart positions. The *Powerage* tour yielded *If You Want Blood, You Got It* (1978) – a punchy, grinding collection of one of the greatest live sets from this era of Heavy Metal. *Highway To Hell* (1979) shifted a million copies in the USA alone. The lyrics often played up Scott's hard reputation as a drinker and sometime petty criminal. He had his last drink on 19 February 1980 – the next morning he was found unconscious in his car and pronounced dead on arrival in hospital.

Scott's death gave a power and validation to the laddish lyrics of the band, who continued in his shadow. Brian Johnson (b. 5 Oct 1947, Newcastle, England) – vocally at least – was a 'like for like' replacement. AC/DC's legendary status rests largely on the albums *Back In Black* (1980) and *For Those About To Rock (We Salute You)* (1981). The former – a UK No.1 – was a requiem for Scott, including the unsentimental 'Have A Drink On Me' and the anthemic 'Hell's Bells'. The 1981 album hit US No.1 and included another affirmation of their faith in Rock in its title track. By this time the band were global stars and they've never looked back. Their winning formula includes a major tour behind each album, unsubtle stage stunts – like the firing of a cannon during 'For Those About To Rock (We Salute You)' – and an image that owes everything to their working class roots. Angus still wears the schoolboy outfit, but by the time of *Flick Of The Switch* (1983) and *Fly On The Wall* (1985), sales were fluctuating.

They remained a major live draw, headlining prestigious events like Castle Donington's Monsters Of Rock festival – in 1981, 1984 and 1991 – and 1985's massive Rock In Rio festival. Each new album – *Who Made Who* (1986), *Blow Up Your Video* (1988), *The Razor's Edge* (1990) and *Ballbreaker* (1995) – added strident anthems to their set. Like early Blues singers, they gave a voice and sound to an audience without much of either. *Beavis And Butthead* might present AC/DC fans as morons, but this band have given an audience of mainly young white males a sound that is almost a rite of passage. The legend of Scott – like that of Jimi Hendrix or Jim Morrison – gives the music an added meaning. His legacy was celebrated by the 1997 box set *Bonfire*.

The simplicity of the sound and image has also been very influential. Metal fans admire Led Zeppelin, but can aspire to be AC/DC. Like other supposedly simple bands – such as Black Sabbath – AC/DC have sent countless hopefuls into guitar shops. Some have gone on to record. Grunge music, in particular, elevated the crunching riff and soundbite lyric to the centre of a musical form. The same riffing assault, fuzzed out and speeded up, is evident in Thrash Metal, while The Beastie Boys popularized the use of AC/DC samples in Rap.

READ *Highway To Hell: The Life And Times Of Bon Scott* (1994), Clinton Walker

SURF www.acdc.rock.com

ACE OF BASE ☉ ✪

WHO Vocals **Linn Berggren** (b. Malin Berggren, 31 Oct 1970, Gothenburg, Sweden), vocals **Jenny Berggren** (b. 19 May 1972, Gothenburg), keyboards **Jonas 'Joker' Berggren** (b. 21 Mar 1967, Gothenburg), keyboards **Ulf 'Buddha' Ekberg** (b. 6 Dec 1970, Gothenburg)

WHEN 1991–

WHERE Gothenburg, Sweden

WHAT Swedish Pop/Reggae fusion

Formed when Ekberg replaced a stagefright-stricken member of the Berggren siblings' band at a gig in Gothenburg, the group toyed with House and Techno as Tech Noir before settling on a Pop/Reggae fusion as Ace Of Base in 1991. After gigs around Gothenburg, they signed with Danish label Mega, having been ignored by the Swedish record industry. Their debut 'Wheel Of Fortune' topped the Danish chart in March 1993, but 'All That She Wants', released in October, placed the group in the international spotlight, earning No.1s in Scandinavia, most of Europe and the UK and a US No.2. *Happy Nation* (1993, repackaged in the USA as *The Sign* in 1994) became the first No.1 by a Swedish act in the USA and earned Ace Of Base an entry – 'Biggest Selling Debut Album' – in the 1995 *Guinness Book Of Records*. Hits 'The Sign', 'Happy Nation', 'Don't Turn Around', 'Living In Danger' and 'Lucky Love' followed, but the pressures of fame weighed heavily on Jenny, who was stalked by a crazed fan in 1994. Their second album, *The Bridge* (1996), failed to reach the commercial heights of its predecessor.

SURF www.aristarec.com

ACID HOUSE

WHAT A faster, 'trippier' form of House. The word 'acid' refers to the distinctive squelches and burps of the Roland TB-303 synthesizer, used to create basslines. American in origin, the sound hit hardest in London, forming the basis of the 90s dance explosion.

WHERE Chicago, London

WHEN 1986–

WHO DJ Pierre 'Acid Trax' (1987), Stakker 'Humanoid' (1988), Hardfloor 'Acperience' (1992), Josh Wink 'Higher State Of Consciousness' (1996)

ACID JAZZ

WHAT Drawn from the 70s hybrid of Funk, Soul and Jazz of artists like Curtis Mayfield, Lou Donaldson and Herbie Hancock. Later practitioners, such as The James Taylor Quartet, The Brand New Heavies, Young Disciples, Jamiroquai, Incognito, D-Influence, Corduroy, Mother Earth and Galliano, added Hip Hop elements and a Pop sheen. Acid Jazz is also a record label, founded by scenemaker Gilles Peterson, later head of competitor Talkin' Loud.

WHERE USA, UK

WHEN 80s–

WHO Young Disciples <u>Road To Freedom</u> (1991), Ronny Jordan <u>The Antidote</u> (1992), Jamiroquai <u>Emergency On Planet Earth</u> (1993), Corduroy <u>Out Of Here</u> (1994)

ADAM & THE ANTS ⊙

WHO Vocals **Adam Ant** (b. Stuart Leslie Goddard, 3 Nov 1954, London, England), guitar/vocals **Marco Pirroni** (b. 27 Apr 1959, London), bass **Kevin Mooney** (b. England), drums **Merrick** (b. Chris Hughes, 3 Mar 1954, London), drums **Terry Lee Miall** (b. 8 Nov 1958, London)

WHEN 1977–1981

WHERE London, England

WHAT Punk chancers to dandy highwaymen

After watching The Sex Pistols play at Hornsey School of Art in 1976, student Stuart Goddard started his own Punk group, The B-Sides, before forming Adam & The Ants (comprising mainly ex-B-Sides at this point). Playing various support slots, they attracted the attention of Derek Jarman, who filmed them for his Punk movie *Jubilee* (1978). After line-up changes and sessions for BBC DJ John Peel, their debut album *Dirk Wears White Sox* (1979) saw them briefly under the influence of Sex Pistols' manager Malcolm McLaren, who in 1980 transplanted Ants members Matthew Ashman, Dave Barbe and Lee Gorman to his new creation, Bow Wow Wow.

After meeting in a London cake shop, Ant formed a partnership with guitarist Pirroni, later recruiting drummers Merrick and Miall and bassist Mooney. This line-up recorded the successful *Kings Of The Wild Frontier* (1980), signalling the start of 'Antmusic': an inspired blend of native American chanting, tribal drumming, Punk and classic Rock 'n' Roll. Visually, the Ants harked back to Glam Rock, resembling a Navaho version of Roxy Music in some of the most lavish videos of the early 80s. Their reign as superstars lasted for one more album, *Prince Charming* (1981), before Ant disbanded the group, continuing with Pirroni as writing partner for *Friend Or Foe* (1982), *Strip* (1983) and *Vive Le Rock* (1985). Pirroni continued as a renowned session musician, while Ant returned, after a five-year hiatus spent acting in America, with *Manners And Physique* (1990) and *Wonderful* (1995), both with Pirroni as guest. Ant also found himself fêted by the likes of Nine Inch Nails and Elastica.

fan A.N.T., c/o Bryan Stanton, 8 Berkeley House, Albany Road, Brentford, Middlesex, TW8 0ND, UK

surf www.uhs.uga.edu/~john/adam_ant/

BRYAN ADAMS ⊙ ◎ ⊙ ✪

WHO b. 5 Nov 1959, Kingston, Ontario, Canada

WHAT Good-time Rocker with mass appeal

An experienced guitarist and pianist, Adams quit school at 16, cashing in his college fund for a piano. After singing with Glam Rockers Sweeney Todd in 1976, Adams struck up a songwriting partnership with drummer Jim Vallance of Prism. They churned out hits for Bachman-Turner Overdrive, Joe Cocker and Bonnie Tyler before striking out with 1979's uncharacteristically disco-ish 'Let Me Take You Dancing'. Returning to straight-ahead Rock, Adams' eponymous 1980 debut garnered little attention.

However, his reputation as a live act – supporting The Kinks, Foreigner and Loverboy – made *You Want It, You Got It* (1982) a moderate success, both in Canada and the USA. 'Straight From The Heart' – his breakthrough US hit – featured on *Cuts Like A Knife* (1983), an emotional, melodic collection which reached US No.8. Further hits 'Cuts Like A Knife' and 'This Time' and gruelling touring ensured the album reached platinum status by the end of 1983. *Reckless* (1985) added to Adams' mega-stardom, giving him first UK hits with 'Run To You', 'Heaven' and 'Summer Of '69'. A string of MTV video classics and the raunchy Tina Turner duet 'It's Only Love' made him a fixture of the US chart. Released by demand from radio stations, 'Heaven' soared to US No.1. Adams opened the US segment of Live Aid and co-wrote Canada's Ethiopian benefit single 'Tears Are Not Enough'. The charity work continued with U2, Lou Reed, Sting and Peter Gabriel on 1986's Conspiracy Of Hope Amnesty International tour of the USA. *Into The Fire* (1987) failed to match previous efforts, reaching a comparatively poor UK No.10 and US No.7. Live, he was successful as ever: high-profile appearances included the East German Peace Festival and Nelson Mandela's 70th Birthday Tribute (1988), and the revival of Pink Floyd's *The Wall* in Berlin, Germany (1990).

Any qualms about Adams' commercial stagnation were cast aside when '(Everything I Do) I Do It For You', from the movie *Robin Hood: Prince Of Thieves* (1991), spent a record-breaking 16 weeks atop the UK chart. *Waking Up The Neighbours* (1991) benefitted accordingly, entering the UK chart at No.1. After relentless touring and hits set *So Far So Good* (1993), he released more of the same with *18 Til I Die* (1996), criticized at the time for suggestive lyrics. Recent years have seen collaborations with Rod Stewart and Sting ('All For Love', 1995), Barbra Streisand ('I Finally Found Someone', 1997) and Davy Spillane (*MTV Unplugged*, 1997).

read *Bryan Adams: Everything He Does* (1995), Sorelle Saidman

fan Bad News, 406-68 Water Street, Vancouver, BC, V6B 1A4, Canada

surf www.geocities.com/Sunset Strip/Towers/4656/

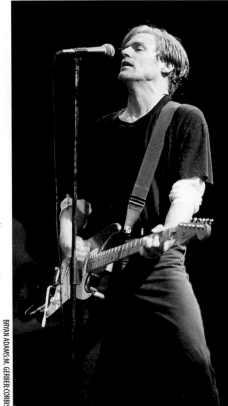

BRYAN ADAMS/M. GERBER.CORBIS

AEROSMITH ✪✪

WHO Vocals **Steven Tyler** (b. Steven Tallarico, 26 Mar 1948, Yonkers, New York, USA), guitar **Joe Perry** (b. Anthony Perry, 10 Sep 1950, Lawrence, Massachusetts, USA), guitar **Brad Whitford** (b. 23 Feb 1952, Reading, Massachusetts), bass **Tom Hamilton** (b. 31 Dec 1951, Colorado Springs, Colorado, USA), drums **Joey Kramer** (b. 21 Jun 1950, The Bronx, New York)

WHEN 1970–

WHERE Boston, Massachusetts, USA

WHAT Funk-fuelled sleaze Rock with a side order of Hip Hop

"If you grew up in the 70s," observed REM's Peter Buck, "you liked Aerosmith." The group's influence riddles Metal and the Rap Rock crossovers that followed their hit union with Run DMC. Acclaim, however, came after years of shaking a Rolling Stones rip-off charge. Not only did drummer-turned-singer Tyler resemble Mick Jagger, but he teamed up with Keef-a-like guitarist Perry. Both bar-band veterans, Tyler even made it into a studio with one act (Chain Reaction), but threw in his lot when invited to join Perry and Hamilton's The Jam Band. They were joined by Tyler's friend Kramer and guitarist Raymond Tabano, the latter giving way to Whitford in 1971. Having toyed with both The Hookers and Spike Jones, they christened themselves Aerosmith, which "sounded cool" (Kramer) and "doesn't mean a thing" (Tyler). *Aerosmith* (1973) included future classics, but didn't trouble chart statisticians. Undaunted, they toured relentlessly, stopping only to record *Get Your Wings* (1974) and *Toys In The Attic* (1975). *Toys* provided their breakthrough: the irrepressible 'Walk This Way'. A classic long before Run DMC's revamp, the song embodied the band's Funk-fuelled Rock. Aerosmith were also a dab hand at ballads, one of which – 'Dream On' – was disinterred from their debut in the wake of 'Walk This Way' and went Top 10. *Rocks* (1976) marked the band's transformation from (in Perry's words) "a bunch of musicians dabbling in drugs to a bunch of addicts dabbling in music." Their decline was slow to show. *Draw The Line* (1977) was patchy, but their live standing was unaffected and culminated in a headliner at the 1978 California Jam II festival in front of 350,000 fans. *Live Bootleg* (1978) is a thrilling testament to Aerosmith in the raw.

By 1979, Tyler and Perry were at war, united only by narcotic indulgence. Guitarist Jimmy Crespo was promoted after uncredited work on *Night In The Ruts* (1979), when his predecessor quit to form The Joe Perry Project. The final straw came when Perry's wife poured milk over Mrs Hamilton. "It's true," cackled Tyler. "We actually broke up over spilled milk." In the fall-out, they issued *Greatest Hits* (1980), including their version of The Beatles' 'Come Together' – the fruit of their appearance in film farrago *Sgt. Pepper's Lonely Hearts Club Band* (1978). Tyler struggled on with Crespo, Kramer, Hamilton and guitarist Rick Dufay (Whitford having quit to form the short-lived Whitford St Holmes) on *Rock In A Hard Place* (1982), a musical highlight but commercial nadir. Tyler plumbed further depths with drink, drugs and bad driving, and Aerosmith seemed condemned to history. However, in 1984 the singer got wind of Alice Cooper's plans to enlist Perry and hastily proposed a reunion. Hauling Whitford back aboard, they tested the live

waters, then issued *Done With Mirrors* (1985), another album whose excellence failed to translate into sales.

The Run DMC hook-up in 1986 could not have been better timed, coinciding with the Hip Hop boom and the resurgence of Metal – many of whose leading lights they had inspired. Bon Jovi led the way, giving way only to Guns N' Roses, who best understood the blend of sleaze and style Aerosmith had hall-marked. Quick to capitalize on this good fortune, Aerosmith enlisted Bon Jovi hit-maker Desmond Child as co-writer and Guns N' Roses as tour support. *Permanent Vacation* (1987) exploded and the band finally made its mark in Britain with a Top 40 album placing (subsequent releases went Top 10).

In a smooth upwards curve, *Pump* (1989) and *Get A Grip* (1993) yielded ever-increasing sales (13 million for the latter) and hits (notably the former's 'Love In An Elevator'). Endorsement by *Wayne's World* and MTV meant they were rarely out of the public eye. Columbia cashed in with *Classics Live 1* (1986) and *Classics Live 2* (1987), *Gems* (1988), *Pandora's Box* (1991), *Pandora's Toys* (1994) and *Box Of Fire* (1994). They headlined the British Monsters Of Rock festival (1993) and Woodstock II (1994). More compilations (1988's *Anthology*, 1994's *Big Ones*), video games, a *Simpsons* cameo, a club opening (Mama Kin's Music Hall in Boston) and even the launch of starlet Alicia Silverstone, who graduated from their videos to celluloid superstardom, added to the Aerosmith profile. Silverstone's partner in the 'Crazy' promo – Liv 'daughter-of-Steven' Tyler – also became quickly established in a highly successful film career. The icing on the cake was Aerosmith's $50 million deal with new label Sony.

With success came renewed inter-band strain. Managerial squabbles prompted reports that the evangelically detoxed Tyler was back in the narcotic saddle, and Kramer in the grip of depression. Happily, they lost only manager Tim Collins (chief architect of the Tyler-gone-bad rumours). *Nine Lives* (1997) yielded neither hits nor sales of traditional proportions, but confirmed their enduring appeal and talent.

READ *Walk This Way* (1997), Aerosmith & Stephen Davis

FAN Aero Force One, PO Box 882494, San Francisco, CA 94188, USA

SURF www.aerosmith.com/

A-HA

WHO Vocals **Morten Harket** (b. 14 Sep 1959, Kongsberg, Norway), keyboards **Magne Furuholmen** (b. 1 Nov 1962, Oslo, Norway), guitar **Pal Waaktaar** (b. 6 Sep 1961, Oslo)

WHEN 1982–

WHERE Oslo, Norway

WHAT Tuneful Nordic Pop

Hearts were set throbbing with 'Take On Me' (1984) and 'The Sun Always Shines On TV' (1985), whose videos mixed live action and animation. *Hunting High And Low* (1985) was followed by heavier *Scoundrel Days* (1986), Bond theme 'The Living Daylights' (1987) and *Stay On These Roads* (1988). *East Of The Sun, West Of The Moon* (1990) gave them a hit with The Everly Brothers' 'Crying In The Rain', but activity subsided after *Memorial Beach* (1993).

SURF www.mason.gmu.edu/~kkasmai/a-ha/a-ha2

AEROSMITH – STEVEN TYLER & JOE PERRY/STEVE DOUBLE/RETNA

"Steven knew how
to keep things tight.
We didn't have a clue
about discipline. For
us the whole thing
was about feel.
So we needed
each other"
Joe Perry

ALICE IN CHAINS ✪✪

WHO Vocals **Layne Staley** (b. 22 Aug 1967, Bellevue, Washington, USA), guitar/vocals **Jerry Cantrell** (b. 18 Mar 1966, Tacoma, Washington), bass **Mike Inez** (b. 14 May 1966, San Fernando, California, USA), drums **Sean Kinney** (b. 27 May 1966, Seattle, Washington)

WHEN 1987–

WHERE Seattle, Washington, USA

WHAT Masterful Metal misery

Despite owing more to Black Sabbath than Sonic Youth, Alice In Chains benefited from the Grunge-ignited spotlight on Seattle. While their debut *Facelift* (1990) was ignored outside the Metal fraternity, post-Nirvana releases sped to the platinum plateau.

The malevolent acoustic EP 'Sap' and the international hit 'Would?' (the latter from the Grunge-era romantic comedy movie *Singles*) preceded the skull-crushing *Dirt* (1992). The album added to a fanbase built on relentless touring and heavy MTV rotation, and rose to US No.6 on its way to triple platinum sales.

But success couldn't stop internal rot. Founder member Mike Starr was replaced by Mike Inez, Layne Staley became alarmingly chemically challenged and 1994's bleakly beautiful *Jar Of Flies* (reissued with 'Sap' for a US No.1) looked like their last gasp.

Staley fuelled split rumours by hooking up with Pearl Jam and Screaming Trees personnel for his side project Mad Season (*Above*, 1995), but the group returned with the US chart-topping *Alice In Chains* (1995). However, live work amounted to a few Kiss supports and an MTV session unleashed as *Unplugged* (1996).

When the unstable Staley mooted more Mad Season and was placed on 'suicide watch', his bandmates prepared solo careers. Jerry Cantrell was first off the mark with *Boggy Depot* in 1998.

Fan Alice In Chains Fan Club, PO Box 61245, Seattle, WA 98121, USA

Surf www.music.sony.com/Music/ArtistInfo/AliceInChains/

ALL SAINTS

WHO Vocals **Melanie 'Mello-Deeeee' Blatt** (b. 25 Mar 1975, London, England), vocals **Shaznay 'Bart' T Lewis** (b. 14 Oct 1975, London), vocals **Nicole 'The Fonz' Appleton** (b. 7 Oct 1974, Canada), vocals **Natalie 'Nona' Appleton** (b. 14 May 1973, Canada)

WHEN 1993–

WHERE All Saints Road, London, England

WHAT R&B Pop babes

Sidestepping the 'manufactured' mantle, All Saints' R&B/Hip Hop/Pop mix supplanted 'girl power' with urban cool (although Melanie Blatt had, as a child, starred in a toothpaste ad with Emma 'Baby Spice' Bunton). After forgotten mid-90s singles on the ZTT label ('Silver Shadow' and 'Let's Get Started'), Blatt and chief songwriter Shaznay Lewis recruited the Appleton sisters and signed to London Records in 1996. Lewis later declined to confirm Pop magazine *Smash Hits*' suggestion that original Saint Simone Rainford left after Blatt threw a fire extinguisher at her.

An infectious Swing anthem, the 1997 hit 'I Know Where It's At' gave no hint they would soar beyond the post-Eternal likes of N-Tyce. But with the Shangri-Las-meets-Gospel-flavoured ballad 'Never Ever', they secured an extraordinary residency in the UK Top 10, finally rising to No.1 in 1998. BRIT awards swiftly ensued.

Amid pin-up status and saturation media coverage (mainly centering on the Saints' relationships with fellow stars like Boyz II Men and Robbie Williams), *All Saints* (1997) rose above the 90s girl/boy band craze. Quirky covers of Red Hot Chili Peppers' 'Under The Bridge' and Labelle's 'Lady Marmalade' nestled amid soulful originals (notably the group-penned 'Heaven') – any of which could continue All Saints' rise to global domination.

Read *All Saints: The Unofficial Biography* (1997), Pop Culture

Surf www.weblink.force9.co.uk/AllSaints/index.

THE ALLMAN BROTHERS BAND ✪

WHO Vocals/keyboards **Gregg Allman** (b. 8 Dec 1947, Nashville, Tennessee, USA), guitar **Duane Allman** (b. 20 Nov 1946, Nashville, d. 29 Oct 1971), guitar/vocals **Forrest Richard 'Dicky' Betts** (b. 12 Dec 1943, West Palm Beach, Florida, USA), bass **Berry Oakley** (b. 4 Apr 1948, Chicago, Illinois, USA, d. 11 Nov 1972), drums **Claude 'Butch' Trucks** (b. 11 May 1947, Jacksonville, Florida), drums **Jai 'Jaimoe' Johanson** (b. 8 Jul 1944, Ocean Springs, Mississippi, USA)

WHEN 1969–

WHERE Macon, Georgia, USA

WHAT Innovators of dramatic Southern Rock

As teenagers, Duane and Gregg Allman played the Blues and, by 1963, were touring bars as The Allman Joys. In 1967, they cut two unremarked albums as Hourglass before splitting. Duane played with Aretha Frankin and Wilson Pickett, then was persuaded, by ex-Otis Redding manager Phil Walden, to form a band.

With fellow sessioneer Johanson, Duane recruited old friend Berry Oakley, locals Betts and Trucks, and Gregg. Relocated to Macon, Georgia, they recorded their self-titled debut in 1969. Gregg wrote the songs, Duane defined the sound: a fusion of Blues, R&B and Country. The twin leads of Duane and Betts, and added muscle of two drummers, distinguished them from contemporaries. *Idlewild South* (1970) reached US No.38. Live, they soared. With the emotionally charged gold album *Live At The Fillmore East* (1971), Duane, who had played the coda on Eric Clapton's 'Layla', secured his reputation as a slide guitar genius.

However, as they began work on their artistic peak, 1972's *Eat A Peach*, tragedy struck. Riding on his motorbike from Oakley's Macon house, Duane swerved to avoid a truck and was killed. Adding pianist Chuck Leavell, *Brothers And Sisters* (1973) made US No.1, was their UK debut (No.42) and yielded the hit 'Ramblin' Man'. In November 1972, Oakley died in a motorbike accident just three blocks from Duane's crash. Drafting Lamar Williams, they struck gold with *Win, Lose Or Draw* (1975), but rifts emerged. In a drugs trial, Gregg testified against a road manager. Incensed by this betrayal, the others ostracized Gregg, then split in 1976.

Gregg, Betts and Trucks reformed in 1978, with guitarist Dan Toler and bassist David Goldflies. *Enlightened Rogues* (1979) made US No.9 but, after later flops, they split again in 1982.

Reformed with Warren Haynes (guitar), Allen Woody (bass) and Johnny Neel (keyboards), then percussionist Marc Quinones, they were inducted into the Rock And Roll Hall Of Fame in 1995.

Read *Midnight Riders: The Story Of The Allman Brothers Band* (1996), Scott Freeman

Surf www.netspace.org/allmans/

MARC ALMOND

WHO b. Peter Marc Almond, 9 Jul 1957, Southport, Merseyside, England

WHAT Melodramatic Torch singer

While still half of Soft Cell, Almond released *Untitled* (1982) and *Torment And Torreos* (1983) as Marc & The Mambas. After Soft Cell's split, he formed The Willing Sinners for *Vermine In Ermine* in 1984. Citing Scott Walker and Jacques Brel as influences, Almond blended dark lyrics with flamboyant, heartfelt performances.

However, *Mother Fist And Her Five Daughters* (1987), *Tenement Symphony* (1991) and *Fantastic Star* (1996) failed to match Soft Cell's success. His biggest hits were covers: Scott Walker's 'Jacky', David McWilliams' 'Days Of Pearly Spencer' and Gene Pitney's 'Something's Gotten Hold Of My Heart', featuring Pitney himself.

Read *Marc Almond* (1995), Jeremy Reed

Surf www.marcalmond.co.uk/foyer.htm

HERB ALPERT ✪✪✪✪✪

WHO b. 31 Mar 1935, Los Angeles, California, USA

WHAT Trumpet-toting MOR mogul

Herb Alpert first recorded as Dore Alpert, before co-writing Sam Cooke hits, including 'Only Sixteen' (1959) and 'Wonderful World' (1960), as Barbara Campbell. Alpert's Dore label released Jan & Dean hits in 1959 and 1960. Co-founding A&M with Jerry Moss in 1962, records with his Tijuana Brass ensemble helped establish the label as America's biggest independent. A take on Bacharach & David's 'This Guy's In Love With You' in 1968 followed a string of Latin-flavoured instrumental hits – dubbed 'Ameriachi' – including 'The Lonely Bull' (1962) and 'A Taste Of Honey' (1965).

After concentrating on A&M for much of the 70s, Alpert rose again with *Rise* (1979), and 1987's *Keep Your Eye On Me*, including 'Diamonds': the US hit starring producers Jam & Lewis' protégée Janet Jackson. The same year, his trumpet playing featured on UB40's 'Rat In Mi Kitchen'. Besides his recording work, Alpert has worked on Broadway productions, launched his own perfume, exhibited his paintings in Europe and founded a new label with Moss – Almo Sounds – following their sale of A&M in 1989. He also runs The Herb Alpert Foundation, a charitable organization dedicated to education, the arts and the environment.

Surf www.geffen.com/almo/herbalpert

AMBIENT

WHAT Ambient was coined by Brian Eno. Eno intended it to act as a 'tint' – altering or enhancing moods rather than dictating them. The slowly evolving textures synonymous with Ambient characterized Eno's <u>Music For Airports</u> (1978), inspired by a visit to Cologne Airport in 1977, where he pondered the kind of music he would like to hear in that environment. Often scorned as mood Muzak, Ambient finally gained acceptance in the late 80s, thanks to acts like Aphex Twin, The Orb, System 7 and Future Sound Of London, who merged Eno-inspired Ambient textures with House, Techno and Psychedelia.

WHERE Europe, USA

WHEN 1977–

WHO Brian Eno <u>Ambient 4: On Land</u> (1982), KLF <u>Chill Out</u> (1990), System 7 <u>System 7</u> (1991), Aphex Twin <u>Collected Ambient Works 85–92</u> (1992), The Orb <u>U.F.Orb</u> (1992), Future Sound Of London <u>Lifeforms</u> (1994), Robert Fripp & David Sylvian <u>Damage</u> (1994)

TORI AMOS ⊙

WHO b. Myra Ellen Amos, 22 Aug 1963, Newton, North Carolina, USA

WHAT Piano-pounding Popstress

TORI AMOS:STEVE DOUBLE:RETNA

Launched as a kooky, one-woman whirlwind à la Kate Bush, Amos' harrowing debut EP 'Me And A Gun' and *Little Earthquakes* (1992) proved she wasn't just another singer/songwriter. Fans quickly unearthed a previous incarnation: her Pat Benatar-esque role fronting Y Kant Tori Read, whose eponymous 1988 album bombed and was played down after Amos' breakthrough. *Under The Pink* (1994) featured hits 'Cornflake Girl' and 'Pretty Good Year' and an implausible cameo by Nine Inch Nails' Trent Reznor.

Furthering her Rock credentials, Amos duetted with Robert Plant on Led Zeppelin tribute *Enconium* (1995). The slow, quiet songs on *Boys For Pele* (1996) weren't the stuff of hits, although Armand Van Helden's chart-topping House makeover of 'Professional Widow' brought her a new audience.

Amos used her transatlantic celebrity to support RAAIN (Rape Abuse And Incest Network), and confirmed her superstar status by appearing on MTV's *Unplugged* (1996). An acknowledged influence on, and supporter of, Alanis Morissette (and favourite of Elton John), Amos furthered her own fortunes with 1998's *From The Choirgirl Hotel*.

(ReaD) *Tori Amos Collectibles* (1997), Paul Campbell

(Fan) Really Deep Thoughts, PO Box 328606, Columbus, OH 43232-8606, USA

(Surf) www.concentric.net/~rdtzine

LAURIE ANDERSON

WHO b. 5 Jun 1947, Chicago, Illinois, USA

WHAT Multi-instrumental performance artist

Best remembered for her single 'O Superman' (1981) – a surprise UK No.2 at eight minutes long – Laurie Anderson is one of America's most prolific and inventive performers, mixing art, film, music and dance since her first unrecorded performance piece 'Duets On Ice' in 1972. *Big Science* (1982) and *Mister Heartbreak* (1984), featuring collaborations with Adrian Belew, Peter Gabriel and William Burroughs, began a critically acclaimed recording career to match her status as a performance artist. Her film *Home Of The Brave* (1986) and subsequent work with Chris Spedding (*Strange Angels*, 1989), Lou Reed (*Bright Red*, 1994) and Brian Eno (*Bright Red* and *The Ugly One With The Jewels*, both 1995) explored Anderson's concern with language, identity, nationality and technology.

In 1997 she coordinated London arts festival Meltdown, and appeared on the star-studded charity single, 'Perfect Day'.

(ReaD) *Stories From The Nerve Bible* (1993), Laurie Anderson

(Surf) www.voyagerco.com/LA/

THE ANIMALS

WHO Vocals/harmonica **Eric Burdon** (b. 11 May 1941, Walker, Tyne and Wear, England), keyboards/vocals **Alan Price** (b. 19 Apr 1942, Fairfield, County Durham, England), bass **Bryan 'Chas' Chandler** (b. 18 Dec 1938, Heaton, Tyne and Wear, d. 17 Jul 1996), guitar **Hilton Valentine** (b. 21 May 1943, North Shields, Tyne and Wear), drums **John Steel** (b. 4 Feb 1941, Gateshead, Tyne and Wear)

WHEN 1962–1983

WHERE Newcastle upon Tyne, England

WHAT Rowdy and respected British beat combo

When Beatlemania opened the floodgates for 'beat' groups, The Animals were ready. Their pedigree included backing Blues legends who visited Newcastle and a successful stint in the Star Club, Hamburg. Produced by Mickie Most, they developed a powerful sound, driving along behind Burdon's rough-edged vocals. Burdon's Blues credentials were impeccable – he was actually born during an air raid! In the summer of 1964, a reworking of the traditional 'House Of The Rising Sun' took The Animals to No.1 on both sides of the Atlantic. Further singles, including 'I'm Crying' (1964) and 'Don't Let Me Be Misunderstood' (1965), hit charts around the world. They also recorded solid albums – *The Animals* (1964), *Animal Tracks* (1965) and *Animalisms* (1966) – a rarity among 60s acts.

Sadly, success paved the way for the 'musical differences' that would become a feature of the expanding Rock industry. Price, whose influence had added melody and restraint to Burdon's wilder desires, left to start a solo career and, in 1966, Burdon rejected commercial material presented by Most. Growing dissent led to a split in 1966, following Burdon's embrace of LSD and hippie culture. The others kept drinking.

Burdon retained the band name for increasingly progressive ventures, such as the highly prized *Winds Of Change* (1968). His solo career included founding the enduring Soul Funk outfit War. Price became a singer/songwriter and Chandler a manager, guiding Jimi Hendrix and Slade to high-profile careers. The 'classic' line-up re-formed twice before Chandler's death, recording *Before We Were So Rudely Interrupted* (1977) for Chandler's label and 1983's *Ark*.

PAUL ANKA

WHO b. 30 Jul 1941, Ottawa, Ontario, Canada

WHAT 50s teen idol singer/songwriter

The first teenager to top the transatlantic charts made his recording debut in 1956 at 15, backed by noted Doo Wop group The Jacks (aka The Cadets). In 1957, Anka's hit-making friends

ANTHRAX

WHO Vocals **John Bush** (b. 24 Aug 1963, Los Angeles, California, USA), guitar

Scott Ian (b. Scott Ian Rosenfeld, 31 Dec 1963, Queens, New York, USA), bass

Frankie Bello (b. 9 Jul 1965, The Bronx, New York), drums **Charlie Benante**

(b. 27 Nov 1962, The Bronx)

WHEN 1981—

WHERE New York, USA

WHAT Politically Correct Thrash Metal

Anthrax's debut *Fistful Of Metal* (1983) promised little, but the replacement of frontman Neil Turbin by Joey Belladonna for *Spreading The Disease* (1985) lit fortune's fuse. With Ian's hooky songs and Belladonna's soaring vocals, Anthrax joined Metallica to lead the Thrash Metal movement. *Among The Living* (1987) and *State Of Euphoria* (1988) took them from the Metal charts to the mainstream and they shed a 'cartoony' image with the Grammy-nominated *Persistence Of Time* (1990) and an arena-filling tour with fellow Thrashers Megadeth and Slayer. A hit reworking of Public Enemy's 'Bring The Noise', from *Attack Of The Killer B's* (1991), prompted a tour with PE themselves. Unenamoured of the Rock Rap revolution, Belladonna quit to be replaced by Bush (ex-Armored Saint). *Sound Of White Noise* (1993) had chart success, but the band split with both Island Records (bowing out with 1994's *Live – The Island Years*) and long-time guitarist Danny Spitz. Pantera riff-monger Dimebag Darrell deputized on *Stomp 442* (1995), proving that although Anthrax's profile had dipped, their sound was as furious as ever.

(Fan) Anthrax NFC, PO Box 254, Kulpsville, PA 19443, USA

(Surf) www.ollusa.edu/student/ucarda/Anthrax.html

APHEX TWIN

WHO b. Richard James, 18 Aug 1971, Limerick, Ireland

WHAT Tank-driving Techno terrorist

James, a child electronics prodigy, experimented with recordings on home-made equipment in the mid-80s. His first releases as Aphex Twin – 1991's 'Analogue Bubblebath' EPs – were followed by the acclaimed *Selected Ambient Works 85–92*, including tracks recorded when he was 14. Signed to Warp in 1993, he recorded the wayward *Surfing On Sine Waves* as Polygon Window. *Selected Ambient Works Vol. II* (UK No.11, 1994) and *I Care Because You Do* (1995) added to the unpredictable legend, as did stunts like buying an ex-army tank, 'playing' sandpaper and food processors during DJ appearances and sampling asthma inhalers on 1995's 'Ventolin'. Straddling the line between experimentalism and absurdity, 1996's *Richard D. James* and the extremely nasty 'Come To Daddy' (1997) continued in typically uncompromising style.

(Surf) www.warp-net.com

The Rover Boys introduced him to their label ABC-Paramount, who snapped up the young singer/songwriter. Soon afterwards, his composition 'Diana' (inspired by his family's 18-year-old babysitter Diana Ayoub) topped US and UK charts and became a rare million-seller in Britain. For the next six years, Anka was seldom away from the hit parade; among his biggest hits were the self-penned ballads 'You Are My Destiny' (1958), 'Put Your Head On My Shoulder', 'Lonely Boy' (both 1959) and 'Puppy Love' (1960), the latter two being revived successfully in the 70s by another teenage idol, Donny Osmond. While in his teens, Anka appeared on every major US music TV show, starred in Las Vegas, headlined at The Copacabana and appeared in the movies *Girls Town* (1959) and *The Longest Day* (1962). In the mid-60s, he concentrated on songwriting and live club work. Against the odds, he had another run of best-sellers in the mid-70s, with the biggest, 'You're Having My Baby' (a 1974 duet with his protégée Odia Coates), topping the US chart. In 1993, Anka, who also penned hits like 'It Doesn't Matter Anymore' (Buddy Holly), 'She's A Lady' (Tom Jones) and 'My Way' (Frank Sinatra), was inducted into the Songwriters Hall Of Fame. *Amigos*, a bilingual record aimed at Latin countries, earned the popular supper-club entertainer another gold disc in 1996, spawning a best-selling duet with leading Latin artist Ricky Martin on 'Diana' – the 10-million-seller that launched his career.

Apple

Apple Records was part of Apple Corps, an organization intended to realize The Beatles' more fanciful ideas: including a London boutique, arts foundation and electronics division – Zapple – supervised by loonball inventor Magic Alex. Although the Fabs remained signed to EMI, 1968's 'Hey Jude' bore the Apple imprint, followed by records by Hot Chocolate, Mary Hopkin, James Taylor, Billy Preston and Badfinger. Apple's London office hosted The Beatles' legendary final roof-top performance, but chaotic administration led to legal and financial problems, exacerbating the group's split in 1970. Apple Corps, however, continues to represent The Beatles' interests.

ARGENT

WHO Vocals/keyboards **Rod Argent** (b. 14 Jun 1945, St Albans, Hertfordshire, England), guitar/vocals **Russ Ballard** (b. 31 Oct 1947, Waltham Cross, Hertfordshire, England), bass **Jim Rodford** (b. 7 Jul 1945, St Albans), drums **Robert Henrit** (b. 2 May 1946, Broxbourne, Hertfordshire, England)

WHEN 1969–1976

WHERE Hertfordshire, England

WHAT Progressive Hard Rockers

Formed by Rod in the wake of previous band The Zombies, Argent were a much heavier, though no less tuneful group, driven by Argent's Hammond organ and guitarist Ballard's highly commercial riff-mongering. *All Together Now* (1972) included their sole US hit 'Hold Your Head Up' and proved to be their commercial peak, but 'Liar' and 'God Gave Rock And Roll To You' were FM radio favourites, and became hits for Three Dog Night (1971) and Kiss (from 1992's *Bill And Ted's Bogus Journey* soundtrack), respectively. Ballard left in 1974, becoming a successful writer and producer, notably for Rainbow ('Since You've Been Gone'), Roger Daltrey and Hot Chocolate. When the group split in 1976, Rod notched up impressive composing, producing and playing credits for The Who, Nanci Griffith and Andrew Lloyd Webber. His musical *Masquerade* played in London in 1982. Rodford and Henrit later joined The Kinks.

JOAN ARMATRADING

WHO b. 9 Dec 1950, St Kitts, West Indies

WHAT Soulful singer/songwriter

Armatrading grew up in England, beginning her musical career with lyricist Pam Nestor in 1972 with *Whatever's For Us,* released on Cube Records. Splitting from Nestor in the early 70s, she signed to A&M, who released *Back To The Night* (1975), followed by her breakthrough album *Joan Armatrading* (1976), which included the UK Top 10 hit 'Love And Affection'. Armatrading's mature songwriting found continued success with *Show Some Emotion* (1977), *To The Limit* (1978), *Me, Myself, I* (1980), *Walk Under Ladders* (1981), *The Key* (1983) and greatest hits collection *Track Record* (1983). After 1985's *Secret Secrets*, her commercial

fortunes wavered. *Sleight Of Hand* (1986), *The Shouting Stage* (1988), *Hearts And Flowers* (1990), *Square The Circle* (1992) and *What's Inside* (1995) were nonetheless well-crafted collections and maintained a loyal fanbase around the world. As a successful black female singer/songwriter, she has influenced many, such as Tracy Chapman and Tasmin Archer, who followed gracefully in her footsteps.

 www.rahul.net/hrmusic/artists/jaart.html

ARRESTED DEVELOPMENT

WHO Vocals **Speech** (b. Todd Thomas, 25 Oct 1968, Milwaukee, Wisconsin, USA), vocals **Aerlee Taree** (b. 10 Jan 1973, Wisconsin), DJ **Headliner** (b. Tim Barnwell, 26 Jul 1967, New Jersey, USA), choreography **Montsho Eshe** (b. 23 Dec 1974, Georgia, USA), drums **Rasa Don** (b. Donald Jones, 22 Nov 1968, New Jersey), 'spiritual advisor' **Baba Oje** (b. 15 May 1932, Laurie, Mississippi, USA)

WHEN 1988–1995

WHERE Georgia, USA

WHAT Mild-mannered Hip Hop

In 1992, Rap was dominated by the LA riots and Ice T's 'Cop Killer' controversy – amidst which, the softly-spoken Arrested Development were a breath of fresh air. 'Tennessee' won over Hip Hop heads, 'People Everyday' snared the mainstream and debut *3 Years, 5 Months And 2 Days In The Life Of…* (1992) won them 1992's Best New Artist Grammy. 'Mr Wendal' – another transatlantic Top 10 hit – carried the momentum into 1993, but interest flagged through *Unplugged* (1993) and *Zingalamduni* (1994) and the band split. Speech's solo career was eclipsed by 'Tennessee' vocalist Dionne Farris' 1995 hit 'I Know'.

ART OF NOISE

WHO Keyboards **Anne Dudley** (b. 7 May 1960, Chatham, Kent, England), keyboards **Jonathan 'JJ' Jeczalik** (b. 11 May 1955), keyboards **Gary Langan**, keyboards **Trevor Horn** (b. 15 Jul 1949, Hertfordshire, England), lyrics **Paul Morley** (b. 26 Mar 1957, Farnham, Surrey, England)

WHEN 1983–1990

WHERE London, England

WHAT Eccentric avant-garde Hip Hop

Horn, Langan, Dudley and Jeczalik, hit-makers behind ABC, conceived AON – named by media manipulator Morley after a 20s futurist manifesto. After debut EP 'Into Battle With…' (1983), transatlantic dancefloors resounded to 1984's Hip Hop-flavoured 'Beatbox' which, added to their anonymous image, erroneously suggested the group was black. *Who's Afraid Of The Art Of Noise?* (1984) yielded UK hit 'Close (To The Edit)', and 'Moments In Love', to which Madonna walked up the aisle with Sean Penn. Jeczalik, Dudley and Langan then jumped ship from Horn's label ZTT to Chrysalis, charting with guitarist Duane Eddy ('Peter Gunn', 1986), TV novelty Max Headroom ('Paranoimia', 1986) and Tom Jones

(1988's Prince cover 'Kiss'). After *In Visible Silence* (1986), *In No Sense? Nonsense!* (1987) and *Below The Waste* (1989), they bowed out with 1990's *The Ambient Collection*, but posthumous compilations *The Fon Mixes* (1992) and *The Drum And Bass Collection* (1997) demonstrated their influence on Dance, notably The Prodigy, who sampled 'Close (To The Edit)' for 'Firestarter'. Post-Art Of Noise, Dudley has enjoyed the most visible career, including the acclaimed collaboration with Killing Joke's Jaz Coleman (*Songs From The Victorius City*, 1990), the quasi-Classical *Ancient And Modern* (1995), orchestral arrangements for Pulp, Boyzone, Elton John and Tina Turner and film scores *The Crying Game* (1992) and *The Full Monty* (1997).

 www.discoveryrec.com/artists/

ASH

WHO Vocals/guitar **Tim Wheeler** (b. 4 Jan 1977, Downpatrick, Northern Ireland), bass **Mark Hamilton** (b. 21 Mar 1977, Lisburn, Northern Ireland), drums **Rick McMurray** (b. 11 Jul 1975, Larne, Northern Ireland)

WHEN 1992–

WHERE Downpatrick, Northern Ireland

WHAT Teenage sensation Pop Punkers

Formerly in schoolboy Metal band Vietnam, Wheeler and Hamilton sacked their unreliable singer and drummer in 1992, recruited drummer McMurray and – juggling recording with school – released their first singles 'Jack Names The Planets', 'Petrol' and 'Uncle Pat' on Irish independent label La La Land in 1994. Signed to English label Infectious, their debut mini-album *Trailer* (1994) was followed by 'Kung Fu', breakthrough hits 'Girl From Mars', 'Goldfinger' and 'Oh Yeah', and the UK No.1 *1977* (1996). 1997 saw the release of *Live At The Wireless* and the addition of former Night Nurse guitarist Charlotte Hatherley (b. 20 Jun 1979, London, England) for the film theme 'A Life Less Ordinary'.

READ *Ash: '77–'97* (1997), Charlie Parker

SURF www.compura.com/martbean/ash/

ASIA ✪

WHO Vocals/bass **John Wetton** (b. 12 Jul 1949, Derby, England), guitar **Steve Howe** (b. 8 Apr 1947, London, England), drums **Carl Palmer** (b. 20 Mar 1947, Birmingham, England), keyboards **Geoffrey Downes**

WHEN 1981–

WHERE Los Angeles, California, USA

WHAT Radio-friendly Rock supergroup

Proving the 'supergroup' didn't die out in the 70s, Asia rose from the ashes of Emerson Lake & Palmer, Yes, King Crimson, Family and Roxy Music. Instantly dismissed in post-Punk Britain, Asia found a home in the USA, where radio lapped up their bombastic AOR. Debut *Asia* (1982) sold over 3 million copies in the USA, spawning two hits, 'Heat Of The Moment' and 'Only Time Will Tell'. Almost as successful, *Alpha* (1983) saw ELP bassist Greg Lake replace Wetton, and the group's stature grew with the TV special *Asia In Asia*, a live performance from the Budokan Theatre, Tokyo, Japan. But *Astra* (1985) stretched the formula too far, prompting Howe's departure, and with new guitarist Mandy Meyer (ex-Krokus) and Wetton returning to replace Lake, the group struggled on before disbanding in 1986. In 1990, Palmer, Downes and Wetton returned with guitarist Pat Thrall for *Then And Now*, while in 1992 Howe reunited with Palmer, Downes and new members John Payne (bass/vocals) and Al Pitrelli (guitar) for *Aqua* and *Asia: Live In Moscow*. The line-up for *Aria* (1994) consisted of Downes, Payne, Pitrelli and drummer Michael Sturgis. Pittrelli quit during a subsequent tour, replaced by ex-Simply Red and future Stone Roses guitarist Aziz Ibrahim.

SURF www.globalnet.co.uk/~asia/

ASWAD

WHO Vocals/guitar **Brinsley Forde** (b. 1952, Guyana), vocals **Donald Griffiths** (b. 1954, Jamaica, West Indies), guitar **Tony Gad** (b. Tony Robinson, 11 Nov 1957, London, England), bass **George Oban**, drums **Angus 'Drummie' Zeb** (b. Angus Gaye, 1959, London, England)

WHEN 1975–

WHERE London, England

WHAT Reggae chart-busters

With their name taken from the Arabic for 'black', Aswad's original line-up (ex-child actor Forde, Drummie, guitarist Donald Benjamin, keyboardist Courtney Hemmings and bassist Ras George Levi Oban) was snapped up by Island, the first high-profile deal for a British Reggae group. Debut *Aswad* (1976) established their popularity, and second album *Hulet* (1980) was recorded by the streamlined line-up of Forde, Drummie and new guitarist Gad. More Reggae hits – 1982's *New Chapter* and *Not Satisfied*, *Live And Direct* (1983), *Rebel Souls* (1984) and *To The Top* (1986) – paved the way for 1988's Pop crossover *Distant Thunder* and UK No.1 'Don't Turn Around'. However, bar 1994's UK No.5 'Shine', later releases succeeded only in the Reggae charts.

Atlantic Records

Atlantic Records, the brainchild of Turkish diplomat's son Ahmet Ertegun and student Herb Abramson, was created in 1947 with a $10,000 loan from Ertegun's dentist. Stick McGhee's 'Drinkin' Wine Spo-Dee-O-Dee' was the label's first success, closely followed by fellow R&B artists The Clovers, Ruth Brown and Ray Charles.

Abramson's departure allowed Billboard magazine reviewer Jerry Wexler to join in 1953, and Soul stars The Drifters, Ben E. King, Aretha Franklin and Wilson Pickett soon followed. Alongside Wexler's production skills, Atlantic recruited the songwriting talents of the legendary Jerry Leiber and Mike Stoller. Ahmet's brother Nesuhi joined in 1956 when the label created a Jazz roster featuring Charles Mingus, John Coltrane and Roland Kirk. When Atlantic's records were released in the UK through Decca in the mid-50s, Bobby Darin became the label's first white star, appearing on sister label Atco. Atco also released Acker Bilk's 'Stranger On The Shore' in America – the first UK record to reach US No.1. A distribution deal with Memphis-based Stax Records linked Atlantic with the hits of Otis Redding, Sam & Dave and Eddie Floyd. Rock and Pop success also came to Atlantic in the 60s with Sonny & Cher, Buffalo Springfield, The Young Rascals and Crosby, Stills, Nash & Young, joined by British acts like Yes, Led Zeppelin, Cream, The Rolling Stones and Bad Company.

Following 70s Soul act successes The Detroit Spinners, Roberta Flack and Sister Sledge, Atlantic reflected the wide range of musical genres emerging throughout the 80s and 90s with artists such as Bette Midler, Foreigner, AC/DC, Phil Collins, Tori Amos and Hootie & The Blowfish. The label celebrated its 40th anniversary in 1988 with a concert at New York's Madison Square Garden featuring, among others, Led Zeppelin. Its Rock heritage was renewed in the 90s by Stone Temple Pilots and matchbox 20, while making room for contemporary acts like Jewel and Lil' Kim.

THE AVERAGE WHITE BAND ✪

WHO Vocals/guitar **Hamish Stuart** (b. 8 Oct 1949, Glasgow, Scotland), guitar **Onnie McIntyre** (b. 25 Sep 1945, Lennoxtown, Scotland), bass/vocals **Alan Gorrie** (b. 19 Jul 1946, Perth, Scotland), drums **Robbie McIntosh** (b. 1950, Scotland, d. 23 Sep 1974), saxophone **Roger Ball** (b. 4 Jun 1944, Dundee, Scotland), saxophone **Malcolm 'Molly' Duncan** (b. 25 Aug 1945, Montrose, Scotland)

WHEN 1971–

WHERE London, England

WHAT Sax-powered Soul from Scotland

Formed by Gorrie and Duncan with the intention of becoming a Scottish Detroit Spinners, The Average White Band (a name suggested by Bonnie Bramlett) were enjoying success with 'Pick Up The Pieces' and their second, eponymously titled album in 1974 when McIntosh died from an accidental heroin overdose at an LA party. Installing their only black member, Steve Ferrone,

AWB enjoyed hits with *Cut The Cake* (1975), *Soul Searching* (1976), *Person To Person* (1977), *Benny And Us* (a collaboration with Ben E. King, 1977), *Warmer Communications* (1978), *Feel No Fret* (1979) and *Shine* (1980). After *Cupid's In Fashion* (1981), AWB split, reforming – minus Stuart, Duncan and Ferrone – in 1989 for *Aftershock*. Stuart became a fixture of Paul McCartney's 90s band. Though accused of stealing ideas from black music, AWB have influenced bands like The Brand New Heavies and been sampled by – among others – TLC, Ice Cube and Arrested Development. They toured again to promote *Soul Tattoo* (1997).

surf www.averagewhiteband.com/

KEVIN AYERS

WHO b. 16 Aug 1944, Herne Bay, Kent, England

WHAT The sound of eccentric England

Leaving Soft Machine in 1968, Ayers began a wayward solo career with 1969's *Joy Of A Toy* before forming the exceptionally weird Whole Earth – with Classical composer David Bedford, saxophonist Lol Coxhill and Mike Oldfield – for *Shooting At The Moon* (1971). *Whatevershebringswesing* (1972) and *Bananamour* (1973) – collaborations with Gong – were punctuated by retreats to the Mediterranean whenever success seemed likely, but 1974's *The Confessions Of Dr Dream And Other Stories* saw a more conventional sound. His live collaboration that year with Oldfield, Nico, John Cale and Brian Eno, *June 1, 1974*, furthered Ayers' leftfield credentials, but *Sweet Deceiver* (1975), *Yes We Have No Mañanas* (1976) and *Rainbow Takeaway* (1977) garnered little acclaim and even fewer sales. Returning to the Mediterranean, the 80s and 90s saw occasional releases, notably 1980's *That's What You Get Babe* and 1992's *Still Life With Guitar*.

fan Why Are We Sleeping?, 112 Parkville Road, Withington, Manchester, M20 4TZ, UK

surf users.globalnet.co.uk/~marwak/index.html

AZTEC CAMERA

WHO Vocals/guitar **Roddy Frame** (b. 29 Jan 1964, East Kilbride, Scotland)

WHEN 1980–

WHERE Glasgow, Scotland

WHAT Jangling Pop prodigy

Aztec Camera, a vehicle for Frame's songwriting, released their debut *High Land Hard Rain* in 1983. Hailed as an instant classic, it demonstrated the well-crafted arrangements and thoughtful lyrics which would typify the 19-year-old's subsequent career. He went on to work with Mark Knopfler (*Knife*, 1984), The Clash's Mick Jones (*Stray*, 1990), Ryuichi Sakamoto (*Dreamland*, 1993) and, on the BRIT award-nominated *Love* (1987), Funk luminaries including Marcus Miller on bass. The third single from *Love*, 'Somewhere In My Heart', peaked at UK No.3.

fan Aztec Camera Information Service, PO Box 321, London, SW7 2JU, UK

surf aoinfo.com?aztec/html

BABYFACE

WHO b. Kenneth Edmonds, 10 Apr 1959, Indianapolis, Indiana, USA

WHAT The man with the golden touch

Despite *Lovers* (1987), *Tender Lover* (1989), *A Closer Look* (1991), *For The Cool In You* (1993), *The Day* (1996) and *MTV Unplugged NYC* (1997), Babyface – his name bequeathed by legendary Funk bass player Bootsy Collins – will not be remembered for his solo albums. Nor will history record early acts The Deele and Manchild as anything other than stepping stones. Instead, he will be celebrated as hitmaker *extraordinaire*: first with production partner Antonio 'LA' Reid (Bobby Brown, Whitney Houston), then solo (Boyz II Men, Whitney Houston again). Among his record-breaking and Grammy-grabbing triumphs are Boyz II Men's 'End Of The Road' (1992): just one of the contributors to combined album and single sales of around 100 million.

Having conquered Soul's peaks (enlisting Aretha Franklin for 1995's star-studded *Waiting To Exhale* soundtrack), he re-routed to Rock (a fruitless collaboration with The Rolling Stones mitigated by hook-ups with Madonna and Eric Clapton), sitcom-scripting (*Schoolin'*) and film production (1997's *Soul Food*). Recent years have brought a share of problems to LA & Babyface's LaFace empire – TLC were almost swallowed by contractual squabbling and Toni Braxton got mutinous – but the hits have continued with Usher.

surf www.all-n-1.com/babyface/lvgindex.html

BABYFACE:TIM HALE:RETNA

BURT BACHARACH:KING COLLECTION:RETNA

Burt Bacharach

A former soldier and musical director for Marlene Dietrich, Bacharach formed an enduring partnership with lyricist Hal David. Perry Como's 1958 sensation 'Magic Moments' established them as first-rate hitmakers. During a break from David, Bacharach penned tunes for The Drifters with lyricist Bob Hilliard, but the duo returned with 60s hits for Frankie Vaughan ('Tower Of Stength'), Gene Pitney ('Twenty Four Hours From Tulsa'), The Walker Brothers ('Make It Easy On Yourself'), Herb Alpert ('This Guy's In Love With You'), Cilla Black ('Anyone Who Had A Heart'), Sandie Shaw ('There's Always Something There To Remind Me'), Dusty Springfield ('I Just Don't Know What To Do With Myself') and Jackie DeShannon ('What The World Needs Now Is Love'). Dionne Warwick, however, was their star interpreter: her bittersweet hits between 1962 and 1971 included 'Don't Make Me Over', 'Anyone Who Had A Heart', 'Walk On By', 'Trains And Boats And Planes', 'Message To Michael', 'Say A Little Prayer' (later a hit for Aretha Franklin), 'Alfie', 'Do You Know The Way To San José' and 'I'll Never Fall In Love Again'. They also penned film themes including <u>Wonderful To Be Young</u> (1962), <u>What's New Pussycat?</u> (1965), whose title track helped launch Tom Jones in the USA, <u>Alfie</u> (1966), <u>Casino Royale</u> (1967) and <u>Butch Cassidy And The Sundance Kid</u> (1969), for which they won two Oscars – for the score, and the extracted 'Raindrops Keep Falling On My Head'. In 1968, they launched a successful Broadway musical, <u>Promises Promises</u>.

Acrimoniously divorced from David, Bacharach's output declined through the 70s, although The Carpenters' version of 'Close To You' and albums of his own – including 1971's <u>Burt Bacharach</u> and <u>Portrait In Music</u> – maintained the legend. With future wife Carole Bayer Sager, Peter Allen and singer Christopher Cross, he penned the Oscar-winning 'Arthur's Theme' (1981) and enjoyed 80s hits with Neil Diamond's 'Heartlight', all-star AIDS charity single 'That's What Friends Are For' (featuring Dionne Warwick, Elton John, Gladys Knight and Stevie Wonder) and the Michael McDonald/Patti Labelle duet 'On My Own'. A 90s renaissance included Deacon Blue's 1990 tribute EP 'Four Bacharach And David Songs' and Gabrielle's 1997 cover of 'Walk On By'. Another vocal fan was Oasis' Noel Gallagher, who joined Bacharach on stage in London in 1996 for a performance of Noel's favourite song, 'This Guy's In Love With You'.

BACHMAN-TURNER OVERDRIVE ✪

WHO Vocals/guitar **Randy Bachman** (b. 27 Sep 1943, Winnipeg, Canada),

guitar **Tim Bachman** (b. 18 Feb 1953, Winnipeg), bass/vocals **C.F. 'Fred' Turner**

(b. 16 Oct 1943, Winnipeg), drums **Robbie Bachman** (b. 18 Feb 1953, Winnipeg)

WHEN 1972–

WHERE Winnipeg, Manitoba, Canada

WHAT Blue-collar AOR

After quitting The Guess Who, cutting solo album *Axe* (1970) and failing to hit big with his next band Black Belt, Randy Bachman formed Bachman-Turner Overdrive – named after its principal members and a trucker's magazine. Rejected by 25 labels, they eventually signed to Mercury for their eponymous 1973 debut, its chugging Rock becoming their trademark. Constant touring paid off, with US hits 'Blue Collar' and 'Taking Care Of Business' from *Bachman-Turner Overdrive II* (1974), but the stuttering US No.1 'You Ain't Seen Nothin' Yet' proved both their commercial peak and undoing. Tim left to become a producer, while later releases failed to match earlier successes, prompting Randy's departure for a solo career in 1977. The group split in 1979, but regrouped periodically throughout the 80s and 90s, sometimes as BTO. Randy Bachman has also toured – sometimes with Turner – as Bachman-Turner Overdrive.

BAD COMPANY ✪

WHO Vocals/guitar/piano **Paul Rodgers** (b. 17 Dec 1949, Middlesbrough,

England), guitar **Mick Ralphs** (b. 31 Mar 1948, Hereford, England), bass

Raymond 'Boz' Burrell (b. 1 Aug 1946, Lincoln, England), drums **Simon Kirke**

(b. 28 Jul 1949, London, England)

WHEN 1973–

WHERE London, England

WHAT Sweat-drenched superstars

Bad Company carried on where Free – who fell apart in summer 1973 – left off. Rodgers and Kirke of Free teamed up with Ralphs, who was increasingly sidelined in Mott The Hoople by Ian Hunter, and Burrell (ex-King Crimson). They had everything going for them: Rodgers was one of the UK's finest Rock singers; they were managed by Peter Grant (who masterminded Led Zeppelin's career) and most of their British Rock rivals were disbanding or keeping a low profile. Their 1974 live debut was soon followed by their first single, 'Can't Get Enough' (UK No.15, US No.5), and an eponymous album (UK No.3, US No.1). In the 1974 *Melody Maker* readers' poll they won 'Brightest Hope', 'Best Single of the Year' and 'Best Male Vocalist'. This winning streak continued in 1975 with *Straight Shooter* (UK/US No.3), propelled by transatlantic hit singles, 'Good Lovin' Gone Bad' and the ballad 'Feel Like Makin' Love', and *Run With The Pack* (1976, UK No.4, US No.5), although concentration on the US market resulted in diminishing domestic success. While always excellent on stage, later recordings sounded tame, and *Burnin' Sky* (1977) fared less well. *Desolation Angels* (1979) and the single 'Rock 'n'

Roll Fantasy' marked a return to form, but disenchantment with playing stadiums and managerial problems took their toll. A three-year silence was broken with the disappointing *Rough Diamonds* (1982). By this time each member had embarked on outside projects and they disbanded the next year. Persuaded by Atlantic Records (parent company of Led Zeppelin's now-defunct Swan Song label with whom they started in the USA) they reformed in 1986 with ex-Ted Nugent Group vocalist Brian Howe (Rodgers having joined Jimmy Page's The Firm). *Fame And Fortune* (1986) enjoyed minor success in the USA, but UK interest had waned and their new synthesizer-dominated sound didn't translate on stage. Burrell left and session bassists were used on *Dangerous Age* (1988), *Holy Water* (1990) and *Here Comes Trouble* (1992). In 1995 vocalist Robert Hart, second guitarist Dave Colwell and ex-Foreigner bassist Rick Wills joined Ralphs and Kirke, and recorded *Company Of Strangers* (1996).

surf www.inetnow.net/~piller/badco.htm

JOAN BAEZ

WHO b. 9 Jan 1941, Staten Island, New York, USA

WHAT Pure-voiced Protest

In 1956 Baez attended a non-violence and civil rights lecture given by Martin Luther King, Jr, which had a profound effect on her career. Her earliest recordings (in 1958) were shelved due to lack of record company interest, but after her family moved to Massachussetts her involvement in the local Folk scene grew. She often appeared at Club 47, a Folk venue in Cambridge, Massachusetts, where she attracted a devoted following. An appearance at the 1960 Newport Folk Festival was followed by her first album *Joan Baez* (1960). The following year she met Bob Dylan and began a lifelong friendship.

Her participation in the civil rights movement began in 1962 when she appeared in concert with a strict no-discrimination racial policy for the audiences. In 1963, a performance of 'We Shall Overcome' was seen by a crowd of nearly 250,000 people at a civil rights rally in Washington, DC. Released as a single, the track charted in the US and UK. Her albums of the period included *Joan Baez Volume Two* (1961), *Joan Baez In Concert* (1962), *Farewell Angelina* (1965), *Any Day Now* (1968) – a collection of Dylan songs – and an unauthorized collection of her 1958 recordings, *Joan Baez In San Francisco* (1965).

More headline appearances at Newport and civil rights rallies followed and she fell foul of the IRS by holding back 60% of her income tax in protest at US involvement in Vietnam. During a series of concerts in Japan, her political comments were deliberately mistranslated and it was claimed that the interpreter was pressured by the CIA. Her husband, David Harris, was arrested in 1969 for draft resistance, serving a twenty-month sentence. The same year, Baez appeared at the Woodstock festival where, on the first day, she performed five songs including 'We Shall Overcome'.

The 70s saw *Come From The Shadows* (1972) – her first for A&M Records – *Where Are You Now, My Son?* (1973) and Spanish-language album *Gracias A La Vida* (1974). Released in 1971, 'The Night They Drove Old Dixie Down' became her biggest-selling single. Baez continued to support not only the civil rights movement but the Nuclear Freeze Movement, Irish Peace People and Amnesty International. She founded and led the Humanitas International Human Rights Committee. Her politics often resulted in concerts being cancelled by local authorities, and she has been subject to death threats and police surveillance.

Diamonds And Rust (1975), featuring the Baez/Dylan biographical title track, was followed by a tour with Bob Dylan as part of his Rolling Thunder Revue, filmed and released as *Renaldo And Clara* in 1978. Throughout the 80s and 90s, Baez continued to tour, record and fight for various causes. *Recently* (1987) was her first studio album for eight years and was nominated for a Grammy. Many awards have been bestowed on Baez over the years – eight gold albums, a gold single, two honorary doctorate degrees, France's Chevalier Légion d'Honneur and six Grammy nominations are only the tip of the iceberg. *Gone From Danger* (1997) was followed by the start of a world tour in October 1997.

READ *And A Voice To Sing With* (1987), Joan Baez

SURF baez.woz.org

BANANARAMA

WHO Vocals **Keren Woodward** (b. 2 Apr 1961, Bristol, England), vocals **Sarah Dallin** (b. 17 Dec 1961, Bristol), vocals **Siobhan Fahey** (b. 10 Sep 1957, London, England)

WHEN 1981–

WHERE London, England

WHAT Sullen all-girl hit machine

Though celebrated for cheery Pop, Bananarama first hit with the grumpy Fun Boy Three on 'It Ain't What You Do It's The Way That You Do It' (1982). Of subsequent smashes, 'Robert De Niro's Waiting' (1984) charted highest. When their star dimmed, they joined Stock, Aitken and Waterman's production line, scoring a transatlantic smash with a technofied take on Shocking Blue's 'Venus' (1986). They graced both the 1984 original and 1989 update of 'Do They Know It's Christmas', although Fahey quit in 1988 to form Shakespear's Sister and eclipsed her former cohorts, despite the latter's hit hook-up with comediennes French & Saunders on 'Help' (1989) and a creditable stab at 90s-style Dance. Now minus Fahey's replacement Jacqui O'Sullivan, Bananarama still thrive as an overseas touring duo.

THE BAND ✪

WHO Vocals/guitar **Robbie Robertson** (b. 5 Jul 1943, Toronto, Ontario, Canada), piano/drums/vocals **Richard Manuel** (b. 3 Apr 1943, Stratford, Canada, d. 4 Mar 1986, Winter Park, Florida, USA), organ **Garth Hudson** (b. 2 Aug 1937, London, Ontario), bass/vocals **Rick Danko** (b. 9 Dec 1943, Simcoe, Canada), drums/mandolin/vocals **Levon Helm** (b. 26 May 1942, Marvell, Arkansas, USA)

WHEN 1967–1976

WHERE Woodstock, New York, USA

WHAT The sound of rural America

"The best band in the

The Band's influential songs remain as fresh and timeless as when they were first recorded. The faraway strains of Nashville radio station WLAC first drew Canadian teenagers Robbie, Rick and Richard to the Blues of America's Deep South. By 1961 they had joined Helm in The Hawks, backing Southern Rockabilly singer Ronnie Hawkins. Adding Hudson, they toured incessantly, splitting from Hawkins in 1963 to form Levon & The Hawks.

The group played a raucous blend of R&B, Soul and Gospel in bars from southern Ontario to Texas before settling in New York in 1965 and releasing 'The Stones I Throw'. Their music caught the attention of Bob Dylan, who invited Robertson and Helm to back him on his first 'electric' concert at Forest Hills, New York. Helm soon quit, stunned by the hostility of Dylan's mortified Folk fans. But The Hawks backed Dylan on his 1966 world tour and Helm rejoined them at Dylan's Woodstock retreat to record *The Basement Tapes* (issued in 1975). These uninhibited sessions had a profound effect: under Dylan's influence, Robertson and Manuel blossomed as songwriters. In 1968, the group – renamed The Band – released their debut *Music From Big Pink*.

In the era of Psychedelia, The Band resurrected the musical heritage of rural America. Lyrics rich in historical and biblical symbolism blended with R&B, Blues, Gospel and Country. Their subjects were small-town characters displaced by a passing way of life; settings were cornfields, the Civil War and carnivals on the edge of town. The Band's raw harmonies and haunting melodies produced a unique musical purity. The album reached No.30 in the US, critics clamoured to define the new sound and their reclusive backwoods lifestyle elevated them to cult status. *The Band* (1969), hailed as a masterpiece, reached US No.9, and delved further into storytelling tradition with an armoury of traditional instruments. Robertson emerged as the principal songwriter; his 'The Night They Drove Old Dixie Down', 'King Harvest (Has Surely Come)' and 'Across The Great Divide' showed devastating maturity. Manuel's prodigious songwriting talent deserted him, and the darker *Stage Fright* (1970), despite reaching US No.5 and UK No.15, reflected the pressures of live performance and success. The disappointing follow-up *Cahoots* (1971) revealed growing rifts and disenchantment.

The live *Rock Of Ages* (1972) was followed by *Moondog Matinee* (1973), a vibrant collection of cover versions. After backing Dylan on his *Planet Waves* and *Before The Flood* albums and tour, they recorded *Northern Lights, Southern Cross* (1975). Their strongest album since *The Band*, it yielded 'Acadian Driftwood', Robertson's heart-rending tribute to his native

Canada. Despite the return to form, Robertson announced he'd had enough and The Band split, playing *The Last Waltz* farewell concert on Thanksgiving Day, 1976. Guests included Bob Dylan, Neil Young, Eric Clapton and Joni Mitchell. The event spawned a live album and Martin Scorcese's documentary film (both 1978).

Danko, Helm and Robertson pursued solo careers while Hudson did session work. Reforming in 1984 without Robertson, tragedy struck when Manuel hanged himself in a Florida motel room in 1986. Danko and Helm reunited in 1991 with three new members, recording *Jericho* (1993) and *High On The Hog* (1996). Both had glimmers of magic, but lacked Robertson's songwriting talent and paled in comparison to *Live At Watkins Glen* (1996), a 1973 concert recording showing The Band at their glorious best.

READ *Across The Great Divide, The Band And America* (1993), Barney Hoskyns

SURF theband.hiof.no/

history of the universe"
George Harrison

THE BANGLES

WHO Vocals/guitar **Susanna Hoffs** (b. 17 Jan 1959, Los Angeles, California, USA), guitar **Vicki Peterson** (b. 11 Jan 1960, Northridge, Los Angeles), bass **Michael Steele** (b. 2 Jun 1959, Los Angeles), drums **Debbi Peterson** (b. 22 Aug 1961, Northridge)

WHEN 1981–1989

WHERE Los Angeles, California, USA

WHAT Go-Go's with more angles

THE BANGLES:JOE DILWORTH:SIN

Psychedelic revivalists Supersonic Bangs found fortune by aping girl-group sensation The Go-Go's. After an Indie single as The Bangs, they were spotted by Go-Go's guru Miles Copeland, who released their self-titled 1982 EP. A deal with CBS followed, the momentum stalled only by bassist Annette Zalinskas' departure, replaced by Steele. After the overlooked *All Over The Place* (1984), Banglemania ensued with the Prince-penned 'Manic Monday' and wacky 'Walk Like An Egyptian' from *Different Light* (1986). A hit cover of Simon & Garfunkel's 'Hazy Shade of Winter' preceded *Everything* (1988), represented chartwise by Garage Rocker 'In Your Room' and epic weepy 'Eternal Flame'. However, just months after the latter became a US/UK No.1 in 1989, inter-band tensions caused them to split. *Greatest Hits* (1990) was a UK smash but a Stateside flop, and solo ventures received even shorter shrift, although Vicki Peterson resurfaced as bassist on the 1995 Go-Go's reunion.

Read *The Bangles* (1989), P. Hogan

Fan Hoffmania, 24 Weapones Valley Road, Scarborough, Y011 2JF, UK

Surf biron.usc.edu/~clare/Bangles.html

BARCLAY JAMES HARVEST

WHO Vocals/keyboards **Stewart 'Wooly' Wolstenholme** (b. 15 Apr 1947, Oldham, Greater Manchester, England), guitar/vocals **John Lees** (b. 13 Jan 1947, Oldham), bass/vocals **Les Holroyd** (b. 12 Mar 1948, Bolton, Greater Manchester), drums **Melvin Pritchard** (b. 20 Jan 1948, Oldham)

WHEN 1966–

WHERE Oldham, Greater Manchester, England

WHAT Melodic 'Pomp' Rock

Formed in 1966, Barclay James Harvest released their eponymous debut album in 1970. By 1971 they were fusing Rock and Classical music on *Once Again* and *Barclay James Harvest And Other Short Stories*. Failure to live up to EMI's expectations with *Baby James Harvest* (1972) saw the band dropped by EMI and sign to Polydor. *Everyone Is Everybody Else* (1974) revived the group's fortunes and by the end of the year they charted for the first time with *Barclay James Harvest Live*. *Time Honoured Ghosts* (1975) and *Octoberon* (1976) enabled the band to make valuable inroads abroad. Further studio albums *Gone To Earth* (1977) and *XII* (1978) were well received, but by 1979, Wolstenholme left due to "musical differences".

Eyes Of The Universe (1979) showcased their more accessible side. *Turn Of The Tide* (1981) prepared the ground for the live in Berlin *A Concert For The People* (1982), which reached No.1 in Germany. Subsequent, accessible releases *Ring Of Changes* (1983) and *Victims Of Circumstance* (1984) both nudged the Top 40 before *Face To Face* (1987) marked a return to the 'traditional' BJH sound. Later that year, the band became the first Western outfit to perform at an open-air concert in East Berlin's Treptower Park.

Another long lay-off preceded *Welcome To The Show* (1990). The band's 25th birthday release, *Best Of Barclay James Harvest* (1992), was followed a year later by *Caught In The Light*, which didn't please Polydor, who dropped them from the UK roster.

In March 1995, after a prolonged legal battle with former arranger Robert John Godfrey (mastermind behind cult sensation The Enid) was finally settled, they recorded 1997's *River Of Dreams*.

Fan Nova Lepidoptera, Hamble Reach, Oslands Lane, Lower Swanwick, Southampton, S031 7EG, UK

Surf www.ftech.net/"harvest /bjh-home

GARY BARLOW ⊙

WHO b. 20 Jan 1971, Frodsham, Cheshire, England

WHAT Boy bandster turned serious singer/songwriter

Uneasy with hormone-drenched hoofing, Gary Barlow disbanded Take That, donned his serious songwriter hat and whipped out 'Forever Love': a UK chart-topper in July 1996 that should have previewed his debut album. However, the latter – scheduled for September 1996 – was overhauled at the behest of Arista label boss Clive Davis (who launched Whitney Houston to superduperdom). Among the results were the Madonna-penned 'Love Won't Wait', which blazed a trail to the top for *Open Road* (1997). Stateside success continued to elude him – despite a short-lived union with The Spice Girls' ex-manager Simon Fuller – but further UK hits, touring, and rivalry with fellow Take That graduate Robbie Williams kept the pot boiling.

Fan Gary Barlow Fan Club, PO Box 153, Stanmore, Middlesex, HA7 2UF, UK

Surf www.ndirect.co.uk/~ricarda.sallmann/garybarlow/

SYD BARRETT

WHO b. Roger Keith Barrett, 6 Jan 1946, Cambridge, England

WHAT Pink Floyd founder, Madcap genius

After Pink Floyd's debut *Piper At The Gates Of Dawn* (1967), their already eccentric leader became intolerably schizophrenic and after *A Saucerful Of Secrets* (1968), Barrett was replaced by Dave Gilmour. His debut solo album, *The Madcap Laughs* (1970), was produced by Gilmour and Floyd bassist Roger Waters. A second album, *Barrett* (1970), was released to mixed reviews.

The short-lived Stars, a group formed around Syd in 1971, lasted only two gigs before Barrett withdrew entirely from music. Events since then are mainly anecdotal: his appearance, bloated and bald, at sessions for Pink Floyd's Barrett tribute *Wish You Were Here* (1975), his reported donations of guitars and other valuables to strangers. *Beyond The Wildwood* (1987) featured Barrett covers by The Shamen among others. A collection of 70s out-takes, *Opel,* was released in 1988 and repackaged with both solo albums and bonus tracks for *Crazy*

Diamond (1993). Living in Cambridge with his family, Barrett reportedly spends his time painting. Despite his musical inactivity, interest in this legend remains undiminished.

(Read) *Crazy Diamond: Syd Barrett And The Dawn Of Pink Floyd* (1991), Mike Watkinson & Pete Anderson

(Fan) Chapter 24, 101 Amersham Road, Terriers, High Wycombe, Buckinghamshire, HP13 5AD, UK

(Surf) www.inkyfingers.com/TERRAPINS/Terrapins.html

BAUHAUS

WHO Vocals **Peter Murphy** (b. 11 Jul 1957, Northampton, England), guitar **Daniel Ash** (b. 31 Jul 1957, Northampton), bass **David Jay** (b. 24 Apr 1957, Northampton), drums **Kevin Haskins** (b. 19 Jul 1960, Northampton)

WHEN 1977–1984

WHERE Northampton, England

WHAT Gothic Punk innovators

Following the release of their debut 'Bela Lugosi's Dead' in 1979, Bauhaus recorded *In The Flat Field* (1980) and several singles for 4AD (including a version of T. Rex's 'Telegram Sam') before signing to Beggars Banquet. Their second album, *Mask* (1981), spawned minor hits, but their biggest success was a version of David Bowie's 'Ziggy Stardust' the following year. *The Sky's Gone Out* (1982) entered the UK charts at No.4 but, after the disappointing *Burning From The Inside* (1983), the band split. Ash, Jay and Haskins became Love & Rockets, whose short-lived Stateside success peaked with 'So Alive' (1989).

(Read) *Bauhaus* (1989), Bruna Zarini

(Surf) www.geocities.com/SunsetStrip/Palms/4349/index.html

THE BAY CITY ROLLERS ⊙ ⊙

WHO Vocals **Leslie McKeown** (b. 12 Nov 1955, Edinburgh, Scotland), guitar **Stuart 'Woody' Wood** (b. 25 Feb 1957, Edinburgh), guitar **Eric Faulkner** (b. 21 Oct 1955, Edinburgh), bass **Alan Longmuir** (b. 20 Jun 1953, Edinburgh), drums **Derek Longmuir** (b. 19 Mar 1955, Edinburgh)

WHEN 1967–

WHERE Edinburgh, Scotland

WHAT Top tartan teenyboppers

Named after a town in Utah, USA, Britain's top 70s teenybopper band in Britain first charted in 1971 with 'Keep On Dancing', which Pop entrepreneur Jonathan King produced and sang on. In 1974, the tartan-clad combo scored nine UK Top 10 hits including the No.1s 'Bye Bye Baby' and 'Give A Little Love'. As their career peaked in Europe, it took off in the USA: their six Top 10 hits included the chart-topping 'Saturday Night'. Despite this success, 'Rollermania' subsided and the "biggest British band since The Beatles" was relegated to the nostalgia circuit.

(Surf) www.baycityrollers.com/

THE BEACH BOYS ⊙ ⊙ ✪ ✪

WHO Vocals **Mike Love** (b. 15 Mar 1941, Los Angeles, California, USA), vocals/guitar **Carl Wilson** (b. 21 Dec 1946, Hawthorne, California, d. 6 Feb 1998), vocals/guitar **Al Jardine** (b. 3 Sep 1942, Lima, Ohio, USA), vocals/bass **Brian Wilson** (b. 20 Jun 1942, Hawthorne), vocals/bass **Bruce Johnston** (b. 27 Jun 1944, Peoria, Illinois, USA), vocals/drums **Dennis Wilson** (b. 4 Dec 1944, Hawthorne, d. 28 Dec 1983, Marina Del Rey, California)

WHEN 1961–

WHERE Hawthorne, California, USA

WHAT Unforgettable, inspirational Pop

Raised in the middle-class Hawthorne district of Los Angeles, Carl, Brian and Dennis Wilson were high school students when they formed a singing group. The brothers were skilled musicians and singers, the prodigiously talented Brian spending his spare time learning arranging and recording in a makeshift garage studio, trying to re-create the complex harmonies of his favourite group, The Four Freshmen. Carl and Dennis were more rebellious: Carl had been expelled from Hawthorne High and Dennis skipped school to spend days surfing. With their cousin Mike Love and Brian's friend Al Jardine, they formed a Freshmen-influenced singing quintet, The Pendletones, named after the type of surfer's shirt which they adopted as stage wear. After several local gigs and name changes – including Kenny & The Cadets (Brian was the aforementioned 'Kenny') and Carl & The Passions – Brian and Mike wrote 'Surfin'' at the suggestion of Dennis, the only genuine surfer Beach Boy. It was released to local success on the tiny Candix label in December 1961, by which time Jardine had been temporarily replaced by fellow Hawthorne teenager David Marks and the group was working under the name The Beach Boys, a name intended to cash in on the surfing fad.

There had been Surf groups before – The Surfaris and Dick Dale had soundtracked countless Californian beach parties – but The Beach Boys perfectly evoked the whirlwind of dating, surfing and hot-rodding that was the affluent teenager's life. Their blend of Dale's party spirit with impeccable Pop harmonies won them a contract with Capitol and national hits with 'Surfin' Safari' (No.14, 1962) and the Chuck Berry steal 'Surfin' USA' (No.3, 1963). Debut album *Surfin' USA* (1963) was a patchwork of standards and old songs by Brian and neighbour Gary Usher but, far from becoming a youth novelty, The Beach Boys moved in strange new directions, as Brian's aching ballad 'Surfer Girl' and his production on 1963's simultaneously released *Surfer Girl* and *Little Deuce Coupe* albums showed.

With the Wilsons' despotic failed songwriter father Murry as manager, The Beach Boys established themselves as the kings of all-American teen Pop with the pristine 'I Get Around', 'Fun Fun Fun' (1964), 'Help Me, Rhonda', 'California Girls' (1965) and their first truly accomplished album, 1964's *All Summer Long*. However, the pressure of constant touring – combined with Murry Wilson's over-ambitious management and bullying – pushed the already fragile Brian into a nervous breakdown. He fired Murry after a fight in 1964 and, following a panic attack on a plane to Texas, decided to retire from live performance,

"I wanted to write music that made other people feel good. Music that helps and heals, because I believe that music is God's voice"

Brian Wilson

BEACH BOYS-KING COLLECTION-RETNA

BRIAN WILSON-HENRY DILTZ-CORBIS

concentrating instead on writing and producing. Brian's replacement – after Glen Campbell's brief stint on tour – was former Bruce & Terry and Rip Chords member Bruce Johnston.

With Brian permanently installed in the studio, lyrics became deeper and the sound broader, taking the trademark close harmonies to complex extremes, as on 1965's Spector-influenced *The Beach Boys Today!* and *Summer Days (And Summer Nights!!)*. Obsessed with topping the sonic achievements of The Beatles' *Rubber Soul* (1965), he immersed himself in recording, experimenting with novel instrumentation – harpsichords, harmonicas, strings, brass, bells, Theremins, even Coca-Cola cans and plastic water bottles – and layered vocal overdubs. Mixing in mono (Brian was deaf in his left ear, so stereo was pointless), harmonies were constructed one voice at a time, stretching not only the primitive studio technology, but also the patience of Brian's sceptical bandmates, who were concerned about his indulgent behaviour and use of LSD. After months of painstaking work, Brian's masterpiece, *Pet Sounds* (1966), emerged: an intimate, dreamy Pop symphony of often contradictory moods, from the heartening 'Wouldn't It Be Nice' and 'Don't Talk (Put Your Head On My Shoulder)', through the ecstatic 'Let's Go Away For A While', 'God Only Knows' and 'Pet Sounds', the confusion of 'That's Not Me' and 'I Just Wasn't Made For These Times' to the despair of 'Caroline No', described by Bruce Johnston as "the death of a quality within him that was so vital… his innocence". Eclipsed by Dylan's *Blonde On Blonde* (1966) and The Beatles' epochal *Revolver* (1966), *Pet Sounds* sold comparatively weakly. Capitol – more interested in promoting lucrative 'best of' compilations – all but ignored the album, insisting on the inclusion of the throw-away 'Sloop John B' and crediting the single release of 'Caroline No' to Wilson alone.

A crestfallen Brian retreated to the studio, working with Van Dyke Parks. *Dumb Angel* (later titled *Smile*) was even more ambitious than its predecessor, with full orchestral arrangements, Theremin solos and a grandiose 'elements suite', which – for the 'Fire' movement – saw the orchestra in firemen's helmets. However, a spate of blazes around Los Angeles, one of them near the studio during the recording of 'Fire', prompted a paranoid Brian to shelve the whole *Smile* project. Legend has it that the tapes of 'Fire' are stored in a fireproof vault, but other *Smile* recordings, such as the Wilson/Parks composition 'Heroes And Villains', surfaced on later Beach Boys albums, including *Smiley Smile* (1967) and *Surf's Up* (1971). The lost potential of *Smile* could be glimpsed in the track Brian spent six months and $16,000 recording in 1966. Released late that year, 'Good Vibrations' – a Psychedelic, Theremin-driven "pocket symphony" – stormed to the top of the US and UK charts, vindicating Brian's efforts, but not convincing the band that his increasingly odd working practices – like writing on a piano in a sandpit for that 'beach vibe'– were anything other than the first signs of madness.

Increasingly un-hip to the burgeoning hippie scene – despite Carl's draft-dodging and Dennis' brief friendship with psycho-killer Charles Manson and family – *Wild Honey*, *Friends* (both 1968), *20/20* (1969) and *Sunflower* (1970), despite flashes of greatness, did little to halt the group's sales decline. With

Brian sidelined, the others took over the bulk of the writing, but Charles Manson's 'Cease To Exist' (re-titled 'Never Learn Not To Love') was regrettably included on *20/20*, along with Brian's *Smile* out-take 'Cabinessence', a weak echo of a genius now a deluded recluse in his Bel Air mansion.

Acceptance into the Rock world came via a move to the Reprise label (home of Neil Young) after 20 albums on Capitol, the formation of their own Brother Records in 1969, a 1970 live jam with The Grateful Dead at New York's Fillmore East and 1971's ironically titled *Surf's Up*, whose melancholic mood and forward-looking environmental messages summed up the fall-out of the hippie movement. Johnston's departure after *Surf's Up* prompted the formation of a new live band, including keyboardist Daryl Dragon, guitarist/bassist/vocalist Blondie Chaplin and drummer Ricky Fataar. Under the direction of new manager (and lyricist) Jack Rieley, the group's reputation as a live act grew, even if audiences preferred older classics to newer material, as the success of later compilations *Endless Summer* (1974) and *Spirit Of America* (1975) proved. Surf throwback *Carl And The Passions* (1972) and the ecological *Holland* (1973) were punctuated by nostalgia-tinged concert tours and repeated attempts to coax Brian back into the studio. Now an overweight exile from every-day life, he spent much of the 70s in a paranoid haze, although *15 Big Ones* (1976) and *The Beach Boys Love You* (1977) saw a short-lived rehabilitation.

Financial difficulties – caused mainly by Murry Wilson's sale of Brian's songs in 1969 and the embezzlement of over $1 million of the group's money by Love's brother Steve – aggravated internal rifts, although Johnston returned for 1979's *L.A. (Light Album)*, their debut for the Caribou label (1978's *M.I.U.* album having been their Brother swan song). While the group's fortunes improved with successful nostalgia tours in the 80s, the soap opera continued with Carl's 1981 departure (he returned a year later) and Brian's psychiatric treatment under the controversial Dr Eugene Landy. Dennis Wilson's death by drowning in 1983 seemed to mark the end, symbolizing the wasted potential of a group who once threatened The Beatles as the greatest group of the 60s. However, Brian's sporadic returns to the group and his 1988 solo album *Brian Wilson* pointed to a renaissance, as did The Beach Boys' collaboration with Rappers The Fat Boys on 1987's 'Wipe Out' and the 1988 US No.1 'Kokomo', from Tom Cruise movie *Cocktail*. The arguments continued, however, with lawsuits between Mike Love and Brian (royalties claims and counter-claims and defamation in Brian's Landy-influenced 1991 autobiography *Wouldn't It Be Nice?*), Sire's refusal to release Brian's *Sweet Insanity* and a restraining order preventing Landy contacting his bewildered client.

Brian, however, seemed to weather the storm, watching daughters Carnie and Wendy climb the charts as part of singing group Wilson Phillips, and collaborating with producer Don Was on 1995's collection of reworkings and archive material *I Just Wasn't Made For These Times*. He also worked with Van Dyke Parks on *Orange Crate Art* (1995) and High Llama Sean O'Hagan on 1998's *Imagination*. Carl's death from cancer in 1998 dealt a heavy blow, but The Beach Boys have already proved the group to be bigger than any individual member.

Read *The Nearest Faraway Place* (1996), Timothy White

Fan Beach Boys Fan Club, Mail Stop 504, 252 Convention Center Drive, Las Vegas, NV 89109, USA

surf www.mindspring.com/~sfrazier/bbfc.htm

BEASTIE BOYS:TONY MOTT:SIN

BEASTIE BOYS ✪ ✪

WHO Vocals/bass **MCA** (b. Adam Yauch, 15 Aug 1967, Brooklyn, New York, USA), vocals/drums **Mike D** (b. Michael Diamond, 20 Nov 1965, New York City), vocals/guitar **Ad-Rock** (b. Adam Horowitz, 31 Oct 1966, New York City)

WHEN 1981–

WHERE New York City, New York, USA

WHAT Hardcore Punks turned funky Hip Hop kings

Formed for Yauch's 14th birthday party, the original Beasties – responsible for the 'Pollywog Stew' EP – included Kate Schellenbach (now of Luscious Jackson) and John Berry in 1982. They were replaced by Horowitz, with whom the Beasties signed to Def Jam. There they persuaded label boss Rick Rubin to sign LL Cool J, then took Rap to the top of the US chart with *Licensed To Ill* (1986). Fulfilling the promise of early singles like 'Rock Hard' (1984), the album fused Hip Hop beats with Heavy Metal riffs, epitomized by the hit 'Fight For Your Right To Party' (in turn fuelling their boisterous live shows). However, *Paul's Boutique* (1989), though well reviewed, sent them into a commercial tailspin. It was ended only by the 'alternative' generation's embracing of *Check Your Head* (1992), a recovery continued by *Ill Communication* (1994). Latterly, the Beasties have become renowned for their outside interests, including Diamond's ever-expanding Grand Royal empire (label, magazine, clothes) and Yauch's campaigning for human rights in Tibet. Fans had to make do with spurious releases like instrumental collection *The In Sound From Way Out* (1996) and 1994's self-explanatory retrospective *Some Old Bullshit*.

surf www.grandroyal.com/BeastieBoys/

THE BEATLES

◉◉◉◉◉◉◉◉◉◉◉◉◉◉◉◉☆☆
☆☆☆☆☆☆☆☆☆☆☆☆☆☆☆☆

WHO Vocals/guitar **John Lennon** (b. 9 Oct 1940, Liverpool, England, d. 8 Dec 1980, New York City, New York, USA), vocals/bass **Paul McCartney** (b. 18 Jun 1942, Liverpool), vocals/guitar **George Harrison** (b. 24 Feb 1943, Liverpool), drums/vocals **Ringo Starr** (b. Richard Starkey, 7 Jul 1940, Liverpool)

WHEN 1958–1970

WHERE Liverpool, England

WHAT The most popular and influential Pop group of all time

The rise of The Beatles in 1963 was the most spectacular event in popular music since the birth of Rock 'n' Roll a decade before. Within a year they achieved two feats previously deemed impossible: surpassing the fame and success of Rock's premier idol Elvis Presley, and thrusting British Pop to worldwide attention. In the seven years between their first chart-toppers and their split in 1970, The Beatles changed the course of Pop and Rock, leaving a body of work rarely rivalled for quality, originality and – as subsequent generations discovered – durability. Their influence on 60s culture was incalculable and passing decades have seen their legacy undiminished, continuing to inspire musicians of every genre.

The starting point of this 20th-century legend was 6 July 1957: the day teenagers John and Paul met at a church fête near their Liverpool homes. Performing that day were Lennon's skiffle band The Quarry Men, who impressed aspiring Rock 'n' Roller McCartney. Introduced by a mutual friend, the pair struck up a relationship and Paul was invited to join the band. As members

came and went, the Quarry Men solidified around these two, who in 1958 recruited Paul's schoolfriend George. They recorded a demo of Buddy Holly's 'That'll Be The Day', and played local dancehalls, parties and talent contests. After a spell as Johnny & The Moondogs, they went through a string of names (including The Nerk Twins and Long John Silver and The Beetles) before becoming The Silver Beetles, soon refined to The Beatles. Stuart Sutcliffe (b. 23 Jun 1940, Edinburgh, Scotland), Lennon's friend from Liverpool Art College, joined on bass and, in August 1960, they took on drummer Pete Best (b. 24 Nov 1941, Madras, India) in time for their first nightclub bookings in Hamburg, Germany. With a repertoire of American R&B, Rock standards and occasional MOR ballads, they survived a gruelling regime of several sets per night before tough audiences. They returned to Liverpool a tight, dynamic Rock 'n' Roll band.

More stints followed in Hamburg, where they also backed singer Tony Sheridan on German single 'My Bonnie'. When Sutcliffe decided to remain with his girlfriend in Hamburg, (he died there of a brain haemorrhage some two years later on 10 April 1962), Paul switched to bass. Back in Liverpool, a residency at the Cavern Club began to build The Beatles' following, hinting at the mayhem to come. Their growing fame was noticed by young businessman Brian Epstein, owner of a record shop near the Cavern, who became their manager. He persuaded them to smarten up their stage appearance, yet they kept the trademark 'Beatle haircuts' invented by student friends in Hamburg.

Epstein tried to interest London record companies in the band but found the going hard, The Beatles' reputation being strictly confined to Liverpool. Teeming with beat groups, the Liverpool circuit was intensely competitive. Most acts played the same material; so, to gain the edge on rivals, The Beatles covered obscure American B-sides and attempted original material. Key influences included Chuck Berry, Little Richard, The Everly

Brothers and Atlantic and Motown artists. Blending imported Soul and Rock with the city's fondness for Country & Western and Folk music, a recognizable Liverpool style emerged, dubbed 'Merseybeat': more raw than star acts like Cliff Richard and The Shadows, specializing in melodic songs driven by rhythm guitars.

On New Year's Day 1962 the group auditioned in London for Decca, a leading label of the day. They were turned down, but Epstein secured another trial with EMI label Parlophone. Staff producer George Martin (whose biggest credits included novelty records by Peter Sellers and The Goons) was impressed by The Beatles' energy and versatility – though not by their songwriting – and signed them. Before their first official session in London, the group and Epstein sacked Best: the drummer had grown detached from the others (and they resented his popularity with fans), while Martin had reservations about his ability. Best's replacement was another Liverpudlian, Ringo Starr, well-known to The Beatles for his work in local band Rory Storm & The Hurricanes. They arrived at EMI's London studios in Abbey Road in September 1962. Martin supplied them with 'How Do You Do It', but reluctantly let them try a Lennon/McCartney composition, 'Love Me Do'. Ironically, Starr's drumming, too, was not thought up to scratch and Martin used session man Alan White. Older and more refined, Martin seemed an odd match for four Northern scruffs, but was very open to new ideas. Over the next seven years he proved the greatest collaborator The Beatles could have hoped for – a skilled arranger who interpreted their untrained musical notions and pushed technology to new heights. With much justice he became known as 'the fifth Beatle'.

Debut 'Love Me Do' proved a modest but encouraging success, reaching UK No.17. Martin acknowledged the strength of John and Paul's songwriting partnership, choosing another original, 'Please Please Me', for the follow-up. With TV and radio exposure, the group's name spread across Britain and, in January 1963, 'Please Please Me' reached No.2. Events acquired growing momentum: nationwide concerts attracted sell-out crowds and,

in May, the band scored its first No.1, 'From Me To You', and released debut *Please Please Me*. Featuring the two singles and their B-sides (the remaining ten tracks were cut in a single day), the album galvanized the UK Pop industry. While it drew heavily on cover versions, which formed most of their early repertoire, resonant new tunes such as 'I Saw Her Standing There' and 'Do You Want To Know A Secret' shattered the assumption that only America could produce classic Pop. In The Beatles' wake came an army of Liverpool acts – many managed by Epstein – including Gerry & The Pacemakers, Cilla Black, The Searchers and The Fourmost. Meanwhile, up and down the country, groups formed as a result of The Beatles' example and, having coined the word 'Beatlemania', the British media fell in love. People of all ages were enchanted by their appearance and witty, cheeky image.

A new single, 'She Loves You', and LP *With The Beatles* (1963) sealed the band's status. They were 'the Fab Four' and a national obsession. The album was a powerful package of memorable Lennon/McCartney songs ('All My Loving' and 'I Wanna Be Your Man') and vibrant R&B covers ('Money', 'Please Mister Postman' and 'You Really Got A Hold On Me'). Its sleeve – a black-and-white portrait of the band in half-darkness – became a defining image of its era. London-based R&B group The Rolling Stones secured their first Top 20 hit with a version of 'I Wanna Be Your Man' and were soon The Beatles' nearest rivals on the British music scene. But the 'mop-tops' seemed unassailable, with the next single – 'I Want To Hold Your Hand' – their most epic and inventive yet and, crucially, the first to break big in America. In February 1964 Beatlemania came to the States: the group played live dates to now-familiar hysteria and made an historic appearance on the Ed Sullivan TV show. Wherever they went, The Beatles seized the popular imagination. Teenage girls were reduced to shrieking fits and tearful declarations of love; boys were moved to imitate the group's image and, often, to become musicians themselves. At a time of rapid social change, The Beatles became the epicentre of the youth movement, part of a

"I can knock The Beatles, but don't let Mick Jagger knock them"

John

wider revolt against formal conventions. It is speculated that America embraced the group in reaction to the trauma of President Kennedy's recent assassination, while in Britain their lowly origins and provincial accents were hailed as harbingers of a less rigid, more classless society. Onlookers soon began to distinguish between the four contrasting, yet complementary, personalities. John, though married to his art-school girlfriend Cynthia (mother of their son Julian), was believed the most rebellious: sharp-tongued to the point of cruelty, the natural leader. Paul was the group's chief heart-throb and its most diplomatic member, a talented songwriter, bass player and vocalist whose tuneful instincts countered Lennon's aggression. George was admired as a guitarist (though his vocal and songwriting talents were necessarily overshadowed) and for his dry, enigmatic wit. Ringo, underrated as a drummer, assumed the role of group clown, admirably down-to-earth even in a

"The Beatles can't save the world. We'll be lucky if we can even save ourselves"

George

group renowned for its common touch. These impressions were fostered in the spring of 1964, when the group teamed up with director Richard Lester for the movie *A Hard Day's Night*, a semi-fictional portrait of the band on tour in Britain. Applauded for the charm and freshness of The Beatles' performances, the film is unpretentious yet stylish, a gem of Rock cinema. Its soundtrack, entirely self-composed, contained two chart-topping singles – the title track and 'Can't Buy Me Love' – as well as McCartney's plangent 'And I Love Her' and 'Things We Said Today'.

Ceaseless overseas work, meanwhile, turned Beatlemania into a worldwide phenomenon. Western Europe, Australia and the Far East were visited and duly conquered. After 'I Feel Fine', yet another album – *Beatles For Sale* (1964) – testified to their amazing work-rate but, apart from 'Eight Days A Week', hinted at fatigue. By early 1965 they were filming again with Richard Lester and casually knocking off their seventh UK No.1, 'Ticket To Ride'. The movie *Help!*, though a box-office triumph, lacked the

sharpness of its predecessor, relying on slapstick routines in exotic locations and a lightweight comic plot. In its title song, Lennon issued a coded cry of distress, at last succumbing to his fame and anxiety. The *Help!* album (1965) also offered the gently orchestrated 'Yesterday', often considered the pinnacle of McCartney's songwriting. The band were honoured by Britain's establishment and awarded MBE medals by the Queen at a ceremony in Buckingham Palace (John later returned his as an anti-establishment gesture). In August, their second US tour included record-breaking shows at New York's giant Shea Stadium – events on a scale then unknown in Pop. Astonishingly, there was no pause in The Beatles' output – they finished the

"It's like if you've been an astronaut and you've been to the moon. What do you do with the rest of your life?"

Paul

year with double A-side 'Day Tripper'/'We Can Work It Out' and *Rubber Soul*. The latter marks a turning point in their work, and the start of a new phase in the Lennon/McCartney partnership. John, in particular, was smitten by the poetic word-play of Bob Dylan (who had also introduced the group to marijuana). To his 'Nowhere Man', 'Girl' and 'Norwegian Wood', he brought a distinctly un-Fab emotional complexity. A gift for words and yearning for self-revelation were Lennon's specialties; McCartney had stronger melodic flair and a penchant for romantic sweetness, as evidenced on 'Michelle'. John could be a plaintive balladeer ('In My Life') and Paul a frantic rocker ('I'm Down'), but the divergence in styles became more apparent. As time wore on they were less apt to collaborate, though their songs retained a joint credit, preferring to consult after writing separately. George, meanwhile, had fallen under the spell of Eastern music while filming *Help!* and startled the Pop world by adorning 'Norwegian

"None of us quite grasped what it was all about. It was washing over our heads like a huge tidal wave"

Ringo

'She Said She Said' and unprecedented strangeness to the unfathomable finale 'Tomorrow Never Knows'. Tape loops, backward tracking, treated vocals and distortion were, if not pioneered, popularized by *Revolver*.

In November 1966, Lennon met Japanese artist Yoko Ono, a minor star of New York's underground scene. Her influence on him, his increasing use of drugs, and deepening distaste for suburban life with wife Cynthia fed a sense of isolation which informed his next composition, 'Strawberry Fields Forever'. Coupled with McCartney's own memoir of Liverpool childhood, the upbeat 'Penny Lane', this double A-side may be The Beatles' greatest 45, but in Britain it was, embarrassingly, denied a No.1 position by Engelbert Humperdinck's 'Release Me'. Undeterred, the band spent early 1967 in EMI's studios crafting the definitive icon of the 'Summer of Love': *Sgt. Pepper's Lonely Hearts Club Band*. Sleeved in a lavish Pop Art design (printing the lyrics was another novelty), it was a psychedelic extravaganza. Though its bizarre departures bewildered many fans, it elevated the group to global figureheads for an emerging hippie counter-culture. Conceived by Paul as a make-believe concert by a fictional music hall act, the album has an illusion of unity, thanks to the curtain-raising title track and its reprise towards the end. Listeners were struck by its extraordinary wholeness, assisted by a running order that merged some tracks into the next, and by the satisfying range of feelings expressed in the songs. The Beatles acquired an almost mystical edge as fans rushed to infer secret meanings in the music. As usual, Lennon supplied the most vivid imagery: his 'Lucy In The Sky With Diamonds' was read as an acid-inspired odyssey. 'Being For The Benefit Of Mr Kite', however, was taken straight from a vintage circus poster, and 'Good Morning Good Morning' reflected his bored withdrawal. Ringo was given a characteristic little-guy role in 'A Little Help From My Friends', while George pursued his Oriental muse in the philosophical 'Within You Without You'. Paul deployed his gift for melody in 'She's Leaving Home', 'Lovely Rita' and 'When I'm 64'. But *Sgt. Pepper's* most astounding moment is its finale, 'A Day In The Life', which married Lennon's drifting melancholy and McCartney's uptempo interlude to orchestral drama.

As highbrow pundits acclaimed *Sgt. Pepper* as a milestone in Western cultural history, the group reinforced their symbolic position through a worldwide satellite broadcast, unveiling universal anthem 'All You Need Is Love'. Having transformed their personal appearance – moustaches, beards, robes and beads replaced the smart suits of yesteryear – they proclaimed a radically different sensibility too, advocating transcendental meditation and, less overtly, mind-altering chemicals as a path to spiritual enlightenment. But on 27 August 1967 they suffered a terrible setback – Epstein was discovered dead in his London flat, victim of an apparent overdose. Without their manager and the solidarity of their touring years, the group began to lose its cohesion, a malady evident in their ill-defined TV movie *Magical Mystery Tour*, dominated by Paul in the face of band apathy. Its screening on Boxing Day 1967 brought general criticism of the whimsical, unfocused plot, but the attendant tracks were often superb, notably Lennon's 'I Am The Walrus' and McCartney's 'Fool On The Hill'. After an Indian sojourn with their guru, the Maharishi, The Beatles unveiled their new company Apple, an idealistic exercise in hippie capitalism (with tax advantages) and launched the label with the landmark 'Hey Jude'/'Revolution'. By summer 1968, John and Yoko had become a public item, and Paul had taken up with American photographer Linda Eastman,

Wood' with a double-tracked sitar. The group explored the possibilities of the studio and transcended the conventions of Pop lyricism, ambitions realized in June 1966 single 'Paperback Writer'/'Rain'. They despaired of live work, the pandemonium making a mockery of their musicianship. Tours were even life-threatening: John incurred the wrath of religious Americans after claiming The Beatles were more popular than Jesus; there was another hair-raising confrontation with anti-Beatle elements in the Philippines. On 29 August 1966, in Candlestick Park, San Francisco, they played the last public gig of their career.

Often regarded as their finest album, *Revolver* (1966) rides this artistic restlessness to dazzling effect. Innovative and bold, it confirmed The Beatles' evolution from tuneful Merseybeat to experimental Rock. Like previous albums, it was squeezed into a tight itinerary of tour dates and promotional duties, yet the group and Martin worked obsessively at finding new sonic textures. In parallel with Brian Wilson, constructing The Beach Boys' epic *Pet Sounds* in Los Angeles (spurred on by *Rubber Soul*), the team used the studio as a medium in its own right, not merely as a way to replicate the band's live sound. Even Ringo's kindergarten shanty showcase 'Yellow Submarine' boasted daring audio trickery. Paul used quasi-classical strings in 'Eleanor Rigby' and pushed his writing to a new level of sophistication with 'Here, There And Everywhere'. John, above all, abolished any vestiges of mop-toppery. Newly converted to 'psychedelic' drug LSD, he brought overpowering tension to the hallucinogenic

undermining the men's professional partnership even further. Another film, the animated fantasy *Yellow Submarine*, was a critical success, but The Beatles' involvement was minimal.

Creative rifts were apparent in their next album, *The Beatles* (1968), commonly called 'the White Album' after its plain, anti-*Pepper* sleeve. The record found all four members on superb form, although it is often considered more the work of solo artists than true collaborators. John contributed songs such as 'Happiness Is A Warm Gun', 'Sexy Sadie' and the avant-garde discord of 'Revolution 9'; Paul's classics included 'Back In The USSR' and 'Helter Skelter'; George excelled on 'While My Guitar Gently Weeps' and Ringo closed proceedings singing Lennon's lullaby 'Good Night'. Hatching an unfulfilled plan to play low-key live dates, they rehearsed new and old material in front of film cameras for the movie which became *Let It Be*. Its highlight – a session on the Apple roof in Saville Row – spawned the 1969 single 'Get Back', featuring American Soul artist Billy Preston, a Beatle pal from Hamburg days who played electric piano and organ on several of the band's final sessions. But the movie ultimately documented a group beset by bickering and soured friendships. Both John and Paul got married in March of that year, the former's adventures (including a honeymoon 'bed-in' with Yoko, for world peace) becoming the subject of new single 'The Ballad Of John And Yoko'. The appointment of New Yorker and Rolling Stones manager Allen Klein as the band's business manager, despite Paul's opposition, made tensions worse.

With their future in doubt, the band reconvened with Martin at EMI's studios to produce a magnificent swan song – *Abbey Road* (1969) – which found The Beatles at a creative peak. George contributed his best songs, 'Something' and 'Here Comes The Sun', John supplied 'Come Together' and the band gelled memorably in the grand medley incorporating Paul's 'Golden Slumbers'. But this was the last music they made as a four-piece. John had already commenced his solo career: after experimental records with Yoko Ono, he formed the ad-hoc Plastic Ono Band, releasing 'Give Peace A Chance', 'Cold Turkey' and 'Instant Karma!'. Paul, too, began work on a solo debut, *McCartney* (1970), and announced, in April 1970, that he was leaving The Beatles, scotching Lennon's plan to initiate the break-up himself. Paul's disaffection had been deepened by the decision – again, against his wishes – to let Phil Spector produce and overdub the *Let It Be* tapes. When the album and movie of that name appeared in May 1970, the group no longer existed.

The new decade saw each ex-Beatle build a solo career, while their financial and legal affairs were fought over in protracted and bitter court cases. Hopes for a reunion, nurtured by fans worldwide, were dashed when Lennon was murdered outside his New York apartment on 8 December 1980. Apple and EMI continued to oversee The Beatles' catalogue: a programme of reissues and compilations culminated, in 1987, in a hugely successful series of CDs. Especially welcomed by collectors was *Live At The BBC* (1994), a compilation of the band's radio sessions from 1962–1965. But the most unexpected sequel was still to come. In 1994, while Apple prepared a documentary TV/video series on The Beatles' story, and George Martin supervised three compilations of unreleased tracks and alternate versions – issued between 1995 and 1996 as *The Beatles Anthology* – the surviving members returned to the studio with producer Jeff Lynne to make the first 'new' Beatle records since 1970. Built on late 70s demos by Lennon, the singles 'Free As A Bird' (originally recorded in 1977) and 'Real Love' (1979) merged his voice with

vocal and instrumental additions by his ex-colleagues. The project prompted mixed feelings: in spite of Yoko's blessing, many felt Lennon would not have approved, and wondered if either song was strong enough to join The Beatles' canon. Others were simply happy to hear the band reunited at all, even in this artificial form. The *Anthology* issues, all warmly received, introduced listeners to Beatle music from first demo 'That'll Be The Day' to final sessions. While confirming the impression given by numerous bootlegs down the years (namely that The Beatles had released almost all their worthwhile songs and had no classics in reserve), the tracks threw light on the band's creative process. In 1996 – as their influence was acknowledged by a new generation of Britpop bands, notably Oasis – The Beatles, once again, became the biggest-earning act in the world.

READ *The Complete Beatles Chronicle* (1992), Mark Lewisohn

FAN London Beatles Fan Club, 4 Oaklands, Constance Road, Whitton, Twickenham, Middlesex, TW2 7JQ, UK

SURF www.lbfc.demon.co.uk/

THE BEAUTIFUL SOUTH ◉ ◉

WHO Vocals **Paul Heaton** (b. 9 May 1962, Birkenhead, Merseyside, England), vocals **Dave Hemingway** (b. 20 Sep 1960, Hull, East Yorkshire, England), vocals **Jacqueline Abbott** (b. 10 Nov 1973, Merseyside), guitar **Dave Rotheray** (b. 9 Feb 1963, Hull), bass **Sean Welch** (b. 12 Apr 1965, Enfield, England), drums **Dave Stead** (b. 15 Oct 1966, Huddersfield, West Yorkshire, England)

WHEN 1989–

WHERE Hull, East Yorkshire, England

WHAT Sweet sounds, harsh words

Formed from the ashes of The Housemartins, Heaton and Hemingway (abandoning drums for vocals) began writing with Rotheray in the late 80s. The original five males recorded hit debut *Welcome To The Beautiful South* (1989, UK No.2), after which guest vocalist Briana Corrigan joined full-time. 'Song For Whoever' and 'You Keep It All In' both made the UK Top 10. Follow-up *Choke* (1990) reached UK No.2 and yielded UK No.1 'A Little Time'. By 1992 the band had banished the ghost of The Housemartins and become household names. *0898* (1992) cemented this position and, as they approached arena-status, they encountered their first problems. Corrigan objected to later lyrics and left. For *Miaow* (1994), Heaton recruited the untried Jacqueline Abbott, who went from a shop assistant to Top 10 star overnight when she provided lead vocals for a cover of Nilsson's 'Everybody's Talkin'' (1994). In 1995, the band scored a UK No.1 with *Carry On Up The Charts – The Best Of The Beautiful South* (1995), of which it was estimated that, within a year, one in seven UK households owned a copy. They managed another UK No.1, *Blue Is The Colour*, in 1996. More UK Top 20 singles – 'Rotterdam (Or Anywhere)' and 'Don't Marry Her' – and an appearance on *Later With Jools Holland* (1997), released on video, ensured the success continued.

SURF www.aber.ac.uk/^rrj5/tbs/bss.html

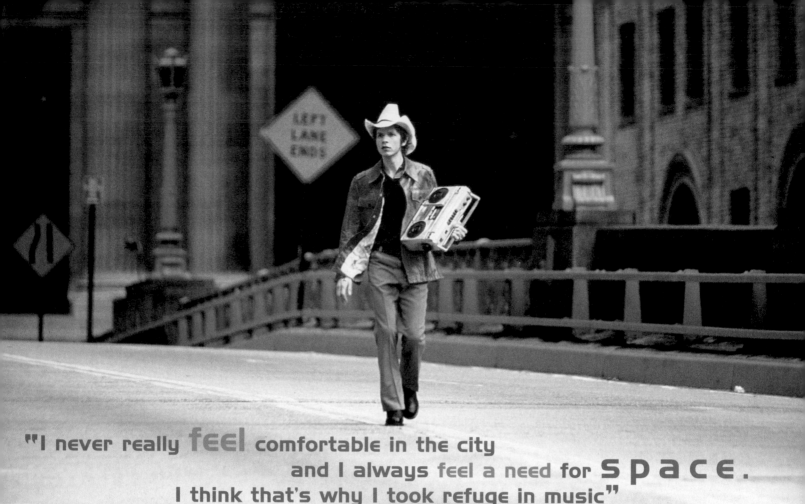

"I never really **feel** comfortable in the city and I always feel a need for **space**. I think that's why I took refuge in music"

BECK

WHO b. Beck David Campbell, 8 Jul 1970, Los Angeles, California, USA

WHAT The Hong Kong Phooey of Hip Hop Folk

Fresh of face but vintage of voice, Beck Hansen's Folk-flavoured Rap crowned him king of post-Grunge 'slacker' Rock. Son of Bluegrass musician David Campbell and Andy Warhol starlet Bibbe Hansen, Beck was raised on American Folk and Blues but, during a spell in New York, immersed himself in Hip Hop. Back in LA, he became known for impromptu performances at local parties and experimented with producer Karl Stephenson for what became debut album *Mellow Gold* (1994), released by Geffen after Beck hit the big time with 'Loser'. Initially released on microscopic Indie Bongload Records in summer 1993, the song attained anthem status after Sonic Youth's Thurston Moore bestowed his Grunge guru blessing upon Beck on MTV's *120 Minutes*. A clause in his Geffen contract allowed Beck to record for other labels, hence the cool but under-bought *Stereopathic Soul Manure* – an anthology of early recordings – and *One Foot In The Grave* (both 1994). Mainstream success came with Noel Gallagher-remixed 'Devil's Haircut' and *Odelay* (1996). His jumble of styles (Woody Guthrie mugged by Run DMC and Gary Numan) and stream-of-consciousness lyrics were given punch by Beastie Boy producers The Dust Brothers. Hits ranged from the Rap rockin' 'Where It's At' to the pastoral, Dylan-sampling 'Jack-Ass'. Beck enlivened many a festival, particularly 1997's Glastonbury, where he added sparkle to the dreary mudbath. Johnny Cash covered his 'Rowboat' in 1996 and a mooted collaboration with Gangsta Rapper Snoop Doggy Dogg confirmed even wimpy white boys can have the Funk.

surf www.geffen.com.beck

JEFF BECK

WHO b. 24 Jun 1944, Wallington, Surrey, England

WHAT The guitarists' guitarist

While contemporaries Jimmy Page and Eric Clapton twinned excellence with excess, Beck quietly assembled a star-studded CV. Having replaced Clapton in the Yardbirds in 1965, he bailed out a year later and made the UK Top 20 with 1967's perennial singalong 'Hi-Ho Silver Lining' and 1969 Donovan collaboration 'Goo Goo Barabajagal (Love Is Hot)'. Thereafter, he concentrated on albums: the Rod Stewart-fronted *Truth* (1968) and *Beck-Ola* (1969), *Rough And Ready* (1971), *Jeff Beck Group* (1972), *Beck, Bogert And Appice* (1973), *Beck, Bogert And Appice Live In Japan* (1973), *Blow By Blow* (1975), *Wired* (1976), *Jeff Beck With The Jan Hammer Group Live* (1977), *There And Back* (1980) and *Flash* (1985). His profile rose courtesy of 1985 US hits with Rod Stewart ('People Get Ready') and Robert Plant's pet project The Honeydrippers ('Rockin' At Midnight'), but returned to cult status with *Jeff Beck's Guitar Shop* (1989), the retrospective *Beckology* (1991), *Frankie's House* (1992) and *Crazy Legs* (1993). His work has encompassed R&B, Psychedelia, Jazz Rock, Rock 'n' Roll and, on a 1986 evisceration of The Troggs' 'Wild Thing', proto-Industrial Heavy Metal – influencing guitarists from Duane Allman to Guns N' Roses' Slash. His career-long guest guitarist sideline stretches from Screamin' Lord Sutch to Kate Bush, while his maverick nature is confirmed by declined invitations to join The Rolling Stones, Pink Floyd and Whitesnake. As he said in 1993, "I'm an awkward son of a bitch when it comes to doing the expected".

read *Guitar Legends* (1995), Chris Gill

surf www.wsvn.com/~staff/beck/

BEE GEES ⊙ ✪ ✪ ✪

WHO Vocals/guitar **Barry Gibb** (b. 1 Sep 1947, Douglas, Isle of Man), vocals/keyboards/bass/guitar **Maurice Gibb** (b. 22 Dec 1949, Douglas), vocals **Robin Gibb** (b. 22 Dec 1949, Douglas)

WHEN 1955–

WHERE Manchester, England

WHAT Velvet-voiced superstar songwriters

The Bee Gees' success demands respect, but because of their image and reliance on radio-friendly Pop, many critics have been unable, or unwilling, to view the act as anything more than clever tunesmiths. Sons of an orchestra leader and singer, the Gibb brothers were singing live in a Manchester cinema when twins Robin and Maurice were only five. The family moved to Australia and by 1962 the boys had a track record of radio, TV, recordings and dates supporting acts like Chubby Checker. Their name, The Bee Gees, was commonly believed to be shorthand for 'Brothers Gibb', but in-depth histories say it came from Bill Good and Bill Gates, two figures instrumental in promoting the act.

By 1966 they were writing their own material and had several Australian hits. Barry's 'Spicks And Specks' was No.1 in Australia when they decided to relocate to England and sign with manager Robert Stigwood and Polydor Records. Although lacking in street cred, their clear diction, classic Pop structures, mellowness and narrative lyrics endeared them to radio producers. Other than pirate stations with poor reception, most of the UK was reliant on BBC radio, and in America, mainstream music still held sway. Many radio producers were afraid of the increasing experimentation of bands like The Beatles. The Bee Gees, harking back to the old and safe method, got played in heavy rotation. In three years they racked up Top 20 hits worldwide, including two UK No.1s with 'Massachusetts' (1967) and 'I've Got To Get A Message To You' (1968). Seasoned performers, they courted the emerging counter-culture with off-beat stories in their lyrics (their second UK chart-topper dealt with the last wish of a condemned man) and their skilfull songwriting soon gained respect. 'To Love Somebody' – still a radio favourite – was the result of Otis Redding seeking out 19-year-old Barry as a writer. By 1970, Janis Joplin, Frank Sinatra, Elvis, Nina Simone and Engelbert Humperdinck had covered Bee Gee songs.

The hits kept coming while the band paid a heavy price. Robin was hospitalized twice – once with nervous exhaustion. Rows and Rock 'n' Roll living raged through their tours. By 1969 Robin was a solo act, Barry had flirted with an acting career and Maurice had married the singer Lulu and was working on solo material. 'How Can You Mend A Broken Heart?' (1971) saw the return of Robin and a US No.1 but, in general, chart positions

were lower and only steady touring kept the band afloat. By 1974 they were suffering variety club dates and the indignity of a rejected album, *A Kick In The Pants Is Worth Eight In The Head*.

Facing oblivion, they dropped 'The' from their name (a small change which seemed to have a large effect, judging from subsequent events) and began work with producer Arif Mardin. Nobody could have expected the impact these sessions would have on the band, and Pop in general. The Mardin/Bee Gees collaboration *Main Course* (1975) featured 'Jive Talkin', returning them to US No.1. Mardin engineered a spookily compressed vocal harmony over a lightweight Disco backing and forced Barry's little-known falsetto to the fore. The band contributed

"We're so **overground, we're underground**"

Barry Gibb

important new ideas, honing a hit formula that still works today: cutting lyrics to fit repetitive melody lines, placing a central idea into the song and using steady and slightly surprising chord progressions. This formula would make them the predominant international act over the next three years. 'You Should Be Dancin'' hit US No.1 in 1976 ahead of their contribution to the best-selling album until *Thriller* and best-selling film soundtrack ever – *Saturday Night Fever* (1977). The album sold over 30 million – topping UK and US charts – and, by early 1978, Bee Gees' stranglehold on US charts matched the 60s achievements of The Beatles. 'How Deep Is Your Love?' 'Stayin' Alive' and 'Night Fever' all hit No.1, the latter also topping the UK chart. With others – like little brother Andy Gibb – taking their songs to US No.1 between the trio's chart-toppers, their dominance was awesome. During one week, Andy held No.1, 'Night Fever' was No.2 and Gibb-written-and-produced 'Emotion', sung by Samantha Sang, held No.3. Even knowledgeable critics swore that Sang didn't exist and was, in fact, Bee Gees in disguise! In 1978, Barry spent 25 weeks at US No.1 as writer or co-writer.

In 1979, 'Too Much Heaven', 'Tragedy' and 'Love You Inside Out' topped US charts – making six consecutive No.1 singles. 'Tragedy' hit UK No.1 and *Spirits Having Flown* topped charts worldwide, including the US and UK. In 1980, the compilation *Greatest* gave them their third consecutive US No.1 album.

It couldn't last. An insular act for many years, the band didn't fully realize what they'd achieved, and their insight into corners of their market was poor. Proof of the band's lack of insight came as early as 1978 when their involvement in the movie *Sgt. Pepper's Lonely Hearts Club Band* saw them and Peter Frampton playing the fictitious band. Soundtrack sales were respectable, but the project is celebrated by bad-movie buffs to this day. From this point on Bee Gees wrote and provided make-overs for other artists. Major names queued up: Barbra Streisand, Dionne Warwick and Diana Ross were rewarded with career highlights. Some of these records were basically Bee Gee cuts with different lead vocalists. The band also worked on their own careers, clocking up further hits including 'You Win Again', which topped the UK chart in 1987. The death of younger brother Andy in March 1988 affected them all and seemed to slow the group down for a time, although the single 'One' (1989), from the album of the same name, reached US No.7. New albums failed to reach previous heights, with *High Civilization* (1991) reaching UK No.24 and *Size Isn't Everything* (1993) reaching UK No.28. However, *Still Waters* took them to No.2 in the UK in 1997.

Their Rock And Roll Hall Of Fame induction (1996) and BRIT award for Lifetime Achievement (1997) were ludicrously overdue, as were their seven Grammys from 16 nominations (while others received awards for performing Bee Gees songs). Some achievements beggar belief – the band composed, and Barry co-produced, the most successful Country single of all time: 'Islands In The Stream' by Kenny Rogers and Dolly Parton. A favourite target for critics whose lists of great songwriters, singles and albums usually omit the Gibb brothers, the band are guilty of nothing other than staying true to their roots.

READ Bee Gees Fan Club, 20505 US 19N, Suite No. 12, 290 Clearwater, FL 34624, USA

SURF www.bgwoc.org/

Beggars Banquet

Founded in 1977 by Martin Mills, Beggars Banquet immediately found success on the burgeoning Punk and New Wave scenes with The Lurkers, The Ramones and Gary Numan, whose 'Are Friends Electric?' provided the label with its first UK No.1 in 1979. Well placed for the British Indie boom of the 80s, the label established itself as a frontrunner with The Fall (who uncharacteristically stayed for seven hit albums), cult heroes The Go-Betweens, The Blue Aeroplanes, Buffalo Tom and The Icicle Works and crypt-dwellers Fields Of The Nephilim and Bauhaus, among others. Meanwhile, sister labels Situation Two, Wiiija and 4AD were formed, the latter releasing recordings by Pixies, Cocteau Twins, Belly and others. The 90s saw The Charlatans and The Prodigy (on Dance off-shoot XL Recordings) swell Beggars Banquet's coffers.

PAT BENATAR ✪

WHO b. Patricia Andrzejewski, 10 Jan 1953, Brooklyn, New York, USA

WHAT Chauvinist-challenging Hard Rockstress

Benatar's debut *In The Heat Of The Night* (1979) began a run of US hits with 'Heartbreaker' – succeeded by 'Hit Me With Your Best Shot' from *Crimes Of Passion* (1980) and 'Fire And Ice' from US No.1 *Precious Time* (1981). In 1982, she married her producer and guitarist Neil Geraldo, and went platinum again with *Get Nervous*. Her Brit breakthroughs – 'Love Is A Battlefield' from *Live From Earth* (1983) and 'We Belong' from *Tropico* (1984) – featured on the hits set *Best Shots* (1987). After final US smash 'Invincible' (1985), her fortunes wound down through *Seven The Hard Way* (1985) and *Wide Awake In Dreamland* (1988). After 1991's bluesy flop *True Love*, she returned to Rock for *Gravity's Rainbow* (1993) and can count on fans to lap up albums like 1997's *Innamorata*.

 SURF www.benatar.com/home.html

GEORGE BENSON ☉ ✪

WHO b. 22 Mar 1943, Pittsburgh, Pennsylvania, USA

WHAT Breezy Jazz guitarist/singer

George Benson sang on US radio before taking up the guitar at 8. After recording for the Amy label and session work in the 50s, he moved to New York and issued acclaimed 60s Jazz albums. In the 70s, he returned to singing and hit with *Breezin'* (1976), a US No.1 collection of Soul/Jazz Fusion which featured Leon Russell's 'This Masquerade' – the first single to top the US Jazz, R&B and Pop charts. *In Flight* (1977), *Weekend In LA* (1978), *Livin' Inside Your Love* (1979) and *Give Me The Night* (1980) made Benson a fixture of US and UK charts. *In Your Eyes* (1983), *20/20* (1984) and *While The City Sleeps…* (1986) were Pop-oriented, but Benson returned to his Jazz roots, collaborating with Dizzy Gillespie, Freddie Hubbard and Lionel Hampton. 1989's *Tenderly* and 1993's *Love Remembers* both topped the US Jazz chart.

GEORGE BENSON/JIM McCRARY/REDFERNS

CHUCK BERRY

WHO b. Charles Edward Anderson Berry, 18 Oct 1926, St Louis, Missouri, USA

WHAT Legendary Rock 'n' Roller

Although it is impossible to pinpoint the first Rock 'n' Roll record, you can be sure that Chuck Berry was the first successful guitar-playing Rock 'n' Roll singer/songwriter. After leaving reform school in 1947, Berry studied hairdressing, cosmetology and the

"If you were going to give Rock 'n' Roll another name you might as well call it Chuck Berry"

John Lennon

guitar. In 1952, his prowess on the latter earned him a place in Blues combo The Johnnie Johnson Trio, which soon became The Chuck Berry Trio. When approaches to Capitol, Mercury and Vee Jay Records proved unsuccessful, he took a tape of his compositions 'Wee Wee Hours' and 'Ida Mae' to Chess. They loved the latter Country-influenced hot-rod Rocker and he re-recorded it for them as 'Maybellene'. It became the biggest R&B hit of 1955, and motored past a handful of covers to reach the US Pop Top 5, earning Berry the Best New R&B Artist award from *Billboard*. In 1956, he clicked with 'Thirty Days', 'No Money Down', 'Roll Over Beethoven', 'Too Much Monkey Business' and 'Brown Eyed Handsome Man'. Berry was also one of the era's outstanding entertainers, and in the late 50s starred in many Rock 'n' Roll shows, performing his distinctive 'duck walk' in low-budget movies. This prolific and profitable period continued with Top 10 hits 'School Day', 'Rock And Roll Music', 'Sweet Little Sixteen' and 'Johnny B. Goode' – perfect pictures of 50s teen life, recorded by countless artists since.

Berry's sales were on the decline when he was arrested in late 1959 for taking a 14-year-old girl across the Mexican border. After a couple of years behind bars, he was freed in late 1963, to find his music back in fashion. He had become an idol of the Beat Boom generation, his songs successfully revived by The Beatles, The Rolling Stones (their debut, 'Come On', came from Berry's catalogue) and The Beach Boys (whose US Top 10 debut, 'Surfin' USA', was a rewrite of 'Sweet Little Sixteen'). Berry also clocked up his first UK Top 10 album entries and added to his hit portfolio in 1964 when 'No Particular Place To Go' reached the transatlantic Top 20. Other prison-penned songs 'Nadine', 'You Never Can Tell' (revived for the movie *Pulp Fiction*) and 'Promised Land' kept his name on the charts.

Despite a big money move to Mercury in 1966, Berry had to wait until he returned to Chess in 1972 for his next hit: a live recording (from the Lanchester Arts Festival) of 'My Ding-A-Ling'. This double-entendre sing-along, based on a 1952 R&B novelty by Dave Bartholomew, became his

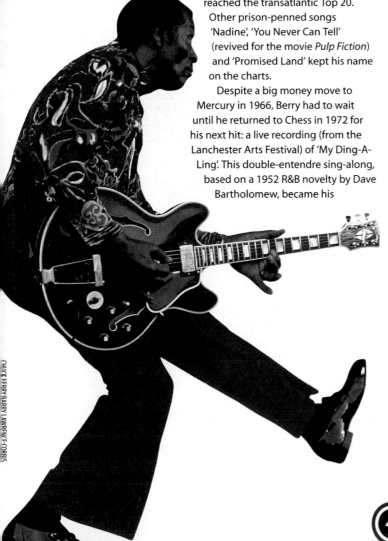

biggest seller and topped charts on both sides of the Atlantic (despite being banned by several radio stations). The follow-up – a re-vamped, ribald version of 1958 B-side 'Reelin' & Rockin' – was his last hit.

Berry's drug problems, sex scandals and tax evasion are no secret. It is also common knowledge that he can be surly and usually refuses to rehearse or play without cash in hand. Nonetheless, he has been a successful headliner for five decades, and staged shows for Presidents Carter and Clinton. Many accolades came Berry's way in the 80s, including a Special Award of Merit from the AMA (American Music Awards) in 1981 and a Lifetime Achievement Grammy in 1985. He was among the first inductees to the Rock And Roll Hall Of Fame and joined the prestigious Songwriters Hall Of Fame in 1986. In 1987, Keith Richards masterminded the film tribute *Hail! Hail! Rock 'n' Roll*. Berry's controversial lifestyle and attitude may have endeared him to few, but history will remember him as one of the most innovative, influential, important and exciting artists in Rock.

READ *Chuck Berry – The Autobiography* (1988), Chuck Berry

SURF shell.ihug.co.nz/~mauricef/frames9.htm

THE B-52's

WHO Vocals **Kate Pierson** (b. 27 Apr 1948, Weehawken, New Jersey, USA), vocals/keyboards **Cindy Wilson** (b. 28 Feb 1957, Athens, Georgia, USA), vocals **Fred Schneider** (b. 1 Jul 1951, Newark, New Jersey), guitar **Ricky Wilson** (b. 19 Mar 1953, Athens, d. 12 Oct 1985), drums **Keith Strickland** (b. 26 Oct 1953, Athens)

WHEN 1976–

WHERE Athens, Georgia, USA

WHAT Eccentric party Pop

The B-52's (named after Kate and Cindy's beehive hairdos) became queens of kitsch New Wave with 1979's 'Rock Lobster'. Devotees included actress Kim Basinger, who once performed as a singer with the band, John Lennon, and David Byrne, who produced *Mesopotamia* (1982). Despite the death of chief writer Ricky, they emerged from cultdom with 1989's *Cosmic Thing* and monster mashes 'Love Shack' and 'Roam'. Pierson guested on fellow Athenians REM's *Out Of Time* (1991). Wilson left (replaced on tour by *Twin Peaks*-tress Julee Cruise), but the resurrection continued with *Good Stuff* (1992). Their devolution into The BC-52's for 1994 movie soundtrack *The Flintstones* confirmed their immersion in the mainstream. Schneider continued a parallel solo career with 1996's Steve Albini-produced *Just Fred*.

READ *Party Out Of Bounds* (1991), Rodger Lyle Brown

SURF www.mulch.demon.co.uk/b52s/

BIG BLACK

WHO Vocals/guitar **Steve Albini** (b. 22 Jul 1962, Pasadena, California, USA), guitar **Santiago Durango** (b. 1959, Medellin, Colombia), bass **Dave Riley** (b. 1961, Michigan, USA)

WHEN 1982–1987

WHERE Chicago, Illinois, USA

WHAT Avant-Punk

Amidst the guitar bands of the 80s, Big Black were distinguished by their abrasiveness and lack of conventional melody. Formed by fanzine writer Steve Albini, who grew up in the wide, open spaces of rural Montana, they took and exaggerated the angular styling of Wire and Gang Of Four and set it to a pummelling drum machine. Two EPs in 1982 – 'Lungs' and 'Bulldozer' – and the mini-album *Racer X* (later released together as *The Hammer Party* in 1987) were recorded with varying line-ups.

Big Black's definitive incarnation recorded *Atomizer* in 1986, which portrayed America as a dysfunctional wasteland. This was re-released in 1986 as *The Rich Man's Eight Track Tape*, including the acclaimed 'Headache' EP. Following records never captured the nihilistic purity of their debut, although 1987's *Songs About Fucking* (including a cover of Kraftwerk's 'The Model') was well received. With typical perversity, they split on its release. The live album *Pigpile* (1992) collected highlights from the band's farewell tour. Subsequently, Albini formed the short-lived and controversially named Rapeman before settling in 1993 with bassist Bob Weston and drummer Todd Trainer in the more low-profile Shellac. He is also a respected producer, having worked with Pixies, Bush, Nirvana, PJ Harvey, Quint and Plant & Page.

BIG COUNTRY ◉

WHO Vocals/guitar **Stuart Adamson** (b. 11 Apr 1958, Manchester, England), guitar **Bruce Watson** (b. 11 Mar 1961, Timmins, Ontario, Canada), bass **Tony Butler** (b. 2 Feb 1957, London, England), drums **Mark Brzezicki** (b. 21 Jun 1957, Slough, Berkshire, England)

WHEN 1982–

WHERE Dunfermline, Scotland

WHAT Caledonian Pomp Rock

Formed by Stuart Adamson after his departure from The Skids, Big Country were a uniquely Scottish-sounding Rock group. Sacking most of the original folky line-up, Adamson recruited session musicians Butler and Brzezicki to complete the group. Like The Alarm and vintage U2, theirs was a majestic post-Punk sound. *The Crossing* (1983) yielded the definitive hit 'In A Big Country' and featured Watson's distinctive bagpipe-like guitar.

The bleaker *Steeltown* (1984) and formulaic *The Seer* (1986) continued their run of success, followed by *Peace In Our Time* (1988), but by Brzezicki's departure in 1989, Big Country were a spent force – despite releasing *Through A Big Country – Greatest Hits* (1990) and *No Place Like Home* (1991). The drummer's return for 1993's *The Buffalo Skinners* did little to reverse their fortunes

and *Why The Long Face* (1995) continued the group's commercial decline. Still popular as a live act, Big Country backed The Kinks' Ray Davies at 1997's Glastonbury Festival in Somerset, England.

ⓕⓐⓝ All Of Us, 201 Gay Street, No. 4, Denton, MD 21629, USA

ⓢⓤⓡⓕ www.intercenter.net/~jnu/bc

BJÖRK

WHO b. Björk Gudmundsdottir, 21 Nov 1965, Reykjavik, Iceland

WHAT Biönic beats, bönkers behaviour

Car alarm-esque vocals and mad public pronouncements have blinded many to the wonder of Björk: a hard-as-nails single mother who makes fantastic records and could probably beat Liam Gallagher in a fight. Long before capturing mainstream attention with 1993's *Debut,* she was a veteran of the internationally ignored Icelandic Pop scene. As an 11-year-old she recorded an eponymous album of covers (including Tina Charles' 'I Love To Love') and her childhood in a Reykjavik commune exposed Björk to a constant stream of musicians. She studied piano and flute but, inspired by Punk, hitched aboard the New Wave bandwagon with Icelandic bands Exodus, Tappi Tikarrass (translated as 'Cork The Bitch's Arse') and the notorious Kukl. The latter metamorphosed into situationist mischief-makers The Sugarcubes.

As the 'Cubes dissolved, she recorded *Gling-Glo* (1991) with Icelandic Jazzman Gudmundar Ingolfsson and collaborated with British technoids 808 State (1991's *EX:EL*). In 1992, Björk returned to Iceland and emerged as deranged diva with the Nellee 'Soul II Soul' Hooper-produced *Debut* (1993), whose musical extremes were represented by hits like the swampy Jazz of 'Human Nature' and dancefloor delight of 'Big Time Sensuality'. Immeasurable hipness and commercial success in 1994 won her two BRIT awards and led to her writing the hit 'Play Dead' for 1994 movie *The Young Americans* and modernizing Madonna with 'Bedtime Story'.

Post (1995) further pressed Björk's claim to the title of the world's most famous Icelander with 'It's Oh So Quiet', the stunning 'Army Of Me' and 'Hyperballad'. A host of celebrity remixers (Underworld and Black Dog among them) pushed Björk back into the club scene with remix collection *Telegraph* (1996), but the strain of stardom began to show that year when she hit the TV news with an attack on a journalist at a Bangkok airport. Worse was yet to come: living in London with her son, Sindri, and Drum 'n' Bass demi-god Goldie, she narrowly dodged death when an acid bomb, mailed by a kamikaze American fan, was intercepted. Subsequent seclusion in rural Spain was spent writing material for what later became the aggressively electronic *Homogenic* (1997), an album heavy with the influence of Björk's new collaborator, LFO genius Mark Bell. Though the singles 'Joga' and 'Bachelorette' failed to scale the heights of earlier classics like 'Violently Happy', an acclaimed tour followed, but was cut short due to her fragile health.

ⓡⓔⓐⓓ *Björkgraphy* (1995), Martin Aston

ⓕⓐⓝ Björk Fan Club, PO Box 4219, London, SW17 7XF, UK

ⓢⓤⓡⓕ www.indian.co.uk/Björk/

"There is [____] of Techno because it's the unknown.
I think it is a very organic thing,
like electricity"

"I'm self-sufficient.
I spend a lot of time on my own
and I shut off quite easily.
When I communicate, I communicate 900%,
then I shut off, which scares people sometimes"

THE BLACK CROWES ✪

WHO Vocals **Chris Robinson** (b. 20 Nov 1966, Atlanta, Georgia, USA), guitar **Rich Robinson** (b. 24 May 1969, Atlanta), guitar **Jeff Cease** (b. 24 Jun 1967, Nashville, Tennessee, USA), bass **Johnny Colt** (b. 1 May 1966, Cherry Point, North Carolina, USA), drums **Steve Gorman** (b. 17 Aug 1965, Hopkinsville, Kentucky, USA)

WHEN 1988–

WHERE Atlanta, Georgia, USA

WHAT Southern-fried, Soul-stirred Hard Rock

While most Metal acts were clinging to Guns N' Roses' coat-tails, The Black Crowes injected swaggering Soul into the genre. The Robinsons (singer Chris and guitarist Rich) honed their art with Punk band Mr Crowe's Garden before changing their name and style in 1988. It was sexy, it was Stonesy, and it found a home on the Def American label. They made their mark with an ace cover of Otis Redding's 'Hard To Handle' and toured until *Shake Your Money Maker* (1990) climbed to the multi-platinum plateau.

Notorious for endorsing marijuana and – after criticizing corporate sponsorship – being kicked off a beer-sponsored ZZ Top tour, the band replaced guitarist Jeff Cease with Marc Ford (b. 13 Apr 1966, Los Angeles, California, USA) for *The Southern Harmony And Musical Companion* (1992). A five-star US No.1, it also confirmed their overseas standing with the epic 'Remedy'.

But *Amorica* (1994) was less well received, its critical mauling reflected by comparatively poor sales. Undeterred, the band supported The Rolling Stones on 1995's *Voodoo Lounge* tour, adding keyboard player Eddie Harsch and percussionist Chris Trujillio to augment their live sound. The band spent a year on the road promoting *Three Snakes And One Charm* (1996), then entered 1998 with new bassist Sven Pipien but minus Ford.

ⓇⒺⒶⒹ *The Black Crowes* (1993), Martin Black

ⓢⓤⓡⓕ www.blackcrowes.com/

BLACK FLAG

WHO Vocals **Henry Rollins** (b. Henry Garfield, 13 Feb 1961, Washington, DC, USA), guitar **Greg Ginn** (b. c.1953), guitar **Dez Cadena**, bass **Chuck Dukowski**, drums **Robo**

WHEN 1977–1986

WHERE Los Angeles, California, USA

WHAT Punishing Jazz Punkers

Founded by guitarist Greg Ginn, Black Flag typified late 70s Hardcore Punk: DIY ethics, hard touring and nihilistic aggression. After years of fluctuating line-ups, the group stabilized in 1981 around Ginn, Chuck Dukowski, Robo (later of The Misfits) and singer Dez Cadena, who switched to rhythm guitar when former ice-cream store manager Henry Rollins joined. Their first full-length album, *Damaged* (1981), which MCA refused to distribute, was released by themselves on Ginn and Dukowski's

SST label, prompting lawsuits from MCA and a two-year delay. After the stop-gap retrospective *Everything Went Black* (1982), they released seven albums before 1986's swan-song, *Who's Got The 10½?*, by which time Cadena was gone and Dukowski and Robo had been replaced by Kira Roessler and Anthony Martinez.

After the split, Ginn concentrated on his solo career, side project Gone and SST, which released recordings by Hüsker Dü, Sonic Youth, Dinosaur Jr and Soundgarden, among others. Rollins formed Rollins Band, also continuing as a solo artist. Black Flag's legacy was compiled on 1987's *Wasted...Again*.

ⓢⓤⓡⓕ www.ipass.net/~jthrush/rollflag.htm

BLACK GRAPE ☉

WHO Vocals **Shaun Ryder** (b. 23 Aug 1962, Little Hulton, Lancashire, England), vocals **Paul 'Kermit' Leveridge** (b. 10 Nov 1969, Manchester, England), guitar **Paul 'Wags' Wagstaff** (b. 28 Dec 1964, Stockport, Lancashire), bass **Danny Saber** (b. 22 Dec 1966, New York City, New York, USA), drums **Ged Lynch** (b. 19 Jul 1968, Oswaldtwistle, England), percussion **Mark 'Bez' Berry** (b. 18 Apr 1964, Manchester)

WHEN 1993–

WHERE Manchester, England

WHAT Loose Funk Rock Punk Hip Hop hybrid

Following the demise of Happy Mondays in 1993, Ryder instigated a short-lived band known as The Mondays, including Bez, Craig Gannon (ex-Smiths) and Gavan Whelan (ex-James), before teaming with ex-Ruthless Rap Assassin Kermit to write and demo songs that would appear on Black Grape's debut *It's Great When You're Straight, Yeah!* (1995). Producer Danny Saber eventually became a fully fledged member and writer. Signed to American label Radioactive, Black Grape's debut single 'Reverend Black Grape' entered the UK Top 10 after an anarchic appearance on *Top Of The Pops*. The album, released in August 1995, shot straight to No.1 in the UK. Further hits were scored with 'In The Name Of The Father', 'Kelly's Heroes' and the non-album track 'Fatneck'. Towards the end of 1995, Bez left the group to devote more time to his family and Kermit was hospitalized with septicemia. However, the Grape bounced back, celebrating the Euro 96 football tournament with 'England's Irie', a collaboration with English comedian Keith Allen and The Clash's Joe Strummer. They also headlined the Tribal Gathering and Reading festivals in England. In 1997, Ryder made his acting debut in *The Avengers* movie, and the group reconvened for *Stupid Stupid Stupid*. However, management wrangles, drug problems and bickering pruned Black Grape when Ryder sacked everyone except Saber.

ⓇⒺⒶⒹ *Shaun Ryder – Happy Mondays, Black Grape & Other Traumas* (1997), Mick Middles

ⓢⓤⓡⓕ www.radioactive.net/BANDS/BLACKG/blackg.html

BLACK SABBATH ⊙

WHO Vocals **John 'Ozzy' Osbourne** (b. 3 Dec 1948, Birmingham, England), guitar **Tony Iommi** (b. 19 Feb 1948, Birmingham), bass **Terry 'Geezer' Butler** (b. 17 Jul 1949, Birmingham), drums **Bill Ward** (b. 5 May 1948, Birmingham)

WHEN 1969–

WHERE Birmingham, England

WHAT The Blues base of the Heavy Metal family tree

The 90s were not kind to Black Sabbath. As their progeny (Metallica, Nirvana, Smashing Pumpkins, Soundgarden, even Ice-T) sold by the truckload, the originals could hardly give albums away, their credibility eroded by labyrinthine line-up changes – a frustrating conclusion to a legend.

Iommi and Ward had played together since adolescence. Recruiting Butler from local band Rare Breed, they advertised for a singer: the successful applicant, a schoolmate of Iommi and bandmate of Butler calling himself Ozzy Zig. The resulting Jazz Blues outfit never amounted to much, due not least to their name: Polka Tulk. "Some famous war or something," said Iommi.

Renamed Earth, the quartet found promoters confusing them with a Pop band of the same name, after relocating to Germany's clubs to hone their craft. Osbourne's technical limitations and Butler's fixation on Z-grade horror limited their artistic scope, but meshed perfectly with their final moniker Black Sabbath – the result a Blues-based grind, topped with Iommi's relentless riffing.

The formula proved irresistible to nihilistic teenyboppers, who kept their debut *Black Sabbath* (1970) and *Paranoid* (1970) on the chart for months, and made the group an arena-filling Stateside draw. Their appeal inspired the 'Rock 'n' Roll made me do it' defence, 'Son of Sam' killer David Berkowitz claiming to have been inspired by Sabbath's 'Lord Of This World'. They even scored a rare Heavy Metal hit with *Paranoid*'s title track. Horrified critics debated whether Sabbath or the similarly uncomplicated Grand Funk Railroad were the worst band in the world.

After *Master Of Reality* (1971) and *Vol. 4* (1972), Iommi tired of one-dimensional sludge and – despite Osbourne's objections – introduced Mellotrons and orchestras to *Sabbath Bloody Sabbath* (1973). The risk paid off and yielded another fine album, *Sabotage*, in 1975. However, beleaguered by business disputes, the compilation *We Sold Our Souls For Rock And Roll* (1976) filled a forced gap. "We didn't even know they were going to put that out," Iommi complained (a pattern repeated with 1977's *Greatest Hits* and 1980's *Live At Last*). Subsequent efforts *Technical Ecstasy* (1976) and *Never Say Die* (1978) sounded stale, and failed to sustain an audience distracted by Punk in the UK and the flashier likes of Kiss and Aerosmith in the USA.

The group turned on itself; Osbourne's self-indulgence prompted his dismissal in 1979 (a trial separation in 1978 had seen vocalist Dave Walker pass through the ranks). A fifteen-year conflict began when both parties enjoyed a resurgence in 1980. Sabbath's trump card was singer Ronnie James Dio, late of Richie Blackmore's Rainbow. With Dio they recorded *Heaven And Hell* (1980), marrying Satanic themes of old to sleeker modern Metal.

The result won over a new generation who considered Iron Maiden the peak of artistry, and Sabbath returned to arenas – albeit without the problem-plagued Ward, replaced by Vinnie 'brother-of-Carmine' Appice. This line-up produced two more

excellent albums: *Mob Rules* (1981) and *Live Evil* (1983). During work on the latter, ego clashes born on tour escalated, Dio and Iommi accusing each other of mixing their contributions higher. The singer decamped, with Appice, to form Dio – a band whose albums tended to out-perform contemporary Sabbath efforts.

Adding fuel to the fire, Sabbath's new manager was Don Arden, estranged father of Osbourne's wife and manager Sharon. The Osbournes attempted to scupper *Live Evil* by releasing their own Sabbath-packed *Speak Of The Devil* (1982) mere months beforehand. Butler and Iommi recalled Ward and, to the horror of fans who had barely stomached Dio's arrival, installed Ian Gillan on vocals for *Born Again* (1983). Joining in the aftermath of a doomed attempt to re-form Deep Purple, Gillan fronted their most underrated album, but unwittingly initiated a farce from which they never fully recovered.

Ward bailed out again, replaced by ELO drummer and fellow Birmingham boy Bev Bevan. On tour, Gillan found his lyric sheets obscured by dry ice. A 'Stonehenge' stage set proved too big for most venues. In the Pyréneés, a gale blew the hall's roof off. Worst, for Sabbath die-hards, the band took to playing Purple's 'Smoke On The Water'. Fact met fiction when the 'rockumentary' spoof *This Is Spinal Tap* came out in 1984 – "I thought they'd had a spy with us," admitted Butler. Gillan defected to the now-revived Purple, and Sabbath were history, resurrected only for Live Aid, where – with no irony intended – the original line-up roared through 'Children Of The Grave'.

Though keen to establish a solo career, Iommi bowed to record company pressure and issued *Seventh Star* (1986) as 'Black Sabbath featuring Tony Iommi'. The Curse of Purple rose again when Iommi's new vocalist Glenn Hughes (ex-Deep Purple Mark 3) proved unfit to tour. The revolving door of personnel – crammed with transient drummers, bassists and keyboard players – blurred as the microphone passed from Ray Gillen to Tony Martin. The latter was welcomed by fans, despite his problems remembering the words to 'Paranoid'.

Iommi, Martin, long-serving keyboard player Geoff Nicholls and journeyman drummer Cozy Powell all appeared on *The Eternal Idol* (1987), *Headless Cross* (1989) and *Tyr* (1990), although bass responsibilities passed from Bob Paisley to Laurence Cottle to Neil Murray. However, with sales hardly threatening to match former glory, Iommi conspired to re-form the last really successful line-up. Dio and Appice, whose fortunes had waned in the late 80s, and Butler, reduced to joining Osbourne's band, happily reboarded the gravy train. The resultant *Dehumanizer* (1992), despite three Grammy nominations, sold poorly and gigs were embarrassingly under-subscribed.

The final straw came when the unwaveringly popular Osbourne invited Sabbath to guest at his intended 'farewell' shows in 1992. Dio refused to appear with a man who had spent years mocking him, and huffed back to solo obscurity, leaving Judas Priest's Rob Halford to take the most temporary job in town. A fully-fledged Sabbath reunion was mooted, but when this was scuppered by Osbourne, Iommi drafted the faithful Martin back in. Appice rejoined Dio and was replaced by Bobby Rondinelli (a former associate of Dio and Ray Gillen, as if the family tree was not incestuous enough). None of these changes restored Sabbath's fortunes, and *Cross Purposes* (1994) was overshadowed by tribute album *Nativity In Black*, starring contemporary Metallers Therapy?, Faith No More and Sepultura.

Butler bid a none-too-fond farewell in 1994 and established a career of his own as G/Z/R – the industrial-flavoured *Plastic Planet* (1995) showing that at least one veteran wasn't stuck in a time warp. Not to be outdone, Iommi recruited Body Count's Ernie C to produce Sabbath's *Forbidden* (1995) – but even a cameo by Ice T couldn't save it from instant obscurity. Fans who'd hoped the resurrected Iommi/Martin/Murray/Powell line-up would produce great things were once again disappointed.

A decade dragging Sabbath through the mud ground to a halt in 1996. The label-less Iommi put the band on ice and announced plans for a first solo album. However, thanks to the lure of the dollar, the oft-attempted reunion took flight in 1997: Osbourne, Iommi, Butler and Faith No More drummer Mike Bordin playing beneath the Sabbath banner on the rapturously received 'Ozzfest' US live extravaganza.

Read *Wheels Of Confusion – The Story Of Black Sabbath* (1996), Steven Rosen

Fan Black Sabbath Fan Club, PO Box 177, Crewe, CW2 7SZ, UK

Surf www.black-sabbath.com

MARY J BLIGE ✪

WHO b. 11 Jan 1971, Atlanta, Georgia, USA

WHAT Queen of Hip Hop Soul

Blending Rap raunch with Soul sensibility (she grew up in both The Bronx and Georgia), Blige's ascension was smoothed by producer Sean 'Puffy' Combs, who helped craft her 1992 smash debut *What's the 411?*. The subsequent backlash – fuelled by innumerable singles, a *411* remix album (1993) and Blige's abrasive personality – was diffused by the silky *My Life* (1994). Having graduated from Stateside sensation to transatlantic star, her success survived a bitter split with Combs. Even without Puffy's Midas touch, *Share My World* (1997) topped the US chart and Blige added a much-needed street sound to the Wembley Stadium-hosted Songs And Vision concert in August 1997.

Fan Mary J. Blige Fan Club, c/o Uptown Records, 729 Seventh Avenue, 12th Floor, New York, NY 10019, USA

Surf www.mcarecords.com/amp16/f.innerview.html

BLONDIE ◉ ◉

WHO Vocals **Deborah Harry** (b. 1 Jul 1945, Miami, Florida, USA), guitar/vocals **Chris Stein** (b. 5 Jan 1950, Brooklyn, New York, USA), guitar **Frank 'The Freak' Infante** (b. New York City, New York), bass **Nigel Harrison** (b. 24 Apr 1951, Stockport, England), drums **Clem Burke** (b. 24 Nov 1955, New York City), keyboards **Jimmy Destri** (b. 13 Apr 1954, Brooklyn, New York)

WHEN 1975–1982

WHERE New York City, New York, USA

WHAT New Wave Pop perfection

The most commercially successful of New York's Punk graduates, Blondie were fronted by one of *the* faces of the 70s, Debbie Harry. Raised by adoptive parents, Harry worked as a beautician, secretary at the BBC in New York, Playboy Bunny and bartender at legendary New York venue Max's Kansas City before joining forgotten Folk ensemble Wind In The Willows. By the early 70s, she was in the girl group-inspired Stilettoes with future Television and Patti Smith Group members Fred Smith and Ivan Kral. When Stein joined in 1973, he and Harry remodelled the group, adding Destri, Burke and bassist Gary Valentine. By 1975, they had settled on the name Blondie and were favourites at New York's premier Punk venue CBGB's, their trashy but melodic Pop Rock mostly written by Stein and Harry. 'X Offender' and their eponymous debut album (1977) were released on Indie label Private Stock before they moved to Chrysalis for *Plastic Letters* (1978). Infante moved to guitar, Harrison replaced Valentine and Blondie scored their first hits – a feminized cover of Randy & The Rainbows' 1963 US hit 'Denise', retitled 'Denis', and Valentine's '(I'm Always Touched By Your) Presence Dear'. Multimillion-selling masterpiece *Parallel Lines* (1978) continued the deluge, with 'Picture This', 'Hanging On The Telephone', 'Sunday Girl' and New Wave Disco monster 'Heart Of Glass'. *Eat To The Beat* (1979) made its mark with 'Dreaming' and 'Atomic'. Harry, now an international sex symbol, eclipsed her bandmates, much to their annoyance; Infante later sued the band for excluding him from group activities. By *Autoamerican* (1980), which pioneered the Rock/Rap crossover on 'Rapture', Blondie was essentially a vehicle for Harry and Stein's songwriting. After Harry's solo debut *Koo Koo* (1981) and *The Best of Blondie* (1981), they reconvened for the underrated *The Hunter* (1982), then split.

Blondie's catchy yet credible Pop, shown in posthumous compilations and remix albums, has had a profound influence on Indie upstarts, notably Sleeper, who covered 'Atomic' on the *Trainspotting* (1996) movie soundtrack. Cited as a pivotal influence by Madonna and Annie Lennox, Harry has collaborated with Stein on more solo albums – *Rockbird* (1985), *Def, Dumb And Blonde* (1989) and *Debravation* (1993) – while acting in movies, including David Cronenberg's *Videodrome* (1982) and John Waters' *Hairspray* (1988), and performs with The Jazz Passengers.

Read *Making Tracks – The Rise And Rise Of Blondie* (1982), Debbie Harry, Chris Stein & Victor Bockris

Fan Picture This, 57 Church Avenue, Humberston, Grimsby, Lincolnshire, DN36 4DJ, UK

Surf www.primenet.com/~lab/blondie.html

"Blondie was pure,
classy Pop
with a confidence
and
attitude that made it
incredibly cool"
Louise Wener
(Sleeper)

BLOOD SWEAT & TEARS ✪✪

WHO Vocals **David Clayton-Thomas** (b. David Thompsett, 13 Sep 1941, Walton-on-Thames, Berkshire, England), guitar/vocals **Steve Katz** (b. 9 May 1945, New York, USA), bass **Jim Fielder** (b. 4 Oct 1947, Denton, Texas, USA), drums **Bobby Colomby** (b. 20 Dec 1944, New York), saxophone/piano **Fred Lipsius** (b. 19 Nov 1943, New York), trombone/keyboards **Dick Halligan** (b. 29 Aug 1943, Troy, New York), horns **Chuck Winfield** (b. 5 Feb 1943, Monessen, Pennsylvania, USA), horns **Lew Soloff** (b. 22 Feb 1944, Brooklyn, New York), horns **Jerry Hyman** (b. 19 May 1947, New York City, New York)

WHEN 1967–

WHERE New York City, New York, USA

WHAT Jazz Rock specialists

Brainchild of ex-Blues Project members Al Kooper (keyboards/ vocals) and Katz, Blood, Sweat & Tears also boasted former Buffalo Springfield bassist Fielder, ex-Odetta drummer Colomby and top New York session players Halligan, Lipsius, Jerry Weiss and Randy Brecker. Signed to Columbia Records, the group released its strong debut, *Child Is Father To The Man*, in 1968. Conflict over control led to the departure of Kooper, Weiss and Brecker. The new line-up (introducing Clayton-Thomas, Soloff, Winfield and Hyman) released an eponymous album in 1969, which topped the US chart and spawned three hits including 'Spinning Wheel'. *Blood, Sweat And Tears 3* (1970) also made No.1. *Blood, Sweat And Tears 4* (1971) was their last strong album, followed by bewildering personnel changes which harmed their output. By the late 70s, only Clayton-Thomas remained of the early line-up and, with him at the helm, they continued on the US nostalgia circuit into the 90s.

 www.forget.se/users/j/jorge/bst.html

THE BLUE NILE

WHO Vocals/guitar **Paul Buchanan** (b. 16 Apr 1956, Edinburgh, Scotland), keyboards **Robert Bell** (b. Glasgow, Scotland), keyboards **Paul Joseph Moore** (b. Glasgow)

WHEN 1981–

WHERE Glasgow, Scotland

WHAT Slow-working emotional landscape artists

Singer and main writer Buchanan was in his mid-20s and editing a theatre magazine when he formed The Blue Nile with friends Bell and Moore. Hi-fi manufacturers Linn used their demo to test record-cutting equipment before creating their own label to distribute the band's debut. Ecstatically reviewed, *A Walk Across The Rooftops* (1984) reached UK No.80.

Perfectionism deferred the follow-up, *Hats*, until 1989. Although beautiful tracks like 'The Downtown Lights' and 'Saturday Night' barely registered as singles, they drew further critical raves and the album peaked at UK No.12 and US No.108.

The following year, the band toured for the first time, in America and Britain. Covers of their songs by Annie Lennox (on whose *Diva* they starred), Rod Stewart and Isaac Hayes supplemented a meagre income. Leaving Linn acrimoniously, they joined Warner. Largely recorded by Buchanan, *Peace At Last* (1996) reaffirmed the heart-wrenching power of his voice and songs, but charted with disappointing brevity. Untroubled to own neither house nor car at 40, Buchanan remained "intoxicated with the idea that you might stumble upon some minor epiphany".

surf www.wbr.com/bluenile/

BLUE ÖYSTER CULT

WHO Vocals/guitar **Eric Bloom** (b. 1 Dec 1944), guitar **Donald 'Buck Dharma' Roeser** (b. 12 Nov 1947), keyboards/guitar/vocals **Allen Lanier** (b. 25 Jun 1946), bass/vocals **Joe Bouchard** (b. 9 Nov 1948, Watertown, New York, USA), drums/vocals **Albert Bouchard** (b. 24 May 1947, Watertown)

WHEN 1969–

WHERE Long Island, New York, USA

WHAT Heavy Metal humorists

When manager Sandy Pearlman (among the first to apply the term 'Heavy Metal' to music) failed to snare Black Sabbath, he fashioned his own Metal monster, Blue Öyster Cult, from late 60s act Soft White Underbelly (aka the Stalk-Forrest Group). *Blue Öyster Cult* (1972), *Tyranny And Mutation* (1973) and *Secret*

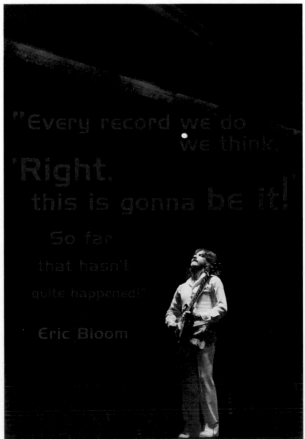

BLUE ÖYSTER CULT/MICHAEL PUTLAND/RETNA

Treaties (1974) sold negligibly – despite the songwriting input of Lanier's Punk poetess girlfriend Patti Smith – but a growing audience made the live On Your Feet Or On Your Knees (1975) a hit. BÖC's success peaked with Agents Of Fortune (1976), its '(Don't Fear) The Reaper' their biggest hit. Spectres (1977), the live Some Enchanted Evening (1978) and Mirrors (1979) filled time before Cultosaurus Erectus (1980) and Fire Of Unknown Origin (1981) benefited from the Metal revival – much of BÖC's work affectionately parodied the genre. Yet another live album, Extraterrestrial Live (1982), was their last hit before the quicksand of personnel turnovers and minor sales claimed another victim. Since The Revolution By Night (1983), Club Ninja (1986) and Imaginos (1988), fans have had to make do with compilations, notably Workshop Of The Telescopes (1995). BÖC are nonetheless celebrated for bringing imagination and irony to Metal.

Ⓕⓐⓝ BÖC Fan Club, PO Box 931324, Los Angeles, CA 90093, USA

ⓢⓤⓡⓕ www.asan.com/users/alexg/boc_faq-2_2.html

BLUES

WHAT The father of Rock 'n' Roll, Blues was first threatened by its bastard son when Elvis covered Arthur 'Big Boy' Crudup's 'That's All Right' in 1954. The genre nonetheless continued to inform Soul, R&B and Rock: The Rolling Stones and post-Beatles superstars John Mayall, Eric Clapton, Peter Green and Led Zeppelin continually harked back to the ominous melancholy of Bluesmen Robert Johnson and Muddy Waters. By the 80s, despite the success of young buck Robert Cray and U2's union with B.B. King, Blues was more likely to be heard in beer commercials than the charts. However, a resurgence of interest in the 90s gave John Lee Hooker his first smashes, revitalized the career of reformed Metaller Gary Moore and inspired prodigies like Jonny Lang.
WHERE Mississippi, USA
WHEN 20s–
WHO Robert Johnson <u>The Complete Recordings</u> (1990), <u>The Simpsons Sing The Blues</u> (1991), John Lee Hooker <u>Mr Lucky</u> (1991), Jonny Lang <u>Lie To Me</u> (1997)

THE BLUES BROTHERS ✪

WHO Vocals/harmonica **Elwood Blues** (b. Dan Aykroyd, 1 Jul 1952, Ottawa, Ontario, Canada), vocals **Joliet 'Jake' Blues** (b. John Belushi, 24 Jan 1949, Wheaton, Illinois, USA, d. 5 Mar 1982, Los Angeles, California, USA)

WHEN 1976–

WHERE "We're the Good Ol' Blues Brothers... Boys... Band... from Chicago."

WHAT Heaven-sent R&B revivalists

Ackroyd and Belushi developed R&B fandom into an act for US TV's Saturday Night Live, a live band (yielding 1978 US No.1 Briefcase Full Of Blues) and a 1980 movie. Despite featuring the legendary likes of Aretha Franklin and Ray Charles, the film flopped and an aborted tour with The Grateful Dead was more 'road to hell' than 'mission from God'. Made in America (1980) failed to match previous sales and the duo hung up their hats and shades. However, the film inspired a Rocky Horror-esque

"It's 106 miles to Chicago. We've got a full tank of gas and half a pack of cigarettes. It's dark and we're wearing sunglasses"
"Hit it"

cult, hence the sequel Blues Brothers 2000 (1998). Returning stars like James Brown were joined by 90s R&B prodigies Erykah Badu and Jonny Lang.

Ⓕⓐⓝ NOMAD, 24 Spinney Close, Stoke-on-Trent, ST9 9PB, UK

ⓢⓤⓡⓕ www.angelfire.com/az/BluesBrothersWorld/index.html

THE BLUETONES ◉

WHO Vocals **Mark Morriss** (b. 18 Oct 1971, Hounslow, Middlesex, England), guitar **Adam Devlin** (b. 17 Sep 1969, Hounslow), bass **Scott Morriss** (b. 10 Oct 1973, Hounslow), drums **Ed Chester** (b. 24 Oct 1971, Darlington, England)

WHEN 1994–

WHERE Hounslow, Middlesex, England

WHAT Backwards-looking Britpop

The Bluetones formed in hometown Hounslow, and lived with fellow Britpoppers Dodgy. Led by the Morriss brothers, the four-piece gathered a substantial following and releases on their own Superior Quality Recordings label sold well. A deal with A&M led to nationwide success: 'Slight Return' debuted at UK No.2. Expecting To Fly (1996) hit No.1 and the singles 'Cut Some Rug' and 'Marblehead Johnson' both reached the UK Top 10. They returned in 1998 with 'Solomon Bites The Worm' and Return To The Last Chance Saloon.

Ⓕⓐⓝ In A Blue Vein, Quarry House, 49 Bracken Park, Scarcroft, Leeds, LS14 3HZ, UK

ⓢⓤⓡⓕ hompages.enterprise.net/bsm/The Bluetones/

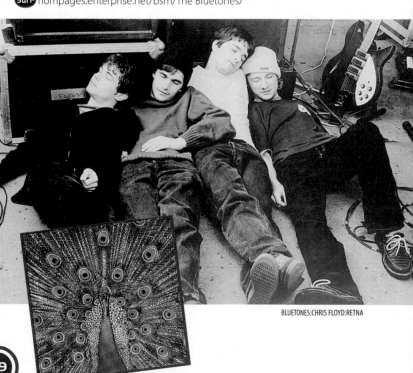

BLUETONES:CHRIS FLOYD:RETNA

"Everything we do has a **subtle jibe** at that suburban way of thinking"

Damon Albarn

BLUR ☉ ☉ ☉

WHO Vocals/guitar/keyboards **Damon Albarn** (b. 23 Mar 1968, London, England), guitar **Graham Coxon** (b. 12 Mar 1969, Rinteln, Germany), bass **Alex James** (b. 21 Nov 1968, Boscombe, Dorset, England), drums **Dave Rowntree** (b. 8 May 1964, Colchester, Essex, England)

WHEN 1988–

WHERE London, England

WHAT The band that put the 'Brit' in Britpop

Drama student and part-time recording studio tea boy Damon Albarn was a veteran of bands in Essex, England, by the time he formed a group with long-time friend Graham Coxon, Alex James and Dave Rowntree in 1988. Coxon and James had met at London's Goldsmiths College, while Rowntree was a fixture of the Essex music scene. After appearances around London in 1990 as Seymour (from J.D. Salinger's novel *Seymour: An Introduction*), they were noticed by Andy Ross, head of EMI subsidiary Food. Ross and his partner Dave Balfe (once bassist for The Teardrop Explodes) offered them a contract on the condition that they change their name. They chose Blur.

Their debut single – the Stone Rosey 'She's So High' – missed the UK Top 40, but the follow-up, 'There's No Other Way', earned an appearance on *Top Of The Pops* in May 1991. Although there were musical similarities, Blur had little in common with the then vogueish 'Madchester' and 'Shoegazer' scenes. Coxon's twisted guitars and Albarn's deadpan vocals turned such comparisons on their head. Blur were shot through with sarcasm and disdain, not only in the mundane suburban stories Albarn told through song, but in their entire attitude to the music scene. With the flawed *Leisure* (1991), they claimed to have "killed Baggy". However, a planned musical coup failed to materialize; by 1992, the Manchester-born Baggy scene was indeed dead, but Blur, too, were on the verge of collapse after a long, uncelebrated US tour and a split with their management. Weak sales of the underrated 'Popscene' and their shambolic, drunken appearance at a charity gig in London seemed to spell the end. Food were close to firing them, shelving tracks they recorded with XTC's Andy Partridge. Blur's thoroughly miserable year was chronicled perfectly in the documentary *Starshaped* (1993).

The horrors of the US tour left Blur – particularly Albarn – with an almost pathological loathing of all things American. Worst was the dominance of Grunge, a scene that filled them with contempt. Accordingly, *Modern Life Is Rubbish* (1993), their 'last chance' from Food, gave not one nod to any American influence, especially since Blur's American label SBK had foolishly suggested they record it with Nirvana knob-twiddler Butch Vig rather than the group's chosen producer, Stephen Street. The foppish sarcasm of old was still there – on grotesque character-based songs like the scornful 'Colin Zeal' – but accompanied by genuine melancholy and nostalgia for a British culture obliterated by American imports. The songwriting (mainly from Albarn) was more crafted and Coxon's guitars more disciplined, leading to occasional comparisons with that other distinctly 'English' band The Kinks. Amid interviews in seaside resorts and photo sessions playing on traditional English stereotypes, neither the album nor the excellent singles 'For Tomorrow' (a skilful steal from Elvis Costello's 'Shipbuilding'), 'Chemical World' and 'Sunday Sunday' amounted to a commercial resurrection. However, Blur were critically reborn as champions of English Pop, especially as they had now replaced their slacker clothes with smart, English Mod-influenced casualwear. Modfather Paul Weller voted *Modern Life Is Rubbish* his favourite album of 1993.

Blur's rehabilitation was completed when 'Girls And Boys' and *Parklife* (1994) crashed into the UK charts. Almost every track celebrated a different aspect of British life: drunken hedonism ('Girls And Boys'), dull days off ('Bank Holiday'), youth unemployment ('Jubilee') and urban alienation ('London Loves'). Even the BBC's shipping forecast was woven into 'This Is A Low'. Save for the vitriolic 'Magic America', *Parklife* refused to acknowledge American culture. Albarn's voice mutated into caricature London cockney, while the songwriting was pure Pop, albeit with a complexity lacking in most of their contemporaries. *Parklife*'s success coincided with new optimism in British Pop: Grunge had died with Kurt Cobain and the music press, weary of American domination, selected Blur – along with Pulp, Suede, Elastica (whose Justine Frischmann was Albarn's girlfriend), The Bluetones and Oasis – to spearhead an English revolt. None of these bands were ashamed to be labelled 'Britpop', least of all Blur, who didn't even bother touring *Parklife* in the States. No American audience could truly empathize with *Quadrophenia* actor Phil Daniels' demented cockney rant on the stomping 'Parklife', the Syd Barrett astrological ramble of James' 'Far Out', or the waltz-time oompahpah of 'The Debt Collector'.

By the time of their legendary appearance at London's Alexandra Palace in October, Blur had helped to prompt a brief but far-reaching Mod revival and had become leading lights in the new mainstream. Sweeping the board at 1995's BRIT and

NME-sponsored BRAT awards, they were challenged only by arch-rivals Oasis. They made no secret of their dislike for each other: Oasis considered Blur contrived and middle class, while Blur ridiculed Oasis' apparent lack of depth. Accepting the 'Best British Act' BRIT award, Albarn graciously asked to share the accolade with their rivals, but the feud escalated to the point of war when both groups scheduled new singles for the same day – 14 August 1995. Albarn fired the first shot, unfavourably comparing Oasis' new single 'Roll With It' to Status Quo, to which Noel Gallagher responded with a range of 'QuOasis' T-shirts. As the standoff continued, the media frenzy reached absurd proportions: for the first time in years, Pop was mentioned on TV news shows. When the dust settled, Blur's 'Country House' was victorious at UK No.1, with Oasis despondent at No.2.

For a while, it appeared Blur had stopped the Oasis machine in its tracks. The Great Escape (1995) – recorded during the stressful period of Parklife's success over the previous 12 months – was intended to be the final part of Blur's 'English trilogy' of albums and was acclaimed as a masterpiece by the music press. But it failed to break in America – perhaps due to the somewhat vague lyrical theme of alienation and downbeat, often tune-free songs. The components were there – Coxon's wayward solos, James' swaggering bass, Albarn's blank storytelling – but there was a pervasive staleness to these new suburban tales, especially the self-parodying 'Ernold Same', recited by British politician Ken Livingstone. The famous Blur irony was working against them, leaving songs like the heartbreaking 'Yuko And Hiro' trapped in a mess of conflicting messages. Only the glorious 'The Universal' (inspired by Albarn's brush with depression and Prozac) and sniping 'Charmless Man' stood out among the confusion.

The album's limitations did little to affect sales – the teenage fans who cherished Parklife's fun and simple beauty remained loyal – but Blur again found themselves vainly chiselling away at the American market while Oasis' epochal (What's The Story) Morning Glory? (1995) scored a direct hit. It would be some time before they could shake off the taunts of failure levelled at them in the music press, who felt Blur had been given what they deserved by working class heroes Oasis. As in their previous dark period in 1992, alcohol played a significant role, fuelling reported rifts between the intense Coxon and the rather more unconcerned James, who could often be found in London clubs with famous friends like artist Damien Hirst. Albarn contributed to 1996's Trainspotting soundtrack and James formed Me Me Me with Elastica's Justin Welch and former Duran Duran and Lilac Time vocalist Stephen Duffy, reaching the UK Top 40 with 1996's 'Hanging Around'.

But these all proved minor distractions. As ever, Blur pulled themselves back from the brink: Coxon and James broke their legendary drinking habits, Albarn and Rowntree learned martial art Tae Kwon Do. During their brief lay-off, Albarn had spent time in Iceland, even buying a share in a bar there. It was here that the fitter, happier Blur did much of the work for Blur (1997), which reconciled their prickly relationship with the British and American music scenes. In a move unthinkable just a year before, Albarn and Coxon publicly expounded the virtues of American groups, especially Pavement and Coxon's beloved Free Jazz experimentalists, John Zorn and Ornette Coleman. No longer constrained by Pop, they set about destroying their own image: allowing Coxon free reign with unhinged guitars,

worrying less about shiny hits and claiming Blur sounded more like their early days as Seymour. Parts sounded almost tortured, especially the garbled shouts of 'Theme From Retro' and teeth-grinding horror of 'Essex Dogs', an exorcism of Albarn's childhood in the suburbs. 'Strange News From Another Star' and 'Look Inside America' maintained the classic Blur melancholy. Coxon made his vocal debut with the Dinosaur Jr-influenced 'You're So Great', and the spiky blasts of 'Chinese Bombs' and 'Song 2' revealed sharp teeth Blur had previously hidden. More surprising than their admission of liking America was the news America liked them: the band made concerted efforts to tour the States and 'Song 2' was adopted by the National Hockey League at ice hockey matches. In Britain, the dreamy 'Beetlebum' entered the chart at No.1, while the other singles from the album, 'Song 2', 'On Your Own' and 'MOR', all made the UK Top 10. Exhaustion set in during an almost year-long world tour, but Coxon made his debut as producer on Chicago band Assembly Line People Program's 1998 debut album, released on his own label, Transcopic.

READ Blur Complete: The Illustrated History (1997), Martin Roach

FAN Blurb, 43 Aspen Close, Stoke-on-Trent, ST7 4HD, UK

SURF www.parlophone.co.uk/blur/

MICHAEL BOLTON ✪✪

WHO b. Michael Bolotin, 26 Feb 1953, New Haven, Connecticut, USA

WHAT Blue-eyed Soulster with a Midas touch

Bolton graduated to superstardom with the transatlantic 1989 smash 'How Am I Supposed To Live Without You'. It vindicated the singer who, despite his 70s act Blackjack and solo output – Michael Bolotin (1975), Every Day Of My Life (1976), Michael Bolton (1983), Everybody's Crazy (1985), The Hunger (1987) and Soul Provider (1989) – had scored only as hit-maker for others, such as Barbra Streisand, Kiss, and Kenny Rogers. His fortunes soared with Time, Love & Tenderness (1991), Timeless (1992), The One Thing (1993), Greatest Hits (1995) and This Is The Time – The Christmas Album (1996). In 1997, he published children's book Secret Of The Lost Kingdom, recorded the theme for Disney's Hercules and released All That Matters.

FAN Fan Emporium, PO Box 679, Branford, CT 06405, USA

SURF www.music.sony.com/Music/ArtistInfo/MichaelBolton/index.html

BON JOVI ◎◎◎◎◎✪✪

WHO Vocals **Jon Bon Jovi** (b. John Francis Jr Bongiovi, 2 Mar 1962, Perth Amboy, New Jersey, USA), keyboards **David Bryan** (b. David Bryan Rushbaum, 7 Feb 1962, Edison, New Jersey), guitar **Richie Sambora** (b. 11 Jul 1959, Perth Amboy), drums **Tico Torres** (b. 7 Oct 1953, Colonia, New Jersey)

WHEN 1983–

WHERE New Jersey, USA

WHAT Stadium Rock in excelsis

Future globe-straddling kings of Rock 'n' Roll, Jon Bon Jovi and David Bryan began in New Jersey bar bands The Rest and Atlantic City Expressway, drawing from Aerosmith and local alumni Southside Johnny and Bruce Springsteen. The latter even jammed with his disciples: "No big deal," claimed JBJ later, "He'd play with anybody." The cowboy-in-waiting also did an apprenticeship at Manhattan's Power Station studios, under his cousin Tony Bongiovi, and appeared on *Star Wars* album *Christmas With the Stars* singing 'R2-D2 We Wish You A Merry Christmas'. The big-time beckoned when 'Runaway', a one-shot solo track, made radio programmers and A&R men sit up. Jon signed to Mercury – contractually, he *is* Bon Jovi – and recruited Bryan, Torres (from Frankie & The Knockouts) and, from The Message, Sambora and bassist Alec Jon Such (b. 14 Nov 1956, Perth Amboy, New Jersey).

Bon Jovi (1984) and *7800° Fahrenheit* (1985) were patchy efforts that nonetheless won respectable reviews and sales. Of more lasting value were the attendant tours and press coverage, which alerted the world to the singer's poster-friendly features. Keen to make the most of their charges, Mercury ordered the band to either write a hit album or see themselves out. Thus the bandwagon was joined by hit writer Desmond Child, who had honed a talent for whoa-hoing choruses with Kiss, headliners on Bon Jovi's first European tour in 1984. The result was *Slippery When Wet* (1986). Leaving no formula uncalculated, it sounded like Journey, Deep Purple, Aerosmith and Springsteen fed through a Pop mincer. Happily, its appearance coincided with American hit radio having been softened up to Hard Rock by Cinderella (themselves BJ 'discoveries') and Def Leppard. Introductory single 'You Give Love A Bad Name' soared to US No.1, followed by 'Livin' On A Prayer', and *Slippery* became the fastest-selling album to that point. A marathon tour climaxed with a headliner at 1987's UK Monsters Of Rock festival, where, in 1985, they had languished in the middle of the bill.

They were back on the road a year later, promoting the classic *New Jersey* (1988). Like *Slippery*, its initial appeal lay in the band's ability to add zest to their steals, but the songs were a class apart: five were hits, two topped the US chart, one ('Bad Medicine') earned praise from Elvis Costello and only a couple mentioned cowboys. However, lest anyone forget that on a steel horse he rode, JBJ closed the decade by putting the band on hold and soundtracking *Young Guns II*. When *Blaze Of Glory* (1990) equalled the band's successes and Sambora issued his own solo album (*Stranger In This Town*, 1991), rumour-mongers honed their epitaphs. Fuelling the fire, JBJ and Sambora squabbled over publishing royalties they earned from Skid Row, a New Jersey band signed to Mercury at their behest, and BJ manager Doc McGhee was convicted of drug-smuggling. McGhee did penance by staging two charity concerts in Moscow in 1989, where the band were dragged into rows between their manager and his other charges Mötley Crüe.

Japanese gigs at the end of 1990 were perceived as the beleaguered band's swan song. JBJ had already widened his options by collaborating with Southside Johnny, Hall & Oates and Canadian guitarist Aldo Nova. But against the odds, the band regrouped. McGhee had been fired, and their own subsidiary label, Jambco (née The Underground), established. Advance speculation centred on a Jesus Jones remix (ultimately unreleased) and Jon's new haircut; however, *Keep The Faith* (1992) was essentially more of the same: no-risk, superlative songs. One of its six singles, 'Dry County', was their most

" I think Jon Bon Jovi should decide what he wants to be. Is he in the Mafia? Is he a cowboy? Is he an Indian? "

Sebastian Bach (Skid Row)

JON BON JOVI:TONY MOTTRAM:RETNA

implausible hit: a lengthy dustbowl elegy that suggested concerns beyond the less cerebral norm.

Unhindered by Grunge, the BJ bandwagon rolled on – albeit without Such, who left in 1995 to be replaced by 'Runaway' bassist Hugh McDonald. After a world-conquering ballad ('Always', 1995), a video with Cindy Crawford ('Please Come Home For Christmas', 1995), a chart-busting best-of (*Crossroads* – the UK's best-seller of 1994) and another, edgier album (*These Days*, 1995), they capped the legend with a stadium tour, including three nights at London's Wembley Stadium – a fitting climax to a decade of Hard Rock hierarchy. Bryan continued a low-key sideline of soundtracks, minor hit-making (Curtis Stigers' 1995 'This Time'), collaborating with Dr John and Sambora, managing Toronto-based band Blaxam and releasing solo album *On A Full Moon* (1994). Sambora weighed in with *Undiscovered Soul* (1998).

Critics hoping to see the back of JBJ have yet to see their wish fulfilled. After an appearance in *Young Guns II* so fleeting that even his grandmother failed to spot him, and failed auditions for *Footloose*, *The Crow 2* and *Heat*, he appeared in *Moonlight And Valentino* (1996), *The Leading Man* and *Homegrown* (both 1997). Filming on location in London, he composed solo album *Destination Anywhere* (1997), produced by Dave Stewart but distinguishable from the band's output mainly by the overwhelming melancholy of the lyrics. It was another success, and coincided with the 'Songs And Vision' concert at Wembley Stadium where he comprehensively upstaged the rest of the bill. Not bad for a kid whose parents had him cut out for a career in hairdressing.

Read *Bon Jovi* (1996), Neil Jeffries

Fan Backstage with Bon Jovi, PO Box 326, Fords, NJ 08863, USA

Surf www.bonjovi.com

BONEY M ⊙⊙⊙

WHO Vocals **Marcia Barrett** (b. 14 Oct 1945, St Catherines, Jamaica), vocals **Maizie Williams** (b. 25 Mar 1951, Montserrat, West Indies), vocals **Liz Mitchell** (b. 12 Jul 1952, Clarendon, Jamaica), vocals **Bobby Farrell** (b. 6 Oct 1949, Aruba, West Indies)

WHEN 1976–

WHERE West Indies via Germany

WHAT Disco chartbusters

Later responsible for Milli Vanilli and Far Corporation, German producer Frank Farian first blessed the world with Boney M. 'Daddy Cool' (1976) was the first of nine UK smashes, of which 'Rivers Of Babylon'/'Brown Girl In The Ring' remained on chart for 40 weeks. Chart-topping albums *Night Flight To Venus* (1978), *Oceans Of Fantasy* (1979) and *The Magic Of…* (1980) confirmed Farian's Midas touch. As the spangly 70s gave way to the earnest 80s, the Boney Magic faded after 'We Kill The World (Don't Kill The World)' (1981). The original quartet dissolved, reappearing in various permutations for minor-selling 80s releases. A 'Boney M Megamix' rightfully restored them to the UK Top 10 in 1992.

Surf muellner.simplenet.com/boneym

BOO RADLEYS ⊙

WHO Guitar/vocals **Sice** (b. Simon Rowbottom, 18 Jun 1969, Wallasey, Merseyside, England), guitar **Martin Carr** (b. 29 Nov 1968, Turso, Highlands, Scotland), bass **Tim Brown** (b. 26 Feb 1969, Wallasey), drums **Rob Cieka** (b. 4 Aug 1968, Birmingham, West Midlands, England)

WHEN 1988–

WHERE Wallasey, Merseyside, England

WHAT The Beatles meets The Jesus & Mary Chain

Taking their name from Harper Lee's novel *To Kill A Mockingbird*, Boo Radleys were just a schoolboy dream until bassist Brown joined founders Sice and Carr in 1988. A demo was noticed by Indie label Action, who financed their noisy debut *Ichabod And I* (1990). Endorsed by DJ John Peel, the group signed to Rough Trade, swapped drummer Steve Hewitt for Cieka and released three EPs, later compiled for 1994's *Learning To Walk*. After 1992's dreamy *Everything's Alright Forever*, critical acclaim translated into sales with The Beach Boys-esque *Giant Steps* (1993) and *Wake Up!* (1995), represented in the UK singles chart with 'Lazarus' and the stomping 'Wake Up Boo!' respectively. Sice recorded solo album *First Fruits* (1996) as Eggman but, having achieved Pop stardom, the Boos stumbled somewhat with 1996's patchy return to noise, *C'mon Kids*.

Surf www.geocities.com/Broadway/3308/boorad.htm

BOOKER T & THE MG's

WHO Keyboards **Booker T Jones** (b. 12 Nov 1944, Memphis, Tennessee, USA), guitar **Steve Cropper** (b. 21 Oct 1941, Ozark Mountains, Missouri, USA), bass **Donald 'Duck' Dunn** (b. 24 Nov 1941, Memphis), drums **Al Jackson Jr** (b. 27 Nov 1935, Memphis, d. 1 Oct 1975, Memphis)

WHEN 1962–

WHERE Memphis, Tennessee, USA

WHAT Premier Soul sessioneers

Booker T & The MG's defined the sound of Memphis Soul in the 60s, both as backing band for Stax label artists Otis Redding, Sam & Dave and Eddie Floyd, and as a hit group in their own right. Cropper and Dunn had played with The Mar-Keys, and Jones and Jackson Jr met on a Willie Mitchell session. The 'MG' stood for 'Memphis Group', though some point also to the popular sports car of that name. A mixed race group (Jones and Jackson were black, Cropper and Dunn white), they were a rarity in the early 60s.

In 1964 the classic line-up fell into place, when Dunn replaced the sacked Lewis Steinberg. They went on to play on scores of Stax hits (many of which Cropper or Jones co-wrote), and toured with the label's other acts. The subtle interplay between Dunn and Jackson, the mellow organ work of Jones, and Cropper's killing guitar lines won enormous respect amongst musicians. This culminated in their 1992 induction to the Rock And Roll Hall Of Fame.

In 1962, The MG's scored instant success with 'Green Onions'. Blues with an insistent keyboard line, it remains their best-known piece. In all, they tallied over a dozen instrumental hits throughout the 60s, including 'Hip Hug-Her', 'Boot-Leg', 'Time Is Tight', and 'Soul Limbo', and covers like The Young Rascals' 'Groovin'. After 1971's *Melting Pot*, Jones became a successful producer in Los Angeles, and released five solo LPs. Cropper's solo collection, *With A Little Help From My Friends*, appeared in 1969, and he remains musically active. He and Dunn played in the 1980 film *The Blues Brothers* and toured as The Blues Brothers Band. Al Jackson was shot dead at his home in 1975, while disturbing an intruder. The surviving members regrouped at Bob Dylan's 1991 tribute concert and for a 1993 tour with Neil Young, and a year later for *That's The Way It Should Be*, which spawned the Grammy award-winning single 'Cruisin'.

ReaD *Sweet Soul Music* (1986), Peter Guralnick

Surf www.rosebudus.com/jones/

THE BOOMTOWN RATS

WHO Vocals **Bob Geldof** (b. 5 Oct 1954, Dublin, Ireland), keyboards **Johnny Fingers** (b. John Moylett, 10 Sep 1956, Ireland), guitar **Gary Roberts** (b. 16 Jun 1954, Ireland), guitar **Gerry Cott** (b. Ireland), bass **Pete Briquette** (b. Patrick Cusack, 2 Jul 1954, Ireland), drums **Simon Crowe** (b. Ireland)

WHEN 1975–1986

WHERE Dublin, Ireland

WHAT Punk turned Pop

The Nightlife Thugs, a quintet of Dublin students, invited Geldof to be their manager before he became their singer. Named The Boomtown Rats after a gang in Woody Guthrie bio-pic *Bound For Glory*, they went to London with a demo during 1976's Summer of Punk. A deal with Ensign reaped instant rewards: 'Looking After No.1' – one of the first New Wave singles to reach the conservative BBC playlist – and their eponymous first album. From the more sophisticated *Tonic For The Troops* (1978) came 'Rat Trap', which was followed to No.1 by 'I Don't Like Mondays', written about an American girl who had shot people at random in a schoolyard – her motive became the song's title. Despite the controversy, it also became their only US smash. *The Fine Art Of Surfacing* (1979) yielded more hits: 'Diamond Smiles' and 'Someone's Looking At You'. Geldof and Fingers became the visual and musical focus of the group: Geldof with his articulate, caustic wit – which made him the delight of TV chat show hosts

and bitter enemy of music journalists – and Fingers with the striped pyjamas he wore onstage.

The Rats became more Funk-oriented on 1981's *Mondo Bongo*. Its hit, 'Banana Republic', savaged their native Ireland, the 'septic isle screaming in a suffering sea'. Increasingly reliant on keyboards and horns, there was no need for two guitarists, and Cott left. The disappointing *V Deep* (1982) sold poorly; by 1984 they were touring universities to fund the equally unimpressive *In The Long Grass*. Its 1985 release was eclipsed by Geldof's masterminding of Band Aid's 'Do They Know It's Christmas'; appearances at Live Aid and Dublin's Self Aid in 1986 marked their farewell. Solo, Geldof suffered the same fate, although he made the UK Top 20 with 1990's 'The Great Song Of Indifference' and remains an articulate, passionate commentator on Pop.

ReaD *Is That It?* (1986), Bob Geldof

Surf www.cs.purdue.edu/homes/jsaid/geldof.html

BOSTON ✪✪

WHO Guitar/keyboards **Tom Scholz** (b. Donald Thomas Scholz, 10 Mar 1947, Toledo, Ohio, USA)

WHEN 1975–

WHERE Boston, Massachusetts, USA

WHAT The archbishops of AOR

Boston's impact on US Rock is best measured by comparing their 1975 classic 'More Than A Feeling' to Nirvana's 'Smells Like Teen Spirit'. The resemblance is ironic, given that Boston's meticulously devised AOR is the very stuff Grunge was supposed to overturn. The group's origins are also far from the sweaty Rock 'n' Roll norm. Technology graduate Scholz recorded a demo in his own 12-track studio, winning a deal with Epic. *Boston* (1978) became the biggest-selling debut in history, a phenomenon that overshadowed all subsequent releases.

Crippled by perfectionism, Scholz recorded only three albums in the next 15 years, a schedule intolerable to singer Brad Delp (one of several shifting sidemen), who quit to form Orion in 1984, and Epic, who sued Scholz in 1983. Consolation for the latter was that the public purchased these sporadic releases – *Don't Look Back* (1978), *Third Stage* (1986), *Walk On* (1994) and *Greatest Hits* (1997) – by the million. Scholz also founded music equipment company Rockman.

Fan Friends of Boston, 4664 Tibbett Ave, Riverdale, NY 10471, USA

Surf www.boston.org/

DAVID BOWIE ⊙⊙⊙⊙⊙⊙⊙⊙⊙

WHO b. David Robert Jones, 8 Jan 1947, Brixton, London, England

WHAT Hugely influential chameleon star man

Even if David Bowie's work *wasn't* still brilliant, we should be on our knees thanking him for past achievements. Oasis' Noel Gallagher proclaimed: "He's written some of the greatest songs in Rock 'n' Roll." The sting in the tail? "I don't think he's done anything since 'Ashes To Ashes'". Damon Albarn of Blur agreed: "I don't think what he's doing now is particularly important." Thirty years after his debut album, Bowie is among the richest and most influential people in Rock. However, recent releases have enjoyed neither sales nor acclaim commensurate with his past achievements and long-term celebrity.

Bowie became familiar with scepticism via underbought singles with early 60s acts Davie Jones & The King Bees and The Manish Boys, then three solo releases on the Pye label. The latter trio did, however, unveil the 'Bowie' banner; devised to avoid confusion with The Monkees' Davy Jones. Of his knife-derived monicker, Bowie explained: "I wanted a truism about cutting through the ties…".

He continued to elude the charts with his Deram label debut *David Bowie* (1967) which, instead of the Who-derived R&B of earlier efforts, took its lead from the English 'music hall' tradition, reaching fresh depths of inanity on the novelty number 'The Laughing Gnome'. Realizing the route to renown was not paved with tenth-rate rip-offs of the likes of Anthony Newley and Ray Davies, Bowie diverted into visual arts, studying mime and acting in roles ranging from an ice-cream commercial to BBC TV play *The Pistol Shot* (1968).

Needing music for his own short film *Love You Till Tuesday* (1968), he produced "a mixture of Salvador Dali, *2001* and The Bee Gees" that the world came to know and love as 'Space Oddity'. A Top 5 UK hit in 1969, it was also the highlight of the confusingly named second album *David Bowie* (aka *Man Of Words/Man Of Music* in the States and, on its worldwide 1972 re-release, *Space Oddity*). However, record buyers steered clear of the album and its successor, *The Man Who Sold The World* (1970). The latter was nonetheless important for introducing both guitarist Mick Ronson – who dominated its long, heavy songs – and Bowie's penchant for cross-dressing (the original sleeve featured Mr Jones in a flowery frock).

The evolution continued with the agenda-setting *Hunky Dory* (1971), with references to Bob Dylan, Andy Warhol, Lou Reed, outer space and teenage angst. These themes were refined into the jackpot-hitting *The Rise And Fall Of Ziggy Stardust And The Spiders From Mars* (1972) which, despite yielding only one hit ('Starman'), crowned Bowie the *grand fromage* of Glam. He fuelled the fire by claiming to be bisexual – an amazing announcement (at the time) only slightly undermined by his stridently heterosexual lifestyle in later years. Blurring the line between Rock and reality, Bowie *became* Ziggy Stardust – an androgynous star from the Glitter galaxy. In 1972, he used this new-found celebrity to resurrect the careers of his inspirations Lou Reed (producing *Transformer*), Iggy & The Stooges (mixing 1973's *Raw Power*) and Mott The Hoople (writing 'All The Young Dudes'). He also visited the USA for the first time with The Spiders From Mars, a trip that inspired the disturbing Hard Rock masterpiece *Aladdin Sane* (1973).

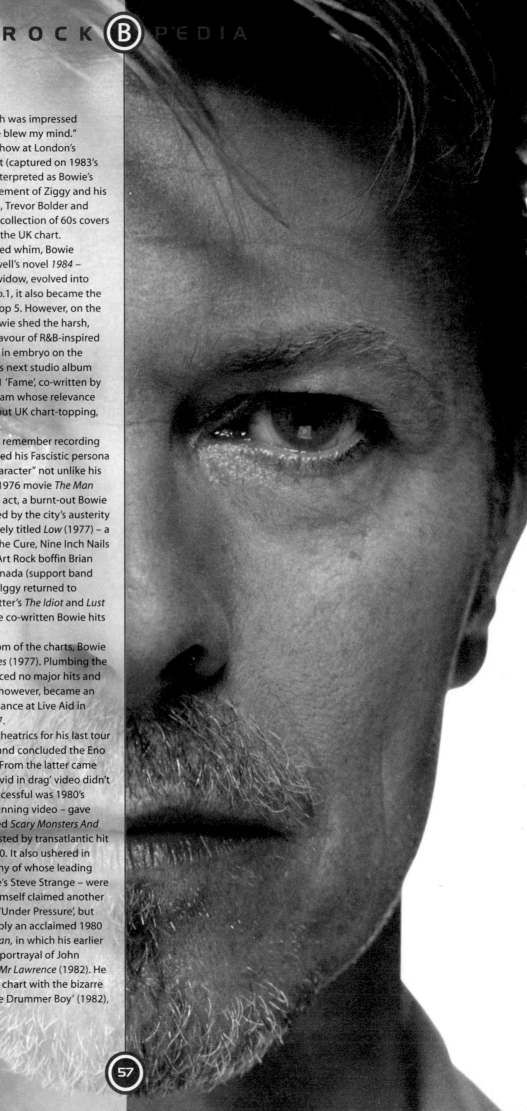

Among witnesses to Ziggy in the flesh was impressed youngster Madonna Louise Ciccone: "He blew my mind." However, Bowie declared a 3 July 1973 show at London's Hammersmith Odeon would be their last (captured on 1983's *Ziggy Stardust: The Motion Picture*). Misinterpreted as Bowie's own farewell, it instead marked the retirement of Ziggy and his band; although Spidermen Mick Ronson, Trevor Bolder and Mike Garson played on *Pin Ups* (1973), a collection of 60s covers that followed *Aladdin Sane* to the top of the UK chart.

Now able to indulge every drug-fuelled whim, Bowie devised a musical version of George Orwell's novel *1984* – which, after intervention from Orwell's widow, evolved into *Diamond Dogs* (1974). Yet another UK No.1, it also became the first of Bowie's three forays into the US Top 5. However, on the accompanying highly theatrical tour, Bowie shed the harsh, humourless sound of *Diamond Dogs* in favour of R&B-inspired "relentless plastic Soul". The latter, heard in embryo on the superb *David Live* (1974), emerged on his next studio album *Young Americans* (1975) with the US No.1 'Fame', co-written by John Lennon – an exposé of celebrity sham whose relevance was compounded by an opportunistic, but UK chart-topping, reissue of 'Space Oddity'.

Blitzed on drugs, Bowie claims not to remember recording *Station To Station* (1976), which introduced his Fascistic persona 'The Thin White Duke' – "a very nasty character" not unlike his role as the alien Thomas Newton in the 1976 movie *The Man Who Fell To Earth*. In a bid to clean up his act, a burnt-out Bowie relocated to Berlin with Iggy Pop. Inspired by the city's austerity and decadent undercurrent, the appositely titled *Low* (1977) – a pivotal influence on gloom merchants The Cure, Nine Inch Nails and Joy Division – began a trilogy with Art Rock boffin Brian Eno. After a jaunt across the USA and Canada (support band Blondie's first Stateside tour), Ziggy and Iggy returned to Germany and promptly produced the latter's *The Idiot* and *Lust For Life* (both 1977), which yielded future co-written Bowie hits 'China Girl' and 'Tonight', respectively.

With Iggy safely returned to the bosom of the charts, Bowie recruited guitarist Robert Fripp for *Heroes* (1977). Plumbing the same emotional depths as *Low*, it produced no major hits and petered out at US No.35. The title track, however, became an anthem – thanks not least to its performance at Live Aid in 1985 – and was covered by Oasis in 1997.

Finally drug-free, Bowie ditched the theatrics for his last tour of the 70s – captured on 1978's *Stage* – and concluded the Eno era with the under-loved *Lodger* (1979). From the latter came 'Boys Keep Swinging', whose sinister 'David in drag' video didn't stop a UK Top 10 placing. Even more successful was 1980's 'Ashes To Ashes' which – helped by a stunning video – gave Bowie his second UK No.1 single. It trailed *Scary Monsters And Super Creeps* (1980) which – further boosted by transatlantic hit 'Fashion' – returned him to the US Top 20. It also ushered in Britain's 'New Romantic' movement, many of whose leading lights – notably Duran Duran and Visage's Steve Strange – were unabashedly Bowie derived. The man himself claimed another smash with 1981's Queen collaboration 'Under Pressure', but otherwise concentrated on acting: notably an acclaimed 1980 Broadway production of *The Elephant Man,* in which his earlier mime lessons paid off with an excellent portrayal of John Merrick, and the movie *Merry Christmas Mr Lawrence* (1982). He returned to the upper reaches of the UK chart with the bizarre Bing Crosby duet 'Peace On Earth – Little Drummer Boy' (1982), then conquered the world with 1983's *Let's Dance*. The title track was a US and UK No.1, and the spectacularly successful 'Serious Moonlight' tour sent ten of his albums into the UK Top 100. At the tail-end of Bowiemania, 1984's *Tonight* and 'Blue Jean' added to the international platinum haul.

Duets with Pat Metheny and Mick Jagger (1985's poignant 'This Is Not America' and exuberant Live Aid tie-in 'Dancing In The Street', respectively) and the beautiful 'Absolute Beginners' (theme for the 1986 movie of the same name) maintained his profile, until he embarked on what looked like a couldn't-care-less crusade. A credibility-crippling appearance in the Jim Henson movie *Labyrinth* was trumped by 1987's career nadir *Never Let Me Down* and the 'Glass Spider' tour – a futile attempt to top the *Diamond Dogs* extravaganza. Attempting to return to his roots, he convened Tin Machine with fellow Iggy cohorts Tony and Hunt Sales, plus guitarist Reeves Gabrels, the latter becoming the longest-serving of Bowie's guitarists (the role-call of which included not only the aforementioned Ronson and Fripp, but also Carlos Alomar, Adrian Belew, Peter Frampton and Stevie Ray Vaughan). The new ensemble made a splash with their Pixies-esque eponymous 1989 debut, but unfairly became an object of derision with *Tin Machine II* (1991) and the live *Oy Vey Baby* (1992). In between, Bowie mounted a money-raking 1990 tour in support of US label Rykodisc's reissue programme and the UK chart-topping compilation *Changesbowie* (1990).

Aiming for world domination once again, *Black Tie White Noise* (1993) reunited Bowie with *Let's Dance* producer Nile Rodgers and Mick Ronson. Propelled to the UK top-spot by the snappy hit 'Jump They Say', it sank in the USA when his new label Savage collapsed. Cheerfully unconcerned, Bowie replaced avarice with art: scoring BBC TV's *The Buddha Of Suburbia* ("The best thing he's done in recent years," decided Pet Shop Boy and keen Bowie-watcher Neil Tennant), exhibiting his paintings at an April 1995 London show and endorsing British sensations Suede. The latter were among a queue of acts at the Temple of Ziggy; other devotees included Nirvana's Kurt Cobain (who covered 'The Man Who Sold The World'), Morrissey (who described *Black Tie White Noise*'s cover of his 'I Know It's Gonna Happen Someday' as "lovely" and supported Bowie in 1995), Elastica's Justine Frischmann (who cited *Scary Monsters* as a favourite) and even Simply Red's Mick Hucknall (who spent school lessons doodling "drawings of Aladdin Sane").

Most important was Nine Inch Nails' Trent Reznor, who invited Bowie along for a US tour and clearly influenced his mentor's arty concept album *1. Outside* (1995). Despite returning Eno to the Bowie brew and coinciding with a 1996 BRIT 'Lifetime Achievement' award, the album spawned no major hits

until Pet Shop Boys remodelled 'Hallo Spaceboy' for a UK No.12. The latter pointed to Bowie's next obsession: Dance mavericks like Tricky and Photek. Sadly, the excellence of the resultant *Earthling* (1997) was drowned by critical derision, mostly because – after pioneering Blue-eyed Soul, Punk and New Romanticism – Bowie seemed to be following rather than leading the pack.

He can now afford to dismiss such criticism, having raised $55 million by floating himself on the stock market. Awarded a star on Hollywood's Walk Of Fame in February 1997, his status was reinforced by another wave of celebrity admirers, notably Placebo (one of several star acts at Bowie's 50th birthday concert at New York's Madison Square Garden), Goldie (on whose 1998 *Saturnz Return* he guested), Ice Cube (who guested on Trent Reznor's remix of the *Earthling* cut 'I'm Afraid Of Americans') and Puff Daddy (who remodelled 'Let's Dance' for his own 'Been Around The World').

Despite claiming to no longer have "that driving need to be an actor", he played Andy Warhol in the 1996 movie *Basquiat* and his *Ziggy*-era out-take 'Velvet Goldmine' inspired a 1998 movie of the same name, starring Ewan McGregor. Meanwhile, his personal multi-media extravaganza continued into 1998: Bowie put two of his lithographs (a self-portrait and a portrait of Iggy Pop) for sale on the Internet.

Even if he never matches the commercial heights of 1973 and 1983, Bowie is more out on a limb now than ever – his music taking risks unthinkable among his megastar contemporaries. Bowie can – as Ziggy predicted – "fall asleep at night as a Rock 'n' Roll Star".

READ *David Bowie – A Chronology* (1983), Kevin Cann

SURF www.davidbowie.com/2.0/

> "I think Bowie was so **innovative** because he was a bit **mad**. He started the character **Ziggy Stardust** and then he said he actually started **believing** he was this character that was like a god"
>
> **Suggs (Madness)**

"What's the name of that band?
The Zero Boys? **Boyzone!**
Now they're really something!
. . . They're hot!
They rock"

Beck

BOY BANDS

WHAT Fired by teen sensations New Edition, vengeful manager Maurice Starr created a white version of his former protégés: the Boston-born New Kids On The Block, whose chiselled looks and radio-friendly R&B became the model. There had been Boy Bands before – The Jackson 5, Latin American phenomenon Menudo (whose members are replaced as soon as they get too old), the pre-Marie Osmonds – but New Kids On The Block sent hormones and sales into overdrive worldwide, and entrepreneurs took notice. It's no coincidence that Take That began their reign just as the Kids bade farewell to fame with 'If You Go Away'. Take That spawned their own imitators, notably 911. Stateside, Backstreet Boys and Hanson took over where New Kids On The Block left off – keeping Pop alive.
WHERE Boston, Massachusetts, USA
WHEN 1984–
WHO New Edition <u>Candy Girl</u> (1983), New Kids On The Block <u>Hangin' Tough</u> (1988), East 17 <u>Around The World</u> (1996), Take That <u>Greatest Hits</u> (1996), Backstreet Boys <u>Backstreet's Back</u> (1997), Hanson <u>Middle Of Nowhere</u> (1997)

BOYZ II MEN ❂❂

WHO Vocals **Nathan 'Alex Vanderpool' Morris** (b. 18 Jun 1971, Philadelphia, Pennsylvania, USA), vocals **Michael 'Bass' McCary** (b. 16 Dec 1971, Philadelphia), vocals **Shawn 'Slim' Stockman** (b. 26 Sep 1972, Philadelphia), vocals **Wanya 'Squirt' Morris** (b. 29 Jul 1973, Philadelphia)

WHEN 1985–

WHERE Philadelphia, Pennsylvania, USA

WHAT Doo Wop meets Hip Hop

Best-selling saviours of the flagging Motown label, Boyz II Men debuted with US No.3 'Motownphilly' from *Cooleyhighharmony* (1991). 'End Of The Road', from Eddie Murphy's 1992 movie *Boomerang*, beat Elvis' title for most weeks (13) atop the US chart – a record they have since broken twice, with 1994's 'I'll Make Love To You' (14 weeks) and the 1995 Mariah Carey collaboration 'One Sweet Day' (16 weeks). Further hits (including 1992's 'Hey Lover' with LL Cool J) and the albums *Christmas Interpretations* (1993), *II* (1994), *The Remix Collection* (1995) and *Evolution* (1997) added to a platinum portfolio.

ReaD *Boyz II Men* (1996), James Earl Hardy

FaN VIP Club, PO Box 884448, San Francisco, CA 94188, USA

SurF fanasylum.com/boyz2men/

BOYZONE ⊙⊙⊙

WHO Vocals **Ronan Keating** (b. 3 Mar 1977, Dublin, Ireland), vocals **Stephen Gately** (b. 17 Mar 1976, Dublin), vocals **Keith Duffy** (b. 1 Oct 1974, Dublin), vocals **Shane Lynch** (b. 3 Jul 1976, Dublin), vocals **Mikey Graham** (b. 15 Aug 1972, Dublin)

WHEN 1993–

WHERE Dublin, Ireland

WHAT Squeaky clean Pop

Handpicked from 300 hopefuls by club owner and manager Louis Walsh, Boyzone conquered Ireland with Detroit Spinners cover 'Working My Way Back To You'. It convinced Walsh to stick with covers, hence the Osmonds revamp and UK breakthrough 'Love Me For A Reason', and the Cat Stevens-penned 'Father And Son' paving the way for the chart-topping *Said And Done* (1995).

The hits continued with 'Words' and the title track from *A Different Beat* (1996) – both UK No.1s – and 'Picture Of You' from *Bean: The Movie* (1997). The latter, combined with Ronan Keating's admission of virginity and co-hosting the Eurovision Song Contest, cemented a wholesome image threatened only by their enthusiasm for Dr Dre and Snoop Doggy Dogg (Keating: "It's hard to deny the beat and funky groove that Rap offers.").

At the close of 1997, they hit with the all-star charity single 'Perfect Day' and a cover of Tracy Chapman's 'Baby Can I Hold You Tonight'. In 1998, Shane Lynch married Eternal's Easther Bennett, Keating's cousin Graham Hopkins drummed with Therapy? and Boyzone took over: *Where We Belong* gave them another No.1, in the same week B*witched – featuring two of Lynch's sisters – topped the UK singles chart with 'C'est La Vie'.

ReaD *Boyzone Go East* (1997), B.P. Fallon

FaN Boyzone Official Fan Club, PO Box 102, Stanmore, Middlesex, HA7 2PY, UK

SurF www.hg4.com/boyzone/

THE BRAND NEW HEAVIES

WHO Vocals **Siedah Garrett**, guitar **Simon Bartholomew** (b. 16 Oct 1965, Ealing, London, England), bass **Andrew Levy** (b. 20 Jul 1966, Ealing), drums/keyboards **Jan Kincaid** (b. 17 May 1966, Ealing)

WHEN 1985–

WHERE Ealing, London, England

WHAT Transatlantic Funksters

Bartholomew, Kincaid and Levy, bandmates since adolescence, played with a succession of vocalists before finding Linda Muriel, who appeared on their first single, 'Got To Give', in 1987. An eponymous debut album, released on Acid Jazz in 1990, featured Jaye Ella Ruth, but US label Delicious Vinyl suggested they re-record tracks with Soul Gospel singer N'Dea Davenport. The revamped 'Dream Come True' was the group's first UK hit in 1992 and album chart success soon followed.

Forays into Hip Hop territory, including 1992's *Heavy Rhyme Experience Vol. 1*, were followed by the massively successful *Brother Sister* (1994), which yielded smash hits 'Dream On Dreamer' and 'Midnight At The Oasis'. Davenport was replaced by former Michael Jackson cohort Siedah Garrett for 1997's *Shelter*, but their fortunes continued to soar.

🏄 www.dvinyl.com/bnh/html/bnh.html1.

BILLY BRAGG

WHO b. Steven William Bragg, 20 Dec 1957, Barking, Essex, England

WHAT Romantic socialist

After the break-up of his first band Riff Raff in 1981, Billy Bragg spent three months in the British army before buying his way out and setting forth as a solo artist. Bragg's mix of politics and romance – as heard on 1984's Go! Discs debut *Life's A Riot With Spy Vs. Spy* and *Brewing Up With Billy Bragg* (1984) – established an earnest image he found difficult to shuffle out of for much of the 80s. On one hand was original, subtle and heartfelt romanticism like 'A New England' (later a UK hit for Kirsty MacColl), 'Levi Stubbs' Tears' (from 1986's *Talking With The Taxman About Poetry*) and 1988's *Workers Playtime*; on the other was his key role in the British Labour Party's 'Red Wedge' youth initiative, his outspoken views on Margaret Thatcher and striking miners and a less-than-glamorous east London vocal bray (sometimes rendering even his most poignant work comical). Typical of this paradox was Bragg's little-known UK No.1 charity single, a splendid version of The Beatles' 'She's Leaving Home', ignored by the media in favour of the insipid flipside, Wet Wet Wet's cover of 'With A Little Help From My Friends'.

After 1990's *The Internationale*, Bragg broadened his appeal with the danceable 'Won't Talk About It' – a hit for Norman Cook's Beats International in 1990 – and *Don't Try This At Home* (1991), a collection of perfect Pop 'n' politics which featured collaborations from ex-Smith Johnny Marr and REM's Peter Buck and Michael Stipe, and yielded the hit 'Sexuality'.

After a lengthy, family-raising sabbatical – punctuated only by a handful of live appearances – Bragg returned in 1996 with typical wit and bile on *William Bloke*.

🏄 www.geocities.com/Athens/Acropolis/1232/Bragg.html

TONI BRAXTON ✪

WHO b. 7 Oct 1967, Severn, Maryland, USA

WHAT Soul saucepot

Discovered by Milli Vanilli songwriter Bill Pettaway, Braxton was launched by hitmakers LA & Babyface. 'Love Shoulda Brought You Home' trailed *Toni Braxton* (1993), source of the international hits 'Another Sad Love Song' and 'Breathe Again'. A subsequent silence ended with 'You're Makin' Me High', the steamy prelude to *Secrets* (1996), her image overhaul confirmed by photo shoots in which she appeared to have forgotten the importance of warm clothes. Braxton's chart profile was equally spectacular – 'Un-break My Heart' being one of *the* hits of 1996.

Her sisters – with whom she sang before LA & Babyface stepped in – struggled on as The Braxtons, denying coat-tail hanging. Meanwhile, Toni's name was connected with bio-pics about singers Eartha Kitt and Frankie Lymon and 50s Hollywood siren Dorothy Dandridge.

🎫 Princess Ashlee Fan Club, Inc, PO Box 4127, Upper Marlboro, MD 20775, USA

🏄 www.geocities.com/ SunsetStrip/3798/main.html

BREAD ⊙

WHO Vocals/bass/guitar **David Gates** (b. 11 Dec 1940, Tulsa, Oklahoma, USA), vocals/guitar **James Griffin** (b. 10 Aug 1943, Cincinatti, Ohio, USA), keyboards/guitar **Larry Knechtel** (b. 4 Aug 1940, Bell, California, USA), drums **Mike Botts** (b. 8 Dec 1944, Sacramento, California)

WHEN 1968–

WHERE Los Angeles, California, USA

WHAT The softest of Soft Rock

Bread were a creative outlet for its two founders, both 'back room' veterans of the LA music scene. In 1962, Gates left a hometown scene that included J.J. Cale and Leon Russell, and – following his 1963 hit for The Murmaids, 'Popsicles And Icicles' – wrote, arranged and produced for Bobby Darin, Elvis Presley and Captain Beefheart. Griffin, raised in Tennessee, also wrote for others, his teen idol recording career having ground to a halt.

A 1967 album by Robb Royer's group Pleasure Faire brought the group together and, signed by Elektra, they debuted with *Bread* (1969). Rich in melody and harmony but underwhelming in sales, it made 1970's *On The Waters* a make-or-break affair, which took off on the back of Gates' Glen Campbell/Jimmy Webb-influenced US No.1 'Make It With You' (at No.5, also their biggest UK hit). More exquisite international hits – mostly ballads by Gates – followed from quirkily diverse albums. The group peaked with 1972's *Baby I'm-A Want You*, by which stage Royer had left (replaced by legendary sessioneer Knechtel) to pursue screenplay writing. Bread burnt out in 1973, with Gates sensing a loss of quality and aborting a sixth album. The epic 'Guitar Man' single, though not their last, provided a fitting swan song.

Regrouping briefly for 1976's respectably successful *Lost Without Your Love*, Bread's members pursued various activities (Gates 'retired' to cattle ranching in 1982 before re-emerging with the excellent but ignored *Love Is Always Seventeen* in 1995), but reunited for a good-natured and apparently final world tour and live album in 1997/98. Periodic 'greatest hits' albums proved even Bread crumbs can have an extended shelf life.

(READ) *Waiting For The Sun: The LA Pop Scene* (1997), Barney Hoskyns

(SURF) www.ktb.net/~insync/BREADtitle.html

BRITPOP

WHAT A press-assisted phenomenon which restored patriotism in the aftermath of Grunge when British Indie Pop bands decided it was the 60s and 70s again. Suede kickstarted it, journalists coined the phrase circa 1994. Blur and Oasis made the most money from it and The Bluetones, Dodgy and a legion of opportunists rode its coat-tails. America was reported "unconcerned".

WHERE UK

WHEN 1994–1997

WHO Suede <u>Suede</u> (1993), Blur <u>Parklife</u> (1994), Oasis <u>Definitely Maybe</u> (1994), Shed Seven <u>Changegiver</u> (1994), Ocean Colour Scene <u>Moseley Shoals</u> (1995), Cast <u>All Change</u> (1995), Pulp <u>Different Class</u> (1995), Sleeper <u>Smart</u> (1995)

BRONSKI BEAT

WHO Vocals **Jimmy Somerville** (b. 22 Jun 1961, Glasgow, Scotland), keyboards **Steve Bronski** (b. 7 Feb 1960, Glasgow), keyboards **Larry Steinbachek** (b. 6 May 1960, London, England)

WHEN 1982–1989

WHERE London, England

WHAT Socially aware falsetto Disco

Bronski Beat came to prominence in June 1984 with their UK Top 10 debut 'Smalltown Boy', the story of a teenage homosexual running away from home for life in the big city. It paved the way for further hits such as 'Why?' and a cover of George Gershwin's 'It Ain't Necessarily So'. *The Age of Consent* (1984) featured a table comparing British sex laws with those of the rest of Europe on its sleeve but, following a collaboration with Marc Almond on a version of Donna Summer's 'I Feel Love', Somerville acrimoniously quit to form The Communards. His replacement was Jon Foster but, after two hits – 'Hit That Perfect Beat' and 'C'mon C'mon' – and *Truthdare Doubledare* (1986), they faded from view, resurfacing briefly in the UK chart with their Eartha Kitt collaboration, 'Cha Cha Heels', in 1989.

ELKIE BROOKS

WHO b. Elaine Bookbinder, 25 Feb 1945, Salford, Greater Manchester, England

WHAT Husky-voiced Blues hollerer

A professional singer since 15, Elkie Brooks' debut, a cover of Etta James' 'Something's Got A Hold On Me', was released on Decca in 1964. After spending most of the 60s on Britain's Jazz scene, she met husband Pete Gage and joined short-lived Fusioneers Dada before forming Vinegar Joe with Gage and Robert Palmer. After two albums, they split in 1974, and Brooks and Palmer went solo. A spell as backing vocalist with American Southern Boogie band Wet Willy preceded her return to England. The well-received but commercially unsuccessful *Rich Man's Woman* (1975) was a final flop before a run of 15 UK hit albums in 20 years, starting with *Two Days Away* (1977) and the hits 'Pearl's A Singer', 'Sunshine

After The Rain' and 'Lilac Wine'. Turning her attention to increasingly MOR collections, *Shooting Star* (1978), *Live And Learn* (1979), *Pearls* (1982), the covers-based *Pearls II* (1982), *Minutes* (1984) and *Screen Gems* (1985) were all creditable successes, but a UK chart renaissance came with *No More The Fool* (1987). Since then, Brooks has remained a popular live artist and returned to her roots with *Nothin' But The Blues* (1994).

 Elkie Brooks Fan Club, 11 Hainthorpe Road, West Norwood, London, SE27 0PL, UK

 www.elkiebrooks.co.uk/

GARTH BROOKS ✪✪✪✪✪

WHO b. Troyal Garth Brooks, 7 Feb 1962, Luba, Oklahoma, USA

WHAT The world's biggest-selling Country artist of the 90s

No one sold more albums in the 90s than distinctively dressed 'hat' act Garth Brooks, who took Country music to new heights and amassed American sales of over 60 million by 1997. The son of little-heralded Country singer Colleen Carroll, he signed with his mother's old label Capitol in 1988 and was an instant success. His eponymous debut album (which has sold over 7 million copies) contained the first of his many Country chart-toppers, 'If Tomorrow Never Comes'. *No Fences* (1990) fared even better with sales now over 13 million, and the third, the 10-million-selling *Ropin' The Wind* (1991), became the first Country album to enter the US Pop chart at No.1. All his subsequent albums also achieved multi-platinum status, and the majority of Brooks' singles have been big Country hits – although, oddly, his singles success has been confined to the Country chart.

Brooks is arguably America's most in-demand live act, selling out scores of stadiums in record-breaking times. Not surprisingly, the singer, who has mined more platinum in the USA than any other American album artist, has also walked away with almost every award in both Country and Pop fields.

 Garth Brooks (1994), Rick Mitchell

BOBBY BROWN ✪

WHO b. 5 Feb 1969, Boston, Massachusetts, USA

WHAT Sultan of Swing

Abandoning R&B teen-stars New Edition, Bobby Brown won few friends with *King Of Stage* (1986). However, teamed with producer Teddy Riley, he took Swingbeat to No.1 with *Don't Be Cruel* (1988). As hit followed hit, Brown graduated from supporting, to eclipsing, New Edition. A US chart-topping duet with Glenn Medeiros ('She Ain't Worth It'), the remix collection *Dance!… Ya Know It!* (1989) and wedlock with Whitney Houston preceded *Bobby* (1992), which exploded with 'Humpin' Around', but fizzled out. The UK hits 'Two Can Play At That Game' and 'Something In Common' couldn't stop a solo career tailspin, and Brown hitched aboard the New Edition reunion (*Home Again*, 1996). That too began promisingly but ground to a halt, and Brown's solo flop *Forever* (1997) put him back at square one.

 www.mcarecords.com/amp15/f.newedition.html

JAMES BROWN

WHO b. 3 May 1928, Barnwell, South Carolina, USA

WHAT "The funkiest man alive" (Ice-T)

James Brown, rightfully known as 'Soul Brother Number One', has amassed more R&B hits during his five decades in show business than any other artist. Only Elvis Presley has enjoyed more US Pop chart entries. Brown had a tough upbringing and even spent time behind bars before helping to form The Famous Flames. In early 1956, with a couple of years of club work behind them, Brown and the group recorded their first single, 'Please, Please, Please', for King Records. This uninhibited, Gospel-inspired gem spent four months on the R&B chart – often alongside Elvis Presley's equally innovative debut hit, 'Heartbreak Hotel'. However, unlike Presley's single, Pop radio stations considered Brown's breakthrough record too wild for airplay. Despite that noteworthy start, he had trouble following this hit, and King were considering dropping him when 'Try Me' gave him his first R&B chart-topper and debut Pop hit in late 1958.

"When we heard we were topping the bill [over James] we couldn't believe it. We tried for two days to get it changed round – I mea[n] you can't follow an act like that"
Mick Jagger

By 1963, he was not only a regular R&B chart visitor, but also regarded as the genre's No.1 entertainer. During his breathtaking stage show, he danced at breakneck speed, screamed, spun feverishly, sweated profusely and even collapsed on cue every night. White audiences finally experienced the unprecedented excitement of Brown's live act via *Live At The Apollo* (1963), which sold over a million and only narrowly missed the top of the US pop charts – an achievement no previous R&B performer could match. His tortured revival of 'Prisoner Of Love' in 1963 helped smash US Pop radio barriers, and groundbreaking Soul singles such as 'Out Of Sight' (1964), the Grammy-winning 'Papa's Got A Brand New Bag' and 'I Got You (I Feel Good)' (both 1965) followed it up the US Pop chart. In 1966, the wrenching 'It's A Man's Man's Man's World' became his first international smash.

Many British bands of the 60s borrowed freely from Brown's repertoire. Some, including The Rolling Stones, attempted to duplicate his act, aiming for similar frantic reactions. His precisely choreographed, fast-moving show was first witnessed in Britain in 1966, when TV's *Ready Steady Go!* devoted a whole edition to him – the first time this had happened. The late 60s saw such innovative sides as 1967's Funk-spawning 'Cold Sweat', 'I Got The Feelin'' (1968) and 'Say It Loud – I'm Black And I'm Proud' (1968), one of many socially aware songs he recorded, which became the anthem of the burgeoning Black Pride movement.

Brown and his band set the Soul music agenda for the 70s, and in that decade he added a further four dozen major R&B hits to his staggering tally. Among the trend-setting tracks were 'Funky Drummer', the million-selling 'Sex Machine' (both 1970) and 'The Payback' (1974).

By Brown's standards, the 80s were a low point, although he scored his biggest international hit with the Grammy-winning 'Living In America' from the movie *Rocky IV* (1986), was elected into the Rock And Roll Hall Of Fame, saw his stage act adopted by artists like Michael Jackson, Prince and Springsteen and heard his work sampled by countless Hip Hop artists. In 1988, while enjoying his biggest success since the mid-70s, he was arrested following an interstate car chase and jailed for six years for a variety of offences. Since his parole in 1991, he has had more awards than hits – Lifetime Achievement trophies from the Grammys and R&B Foundation among them. Other accolades recently received include his own star on both the Hollywood Rock Walk and the prestigious Hollywood Walk Of Fame and a bridge and street named after him. Brown, who changed the course of R&B on several occasions, is justifiably known as 'The Hardest Working Man In Show Business'. He can also lay claim to being 'The Godfather of Soul, Funk, Disco and Hip Hop', and is arguably the most influential and important African-American entertainer of the 20th century.

Ⓡᴇᴀᴅ *James Brown: The Godfather Of Soul* (1997), James Brown & Bruce Tucker

ⓈᴜʀF www.onlinetalent.com/MRBrown_homepage.html

JACKSON BROWNE ✪

WHO b. 9 Oct 1948, Heidelberg, Germany

WHAT Politically conscious singer/songwriter

The son of army parents, Browne first came to prominence as a guitarist for Nico, who included three of his songs on her debut *Chelsea Girls* (1968). Shortly after, he signed to media mogul David Geffen's Asylum Records label, and became one of the pivotal figures of the 'California Cowboy' Country Rock scene of the early 70s, co-writing The Eagles' breakthrough hit 'Take It Easy'. A versatile songwriter, his material was covered by artists as disparate as The Byrds, Joe Cocker and The Jackson 5.

His own early albums *Jackson Browne* (1972), *For Everyman* (1973) and *Late For The Sky* (1974) were literate and melodic but intensely introspective affairs, a tendency which reached its apogee with the shadow cast over *The Pretender* (1976) by the suicide of his wife Phyllis. His popularity grew with the US Top 3/UK Top 30 live album *Running On Empty* (1978), peaking with his only chart-topper, *Hold Out* (US No.1, 1980).

Thereafter, Browne became increasingly involved with political matters, playing benefits for various left-of-centre, pro-ecology causes. In 1979, he organized the Musicians United for Safe Energy (MUSE) concert at which performances by Bruce Springsteen, Crosby, Stills & Nash, James Taylor, Carly Simon and others were recorded for the *No Nukes* (1980) album. Throughout the 80s, he continued to debunk what he viewed as the selfishness of America: *Lawyers In Love* (1983) satirized the yuppie lifestyle, and *Lives In The Balance* (1986) attacked the Reagan administration's policy on Central America. He scored his biggest singles success with 1982's 'Somebody's Baby'.

The break-up of his relationship with actress Daryl Hannah in 1992 prefigured a return to his earlier confessional style on *I'm Alive* (1993), though he continued to support political causes. In 1996, he released *Looking East* – whose co-writers included eels cohort Mark Goldenberg – and moved to Barcelona, Spain.

Ⓡᴇᴀᴅ *Jackson Browne – The Story Of A Hold Out* (1982), Rich Wiseman

ⓈᴜʀF www.pics.com/~spyder/webdoc12.htm

JEFF BUCKLEY

WHO b. 17 Nov 1966, Orange County, California, USA, d. 4 Jun 1997, Memphis Harbour, Tennessee, USA

WHAT Epic electric Folk Rock

Son of the equally tragic Tim Buckley – whom he barely knew – Jeff became known as a powerful singer/songwriter with the mini-album *Live At Sin-E* in 1994. Buckley's multi-octave voice and post-Grunge material, such as the ethereal 'So Real' and Led Zeppelin-esque 'Eternal Life', were featured on 1995's epic *Grace*, which earned plaudits similar to those of his famous father.

After two years of touring, Buckley and band moved to Memphis in early 1997 to rehearse and record *Grace*'s long-awaited follow-up but, on 29 May while swimming in Memphis Harbor, he was swept into the wake of a passing boat and drowned. His body was found on 4 June. The posthumous *Sketches (For My Sweetheart The Drunk)* in 1998 was assembled from his recordings for an album called *My Sweetheart The Drunk*. It included tracks with Television guitarist Tom Verlaine and an improbable cover of Genesis' 'Back In New York City'.

ⓈᴜʀF www.goodnet.com/~gkelemen/jeffhome.html

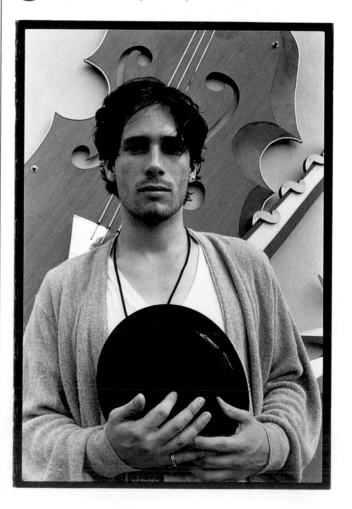

TIM BUCKLEY

WHO b. 14 Feb 1947, Washington, DC, USA, d. 29 Jun 1975, Santa Monica, California, USA

WHAT Avant-garde Folkster

Tim Buckley's career began in the 60s, playing with school friend and future Buffalo Springfield and Blood, Sweat & Tears bassist Jim Fielder, before joining Elektra's Folk roster in 1966 for his eponymous debut album. *Goodbye And Hello* (1967) and *Happy Sad* (1969) demonstrated a more anguished, tense approach in Buckley's music, while his four-octave voice took on troubadour inflections, rather like Greenwich Village songwriter Fred Neil, whose 'Dolphins' became one of Buckley's best recorded moments. Touted as a potential megastar, he followed his own wayward muse, with a series of uncompromising albums – *Blue Afternoon* (1970), *Lorca* (1970), *Star Sailor* (1971), *Greetings From LA* (1972), *Sefronia* (1973) – and live shows heavy on free-form experimentation.

Look At The Fool (1974), however, was Buckley's last album. After a 1975 show in Dallas, he died of a heroin overdose. He was survived by son Jeff, also fêted before his death in 1997. Tim's romantically young death prompted a resurgence of interest in his music during the 80s and 90s, including This Mortal Coil's 1983 hit cover of 'Song To The Siren' (later sampled by The Chemical Brothers) and a plethora of archive releases, including the 1994 compilation *Morning Glory*.

 pantheon.cis.yale.edu/~bodoin/tbarchives.html

BUFFALO SPRINGFIELD

WHO Guitar/vocals **Stephen Stills** (b. 3 Jan 1945, Dallas, Texas, USA), guitar/vocals **Richie Furay** (b. 9 May 1944, Dayton, Ohio, USA), guitar/vocals **Neil Young** (b. 12 Nov 1945, Toronto, Ontario, Canada), bass **Bruce Palmer** (b. 9 Sep 1946, Liverpool, Nova Scotia, Canada), drums/vocals **Dewey Martin** (b. 30 Sep 1942, Chesterville, Ontario)

WHEN 1966–1968

WHERE Los Angeles, California, USA

WHAT Short-lived early Country Rock innovators

Best known for the Pop anthem 'For What It's Worth', featured in numerous TV documentaries and movies, Buffalo Springfield left an undeniable mark on Rock, despite only a two-year existence. In that time, they were in the vanguard of Folk and Country Rock, and led the way for the 70s Californian Rock scene (The Eagles being among their disciples).

The band was founded by Stills and Furay with Young, whom they had met a year earlier, and Palmer, after a fortuitous meeting in a traffic jam on Sunset Boulevard. Adding drummer Martin, the band – named after a steamroller parked outside their house – soon caused a stir as a live act. Their debut performance at the Orange County Fairgrounds, San Bernardino, on 15 April 1966, was well received, and led to support slots with The Byrds and The Rolling Stones. Record companies flocked to

> **" Things got pretty hot on stage** and, when Neil and Stephen got into the dressing room, they started **swinging** at each other with their guitars.
>
> ## It was like two old ladies goin' at it with their purses **"**
>
> ### Dewey Martin

sign them and, on accepting Atlantic Records' offer, they began work on their debut, released that December. *Buffalo Springfield* (1966) was refreshingly new – its rich tapestry of acoustic and electric guitars and breezy vocals set a benchmark for others to copy. Shortly afterwards, Stills' catchy 'For What It's Worth' (a comment on the Sunset Strip riots) became the group's biggest hit, at US No.7, in February 1967.

Their success was short-lived. Internal differences (particularly between Stills and Young), and Palmer's drug use (culminating in a series of arrests and deportations), plagued the band for most of 1967. Young's old friend, Ken Koblun, and future Blood, Sweat & Tears bassist Jim Fielder were employed to fill the gap just as the single was taking off. More disruptions ensued when, within days of Palmer's return, Young announced his decision to go solo. Guitarist Doug Hastings (later in Rhinoceros) joined for an appearance at The Monterey International Pop Festival on 16 June, as did itinerant Byrd, David Crosby, for a 45-minute set.

Young returned for the long-awaited *Buffalo Springfield Again* (1967), a vast improvement on their debut, reflecting the maturity and eclecticism of a group finding its feet after a year of turmoil. Stills' contributions 'Rock 'n' Roll Woman' and 'Bluebird' and Young's 'Expecting To Fly' were all minor hits, while the album peaked at US No.44. Tours supporting The Beach Boys briefly enhanced the group's profile, although Palmer's subsequent arrest on drugs charges quickly sealed their fate. His replacement, recording engineer Jim Messina, helped piece together a third album, *Last Time Around*, released posthumously after their final concert at the Long Beach Arena on 5 May 1968. Ironically, this was their best-seller, peaking at US No.42.

Since then, members of Buffalo Springfield have gone on to varying degrees of success: Stills in Crosby, Stills, Nash & Young, and an illustrious solo career, and Furay and Messina in Poco (which gave birth to Loggins & Messina) being the most successful. Palmer and Martin, whose solo careers faltered, formed tribute band Buffalo Springfield Revisited in 1985, which led to short-lived reunions with the other original members (including an appearance at Atlantic Record's 40th Birthday shindig at New York's Madison Square Garden in 1988).

Despite their early demise, Buffalo Springfield's influence is evident in contemporary US Rock and a revamped 'For What It's Worth' provided Dance group Oui 3 with their first hit in 1993. Their pivotal role was acknowledged when, in May 1997, the group were inducted into the Rock And Roll Hall Of Fame. Stills became the first musician to be honoured twice in the same year, having already been nominated with Crosby, Stills & Nash.

READ *For What It's Worth – The Story Of Buffalo Springfield* (1997), John Einarson with Richie Furay

SURF JEinarso@mbet.mb.ca

BUSH ☆

WHO Vocals/guitar **Gavin Rossdale** (b. 30 Oct 1967, London, England), guitar **Nigel Pulsford** (b. 11 Apr 1965, Newport, Gwent, Wales), bass **Dave Parsons** (b. 2 Jul 1966, Uxbridge, Middlesex, England), drums **Robin Goodridge** (b. 10 Sep 1966, Crawley, West Sussex, England)

WHEN 1992–

WHERE Shepherd's Bush, London, England

WHAT Intense, moody, anthemic, discordant Grungesters

Bush grew when Nigel Pulsford met Gavin Rossdale backstage at a Bryan Adams gig in November 1991. Shared interests emerged and, teaming up with Dave Parsons (ex-Transvision Vamp) and Robin Goodridge in 1992, they spent two years demoing songs while gigging around London pubs as Future Primitive. Their break came when Rob Kahane, president of the LA-based Trauma Records, heard their demo and offered them a two-album deal. Renaming themselves Bush, they recorded their debut *Sixteen Stone* in late 1994.

Influential LA radio station K-ROQ placed the album opener 'Everything Zen' on heavy rotation, and interest grew. Heading Stateside in January 1995, Bush never looked back. America loved the power and intensity of tracks like 'Everything Zen', 'Comedown' and 'Little Things', with lyrics of disaffection and loss shrouded in rousing guitar-drenched choruses. While Bush played 230 US gigs in 15 months, *Sixteen Stone* sold 8 million copies, peaking at No.4 in the *Billboard* charts. The follow-up, *Razorblade Suitcase* (1997), entered at the top of the US chart.

At home, Bush were ridiculed as Nirvana copyists. While similarities were undeniable, Rossdale's vocal intensity married with Pulsford's twisted guitar onslaughts established Bush as a band of individual merit. While domestic success didn't compare to their arena status in the USA, the band built a fanbase by touring small UK clubs – the prelude to larger venues and triumphant festival dates.

In February 1997, *Razorblade Suitcase* reached UK No.4, while 'Swallowed' peaked at No.7. The latter was remixed by Goldie for *Deconstructed* (1997), a collection of remodels that also included their Tricky-helmed cover of Joy Division's 'In A Lonely Place'. The starry associations continued with Rossdale dating No Doubt's hard-rockin' Gwen Stefani and getting a Grunge seal of approval from Courtney Love.

Fan amBush, PO Box 11306, London, WC1E 7AJ, UK
Surf www.bushnet.com/

KATE BUSH ◉◉◉

WHO b. 30 Jul 1958, Bexleyheath, Kent, England

WHAT Gentle philosopher and saucy sensualist

Kate began her recording career as 'the company's daughter' at EMI, but went on to create a unique role in the corporate music industry as homeworker-superstar. She grew up cosseted by her family in a 350-year-old farmhouse on London's southern outskirts. Her father, a doctor, played Classical piano, brother John was a poet and photographer (his pictures adorn her album sleeves) and brother Paddy a skilled maker and player of stringed instruments (later appearing regularly on her records).

Bush taught herself piano and soon discovered a gift for composition. At 16, she had written 200 songs. Through family connections, her fertile imagination and strange soar-and-swoop vocal style were brought to the attention of Pink Floyd's Dave

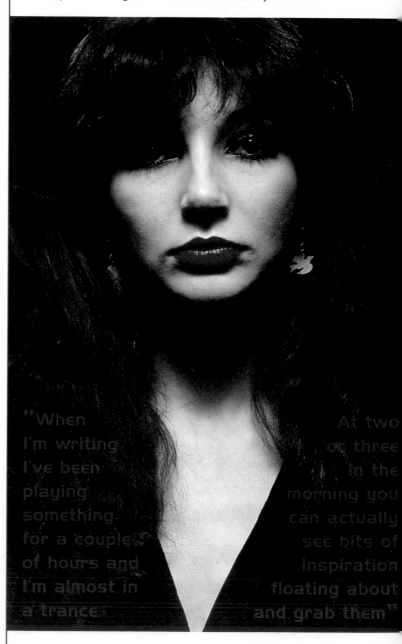

"When I'm writing I've been playing something for a couple of hours and I'm almost in a trance. At two or three in the morning you can actually see bits of inspiration floating about and grab them"

Gilmour, who insisted that an EMI executive listen. Impressed, the company innovatively offered her a £3,500 advance to take a couple of years away from school to concentrate on her music career. She studied dance with Lindsay Kemp and mime with Adam Darius, both noted teachers, and served a rudimentary apprenticeship with the K.T. Bush Band, purveyors of Rolling Stones and Soul covers. The line-up included bassist Del Palmer, who became Kate's long-term boyfriend. In 1978, she released her first single, the extraordinary 'Wuthering Heights'. A wild, screechy tale drawn from the Emily Brontë novel, it crashed through Pop's weirdness barrier to make UK No.1 for a month. A hit all over Europe as well, it paved the way for *The Kick Inside* (UK No.3), which sold a million domestically.

Her unmistakable four-octave voice and uninhibited spirit in going flat-out for grotesque or comic effect grabbed listeners by the shirtfront. But *The Kick Inside* showed that behind the quirky sounds lay forthright approaches to sex and sensuality. 'Them Heavy People' acknowledged Gurdjieff's influence on her spiritual/mystical views, but the beauty of sex was her unbridled theme in 'Moving', 'Saxophone Song' and 'Feel It'. Other intimate matters touched upon were period pains and brother-sister incest ('The Kick Inside'), carried off with such candour that neither prurient speculation nor puritan outrage ensued.

A period of frantic activity followed. Under business pressure, later that year she wrote and recorded the follow-up, *Lionheart*, in two months, an extraordinary effort in the circumstances. The following April she toured the UK and Europe for the first time, devising dance routines for every song. The 2½-hour show, with 17 costume changes, won enraptured reviews. But after the 28 gigs she never played live again, bar the occasional charity concert spot, her explanation being the unbearable exhaustion she suffered. She was also deeply affected by the death of her lighting director, Bill Duffield, in a backstage accident on the tour preview night ('Blow Away' on *Never For Ever* is dedicated to him). Subsequently, her visual creativity was confined to often stunning video productions.

Bush took control of her working life by forming a company, Novercia, to handle her affairs, with herself as head, her parents and brothers the only directors. Her third album *Never For Ever* (1980) entered the UK chart at No.1, boosted by Top 20 hits with her first political songs, 'Breathing' (an unborn baby's experience of nuclear war) and 'Army Dreamers' (a mother mourning her soldier son's death). More characteristically, the sleeve illustration portrayed a cornucopia of animals – 'the creatures of her imagination', her songs – gushing from beneath her skirt.

Her self-production debut, *The Dreaming* (1982), proved her first commercial failure. Its only substantial hit, 'Sat In Your Lap', came out more than a year in advance and the album seemed

to baffle industry types and fans alike. Bush later reflected: "That was my 'She's gone mad' album... There's a lot of anger in it. A lot of 'I'm an artist, right!'" In response, she upgraded her studio at the Bush family home, installing a Fairlight synthesizer/sampler, so that she could record albums there, securing the privacy she craved and minimizing EMI's control via budgeting. *Hounds Of Love* (1985) entered the UK chart at No.1. It was preceded by the racing, percussive single, 'Running Up That Hill' (UK No.3) – influenced by her friend Peter Gabriel's method of writing from rhythm rather than chords or melody – and sustained by 'Cloudbusting', with its elaborate video starring Donald Sutherland. It featured a 'concept' second side which explored Bush's fascination with Shakespeare's Ophelia (*Hamlet*) and escapologist Houdini's account of nearly drowning under ice. Critical eulogies resumed. It was her best-seller in America, reaching No.30.

The following year, Bush duetted with Gabriel on his UK No.9 'Don't Give Up'. Then *The Whole Story* (1986) anthology became her third UK No.1. Thereafter, it seemed that a mixture of perfectionism and self-doubt held her back. *The Sensual World* (1989) had its moments, but musically it was less compelling and distinctive than its predecessors. Another

kate bush

long silence prevailed while Bush weathered the worst emotional pain of a life which had been defined by certain constants. During the early 90s her mother, Hannah, died and she broke up with Del Palmer. *The Red Shoes* (1993) reflected both events. Again a commercial disappointment, it was nonetheless more raw and heartfelt than anything she'd written before, as she mourned her losses – noting that "just being alive, it can really hurt" in 'Moments Of Pleasure' – and howled her anger, thrashing her own bass and guitar accompaniment in 'Big Stripey Lie'. Intriguing Soul and Funk variants cropped up on 'Constellation Of The Heart' and 'Why Should I Love You?', a long-rumoured collaboration with Prince. Anguished as it was, the album still implied a vivid future.

After the release of a 50-minute self-produced movie, *The Line, The Cross And The Curve* (1994), based on tracks from *The Red Shoes*, Bush withdrew from public view once more to record at home. Meanwhile, her inspirational effect on female artists continued to be heard in the work of Tori Amos, Sinead O'Connor, Jane Siberry and Björk, among others.

READ *Kate Bush: A Visual Documentary* (1988), Kevin Cann & Sean Mayes

FAN Homeground, PO Box 120, Welling, Kent, DA16 3DS, UK

SURF fly.hiwaag.net/~cbullard/index.html

BUTTHOLE SURFERS

WHO Vocals **Gibby Haynes** (b. Gibson Haynes, c.1957), guitar **Paul Leary**, drums **King Coffey**

WHEN 1981–

WHERE San Antonio, Texas, USA

WHAT Warped psychedelic Punk

A cocktail of Psychedelia, Punk and weirdness gave Buttholes' a long and surprisingly successful career. Signed to Alternative Tentacles (whose head Jello Biafra masterminded fellow shockers Dead Kennedys), they unleashed their experimentalism on *The Butthole Surfers* (1984) and in blood-'n'-sex-crazed gigs. Moving to Blast First, then to Capitol, they refined sound and personnel with ensuing years and albums, culminating in the acclaimed *Locust Abortion Technician* (1987), the Led Zeppelin-twisting, proto-Grunge *Hairway To Steven* (1988) and UK hits *Piouhgd* (1991) and *Independent Worm Saloon* (1993). Their mainstream ascent was confirmed by a production credit for Zep bassist John Paul Jones on the latter, Haynes' union with celluloid sex-bomb Johnny Depp for critically slaughtered *P* and a slot on the *Beavis & Butthead Do America* soundtrack alongside LL Cool J. Coffey found fame with side project Drain, but they resolved not to split – said Leary, "What else are we gonna do?"

surf www.buttholesurfers.com

BUZZCOCKS

WHO Vocals/guitar **Pete Shelley** (b. Peter McNeish, 17 Apr 1955), guitar **Steve Diggle**, bass **Steve Garvey**, drums **John Maher**

WHEN 1976–

WHERE Manchester, England

WHAT Punk-powered Pop

Inspired by The Sex Pistols, Buzzcocks carved a niche in Punk with the seminal 'Spiral Scratch' EP, released on their New Hormones label in January 1977. After playing The Clash's 1977 'White Riot' tour, original vocalist Howard Devoto quit for Magazine, and Shelley took over on vocals for 'Orgasm Addict', first of a run of Pop classics including 1978 hits 'What Do I Get?', 'Promises' and their biggest hit 'Ever Fallen In Love (With Someone You Shouldn't've)'. After the Shelley-dominated *Another Music In A Different Kitchen* (1978), *Love Bites* (1978) was less Punk, more polish. The magic faded with *A Different Kind Of Tension* (1979), with its singles failing to chart and an aborted tour, and Shelley turned to drugs. He split the group in February 1981 and embarked on a solo career, whose highlight was *Homosapien* (1981). Diggle and Maher soldiered on as Flag Of Convenience, then, controversially, as Buzzcocks FOC.

The box set *Product* (1989) prompted a reformation. Joined by former Smiths drummer Mike Joyce, they issued *Trade Test Transmissions* (1993) and played support at Nirvana's final gigs.

read *Buzzcocks – The Complete History* (1995), Tony McGartland

 surf ender.fim.ucla.edu/SecretPublic.html

THE BYRDS

WHO Vocals/tambourine/guitar **Gene Clark** (b. Harold Eugene Clark, 17 Nov 1944, Tipton, Ohio, USA, d. 24 May 1991, Sherman Oaks, California, USA), guitar/vocals **Roger McGuinn** (b. James Joseph McGuinn III, 13 Jul 1942, Chicago, Illinois, USA), guitar/vocals **David Crosby** (b. David Van Cortland, 14 Aug 1941, Los Angeles, California, USA), bass/vocals **Chris Hillman** (b. 4 Dec 1944, Los Angeles), drums **Michael Clarke** (b. Michael James Dick, 3 Jun 1946, Spokane, Washington, USA, d. 19 Dec 1993, Treasure Island, Florida, USA)

WHEN 1964–1973

WHERE Los Angeles, California, USA

WHAT Jingle-jangle legends

Jim McGuinn, David Crosby and Gene Clark were playing Folk on the Los Angeles coffee house circuit as The Jet Set when they recruited rhythm section Chris Hillman and Michael Clarke in 1964. Most of them had colourful musical histories in the Folk, Country, Bluegrass, Blues and Jazz scenes – notably McGuinn's stints with The Limeliters, Bobby Darin and Judy Collins – but saw a future in which these diverse influences would somehow propel them to the heights of The Beatles, McGuinn's pet obsession (along with aircraft). All of them, in fact, were hooked on the Fab Four and, after a trip to the cinema to see *A Hard Day's Night* (1964), The Jet Set became The Beefeaters for debut 'Please Let Me Love You'. Released on Elektra – whose boss Jac Holzman also financed demos, later released as 1973's *Preflyte* – the single demonstrated the beginnings of their unique, Folk-filtered vision of Rock 'n' Roll.

Touted as 'LA's answer to London', The Beefeaters won the support of Beatles publicist Derek Taylor and Jazz trumpeter Miles Davis, secured a contract with Columbia and adopted a sensible name – The Byrds: a deliberately misspelt tribute to their Merseybeat mentors and to aviator Admiral Byrd. At the insistence of producer Terry Melcher and manager Jim Dickson, they reluctantly agreed to record Bob Dylan's then unreleased 'Mr Tambourine Man'. Still finding their feet musically (the impoverished Clarke was accustomed to drumming on cardboard boxes), the group were replaced by session players.

Bar Crosby and Clark's vocal harmonies, the only Byrd on the recording was McGuinn, whose half-Dylan, half-Lennon vocals and shining 12-string Rickenbacker arpeggios sealed The Byrds' fate (the song always overshadowed later achievements) and took Dylan's Folk Rock fusion to another level. Topping both the UK and US charts in 1965, 'Mr Tambourine Man' marked a pivotal moment in Pop – by merging Dylan's abstract imagery with Lennon and McCartney's Pop sheen, the energy of Rock and emotion of Folk had been united.

Later bands like Buffalo Springfield, Love, Jefferson Airplane and The Doors followed their lead in more psychedelic directions. The Byrds' *Mr Tambourine Man* (1965) also included majestic covers of Dylan's 'Spanish Harlem Incident', 'All I Really Want To Do' and 'Chimes Of Freedom' and two Gene Clark-penned classics – 'I Knew I'd Want You' and 'Feel A Whole Lot Better'. Festooned with impeccable harmonies and McGuinn's inspired guitar, the album was also a best-seller, inspiring The Beatles' *Rubber Soul* (1965) and Dylan himself.

"Of course it was a drug song. We were stoned when we wrote it"

David Crosby

"42 or 43,000 feet, or about eight miles high, is the altitude for military aircraft – and that led people to believe it was about drugs and not aeroplanes"

Roger McGuinn

However, the hastily released follow-up *Turn! Turn! Turn!* (1966) failed to match its predecessor, despite the US No.1 title track and Clark and McGuinn's double A-side 'Set You Free This Time'/'It Won't Be Wrong'. Clark quit in early 1966 after touring pressures caused his fear of flying to become an issue. *Fifth Dimension*, released at the end of the year, was a return to form, especially on the spaced-out '5D (Fifth Dimension)', 'Mr Spaceman' and the proto-psychedelic 'Eight Miles High'. The latter, inspired by a miserable visit to London (hence the reference to The Small Faces), featured a fierce McGuinn opening riff inspired by Jazz saxophonist John Coltrane. Released in May 1966, 'Eight Miles High' immediately fell foul of straight-laced radio stations, convinced that the song glorified drugs. The band innocently claimed the title referred to the cruising altitude of jet aircraft and echoed The Beatles' 'Eight Days A Week'.

Younger Than Yesterday (1967) sold only moderately, despite being their most rounded album; with the sarcastic, reportedly Monkees-inspired 'So You Want To Be A Rock 'n' Roll Star' nestling alongside more jangling Dylan covers ('Younger Than Yesterday', 'My Back Pages'), McGuinn's usual inventiveness ('CTA 102') and Hillman's inspired Pop ('Have You Seen Her Face', 'Time Between' and 'Thoughts And Words'). Most startling, however, were the Crosby/McGuinn composition 'Renaissance Fair' and Crosby's solo offerings – the Raga Rock drone of 'Mind Gardens' and the supremely downcast 'Everybody's Been Burned'.

Crosby was now fraternizing with Buffalo Springfield and Jefferson Airplane and was becoming involved in the revolutionary Haight-Ashbury counter-culture, much to the annoyance of the more conservative McGuinn. Crosby's ego was also a problem, with concerts stalled by marathon tune-up sessions and rambling political sermons. The final straw came when Crosby's 'Triad' – a celebration of three-way sex – was rejected for *The Notorious Byrd Brothers* (1968). Fired and replaced by a horse on the cover's group photo, he headed for 70s superstardom with Crosby, Stills & Nash.

Claiming to have conquered his fear of flight, Clark returned for three disastrous weeks, before his phobias returned. Despite the loss of Crosby, *The Notorious Byrd Brothers* was hailed as a masterpiece, combining the usual Byrds sound with pedal steel guitars, horn sections and futuristic Moog explorations. However, the album failed to halt a commercial decline, prompting Clarke to quit. He returned with Firefall in the 70s.

Reduced to Hillman and McGuinn – 'Jim' was now 'Roger' following his conversion to the religious cult Subud – they recruited Hillman's cousin Kevin Kelley on drums and keyboard player/guitarist/singer Gram Parsons, formerly of fêted Folksters The Shilos and The International Submarine Band. McGuinn's idea for an electronic Jazz album was scuppered when Parsons took control and moved the group to Nashville, where they played to a bemused Grand Ole Opry audience, having drafted in former Parsons sidemen Jay Dee Manness, Jon Corneal, Sneaky Pete Kleinow, Doug Dillard and Earl P. Ball. A European tour preceded the new album, dominated by Parsons until his lead vocals were re-recorded by McGuinn after legal threats from Parsons' original label LHI. Parson's original vocals were eventually released on 1990's *The Byrds* retrospective box set.

Parson's impact was nonetheless evident on *Sweetheart Of The Rodeo* (1968), which paved the way for the early 70s commercial phenomenon, Country Rock. However, acclaim failed to stimulate sales and, having helped The Byrds break more barriers, Parsons tired of conflicts with McGuinn and left on the eve of a controversial South African tour. Hillman followed, joining Parsons in Country Rock legends The Flying Burrito Brothers (and later, Manassas with Stephen Stills), leaving McGuinn the only original Byrd.

Mustering a new line-up, McGuinn recruited brilliant guitarist Clarence White, drummer Gene Parsons and bassist John York. White had already contributed to three previous Byrds albums and been in Nashville West with Parsons, while York had played for The Mamas & The Papas. However, despite the occasional glimmer of former glories (like the Gospel-tinged 'Jesus Is Just Alright' from 1969's *Dr Byrds And Mr Hyde* and the epic 'Chestnut Mare' from 1970's *Untitled*), *Ballad Of Easy Rider* (1969) and *Byrdmaniax* (1971) added nothing to The Byrds' legacy. York was replaced with Skip Battin in 1969 and the next incarnation, from 1969–1972, despite being the band's most stable and best performing line-up, led to McGuinn finally laying The Byrds to rest with 1972's *Farther Along* (save for 1973's forgettable but lucrative reunion *Byrds*, recorded by the original line-up).

After the low-key *Roger McGuinn* (1973), *Peace On You* (1974) and *Roger McGuinn And Band* (1975), McGuinn's solo career assumed a higher profile with a stint on Dylan's Rolling Thunder Revue tour, where he met former David Bowie sidekick Mick Ronson, producer of McGuinn's *Cardiff Rose* (1976). *Thunderbyrd* (1977) saw him convene a band of the same name and in 1979, McGuinn, Clark And Hillman's eponymous album saw a slight upswing in their commercial fortunes. However, Clark was largely absent from *City* (1980).

In the 80s, The Byrds' blueprint was adopted by REM while the originators squabbled. Hillman led The Desert Rose Band, while Clark and Clarke toured as The Byrds, much to the displeasure of Crosby, Hillman and McGuinn, who regrouped in a vain effort to reclaim rights to the name. McGuinn's *Back From Rio* (1991) saw guest appearances from Tom Petty and Elvis Costello and coincided with The Byrds' induction into the Rock And Roll Hall Of Fame. Gene Clark died a few months later, but Michael Clarke continued to tour as The Byrds until his death in 1993. McGuinn's solo career continued with *Live From Mars* in November 1996.

(Read) *Timeless Flight Revisited* (1997), Johnny Rogan

(Surf) www.geocities.com/SunsetStrip/palms/2522/byrds.html

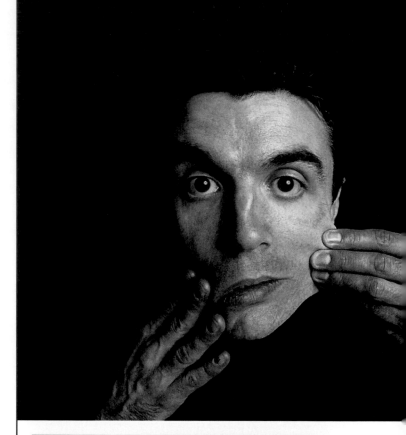

DAVID BYRNE

WHO b. 14 May 1952, Dumbarton, Scotland

WHAT Ex-Talking Heads Rock experimentalist

During his reign as the head of Talking Heads, Byrne periodically made solo projects, the first being *My Life In The Bush Of Ghosts* (1981) with Brian Eno, which merged electronic sounds with ethnic percussion and rhythms. Byrne has always conjured unique magic from seemingly disparate influences, such as the theatrical scores *The Complete Score From The Broadway Production Of 'The Catherine Wheel'* (1981) and *Music For 'The Knee Plays'* (1985), and his movie work, *Married To The Mob* (1988) and *The Last Emperor* (1988) with Ryuichi Sakamoto and Cong Su. The Talking Heads movie *True Stories*, which he wrote and produced, yielded his own separate soundtrack album, *Sounds From True Stories* (1986), featuring The Kronos Quartet.

After Talking Heads' final album *Naked* (1988), Byrne formed the Luaka Bop label in 1989 to release his own skewed Pop, as well as albums by Brazilian, Cuban and Asian musicians. After touring with a 14-piece Latin band for *Rei Momo* (1989), he produced a documentary about Yoruban dance rituals, *IléAiyé (The House Of Life)* (1989), and an orchestral score with Robert Wilson, *The Forest* (1991). *Uh-Oh* (1992) retained strong Brazilian and Cuban elements, but with a slight return to straightforward Rock, a shift that continued with the underbought *David Byrne* (1994). *Feelings* (1997), a partial collaboration with British Trip Hop group Morcheeba, experimented with sampling and Drum 'n' Bass. He has also produced other artists, including The B-52's (1982's *Mesopotamia*) and Fun Boy Three (1983's *Waiting*) and presented exhibitions of his own photography.

(Surf) www.talking-heads.net/davidbyrne/index.html

C+C MUSIC FACTORY

WHO Producer **Robert Clivillés** (b. 30 Aug 1964, New York, USA), producer

David Cole (b. 3 Jun 1962, Johnson City, Tennessee, d. 24 Jan 1995)

WHEN 1987–1995

WHERE New York, USA

WHAT Massive House chart-busters

Clivilles and Cole brought House to America's heartlands with the chart-topping title track of *Gonna Make You Sweat* (1991), their stylish visuals and production distinguishing them from predecessors like Technotronic's 'Pump Up The Jam'. After 1987's 'Do It Properly' (by 2 Puerto Ricans, A Black Man And A Dominican), they progressed from upfront Dance to nouveau Disco (epitomized by Whitney Houston's C+C-helmed 'I'm Every Woman'). Connoisseurs applauded work with US trio Seduction, 'Things That Make You Go Hmmm…' gave House a sly slant and their storming 'Deeper Love' briefly revitalized Aretha Franklin's career. C+C continued in a funkier vein on *Anything Goes* (1994), but ended when Cole died of meningitis. Clivillés' subsequent mix mastery – notably his work with Mariah Carey – keeps C+C's legacy alive.

surf www.galactica.it/101/black/accmscf.html

J.J. CALE

WHO b. Jean Jacques Cale, 5 Dec 1938, Oklahoma City, Oklahoma, USA

WHAT Laid-back loner of Country Blues

J.J. Cale followed fellow Oklahoma musician Leon Russell to Los Angeles in the early 60s to play sessions and tour with the Delaney & Bonnie band, before making (as The Leathercoated Minds) the bogus psychedelic album *A Trip Down Sunset Strip* (1967). Returning to Oklahoma, he signed to Russell's Shelter label. After Eric Clapton had a US hit with Cale's song 'After Midnight' in 1970, his debut *Naturally* (1972) was a cult success, providing Cale with his first hit 'Crazy Mama' (US No.22).

A master of Rockabilly Blues, his engaging, laid-back style varied little through *Really* (1972), *Okie* (1974), *Troubadour* (1976), *5* (1979), *Shades* (1981), *Grasshopper* (1982), *8* (1982) and the film score *La Femme De Mon Pote* (1984). His fluid guitar proved influential on Clapton (who also recorded his 'Cocaine' in 1977) and Dire Straits' Mark Knopfler. Shy and reclusive, Cale retired for several years in the mid-80s before returning with the acclaimed *Travel-Log* (1989). *Number 10* (1992), *Closer To You* (1994) and *Guitar Man* (1996) later appeared, along with a third retrospective compilation, *Anyway The Wind Blows* (1997).

JOHN CALE

WHO b. 9 Mar 1942, Crynant, West Glamorgan, Wales

WHAT Influential, multi-skilled, Rock experimentalist

After studying viola and keyboards in London, Cale moved to the USA in 1963 to study modern composition. Settling in New York, he worked with avant-gardists John Cage and La Monte Young and met Lou Reed, with whom he formed The Velvet Underground in 1964. Leaving the band in 1968, he worked as a producer and A&R man for several record labels, while his own albums veered between stark melancholy (1970's debut *Vintage Violence*), experimentalism (1971's Terry Riley collaboration *Church Of Anthrax*) and Classical (1972's *The Academy In Peril*). *Paris 1919* (with Little Feat's Lowell George) in 1973 and *Fear* (1974) saw Cale at his wayward best, but the pressures of other work – including collaborations with Brian Eno, Kevin Ayers, Nick Drake and Nico, soundtracks for Andy Warhol and Roger Corman, production for Iggy Pop, Patti Smith, Jonathan Richman and Squeeze – saw a decline in his own work.

However, he was hailed as a major influence on Punk, a status confirmed with the consummate *Guts* (1977), *Sabotage! Live!* (1979) and frenzied concerts, one of which culminated in the on-stage beheading of a chicken. In the 80s, he continued producing (including Happy Mondays' 1987 album debut) and re-established himself as a composer with *Honi Soit* (1981), *Music For A New Society* (1982) and *Artificial Intelligence* (1985). After *Words For The Dying* (1989) and Brian Eno collaboration *Wrong Way Up* (1990), Cale reunited with Reed for the Andy Warhol tribute *Songs For Drella* (1990) and a short-lived Velvets reunion in 1993. His solo albums continued with *Last Day On Earth* (1994), *Walking On Locusts* (1996) and *Eat/Kiss* (1997).

surf faraday.ucd.ie/~eoin/johncale.html

GLEN CAMPBELL ✪

WHO b. 22 Apr 1936, Delight, Arkansas, USA

WHAT Session guitar ace turned Country megastar

Leaving school in 1953 to pursue a music career, Glen Campbell toured extensively with The Dick Hills Band and his own Glen Campbell & The Western Wranglers. Urged by Albuquerque DJ Jerry Naylor, he moved to LA in 1960, found work as a session guitarist and temporarily joined The Champs. Juggling a session career – he estimated he played on 586 in 1963 – with his own recordings, his debut 'Turn Around, Look At Me' started a string of singles. After a stint in The Beach Boys in 1965, he charted with US Country hit 'Burning Bridges' before crossing into Pop charts in the late 60s with John Hartford's 'Gentle On My Mind' (1967) and Jimmy Webb-penned classics 'By The Time I Get To Phoenix' (1968), 'Wichita Lineman' and 'Galveston' (both 1969).

In the 70s, Campbell was a superstar, branching into movies – *Norwood* (1969) and *True Grit* (1969) – while hosting his own TV show, *The Glen Campbell Good Time Hour* (1969–1972). The hits continued with 'Rhinestone Cowboy' (1975) and 'Southern Nights' (1977), while he appeared on TV specials and worked for charities and other causes, including the American National Reading Council and the National Migraine Foundation. Few Country stars have crossed over like Campbell, who has funded a college scholarship, represented America as Bicentennial Ambassador Of Goodwill, deputized for talk-show host Johnny Carson, performed at the request of HRH Elizabeth, the Queen Mother, and been given his own Walk Of Fame star in Hollywood. He remains popular on Country and Gospel charts and on the live circuit, where he performs 200 concerts a year.

READ *Rhinestone Cowboy: An Autobiography* (1994), Glen Campbell

FAN Glen Campbell International Fanclub, 10351 Santa Monica Boulevard, Suite 300, Los Angeles, CA 90025, USA

SURF www.glencampbellshow.com

CAN

WHO Vocals **Damo Suzuki** (b. Kenji Suzuki, 16 Jan 1950, Japan), guitar/violin **Michael Karoli** (b. 29 Apr 1948, Straubing, Germany), keyboards **Irmin Schmidt** (b. 29 May 1937, Berlin, Germany), bass **Holger Czukay** (b. 24 Mar 1938, Free City of Danzig (now Gdansk), Poland), drums **Jaki Liebezeit** (b. 26 May 1938, Dresden, Germany)

WHEN 1968–1989

WHERE Cologne, Germany

WHAT Krautrock titans

Former students of composer Karlheinz Stockhausen, Schmidt and Czukay decided to form a Rock band after being introduced to The Velvet Underground (Can's closest musical counterpart) by Karoli. Alongside former Jazz drummer Liebezeit they recruited original vocalist, black American Malcolm Mooney, who gave the group its name and appeared on their debut *Monster Movie* (1969). However, Mooney left in December 1969,

alienated by life in West Germany. His replacement, Damo Suzuki, fronted the excellent *Tago Mago* (1971) and *Ege Bamyasi* (1972). However, he too quit, in 1972, to become a Jehovah's Witness, leaving the others to share vocal duties. Ex-Traffic members Rosko Gee and Reebop Kwaku-Baah on bass and percussion added a funky edge to Can's increasingly directionless sound. 'I Want More' (1976) became their only UK hit, but Can folded in 1978, reforming briefly in 1989 for *Rite Time*. Meanwhile, The Fall, The Stone Roses, Primal Scream and Julian Cope credited them as inspiration. Tracks from Can's extensive back catalogue were remixed for *Sacrilege* (1997).

READ *The Can Book* (1989), Patrick Bussy & Andy Hall

SURF www.io.com/~jwc/rock/can.html

CANNED HEAT

WHO Vocals/harmonica **Bob 'The Bear' Hite** (b. 26 Feb 1945, Torrance, California, USA, d. 5 Apr 1981), guitar/vocals/harmonica **Al 'Blind Owl' Wilson** (b. 4 Jul 1943, Boston, Massachussetts, USA, d. 3 Sep 1970), guitar **Henry Vestine** (b. 25 Dec 1944, Washington, DC, USA), bass **Larry Taylor** (b. 26 Jun 1942, New York, USA), drums **Fito de la Parra** (b. 8 Feb 1946, Mexico City, Mexico)

WHEN 1966–

WHERE Los Angeles, California, USA

WHAT Country Blues Boogie

Featuring heavyweight frontman Bob Hite, Canned Heat signed to Liberty after playing 1967's Monterey Festival. They released *Canned Heat* (1967) and hit with 'On The Road Again' in the US and UK. *Boogie With Canned Heat* (1968) gained their highest US placing (No.16), its hit 'Going Up The Country' later featured in the movie *Woodstock*. Peaking at the turn of the decade with 'Let's Work Together', which reached UK No.2, Wilson's death in 1970 triggered a creative decline, but even Hite's death in 1981 didn't stop them recording and performing into the late 90s.

Capitol Records

Songwriters Johnny Mercer and Buddy DeSylva united with record retailer Glenn Wallichs to form America's first West Coast-based label in 1942. Having hit with Ella Mae Morse's 'Cow Cow Boogie', and despite difficulty obtaining shellac for record production during World War II, Capitol invested in artists like Nat 'King' Cole, Peggy Lee and Frank Sinatra. By 1955, it was America's fourth most successful label. Brit giant EMI made Capitol its US outlet and their LA landmark building, the Capitol Tower (built to resemble a stack of records), opened in 1956. The label launched Gene Vincent, The Kingston Trio and The Beach Boys, but faltered with its parent company's brightest stars, declining to release the first Beatles recording in America. After pressure from EMI, Capitol scored nearly 40 US No.1 albums and singles with the Fab Four. Their success attracted 70s stars The Band, Helen Reddy, Grand Funk Railroad, Pink Floyd, Steve Miller and Glen Campbell. The 80s and 90s saw Rock, Soul and Country signings including Heart, Bonnie Raitt, Tina Turner, Crowded House, Meredith Brooks and Garth Brooks.

CAPTAIN BEEFHEART

WHO b. Donald Van Vliet, 15 Jan 1941, Glendale, California, USA

WHAT The most maverick of mavericks (with enduring cult appeal)

Don Van Vliet was a noted sculptor before venturing into music and has now become a collectible and respected painter. Supposedly christened Captain Beefheart by schoolfriend Frank Zappa, Vliet formed The Magic Band in 1964. Early recordings featured the Captain's edgy but powerful voice performing gymnastics in front of a rolling backing. A&M released their first single 'Diddy Wah Diddy', a Bo Diddley cover, but rejected subsequent recordings for their downbeat lyrics. *Safe As Milk* (1967) and *Strictly Personal* (1968), released on Kama Sutra, featured disjointed Blues and off-the-wall lyrics, aligning the Captain with the hippie crowd. But in 1969, signed to Zappa's label Straight, the Zappa-produced masterpiece *Trout Mask Replica* left such notions behind. Its surreal lyrics and angular musical accompaniments replaced musical conventions with frenzied, impressionistic soundscapes, making it one of the most creative and mind-blowing albums ever. Beefheart reportedly crumpled a piece of paper next to guitarist Zoot Horn Rollo's ear and instructed him to 'Play like that'. Live appearances were equally manic – although Beefheart failed an audition for Zappa's band and thereafter spoke of him in strained terms.

Although Beefheart never completely recaptured *Trout*'s power, *Lick My Decals Off, Baby* (1971), *The Spotlight Kid* (1972) and the more commercial *Clear Spot* (1973) developed its ideas. The latter included 'Big Eyed Beans From Venus' – an eccentric gem loved by people who understand little else in Beefheart's catalogue. *Unconditionally Guaranteed* and *Blue Jeans And Moonbeams* (1974), apparently aimed at the mainstream, were poorly received and Beefheart became disillusioned with Rock. After 1978's 'comeback' *Shiny Beast (Bat Chain Puller)*, his last great moments in music came with albums which used ideas and sounds first developed for *Trout*. *Doc At The Radar Station* (1980) and *Ice Cream For Crow* (1982) showed the Captain in command of his own incredible sound and intoning some of his best lyrics in years. He has released nothing since then – apart from a procession of respected and valuable paintings, mainly produced at his Mojave Desert home.

Too much of an iconoclast to make serious commercial headway, Beefheart's disillusionment with a business that added unwanted production gloss to his ideas and forced him to squash his massive sound into sets supporting other acts was predictable. He remains a respected and discussed figure – influencing artists as implausible as Kate Bush and PJ Harvey – and the subject of some great stories: Beefheart's incredible voice once broke a studio microphone and he called a tree surgeon during the *Trout* sessions because he was concerned his music was harming nearby trees.

READ *Captain Beefheart: The Man And His Music* (1989), Colin Webb

SURF farcry.neurobio.pitt.edu/cb.html

THE CARDIGANS

WHO Vocals **Nina Persson** (b. 1975), guitar **Peter Svensson** (b. 1974), guitar/keyboards **Olaf-Lasse Johansson** (b. 1973), bass **Magnus Sveningsson** (b. 1972), drums **Bengt Lagerberg** (b. 1973)

WHEN 1992–

WHERE Jönköping, Sweden

WHAT Bittersweet Indie Pop

While sharing a flat in Malmö, Sweden, The Cardigans recorded debut *Emmerdale* (1994) as a tribute to the British TV soap opera. Their flowery, Jazz-tinged Indie Pop disguised some ugly themes: 1995's outwardly cute *Life* included an easy-listening cover of Black Sabbath's 'Sabbath Bloody Sabbath'; they also neutered Ozzy & Co's 'Iron Man'. Spearheading a 90s Swedish Rock renaissance (along with fellow Scandinavians The Wannadies), their commercial breakthrough came with *First Band On The Moon* (1996), from which 'Lovefool' hit the US and UK charts, via its inclusion in the movie *Romeo & Juliet* (1997). 'It's War' was included on the 1997 soundtrack *A Life Less Ordinary*, while the dubious *A Tribute To The Cardigans* (1997) saw lots of bands most people have never heard of (Groove Tunnel?!) re-interpreting their past classics, confirming the band's ascent to greatness.

SURF churchill.gryphon.com/cardigans/main/

MARIAH CAREY ⊙ ⊙ ✪ ✪ ✪ ✪

WHO b. 27 Mar 1970, Long Island, New York, USA

WHAT Songbird supreme

Envisaged as 'the next Whitney Houston', Carey began more like Madonna – fleeing a troubled family background to New York City. There she demoed, waitressed and sang before being signed by Columbia Records president Tommy Mottola. 'Vision Of Love', from *Mariah Carey* (1990), and the title track of *Emotions* (1991) sandwiched a record-breaking run of five consecutive US chart-toppers. 'I'll Be There' from *MTV Unplugged* (1992) and 'Dreamlover' and 'Hero' from *Music Box* (1993) continued the Stateside sensation, while the latter album and 'Without You' were her first UK No.1s. In November 1993, a backlash – simmering since she married Mottola earlier that year – exploded with savage reviews of her first tour. Undeterred, Carey released the critic-baiting *Merry Christmas* (1994), then smashed US chart records again with 'Fantasy', 'One Sweet Day' and *Daydream* (1995). At the height of her commercial supremacy, Carey dumped Mottola (now president of Sony), established her own label (Crave) and stuck with a winning formula on *Butterfly* (1997).

READ *Mariah Carey – Her Story* (1995), Chris Nickson

Fan Mariah Carey Fan Club, PO Box 679, Branford, CT 06405, USA

surf www.music.sony.com/Music/ArtistInfo/MariahCarey/

BELINDA CARLISLE ⊙

WHO b. 17 Aug 1958, Hollywood, California, USA

WHAT Ex-Go-Go bad girl made good

When illness prevented her joining Punk legends The Germs, Carlisle gigged with the unlamented Black Randy & The Metro Squad, then found fame with party girls The Go-Go's. After their split in 1984, Carlisle became an MTV star, making a splash with 'Mad About You' (US No.3), from debut *Belinda* (1986). Most celebrated of the ensuing AOR is 1987 chart-topper 'Heaven Is A Place On Earth'. After a turbulent 1994 Go-Go's reunion, Carlisle moved to the south of France and left Virgin after five albums: *Heaven On Earth* (1987), *Runaway Horses* (1989), *Live Your Life Be Free* (1991), *The Best Of Belinda Volume 1* (1992) and *Real* (1993). She resumed her solo career in style with former Go-Go's label IRS: pushing a UK hit tally to 21 with three singles from *A Woman And A Man* (1996).

Fan 3907 W. Alameda Ave, #200 Beverly Hills, CA 91505, USA

surf www.geocities.com/SunsetStrip/Palms/2202/

MARY-CHAPIN CARPENTER

WHO b. 21 Feb 1958, Princeton, New Jersey, USA

WHAT Country queen

In ten years of heavy gigging and drinking before her first album, Carpenter progressed from nervy club nights to bar circuit engagements. Having kicked the bottle and concentrated on writing, a 1986 demo won a deal with Columbia and became her acclaimed debut *Hometown Girl* (1987). Success ensued with *State Of The Heart* (1989), while 1990's *Shooting Straight In The Dark* and a scene-stealing Country award show performance paved the way for platinum-sellers *Come On Come On* (1992) – featuring fellow Country queens Shawn Colvin, Indigo Girls and Rosanne Cash – and *Stones In The Road* (1994). *A Place In The World* (1996) followed a huge-grossing 1995 tour, and two of her songs were developed into children's books: *Dreamland* and, in 1998, *Halley Came To Jackson*.

Fan WMCC, PO Box 2515, Cinnaminson, NJ 08077, USA

surf www.dopig.uab.edu/people/ctichenor/chapin.html

THE CARPENTERS ⊙ ⊙ ✪

WHO Vocals/drums **Karen Carpenter** (b. 2 Mar 1950, New Haven, Connecticut, USA, d. 4 Feb 1983, Downey, California, USA), vocals/keyboards **Richard Carpenter** (b. 15 Oct 1946, New Haven)

WHEN 1968–1983

WHERE Downey, California, USA

WHAT Sumptuous vocal harmony Pop with a tragic ending

Brother and sister Richard and Karen Carpenter's unabashed, middle-of-the-road Pop – a sales phenomenon in the early 70s –

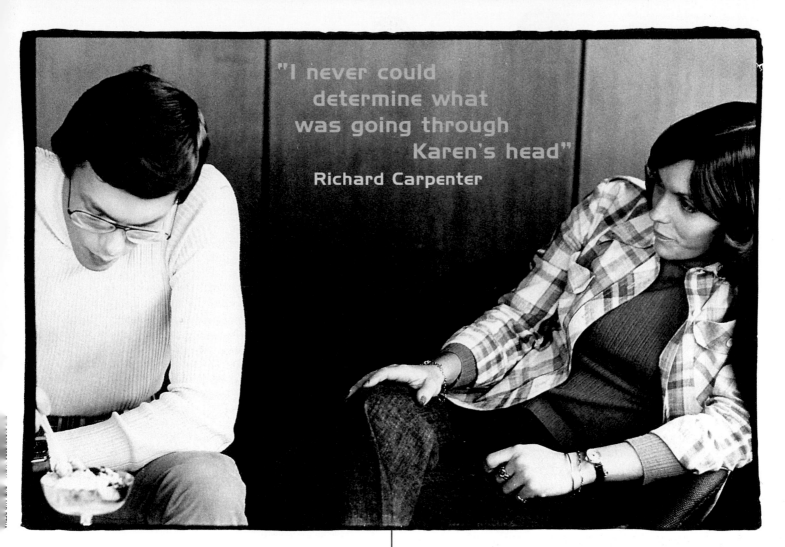

"I never could
determine what
was going through
Karen's head"
Richard Carpenter

has withstood the rigours of fashion and, in the wake of Karen's tragic death in 1983, been critically reappraised. Karen's angelic voice lingers in the memories of all who have heard it wing its way on a gentle breeze of pure Pop.

Karen drummed with a school marching band and Richard started learning the piano aged 12. Both had also been choristers but first played together in 1963, when they formed a Jazz trio with Richard's California State University friend Wes Jacobs. The director of Richard's college choir recommended he send a tape of the trio to session bassist Joe Osborn, who released a recording (credited to Karen, featuring Richard and Jacobs) in June 1966. After winning a 'Battle Of The Bands' competition at The Hollywood Bowl, they were approached by RCA, who recorded a demo, but later dropped them. The trio split when Jacobs left to study in New York, but Richard and Karen continued with four other Cal State students as The Summerchimes, a vocal harmony group rechristened the slightly more hip Spectrum before folding in 1968.

Continuing as a duo, Karen and Richard were recruited by Ford Motor Company jingle composers John and Tom Bahler of the group Going Thing, with whom they signed to the J. Walter Thompson advertising agency. However, they were poached by Herb Alpert, who signed them to his A&M label in April 1969 and released their debut album *Offering* (1969) a few months later. The album did little business until retitled *Ticket To Ride*, to cash in on the moderate 1970 success of their Beatles cover.

Their commercial breakthrough came soon after, courtesy of songwriting legend Burt Bacharach, who had already asked them to perform a medley of Bacharach & David songs at a benefit concert. The Carpenter's reworking of the little-known '(They Long To Be) Close To You' hit US No.1 in July 1970, while the album *Close To You* (1970) reached US No.2 and set the

standard for a long run of sentimental covers and self-penned hits, including 'We've Only Just Begun', 'Rainy Days And Mondays', 'Superstar', 'Sing', 'Yesterday Once More', 'Top Of The World', 'I Won't Last A Day Without You', 'Please Mr Postman' and 'Only Yesterday', as well as concert appearances around the world and the 1971 NBC TV series *Make Your Own Kind Of Music*.

The Carpenters' heyday was the early 70s, but they had hits later in the decade with 1976's 'There's A Kind Of Hush (All Over The World)' and 1977's 'Calling Occupants Of Interplanetary Craft (The Recognized Anthem Of World Contact Day)'. However, the group's workload took its toll on Richard, who became addicted to Qualuudes. Karen's health was an even greater cause for concern: she dieted compulsively and was now painfully thin. While Richard recovered, she began work on a solo album with producer Phil Ramone, but abandoned it to contribute to The Carpenters' *Made In America* (1981).

Returning only briefly to the US Top 20 with 'Touch Me When We're Dancing' in 1981, The Carpenters' final recordings were in 1982. On 4 February 1983, Karen was found unconscious at her parents' home and rushed to hospital where she died of cardiac arrest linked to anorexia. A TV biopic, *The Karen Carpenter Story*, topped the US ratings when it was shown in 1989 and numerous compilations testify to The Carpenters' unique and fragile sound (and their sensational commercial success). In 1994, fans of The Carpenters – including such unlikely artists as Sonic Youth and Babes In Toyland – covered a selection of their songs for the tribute album *If I Were A Carpenter*. More traditional treatments came on Richard's *Pianist–Arranger–Composer–Conductor* in 1998.

READ *Karen Carpenter* (1995), Ray Coleman
SURF www.mirai.or.jp/~gda/cp/index3.htm

CARTER THE UNSTOPPABLE SEX MACHINE•STEVE DOUBLE•RETNA

CARTER THE UNSTOPPABLE SEX MACHINE ⊙

WHO Vocals/guitar **Jim Bob** (b. James Morrison, 22 Nov 1960, London, England), guitar/keyboards **Fruitbat** (b. Les Carter, 12 Dec 1958, London)

WHEN 1987–1998

WHERE London, England

WHAT The Punk Pet Shop Boys

Jim Bob and Fruitbat told pun-laden, yet dark, south London fables using guitars mixed with samples and sequences. 'Bloodsport For All' (1992) was an attack on army bullying and racism, but its release at the beginning of the Gulf War caused the BBC to ban it. Other unlikely Pop subjects included child abuse and slum landlords. After five LPs, including the No.1 *1992: The Love Album*, and nine Top 40 singles (including the Top 10 hit 'The Only Living Boy in New Cross'), the duo expanded to include live musicians, only to call it a day in January 1998 after their final album, *I Blame The Government*.

ⓕⓐⓝ Club Carter, PO Box 709, London, SE19 1JY, UK

ⓢⓤⓡⓕ www.users.dircon.co.uk/~fruity/

JOHNNY CASH ✪

WHO b. 26 Feb 1932, Kingsland, Arkansas, USA

WHAT Black-clad Country singer/songwriter

After a spell in the US Air Force and a short career as an electrical appliance salesman, Cash became a stablemate of Elvis, Carl Perkins and Jerry Lee Lewis at Sun Studios in Memphis. His 1955 debut, 'Hey Porter', was a local hit, starting a string of successes, including 'Folsom Prison Blues' and his first Pop hit 'I Walk The Line'. Though keen to do Gospel music, Sun owner Sam Phillips felt there was no market for such material; Cash finally got the opportunity in 1958, when he switched to Columbia and recorded an album of Gospel songs. 'Ride This Train' (1960) and *Blood, Sweat And Tears* (1963) preceded the controversial *Bitter Tears* (1964), highlighting mistreatment of American Indians. In the mid-60s his career hit a low, not helped by addiction to prescription drugs. Rare hits during this period were 'Ring Of Fire' (1963) and 'It Ain't Me Babe' (1965), the former co-written by June Carter who, in 1968, became Cash's second wife. Their daughter, Carlene Carter, also became a singer/songwriter star and married Nick Lowe, who later wrote Cash's 'A Beast in Me'.

A live album recorded at the notorious Folsom Prison in 1968 became one of his biggest sellers and restarted his career. He repeated the success with a 1969 concert at San Quentin, from which 'A Boy Named Sue' gave Cash his first UK Top 20 hit. Networked TV shows followed and he swept the boards at the 1969 Country Music Association awards ceremony, collecting five. Cash also had a successful acting career, appearing in a remake of the John Ford classic *Stagecoach* (1966), *A Gunfight* (1970), in which he co-starred with Kirk Douglas, and *The Pride Of Jesse Hallam* (1982), as well as TV cameos in *Little House On The Prairie* and *Dr Quinn – Medicine Woman*.

THE CARS

WHO Vocals/guitar **Ric Ocasek** (b. Richard Otcasek, 23 Mar 1949, Baltimore, Maryland, USA), vocals/guitar **Elliot Easton** (b. Elliot Shapiro, 18 Dec 1953, Brooklyn, New York, USA), vocals/bass **Ben Orr** (b. Benjamin Orzechowski, 9 Aug 1955, Cleveland, Ohio, USA), vocals/keyboards/percussion/saxophone **Greg Hawkes** (b. Baltimore), drums **David Robinson** (b. 2 Apr 1953, Boston, Massachusetts, USA)

WHEN 1976–1988

WHERE Boston, Massachusetts, USA

WHAT New Wave motor cool

Convened in the early 70s, The Cars were christened by Robinson when he joined in 1976. Their eponymous debut (1978) yielded international hits 'My Best Friend's Girl' and 'Just What I Needed'. Subsequent success was confined largely to the USA, although they returned to the world stage when 'Drive', from 1984's *Heartbeat City*, soundtracked an emotive film clip at Live Aid and reached US No.3 and UK No.5. The band split in 1988, leaving a legacy of polished Pop Rock and innovative videos.

ⓡⓔⓐⓓ *Frozen Fire – The Story Of The Cars* (1985), Toby Goldstein

ⓕⓐⓝ frozen-fire-request@cs.hmc.edu

ⓢⓤⓡⓕ www.usats.com/dale/thecars/

He has recorded with a range of artists including Neil Young, U2 and Bob Dylan. In fact, Cash was instrumental in Dylan's signing to Columbia and wrote the sleevenotes for Dylan's *Nashville Skyline*, winning one of his eight Grammy Awards. In 1986 he teamed up with Willie Nelson, Waylon Jennings and Kris Kristofferson to form The Highwaymen, who released three successful albums and toured together.

After 30 years, Columbia unwisely dropped him from their roster. During a short spell on Mercury, he reunited with Jerry Lee Lewis, Carl Perkins and Roy Orbison on the Memphis homecoming *Class Of '55*. Finally finding a sympathetic home at Rick Rubin's American label, he recorded the acclaimed *American Recordings* (1994) and *Unchained* (1996) – the latter including covers of Beck and Soundgarden songs. His contemporary credentials were furthered by a show-stopping cameo on U2's 'The Wanderer' (from 1993's *Zooropa*), an appearance on the *Dead Man Walking* soundtrack (1996) and a collaboration with members of young Country bucks The Jayhawks. An enduring legend despite failing health, the 'Man In Black' (a title derived from his 1971 anti-Vietnam song and a reminder of life's dark side) is the only living artist to be inducted into the Rock And Roll, Country Music and Songwriters Halls Of Fame.

Read *Cash* (1997), Johnny Cash & Patrick Carr

Fan 'The Man In Black', Peter Lewry, 100 Boxgrove, Goring-By-Sea, West Sussex, BN12 6LX, UK

Surf www.johnnycash.com/

DAVID CASSIDY ◉

WHO b. 12 Apr 1950, New York City, New York, USA

WHAT Teen idol with talent to spare

From 1970–1974, Cassidy appeared in *The Partridge Family*, a TV show about a family Pop group. Consequent chart success included UK No.1s 'How Can I Be Sure' (1972), 'Daydreamer/The Puppy Song' (1973) and *Dreams Are Nuthin' More Than Wishes* (1973). Cassidy's talents were greater than the part demanded, evidenced by an accomplished version of 'For What It's Worth' on *Cassidy Live* (1974). In 1975 he recruited stars such as Beach Boy Carl Wilson to cut mainly self-penned material, but his reputation ensured critical and commercial failure. An award-nominated role in US TV's *A Chance to Live* (1978) helped fill the gap before the smooth AOR of *Romance* (1985). US success returned with *David Cassidy* (1990) and *Didn't You Used To Be David Cassidy?* (1992) and he still acts, writes, records and performs. *When I'm A Rock 'n' Roll Star* (1996) compiled his 70s Country Rock work. Throughout 1998, he starred in Las Vegas musical *EFX* – the world's most expensive stage production.

Read *Come On, Get Happy: Fear And Loathing* (1994), David Cassidy

Fan International David Cassidy Fanclub, The Old Post House, The Street, Litlington, East Sussex, BN26 5RD, UK

Surf members.aol.com/bewit/1164/private/dav

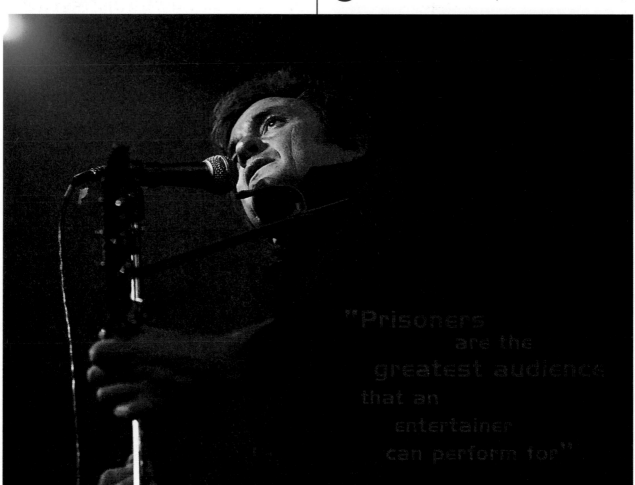

"Prisoners are the greatest audience that an entertainer can perform for"

CAST

WHO Vocals/guitar **John Power** (b. 14 Sep 1967, Liverpool, England), guitar **Liam 'Skin' Tyson** (b. 7 Sep 1969, Liverpool), bass **Peter Wilkinson** (b. 9 May 1969, Liverpool), drums **Keith O'Neill** (b. 18 Feb 1969, Liverpool)

WHEN 1993–

WHERE Liverpool, England

WHAT Bubbling Britpop loons

Cast were named after a line in The La's last song 'Looking Glass', "the change is cast...". Having left The La's in 1991, Power spent a year writing before recruiting bassist Wilkinson, drummer Russell Brady and a parade of guitarists, including fellow La's man Peter 'Cammy' Cammel. With guitarist Tyson and drummer O'Neill, Cast secured gigs with Elvis Costello and Oasis, and a deal with Polydor. 'Fine Time' entered the UK Top 20 in July 1995, and *All Change* (1995) sold a million. Hits including 'Flying' and 'Walkaway', and a hectic live schedule, boosted Cast's profile. The more diverse *Mother Nature Calls* (1997) received less favourable reviews, but still entered the UK Top 3 and delivered a stream of Top 20 sing-along hits: 'Free Me', 'Guiding Star', 'Live The Dream' and 'I'm So Lonely'.

surf www.cast.co.uk

CATATONIA ⊙

WHO Vocals **Cerys Matthews** (b. 11 Apr 1969, Cardiff, Wales), guitar **Mark Roberts** (b. 3 Nov 1969, Colwyn Bay, Wales), guitar **Owen Powell** (b. 9 Jul 1967, Cambridge, England), bass **Paul Jones** (b. 5 Feb 1960, Colwyn Bay), drums **Aled Richards** (b. 5 Jul 1969, Carmarthen, Wales)

WHEN 1993–

WHERE Cardiff, Wales

WHAT Sharp, pretty Welsh Indie Popsters

Mark Roberts found Cerys Matthews busking Jefferson Airplane songs and asked her to form a band. On Welsh Indie label Crai, they released 'For Tinkerbell', 'Hooked' and 'Whale'. With 1995's 'Bleed', released on the Nursery label, acclaim translated into sales and Catatonia were snapped up by Blanco Y Negro. Hard touring left Indie also-rans Marion, Salad and Puressence trailing in their wake and the band embarked on their debut album with Blur/Smiths producer Stephen Street. *Way Beyond Blue* (1996) was packed full of sly lyrics wrapped in deceptively pretty melodies, notably the hit 'You've Got A Lot To Answer For'.

They took a harder turn with 1997's rabble-rousing 'I Am The Mob', but finally broke into the national consciousness with the *X-Files*-flavoured 'Mulder And Scully' – a UK No.3 that propelled *International Velvet* (1998) up the charts. Matthews' striking looks and voice made her a media magnet and were showcased on her 1998 duet with Space, 'The Ballad Of Tom Jones'.

fan Catatonia, Trinity Street, 3 Alveston Place, CV32 4SN, UK

surf www.wea.co.uk/blanco/catatonia_biog.htm

NICK CAVE & THE BAD SEEDS

WHO Vocals/keyboards **Nick Cave** (b. 22 Sep 1957, Wangarrata, Australia), multi-instrumentalist **Mick Harvey** (b. 29 Sep 1958, Rochester, Australia), guitar/vocals **Blixa Bargeld** (b. 12 Jan 1959, Berlin, Germany), bass **Conway Savage** (b. 27 Jul 1960, Foster, Australia), drums **Thomas Wydler** (b. 9 Oct 1959, Zurich, Switzerland), keyboards **Martyn P. Casey** (b. 10 Jul 1960, Chesterfield, England)

WHEN 1983–

WHERE London, England

WHAT Tales from the dark side

Heroin abuse, riotous audiences, critical backlashes and volatile line-ups have proved only temporary setbacks to The Bad Seeds – convened by Nick Cave and Mick Harvey (formerly of hellish Punkers The Birthday Party) and Blixa Bargeld (also a member of German noise terrorists Einstürzende Neubauten).

Cave began his career (with Harvey and bassist Tracy Pew, guitarist Rowland S. Howard and drummer Phil Calvert) in late 70s Australia as The Boys Next Door, who released one album, *Door, Door* (1978), before mutating into The Birthday Party in 1980. The band relocated to London, signed to 4AD and released their first EP, 'Prayers On Fire', in 1981. With Cave cast as a Gothic Elvis, backed by monstrous basslines, raging drums and jagged guitars, the band's chaotic live performances were unique in dreary post-Punk London. *Junkyard* (1982) and the EPs 'The Bad Seed', 'The Birthday Party' and 'Mutiny!' (all 1983) followed, the first inspiring the name of Cave's next band when The Birthday Party was over in 1983.

Nick Cave & The Bad Seeds' 1984 debut *From Her To Eternity* revealed subtlety The Birthday Party lacked, notably on crooning covers of Leonard Cohen's 'Avalanche' and Elvis' 'In The Ghetto'. The King reappeared as inspiration for the savage 'Tupelo' from

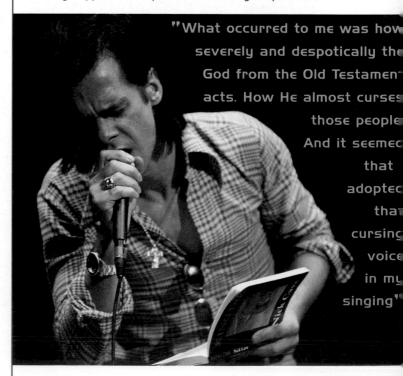

"What occurred to me was how severely and despotically the God from the Old Testament acts. How He almost curses those people. And it seemed that adopted that cursing voice in my singing"

1985's *The Firstborn Is Dead*, which preceded covers collection *Kicking Against The Pricks* (1986). Their first masterpiece, however, was 'Your Funeral… My Trial' (1986), an all-original, double EP which tempered the sonic and lyrical violence with inspired songwriting. This upturn was confirmed by Cave's books *King Ink* (1988) and *And The Ass Saw The Angel* (1989) and 1988's *Tender Prey*, which included the classic 'The Mercy Seat' – the final murmurs of a prisoner waiting for the electric chair. Films also proved fruitful for Cave & The Bad Seeds, with soundtrack contributions including Wim Wenders' *Wings Of Desire* (1987), *Until The End Of The World* (1991) and *Faraway, So Close* (1993) and Peter Sempel's *Dandy* (1989). Cave also appeared in *Ghosts… Of The Civil Dead* (1989) and *Johnny Suede* (1991).

After 1990's *The Good Son* (which yielded the exquisitely crafted ballad 'The Ship Song' and saw Cave kick a debilitating heroin addiction), they finally cracked the UK Top 30 with *Henry's Dream* (1992). Cave's 1992 duet with Shane MacGowan ('What A Wonderful World'), however, did not unduly challenge Whitney Houston for the Christmas No.1, and 1993's *Live Seeds* never looked likely to rival *Frampton Comes Alive*. Strong sales returned for *Let Love In* (1994) before Cave enjoyed his biggest hit with the Kylie Minogue duet 'Where The Wild Roses Grow' (UK No.11). The latter trailed *Murder Ballads* (1996), from which 'Henry Lee' – with Polly Harvey – was another hit. His relationship with the latter reportedly extended beyond the studio, a subject broodingly examined on 1997's *The Boatman's Call*, alongside songs about former loves Viviane Carneiro (mother of Cave's son Luke) and Anita Lane – a long-time inspiration and former Bad Seed. Elsewhere, Cave collaborated on ex-Magazine, Birthday Party and Bad Seeds bassist Barry Adamson's *Oedipus Schmoedipus* (1996) and joined Mick Harvey and Bargeld on the 1996 film soundtrack *To Have & To Hold*. In 1997, Mick Harvey released a second collection of Serge Gainsbourg covers, *Pink Elephants* – the sequel to 1995's *Intoxicated Man*.

ReaD *Bad Seed* (1995), Ian Johnston

Surf www.zephyr.net/users/cave/

TRACY CHAPMAN ◉ ◉ ✪

WHO b. 20 Mar 1964, Cleveland, Ohio, USA

WHAT Quiet protest singer

Dogged by Joan Armatrading comparisons, Tracy Chapman can best be likened to the black 'first lady of American Folk', Odetta. Acclaimed in Folk circles – notably by 10,000 Maniacs' Natalie Merchant – Chapman exploded with a scene-stealing cameo at 1988's Nelson Mandela tribute concert at London's Wembley Stadium. 'Fast Car' crashed transatlantic charts, millions bought *Tracy Chapman* (1988), she toured with Sting and Springsteen, and her mantelpiece groaned under three Grammys. The momentum carried *Crossroads* (1989) to platinum sales, but *Matters Of The Heart* (1992) underachieved critically and commercially. She returned in style with the triple platinum *New Beginning* (1996) and the Grammy-winning hit 'Give Me One Reason'. In 1997, she played the all-female, summer sensation Lilith Fair tour and duetted with B.B. King on his *Deuces Wild*. Meanwhile, her 'Baby Can I Hold You' became a hit for Boyzone.

Surf www.elektra.com/alternative_club/chapman/chapman.html

THE CHARLATANS ◉ ◎ ◉

WHO Vocals **Tim Burgess** (b. 30 May 1967, Salford, Greater Manchester, England), guitar **Mark Collins** (b. 14 Aug 1965), bass **Martin Blunt** (b. 21 May 1964), drums **Jon Brookes** (b. 21 Sep 1968), keyboards **Rob Collins** (b. 23 Feb 1963, d. 23 Jul 1996)

WHEN 1988–

WHERE Northwich, England

WHAT Madchester survivors

The Charlatans emerged from West Midlands bands The Electric Crayons, Makin' Time and The Gift Horses. After Burgess joined in 1989, 'Indian Rope' led to a deal with Beggars Banquet. 'The Only One I Know' (1990) swept them up in the 'Madchester' scene despite critical crucifixion of their ubiquitous psychedelic organ sound, courtesy of mainstay Rob Collins. Their debut album *Some Friendly* went to UK No.1, but *Between 10th And 11th* (1992) failed to match their opening success. In 1993, while Burgess romped with St Etienne on 'I Was Born On Christmas Day', Collins spent time in jail for his part in an armed robbery. After 1994's Britpop rebirth *Up To Our Hips*, they reclaimed the UK No.1 with *The Charlatans* (1995). Meanwhile, Burgess graced The Chemical Brothers' 1995 hit 'Life Is Sweet'. In July 1996, while the band were recording their fifth album, Collins was killed in a car crash. However, the group's success story continued with *Tellin' Stories* (1997), another UK No.1. *Melting Pot* (1998) – named after the band's favourite Northwich café – collected their best moments.

fan '109', PO Box 94, Northwich, Cheshire, CW9 5TS, UK

surf www.ifi.uio.no/^eirkig/charlatans.html

RAY CHARLES ✪

WHO b. Ray Charles Robinson, 23 Sep 1930, Albany, Georgia, USA

WHAT Genius of R&B, Jazz, Soul, Pop and Country

This blind singer/songwriter/producer/arranger/band leader and pianist played in a Country band before first making his mark as leader of hitmaking R&B act The Maxim Trio in 1949. In the early 50s he built up a following via his singles on Swing Time and his live shows with Lowell Fulson's band. When Atlantic bought out his contract for $2,500, he formed his own band and soon transformed from a 'cool' balladeer to a fervent Gospel-based vocalist and respected Jazz musician. Probably the first R&B act to produce himself, Charles recorded many seminal Soul sides for Atlantic, including 'I Got A Woman', 'Drown In My Own Tears', 'Hallelujah I Love Her So' (all 1954) and the vocally abandoned call-and-response classic 'What'd I Say' (1959) – his first major Pop hit.

In 1960, ABC-Paramount signed him to a staggering $50,000-a-year deal. In the first two years he topped the US best-sellers list with 'Georgia On My Mind', 'Hit The Road Jack' and the worldwide smash 'I Can't Stop Loving You', the latter from his boundary-stretching album *Modern Sounds In Country And Western Music* (1962) – the first R&B album to reach No.1. Laying the foundations for the 60s Soul boom, Charles was seldom out of the R&B and Pop charts in that decade, with his versions of Country songs 'You Don't Know Me', 'You Are My Sunshine', (both 1962), 'Take These Chains From My Heart', 'Busted' (both 1963) and 'Crying Time' (1966) selling particularly well. Oddly though, he did not become a Country hitmaker until the mid-80s, when he also sang on the 4-million-selling 'We Are The World' (1985) by USA For Africa.

The first popular entertainer to be tagged a 'genius' has had his compositions recorded by many major stars, and numerous Rock and R&B stars have aped his raspy vocal style. Charles, who has a shelf full of Grammy awards (including one for Lifetime Achievement), was among the first members of the Rock And Roll Hall Of Fame and is unique in having reaped so much success in so many diverse areas of music.

read *Brother Ray – The Ray Charles Story* (1992), Ray Charles & David Ritz

CHEAP TRICK

WHO Vocals **Robin Zander** (b. 23 Jan 1953, Loves Park, Illinois, USA), guitar **Rick Nielsen** (b. 22 Dec 1946, Rockford, Illinois), bass **Tom Petersson** (b. 9 May 1950, Rockford), drums **Bun E. Carlos** (b. 12 Jun 1951, Rockford)

WHEN 1974–

WHERE Chicago, Illinois, USA

WHAT Wacky New Wave Rock

After rigorous touring, Cheap Trick hit big in Japan, where they became heroes overnight. Popularity in America came after the release of *Cheap Trick At Budokan* (1978) and support slots were exchanged for huge headline gigs. Their well-known US hit, 'I Want You To Want Me', followed, reaching No.7. Cheap Trick's peculiar take on Metal is best shown on covers like 'Ain't That A Shame' and in their unique appearance: Nielsen's baseball cap and cartoon high kicks contrasting with the long-haired good looks of Zander and Petersson. As their popularity waned, Petersson departed, only to rejoin in 1988 before 'The Flame' surprisingly topped the US chart. As befits an acknowledged influence on Nirvana, a promotional album – *Cheap Trick*, with attached single, 'Say Goodbye' – came out on Sub Pop in 1997.

 member.aol/melkel/index.html

CHUBBY CHECKER

WHO b. Ernest Evans, 3 Oct 1941, Philadelphia, Pennsylvania, USA

WHAT The King of the Twist

Chubby Checker is a record breaker. His recording of 'The Twist' is the only single to have topped the US chart on two separate occasions, and he was the first Rock artist to place four albums simultaneously in the US Top 10.

Despite reaching the US Top 40 with novelty debut 'The Class' (containing his impersonations of Elvis Presley and Fats Domino), Checker's next two singles achieved negligible sales. Top DJ Dick Clark, who had pushed his first hit, suggested Checker cover 'The Twist', and included his version on *American Bandstand* in preference to Hank Ballard's original. It topped the US chart in September 1960 and astoundingly returned to the summit 15 months later when adults discovered the dance. The Twist went on to become the Rock era's most popular dance, although it was his sequel – another Ballard-influenced track, 'Let's Twist Again' – which got the whole world twisting in 1962.

Checker later successfully extolled the virtues of such dances as the Hucklebuck, Pony, Mess Around, Fly, Limbo, Popeye, Birdland, and the Freddie (often after other acts launched them). In 1988, Checker, who has never lacked for club work, re-charted internationally with an update of 'The Twist' in the company of Rappers The Fat Boys. He may not have been among the most original artists of his era, but in the early 60s Checker was the world's No.1 dance instructor.

THE CHEMICAL BROTHERS ⊙

WHO Keyboards **Tom Rowlands** (b. 11 Jan 1971, Kingston upon Thames, Surrey, England), keyboards **Ed Simons** (b. 9 Jun 1970, Oxford, England)

WHEN 1989–

WHERE Manchester, England

WHAT Techno for headbangers

THE CHEMICAL BROTHERS/STEVE DOUBLE/SIN

Tom Rowlands and Ed Simons met at university and formed a DJ duo. Naming themselves The Dust Brothers (a tribute to the Amercian Hip Hop producers), they began performing around Manchester and started their own club. Tom was moonlighting with his own band, Ariel, which fell apart around the time of The Dust Brothers' first recording, 'Song To The Siren', was released on their own Diamond label in 1992. This led to a contract with Dance label Junior Boys Own in 1993 and they became resident DJs at London's hip Heavenly Sunday Social club, while continuing to release low-budget, Techno and Breakbeat singles, such as 1994's seminal 'Chemical Beats'. Dust Brothers remixes were also heavily in demand and knobs were duly twiddled for The Charlatans, Primal Scream and The Prodigy, among others.

Faced with a lawsuit from their US namesakes in 1995, they considered The Grit Brothers (a suggestion from Ed's grandma) before settling on The Chemical Brothers. Their genre-defining debut *Exit Planet Dust* (1995) fused elements of Dub, Techno, Funk and Rock into an explosive 'Big Beat' style, but also found room for Charlatan chap Tim Burgess and folkstress Beth Orton.

Chemical Brothers fan Noel Gallagher co-wrote and sang on their UK No.1 'Setting Sun', a 90s remodelling of The Beatles' 'Tomorrow Never Knows'. Featuring another cameo from Beth Orton, the chart-topping *Dig Your Own Hole* (1997) was preceded by the monstrous 'Block Rockin' Beats' and appreciation from the USA, where – with Orbital, Underworld and The Prodigy – the group spearheaded the 'Electronica' boom of the late 90s.

surf raft.vmg.co.uk/chemicalbros/

CHER ⊙⊙

WHO b. Cherilyn Sarkasian LaPier, 21 May 1946, El Centro, California, USA

WHAT Rock Movie Star

With her husband Sonny Bono, Cher shot to fame when 'I Got You Babe' topped transatlantic charts in 1965. The loving face of anti-establishmentarianism, the duo scored hits on Atlantic between 1965 and 1968, characterized by Bono's Spectorish production, derivative songwriting and slightly off-key sound.

Cher's 1966 solo hit 'Bang Bang My Baby Shot Me Down' portrayed her as poor and misunderstood, a theme continued by her biggest hit after she signed to MCA in 1971: 'Gypsies, Tramps And Thieves'. The single became a million-seller on the back of US TV's *The Sonny & Cher Comedy Hour*. Best-selling *Cher* (1972) was followed by No.1s 'Half Breed' (1973) and 'Dark Lady' (1974).

Splitting from Bono in 1973, Cher became an icon of female independence. She met and married Gregg Allman in 1976 and got rockier on *Allman And Woman: Two The Hard Way* (1977). The album, like the marriage, failed. As the 70s faded, she flirted with Disco (1979's hit 'Take Me Home') and Metal (1980's *Black Rose*).

Her career was revitalized in 1987 with Oscar-winning acting in *Moonstruck* and the *Cher* album, featuring hits penned by Michael Bolton and Jon Bon Jovi. The careers dovetailed when 'The Shoop Shoop Song', from her hit movie *Mermaids*, made No.1 in 1991. Success continued with *Heart Of Stone* (1989), the UK No.1s *Love Hurts* (1991) and *Greatest Hits 1965–1992* (1992), and 'Walking In Memphis' from *It's A Man's World* (1995).

Sonny Bono died in a skiing accident on 5 January 1998.

ⓡⓔⓐⓓ *Totally Uninhibited: The Life And Times Of Cher* (1991), Lawrence J. Quirk

ⓢⓤⓡⓕ www.inch.com/~harbur/cher/index.html

NENEH CHERRY

WHO b. Neneh Mariana Karlsson, 10 Mar 1964, Stockholm, Sweden

WHAT Bohemian Rap star

Whitney, Kylie, Tiffany… sinking in sugar, mid-1989 transatlantic charts were spiced up by a pregnant Hip Hop bombshell with a patchwork background and neat line in put-downs: "Whaddya expect? The guy's a gigolo, man – y'knowhatimean?" Neneh's parentage (Jazz trumpeter Don Cherry) and pedigree (three albums with early 80s Funksters Rip, Rig & Panic) were rendered irrelevant by her new cohorts: stylist Jamie Morgan, his associate Cameron McVey (later Mr Cherry), Bomb The Bass mastermind Tim Simenon and Wild Bunch supremo Nellee Hooper.

Together, they fashioned the single 'Buffalo Stance' and album *Raw Like Sushi* (1989) into world-beating breaths of fresh air. Twelve months and four hits later, motherhood took priority. In 1990, a creepy take on 'I've Got You Under My Skin' for the AIDS benefit *Red Hot + Blue* and a one-off Rip, Rig & Panic reunion were her sole outings for three years.

Homebrew (1992) boasted REM's Michael Stipe, Gang Starr and Portishead's Geoff Barrow. This all-star cast, while not enough to save a commercial

---

Polish brothers Leonard and Phil Chess formed Aristocrat – label home of Muddy Waters – in Chicago in 1947. Renamed Chess, it flourished with product leased from labels like Sun and its own stars Howlin' Wolf, Little Walter, Willie Dixon and Chuck Berry, who inspired the likes of the Stones and John Mayall. Chess launched subsidiaries Checker (Bo Diddley, Sonny Boy Williamson) and Argo (Ramsey Lewis, Wes Montgomery), but in the early 60s the brothers turned their sights on radio. Koko Taylor and Fontella Bass kept Chess in the charts but, after Leonard's death in 1969, the label was sold to tape company GRT. Chess recordings survived further changes in ownership until the catalogue was acquired by MCA in 1985.

flop, confirmed Neneh as a talent magnet, other collaborators including The Jungle Brothers, Tricky, Massive Attack and – on the 1995 charity UK chart-topper 'Love Can Build A Bridge' – Cher, Chrissie Hynde and Eric Clapton. Accordingly, '7 Seconds', a 1994 duet with Youssou N'Dour, returned her to the spotlight, rising to No.3 in its five months on the UK chart.

In 1997 came *Man*, from which 'Woman' (1996) – featuring ex-Suede guitarist Bernard Butler – pitched her into the Top 10 alongside The Spice Girls (confessed fans of Neneh). "I'm the kind of woman that was built to last," sang Ms Cherry – no 'girl power' required. Meanwhile, Cameron McVey was one of the writer/ producers behind fresh female sensations All Saints.

ⓢⓤⓡⓕ www.sheenaweb.com/neneh/

CHIC

WHO Vocals **Alfa Anderson** (b. 7 Sep 1946), vocals **Luci Martin** (b. 10 Jan 1955), guitar **Nile Rodgers** (b. 19 Sep 1952), bass **Bernard Edwards** (b. 31 Oct 1952, Greenville, North Carolina, USA, d. 18 Apr 1996, Tokyo, Japan), drums

Tony Thompson (b. 15 Nov 1954)

WHEN 1976–1996

WHERE The Bronx, New York, USA

WHAT Distilled Disco

Rodgers and Edwards paid dues in Soul and R&B bands before forming Fusion trio The Big Apple Band with Thompson, ex-Labelle. Renamed Chic, they recruited vocalist Norma Jean Wright and switched to Disco for 1977 debut *Chic*, propelled by million-seller 'Dance Dance Dance (Yowsah, Yowsah, Yowsah)'. With Martin replacing Wright, *C'est Chic* (1978) and *Risqué* (1979) yielded mega-hits 'Everybody Dance', 'Le Freak', 'I Want Your Love' and the classic 'Good Times'. The latter helped kickstart Hip Hop (when sampled by Grandmaster Flash and The Sugarhill Gang) and revitalized Queen's Stateside fortunes (courtesy of the *très* Chic 'Another One Bites The Dust').

Rodgers and Edwards became a production powerhouse, transforming Sister Sledge into divas with 1979's *We Are Family* and launching Diana Ross into the 80s with 'Upside Down'. Their own fortunes declined through *Real People* (1980), *Tongue In Chic* (1982) and *Believer* (1983). Edwards produced ABC, Rod Stewart, Gladys Knight, Robert Palmer and Duran Duran offshoot Power Station (also featuring Thompson), while Rodgers sold millions with Bowie, Madonna and Duran Duran. They periodically reunited as Chic until Edwards' sudden death in Japan in 1996.

CHICAGO ✪✪✪✪✪

WHO Vocals/guitar **Terry Kath** (b. 31 Jan 1946, Chicago, Illinois, USA, d. 23 Jan 1978), vocals/bass **Peter Cetera** (b. 13 Sep 1944, Chicago), vocals/keyboards **Robert Lamm** (b. 13 Oct 1944, Brooklyn, New York, USA), saxophone **Walter Parazaider** (b. 14 Mar 1945, Chicago), drums **Danny Seraphine** (b. 28 Aug 1948, Chicago), trombone **James Pankow** (b. 20 Aug 1947, Chicago), trumpet **Lee Loughname** (b. 21 Oct 1941, Chicago)

WHEN 1966–

WHERE Chicago, Illinois, USA

WHAT From brassware to ballads

Originally The Missing Links, then The Big Thing, Chicago Transit Authority released their self-titled debut in 1969 on Columbia. Streamlined to Chicago, they moved from Jazz Rock to Pop Rock. *Chicago II* (1970) began a series of numerical titles, up to *Chicago 21* (1991). Exceptions were the live set *Chicago At Carnegie Hall* (1971) and *Hot Streets* (1978). The band had five consecutive US chart-toppers: *Chicago V* (1972), *Chicago VI* (1973), *Chicago VII* (1974), *Chicago VIII* (1975) and the hits set *Chicago IX* (1975). Only *Chicago V* charted in the UK, reaching No.24.

Transatlantic hits included the classic 'If You Leave Me Now' (1976) and '25 Or 6 To 4' (1970). Chicago added Brazilian percussionist Laudir de Oliveira in 1974, and won a Grammy for *Chicago X* in 1977. Kath's death in a bizarre gun accident led to a succession of line-up changes and moderately selling albums. Despite occasional hits, Chicago's glory days were over – a fate confirmed when Cetera left in 1985 to pursue solo success.

Belated credibility called in 1995 when Bucketheads sampled Chicago's disastrous Disco stab 'Street Player' (1979) for Dance hit 'The Bomb (These Sounds Fall Into My Mind)'.

(ReaD) *Chicago Is Forever* (1997), Chicago True Advocates

(Fan) Chicago True Advocates, PO Box 195, Landing, NJ 07850, USA

(Surf) www.chicrecords.com/

Chrysalis was formed in 1969 by Rock managers Chris Wright and Terry Ellis, and debuted with their clients Jethro Tull and Ten Years After. The success of Leo Sayer prompted the establishment of a US operation in the late 70s when Nick Gilder and Blondie brought further Stateside success. Chrysalis forged through the 80s with Ultravox, Spandau Ballet, Billy Idol, Huey Lewis and Sinead O'Connor, adding The Proclaimers, Arrested Development, Babybird, Simple Minds and Robbie Williams in the 90s. Wright and Ellis quit, but the former, who sold the label to EMI music, remains head of Chrysalis Group.

CLANNAD

WHO Vocals/harp **Maire Brennan** (b. 4 Aug 1952, Dublin, Ireland), vocals/guitar **Pol Brennan**, vocals/bass/keyboards **Ciaran Brennan** (b. 4 Mar, Dublin), mandolin/vocals **Padraig Duggan** (b. 23 Jan, Gweedore, Ireland), guitar/vocals **Noel Duggan** (b. 23 Jan, Gweedore)

WHEN 1970–

WHERE Gweedore, Ireland

WHAT Prototypical Celtic spiritualists

Born to a musical family (father Lee owned a pub and fronted a showband), Ciaran formed Clannad as a trio with his uncles Padraig and Noel in 1970. His sister Maire joined, initially as harpist, in 1971, with brother Pol following shortly after as the group's 'Pop idol' frontman. The Philips label snapped up Clannad at the 1970 Letterkenny Folk Festival, but – embarrassed by the group's use of the then unfashionable Gaelic language – delayed their debut until 1973. That album, the Pentangle-esque *Clannad*, helped revitalize Irish music for the Rock generation. Clannad toured extensively in Europe, releasing further Gaelic-language albums via one-off deals with Irish independents, climaxing with *Fuaim* (1982), the best of their early period and their sole recording with sister and future solo star Enya.

The modern Clannad era of big production values and original material was ushered in with 'Theme To Harry's Game', a UK No.5 in 1982, and the resulting security of a major label contract. In 1984, *Legend* (music from TV's *Robin of Sherwood*) expanded their audience, while *Macalla* (1985) – featuring 'In A

Lifetime', a UK No.17 with U2's Bono – remains their definitive collection. *Sirius* (1987) was an ill-advised attempt to break America; the real US breakthrough, ironically, arrived in 1990 when 'Harry's Game' soundtracked a TV car ad. Subsequent albums have maintained the formula, and Clannad are celebrated as pioneers of the mainstream acceptance of all things Celtic.

READ *Irish Rock* (1987), Mark Prendergast

ERIC CLAPTON ⊙✪✪✪

WHO b. Eric Patrick Clapton, 30 Mar 1945, Ripley, Surrey, England

WHAT Guitar 'God'

Patricia Clapton was 16 when she gave birth to Eric after an affair with a married Canadian serviceman. His grandmother, Rose, and her husband, Jack Clapp, raised him as their son and reluctantly bought him a guitar when Clapton was 13. They had hoped his considerable drawing skills would lead to a safer career as a commercial artist. A growing obsession with playing the Blues hindered his graphic art studies at Kingston College of Art, from which he was dismissed in 1962. As this coincided with a growing London Blues scene, his timing was fortuitous. Clapton haunted local clubs – watching, occasionally playing.

His grandfather, impatient with Clapton's lack of direction, insisted he work with him for several months, helping him with his bricklaying work. The purchase of an electric guitar spurred him to join his first band, Rhode Island Red & The Roosters (shortened to The Roosters) in 1963. They lasted six months (lack of transport being a problem) and Clapton had a brief stint with Casey Jones & The Engineers before joining the fledgling Yardbirds in October 1963.

❝ You know it's the Blues when he plays it
B.B. King ❞

By 1965, Blues purist Clapton was growing tired of the Yardbirds' shift towards Pop and teamed up with John Mayall's Bluesbreakers. His reputation as a virtuoso Blues guitarist was growing steadily, although he was embarrassed by the "Clapton is God" graffiti seen in London at the time. Within a year, he was restless and formed Cream with Jack Bruce and Ginger Baker. The trio had considerable success with their tours and album releases but, by the end of 1968, Clapton had had enough of the constant fighting between Bruce and Baker and the group disbanded. During that period, he contributed a memorable guitar solo to George Harrison's 'While My Guitar Gently Weeps'.

In an attempt to take a brief respite from music, Clapton bought a mansion in Surrey, but his holiday didn't last long as he was soon talking to Steve Winwood about forming a new band. They were joined by Ginger Baker and ex-Family bassist Rick Grech, and the press were immediately speculating about

this latest 'supergroup'. Such assumptions caused an amused Clapton to name the group Blind Faith, and the under-rehearsed members were rushed into their first performance, a free concert in London's Hyde Park. An ill-fated American tour was organized, which proved the undoing of the band, although their self-titled LP topped both the UK and US charts.

During the tour, Clapton became close to the support band, Delaney & Bonnie & Friends, who encouraged Clapton to develop his singing. He toured with them in England before taking their backing band with him to Los Angeles to record his first solo album, *Eric Clapton* (1970), squeezing in appearances with John Lennon's Plastic Ono Band in Toronto and London the year before. The newly christened Derek & The Dominos recorded *Layla And Other Assorted Love Songs* (1970) in Miami, with Duane Allman dropping in to contribute to the title song, which was inspired by Clapton's infatuation with George Harrison's wife, Patti.

The band soon disintegrated amidst drug problems and, by 1971, Clapton was a virtual recluse and addicted to heroin. In 1973, his friend and admirer Pete Townshend stepped in to help, organizing the star-studded 'comeback' show captured on *Eric Clapton's Rainbow Concert* (1973). His rehabilitation was completed with a first US No.1, *461 Ocean Boulevard*, which gave him his first UK Top 10 hit since 'Layla' – a cover of Bob Marley's 'I Shot The Sheriff' that also topped the US chart.

He also began a relationship with Patti Harrison, whose marriage had already been rocky. Although alcohol replaced heroin, Clapton toured and recorded albums that puzzled critics but sold well, including *There's One In Every Crowd* (1975), *E.C. Was Here* (1975), *No Reason To Cry* (1976), *Slowhand* (1977) and *Backless* (1978). Hits from the period included 1977's future standard 'Lay Down Sally' – whose co-writer, Marcella Detroit, later made her own mark as half of 80s stars Shakespear's Sister.

Clapton's drinking contributed to drunken racist remarks during a 1976 gig, which led to public protest and which he immediately regretted. Despite nearly dying from ulcers in 1981, it was months before he went into rehabilitation.

In the 80s, Clapton transformed from musicianly legend to top-flight superstar. In 1985, *Behind The Sun* returned him to the UK Top 10, followed by *August* (1986), *The Cream Of Eric Clapton* (1987) and *Journeyman* (1989). Constant touring, session work (notably a scene-stealing performance on Roger Waters' 1984 *The Pros And Cons Of Hitch Hiking*) and high-profile appearances included an annual residency at the Royal Albert Hall in London, commemorated on *24 Nights* (1991). In 1991, however, he was devastated by the death of his 4-year-old son, Conor, who fell from a window. The ballad inspired by his son, 'Tears In Heaven' – originally written for the movie *Rush* – was movingly performed on an *Unplugged* appearance; the 7-million-selling album of which gave him his second US chart-topper and contributed to a haul of six Grammys in 1992.

In 1994, Clapton recorded an album of Blues standards, *From The Cradle*, which topped both the UK and US charts and won another Grammy. He was awarded an OBE in 1995, but attracted more attention by flirting with Rock chick Sheryl Crow. He returned to music in 1998 with *Pilgrim*.

READ *Crossroads – The Life And Music Of Eric Clapton* (1995), Michael Schumacher

FAN Where's Eric, 74 Lowbrook Drive, Maidenhead, SL6 3XR, UK

SURF mars.superlink.net/user/wnuck/clapton.html

THE DAVE CLARK FIVE

WHO Drums **Dave Clark** (b. 15 Dec 1942, Tottenham, London, England), vocals/keyboards **Mike Smith** (b. 12 Dec 1943, Edmonton, London), guitar **Lenny Davidson** (b. 30 May 1944, Enfield, Middlesex, England), guitar **Rick Huxley** (b. 5 Aug 1942, Dartford, Kent, England), saxophone/guitar **Denis Payton** (b. 11 Aug 1943, Walthamstow, London, England)

WHEN 1958–1973

WHERE London, England

WHAT 60s British Invasion superstars

The quintet released singles on Ember, Piccadilly and Columbia before the stomping 'Glad All Over' headed the UK chart in 1964 and gave them the first of nine UK and 14 US Top 20 entries. Among the photogenic act's best remembered recordings are their 1965 revival of 'Over And Over' (a US No.1 which was overlooked in Britain) and the Clark and Smith compositions 'Bits And Pieces', 'Everybody Knows' and the theme song from their debut film *Catch Us If You Can* (all 1964). The mod-dressed combo's American popularity can also be judged by the fact that half a dozen of their albums also cracked the US Top 20, and that they appeared more times on Ed Sullivan's prestigious TV show than any other artist. An American reviewer noted, "The group have considerably more volume than The Beatles, and so have their fans". However, by 1968 the fivesome's fervent following had declined and in 1973, with sales of over 50 million records behind them, they disbanded. Dave Clark has since become a highly successful music business entrepreneur, and owns the rights to British TV series *Ready Steady Go!*, the hit musical *Time* and the group's recordings.

THE CLASH

WHO Vocals/guitar **Joe Strummer** (b. John Mellors, 21 Aug 1952, Ankara, Turkey), guitar **Mick Jones** (b. 26 Jun 1953, London, England), bass **Paul Simonon** (b. 15 Dec 1955, London), drums **Nicky 'Topper' Headon** (b. 30 May 1955, Bromley, Kent, England)

WHEN 1976–1986

WHERE London, England

WHAT Raw guitar power barbed with sharp hooks

The Clash did more than any other act to define the style, principles and limitations of Punk. At first overshadowed by The Sex Pistols, they survived to create controversy and compelling music long after the Pistols self-destructed and were one of the few Punk bands to rival the excitement of the Pistols' live shows.

Jones, Simonon and Headon first played together in proto-Punk band The London SS in the mid-70s, which proved as short-lived as their name was dreadful, and in early 1976 the guitarist and bassist joined forces with Strummer, who'd spent three years playing Pub Rock with The 101'ers.

The first incarnation of The Clash also included guitarist Keith Levene, later of Public Image Ltd, and drummer Terry Chimes. Both left before the band signed to CBS, but Chimes nonetheless played on their debut album, credited as Tory Crimes on the sleeve. The deal with CBS had been secured by another key figure in The Clash story: charismatic manager Bernie Rhodes, who would be sacked by the band in late 1978, then reinstated in 1981. Recorded in three weekends with engineer Mickey Foote acting as producer, *The Clash* (1977) was fast, furious and thrilling, its raw guitar power barbed with sharp hooks. The lyrics of Strummer and Jones' songs were almost unintelligible, but the

many who cared to decipher them heard vivid descriptions of urban decay and conflict. 'White Riot' (1977) was the first single, and became one of the great Punk anthems, and a cover of Junior Murvin's reggae hit 'Police And Thieves' showed the breadth of the band's vision. *The Clash* reached the UK Top 20 and won huge critical acclaim; *Rolling Stone* calling it "the definitive Punk album" long before it was released in America.

In a bid to make The Clash palatable to American fans, CBS persuaded the band to work with producer Sandy Pearlman on *Give 'Em Enough Rope* (1978). By the time it was recorded, Headon had been brought back to complete the definitive Clash line-up. The band's incendiary live shows were immortalized in the semi-documentary, semi-drama film *Rude Boy* (1980). Pearlman, best known for his work with Blue Öyster Cult, smoothed the jagged edges from The Clash's sound without destroying the power of tracks like 'Safe European Home' and 'Guns On The Roof'. The album hit UK No.2 and yielded the band's first UK Top 20 single, 'Tommy Gun', but failed to provide the hoped-for breakthrough in America.

The Clash therefore refused to compromise on their next album. The producer was the band's own choice – Guy Stevens, an eccentric but inspirational character who'd produced the first Clash demos. The reunion with Stevens sent the band into creative overdrive, and they demanded that the album be a double. Their judgement was correct on every count. *London Calling* (1979) was that rare thing, a double album that justified the extra running time, and in early 1980 it climbed the *Billboard* Top 30, while The Clash played to packed houses across America.

At this point The Clash *did* become over-ambitious, with a triple-album set on which quality control slipped. *Sandinista!* (1980) had its highlights, notably 'The Call-Up' and 'Hitsville UK', but as a whole tried the patience of their most loyal admirers.

The Clash rediscovered their focus with producer Glyn Johns on *Combat Rock* (1982). Showing both diversity and discipline, the album included two international hits: the double A-side 'Should I Stay Or Should I Go?'/'Straight To Hell' and 'Rock The Casbah'. However, May 1982 – the month of the album's release – also saw the beginning of the end for the band. Headon was sacked, officially owing to "a difference of political direction", but actually because of drug problems that eventually led to an eighteen-month jail sentence in late 1987. Chimes rejoined The Clash for their biggest US tour, which included a series of shows supporting The Who. The following year he quit again, to be replaced by Pete Howard.

The band's big decline began in September 1983, when Strummer and Simonon sacked Jones for drifting apart from the original idea of The Clash. (Jones resurfaced with Big Audio Dynamite.) Strummer later admitted: "I stabbed him in the back." Guitarists Vince White and Nick Sheppard were recruited, and Strummer and Rhodes co-wrote *Cut The Crap* (1985). Critical consensus suggested two words of the title were superfluous. The album sold poorly, and the band finally split in early 1986.

There was one last twist left in the tale of The Clash. While together, the band hit the UK singles chart on 17 occasions without once reaching the Top 10, their success inhibited by the band's refusal to appear on *Top Of The Pops*. However, in 1991, 'Should I Stay Or Should I Go?' was chosen as the soundtrack for a Levi jeans commercial, prompting the single's re-release; the TV exposure gave The Clash a posthumous No.1. To their credit, the ex-members resisted the temptation of a reunion, preferring to keep The Clash as a (mostly) glorious memory.

read *A Riot Of Our Own* (1997), Johnny Green & Garry Barker

surf www.primenet.com/~jendave/clash/clash.htm

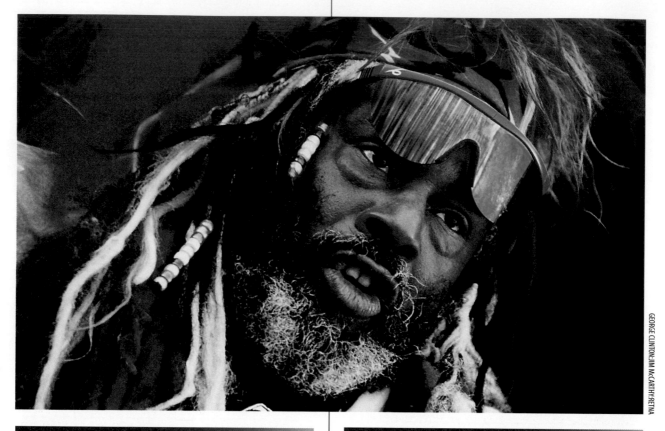

PATSY CLINE

WHO b. Virginia Patterson Hensley, 8 Sep 1932, Winchester, Virginia, USA, d. 5
Mar 1963, near Camden, Tennessee, USA

WHAT Sweet dreaming Country legend

After several years on the honky-tonk circuit, Cline first tasted
fame in 1955 when she won on the star-making TV show *Arthur
Godfrey's Talent Scouts*, singing her fifth single, 'Walkin' After
Midnight'. The record rocketed into both the US Country and
Pop Top 20s and she was voted Most Promising Female Country
Singer of 1957. Nonetheless, her record sales declined until
1961, when 'I Fall To Pieces' reaped her first gold disc. The
follow-up later in the year, Willie Nelson's composition 'Crazy'
(later voted America's Most Popular Country Song of all time),
fared even better and 'She's Got You' (1962) followed them into
the US Top 20. However, tragedy struck in March 1963, when
she died alongside Country stars Hawkshaw Hawkins and
Cowboy Copas in a light aircraft crash. Her funeral was attended
by 25,000 grieving fans.

In America, her records continued to sell well and her *12
Greatest Hits* album topped the Country chart for an
unprecedented four years, selling over 7 million copies. In
Britain, Country's most respected and important female artist
sold more records in the 90s than ever before, with 'Crazy'
finally reaching the Top 20 in 1991. Not unexpectedly, the
emotive song stylist, whose life story was made into the movie
Sweet Dreams (1985), became the first female inducted into the
Country Music Hall Of Fame.

READ *I Fall To Pieces: The Music And Life Of Patsy Cline* (1995),
Mark Bego

GEORGE CLINTON

WHO b. 22 Jul 1941, a galaxy far, far away

WHAT Dr Funkenstein

A thirty-year crusade "to rescue Dance music from the blahs"
began in 1967. After a decade of Doo Wop oblivion, The
Parliaments scored a US hit with '(I Wanna) Testify'. It vindicated
their leader, George Clinton, whose only success to date was
placing his 'I'll Bet You' on a Jackson 5 album. However, when
the band became entangled in legalities, Clinton seized the
opportunity to found the 'P-Funk' dynasty. Equal parts social
commentary and comic book insanity, the style 'P-Funk' became
a quasi-mystical *thang* analogous to *Star Wars*' 'The Force'.

In 1970, the group recorded both as Parliament (*Osmium*,
revamped in 1990 as *Rhenium*) and the wiggier, Hendrix-derived
Funkadelic (*Funkadelic*). The latter hit an acid-fried stride with
Free Your Mind And Your Ass Will Follow (1971), *Maggot Brain*
(1971), *America Eats Its Young* (1972) and *Cosmic Slop* (1973), all
on the Westbound label. Parliament resurfaced on Casablanca
with *Up For The Down Stroke* (1974), furthering the cause with
Chocolate City (1975), *Mothership Connection* and *The Clones Of
Dr Funkenstein* (both 1976), then *Live-P Funk Earth Tour* and
Funkentelechy Vs The Placebo Syndrome (both 1977). From the
latter came the awesome US Soul chart-topper 'Flashlight'.
Funkadelic, meanwhile, streamlined its sound through *Standing
On The Verge Of Getting It On* (1974), *Let's Take It To The Stage*
(1975) and *Tales Of Kidd Funkadelic* (1976).

The key to P-Funk's evolution from guitar-grounded sludge
to bass-boosted stardust was Bootsy Collins, who jumped the
James Brown juggernaut in search of freedom and recognition.
Clinton rewarded him with the spin-off Bootsy's Rubber Band,

whose three albums (and other P-Funk products) featured keyboardist Bernie Worrell, who later gave Talking Heads more bounce to the ounce.

P-Funk conquered the universe in 1978: Funkadelic's *Hardcore Jollies* was followed by *One Nation Under A Groove*, whose title track ruled the US Soul chart and even made the UK's staid hit parade. Female funkstresses Parlet debuted with *Pleasure Principle*, the Bootsy-produced Brides Of Funkenstein kicked off with the hit 'Disco To Go' from *Funk Or Walk*, and Parliament rounded off the year atop the Soul chart with 'Aqua Boogie (A Psychoalphadiscobetabioaquadoloop)' from *Motor Booty Affair*. The momentum continued into 1979, courtesy of Parliament's *Gloryhallastoopid (Pin The Tale On The Funky)*, albums by the Brides and Parlet, and Funkadelic's '(Not Just) Knee Deep' from *Uncle Jam Wants You*.

However, the empire fell in the 80s. Though Parlet bubbled along with *Play Me Or Trade Me* (1980), Parliament sank with *Trombipulation* (1980). Mutinous sidemen, led by Clarence 'Fuzzy' Haskins, created a *faux* Funkadelic, scoring minor hits with *Connections And Disconnections* and its title track (1981). Clinton successfully sued for custody of the name, but charted only marginally higher with *The Electric Spanking Of War Babies* (1981) and *its* title track, featuring Sly Stone. He fared better with solo debut *Computer Games* (1982) – whose hit 'Atomic Dog' is, said Public Enemy's Chuck D, "Every Rapper's favourite record". However, sales dwindled through *You Shouldn't-Nuf Bit Fish* (1983), *Some Of My Best Jokes Are Friends* (1985) and *R&B Skeletons In The Closet* (1986). The P-Funk All-Stars' *Urban Dancefloor Guerrillas* (1983) was the last gasp of his Uncle Jam vanity label, which had struck gold with Zapp frontman Roger Troutman. Although heralded as a hero by younger stars – including Red Hot Chili Peppers, whose *Freaky Styley* (1985) he produced – Clinton ran aground on bankruptcy and bad habits.

Prince lent a hand – signing him to Paisley Park, releasing the nondescript *The Cinderella Theory* (1989) and featuring him on *Graffiti Bridge* (1990) – but Clinton's Second Coming began only when the well of James Brown samples ran dry, and Rappers like Digital Underground took to plundering P-Funk. Most richly rewarded was Dr Dre, who detonated the 'G-Funk' explosion with *The Chronic* (1992) – after which, no record was complete without boingy Bootsy bass, Worrell-esque whirls or a dip into Clinton's lexicon of ludicrousness. Ice Cube went the whole hog by reworking 'One Nation Under A Groove' with Clinton himself for the misleadingly monickered 'Bop Gun', a transatlantic hit in 1993.

Clinton celebrated with the five-album *Family Series* (1992–93), his solo comeback *Hey Man… Smell My Finger* (1993), two volumes of the DJ-friendly *Sample Some Of Disc, Sample Some Of DAT* (1993), a collaboration with UK Indie band Primal Scream (*Give Out But Don't Give Up*, 1994) and a Parliafunkadelicment revival on *Dope Dogs* (1995). Old labels cashed in with reissues and compilations.

The final proof of P-Funk's corruption of the mainstream came when Pop princesses The Spice Girls sampled Digital Underground. There was no need for Clinton to title a reunion of his old cronies *The Awesome Power Of A Fully Operational Mothership* (1997) – the evidence was all around.

READ *No.1 Bimini Road – Authentic P-Funk Insights* (1996), Diem Jones

FAN The P-Funk Fan Club, PO Box 1895, Newark, NJ 07101-1895, USA

SURF www.gnofn.org/-1nation

EDDIE COCHRAN

WHO b. 3 Oct 1938, Oklahoma, USA, d. 17 Apr 1960, Wiltshire, England

WHAT Rock 'n' Roll innovator and icon

As a star, Eddie lived and recorded in Los Angeles, but he grew up in the Midwest, which influenced his early involvement in Country music. At 16, he played guitar with unrelated Country singer Hank Cochran in The Cochran Brothers, touring the USA and making local TV appearances. Hearing Elvis Presley converted Eddie to Rock 'n' Roll and, in 1956, he joined forces with Jerry Capeheart to write for other artists and worked as a session guitarist. While recording movie music in August 1956, he was offered the role of a singer in the movie *The Girl Can't Help It* (1956). Described as the James Dean of Rock 'n' Roll, his good looks helped secure the role for which he performed '20 Flight Rock'. Happiest just playing guitar, Eddie later said, "I thought it was a joke – I didn't know if I could sing". A record contract followed and, in April 1957, the gimmicky, echo-laden 'Sitting in the Balcony' was his first US hit. With the punchy teenage angst of 'Summertime Blues', co-written with Capeheart, Eddie got his biggest US and first UK hit in late 1958. Showing remarkable confidence for a 19-year-old, Eddie performed all instruments and vocals, including the bass voice. 'C'mon Everybody' and 'Something Else', both 1959, also became Rock 'n' Roll standards – notably demolished by The Sex Pistols in 1979. Like his close friend Buddy Holly, Eddie was also interested in record production and left his mark on several Gene Vincent tracks, notably 'Pistol Packin' Mama'.

In 1960 Eddie played a UK sellout tour with Vincent and enjoyed fan mania he never achieved in the USA. The adulation and hell-raising presence of Vincent led to occasional excess. In London, they kicked a hotel door off its hinges and, on the underground, Eddie pulled the communication cord on a train as a prank, waited for the guard to arrive and calmly paid the £5 fine for 'improper use'. At the end of the tour, rushing to London from Bristol, Eddie's taxi span out of control into a lamp-post. Co-passengers Gene Vincent and Sharon Sheeley recovered, but Eddie suffered severe head injuries and died the next day.

Cochran's influence has been acknowledged by many British Rock acts, particularly The Beatles – who saw him play in Liverpool in 1960 – The Who and the aforementioned Pistols.

 SURF www2.geocities.com/SunsetStrip/Alley/1087/cochran.html

JOE COCKER

WHO b. 20 May 1944, Sheffield, South Yorkshire, England

WHAT Raw, soulful singer and 60s survivor

Cocker began his career in 1961 as Vance Arnold, fronting The Avengers, and as a solo artist released a flop cover of The Beatles' 'I'll Cry Instead' (1964). He subsequently formed Joe Cocker's Big Blues, which toured American Air Force bases in France, but was then inactive for a year. Finding a musical soulmate in Chris Stainton (bass, keyboards), he formed The Grease Band with him in 1966. The band's second single – a reworking of The Beatles' 'With A Little Help From My Friends', recorded with guitarist Jimmy Page – became a UK No.1 in 1968.

Cocker's tonsil-shredding, Ray Charles-influenced vocals and his live appearances, in which he grimaced grotesquely and his limbs flailed apparently uncontrollably, were utterly compelling. The Grease Band evolved to feature Stainton (keyboards), Henry McCullough (guitar), Alan Spenner (bass), and Bruce Rowland (drums), and the band's stunning Woodstock appearance helped them crack America, where their albums *With A Little Help From My Friends* (1969) and *Joe Cocker!* (1969) were more successful than in the UK. Leon Russell's 'Delta Lady' was another major hit, but after a further exhausting US tour Cocker split from the band. Anticipating a much-needed rest, he found instead his management threatening legal action if he didn't tour again immediately. Leon Russell – perhaps helpfully, perhaps opportunistically – convened a huge band to back Cocker, many of whom had been associated with Delaney & Bonnie, including Jim Gordon (drums), Carl Radle (bass), Bobby Keys (saxophone) and Rita Coolidge (vocals). The resulting tour, with Russell arguably stealing the show, produced a live double album (1970) and film (1971), both named *Mad Dogs And Englishmen*, but Cocker allegedly finished the tour with less than $1,000 profit.

Unhappy and apparently burnt out, Cocker retired for 18 months. Subsequent albums like *I Can Stand A Little Rain* (1974), including the classic 'You Are So Beautiful', and *Jamaica Say You Will* (1975) were inconsistent, with Cocker suffering serious drink and drug problems, and his career began to fade badly. Amazingly, 'Up Where We Belong', a duet with Jennifer Warnes for the movie *An Officer And A Gentleman*, became a huge hit (1983), and Cocker's career was reborn. His personal problems seemingly under control, he appeared at prestigious events such as the Prince's Trust Gala, Nelson Mandela's Birthday Concert and President Bush's Inauguration. Although his voice had lost some range, Cocker remained a soulful vocalist, and albums like *One Night Of Sin* (1989) and *Night Calls* (1992) were among his most successful ever.

ReaD *With A Little Help From My Friends* (1990), J.P. Bean

SUrf www.cocker.com/

COCTEAU TWINS

WHO Vocals **Elizabeth Fraser** (b. 29 Aug 1963, Grangemouth, Scotland), guitar/keyboards/production **Robin Guthrie** (b. 4 Jan 1962, Grangemouth), bass/keyboards **Simon Raymonde** (b. 3 Apr 1962, London, England)

WHEN 1981–

WHERE Grangemouth, Scotland

WHAT Pure, glittering, ethereal, shimmering sound

Cocteau Twins were staples of 80s Indie, with much-copied vaporous guitar and vocals married to subtle electronic washes and rhythms. Their debut *Garlands* (1982) garnered unanimous critical praise, continued by 1983's EP 'Lullabies' and *Head Over Heels*. Fraser scraped the chart with This Mortal Coil on a classic cover of Tim Buckley's 'Song To The Siren'. Replacing bassist Will Heggie with Simon Raymonde, *Treasure* (1984), *Victorialand* (1986), the Harold Budd collaboration *The Moon And The Melodies* (1986) and *Blue Bell Knoll* (1988) elaborated the Cocteaus' abstract brief, especially Fraser's vocals, more reliant on texture than lyrics. *Heaven Or Las Vegas* (1990), their biggest

UK hit (No.7), was their last for 4AD, the label they typified in the 80s. The Fontana-released *Four Calender Cafe* (1993) and *Milk And Kisses* (1996) – with lyrics that could be heard for a change – proved disappointing. Their influence can be found in early releases by Lush and the soundscapes of Future Sound Of London, on whose *Lifeforms* (1994) Fraser appeared. All three contributed to Spooky's *Found Sound* (1996) and Raymonde released solo album *Blame Someone Else* in 1997.

Surf www.cocteautwins.com

LEONARD COHEN

WHO b. Leonard Norman Cohen, 21 Sep 1934, Montreal, Canada

WHAT Laconic, lovelorn troubadour

Inspired by Spanish poet Federico Garcia Lorca, Cohen began writing poetry at the age of 15. At University in Montreal, he won prizes in creative writing and literature, and had his first anthology, *Let Us Compare Mythologies* (1956), published. As with later lyrics, his poetic themes were love, sex, guilt, war, personal and religious identity, and the Nazi Holocaust.

With the help of Canadian Arts Council scholarships, Cohen relocated to the Greek island Hydra in 1960, where he settled down to write books. There he met the first of several female

"Give me a Leonard Cohen afterworld"
Kurt Cobain

Cohen songs, *Famous Blue Raincoat* (1986), his *I'm Your Man* (1988) was acclaimed as the best of his career. It also affected a major sea-change in public perception of Cohen, now acknowledged as a droll ironist thanks to songs like 'Everybody Knows' and 'Tower Of Song'. *The Future* (1992) and *Cohen Live* (1994) cemented that reputation, with Cohen's shows being rapturously received, especially in Europe. In 1991, he was made an Officer Of The Order Of Canada, and in 1993 he received the Governor-General's Performing Arts Award. Two of his songs were included in Trent Reznor's soundtrack *Natural Born Killers* (1994). Having spent most of his career shuttling between New York, Los Angeles, Montreal and Hydra, the late 90s found Cohen spending long periods meditating at the monastery run by his friend, Zen master Joshu Sasaki Roshi on Mt Baldy, California.

read *Leonard Cohen: A Life In Art* (1994), Ira Nadel

surf www.leonardcohen.com/

LLOYD COLE & THE COMMOTIONS

WHO Vocals/guitar **Lloyd Cole** (b. 31 Jan 1961, Buxton, Derbyshire, England), guitar **Neil Clark** (b. 3 Jul 1955), bass **Lawrence Donegan** (b. 13 Jul 1961), drums **Stephen Irvine** (b. 16 Dec 1959), keyboards **Blair Cowan**

WHEN 1982–1988

WHERE Glasgow, Scotland

WHAT Introspective guitar Pop

While studying in Glasgow in the early 80s, Cole formed The Commotions with Blair Cowan and Neil Clark. After early line-up changes, the band stabilized with the addition of Lawrence Donegan and Stephen Irvine. Their debut *Rattlesnakes* (1984) demonstrated Cole's sharp insights and clever lyrics, notably on the hit 'Perfect Skin'. After two more successful albums – 1985's *Easy Pieces* (which yielded peak UK hits 'Brand New Friend' and 'Lost Weekend') and *Mainstream* (1987) – and Cole's songwriting collaboration with Sandie Shaw (on 1986's 'Are You Ready To Be Heartbroken'), the band parted company in 1988.

Cole went solo and relocated to New York, failing to recapture earlier commercial success with *Lloyd Cole* (1990), *Don't Get Weird With Me, Babe* (1991), *Bad Vibes* (1993) and *Love Story* (1995), despite all-star casts including Power-popper Matthew Sweet, ex-Voidoid Robert Quine, and former Fairground Attraction member and Morrissey cohort Mark Nevin.

surf www.best.com/^drumz/cole/

muses, Norwegian Marianne Jensen, who inspired 'So Long, Marianne'. Over the next few years, he published three more volumes of poetry and two 'experimental' novels, *The Favourite Game* (1963) and *Beautiful Losers* (1966). As his literary fame grew, he was the subject of documentary film *Ladies And Gentlemen… Mr Leonard Cohen* (1965) before being 'hijacked' by the burgeoning New York Folk scene and signed by John Hammond Sr to Columbia, for whom he recorded *Songs Of Leonard Cohen* (1968), featuring his first single, 'Suzanne'.

His painfully honest and painstakingly wrought songs, delivered in a lugubrious baritone to the accompaniment of flamenco-inspired guitar, gave him a reputation as a gloomy existentialist 'bedsit balladeer', a reputation which deepened through the 70s as *Songs From A Room* (1969), *Songs Of Love And Hate* (1971) and *Live Songs* (1973) dealt with alienation, suicide and depression alongside love and religious musings.

In 1973, he toured the Holy Land, playing shows for Israeli troops engaged in the Yom Kippur War with Egypt, inspiring 'Lover Lover Lover' on *New Skin For The Old Ceremony* (1974). Also on the album was 'Chelsea Hotel No 2', a reminiscence of his late 60s relationship with Janis Joplin. Produced by the eccentric Phil Spector, *Death Of A Ladies' Man* (1977) was an ill-judged attempt to beef up Cohen's sound, though notable for the presence of Bob Dylan on 'Don't Go Home With Your Hard-On'.

Facing diminishing returns, Cohen took an extended sabbatical after *Recent Songs* (1979), though his 30-minute feature film *I Am A Hotel* (1984) won a prize at the Montreux TV Festival. The following year, *Various Positions* (1985) announced a change of direction, with Cohen utilizing modern music technology. Following the success of Jennifer Warnes' album of

"I suppose
Phil Collins offers
'something for everybody'
and in hipdom that's not cool.
But in the real world,
there's no shame
in that at all"
Phil Collins

PHIL COLLINS ⊙⊙⊙⊙⊙☆☆

WHO b. 31 Jan 1951, Chiswick, London, England

WHAT Workaholic superstar, drummer, actor and producer

When the young Phil Collins joined Progressive Rock band Genesis as their drummer in 1970, few could have predicted he would later become a major international star in his own right. A versatile drummer and competent backing vocalist, Collins remained in the background until, in a surprise move, he took over as the band's lead vocalist when Peter Gabriel quit in 1975.

A Trick Of The Tail, released in 1976, became the first Genesis album to feature Collins as lead vocalist and, far from drifting into obscurity as many had forecast, the band gained in strength, going on to enjoy substantial sales success. A workaholic, Collins found the need to diversify and, alongside his work with Genesis, drummed with Jazz Rock band Brand X, appearing on several of their late 70s albums.

In 1981 he released his first solo album, *Face Value*. A collection of mainly melancholy, self-composed ballads, it drew on the feelings of despair and bitterness he suffered following the collapse of his marriage in 1979, and struck a chord with both British and American record buyers, topping the UK chart and becoming a US Top 10 hit. 'In The Air Tonight', a particularly atmospheric song taken from the album, became his first single, reaching UK No.2 and US No.19.

Collins continued to enjoy major international success with Genesis, also finding time to guest as drummer on albums by, among others, Brian Eno, Robert Fripp, Eric Clapton, Peter Gabriel and Robert Plant. In 1982 he released *Hello, I Must Be Going*, his second solo album. Very much in the style of its predecessor, it reached UK No.2 and US No.8, also yielding his first UK No.1 single with a cover of The Supremes' 'You Can't Hurry Love'. In the same year, he played at the inaugural Prince's

Trust Rock Gala in London, continuing his involvement with the charity when the concert became an annual event. In 1984, he performed on the Band Aid charity hit 'Do They Know It's Christmas?' and, at the subsequent Live Aid concerts at London and Philadelphia the following year, he flew across the Atlantic by Concorde, enabling him to perform at both events. By this time he had become a high-flying figure, and the 1985 release of his third solo album, *No Jacket Required*, saw him top both the UK and US charts. The musical formula remained unchanged, with his intense, melodramatic songs proving even more popular in the USA than at home, as his numerous US No.1s bear witness.

In 1988, in addition to his solo and band work, he returned to acting. As a child he had appeared in several minor film roles and played The Artful Dodger in the London stage production of *Oliver!*; as an adult he appeared in TV programmes (including *Miami Vice*) and movies. Of the latter, *Buster* (1988) and *Frauds* (1992) saw him progress to starring roles.

Multi-talented, he has written songs for movie soundtracks and has also been in demand as a record producer, working on recordings by Frida Lyngstad (of Abba), Eric Clapton, David Crosby, John Martyn, Howard Jones and others.

Collins has not always been critically fashionable, but the production of his music has always been classy and, with his instantly recognizable voice, his undemanding songs of heartbreak and spurned love have remained consistently popular. ...*But Seriously* (1989) became another transatlantic chart-topper, but subsequent albums *Both Sides* (1993) and *Dance Into The Light* (1996) suggested that Collins was perhaps past his commercial prime. The 90s have seen major changes in his life. Divorced from his second wife, finally leaving Genesis and moving to live in Switzerland might indicate a slowing down in a relentless career.

READ *Phil Collins: The Definitive Biography* (1997), Ray Coleman

SURF members.aol.com/DenFraz/pcollins.html

The world's oldest record label, founded in 1887 as the Columbia Phonograph Company, launched the long-playing record in 1947. Its early stars included Blues singers Bessie Smith and Robert Johnson, who were succeeded by the lighter likes of Doris Day, Paul Anka, Frankie Lymon, Johnnie Ray, Andy Williams and Johnny Mathis in the 50s – by which time the label had evolved into CBS (Columbia Broadcasting System). In the 60s, it was a Rock and Folk market leader with The Byrds, Bob Dylan and Simon & Garfunkel; a mega-selling roster bolstered by subsequent acquisitions Bruce Springsteen, Michael Jackson, Meat Loaf, Billy Joel, Shakin' Stevens and George Michael. Although the latter quit in a furious flurry, Mariah Carey, Celine Dion, Jamiroquai, Kula Shaker and Manic Street Preachers kept sales buoyant into the 90s.

In 1987, the label was bought by Japanese giant Sony, who (legally unable to use the CBS name) bought the Columbia label from EMI – to whom it had been sold in the 30s. Cliff Richard, The Shadows, Helen Shapiro, Gerry & The Pacemakers, The Animals, The Dave Clark Five, The Yardbirds and Herman's Hermits were all released on EMI's Columbia, but confusion with the American Columbia label contributed to EMI's dropping of the name for Pop purposes even before Sony's acquisition of the rights.

THE COMMODORES

WHO Vocals/keyboards **Lionel Richie** (b. 20 Jun 1949, Tuskegee, Alabama, USA), guitar **Thomas McClary** (b. 6 Oct 1950), multi-instrumentalist **Milan Williams** (b. 28 Mar 1949, Mississippi), trumpet **William King** (b. 30 Jan 1949, Alabama), bass **Ronald LaPraed** (b. 4 Sep 1946, Alabama), drums **Walter 'Clyde' Orange** (b. 10 Dec 1947, Florida, USA)

WHEN 1967–

WHERE Tuskegee, Alabama, USA

WHAT Three Times A Lady'-lovin' Funk balladeers

Even though the band's 1969 debut album on Atlantic and their first handful of Motown singles slipped out unnoticed, The Commodores became one of the 70s' most popular recording acts.

Originally making their name as hard-hitting Funksters with tracks like 'Machine Gun' and 'Slippery When Wet', they later became one of the era's best-known ballad acts. Among the sextet's transatlantic hits were million-sellers 'Easy' (covered by Faith No More), 'Three Times A Lady' and 'Still' – all penned by lead singer Lionel Richie.

In 1982, he left and was replaced by Englishman J.D. Nicholas, who shared lead vocals on the Grammy-winning 'Nightshift' – The Commodores' only major hit without Richie. The group subsequently recorded for Polydor and SBK with minor success.

THE COMMUNARDS

WHO Vocals **Jimmy Somerville** (b. 22 Jun 1961, Glasgow, Scotland), keyboards **Richard Coles** (b. 23 Jun 1962, Northampton, England)

WHEN 1985–1988

WHERE London, England

WHAT High-pitched and pointed Pop

After an acrimonious split from Bronski Beat, Somerville joined former Royal College of Church Music student Coles to form The Communards. Musically similar to Bronski Beat, their debut 'You Are My World' became a minor hit in November 1985. Having assembled a female-dominated backing band, they appeared on the Labour Party-sponsored Red Wedge UK tour alongside The Style Council and Billy Bragg in February 1986. Their first major success arrived later that year with a UK No.1 version of Harold Melvin's 'Don't Leave Me This Way'. The duet with vocalist Sarah-Jane Morris, whose husky baritone contrasted with Somerville's falsetto, helped *Communards* (1986) reach the UK Top 10. Further hits included a cover of Gloria Gaynor's 'Never Can Say Goodbye', and 'For A Friend', dedicated to an associate who had died of AIDS. Both came from the best-selling *Red* (1987), as did final hit 'There's More To Love (Than Boy Meets Girl)' in June 1988, after which Somerville went solo and Coles returned to Classical music.

SURF bela.fei.tuke.sk/~benor/communards/index.html

RY COODER

WHO b. Ryland Peter Cooper, 15 Mar 1947, Los Angeles, California, USA

WHAT Definitive Blues slide guitarist

Cooder first performed at Los Angeles' Folk club Ash Grove aged 16. Forming his first band, The Rising Sons, with Taj Mahal in 1966, he recorded with Captain Beefheart, Little Feat and The Rolling Stones (on 1969's *Let It Bleed*). However, relations with the latter soured after a dispute with Keith Richards over ownership of the guitar riff which became 'Honky Tonk Women'.

Cooder's eponymous solo debut (1971), blending Rock, Blues and Folk, signalled his fascination with fusing styles. *Paradise And Lunch* (1973) mixed Gospel, Reggae and regional styles with imaginative abandon. Acclaimed *Chicken Skin Music* (1975) added Tex-Mex influences to the eclectic musical brew.

Releasing an album almost every year in the 70s, Cooder achieved modest success at home and cult status in Europe. *Bop Till You Drop* (1979) made the UK Top 40 and heralded a return to R&B, continued by *Borderline* (1980). But poor reviews and sales of 1982's *The Slide Area* suggested his style had become jaded. Losing money on a European tour, he returned, disenchanted, to his Santa Monica home and concentrated on soundtracks. After *Performance* (1979) and *The Long Riders* (1980), he graced *Goin' South* and *Geronimo* in 1984, *Alamo Bay* (1985) and *Crossroads* (1986). Haunting work on *Paris, Texas* (1985) won most praise, his acoustic bottleneck guitar echoing the movie's melancholy.

Cooder turned to World Music in the 90s. After a union with Ali Farka Toure, 1994's *Talking Timbuktu*, a 'dream orchestra' of Cuban Blues idols appeared on *Buena Vista Social Club* (1997), which he described as the best musical experience of his life.

surf www.dpac.tas.gov.au/~neilm/Ry.html

NORMAN COOK

WHO b. Quentin Cook, 31 Jul 1963, Brighton, England

WHAT Many-monikered Dance-master

When The Housemartins folded, bassist Norman Cook launched a five-year mission to seek out strange new worlds. After 1989 hits 'Won't Talk About It', with Billy Bragg, and 'For Spacious Lies', he formed Beats International, added a Clash bassline to an old SOS Band gem, called it 'Dub Be Good To Me' and sailed to the UK top spot in 1990. *Let Them Eat Bingo* and a sublime revamp of 'Won't Talk About It' with Lindy Layton followed its hit footsteps, but Beats bowed out after *Excursion On The Version* (1991). Enter Freakpower, whose Isley Brothers pastiche 'Turn On Tune In Cop Out' (from 1994's *Drive Thru Booty*) hit after soundtracking a Levi's ad. When the Freaks ran out of power, Cook returned to his pre-Housemartins DJ life: hence pseudonymous chart-busters Pizzaman (1995's 'Happiness'), Mighty Dub Katz (1997's 'Magic Carpet Ride') and Fatboy Slim (1996's 'Going Out Of My Head' from *Better Living Through Chemistry*). The Cook recipe – Hip Hop beats and psychedelic lunacy – put him at the epicentre of the 'Big Beat' explosion, alongside fellow drum freaks Lionrock, The Chemical Brothers and Brighton label Skint. He reaped rewards in 1998 with storming remixes of Wildchild's 'Renegade Master' and Cornershop's UK No.1 'Brimful Of Asha'. If you want to know how he did it, check out Cook's 1992 sample set *Skip To My Loops*.

surf www.skint.net/

SAM COOKE

WHO b. 22 Jan 1931, Clarksdale, Mississippi, USA, d. 11 Dec 1964

WHAT *The* Soul singer

Cooke fronted the successful Gospel group The Soul Stirrers from 1950–1956, and was considered "the first bobby-sox idol in Gospel music". However, Gospel followers frowned on 'selling out' – when he released the poppy 'Loveable' (based on The Soul Stirrers' 'Wonderful') as Dale Cook, it created a furore that resulted in him leaving the group. In 1957, he moved from Specialty Records to Keen and his third release for them, 'You Send Me', shot to the top of the US chart. In the late 50s, he appeared on top US TV shows and headlined Rock and R&B package shows. Among his best-known 50s recordings were his compositions 'Only Sixteen' (a UK No.1 by Craig Douglas) and 'Wonderful World' – amazingly, a European chart-topper in 1986 after the song was heard in a TV advert for Levi jeans.

In 1960, RCA paid a reported $100,000 for his contract, dwarfing their record payment for Elvis Presley's signature. Cooke rewarded their faith by clocking up a string of smashes, including the self-penned transatlantic hits 'Chain Gang' (1960), 'Cupid' (1961), 'Twistin' The Night Away' (1962) and 'Another Saturday Night' (1963). Rightly regarded as one of the fathers of Soul, Cooke also recorded Easy Listening and was equally popular with the Copacabana crowd. An astute businessman, he also ran a successful label and publishing company.

In late 1964, still at the peak of his career, he was shot and killed in strange circumstances by a motel manageress in Los Angeles. Since then, many artists have recorded his songs and his influence can be heard in countless R&B acts. This prolific performer was among the first inductees to the Rock And Roll Hall Of Fame, and is also in the Songwriters Hall Of Fame.

read *You Send Me – The Life And Times Of Sam Cooke* (1995), Wolff, Crain, White, Tenenbaum

COOLIO

WHO b. Artis Ivey Jr, 1 Aug 1963, South Central Los Angeles, USA

WHAT Pop Gangsta

Rapping since high school, Coolio ("My homeboy asked me: Who do you think you are, Coolio Iglesias?") was derailed by crack. Cleaned up and firefighting for a living, he made up for a lapsed education and – after a spell with WC & The Maad Circle – embarked on solo superstardom. The fabulous Lakeside revamp 'Fantastic Voyage' propelled *It Takes A Thief* (1994) into the US Top 10, before the world surrendered to the title track of *Gangsta's Paradise* (1995) – a gritty update of Stevie Wonder's 1976 'Pastime Paradise'. He went for the commercial jugular with a *Batman And Robin* (1997) cameo and the classically based hit 'C U When U Get There' from *My Soul* (1997). Collaborators on the latter, 40 Thevz, were among the first signings to his LA-based label Crowbar in 1997.

surf home1.swipnet.se/~w-10840/

ALICE COOPER ✪

WHO b. Vincent Damien Furnier, 4 Feb 1948, Detroit, Michigan, USA

WHAT Shock Rock

More frightening than Marilyn Manson, kookier than Kiss and funnier than Freddy Krueger, Alice Cooper inspired all three. The wholesome name for this horror/Rock hybrid was summoned at a ouija board session, presaging the demon-dusted Psychedelia of *Pretties For You* (1969) and *Easy Action* (1970). Both were issued on Frank Zappa's Straight label, who signed Alice – then a group, rather than solo star – on the strength of a club-clearing reputation as the worst band in LA (they'd moved from Arizona to "drive a stake through the heart of the love generation"). Neither Alice nor other Straight stuff amounted to much, and the label and its roster were sold to Warner Bros.

Warner's investment paid off when Alice twinned with producer Bob Ezrin. Through *Love It To Death* (1971), *Killer* (1971) and *School's Out* (1972), they developed a blend of mock-Broadway drama, trashy riffing and seedy lyrics. These vaguely conceptual affairs were complemented by hammy horror shows: a senses-shaking experience that spawned No.1s in Britain (the title track of *School's Out*) and America (1973's *Billion Dollar Babies*, featuring Donovan and Marc Bolan). Their leader's sick satire of American excess – sex, money, murder – made Alice Cooper a household name, but his celebrity divided the band. Coupled with Ezrin's departure, *Muscle Of Love* (1973) suffered accordingly. Leaving *Alice Cooper's Greatest Hits* (1974) as their epitaph, the band split: guitarist Michael Bruce, bassist Dennis Dunaway and drummer Neal Smith struggled bitterly as Billion Dollar Babies, while guitarist Glen Buxton continued a cycle of abuse that ended with his death in 1997.

Meanwhile, Alice became a superstar with *Welcome To My Nightmare* (1975). Ezrin returned, Vincent Price guested, the *Nightmare* tour was his most theatrical and Alice belied his 'shock Rock' tag with the pro-feminist US No.12 'Only Women Bleed' – the latest example of a ballad tradition that had already yielded hits with 'Hello Hurray' and 'Teenage Lament '74'.

The momentum carried the self-mocking *Alice Cooper Goes To Hell* (1976), but Kiss stole his Stateside thunder and Punk swept Britain – ironically, Johnny Rotten auditioned for The Sex Pistols bawling Alice's 1971 hit 'I'm Eighteen'. Alice's reliance on alcohol made *Lace And Whiskey* (1977) an unfortunate intro to his post-platinum years. *Lace*'s 'You And Me' returned him to the US Top 10 for the first time since 1972, but neither that album nor *The Alice Cooper Show* (1978) were hits. The cool ghoul was reduced to appearing on US TV's *Hollywood Squares* and *The Muppets*.

From self-imposed exile in an asylum, he returned to relative sobriety and the charts with 'How You Gonna See Me Now'. Its parent album, *From The Inside* (1978), was a chillingly dramatized account of asylum life, with input from Elton John's lyricist Bernie Taupin. However, sales declined to barely chart-troubling levels with the new wavey *Flush The Fashion* (1980), *Special Forces* (1981), *Zipper Catches Skin* (1982) and *Da Da* (1983). Despite minor hits and a faithful live following, Alice became best known as golf's least plausible advocate.

By the mid-80s, Heavy Metal had become fashionable again, thanks to Cooper copyists like Twisted Sister. Alice cashed in with the shamelessly nostalgic The Nightmare Returns tour and, after the insipid *Constrictor* (1986), the strong hit albums *Raise*

Your Fist And Yell (1987), *Trash* (1989) and *Hey Stoopid* (1991). With input drawn from Bon Jovi and Guns N' Roses, he jostled the imitators in transatlantic charts, notably with *Trash*'s horrible hit 'Poison'. His demonic deification was completed by a scene-stealing cameo on Guns N' Roses' 'The Garden' (1991), the prostation of Wayne and Garth at his feet in the movie *Wayne's World* (1992) and a duet with White Zombie's Rob Zombie on the *X-Files* album *Songs In The Key Of X* (1996).

Sadly, his own *The Last Temptation Of Alice Cooper* (1994) – a superb return to conceptual, gory glory – got somewhat lost and Alice has been a low-key presence in Rock since, with only the compilations *Classiks* (1995) and *A Fistful Of Alice* (1997) breaking the silence. However, the success of Marilyn Manson (for whom Alice expressed reserved enthusiasm) proved the Cooper recipe – make-up, blood, trash Rock – was still bubbling.

READ *No More Mr Nice Guy: The Inside Story Of The Alice Cooper Group* (1996), Michael Bruce

SURF www.pathcom.com/'omega/aliceop.ht

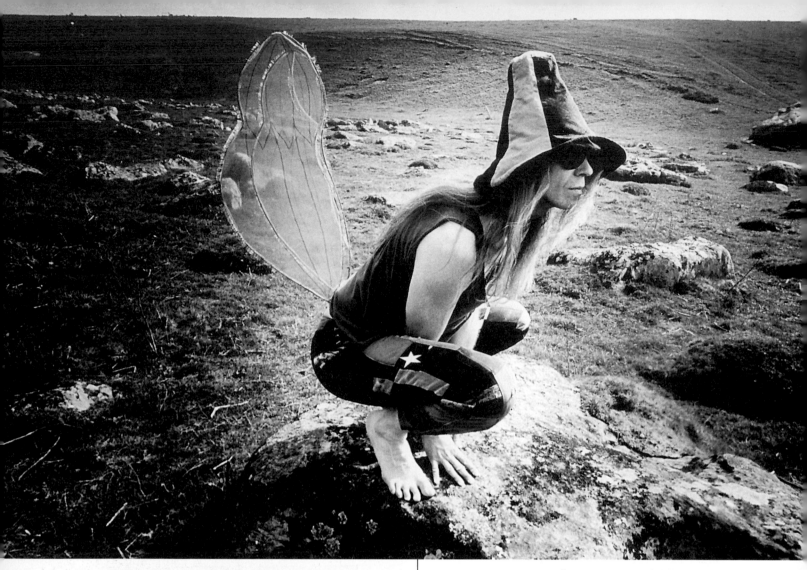

JULIAN COPE

WHO b. 21 Oct 1957, Deri, Mid Glamorgan, Wales

WHAT Ex-Teardrop Explodes singer turned Spacerock eco warrior

Following the demise of The Teardrop Explodes the previous year, Cope's first solo effort, 'Sunshine Playroom', appeared in late 1983, a typically off-the-wall release taken from his debut *World Shut Your Mouth* (1984). This was followed by the even more bizarre *Fried* (1984), the sleeve featuring a naked Cope wearing a giant turtle shell on his back. However, after Mercury refused to release *Skellington* in 1984, he found himself freed from his record contract and retreated to his Tamworth home to recuperate from severe drug problems.

When he eventually resurfaced in late 1986, newly signed to Island, the sound was more straightforward Rock Pop. 'World Shut Your Mouth' and *Saint Julian* (1987) propelled him high in the UK charts. However, *My Nation Underground* (1988) disappointed many and Cope disappeared again for a few years. A pair of fan-club-only albums – *Skellington* and *Droolian* (both 1990) – gave some indication as to where Cope was heading musically. The ambitious *Peggy Suicide* (1991) showed a return to form and made up a trilogy alongside the similarly eco-themed *Jehovahkill* (1992) and *Autogeddon* (1994).

Ironically, Cope had been dropped by Island in 1993, and the Echo released *Autogeddon* went on to be his highest-charting album since 1987. 'Try Try Try' was his biggest hit single for years and *20 Mothers* (1995) was a hugely accomplished work. *Interpreter*'s (1996) space/alien theme was exemplified by the single 'I Come From Another Planet, Baby'. Cope is also an ecological activist who has used his position to voice concern on various issues and joined in the protest at the controversial Newbury By-Pass road-building programme.

read *Head On* (1994), Julian Cope

fan Julian Cope, c/o Outlaw, 145 Oxford Street, London, W1, UK

surf american.recordings.com/American_Artists/Julian_Cope/cope_home

ELVIS COSTELLO

WHO b. Declan Patrick MacManus, 25 Aug 1954, Paddington, London, England

WHAT Eclectic musical chameleon and leading singer/songwriter

Bouncing from London to Liverpool and back again, teenager Declan MacManus played solo, then formed Flip City. When they folded in 1975, MacManus went solo again and adopted his grandmother's maiden name to become D.P. Costello. When marching into record company offices and playing to anyone who would listen reaped no rewards, he hand-delivered a demo to the newly formed Stiff label. The direct approach finally paid dividends when Costello was signed. 'D.P.' was replaced by the iconoclastic 'Elvis'.

His debut *My Aim Is True* (1977), recorded in 24 hours, featured Country Rock outfit Clover as a backing band, while The Rumour's Steve Goulding, Andrew Bodnar and Steve Nieve featured on UK single 'Watching The Detectives'. To form a permanent group, Costello recruited Nieve (keyboards) plus

Bruce and Pete Thomas (bass and drums respectively), aka The Attractions. Though not exactly 'Punk', Costello's 'vengeful nerd' image and bitter songs were 'New Wave' enough to join the vanguard.

This Year's Model (1978) attacked the 'fake' fashion and music worlds in the hits 'Pump It Up' (later covered by The Wildhearts) and '(I Don't Want To Go To) Chelsea'. Armed Forces (1979) continued Costello's UK success, peaking at No.2 and spawning his top-selling single 'Oliver's Army'. His US success screeched to a halt when, after a 1979 gig in Ohio, a 'tired and emotional' Costello squared up against American stars Stephen Stills and Bonnie Bramlett. Taking exception to the suggestion that English artists couldn't match the depth of American black performers, Costello described Ray Charles as a "a blind, ignorant nigger". Bramlett knocked him to the ground and, despite Costello's shamefaced claim that he'd simply wanted to outrage his antagonists, he received death threats and Armed Forces was taken off radio playlists. Not until 1981 was Costello to tour the USA again.

His remorse was reflected in Get Happy!! (1980). It had a 'blacker', more soulful feel, drawing on Stax and Motown, and contained R&B legends Sam & Dave's 'I Can't Stand Up For Falling Down' – the first cover on a Costello album. Costello again reached UK No.2, did poorly Stateside and, drained by the end of 1980, almost quit show business. Within months, however, he was back with Trust (1981), whose songs evoked the mood of sleazy 40s nightclubs. One, 'Different Finger', heralded the change made on Almost Blue (1981).

Deciding his state of mind could be better expressed through cover versions, Costello planned a collection of melancholy songs from different genres, but his passion for Country triumphed. He collaborated with legendary producer Billy Sherrill on songs from Country greats including Jerry Chestnut, whose 'Good Year For The Roses' provided an unlikely hit. The making of Almost Blue was recorded by UK TV, capturing the strained relationship between Sherrill and his 'Punk' charges.

Imperial Bedroom (1982) marked another change of style, containing references to producer Geoff Emerick's former clients The Beatles (he worked on Sgt Pepper). An album chart high-flyer, its singles flopped. To redress this, Punch The Clock (1983) featured Elvis in a softer 'come hither' pose on the sleeve. Benefiting from punchier playing and Pop producers Clive Langer and Alan Winstanley (who worked with Madness), it fared better although, ironically, most commercially successful was the out-take 'Pills And Soap', credited to The Imposter.

By 1984, Costello had broken with his wife. Goodbye Cruel World (1984) was so confessional that the singer admitted a priest would have been more appropriate than a producer. Subsequently, Costello split with The Attractions, produced The Pogues (whose bass player Cait O'Riordan became the new Mrs Costello) and toured the world with T-Bone Burnett as The Coward Brothers. Burnett was heavily involved in Costello's King Of America (1986). An Attractions reunion was mooted (alongside The Confederates, boasting Rock 'n' Roll giants Jerry Scheff and James Burton), but they failed to gel with the new Costello/Burnett axis, making only one appearance. They did grace the brooding Blood And Chocolate (1986) but, in 1987, Costello again parted with his regular band and signed with Warner for Spike (1989), his most commercially successful album. Mighty Like A Rose (1991) contained great songs, but failed to dazzle customers, fuelling speculation that Costello had lost his

way. However, a collaboration with Classical quartet The Brodsky Quartet on The Juliet Letters (1993) invigorated his career. Costello confounded critics when he and the re-enlisted Attractions released the feisty return-to-form Brutal Youth (1994).

Kojak Variety (1995), featuring more covers, followed. Two years on, All This Useless Beauty featured tracks he'd written for others, notably Roger McGuinn and Johnny Cash. Costello's break with Warner was marked by the eclectic selection Extreme Honey (1997), a fine companion to earlier compilations The Best Of Elvis Costello (1985) and Girls,Girls,Girls (1989).

(READ) Let Them All Talk (1998), Brian Hinton

(FAN) Beyond Belief: Mark Perry, 6 Hillside Grove, Taunton, Somerset, TA1 4LA, UK

(SURF) east.isx.com/~schnitz/elvis.html

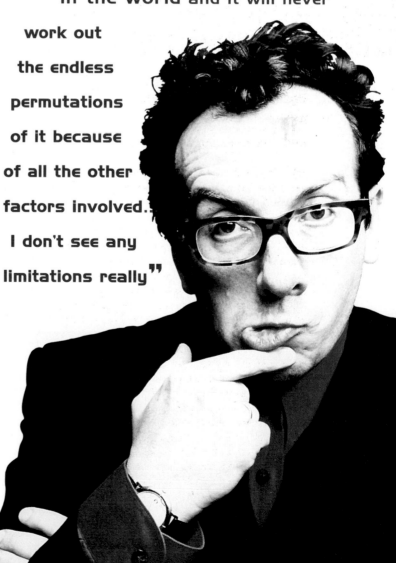

"The great thing about music is that you can get the biggest computer in the world and it will never work out the endless permutations of it because of all the other factors involved... I don't see any limitations really"

ELVIS COSTELLO/PATRICK ROCHON/RETNA

Festival favourites Country Joe's early albums *Electric Music For The Mind And Body* (1967) and *I-Feel-Like-I'm-Fixin'-To-Die* (1967) were psychedelic classics, and the high-spirited 'Fish Cheer' ("Gimme an F, Gimme an I… What's that spell?"), reinvented as the 'F**k Cheer', was a highlight of *Woodstock* (1969). *Together* (1968), with songwriting shared, disappointed, but with McDonald resuming control, and everyone except Melton replaced, *Here We Are Again* (1969) and *C. J. Fish* (1970) were excellent. The original members' *Reunion* (1977) was weak, but McDonald has released over 20 fine solo albums.

(surf) www.well.com/user/cjfish/

COUNTRY ROCK

WHAT A fusion of traditional Country Music with Rock 'n' Roll, combining elements of Bluegrass, Folk, Blues and Pop. Pioneers of a sound incorporating pedal steel guitar and fiddle into the traditional drums, bass, rythmn and lead guitar line-up included The International Submarine Band, Gram Parsons and The Everly Brothers. These in turn influenced The Byrds, Dillard & Clark, Poco and The Flying Burrito Brothers. A less Country more Rock second wave was led by The Eagles, America, Brewer & Shipley, Emmylou Harris, Linda Ronstadt and Loggins & Messina as the 70s began. True practitioners such as The Remmingtons, The Desert Rose Band, The Cowboy Junkies, Jason & The Scorchers, Restless Heart and Electric Range show from their aptly selected names where their influences lie.. Country Rock-influenced contemporary bands include REM, Teenage Fanclub and The Lemonheads.

WHERE California, USA

WHEN 1967–

WHO The Byrds <u>Sweetheart Of The Rodeo</u> (1968), The Flying Burrito Brothers <u>Gilded Palace Of Sin</u> (1969), Bob Dylan <u>Nashville Skyline</u> (1969), Poco <u>Pickin' Up The Pieces</u> (1969), Gram Parsons <u>G.P.</u> (1969)

THE CRANBERRIES ◉

WHO Vocals/guitar **Dolores O'Riordan** (b. 6 Sep 1971, Limerick, Ireland), guitar **Noel Hogan** (b. 25 Dec 1971, Moycross, Ireland), bass **Michael Hogan** (b. 29 Apr 1973, Moycross), drums **Feargal Lawlor** (b. 4 Mar 1971, Limerick)

WHEN 1990–

WHERE Limerick, Ireland

WHAT Lilting guitar Pop

One of Ireland's greatest contemporary success stories took shape in 1990, when Dolores O'Riordan joined The Cranberry Saw Us – their punning moniker a legacy of former singer Niall Quinn, noted for his humorous lyrics. The new female vocalist – her sincere, plaintive voice largely untouched by Rock 'n' Roll – seemed more interested in Gregorian chants she had learnt at Church and Country tunes she heard when accompanying her father to a local bar. The final strand of her musical upbringing was the quietly adorned style of traditional Irish singing.

Brothers Noel and Michael Hogan, plus drummer Lawlor, were aficionados of British Indie acts The Sundays and The

COUNTING CROWS ✪

WHO Vocals/piano **Adam Duritz** (b. 1 Aug 1964, Baltimore, Maryland, USA), guitar **David Bryson** (b. 5 Oct 1961, San Francisco, California), guitar **Dan Vickrey** (b. 26 Aug 1966, Walnut Creek, California, USA), keyboards **Charlie Gillingham** (b. 12 Jan 1960, Torrance, California), bass **Matt Malley** (b. 4 Jul 1963), drums **Ben Mize** (b. 2 Feb 1971)

WHEN 1989–

WHERE San Francisco, California, USA

WHAT Country Rock's Pearl Jam

Named after an old English rhyme, Duritz and Bryson performed as an acoustic duo before recruiting Malley, Gillingham and drummer Steve Bowman to record a demo. A 1992 showcase gig landed a deal with Geffen, for whom they recorded their debut with producer T-Bone Burnett. *August And Everything After* (1993) began a slow climb to the US Top 5 while the Crows – now joined by Vickrey – opened for Midnight Oil, Suede, The Cranberries and Cracker. Becoming MTV favourites with 'Mr Jones', they toured as headliners, unhindered by Bowman's departure (to 'Frisco band Third Eye Blind). Duritz's 'tortured artist' image was propagated by volatile entwinings with actresses, including *Friends*' Jennifer Aniston and Courteney Cox. *Recovering The Satellites* (1996) reminded people why the Crows were supposed to be famous.

(fan) Counting Crows, PO Box 5008, Berkeley, CA 94705, USA

(surf) www.countingcrows.com/

COUNTRY JOE & THE FISH

WHO Vocals/guitar **Country Joe McDonald** (b. 1 Jan 1942, El Monte, California, USA), guitar/vocals **Barry Melton** (b. 14 Jun 1947, Brooklyn, New York, USA), organ/guitar **David Cohen** (b. 1942, Brooklyn), bass/harmonica **Bruce Barthol** (b. 1947, Berkeley, California), drums **Gary 'Chicken' Hirsh** (b. 1940, California)

WHEN 1965–1970

WHERE Berkeley, USA

WHAT Acid Rock, satire, mischievous fun

Smiths, who influenced their playing style, allowing plenty of space for O'Riordan's already impressive skills. Their 1990 demo 'Nothing Left At All' created interest in Ireland and they signed to Island Records the following year, although their first EP, 'Uncertain', was released on the Xeric imprint in November 1991.

After agonizing delays, their debut album *Everybody Else Is Doing It, So Why Can't We?* appeared in March 1993 to a lukewarm reception. The band spent much of the rest of the year touring America – eclipsing sometime headliners Suede – and, within a year of the album's release, had sold 2 million copies there. This success was replicated in Britain, encouraged by hit reissues of 'Dreams' and 'Linger'. By June 1994, the album topped the UK chart. *No Need To Argue*, released in October, preceded a tour involving 2,000 shows in 23 countries, as the phenomenal sales continued. O'Riordan's lyrics were more controversial – 'Zombie' berated the terrorist mindset in Ireland.

O'Riordan had become a full-blown celebrity. Her marriage to the band's Canadian tour manager, Don Burton, in July 1994 was overrun by the world's media. In August that year, The Cranberries were the youngest act to play the American festival 'Woodstock 2'. Their third album *To The Faithful Departed* (1996) was co-produced by Bruce Fairbairn, famous for his work with Aerosmith, AC/DC and Van Halen. Despite the harder sound, British reviewers were largely critical of the record, especially the simplistic lyrics to 'I Just Shot John Lennon', 'War Child' and 'Bosnia'. Despite cancelled tours and health problems, the band continued with massive sales which, by the end of 1997, exceeded 27 million worldwide.

Read *The Cranberries: In Your Head* (1996), Stuart Bailie

Fan The Cranberries, PO Box 180, Limerick, Ireland

Surf www.cranberries.com

CRASH TEST DUMMIES

WHO Vocals/guitar **Brad Roberts** (b. 10 Jan 1964, Winnipeg, Manitoba, Canada), bass **Dan Roberts** (b. 22 May 1967, Winnipeg), drums **Mitch Dorge** (b. 15 Sep 1960, Winnipeg), keyboards **Ellen Reid** (b. 14 Jul 1966, Selkirk, Manitoba), harmonica **Benjamin Darvill** (b. 4 Jan 1967, Winnipeg)

WHEN 1990–

WHERE Winnipeg, Manitoba, Canada

WHAT Oh-so-clever Folk Rock

Crash Test Dummies were formed to relieve the boredom of Canadian winters. Brothers Brad and Dan Roberts recruited Reid, Darvill and original drummer Vince Lambert for 1991's debut *The Ghosts That Haunt Me*, which established the band as major domestic stars. With new drummer Dorge, 1994's *God Shuffled His Feet* proved their commercial peak, with the eccentric hits 'Mmm, Mmm, Mmm, Mmm' and 'Afternoons And Coffee Spoons' propelling the album to UK No.2 and US No.9. Producer and ex-Talking Head Jerry Harrison gave the Dummies' traditional Rock a Headsy finish – a far cry from their embryonic Alice Cooper cover days. After a break punctuated only by a cover of XTC's 'The Ballad Of Peter Pumpkinhead' for the 1995 Jim Carrey movie *Dumb And Dumber*, their third album, *A Worm's Life* (1996), failed to match former heights.

Read *Superman's Song: The Story Of Crash Test Dummies* (1995), Stephen Ostick

Surf www.crashtestdummies.com/

RANDY CRAWFORD

WHO b. Veronica Crawford, 18 Feb 1952, Macon, Georgia, USA

WHAT Powerful Southern Soul

Crawford polished her craft at club gigs from Cincinatti to St Tropez, but made her name in mid-70s New York, where she sang with Jazzmen George Benson and Cannonball Adderley. She fronted R&B veterans The Crusaders on transatlantic biggie 'Street Life' (1979), and follow-ups 'One Day I'll Fly Away' (1980), 'You Might Need Somebody' (1981) and 'Rainy Night In Georgia' (1981) became Soul standards. *Secret Combination* (1981) remained on the album chart for 60 weeks, after which her profile dipped, despite a return to the Top 10 with 'Almaz' (1986).

Naked And True (1995) brought Crawford full circle: it included Benson's 'Give Me The Night', and confirmed her Soul heritage by featuring Funkadelicists Bootsy Collins, Bernie Worrell and The Fred Wesley Horns. However, she enjoyed her highest profile of the decade when rising starlet Shola Ama covered 'You Might Need Somebody' in 1997.

ROBERT CRAY

WHO b. 1 Aug 1953, Columbus, Georgia, USA

WHAT Sultan of Blues

The 80s 'Blues revival' revolved around Robert Cray. His blend of Soul vocals and Blues guitar won approval both from the 'old guard' – Eric Clapton, Tina Turner, Diana Ross – and a younger audience, who pushed him into the platinum bracket.

Cray and bassist Robert Cousins united in 1974, graduating from admirers to bandmates of Bluesman Albert Collins. With keyboardist Peter Boes and drummer David Olson, they launched The Robert Cray Band in 1980 with *Who's Been Talkin'*. After the Tomato label collapsed, they signed to Hightone for *Bad Influence* (1983) and *False Accusations* (1985), then peaked with the first of a string of hit albums for Mercury; *Strong Persuader* (1986) added The Memphis Horns and reached the US Top 10. Sales ticked over for *Don't Be Afraid Of The Dark* (1988),

Midnight Stroll (1990), *I Was Warned* (1992) and *Shame And Sin* (1993), dwindling only with 1995's *Some Rainy Morning*. Along the way, Cray repaid Collins, backing on the latter's *Showdown* (1985), and mingled with the R&B hierarchy: appearing in Chuck Berry bio-pic *Hail! Hail! Rock And Roll* (1986), touring with Clapton and duetting with John Lee Hooker (1989). He returned with a new band for 1997's *Sweet Potato Pie*.

surf imusic.com/showcase/contemporary/rcray.html

CREAM ◉✪

WHO Guitar/vocals **Eric Clapton** (b. 30 Mar 1945, Ripley, Surrey, England), bass/vocals **Jack Bruce** (b. John Symon Asher Bruce, 14 May 1943, Lanarkshire, Scotland), drums **Ginger Baker** (b. Peter Baker, 19 Aug 1939, Lewisham, London, England)

WHEN 1966–1968

WHERE London, England

WHAT Pioneering power trio

Unburdened by modesty, Ginger Baker, Jack Bruce and Eric Clapton named themselves Cream as a reflection of their peerless instrumental prowess.

All were veterans of the late 50s/early 60s R&B revival in London. Baker, the eldest, had drummed with homegrown Jazz and Blues outfits, including Alexis Korner's Blues Incorporated and The Graham Bond Organisation, where he shared rhythm duties with classically trained bassist Bruce, who had moved to Manfred Mann. Clapton, the youngest, acquired the sobriquet 'God' as guitarist for The Yardbirds and, later, John Mayall's Bluesbreakers. After Baker met Clapton at a Bluesbreakers show in Oxford, England, the two floated the idea for a new group, Clapton suggesting Bruce as the third member. When Bruce quit Manfred Mann on 16 July 1966, Cream was duly formed.

Their first performance (billed under their individual names) was at 1966's Windsor Jazz & Blues Festival, forerunner of the Reading Festival. Their low-key debut 'Wrapping Paper' caused few ripples, but the follow-up 'I Feel Free' was an immediate hit, reaching UK No.11 in 1967. Like much of Cream's work, it was composed by Bruce with Jazz poet Pete Brown, who later had a modicum of success with his own bands Battered Ornaments and Piblokto!. The trio's debut album *Fresh Cream* (1967) mixed Bruce/Brown originals with Blues standards like Skip James' 'I'm So Glad' and Willie Dixon's 'Spoonful', but it was *Disraeli Gears* (1967), featuring the hit 'Strange Brew' and the band's most famous riff, 'Sunshine Of Your Love', which brought the band their breakthrough on both sides of the Atlantic.

Cream's reputation was built on tireless touring through 1967, during which tracks were expanded to marathon 'neocontrapuntal' jams, based on the Jazz principle of theme and variations. At their best, these loud improvisations were exhilarating affairs, but they could also be tedious in the extreme: only those possessed of concrete buttocks could sit through Baker's 17-minute drum solo 'Toad'. Their third album, *Wheels Of Fire* (1968), was a double set, featuring one album of studio material and another devoted to four lengthy live tracks. But turbulent relations between the members came to a head as *Wheels Of Fire* brought them their greatest success and the band announced they would break up.

Their final shows, at London's Royal Albert Hall on 25 and 26 November 1968, were filmed for TV, but such was Cream's popularity, especially in America, that two further live albums, *Live Cream* (1970) and *Live Cream Vol. 2* (1972), and a final studio set, *Goodbye Cream* (1969), all charted high, the latter their only UK No.1. After their break-up, Baker and Clapton hooked up with ex-Family bassist Rick Grech and Traffic singer/keyboardist Steve Winwood in another supergroup, the short-lived Blind Faith. All three Cream members have pursued solo careers with varying success, re-forming in 1993 only to play three numbers at their induction into the Rock And Roll Hall Of Fame. An ill-fated reformation of sorts came in 1994 when Baker and Bruce recruited Gary Moore to become BBM for Around The Next Dream – a project that lived up to Cream's turbulent tradition.

Cream's influence, however, was immediate and far-reaching, as Led Zeppelin, Jimi Hendrix and The Allman Brothers Band helped develop Hard Rock from their original template.

read *Strange Brew* (1994), Chris Welch

surf www.fas.harvard.edu/~daraujo/cream.html

"**The Cream never really played that much Blues.** I think we aimed to **start a revolution** in musical thought. We set out to **change the world, to upset people, and to shock them...** Our aim was to get **so far away** from the original line that you're playing something that's **never been heard before**"

Eric Clapton

Creation

Formed in 1983 by Alan McGee, Creation became a titan of the Indie scene of the 80s and 90s. McGee moved to London in 1982 to start a venue (The Living Room) and a label, Creation, named after an obscure English 60s group. Limited edition, low-budget singles established a cult following, but McGee's first major signings were fellow Scots The Jesus & Mary Chain, whose feedback-drenched assault merged his twin loves, Psychedelia and Punk. With fellow Creation artists The Pastels, Primal Scream, My Bloody Valentine and The House Of Love, they established a sometimes nostalgic house style which shaped mid- to late-80s Indie. In the 90s, the label's domination grew (despite financial difficulties which prompted a partial sellout to Sony) with the success of Teenage Fanclub, Sugar, Ride, The Boo Radleys and the evergreen Primal Scream. Nothing, however, matched the seismic impact of Oasis – not even a reissue of William 'Captain Kirk' Shatner's classic <u>The Transformed Man</u> on Creation offshoot Rev-Ola.

CREEDENCE CLEARWATER REVIVAL ⊙ ✪ ✪

WHO Vocals/guitar **John Fogerty** (b. 28 May 1945, Berkeley, California, USA), guitar **Tom Fogerty** (b. 9 Nov 1941, Berkeley, d. 6 Sep 1990), bass **Stuart Cook** (b. 25 Apr 1945, Oakland, California), drums **Doug Clifford** (b. 24 Apr 1945, Palo Alto, California)

WHEN 1967–1972

WHERE Berkeley, California, USA

WHAT Bayou-based Rock

Tommy Fogerty & The Blue Velvets played clubs and bars before signing to the Fantasy label in 1964. Renamed The Golliwogs, they released British-sounding flop singles before temporarily folding when John Fogerty and Clifford were drafted in 1966. Returning from National Service, John renamed the band Creedence Clearwater Revival, after family friend Creedence Nuball, a beer commercial and the band's new musical direction.

Fogerty conjured a nostalgic vision of America's Deep South, which he had never even visited. The Bayou and the Mississippi fuelled his lyrics. Sun-era Rock 'n' Roll and carefully constructed 'jamming' forged the sound. With John's rasping vocals, they built an impressive live reputation. Debut *Creedence Clearwater Revival* (1968) began a succession of million-sellers which made them one of the biggest bands in America over the next two years. Their raucous cover of Dale Hawkins' 'Suzie Q' reached US No.11 and 'Proud Mary' – the tale of a Mississippi steamboat, written by John Fogerty on the day of his Army discharge – hit US No.2. Covered by Elvis Presley, it also became a hit for Ike and Tina Turner. Thereafter, Fogerty dominated the songwriting.

Follow-up *Bayou Country* (1969) saw the band honing their 'swamp Rock'. It reached US No.7 while 'Bad Moon Rising' became a UK No.1. *Green River* (1969) topped the US chart; 'Down By The River' and the title track were both Top 5 US hits.

A festival favourite, the band played Woodstock and widened their appeal to mainstream audiences. *Willy And The Poor Boys* (1970) reached US No.3 while 'Travelling Band' and 'Up Around

The Bend' made the US and UK Top 10. To cap a productive year, *Cosmo's Factory* (1970) topped the US and UK album charts.

But by 1971, the band were in decline. Amid fierce internal bickering and contractual disputes, they released the disappointing *Pendulum*. Tom Fogerty quit and, in October 1972, after the dismal *Mardi Gras*, Creedence split.

John achieved sporadic success with 1975's 'Rockin' All Over The World' and 1985's US No.1 *Centerfield*. Tom died in 1990, three years before their induction into the Rock And Roll Hall Of Fame, and John's refusal to allow Clifford or Cook onstage for the finale jam revealed unreconciled rifts. In 1997, he released *Blue Moon Swamp* and fulfilled a thirty-year urge to visit Mississippi, which he had immortalized in his songs.

CROSBY STILLS NASH & YOUNG ✪✪✪

WHO Vocals/guitar/keyboards **David Crosby** (b. David Van Cortland, 14 Aug 1941, Los Angeles, California, USA), vocals/guitar/keyboards **Stephen Stills** (b. 3 Jan 1945, Dallas,Texas, USA), vocals/guitar/keyboards **Graham Nash** (b. 2 Feb 1942, Blackpool, England), vocals/guitar/keyboards **Neil Young** (b. 12 Nov 1945, Toronto, Ontario, Canada)

WHEN 1968–

WHERE Laurel Canyon, California, USA

WHAT (In)harmonious hippie leaders

Depending on who you believe, Crosby, Stills & Nash first sang three-part harmony together in Laurel Canyon, California, in Mama Cass' dining room (so says Stills) or nearby at Joni Mitchell's place (according to Crosby). There is little doubt, however, that Cass was the CSN catalyst, having introduced Nash to Crosby. Former Byrd Crosby and Stills (ex-Buffalo Springfield) decided to 'steal' Nash from Manchester Pop band The Hollies. After a February 1968 Hollies show at the Whisky-A-Go-Go in Los Angeles, the trio settled on a loose musical relationship that would see them record collectively and as solo artists.

Debut album *Crosby, Stills And Nash* (1969) contained thoughtful and political writing from all three, including the hippie summer hit 'Marrakesh Express', a Nash song The Hollies had rejected, which had led to his defection. Rehearsed in London and Long Island, New York, the album was awash with fine acoustic and electric playing from Stills but, above all, it was the harmonies that encouraged 2 million US sales in its first year. CSN were the 'standard bearers' for the hippie movement and whether it was the shooting of Bobby Kennedy ('Long Time Gone') or escape to a hippie idyll ('Wooden Ships'), their lyrics spoke for many in the midst of the anti-Vietnam war movement. In August 1969, the trio played the massive Woodstock festival – only their second live appearance – for a paltry $5,000. Stills had already enlisted his Buffalo Springfield sparring partner Neil Young to add extra guitar and keyboards for live performances. Young insisted he be fully credited, and three became four as Crosby, Stills, Nash & Young before they played the Big Sur Folk Festival in September.

The decade should have ended on a high; *Crosby, Stills And Nash* went gold in the USA in October but, on the same day, Crosby's girlfriend, Christine Hinton, was killed in a road accident while taking their cats to the vet. More despair followed in December as a fan was murdered at Altamont, where CSN&Y shared the bill with The Rolling Stones, and the 60s finished on a depressingly violent note.

Déjà Vu (1970), recorded amid escalating tension between the four, was a group album in name only, most of its tracks being solo offerings with added group harmonies. However, the quality and diversity of the music guaranteed a quick leap to the top of the US album chart. Nash's 'Teach Your Children' and the cosy 'Our House' were the album's sing-along Top 30 singles, countered by the dark melancholy of Stills' '4+20' and Young's 'Helpless'. Crosby's hippie rant 'Almost Cut My Hair' employed a harder electric edge, used again to chilling effect on Young's 'Ohio' (not on the album), a shocked response to the killing of four Kent State University student demonstrators by National Guardsmen. Giant popularity was matched by four giant-sized egos. The songs kept coming, but it was their respective solo albums that benefited, following the break-up of CSN&Y in July

1970. Despite the split, they returned to the top of the charts a year later with the aptly titled live album *4-Way Street*. Various concert permutations of the group (most commonly Crosby and Nash) continued to cash in on the success, but public demand for a new Crosby, Stills, Nash & Young studio album was ignored until a 1973 get-together in Hawaii. Tracks were recorded, a title agreed (*Human Highway*) and even a cover photo taken before another four-way fall-out.

By 1974 they had patched up their differences sufficiently to consider what cynics suggested was a last chance cash-in: Rock's first stadium tour. It trundled across the States, grossing an estimated $11 million, and ended with a four-hour show at England's Wembley Stadium. A greatest hits album, *So Far – The Best Of*, their third consecutive US No.1, coincided with the tour.

Work on a new album, however, ended in acrimony, with new material diverted to The Stills Young Band's *Long May You Run* (1976) and Crosby & Nash's *Whistling Down The Wire* (1976). By 1977, Young had departed for a full-time solo career, but Crosby, Stills & Nash at last managed a new album, *CSN*. Strong on harmonies, it lacked the songwriting strength of previous releases but peaked at US No.2 with the gentle 'Just A Song Before I Go' becoming their biggest hit (US No.7). Subsequently, the three were content to re-form every so often for shows filled with old classics. One such reunion saw them at the Musicians United For Safe Energy (MUSE) benefit at Madison Square Garden, New York City, in September 1979. These 'No Nukes' concerts with Bruce Springsteen, among others, proved they could still wow an audience – but Crosby's drug problems were beginning to eclipse his musical ability, as his negligible input to 1982's *Daylight Again* proved. Notable mainly for Nash's 'Wasted On The Way' and Stills' 'Southern Cross', *Daylight Again* was padded by outside writers and vocalists (such as Art Garfunkel and The Eagles' Timothy B. Schmit) for the first time and, despite reaching US No.18, failed to make the UK chart. *Allies* (1983), a live album with two new studio tracks, put together again without Crosby, followed.

In December 1985, a few months after a lacklustre CSN&Y performance at Live Aid, Crosby – following arrests for drugs and firearms offences – was jailed in Texas, a sentence which probably saved his life. Tales of prison life and chemical dependency were graphically related in the book *Long Time Gone*. His enthusiasm and songwriting skill returned and the frighteningly personal 'Compass' graced a new CSN&Y album *American Dream* (1988). This short-lived association with Young proved CS&N still had something to offer, even though it was the ever popular live performances, rather than recordings, that fans warmed to. *Live It Up* (1990) and *After The Storm* (1994) were lightweight compared to 1991's boxed retrospective, *CSN*.

Crosby celebrated his 53rd birthday with Stills and Nash at Woodstock II in 1994, but was plagued by ill-health before a liver transplant that November. Crosby has been an outstanding example of Rock lifestyle survival. During the 90s, his beaming face – complete with the famous walrus moustache – popped up in Steven Spielberg's movie *Hook* (1991) and TV appearances with *Roseanne* and *The Simpsons*. A recipe of acoustic songs and lengthy anecdotes kept Crosby, Stills and Nash alive on the concert circuit, despite their lack of a recording deal. They were inducted into the Rock And Roll Hall Of Fame in 1997.

READ *Crosby, Stills, Nash & Young: The Visual Documentary* (1996), Johnny Rogan

Fan So Far, 2 Woodbine Cottages, Melin Ct, Resolven SA11 4BA, UK

SHERYL CROW

WHO b. 11 Feb 1962, Kennett, Missouri, USA

WHAT She rocks, she rolls (like a Rolling Stone)

For Sheryl, success came relatively late in life, at 31. After attending the University of Missouri, dating a young Brad Pitt and graduating with a degree in Classical piano, she moved to St Louis and joined a covers band called Kashmir. Here she received her first break, singing a McDonald's jingle. Oddly unfulfilled by such endeavours, she moved to Los Angeles and became a backing singer and writer for artists including Rod Stewart, Eric Clapton (remember this name, you'll be seeing it again) and Stevie Wonder. She held a similar position on Michael Jackson's 1987/1988 *Bad* tour – hence the reference to MJ manager "Frank Dileo's dong" in a later lyric – before taking Don Henley's advice to work on her own stuff.

After an aborted first attempt at a solo debut – she feared it had been over-produced – *Tuesday Night Music Club* emerged in 1993. The album had been recorded at her friend Bill Bottrell's studio on, not surprisingly, Tuesday nights, with a loose bunch of musicians who gelled into a Country-tinged, bar band-esque affair. The slow-burning album eventually scaled the multi-platinum heights of transatlantic charts thanks to the radio-friendly 'All I Wanna Do'. Another of its hits, the beautiful 'Strong Enough', appeared in the Brad Pitt movie *Kalifornia* (1995).

After tireless touring and appearances on Led Zeppelin, The Carpenters and *X-Files* tribute albums, she recorded and produced *Sheryl Crow* (1996). A radical image change from curly-haired girl-next-door to leather-clad sex symbol accompanied a raunchy overhaul of the music – evidenced by the Rolling Stones-aping opening single 'If It Makes You Happy' and its brain-bending video. Further hits 'Everyday Is A Winding Road', 'A Change Would Do You Good' and 'Home' kept the album high in the charts while she roamed the world again – occasionally accompanied by beau Eric Clapton.

Crow's apparent bid for world domination continued in 1997 with the Bond movie theme 'Tomorrow Never Dies', a boundary-crunching cameo on Salt-N-Pepa's *Brand New* and support slots on the Stones' *Bridges To Babylon* tour – earning the rarely bestowed respect of Keith Richards. At the younger end of the live spectrum, she joined Sarah McLachlan's triumphant 'fem-fest' Lilith Fair – an all-women affair that confounded business predictions by selling out across America.

Surf www.geocities.com/hollywood/hills/1192/sheryl.html

CROWDED HOUSE ⊙

WHO Vocals/guitar **Neil Finn** (b. 27 May 1958, Te Awamutu, North Island, New Zealand), bass **Nick Seymour** (b. 9 Dec 1958, Benalla, Victoria, Australia), drums **Paul Hester** (b. 8 Jan 1959, Melbourne, Victoria)

WHEN 1985–1996

WHERE Melbourne, Australia

WHAT Exquisite, sweet, melancholy Pop

Crowded House emerged from Split Enz, an idiosyncratic Art Rock sextet founded by Neil Finn's older brother Tim (vocals/keyboards/guitar, b. 25 Jun, 1952, Te Awamutu). Tim ended Split Enz's thirteen-year run in 1985 when he went solo and settled in England with actress Greta Scacchi. Neil, who joined the Enz and attendant sibling rivalry at 18, was then based in Melbourne. He enlisted bassist Seymour and Enz drummer Hester to form The Mullanes. Signed by Capitol in America on the strength of Neil's songs, the trio decamped to Los Angeles, lived in a crowded house, renamed themselves, and recorded a self-titled album produced by Mitchell Froom. Released in 1986, its glorious songs of love and pain, uncluttered arrangements and stunning harmonies were so little noticed that Crowded House played acoustic gigs in restaurants to attract attention – acquiring a reputation for repartee, slapstick, striptease and audience participation.

American radio discovered them in 1987. Neil's heart-stopping compositions 'Don't Dream It's Over' and 'Something So Strong' reached the US Top 10 and *Crowded House* rose to No.12. But the glimpse of glory proved short-lived. *Temple Of Low Men* (1988) – arguably their best – stiffed everywhere. "Too melancholy" was the received explanation. Crowded House slid into rarely resolved unrest. Tim left Europe – career stalled and marriage over – for Australia and, with Neil, who had also returned, began to write a Finn brothers' album in January 1990.

When Capitol in LA told Crowded House the advance tape of their third album didn't pass muster, Neil turned to his recent writing spree with Tim. Then Hester and Seymour got back to the studio, the chartbusting subtleties of 'Weather With You', 'Four Seasons In One Day' and 'It's Only Natural' were on the tracklist and Crowded House had a new member, Tim Finn.

Woodface (1991) altered their commercial geography. It failed to recapture America, but a long stay in the British charts,

"Songwriting is a mystery. And it's a mystery to me that it's a mystery. But that sounds stupid"

Neil Finn

peaking at No.6, was matched in many countries. However, Tim's "animal intensity", as Neil put it, upset the band's stage act. That November, before a Glasgow gig, he left by mutual consent. For *Together Alone* (1993), Neil moved back to New Zealand, British dance specialist Youth replaced Mitchell Froom as producer, and keyboardist Mark Hart joined. It maintained *Woodface*'s success: critical acclaim, UK No.4, American indifference. But during sessions in New Zealand, Hester recalled, "personal relationships really took a beating".

In April the following year, he cracked and quit. Crowded House completed their commitments with a stand-in, but their farewell began the moment Hester left. Neil announced the quietus officially in June 1996 and the last rites were celebrated in front of 150,000 people beside the Sydney Harbour Bridge and Opera House on 24 November. Hester rejoined for the night and for the new tracks on *Recurring Dream: The Best Of Crowded House* (1996), the band's only UK No.1. Afterwards, Seymour and Hester lay doggo, Hart returned to Supertramp from whence he came and Tim ploughed on with his solo endeavours and finally completed an album with his brother (*Finn*, 1995).

(READ) *Something So Strong* (1997), Chris Bourke

(FAN) PO Box 21, Freepost, London, W10 6BR, UK

(SURF) www.etext.org/Mailing.lists/house/

THE CULT ⊙

WHO Vocals **Ian Astbury** (b. Ian Lindsay, 14 May 1962, Heswell, Merseyside, England), guitar **Billy Duffy** (b. William H. Duffy, 12 May 1959, Manchester, England)

WHEN 1982–1995

WHERE Bradford, England

WHAT Goth-spawned mystical Rock pigs

As their name shrank, sales skyrocketed. Short-lived Goths Southern Death Cult became Death Cult in 1983, comprising their founder Ian Astbury, ex-Ritual members Jamie Stewart (bass) and Ray Mondo (drums), and Billy Duffy, formerly of Theatre Of Hate and Ed Banger & The Nosebleeds (a Punk group celebrated only for launching Smiths singer Morrissey). After two singles on Indie label Situation 2 (who released Southern Death Cult's 'Fat Man' and an eponymous 1983 anthology), the group installed the first of several new drummers (Nigel Preston, ex-Sex Gang Children) and abridged their name to The Cult for *Dreamtime* (1984) and minor hit 'Resurrection Joe'.

Preston was temporarily replaced by Big Country's Mark Brzezicki – aka 'Mark Unpronounceablename' to readers of British Pop magazine *Smash Hits* – for *Love* (1985), on which 60s Psychedelia embellished their unfashionable blend of Doors-style mysticism and Gothic Indie. Lambasted by the music press, the band won over Rock fans, and the storming 'She Sells Sanctuary', 'Rain' and 'Revolution' followed the album up the UK charts. A 1986 world tour – with new drummer Les Warner – promoted them to arena-filling headliners.

With the AC/DC-style raunch of 1987's Rick 'Def Jam' Rubin-produced *Electric*, The Cult finally bade farewell to bemused British Indie fans, moved to Los Angeles, hung out with Guns N'

Roses (recruiting GN'R's future drummer Matt Sorum) and became a pastiche Metal band. The makeover was confirmed by Duffy's leather-clad, Les Paul-wielding cover pose on *Sonic Temple* (1989), but rockist indulgence (drugs, drinking, brawls) destabilized the group, a situation exacerbated by Stewart's departure in 1990. In 1991, the patchy *Ceremony* (packed with Astbury's trademark shamanism) prompted an ill-advised foray into electronic territory, premiered on 'The Witch' from 1993's UK No.1 *Pure Cult* compilation and elaborated on 1994's largely ignored swan song, *The Cult*. After their split, Duffy briefly joined ex-Wonder Stuff singer Miles Hunt's Vent 414, formed the short-lived Interstate (with Love drummer Brzezicki and ex-Mission bassist Craig Adams) and toured with Iggy Pop, while Astbury formed the predictably raunchy The Holy Barbarians.

surf www.coastnet.com/~jtaylor/cult.html

CULTURE CLUB ◉

WHO Vocals **Boy George** (b. George O'Dowd, 14 Jun 1961, Bexley, Kent, England), guitar/keyboards **Roy Hay** (b. 12 Aug 1961, Southend-on-Sea, Essex, England), bass **Mikey Craig** (b. 15 Feb 1960, London, England), drums **Jon Moss** (b. 11 Sep 1957, London)

WHEN 1981–1986

WHERE London, England

WHAT New Romantic Pop burn-outs

Bowie fanatic O'Dowd was a well-known face on London's early-80s New Romantic scene, brushing with fame as an early member – under the name Lieutenant Lush – of the Malcolm McLaren-managed Bow Wow Wow. In 1981, he formed Sex Gang Children with (ex-Adam & The Ants/ Damned drummer) Moss, Hay and Craig. Renamed Culture Club, the group signed to Virgin, and after two flops hit the UK No.1 with 'Do You Really Want To Hurt Me'. Viewers of BBC's *Top Of The Pops* had seen nothing like it: was it a girl or a boy? Parents were dismayed to find their children idolizing this *thing*. Through the tabloid press and TV chat shows, they learned 'it' was Boy George: a cheerfully outspoken Pop star who, he claimed, "preferred a cup of tea to sex".

Culture Club's music was inspired and eccentric. Their debut *Kissing To Be Clever*

(1982) was an international success, and 1983's *Colour By Numbers* spawned the hits 'Church Of The Poison Mind', 'Victims', 'It's A Miracle' and the UK/US No.1 'Karma Chameleon'.

However, things went quickly downhill. The lacklustre *Waking Up With The House On Fire* (1984) included the insipid 'The War Song', and the band's first flop in years, 'The Medal Song'. *From Luxury To Heartache* (1986) proved their final album: the group crumbled after the break-up of George and Moss's relationship, while George's much publicized heroin addiction meant Culture Club's passing was hardly noticed. Moss and Hay went on to less high-profile groups, while Craig became a producer. George became an acclaimed DJ, sporadically successful solo artist (scoring highest with 1987's UK No.1 'Everything I Own') and newspaper columnist. In 1998, despite years of bitchy backbiting, the four reunited for a financially motivated US tour.

read *Take It Like A Man* (1995), Boy George & Spencer Bright

fan Distant Dream, 42 Winter Grove, Parr, St Helens, Merseyside, WA9 2JS, UK

surf www.vmg.co.uk/boygeorge/

I started wearing [lipstick] because it made me feel **confident** and more **attractive.** I'm completely **featureless** without it. But on stage I always used to lean my mouth on the mike and **shut my eyes** so I wouldn't have to see the people. And at the end I'd come off with lipstick smeared **all over my face,** so I thought I might as well go on with it like that and make it **look intentional**

THE CURE ⊙

WHO Vocals/guitar **Robert Smith** (b. 21 Apr 1959, Blackpool, Lancashire, England), guitar **Porl Thompson** (b. 8 Nov 1957, London, England), bass **Simon Gallup** (b. 1 Jun 1960, Duxhurst, Surrey, England), drums **Boris Williams** (b. 24 Apr 1957, Versailles, France)

WHEN 1976–

WHERE Crawley, West Sussex, England

WHAT Grand masters of Goth

In trademark smeared lipstick, sneakers and saggy sweater, The Cure's Robert Smith is the grand old duke of Goth. With 10,000 men in tow, he marched to the top of the hill and… stayed there. Despite mind-boggling line-up changes, mega-selling albums, Hell and high water, The Cure have remained firmly idiosyncratic throughout their lengthy and complex history.

Initially The Easy Cure, schoolfriends Smith, Laurence 'Lol' Tolhurst and bassist Michael Dempsey were augmented by singer Peter O'Toole and guitarist Porl Thompson. In 1978, they reverted to the original trio, dropped the 'Easy' and cut 'Killing An Arab' – inspired by Albert Camus' novel *L'Etranger*. Polydor's Chris Parry landed them a deal with UK Indie Small Wonder and the track was released as The Cure's debut in December 1978. Critics raved, but the single failed to chart.

However, their debut for Parry's new label Fiction – *Three Imaginary Boys* (1979) – made UK No.44. On tour with Siouxsie & The Banshees, Smith replaced AWOL Banshees guitarist John McKay, launching a union that peaked with Smith and Banshee Steve Severin forming The Glove for 1983's *Blue Sunshine*.

In 1980, Simon Gallup replaced Dempsey and Matthieu Hartley joined on keyboards. Despite its icy gloom – typified by the excellent 'A Forest' – *Seventeen Seconds* (1980) reached UK No.17. Then Hartley resigned, leaving the remaining trio to record *Faith* and movie soundtrack *Carnage Visors* (both 1981).

Pornography (1982) plumbed the depths of bleakness and soared into the UK Top 5. However, bickering prompted Gallup's defection to The Cry with Hartley. Tolhurst, meanwhile, swapped drums for keyboards, making way for ex-Wreckless Eric drummer Steve Goulding on 'Let's Go To Bed', a Pop confection that belied their doom 'n' gloom reputation and initiated a long association with video director Tim Pope.

When Smith rejoined the Banshees for a 1983 tour, a permanent transfer was mooted. However, the counsel of Parry and the success of The Cure's 'The Walk' and 'Love Cats' persuaded Smith that The Cure, rebuilt with drummer Andy Anderson and bassist Phil Thornalley, were indeed his first love.

However, 1984 proved traumatic. After a UK tour to promote *three* new albums – the compilation *Japanese Whispers*, *The Top* (which spawned the fluttery, Syd Barrett-esque hit 'Caterpillar') and *Concert: The Cure Live* – Smith was scheduled to tour again with the Banshees, but collapsed from exhaustion.

He recruited drummer Boris Williams, welcomed back Simon Gallup and Porl Thompson and crafted a classic: *The Head On The Door* (1985). It was heralded by the storming 'In Between Days' and 'Close To Me', whose accompanying Pope-directed video packed the band into a wardrobe and pushed them over a cliff.

Their stock was raised by *Standing On The Beach – The Singles* (1986). When *Kiss Me, Kiss Me, Kiss Me* (1987) appeared, The Cure were as hot as its smouldering orange artwork, which beckoned buyers into a world in which Smith cudgeled and caressed them into submission. For every howl on tracks like 'The Kiss', there was a delicious dollop of romance, as in 'Just Like Heaven' or 'Catch'. In the ensuing two-year hiatus, Smith cemented one long-term relationship – marrying his childhood sweetheart Mary – and dissolved another: the increasingly unreliable Tolhurst was fired and replaced by Roger O'Donnell.

Gloom recaptured the upper hand on *Disintegration* (1989). However, overwhelming bleakness proved no commercial obstacle: it soared to US No.12, where The Cure were now a stadium-filling sensation, yet *still* hip. In 1990, Smith embraced Dance, employing DJs to remix classics for *Mixed Up*.

Wielding a Best British Group BRIT award, they released *Entreat* (1991) – a live set entirely culled from *Disintegration* – whose profits were split between ten charities. This virtue was rewarded when *Wish* (1992) – with ex-roadie Perry Bamonte on keyboards and guitar – topped the UK chart and climbed to US No.2, trailed by the hits 'Friday I'm In Love' and 'High'. The live albums *Show* and *Paris* followed in 1993 – without the services of Porl Thompson, who later joined Page & Plant. More woe came in 1994, when Smith and Parry endured (but won) a court case brought against them, for alleged underpayment, by Tolhurst.

In 1995, Roger O'Donnell returned and Jason Cooper replaced the long-serving Williams, while the band recorded 23 new songs for the surprisingly under-bought *Wild Mood Swings* (1996). Though Smith's inspiration showed signs of waning, 1997's hits set *Galore* proved how many times The Cure have touched greatness.

ʀᴇᴀᴅ *Ten Imaginary Years* (1987), Steve Sutherland & Robert Smith

ꜰᴀɴ The Cure, PO Box 211, Hayes, Middlesex UB4 9N2, UK

ꜱᴜʀꜰ thecure.com

CYPRESS HILL ✪

WHO Vocals **B-Real** (b. Louis Freeze, 2 Jun 1970, South Gate, Los Angeles, USA), vocals **Sen Dog** (b. Senen Reyes, 20 Nov 1965, Cuba), DJ/producer **DJ Muggs** (b. Lawrence Muggerud, 28 Jan 1968, New York, USA)

WHEN 1984–

WHERE Los Angeles, USA

WHAT Smokin' Latino Hip Hop

Cypress Hill set their agenda with early songs like 'Trigga Happy Nigga' and 'Light Another', which expound the virtues of guns and press for the legalization of marijuana. The latter, reworked as Rap classic 'How I Could Just Kill A Man', propelled *Cypress Hill* (1991) to platinum status. On 1992's US Lollapalooza tour, they appeared alongside Pearl Jam, with whom they collaborated on the 1993 *Judgement Night* soundtrack. The resultant Rock/Rap fanbase made *Black Sunday* (1993) a transatlantic chart-stormer.

But after *III – Temples of Boom* (1995), the group splintered: Muggs declined to tour and Sen Dog bailed out altogether. In 1997, solo projects *Muggs Presents… The Soul Assassins* and B-Real's *The Psycho Realm* plugged the subsequent gap.

ꜱᴜʀꜰ www.music.sony.com/Music/ArtistInfo/CypressHill/index.html

" have a lot to say, & we say it fast "

Rat Scabies

DAFT PUNK

WHO Keyboards **Thomas Bangaltier** (b. 1 Jan 1975), keyboards **Guy-Manuel De Homem Christo** (b. 8 Feb 1974)

WHEN 1993–

WHERE Paris, France

WHAT D.I.Y. D.I.S.C.O.

While the USA flipped for Electronica, France resumed nuclear testing, this time in Britain, with a fearsome blend of Disco, Hip Hop, Techno, Funk and Kiss called Daft Punk. Inspired by the early 90s Indie Dance scene (defining moment: Primal Scream's 'Loaded'), Bangaltier (son of Ottowan's 'D.I.S.C.O.' writer Daniel Vangarde) and De Homem Christo formed Darlin', Beach Boys fanciers signed to Stereolab's Duophonic label and described by *Melody Maker* as "Daft Punk".

When Bangaltier received a sampler for his 18th birthday, they threw away the guitars and emerged from their bedroom studio with the wonderfully primitive 'The New Wave' (1994) on Scottish label Soma. By 1997, they had remixed The Chemical Brothers and Gabrielle, graced the soundtrack to Playstation game *Wipeout 2097* and scaled UK charts with re-released

second single 'Da Funk' and *Homework* (1997) – pick 'n' mix samples and noise which yielded super hits 'Around The World' and 'Burnin'' and sparked a 'Parisian Techno' boom (grateful beneficiaries included Air).

SURF www.geocities.com/SiliconValley/Heights/1275/DaftPunk.html

THE DAMNED

WHO Vocals **Dave Vanian** (b. David Letts, 12 Oct 1956, Hemel Hempstead, England), guitar **Brian James** (b. Brian Robertson, 18 Feb 1955, Brighton, England), bass **Captain Sensible** (b. Ray Burns, 24 Apr 1955, Croydon, England), drums **Rat Scabies** (b. Chris Miller, 30 Jul 1957, Kingston upon Thames, England)

WHEN 1976–

WHERE London, England

WHAT Amphetamine-fuelled Punk pioneers

James and Scabies, formerly members of London SS alongside Mick Jones and Tony James (later of The Clash and Generation X respectively), united with Johnny Moped guitarist Sensible to form The Damned in May 1976. Having worked as a grave digger, Vanian adopted a 'Hammer Horror' image and joined in time for their debut supporting The Sex Pistols at London's 100 Club. Signed to Indie label Stiff, their 'New Rose' (1976), coupled with a breakneck version of The Beatles' 'Help!', is considered by many to be the first Punk record. Its healthy sales encouraged Island Records to take on Stiff's distribution. *Damned Damned Damned* (1977) entered the UK Top 40, and was produced by Nick Lowe, who encountered them after fighting with Scabies on a coach travelling to a French Punk festival. The sleeve featured a picture of Punk contemporaries Eddie & The Hot Rods – a typical Stiff in-joke. After *Music for Pleasure* (1977), the band split, James taking the name Damned with him.

Scabies, Sensible (now on guitar) and Vanian spent much of 1978 playing as The Doomed with temporary bass players, such as Motorhead's Lemmy, before legally re-acquiring the Damned name. With bassist Alistair 'Algy' Ward (later of Metal flops Tank), they charted with 'Love Song' from *Machine Gun Etiquette* (1979), *The Black Album* (1980) and *Strawberries* (1982). Sensible pursued a parallel solo career: an English version of Plastic Bertrand's 1978 hit 'Ça Plane Pour Moi' and 'This Is Your Captain Speaking' were followed by a UK chart-topping remake of 'Happy Talk' from the musical *South Pacific*. Sensible left The Damned in 1984.

With guitarist Roman Jugg and bassist Bryn Merrick, they abandoned frenetic Punk for psychedelic Pop in *Phantasmagoria* (1985), spawning the UK hits 'Grimly Fiendish' and 'The Shadow Of Love'. A version of Barry Ryan's 'Eloise' became their biggest hit, reaching the UK Top 3 in March 1986. But after a handful of minor hits and *Anything* (1986), they called it a day in early 1989.

The split proved short-lived when the original line-up re-formed to support The Ramones in 1991 and play on the Punk nostalgia circuit. Less celebrated than The Clash and the Pistols, The Damned are nonetheless fondly remembered, with celebrity admirers including Dinosaur Jr and Guns N' Roses.

SURF www.geocities.com/sunsetstrip/towers/4359/damned.html

TERENCE TRENT D'ARBY ◎

WHO b. 15 Mar 1962, New York City, New York, USA

WHAT Eccentric Soul singer

Terence Trent D'Arby came to prominence in April 1987 when 'If You Let Me Stay' became a huge UK hit. Despite claiming he was "brought up by wolves", D'Arby was a boxing champion in Florida before enlisting in the US Army. He was stationed in Frankfurt, Germany, in the 3rd Armoured Battalion, Elvis Presley's old regiment. Joining local Funk outfit Touch in 1982, he left after being discharged from the army in mid-1983 and relocated to London, England.

Debut *Introducing The Hardline According To Terence Trent D'Arby* (1987) received major critical acclaim. Produced by Martyn Ware of Heaven 17, it reached UK No.1 and US No.4 – going platinum both places – and spawned the chart-topping 'Wishing Well'. After a two-year silence, interrupted only by 'The Birth Of Maudie', credited to 'The Incredible EG O'Reilly', *Neither Fish Nor Flesh* (1990) appeared, to critical derision and negligible sales. 'To Know Someone Deeply Is To Know Someone Softly' barely scraped the charts. After appearing with Ware's BEF on *Music Of Quality And Distinction Vol.2* (1991), performing Bob Dylan's 'It's Alright Ma, I'm Only Bleeding', he recovered commercially with *Symphony Or Damn* (1993), scoring with 'She Kissed Me' and the Des'ree duet 'Delicate'. The album was entirely written and produced by D'Arby, who declared:

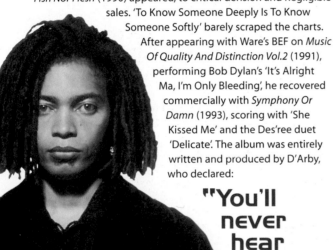

"You'll never hear a crap song from me! I'm a genius!"

Vibrator (1995), again written/produced by D'Arby, reached UK No.11. Snapped up by Java Records (a joint venture by Capitol and Alanis Morissette's producer-turned-media-mogul Glen Ballard), he appeared as an A&R man in the film *Clubland* (1998).

🏄 www.home3.inet.tele.dk/hgaarde/TTDarby/

MILES DAVIS

WHO b. 26 May 1926, Alton, Illinois, USA, d. 28 Sep 1991, Santa Monica, California, USA

WHAT Boundary-breaking Jazz innovator

Davis' influence on Jazz, and music in general, is immeasurable. Only his beloved Duke Ellington had the same innovation. Only Louis Armstrong and Dizzy Gillespie spawned as many imitators as Miles' cool, understated trumpet style, though neither shared his daring.

Davis was 19 when he began playing trumpet with the star of Bebop, Charlie Parker. *Birth Of The Cool* (1957), a compilation of early recordings made after he left Parker's band, is a classic. Collaborations in the 50s with fellow legends-to-be John Coltrane and Gil Evans – and the inspirational albums *Miles Ahead* (1957), *Kind Of Blue* (1959) and *Sketches Of Spain* (1960) – gave way to a great mid-60s quintet with Herbie Hancock and Wayne Shorter. Davis' body of work already ensured his reputation would outlive him. Yet rather than rest on his laurels, he alienated purists by going electric.

Professing admiration for Jimi Hendrix and Sly Stone, his recordings from 1968 to his 'retirement' in 1975 saw Jazz mutate into Rock without compromising its exploratory spirit. Electric piano dominated *In A Silent Way* (1969), while the heavier *Bitches Brew* and *Jack Johnson* (both 1970) showcased guitarist John McLaughlin. Fusion was born, and its flagship band Weather Report grew from Miles' group of the period.

Live-Evil (1971) and the following year's *On The Corner* introduced wah-wah trumpet, the latter amidst African and Indian influences. A slew of expansive live albums saw out this chapter, eventually drawn to a close by illness. From 1980 until his death from a stroke and pneumonia, Davis embraced mostly slick Pop Jazz, jamming and recording with celebrity disciple Prince. He also recorded material by Cyndi Lauper and Scritti Politti and continued his experimental collaborations up until the very end, as seen in the posthumous release of Jazz Hip Hop project *Doo-Bop* (1992), recorded with Rapper Easy Mo Bee.

📖 *Miles Davis: A Critical Biography* (1982), Ian Carr

🏄 miles.rtvf.nwu.edu/miles/milestones.html

THE SPENCER DAVIS GROUP

WHO Vocals/guitar/keyboards **Steve 'Stevie' Winwood** (b. 12 May 1948, Birmingham, England), guitar **Spencer Davis** (b. 17 Jul 1937, Swansea, Wales), bass **Mervyn 'Muff' Winwood** (b. 15 Jun 1943, Birmingham), drums **Pete York** (b. 15 Aug 1942, Redcar, North Yorkshire, England)

WHEN 1962–1969

WHERE Birmingham, England

WHAT Classic British R&B

Stevie started playing on stage wearing short trousers and was once sent home from a pub gig for being underage. He and brother 'Muff' first played guitar in their father's dance orchestra in 1956. They went their own way in 1960, playing Jazz, then Blues. Blues specialist Spencer Davis joined them the same year and, due to his age and willingness to be a spokesman, the group was named after him. Davis initially sang most of the lead vocals, but Stevie's vocals got a better response. The latter owed much to Ray Charles – he sang Charles' songs like 'Georgia On My Mind' and 'What I'd Say' – and many who heard early Spencer Davis Group singles thought they were black!

By 1964 they had become Birmingham's top Blues band. Chris Blackwell (future owner of Island Records) became their manager and got them a record deal. The first album of Blues covers, in 1965, was lightweight compared to contemporaries like The Rolling Stones, but the second single, R&B cover 'I Can't Stand It', made a good impression, despite a low chart placing (UK No.41). In 1965 the group's main success was as a popular UK live act, often playing seven nights a week, with Eric Clapton occasionally joining them onstage for Blues jams.

Chart success came when the band switched to Pop. The punchy 'Keep On Running' – one of the first uses of fuzz guitar – knocked The Beatles from UK No.1 in January 1966. It was written by Jamaican singer Jackie Edwards, as was the next single 'Somebody Help Me' (UK No.1). The more complex, self-penned singles 'Gimme Some Lovin'' (UK No.2, US No.12), released in 1966, and 1967's 'I'm A Man' (UK No.9, US No.10), were arguably the group's best artistic achievements.

Stevie's growing ability outstripped Muff and Davis and he split in April 1967 to form the more experimental Traffic, but rarely recaptured the excitement of those early hits. Muff quit to become a successful A&R man. Davis struggled on with York and fluctuating replacements until 1969, but their records suffered murky production and weak songwriting, and lacked Stevie's distinctive voice.

CHRIS DE BURGH ⊙

WHO b. Christopher John Davidson, 15 Oct 1948, Argentina

WHAT Unfashionable MOR romantic

Discovered by songwriters Doug Flett and Guy Fletcher, Chris De Burgh signed to A&M in 1974, setting his sights on the soft end of the Rock market with *Far Beyond These Castle Walls*, *Spanish Train And Other Stories* (both 1975), *At The End Of A Perfect Day* (1977) and *Crusader* (1979). International successes included 1980's *Eastern Wind* – Norway's second-biggest selling album after The Beatles' *Abbey Road*. In Britain, where he was known mostly for 'A Spaceman Came Travelling' (1976) and lobbying A&M to drop The Sex Pistols, De Burgh did not bother the charts until 1982's *The Getaway* and the single 'Don't Pay The Ferryman'. *Man On The Line* (1984) sold even better, but it was 1986's *Into The Light* – prefaced by 'The Lady In Red' – which sent De Burgh stellar, reaching UK No.2 and US No.25.

Flying Colours (1988), *Power Of Ten* (1992) and *This Way Up* (1994) scaled similar heights, but De Burgh's wholesome image slipped amid publicity over his alleged adultery, with compilation *Beautiful Dreams* (1995) falling outside the UK Top 30. De Burgh was among the artists invited to perform at a concert in memory of Diana, Princess of Wales at Althorp on 27 June 1998.

surf www.tuns.ca/~nicholsd/music/cdeb.html

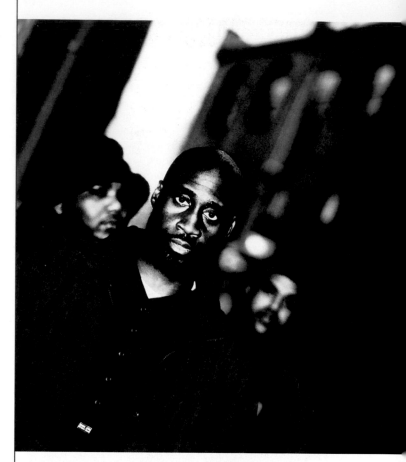

DE LA SOUL

WHO Vocals **Posdnuos** (b. Kelvin Mercer, 17 Aug 1969, Brooklyn, New York, USA), vocals **Trugoy The Dove** (b. David Jolicoeur, 21 Sep 1968, Brooklyn), vocals **Mase** (b. Vincent Mason Jr, 24 Mar 1970, Brooklyn)

WHEN 1987–

WHERE Long Island, New York, USA

WHAT Hippie Hop turned grumpy Rap

De La Soul, steered by producer Prince Paul of Hip Hop pioneers Stetsasonic, were snapped up by the Tommy Boy label in 1988. The Funkadelic-fuelled 'Me Myself And I' from *3 Feet High And Rising* (1989) replaced Rap's bitches and firearms with beads and flowers. Like-minded acts The Jungle Brothers, Queen Latifah, A Tribe Called Quest and Monie Love united in an informal 'Native Tongues' collective, hence the delightful De La Soul/Queen Latifah hit 'Mama Gave Birth To The Soul Children' (1990).

However, chirpy hits like 'Ring Ring Ring (Ha Ha Hey)' from *De La Soul Is Dead* (1991) barely masked their growing cynicism. After the indifferently received *Buhloone Mindstate* (1993), Prince Paul quit to concentrate on The Gravediggaz, with fellow Rap superproducer and Wu Tang mastermind RZA. De La Soul collaborated with Teenage Fanclub on the acclaimed *Judgement Night* (1993) soundtrack cut 'Fallin'' and kept the faithful happy with *Stakes Is High* (1996). Although A Tribe Called Quest have enjoyed greater success, De La Soul helped put Rap on the map.

surf people.clarkson.edu/~currieat/dela/tongue.html

DEACON BLUE ⊙⊙

WHO Vocals **Ricky Ross** (b. 22 Dec 1957, Dundee, Scotland), vocals **Lorraine McIntosh** (b. 13 May 1964, Glasgow, Scotland), guitar **Graeme Kelling** (b. 4 Apr 1957, Paisley, Scotland), keyboards **Jim Prime** (b. 3 Nov 1960, Kilmarnock, Scotland), bass **Ewen Vernal** (b. 27 Feb 1964, Glasgow), drums **Dougie Vipond** (b. 15 Oct 1966, Johnstone, Scotland)

WHEN 1985–1994

WHERE Glasgow, Scotland

WHAT Rock from Raintown

Hand on heart and eye on the chart, Ross missed the target with solo album *So Long Ago* (1983) but hit with Deacon Blue's debut *Raintown* (1987) – named after their home, Glasgow (the band name came from Steely Dan's 'Deacon Blues'). Though its success was better measured in airplay and acclaim than sales, the album clung to the UK chart for 77 weeks, buoyed by classy singles like 'Dignity' and the repackaged reissue *Raintown & Riches* (1988). The "woo-woo"-ing chorus of 'Real Gone Kid', however, went Top 10 and *When The World Knows Your Name* (1989) toppled Madonna from the UK No.1 spot. Giddy with success, the group sanctioned B-sides collection *Ooh Las Vegas* (1990) – a moderate success, but definite case of overkill.

More modest (and self-explanatory) was EP 'Four Bacharach And David Songs' (1990) – their biggest UK hit (No.2) – which set the tone for the more reflective *Fellow Hoodlums* (1991). In contrast, *Whatever You Say, Say Nothing* (1993) was helmed by voguish Dance producers Steve Osborne and Paul Oakenfold. 'Your Town' (1992), an Osborne/Oakenfold-produced single, entered the Dance chart but eroded much of their fanbase.

Faced with domestic decline, an invisible international profile and the increasing dominance of partners Ross and McIntosh, the group split, leaving *Our Town – The Greatest Hits* (1994) as their chart-topping epitaph. Neither Ross' solo albums – *What You Are* (1996) and *New Recording* (1997) – nor CBS' barrel-scraping *Riches & More* (1997) scaled similar heights.

Read *Just What I Feel* (1995), Dave Bowler & Bryan Dray

Surf www.geocities.com/SunsetStrip/7849/index.html

DEAD KENNEDYS

WHO Vocals **Jello Biafra** (b. Eric Boujet, 17 Jun 1958, Boulder, Colorado, USA), guitar **East Bay Ray** (b. Ray Glasser, Castro Valley, California, USA), bass **Klaus Flouride** (b. Detroit, Michigan, USA), drums **Darren Peligro** (b. East St Louis, Illinois, USA)

WHEN 1978–1986

WHERE San Francisco, California, USA

WHAT Antagonistic Hardcore Punks

Arriving in San Francisco in mid-1978, Biafra gave the finger to his new home state with 'California Über Alles' (1979) – a scathing attack on California governor Jerry Brown. He also stood in 1979's San Francisco mayoral elections, finishing fourth out of ten.

After debut *Fresh Fruit For Rotting Vegetables* (1980), the band hit the UK chart with 'Too Drunk To Fuck', described as "that song by the Dead Kennedys" on *Top Of The Pops*. Peligro replaced original drummer Bruce 'Ted' Slesinger for *Plastic Surgery Disasters* (1982), *Frankenchrist* (1985) and *Bedtime For Democracy* (1986). A career-ruining court case over the alleged obscenity of a poster included with *Frankenchrist* made Biafra a fervent anti-censorship campaigner. Following the band's demise, he has recorded with the likes of Ice-T, DOA, NoMeansNo and Ministry, while Dead Kennedys have been a lasting influence on contemporary US Punk bands.

Read *Kennedys, The Unauthorized Version* (1983), Marion Kester & F-Stop Fitzgerald

Surf www.geocities.com/SunsetStrip/6558/DKPAGE.HTM

Death Row

Once Rap's mightiest mover, Death Row was founded by Dr Dre and Marion 'Suge' Knight, who forcibly persuaded NWA leader Eazy E to relinquish Dre from his Ruthless Records. The Doctor's <u>The Chronic</u> (1992) unleashed Snoop Doggy Dogg and associated releases – including Tha Dogg Pound's <u>Dogg Food</u> (1995) and the superb soundtrack <u>Above The Rim</u> (1994) – became guaranteed US smashes. But commercial domination was no protection against corporate wrath. Under heat from anti-Rap campaigners, industry giant Time Warner jettisoned Death Row distributor Interscope. Entertaining rivalry with Ruthless was replaced by bitter war with Puff Daddy's Bad Boy label, a dispute implicated in the murders of Death Row's Tupac Shakur and Bad Boy's Notorious BIG. Alarmed that his protegés were spending more time in court than in the studio, Dre jumped ship to his Aftermath label and Knight – on parole for violence – was jailed in 1995, rendering the company's renaming as 'The New And "Untouchable" Death Row Records' somewhat ironic. Amidst lawsuits, Snoop's departure and fragile distribution deals, the label was buoyed by posthumous Shakur releases, but <u>Death Row's Greatest Hits</u> (1996) looked suspiciously like an epitaph.

Decca

Launched by British stockbroker Sir Edward Lewis in 1929, Decca's first successes included Bing Crosby and Al Jolson. An American division triumphed with Crosby's 30-million-selling 'White Christmas' and Louis Armstrong. After MCA purchased US Decca, Lewis founded London Records in 1947 as his US outlet; hits by Lonnie Donegan, Tommy Steele and Billy Fury, The Rolling Stones, The Moody Blues, Tom Jones and Engelbert Humperdinck ensued. Among the most successful was The Tornados' classic 'Telstar' (1962). London also leased small US labels' catalogues for release by Decca in the UK, including Little Richard, The Everly Brothers, Del Shannon, The Crystals and The Ronettes. Decca faded during the 70s and, following Lewis' death in 1980, was purchased by Polygram, renamed London Recordings, and carried on strong with New Order, The Communards, Shakespear's Sister, Run DMC, East 17 and All Saints.

DEEP PURPLE ☉☉☉

WHO Vocals **Ian Gillan** (b. 19 Aug 1945, Hounslow, England), guitar **Ritchie Blackmore** (b. 14 Apr 1945, Weston-super-Mare, England), keyboards **Jon Lord** (b. 9 Jun 1941, Leicester, England), drums **Ian Paice** (b. 29 Jun 1948, Nottingham, England), bass **Roger Glover** (b. 30 Nov 1945, Brecon, Wales)

WHEN 1968–

WHERE Hertfordshire, England

WHAT Classical meets Heavy Metal

According to many Rock archaeologists, the birth of Heavy Metal can be traced back to 1970 and two British bands: Black Sabbath, with their eponymous debut and *Paranoid*, and Deep Purple with their fifth album *In Rock*. Hendrix? Led Zeppelin? Blue Cheer? Just loud, plugged-in Blues with some Psychedelia, Garage Rock or Ethno-Folk thrown in. No, it was Black Sabbath who gave Metal its catatonically slow, dark heaviness and Deep Purple who added the progressive flash and brilliance. The four seminal albums that the so-called 'classic Mark II line-up' (listed above) recorded in two years at the start of the 70s – *In Rock* (1970), *Fireball* (1971), *Machine Head* (1972) and *Made In Japan* (1972) – established Deep Purple's reputation and fortune, while simultaneously making Metal the decade's dominant genre.

Prior to 1969's Mark II recruitment of Episode Six's bassist Roger Glover and vocalist Ian Gillan (who'd also sung the lead in the stage musical *Jesus Christ Superstar*), Deep Purple had been an undistinguished underground band in the Vanilla Fudge vein, slogging through Europe's club circuit without much success. However, they had had two hits in the States with cover versions of already well-known Pop songs: Joe South/Billy Joe Royal's 'Hush' and Neil Diamond's 'Kentucky Woman' (both featuring Rod Evans, ex-Maze, on vocals). By that time the year-old band – evidently starting as it meant to go on – had been through a number of changes. Their name started out as Roundabout; they then toyed with Concrete God before settling on the name of Ritchie Blackmore's granny's favourite song. The line-up was originally based around Chris Curtis – former drummer with The Searchers, now a vocalist – plus Blackmore, Lord, Dave Curtis and Bobby Woodman. Within months, both Curtises were out, and Paice, Evans and bassist Nick Simper were in, some for longer periods than others.

On the strength of their hit singles, debut *Shades Of Deep Purple* (1968) made the US Top 30 (although it got nowhere in Britain). But, despite touring the States extensively, they were unable to repeat their success with the average Pop Rock of *The Book Of Taliesyn* (1969) and *Deep Purple* (1969) or the quite dreadful, if ambitious, *Concerto For Group And Orchestra* (1970), performed live with the Royal Philharmonic Orchestra. Then *Deep Purple In Rock* (1970) came along like a bolt from the blue. The band's Hard Rock style sounded self-assured and powerful;

songs like 'Child in Time' showcased Gillan's formidable vocal range and trademark screams, along with Blackmore's and Lord's virtuoso guitar-keyboard duels. The album shot to the No.4 slot on the UK chart, followed by two big UK hit singles: 'Black Night' and 'Strange Kind Of Woman'.

For the follow-up, *Fireball* (1971), the band piled into an old farmhouse in middle-of-nowhere Devon, with wives, babies, animals and roadies in tow and a Revox tape machine to record their writing sessions for the first time. Before emerging with a second masterpiece, they drank a lot, held seances, and came very close to killing each other. One night Glover awoke to find Blackmore hovering over him, axe in hand, after breaking down his bedroom door. "Even at its friendliest," said Glover, "Deep Purple was a sharp place to be. There was a lot of challenging one another. Those frictions were healthy at first – it made us better, more competitive players. But by the time *Fireball* was done, it was starting to become destructive."

Fireball topped the UK charts, just failing to make the US Top 30. And the band set out on the first of a series of lengthy tours, each show walking an ever more fraying tightrope between triumph and utter disaster: Gillan was hospitalized for exhaustion and the trademark on-stage musical duelling spilled increasingly off-stage. But they made it back into the studio at the end of 1971, and *Machine Head* (1972) was released to massive acclaim – in the UK, Europe, USA and Japan. Classic tracks included 'Highway Star', 'Space Truckin'' and the song with the riff that made a million adolescent boys pick up an electric guitar – 'Smoke On The Water' – written after the band's near-disastrous gig with Frank Zappa in Montreux in 1971 when the building caught fire. These songs and more were resurrected in an even more powerful form on the double live album *Made In Japan* (1972), which captured the band at its peak, following three years of almost non-stop gigs.

But Deep Purple's internal tensions had come to a head. After releasing the less stunning *Who Do We Think We Are* (1973), Gillan quit the band during their Japanese tour, with Glover following a month later. Enter Deep Purple Mark III. Answering the band's ad for a new vocalist were the previously unknown David Coverdale (b. 22 Sep 1949, Saltburn, England), a semi-pro musician and assistant in a posh Yorkshire menswear shop; and ex-Trapeze bassist Glenn Hughes (b. 21 Aug 1952, Penkridge, Staffordshire, England). The first album to feature the new Purple members, *Burn* (1974), was a transformation: although still stylistically experimental and guitar-heavy – at this time the band was officially recognized

> *The best music always seems to be a mix of hitherto unmixable styles – black and white, Country & Western and the Blues – so I suppose Classic meets Rock is Deep Purple's legacy*
>
> **Roger Glover**

by *The Guinness Book Of Records* as the loudest band in the world – Gillan's distinctive vocals were conspicous by their absence, and the album reflected the two new men's Blues, Funk and Soul influences. This did not make Blackmore happy. But, instead of waging battle, he seemed to lose interest – you can hardly hear him on *Stormbringer* (1975) – and it was no surprise when in 1975 he quit to form his own band, Rainbow.

His replacement was ex-James Gang guitarist, Tommy Bolin (b. 18 Apr 1951, Sioux City, Iowa, USA, d. 4 Dec 1976, Miami, Florida, USA), who debuted with the band on the relatively successful *Come Taste The Band* (1975). But, although he'd been recommended by Blackmore, the guitar virtuoso's Jazz Soul style proved incompatible with Deep Purple's heavy sound. In 1976 – having sold over 15 million albums – the band folded. Coverdale formed Whitesnake; Lord and Paice – who already had solo albums in the stores – formed Paice, Ashton & Lord with Tony Ashton; Glenn Hughes (whose soulful vocals were heard on Purple's last album) briefly returned to Trapeze before launching a solo career; and Bolin died of a heroin overdose.

Rumours of a re-formation started to circulate in the press almost from the moment the band broke up, despite the solo success of at least some former members (Rainbow and Whitesnake especially). But the nearest thing to a reunion came when Blackmore, Lord, Paice and Glover got together in 1980 to take legal action against a band billing itself as Deep Purple – put together by Mark I members Rod Evans and Nick Simper –

which had embarked on a US arena tour. Meanwhile, a slew of reissues, live albums and compilations kept the Purple name and legacy alive – *Deep Purple Live/Made In Europe* (1976), *The Mark II Purple Singles* (1979), *Deepest Purple/The Very Best Of Deep Purple* (1980), *In Concert* (1980), and *Deep Purple Live In London* (1982) – until a rumoured $2-million-apiece offer for each member of the Mark II line up bore fruit in 1984 with the acclaimed reunion album *Perfect Strangers* – rightly nicknamed by Blackmore, "At Last The 1974 Album".

Enthused with its reception, Deep Purple took to the road – headlining the Knebworth Fayre in 1985 – and stopped only to record the weaker *The House Of Blue Light* (1987). But despite talk of a new "maturity", the old acrimony was soon back. Again Gillan was first to go – following the live *Nobody's Perfect* (1988). Ironically, ex-Rainbow vocalist Joe Lynn Turner was drafted in for *Slaves & Masters* (1990). Gillan rejoined for *The Battle Rages On* (1993), then quit. Blackmore followed suit. He was replaced briefly by American maestro Joe Satriani, then more permanently by Steve Morse. Gillan, meanwhile, reappeared once again for the 1996 album *Purpendicular*.

READ *Illustrated Biography* (1984), Chris Charlesworth

FAN The Deep Purple Appreciation Society, PO Box 254, Sheffield, S6 1DF, UK

SURF www.rpmrecords.co.uk/dpas

Def Jam

In the mid-80s, Def Jam (and its raison d'être Rap) transformed from the biggest underground sensation in the world to a mainstream monolith. The bizarre pairing of white college kid Rick Rubin and black promoter Russell Simmons took the sound of the streets – a soundclash of Rock and Rap – to the top of the charts. Their Rap credentials were secured with their first release, LL Cool J's 'I Need A Beat', in 1984. Platinum sales ensued. CBS took over their distribution and Rubin had the bright idea of adding Metal guitars to his protegés' snarling beats and rhymes. The results – including The Beastie Boys' Licensed To Ill – were eclipsed for sheer power only by the cataclysmic Public Enemy, their banner carriers in the late 80s. By the 90s, the empire had crumbled just a little: Rubin – now more enamoured of the likes of Slayer – formed the Def American label which, transformed into American Recordings (after Rubin ceremonially ditched the outdated 'Def'), made millions from the most eclectic signings (The Black Crowes next to Sir Mix-A-Lot, Johnny Cash next to Donovan). Meanwhile, Simmons ploughed on with Def Jam, coasting mainly on the platinum consistency of LL Cool J, before hitting a mid-90s renaissance with Foxy Brown, Method Man and Redman. "You create your own musical identity," said Simmons in 1990, "and do something special."

DEF LEPPARD ⊙ ⊙ ✪ ✪

WHO Vocals **Joe Elliott** (b. 1 Aug 1959, Sheffield, England), guitar **Vivian Campbell** (b. 25 Aug 1962, Belfast, Northern Ireland), guitar **Phil Collen** (b. 8 Dec 1957, London, England), bass **Rick Savage** (b. 2 Dec 1960, Sheffield), drums **Rick Allen** (b. 1 Nov 1963, Sheffield)

WHEN 1977–

WHERE Sheffield, England

WHAT Heavy British steel

Their route to multi-platinum megastardom littered with death and disaster, Def Leppard found success easier than survival. Their triumph is due largely to ambitious frontman Elliott, who joined Savage, guitarist Pete Willis and drummer Tony Kenning in schoolboy band Atomic Mass. He rechristened them Deaf Leopard (in honour of Led Zeppelin), streamlined the name in 1978 and recruited 'Steamin' Steve Clark (b. 23 Apr 1961, Sheffield, England, d. 8 Jan 1991) in emulation of the twin-guitar format of heroes Thin Lizzy, UFO and Judas Priest.

Frank Noon replaced Kenning for debut EP 'Getcha Rocks Off'– celebrated for the galloping title track – before baby-faced basher Allen secured the drum stool. Media interest enabled Leppard to ride the 'New Wave of British Heavy Metal' to a 1979 Vertigo deal. An EP reissue and debut *On Through The Night* (1980) won transatlantic sales and US support slots but, on their return, they were greeted not as conquering heroes but sellouts.

Distancing themselves from the meat-and-potatoes Metal of contemporaries Iron Maiden and Saxon, Leppard hired Robert John 'Mutt' Lange as producer. AC/DC and Foreigner had been recent beneficiaries of his platinum touch, now applied to *High*

'N' Dry (1981). Despite being Def Leppard's lowest-charting UK album (No.26), it furthered their skyward Stateside curve, especially when the fledgling MTV took the band to its bosom. The contrast between American acclaim and domestic apathy, coupled with relentless touring, drove the band to breaking point. First to crack was Willis, fired in 1982. His replacement, Collen, formerly of second-leaguers Girl, arrived just in time to make his mark on *Pyromania* (1983). Scraping the UK Top 20, the album exploded in America, thanks to the smash 'Photograph' – inspired by a picture of Marilyn Monroe on Elliott's bathroom door. Leppard ascended to headlining status, and *Pyromania* remained in the US Top 10 for months, at one point held off the top only by Michael Jackson's *Thriller*. Flushed with success, the band embarked on their most turbulent period. The overworked Lange left, and Meat Loaf mastermind Jim Steinman was hired.

Despite a mutual interest in bombastic Hard Rock, Leppard and Steinman were a marriage made in hell, grumpily parting company after three fruitless months of recording. Even worse, drummer Allen lost an arm in a car crash in December 1984 but, after an awe-inspiring recovery, resumed work two months later. Lange also returned, and the band set about topping *Pyromania*. "We actually sat in the studio at one time," explained Elliott, "and said… 'Tell me one good reason why a white English Rock band can't sell 10 million albums'."

The UK finally took Leppard to its heart at the 1986 Monsters Of Rock festival, six years after a 'bottling' on stage at the Reading Festival. "I've never seen so many hands go up in the air!" recalled Allen. "I just sat there behind the drums and burst into tears…". A year later, *Hysteria* topped the UK chart, and remained on the list for two years. This, however, could not rival its impact Stateside, where it sold 12 million, becoming both

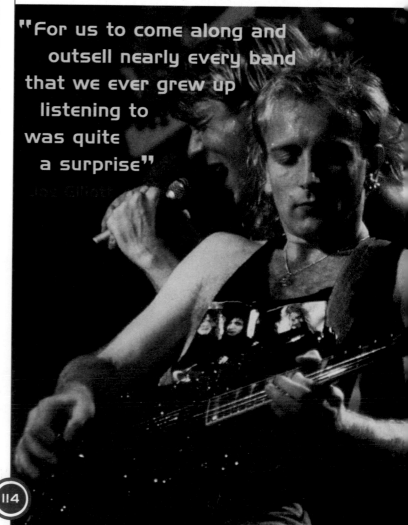

"For us to come along and outsell nearly every band that we ever grew up listening to was quite a surprise"
Joe Elliott

one of the biggest-selling albums ever by a UK group in America and the first million-selling Metal CD. Six hits kept it in the US Top 10 until 1989. However, tragedy again followed triumph: succumbing to alcoholism, Clark died in London on 8 January 1991. Soldiering on, they released the splendidly stupid 'Let's Get Rocked' as a trailer to *Adrenalize* (1992). Although never approaching the heights of *Hysteria*, it entered at the top of the US chart, selling 2 million in its first week. Meanwhile, Lange cleaned up with Bryan Adams' Leppard-like *Waking Up The Neighbours* (1991). Clark was replaced by the well-travelled Campbell, with whom they played the Freddie Mercury Tribute Concert at London's Wembley Stadium in 1992 and a career-capping homecoming at Sheffield's Don Valley Stadium. Sales ticked over with odds 'n' sods collection *Retro-Active* (1993) and hits set *Vault* (1995). The former's hit 'Two Steps Behind' confirmed their knack for ballads, a talent first revealed by *High 'N' Dry's* 'Bringin' On The Heartbreak' and crowned by their biggest UK smash, 'When Love And Hate Collide' (1995).

Proving that Leppard and luck would never go together, *Slang* (1996) was their least successful album for a decade, its adventurous blend of classic AOR and gritty Grunge passing largely unremarked. The band could, however, content themselves with having redefined the term 'against all odds'.

Read *Animal Instinct: The Def Leppard Story* (1992), David Fricke

Surf www.geocities.com/"defleppard/index2.html

DEFTONES

WHO Vocals **Chino Moreno**, guitar **Stephen 'Stef' Carpenter**, bass **Chi Cheng**, drums **Abe Cunningham**

WHEN 1988–

WHERE Sacramento, California, USA

WHAT Riffs 'n' rhythm from 'the coolest band in the world'

Whirr with us back to 1988: Britain is in the grip of Acid House and Bros. America, meanwhile, is reeling to the 'Skate Punk' sounds of Suicidal Tendencies and Very Heavy Metal of Danzig and Metallica. Or at least it is on the West Coast, where skateboarders Chino, Stef, Abe and Chi goof about in a garage. Further fuelled by the local 'Funk Metal' scene – whose banner carriers were Fishbone and Primus – Deftones devised a blend of hard riffing, sparky rhythms and oblique lyrics. (On tour with Korn later, Deftones were surprised to find this formula had occurred to other bands too.)

Touring far and wide paid off when they were spotted in LA and signed to Madonna's label Maverick. Suddenly, Deftones were everywhere: in record stores with *Adrenaline* (1995), on MTV with '7 Words', on screen in *The Crow: City Of Angels* (1996), on the soundtrack of *Escape From LA* (1996) and on tour with the likes of White Zombie. With *Around The Fur* (1997) – which added PJ Harvey to the list of influences – Deftones graduated from Metallica fans to rivals, smashing into Metal magazines' 'Best Band' poll results. Among the Rock acts commissioned for

1997 remixes by Puff Daddy, they also demonstrated an implausible affection for wimpy Brit acts by guesting on tributes to The Smiths, Duran Duran and Depeche Mode.

Fan The Deftones Fan Club, PO Box 245039, Sacramento, CA 95824-5039, USA

Surf www.wbr.com/maverick/deftones/

DESMOND DEKKER

WHO b. Desmond Dacres, 16 Jul 1942, Kingston, Jamaica

WHAT First truly international Reggae star

Dekker's huge success in the mid to late 60s was somewhat unlikely. Singing from the side of his mouth in a patois indecipherable to many fans, he nevertheless scored a huge string of hits in the UK and Europe, and had one smash in America with 'Israelites', a UK No.1 in 1969. Dekker began singing for producer and future mentor Leslie Kong in 1963, hitting in Jamaica with the tough but moral Ska song 'Honour Your Father And Mother'. By 1966 – with backing vocalists The Aces, who briefly included his brother George, and working in the Jamaican Rock Steady style – he scored a UK No.14 with '007 (Shanty Town)', linking Jamaican rude boys and James Bond.

'Israelites', about the poor, 'It Miek' and 'Pickney Gal', both about his family, and a cover of Jimmy Cliff's 'You Can Get It If You Really Want' made him *the* Reggae act in the UK between 1969 and 1970. But when Kong died of heart failure in 1971, Dekker's career stalled and, despite being signed to the fashionable Stiff label in 1980 and regular reissues of his classic 45s, it remained that way.

DEL AMITRI

WHO Vocals/bass **Justin Currie** (b. 11 Dec 1964, Glasgow, Scotland), guitar **Iain Harvie** (b. 19 May 1962, Glasgow), guitar **David Cummings**

WHEN 1980–

WHERE Glasgow, Scotland

WHAT Melancholic soft Rock

Spawned by the crowded, early 80s Glasgow Indie scene, Del Amitri (Greek for 'from the womb') were initially compared to contemporaries Orange Juice and Joy Division, albeit with a pastoral, acoustic slant on the melancholic music of the day. 'Sense Sickness' (1983) was followed by an unhappy period with Chrysalis, who dropped them after an eponymous debut in 1985. They spent the remainder of the 80s building a loyal live following until *Waking Hours* (1989) and 'Nothing Ever Happens' brought their latterly adopted Country Rock to public attention.

Original guitarist Bryan Tolland and drummer Paul Tyagi were replaced by Cummings, McDermott and Alston for the highly successful *Change Everything* (1992). McDermott was gone for 1995's *Twisted*, while *Some Other Sucker's Parade* (1997) saw core members Currie and Harvie augmented by Alston, drummer Mark Price and ex-Godfathers guitarist Kris Dollimore.

Surf del-amitri.linex.com/

JOHN DENVER ✪✪✪

WHO b. John Henry Deutschendorf Jr, 31 Dec 1943, Roswell, New Mexico, USA, d. 12 Oct 1997, Monterey, California, USA

WHAT Environmentally friendly, clean-cut Folk superstar

College drop-out John Denver moved to LA in the 60s and joined The Chad Mitchell Trio before his solo debut *Rhymes And Reasons* (1969). Its 'Leaving On A Jet Plane' was a hit for Peter, Paul & Mary that year, and prompted a lawsuit when New Order nicked it for 'Run' in 1989. Denver's superstardom began with early 70s smashes 'Take Me Home, Country Roads' (US No.2, 1971), *Rocky Mountain High* (1972), No.1s 'Annie's Song', and 'Sunshine On My Shoulders' (both 1974), 'Thank God I'm A Country Boy' and 'I'm Sorry' (both 1975), and TV and movie appearances. His first No.1 album, *John Denver's Greatest Hits* (1973), stayed in the US charts for two years, and he had two more No.1s with *Back Home Again* (1974) and *Windsong* (1975). Denver rounded off the 70s with *John Denver & The Muppets* (1979), a Christmas album recorded with his popular furry friends.

He endorsed environmental causes, including the anti-nuclear movement, and applied to NASA to become an astronaut. In 1987, he participated in concerts in the former Soviet Union for victims of the Chernobyl disaster. Although his commercial fortunes waned, Denver performed and recorded regularly. Sadly, *Love Again* (1996) was his final release: he was killed in a plane crash in California.

surf home.clara.net/jthorogood/freespirit/

DEPECHE MODE ◉◉✪

WHO Vocals **Dave Gahan** (b. 9 May 1962, Epping, Essex, England), keyboards/guitar **Martin Gore** (b. 23 Jul 1961, Dagenham, Essex), keyboards **Andy Fletcher** (b. 8 Jul 1961, Nottingham, England), keyboards **Alan Wilder** (b. 1 Jun 1959, London, England)

WHEN 1980–

WHERE Basildon, Essex, England

WHAT Pop Doom and Gloom

In May 1980, via school and Boys Brigade connections in Basildon, Essex, England, where they all grew up, Gore and Fletcher formed Composition Of Sound with Vince Clarke (b. 3 Jul 1960, South Woodford, London, England). As a post-Punk guitar combo,

they floundered until Gore bought a Moog. Clarke appropriated it to complement his particular songwriting talent. They spotted Gahan, then a design student, with another group at the scout hut where they rehearsed and promptly co-opted him. His first significant contribution was to pluck the name Depeche Mode – 'fast fashion' – from the cover of a French magazine.

Influenced by Kraftwerk and German producer Giorgio Moroder, they moved to an all-keyboard line-up and slipped easily into the New Romantic or Futurist movement – protesting independence while availing themselves of its publicity value. An early 'Futurist night' residency at the Bridgehouse in London's East End led to Daniel Miller, owner of the embryonic Mute label, signing them on a handshake deal which stayed the course of their career. With an early song, 'Photographic', on the New Romantic compilation *Some Bizarre Album* in March 1981 raising their profile, they soon scored the first of 32 UK Top 30 singles, 'New Life' and 'Just Can't Get Enough'. Debut album *Speak And Spell* reached UK No.10. That December, however, Clarke, who disliked life on the road, left at the end of a British tour (going on to huge successes with Yazoo and Erasure).

> **"There's two extreme views of Depeche Mode in England. We're either Pop, or doom and gloom. Actually, we're both"**
> Andy Fletcher

Because Clarke had written nearly all their songs, Depeche Mode's demise was predicted. But they recruited the technical and keyboard skills of Wilder, who had recorded two unremarkable albums with The Hitmen. Gore stepped up to show he, too, could come up with bippity-bop chart songs like 'See You' and 'The Meaning Of Love', before exploring the more varied directions presaged by 1982's 'Leave In Silence', which referred ambiguously to a difficult relationship and/or the Falklands war. *A Broken Frame* (1982) began a long period of commercial consolidation. *Construction Time Again* (1983), *Some Great Reward* (1984), *The Singles 1981–85* (1985), *Black Celebration* (1986) and *Music For The Masses* (1987) and key singles including 'Everything Counts', 'Master And Servant' and 'People Are People' steadily advanced their cause in Britain, Europe and America.

Gore constantly urged this growing audience into leftfield, reflecting his interest in both German Industrial sounds (especially Einstürzende Neubauten) and a sexuality which he displayed by wearing leather skirts and writing lyrics such as "Domination's the name of the game/In bed or in life" ('Master And Servant'). Once lightweight popsters, in America they came to be acknowledged for their influence on Techno by key figures like Todd Terry and Derrick May.

Their standing, won by adventurous music and hard touring, was confirmed when their concert at Pasadena Rose Bowl, California, on 18 July 1988, drew 66,000 and then reached a worldwide audience through the live album and video *101*, directed by D.A. Pennebaker (legendary for Bob Dylan's *Don't Look Back* 'rockumentary'). After a brief interlude in which Gore and Wilder put out solo records, *Violator* (1990) went to UK No.2, US No.7, and sold 6 million worldwide. The World Violation tour,

seen by 1.2 million over eight months, was triumphant, but also proved the turning point into the band's 90s horror story.

During the break between tour and new album, Gahan went from fresh-faced lad to Rock monster. While Gore and Fletcher were marrying and having children, he left his wife and 5-year-old son, moved to Los Angeles, acquired a beard, tattoos and a new American wife and took up heroin. In March 1992, when he flew to Madrid to record, the others were shocked by what they saw. "The looks on their faces *battered* me," Gahan later recalled.

Songs Of Faith And Devotion (1993) – followed by *Songs Of Faith And Devotion Live* (1993) – entered both the British and American charts at No.1, but this crowning success resulted in stressfully extended touring. Gahan took a near-fatal overdose, Gore was hospitalized by a cerebral seizure, and Fletcher – who had taken on the business side of the band – had to fly home and spend a month in a psychiatric hospital to combat depression and 'obsessive compulsive disorder'. (Darryl Bamonte, brother of The Cure's Perry, stood in for him.)

In the aftermath, Wilder left, Gore and Fletcher embraced healthier lifestyles, and Gahan carried on 'partying'. In August 1995, after a failed sojourn in a rehabilitation clinic, he attempted suicide. The following spring, when he joined the others in New York to record a new album, his voice had gone. Gore and Fletcher told him to "go home to LA and sort yourself out". Instead, he took to injecting 'speedballs' of heroin and cocaine until, on 28 May 1996, another near-fatal overdose finally triggered the will to stop.

With Gahan abstaining from drugs and alcohol, and receiving therapy while under threat of a suspended jail sentence for possession, Depeche Mode completed *Ultra* (1997, UK No.1 and US No.4), in many ways a grim reflection on what they had been through. Firmly guided by Fletcher, they refused to tour. Sales declined accordingly, but the band stood by the view that a commercial dip was the least of their worries.

Meanwhile, Gahan tried to recruit Marilyn Manson for 1998's Depeche Mode tribute album *For The Masses*, the cast of which also features Smashing Pumpkins and Monster Magnet.

(READ) *Depeche Mode: Some Great Reward* (1994), Dave Thompson

(FAN) BONG, PO Box 1281, London, N1 9UX, UK

(SURF) dm_fan_club@mutelibtech.com

DES'REE

WHO b. Des'ree Weekes, 30 Nov 1968, London, England

WHAT Funky Folkstress

When the star-crossed lovers first meet in the 1997 movie *William Shakespeare's Romeo And Juliet*, they do so to the strains of 'Kissing You' by Des'ree. The south Londoner has maintained a peripheral popularity since her 1991 debut 'Feel So High' from *Mind Adventures* (1992). Hailed as a pioneer of 'Folk Funk' – one of the music press' less durable pigeonholes – she scaled charts with the Terence Trent D'Arby duet 'Delicate' (1993) and, from her second album *I Ain't Movin'* (1994), 'You Gotta Be'. The latter hit the US Top 5 in 1995 – and could be said to have done so again in 1997 courtesy of Janet Jackson's remarkably similar 'Got Till It's Gone'.

 www.music.sony.com/Music/Images/Desree/Bio.gif

Homo'/'Mongoloid' (1977), the Eno-produced *Q: Are We Not Men? A: We Are Devo!* (1978) yielded a peculiar near-hit cover of The Rolling Stones' 'Satisfaction'. *Freedom Of Choice* (1980) bequeathed their biggest hit, 'Whip It'. The concept paled with *New Traditionalists* (1981) and *Oh No! It's Devo* (1982) and they split in 1985. Mark Mothersbaugh worked as a TV composer until they reformed (with drummer Myers replaced by David Kendrick) for *Total Devo* (1988) and *Smooth Noodle Maps* (1990).

Aside from a 1991 European tour, little further was heard (except Nirvana's cover of their 'Turnaround' on 1992's *Incesticide*) until Devo's contribution to the *Mighty Morphin Power Rangers* soundtrack (1995), their cover of Nine Inch Nails' 'Head Like A Hole' for the *Supercop* soundtrack (1996), Mothersbaugh's excellent kids' cartoon theme *Rugrats* and appearances on 1996's Lollapalooza tour and in US TV's *Ellen*.

 www.akula.com/~drazz/devo/

DEVO

WHO Vocals/keyboards/guitar **Mark Mothersbaugh**, guitar/vocals **Bob 'Bob I' Mothersbaugh**, bass **Jerry Casale**, drums **Alan Myers**, keyboards/guitar/vocals **Bob 'Bob II' Casale**

WHEN 1972–

WHERE Akron, Ohio, USA

WHAT New Wave flowerpot men

Genetic and social 'devolution' topped the incomprehensible agenda of Mark Mothersbaugh and Jerry Casale when they formed arch-experimentalists Devo: a cult success in boiler suits and flowerpot headgear. After the award-winning short film *The Truth About De-Evolution* (1975) and self-financed 'Jocko

DEXY'S MIDNIGHT RUNNERS

WHO Vocals/guitar **Kevin Rowland** (b. 17 Aug 1953, Wolverhampton, England), guitar **Al Archer**, bass **Pete Williams**, drums **Andy Growcott**, keyboards **Pete Saunders**, trombone **'Big' Jimmy Patterson**, alto sax **Steve 'Babyface' Spooner**, tenor sax **Jeff 'J.B.' Blythe**

WHEN 1978–1987

WHERE Birmingham, England

WHAT Wayward Celtic Soul brothers

Born of Irish parents, Rowland debuted in Lucy & The Lovers, then Birmingham Punk band The Killjoys. After the latter's 1977 flop 'Johnny Won't Get To Heaven', he and Archer formed Dexy's Midnight Runners – Northern Soul slang for the drug Dexedrine, ironic for a clean-living group of cross-country runners.

In the prevailing Punk climate, Dexy's were distinguished by their woolly-hatted, workmen-jacketed, sports bag-carrying image, inspired by Martin Scorsese's movie *Mean Streets* (1973). Musically, they were even more out of step: 1980's debut 'Dance Stance' was a homage to 60s Soul with lyrics protesting anti-Irish prejudice. 'Geno' – a tribute to British Soulster Geno Washington – saw future Style Councillor Mick Talbot replace keyboardist Saunders, but the group puzzled observers when Rowland seized master tapes of *Searching For The Young Soul Rebels* (1980) as leverage in negotiations with EMI. The deliberately uncommercial 'Keep It (Part 2)' aggravated internal rifts and prompted Patterson and Rowland to move to Phonogram while the others continued as The Bureau.

With fresh sidemen, Rowland and Patterson's late 1981 shows unveiled fiddle trio The Emerald Express and a 'Celtic' Folk element, which characterized *Too-Rye-Ay* (1982) and UK No.1 'Come On Eileen'. Following Patterson's acrimonious exit, only guitarist Billy Adams, Express member Helen O'Hara and new recruit Nick Gatfield appeared on 1985's baffling but excellent *Don't Stand Me Down* (1985), which saw *Too-Rye-Ay*'s dungarees and grime replaced by business suits. After final hit 'Because Of You' (theme for British TV's *Brush Strokes*), Rowland disappeared, emerging only for solo album *The Wanderer* (1988) and occasional live appearances. Gatfield became an A&R man at EMI, signing Radiohead before becoming MD at Polydor.

NEIL DIAMOND ◉

WHO b. 24 Jan 1941, Brooklyn, New York, USA

WHAT Gospel-esque MOR forever-lasting diamond

Having recorded with his friend Jack Parker as Neil & Jack, Diamond quit college in 1962 and joined music publisher Sunbeam as a songwriter. After another bid for stardom in 1965 with 'Clown Town', songwriters Barry and Ellie Greenwich signed him to their writing and publishing company and secured a deal with Atlantic subsidiary Bang for his debut hits 'Solitary Man', 'Cherry Cherry' and 'I Got The Feelin' (Oh No No)' in 1966. He scored his first songwriting US No.1 with The Monkees' 'I'm A Believer'. Solo hits continued with 'You Got To Me', 'Girl, You'll Be A Woman Soon', 'Thank The Lord For The Night Time' and 'Kentucky Woman'. But with second album *Just For You* (1967), Bang's interest waned, prompting Diamond's move to California and the Uni (later MCA) label for the flop *Velvet Gloves And Spit* (1968). Exhaustive touring and a string of late 60s/early 70s hits – 'Brother Love's Travelling Salvation Show', 'Sweet Caroline' and the US No.1s 'Cracklin' Rosie' and 'Song Sung Blue' – thrust Diamond into the major league with *Moods* and *Hot August Night* (both 1972). Signed to Columbia for a record-breaking $5 million, Diamond's soundtrack *Jonathan Livingston Seagull* (1973) was more profitable than the movie. An appearance at The Band's Last Waltz concert in 1976 led to Robbie Robertson producing the monstrously successful *Beautiful Noise* (1976).

Ever the all-round entertainer, Diamond duetted with Barbra Streisand on 1978's 'You Don't Bring Me Flowers', made top-rated TV specials and starred in a 1980 remake of Al Jolson's *The Jazz Singer*, which produced a multi-platinum soundtrack and hits including 'Love On The Rocks'. His profile was maintained with tours and *Heartlight* (1982), *Primitive* (1984), *Headed For The Future* (1986), *Hot August Night II* (1987) and *The Best Years Of Our Lives* (1989). Covers by UB40 ('Red Red Wine') and Urge Overkill ('Girl, You'll Be A Woman Soon' from 1994's *Pulp Fiction* soundtrack) yielded fat royalty cheques.

Fan Diamond Connection, PO Box 2764, Witham, Essex, CM8 2SF, UK

Surf www.worldaccess.nl/~hogensti

BO DIDDLEY

WHO b. Otha Ellas Bates, 30 Dec 1928, McComb, Mississippi, USA

WHAT Evergreen Rock 'n' Roll and R&B innovator

Chess Records launched Diddley into the first wave of Rock 'n' Roll. Alternating hard-driving Blues with catchy standards like 'I'm A Man' (1955), Bo exploded live. Overlaying scratchy rhythms on scatter-gun beats, he could reduce audiences to a jiving mass in seconds. Singles-wise, the US No.20 'Say Man' (1959) did best. Albums-wise Diddley did well, especially in Britain, where four collections charted: 1963's *Bo Diddley, Bo Diddley Is A Gunslinger* and *Bo Diddley Rides Again* and 1964's *Bo Diddley's Beach Party*.

By the mid-60s a new generation had captured the charts. Some, like The Rolling Stones, clearly drew on Diddley – who survived better than most 50s stars because his live work remained brilliant. In the past 30 years, Bo has left club audiences reeling, gained coveted support slots including The Clash's first US tour and dates with the Stones and shared festival bills with John Lennon. Meanwhile, his albums – notably 1996's *A Man Amongst Men* – have seen the likes of Keith Richards and Bon Jovi's Richie Sambora backing the great man.

Various admirers include Australian actor Craig McLachlan, who took 'Mona' into the UK chart; The Smiths, who lifted a riff for 'How Soon Is Now'; Buddy Holly, who covered 'Bo Diddley'; and U2, whose 'Desire' was pure Bo. However, Diddley's genius remains elusive. In the scratchy rhythms and chugging beat of his best work, Diddley hinted at a power that others still seek and his live work set standards most can only envy.

** READ** *Bo Diddley: Living Legend* (1997), George R. White

SURF www.codeblue.records.com/diddley.html

DINOSAUR JR

WHO Vocals/guitar **J. Mascis** (b. Joseph D. Mascis, 10 Dec 1965, Amherst, Massachusetts, USA), bass **Lou Barlow** (b. 17 Jul 1966, Northampton, Massachusetts), drums **Murph** (b. Emmett 'Patrick' J. Murphy, 21 Dec 1964)

WHEN 1984–1997

WHERE Amherst, Massachusetts, USA

WHAT Lethargic Grunge pioneers

Formed from the remnants of Hardcore Punk band Deep Wound by Barlow and lethargic guitar wiz Mascis, Dinosaur Jr began as plain Dinosaur for their eponymous 1985 debut album.

Pressured to change their name by West Coast band The Dinosaurs, they added the diminutive suffix for 1987's proto-Grunge classic *You're Living All Over Me*. The startling blend of noise and melody on 1988's underground smashes 'Freak Scene' and *Bug,* released on Blast First, paved the way for Nirvana.

Following Barlow's acrimonious exit to form Sebadoh, Mascis initiated a revolving personnel policy (including ex-Screaming Trees bassist Donna Biddell and US Indie journeymen Don Fleming and Jay Spiegel) for 1988's Cure cover 'Just Like Heaven' and 1991's comeback EP 'The Wagon', but played everything on the disappointing *Green Mind* (1991). *Where You Been* (1992) added ex-Snakepit bassist Mike Johnson and welcomed back part-time drummer Murph, who was gone again for 1994's *Without A Sound*. After touring 1997's *Hand It Over*, the group split, Mascis and Johnson going solo. Barlow soundtracked *Kids* (1996) as trip hoppy alter-ego Folk Implosion.

SURF www.iwaynet.net/~keeblin/dinosaur.html

CELINE DION ☉☉☉✪

WHO b. 30 Mar 1968, Charlemagne, Quebec, Canada

WHAT La chanteuse de plus grand succès

Long before conquering the world, talented teenager Céline Dion became a French-Canadian star with *La Voix Du Bon Dieu* (1981), *Céline Chante Noël* (1981), *Tellement J'ai D'Amour* (1982), *Chants Et Contes De Noël* (1983), *Les Chemins De Ma Maison* (1983), *Melanie* (1984), *En Concert* (1985), *C'est Pour Toi* (1985), *Incognito* (1987) and the compilations *Les Plus Grands Succès De Céline Dion* (1984), *Les Oiseaux Du Bonheur* (1984) and *Les Chansons En Or* (1986).

Sights set on international fame, she won the Eurovision Song Contest in 1988 and broke the US Top 5 with 'Where Does My Heart Beat Now' from her English-language debut *Unison* (1990). In 1991, she recorded *Dion Chante Plamondon*, songs by French-Canadian Pop writer Luc Plamondon, then guested on *Tycoon* – an English adaptation of Plamondon's Rock opera *Starmania* – alongside Cyndi Lauper, Kim Carnes, Tom Jones,

Ronnie Spector and Nina Hagen. The Disney theme 'Beauty And The Beast', featuring Soul crooner Peabo Bryson, established her worldwide and appeared on *Céline Dion* (1992), as did the US hit 'If You Asked Me To', but it was *The Colour Of My Love* (1993) that launched her into the superstar sphere. 'The Power Of Love' reached US No.1 and 'Think Twice' became one of only a handful of million-selling UK singles by women.

The retrospective *Les Premières Années* (1993), the live *A L'Olympia* (1994) and the French collection *D'Eux* (1995) kept the market bubbling before *Falling Into You* became 1996's best-selling album, powered by hits like 'It's All Coming Back To Me Now'. *Live A Paris* (1996) added to her sprawling discography, while *Let's Talk About Love* (1997) and the Barbra Streisand duet 'Tell Him' trampled transatlantic charts. Powering into 1998, Dion sang the transatlantic chart-topping *Titanic* movie theme 'My Heart Will Go On' and guested on the star-studded *Sesame Street* project *Elmopalooza*.

(Fan) Céline Dion International Fan Club, PO Box 551, Don Mills, Ontario, Canada M3C 2T6

(surf) www.celineonline.com/

DIRE STRAITS ☉☉☉☉✪

WHO Vocals/guitar **Mark Knopfler** (b. 12 Aug 1949, Glasgow, Scotland), guitar **David Knopfler** (b. 27 Dec 1952, Glasgow), bass **John Illsley** (b. 24 Jun 1949, Leicester, England), drums **Pick Withers** (b. 4 Apr 1948, Leicester)

WHEN 1977–

WHERE London, England

WHAT Laid-back world conquerors

Sons of an architect, Mark and David Knopfler grew up in Newcastle upon Tyne, England. Before playing in anything more than beer-money bands, Mark was a journalist, literature student, market gardener, warehouseman, labourer and teacher. He worked passionately at his guitar, synthesizing Blues and Country into his own style. By mid-1977, he was ready to be heard. He asked his brother, then a social worker in Deptford, south London, to join him in a new band. David brought along his flatmate John Illsley who, in turn, knew Pick Withers.

A year on from The Sex Pistols' eruption, the musicianly cool of Dire Straits, fronted by Knopfler's J.J. Cale-like growl, looked unpromising. But they scraped together £120 to demo a song called 'Sultans Of Swing'. Renowned BBC DJ Charlie Gillett aired it. Phonogram A&R man John Stainze was listening. He went to a gig and signed them to Phonogram subsidiary Vertigo that October. Crucially, Stainze introduced them to agent Ed Bicknell who, instantly enamoured, asked to manage them; one of the rare band-manager matches made in heaven was solemnized.

Dire Straits began 1978 as support act on a Talking Heads European tour. Within 12 months, initially unremarked at home, their self-titled debut had started its long run to US No.2. The following March, Bob Dylan invited Knopfler and Withers to play

"I don't feel pressure.
They say, 'How can you follow
Brothers In Arms?'
But it's only a record,
    only a band playing and touring.

It's not the Second Coming"

Mark Knopfler

on his first 'born-again' album, *Slow Train Coming*. While Dire Straits recorded *Communiqué* (1979), 'Sultans Of Swing' belatedly hit the UK Top 10 and the first album rose to No.5. Both albums charted worldwide.

Often stretching Country Blues basics to epic dimensions – notably 1982's 14-minute 'Telegraph Road'– *Making Movies* (1980), *Love Over Gold* (1982, their first Mark Knopfler production and UK No.1) and *Alchemy – Dire Straits Live* (1984) did well worldwide, though merely marked time in America. Knopfler also established himself as a 'star guest' (on Steely Dan, Van Morrison and Phil Everly albums), producer (Dylan's *Infidels*, Aztec Camera's *Knife*), and soundtrack composer (*Local Hero, Cal, Comfort And Joy*).

When David (1980) and Withers (1982) left, the band slimmed to Mark and Illsley, plus help (although long-serving keyboard players Alan Clark and Guy Fletcher were acknowledged as musical, if not contractual, Straits). In 1984, both David and Illsley released flop solo albums. Then came the phenomenon. Deceptively dark, *Brothers In Arms* (1985) was fired into orbit by two punchy, radio-adhesive singles: 'Money For Nothing' with Sting (UK No.4, US No.1) and 'Walk Of Life' (UK No.2, US No.7).

A world tour grew to 248 shows, with 3 million tickets sold. The album topped charts in 25 countries, with 23-million-plus sales. It benefited from, and helped generate, the new market for CDs.

A year on the road left the band exhausted. While Vertigo bided their time with hits compilation *Money For Nothing* (1988), Illsley recorded solo and painted. Knopfler diversified into therapeutic stints with Eric Clapton's road band, more soundtrack work (*The Princess Bride, Last Exit To Brooklyn*), production (Willy DeVille, Randy Newman), a duets album with Nashville guitarist Chet Atkins (*Neck And Neck*, 1990) and an album and tour with his hobby band, The Notting Hillbillies (*Missing… Presumed Having A Good Time*, 1990).

Dire Straits re-emerged only for Prince's Trust concerts and the Nelson Mandela 70th Birthday Tribute (1988). Finally, in 1991, they released the UK No.1 *On Every Street*. Returning to the short-song format of their early days, it mixed cheery shuffles and bleaker ruminations but lacked hits and, despite another successful global tour, confirmed the band's time had passed.

Their history was further documented by *On The Night* (1993, live from the *On Every Street* tour) and *Live At The BBC* (1995, recorded 1978). With the band resting, rather than officially deceased, Knopfler decided to record solo in future. His *Golden Heart* was released in 1996.

READ *Mark Knopfler* (1991), Myles Palmer

surf www.users.winesy.se/daniel/index.html

DISCO

WHAT Despite pioneering hit 'Rock Your Baby' by George McCrae (1974), Disco's roots were in Soul: the lover-man raps of Isaac Hayes and Barry White and the sweeping strings of Gamble & Huff's 'Philly Sound' productions (Harold Melvin, The O'Jays, The Three Degrees). Grown from club novelty to galactic phenomenon, it joined Punk in challenging dinosaur Rock's domination; hence the 25-million-selling <u>Saturday Night Fever</u> (1977) and attendant gems like Yvonne Elliman's 'If I Can't Have You' and The Trammps' 'Disco Inferno'. Italian producer Giorgio Moroder pioneered a more electronic variant whose early highlight – 'I Feel Love' by Donna Summer – was a landmark on the road to House. Eroded by over-exposure and the emergence of Hip Hop, Disco's legacy is both ironic (U2's 'Discotheque') and inspirational (George Michael's 'Fastlove').

WHERE New York gay clubs

WHEN 1974–

WHO Barry White <u>Can't Get Enough</u> (1974), Rose Royce <u>Car Wash</u> (1976), Chic <u>C'est Chic</u> (1978), Village People <u>Macho Men</u> (1978), Donna Summer <u>Bad Girls</u> (1979)

Disc Jockeys

When dinosaurs ruled the earth, Disc Jockeys spun records on the radio and chatted a bit. Though such beings survive to this day, 'DJ' now refers more to the faceless overlords of Dance. In the late 80s, the advent of House transformed the likes of Mark 'S'Express' Moore and Tim 'Bomb The Bass' Simenon from geeks to visionaries (a trend well established in Rap by Grandmaster Flash, Run DMC's Jam Master Jay and Gang Starr's DJ Premier). The result was that Andrew Weatherall, Paul Oakenfold and Gary Clail not only put out their own records (notably Weatherall's band Sabres Of Paradise) but were also invited to produce, remix and DJ for the megastarry likes of U2. At the other end of the spectrum, club denizens made gods out of the record-spinning likes of Boy George, Sasha and John Digweed.

DJ SHADOW

WHO b. Josh Davis, 1973

WHAT "The Jimmy Page of the sampler"

Although Trip Hop is commonly traced to English city Bristol, its birthplace was, in fact, the sleepy Californian town of Davis where DJ Shadow – for whose 'In/Flux' single the term was first used – grew up. In his teens, Josh Davis shunned Rock for Hip Hop, turntables and his source material: battered, secondhand vinyl. At university, he joined artist collective Sole Sides and – via a remix for African group Zimbabwe Legit – signed to Mo'Wax and became DJ Shadow. 'In/Flux' (1993), 'Lost And Found' (1994) and 'What Does Your Soul Look Like?' (1995) established his all-sampled sound – everything from obscure Funk and Soul records to movie soundtracks and U2's 'Sunday Bloody Sunday' cut 'n' pasted into impossibly detailed collages – perfected on the monstrous *Endtroducing* (1996), 'Midnight In A Perfect World' and 'Stem'. Critical adulation, production work

for Paris, DJ Krush, Depeche Mode and Massive Attack, a support slot with Radiohead (and collaboration with Thom Yorke for Mo'Wax boss James Lavelle's U.N.K.L.E. project) and a movie soundtrack for Wim Wenders' *The End Of Violence* (1997) preceded 'High Noon', Q-Bert remix collection *Camel Bobsled Race* (1997) and limited-edition album *Preemptive Strike* (1998).

surf www.spy.net/~hoover/shadow.html

DODGY

WHO Vocals/bass **Nigel Clarke** (b. 18 Sep 1966, Redditch, England), guitar **Andy Miller** (b. 18 Dec 1968, London, England), drums **Mathew Priest** (b. 3 Apr 1970, Birmingham, England)

WHEN 1990–

WHERE London, England

WHAT Melodic 60s-influenced Popsters

After playing in various Birmingham bands, Mathew Priest and Nigel Clarke relocated to London and met Andy Miller after placing an advert saying "Wanted: Jimi Hendrix". Establishing The Dodgy Club, a mix of DJs and live acts (including Oasis and Folk singer Ralph McTell) alongside the band themselves, they signed to A&M and released the poorly purchased *Dodgy Album* in 1993. *Homegrown* (1994) featured their first Top 40 hit 'Staying Out For The Summer' and the group became a fixture at British festivals. They even took a circus tent around the country, providing a 'mobile festival' to promote *Free Peace Sweet* (1996), which spawned the summer anthem 'Good Enough' and rocky 'In A Room'. Clarke's departure in early 1998 prompted a sabbatical, but the band resolved to continue with guest vocalists.

FATS DOMINO

WHO b. Antoine Domino, 16 Feb 1928, New Orleans, Louisiana, USA

WHAT R&B Rock 'n' Roll legend

The biggest-selling R&B artist of the 50s, Domino kickstarted the genre with debut 'The Fat Man' (1949). He had five years of hits under his belt before 'Ain't That A Shame' introduced him to the US Pop chart in 1955. Subsequent smashes included 'Blueberry Hill' , 'I'm In Love Again' (both 1956), 'I'm Walkin'' (1957), 'I Want To Walk You Home', 'Be My Guest' (both 1959) and 'Walking To New Orleans' (1960) – all sung in his unique Creole style, featuring rhymes other performers would not even attempt.

Although his big hits stopped in 1962, Fats Domino remains revered (hence The Beatles' Domino-ish 'Lady Madonna'). In the 90s, his 'Land of 1,000 Dances' mutated into Ini Kamoze's 'Here Comes The Hotstepper' and 'It Keeps Rainin'' was a hit for Bitty McLean. With over 50 million sales and sellout shows, Domino, one of Rock 'n' Roll's most successful survivors, was among the first handful of acts inducted into the Rock And Roll Hall Of Fame and also received a Lifetime Achievement Grammy award.

FATS DOMINO/JAK KILBY/RETNA

LONNIE DONEGAN

WHO b. Anthony Donegan, 29 Apr 1931, Glasgow, Scotland

WHAT The King of Skiffle

One of *the* 50s stars, Donegan's stage name was a tribute to his idol, Bluesman Lonnie Johnson. A banjo-player in Jazz bands, Donegan switched to guitar for numbers during intervals at club dates. A highlight of his act, Leadbelly's 'Rock Island Line', became a smash in Britain and, rarely for the time, the USA.

From 1956–1962 his Skiffle formula – reworking Folk and Blues songs – yielded over 30 hits, including No.1s in 1957 with 'Cumberland Gap' and 'Gamblin' Man'/'Puttin' On The Style'. His last international hit, 'Does Your Chewing Gum Lose Its Flavour?' (1959), moved him towards family entertainment, culminating in final chart-topper 'My Old Man's A Dustman' (1960).

Donegan almost single-handedly popularized Skiffle and inspired countless teenagers. A 1978 re-recording of his hits, *Puttin' On The Style*, produced by Adam Faith, featured Elton John, Brian May and Ron Wood. Despite heart surgery in 1985, Donegan was still playing occasional dates a decade later.

READ *Skiffle: The Definitive Inside Story* (1997), Chas McDevitt

DONOVAN

WHO b. Donovan Leitch, 10 May 1946, Glasgow, Scotland

WHAT Flowery Folk – 'The British Dylan'

From childhood in Glasgow, to adolescence in England, Donovan dropped out of college, wound up in Cornwall and began playing Folk clubs and pubs around the country. A demo secured a short residency on British Pop show *Ready Steady Go!* in 1965.

His 1965 single 'Catch The Wind' reached UK No.4, five places above Bob Dylan's simultaneous British debut 'The Times They Are A-Changin''. Much was made of Donovan's similarity to Dylan, and the two met on camera in D.A. Pennebaker's Dylan documentary *Don't Look Back* (1965), when Donovan played him 'To Sing For You' and requested that the nasal Folkster sing him 'It's All Over Now, Baby Blue'. In any case, Donovan's music was very English – harps, flutes and strings complementing guitars.

The 1965 hits 'Colours' and 'Universal Soldier' trailed experimental records with producer Mickie Most. 'Sunshine Superman' (1966), Donovan's US breakthrough, reached US No.1 and featured future Led Zeppelin founders John Paul Jones and Jimmy Page. Ensuing hits included 1966's 'Mellow Yellow' (featuring Paul McCartney's whispering), 'Epistle To Dippy', 'There Is A Mountain' and 'Wear Your Love Like Heaven' (all 1997). In 1968, Donovan joined The Beatles on a transcendental meditation course and returned seriously psychedelic with 'Jennifer Juniper', 'Hurdy Gurdy Man', 'Atlantis' and his last UK hit, 'Barabajagal (Love Is Hot)' with The Jeff Beck Group in 1969.

Subsequent work yielded diminishing returns despite its general excellence – notably the soundtrack to Franco Zeffirelli's *Brother Sun, Sister Moon* (1973). After a four-year absence from the stage, he returned with the concept album and show *7-Tease* (1974), but spent most of the 70s and 80s in obscurity.

Critical and commercial re-appraisal came in 1990, thanks to the patronage of Happy Mondays (whose Shaun Ryder married Donovan's daughter Ione Skye) and children's entertainers Trev & Simon, with whom he re-recorded 'Jennifer Juniper'. *Rising* (1990) did respectable business, as did the Rick Rubin-produced *Count On Me* (1994) and *Sutras* (1997). The Leitch clan spawned another star in the 90s, when Donovan's fashion-model son, also named Donovan, formed Glam wannabes Nancy Boy.

FAN Donovan's Friends, PO Box 1119, London, SW9 9JW, UK

SURF www.dur.ac.uk/~d416bb/don/

JASON DONOVAN ☉

WHO b. 1 Jun 1968, Malvern, Melbourne, Victoria, Australia

WHAT Jason, the amazing technicolour dreamboat

Jason Donovan followed his then-belle and *Neighbours* co-star Kylie Minogue into the UK charts with, notably, three No.1s: 'Too Many Broken Hearts', 'Sealed With A Kiss' (both 1989) and 'Any Dream Will Do' (1990). The latter was the fruit of his stint in *Joseph & The Amazing Technicolour Dreamcoat* – the 1991 cast recording of which was, like Donovan's *Ten Good Reasons* (1989), a UK No.1. Thereafter, his halo slipped: "He's becoming more crazy," reported Kylie. "Nice crazy. But he's a nutter sometimes."

THE DOOBIE BROTHERS ✪

WHO Vocals/guitar **Tom Johnston** (b. Visalia, California, USA), vocals/guitar **Pat Simmons** (b. 23 Jan 1950, Aberdeen, Washington, USA), guitar **Jeff 'Skunk' Baxter** (b. 13 Dec 1948, Washington, DC, USA), bass/vocals **Tiran Porter** (b. Los Angeles, California), keyboards/vocals **Michael McDonald** (b. 2 Dec 1952, St Louis, Missouri, USA), drums **John Hartman** (b. 18 Mar 1950, Falls Church, Virginia, USA), drums **Michael Hossack** (b. 18 Sep 1950, Paterson, New York, USA)

WHEN 1970–

WHERE San Jose, California, USA

WHAT Rhythmic Country Rockers turned Soul brothers

There are two different Doobie Brothers, the band being a rare example of a completely successful style make-over. Formed around the songs and harmonies of guitarists Tom Johnston and Pat Simmons, the original Doobies – the name derives from a slang term for a joint – excelled at sprightly Country Rock hit anthems like 'Listen To The Music' and 'Long Train Runnin'' (1973), securing the platinum-selling albums *Toulouse Street* (1972) and *The Captain And Me* (1973).

After guesting on *What Were Once Vices Are Now Habits* (1974), Steely Dan guitarist Jeff 'Skunk' Baxter joined the group permanently, toughening the band's style – though, ironically, it was the folksy, almost a cappella 'Black Water' which furnished their first US No.1 the next year. In 1975, the year of their most successful UK album, the cowboy-themed *Stampede* (UK No.14), Johnston retired due to illness. At Baxter's suggestion, the band recruited session singer McDonald, whose sleek, Soul-tinged vocals added a new dimension to *Takin' It To The Streets* (1976) and *Livin' On The Fault Line* (1977). Johnston briefly rejoined before pursuing a less successful solo career. With McDonald in the ascendant, the Doobies peaked again, winning four Grammys with the funky *Minute By Minute* (US No.1, 1979) and its No.1 'What A Fool Believes'. Despite the success of *One Step Closer* (US No.3, 1980) and its Top 5 single 'Real Love', the lure of solo careers pulled the band apart, albeit in an orderly fashion which allowed a farewell tour and live album to be slotted alongside Simmons' and McDonald's projects.

McDonald went on to have several hits, including a chart-topping duet with Patti Labelle, 'On My Own' (US No.1, UK No.2, 1986), while the original line-up re-formed in 1988, experiencing diminishing returns with *Cycles* (1989) and *Brotherhood* (1991). In 1994, a Dance remix of 'Long Train Runnin'' reached UK No 7.

surf www.doobiebros.com/indexMacEx.html

THE DOORS ✪

WHO Vocals **James Douglas 'Jim' Morrison** (b. 8 Dec 1943, Melbourne, Florida, USA, d. 3 Jul 1971, Paris, France), guitar **Robbie Krieger** (b. 8 Feb 1946, Los Angeles, California, USA), keyboards **Ray Manzarek** (b. 2 Dec 1939, Chicago, Illinois, USA), drums **John Densmore** (b. 1 Dec 1944, Los Angeles)

WHEN 1965–1973

WHERE Los Angeles, California, USA

WHAT Hot, sexy, poetic, apocalyptic Rock

The detached coldness of Jim Morrison's lyrics can be traced to the upheaval of his childhood, caused by his father's numerous postings with the US Navy. At school, he developed a love of breaking taboos and shocking people. Typically, in his first interviews as a Pop star, he lied that his parents were dead.

Morrison's initial passion was for literature, in which he excelled at school (he had an IQ of 149). From poet William Blake's quote "If the doors of perception were fully cleansed we should see life as it really is" he named The Doors. He found the quote in Aldous Huxley's book *The Doors Of Perception*, which described the effects of the drug mescalin. As a teenager, he visited the Blues clubs of Washington, DC, and was a fan of Elvis Presley, though he was 21 before he started singing.

After graduating, he spent the summer of 1965 at Venice Beach sleeping on a roof, writing poetry and taking LSD. With fellow student Ray Manzarek – to whom he recited the words of 'Moonlight Drive' – he worked out arrangements for 'Hello I Love You', 'Moonlight Drive', 'Soul Kitchen', 'People Are Strange', 'My Eyes Have Seen You' and 'End Of The Night'. This period was one of Morrison's most creative: lyrics written in 1965 dominate the first two Doors albums, and appear sporadically thereafter, e.g. 'Summer's Almost Gone' and 'The Cars Hiss By My Window'.

In 1965, Manzarek was in covers group Rick & The Ravens with his brothers, though he had Classical piano training and also played Jazz. Morrison joined, but the others left in dismay at his lyrics and behaviour. Manzarek's ability to cope with Morrison's drug and alcohol abuse and resultant mood swings sealed their partnership. Drummer Densmore and flamenco-trained guitarist Krieger were recruited from Manzarek's transcendental meditation classes. Struggling to find a bassist, they decided they had a more unique sound without.

The band's break came in early 1966 when they secured a residency at LA club The London Fog. For three months they played six nights a week. Although eventually fired for not pulling crowds, The Doors polished their set, using the repetition to work out long arrangements for 'The End' and 'When The Music's Over'. Their set also included standards such as Willie Dixon's 'Little Red Rooster', Them's 'Gloria' and The Kingsmen's 'Louie Louie'. In May 1966 a new residency began at the prestigious Whisky-A-Go-Go club. Here

> **"We're more interested in the dark side of life, the evil thing, the night time"**
>
> **Jim Morrison**

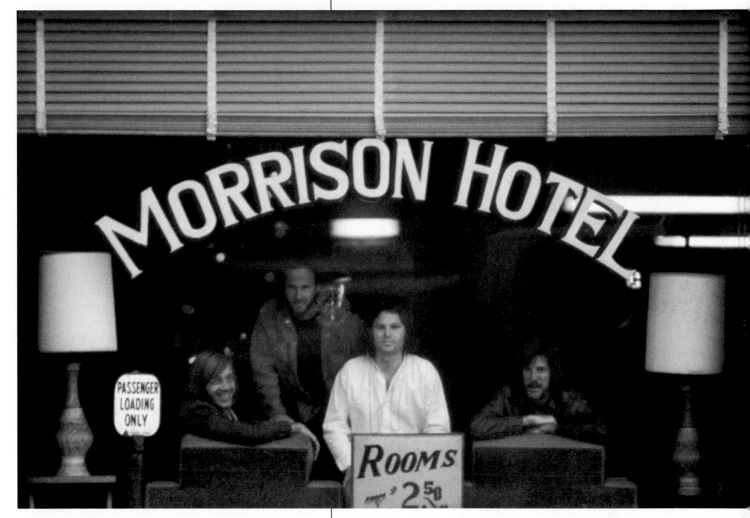

Morrison worked out the Oedipal lyrics to 'The End', which got them fired in July. Fortunately, The Doors had by this time gained big exposure, frequently out-performing headliners Them and The Byrds, leading to a contract with Elektra.

The Doors (US No.2), released in January 1967, featured the best of their well-honed live set. 'Break On Through (To The Other Side)' was the first single, but 'Light My Fire', written by Krieger, brought their first singles chart success, becoming a US No.1 in July 1967. *Strange Days* (US No.3), in late 1967, was largely a recording of the remainder of their early live set.

With Morrison now a sex symbol in trademark tight leather, The Doors became an arena-filling sensation. The next three years were spent on regular tours of the USA and one European visit in 1968. Morrison, disenchanted with the Pop spectacle, started taunting the audience and on occasions inciting them to riot. His drinking and drug-taking badly affected his singing and input at recording. An exasperated Densmore briefly quit when Morrison fell asleep and urinated in a drunken stupor in the studio. He was arrested several times for drunkenness and, in Miami in 1969, was charged with exposing himself on stage. A court case dragged on until October 1970, when he was sentenced for 'profanity' and 'indecent exposure'.

Morrison's disillusionment and drunkenness were largely to blame for the lacklustre *Waiting For The Sun* (1968 – still a US No.1), which scraped the barrel with songs written in 1965 and 1966, while new songs such as 'Five To One' came close to self-

parody. However, *The Soft Parade* (1969) produced US hits 'Tell All The People' and 'Touch Me', both written by Krieger. Morrison talked of quitting the group for movies or going to Paris to concentrate on poetry and novels.

Morrison Hotel (1970) was hailed as a major comeback. The intricate and orchestral productions of the previous two albums were replaced by performances recorded live in the studio, with a bassist. This style was again used successfully on *LA Woman* (1971), whose title track and hits 'Riders On The Storm' and 'Love Her Madly' re-established The Doors' reputation.

On bail and appealing against his jail sentence, Morrison left for Paris in March 1971. There he wrote and drank heavily. On 3 July he was found dead in the bath by his girlfriend Pamela Courson. His death was officially recorded as heart failure.

The remaining Doors continued as a trio until 1973, releasing the unloved *Full Circle* (1971) and *Other Voices* (1972). They regrouped to add backing music to poetry recorded by Morrison, released as *An American Prayer* in 1979. That year the powerful use of 'The End' in the movie *Apocalypse Now* brought a reawakened interest in The Doors. This led to the Oliver Stone movie *The Doors* in 1991 – a dramatization of their career which returned their music to the charts.

ReaD *No One Here Gets Out Alive* (1975), Jerry Hopkins & Danny Sugarman

Surf www.jps.net/cjam/journey.html

DR DRE

WHO b. Andre Young, 18 Feb 1965, south-central Los Angeles, California, USA

WHAT The Quincy Jones of Rap

Graduating from early outfit World Class Wreckin' Cru to Rap revolutionaries NWA, Dr Dre became one of Hip Hop's most respected and successful producers. He transformed the genre with solo debut *The Chronic* (1993), which revamped George Clinton's P-Funk for a new generation. Protegés Snoop Doggy Dogg and Warren G and the Dre-helmed soundtracks *Above The Rim* and *Murder Was The Case* swamped 1994's US charts.

However, shortly after Death Row – the label he'd co-founded – signed doomed superstar Tupac Shakur, Dre quit the increasingly dangerous world of Gangsta Rap. 'Been There, Done That', he bragged on fresh set *The Aftermath* (1996). He then extended his platinum touch selectively (beneficiaries including BLACKstreet and Foxy Brown), ensuring a longevity that has eluded many contemporaries.

Fan Aftermath Entertainment, 15060 Ventura Boulevard, Suite 225, Sherman Oaks, CA 91403, USA

surf www.aftermath.com

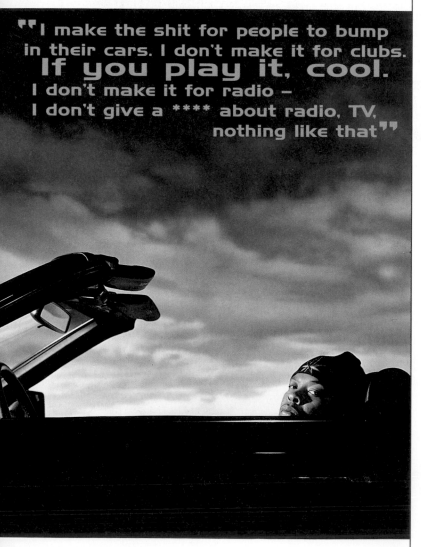

"I make the shit for people to bump in their cars. I don't make it for clubs. If you play it, cool. I don't make it for radio – I don't give a **** about radio, TV, nothing like that"

DR FEELGOOD ⊙

WHO Vocals/guitar **Lee Brilleaux** (b. Lee Collinson, 10 May 1952, Durban, South Africa, d. 7 Apr 1994, Canvey Island, Essex, England), guitar **Wilko Johnson** (b. John Wilkinson, 12 Jul 1947), bass **Sparko** (b. John Sparks, 22 Feb 1953), drums **The Big Figure** (b. John Martin, 8 Nov 1946)

WHEN 1971–1994

WHERE Canvey Island, Essex, England

WHAT Godfathers of Pub Rock

Formed from the ashes of R&B bands The Fix and The Roamers, Dr Feelgood debuted with *Down By The Jetty* (1975), unusual for its mono recording, and broke the UK chart with *Malpractice* (1975). Ever popular live, playing mainly in and around London, the band became forerunners of the media-coined 'Pub Rock' movement. Their live set *Stupidity* (1976) topped the UK chart, but their momentum was halted when the robotic Johnson left, taking his distinctive guitar sound with him. John Mayo joined for *Sneakin' Suspicion* (1977) and Feelgood flourished through the late 70s, notably with 1979's UK Top 10 hit 'Milk And Alcohol', allegedly penned by band comrade Nick Lowe after witnessing bluesman John Lee Hooker in concert.

The band fragmented in 1982, but Brilleaux persevered with fluctuating line-ups until his untimely death from throat cancer.

Read *Down By The Jetty* (1997), Tony Moon

surf ourworld.compuserve.com/homepages/dr_feelgood_info_service/feelgood.htm

DR JOHN

WHO b. Malcolm 'Mac' Rebennack, 21 Nov 1941, New Orleans, Louisiana, USA

WHAT Growling New Orleans R&B Pianist

First a producer for the Ace label in the late 50s, Rebennack spent much of the 60s touring and playing guitar on countless sessions. A nightclub fracas (in which one of his fingers was shot off) forced him to revert primarily to piano, which he had learnt from New Orleans pianists Professor Longhair and James Booker.

His debut *Gris Gris* (1968) introduced his psychedelic voodoo persona Dr John. Containing his most famous song, 'I Walk On Guilded Splinters', its spooky blend of swampy R&B, percussion and voodoo proclamations proved a cult hippie hit, though subsequent albums returned to a more traditional New Orleans sound. The acclaimed *Gumbo* (1971) included Big Easy standards like 'Iko Iko' and 'Tipitina'. A collaboration with the city's top producer Allen Toussaint brought the Doctor hits with the funky 'Right Place, Wrong Time' (US No.9, 1973) and the albums *In The Right Place* (US No.24, 1973) and *Desitively Bonnaroo* (1974).

His career has since encompassed solo piano albums such as *Dr John Plays Mac Rebennack* (1982), collections of reworked Jazz standards like *In A Sentimental Mood* (1989) and further hometown homages like *Goin' Back To New Orleans* (1992).

Trippin' Live (1997) was nominated for a Grammy, and a year on he could count Paul Weller, Supergrass, Primal Scream and Spiritualized among his collaborators.

READ *Under A Hoodoo Moon* (1994), Dr John & Jack Rummel

SURF www.drjohn.com/

NICK DRAKE

WHO b. 18 Jun 1948, Burma, d. 25 Nov 1974, Birmingham, England

WHAT Shy, tortured Folk Rock poet

Although chart success eluded him, interest in Nick Drake lingers long after his death. Recommended to producer Joe Boyd by Fairport Convention's Ashley Hutchings in 1968, Drake recorded his debut for Island between lectures at Cambridge University.

Although critically acclaimed, sales of *Five Leaves Left* (1969) suffered from Drake's reluctance to meet the press and perform live. With the plush *Bryter Layter* (1970) and darker *Pink Moon* (1972), he became increasingly introverted and depressed, and died from an overdose of antidepressants at 26. Buried in the village churchyard at Tanworth-in-Arden, England, where he grew up, Drake is better known now than during his short life. Boyd's 1992 compilation of Drake's work, *Way To Blue*, is a marvellous introduction to a unique musician.

READ *Nick Drake: The Biography* (1997), Patrick Humphries

FAN Pink Moon, 34 Kingsbridge Road, Walton-on-Thames, Surrey, KT12 2BZ, UK

SURF www.algonet.se/~iguana/DRAKE/DRAKE.html

THE DRIFTERS

WHO Vocals **Clyde McPhatter** (b. 15 Nov 1931, Durham, North Carolina, USA, d. 13 Jun 1972, Teaneck, New Jersey), vocals **Johnny Moore** (b. 1934, Selma, Alabama, USA), vocals **Ben E. King** (b. Benjamin Earl Nelson, 23 Sep 1938, Henderson, North Carolina), vocals **Rudy Lewis** (b. 27 May 1935, Chicago, Illinois, USA, d. 20 May 1964)

WHEN 1953–

WHERE New York, USA

WHAT R&B perennials

Clyde McPhatter left R&B's celebrated Billy Ward & The Dominoes to make groundbreaking, Gospel-influenced gems with The Drifters' 'Money Honey' (1953), 'Such A Night', 'Honey Love', 'White Christmas' (all 1954) and 'What'cha Gonna Do' (1955). When he was drafted, his replacements included Moore, heard on mid-50s hits 'Ruby Baby' (1955) and 'Fools Fall In Love' (1957).

Their manager disbanded the group in 1958, replacing them with the Ben E. King-fronted Five Crowns. King's reign saw their biggest American hits – the innovative, string-soaked 'There Goes My Baby' (1959) and transatlantic smash 'Save The Last Dance For Me' (1960). When King went solo, Lewis sang lead on the influential 'Up On The Roof' (1962) and 'On Broadway' (1963) before succumbing to a heart attack in 1964.

Moore drifted back and led mid-60s favourites 'Under The Boardwalk' (1964), 'Saturday Night At The Movies' (1964), 'At The Club' (1965) and 'Come On Over To My Place' (1965).

When reissues of the last three scaled the UK chart in the early 70s, the group relocated to Britain and notched up five further, Moore-fronted Top 10 entries, including 'Like Sister And Brother', 'Kissin' In The Back Row Of The Movies' (both 1973) and 'There Goes My First Love' (1975).

In 1987, the Rock And Roll Hall Of Fame inducted McPhatter. One year later he was joined by The Drifters, who could have filled the stage if every past member had attended!

READ *Save The Last Dance For Me: The Musical Legacy Of The Drifters 1953–1993* (1997), Tony Allan & Faye Treadwell

DRUM 'N' BASS/JUNGLE

WHAT Jungle grew from the British Hardcore rave scene, mixing Dub, Reggae and Hip Hop samples into a hybrid of furious beats and prolapse-inducing sub-bass. The aggressive sound of pioneers General Levy, Fabio (who named the style) and Grooverider was given an epic twist by Goldie and his Metalheadz stable of early 90s artists, including Photek and Dillinja. LTJ Bukem, long-time exponent A Guy Called Gerald and Mercury Prize-winner Roni Size added prettier Jazz elements, with the style gaining alternative monikers Intelligent and finally Drum 'N' Bass. It once looked like the future, but when David Bowie (1997's <u>Earthling</u>) and even Eric Clapton 'went' Drum 'N' Bass (as T.D.F. on 1997's <u>Retail Therapy</u>), the style lost some of its underground appeal. Drum 'n' Bass has yet to make much of an impact Stateside, where artists like Goldie were absorbed into the Trip Hop/Electronica bubble.
WHERE UK
WHEN 90s–
WHO Goldie <u>Timeless</u> (1995), A Guy Called Gerald <u>Black Secret Technology</u> (1996), Baby D <u>Deliverance</u> (1996), Various <u>Platinum Breaks</u> (1996), LTJ Bukem <u>Earth</u> (1996), Roni Size & Reprazent <u>Nu Forms</u> (1997)

DUB

WHAT Dub began when producers in Jamaica utilized the instrumental track of a vocal record for a B-side to save money, calling them 'Versions'. Talking artists such as U-Roy used them as their own backing tracks, then producers such as Lynford Anderson and Lee 'Scratch' Perry went a step further, adding spacey effects and echo-strewn songs such as Perry's 'Clint Eastwood' (1969). Electronics engineer King Tubby became champion of the genre in the mid-70s, making the classic <u>King Tubby Meets Rockers Uptown</u> (1977) with melodica maestro Augustus Pablo. Although Dub fell from favour in 80s Jamaica, UK producers such as Mad Professor and Jah Shaka kept it alive, and it had a huge influence on Techno. Dub's Reggae renaissance came in the 90s via the British New Roots movement and engineer Bobby Digital in Jamaica.
WHERE Jamaica
WHEN 1969–
WHO Lee Perry & The Upsetters <u>Blackboard Jungle Dub</u> (1974), Augustus Pablo <u>King Tubby Meets Rockers Uptown</u> (1977), Joe Gibbs & The Professionals <u>African Dub Chapter 3</u> (1978)

DUBSTAR

WHO Vocals **Sarah Blackwood** (b. 6 May 1971, Halifax, England), keyboards

Steve Hellier (b. 14 May 1969, Kent, England), guitar **Chris Wilkie** (b. 25 Jan

1973, Gateshead, England)

WHEN 1993–

WHERE Gateshead, England

WHAT Unhappy hitmakers

Despite their muscular moments, The Smiths inspired a generation of moping students like Hillier and Wilkie, whose unfortunately named The Joans evolved into the Sarah Blackwood-fronted Dubstar. Finding a sympathetic ear at Blur's label Food, they debuted with the lovely 'Stars' in 1995. A cover of the ultra-unknown Brick Supply's 'Not So Manic Now' made the UK Top 20, and the parent album *Disgraceful* (1995) went gold, despite complaints about its suggestive cover. They even earned appreciation from Johnny Marr, mitigating the unfavourable comparisons. A tour with Erasure preceded 'No More Talk', which in turn trailed *Goodbye* (1997). Small but secure at home, Dubstar sought to raise overseas sales above vanishing point by appointing Soft Cell mastermind Stevo as manager and filleting their albums for the US release *Cathedral Park* (1997).

Fan Dubstar, Freepost, PO Box 460, Buckinghamshire, HP12 4BR, UK

Surf www.gre.ac.uk/~mr10/actual/dubstar.html

DURAN DURAN ⊙

WHO Vocals **Simon Le Bon** (b. 27 Oct 1958, Bushey, England), keyboards

Nick Rhodes (b. Nicholas Bates, 8 Jun 1962, Birmingham, England), guitar

Warren Cuccurullo (b. 8 Dec 1956, Brooklyn, New York, USA)

WHEN 1978–

WHERE Birmingham, England

WHAT Hits, haircuts and videos

Though harsh on Progressive Rock dinosaurs, Punk grudgingly respected Art Rockers like Roxy Music – hence bassist John Taylor and Nick Rhodes hatched a band inspired by The Sex Pistols and sounding like Roxy. Named after the villain in 60s flick *Barbarella*, their early bandmates included Steven 'Tin Tin' Duffy (the future Lilac Time leader, solo chart star and mate of Blur).

The world-conquering line-up – including drummer Roger Taylor (no relation), guitarist Andy Taylor (likewise) and former choirboy Le Bon – hit with 'Planet Earth', 'Careless Memories' and 'Girls On Film' from *Duran Duran* (1981). Their futuristic Dance Rock was good, but the 'New Romantic' image – candyfloss with cheekbones – was even better. *Rio* (1982) matched visual extravagance with musical might; its hits conquered America as Duranmania enveloped the MTV generation (including Courtney

Love, who later covered 'Hungry Like The Wolf' live with Hole). However, *Seven And The Ragged Tiger* (1983), despite yielding the transatlantic No.1 'The Reflex', sounded drained of inspiration. Fittingly, their first major US tour – source of the live album *Arena* (1984) – was sponsored by Coke.

This success, including the Bond movie theme and US No.1 'A View To A Kill', masked division, and Live Aid was the quintet's last outing. Taylors John and Andy recruited singer Robert Palmer and Chic drummer Tony Thompson for The Power Station, whose self-titled 1985 album yielded the hits 'Some Like It Hot' and 'Get It On'. Le Bon and Rhodes fared poorer as Arcadia with *So Red The Rose* (1985), while Roger Taylor disappeared altogether. Further tensions during work on Duran comeback *Notorious* (1986) saw Andy Taylor quit for a solo career. (He later produced British Hard Rock outfit Thunder.) He was replaced by Warren Cuccurullo (ex-Frank Zappa and Missing Persons), while producer Nile Rodgers (of Chic) dominated the hit 'Notorious' (1986). However, 'Skin Trade' (1987) was their first single in five years to miss the UK Top 10, and barely scraped the US Top 40.

By 1988, not even transatlantic smashes 'I Don't Want Your Love' and 'All She Wants Is' could save *Big Thing* from a negligible chart run. The hits collection *Decade* (1989) and *Liberty* (1990) restored them to the UK Top 10, but bombed Stateside. As celebrity wives Yasmin Le Bon and Amanda de Cadenet (Mrs John Taylor) eclipsed their husbands, it was assumed the Pop graveyard had claimed another corpse.

They stormed back with the classic 'Ordinary World' from *Duran Duran* (1993), aka *The Wedding Album*, but their second 1993 hit, 'Come Undone', presaged another downturn: the covers collection *Thank You* (1995) was swept asunder amid critical derision. John Taylor briefly revived The Power Station, then convened The Neurotic Outsiders with Sex Pistol Steve Jones and Guns N' Roses' Duff McKagan and Matt Sorum. He quit Duran in 1997, leaving them to revive the 80s with a controversy-courting video for 'Electric Barbarella' from *Medazzaland* (1997).

Meanwhile, 1997's *The Duran Duran Tribute Album* (featuring Deftones) testified to the enduring affection of Durannies.

Read *Duran Duran: The First Four Years Of The Fab Five* (1984), Neil Gaiman

Fan MDD, PO Box 2058, Philadelphia, PA 19103, USA

Surf pawprint-std.com/duran/

IAN DURY

WHO b. 12 May 1942, Upminster, Essex, England

WHAT Crafty Cockney cum tragi-comic wordsmith

A Pop star for just two years, but one of the great British lyricists, Dury's coarsely elegant rhymes could document a relationship in four lines: "Home improvement expert Harold Hill of Harold Hill/Of do-it-yourself dexterity and double-glazing skill/Came home to find another gentleman's kippers in the grill/So he sanded off his winkle with a Black & Decker drill" ('This Is What We Find'). Or could make six exuberant words say it all: "Two fat persons click click click!" ('Hit Me With Your Rhythm Stick').

Dury cut a unique figure after childhood polio left him with a withered leg and severe limp. A graduate of London's Royal College of Art, then a design teacher, he formed Kilburn & The High Roads when he was 28. Pub Rock heroes, they recorded two salty, unsuccessful albums (*Wotabunch*, belatedly released in 1978, then *Handsome*, 1975). The Kilburns expired in 1976 and Dury took a year out to write with their keyboard player, Chaz Jankel. Signed to Stiff, Dury's first solo single, 'Sex And Drugs And Rock And Roll', proved iconic but uncommercial. In 1977 he formed The Blockheads, a band of seasoned veterans, to play the 'Stiff Live Stiffs' tour with Elvis Costello and Nick Lowe – collectively, Pub Rock's credible answer to Punk.

For two years Dury was unstoppable. The literate stomp of *New Boots And Panties!* (1978, UK No.5) and *Do It Yourself* (1979, UK No.2) did very well, despite omitting the hits 'What A Waste', 'Hit Me With Your Rhythm Stick' (UK No.1) and 'Reasons To Be Cheerful (Part 3)'.

Inexplicably, the bottom then dropped out of the market for Dury. *Laughter* (1980), as fierce and funny as ever, stalled at UK No.48. The undistinguished *Lord Upminster* (1981) and *4,000 Weeks Holiday* (1984), both on Polydor, flopped and Dury got by on acting and TV ads. After Blockhead reunion gigs celebrated by the live *Warts And Audience* (1989), he released *The Bus Driver's Prayer & Other Stories* (1992) on Demon. Utterly brilliant, it passed unremarked and soon Dury was dropped again. His vibrant influence lives on through peculiarly English bands such as Madness, Carter The Unstoppable Sex Machine and Blur.

Surf www.bestiff.demon.co.uk/Artists/IanDury.html

BOB DYLAN ☉☉☉☉☉☉☉ ✪✪✪

WHO b. Robert Allen Zimmerman, 24 May 1941, Duluth, Minnesota, USA

WHAT Rock and Folk's mythical leader and songwriter supreme

Rock took a left turn in 1965. The Beatles stopped asking to hold hands and cried 'Help'. The Rolling Stones replaced R&B recycling with the roaring '(I Can't Get No) Satisfaction'. Meanwhile, Bob Dylan – who inspired both transformations – unleashed the sloganeering 'Subterranean Homesick Blues', of which Radiohead's 'Subterranean Homesick Alien' is only the most explicit descendant. As well as inspiring the wordplay of these Rock icons, Dylan must be one of the most covered singer/songwriters of all time.

Despite his mythical status, Dylan's early years were fairly uneventful. When he was 6, his family moved to the small mining town of Hibbing, Minnesota, near the Canadian border. In between helping out at his father's electrical store, Dylan taught himself to play piano, then harmonica, then guitar. First transfixed by Hank Williams, Johnnie Ray, Elvis and Little Richard (he spent much of his teenage years banging away at the piano and howling), he was converted to Folk – particularly Woody Guthrie – at the University of Minnesota in 1959. The genre gave a natural home to his wheezy vocals, his driving harmonica and acoustic guitar playing. Adopting the name Bob Dylan (probably inspired by poet Dylan Thomas), he replaced studies with gigging. Fired with the dream of meeting Woody, then wasting away in a New Jersey hospital with a long-term illness, he went East to meet his hero in January 1961.

Guthrie took to Dylan immediately and they became friends. 'Song To Woody' – one of Dylan's first self-penned songs to capture the attention of other Folk singers – later appeared on his first album. Relocating to New York's Greenwich Village, Dylan began to spin his own myth. Denying his past, he told many that he was a roaming orphan from New Mexico. He spent most of 1961 living in other people's homes, supported by new friends and fellow Folk musicians such as Dave Van Ronk, Phil Ochs, Jack Elliott and Eric Anderson. By the end of the year he was an acclaimed fixture on the club circuit, adopted by manager Albert Grossman and talent-spotted by Columbia Records' John Hammond. However, the grim Folk and Blues homages of debut *Bob Dylan* (1962) found few buyers in a market dominated by the Easy Listening likes of Bert Kaempfert, Henry Mancini and *Blue Hawaii*-era Elvis.

"It's not me, it's the songs. I'm just the postman, I deliver the songs"

The same fate might have befallen *The Freewheelin' Bob Dylan* (1963) had it not been for Peter, Paul & Mary's sweet cover of the album's 'Blowin' In The Wind', a transatlantic hit in the summer of 1963. The album topped the UK chart, and the song – alongside other Protest classics such as 'Masters Of War', 'Pawn In Their Game' and 'A Hard Rain's A-Gonna Fall'– catapulted Dylan to the position of Folk's foremost Protest songwriter. With poetry unmatched by his contemporaries, Dylan articulated the feelings of a disaffected generation who believed in a better world.

The Times They Are A-Changin' (1964) included more of the Protest songs that people had come to expect – such as 'The Lonesome Death Of Hattie Carroll' and the title track (a major anthem for 60s youth culture) – but songs like 'Boots Of Spanish Leather' and 'One Too Many Mornings' reflected a growing obsession with deciphering his relationships.

The pressure on Dylan to live up to the expectations of many in the Folk scene and civil rights movement (which had adopted him as its singing spokesman) began to take its toll, and he felt

"No one's free,
even the
birds are chained
to the sky"

In 1966, John Lennon's more oblique lyrics on The Beatles' *Rubber Soul* and *Revolver* were among the high-profile Dylan derivations, while the man himself recruited The Hawks (later The Band) for further flame-fanning electric performances.

Blonde On Blonde (1966) justified the hype, blending the hits 'Just Like A Woman' and 'Rainy Day Women #12 & 35' with epic ballads like 'Sad Eyed Lady Of The Lowlands'. Having raised the prestige of song lyrics among academics and intellectuals, Dylan was dissected in classrooms by curious students and analysed in bedrooms by obsessive fans. The influence on Dylan of poets like Arthur Rimbaud and Allen Ginsberg (a contemporary and friend) gave his lyrics a complexity and breadth that most songwriters had never even imagined, much less attempted.

Despite disappointing some of his Folk fans, Dylan acquired new worshippers who kneeled at the altar of his mysterious lyrics and raw, uncompromising sound. However, the effect of fame on Dylan's personal life became crippling. Only 21 when he wrote 'Blowin' In The Wind', he had barely arrived before being hailed a sage. By the age of 25, the pedestal fans had placed him on had begun to affect him. Stories of Dylan's tantrums, cruelty and inability to accept any criticism accumulated.

Dylanmania had clearly hit its height when his serious motorcycle crash in July 1966 was widely analysed for significance. Although Dylan disciples saw it as his crucifixion – the inevitable result of having gone so far and risen so high – the most mundane explanation was a documented inability with motor vehicles. Whatever the reason, the accident allowed Dylan to dismount the treadmill. Columbia plugged the gap with *Bob Dylan's Greatest Hits* (1966) while he recorded the mellow *John Wesley Harding* (1967) – yielding the uncharacteristically gentle 'I'll Be Your Baby Tonight' and 'All Along The Watchtower' (popularized by Jimi Hendrix's explosive 1967 recording) – and *The Basement Tapes* (belatedly released in 1975), both with The Band. Privacy had always been important to Dylan – he kept his marriage a secret at first and would distract journalists who strayed into the personal realm – but now it was paramount. Holed up in the small town of Woodstock, in upstate New York, with his wife Sara, her daughter Maria, and his two sons with Sara – Jesse and Seth – the only other people he would see were old friends like Eric Anderson and chosen musicians, mainly members of The Band.

Putting speed-crazed Rock on the back-burner, Dylan 'went Country' for *Nashville Skyline* (1969), featuring Country legend Johnny Cash. The hit 'Lay Lady Lay' – with his nasal whine replaced by a more soothing croon – returned him to the upper reaches of transatlantic single charts and became an enduring favourite (capable of reducing the youthful Madonna to tears). However, 1970's *Self Portrait* and *New Morning* – despite continuing a run of UK album chart-toppers – yielded no hits and spent uncharacteristically fleeting periods in the US chart.

Many Dylan fanatics felt he had sold out, no longer spinning his iconoclastic web of lyrics or sounding his raucous horn of battle. In 1971, neither his much-trumpeted book *Tarantula* nor a post-crash return to the stage at George Harrison's Concert for Bangla Desh did much to restore his reputation. Columbia weighed in again with *Bob Dylan's Greatest Hits, Vol. II* (1971), while Dylan agreed to appear in and score Sam Peckinpah's Western *Pat Garrett And Billy The Kid* (1973), the only worthwhile result of which was the evergreen 'Knockin' On Heaven's Door' (which he after played for the Pope at The Eucharist Congress in Bologna, Italy, in 1997). The wretchedness was

confined by the growing demands of those who looked to him to lead them into a promised land of equality and freedom. Disillusionment sparked by President Kennedy's assassination in 1963 and Dylan's own changing views led to *Another Side Of Bob Dylan* (1964), its title self-explanatory. It initiated his farewell to both Folk ('It Ain't Me Babe') and girlfriend/*Freewheelin'* cover co-star Suze Rotolo ('Ballad In Plain D'). The latter was replaced by Joan Baez (the 'Queen of Folk' who had been instrumental in promoting Dylan by performing his songs and taking him on tour), the former by the strident Rock of *Bringing It All Back Home* (1965). 'Subterranean Homesick Blues' was followed up the charts by The Byrds' cover of Dylan's 'Mr Tambourine Man'.

By now it was apparent that Dylan had escaped the Folk fold and embarked upon a journey that would give both intellectual and emotional depth to the future of Rock. Baez accused Dylan of abandoning his people. He replied they were *her* people, not his. Those who refused to release him from his unsigned contract as Folk's Messiah booed at concerts where he exposed his new Rock sound.

Undaunted by purists' protests, Dylan continued the Folk Rock advance on *Highway 61 Revisited* (1965), source of his biggest US hit, 'Like A Rolling Stone'. Now that his protest had become more personal, this song and others – such as 'Queen Jane Approximately', 'Tombstone Blues', 'Desolation Row' – were full of painful realizations and a brooding bitterness. The chilling 'Ballad Of A Thin Man' was a scathing attack on music journalists, an antipathy reflected in the D.A. Pennebaker documentary *Don't Look Back* (1965), depicting Dylan's infamous English tour, which led to Baez's Big Zim swan song (Sara Lowndes soon became Mrs Dylan and inspiration for much lyrical muck-raking).

compounded when he briefly defected to the Asylum label, prompting Columbia to release the out-takes set *Dylan* (1974), which charted fleetingly in the USA and not at all in the UK.

Fired up again, he reunited with The Band for *Planet Waves* (1974) – his first US No.1 – and a spectacularly over-subscribed US tour. From the latter came the live *Before The Flood* (1974), his second and last album for Asylum. He returned to Columbia for *Blood On The Tracks* (1975), which – though inspired by domestic turmoil and re-recorded at the eleventh hour – is one of his classics. *Desire* (1976), with violin added to the Dylan sound, followed *Blood* to the top in the USA, and the Rolling Thunder Revue tour returned Joan Baez and The Byrds' Roger McGuinn to the Dylan fold. However, the underwhelming live album *Hard Rain* (1976) and incomprehensible tour film *Renaldo And Clara* (1978), coupled with divorce, began a decline from which Dylan would take a long time to recover. *Street Legal* (1978) was hardly a great comeback and, although he remained a huge concert draw, *Bob Dylan At Budokan* (1978) suggested his appeal was based more on legend than music.

Floundering for direction again, he converted to Christianity, overcame the consequent amazement with the million-selling *Slow Train Coming* (1979), alienated the faithful with evangelical gigs and watched *Saved* (1980) disappear into a commercial black hole from which his Stateside chart status never returned. Despite the improved songwriting of *Shot Of Love* (1981), *Infidels* (1983) and *Empire Burlesque* (1985), Dylan seemed aimless. His increasingly hit-and-miss shows yielded another disposable live album, *Real Live* (1984), and a ramshackle appearance at Live Aid prompted concern about his sanity.

Increasingly out of touch with his former self, he was reportedly taught how to sing like the Dylan of old by Stevie Wonder on the recording of USA For Africa's 'We Are The World' (1985). A fleeting reunion with common sense saw him recruit Tom Petty & The Heartbreakers as a live band, but any goodwill this might have engendered was undone by *Knocked Out Loaded* (1986) and an unforgivably sloppy association with The Grateful Dead. The success of *Dylan And The Dead* (1989) can be attributed only to US record-buyers' taste for nostalgia; similarly, 1985's retrospective *Biograph* was Dylan's sole platinum seller of the 80s. A credibility-crippling appearance in the critically derided 1987 movie *Hearts Of Fire* was his lowest low. *Down In The Groove* (1988) and yet another volume of *Greatest Hits* sank without trace.

Apparently working to his own single-minded agenda, Dylan briefly surfaced with *The Traveling Wilburys: Volume One* (1988), as part of a supergroup featuring the writing and musicianship of himself, George Harrison, Tom Petty, Jeff Lynne and the late Roy Orbison, which was generally well received, then embarked on his 'Never-Ending Tour', which played to dwindling audiences.

A 1963 claim that "I don't give a damn about the melodies" proved prophetic as he reworked much-loved music with either indifference or hostility. Songwriting reclaimed the upper hand on his Daniel Lanois-produced chart comeback *Oh Mercy* (1989) and *Under The Red Sky* (1990), but Folk and Blues covers reigned for *Good As I Been To You* (1992) and *World Gone Wrong* (1993). In between, *The Traveling Wilburys: Volume Three* (1990) and box set *The Bootleg Series 1961–1991* kept Bobophiles busy.

Confirming his apparently terminal dislocation from contemporary music, reports of a 30th anniversary tribute concert at New York's Madison Square Garden in 1992 were dominated not by Dylan but the fate of ill-received acolyte Sinead O'Connor. The concert witnessed Dylan replacing his usually impeccable phrasing with a seemingly perverse sense of word emphasis and an unintelligible mumbling of his most well-loved lyrics. In 1995, *Unplugged* proved once and for all that, for Dylan, live albums were best avoided.

With expectations at a terminal low, *Time Out Of Mind* (1997), again produced by Daniel Lanois, was seen as a return to form, lauded by the likes of Elvis Costello and receiving three Grammy nominations. It revived his commercial fortunes Stateside, but serious health problems ensured the rejoicing was short-lived. True to form, Columbia ensured an epitaph was available if

bob dylan

needed, with *The Best Of Bob Dylan* (1997). He recovered to play some of his best-received shows in a decade, including that Papal performance. He also worked with playwright Sam Shepard on songs in 1997 (perhaps harping back to the old days when girlfriend Suze had introduced him to the plays of Bertolt Brecht, said to have influenced early Dylan material).

Meanwhile, his youngest son Jakob scored hit albums with his band The Wallflowers – *The Wallflowers* (1992) and *Bringing Down The Horse* (1996) – the latter reaching the Top 10 and going multi-platinum. A redemptive year for Dylan, 1997 ended with his nomination for the Nobel Prize for Literature. As if the strength of Dylan's songwriting needed reinforcing, an album of 18 Dylan songs, *And The Times They Were A-Changin'*, including such major artists as Eric Clapton and Rod Stewart, was released on Polygram in January 1998. Despite all the accolades (such as three Grammys in the February 1998 ceremony, including Best Album), Dylan – a charismatic and wilful character, with one of Rock's most illustrious back catalogues – continues to do whatever he wants, whenever he wants.

Read *No Direction Home: The Life And Music Of Bob Dylan* (1997), Robert Shelton

Fan Isis, c/o Derek Barker, PO Box 132, Coventry, CV3 5RE, UK

Surf www.bobdylan.com/about/

THE EAGLES ✪✪✪✪✪

WHO Vocals/guitar/keyboards **Glenn Frey** (b. 6 Nov 1948, Detroit, Michigan, USA), vocals/drums **Don Henley** (b. 22 Jul 1947, Gilmer, Texas, USA), vocals/guitar/mandolin/banjo **Bernie Leadon** (b. 19 Jul 1947, Minneapolis, Minnesota, USA), vocals/guitar **Don Felder** (b. 21 Sep 1947, Topanga, California, USA), vocals/guitar **Joe Walsh** (b. 20 Nov 1947, Wichita, Kansas, USA), vocals/bass **Timothy B. Schmit** (b. 30 Oct 1947, Sacramento, California)

WHEN 1971–

WHERE Los Angeles, California, USA

WHAT From Country Rock to commercial superstars

Regarded as the personification of young West Coast America in the 70s, The Eagles were formed when the original four members met as part of Linda Ronstadt's backing band. Frey had played with various Detroit bands, including one fronted by Bob Seger, and Longbranch Pennywhistle with long-time writing partner John David Souther; Henley had been a member of Shiloh; Leadon with The Flying Burrito Brothers, and Dillard & Clark; and Meisner with Poco and Rick Nelson's Stone Canyon Band. After signing to David Geffen's new Country Rock-oriented label Asylum, they impressed British producer Glyn Johns with their versatility and harmonies. He brought them to London to record their 1972 eponymous debut album, which yielded three US chart hits – 'Take It Easy', co-written by Frey and Jackson Browne, 'Witchy Woman', and 'Peaceful Easy Feeling'. None charted in the UK, although they attracted a considerable British following, particularly among critics. It was rumoured that Richard Thompson of Fairport Convention was invited to become a member in the early days.

Their second album, the semi-concept *Desperado* (1973) – also recorded in London with Johns – sold less well, although it included 'Tequila Sunrise' and the title track, a 'cowboy classic' covered by Linda Ronstadt, The Carpenters and Bonnie Raitt. Director Sam Peckinpah expressed interest in developing the song's story into a movie. During sessions for their third album, the group fell out with Johns and returned to the USA to seek another producer. They chose Bill Szymczyk, partly because his work on Joe Walsh's solo album had impressed them, and partly because they and Walsh had a common manager in Irving Azoff.

Resuming sessions, a chance meeting and jam with guitarist and studio engineer Don Felder led to his joining as a fifth member. His guitar work added a whole new dimension to the sound and, according to Frey, "he just blew us all away". Released in 1974, *On The Border* reached US No.17, produced further minor hits in 'Already Gone', 'James Dean' and, the following year, unleashed the first of five chart-toppers: the ballad 'Best Of My Love'. The album also gave them their UK chart debut at No.28. However, their real British breakthrough came with a one-off gig at Wembley Stadium in June 1975, upstaging headliner Elton John, to promote fourth album *One Of These Nights*. Spending nearly a year in the US album chart, as well as topping it for five weeks, it spawned three transatlantic hits: the title track (which reached US No.1), 'Lyin' Eyes', and 'Take It To The Limit'. Musically, it marked the group's transition from Country to Rock.

A disillusioned Leadon left at the end of the year to form the Bernie Leadon-Michael Georgiades Band. He was replaced by Walsh, also on the bill at Wembley, who had been a bigger draw in some parts of the USA than the band. Observers felt his stay with the group would be only temporary. Anxious that Walsh's stay might be short-lived, Asylum rushed out their *Greatest Hits 1971–1975*, which went on to sell more than 24 million copies. Walsh's guitar 'flash' gave the band a new lease on life and they went from strength to strength. *Hotel California* (1976) was their enduring classic, with global sales of over 7 million by the end of 1977. The first single from it, 'New Kid In Town', and the title track both topped the US chart; the latter became their only UK Top 10 single; and the funkier 'Life In The Fast Lane' reached US No.11. At the end of 1977 Meisner left and was replaced by Schmit, who had coincidentally replaced him in Poco.

Hotel California was hard to follow, and the group suffered a critical backlash. In the wake of Punk, they were criticized for sounding outdated and irrelevant. After releasing a non-album single in 1978, a cover version of Charles Brown's Doo Wop classic 'Please Come Home For Christmas', sessions for their last album were marked by internal friction. *The Long Run* (which they sometimes referred to irreverently as 'The Long One', as time in the studio seemed never-ending) was released in late 1979. It reached US No.1, UK No.4 and gave them a fifth and final US No.1 single, 'Heartache Tonight', but was a critical disappointment. A live album was released a year later, but the group had gone their separate ways by then. They were tired of the megastar lifestyle; they had discovered "lyrics are not a replenishable source"; and above all, "it had stopped being fun". In 1982, Henley, asked if they would ever get together again, replied, "When hell freezes over."

During the 80s all pursued solo careers with varying success. Simultaneous UK Top 20 chart entries in 1985 for Henley ('The Boys Of Summer') and Frey ('The Heat Is On') led to renewed interest in their back catalogue and another successful compilation album. In 1993, the 1979 line-up returned to the studio to play on an Eagles tribute album, *Common Thread*, backing Country singer Travis Tritt. Soon afterwards they ended years of speculation by agreeing to reform, and a live show was recorded for MTV, featuring 11 songs from the back catalogue. Introducing the first number, Frey quipped, "For the record, we never broke up – we just took a 14-year vacation". The performance and four new studio tracks, including the singles 'Get Over It' and 'Love Will Keep Us Alive', appeared on *Hell Freezes Over* (1994), and the group played live dates in the USA and Europe during the next two years.

READ *The Long Run* (1995), Marc Shapiro

FAN Wasted Times, L & M, 401 N. 6th St, #108, McAllen, Texas 78504, USA

SURF members.aol.com/ivyrain/fastlane.htm

" **The theme of all our albums...** is looking for **it**, whether **it** be a woman, or peace of mind, or satisfaction, or success, riches or happiness, or any of that "

Don Henley

EARTH WIND & FIRE ✪✪

WHO Vocals/drums **Maurice White** (b. 19 Dec 1941, Chicago, Illinois, USA), vocals/percussion **Philip Bailey** (b. 8 May 1951, Denver, Colorado, USA), bass **Verdine White** (b. 25 Jul 1951), percussion **Ralph Johnson** (b. 4 Jul 1951)

WHEN 1970–

WHERE Los Angeles, California, USA

WHAT Excitement, wonder & Funk

Although their spangly symbolism suggested otherworldly origins, Earth Wind & Fire came from White's frustrated ambition. After a 1962–1967 tenure as 'staff drummer' at R&B label Chess (he'd played with Ramsey 'The In Crowd' Lewis), he formed The Salty Peppers, which evolved into EWF. Debut *Earth Wind And Fire* and *The Need Of Love* (both 1971) were under-purchased.

More profitable were acquiring singing percussionist Bailey (other associates included future solo sax star Ronnie Laws), defecting from Warner to CBS for *Last Days And Time* (1972), charting with *Head To The Sky* (1973), growing with *Open Our Eyes* (1974), exploding with US No.1 'Shining Star', and competing with the similarly spectacular but markedly less spiritual George Clinton. ("Earth, Wind and no Fire," he sniped.)

EWF rejuvenated Ramsey Lewis' career with *Sun Goddess* (1974), scored US No.1s with 1975's *That's The Way Of The World* and *Gratitude*, and broke the UK with 'Saturday Nite' from *Spirit* (1976). For two years, they ruled: *All 'N All* (1977) sold millions; protegées The Emotions scored with 'Best Of My Love' and EWF collaboration 'Boogie Wonderland'; Michael Jackson took notes at their magical shows; and the silver lining of celluloid raincloud *Sgt. Pepper's Lonely Hearts Club Band* (1978) was EWF's Fab-Funked 'Got To Get You Into My Life'. *The Best Of…* (1978), *I Am* (1979), *Faces* (1980) and *Raise* (1981) kept hits coming, but the band cracked amid White's extra-curricular productions.

EWF's *Powerlight* (1983) and *Electric Universe* (1984) were eclipsed by Bailey's solo career, which peaked with the 1984 Phil Collins duet 'Easy Lover'. White successfully resurrected EWF for *Touch The World* (1987), after which *Heritage* (1990), *The Eternal Dance* (1992), *Millennium* (1993) and *In The Name Of Love* (1997) kept the band on the road and in the hearts of the faithful.

 www.ewf.org/

EAST 17 ☉

WHO Vocals **Tony Mortimer** (b. 21 Oct 1970, Stepney, London, England), vocals **Terry Coldwell** (b. 21 Jul 1974, Islington, London), vocals **John Hendy** (b. 26 Mar 1971, Barking, Essex, England), vocals **Brian Harvey** (b. 8 Aug 1974, Edmonton, London)

WHEN 1990–

WHERE Walthamstow, London, England

WHAT The Rolling Stones to Take That's Beatles

Hellbent on stardom, Tony Mortimer badgered Pet Shop Boys manager Tom Watkins for a gig. Watkins offered him a job as a dancer for Faith Hope & Charity (featuring TV starlet Dani Behr), before being convinced by Mortimer's demo 'Deep'. Drafting in schoolfriends John, Brian and Terry, the band signed to London Records on April Fool's Day 1992. Drug connotations forced the expansion of original moniker E17 (their hometown postcode), but proved no obstacle to Top 10 debut 'House Of Love' from *Walthamstow* (1993). Harvey cemented their 'bad boy' image with a cannabis bust. *Steam* (1994) spawned the UK No.1 'Stay Another Day', but *Up All Night* (1995) was overshadowed by reported dissension. After classy Gabrielle duet 'If You Ever' and hit collection *Around The World* (1996), Harvey was sacked for endorsing Ecstasy and Mortimer quit to join Sub Zero. With Harvey reinstated, East 17 began 1998 looking for a new deal.

read *East 17 Talkback* (1995), Carl Jenkins

fan The K-9 Club, PO Box 153, Stanmore, Middlesex, HA7 2HF, UK

surf oracle.dsuper.net/~pfte/

ECHO & THE BUNNYMEN

WHO Vocals **Ian McCulloch** (b. 5 May 1959, Liverpool, England), guitar **Will Sergeant** (b. 12 Apr 1958, Liverpool), bass **Les Pattinson** (b. 18 Apr 1958, Liverpool), drums **Pete De Freitas** (b. 2 Aug 1961, Port of Spain, Trinidad, d. 15 Jun 1989, Liverpool)

WHEN 1978–

WHERE Liverpool, Merseyside, England

WHAT Romantic, psychedelic, post-Punk weird Pop

Alongside fellow Liverpudlians The Teardrop Explodes, The Icicle Works and Pete Wylie's various Wah! incarnations, Echo & The Bunnymen led Liverpool's early 80s 'Neopsychedelia' scene. After a brief stint with Julian Cope and Wylie as The Crucial Three, McCulloch met fellow Doors fan Sergeant in 1978 and started writing songs with a drum machine christened 'Echo'. Pattinson was recruited and the trio (plus Echo) made their live debut as Echo & The Bunnymen at Liverpool club Eric's in late 1978.

After 'The Pictures On My Wall', on Liverpool's Zoo label, and 'Monkeys', on a Liverpool scene compilation in 1979, they signed to Sire and replaced Echo with De Freitas for 'Rescue' in 1980. Produced by Liverpool luminaries Ian Broudie (Big In Japan and The Lightning Seeds), Bill Drummond (Big In Japan, founder of Zoo, the group's manager and later half of KLF) and Dave Balfe (The Teardrop Explodes), *Crocodiles* (1980) was an immediate success, fusing the tense darkness of early 80s Indie with classic

Pop, as in 'Do It Clean' (later covered by Hole). This musical clash was mirrored by apocalyptic stage sets and army clothing.

Heaven Up Here (1981) gave the group their first US success. A dark, experimental set, its self-conscious atmospherics were eclipsed by *Porcupine* (1983), the Bunnymen's breakthrough, with glittering psychedelic Pop and Eastern strings on hits 'The Back Of Love' and 'The Cutter'. The group toured extensively, even playing in the remote Scottish Hebrides in July 1983, where McCulloch fought with a local over his ballet shoes. *Ocean Rain* (1984), even more successful than *Porcupine*, showed a focused, romantic style on the classic 'The Killing Moon'. After hits set *Songs To Learn And Sing* (1985), they crumbled, with De Freitas and McCulloch experiencing drug problems. When De Freitas disappeared on a drug-fuelled road trip, he was replaced by ex-Haircut 100 drummer Blair Cunningham for 1986's tours. In 1987, after a lacklustre cover of The Doors' 'People Are Strange' on *The Lost Boys* soundtrack, *Echo And The Bunnymen,* having been recorded twice, was released – their biggest international hit, yet possibly their weakest effort, save for brilliant single 'The Game'.

After 1988's tour with New Order, McCulloch quit to start a largely unsuccessful solo career and was replaced by Noel Burke. De Freitas, tragically killed in a motorcycle accident in Liverpool, was also replaced, by Damon Reece, for the heavily psychedelic *Reverberation* (1990) before they split up. After two solo albums, Sergeant reunited with McCulloch in Electrafixion for *Burned* (1995). Then, Echo & The Bunnymen re-formed with Pattinson, drummer Michael Lee and Owen Vyse on keyboards for *Evergreen* (1997), yielding 'Nothing Lasts Forever'. An anthology, *Ballyhoo* (1997), included most of their 80s singles.

READ *Never Stop* (1989), Dave Thompson

FAN Chris Adams/Watchtower, PO Box 471, Cambridge, MA 02142-0004, USA

SURF www.dez.com/doug/bunnymen.html

ECHOBELLY

WHO Vocals **Sonya Aurora Madan**, guitar **Glenn Johansson**, bass **Alex Keyser**, drums **Andy Henderson** (b. 4 Aug 1966)

WHEN 1993–

WHERE London, England

WHAT Sparky Indie Pop

Echobelly's curious mix of characters made them press darlings and Morrissey favourites (his former group The Smiths were an evident influence). With a Swedish skinhead (Glenn Johansson), black lesbian (ex-Curve guitarist Debbie Smith, b. 6 Aug 1968, London England) and female Asian singer, column inches flowed. The well-received debut EP 'Bellyache' (1993) was followed by the hit album *Everybody's Got One* (1994). A 'double-header' tour with Oasis increased their coverage and 'I Can't Imagine The World Without Me' made it to the UK Top 40. This success was boosted by *On* (1995) and hits 'Car Fiction' and 'Great Things'. Legal wranglings forced an eighteen-month break before they came back with *Lustra* (1997); afterwards, Smith departed.

FAN More, 29 Auchinbaird, Salichie, FK10 3HA, Scotland, UK

SURF www.urban.or.jb/home/echobell/

DUANE EDDY

WHO b. 26 Apr 1938, Corning, New York, USA

WHAT The titan of 'Twang'

Eddy's revolutionary 'twangy' guitar sound (achieved by playing the bass strings of his Gretsch through an echo chamber) was first successful on minor hit 'Moovin' N' Groovin" in 1958. More transatlantic hits followed: the million-selling 'Rebel-Rouser' (1958), 'Forty Miles Of Bad Road', 'Peter Gunn' (both 1959), 'Shazam' and string-filled movie theme 'Because They're Young' (both 1960), all featuring fellow Arizona-based musicians Steve Douglas (sax) and Mike Bermani (drums) from Kip Tyler's Flips, who became his backing band The Rebels. Mostly composed with producer Lee Hazlewood, many songs featured a rocking sax break and 'rebel yells' from The Sharps (aka The Rivingtons).

Despite many appearances on Dick Clark's US TV shows, he was more popular in Britain. The first Rock instrumentalist to reach superstardom (and probably the first to record in stereo), Eddy added to his UK hit tally after US popularity waned, returning to the UK Top 10 with a reworking of 'Peter Gunn' (with Art Of Noise) in 1986. Added to the Rock And Roll Hall Of Fame in 1994, this influential guitarist's music appeared on hit soundtracks *Forrest Gump*, *Natural Born Killers* (both 1994) and *Broken Arrow* (1996).

ECHOBELLY/KEVIN CUMMINS-LH

DAVE EDMUNDS

WHO b. 15 April 1944, Cardiff, Wales

WHAT Rockabilly guitarist, singer, producer and songwriter

Inspired by early Rock 'n' Roll, Edmunds formed The Human Beanz, which became Love Sculpture in 1967, and split up in 1969. He began a solo career with hit covers 'I Hear You Knockin'' (UK No.1, 1971), 'Baby I Love You' (1972) and 'Born To Be With You' (1973) and built Rockfield studios in Wales, where he produced artists like Del Shannon and The Flamin' Groovies.

Recording the soundtrack and starring in *Stardust* (1974), he united with bassist Nick Lowe. They played on each other's 70s records including Edmunds' *Tracks On Wax* (1979), with hits 'Girls Talk' (written by Elvis Costello) and 'Queen Of Hearts'. They also formed the short-lived Rockpile in 1980, for *Seconds Of Pleasure*. Success in the 80s came as a producer, waggling faders for The Stray Cats, k.d. lang and The Everly Brothers, and twanging guitar for Paul McCartney. In 1990, he played in a John Lennon tribute concert in Liverpool and fronted an all-star revue band on *Closer To The Flame*. In 1996, he recorded 'It Doesn't Matter Anymore' for tribute album *notfadeaway: remembering buddy holly*.

EELS

WHO Vocals/guitar/keyboards **Mark 'E' Everett** (b. Virginia, USA), bass/vocals **Tommy Walter**, drums/vocals **Butch Norton**

WHEN 1995–

WHERE Los Angeles, California, USA

WHAT 'Surreel'

Trouble magnet Everett – having troubled few cash registers with flop solo albums *A Man Called E* (1992) and *Broken Toy Shop* (1993) – formed eels with Norton and Walter in 1995. Signed and produced by Michael Simpson (A&R man for Geffen subsidiary Dreamworks and half of Beck's producers The Dust Brothers), the surreal dirge 'Novocaine For The Soul' went Top 10 and *Beautiful Freak* (1996) went platinum. After a Lollapalooza stint and further hits, Walter came clean about the obvious (and hotly-denied) Beck influence; oddly, he was an eel no longer after 1997. Everett's co-writer Mark Goldenberg contributed to *Left Of The Middle* (1997) by Australian songstress Natalie Imbruglia. Eels endorsees, revealed Everett, include Tricky: "He said, 'You guys are dope'. Or maybe he said, 'You guys are dopes'."

surf rawk.simplenet.com/eels/

808 STATE

WHO Keyboards **Graham Massey** (b. 4 Aug 1960), keyboards **Andrew Barker** (b. 9 Mar 1968), keyboards **Darren Partington** (b. 1 Nov 1969)

WHEN 1988–

WHERE Manchester, England

WHAT Techno innovators

Formed by Graham Massey, Martin Price and DJ Gerald Simpson, 808 State (named after a drum machine) issued the experimental *Newbuild* (1988) before scoring a first hit with 1989's epic 'Pacific State' from *Quadrastate*. Inspired by Acid House, they blended guitars, synthesized saxophones and production tricks with Techno. Simpson left for solo success as A Guy Called Gerald but, with DJs Andrew Barker and Darren Partington, and the explosion of 'Madchester', 808 crossed over to an Indie audience with 1990's 'Cubik' and – with Rapper MC Tunes – 'The Only Rhyme That Bites' and the Stone Roses-pilfering 'Tunes Splits The Atom'.

808 STATE:MATT ANKER:RETNA ©

Price left before *EX:EL* (1991), featuring New Order's Bernard Sumner and Björk, for whom Massey later co-wrote and produced *Post* (1995). Now established remixers (employers included David Bowie, The Shamen, Primal Scream and Electronic), 1992's *Gorgeous* was more sumptuous (but less commercially successful), while the fan club-only *State To State* returned to pure danceability. With cameos from Manic Street Preachers' James Dean Bradfield and Icelandic vocalist Ragga, *Don Solaris* (1996) saw their reputation grow. Tunes reappeared in 1997 with The Dust Junkys.

surf www.808state.com

EINSTÜRZENDE NEUBAUTEN

WHO **Blixa Bargeld** (b. 12 Jan 1959, Berlin, Germany), **Marc Chung**, Alexander Van Borsig, N.U.Unruh, F.M.Einheit

WHEN 1980–

WHERE Berlin, Germany

WHAT Industrial-strength Industrialists

Originating from the Berlin arts group Geniale Dilletanten, Einstürzende Neubauten (German for 'Collapsing New Buildings') picked up where Faust and Throbbing Gristle left off, taking abrasive Industrial noise to extremes with mangled guitars, scrap metal and power tools. After early performances on Berlin's streets (the sound of Blixa Bargeld hurling himself at a concrete bridge has to be heard to be believed), they poured the whole terrifying mess into early albums *Kollaps* (1981), *Drawings Of Patient O.T.* (1983), *Strategies Against Architecture* (1984) and the excellent *Half-Man* (1985). Though slowed in the 90s by Bargeld's part-time role as guitarist with Nick Cave & The Bad Seeds, Neubauten's uncompromising approach proved inspirational to Nine Inch Nails and continued with 1997's *Ende Neu*, which featured guest remixers John Spencer and Alec Empire.

fan Einstürzende Neubauten, PO Box 20207, London Terrace Station, New York, NY 10011, USA

joined in 1996. A long period of inactivity followed, punctuated only by Welch's side project (with Blur's Alex James and Stephen Duffy) Me Me Me and Frischmann's live appearance as part of avant-garde supergroup The Brood and with Suede.

surf www.actwin.com/lineup/

ELECTRIC LIGHT ORCHESTRA ◉◉

WHO Vocals/guitar/keyboards **Jeff Lynne** (b. 30 Dec 1947, Birmingham, England), bass/vocals **Kelly Groucutt** (b. 8 Sep 1945, Birmingham), drums **Bev Bevan** (b. 25 Nov 1946, Birmingham), keyboards **Richard Tandy** (b. 26 Mar 1948, Birmingham), violin **Mik Kaminski** (b. 2 Sep 1951, Harrogate, England), cello **Melvyn Gale** (b. 15 Jan 1952, London, England), cello **Hugh McDowell** (b. 31 Jul 1953, London, England)

WHEN 1971–

WHERE Birmingham, England

WHAT Beethoven meets The Beatles

Electric Light Orchestra began as the brainchild of Roy Wood, who envisioned an ambitious new outfit combining Classical and electric instruments. He recruited admired songwriter Lynne to the final incarnation of his band The Move, and the pair plotted its transmogrification into ELO. With horns and violin augmenting the multi-instrumental talents of both frontmen – which stretched to woodwind and piano as well as guitar, bass

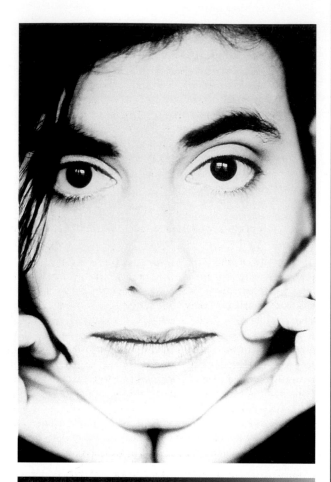

ELASTICA ◉

WHO Vocals/guitar **Justine Frischmann** (b. 16 Sep 1969, Twickenham, England), guitar/vocals **Donna Matthews** (b. 2 Dec 1971, Newport, Wales), bass **Annie Holland** (b. 26 Aug 1965, Brighton, England), drums **Justin Welch** (b. 4 Dec 1972, Nuneaton, England)

WHEN 1992–

WHERE London, England

WHAT Punk-powered Pop

Frustrated with her marginalized role in an early incarnation of Suede, guitarist Frischmann quit, and began jamming with former occasional Suede drummer Welch in June 1992 with Justine's boyfriend – Blur's Damon Albarn – on bass. Bassist Holland arrived later in the month and, in September, guitarist Matthews completed the line-up. After flirting with several names – including Vaseline and Onk – the band settled on Elastica in 1993, releasing debut 'Stutter' in November.

Elastica (1994) saw the band become one of the most interesting and successful fixtures of the burgeoning Britpop scene, although Wire and The Stranglers took action for alleged plagiarism over hits 'Lineup' and 'Connection' (Wire's 'I Am The Fly' and 'Three Girl Rumba') and 'Waking Up' (The Stranglers' 'No More Heroes'). Holland left before an appearance on 1995's Lollapalooza tour, temporarily replaced by Abby Travis, before new bassist Sheila Chipperfield and keyboard player Dave Bush

and vocals – and Move founder Bevan on drums, their self-titled debut (aka *No Answer*) was released in 1971. It unleashed a UK hit with Lynne's '10538 Overture', but Wood was saddened that Lynne's songwriting talents were overlooked in favour of his own and, to everyone's astonishment, decided to leave in July 1972.

Bassist Michael D'Albuquerque, cellist Mike Edwards, and keyboardist Richard Tandy (a one-time Move member) were taken on to turn the studio project into a touring band. With Lynne firmly in the driving seat, ELO produced innovative albums which drew on exciting instrumentation (featuring synthesizers, multi-layered vocals and eventually full orchestras) as well as the rustic whimsy of Lynne's songwriting.

By *Face The Music* (1975), the string section had settled on two cellists (Gale and McDowell) and a violinist (Kaminski), while the extrovert Groucutt had replaced D'Albuquerque on bass. Increasing success in the States – the symphonic *Eldorado* (1974) went gold – countered faltering interest at home, which seemed to have peaked with their mock-Classical make-over of 'Roll Over Beethoven' (1973). But with Lynne's output becoming punchier and the band's string-driven sound finally percolating the British airwaves, they began to deliver on their early promise. In the latter half of the 70s, hits like 'Evil Woman' (1975), 'Telephone Line' (1977), 'Mr Blue Sky' (1978) and 'The Diary Of Horace Wimp' (1979) made ELO a near-constant chart presence, and *A New World Record* (1976) brought them their first UK gold disc.

Out Of The Blue (1977) was their most complete statement so far, and its follow-up, *Discovery* (1979), rose to No.1 on a tide of ELOmania. Although the creative edge was slipping, there was enough momentum to generate a No.1, 'Xanadu' (with Olivia Newton-John), and another best-seller, *Time* (1981). After *Secret Messages* (1983), Bevan quit to join Black Sabbath, Groucutt sued for back pay and Lynne called it a day, later establishing himself as a producer, working with the three Beatles in the 90s, and recording as a Traveling Wilbury.

There was one final flowering of ELO when Lynne, Bevan and Tandy reunited for *Balance of Power* (1986). Bevan subsequently tried to lead his own ELO Part 2, but their self-titled album (1991) and accompanying tour failed to create much interest.

> "ELO had to be the most boring band in the world to work with. It was like working with old age pensioners"
>
> Sharon 'Mrs Ozzy' Osbourne

 www.hk.super.net/~bluesky

ELECTRONIC

WHO Vocals/guitar/keyboards **Bernard Sumner** (b. Bernard Dicken, 4 Jan 1956, Salford, England), guitar/keyboards **Johnny Marr** (b. John Maher, 31 Oct 1963, Ardwick, England)

WHEN 1989–

WHERE Manchester, England

WHAT House beats and jangly Pop

Ex-Smiths guitarist Johnny Marr and New Order's singer Bernard Sumner are the painfully slow-working Electronic, intended initially as a side project. 'Getting Away With It' (1989) – the first of five Top 20 hits – featured Pet Shop Boy Neil Tennant and combined Marr's knack for ingenious chords and jangly guitars with Sumner's trademark synthesized melancholy. Electronic promised great things with 'Get The Message' in 1991 and their eponymous debut album peaked at UK No.2. After a lengthy break to accommodate New Order's *Republic* (1993) and Marr's collaboration with The The, Electronic reconvened with ex-Kraftwerk member Karl Bartos for *Raise The Pressure* (1996), a predictably tasteful collection of House beats and jangly Pop.

surf slashmc.rice.edu/ceremony/electronic/electronic.html

EMERSON LAKE & PALMER ⊙

WHO Vocals/guitar/bass **Greg Lake** (b. 10 Nov 1948, Bournemouth, England), keyboards **Keith Emerson** (b. 2 Nov 1944, Todmorden, Yorkshire, England), drums/percussion **Carl Palmer** (b. 20 Mar 1947, Birmingham, England)

WHEN 1970–

WHERE England

WHAT Progressive Rock supergroup

Lake came from King Crimson, Palmer from Atomic Rooster and Emerson from The Nice: a combination of musical ability and Rock roots that took Emerson, Lake & Palmer into the growing market for Progressive Rock. They recorded Classical works in a Rock style, composed music with complex structures and timings and delivered the lot live with showmanship that kept crowds enthralled over 20-minute tracks.

DJ Alan Freeman helped to push UK hit albums, including *Emerson, Lake And Palmer* (1970), the No.1 *Tarkus* (1971), *Pictures At An Exhibition* (1971), *Trilogy* (1972) and *Brain Salad Surgery* (1973). Sales were also impressive in the USA, with the live triple *Welcome Back My Friends To The Show That Never Ends, Ladies And Gentlemen… Emerson, Lake And Palmer* (1974) topping its predecessors with a No.4 place.

What their fans saw as ambition, others saw as arrogance. The title of the live album was – apparently – a deliberate attempt to give chart compilers a typographical problem from a band who took high chart placings for granted.

EMF

WHO Vocals **James Atkin** (b. 28 Mar 1969, Cinderford, England), guitar **Ian Dench** (b. 7 Aug 1964, Cheltenham, England), keyboards **Derry Brownson** (b. 10 Nov 1970, Gloucester, England), bass **Zachary Foley** (b. 9 Dec 1970, Gloucester), drums **Mark Decloedt** (b. 26 Jun 1969, Gloucester)

WHEN 1989–1995

WHERE Cinderford, Gloucestershire, England

WHAT The short-lived emperors of Indie Dance

EMF found themselves in the UK Top 3 with 'Unbelievable' less than a year after playing their first concert. *Schubert Dip* (1991) attracted controversy over the song 'Lies', which contained a sample of John Lennon's assassin, Mark Chapman, reciting from Lennon's 'Watching The Wheels'; resulting in an out-of-court settlement to Yoko Ono and the sample's removal.

'Unbelievable' topped the US charts. Subsequent albums *Stigma* (1992) and *Cha Cha Cha* (1995) failed to match this success, but EMF scored a final UK hit with their 1995 version of The Monkees' 'I'm A Believer', featuring vocals by British comedy duo Vic Reeves and Bob Mortimer. Although EMF disappeared out of sight, appreciation for them lives on in some unlikely people, such as Pavement's Steve Malkmus.

The self-indulgent *Works* (1977) compiled solo work with new ELP tracks, including an unlikely UK No.2 with a reworking of Aaron Copeland's 'Fanfare For The Common Man'. The hit notwithstanding, Emerson Lake & Palmer were rapidly losing touch with Rock fans and critical support. *Love Beach* (1978) was song-based, flirted with Disco and hit the bargain bins after staggering into the lower reaches of the chart. General opinion was that ELP were finished and *In Concert* (1979) made sense only as a contractual obligation.

The early 80s brought a handful of solo projects and Palmer's high-profile addition to the ranks of AOR specialists Asia. ELP's influence on Rock appeared minimal and their collective past appeared to inhibit the solo careers of Emerson and Lake. The advent of CD and a market for classic Rock invigorated sales to a small degree and in 1986 Cozy Powell was drafted in to drum on a new album and tour – maintaining the ELP moniker and some of the classic sound. Songwriter Robert Berry joined for *To The Power Of Three* (1988), their least successful release.

However, by 1992, 70s Rock dinosaurs were undergoing something of a rehabilitation and the original trio reformed for *Black Moon* (1992), *Live At The Royal Albert Hall* (1993) and *In The Hot Seat* (1994), all rockier and more concise than the classic work, but drawing heavily on ELP's established style. Touring and high-profile repackaging in the form of the massive *Return Of The Manticore* (1993) also rallied the faithful. There is a certain irony that a band labelled as 'Progressive' should find themselves trading off a sound that is little changed in over 25 years, but ELP's 90s return has re-established the musical credentials of an outfit which helped define Prog Rock and break through boundaries between music genres.

surf www.dynrec.com/el

EMI

Electric and Musical Industries Ltd was founded in 1931 when competitors The Graphophone Company and The Columbia Gramophone Company settled their differences with a merger – an agreement traced to 1897. However, an EMI label was not established until 1972, when Marc Bolan's 'Metal Guru' became the new imprint's first hit.

EMI used HMV, Columbia, Parlophone and, from 1969, Harvest as its main labels until HMV was re-established as a Classical label and problems were encountered with the lack of worldwide rights for Columbia. EMI launched Pilot, Steve Harley & Cockney Rebel and Queen alongside established stars Cliff Richard and The Shadows, who transferred from the Columbia label. Kate Bush, The Sex Pistols (who wrote the vitriolic 'EMI' about their brief association), Olivia Newton-John, Sheena Easton, Whitesnake, Iron Maiden, The Rolling Stones, Duran Duran and Diana Ross were subsequent signings.

In the 90s, Eternal, Shampoo, Chumbawamba, Terrorvision and Louise, plus former Harvest stalwarts Pink Floyd, head the EMI roster. The company's interest in Chrysalis, Capitol, Virgin and Apple meant that Smashing Pumpkins and Garth Brooks joined perennial money-spinners The Beatles in EMI's 100th Birthday shenanigans in 1997.

> "By and large what I write is a
> ## figment of my imagination
> and it has to be fairy-tale-like"
>
> Greg Lake

EN VOGUE

WHO Vocals **Terry Ellis** (b. 5 Sep 1966, Houston, Texas, USA), vocals **Cindy Herron** (b. 26 Sep 1965, San Francisco, California, USA), vocals **Maxine Jones** (b. 16 Jan 1965, Paterson, New Jersey, USA), vocals **Dawn Robinson** (b. 28 Nov 1968, New London, Connecticut, USA)

WHEN 1988–

WHERE Oakland, California, USA

WHAT Funky divas

One-hit wonders with Timex Social Club and Club Nouveau, producers Denzil Foster and Thomas McElroy scored third time out with a group inspired by platinum gals Exposé. En Vogue's debut *Born To Sing* (1990) yielded three No.1s on the US R&B chart, one of which – 'Hold On' – became an international success. As charts were swamped by similar 'New Jill Swing' acts, En Vogue set fresh standards with the triple-platinum Curtis Mayfield-flavoured *Funky Divas* (1992), duetted with Salt-N-Pepa on the fabulous 'Whatta Man' and acrimoniously supported Luther Vandross. Amid split rumours, they temporarily disbanded (hence Ellis' 1995 solo *Southern Gal*), but returned in

style with 1997's transatlantic chart limpet 'Don't Let Go (Love)'. Robinson departed (reappearing with Rap supergroup The Firm) and the remaining trio released *EV3* (1997).

surf www.elektra.com/randb_club/en_vogue/envogue.html

BRIAN ENO

WHO b. Brian Peter George St John Le Baptiste de la Salle Eno, 15 May 1948, Woodbridge, Suffolk, England

WHAT "Non-musician", producer, artist

Born into a line of postmen, Eno broke with family tradition and forayed into Pop – a tape of poetry and slow-motion metallic clangs – in 1965, while studying at Winchester College of Art.

Although raised on Doo Wop and Rock 'n' Roll, he took his working methods (repetition, improvisation, chance discovery) from avant-garde artists La Monte Young, John Cage and Steve Reich. He graduated through early bands Merchant Taylor's Simultaneous Cabinet and Maxwell Demon to Cornelius Cardew's Scratch Orchestra (participating in 1971's *The Great Learning*) and The Portsmouth Sinfonia, whose varying competence made notorious their versions of popular Classical

pieces. He later produced the Sinfonia's *The Popular Classics* (1973) and *Hallelujah* (1974).

Eno co-founded Roxy Music in 1971 with fellow Winchester alumnus Andy Mackay, mangling their sound through his synthesizers on *Roxy Music* (1972) and *For Your Pleasure* (1973). After the on-stage realization that he was thinking more about his laundry than his playing, Eno quit. His first post-Roxy release was 1973's *No Pussyfooting*, on which Robert Fripp's guitars were 'sculpted' with Eno's tape delays and filters. Further collaborators included Cluster (1977's *Cluster And Eno* and 1978's *After The Heat*) and Nico, John Cale and Kevin Ayers (1974's *June 1, 1974*).

The skewed Pop of Eno's 1974 solo debut, *Here Come The Warm Jets* (a euphemism for urinating), featuring Fripp, Chris Spedding and Eno's Roxy pals, was followed by spiky *Taking Tiger Mountain (By Strategy)* in 1975. Ill-health forced a rest, prompting the calmer *Another Green World* (1975). Further convalescence – he was knocked down by a car – led seemingly accident-prone Eno to invent Ambient, casting himself as planner rather than musician on loop-laden *Discreet Music* (1975), a blueprint refined on the 'Ambient' series: *Music For Airports* (1978), *The Plateaux Of Mirror* (1980), *Day Of Radiance* (1980) and *On Land* (1982). Developing this 'systems' approach, in 1975 Eno and artist Peter Schmidt devised 'Oblique Strategies', a set of *I Ching*-like cards with instructions and solutions, designed to ease creative crises.

The edgier *Before And After Science* (1977) coincided with Eno's first superstar production work, which often extended to co-writing. Unions with David Bowie (the classic 'Berlin' trilogy) and Talking Heads preceded the African-influenced David Byrne collaboration *My Life In The Bush Of Ghosts* (1981). In 1978, he compiled the EP 'No New York', showcasing DNA, Mars, Teenage

Jesus & The Jerks and The Contortions – representatives of New York's underground No Wave scene. Other notable credits include Ultravox!'s eponymous 1978 debut and Devo's *Q: Are We Not Men? A: We Are Devo!* (1977). In the 80s, Eno garnered awards for atmospheric productions (with long-time associate Daniel Lanois) on U2's *The Unforgettable Fire* (1984) and *The Joshua Tree* (1987), on which his idiosyncrasies became the mainstream. Further albums with Lanois, by brother Roger Eno, Harold Budd and Michael Brook were fruits of his production company, Opal.

Returning to Pop with the John Cale collaboration *Wrong Way Up* (1990), he was lauded for the resurgence of Ambient as a Dance sub-genre (courtesy of The Orb, System 7 and Future Sound Of London) and U2's electronic rebirth on *Achtung Baby* (1991) and *Zooropa* (1993). Solo releases continued with the acclaimed *Nerve Net* (1992), *The Shutov Assembly* (1992), *Neroli* (1993) and the Derek Jarman soundtrack *Glitterbug* (1994), later released in modified form as the Eno/Jah Wobble album *Spinner* (1995). His 1995 work – including David Bowie's *Outside*, U2's *Passengers*, an art exhibition with Laurie Anderson and a student group and the *Generative Music* CD ROM (1996) – was chronicled in the excellent book *A Year (With Swollen Appendices)*, the highlights of Eno's diary, with added essays and stories. In 1997, Eno and family moved temporarily to St Petersburg, Russia, but recording continued with *The Drop* (1997).

Read *A Year (With Swollen Appendices)* (1996), Brian Eno

Surf www.hyperreal.org/music/artists/brian_eno/

ENYA ⊙

WHO b. Eithne Ni Bhraonain, 17 May 1961, Gweedore, County Donegal, Ireland

WHAT Ethereal Pop hymns

Enya (a phonetic spelling of her first name Eithne) broadened her traditional Gaelic background when she studied Classical music at school. Clannad – a group comprising two of her brothers, two uncles and a sister – provided a platform for her keyboard skills, but after two years she left the band, together with manager Nicky Ryan. An unconventional talent, isolated from all contemporary Rock and Pop influence, she was given time and space to develop when Ryan and his wife Roma invited her to live and work in their Dublin house/studio. Rewards came when a score for David Puttnam's 1985 film *The Frog Prince* led to her first solo album, *Enya*, in 1987, including music composed for a UK TV series, later re-packaged as *The Celts* (1992). Her first WEA release was *Watermark* (1988), which gave her the UK No.1 'Orinoco Flow' and wider exposure when tracks were used in the films *Green Card* (1990), *LA Story* (1991) and *Far And Away* (1992).

Despite not touring, Enya's appeal was reaching a peak, and *Shepherd Moons* (1991) sold over 4 million copies in the USA and topped the UK charts. Having perfected a unique sound, no attempt was made to change the winning formula: the waves of calming harmonies changed little from one album to the next.

The Memory Of Trees (1995), despite the wait, contributed to a staggering total career sale of 33 million albums. *Paint The Sky With Stars: The Best Of Enya* was released in 1997.

Fan Enya Fan Club, Jim Waters, 282, Briar Road, Bellingham, WA 98225, USA

Surf sunsite.auc.dk/enya/main.htm

BRIAN ENO/MARTIN GOODACRE-RETNA

Brian Epstein

It's hard to conceive of a world where The Beatles never happened, but without Brian Epstein (b. 19 Sep 1934, Liverpool, England, d. 27 Aug 1967) such a world would be a likelihood. They were local heroes when the Liverpool record shop owner, intrigued by customer requests, had his world rocked by one of their lunchtime performances at The Cavern in November 1961. A month later, Epstein insisted he become their manager and The Beatles' bumpy career turned skywards. Fair and loyal, Epstein upped the ante in concert fees and contractual freedom, and rewrote the rule book to deal with the unprecedented phenomenon he'd helped unleash. Though often remembered for his failures, such as the loss of The Beatles' merchandising rights, Epstein's tenacity and perceptiveness were essential ingredients in the group's success.

Three days before his contract with The Beatles was up for renewal, Epstein, manager of the world's most successful band, died alone of an accidental drugs overdose. Others also rose to stardom under his tutelage: Gerry & The Pacemakers, Billy J. Kramer and Cilla Black.

READ A Cellarful Of Noise (1964), Brian Epstein & Derek Taylor

ERASURE ⊙⊙⊙⊙⊙

WHO Vocals **Andy Bell** (b. 25 Apr 1964, Peterborough, Cambridgeshire, England), keyboards/guitar **Vince Clarke** (b. 3 Jul 1960, South Woodford, London, England)

WHEN 1985–

WHERE London, England

WHAT The Status Quo of Synth Pop

Vince Clarke – shy synth-prodder in Depeche Mode, Yazoo and The Assembly – intended to record a solo album using various vocalists. One applicant was flamboyant Andy Bell, whose voice was strikingly similar to Alison Moyet, Clarke's partner in Yazoo. Signed to Mute, 'Who Needs Love like That?' was a minor hit and *Wonderland* (1986) scraped the lower reaches of the UK chart. Tireless touring paid off: *The Circus* (1987) followed 'Sometimes' to the Top 10 and made inroads in the US – a process completed when 'Chains Of Love' from the UK chart-topping *The Innocents* (1988) reached US No.12. Meanwhile, the 'Crackers International' EP sold over half a million in Britain and BRIT awards beckoned.

    Wild! (1989) and *Chorus* (1991) kept hits coming and 1992's 'Abba-esque' EP (led by an electronic 'Take A Chance On Me') hit new heights of camp. Bell was already notorious for flamboyant stagewear (a rubber leotard, Dr Marten boots encrusted with rubies, etc). Now Clarke was coaxed from his shadow as the duo dressed as Abba's Agnetha and Frida for the video, scored their first UK No.1 in July 1992 and prompted the Abba tribute band Björn Again's 'Erasure-ish' EP. Singles set *Pop!* (1992) and *I Say I Say I Say* (1994) were No.1s, but *Erasure* (1995) and *Cowboy* (1997) showed their synthesized Disco beginning to wane.

fan All Through The Years, 96 St Albans Road, Arnold, Nottingham, NG5 6GW, UK

surf www.gac.edu/~dlundber/erasure.html

GLORIA ESTEFAN ⊙⊙

WHO b. Gloria Maria Fajardo, 1 Sep 1957, Havana, Cuba

WHAT Latina diva

The daughter of a Cuban revolutionary, Gloria evolved from a shy teenager keen on psychology to Latin music's biggest crossover success story. She was propelled into the spotlight by Emilio Estefan, whose band The Miami Latin Boys were rechristened Miami Sound Machine on her arrival in 1975. *Live Again/Renacer* (1977), *Miami Sound Machine* (1978), *Imported* (1979), *Otra Vez* (1981), *Rio* (1982) and *A Toda Maquina* (1984) made them Latin music stars, prompting Emilio (now Gloria's husband) to set sights on English-speaking record-buyers. 'Dr Beat' from *Eyes Of Innocence* (1984) and 'Conga' from *Primitive Love* (1986) achieved the dream and made his wife a global star – by *Let It Loose* (1987) they were billed as Gloria Estefan & Miami Sound Machine.

    The US No.1 'Anything For You' proved Gloria as adept at Madonna-esque ballads as bouncy Latinbeat, returning her to the UK Top 10 (where *Let It Loose* was repackaged as the No.1 *Anything For You*); subsequent albums were credited to her alone. After her commercial peak *Cuts Both Ways* (1989) – a UK No.1 and source of the US No.1 'Don't Wanna Lose You' – Gloria survived a near fatal coach crash, returning with another US No.1, 'Coming Out Of The Dark', from *Into The Light* (1991). *Greatest Hits* (1992) and *Christmas Through Your Eyes* (1993) rounded off her global popularity. She went Spanish again for *Mi Tierra* (1993) and *Abriendo Puertas* (1995), while covers set *Hold*

Me, Thrill Me, Kiss Me (1994) returned her to transatlantic Top 10s. Confirming her international profile, she performed the Olympic theme 'Reach', from *Destiny* (1996), at the Atlanta games.

READ *Gloria Estefan: The Pop Superstar From Tragedy To Triumph* (1997), Anthony M. DeStefano

surf www.almetco.com/estefan/gloria-1.html

ETERNAL

WHO Vocals **Easther Bennett** (b. 11 Dec 1972, Croydon, south London, England), vocals **Vernie Bennett** (b. Vernett Bennett, 17 May 1971, Croydon), vocals **Kéllé Bryan** (b. 12 Mar 1975, south London)

WHEN 1992–

WHERE London, England

WHAT South London Soul sensations

While predecessors like Mica Paris floundered, Eternal have kept home-grown British Soul alive. They hit big with UK No.4 'Stay', the first of six singles that kept *Always And Forever* (1993) on the UK chart for over a year. Stateside success – bar a Top 20 entry with 'Stay' in 1994 – proved elusive, blamed in some quarters on the credibility-dampening presence of white co-vocalist Louise Nurding. Her exit in mid-1995 for solo sauciness proved a mere flicker of the Eternal flame: *Power Of A Woman* (1995) spawned five UK Top 10 hits and *Before The Rain* (1997) yielded the UK chart-topping 'I Wanna Be The Only One', featuring Soul veteran and long-time Eternal contributor Bebe Winans. It paved the way for *Greatest Hits* (1997), released amid strenuously denied split rumours. Undaunted by such scandal, Easther Bennett expressed a wish to "try something really wacky" next time out: "A duet with The Prodigy or anything like that...."

Fan PO Box 460, High Wycombe, Buckinghamshire, HP12 4BR, UK

surf eternal.electronic.co.uk/

Eurovision Song Contest

Long before the European Union, international boundaries were challenged by Pop power. The European Broadcasting Union (dubbed 'Eurovision') needed a show that would, for one evening, unite Europe. Inspired by Italy's San Remo Music Festival, advances in telecommunications and dreams of global harmony, they devised the Eurovision Song Contest, in which up to 25 countries jostle to find a new song worthy of the crown 'Grand Prix d'Eurovision'. The show gripped the public imagination and, held every year since its 1956 debut, has become the Earth's most viewed musical event, with an audience of up to 600 million.

The first winner was Switzerland's Lys Assia and 'Refrains'. More celebrated entrants include Julio Iglesias (Spain, 1970), Cliff Richard (UK, 1968/1973), Nana Mouskouri (Luxembourg, 1963), Olivia Newton-John (UK, 1974), Françoise Hardy (Monaco, 1963), Gina G (UK, 1996), Abba (Sweden, 1974) and Céline Dion (Switzerland, 1988). Winning songs often became hits, like Sandie Shaw's 'Puppet On A String' (1967), Brotherhood Of Man's 'Save Your Kisses For Me' (1976), Bucks Fizz's 'Making Your Mind Up' (1981) and Abba's 'Waterloo' (1974) – the first smash by the band who defined Eurovision's quest for Pop nirvana. Others lost, but – like Cliff's 'Congratulations', Dominico Modugno's 'Volare' and Vicky Leandros' 'L'Amour Est Bleu' – became evergreens.

Ireland holds a record seven victories; their Johnny Logan won twice with 1980's 'What's Another Year' and 1987's 'Hold Me Now'. Even the non-competing Irish interval act Riverdance became a phenomenon after its unveiling at 1994's contest. Surprise results include 1995's winner, the New Age hit 'Nocturne' by Norway's Secret Garden – a rare victory for a country usually damned by judges. Other cultural differences often prompt the verdict 'nul points', but claims that this reflects political tension are strenuously denied. The winning UK entry in 1997, 'Love Shine A Light', briefly revived the career of 80s stars Katrina & The Waves. Often dismissed as outmoded or kitsch (step forward Dutch group Teach-In's 1975 triumph 'Ding-A-Dong'), the event's longevity attests to its value as a peace-promotin' entertainment spectacular. Its cult status is upheld by over 20 Eurovision fan clubs worldwide.

READ The Complete Eurovision Song Contest Companion (1998), Jonathan Rice, Tim Rice, Paul Gambaccini & Tony Brown

FAN Eurosong News, Alte Hafenstr. 37-38, DE-28757 Bremen, Germany.

SURF www.pilgrims_rest.demon.co.uk/eurosong.htm.

EURYTHMICS ☉☉☉

WHO Vocals **Annie Lennox** (b. 25 Dec 1954, Aberdeen, Scotland), multi-instrumentalist **David Stewart** (b. 9 Sep 1952, Sunderland, England)

WHEN 1981–1989

WHERE London, England

WHAT Weird and wonderful Pop Synth Symphonies

Despite the disintegration of both their post-Punk band The Tourists and their own relationship, Stewart and Lennox became an international sensation and an implausible influence on 90s Heavy Metal horrors Marilyn Manson. Their debut *In The Garden* (1981) failed to match even The Tourists' meagre album chart success, but 1982's 'Love Is A Stranger' made minor ripples, its impact spread by the duo's outlandish TV appearances: while Stewart lurked in the background, the strikingly androgynous Lennox camped archly in the spotlight.

The sinister sing-along 'Sweet Dreams (Are Made of This)' soared to UK No.2 and US No.1, and for two years Eurythmics were unstoppable. *Sweet Dreams (Are Made Of This)* (1983), the UK chart-topper *Touch* (1983), 1984's movie soundtrack *1984 (For The Love Of Big Brother)* and *Be Yourself Tonight* (1985) spawned smash after smash, from the synth classics 'Here Comes The Rain Again' and 'Who's That Girl' to the R&B-flavoured 'There Must Be An Angel (Playing With My Heart)' and 'Sisters Are Doin' It For Themselves' (the latter a duet with Aretha Franklin).

They became an international live attraction – hence the stadium Rock-styling of *Revenge* (1986) – but then began a slow commercial decline. *Savage* (1987) retreated to their original, colder sound and became a fan favourite, but flopped Stateside. They recovered with 1989's *We Too Are One* (UK No.1, US No.34), but Lennox and Stewart were increasingly straining at the leash. Although they never officially split, the posthumous nature of UK No.1 *Greatest Hits* (1991) and *Live 1983–1989* (1993) was confirmed by Lennox's spectacular solo career and Stewart's bewildering variety of ventures. The latter included helming Vegas (with Terry Hall) and The Spiritual Cowboys, setting up the Anxious record label to showcase acts like Curve, producing Mick Jagger and Tom Petty, helping launch Alisha's Attic and Shakespear's Sister (whose Siobhan Fahey guested as part of Bananarama in Eurythmics' 'Who's That Girl' video and became Mrs Stewart), and duetting with saxophonist Candy Dulfer on 'Lily Was Here'.

Marilyn Manson's 1997 cover of 'Sweet Dreams' testified to the impact Eurythmics had on 80s Pop – a legacy reinforced by a 1998 remix collection featuring, among other fashionable names, Sneaker Pimps' revamp of 'Never Gonna Cry Again'.

Coincidentally, Stewart and Lennox reunited for a one-off gig to bid farewell to a BMG record company big-wig, but a longer-term reunion is said by both to be unlikely.

ReaD *Eurythmics: Sweet Dreams* (1996), Johnny Waller & Steve Rapport

surf imv.aau.dk/~vibber/Eurythmics/Index.html

THE EVERLY BROTHERS

WHO Vocals/guitar **Don Everly** (b. Isaac Donald Everly, 1 Feb 1937, Brownie, Kentucky, USA), vocals/guitar **Phil Everly** (b. 19 Jan 1939, Chicago, Illinois, USA)

WHAT Harmony-based vocal duo

After an unsuccessful recording debut with Columbia in early 1956, Don and Phil were signed by the New York label Cadence where they recorded a song by Felice and Boudleaux Bryant. 'Bye Bye Love', a track rejected by several other artists, became a Top 10 hit in both the US and UK. Their vocal style, with acoustic guitars over a Rock 'n' Roll beat, was to become an Everly Brothers trademark and influence Paul McCartney and Graham Nash among others.

'Wake Up Little Susie' gave them their first US chart-topper in 1957. Their first UK No.1, 'All I Have To Do Is Dream', released in 1958, was followed with a run of hits including 'Bird Dog' (1958), 'Problems' (1959), and '('Til) I Kissed You' (1959). Their first record to be recorded outside of Nashville was 'Let It Be Me', recorded in New York in 1959. Then came their biggest selling single, 'Cathy's Clown' (1960), selling over 3 million copies worldwide and a No.1 in both the US and UK, where it stayed for eight weeks.

The Everlys' albums followed the same style. *It's Everly Time!* (1960), *The Fabulous Style Of The Everly Brothers* (1960) and *A Date With The Everly Brothers* (1961) were hits on both sides of the Atlantic, although *Instant Party* (1962) was their last hit album for eight years.

Personal problems saw them break up in 1973. Solo projects and the success of a compilation, *Walk Right Back With The Everlys* (1975), renewed interest in their music. In 1983, they put their differences behind them and played a reunion concert: on 23 September at the Royal Albert Hall. The recorded and filmed show was a great success.

Still a big concert draw all over the world, the Everlys now record and tour regularly.

ReaD *Ike's Boys – Story Of The Everly Brothers* (1990), Phyllis Karpp

EVERYTHING BUT THE GIRL

WHO Vocals **Tracey Thorn** (b. 26 Sep 1962, Brookman's Park, Hertfordshire, England), guitar/keyboards **Ben Watt** (b. 6 Dec 1962, London, England)

WHEN 1984–

WHERE Hull, England

WHAT Acoustic earnestness turned Trip Hop

Meeting at Hull University in the early 80s, Ben Watt and Tracey Thorn both recorded solo albums on the Cherry Red label (Thorn also recorded two albums with The Marine Girls) before forming Everything But The Girl, signing to Blanco Y Negro, and guesting on The Style Council's *Café Bleu* (1984). Early albums like the Jazz-inflected *Eden* (1984), the Smiths-esque *Love Not Money* (1985) and the ambitiously orchestrated *Baby The Stars Shine Bright* (1986) sold well, but it was not until *Idlewild* (1988) spawned a hit cover of Danny Whitten's 'I Don't Want To Talk About It' (previously covered by Rod Stewart) that EBTG

EXTREME

WHO Vocals **Gary Cherone** (b. 26 Jul 1961, Malden, Massachusetts, USA), guitar **Nuno Bettencourt** (b. 20 Sep 1966, Azores, Portugal), bass **Pat Badger** (b. 22 Jul 1967, Boston, Massachusetts), drums **Paul Geary** (b. 24 Jul 1961, Medford, Massachusetts)

WHEN 1985–1996

WHERE Boston, Massachusetts, USA

WHAT Van hot chili queens

Nuno Bettencourt's confessed ambition was to be "like Queen". Along the way, he was first "like Van Halen" – *Extreme* (1989), produced by Queen engineer Mack, set guitar magazines a-quiver at his wheedly-weeing fret-burning – then "like Red Hot Chili Peppers", craftily flogging the Funk-rocking *Pornograffitti* (1990) on the back of acoustic tearjerker 'More Than Words'. The whole world bought it and old bubblehead Brian May awarded a royal seal of approval at the 1992 Freddie Mercury tribute extravaganza. Finally, Bettencourt made his own *Night At The Opera* with the pomp-rocking *III Sides to Every Story* (1992) – only to see the whole world buy REM's *Automatic For The People* instead. Extreme persevered with *Waiting For The Punchline* (1995) before singer Gary Cherone boarded the good ship Van Halen, drummer Paul Geary's replacement Mike Mangini hooked up with Steve Vai and Bettencourt went a-wheedly-weeing alone on *Schizophonic* (1997).

(Fan) Seashells For Souls, Essington House, North Tawton, Devon, EX20 2EX, UK

(Surf) www.kramerskorner.com/extreme.html

became a major chart act. *The Language Of Life* (1990) spawned another hit with 'Driving', but *Worldwide* (1991) brought them to a halt as Watt fought a near fatal illness. The lull was broken with 1992's 'Covers' EP, and hits set *Home Movies – The Best Of Everything But The Girl* (1993).

Watt and Thorn's appearances on Massive Attack's *Protection* (1994) heightened EBTG's credibility, but the duo's return with the Dub-meets-Nick Drake of *Amplified Heart* (1994) went uncelebrated until House DJ Todd Terry transformed 'Missing' into a triumphantly downbeat anthem. The single became a worldwide success in 1995 and remained in the UK Top 10 for more than three months.

Meanwhile, guitars were binned in favour of samplers and the heavily Drum 'n' Bass-influenced *Walking Wounded* (1996) became their biggest success, producing three hits – 'Walking Wounded', 'Wrong' and 'Single' – and making Everything But The Girl one of the few groups of their Indie ilk to survive the Dance revolution.

(Fan) Everything But The Girl, PO Box 2884, London, W6 0ZZ, UK

(Surf) www.ebtg.com

THE FACES ⊙

WHO Vocals **Rod Stewart** (b. Roderick Stewart, 10 Jan 1945, Highgate, London, England), guitar **Ron Wood** (b. 1 Jun 1947, Middlesex, England), bass **Ronnie Lane** (b. 1 Apr 1946, Plaistow, London, d. 4 Jun 1997, Colorado, USA), drums **Kenney Jones** (b. 16 Sep 1948, Stepney, London), keyboards **Ian McLagan** (b. 12 May 1945, Middlesex)

WHEN 1969–1975

WHERE London, England

WHAT Good-time Rock 'n' Roll

After Steve Marriott left The Small Faces in 1969, the remaining members – Lane, Jones and McLagan – joined Jeff Beck Group refugees Wood and Stewart to form The Faces. Debuting at a 1970 Cambridge University ball (under the pseudonym Quiet Melon), they became one of the best live acts of the 70s.

They were loud, boozy and shambolic on stage – and often offstage too: sessions for their lacklustre debut *First Step* (1970) rarely got beyond pre-studio drinking marathons in the bar next door. The partly live *Long Player* (1971) and excellent *A Nod's As Good As A Wink... To A Blind Horse* (1971) firmly established their raucous brand of good-time Rock 'n' Roll. Tracks like 'Had Me A Real Good Time' (1971) and the hits 'Stay With Me' (1972), 'Cindy Incidentally' and 'Pool Hall Richard' (both 1973) evoked their live spirit, while Lane's gentler, rootsy melodies – 'Stone', 'Richmond', 'Debris' – added variety.

From the first night of their first American tour – supporting Savoy Brown in Detroit – The Faces were well received in the States. However, by 1973, despite worldwide success, Stewart's tendency to keep the best material for his increasingly successful solo career aggravated personality clashes within the band. The crunch came when British Pop weekly *Melody Maker* printed an off-the-record comment from the singer that their fourth album, *Ooh La La* (1973), was "a bloody mess" and inferior to his own forthcoming album.

Ironically, Stewart's popularity made this patchy collection their only UK No.1, but Lane, who particularly resented The Faces becoming Stewart's stooges, resigned in protest. He formed Slim Chance, who released several albums (notably 1974's *Anymore For Anymore*) and had two 1974 hits, 'How Come' and 'The Poacher' (later covered live by Lane lovers Paul Weller and Ocean Colour Scene), but his career was tragically curtailed by the multiple sclerosis which finally killed him in 1997.

With ex-Free guitarist Tetsu Yamauchi, The Faces released two more chart singles including 'You Can Make Me Dance Sing Or Anything (Even Take The Dog For A Walk, Mend A Fuse, Fold Away The Ironing Board Or Any Other Domestic Short Comings)' (1974) and a weak live album, *Overture And Beginners* (1974), before Stewart left to pursue his solo career and the group split.

Wood joined The Rolling Stones, Jones replaced Keith Moon in The Who and McLagan played with Stewart, the Stones and Bruce Springsteen. *The Best Of The Faces* was released in 1977 and the group re-formed – without the seriously ill Lane – for a one-off performance at 1993's BRIT awards.

FAIRPORT CONVENTION

WHO Vocals/guitar **Richard Thompson** (b. 3 Apr 1949, London, England), guitar **Simon Nicol** (b. 13 Oct 1950, London), guitar **Ashley Hutchings** (b. 26 Jan 1945, London), vocals **Sandy Denny** (b. Alexandra Denny, 6 Jan 1948, Wimbledon, London, d. 21 Apr 1978, London), bass **Dave Pegg** (b. 2 Nov 1947, Birmingham, England), drums **Dave Mattacks** (b. Mar 1948, London), violin **Dave Swarbrick** (b. 5 Apr 1941, London)

WHEN 1966–

WHERE London, England

WHAT English Folk Rock pioneers

Formed by Richard Thompson, Simon Nicol, Ashley Hutchings, vocalist Judy Dyble, guitarist/vocalist Ian Matthews and drummer Martin Lamble, Fairport Convention devised an English version of the Folk Rock of American artists like Bob Dylan.

Following patchy debut *Fairport Convention* (1967), Sandy Denny replaced Dyble, and the more accomplished *What We Did On Our Holidays* (1968) reflected their growing confidence.

Unhalfbricking (1969) crystallized the group's sound, largely thanks to the addition of violinist Dave Swarbrick, an English Folk mainstay best known for work with Martin Carthy. The album included Fairport's only hit, a Gallicized version of Dylan's 'If You Gotta Go, Go Now' called 'Si Tu Dois Partir'. A lengthy raga Folk treatment of the traditional 'A Sailor's Life' hinted at the group's future. Matthews left to pursue Country Rock with Matthews Southern Comfort, who had a UK No.1 with Joni Mitchell's 'Woodstock' (1970), and Lamble was killed on 14 May 1969 when the group's van crashed.

With new drummer Dave Mattacks, the predominantly traditional *Liege & Lief* (UK No.17, 1969) was successfully

promoted as the "first British Folk Rock album ever", but musical differences caused a split: Denny, who wished to pursue a more contemporary style, left to form Fotheringay, while the more traditional Hutchings departed to form Steeleye Span.

Dave Pegg came in on bass, cementing one of the most reliable and enduring English rhythm sections with Mattacks, and Fairport's success continued through *Full House* (1970) and *Angel Delight* (1971). But in 1971, Thompson, the band's most gifted musician and songwriter, left to develop a solo career, and following the disappointing convict-themed concept album *Babbacombe Lee* (1971), Nicol also departed.

Australians Trevor Lucas and New Yorker Jerry Donahue were recruited as replacement guitarists, but *Rosie* (1973), *Nine* (1973) and *Rising For The Moon* (1975) brought diminishing returns. They announced a short-lived split in 1979.

Fairport's subsequent career became a dizzying round of departures, arrivals and reunions, although they made a fleeting return to the UK chart with *Red And Gold* in 1989. Always strong performers, the group have released four live albums, and host the Cropredy Folk Festival in the UK every August.

Star guests at Cropredy have included Richard Thompson, Jethro Tull, Robert Plant and All About Eve's Julianne Regan. The latter – a graduate from the UK's Goth genre – was clutched to the bosom of Denny fans still mourning her death in April 1978. Denny was further celebrated with a namecheck on The Spice Girls' 'The Lady Is A Vamp' from *Spiceworld* (1997).

READ *Meet On The Ledge* (1982), Patrick Humphries

SURF www.novpapyrus.com/fairport/

ADAM FAITH

WHO b. Terence Nelhams, 23 Jun 1940, London, England

WHAT Singer, actor and financial adviser

Faith came to fame in 1957 with Skiffle group The Worried Men, who played London's famous 2 i's coffee bar and appeared on *6-5 Special*. When his first two solo singles on HMV flopped, Faith briefly united with Freddy Lloyd as Terry & Freddy, before joining BBC TV's *Drumbeat*. After 'Ah! Poor Little Baby' (1959) on Top Rank narrowly missed the hit parade, he signed with Parlophone for the Buddy Holly-influenced 'What Do You Want' (1959), which topped the chart and started his unprecedented run of seven successive Top 5 singles. Like many of the diminutive star's hits, it was penned by Johnny Worth and arranged by John Barry – two other *Drumbeat* regulars.

In the early 60s, Faith starred in a handful of movies and scored 14 consecutive Top 20 entries with original songs (a rarity at the time). Hits included 'Poor Me' (1960) – the title of his first autobiography – 'Someone Else's Baby' (1960) and 'Made You'. Faith's distinctive voice and striking looks made him one of the most popular British teen idols in the pre-Beatles era.

He remained active in show business: managing Leo Sayer, appearing in more movies and top-rated British TV series like *Budgie* and *Love Hurts*, as well as making a name for himself as an astute financial adviser.

READ *Acts Of Faith* (1997), Adam Faith

FAITH NO MORE

WHO Vocals **Mike Patton** (b. 27 Jan 1968, Eureka, California, USA), guitar **Jim Martin** (b. 21 Jul 1961, Oakland, California), bass **Billy Gould** (b. 23 Apr 23 1963, Los Angeles, California), drums **Mike 'Puffy' Bordin** (b. 27 Nov 1962, San Francisco, California), keyboards **Roddy Bottum** (b. 1 Jul 1963, Los Angeles)

WHEN 1981–1998

WHERE San Francisco, California, USA

WHAT Funk, filth and fighting

A rare example of band squabbles *improving* music, the dysfunctional Faith No More remain one of Rock's oddities. Early turbulence was exemplified by the tenure of Courtney Love as vocalist (for six gigs, say the band; for a year, says Courtney).

They stabilized with singer Chuck Moseley, signed to Indie label Mordam and released patchy 1985 debut *We Care A Lot* (aka *Faith No More* in the UK). Moving to Slash Records for 1987's miserable *Introduce Yourself* (which nevertheless included the early gem 'We Care A Lot'), Faith No More joined Red Hot Chili Peppers and Fishbone in the Funk Metal vanguard. However, characteristic bickering saw Moseley replaced by Patton of cult Hardcore growlers Mr Bungle.

The Real Thing (1989) was more melodic, but Patton's lyrics – spanning the spectrum from death to defecation – ensured that the likes of 'Epic' became adolescent anthems. FNM's live grind and Patton's manic performances were commemorated on 1991's *Live At The Brixton Academy* and video *You Fat Bastards*.

Angel Dust (1992) proved their masterpiece: Patton's guttural vocals (his voice dropped almost a full octave after *The Real Thing*), monstrous riffing (notably the savage 'Jizzlobber') and once grotesque humour now just plain grotesque. A creepily faithful 1993 cover of The Commodores' 'Easy' (issued with 'Be Aggressive' as 'I'm Easy') and *Judgement Night* soundtrack cut 'Another Body Murdered' (with Samoan Hip Hop hardmen Boo-Yaa Tribe) proved Martin's swan song – ousted in favour first of Bungle guitarist Trey Spruance, then former roadie Dean Menta.

The band were happier minus Martin, but fans shunned the earnest (albeit equally harsh and idiosyncratic) *King For A Day… Fool For A Lifetime* (1995). Side projects – Bordin with Ozzy Osbourne, Patton with Mr Bungle and Bottum with Imperial Teen – fuelled 'split' rumours, but FNM returned with new guitarist Jon Hudson and the decidedly tired *Record Of The Year* (1997).

surf www.fnm.com/

MARIANNE FAITHFULL

WHO b. 29 Dec 1949, Hampstead, London, England

WHAT Lived-in voice and legendary vice

A 'Good girl gone bad' tag has dogged Marianne Faithfull for much of three decades. It also overshadows her fine music, which began when The Rolling Stones' manager Andrew Loog Oldham plucked her from high society and commissioned Mick Jagger and Keith Richards to compose an appropriate song. Un-Stonesy heartbreaker 'As Tears Go By' became her first hit and

"I've gone through life standing there saying, 'Look at me, aren't I pretty? Please buy me.' Which is what I did as a Pop singer, and I've done it with every man since, and I don't like to be like that anymore"

MARIANNE FAITHFULL/PHOTOFEST/RETNA

signature tune. She and Jagger became the toast of 'Swinging London', and her transformation from convent girl to 'It girl' was cemented by a scantily clad cameo in Richards' first major drugs bust. Her discography began strongly in 1965 with *Come My Way* and *Marianne Faithfull*, but was eclipsed by her acting career (notably 1968's compellingly awful *Girl On A Motorcycle*) and doomed entanglement with Jagger. Pressures of the latter led her to dangerous extremes: the harrowing 'Sister Morphine' (for which she initially received no credit when the Stones put it on *Sticky Fingers*) says it all.

After a failed suicide bid, she slipped into the arms of heroin and wasted much of the 70s before a resurrection with *Broken English* (1979). No longer an angel with a voice to match, Faithfull was instead an elegant interpreter, a transition confirmed by her covers collection *Strange Weather* (1987). An in-demand collaborator, Faithfull's admiring associates have ranged – in 1997 alone – from Metallica to Blur's Alex James.

read *Faithfull* (1994), Marianne Faithfull & David Dalton

surf www.planete.net/~smironne/

THE FALL

WHO Vocals **Mark E. Smith** (b. 5 Mar 1957, Manchester, England), guitar

Craig Scanlon, bass **Stephen Hanley**, drums **Karl Burns**

WHEN 1977–

WHERE Manchester, England

WHAT Irritable, influential iconoclasts

Tied to a dull office job in Manchester docks, Mark E. Smith tried out as vocalist in local Rock groups – all of whom turned him down, such was his dissimilarity to Robert Plant and Paul Rodgers. Inspired by Punk and Krautrock, he gathered guitarist Martin Bramah and bass player Tony Friel, christened them The Fall (after an Albert Camus novel), added drummer Karl Burns and keyboard player Una Baines, and set about inflicting his jaundiced wit on an unsuspecting and largely unappreciative world. One of Rock's most wayward careers had begun.

After 1977 gigs on the resolutely un-Punk working men's club circuit, The Fall recorded their first of many BBC radio sessions for superfan John Peel (the best of which were compiled on 1998's *Peel Sessions*) and released their debut EP 'Bingo Master's Breakout' (1978) on the microscopic Step Forward label. *Live At The Witch Trials* and *Dragnet* (both 1979) demonstrated nearly every Fall facet: a fluid line-up (Out: Baines and replacement Yvonne Pawlett, Friel, Bramah, Burns; In: Craig Scanlon, Marc Riley, Steve Hanley, Mike Leigh), unclassifiable music (elements of Gary Glitter-esque Glam, Rockabilly, Krautrock, Punk), slang-strewn lyrics and, most famously, Smith's caustic vocal style-uh, where each line ended in a disdainful drawl-uh.

They signed to Rough Trade for 1980's formidable live *Totale's Turns (It's Now Or Never)* and *Grotesque (After The Gramme)* and the mini-album *Slates* (1981), but decamped to the obscure Kamera label for 1982's double-drummer masterpiece *Hex Enduction Hour*, with Leigh and the returned Burns, and weaker *Room To Live*. By 1983's more upbeat, Rough Trade-released *Perverted By Language*, Smith had recruited guitarist and future wife Brix, whose Pop sensibilities balanced his rampant inventiveness. Still firmly idiosyncratic, The Fall steered nearer the mainstream with *The Wonderful And Frightening World Of The Fall* (1984), *This Nation's Saving Grace* (1985; goodbye Paul Hanley, hello Simon Rogers), *Bend Sinister*

(1986; goodbye Burns, hello Simon Wolstencroft) and *The Frenz Experiment* (1988; hello keyboard player Marcia Schofield). Surprise hit versions of The Kinks' 'Victoria' and R. Dean Taylor's 'There's A Ghost In My House' nestled beside customary paranoia and bile. They took another unexpected turn with Michael Clark ballet soundtrack *I Am Kurious Oranj* (1988).

After 1989's *Seminal Live* (half-live, half-studio) came a return to form with the excellent *Extricate* (1990; hello again Bramah). Close to

biography and charged with atypical emotional range, it dwelt on Smith's split with Brix (who had also left the band, resuming side project The Adult Net) in 'Sing! Harpy', and on his father's death in the lyrical, evocative 'Bill Is Dead'.

Shift Work (1991) proved another unexpected late peak, with a slimmed-down line-up of Smith, Scanlon, Hanley, Wolstencroft and fiddle player Kenny Brady. *Code: Selfish* (1992), *The Infotainment Scan* (1993; hello keyboard player David Bush) and *Middle Class Revolt* (1994) were multi-textured and mellower (including *Infotainment*'s cover of Sister Sledge's 'Lost In Music'),

"God is fond of The Fall"

but Smith descended into self-parodic interviews – ranting about music, politics, 'kids today', etc – and public bust-ups with his colleagues. The Fall trudged on regardless, briefly welcoming Brix back on *Cerebral Caustic* (1995) and, in 1996, the shambolic live album *The Twenty Seven Points* (featuring 28 tracks) and *The Light User Syndrome* (goodbye long-term guitarist Scanlon and Bush, hello keyboard player Julia Nagle and hello again Karl Burns). *Levitate* (1997) was, in great Fall tradition, an eclectic epic – merging Surf Rock, Drum 'n' Bass and Krautrock. It also saw the exit of Wolstencroft, the re-departure of Brix and arrival of guitarist Tommy Crooks.

As well as the musicians who have graced the barrage of Fall albums, Smith has collaborated with Coldcut, Tackhead, Inspiral Carpets, Long Fin Killie, DOSE, Edwyn Collins and Elastica. At *NME*'s 1998 Brat awards, he was given a 'godlike genius' award. Although Smith proclaimed their influence on everyone, notable disciples include Pavement, Elastica and Happy Mondays.

(READ) *Paintwork: A Portrait Of The Fall* (1989), Brian Edge

(FAN) The Biggest Library Yet, 106 Fleet Road, London, NW3 2QX, UK

(SURF) www.dcs.ed.ac.uk/home/cxl/fall/

FAMILY

WHO Vocals **Roger Chapman** (b. 8 Apr 1942, Leicester, England), guitar **Charlie Whitney** (b. 24 Jun 1944, Skipton, North Yorkshire, England), bass **Rick Grech** (b. 1 Nov 1946, Bordeaux, France, d. 17 Mar 1990), drums **Rob Townsend** (b. 7 Jul 1947, Leicester), saxophone **Jim King** (b. Jan 1947, Kettering, England)

WHEN 1967–1973

WHERE Leicester, England

WHAT Raucous, warbling Prog Rock

Evolving from 60s band The Farinas, Family established Prog Rock credentials with seven, strong UK Top 40 albums. *A Song For Me* (1970) was most successful, its UK No.4 position matched by 'In My Own Time', which showcased singer Chapman's distinctive vibrato. Despite heavy touring, Family's fluctuating personnel and lack of US success prompted their split in 1973.

Chapman and Whitney formed Streetwalkers (which also boasted ex-Jeff Beck guitarist Bob Tench), while Townsend – and later Family member Tony Ashton – joined Medicine Head.

 members.aol.com/songforme/index.htm

THE FARM ⊙

WHO Vocals **Peter Hooton** (b. 28 Sep 1962, Liverpool, England), guitar **Steve Grimes** (b. 4 Jun 1962, Liverpool), guitar **Keith Mullen**, bass **Carl Hunter** (b. 14 Apr 1965, Bootle, England), drums **Roy Boulter** (b. 2 Jul 1964, Liverpool), keyboards **Ben Leach** (b. 2 May 1969, Liverpool)

WHEN 1983–

WHERE Liverpool, England

WHAT Bouncy, socially aware Indie Dance

Originally The Excitements, The Farm's nucleus of Hooton and Grimes recruited Hunter, Boulter, Leach and Mullen in 1986, following the death of original drummer Andy McVann. With a string of Indie hits behind them, mainstream success beckoned in 1990 with 'Stepping Stone', 'Groovy Train' and anti-war anthem 'All Together Now', the latter based on Pachelbel's 'Canon And Gigue In D Major' (later re-used by Coolio on his 1997 hit 'C U When U Get There').

The UK chart-topping *Spartacus* (1991) cast The Farm among the most Pop-oriented of the 'Baggy' Indie Dance bands, but subsequent singles failed to reach the UK Top 20. Despite a hit cover of The Human League's 'Don't You Want Me', *Hullabaloo* (1994) failed to chart. Taking a sabbatical, Hunter became a designer, Leach played with former Madness singer and Farm manager Suggs, and Boulter wrote TV scripts. Hooton, Grimes and Mullen began 1996's Dance-oriented studio project Mondial.

fan Top Floor, 29 Hamilton Square, Birkenhead, Merseyside, L41 6AZ, UK

surf www.du.edu/~dhaley/farm/farm.html

FAUST

WHO Guitar/bass **Jean Hervé Peron**, percussion **Werner 'Zappi' Diermeier**, percussion **Arnulf Meifert**, keyboards **Rudolf Sosna**, keyboards **Joachim Irmler**, tapes **Gunter Wüsthoff**, production **Uwe Nettlebeck**, engineer **Kurt Graupner**

WHEN 1968–

WHERE Hamburg, Germany

WHAT Mythical Krautrockers

Faust were formed by Nettlebeck – a German counter-culture journalist and reported friend of the Red Army and Baader-Meinhof terrorist groups – recruited by the Polydor label to add credibility to their roster. Moving some Hamburg musicians into a schoolhouse in Wümme, which became their commune and studio, they set about creating iconoclastic 'free' Rock, eventually producing debut *Faust* (1971).

A cult following, particularly in England, saw the more conventional *Faust So Far* (1972) and Tony Conrad collaboration *Outside The Dream Syndicate* (1973) partly recoup colossal costs, but 1973's Krautrock classic *The Faust Tapes* – sold in the UK by Virgin for the price of a single – was a mega-selling money loss.

After a chaotic UK tour – instruments included pneumatic drills and pinball machines – and *Faust 4* (1973), the group dispersed. Faust's legend grew with reissues and archive releases, and their evident influence on Julian Cope, The Fall and Einstürzende Neubauten. Mainstays Jean Hervé Peron, Zappi Diermeier and Joachim Irmler reconvened in various permutations for 1996's *Rien* and *Untitled*, and 1997's *You Know FaUSt*, *Edinburgh '97* and *Faust Wakes Nosferatu*.

surf www.adweb.co.uk/andyw/faust/

JOSÉ FELICIANO

WHO b. 10 Sep 1945, Lares, Puerto Rico

WHAT Latin-style Easy Listening

Born blind, Feliciano learned guitar during his childhood in New York before earning a reputation on the Greenwich Village scene there and signing to RCA. Early recognition was limited to the Latin charts (where three Spanish-language albums triumphed). With 1968's *Feliciano!*, the multi-lingual star broke into US and UK charts, including Latin versions of The Doors' 'Light My Fire' and The Mama & The Papas' 'California Dreamin'.

Despite this emphasis on covers (including a controversial version of 'The Star Spangled Banner' at the 1968 World Series baseball tournament), Feliciano wrote both the Bruce Ruffin UK hit 'Rain' (1971) and the theme for 70s American sit-com *Chico & The Man* (1975). Stateside fame expanded to TV appearances (*Kung Fu* and *McMillan & Wife*) and movies (the soundtrack to 1969's *MacKenna's Gold*).

Feliciano's unique Latin take on Rock led to six Grammy awards and gold and platinum albums around the world.

surf www.areacom.it/html/arte_cultura/feliciano/index.htm

"I don't think I'm so much of a smoothie. I'm more of a rough diamond-type, really"

BRYAN FERRY ◉ ◉

WHO b. 26 Sep 1945, Washington, Tyne and Wear, England

WHAT Suave matinee idol of Rock

Having begun his solo career while still fronting Roxy Music, Ferry was well placed to survive the band's long inactivity and eventual dissolution. Within a year of Roxy's self-titled debut, the singer released 1973's *These Foolish Things*, applying his mannered warble to covers ranging from Bob Dylan's 'A Hard Rain's A-Gonna Fall' to The Beach Boys' 'Don't Worry Baby'.

Ferry's delivery had an affecting tug, projecting vulnerability amid the elegant, lounge-lizard image. The approach was successfully repeated for *Another Time, Another Place* (1974), revisiting his Soul fan roots in 'The 'In' Crowd' and perfecting his retro sophistication in the supper-club standard 'Smoke Gets In Your Eyes'. *Let's Stick Together* (1976) broadened the formula to include reworkings of Roxy songs as well as stabs at classic Pop and R&B. The album's title track, built around Wilbert Harrison's Blues number 'Let's Work Together', became a hit, assisted by a video starring his then girlfriend, Jerry Hall. By 1977, *In Your Mind* presented all-new Ferry material, like the single 'Tokyo Joe', but he found his true artistic focus in the outstanding *The Bride Stripped Bare* (1978), a melancholic work reflecting his split with Hall, who had taken up with Mick Jagger. In the early 80s he concentrated on the revived Roxy Music, but made a chart-topping return to solo form with *Boys And Girls* (1985), featuring the hit 'Slave To Love'.

A notoriously slow worker, his later releases have been infrequent – after *Bête Noire* (1987) he made another covers album, *Taxi* (1993), then *Mamouna* in 1994. All were dependably smooth, but lacked the vitality of earlier albums.

read *Bryan Ferry Story* (1976), Rex Balfourd

fan Bryan Ferry and Roxy Music Information Service, PO Box 829, Dumbarton G82 1BG, UK

surf www.cco.caltech.edu/~bryan/roxy/

FINE YOUNG CANNIBALS ◉ ✪

WHO Vocals **Roland Gift** (b. 28 Apr 1961, Birmingham, England), guitar

Andy Cox (b. 25 Jan 1956, Birmingham), bass/keyboards **David Steele** (b. 8 Sep 1960, Isle of Wight, England)

WHEN 1985–1992

WHERE Birmingham, England

WHAT Ska Soul Pop pourri

Founded by English Beat members Steele and Cox, FYC (their reputation outweighing a minuscule output) achieved instant cult status thanks to a launch on British TV's *The Tube*. Gift's Soul-inflected vocals and Steele and Cox's loose-limbed dancing propelled debuts 'Johnny Come Home' and *Fine Young Cannibals* (both 1985) into the UK charts, followed by covers of Elvis' 'Suspicious Minds' (1986) and Buzzcocks' 'Ever Fallen In Love' (1987), the latter from Jonathan Demme's movie *Something Wild*.

After more movie work (1997's *Tin Men* soundtrack and Gift's 1987 acting debut, *Sammy And Rosie Get Laid*), FYC went into hibernation during which Cox and Steele scored 1988 House hits 'Tired Of Getting Pushed Around' and 'Heat It Up' as Two Men, A Drum Machine And A Trumpet. Not until 1989 did Gift's quavering quacks grace new material: the polished *The Raw And The Cooked* (notching up 8 million sales), US No.1s 'She Drives Me Crazy' (whose video shamelessly aped New Order's 'True Faith') and 'Good Thing' and dancefloor re-jiggle *The Raw And The Remix* (1990). With Gift again distracted by acting – including *Scandal* (1989) – FYC splintered. An aborted final album was recycled for the hits set *The Finest* (1996).

surf www.dsv.su.se/~mats-bjo/fyc/fychome.html

ROBERTA FLACK ✪

WHO b. 10 Feb 1937, Black Mountain, North Carolina, USA

WHAT Softly-singing Soulstress

The formidable Ms Flack, a high-school music teacher, was singing in clubs in Washington, DC, when musician Les McCann spotted her in 1968. Signed to Atlantic and teamed with former classmate Donny Hathaway, Flack recorded her 1969 debut *First Take* in a day. One of its cuts – 'The First Time Ever I Saw Your Face' – became a 1972 US No.1, boosted by its exposure in the Clint Eastwood movie *Play Misty For Me*, taking *First Take* to the top of the US album chart for five weeks. The following year 'Killing Me Softly' topped the US charts, at last fulfilling early comparisons to the Queen of Soul, Aretha Franklin.

Flack spent the rest of the 70s duetting with Hathaway and scoring hits like 'Where Is The Love' (1973), 'Feel Like Makin' Love' (1974) and 'The Closer I Get To You' (1978), until Hathaway took his own life in 1979. 'Back Together Again', one of their final duets, reached UK No.3 in 1980. She teamed up with Peabo Bryson for her biggest UK hit, 'Tonight I Celebrate My Love', which reached UK No.2 in 1983, and became a name to drop again when Hip Hop chartbusters The Fugees revived 'Killing Me Softly' in 1996 with worldwide success.

FLEETWOOD MAC ⊙⊙⊙⊙ ★★★★

WHO Vocals/guitar **Lindsey Buckingham** (b. 3 Oct 1949, Palo Alto, California, USA), vocals **Stevie Nicks** (b. 26 May 1948, Phoenix, Arizona, USA), vocals/keyboards **Christine McVie** (b. Christine Perfect, 12 Jul 1943, Birmingham, England), bass **John McVie** (b. 26 Nov 1945, London, England), drums **Mick Fleetwood** (b. 24 June 1942, Redruth, Cornwall, England)

WHEN 1967–

WHERE London to California

WHAT Rock's longest-running "musical soap opera" (Lindsey Buckingham)

Fleetwood Mac's roots can be traced to John Mayall's Bluesbreakers in early 1967. Mayall gave guitarist Peter Green studio time as a present and the results included a track called 'Fleetwood Mac' – derived from his favourite rhythm section, fellow Bluesbreakers Fleetwood and McVie. In July 1967, Green left the Bluesbreakers, taking Fleetwood with him, although it took McVie a few more months to leave the security of Mayall's group.

fleetwood mac

Mike Vernon – former Decca house producer – signed Green to his specialist label, Blue Horizon, and recommended guitarist Jeremy Spencer of Birmingham-based Blues outfit The Levi Set. Spencer could emulate Elmore James' slide guitar, although this later became a limitation. An ad in *Melody Maker* secured bass player Bob Brunning, although Green still had his sights on McVie. The group's auspicious debut was at the Windsor Jazz & Blues Festival on 13 August 1967. Their first single 'I Believe My Time Ain't Long' – essentially Elmore James' 'Dust My Broom' with new words by Spencer – preceded *Peter Green's Fleetwood Mac* (1968), which reached UK No.4.

Subsequent 1968 singles 'Black Magic Woman' and 'Need Your Love So Bad' – strong songs dominated by Green's guitar – failed to make the UK Top 30. The latter featured a string arrangement scored by Mickey Baker of Mickey & Sylvia fame. Next up that year was the group's only UK No.1 'Albatross' – a sea-change from their Blues roots – featuring fine playing from recent guitar recruit Danny Kirwan, whose rich, easy-going style echoed American West Coast Rock.

In 1969, during their second American tour, they recorded at famous Chess Studios in Chicago with their Blues heroes Willie Dixon, Otis Spann and Shakey Horton. Blue Horizon issued the

material nearly a year later. In September 1969, the band signed with Warner Bros for the heavier *Then Play On* (1969). The album contained Green's masterpiece 'Oh Well Parts 1 & 2', but success was short-lived. Green grew anxious about fame and fortune, even suggesting the group give all their money to charity. In Munich, during their 1970 European tour, he was introduced to a group of German hippies and LSD: a perilous combination that spelt the end of his involvement with Fleetwood Mac. Green's final recording with the group (bar a cameo on 1979's *Tusk*) was the single 'The Green Manalishi'. He left in May 1970.

Green's exit was the first of many radical line-up changes. En route to LA for a third American tour, Spencer decided to quit. Having left a hotel to get food, he never returned and was traced to religious cult The Children Of God, where his hair had been shaved and name changed. Equally oddly, Green deputized on the remaining tour dates. Kirwan was next to go, fired by Fleetwood for excessive drinking and bad behaviour. McVie's wife Christine joined in 1970, although she had worked on *Mr Wonderful* (1968) and designed the cover for *Kiln House* (1970). Bob Welch joined in 1971, Bob Weston and Dave Walker in 1972, although the latter two were gone within 12 months. Each new line-up brought new ideas and styles to the group, but *Future Games* (1971), *Bare Trees* (1972), *Penguin* (1973) and *Mystery To Me* (1974) made little impact on the charts.

This period also saw the strangest event in the group's history: after Weston's departure, the group took a break. Manager Clifford Davis assembled a 'new' Fleetwood Mac, claiming he owned the name. Legal battles ensued, during which the real Fleetwood Mac relocated to California to renegotiate a deal with Warner Bros and repair the damage.

With the problem resolved, Fleetwood took over their management and they recorded *Heroes Are Hard To Find* (1974), the last to feature Welch. His going solo in 1974 left the band without a frontman. Searching for a studio to record their next album, Fleetwood was played an album called *Buckingham Nicks* (1973) to demonstrate the quality of Sound City Studios. Impressed by Buckingham, he was told that its makers were, coincidentally, in the next studio. Discovering Buckingham wouldn't join without Nicks, he was persuaded to recruit both over dinner a few weeks later, triggering a world-conquering sales phenomenon and trauma-charged soap opera.

West Coast cool ousting lingering Blues, *Fleetwood Mac* (1975) topped the US chart 15 months after its release. It spawned hits like 'Over My Head', heavily exposed on FM radio in the USA, and 'Rhiannon', an enduring live favourite. Prior to the album's release, they went on the road to introduce the new members. Nicks promptly became the focus of the band,

> **"I think the only ones who didn't have an affair were me and Mick"**
> John McVie

inspiring future stars as disparate as Courtney Love (who later covered her 'Gold Dust Woman' with Hole) and Belinda Carlisle.

Amid success, however, Buckingham and Nicks broke off their relationship and the McVies decided to divorce – the besieged background to *Rumours* (1977). The original title was *Yesterday's Gone*, changed after McVie's comment that the songs sounded like a bunch of rumours. Having spent 31 weeks atop the US chart, it became their biggest-selling album and one of the best-sellers of all time.

'Go Your Own Way', 'Don't Stop', 'Dreams' and 'You Make Loving Fun' were hits and 'The Chain' became equally famous as the theme to BBC TV's motor-racing coverage. One of the USA's biggest draws, Mac spent most of 1977 and 1978 on the road.

Delayed by perfectionism and excess, the follow-up emerged as *Tusk* (1979). Its uncommercial length and musical boldness put Warner Bros staff in fear of their bonuses: even sales of over 4 million were a failure compared to *Rumours*. However, the title track became the group's first UK Top 10 hit in nearly nine years.

A gruelling year-long world tour nearly caused their break-up. In 1981, Buckingham – the band's musical driving force – hit with 'Trouble' from his *Law And Order*, while Nicks initiated a starry solo career with *Bella Donna* (followed, with varying fortunes, by 1983's *The Wild Heart*, 1985's *Rock A Little*, 1989's *The Other Side Of The Mirror*, 1991's hits set *Timespace*, 1994's *Street Angel* and 1998's box set *Enchanted*). Solo efforts by Fleetwood and Christine McVie went largely uncelebrated.

They regrouped long enough for *Mirage* (1982) – a *Rumours* retread that spawned the UK hit 'Oh Diane' and US hit 'Gypsy' – but splintered after another tense tour.

Christine's work on movie soundtrack *A Fine Mess* (1985) reunited the group. Asked to record 'Can't Help Falling In Love', she enlisted her bandmates, from which sessions evolved *Tango In The Night* (1987), their biggest success since *Rumours*. Though jam-packed with hits – 'Big Love', 'Seven Wonders', 'Little Lies', 'Family Man', 'Everywhere' and 'Isn't It

Midnight' – it wasn't enough to appease the restless Buckingham.

On tour, he was replaced by Rick Vito and Billy Burnette, a substitution maintained by *Behind The Mask* (1990), another UK No.1, although there were no hits this time around. Disillusioned, Christine McVie and Nicks played their last shows with the band in December 1990. Vito followed a year later.

Thereafter, they reunited only for four tracks on the 25th anniversary set *The Chain* (1992), although the classic quintet appeared, at the request of President Clinton, at his inaugural party. Their performance of 'Don't Stop', the song chosen as his campaign anthem, was the first time they had appeared together in nearly a decade.

With a new line-up boasting ex-Traffic member Dave Mason and Becca Bramlett, daughter of Delaney & Bonnie, Fleetwood and McVie recorded *Time* (1995). Despite a guest appearance by Buckingham, it was a commercial disaster, charting low and fleetingly. A nostalgia package tour with Pat Benatar and REO Speedwagon did little to help and the band split in 1996.

However, another soundtrack oiled the cogs of conciliation: Fleetwood, Buckingham and Nicks reunited for 'Twisted', from the movie *Twister* (1996), then Buckingham agreed to postpone a torturously overworked solo album and celebrate *Rumours'* 20th anniversary with Fleetwood, Nicks and the McVies. They taped a spectacular show for MTV – issued as the US No.1 *The Dance* (1997). Its heartwarming highlights included the mad marching-band stomper 'Tusk' and the Buckingham-Nicks duet 'Landslide' (a tune beloved of Billy Corgan, whose cover of it graces Smashing Pumpkins' *Pisces Iscariot*). They went back on the road in September 1997: a Stateside stadium sensation that proved domestic drama is no obstacle to the might of melody. In 1998, they received a BRIT award for Lifetime Achievement.

READ *Fleetwood Mac – Behind The Masks* (1991), Bob Brunning

FAN Crystal, Aine Foley, 46 St. John's Avenue, Clondalkin, Dublin 22, Ireland

SURF www.cyberpenguin.net/penguin/

THE FLYING BURRITO BROTHERS

WHO Vocals/guitar/keyboards **Gram Parsons** (b. Ingram Cecil Connor III, 5 Nov 1946, Winter Haven, Florida, USA, d. 19 Sep 1973, Yucca Valley, California, USA), vocals/guitar **Chris Hillman** (b. 4 Dec 1944, Los Angeles, California), guitar **Sneaky Pete Kleinow** (b. 1934, South Bend, Indiana), bass **Chris Ethridge**, drums **Michael Clarke** (b. Michael James Dick, 3 Jun 1946, Spokane, Washington, USA, d. 19 Dec 1993, Treasure Island, Florida)

WHEN 1968–1993

WHERE Los Angeles, California, USA

WHAT Seminal Country Rock

Having pioneered Country Rock with The Byrds, Parsons and Hillman defined the genre with *The Gilded Palace Of Sin* (1969).

After Parsons' departure in 1970, they still excelled live and on record, best illustrated by *Last Of The Red Hot Burritos* (1972) but, when Hillman left in 1973, decline set in. Various line-ups performed as The Burrito Brothers, The Flying Brothers and, finally, into the 90s as The Flying Burrito Brothers once again.

The Burritos' legacy is best measured by Parsons' influence on his contemporaries. Having transformed The Byrds, he pursued the Country Rock quest with his new band. The Eagles – who numbered one-time Burrito guitarist Bernie Leadon in their ranks – were only the most successful of their descendants.

In 1992, in one of those odd coincidences that are the very stuff of Rock arcana, Indie poppers Belly covered the Burritos' 'Hot Burrito #1' while Dinosaur Jr had a bash at 'Hot Burrito #2'.

FOCUS

WHO Vocals/keyboards/flute **Thijs Van Leer** (b. 31 Mar 1948, Amsterdam, The Netherlands), guitar/lute/bass **Jan Akkerman** (b. 24 Dec 1946, Amsterdam), bass **Bert Reuter** (b. 26 Nov 1946, Amsterdam), drums **Pierre Van Der Linden** (b. 19 Feb 1946, Amsterdam)

WHEN 1969–1976

WHERE Amsterdam, The Netherlands

WHAT Progressive yodelling

Originally a trio, Focus focused when Akkerman – a locally famed guitar prodigy – was poached from psychedelic Rock outfit Brainbox. Debuting, albeit obscurely, on the Dutch soundtrack recording of *Hair*, they hit their (largely wordless) stride with *In And Out Of Focus* (1971). Touring and media interest – notably BBC TV's *Old Grey Whistle Test* – made Focus an international sensation. In 1972, *Moving Waves* and *Focus 3* made the UK Top 10, while 1973's yodelling classic 'Hocus Pocus' and 'Sylvia' made UK No.20 and No.4 – the former also reaching US No.9.

However, Focus failed to maintain status and inspiration, with Akkerman quitting on the eve of a 1976 UK tour and prior to a bizarre swan-song album featuring P.J. Proby. Akkerman and Van Leer, however, continue to make European solo albums.

surf members.aol.com/akkernet

FOLK ROCK

WHAT Folk Rock refers to both American artists – Bob Dylan, The Byrds, The Mamas & The Papas – who electrified the previously acoustic protest genre, and a largely English fusion of Rock and traditional music. Pentangle, Davey Graham and Ashley Hutchings – founder of Fairport Convention, Steeleye Span and The Albion Band – can be credited with defining and popularizing the British brand of Folk Rock, and with influencing Led Zeppelin, Jethro Tull and Wishbone Ash.

WHERE USA, UK

WHEN 60s–

WHO Bob Dylan <u>Bringing It All Back Home</u> (1965), The Byrds <u>Turn! Turn! Turn!</u> (1966), The Mamas & The Papas <u>If You Can Believe Your Eyes And Ears</u> (1966), Fairport Convention <u>Liege & Lief</u> (1969), Steeleye Span <u>Hark! The Village Wait</u> (1970), Beth Orton <u>Trailer Park</u> (1996)

FOO FIGHTERS

WHO Vocals/guitar **Dave Grohl** (b. 14 Jan 1969, Warren, Ohio, USA), guitar **Franz Stahl**, bass **Nate Mendel**, drums **Taylor Hawkins**

WHEN 1994–

WHERE Seattle, Washington, USA

WHAT Post-Grunge gods

In the aftermath of Nirvana, drummer Dave Grohl worked on the *Backbeat* (1994) soundtrack, toured with Tom Petty (and came close to joining Petty's backing band The Heartbreakers full-time), then exploded into the spotlight with *Foo Fighters* (1995) – named after World War II pilots' terminology for UFOs. Though reassuringly Nirvana-ish, notably on 'Alone+Easy Target', it demonstrated a melodic flair barely hinted at by the melancholy 'Marigold', his sole solo writing credit with the band.

Having recorded the album more or less singlehandedly, Grohl, now a guitar-playing frontman, recruited ex-Germs/Nirvana guitarist Pat Smear and – from Sub Pop hopefuls Sunny Day Real Estate – bassist Nate Mendel and drummer William Goldsmith. Hits (notably 1995's UK smash 'This Is A Call') and thrilling shows (such as a chaotic appearance at England's Reading Festival in 1995) pushed them to platinum sales, after which Goldsmith was replaced by Alanis Morissette drummer Taylor Hawkins.

Following *The Colour And The Shape* (1997), their headliner at Seattle's Bumbershoot Festival marked not only Smear's farewell but a one-off reunion with Nirvana bassist Krist Novoselic (on a cover of Led Zeppelin's 'Communication Breakdown').

With new guitarist Franz Stahl (a veteran from one of Grohl's former bands, Scream), the Foos' melodic Metal, witty videos and collaborations (a tour with Prodigy and a wall-crumbling makeover of Puff Daddy's 'It's All About The Benjamins' in 1998) continue to distinguish them from the post-Grunge hordes.

fan Foo Fighters, PO Box 19700, Seattle, WA 98109, USA

surf www.foofighters.com/foo/

FOREIGNER ⊙ ✪

WHO Vocals **Lou Gramm** (b. Lou Grammatico, 2 May 1950, Rochester, New York, USA), guitar **Mick Jones** (b. 27 Dec 1944, London, England), guitar/keyboards **Ian McDonald** (b. 25 Jun 1946, London), bass **Ed Gagliardi** (b. 13 Feb 1952, New York), drums **Dennis Elliot** (b. 18 Aug 1950, London), keyboards **Al Greenwood** (b. 20 Oct 1951, New York)

WHEN 1976–

WHERE New York, USA

WHAT Anglo-American Arena Rock sensation

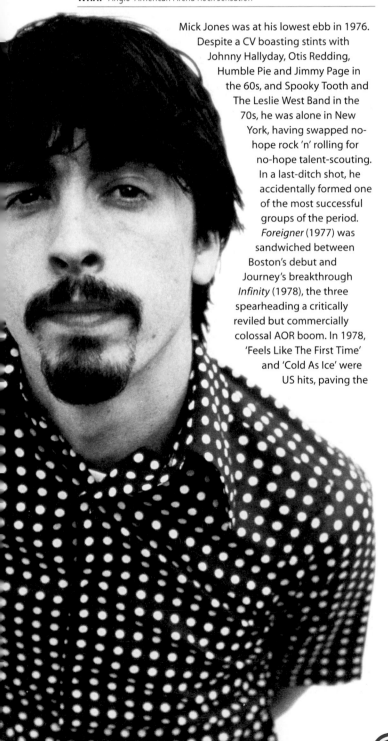

Mick Jones was at his lowest ebb in 1976. Despite a CV boasting stints with Johnny Hallyday, Otis Redding, Humble Pie and Jimmy Page in the 60s, and Spooky Tooth and The Leslie West Band in the 70s, he was alone in New York, having swapped no-hope rock 'n' rolling for no-hope talent-scouting. In a last-ditch shot, he accidentally formed one of the most successful groups of the period. *Foreigner* (1977) was sandwiched between Boston's debut and Journey's breakthrough *Infinity* (1978), the three spearheading a critically reviled but commercially colossal AOR boom. In 1978, 'Feels Like The First Time' and 'Cold As Ice' were US hits, paving the way for *Double Vision* (1978) and its smashes 'Hot Blooded' and the title track. Rick Wills replaced Gagliardi for their heaviest album, *Head Games* (1979), which failed even to chart in the UK. In the aftermath, Greenwood and McDonald departed – Jones being the sole constant in future line-ups.

'Urgent' (1981), distinguished by Junior Walker's scorching sax, gave them another US hit, before transatlantic sensation 'Waiting For A Girl Like You' led *4* (1981) to multi-platinum US sales and over a year on the UK chart. They capitalized on this upsurge with the best-of set, *Records* (1982). *Agent Provocateur* (1984), trailed by US/UK No.1 'I Want To Know What Love Is', was another world-beater, but fragile relations between Jones and Gramm deteriorated. *Inside Information* (1987) spawned yet more US smashes – 'Say You Will' and 'I Don't Want To Live Without You' – but couldn't keep Gramm from promoting a tentative solo career into a full-time concern. Jones plumbed the depths with his own, eponymous 1989 album, but enjoyed more success in collaborations with Billy Joel and Eric Clapton.

However, when both Gramm's new act Shadow King and Foreigner's *Unusual Heat* (1991) – featuring Johnny Edwards on vocals – sank without trace, they reunited. Though their commercial standing had plummeted, *The Very Best… And Beyond* (1992) and *Mr Moonlight* (1994) proved their craftsmanship to be intact.

Fan Hard To Handle Management, 1133 Broadway, Suite 1301, New York, NY 10010, USA

Surf www.geocities.com/SunsetStrip/8471/index.htm

4AD

4AD loomed large over 80s Indie, propelling Pixies, Throwing Muses, Lush, Cocteau Twins and The Breeders chartwards, but keeping an alternative cool. Founded in 1980 by Beggars Banquet personnel Ivo Watts-Russell and Peter Kent, the label traded as Axis for early releases (notably Bauhaus), but secured Goth credentials as 4AD with The The and The Birthday Party. Clothed in Vaughan Oliver's sumptuous designs, the Watts-Russell discoveries Cocteau Twins (and fellow etherealists Dead Can Dance) typified the label's abstract approach and guested in the 4AD 'supergroup' This Mortal Coil. An introverted period in the mid-80s (when proto-Dance experimentalists Colourbox and X-Mal Deutschland reigned supreme) gave way to credible commercialism: Pixies and Throwing Muses revealed a hitherto hidden American Rock tendency and A.R. Kane/Colourbox offshoot M/A/R/R/S stormed UK and US charts with 1987's excellent 'Pump Up The Volume'. After an early 90s surge with Lush, The Breeders and Belly, 4AD withdrew into its ambient fog, save for albums by former Muses Tanya Donelly and Kristin Hersh.

"I really like the Foo Fighters because their essence is what I remember as the essence of Dave's drumming – powerful and heavy yet also fun-loving"

Krist Novoselic (Nirvana)

THE FOUR SEASONS ⊙

WHO Vocals **Frankie Valli** (b. Francis Castelluccio, 3 May 1937, Newark, New Jersey, USA), vocals **Bob Gaudio** (b. 17 Nov 1942, The Bronx, New York, USA)

WHEN 1956–

WHERE Newark, New Jersey, USA

WHAT Falsetto majesty

From Newark band The Varietones, Frankie Valli, Hank Magenski and brothers Nick and Tommy De Vito formed The Four Lovers, who enjoyed a minor hit with Otis Blackwell's '(You're The) Apple Of My Eye' (1956) – compensation for not recording 'Don't Be Cruel', which Blackwell had earmarked for Elvis.

After a stint at Philadelphia label Swan, briefly The Beatles' US home, 1960 saw them rechristened The Four Seasons. In the first of many line-up changes, Gaudio joined and wrote their US No.1 hit 'Sherry' (1962), lodging Valli's falsetto in Rock history. In 1963, No.1s 'Big Girls Don't Cry' and 'Walk Like A Man' confirmed The Four Seasons as challengers to The Beach Boys and Beatles' domination. Million-sellers abounded: 'Dawn (Go Away)', 'Rag Doll' (both 1964), 'Let's Hang On' (1965), 'Workin' My Way Back To You' (1966). Valli scored solo with 'The Proud One' (1966) and 'Can't Take My Eyes Off You' (1967). However, success was derailed by 1969's psychedelic *Genuine Imitation Life Gazette*.

In the 70s, cabaret hell beckoned. However, Valli's 1974 solo single 'My Eyes Adored You' was a career-saving smash. The Bay City Rollers and The Osmonds continued the renaissance with Valli/Four Seasons covers, while their own *Who Loves You* (1975) – notably the title track and 'December '63 (Oh What A Night)' – capitalized on the nostalgia and Disco markets (albeit minus Gaudio). After *Helicon* (1976), Valli split to concentrate on his solo career, which flared with 1978's US No.1 theme from *Grease*.

Reunions in the 80s (sometimes starring six Four Seasons) preceded the original line-up's 1990 induction to the Rock And Roll Hall Of Fame. 'December '63' saw action again in the 90s: used in movie weepy *Forrest Gump* (1994) and covered by the magnificent Clock in 1996.

SURF www.srv.net/~roxtar/fvalli.html

THE FOUR TOPS ⊙

WHO Vocals **Levi Stubbs** (b. 6 Jun 1936, Detroit, Michigan, USA), vocals **Abdul 'Duke' Fakir** (b. 26 Dec 1935, Detroit), vocals **Renaldo 'Obie' Benson** (b. 1937, Detroit), vocals **Lawrence Payton** (b. 1938, Detroit, d. 1997)

WHEN 1953–

WHERE Detroit, Michigan, USA

WHAT Solid, soulful and sporadically sublime

Originally The Four Aims, this quartet retained the same line-up for 44 years and set standards for vocal drama that few matched. Their early act involved close-harmony singing and a willingness to perform anywhere. Detroit label Motown opened doors for local talent and The Four Tops were soon signed. Producers/writers Holland-Dozier-Holland's hits showcased Stubbs' impassioned lead vocals and the others' strong support. 'I Can't Help Myself' (1965) and 'Reach Out, I'll Be There' (1966) both hit US No.1, the latter repeating the feat in the UK and setting new standards for sound, its ambitious production using everything from flutes to Arab drums. Their powerful and danceable sound proved surprisingly adaptable, taking in Psychedelia, MOR and Gospel with ease. Among a succession of hit albums, *Greatest Hits* (1968) spent over a year on the UK chart, reaching No.1 in the process. Their production team's exit from Motown and the label's shift to Los Angeles led the Tops to ABC, for whom they cut more hits before moving towards the nostalgia circuit as changing fashions cut them adrift from the Pop audience.

A professional, hard-working quartet, their business-like approach was at odds with the political consciousness of 70s black music. Benson co-wrote the seminal 'What's Goin' On' for Marvin Gaye, but The Four Tops never cut anything as blatant.

In 1988, 'Loco In Acapulco', from the soundtrack to *Buster*, and 'Indestructible' showed the old power in good shape after 35 years. By the time of Payton's death, the influence and quality of The Four Tops were widely accepted and obituaries extended from music magazines to the daily press.

SURF wormhole.map.com/'freek/fourtops/html

Kim Fowley

KIM FOWLEY:LFI

Ubiquitous in Rock since the 50s, Kim Fowley is a songwriter, producer, manager, organizer and troublemaker. Born on 21 July 1939 in Los Angeles, California, USA, Fowley was the son of Douglas, who played Doc on US TV's Wyatt Earp, while his step-grandfather was composer Rudolf Friml. After meeting a young Brian Wilson in 1957, he began writing songs and joined local group The Jayhawks.

In 1959, Fowley became a DJ in Boise, Idaho, producing Paul Revere & The Raiders and The Hollywood Argyles' 1960 US No.1 'Alley Oop'. More hits followed with B. Bumble & The Stingers' Tchaikovsky pastiche 'Nutrocker' and The Rivingtons' 'Papa-Oom-Mow-Mow' (as horrifically featured in Stanley Kubrick's 1987 movie Full Metal Jacket). In 1963, Fowley hit with his own group The Murmaids' 'Popsicles and Icicles'. In England, he worked with P.J. Proby, appeared on TV's Ready Steady Go! and produced Slade, Traffic's Jim Capaldi and Dave Mason, Family and Soft Machine. Stateside, he became immersed in Psychedelia: organizing love-ins, recording his Love Is Alive And Well (1967), singing on Frank Zappa's Freak Out (1967) and producing The Seeds and The Fraternity Of Man's 'Don't Bogart That Joint'.

In 1969, Fowley produced Gene Vincent's I'm Back And I'm Proud, then worked with Warren Zevon, Helen Reddy and Jonathan Richman & The Modern Lovers. He was also a successful songwriter for The Beach Boys, The Byrds, Them, Leo Kottke and Cat Stevens. Despite more albums, it is as a writer, producer and impresario that Fowley is best known. In 1976, with lyricist Kari Krome, he masterminded The Runaways, featuring Joan Jett and Lita Ford. Opportunistic instincts intact, Fowley formed a new Runaways in 1987 with an entirely different line-up.

PETER FRAMPTON ✪

WHO b. 22 Apr 1950, Beckenham, Kent, England

WHAT Teen idol turned guitar hero

As guitarist for British hit-makers The Herd, Peter Frampton was voted 'The Face of 1968'. This iconic status was reinforced when, as Wayne's World II had it, Frampton Comes Alive was "issued at birth" to Stateside suburb-dwellers.

After five albums with Humble Pie and flop solo debut Wind Of Change (1972), America embraced the lush Frampton's Camel (1973), Something's Happening (1974) and Frampton (1975). Constant touring presaged the Frampton Comes Alive! (1976) phenomenon, whose live hits 'Show Me The Way' (featuring a squawking 'TalkBox' later deployed on Bon Jovi's 'Livin' On A Prayer'), 'Baby I Love Your Way' and 'Do You Feel Like We Do' made it one of the albums of the 70s.

I'm In You (1977) was his last platinum-seller and – unlike co-stars Aerosmith, Bee Gees and Earth, Wind & Fire – he barely survived 1978's movie flop Sgt. Pepper's Lonely Hearts Club Band. After Where I Should Be (1979), charts found no room for Breakin' All The Rules (1981), The Art Of Control (1982), Premonition (1986) or When All The Pieces Fit (1989). Premonition did, however, catch the ear of old schoolmate David Bowie, who invited Frampton onto his 1987 'Glass Spider' tour. After a tentative reunion with Humble Pie's Steve Marriott, ended by the latter's death in 1991, he resumed a low-key career with Peter Frampton (1994) and Frampton Comes Alive II (1995), and united with Foreigner and REO Speedwagon for 1995's thrilling 'Can't Stop Rockin' tour.

ⓇⒺⒶⒹ Peter Frampton (1979), Irene Adler

Ⓕⓐⓝ Frampton, c/o Rock Around The World, PO Box 352, Woodland Hills, CA 91365, USA

ⓈⓊⓇⒻ www.frampton.com/

FRANKIE GOES TO HOLLYWOOD ⊙

WHO Vocals **William 'Holly' Johnson** (b. 19 Feb 1960, Khartoum, Sudan), backing vocals/dancing **Paul Rutherford** (b. 8 Dec 1959, Liverpool, England), guitar **Brian 'Nasher' Nash** (b. 20 May 1963, Liverpool), bass **Mark O'Toole** (b. 6 Jan 1964, Liverpool), drums **Peter 'Ped' Gill** (b. 8 Mar 1964, Liverpool)

WHEN 1982–1987

WHERE Liverpool, England

WHAT Sex and Dance and Rock 'n' Roll

From the fertile late-70s Liverpool band Big In Japan (featuring KLF's Bill Drummond and Lightning Seed Ian Broudie) came 'dirty Disco' diva Holly Johnson. Spurning solo obscurity, he formed Frankie Goes To Hollywood, officially named after a headline about Frank Sinatra. Embellished by the scantily clad Leather Pets and sideman Paul Rutherford, a performance on UK TV show *The Tube* snared superstar producer Trevor Horn, who made Frankie the flagship of his label ZTT. A BBC ban sent 'Relax' supernova in early 1984, followed by 'Two Tribes', whose nine-week stay atop the chart was bolstered by a blood-crazed video.

The spectacular *Welcome To The Pleasuredome* and a third No.1, 'The Power Of Love', confirmed Frankie as *the* phenomenon of 1984. In January 1985, 'Relax' cruised to No.10 in America – uniting transatlantic teenagers in 'Frankie Say' T-shirts. As their domination peaked, war erupted between 'The Lads' (Nash, Gill and O'Toole) and Johnson, exacerbated by ego-clashes at ZTT.

Liverpool limped out in October 1986; its sales and singles

signalling Frankiemania's demise. Only Johnson enjoyed subsequent success – although his albums (notably 1989's UK No.1 *Blast*) were overshadowed when he was diagnosed HIV-positive. ZTT's tenth anniversary sent Frankie reissues and hits album *Bang!* (1993) into the UK chart, heart-warming nostalgia quickly deadened by 1994's redundant remix collection *Reload*.

READ *A Bone In My Flute* (1994), Holly Johnson

FAN FGTH Fan Base, PO Box 223270, 57038 Siegen, Germany

SURF www.cs.unimaas.nl/~antal/fgth/fgth-home.html

ARETHA FRANKLIN

WHO b. 25 Mar 1942, Memphis, Tennessee, USA

WHAT Queen of Soul

Aretha was raised by her father, the Reverend C.L. Franklin, after her mother left when she was 6. The Franklins were one of Detroit's most prominent black families, and Aretha was given singing lessons by legends like Mahalia Jackson, The Ward Sisters, Frances Steadman, Marion Williams and James Cleveland, all friends of her father. Aretha taught herself piano and toured the Gospel circuit with her father, but didn't consider a singing career until she heard another family friend, Clara Ward, sing 'Peace In The Valley' at a funeral.

Her first recordings, for Chicago's Checker label, were made at her father's church when she was 14, but she signed to Columbia for her first R&B hits: 'Today I Sing The Blues' (1960), 'Won't Be Long' and 'Operation Heatbreak' (both 1961).

Crossover success remained elusive until her defection to Atlantic in 1966. Over the next three years, with producers Jerry Wexler, Arif Mardin and Tom Dowd, and musicians King Curtis and The Muscle Shoals Sound Rhythm Section, she initiated a classic streak with 1967's 'I Never Loved A Man (The Way I Love You)'. An anthemic revamp of Otis Redding's 'Respect' (1967) was followed up the charts by Carole King's '(You Make Me Feel Like) A Natural Woman' and, in 1968, Don Covay's 'See Saw' and 'Chain Of Fools' and Bacharach & David's 'I Say A Little Prayer'.

Four US Top 5 albums – 1967's *I Never Loved A Man The Way I Love You* and *Aretha Arrives*, and 1968's *Aretha: Lady Soul* and *Aretha Now* (the latter also a UK smash) – testified to her popularity. By the end of the 60s, Franklin had been crowned 'Lady Soul', but was dogged by controversy – including arrests for reckless driving and disorderly conduct – and an unhappy relationship with manager Ted White, whom she married in 1962.

However, classics kept coming. On Pop covers collection *This Girl's In Love*

With You (1970), she made The Band's 'The Weight' – featuring Duane Allman on slide guitar – her own. Other classics given Lady Soul's loving touch included Simon & Garfunkel's 'Bridge Over Troubled Water' and Ben E. King's 'Spanish Harlem' – both featured on *Aretha's Greatest Hits* (1971).

There was critical acclaim for *Spirit In The Dark* (1970), sales success for *Aretha Live At Fillmore West* (1971) and both for *Young, Gifted & Black* (1972). The latter featured two US smashes: 'Rock Steady', an ahead-of-its-time Funk gem, and 'Day Dreaming', a little slice of heaven. However, after the double-platinum Gospel set *Amazing Grace* (1972) and the transatlantic hit 'Until You Come Back To Me', from *Let Me In Your Life* (1974), Franklin drifted.

Despite its hit 'Angel' (written by one of Aretha's greatest collaborators, her sister Carolyn), 1973's *Hey Now Hey (The Other Side Of The Sky)* was a flop hook-up with producer Quincy Jones. *With Everything I Feel In Me* (1974) and *You* (1975) were just flops.

Recovering with the Curtis Mayfield-produced *Sparkle* (1976), she slipped again with *Sweet Passion* (1977), *Almighty Fire* (1978) and *La Diva* (1979). The latter, an ill-advised stray into Disco, was her last album for Atlantic before switching to Arista, who set her to work on poppier stuff with *Aretha* (1980) and *Love All The Hurt Away* (1981). The policy paid off when the Luther Vandross-produced *Jump To It* (1982) returned her to the charts – albeit in a fairly low position. After the Vandross-produced *Get It Right* (1983) bombed, Arista took charge, recruiting cream-of-the-crop sessioneers and producer Narada Michael Walden for *Who's Zoomin' Who* (1985). Thanks to hits like the title track and 'Freeway Of Love', it was a million-selling resurrection. Hits with Eurythmics (1985's 'Sisters Are Doin' It For Themselves') and George Michael ('I Knew You Were Waiting (For Me)', from 1986's *Aretha*) confirmed the comeback and, in 1987, she became the first woman inducted to the Rock And Roll Hall Of Fame.

However, Franklin again fell victim to stylistic indecision. *One Lord, One Faith, One Baptism* (1988) was a sensational return to Gospel, *Through The Storm* (1989) an underwhelming return to Pop, despite its hit title track duet with Elton John. The latter was among the guests on the 1993 TV special *Aretha Franklin: Duets* with Gloria Estefan, George Michael, Smokey Robinson and Rod Stewart. The best of this genre-hopping was her storming 1994 makeover of C+C Factory's 'A Deeper Love'.

Three decades after her 1968 landmark *Aretha: Lady Soul*, Franklin made a star-studded comeback. Her previous effort, *What You See Is What You Sweat* (1991), had been outsold 2:1 by *Greatest Hits (1980–1994)*. Now the Hip Hop glitterati, including Puff Daddy, were gathered for *A Rose Is Still A Rose* (1998). Its title track was written by Fugee star Lauryn Hill, who told *Billboard*:

"After she left the session, we ran into the booth and tried to soak up her energy. It smelled like church. It was pure and filled with life..."

Franklin's renaissance continued with the reprisal of her role as a harassed diner owner in *Blues Brothers 2000* and a roof-raising cameo at the 1998 Grammy award ceremony, where she deputized for Luciano Pavarotti on a soaring 'Nessun Dorma'.

READ *Aretha Franklin* (1990), Mark Bego

SURF www.wallofsound.com/artists/arethafranklin/index.html

FREE

WHO Vocals **Paul Rodgers** (b. 17 Dec 1949, Middlesborough, Cleveland, England), guitar **Paul Kossoff** (b. 14 Sep 1950, London, England, d. 19 Mar 1976), bass **Andy Fraser** (b. 3 Jul 1952, London), drums **Simon Kirke** (b. 29 Jul 1949, London)

WHEN 1968–1973

WHERE London, England

WHAT Classic British R&B

In singer Paul Rodgers and guitarist Paul Kossoff, Free possessed two of British R&B's all-time greats. They met by chance on London's 'Blues boom' gig circuit. Kossoff, son of actor David, was with drummer Simon Kirke in Black Cat Bones when he spotted Rodgers fronting fellow black music fans Brown Sugar. Blues veteran Alexis Korner recommended 15-year-old prodigy Andy Fraser – just sacked by John Mayall – for bass.

On 19 April 1968, in Battersea, London, they rehearsed and wrote for the first time. Soon, they were off on a six-gigs-a-week schedule maintained for the next two years. In July, Chris Blackwell signed them to his Island label. *Tons Of Sobs* (1968) and *Free* (1969) sold modestly and constant touring produced good money (handled by the precociously astute Fraser).

Rodgers' and Fraser's 'All Right Now' turned their lives upside down. With its distinctive bassline, guitar break and summery sway, it reached UK No.2, highlighted Free's set at the second Isle Of Wight Festival and lifted parent album *Fire And Water* to UK No.2 and US No.17. However, Free's friendship proved vulnerable to fame. A power struggle between Fraser and Rodgers developed and, ten months after 'All Right Now', the band split – just weeks before their cheery 'My Brother Jake' hit UK No.4.

The rest of Free's story veered between shambolic and tragic. Fraser's band Toby and Rodgers' Peace went nowhere, as did Kossoff, Kirke, Tetsu & Rabbit's self-titled album (1971). Despairing at Free's demise, Kossoff slid into narcotic oblivion (tranquilizers first, heroin later). Partly to restore their own fortunes, but also hoping to help Kossoff, Free re-formed in January 1972. *Free At Last* did well (UK No.9), but Kossoff's playing was painfully erratic and the rift between Fraser and Rodgers beyond repair. The bassist left that July. With Kossoff collapsing on stage, missing overseas tours and playing only sporadically on *Heartbreaker* (1973), Free disbanded at the end of their 1973 US tour, after a last hit with 'Wishing Well' (UK No.7).

Fraser's subsequent groups failed and, in the mid-70s, he moved Stateside to earn a comfortable living as a songwriter. Rodgers and Kirke founded Bad Company and secured a place in the big league. Kossoff toured and recorded with Back Street Crawler but, after drug-related misadventures, died of heart failure on a Los Angeles–New York flight.

Although Free's legacy is often boiled down to 'All Right Now' (hence *The Best Of Free – All Right Now*, a Top 10 hit in 1991), their loose-limbed take on Rock lives on in the likes of Reef and even Pearl Jam's less angsty moments.

(fan) Free Appreciation Society, c/o David Clayton, 39 Staverton Road, Bilborough, Nottingham, NG8 4ET, UK

(surf) www.inetnow.net/-piller/freebe.hem

Alan Freed

Alan Freed was a revolutionary 50s American radio DJ, widely credited with popularizing Rock 'n' Roll. Born on 15 December 1922, in Johnstown, Pennsylvania, USA, Freed played trombone and led a Jazz band at high school in Ohio. After college, he worked at several radio stations, settling at WJW in Cleveland, Ohio, in 1950. On his show Moondog's Rock 'n' Roll Party, he played black R&B records to a predominantly white audience, rechristening the sound 'Rock 'n' Roll'. A riotous 1952 'Moondog Ball' in Cleveland was cancelled when thousands gatecrashed the arena. Moving to New York station WINS in 1954, Freed added to his notoriety with wild concerts at the Brooklyn Paramount. His manic broadcasting put WINS among the most popular stations and, as Rock 'n' Roll gained momentum, Freed tried to copyright the term.

While receptive to white stars such as Elvis, and appearing in movies such as Rock Around The Clock (1956) and Mr Rock 'N' Roll (1957), Freed remained loyal to R&B, earning him many enemies. A riot at a Boston show led to incitement charges which, although dropped later, bankrupted him with legal fees. In 1959, Freed was accused of 'payola': accepting money from record companies in return for airplay. (He earned a co-writer credit on Chuck Berry's 'Maybelline' for such services.) He was charged with 26 counts of bribery, for which he was fined and given a suspended sentence. His career in tatters, Freed was excluded from a scene he had helped to create, while other DJs continued to profit from payola. Awaiting trial on tax evasion charges, he died on 20 January 1965, in Palm Springs, Florida.

ROBERT FRIPP

WHO b. 16 May 1946, Wimborne, Dorset, England

WHAT Guitar craftsman

Head honcho of King Crimson, Robert Fripp also produced an erratic but frequently more interesting bunch of solo albums and collaborations. Two of the earliest were with Brian Eno: the frightening *No Pussyfooting* (1973) and more restrained *Evening Star* (1975). In 1974, he quit the music biz to hibernate and re-learn the guitar from scratch, a process he dubbed 'Guitarcraft'.

Exposure (1977) was a brilliant return to form. Collaborators included Peter Hammill, Peter Gabriel (with whom he toured and whose second solo album he produced) and Daryl Hall. His patented 'Frippertronics' – soloing over taped guitar loops – was showcased on late 70s albums, notably *Let The Power Fall* (1978). He formed short-lived Pop act The League Of Gentlemen with Barry Andrews from XTC in 1981, before re-forming Crimson. He also married (in 1986), recorded and toured with Toyah Willcox.

The late 80s found him concentrating on an American Guitarcraft school, source of bandmates and Fripp clones, and continuing a decade-long diatribe against the music biz. Despite this antipathy, he returned to the UK chart with 1993's David Sylvian collaboration *The First Day*. Frippertronics has evolved into the New Age-ish 'Soundscapes', captured on a welter of live releases on his own Discipline Global Mobile label and a cameo on Ambient noodlers Future Sound Of London's *Lifeforms* (1994).

read *Robert Fripp: From King Crimson To Guitar Craft* (1991), Eric Tamm

Fan We'll Let You Know, 3 Kings Drive, Bradford, BD2 1PX, UK

surf www.discipline.co.uk/

THE FUGEES ✪

WHO Vocals **Lauryn 'L-Boogie' Hill** (b. 19 Oct 1975, East Orange, New Jersey, USA), vocals/guitar **Wyclef** (b. Jeannel Wyclef Jean, 17 Oct 1972, Haiti), vocals **Pras** (b. Samuel Prakazrel Michel, 19 Oct 1972, Haiti)

WHEN 1987–

WHERE New York, USA

WHAT Rap, Reggae, riches

Amidst Gangsta Rap's guns 'n' gloom, Fugees offered optimistic lyrics and music based on acoustic instruments rather than P-Funk samples. The world shrugged and ignored *Blunted On Reality* (1993). Undaunted, the former 'Tranzlator Crew' refined the 'Refugee Camp' manifesto that blossomed on *The Score* (1996). The infectious 'Fu-Gee-La' paved the way for global phenonemon 'Killing Me Softly' (a Reggaefied take on Roberta Flack's 'Killing Me Softly With His Song'). Second UK No.1 'Ready Or Not' proved it wasn't a fluke. United with fellow Rappers Nas and Cypress Hill, they toured the most theatrical Funk show since George Clinton, then rounded off the year with a cover of 'No Woman, No Cry' and remix album *Bootleg Versions* (1996).

The hits continued into 1997 with the Abba-sampling 'Rumble In The Jungle', Lauryn's lovesexy 'The Sweetest Thing', Pras' 'Avenues' (based on Eddy Grant's 'Electric Avenue') and the kaleidoscopic, million-selling *Wyclef Jean Presents The Carnival Featuring Refugee Allstars*. Among the hits from the latter were 'Gone Till November', whose lyric quoted 'Knockin' On Heaven's Door' and whose video featured, spookily enough, Bob Dylan.

In 1998, Fugee finesse was extended to R&B divas both modern and veteran. Wyclef produced R&B starlets Destiny's Child and guested in their video for the sensational 'No, No, No', while Lauryn wrote the proud 'A Rose Is Still A Rose' for Aretha Franklin. "She was right on the target with the message," said Aretha. "It was two powerful sisters working together."

surf www.geocities.com/SouthBeach/2903/fugees.htm

FUN LOVIN' CRIMINALS

WHO Vocals/guitar **Huey** (b. New York City, New York, USA), keyboards/bass/trumpet **Fast** (b. New York), drums **Steve** (b. New York)

WHEN 1993–

WHERE New York, USA

WHAT Mob-obsessed Hip Hop Rock

On their debut EP 'The Grave And The Constant', Fun Lovin' Criminals blended Hip Hop, Jazz and Blues. Their breakthrough, 'Scooby Snacks' (1996), added Tarantino movie samples to the mix, paving the way for the cool lifestyle essential *Fun Lovin' Criminals* (1996). The hits 'The Fun Lovin' Criminal', 'The King Of New York' and a cover of 10cc's 'I'm Not In Love' kept the momentum going into 1997. Huey sang on the star-stuffed UK No.1 'Perfect Day' and added a touch of romance to the Criminal world by stepping out with Saffron of Republica.

 Fun Lovin' Criminals Fan Club, 401 Hillscross Avenue, Morden, Surrey, SM4 4BZ, UK

 www.geocities.com/SiliconValley/Heights/7725/flc.htm

FUNK

WHAT The straightjacket of Soul could only contain James Brown for so long. In 1967, his boundary bombing extended beyond exhilarating live shows to heart-stopping hits like 'Cold Sweat'. Heartfelt harmonies were toppled by bass-driven lust – hence 1970's key classic 'Get Up (I Feel Like Being A Sex Machine)'. George Clinton and Sly Stone added psychedelic lunacy to the stew: the flamboyant counterpart to R&B in 70s black music. Their legacy lives on in innumerable Hip Hop samples and impressionable white boys like Red Hot Chili Peppers and The Brand New Heavies.
WHERE USA
WHEN Late 60s–
WHO Sly & The Family Stone <u>Greatest Hits</u> (1970), The Gap Band <u>Gap Band IV</u> (1982), George Clinton <u>Computer Games</u> (1982), James Brown <u>In A Jungle Groove</u> (1986)

BILLY FURY

WHO b. Ronald Wycherly, 17 Apr 1941, Liverpool, England, d. 28 Jan 1983

WHAT One of Britain's greatest pre-Beatles Rock 'n' Roll stars

Ronald Wycherly was spotted at a gig in Liverpool by impresario Larry Parnes, who christened him Billy Fury. He began touring and released his first hit for Decca, 'Maybe Tomorrow', in 1959. In March 1960, he hit UK No.9 with his own composition, 'Colette', followed by 'That's Love' and his first album, *The Sound Of Fury* (1960). After more hits and sacking his band The Blue Flames – which included keyboardist Georgie Fame – Fury abandoned Rock 'n' Roll for MOR hits such as 'Halfway To Paradise' and 'Jealousy' (both 1961).

After appearing in the movie *I've Gotta Horse* (1965) and more UK hits, Fury began a lengthy absence from the charts in 1966 and underwent surgery for heart problems. In 1973, he came out of semi-retirement to play Rock 'n' Roller Rocky Tempest in the movie *That'll Be The Day*. In 1982, making a TV show and recording songs for a comeback, Fury was hospitalized after a heart attack. He died of heart disease in January 1983, aged 41.

 Half Way To Paradise (1996), Spencer Lee

 Now Dig This, 19 South Hill Road, Bensham, Gateshead, Tyne and Wear, NE2 2XR, UK

FUSION

WHAT Often tarred as musicianly meandering, Fusion refers to a blend of Rock and Jazz. Miles Davis led the way, followed by John McLaughlin, Billy Cobham and Chick Corea, blasting off into sometimes exhilarating, sometimes interminable 'explorations' (hence Spinal Tap's 'Jazz Odyssey'). Though now a commercial dead duck, elements of Fusion survive in Acid Jazz acts like Jamiroquai.
WHERE USA
WHEN 60s–
WHO Miles Davis & John McLaughlin <u>Jack Johnson</u> (1970), Soft Machine <u>Third</u> (1970), Weather Report <u>Street Nighter</u> (1973), Joni Mitchell <u>Mingus</u> (1979)

PETER GABRIEL ◉◉

WHO b. 13 Feb 1950, Chobham, Surrey, England

WHAT Musical Merlin of multi-media

After recording the mysterious novelty single 'You'll Never Know' with English comedy actor Charlie Drake, and a cover of The Beatles' 'Strawberry Fields Forever' for the soundtrack *All This And World War II* (1976), Gabriel began recording his first album. *Peter Gabriel* (1977) – the first of four eponymous albums – was more focused and personal than his work with Genesis. Despite the shift in approach, he immediately established himself as a chartworthy artist with the single 'Solsbury Hill' (1977).

Peter Gabriel (1978), produced by Robert Fripp, was weakened by the conflict between Fripp's improvisational athleticism and Gabriel's painstakingly crafted compositions. More successful artistically, rather than commercially, was Fripp's *Exposure* (1979), on which Gabriel sang. He spent most of 1979 planning a movie of *The Lamb Lies Down On Broadway,* which came to nothing.

Meanwhile, a new album was underway, with Phil Collins, Fripp, keyboard player Larry Fast and bassist Tony Levin. Producer Steve Lillywhite, fresh from sessions with Siouxsie & The Banshees, corralled Gabriel's experimental leanings, led by his new Fairlight CMI – one of the first sampler/sequencers. *Peter Gabriel* (1980) saw cameos from Kate Bush, who sang on the hit 'Games Without Frontiers', and Paul Weller. 'Biko', an anthemic protest song about the injustices of the South African apartheid system and death of political activist Steve Biko, contained samples of African funeral drumming. Although only a minor hit, the song symbolized the 80s' anti-apartheid effort, and Gabriel's championing of what became known as World Music.

He furthered the cause in July 1982 with the first of his World Of Music, Arts & Dance (WOMAD) festivals in Somerset, England, which united diverse musicians together from all over the world and left Gabriel with a £200,000 debt. Genesis helped out with a reunion gig later that year. In September 1982, his last self-titled album – retitled *Security* in America by Gabriel's US label Geffen – used more ethnic instrumentation, including Ethiopian pipes and Ghanaian percussion. Amid spooky drones and drums, the funky 'Shock The Monkey' gave Gabriel his first US hit.

He reunited once more with Genesis in May 1983 to collect an Ivor Novello award for 'Outstanding Contribution To British Music' and released *Peter Gabriel Plays Live* (1983).

Turning to movies, Gabriel contributed the eerie 'Walk Through The Fire' to *Against All Odds* (1984), the boppy 'Out Out' to *Gremlins* (1984) and an entire score to *Birdy* (1985). He also established his involvement with the human rights movement, contributing to Artists United Against Apartheid album *Sun City* (1985) and the single 'Sun City'.

Gabriel's international megastardom came in 1986 with the smash 'Sledgehammer' and its ground-breaking animated video. At last combining innovation with commercialism, he even gave his next album a name, *So* (1986) – which mixed his experiments in texture with catchy Pop songs. Further singles from the album included 'Don't Give Up' with Kate Bush, the US-only 'In Your Eyes' and 'Big Time'. Further charity work included an American tour, 'A Conspiracy Of Hope', with U2, Sting, Bryan Adams and Lou Reed, a huge anti-apartheid concert in London, and the contribution of 'Biko', now an anti-apartheid anthem, to the Amnesty International benefit album, *Conspiracy Of Hope.*

Much of 1988 was spent playing shows worldwide, including Nelson Mandela's 70th birthday tribute at Wembley Stadium, London, and the 'Human Rights Now!' tour for Amnesty with Sting, Bruce Springsteen, Tracy Chapman and Youssou N'Dour.

In 1989, after collaborating with Youssou N'Dour on his *Set* album, Gabriel's soundtrack to the controversial Martin Scorsese movie *The Last Temptation Of Christ*, entitled *Passion*, was issued.

On 16 April 1990, Gabriel again resurrected 'Biko' when he played the second Nelson Mandela tribute concert at Wembley Stadium. In 1991, Gabriel released the hits set *Shaking The Tree* and organized events such as WOMAD (an annual event since 1982) and a 'recording week' for over 100 musicians from around the world as part of his Real World organization, which consists of an advanced studio in Wiltshire, England, and a record label releasing the works of international musicians.

The wrenching 'Digging In the Dirt' trailed *Us* (1992), which married *So*'s tasteful sound to darker lyrics, dwelling on troubled relationships (including one with actress Rosanna Arquette). He diversified into CD ROMs: *XPLORA 1* (1994) combined video, stills and audio to enable entrance into an interactive Real World environment, including a photo album, a journey through the WOMAD festival, the opportunity to remix 'Digging In The Dirt' and a jam session with Brian Eno. *EVE* (1996) is an adventure which interweaves contemporary art with Gabriel's music. Long-term plans include his plan, with Brian Eno, to open a Real World theme park and a Millennium project called 'The Clock Library'.

ReaD *Peter Gabriel: An Authorised Biography* (1988), Spencer Bright

Fan Real World Notes, PO Box 35, Corsham, Wiltshire, SN13 8SZ, UK

Surf realworld.on.net

GALLAGHER & LYLE

WHO Vocals/guitar/keyboards Benny Gallagher (b. Largs, Ayrshire, Scotland), vocals/guitar Graham Lyle (b. Largs)

WHEN 1972–1979

WHERE Largs, Ayrshire, Scotland

WHAT Swinging Scottish Folk

Gallagher and Lyle joined forces in 1964, initially as songwriters. Recognition came in 1968 when they were signed by The Beatles to write for Apple artists like Mary Hopkin. In 1970, they joined McGuinness Flint and penned the folkish UK Top 10 hits 'When I'm Dead And Gone' and 'Malt And Barley Blues'. In 1972, they went solo as Gallagher & Lyle, but not until their fifth album *Breakaway* (1976) did they chart again with the hits 'Heart On My Sleeve' and 'I Wanna Stay With You'. However, their mellow, radio-friendly sound was only briefly in vogue, elusive further success prompting their split in 1979. Lyle formed a new songwriting partnership with Terry Britten, their hits including 'What's Love Got To Do With It?' for Tina Turner in 1984.

RORY GALLAGHER

WHO b. 2 Mar 1949, Ballyshannon, Donegal, Ireland, d. 14 Jun 1995

WHAT Down-to-earth Blues guitar showman

Rory Gallagher's youthful idolization of Lonnie Donegan ("Because he played with such guts") led him to a profound love of Blues. He later said:

"Hardly a day goes by without me sticking on a Muddy Waters record"

After an apprenticeship with The Fontana Showband – later The Impact – Gallagher formed Taste in 1966 with drummer Norman Damery and bassist Eric Kitteringham. But, in Belfast in 1968, he found the perfect partnership with drummer John Wilson (ex-Them) and bassist Richard 'Charlie' McCracken. Taste rapidly cracked the British and European club and festival circuit: Gallagher, a charismatic frontman, thrillingly matched by Wilson and McCracken's exciting and unpretentious musicianship.

Taste (1969) and *On The Boards* (1970) were acclaimed and a prestigious US tour supporting Blind Faith augured well. But management hassles estranged Gallagher from his colleagues and the band sundered amid great bitterness. *Live Taste* (1971) and *Live At The Isle Of Wight* (1972) were released posthumously.

Wilson and McCracken formed Stud, recording three Progressive albums. McCracken later played with Spencer Davis; Wilson became Northern Ireland's top session drummer.

Gallagher returned to Belfast and recruited Wilgar Campbell (drums) and Gerry McAvoy (bass). With a slowly evolving line-up, he became renowned as a down-to-earth, hard-working performer whose rejection of the trappings of stardom was symbolized by his invariable jeans and workshirt and ever-present battered Fender Stratocaster.

He recorded with heroes like Muddy Waters, Albert King and Lonnie Donegan and worked with The Rolling Stones on their

GABRIELLE

WHO b. Louise Gabrielle Bobb, 16 May 1970, south London, England

WHAT Motownish UK chartbuster

Gabrielle won over the world with 'Dreams' (1993), a UK No.1 and US No.26. Her distinctive, eye-patched image and further hits 'Going Nowhere', 'I Wish' and 'Because Of You' helped her debut album *Find Your Way* (1993) into a million homes, and won her the 1994 BRIT award for Best British Newcomer.

After spending a year on motherhood, she returned in style with the Motownish 'Give Me A Little More Time' and beautiful 'If You Really Cared' from *Gabrielle* (1996), which added En Vogue's helmsmen Thomas McElroy and Denzil Foster to her production team. She rounded off a successful comeback with a hit cover of Swing stars Shai's 'If You Ever' – a collaboration with Pop bad lads East 17 (UK No.2, 1996). A hit cover of Burt Bacharach's 'Walk On By' and a BRIT award for Best Female ensured the success continued into 1997.

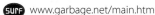
Black And Blue sessions in 1975 but, although albums like *Live! In Europe '72* (1972), *Blueprint* (1973) and *Irish Tour '74* (1974) charted, Gallagher never achieved major stardom.

It looked as if Gallagher, like his Blues mentors, would be on the road forever. But, in the 80s, though still popular, he became plagued by doubts and obsessive about details, admitting "I agonize too much". His health declined and he died of complications following a liver transplant in 1995.

READ *Irish Rock* (1987), Mark J. Prendergast

FAN 22 Killybrack Mews, Omagh, Northern Ireland

SURF www.btinternet.com/~rory.gallagher

GANGSTA RAP

WHAT The grand tradition of music clashes (Beatles v. Stones, Oasis v. Blur) reached a lethal low in the mid-90s. Rival Rap label bosses Suge Knight (Death Row) and Sean 'Puffy' Combs (Bad Boy) got irate, then figureheads Tupac Shakur and The Notorious BIG got dead. Simmering resentment between Puffy's New York and Knight's California was gleefully reported as an East v. West Coast war – the flames fanned by releases like Ice Cube's battle-crazed <u>Westside Connection</u> (1996). It was a messy end to Gangsta's first decade, in which the genre progressed from cause célèbre (Ice-T), through chart champ (Dr Dre), to cliché (Snoop Doggy Dogg). Though the music evolved from hard-as-nails Hip Hop and George Clinton-esque G-Funk to radio-friendly R&B, the themes remained unchanged – Gangsta's guns, drugs and sex being essentials of the 'playa' lifestyle espoused by platinum-sellers Foxy Brown, Jaÿ-Z and Master P.
WHERE Los Angeles, California, USA
WHEN 1987–
WHO The Notorious BIG <u>Ready To Die</u> (1994), The Firm <u>The Album</u> (1997), Various <u>Gang Related (The Soundtrack)</u> (1997)

GARBAGE ⊙

WHO Vocals/guitar **Shirley Manson** (b. Edinburgh, Scotland), guitar/bass/keyboards **Steve Marker** (b. USA), guitar/bass/keyboards **Duke Erikson** (b. Doug Erikson, USA), drums/keyboards **Butch Vig** (b. Bryan Vig, Viroqua, USA)

WHEN 1993–

WHERE Wisconsin, USA

WHAT The Grunge M People

Vig (producer of Nirvana, Smashing Pumpkins, Sonic Youth), Erikson and Marker, having fruitlessly tried to escape studio production with their groups Spooner and Firetown, found the key with Manson, formerly of Indie also-rans Goodbye Mr MacKenzie and Angel Fish. She joined them in Garbage, named after a friend's verdict on their music. After two limited-edition singles in 1994 – 'Vow' and 'Subhuman' – their Goth Grunge conquered the UK and US charts in 1995 with 'Only Happy When It Rains' and 'Queer' from debut *Garbage* (1995), which also yielded the hits 'Stupid Girl' and 'Milk' – a collaboration with Tricky – in 1996. *Version 2.0* made UK No.1 in 1998.

FAN Garbage Zone, 300 Queen Anne Ave. N., Suite 332, Seattle, WA 98109, USA

SURF www.garbage.net/main.htm

"This whole band thing... I keep thinking it's all gonna go **horribly wrong.** I'm just waiting for someone to jump out at me, **laughing** that they had me going**"**

MARVIN GAYE

WHO b. Marvin Pentz Gay Jr, 2 Apr 1939, Washington, DC, USA, d. 1 Apr 1984, Los Angeles, California, USA

WHAT Sadly missed Soul pioneer

With a childhood background of singing and playing the organ at his father's church, Marvin received an honourable discharge from the US Air Force in 1957 and joined Doo Wop group The

Marquees, who recorded the flop Okeh singles 'Hey Little Schoolgirl' (produced by Bo Diddley) and 'Baby You're My Only Love' before being absorbed into The Moonglows by their leader Harvey Fuqua. Gaye sang with the rechristened Harvey & The Moonglows, who released 'Almost Grown' on Chess in 1959. He and Fuqua then left for Detroit, where Fuqua set up two labels, Tri-Phi and Harvey, later absorbed into Motown when Fuqua married into the family of Motown boss Berry Gordy.

Gaye also married into the Motown mob (his wife Anna was Gordy's sister). In 1961, having drummed on several singles – including The Marvelettes' 'Please Mr Postman' – he recorded his Motown debut, *The Soulful Moods Of Marvin Gaye* (1961), a collection of Jazz-inflected croons intended – according to friend Smokey Robinson – to establish him as a black Sinatra. The album and extracted singles flopped, but 1962's 'Stubborn Kind Of Fellow' set in motion a train of hits, combining Gaye's Gospel background with Motown's famous Soul sheen on 'Hitch Hike', 'Pride And Joy' and 'Can I Get A Witness' (all 1963).

Gaye became one of Motown's flagship artists, notching up hits throughout the 60s, including 'You're A Wonderful One', 'Once Upon A Time' (his debut UK hit), 'What's The Matter With You Baby', 'Try It Baby', 'How Sweet It Is (To Be Loved By You)' (all 1964), 'I'll Be Doggone', 'Ain't That Peculiar' (both 1965) and a string of duets with Mary Wells ('Once Upon A Time' from 1964's *Together*), Kim Weston ('What Good Am I Without You', 'It Takes Two' and the 1967 album *Take Two*) and his most enduring vocal foil, Tammi Terrell, with whom he recorded the classics 'Ain't Nothing Like The Real Thing' (1968), 'The Onion Song' (1969) and two albums, *United* (1967) and *Easy* (1969).

The ever progressive Gaye stretched Motown's 3-minute Pop format to the limit, especially on 'I Heard It Through The Grapevine' (1969). The song had already been recorded by labelmates Gladys Knight & The Pips, but Gaye's darker version – with help from producer Norman Whitfield – was so far from the label's formula, even Berry Gordy was unconvinced. Gaye proved him wrong when the single became the label's biggest seller of its twenty-year history.

Terrell's death from a brain tumour in 1970 sent Gaye into semi-retirement, during which he tried out for American football team The Detroit Lions and recorded an album which did little to help his creative disagreements with Gordy. Gaye had often declared his discomfort with the Motown regime and his lack of control over the material he recorded, especially as he saw himself as a Jazz singer. He had already proved himself as a writer with William Stevenson on Martha & The Vandellas' 'Dancing In The Street' (1964) and his long-awaited new album was entirely self-composed. *What's Going On* (1971) – a softly-voiced song-cycle about poverty, war and ecology – was immediately rejected by Gordy, who even now maintains his bewilderment at the album. Again, Gaye proved him wrong – the album reached US No.6, spawned three hits – 'What's Going

"Marvin Gaye is our John Lennon. The longer he's gone, the more young people appreciate his art. What's Going On was a work of genius far ahead of its time"

Janet Jackson

On', 'Inner City Blues (Make Me Wanna Holler)' and 'Mercy Mercy Me (The Ecology)' – and paved the way for fellow Motown artist Stevie Wonder to move into similarly conceptual areas.

Gaye showed no sign of stagnation with his eerie score for 1972 movie *Trouble Man* and the erotic Soul of *Let's Get It On* (1972) and *I Want You* (1976). The duets continued, this time with Diana Ross on 'You're A Special Part Of Me' (1973), 'My Mistake (Was To Love You)', 'Don't Knock My Love', 'You Are Everything' and 'Stop Look Listen (To Your Heart)' (all 1974), and the album *Diana And Marvin* (1974). But personal problems marred his success, including a bitter divorce with Anna Gordy – paid for by the confessional *Here, My Dear* (1978) – bankruptcy and cocaine addiction. Moving to Hawaii to escape his tax debts, he reportedly attempted suicide.

Still on the run from American tax investigators, Gaye moved to Europe in the early 80s, dividing his time between England and Belgium, where he began to restructure his life after years of drug abuse and the collapse of his second marriage. *In Our Lifetime* (1981) was another inspired blend of Funk, Jazz and Soul and his last album for Motown. The Columbia-released *Midnight Love* (1982) included another classic: the career-saving 'Sexual Healing', which won him a Grammy in 1983. Gaye returned to the USA, but once more descended into cocaine-induced paranoia and depression. Living with his parents in LA, he threatened suicide several times. Feuding with his father peaked when, during a violent argument on 1 April 1984, the eve of Marvin's 45th birthday, Gaye Senior shot his son at point-blank range, killing him instantly.

His posthumous releases included out-takes sets *Dream Of A Lifetime* (1985), *Motown Remembers Marvin Gaye* (1986) and *Romantically Yours* (1986). In 1987, he was inducted into the Rock And Roll Hall Of Fame. The tribute album *Inner City Blues: The Music Of Marvin Gaye* (1995) included Madonna (with Massive Attack), Neneh Cherry, Stevie Wonder and Boyz II Men. In 1996, Gaye received a Lifetime Achievement Grammy award.

READ *Divided Soul* (1991), David Ritz

SURF www.sedgsoftware/marvin

GLORIA GAYNOR

WHO b. 7 Sep 1949, Newark, New Jersey, USA

WHAT Disco survivor

After several attempts to get into the music industry, Gaynor toured with New Jersey group The Soul Satisfiers before relocating to New York and signing to Columbia for 1973's dancefloor-aimed 'Honey Bee'. Moving to MGM in 1975, she hit US No.9 with *Never Can Say Goodbye* – whose title track had previously charted via recordings by The Jackson 5 and Isaac Hayes. After a career downturn with *Experience Gloria Gaynor* (1975), *I've Got You* (1976), *Glorious* (1977) and *Gloria Gaynor's Park Avenue Sound* (1978), she returned triumphant with 1979's platinum-selling *Love Tracks*, from which 'I Will Survive' swept to US No.1 and became a perennial Disco and karaoke favourite.

Subsequent releases – including *Gloria Gaynor* (1982), *I Am What I Am* (1984) and *Love Affair* (1992) – reflected her conversion to Christianity and failed to reach such dizzying heights, but covers by Chantay Savage (1996) and Cake (1997) confirmed the enduring appeal of her survival anthem.

Founded by former Asylum executive David Geffen and bankrolled by WEA, Geffen opened in 1979 with proven sellers Elton John and Donna Summer, but scored high with John Lennon's final album <u>Double Fantasy</u> (1980). A mid-80s dry spell ended in 1987 with triple-header Metal hit fest <u>Permanent Vacation</u> (Aerosmith), <u>1987</u> (Whitesnake) and <u>Appetite For Destruction</u> (Guns N' Roses). The label was also rejuvenated by Peter Gabriel, XTC, Kylie Minogue, Cher (a former belle of the label's head), Edie Brickell, Don Henley and Joni Mitchell (another former belle, who wrote 'Free Man In Paris' about David Geffen). When acquired by MCA in 1989, Geffen was the USA's third biggest label. Geffen remained president, and offshoot DGC got a licence to print money with Nirvana's <u>Nevermind</u> (1991) and other signings Hole, Beck, Aimee Mann and Weezer. Geffen finally left the company in 1995, founding SKG Dreamworks – home to George Michael and eels – with Steven Spielberg.

Geffen

THE J. GEILS BAND ✪

WHO Vocals **Peter Wolf** (b. Peter Blankfield, 7 Mar 1946, The Bronx, New York, USA), guitar **Jerome Geils** (b. 20 Feb 1946, New York City, New York), bass **Danny Klein** (b. 23 May 1946, New York City), drums **Stephen Bladd** (b. 13 Jul 1942, Boston, Massachusetts, USA), keyboards **Seth Justman** (b. 27 Jan 1951, Washington, DC, USA), harmonica **Magic Dick** (b. Richard Salwitz, 13 May 1945, New London, Connecticut, USA)

WHEN 1967–1985

WHERE Boston, Massachusetts, USA

WHAT Boston's biggest bar band

When the psychedelic bandwagon 'The Bosstown Sound' failed to make superstars of Peter Wolf's group The Hallucinations, he devoted himself to R&B with The J. Geils Band. They became a live sensation, snottily blanking Boston contemporaries Aerosmith, although the latter promptly eclipsed them.

The J. Geils Band discography began strongly with an acclaimed, eponymous debut (1971) and US No.10 *Bloodshot* (1973), but chart placings petered out and the band became more famous for Wolf's relationship with actress Faye Dunaway. (They married in 1974 and divorced five years later.)

Quitting the Atlantic label for EMI, they emerged from the doldrums with *Love Stinks* (1980) and finally exploded with the Funk Rock monster *Freeze Frame* (1981) – the album and transatlantic hit 'Centerfold' were US No.1s. However, the live *Showtime!* (1982) was their chart swan song, Wolf was fired in late 1983 and they split after *You're Gettin' Even While I'm Gettin' Odd* (1984). Wolf had a sporadic solo career – whose highlights were 1984's *Lights Out*, co-produced by electro whizkid Michael Jonzun, and 1987's irrepressible 'Come As You Are' – while Magic Dick and Geils reunited in 1993 to form Bluestime. Seth Justman used the quirky production flourishes he'd honed through *Freeze Frame* on Debbie Harry's *Rockbird* (1986).

SURF www.allmusic.com/cg/amg.exe

GENERATION X

WHO Vocals **Billy Idol** (b. William Broad, 30 Nov 1955, Stanmore, Middlesex, England), guitar/vocals **Bob Andrews**, bass/vocals **Tony James** (b. 1956), drums **John Towe**

WHEN 1976–1981

WHERE London, England

WHAT Pretty Punks

Refugees from Punk hipsters Chelsea, Billy Idol, Tony James and John Towe recruited guitarist Bob Andrews for Generation X, who made their debut at premier London Punk venue The Roxy in December 1976, despite owing more to Eddie Cochran and Slade than to The Stooges and Ramones. In the sneering, bleach-blond Idol, the group had a natural star whose looks propelled their debut 'Your Generation' into the UK Top 40. Towe left afterwards for The Adverts (replaced by ex-Subway Sect drummer Mark Laff), but with 'Ready Steady Go' and *Generation X* (1978), they blossomed from Punk also-rans to New Wave Popsters, garnering grudging respect from the press.

The Ian Hunter-produced *Valley Of The Dolls* (1979) and the singles 'King Rocker' and 'Valley Of The Dolls' pointed towards a successful, if slightly bland, future but, by 1980's classic ode to masturbation 'Dancing With Myself' (credited to 'Gen X'), tension was brewing: Laff quit and was replaced first by Clash drummer Terry Chimes, then fellow ex-Chelsea man James Stephenson. One last album (1981's forgettable *Kiss Me Deadly*) and it was all over – Idol embarked on a successful solo career in the USA, while James founded the reviled Sigue Sigue Sputnik and eventually joined The Sisters Of Mercy.

GENESIS ⊙⊙⊙⊙⊙⊙

WHO Vocals/drums **Phil Collins** (b. 31 Jan 1951, Chiswick, London), guitar/bass **Mike Rutherford** (b. 2 Oct 1950, Guildford, Surrey), keyboards **Tony Banks** (b. 27 Mar 1950, East Heathly, Sussex, England)

WHEN 1967–

WHERE Godalming, Surrey, England

WHAT English Prog Rockers turned Pop hit-makers

Genesis began as a union of members of two fledgling outfits, The Garden Wall and The Anon. Vocalist Peter Gabriel, guitarist Anthony Phillips, bassist Mike Rutherford, keyboard player Tony Banks and drummer Chris Stewart were pupils at Charterhouse School in Surrey. In 1967 they sent a demo to music impresario Jonathan King (an ex-Charterhouse pupil), who was sufficiently impressed to sign them and record their debut *From Genesis To Revelation* (1969), also coming up with the name 'Genesis'. The band briefly used the name 'Revelation' so as not to be confused with an American group named Genesis. The latter disbanded, and Genesis reverted to their original name.

Undaunted by commercial failure and King's consequent lack of interest, Genesis persevered with *Trespass* (1970), featuring new drummer John Mayhew. Melodic and flowery, it indicated the Progressive Rock direction the band was following, but again achieved little success. Within a year, Phillips left to pursue a low-key solo career in TV soundtracks and New Age noodling.

New drummer Phil Collins and guitarist Steve Hackett joined Gabriel, Banks and Rutherford for *Nursery Cryme* (1971), which set their Art Rock agenda with tracks like 'The Return Of The Giant Hogweed' and the live favourite 'The Musical Box'.

Key to Genesis' evolution was Gabriel's inventive theatricality, which made for weirdly witty lyrics and live shows. An early peak was 'Supper's Ready' from their UK chart debut *Foxtrot* (1972). In its pun-laden vision of the apocalypse lie the seeds of countless Progressive clichés, which were most wholeheartedly embraced by Marillion. Having attracted an earnestly fanatical following, the band broke the UK Top 10 with *Genesis Live* (1973). An icky sleeve note by Gabriel (the tale of a woman who unzips her body) confirmed a cosmic jokiness that distinguished Genesis from contemporaries like Yes and Emerson, Lake & Palmer.

They made good on their burgeoning reputation with the excellent *Selling England By The Pound* (1973). Their first album to chart in the US, it reached the UK Top 3 and yielded the hit 'I Know What I Like (In Your Wardrobe)', a UK No.21 in April 1974.

This success gave them licence to go completely mad on *The Lamb Lies Down On Broadway* (1974). In the tradition of the time, it was a double-album concept affair – but its incomprehensible story was rendered palatable by some of their best-ever songs, including the spine-tingling title track, the proto-electronic 'Back In NYC', the beautiful 'Carpet Crawlers' and the climactic 'In The Cage'. However, ambition bested them: a multi-media live show was dogged by technical mishap and Gabriel became distracted by plans for a *Lamb* movie. Having strained the patience of his cohorts, whose interest in theatrics tended to take second place to musicianship, Gabriel quit the band in 1975.

His was a hard act to follow, but pundits were confounded when Collins stepped forward and assumed the frontman role with remarkable confidence and ability (he sounded similar and had formerly sung background vocals while Gabriel took lead).

A Trick Of The Tail (1976) proved Collins was up to the task: it received excellent reviews, was their first gold disc in America and spent most of 1976 on the UK chart. The unspectacularly pleasant *Wind And Wuthering* (1976) and the live *Seconds Out* (1977) kept the faithful happy – but not Hackett, who quit for a solo career (which peaked with 1980's *Defector*, a UK No.9).

The remaining trio soldiered on with *And Then There Were Three* (1978) – which, despite disappointing die-hard fans and being among their least interesting albums, struck a chord with a wider public. The hit 'Follow You Follow Me' pushed them to platinum sales and paved the way for global conquest.

The world was theirs with *Duke* (1980) and *Abacab* (1981), both UK No.1s and US platinum-shifters.

Genesis' lengthy quest for a balance between Tony Banks' arty leanings, Rutherford's tunefulness and Collins' commercial instincts paid off with *Duke*'s 'Misunderstanding' and 'Turn It On Again' and *Abacab*'s title track – all transatlantic hits. The band's profile also profited from Collins' awesomely successful, parallel solo career – although there were hints that the division between the two was blurring.

DUKE
GENESIS

> "I suppose Genesis have had their **wild moments,** but we've always been seen as a **rather gentlemanly** band"

Mike Rutherford

However, after the superfluous *3 Sides Live* (1982), *Genesis* (1983) took a darker direction with the disturbing hit 'Mama' and the ghostly 'Home By The Sea'. More representative of their longer-term plans were the hits 'That's All' and 'Illegal Alien' – chirpy numbers that presaged 1986's Pop juggernaut *Invisible Touch*. It was another UK No.1 and a multi-million-seller in the USA, where the title track topped the chart. Its further smashes – 'Throwing It All Away', 'Land Of Confusion', 'Tonight, Tonight, Tonight' and 'In Too Deep' – sent them spiralling into the stadium circuit, maintained by *We Can't Dance* (1991) and its hits 'No Son Of Mine' and 'I Can't Dance'.

Genesis' tendency to commemorate their every move began to look like self-parody with *Live – The Way We Walk Volume One: The Shorts* (1992) and *Live – The Way We Walk Volume Two: The Longs* (1993). Sadly, an October 1982 reunion with Gabriel at the UK's Milton Keynes Bowl – a benefit for the singer's beleaguered WOMAD project – is commemorated by bootlegs only.

Solo stuff enjoyed varying fortunes. Collins and Gabriel were rarely short of chart-topping tunes and dollar-reaping albums. Hackett plugged away for years before scaling the US chart with *GTR* (1986), an AOR-ish collaboration with fellow Prog guitar hero Steve Howe of Yes. Equally shamelessly, he traded on former glories with the remake-fest *Genesis Revisited* (1996).

Rutherford coasted on Genesis' coat-tails with *Smallcreep's Day* (1980) and *Acting Very Strange* (1982), before hitting his stride with the band and album *Mike And The Mechanics* (1986).

The latter had a stab at challenging Collins' supremacy with the huge US hits 'Silent Running', 'All I Need Is A Miracle' and the chart-topping title track from *The Living Years* (1988). Their *Word Of Mouth* (1991) and *Beggar On A Beach Of Gold* (1995) kept sales bubbling well above the underbought levels of Tony Banks, the unluckiest man in Genesis. His *A Curious Feeling* (1979) and *The Fugitive* (1983) scraped the charts, but not even megastar guests like Fish from Marillion and That Bloke Out Of Wang Chung could save DOA's like *Bankstatement* (1989) and *Still* (1991).

Fish's name came up again when Rutherford and Banks found themselves auditioning lead singers after Collins grew tired of reconciling Pop sensibilities with the others' more experimental leanings and quit in 1996. However, after lengthy auditions, they settled on Ray Wilson, who briefly shot to stardom with Stiltskin (their Levi ad signature song 'Inside' was a UK chart-topper in 1994). Although the substitution failed to return their commercial success to former heights, *Calling All Stations* (1997) was a polished variation on the Gabriel-era formula of oblique lyrics and sweeping sounds. A UK No.2 placing and well-received shows confirmed Genesis had come from revelation, through revolution, to resolution.

READ *Genesis* (1992), Dave Bowler & Bryan Dray

FAN The Waiting Room, 174 Salisbury Road, Liverpool, L5 6RQ, UK

SURF www.genesis-web.com

GERRY & THE PACEMAKERS

WHO Vocals/guitar **Gerry Marsden** (b. 24 Sep 1942, Liverpool, England), bass **Les Chadwick** (b. 11 May 1943, Liverpool), piano **Les Maguire** (b. 27 Dec 1941, Wallasey, Merseyside, England), drums **Freddie Marsden** (b. 23 Nov 1940, Liverpool)

WHEN 1959–1967

WHERE Liverpool, England

WHAT Masters of Merseybeat

Gerry & The Pacemakers were the first Liverpool group to top the UK chart and the first act ever to reach No.1 with their first three British releases (a record not equalled for 20 years). Like The Beatles, they honed their skills at Liverpool's Cavern and in the cellar clubs of Hamburg, were managed by Brian Epstein, produced by George Martin and their first No.1, 'How Do You Do It?' (1963), had even been recorded previously by the Fab Four.

Voted Best New Act of 1963, they completed their trio of toppers with 'I Like It' and 'You'll Never Walk Alone' (both 1963). They helped lead the British Invasion of America: among their transatlantic Top 20 hits were the self-penned 'Don't Let The Sun Catch You Crying' (1964) and 'Ferry 'Cross The Mersey' (1965), the theme from their first film of the same name (1964). The group, who were the flagship of the Merseybeat sound, sank with that style and disbanded in 1967. Effervescent lead singer Marsden remained in the public eye, however, and in the 80s sang on two charity chart-toppers, reviving the group's earlier show-stoppers, 'You'll Never Walk Alone' and 'Ferry 'Cross The Mersey'.

Glastonbury

The Glastonbury Festival is one of the most enduring and well-loved Rock festivals in the world. Farmer and organizer Michael Eavis conceived the event after witnessing Led Zeppelin, Jefferson Airplane, Pink Floyd and Santana at the 1970 Bath Blues Festival in England. The first 'Glastonbury Fayre' was arranged for 19 September 1970, with The Kinks as headliners. When they sent Eavis a doctor's sick note excusing their non-appearance, Marc Bolan's T. Rex were drafted in as replacements and 1,500 fans turned up. A local Hell's Angels group provided dubious security, between them exhausting Eavis' free milk supplies and landing him heavily in debt. Andrew Kerr was organizer for the 1971 festival, with Bill Harkin constructing the now famous 'Pyramid Stage' (also a cowshed for Eavis), for a bill including Hawkwind, Traffic, Joan Baez, Fairport Convention and David Bowie, with an estimated attendance of 12,000. One of the few festivals remaining loyal to the hippie philosophies that inspired it, the Glastonbury Festival has always been a patron of charities, including CND and, more recently, Greenpeace. By the 90s, the festival was huge, with hundreds of acts, including circus performers and comedians as well as bands. The festival's 25th anniversary, in 1995, boasted Oasis, Pulp, Orbital, Massive Attack, Portishead, Sinead O'Connor, PJ Harvey, Page & Plant, The Lightning Seeds, Supergrass, The Prodigy and Ash, among many others.

GLAM ROCK

WHAT When frumpy mods Slade and hippie wannabe Marc Bolan failed to set charts alight, they followed David Bowie's lead: dabbing on glitter, pulling on platform boots and promptly plundering the hearts and wallets of a generation of teenyboppers. Glam's hallmarks were lyrical ludicrousness, musical unsophistication and visual excess, epitomised by Gary Glitter (hence the offshoot 'Glitter Rock'), satirized by David Bowie's 'Rebel Rebel' and appropriated by Kiss. The genre died at the feet of Punk, although a mid-80s revival under the Heavy Metal umbrella spawned Poison, Guns N' Roses and, to their subsequent embarrassment, Pantera.

WHERE UK

WHEN 1971–1975

WHO T. Rex <u>Electric Warrior</u> (1971), David Bowie <u>The Rise And Fall Of Ziggy Stardust And The Spiders From Mars</u> (1972), Gary Glitter <u>Glitter</u> (1972), Sweet <u>Desolation Boulevard</u> (1974), Slade <u>Wall Of Hits</u> (1991), Poison <u>Look What The Cat Dragged In</u> (1986)

GARY GLITTER

WHO b. Paul Gadd, 8 May 1940, Banbury, Oxfordshire, England

WHAT Glam Rock Elvis

He'd been a TV Pop show warm-up man and made desperate Pop singles under desperate names – including Rubber Bucket. Glam Rock, with its stick-on charm and Rock 'n' Roll roots, was a godsend for Glitter, who first donned a spangly suit in 1972. With a sound half-way between a football terrace and the Rock 'n' Roll beat of early Elvis, Glitter hit the UK charts with 1973's tribal-thumping 'Rock And Roll (Parts 1 & 2)', 'I Didn't Know I Loved You (Till I Saw You Rock 'N' Roll)', 'Do You Wanna Touch Me? (Oh Yeah)', 'Hello Hello I'm Back Again' and the No.1s 'I'm The Leader Of The Gang (I Am)' and 'I Love You Love Me Love' in 1973.

Further hits, including third No.1 'Always Yours' (1974), kept his reign as Glam's camp king secure – although America remained unmoved, purchasing only 'Rock And Roll Part 2' and 'I Didn't Know I Loved You…' in chart-worthy quantities. The former became a sports stadium favourite and resurfaced in barely-disguised form as KLF's 1988 hit 'Doctorin' The Tardis'.

A trouper to the end, Glitter soldiered through bankruptcy and terminal unfashionability to return to the UK chart with 1984's 'Dance Me Up' and the Top 10 smash 'Another Rock And Roll Christmas'. He continues to play the part with annual 'Gang' shows combining Glam and pantomime to perfection.

Never taking himself seriously, Glitter's gigging kept him in the public eye, helping him survive damaging tabloid stories about his private life. Vocally, he never needed to be great, although he's pretty good on the original *Jesus Christ Superstar* (1972), where he's billed as 'Paul Raven'. Sadly, his cameo in The Spice Girls' movie classic *Spiceworld* (1997) amounted to nothing.

fan Our Gang Gary Glitter Official Fan Club, PO Box 927, Edgbaston, Birmingham, B16 0EB, UK

surf www.ourworld.compuserve.com/homepages/vanderhinden/gg1400

"I can't stand people not looking at me when I'm on stage"

THE GO-GO'S ☆

WHO Vocals **Belinda Carlisle** (b. 17 Aug 1958, Hollywood, California, USA), guitar **Charlotte Caffey** (b. 21 Oct 1953, Santa Monica, California), guitar **Jane Wiedlin** (b. 20 May 1958, Oconomowoc, Wisconsin, USA), bass **Kathy Valentine** (b. 7 Jan 1959, Austin, Texas, USA), drums **Gina Schock** (b. 31 Aug 1957, Baltimore, Maryland, USA)

WHEN 1978–1985

WHERE Los Angeles, California, USA

WHAT New Wave darlings

Despite charting with chirpy New Wave, The Go-Go's were California Punks at heart. Their ascent to multi-platinum status with the US No.1 *Beauty And The Beat* (1981) was matched by a cocaine-driven descent, including being banned from Ozzy Osbourne's dressing room for rowdiness. Convening as The Misfits (unrelated to the same-named Metallers), they burned bright with *Beauty* hits 'We Got the Beat' and 'Our Lips Are Sealed', but fizzled out with *Vacation* (1982) and *Talk Show* (1984).

Carlisle cleaned up for solo stardom (aided by Caffey) while Wiedlin recorded and acted. Reunions for *Greatest Hits* (1990) and *Return To The Valley Of The Go-Go's* (1994) eventually ended acrimoniously, but The Go-Go's clearly influenced acts like The Bangles and Cyndi Lauper and are fondly remembered by the pre-MTV generation. Caffey's later band The Graces helped springboard Meredith 'Bitch' Brooks to stardom.

FAN Beatnik Beat, PO Box 129, Southport, PR8 6UW, UK

SURF www.geocities.com/SunsetStrip/3981/

GOLDEN EARRING

WHO Vocals/guitar **George Kooymans** (b. 11 Mar 1948, The Hague, The Netherlands), bass/keyboards/harmonica **Rinus Gerritsen** (b. Marinus Gerritsen, 9 Aug 1946, The Hague), vocals/flute/saxophone **Barry Hay** (b. 16 Aug 1948, Faizabad, India), drums **Cesar Zuiderwijk** (b. 18 Jul 1950, The Hague)

WHEN 1961–

WHERE The Hague, The Netherlands

WHAT Hard Rock from The Hague

Formerly The Tornados, The Golden Earrings were formed by Kooymans and Gerritsen, still schoolboys when the bubblegum of 'Please Go' and *Just Earring* charted in their native Holland in 1964. By 1968, they were the hard rockin' Golden Earring. Little known in the USA and UK, the European success of 1972's 'Back Home' and *Together* caught the attention of The Who, who signed them to their Track label, releasing the compilation of Dutch hits *Hearing Earring* (1973).

Moontan (1974) was their international peak, its classic 'Radar Love' reaching US No.20 and UK No.7. While later releases failed to storm the USA, European success continued with *Switch* (1975), *Contraband* (1977), *Grab It For A Second* (1979), *Prisoner Of The Night* (1980) and *N.E.W.S.* (1984), among others. 'Twilight Zone' (from 1983's *Cut*) repeated the success of 'Radar Love', but Golden Earring otherwise remain the most successful Rock group you've never heard of.

SURF www.mdc.net/~dlynch/earring.htm

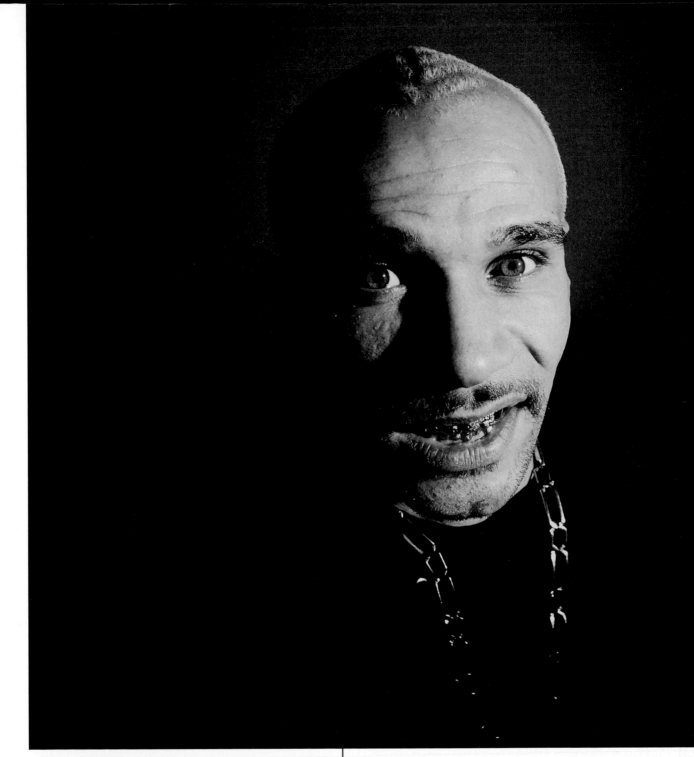

GOLDIE

WHO b. Clifford Price, 1965, Wolverhampton, England

WHAT Drum 'n' Bass dominator

From a misspent childhood, Clifford Price, aka Goldie, gravitated to the uncelebrated British Hip Hop scene. Dabbling in dancing and graffiti, he joined local Wolverhampton crew B-Boys.

After a trip to New York with future Massive Attack member 3-D, Goldie moved to his father's home in Miami, earning a living making and selling engraved gold tooth caps – hence the nickname. On his return to Britain, he immersed himself in the early-90s House and Hardcore scenes, acting as an A&R scout for the Reinforced label.

Recording as Rufige Kru, Goldie – with contemporaries like Fabio and Grooverider – created a sinister new sound, combining Hardcore's breakneck speed with butchered Hip Hop, Funk and Reggae. By 1994, Rufige Kru recordings like 'Rollin' Like A Scottie', 'Manslaughter' and 'Fury' had become Jungle classics.

Meanwhile, Goldie recorded as MetalHeadz: the acclaimed 'Terminator' EP and aching 'Angel' paving the way for his commercial breakthrough 'Inner City Life'. *Timeless* (1995) was confirmation of Jungle's explosion, opening the floodgates for later conquerors Roni Size and LTJ Bukem (and artists like Photek, signed to Goldie's Metalheadz label), but Goldie was swift to disassociate himself from a rash of imitators as the scene became increasingly split between its underground past and commercialized future.

Celebrity beckoned, including a well-publicized romance with Björk and a stint as a credible clothes horse. Splitting with long-time collaborator Rob Playford, 1997's 'Digital' (with Hip Hop preacher KRS-1) prefaced the crazed Noel Gallagher hook-up 'Temper Temper' and long-overdue *Saturnz Return* (1998): a bold move away from Drum 'n' Bass which included Goldie's first vocals, his orchestral epic 'Mother' and David Bowie on 'Truth'.

Berry Gordy

Born in 1929 in Detroit, Berry Gordy abandoned songwriting for professional boxing before joining the US Army during the Korean war. Discharged in 1953, he returned to Detroit, opened a Jazz record store, then worked in a Ford factory when the shop bankrupted him. His fortunes improved when he penned Jackie Wilson's hits 'Reet Petite' (1957) and 'Lonely Teardops' (1958) and Marv Johnson's 'You Got What It Takes' (1959). In 1960, he founded Motown, whose enormous success established him as a pioneering black music executive. He cast Motown protégée Diana Ross as Billie Holiday in the acclaimed biopic <u>Lady Sings The Blues</u> (1972), but watched helpless as <u>Mahogany</u> (1975) bombed. However, executive producer credits on the blockbusters <u>Dirty Dancing</u> (1987) and <u>Coming To America</u> (1988) proved less humiliating. Gordy's involvement with Motown declined to the point where he sold out to MCA, but his candid autobiography <u>To Be Loved</u> (1995) is testimony to his legendary status.

GOTH

WHAT From Punk's ashes rose the black-clad likes of Bauhaus and The Cure. They took Joy Division-esque despair to cartoon extremes, inspiring the self-parodic Sisters Of Mercy. 'Goth' – derived from a literary genre characterized by gloom and grotesqueness – quickly became a term of abuse, aggravating Nick Cave in particular. However, its portentous bass, droning synths and Dracula-esque trappings spawned the MTV-era horror of Nine Inch Nails, Marilyn Manson and <u>The Crow</u>.
WHERE Transylvania/Hades/Leeds, UK
WHEN 1977–
WHO The Cure <u>Pornography</u> (1982), Alien Sex Fiend <u>Who's Been Sleeping In My Brain?</u> (1983), The Mission <u>Children</u> (1988), Fields Of The Nephilim <u>The Nephilim</u> (1988), Various <u>The Crow</u> (1994)

Bill Graham

Born Wolfgang Grajonca in Germany in 1931, Bill Graham arrived in the USA as a refugee. After serving in the Korean war, he waited tables, drove taxis, studied drama, managed a mime troupe, then began promoting Rock gigs at a San Francisco skating rink he renamed The Fillmore. The latter became the centre of the late 60s hippie scene, featuring the likes of Jefferson Airplane and The Grateful Dead. As the scene grew, so too did the Fillmore chain: in 1968, the Fillmore West was followed by New York's Fillmore East. Accused of exploiting the hippie scene, Graham confounded critics by staging benefit concerts and putting black and white artists on the same bills. Disenchanted with the industry, he even closed the Fillmores in 1971. After brief retirement, he assumed management and promotional duties for Bob Dylan and The Grateful Dead and organized events such as The Band's 'Last Waltz' concert in 1976, the American Live Aid operation and Amnesty International's 1986 'Conspiracy Of Hope' tour. Graham was killed in a helicopter crash, returning from a concert, in October 1991.

THE GRATEFUL DEAD

WHO Vocals/guitar **Jerry Garcia** (b. Jerome John Garcia, 1 Aug 1942, San Francisco, California, USA, d. 9 Aug 1995, Forest Knolls, California), guitar **Bob Weir** (b. Robert Hall, 16 Oct 1947, San Francisco), organ **Ron 'Pigpen' McKernan** (b. 8 Sep 1945, San Bruno, California, d. 8 Mar 1973, Corte Madera, California), bass **Phil Lesh** (b. Philip Chapman, 15 Mar 1940, Berkeley, California), drums **Bill Kreutzmann** (b. 7 Apr 1946, Palo Alto, California), drums **Mickey Hart** (b. 11 Sep 1943, Long Island, New York, USA)

WHEN 1965–1995

WHERE San Francisco, California, USA

WHAT Acid Rock Odysseys

Through three decades, The Grateful Dead epitomized hippie idealism, from their anarcho-communalist origins in San Francisco to the development of an independent business dealing directly with their extensive fanbase of 'Deadheads'.

Though caricatured as dreamers and financial incompetents, The Dead became so efficient that, despite erratic album sales, they remained one of America's major concert attractions, even with a six-year gap between album releases. When they brought down the final curtain in December 1995, their corporation's annual revenue topped $50 million.

The band's roots lay in the Folk and Blues boom of the early 60s: Garcia, Weir and McKernan got together in 1964 as Mother McCree's Uptown Jug Champions. When Lesh and Kreutzmann joined the following year, the group went electric as The Warlocks, adopting the name The Grateful Dead in 1966 as the hippie movement took off in their Haight-Ashbury backyard.

Originally playing a mixture of R&B and Folk Rock, they developed a more free-form improvisational style which matched the drug-fuelled euphoria of the times, often playing for hours at free concerts and San Francisco venues such as the Carousel (later the Fillmore) and Avalon. Their commune at 710 Ashbury, San Francisco, was one of the centres of the burgeoning hippie culture, and the band became a staple at the era's defining moments, including the 1967 Monterey Pop Festival and both Woodstock and Altamont (where they disastrously recommended the Hell's Angels as security to headliners The Rolling Stones) in 1969. In July 1973, playing alongside The Band and The Allman Brothers Band, they drew the largest audience of all time – 600,000 – to a concert at Watkins Glen, New York.

Garcia's writing partner, the poet Robert Hunter, had taken part in LSD experiments, and the group became the new drug's earliest and most ardent devotees, playing at the Trips Festivals and Acid Tests organized by charismatic writer Ken Kesey. With acid chemist Owsley Stanley III as their sound engineer and equipment designer, they were assured a constant supply of LSD with which they would dose unsuspecting visitors. When Warner Bros boss Joe Smith signed them, he was careful not to accept any drinks they offered.

Things were moving at such a pace that their first album *The Grateful Dead* (1967) was out of date by the time it was released. *Anthem Of The Sun* (1968) more accurately reflected their meandering psychedelic style. An extended suite painstakingly (and expensively) assembled from 17 live shows, sundry studio recordings and fragments of *musique concrète*, it was a commercial disaster which left the band in debt to Warners for years, though it has since been acknowledged as a classic of its kind. *Aoxomoxoa* (1969) was more controlled though equally unsuccessful, but *Live Dead* (1969) afforded the group their greatest breakthrough with lengthy but involving versions of 'Turn On Your Lovelight' and 'Dark Star'. The latter became a staple of their live set, reaching its apotheosis with the release of *GrayFolded* (1995), on which avant-garde composer John 'Plunderphonics' Oswald sampled and spliced dozens of live versions of the tune into two 45-minute pieces.

Influenced by The Band's revival of rootsy Rock, the group adopted polished Country Rock for *Workingman's Dead* (US No.27, 1970) and *American Beauty* (US No.30, 1970). Both drew on their history with, respectively, 'Uncle John's Band' and the anthemic 'Truckin'; the latter recounting the turmoil of a year in which the group was busted for drugs in New Orleans and had been forced to sack their manager Lenny Hart (drummer Mickey's father) for embezzlement. The group's burgeoning popularity, however, enabled a second live double album, *Grateful Dead* (aka *Skull & Roses*), to crack the US Top 30 in 1971. Emboldened by its success, they went one further the following year with *Europe '72* (US No.24, 1972), a triple album culled from their first major European tour, which even hardened Deadheads regarded as over-indulgent and tedious. The Dead's dedication to uncharted exploration was both appealing *and* frustrating: while their improvisational spirit could lead them up annoyingly featureless blind alleys, without it they tended to lapse into complacent Soft Rock, particularly when McKernan's death from liver failure in 1973 deprived the band of a positively unpredictable element. (He was replaced by Keith Godchaux, who brought along his wife Donna as an extra vocalist.)

The group's 1972 decision to start their own labels, Grateful Dead (for band releases) and Round (for solo projects), was typically ahead of its time, but *Wake Of The Flood* (US No.18, 1973), *From The Mars Hotel* (US No.16, 1974) and *Blues For Allah* (US No.12, 1975) were lacklustre affairs, despite their chart placings. Various offshoots included two self-titled solo albums from *Garcia* (1972 and 1974), and offerings from his Bluegrass ensemble Old And In The Way (1975), Hart's *Diga Rhythm Band* (1976) of eclectic percussionists, Weir's *Ace* (1972) and *Kingfish* (1976), Robert Hunter's *Tales Of The Great Rum Runners* (1974) and *Tiger Rose* (1975), and Lesh's experimental electronic album, *Seastones* (1975). Another splinter-group – Country Rock outfit New Riders Of The Purple Sage – developed a flourishing career

away from the Dead. But as the members diversified, the parent group lost impetus. Another live double, *Steal Your Face* (1976), failed even to chart and, in an attempt to revitalize their career, the band signed to Arista.

Things went from bad to worse with *Terrapin Station* (US No.28, 1977), the abysmal *Shakedown Street* (US No.41, 1978) and *Go To Heaven* (US No.23, 1980). The situation wasn't helped by three benefit gigs at the Great Pyramid for Egypt's Department of Antiquities, the last timed to coincide with September 1978's lunar eclipse. Transporting Owsley's custom-built 23-ton sound system to Africa and back reputedly cost the group $500,000.

Only their live reputation and appetite for touring enabled the Dead to continue profitably into the 80s. They eschewed studio recording until 1987 when, aided by an engaging video featuring puppet skeletons of the band, they won a first Top 10 hit with the catchy, autobiographical 'Touch Of Grey' (US No.9).

Its parent album, *In The Dark* (US No.6, 1987), was the most successful of their career, and though that year's tour backing Bob Dylan – never the strictest enforcer of musical structure himself – resulted in the predictably unfocused *Dylan And The Dead* (1989), the group remained among the biggest draws in America, with the 90s spent touring and releasing a

the grateful dead

plethora of live albums and merchandise including comics, golf and ski equipment, backpacks, books and dolls. The results were astonishing: in the last five years of their existence, the Dead sold over $226 million of tickets. Even a range of Garcia-designed neckties grossed $10 million in 1992, with Hillary Clinton buying some as Presidential Christmas presents. The group donated vast sums to ecological and musical causes, and sponsored the Lithuanian basketball team to appear in the 1992 Olympics, where they wore Dead-designed outfits.

The band called it a day when their guiding spirit Garcia, whom diabetes and persistent heroin usage had long rendered frail, suffered a fatal heart attack in a drug treatment centre in 1995. In tribute, a tie-dyed Grateful Dead flag was flown at half-mast over San Francisco's City Hall, two Arizona astrophysicist Deadheads named an asteroid after him, and his ashes were sprinkled in the Ganges and the San Francisco Bay.

The surviving members – bar drummer Kreutzmann – reunited in 1996 for a summer tour as The Other Ones, with guest keyboard player Bruce Hornsby.

READ *Dark Star: An Oral Biography Of Jerry Garcia* (1996), Robert Greenfield

SURF grateful.dead.net/

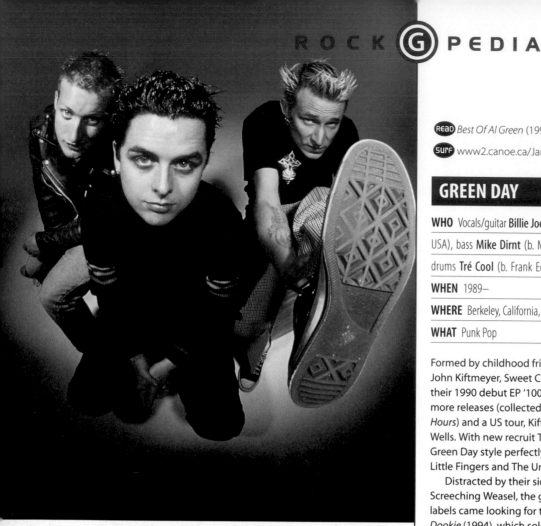

GREEN DAY

WHO Vocals/guitar **Billie Joe Armstrong** (b. 17 Feb 1972, San Pablo, California, USA), bass **Mike Dirnt** (b. Mike Pritchard, 4 May 1972, Berkeley, California), drums **Tré Cool** (b. Frank Edwin Wright III, 9 Dec 1972, Willits, California)

WHEN 1989—

WHERE Berkeley, California, USA

WHAT Punk Pop

Formed by childhood friends Armstrong and Dirnt and drummer John Kiftmeyer, Sweet Children became Green Day just before their 1990 debut EP '1000 Hours', on US Indie label Lookout. After more releases (collected on 1991's *1,039/Smoothed Out Slappy Hours*) and a US tour, Kiftmeyer quit for college and The Ne'er Do Wells. With new recruit Tré Cool, 1992's *Kerplunk* outlined the Green Day style perfectly: heavy doses of The Ramones, Stiff Little Fingers and The Undertones blended with snappy Pop.

Distracted by their side-projects Pinhead Gunpowder and Screeching Weasel, the group were unprepared when major labels came looking for them, and for the massive success of *Dookie* (1994), which sold over 10 million worldwide (thanks partly to the heavily rotated 'Basket Case'). Bewildered by their own success, they stumbled with 1995's *Insomniac* amid rumours of a split, but stabilized with the relatively low-key *Nimrod* (1997).

They left their multi-media mark in 1998 on the *Godzilla* movie soundtrack (with a remix of *Insomniac*'s 'Brain Stew') and a cartoon cameo in *King Of The Hill* as Cane & The Stubborn Stains.

AL GREEN

WHO b. Al Greene, 13 Apr 1946, Forrest City, Arkansas, USA

WHAT Honey-voiced Soul and Gospel superstar

Dismayed by his growing interest in R&B, Al's father fired him from the Greene Brothers Gospel group. Al then formed The Creations, who played the club circuit in the mid-60s. In 1967, the group set up the Hot Line Music Journal label, whose first release, 'Back Up Train' (credited to Al Greene & The Soul Mates), steamed into the R&B Top 10. However, it was a one-off hit and the label folded. Al dropped the 'E' from his surname and embarked on a solo career.

In 1969, producer Willie Mitchell signed him to the Memphis-based Hi label and in 1971, after a handful of R&B successes, Green's amazing run of crossover hits began with 'Tired Of Being Alone'. He followed that transatlantic Top 10 entry with 'Let's Stay Together' (1971), which topped the US Pop and R&B charts.

For the next three years, Green and Mitchell struck gold with classics like 'Look What You Done For Me' and the title track from *I'm Still In Love With You* (1972), 'Call Me (Come Back Home)', 'Here I Am (Come And Take Me)' and 'You Ought To Be With Me' from *Call Me* (1973) and 'Sha La La (Make Me Happy)' from *Al Green Explores Your Mind* (1974). Over five gold albums, he transformed from a post-Otis Redding funkateer to a soft Soul loverman, before a religious conversion led to him becoming a full-time preacher and Grammy-winning Gospel singer in 1979 (the same year Talking Heads scored a hit with his 'Take Me To The River').

He scored a transatlantic hit with the 1988 Annie Lennox duet 'Put A Little Love In Your Heart', was inducted into the Rock And Roll Hall Of Fame in 1995 and was heard by over a billion people worldwide when he helped to close the 1996 Atlanta Olympics.

GRUNGE

WHAT No one paid much attention when Punk-crazed kids like Melvins, Dinosaur Jr and Mudhoney fused adolescent inspirations Neil Young, Black Sabbath, Hüsker Dü and Black Flag to create Grunge. However, when Soundgarden, Nirvana and Pearl Jam added radio-friendly melodies and choruses, a globe-gobbling phenomenon was spawned. Overnight, plaid shirts, split ends, lyrical angst and monstrous riffing were jostling Michael Jackson at chart peaks. Though Grunge trampled into Indie and Pop, its most cataclysmic impact was on Heavy Metal: Glam poodles like Mötley Crüe were supplanted by ersatz grungers like Stone Temple Pilots. It also shot a new breed of girl groups to the top of the pile: Hole, L7, Babes In Toyland and – in the 'Riot Grrrl' uprising – Bikini Kill and Huggy Bear. The death of Kurt Cobain ended Grunge's glory, but it lives on, to the dismay of purists, with mega-sellers Offspring and Bush.

WHERE USA

WHEN 90s

WHO Babes In Toyland <u>Spanking Machine</u> (1990), Mudhoney <u>Every Good Boy Deserves Fudge</u> (1991), Nirvana <u>In Utero</u> (1993), Pearl Jam <u>Vitalogy</u> (1994), L7 <u>Bricks Are Heavy</u> (1992), Offspring <u>SMASH</u> (1994)

GUNS N' ROSES ☉ ✪ ✪

WHO Vocals **Axl Rose** (b. William Bailey, 6 Feb 1962, Lafayette, Indiana, USA), guitar **Izzy Stradlin** (b. Jeffrey Isbell, 8 Apr 1962, Lafayette), guitar **Slash** (b. Saul Hudson, 23 Jul 1965, Stoke-on-Trent, Staffordshire, England), bass **Duff McKagan** (b. Michael McKagan, 5 Feb 1964, Seattle, Washington, USA), drums **Steven Adler** (b. 22 Jan 1965, Cleveland, Ohio, USA)

WHEN 1985–

WHERE Hollywood, California, USA

WHAT The most dangerous (and worst-dressed) Metal band in the world

An early Guns N' Roses ad claimed "They're living fast and they'll die young", but despite intravenous indulgence and critical wishful thinking, they burned bright… then disappeared, apparently stalled by, of all things, artistic indecision.

Lured by the bright lights, country boys Axl Rose and Izzy Stradlin first bid for glory in Hollywood Rose and LA Guns. Fellow pilgrim Duff McKagan – having concluded (inaccurately, as it turned out) that one could "get to the top in Seattle and still be nowhere" – joined Road Crew, whose guitarist, Slash, had auditioned unsuccessfully for Poison and the embryonic GN'R ("Too Bluesy," they said). In 1985, McKagan defected to Rose and Stradlin's band, followed by Slash and Road Crew drummer Adler when early GN'R personnel Rob Gardner and Tracii Guns bailed out. The self-financed 'Live ?!*@ Like A Suicide' EP (1986) catapulted them onto Metal magazine covers. Writers and band alike hero-worshipped deceased Glam stars Hanoi Rocks, who brought 70s-style raunch to the 80s. About the only thing GN'R *didn't* owe to Hanoi was Rose's squawking voice (alternated with a more palatable Iggy Poppish croon).

In July 1986, they signed to Geffen and recorded *Appetite For Destruction* (1987), whose controversial cover painting of a robot menacing a Girl Scout initially had more impact than its white-hot anthems. GN'R's press coverage was quite disproportionate to their success: excesses were gleefully detailed and Metal magazine *Kerrang!* dubbed them Lines N' Noses. Two support slots fuelled the fire: a debauched jaunt with Mötley Crüe, then a stadium tour with the cleaned-up Aerosmith (whose Joe Perry and Steven Tyler bequeathed their 'Toxic Twins' mantle to the young Guns).

Appetite sold modestly for nearly a year, exploding when MTV fell in love with 'Sweet Child O' Mine'. The single and album topped the US charts, with a knock-on effect across the Atlantic. Never expecting to be bigger than Motörhead, GN'R were suddenly up with U2 and Bon Jovi: the album became the biggest-selling debut since *Boston* and eventually sold over 21 million. The ongoing Aerosmith tour and a stream of singles kept the pot boiling, before they blew the lid off with *GN'R Lies* (1988): their debut EP repackaged with new tracks. It made Guns N' Roses the first band in 15 years to place two albums simultaneously in the US Top 5 and yielded a tender anthem in 'Patience', yet achieved notoriety thanks to the minority-baiting 'One In A Million'. Critics railed, sales soared.

In the aftermath, Slash and Adler upped their indulgence, to the dismay of the comparatively clean Rose, whose obsessiveness further delayed a follow-up. Their resurrection at 1990's Farm Aid charity gig dispelled split rumours, although

Adler then achieved what *Q* magazine hailed as the awesome feat of being fired from GN'R for taking too many drugs. Slash poached replacement Matt Sorum (b. 19 Nov 1960, Long Beach, California, USA) from The Cult, and their ranks were swelled by keyboardist Dizzy Reed; the new line-up debuting at Brazil's Rock In Rio festival in 1991. *Use Your Illusion I* and *II* finally appeared that September, topping charts worldwide and eventually selling over 16 million each.

Stradlin, meanwhile, recovered from alcoholism, but promptly lost interest in the band he'd created. "I expressed my feelings to Axl," he explained, "and the very next night on MTV I saw that I was going to be replaced… I took that as an indication that I'd really pissed him off." Despite a well-received set with new band The Ju Ju Hounds in 1992, he seemed to be happiest out of the spotlight.

His replacement was Gilby Clarke (b. 17 Aug 1962, Cleveland, Ohio, USA), with whom GN'R embarked on a two-year tour, controversy dogging their every move. Dates with Metallica included a riot in St Louis, and ended with Rose and Metallica's James Hetfield at each other's throats. Critics – who slammed the band's teleprompters, backing singers and horn section –

Thereafter, GN'R – or, more precisely, the despotic Rose – tested the patience of even loyal followers. Clarke was replaced by Paul Huge, reportedly roundly loathed by Slash. The latter's attempt to reconcile with the singer yielded one hit – a cover of Stones anthem 'Sympathy For The Devil' (1995) – after which GN'R effectively ceased to be. Clarke issued *Pawnshop Guitars* (1994) and Slash scored with *It's Five O'Clock Somewhere* (1995), but – incensed by the latter's side-line Slash's Snakepit – Axl fired the guitarist in 1996; rumoured replacements included Sex Pistol Steve Jones. Recording plans were scuppered when hoped-for producer Moby declined to relocate to the West Coast and, in 1997, a *Q* enquiry to GN'R's record company about the band's plans was met with "Have they got back together?"

READ *Over The Top – The True Story Of Guns N' Roses* (1993), Mark Putterford

SURF www.teleport.com/~boerio/gnr/index.html

ARLO GUTHRIE

WHO b. 10 Jul 1947, Coney Island, New York, USA

WHAT Breezy Folk with political bite

Following in the footsteps of his father Woody, Arlo began playing harmonica aged 3 and guitar at 6. After attending college in Montana, he played the East Coast coffeehouse circuit. An acclaimed performance at Newport Folk Festival was followed by his debut *Alice's Restaurant* (1967), which reached US No.17 just weeks after Woody died. The album – which wove anti-Vietnam protests with whimsical Folk – was made into a movie in 1970 with Guthrie playing himself.

A performance at Woodstock increased Arlo's following, but future albums failed to match his earlier success. In 1972, he hit the US chart again with 'City Of New Orleans', but abandoned this more commercial style for a simpler approach. Guthrie launched Rising Son Records in the 80s and, in 1992, a collection of Woody's songs, performed by his children – *Twenty Grow Big Songs* – was nominated for a Grammy award.

WOODY GUTHRIE

WHO b. 14 Jul 1912, Okemah, Oklahoma, USA, d. 3 Oct 1967, Queens, New York, USA

WHAT Protest pioneer

With the bold "This machine kills fascists" on his guitar, Woody Guthrie expressed political views through innovative and passionate songs. Having inherited the skills of his banjo-playing father, Guthrie became known for impromptu shows and also collaborated with Blues legend Leadbelly. While his songs failed commercially, their political awareness gave Folk new direction.

Having tackled issues such as America's Great Depression and World War II, he wrote regularly for a Communist newspaper, but his influence and popularity grew only in his last years. Suffering from a disease of the nervous system, Guthrie was visited by Bob Dylan, just one of the artists inspired by his groundbreaking music. Others, including U2 and Bruce Springsteen, contributed to the 1988 tribute *Folkways: A Vision Shared*.

were lambasted in Rose's on-stage tirades. In a final twist, Stradlin deputized for Clarke after the latter broke his hand, reputedly earning a million dollars for five gigs. "I'm getting more and more confused about who's who," grumbled Roddy Bottum of support band Faith No More. "There's Dizzy and Iggy and Lizzy and Tizzy and Gilby and Giddy…"

Often overlooked was the music itself. The *Illusion* sets – heart-stopping headbangers laced with subdued smoulderers – yielded seven hits (including the *Terminator II* movie theme 'You Could Be Mine' and Wings cover 'Live And Let Die') and impressive videos; while a version of 'Knockin' On Heaven's Door', from their acclaimed appearance at the 1992 Freddie Mercury tribute gig, gave GN'R their biggest UK hit.

When the tour wound down in mid-1993, fans had only a few months to kill before new stuff emerged. McKagan's *Believe In Me* appeared in October, but was promptly upstaged by GN'R's *The Spaghetti Incident?*, a much-mooted covers collection. Envisaged as a Punk EP, it expanded to include Nazareth and The Skyliners, the latter's 1959 classic 'Since I Don't Have You' becoming GN'R's most implausible hit. Again, however, the gripping music was eclipsed by controversy, this time concerning the inclusion of 'Look At Your Game Girl', written by murderer Charles Manson.

HAIRCUT 100

WHO Vocals/guitar **Nick Heyward** (b. 20 May 1961, Beckenham, England), guitar **Graham Jones** (b. 8 Jul 1961, Bridlington, England), guitar **Phil Smith** (b. 1 May 1959, Redbridge, England), bass **Les Nemes** (b. 5 Dec 1960, Croydon, England), drums **Blair Cunningham** (b. 11 Oct 1957, Harlem, New York, USA), percussion **Mark Fox** (b. 13 Feb 1958)

WHEN 1981–1983

WHERE London, England

WHAT Carefree funky Pop

Haircut 100's angular Pop hit immediately when 'Favourite Shirts (Boy Meets Girl)' charted in 1981, helped by pin-up singer Nick Heyward. After hits 'Love Plus One', 'Fantastic Day', 'Nobody's Fool' and *Pelican West* (all 1982), plans were made for a TV series. However, stardom took its toll on Heyward, who quit soon after.

Percussionist Mark Fox led their final album *Paint And Paint* (1983), while Heyward went solo with *North Of A Miracle* (1983), *Postcards From Home* (1986), *I Love You Avenue* (1988), *From Monday To Sunday* (1993), *Tangled* (1995) and *World's End* (1997).

BILL HALEY

WHO b. 6 July 1925, Highland Park, Detroit, Michigan, USA, d. 9 Feb 1981

WHAT The first Rock 'n' Roll star…?

Although not the first to record with a Rock 'n' Roll beat, Haley was first to make the sound internationally successful. With The Down Homers, Haley recorded 'We're Recruiting'. In the late 40s he formed The Four Aces Of Western Swing, and in 1950 launched Bill Haley & The Saddlemen, whose Country R&B mix was tagged 'Cowboy Jive'. Their pioneering tracks included 1951's 'Rocket 88' and 1952's 'Rock The Joint'. When the latter, dubbed 'the blueprint for Rockabilly', outsold earlier efforts, Haley ditched Country and renamed his band The Comets. Their Haley-penned 'Crazy Man Crazy' reached the US Top 20 in 1953. Follow-up, 'Fractured' and 'Live It Up', also dented the US chart.

Intended as a B-side, the hastily recorded version of their live favourite 'Rock Around The Clock' (previously recorded by Sunny Dae), was fairly successful in early 1954 before a slicker cover of Joe Turner's 'Shake, Rattle & Roll' introduced Haley to the transatlantic Top 10. 'Dim, Dim The Lights' and 'Mambo Rock' (both 1955) followed it into the US chart before '(We're Gonna) Rock Around The Clock' (reissued after inclusion in the 1955 movie *Blackboard Jungle*) shot to the top in the UK and USA, becoming the first single to sell over a million in Britain. When three Comets left to form The Jodimars, guitarist Franny Beecher, saxophonist Rudy Pompilli and drummer Ralph Jones joined guitarist Billy Williamson, pianist/accordionist Johnny Grande and bassist Al Rex to form the best known line-up of The Comets.

Amongst their other hits were 'Razzle Dazzle' (1955), 'The Saints Rock 'N Roll' (1956) and the R&B songs 'Burn That Candle' (1955), 'Rip It Up' and 'See You Later, Alligator' (both 1956). In 1956, Haley & The Comets starred in the low-budget, big-earning movies *Rock Around The Clock* and *Don't Knock The Rock* and had five singles simultaneously in the UK Top 20. They smashed box-office records around the world, received unprecedented media coverage for their riotous 1957 British tour and were "treated like royalty" according to Haley. Nevertheless, by spring 1957, sales had slumped, their one-dimensional style and 30-something appearance blamed for the drastic decline.

The kiss-curled Haley was a prominent figure in Rock 'n' Roll revivals of the 60s and 70s and played to packed houses around the world until his death in 1981. He will always be remembered for '(We're Gonna) Rock Around The Clock', which amassed sales of over 25 million and changed the face of popular music.

READ *Sound And Glory* (1990), John W. Haley & John Von Hoelle

HALL & OATES

WHO Vocals/keyboards/guitar **Daryl Hall** (b. Daryl Franklin Hohl, 11 Oct 1948, Pottstown, Pennsylvania, USA), vocals/guitar **John Oates** (b. 7 Apr 1949, New York City, New York, USA)

WHEN 1969–

WHERE Philadelphia, Pennsylvania, USA

WHAT Blue-eyed Soul's banner-carriers

Among white boys playing black Soul, Hall & Oates were market leaders. Hall's early association with 'Philly Sound' producers Kenny Gamble, Leon Huff and Thom Bell included backing vocals for The Delfonics and The Stylistics. When his own band Gulliver fell short of this illustrious company, he and student friend Oates formed a Folk duo and signed to Atlantic. During *Whole Oates* (1972), *Abandoned Luncheonette* (1973) and *War Babies* (1974), Soul supplanted Folk before they fled Atlantic to RCA in 1975.

'Sara Smile' and *Daryl Hall & John Oates* (1976) rose up the US chart, prompting Atlantic's hit reissue of the classic tear-jerker 'She's Gone' from *Abandoned Luncheonette*. The upward curve continued with *Bigger Than Both Of Us* (1976) and US No.1 'Rich Girl', but declined through *Beauty On A Back Street* (1977), *Livetime* (1978), *Along The Red Ledge* (1978) and *X-Static* (1979). Hall took tentative solo steps with the Robert Fripp-produced *Sacred Songs* (1980). However, US No.1 'Kiss On My List', from *Voices* (1980), launched a blockbusting purple patch. *Private Eyes* (1981), *H₂O* (1982), hits set *Rock 'N' Soul, Part 1* (1983) and *Big Bam Boom* (1984) were the mega-selling sources of US chart-toppers 'Private Eyes', 'Maneater', 'I Can't Go For That' (revamped by De La Soul as 'Say No Go' and sampled by Rap artists such as Heavy D) and 'Out Of Touch'. In 1984, the RIAA announced that they were the most successful duo ever. This platinum-

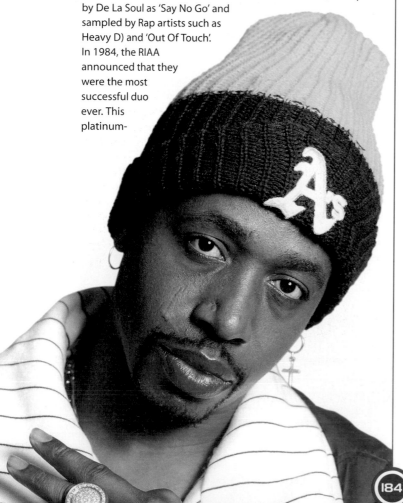

plaudited superduperdom enabled them to reunite estranged Temptations legends David Ruffin and Eddie Kendricks for the excellent *Live At The Apollo* (1985) and a Live Aid performance, but presaged a trial separation and the resumption of Hall's underwhelming solo career. Despite the successful comeback *Ooh Yeah!* (1988), the relative failure of *Change Of Season* (1990) prompted Hall to go it alone again with *Soul Alone* (1993), yielding Top 30 hit 'Stop Loving Me, Stop Loving You'. More minor hits (including collaborations with Sounds Of Blackness and Dusty Springfield) led to a reunion on *Marigold Sky* (1997).

(ReaD) *Dangerous Dances* (1984), Nick Tosches

(Fan) In Touch, 18 Twickenham Drive, Wirral, L46 1RL, UK

(Surf) www.h-and-onews.demon.co.uk

HAMMER ✪

WHO b. Stanley Kirk Burrell, 30 Mar 1963, Oakland, California, USA

WHAT Rap goes Pop

Ridiculed for his hook-hijacking, egomania and voluminous trousers, MC Hammer nonetheless opened lots of doors for Rap. After his Indie label debut *Feel My Power* (repackaged by Capitol as 1989's *Let's Get It Started*), he dominated the USA in 1990 with revamps of Rick James ('U Can't Touch This'), The Chi-Lites ('Have You Seen Her') and Prince ('Pray'), while the 10-million-selling *Please Hammer Don't Hurt 'Em* (1990) spent 21 weeks at No.1.

After his final smash 'Addams Groove', stratospheric success waned through *Too Legit To Quit* (1991), *The Funky Headhunter* (1994), *Inside Out* (1995) and *Family Affair* (1997), despite his shedding the unfashionable 'MC'. Hammer persevered through bankruptcy, with a more restrained lifestyle and wardrobe.

(ReaD) *Hammer: 2 Legit 2 Quit (Taking Part)* (1992), Linda Saylor-Marchant

(Surf) www.mchammer.com/pg3.html

HANOI ROCKS

WHO Vocals/saxophone **Michael Monroe** (b. Matti Fagerholm, 17 Jun 1962), guitar **Andy McCoy** (b. Antti Hulkko, 11 Oct 1962, Pelkosenniemie, Finland), guitar **Nasty Suicide** (b. Jan Stenfors, 4 Sep 1963), bass **Sam Yaffa** (b. Sami Takamaki, 4 Aug 1963), drums **Razzle** (b. Nicholas Dingley, Isle of Wight, England)

WHEN 1980–1985

WHERE Finland

WHAT Trash Metal titans

Just as The New York Dolls reaped few rewards by pioneering Glam Punk, so their musical (and sartorial) heirs Hanoi Rocks benefited little by flying the Glam Metal flag. Early albums and energetic shows won them a cult following, but 1983's *Back To Mystery City* (produced by Mott The Hoople alumni Dale Griffin and Overend Watts) was Hanoi's commercial breakthrough.

However, shortly after their biggest success – *Two Steps From*

The Move (1984) – a car crash claimed the life of Razzle (earning a jail sentence for drunk driver Vince Neil of Mötley Crüe) and the group disintegrated. McCoy formed Cherry Bombz with Clash survivor Terry Chimes and Anita Chellemah of UK novelty act, Toto 'I Eat Cannibals' Coelo. Monroe achieved his highest profile through collaborations with Guns N' Roses, whose debt to Hanoi showed in their Hard Rock and hairstyles.

surf pilleri.spt.fi/~jukka/

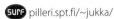
HAPPY MONDAYS

WHO Vocals **Shaun 'X' Ryder** (b. 23 Aug 1962, Little Hulton, Lancashire, England), guitar **Mark 'Cow' Day** (b. 29 Dec 1961, Manchester, England), bass **Paul 'Horse' Ryder** (b. 24 Apr 1964, Manchester), drums **Gary 'Ronnie' Whelan** (b. 12 Feb 1966, Manchester), keyboards **Paul 'Penis' Davis** (b. 7 Mar 1966, Manchester), dancing/percussion/"Madchester vibes in the area" **Mark 'Bez' Berry** (b. 18 Apr 1964, Manchester)

WHEN 1980–1993

WHERE Manchester, England

WHAT Anarchic, drug-addled Funk

Happy Mondays ushered in the early 90s 'Baggy' scene – a revolutionary mix of Dance and Indie – and injected genuine danger into the music industry. Record label boss Tony Wilson called them 'scum', but that's what made them great.

Formed in 1980, the Ryders' stand-up comic father Derek became their road manager. They recruited Paul Davis in 1983 and called themselves Happy Mondays (a reaction to New Order's 'Blue Monday') in 1984. Signed to Manchester label Factory in 1985, their debut 'Delightful' laid out their agenda: stoned Funk, teetering wonderfully on the brink of collapse. Although not great players, the music, particularly Shaun Ryder's lyrics and ragged vocals, was inspired. Best of all was new recruit Bez, who did little but dance his unique loping dance. He was there only for fun, a concept lost on John Cale, who was driven to despair producing 1987's chaotic *Squirrel & G-Man Twenty Four Hour Party People Plastic Face Carnt Smile (White Out)*.

'Wrote For Luck' from *Bummed* (1988) flexed their psychedelic Funk, making it ripe for dance remixes by Paul Oakenfold and Erasure's Vince Clarke. Poised between their Indie origins and the Acid House boom, they were to spearhead a revolution (building on the foundations of Factory forerunners like A Certain Ratio): the seamless merging of Rock and Dance. With their 'Madchester Rave On' EP, the Manchester-led Indie Dance scene (or 'Baggy') began its domination. 'Step On', their cover of John Kongos' 1971 hit 'He's Gonna Step On You Again', made UK No.5, as did 'Kinky Afro', ushering in success that ultimately destroyed the band.

Pills 'N' Thrills And Bellyaches (1990) was uncharacteristically polished and – despite reaching UK No.4 and US No.89 – lacked the power of previous efforts. 'Baggy' was dying, proved by poor attendance at their stadium show in June 1991 at Elland Road, Leeds, England, issued as *Live* (1991). By year's end, the Mondays had lapsed into self-parody, releasing the moribund 'Judge Fudge', sparking a backlash with homophobic statements, and appearing in Malcolm McLaren's *The Ghosts Of Oxford Street* TV special, performing The Bee Gees' 'Staying Alive'.

Working with Talking Heads' Tina Weymouth and Chris Frantz in the West Indies, Ryder 's drug habit reached breaking point and Bez broke his arm twice. … *Yes Please!* (1992) showed signs of recovery, but too late for the band and Factory, which folded soon after its release. The Mondays finally split while negotiating a new deal with EMI. Ryder returned with Bez in Black Grape.

surf gladstone.uoregon.edu/~cymru/mondays.html

STEVE HARLEY & COCKNEY REBEL

WHO Vocals/guitar **Steve Harley** (b. Steven Nice, 27 Feb 1951, London, England), guitar **Jim Cregan** (b. 9 Mar 1946), bass **George Ford**, drums **Stuart Elliott**, keyboards **Duncan Mackay** (b. 2 July 1950)

WHEN 1973–

WHERE Beckenham, Kent, England

WHAT Wordy, melodramatic Rock

Journalist and part-time Folk singer Steve Harley convened the original Cockney Rebel with bassist Paul Jeffreys, Stuart Elliott, guitarist/violinist Jean Paul Croker and keyboard player Milton Reame James. Debut *Human Menagerie* (1973) established a cult following and included their classic 'Sebastian'. The line-up lasted for 1974's chart breakthrough *The Psychomodo* – before Harley brought in Cregan, Ford and MacKay for *The Best Years Of Our Lives* (1975) and Cockney Rebel's best-known hit, 'Make Me Smile (Come Up And See Me)'. But, commercially, it was a slow downhill ride with *Timeless Flight* (1976) and *Love's A Prima Donna* (1976).

Harley disbanded the group in 1977, releasing solo offerings *Hobo With A Grin* (1977) and *The Candidate* (1979) before being dropped by EMI. After a spell away from the public eye, he returned to the UK Top 10 in 1986 with Sarah Brightman on the title song from Andrew Lloyd Webber's *Phantom Of The Opera*.

Cockney Rebel returned to the news in 1988 when original bassist Paul Jeffreys was killed in the Lockerbie air disaster, and Harley has re-formed the group (with various line-ups) several times since the late 80s.

fan Steve Harley & Cockney Rebel Fan Club, 250 Spencers Croft, Harlow, Essex, CM18 6JN, UK

surf www.clickfun.com/steveharley/

ROY HARPER

WHO b. 12 Jun 1941, Manchester, England

WHAT Uncompromising Rock guru

Roy Harper is one of Rock's few genuine mavericks. After troubled teenage years in the RAF, a mental hospital and prison, mid-60s gigs at London Folk clubs led to the reputation-boosting albums *Come Out Fighting Genghis Smith* (1967), *Folkjokeopus* (1969) and *Flat, Baroque And Berserk* (1970), featuring the politically explicit 'I Hate The White Man' and his first electric track, 'Hell's Angels'.

Stormcock (1971) and *Lifemask* (1973), acclaimed at the time, now seem self-indulgent and pretentious. Live, Harper veered from engaging insight to stoned rambling, but remained highly regarded by fellow musicians. He guested on Pink Floyd's *Wish You Were Here* (1975); Paul and Linda McCartney appeared on his highest-charting album, *Bullinamingvase* (No.25, 1977); Kate Bush sang on *The Unknown Soldier* (1980); and Jimmy Page, who raised his mate to guru status with 'Hats Off To Harper' on *Led Zeppelin III* (1970), collaborated on the career-revitalizing *Whatever Happened To Jugula?* (1985), among others. Much of this material reflected his inner turmoil and uncompromising opinions, while retaining affection for English tradition: 'When An Old Cricketer Leaves The Crease' on 1975's *HQ*, for instance, was dedicated to players Geoff Boycott and John Snow.

Despite intermittent ill-health – a lung disorder almost killed him in the mid-70s – he continues playing and, in 1993, began reissuing his back catalogue on his own Science Friction label.

Fan Science Friction, PO Box 979, Sheffield, S8 8YW, UK

Surf www.royharper.com

EMMYLOU HARRIS

WHO b. 2 Apr 1947, Birmingham, Alabama, USA

WHAT Cool Country elegance

Emmylou Harris' musical career began after her family moved to Washington, DC, where she spent the latter half of the 60s playing Folk clubs on the East Coast. In 1969 she released *Gliding Bird*, a commercial flop and, in the early 70s, joined ex-Byrds and Flying Burrito Brothers vocalist Gram Parsons to appear on two albums and tour as part of his Fallen Angels Band.

Following his tragic death in 1973, Emmylou recorded *Pieces Of The Sky* (1975), the first of a series of Country Rock successes. *Elite Hotel* (1976) gave Emmylou her only UK hit with Lennon and McCartney's 'Here, There And Everywhere'. Her exploration of Country and Bluegrass resulted in *Blue Kentucky Girl* (1979) and *Roses In The Snow* (1980), the latter featuring a Bluegrass version of Simon and Garfunkel's 'The Boxer'.

Parsons' influence has stayed with Emmylou throughout her career and on the live album, *Last Date* (1982), she featured three of his songs. In 1987, *Trio*, her long-awaited collaboration with Linda Ronstadt and Dolly Parton, was released. A slight departure in the 90s found Emmylou working with producer Daniel Lanois on the critically acclaimed *Wrecking Ball* (1995).

Surf www.telalink.net/~kate/index.html

GEORGE HARRISON ✪✪

WHO b. 24 Feb 1943 Liverpool, England

WHAT The mystic Beatle, still a Dark Horse

Overshadowed by John Lennon and Paul McCartney, and lacking the common touch of Ringo Starr, George Harrison had the lowest profile of any Beatle. But 'The Quiet One' played a spectacular part in the band's studio swan-song *Abbey Road* (1969) with his songs 'Something' and 'Here Comes The Sun'. He had already dabbled outside the band with the experimental solo albums *Wonderwall Music* (1969) and *Electronic Music* (1969), as well as pursuing his interest in Eastern philosophy by producing 'Hare Krishna Mantra', a Top 20 hit for the Radha Krishna Temple.

> **" I don't want to be in the business full-time because I'm a gardener. I plant flowers and watch them grow "**

Hopes were high for George's post-Beatles career when he kicked off with the ambitious triple-album *All Things Must Pass* (1970), produced by Phil Spector and featuring the No.1 'My Sweet Lord'. In 1971 he used his influence to stage the New York Concerts For Bangla Desh, co-starring Bob Dylan and Indian musician Ravi Shankar. The events raised funds for victims of war and famine, foreshadowing later Rock benefits such as Live Aid; they also spawned another triple album. Harrison scored a second US No.1 with 'Give Me Love (Give Me Peace On Earth)' from 1973's *Living In The Material World*, which emphasized his spiritual concerns (Oasis fans may note the song 'Be Here Now').

But from this point Harrison's fortunes faltered: *Dark Horse* (1975) was less well received, while his wife Patti left him for his friend Eric Clapton. *Extra Texture: Read All About It* (1975) was an undistinguished end to his time on The Beatles' Apple label. With his own Dark Horse imprint, he signed to A&M, but was sued by that company for late delivery of *Thirty Three And A Third* (1976). He was later rescued by Warner Bros who bought him out of the deal. His troubles continued with a serious bout of hepatitis and a festering lawsuit from the publishers of the 1963 Chiffons hit, 'He's So Fine', who claimed its copyright was infringed by 'My Sweet Lord'. A New York court eventually upheld the charge, finding Harrison culpable of "unconscious" plagiarism.

Harrison's other pursuits included racing cars and his company HandMade Films, who sponsored successful movies including *Monty Python's Life Of Brian* (1979) and *The Long Good Friday* (1980). Later albums had uneven success, although 1987's *Cloud Nine* spawned a US No.1 with 'Got My Mind Set On You', and led to sessions with Dylan, Roy Orbison, Tom Petty and Jeff Lynne who formed mock supergroup The Traveling Wilburys.

In 1992 George played an Albert Hall show in support of Britain's mystically inclined Natural Law Party, with no tangible benefit to their electoral fortunes, and in 1995 joined surviving Beatles Paul and Ringo for the hits 'Free As A Bird' and 'Real Love'. His media appearances remained rare, and his musical output dried up, suggesting 'The Quiet One' had reverted to type.

Surf home.dti.net/warr/harrison.html

ALEX HARVEY

WHO b. 5 Feb 1935, Glasgow, Scotland, d. 4 Feb 1981, Zeebruggen, Belgium

WHAT Thuggish theatrical Rock

Scotland's answer to English proto-Rock 'n' Roller Tommy Steele, Alex Harvey switched to R&B in the late 50s, building a following around Glasgow and Edinburgh with The Alex Harvey Soul Band and backing visiting US stars Eddie Cochran and Gene Vincent.

After a residency in Hamburg (hence 1963's live *Alex Harvey And His Soul Band*), he recorded 1964's *The Blues* with brother Leslie, formed Blues Council and flirted with Psychedelia in Giant Moth – rewarded by a job in the house band for the musical *Hair*. More ill-fated ventures included 1969's *Roman Wall Blues*, until he devised The Sensational Alex Harvey Band in 1972. Theatrical shows notable for guitarist Zal Cleminson's clown-like make-up paid off when *The Impossible Dream* (1974) and a melodramatic 1975 cover of Tom Jones' 'Delilah' were followed up charts by 1975's *Tomorrow Belongs To Me,* then *The Sensational Alex Harvey Band Live* and 1976's *Penthouse Tapes* and *SAHB Stories*.

Retiring from hell-raising in 1977, Harvey released the solo album *The Mafia Stole My Guitar* (1979) and toured sporadically until his death from a heart attack in 1981.

surf members.aol.com/dwademcd/sahb/index.html

PJ HARVEY

WHO Vocals/guitar **Polly Harvey** (b. 9 Oct 1969, Yeovil, Somerset, England), bass **Stephen Vaughan** (b. 22 Jun 1962, Wolverhampton, England), drums **Rob Ellis** (b. 13 Feb 1962, Bristol, England)

WHEN 1991–

WHERE Yeovil, Somerset, England

WHAT In-your-face femininity

Polly Jean Harvey's self-named power trio debuted with 1991's 'Dress'. Acclaim for their abrasive sound and lyrical frankness preceded chart success with 1992's 'Sheela-Na-Gig' and *Dry*. *Rid of Me* (1993) was even harsher; produced by Steve Albini, it boosted Harvey to international renown (and a spot on 1995's *Batman Forever* soundtrack). *4-Track Demos* (1993) highlighted intricacies hidden by Albini's sandblasting production.

The trio dissolved under pressure. Continuing solo, Harvey's more mainstream *To Bring You My Love* (1995) mixed Nick Cave-esque Americana with uncharacteristic campness. After *Dance Hall At Louse Point* (1996) – with friend and guitarist John Parish – she reunited with Rob Ellis for *Soundtrack To Spleen* (1996), duetted with Nick Cave (1996) and Tricky (1997) and played Christ's bodyguard in Hal Hartley's movie *The Book Of Life* (1998).

surf polygram.com/polygram/island/artists/harvey-pj/PJBio.html

HAWKWIND

WHO Vocals/guitar/keyboards **Dave Brock** (b. 20 Aug 1941, Isleworth, England), vocals **Robert Calvert** (b. 9 Mar 1945, Pretoria, South Africa, d. 14 Aug 1988, Kent, England), saxophone/vocals **Nik Turner** (b. 26 Aug 1940, Oxford, England)

WHEN 1969–

WHERE London, England

WHAT Hippie sci-fi Metal

After Group X and Hawkwind Zoo, Brock and Turner settled on their final name for *Hawkwind* (1970). Free-festival stalwarts, their thumping bass and keyboard wash is epitomized by 1972's UK hit 'Silver Machine' and their sole Top 10 album *Space Ritual Live* (1973). The celebrated *Warrior On The Edge Of Time* (1975) featured recurrent collaborator, Sci-Fi author Michael Moorcock, while idiosyncratic poet Robert Calvert added a gloriously off-key focus to albums like *Quark, Strangeness And Charm* (1977).

Chronicle Of The Black Sword (1985) added enough riff power to impress headbangers and *Electric Teepee* (1992) attuned them to 90s New Age-ism. Despite a counter-culture image, they have racked up 20 UK hit albums. Their legacy includes soundalikes The Ozric Tentacles and the legend that is Motörhead mainman and former Hawkwind bassist Ian 'Lemmy' Kilminster.

read *Hawkwind: The Never Ending Story Of The Psychedelic Warlords* (1993), Brian Tawn & Gigi Marinoni

surf www.hawkwind.com/

ISAAC HAYES ✪

WHO b. 20 Aug 1942, Covington, Tennesse, USA

WHAT Hot buttered Soul

Less legend than Love God, Hayes graduated from self-taught musical apprenticeship to an in-house position at the classic-spawning Stax label. There he united with David Porter as 'The Soul Children', composers of gems like 'B-A-B-Y' for Carla Thomas and 'Soul Man' for their principal mouthpieces, Sam & Dave.

The latter's split precipitated Hayes and Porter's separation and, after his solo debut *Presenting Isaac Hayes* (1967), he issued the iconic *Hot Buttered Soul* (1969). As if epic arrangements of 'Walk On By' and 'By The Time I Get To Phoenix' weren't impressive enough, there was the singer's shaven-headed, perma-shaded, gold-bedecked, chocolate-throated loverman image, maintained by 1970's *The Isaac Hayes Movement* and *To Be Continued*. Hayes lit more fires with the US chart-topping soundtrack to *Shaft* (1971), from which 'Theme From Shaft' became his British breakthrough and a US No.1.

Black Moses (1971) was a bigger and better variation on the old formula: R&B raunch like 'Never Gonna Give You Up' blended with implausible revamps like The Carpenters' '(They Long To Be) Close To You'. Audible laughter on *Live At The Sahara Tahoe* (1973) proved even Hayes didn't take this stuff seriously and *Joy* (1973) kept gold records coming.

After scoring the 1974 movies *Tough Guys* and *Truck Turner* (and starring in the latter), Hayes quit Stax for his own Hot Buttered Soul label. However, *Chocolate Chip* (1975) was his last major hit: the blatantly Isaac-influenced Barry White was loverman *du jour* and Disco swept Soul aside. Hayes rode the bandwagon with *Groove-A-Thon* (1975) and the UK hit title track from *Disco Connection* (1976), but succumbed to bankruptcy.

A clutch of largely ignored releases ensued, including the Dionne Warwick collaboration *A Man and A Woman* (1977), before Hayes hit the comeback trail. *Royal Rappin'* (1979) was an acclaimed head-to-head with Millie Jackson, *Don't Let Go* (1979) returned him to US charts and The Blues Brothers revived 'Soul Man' (Lou Reed charted with another cover of the song in 1987).

In the 80s, Hayes put filming first – notably starring in *Escape From New York* (1981). His influence lived on in House (his 'I Can't Turn Around' became Farley 'Jackmaster' Funk's 1986 anthem 'Love Can't Turn Around'), R&B (the black, bald and bold R. Kelly) and Hip Hop (in 1994, Portishead's 'Glory Box' and Tricky's 'Hell Is Round The Corner' used the same Hayes sample).

He made an acclaimed comeback with 1995's *Branded* and its instrumental counterpart *Raw And Refined*, an unashamed revival of the hot buttered recipe. Ike's iconic status has been further reinforced by his cameo in Tupac Shakur's 'Temptations' video (1995), his *Shaft* spoofs on the *Beavis & Butthead Do America* soundtrack (1996) and TV's *The Fresh Prince Of Bel Air*, and his voicing of a character in the cult cartoon *South Park*.

SURF hem.passagen.se/oleh3376/

"I can do a lot on the planet via my music"

HEART ☆

WHO Vocals **Ann Wilson** (b. 19 Jun 1950, San Diego, California, USA), guitar/vocals **Nancy Wilson** (b. 16 Mar 1954, San Francisco, California), guitar **Howard Leese** (b. 13 Jun 1951, Los Angeles, California)

WHEN 1966–

WHERE Seattle, Washington, USA

WHAT Godmothers of Grunge

Seattle-ites to the core, Ann and Nancy Wilson began in Grunge's hometown and ended up singing with Alice In Chains. Originally bar band The Army, Heart was founded by guitarist Roger Fisher and bassist Steve Fossen. The Wilsons added acoustic ballads to powerhouse riffing to produce the US million-sellers *Dreamboat Annie* (1976), *Little Queen* (1977), *Magazine* (1978), *Dog & Butterfly* (1978), *Bebe Le Strange* (1980) and *Greatest Hits/Live* (1980).

The 80s brought a broken Heart: Fossen and Fisher departed, and *Private Audition* (1982) and *Passionworks* (1983) bombed. Undaunted, they recruited bassist Mark Andes and drummer Denny Carmassi, hired crack hitmakers like Bernie Taupin, donned post-Prince frills and shot to the top of the US chart with *Heart* (1985), its smashes including the No.1 'These Dreams'. *Bad Animals* (1987), *Brigade* (1990) and hits like 'Alone' and 'All I Wanna Do Is Make Love To You' carried the resurrection overseas.

But the uncelebrated *Rock The House Live* (1991) and *Desire Walks On* (1993) prompted another rethink when Carmassi and Andes left the band – hence, 1995's live acoustic *The Road Home* and promotion of hobby band The Lovemongers (unveiled on 1992's *Singles* soundtrack Zep cover 'The Battle Of Evermore') to a full-time venture on *Whirlygig* (1997). Alice In Chains guest slots on *Sap* (1991) and *Dirt* (1992) maintained their Seattle cool.

(Fan) Heartmongers Fan Club, 9805 N.E. 116th Street, Box #7328, Kirkland, Washington, 98034, USA

(surf) www.annandnancy.com/

HEAVEN 17

WHO Vocals/keyboards **Glenn Gregory** (b. 16 May 1958, Sheffield, England), keyboards **Martyn Ware** (b. 19 May 1956, Sheffield), keyboards **Ian Craig Marsh** (b. 11 Nov 1956, Sheffield)

WHEN 1980–

WHERE London, England

WHAT Shiny, happy Synth Pop people

Having flounced from The Human League, Ian Craig Marsh and Martyn Ware moved to London to form the production company BEF (British Electric Foundation) and issued 1981's cassette-only *Music For Stowaways*, produced for use on personal stereos.

Adding Glenn Gregory, they formed Heaven 17, named after a group in Anthony Burgess' novel *A Clockwork Orange*. The club hit '(We Don't Need This) Fascist Groove Thang' had its fortunes thwarted by a BBC ban: Radio 1 objected to its lyrical jabs at then US President Ronald Reagan. Real success began with

Penthouse And Pavement (1981) and 'Temptation' from their UK No.4 *The Luxury Gap* (1983). In between, BEF's *Music Of Quality And Distinction* (1982) – despite boasting guests such as Billy MacKenzie (Associates), Tina Turner and Gary Glitter – flopped.

How Men Are (1983) fell short of Heaven 17's earlier success, but they helped revive Tina Turner's career by producing 'Let's Stay Together', and made 'Soul Deep', with The Style Council, in aid of striking coal-miners. Music for an aborted French movie formed part of *Pleasure One* (1986), and they resurfaced in 1988 with the disappointing *Teddy Bear, Duke & Psycho*.

BEF's *Music Of Quality And Distinction Volume 2* (1991), starring Terence Trent D'Arby and Chaka Khan, spawned a minor hit with Lalah Hathaway's take on 'Family Affair'. A remixed 'Temptation' hit the charts in 1992, followed by anthology *Higher And Higher*. In 1997, the group was reactivated for *Bigger Than America*.

HEAVY METAL

WHAT "I sure as hell don't think Metallica's Metal, or Guns N' Roses… or Kiss… It just doesn't deal with the ground opening up and little dwarves coming out riding dragons." Though wary of the tag, Gene Simmons and his band Kiss embody many Metal hallmarks – blood and thunder shows, loud guitars, critical disdain and huge popularity. Traced to author William Burroughs, the term was popularized by Steppenwolf's 'Born To Be Wild'. "Heavy Metal thunder" evoked the Harleys of <u>Easy Rider</u> (1969), on whose soundtrack it appeared, but described a genre initiated by riffmeisters Link Wray and The Kinks, developed by Jimi Hendrix and The Yardbirds and taken to the top by Black Sabbath. Led Zeppelin and Deep Purple kept the flag flying, followed Stateside by Aerosmith and Kiss. In 1977, Van Halen stormed in, their legacy mid-80s bands like Poison. When radio resistance crumbled, even the uncompromising Guns N' Roses ascended the platinum pile. Metal's broad church now welcomes Pantera and Prodigy, Nine Inch Nails and No Doubt. No longer defined by Satanism and sex, it retains the world's biggest, most loyal audience.

WHERE UK, USA

WHEN 1969–

WHO Montrose <u>Montrose</u> (1973), Accept <u>Restless And Wild</u> (1982), Exodus <u>Bonded By Blood</u> (1985), Mother Love Bone <u>Stardog Champion</u> (1992), Korn <u>Life Is Peachy</u> (1996)

JIMI HENDRIX ✪

WHO b. Johnny Allen Hendrix, 27 Nov 1942, Seattle, Washington, USA, renamed James Marshall Hendrix, d. 18 Sep 1970, London, England

WHAT Guitar genius

Of the Rock stars whose premature deaths marked the passage from 60s idealism to 70s cynicism, Hendrix exerts the greatest influence from beyond the grave. Posthumous releases by the flamboyant guitarist outnumber by about 60:1 the handful of albums issued during his lifetime, and his gymnastic style remains the bench-mark by which Rock guitarists are measured.

Although left-handed, Hendrix learned to play on a normally strung guitar turned upside down, teaching himself the rudiments of Blues by listening to Robert Johnson and B.B. King.

Volunteering for the 101st Airborne Division in 1961 (to avoid being drafted into a less glamorous unit), he was discharged a year later after injuring his back.

Between 1963 and 1965, he worked in R&B bands backing Wilson Pickett, Solomon Burke, Sam Cooke, The Isley Brothers, James Brown and Little Richard.

After a dispute over money led to his departure from Richard's Upsetters, Hendrix moved to New York and joined Curtis Knight & The Squires, with whom he recorded mediocre tracks that would be endlessly recycled on dire albums like *Get That Feeling* (1967). He also signed a poor contract with record company boss Ed Chalpin, a subsequent thorn in Hendrix's side.

With his own band, Jimmy James & The Blue Flames, Hendrix developed a reputation at local clubs such as Greenwich Village's Cafe Wha?. He was spotted by Animals bassist Chas Chandler, who became his manager and transplanted him to England to launch a solo career. In 'swinging London', he was a sensation: technically peerless, his years of touring had taught him showmanship which had been *de rigueur* for more extrovert R&B guitarists since T-Bone Walker astonished 40s audiences by playing guitar behind his head while doing the splits. Playing the guitar with his teeth, using the microphone stand as a slide and making innovative use of feedback and distortion (courtesy of new Marshall amplifiers), Hendrix cut a dashing, dynamic figure. His brocade jackets, chiffon scarves, crushed-velvet trousers and huge afro distinguished him from contemporary black musicians, most of whom stuck to tight suits or tuxedos.

With bassist Noel Redding (b. David Redding, 25 Dec 1945, Folkestone, England) and ex-Georgie Fame & The Blue Flames drummer Mitch Mitchell (b. John Mitchell, 9 Jun 1947, Ealing, London), The Jimi Hendrix Experience's first single 'Hey Joe' (1966) was an immediate success. Its tale of murderous revenge, combined with Hendrix's electric dandy look, polarized opinion along generational lines: parents spluttered apoplectically at his TV appearances, as Hendrix became an icon of social and sexual liberation for their offspring. Late in 1966, he signed a four-year management deal with Mike Jeffrey, who in March 1967 committed him to a five-year, $1-million recording contract with Reprise in America.

> "Some girlfriend rang up and said, 'You've got to hear this guy, Jimi Hendrix.' And I went, Oh really? She said, 'Yeah, I was at the club last night. It was unbelievable.' And I went, Thanks. That's all you want to hear about first thing in the morning... someone else's outrageous guitar playing. So I went along to see Hendrix. It was unbelievable. I just went away thinking I'd better think of something else to do"
>
> Jeff Beck

With European and UK shows enhancing his reputation, Hendrix scored again with the psychedelic classic 'Purple Haze' (1967) and the bluesier ballad 'The Wind Cries Mary' (1967), while the Experience's debut *Are You Experienced?* (US No.5, 1967) was prevented from reaching the top only by The Beatles' *Sgt. Pepper's Lonely Hearts Club Band*. Following a visceral performance at the Monterey Pop Festival in June, the climax of which saw Hendrix igniting his lighter fuel-doused guitar, the album spent more than 100 weeks on the US chart. The live *Monterey International Pop Festival* (1970) featured a side apiece from Hendrix and Otis Redding but, despite acclaim from the festival's hip young audience, the guitarist was booed at shows supporting The Mamas & The Papas and The Monkees. Hendrix was dropped after only eight shows, when his erotically charged performance proved too red in tooth and claw for Monkees' fans.

Having played 180 dates that year, 1967 concluded with another hit, 'Burning Of The Midnight Lamp', and *Axis: Bold As Love* (1968). But cracks began to show: following a fight with Redding in a Swedish hotel in January 1968, Hendrix spent a night in jail. He was also increasingly frustrated with others' perception of him as a showman and guitar trickster; feeling this obscured his artistry, he began toning down the stage antics. The compilation *Smash Hits* (1969) was followed by a 47-date American tour, before a definitive version of Dylan's 'All Along The Watchtower' (1968) paved the way for his masterpiece *Electric Ladyland* (UK No.6, US No.1, 1968), recorded with the Experience and "heavy friends" like Stevie Winwood, Al Kooper, Buddy Miles and Jefferson Airplane's Jack Casady. Against Hendrix's wishes, the artwork of the UK release featured a bevy of naked women, a tacky publicity stunt. In America, where the album boasted a more tasteful, psychedelic sleeve, Hendrix was named Artist Of The Year by *Billboard* magazine.

In 1969, the Experience disbanded when Redding quit to form Fat Mattress. With a temporary aggregation called Gypsy Sun & Rainbows, consisting of Hendrix, Mitchell, rhythm guitarist Larry Leeds, percussionists Juma Sultan and Jerry Velez, and old army buddy Billy Cox on bass, Hendrix played Woodstock. His amazing version of 'The Star-Spangled Banner', though witnessed by only a few spectators, became the highlight of the subsequent film and album. The rest of 1969 was spent recording, with friends like Stephen Stills and Jazz guitarist John McLaughlin, and rehearsing a new group, Band Of Gypsys, comprising himself, Cox and drummer Buddy Miles. A lacklustre live album by this outfit, *Band Of Gypsys* (UK No.6, US No.5, 1970), was ultimately given to Ed Chalpin – who also received a $1-million payment and a percentage of the guitarist's future earnings – to settle a long-running lawsuit arising from Hendrix's

1965 contract. Band Of Gypsys proved short-lived, breaking up during a January 1970 concert at Madison Square Garden.

Waiting for the lawsuit to be settled, Hendrix's royalties had been frozen, delaying construction of his New York recording studio Electric Lady until June, when he finally got to record there. After another US tour, this time with Cox and Mitchell, he played concerts in Maui, Hawaii – where a film, *Rainbow Bridge*, was made of his performance – and at England's Isle Of Wight Festival, which provided the live album *Jimi Hendrix At The Isle Of Wight* (1971). The 'soundtrack' to *Rainbow Bridge* (1971), however, contained no material recorded in Hawaii. A smattering of European shows culminated in a final appearance at Ronnie Scott's Club in London, jamming with Eric Burdon & War.

On the evening of 18 September 1970, he was found dead at the London flat of his girlfriend Monika Danneman, having choked on his vomit while sleeping. His final words, "I need help bad, man," were left on Chandler's answering machine. The rush-released 'Voodoo Chile (Slight Return)' (1970) gave Hendrix his only UK chart-topper.

Material recorded for a concept album provisionally titled *The First Rays Of The New Rising Sun* became Hendrix's final studio album *Cry Of Love* (UK

jimi hendrix

No.2, US No.3, 1971), the first of a glut of posthumous releases (though at least this contained material he considered complete). Throughout the 70s, albums appeared on which Hendrix's guitar and vocals had been overdubbed with backings by producer/engineer Alan Douglas: *War Heroes* (1972), *Loose Ends* (1974), *Crash Landing* (1975) and *Midnight Lightning* (1975). A further deluge of live recordings was also released, notably *Hendrix In The West* (1972), *Radio One* (1989), the complete *Woodstock* (1994) and the box set *Stages* (1992), while compilations such as *Cornerstones* (1990) and *The Ultimate Experience* (1993) chart periodically. The more selective *Blues* (1994) attempted to rescue the guitarist from his garish Heavy Metal antecedents by showcasing Hendrix's R&B leanings.

Various factions, including Alan Douglas and Hendrix's family, have waged long legal tussles over rights to his estate. Studio out-takes and material originally from albums like *Rainbow Bridge* and *Cry Of Love* have been re-combined on albums such as *Voodoo Soup* (1995), *First Rays Of The New Rising Sun* (1997) and *South Saturn Delta* (1997). Decades after his death, Hendrix continues to generate around 3 million album sales per year.

(READ) *Crosstown Traffic* (1990), Charles Shaar Murray

(FAN) Experience Hendrix, PO Box 4459, Seattle, WA 98104, USA

(SURF) www.jimi-hendrix.com/

DON HENLEY

WHO b. 22 Jul 1947, Gilmer, Texas, USA

WHAT AOR with a conscience

Cynical, self-obsessed and a drummer, Henley wasn't a natural 80s superstar. Even a pivotal role in 70s megastars The Eagles couldn't push his solo debut *I Can't Stand Still* (1982) past an un-mega US No.26. However, the hit 'Dirty Laundry' signalled an edgy departure from The Eagles' breeziness. The rueful radio favourite 'Boys Of Summer' completed the transformation and propelled *Building The Perfect Beast* (1984) to triple platinum.

The End Of The Innocence (1989) became his biggest album, thanks partly to Bruce Hornsby (who co-wrote the hit title track) and Axl Rose (who co-bellowed 'I Will Not Go Quietly'). Rose recruited Henley for an award show performance when Guns N' Roses drummer Steven Adler stayed in bed. Thereafter, Henley devoted energies to conservation charity work, resurfacing only for Eagles reunion *Hell Freezes Over* (1994) and the subsequent mega-bucks tour. Fans made do with hits set *Actual Miles* (1995).

READ *Heaven Is Under Our Feet* (1992), Don Henley & Dave Marsh

SURF members.aol.com/ivyrain/don.htm

HERMAN'S HERMITS

WHO Vocals **Peter Noone** (b. 5 Nov 1947, Davyhulme, Manchester, England), guitar **Derek 'Lek' Leckenby** (b. 14 May 1946, Leeds, England, d. 4 Jun 1994, Moses Lake, Washington, USA), bass **Karl Green** (b. 31 Jul 1947, Salford, England), drums **Barry 'Bean' Whitwam** (b. 21 Jul 1946, Manchester)

WHEN 1963-1994

WHERE Manchester, England

WHAT British Invasion idols of the 60s

The early 60s 'British Invasion' of America was spearheaded by The Beatles, The Stones… and Herman's Hermits. Their No.1 UK debut 'I'm Into Something Good' (1964) was also the first of 14 Stateside smashes, including 1965's chart-toppers 'Mrs Brown You've Got A Lovely Daughter' and 'I'm Henry The VIII I Am'.

However, the group existed only as a vehicle for teen idol and former child actor Noone; manager Mickie Most didn't even let the Hermits play on their own records (session players included Led Zeppelin's Jimmy Page and John Paul Jones). Noone quit in 1970 for an erratic solo career, and the Hermits drifted round the cabaret circuit in various forms until Leckenby's death in 1994.

SURF members.aol.com/bocad/hh.htm

STEVE HILLAGE/SYSTEM 7

WHO b. 2 Aug 1951, London, England

WHAT The hippie guitar hero who refused to die

Steve Hillage quit a Canterbury University philosophy course to flit across the cosmic vanguard – Uriel, Egg, Khan and Kevin

Ayers' Decadence – before joining Gong in 1973. Their keyboard player, Miquette Giraudy, became his life partner.

Despite rumours that he would replace Mick Taylor in The Rolling Stones, he went solo in1975. His eight Virgin albums reflected a belief in music as "the marriage of religion and science" – and, incidentally, of guitars and synthesizers. *L* was the most successful album, reaching UK No.10 in 1976.

He retired as a performer in 1983 and worked as a producer (Simple Minds, Robyn Hitchcock) until re-emerging in 1990, with Giraudy, leading Ambient assemblage System 7. Their best – *Point 3* (1994) and *Power Of Seven* (1996), including collaborations with the likes of Techno pioneers Derrick May and Marshall Jefferson and The Orb's Alex Paterson – won Hillage a whole new reputation for post-guitar adventurousness.

READ *Gong Dreaming II – Gong* (1998), Daevid Allen

FAN Gas (Gong Fan Club), PO Box 87J, Glastonbury, Somerset, BA6 9FE, UK

SURF www.easynet.co.uk/system7/

HIP HOP

WHAT "Hip Hop," says Public Enemy's Chuck D, "is the culture of whatever black people create." Before Rap, that included block parties ruled by DJs like Afrika Bambaataa and Grandmaster Flash, graffiti, scratching and breakdancing. From Hip Hop came 'Electro' – electronic dance music owing as much to Kraftwerk as to James Brown. However, when Flash dropped the groundbreaking 'reality rap' single 'The Message' in 1982, Hip Hop's 'b-boys' switched from party to protest and Rap swiftly swamped the genre.

WHERE Harlem, The Bronx, New York, USA

WHEN 1976–

WHO Various <u>Genius Of Rap</u> (1987), Various <u>Classic Electro Mastercuts</u> (1994), Various <u>Beat Classic</u> (1997)

ROBYN HITCHCOCK

WHO b. 3 Mar 1953, London, England

WHAT Melancholy and the infinite Syd-ness

After The Soft Boys split in 1981, their leader Robyn Hitchcock went solo, releasing *Black Snake Diamond Role* that year. After *Groove Decay* (1982) and *I Often Dream Of Trains* (1984), he recruited backing band The Egyptians.

A large US fanbase lapped up *Fegmania!* (1985), *Gotta Let This Hen Out!* (1985) and *Element Of Light* (1986). Thanks to support from REM, A&M signed him for *Globe Of Frogs* (1988), source of the US alternative hit 'Balloon Man'. *Queen Elvis* (1989) and *Perspex Island* (1991) featured REM personnel and bookended 1990 solo album *Eye*. After *Respect* (1993), Hitchcock disbanded The Egyptians and signed to Warner for *Moss Elixir* (1996).

Though never a mainstream success, Hitchcock's Syd Barrett-esque music and image inspire a devotional following. His film collaboration with director Jonathan Demme, *Storefront Hitchcock*, was released in March 1998.

SURF web.syr.edu/~jojones/hitchcock.html

HOLE

WHO Vocals/guitar **Courtney Love** (b. Love Michelle Harrison, 9 Jul 1965, San Francisco, California, USA), guitar **Eric Erlandson** (b. 9 Jan 1963, Los Angeles, California), bass **Melissa Auf Der Maur** (b. 17 Mar 1972, Montreal, Canada), drums **Patty Schemel** (b. 24 Apr 1967, Seattle, Washington, USA)

WHEN 1989–

WHERE Los Angeles, California, USA

WHAT The 90s' greatest rabble-rousing Rock Star

A troubled child and juvenile delinquent, Courtney Love moved in star circles long before becoming one herself. Inspired by The Sex Pistols, she formed a short-lived band in Portland, Oregon, USA, then relocated to England – via Japan and Ireland – in 1981, where she hung out in Liverpool with Echo & The

Bunnymen and Julian Cope. "She was amazingly horrible," Cope told *Select* magazine. "One of those people that you want to talk about all the time, but being around her's unbearable."

Back in the USA, Love – now 17 – passed through a formative Faith No More in San Francisco, before returning to Portland to form Sugar Baby Doll with Jennifer Finch (later of Grunge queens L7) and Kat Bjelland. She moonlighted with cameos in Alex Cox's movies *Sid And Nancy* (1986) and *Straight To Hell* (1987).

Sugar Baby Doll gave way to the Minneapolis-based Babes In Toyland, featuring Love, Bjelland and drummer Lori Barbero – a union split when Kat and Courtney feuded over credit for the 'kinderwhore' look (frilly frocks offset by boots and bad attitude) and vied for the attention of a rising star called Kurt Cobain.

While the Babes went on to better things (notably 1992's *Fontanelle*), Love moved to Los Angeles and recruited guitarist Eric Erlandson, bassist Jill Emery and drummer Caroline Rue for Hole. Their grungey EPs 'Rat Bastard' (1990) and 'Dicknail' (1991) made them press darlings, especially in England, where *Pretty On The Inside* (1991) reached No.59. The breathtaking album veered giddily from sheet-metal riffing to a radio playing Fleetwood Mac's 'Rhiannon'. On tour, Love added Leadbelly's 'Where Did You Sleep Last Night' to Hole's set – a brainwave that evidently made a strong impression on Kurt Cobain (he did the same thing for Nirvana's *Unplugged* set). Other songs given a Hole overhaul included The Crystals' amazing 'He Hit Me And It Felt Like A Kiss'.

Cobain and Love were now entwined, enshrined by media labels like 'Grunge's Sid and Nancy' and 'Love's young nightmare'. High-profile harassment was assured by their marriage in 1992 and the birth of their daughter amid rumours of heroin use.

Meanwhile, drummer Patty Schemel and bassist Kristen Pfaff replaced Rue (couldn't play fast enough, apparently) and Emery (who resurfaced years later in Mazzy Star). Schemel's previous band found their name immortalized as 'Doll Parts', a ballad on Hole's next album. A flawless collection – *Pretty*'s crunch corralled into glorious songs – *Live Through This* (1994) should have been Love's triumph. Instead, it became the ghastly soundtrack to Cobain's suicide in April and Pfaff's heroin-linked death in June.

Grief-stricken, Love thrust Hole (with new bassist Melissa Auf Der Maur) into a punishing world tour, punctuated by a drug overdose and assaults on audience members and fellow stars. But by its close, she had returned to earth, even playing Nirvana's 'Pennyroyal Tea' while daughter Frances danced on stage.

She found a new home in movies. First was helming the *Tank Girl* soundtrack (1995), an apparent bid to rival Trent Reznor's *Natural Born Killers* (Love had toured and slept with Reznor, and wasted no opportunity to express how disappointing both experiences were). More rewardingly, she appeared in *Feeling Minnesota* (1996) and *Basquiat* (1996), then made an acclaimed, Golden Globe-nominated turn in *The People Vs. Larry Flynt* (1996).

Rarities set *My Body The Hand Grenade* (1997) filled time while Love prepared a new album, aided by Smashing Pumpkins' Billy Corgan and Nine Inch Nail Chris Vrenna. She even ended a feud with Madonna, simmering since The Big M fruitlessly bid to sign Hole to her label Maverick. After a joint *Rolling Stone* cover story, Madonna confirmed Love's entry into Versace-modelling stardom with "God bless her! Now we're all in the same club".

READ *Courtney Love – The Real Story* (1997), Poppy Z. Brite

FAN E Coli La La, 36 St. Margaret's Avenue, South Harrow, Middlesex, HA2 8DA, UK

SURF dollparts.simplenet.com/

Long before being inducted into the Rock And Roll Hall Of Fame in 1990, Brian Holland (b. 15 Feb 1941, Detroit, Michigan, USA), Lamont Dozier (b. 16 Jun 1941, Detroit) and Eddie Holland (b. 30 Oct 1939, Detroit) etched themselves into musical history. In-house hit-makers at Motown, they penned and produced 60s jewels like Martha & The Vandellas' 'Heat Wave' (1963), Marvin Gaye's 'How Sweet It Is (To Be Loved By You)' (1964), The Four Tops' 'Reach Out I'll Be There' and The Isley Brothers' 'This Old Heart Of Mine' (both 1966).

Their shiniest stars were The Supremes, 17 of whose hits bore the HDH seal. 'Where Did Our Love Go' (1964), 'Stop! In The Name Of Love' (1965), 'You Can't Hurry Love' and 'You Keep Me Hanging On' (both 1966) highlighted their gift for marrying drama and romance, a timeless twosome.

The Holland brothers' long association with Motown mastermind Berry Gordy soured in 1968 and the trio established the Invictus/Hot Wax label. Subsequent additions to their legacy included Chairmen Of The Board's 'Give Me Just A Little More Time'. In the 70s they gave way to Soul successors like Gamble & Huff and Thom Bell, but their genius was rarely rivalled and never eclipsed.

THE HOLLIES

WHO Vocals **Allan Clarke** (b. 5 Apr 1942, Salford, England), guitar **Tony Hicks** (b. 16 Dec 1943, Nelson, Lancashire, England), guitar **Graham Nash** (b. 2 Feb 1942, Blackpool, Lancashire), bass **Eric Haydock** (b. 3 Feb 1943, Stockport, Lancashire), drums **Bobby Elliott** (b. 8 Dec 1942, Burnley, Lancashire)

WHEN 1962–

WHERE Manchester, England

WHAT Manchester's answer to The Beatles

Formed by Clarke and Nash, The Deltas signed to Parlophone in 1963, added Hicks and became The Hollies. '(Ain't That) Just Like Me' initiated a stunning run of harmonized 60s classics, including 'Stay' (1963), 'Just One Look' (1964), 'I'm Alive' (UK No.1, 1965) and 'Carrie-Anne' (1967) – during which drummer Don Rathbone replaced Elliott. *Stay With The Hollies* (1964) reached UK No.2, but US success proved elusive until 'Bus Stop' (1966) made the Top 5.

Stylistic indecision proved their undoing: after 1967's weak-selling psychedelic efforts 'King Midas In Reverse', *Evolution* and *Butterfly*, desperation prompted the covers collection *Hollies Sing Dylan* (1969). Unimpressed, Nash upped sticks for 70s excess with Crosby, Stills & Nash.

In came Terry Sylvester (from fellow British beat boomers The Swingin' Blue Jeans), with whom 'He Ain't Heavy, He's My Brother' became the group's anthem, returning to No.1 in 1988 after its resurrection in a TV commercial. The hits continued, notably with 1972's US No.2 'Long Tall Woman (In A Black Dress)'. Clarke went solo, but returned in 1973 when replacement Michael Rickfors was axed due to his strong Scandinavian accent.

Rehabilitation came with 'The Air That I Breathe' (1974) but 1981's Disco medley 'Holliedaze' confirmed their descent into cabaret oblivion. Various line-up changes included the addition

of Bread guitarist James Griffin before Nash, Clarke, Hicks and Elliott regrouped in 1983 for *What Goes Around*, yielding a minor US hit cover of The Supremes' 'Stop! In The Name of Love'. Nash drifted back to CSN, leaving the remaining three to tour and occasionally record.

The tribute album *Sing Hollies In Reverse* (1995) featured The Posies, REM producer Mitch Easter and future eels mainman E.

surf www.proweb.co.uk/~rhaywood/

BUDDY HOLLY ⊙ ⊙

WHO b. Charles Hardin Holley, 7 Sep 1936, Lubbock, Texas, USA, d. 3 Feb 1959, Clear Lake, Iowa, USA

WHAT Specs 'n' bugs 'n' Rock 'n' Roll

Buddy Holly took to the guitar in his early teens, performing Country and Blues songs at schools and local dances. A 1955 support slot with Elvis Presley in Lubbock converted him to Rock 'n' Roll. He impressed Presley's manager, whose support won Holly a deal with Decca. However, disastrous 1956 sessions in Nashville yielded Country-style flops 'Blue Days Black Nights' and 'Modern Don Juan' and Holly was dropped.

Undeterred, he recorded a demo at Norman Petty's studio in Clovis, New Mexico, who took it to New York and sold the tracks to Coral Records (ironically a subsidiary of Decca), who released the transatlantic No.1 'That'll Be The Day' in May 1957. Holly's melodic invention, hiccuping vocals, Fender Stratocaster and horn-rimmed specs made him a pivotal Pop sensation. An early Rock 'n' Roll missionary to Britain, he influenced a generation of beat boomers, including The Beatles and The Rolling Stones.

With The Crickets – drummer Jerry Allison, bassist Joe B Mauldin and, in the early days, guitarist Niki Sullivan – Holly returned to Clovis to record 1957's classics 'Words Of Love', 'Everyday', 'Oh Boy', 'Not Fade Away', 'Peggy Sue', 'Listen To Me' and 1958's 'It's So Easy'. Holly's creativity was matched by Petty's experimentation ('Words Of Love' pioneered double-tracked vocals). Holly worked for his brother's tiling business until July 1957 when 'That'll Be The Day' became a hit. They spent 1958 in exhausting tours of North America, the UK and Australia.

Having recorded the hits 'Maybe Baby', 'Rave On' and 'Think It Over', Holly split from the Crickets in mid-1958 and that autumn recorded with an orchestra on 'It Doesn't Matter Anymore' and 'True Love Ways'. Lyrics for the latter and 'Peggy Sue Got Married' demonstrated his growing sophistication.

In August 1958, he married Maria Santiago and moved to New York. Impoverished by an unfavourable situation with the now estranged Petty, he undertook a mismanaged US tour in deep winter, with a new band. On 2 February 1959 – fed

up with travelling on a cold, dilapidated tour bus – Holly and fellow stars The Big Bopper and Ritchie Valens hired an aircraft. The plane crashed in light snow around 1:00 am on 3 February, soon after take off, killing them all.

His potential barely fulfilled, Holly's death at 22 was among Rock 'n' Roll's greatest tragedies. However, posthumous hits like 'Brown-Eyed Handsome Man' (1963), innumerable compilations, 1978 bio-pic *The Buddy Holly Story* and the long-running musical *Buddy* have kept his legend alive.

READ *Buddy Holly: The Real Story* (1995), Ellis Amburn

FAN British Buddy Holly Society, 'Bramwell' Roke, Wallingford, Oxon OX10 6JD, UK

SURF www.visuallink.net/kdwilt/bio.html

JOHN LEE HOOKER

WHO b. 22 Aug 1920, Clarksdale, Mississippi, USA

WHAT Granddaddy of Blues

Born in the Mississippi heartland of Country Blues, John Lee Hooker drifted north to Detroit during World War Two, scoring a million-seller in 1948 with 'Boogie Chillen'. It set the pattern for Hooker's unique sound: deep, mumbled vocals over a shuffling beat and clanging guitar riffs. His sudden popularity was reinforced by follow-ups like 'I'm In The Mood' (1965), but as black audiences turned away from Blues, so Hooker's fortunes waned until his rediscovery by white 60s Rock bands.

Now a cult hero, he toured Britain in 1964, enjoying hits with the reissued singles 'Boom Boom' and 'Dimples'. In the USA, he teamed up with Boogie act Canned Heat for 1971's *Hooker 'n' Heat*, before entering another period of relative obscurity.

His comeback, *The Healer* (1989), whose guests included Carlos Santana and Bonnie Raitt, brought Hooker a new generation of fans. Prolific in his old age, his albums include *Mr Lucky* (1991), *Boom Boom* (1992), *Chill Out* (1995) and *Don't Look Back* (1997), with Van Morrison and Keith Richards among his acolytes. Long-time admirer Pete Townshend recruited him for his *The Iron Man* (1989). Hooker became so celebrated as a Blues figurehead that he lent his face and music to commercials for anything from jeans to cognac. Levi's ad theme 'Boom Boom' (a 1962 US hit) scaled the UK chart three decades later to No.16.

READ *John Lee Hooker: Boogie Man* (1998), Charles Shaar Murray

SURF www.rosebudus.com/hooker/

HOOTIE & THE BLOWFISH ✪✪

WHO Vocals/guitar **Darius Rucker** (b. 13 May 1966, Charleston, South Carolina, USA), guitar **Mark Bryan** (b. 6 May 1967, Silver Spring, Maryland, USA), bass **Dean Felber** (b. 9 Jun 1967, Bethesda, Maryland), drums **Jim 'Soni' Sonefeld** (b. 20 Oct 1964, Lansing, Michigan, USA)

WHEN 1986–

WHERE Columbia, South Carolina, USA

WHAT Southern super-sellers

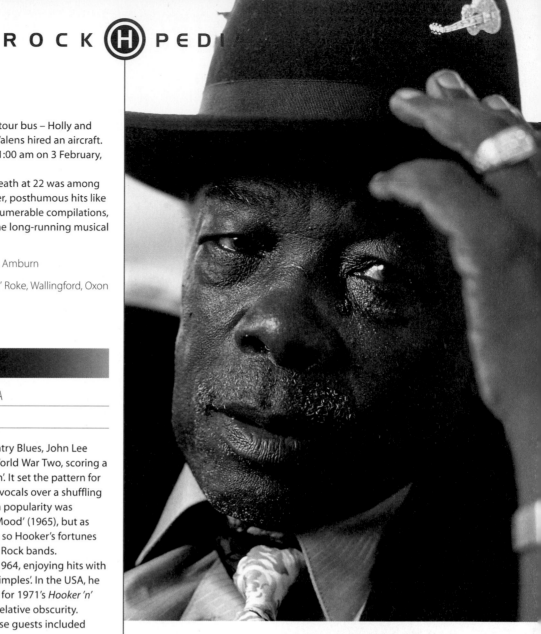

Despite a self-confessedly awful name (inspired by two college friends), Hootie & The Blowfish became a phenomenon, their uncomplicated Southern Rock refined on independent releases *Hootie & The Blowfish, Time* (both 1991) and *Kootchypop* (1993). The cream of these formed their Atlantic debut *Cracked Rear View* (1994), which – reinforced by hearty hit 'Hold My Hand' and relentless touring – became a mega-platinum monster.

Hootie joined all-star casts on 1995's movie soundtrack *White Man's Burden* (with Roy Orbison's 'Sweet Dream Baby'), the Led Zeppelin tribute *Encomium* (with 'Hey Hey What Can I Do') and TV soundtrack *Friends* (with 80s alternative act 54-40's 'I Go Blind'); and were name-checked in the latter – Courteney Cox's character explaining a backstage-bestowed lovebite as "the work of a Blowfish". The band also established its own Breaking Records label.

However, *Fairweather Johnson* (1996) – despite yielding the engaging hit 'The Old Man And Me', having its release promoted with an *MTV Unplugged* session and topping the US chart in its first week – sold less spectacularly. While The Dave Matthews Band became the newest torch-carriers for rootsy Rock, the Blowfish retreated to plan a 1998 comeback.

READ *Hootie! How The Blowfish Put The Pop Back In Pop Rock* (1997), Mike Miller

FAN Fishco, PO Box 5656, Columbia, South Carolina 29250, USA

SURF www.hootie.com/

HOT CHOCOLATE

WHO Vocals **Errol Brown** (b. 12 Nov 1948, Kingston, Jamaica), guitar **Harvey Hinsley** (b. 19 Jan 1948, Northampton, England), bass **Patrick Olive** (b. 22 Mar 1947, Grenada), drums **Tony Connor** (b. 6 Apr 1947, Romford, Essex, England), keyboards **Larry Ferguson** (b. 14 Apr 1948, Nassau, The Bahamas)

WHEN 1969–1987

WHERE London, England

WHAT A sweet taste of the 70s

After a fruitless tenure on The Beatles' Apple label, Hot Chocolate found success with RAK Records' Mickie Most. He abbreviated their name from The Hot Chocolate Band and oversaw the release of their first hit, 1970's 'Love Is Life'.

Rarely off the UK chart thereafter – 'So You Win Again' was a 1977 chart-topper – they scored Stateside with 'Emma' (1975), 'You Sexy Thing' (1975) and 'Every 1's A Winner' (1978). With their seductive lead singer Errol Brown a sort of sweet substitute for harder-hitting Soul love gods like Isaac Hayes, Hot Chocolate became as entwined with 70s Pop culture as *Star Wars*. However, after a final flurry of hits, including 1982's heartbreaking 'It Started With A Kiss', the group dissolved in the mid-80s.

They have since enjoyed an Abba-esque resurgence of credibility: Urge Overkill, PJ Harvey and Sisters Of Mercy all added Chocolate to their live sets, while a remixed 'You Sexy Thing' scaled the UK Top 10 in 1987. Another revival came when 'You Sexy Thing' resurfaced in the 1997 movie *The Full Monty*.

HOTHOUSE FLOWERS

WHO Vocals/keyboards **Liam O'Maonlai** (b. 7 Nov 1964, Dublin, Ireland), guitar **Fiachna O'Braonain** (b. 27 Nov 1965, Dublin), bass **Peter O'Toole** (b. 1 Apr 1965, Dublin), drums **Jerry Fehily** (b. 29 Aug 1963, Bishops Town, Ireland), saxophone **Leo Barnes** (b. 5 Oct 1965, Dublin)

WHEN 1986–

WHERE Dublin, Ireland

WHAT Celtic Gospel

Originally The Incomparable Benzini Brothers, street performers Liam O'Maonlai and Fiachna O'Braonain were spotted on Irish TV in 1986 by U2's Bono. Their first single on U2's Mother label, 'Love Don't Work This Way', attracted the attention of London Records and their debut *People* (1988) made UK No.2.

Home (1990) and *Songs From The Rain* (1993) preceded a five-year hiatus during which Fehily and Barnes left and the others dabbled in side projects – O'Maonlai joined Crowded House-person Tim Finn and Irish troubadour Andy White in Alt, while other drinking partners/collaborators included Michelle Shocked, Sinéad O'Connor, Maria McKee and Def Leppard's Joe Elliott. The Flowers remain in bloom.

 World Information Service for Hothouse Flowers, PO Box 152, Seaford, Victoria, Australia 3198

surf www.itc.icl.ie/~sean/hhf/

HOUSE

WHAT House came from nowhere to change everything. It first soundtracked gay discos in Chicago, blending euphoric Soul with mechanized beats. DJs Frankie Knuckles, Farley 'Jackmaster' Funk, Steve 'Silk' Hurley and Marshall Jefferson battled to patent the sound. Farley was first on record with 'Love Can't Turn Around', Jefferson was first to hit with 'Move Your Body (The House Anthem)'. Hurley's 'Jack Your Body' (1987) was first to hit No.1. All but ignored in the USA, House found a home in Europe. In Britain, its effect was as revolutionary as Punk, as Krush, Coldcut, Bomb The Bass and S-Express stormed charts. On the continent, Italo-House gave rise to classics like Black Box's 'Ride On Time'. House also rocked Rock: The Beloved, KLF, Primal Scream and Happy Mondays were just some of those who crashed the party. Even U2 hitched aboard, with the pulsating likes of 'Lemon'. Meanwhile, House spawned Garage (slick, equally indebted to House's robotic brother Techno), Handbag (faithful to House's gay origins, very slick), Progressive (synth-wibbling like Orbital and Banco De Gaia), Euro-House/Euro-Cheese (anything grown-ups hate, like Whigfield's 'Saturday Night'). See? It changed everything.

WHERE Chicago, London, Milan

WHEN Mid-80s–

WHO Bomb The Bass <u>Into The Dragon</u> (1988), Ten City <u>Foundation</u> (1988), Aqua <u>Aquarium</u> (1995)

THE HOUSEMARTINS

WHO Vocals **Paul Heaton** (b. 9 May 1962, Birkenhead, England), guitar **Stan Cullimore** (b. Ian Cullimore, 6 May 1962, Hull, England), bass **Norman Cook** (b. Quentin Cook, 31 Jul 1963, Brighton, England) drums **Dave Hemingway** (b. 20 Sep 1960, Hull)

WHEN 1984–1988

WHERE Hull, England

WHAT Socialist Pop harmonies

After gigging with original bassist and drummer Ted Key and Hugh Whitaker, The Housemartins signed to Go! Discs for their debut 'Flag Day' in 1985. By the time of their first UK hit 'Happy Hour', Key had been replaced by Cook. *London 0 Hull 4* (1986) repeated the hit's success, and their a capella take on Isley Jasper Isley's 'Caravan Of Love' was 1986's UK Christmas No.1.

In 1987 Whitaker left due to "ideological differences". Joined by Hemingway, the group reinforced their socialist political stance by appearing on the Labour Party-sponsored 'Red Wedge' UK tour. More hits followed, as well as *The People Who Grinned Themselves To Death* (1987) – a reference to the ever-smiling British Royal Family. In 1988, the group announced their split, informing the media that "in a world of Rick Astley, Shakin' Stevens and Pet Shop Boys, they simply weren't good enough". A further example of their self-deprecating humour was the compilation *Now That's What I Call Quite Good* (1988).

Heaton and Hemingway resurfaced with mega-sellers The Beautiful South and Cook re-entered the world of Dance.

WHITNEY HOUSTON ⊙ ⊙ ✪ ✪ ✪

WHO b. 9 Aug 1963, Newark, New Jersey, USA

WHAT Soul sister superstar

Long before she played a fictional superstar in *The Bodyguard*, Whitney Houston's rise looked like a fairy story. Born into a Soul dynasty that boasts Gospel star Cissy Houston (her mother) and Dionne Warwick (her cousin), Houston graduated to backing the likes of Chaka Khan and The Neville Brothers.

After a cover-grabbing modelling career in the early 80s, she was groomed for musical megastardom. A minor hit with Teddy Pendergrass – 'Hold Me' (1984) – gave no clue to the scale of success she was to enjoy on her own. In 1985, 'You Give Good Love' made the US Top 3, then 'Saving All My Love For You' topped the US and UK charts. Deposing Madonna as 'Queen of Pop', she would thereafter be rivalled only by Mariah Carey.

An astute mix of Dance confections such as 'How Will I Know' (1986) and 'I Wanna Dance With Somebody' (1987) and lung-busting ballads like 'Greatest Love Of All' (1986) and 'Where Do Broken Hearts Go' (1988) added up to a record-breaking seven consecutive US No.1s. Her second album, 1987's *Whitney* (successor to 1985's equally innovatively titled *Whitney Houston*) was the first by a woman to enter at No.1 in the US chart.

I'm Your Baby Tonight (1990) was a relative disappointment, yielding 'only' two US chart-toppers – the title track and 'All The Man That I Need'. But any disenchantment was quickly assuaged by 'I Will Always Love You', from *The Bodyguard* soundtrack (1992): a ten-week UK No.1 and the top single in *Billboard*'s 'Hot 100' history. The album also joined the all-time best-sellers, and Houston made a creditable transition into acting.

The latter has come to dominate her career and fans anxious for new material have had to content themselves with soundtrack cuts like the soothing 'Exhale (Shoop Shoop)' (from *Waiting To Exhale*, 1995) and the effervescent, Annie Lennox-composed 'Step By Step' (from *The Preacher's Wife*, 1996). She teamed with young Swing star Brandy in a 1997 US TV version of *Cinderella* and Will Smith for *Anything For Love* (1998).

Houston also duetted with her husband Bobby Brown on 1994's 'Something In Common' – a cheery launch for a marriage that has since had to endure intense media scrutiny. Houston's long-mooted 'greatest hits' set has yet to appear, but extra reserves of platinum are doubtless being mined in preparation.

READ *Diva: The Totally Unauthorised Biography Of Whitney Houston* (1995), Jeffery Bowman

FAN Whitney Houston Platinum Club, PO Box 885288, San Francisco, CA 94188, USA

SURF fanasylum.com/whitney/

"When I used to watch my mother sing,

which was usually in church,

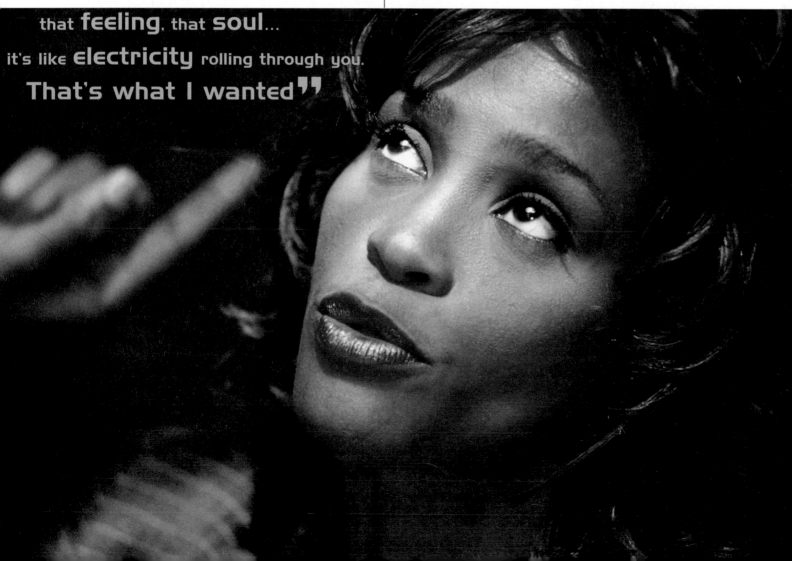

that **feeling**, that **soul**...

it's like **electricity** rolling through you.

That's what I wanted"

THE HUMAN LEAGUE

WHO Vocals/keyboards **Philip Oakey** (b. 2 Oct 1955, Leicester, England), vocals **Susanne Sulley** (b. 26 Mar 1963, Sheffield, England), vocals **Joanne Catherall** (b. 18 Sep 1962, Sheffield)

WHEN 1977–

WHERE Sheffield, South Yorkshire, England

WHAT Synth Pop sparklers

Taking their name from sci-fi board game Starforce, Martyn Ware and Ian Craig Marsh formed The Human League with hospital porter Philip Oakey. Ice-cream salesman Philip Adrian Wright joined as 'visual director', enlivening early gigs with Pop Art slide shows. Indie singles 'Being Boiled'/'Circus Of Death' (1978) and 'The Dignity Of Labour Pts I-IV' (1979) preceded a move to Virgin.

After their major-label debut 'I Don't Depend On You' (1979), credited to The Men, *Reproduction* (1979) scraped the UK Top 40. An electronic overhaul of Gary Glitter's 'Rock And Roll Part 2', from the 'Holiday 80' EP, got them on *Top Of The Pops*, but Marsh and Ware flounced off to form Heaven 17 after *Travelogue* (1980). In stepped keyboard player Ian Burden and singers Sulley and Catherall, but it took a visit to the girls' school and Sunday lunch at Catherall's parents before the latter were permitted to join.

In May 1981, they exploded with 'The Sound Of The Crowd'. Ex-Rezillo Jo Callis joined on keyboards for further hits 'Love Action (I Believe In Love)' and 'Open Your Heart'. *Dare* (1981) and 'Don't You Want Me' topped Christmas charts, a feat repeated Stateside, despite universal discomfort at the freakishly fringed Oakey. After a re-release of 'Being Boiled', 1982 hits 'Mirror Man' and '(Keep Feeling) Fascination' and a Disco revamp of *Dare* (*Love And Dancing,* by the League Unlimited Orchestra), *Hysteria* (1984) dulled their glow. However, Oakey's collaboration with Giorgio Moroder (whose 'I Feel Love' with Donna Summer was a key influence), 'Together In Electric Dreams' (1984), fared better.

Crash (1986), masterminded by miracle workers Jam & Lewis, produced the worldwide smash 'Human' but, after *Greatest Hits* (1988), *Romantic?* (1990) did little to restore their fortunes. Finally abandoning Rock and R&B, they returned to the Synth Pop they did best on *Octopus* (1995), trailed by the biggie 'Tell Me When'.

 www.escritoire.demon.co.uk/human.htm

HUMBLE PIE

WHO Vocals/guitar/keyboards/harmonica **Steve Marriott** (b. 30 Jan 1947, London, England, d. 20 Apr 1991), vocals/guitar **Peter Frampton** (b. 22 Apr 1950, Beckenham, Kent, England), bass **Greg Ridley** (b. 23 Oct 1947, Carlisle, England), drums **Jerry Shirley** (b. 4 Feb 1952, England)

WHEN 1968–1982

WHERE London, England

WHAT "Spittin', arse-kickin' Rock 'n' Roll, man" (Steve Marriott)

After quitting The Small Faces, Steve Marriott joined forces with ex-Herd member Peter Frampton who, with Jerry Shirley, was in search of a guitarist for a new band. Recruited ex-Spooky Tooth member Greg Ridley in late 1968, the line-up was complete.

Their debut, *As Safe As Yesterday Is* (1969) – with its UK No.4 single 'Natural Born Bugie' – displayed Frampton's Jazz roots, its softer sound contrasting with the crunching Rock Marriott later adopted. After a UK tour and the release of *Town And Country* (1969), their label, Immediate, went bankrupt. Left with little money or support, the band were saved by A&M. *Humble Pie* (1970) and *Rock On* (1971) followed, but it was not until the riotous live album *Performance – Rockin' The Fillmore* (1971) that Humble Pie broke into the US charts, reaching No.21. The difference in styles led to Frampton's departure in 1971, beginning a solo career which elevated him to superstar status.

Humble Pie continued as a trio before enlisting ex-Colosseum guitarist Dave Clempson. *Smokin'* (1972) proved the band's most successful release, reaching US No.6. Backing singers The Blackberries were added in 1973, but the next three albums made little impact. The group disbanded in 1975 and the Steve Marriott All-Stars' *Marriott* (1976) failed to chart. In 1979, Marriott re-formed Humble Pie with Shirley and new recruits Anthony Jones and Bobby Tench, but the group split again two years later.

Marriott died in a 1991 house fire, depriving the world of a truly inspirational vocalist. However, his influence lives on and, while Humble Pie were never at the forefront of the 70s scene, their influence can be heard in the Rock and Soul of Paul Weller.

 www.dhc.net/~schow/humblepie/humblepie.htm

HÜSKER DÜ

WHO Guitar/vocals **Bob Mould** (b. 12 Oct 1960, Malone, New York, USA), bass **Greg Norton** (b. 13 Mar 1959, Rock Island, Illinois, USA), drums/vocals **Grant Hart** (b. Grantzberg Hart, 18 Mar 1961, St Paul, Minnesota, USA)

WHEN 1979–1988

WHERE Minneapolis, Minnesota, USA

WHAT Hardcore songs and stories

Hüsker Dü (Swedish for "Do you remember?") were initially distinguished from the Black Flag-descended Hardcore hordes only by their astonishing speed, captured on *Land Speed Record* (1981) and *Everything Falls Apart* (1982). Their breakthrough – the double, concept album *Zen Arcade* (1984) – broke all the 'rules' of the genre. Acclaim translated into sales with the epic *Warehouse: Songs And Stories* (1987), but the band were torn apart by internal tension and Grant Hart's heroin addiction.

After the split, Bob Mould issued the glum *Workbook* (1989) and *Black Sheets Of Rain* (1990) before returning roaring riffs and choruses to centre stage. The gigantic *Copper Blue* (1992) initiated the shooting star career of Sugar, who rode the crest of Grunge – a genre Hüsker Dü helped to spawn – and lasted through the nerve-rattling *Beaster* (1993) and *File Under Easy Listening* (1994). Mould resumed his solo career with *Bob Mould* (1996). Meanwhile, Hart formed Nova Mob (whose most ambitious outing was 1991's *The Last Days Of Pompeii*) and Greg Norton moved into food catering.

 www.ncl.ac.uk/~n4262587/husker.html

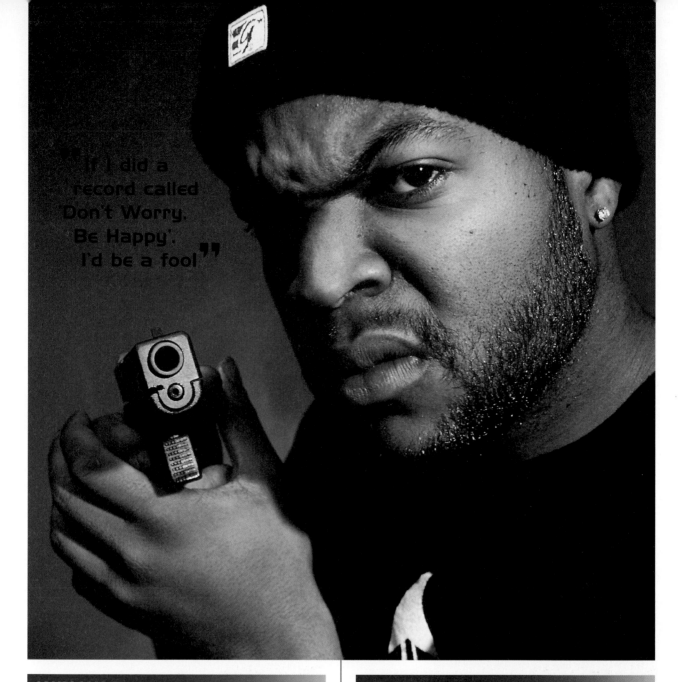

"If I did a record called
'Don't Worry,
Be Happy',
I'd be a fool"

JANIS IAN ✪

WHO b. Janis Eddy Fink, 7 May 1951, New York City, New York, USA

WHAT Urban introspection

Janis Ian began writing and performing in her early teens. Her 1967 debut 'Society's Child (Baby I've Been Thinking)', a bitter song about racism and hypocrisy, was widely banned by US radio stations until championed by conductor Leonard Bernstein, reaching US No.14. Her eponymous first album (1967) also sold well, but after less successful follow-ups she retired temporarily from music.

A new deal in 1974 brought critical and commercial success with *Stars*, and 1975's US No.3 'At Seventeen' and US No.1 *Between The Lines*. She had minor UK hits with 'Fly Too High' and 'The Other Side Of The Sun' from *Night Rains* (1979), featuring Disco wizard Giorgio Moroder and Jazz pianist Chick Corea.

Her career suffered later with management problems and the failure of a second marriage, after which she announced she was gay. A return with *Breaking Silence* (1992) and *Revenge* (1995) showed her songs to be as incisive as ever.

 www.songs.com/janisian

ICE CUBE

WHO b. O'Shea Jackson, 15 Jun 1969, Los Angeles, California, USA

WHAT Gangsta Rap's self-proclaimed 'Nigga Ya Love To Hate'

Sprung from Gangsta Rap supergroup NWA, Ice Cube defected from his native California to hook up with East Coast supremos Public Enemy. With Public Enemy producers The Bomb Squad at the helm, his debut *AmeriKKKa's Most Wanted* (1990) initiated a string of smashes – *Kill At Will* (1990), *Death Certificate* (1991), *The Predator* (1992), *Lethal Injection* (1993) and sidekicks Da Lench Mob's *Guerillas In Tha Mist* (1992) – that testified to Cube's lyrical dexterity and business acumen, not to mention a contrived image that recast a suburban student as a gun-totin' gangsta. "They're not really livin' like that," objected Ice T. "There's a point where Ice Cube has to admit he lives with his mother."

In the mid-90s, when he began to be eclipsed by younger G's, Cube put Rap on hold and concentrated on movies. Acclaimed turns in *Boyz N The Hood* (1991) and *Trespass* (1992) preceded *Higher Learning* (1995), *The Glass Shield* (1995), the self-penned *Friday* (1996), *Dangerous Ground* (1997) with Liz Hurley, *Anaconda* (1997) and directorial debut *The Player's Club* (1997).

He returned to music with *Westside Connection* (1996), an ill-advisedly antagonistic contribution to the East/West Coast conflict that had flared around Tupac Shakur and The Notorious BIG. A highly entertaining dispute with long-time collaborators Cypress Hill (they said he stole a hook) added to the furore.

In between films and feuding, stop-gap collections *Bootlegs & B Sides* (1994) and *Featuring…* (1997) paved the way for *War And Peace* (1998). A long-mooted album-length collaboration with former NWA cohort Dr Dre (titled *Helter Skelter*) never materialized, although the pair's 'Natural Born Killaz' was a hit highlight from the *Murder Was The Case* soundtrack (1995).

surf members.aol.com/ALTHUG1/home.html

ICE-T

WHO b. Tracy Marrow, c.1958, Newark, New Jersey, USA

WHAT Original Gangsta

East Coast-born Ice-T found fortune in the West. Early LA-based ventures included his 1983 debut 'The Coldest Rapper' and two breakdance movies. More memorably, Ice popularized Gangsta Rap with the censor-baiting violence and profanity of *Rhyme Pays* (1987), *Power* (1988) and *The Iceberg: Freedom Of Speech… Just Watch What You Say* (1989). The flames burned hottest in 1991, with his acclaimed role in the movie *New Jack City* and the stone-cold classic *O.G. Original Gangster*. From the latter, his band Body Count evolved from Thrash Metal one-off to a full-blown project, whose self-titled debut (1992) included 'Cop Killer'. With police and politicians in uproar, the track became an international *cause célèbre*.

Rap fans, however, lost interest, largely ignoring *Home Invasion* (1993) and other releases on his Rhyme Syndicate label. His multi-media career continued with the frank manifesto *The Ice Opinion*, Body

Count's *Born Dead* (1994) and *Violent Demise* (1998), TV roles and a kangaroo-costumed cameo in 1995's *Tank Girl* movie. Although *VI: Return Of The Real* (1996) again received short shrift, Ice remains an articulate commentator on both Rap and end-of-the-millennium existence. Fellow Rap prophet The RZA (Wu-Tang Clan) helped out on *The Seventh Deadliest Sin* (1998).

read *The Ice Opinion* (1994), Ice T & Heidi Siegmund

surf www.sasquatch.com/~zane/ice.html

THE ICICLE WORKS

WHO Vocals/guitar **Ian McNabb** (b. Robert Ian McNabb, 3 Nov 1960, Liverpool, England), bass **Chris Layhe**, drums **Chris Sharrock**

WHEN 1980–1990

WHERE Liverpool, England

WHAT Post-Punk Psychedelia

Named after a sci-fi novel, The Icicle Works joined Liverpool's early 80s 'Neo-Psychedelia' wave, which also propelled Echo & The Bunnymen and The Teardrop Explodes to stardom. Slightly less stellar but acclaimed nonetheless, The Icicle Works' biggest UK hit was 1983's 'Love Is A Wonderful Colour'. Their debut *Icicle Works* (1984) reached the US Top 40, as did the extracted 'Birds Fly (Whisper To A Scream)', but *The Small Price Of A Bicycle* (1985), *If You Want To Defeat His Enemy Sing His Song* (1987) and *Blind* (1988) formed fewer ripples.

Sharrock departed (to The La's and, later, Lightning Seeds), as did Layhe. Ringo Starr's son Zak briefly occupied the drumstool, while various keyboardists, bassists and a guitarist passed through before the band bowed out with *Permanent Damage* (1990). McNabb's solo career included *Truth And Beauty* (1993), *Head Like A Rock* (1994) – featuring Neil Young's band Crazy Horse – and *Merseybeast* (1996).

surf www.dm.net/~sharan/musiconline/icicleworks.html

BILLY IDOL

WHO b. William Broad, 30 Nov 1955, Stanmore, Middlesex, England

WHAT Sneering, ever-youthful MTV rocker

After Generation X split in 1982, singer Billy Idol fled to New York, into the arms of Kiss manager Bill Aucoin, producer Keith Forsey and guitarist Steve Stevens. His debut EP 'Don't Stop' (1981) preceded the 1982 smash 'Hot In The City', which affixed Idol's sneer to MTV and pushed *Billy Idol* (1982) up the US chart.

UK success ensued with 1984's 'Eyes Without A Face', a Synth Rock chiller from *Rebel Yell* (1983), source also of the hits 'White Wedding' and 'Rebel Yell'. By 1986's *Whiplash Smile*, his pastiche dumb rock 'n' rolling had become dangerous indulgence, hence a 1990 motorcycle crash. Little acting was required for his hell-raising role in Oliver Stone's 1991 biopic *The Doors*. Fatherhood and respectable sales of the less studied *Charmed Life* (1990) seemed to stabilize him, but 1993's *Cyberpunk* (a concept album inspired by sci-fi author William Gibson) sank without trace.

surf www.geocities.com/SunsetStrip/6464/

THE INCREDIBLE STRING BAND

WHO Vocals/guitar/etc **Mike Heron** (b. 12 Dec 1942, Edinburgh, Scotland), vocals/guitar/etc **Robin Williamson** (b. 24 Nov 1943, Edinburgh)

WHEN 1965–1974

WHERE Glasgow, Scotland

WHAT Hippie Folk

Mixing Celtic Folk with genuine invention, The Incredible String Band rode the first wave of hippiedom. A psychedelic sleeve for *5000 Spirits Or The Layers Of The Onion* (1967) fostered a 'far out' image, while *The Hangman's Beautiful Daughter* (1968) exhibited the hallmarks of a Progressive epic: mystical lyrics, odd timings and exotic instrumentation. Folk roots anchored the work, but inventive writing gave the band its own identity. Others like Dr Strangely Strange and Tyrannosaurus Rex achieved a similar effect, but only the Incredibles notched up the sales.

As the 60s faded, they remained unique until their fluid line-up split up in 1974. Robin became a modern-day bard (harpist, storyteller), while Mike pursued commercial Folk Rock. The duo briefly reunited in the 90s and a faithful fanbase, including Pet Shop Boy Neil Tennant, campaigned for a full-scale ISB reunion.

Fan BeGLAD, 11 Ratcliffe Road, Sheffield S11 8YA, UK

surf dspace.dial.pipex.com/town/square/ac455/index.htm

INDIE

WHAT A by-product of Punk's DIY ethic was the growth of independent record labels: free from giants like EMI and Sony, founded by fans and motivated by passion not profit. Championing artists ignored by majors, the 'Indies' infiltrated the mainstream with Ian Dury (Stiff) and Joy Division (Factory), but clung to 'alternative' cool. Gradually, 'Indie' referred less to business than style. Chart compilers stuck to the official definition (hence Kylie Minogue could appear alongside Alien Sex Fiend), but public perception of 'Indie' was a bunch of whining guitar bands, be they The Smiths, The Cure or, Stateside, Sonic Youth and Hüsker Dü. These spawned legions of soundalikes and stimulated ersatz 'Indie' offshoots from major labels, such as EMI's Food (Blur, Dubstar) and Geffen's DGC (Sonic Youth, Nirvana). With 'Indie' and 'Alternative' reduced to marketing terms, genuine Indie labels can barely compete, and sympathetic retailers have been obliterated by chain stores. Former titans Stiff, Factory and Rough Trade were bankrupted by their independence, and the maverick Creation was forced into the arms of Sony. Meanwhile, Indie – particularly in Britain – has entertained itself with press-led parlour games: C86, Baggy, Grunge, Crusty, Grebo, Shoegazing, The New Wave Of New Wave, Transit-Core and Riot Grrrl were just some of the thankfully short-lived sub-genres.
WHERE UK, USA
WHEN Late 70s–
WHO Joy Division Unknown Pleasures (1979), The Smiths The Queen Is Dead (1986), Sonic Youth Daydream Nation (1988), The Fall Extricate (1990), Mogwai Young Team (1997), Sneaker Pimps Becoming X (1997), Peter Andre Time (1997)

INDUSTRIAL

WHAT Rooted in the experimental violence of 60s/70s German Progressive Rock, 'Industrial' was first coined in 1976 by British noise anarchists Throbbing Gristle. Industrial began as 'anti-music', mixing electronics with found sounds, often originating from machinery. Musical and visual extremity remained a central theme – Gristle's grinding assault was accompanied by films of pornography, fascism and death. Post-Punk practitioners Cabaret Voltaire, Foetus and Einstürzende Neubauten emphasized electronics and atonality, the former heavily influencing later technological industrialists like Skinny Puppy and Front 242. The most commercial Industrial artists are Ministry and Nine Inch Nails, who edged the style closer to Metal, while elements of the genre popped up in Depeche Mode.
WHERE Europe, USA
WHEN 70s–
WHO Throbbing Gristle D.O.A. (1978), Cabaret Voltaire Mix-Up (1979), Einstürzende Neubauten Drawings Of Patient O.T. (1983), Ministry The Land Of Rape And Honey (1988), KMFDM Naive (1990), Various Hot Wired Monstertrux (1993), Nine Inch Nails Further Down The Spiral (1995)

INSPIRAL CARPETS

WHO Vocals **Tom Hingley** (b. 9 Jul 1965, Oxford, England), keyboards/vocals **Clint Boon** (b. 28 Jun 1959, Oldham, England), guitar **Graham Lambert** (b. 10 Jul 1964, Oldham), bass **Martyn 'Bungle' Walsh** (b. 3 Jul 1968, Manchester, England), drums **Craig Gill** (b. 5 Dec 1971, Manchester)

WHEN 1986–1994

WHERE Oldham, England

WHAT Organ-driven Indie Pop

Inspiral Carpets joined 'Madchester' market leaders Happy Mondays and The Stone Roses as purveyors of danceable Pop, distinguished mainly by Clint Boon's 60s-sounding Farfisa organ.

After their debut EP, 'Plane Crash' (1988), they replaced vocalist Stephen Holt with Tom Hingley, rejecting a then unknown Noel Gallagher, who instead joined their road crew. A cult following grew with the 1989 classics 'Trainsurfing' and 'Move' (and their notorious T-shirt slogan 'Cool As Fuck'), then blossomed when the Inspirals signed to Mute, who maintained the band's Cow Records imprint on their 1990 breakthrough 'This Is How It Feels' and their album debut *Life* (UK No.2, 1990).

After the glorious 'She Comes In The Fall' and 'Island Head' EP, they spurned Pop's primary colours for the surprisingly dark *The Beast Inside* (1991). In 1992, despite the success of 'Dragging Me Down', *Revenge Of The Goldfish* marked a commercial downturn, accelerated by the noisier *Devil Hopping* (1994), which featured the spectacular 'Saturn 5' and, with Fall übermensch Mark E. Smith, 'I Want You'.

Inspiral Carpets bowed out with hits set *The Singles* (1995), Hingley formed The Lovers and Boon went solo. Former roadie Gallagher had long since set about conquering the universe.

surf www.mutelibtech.com/mute/inspiral/inspiral.htm

"Pop eats its young,
that's for sure"

INXS ☉

WHO Vocals **Michael Hutchence** (b. 22 Jan 1960, Sydney, Australia, d. 22 Nov 1997, Sydney), guitar/keyboards **Andrew Farriss** (b. 27 Mar 1959, Perth, Western Australia), guitar/saxophone **Kirk Pengilly** (b. 4 Jul 1958, Sydney), guitar **Tim Farriss** (b. 16 Aug 1957, Perth), bass **Garry Gary Beers** (b. 22 Jun 1957, Sydney), drums **Jon Farriss** (b. 10 Aug 1961, Perth)

WHEN 1977–1997

WHERE Sydney, New South Wales, Australia

WHAT Funk-rocking wizards of Oz

Battle-hardened by Australian bar gigs, the six-strong INXS remained unchanged after convening as The Farriss Brothers. They debuted their new name in 1979 and released *INXS* in 1980. A relentless road campaign – Una Brilliante Band De Musica Amenizara Espectaculo Tour – sent *Underneath The Colours* (1981) and *Shabooh Shoobah* (1982) up their homeland chart.

They invaded America in 1983: 'The One Thing' became an MTV favourite, unhindered by Hutchence's gorgeousness. The takeover continued with high-profile shows, a mini-album of *Shabooh* remixes (1983's *Dekadance*) and work with Chic production whiz Nile Rodgers. The result was *The Swing* (1984): a double-platinum Australian No.1, from which 'Original Sin' took them tantalizingly close to a major international breakthrough. Boosted by their Live Aid slot and transatlantic hit 'What You Need', *Listen Like Thieves* (1985) did the trick, breaching the UK Top 50 and going platinum Stateside.

In a brief break, Hutchence starred in Australian underground movie *Dogs In Space* (1986), scoring a solo hit with the soundtrack's 'Rooms For The Memory'. Andrew and Jon Farriss produced Australian stars Jenny Morris and Richard Clapton respectively. Band activities resumed for global gargantuan *Kick* (1987). 'Need You Tonight' (No.1), 'Devil Inside', 'New Sensation' and 'Never Tear Us Apart' were US smashes, while 'Mystify' became one of their biggest and best-loved UK hits.

Further individual ventures – including Hutchence's *Max Q* (1989) album and role in *Frankenstein Unbound* (1990) – preceded the reconvened band's *X* (1990). Trailed by the hit 'Suicide Blonde' – inspired by Hutchence's girlfriend Kylie Minogue – the album rode *Kick*'s coat-tails to platinum status. The X Factor World Tour culminated in the Wembley Stadium extravaganza Summer XS. The triumphant *Live Baby Live* (1991) capped a celebratory year.

Though they remained stars in Australia and Europe, their American profile plummeted. The sumptuous *Welcome To Wherever You Are* (1992) was a deserved UK No.1, but failed even to match *X*'s measly million Stateside. By *Full Moon, Dirty Hearts* (1993), Hutchence's new love, supermodel Helena Christensen, was more newsworthy, and a tabloid feeding frenzy ensued when she gave way to Bob Geldof's ex, Paula Yates. *The Greatest Hits* (1994) filled a long silence before *Elegantly Wasted* (1997), which took none of the risks of its immediate predecessors.

Hutchence had been working on a solo album with producer and Gang Of Four guitarist Andy Gill when, at the beginning of INXS's 20th anniversary Australian tour, he was found hanging by a belt in his hotel room – a sad end for a man and band who had always infused their Rock 'n' Roll clichés with fresh sparkle.

(ʀᴇᴀᴅ) *INXS: The Official Inside Story Of A Band On The Road* (1992), Ed St John

(ꜰᴀɴ) What You Need, 17 Ink Pen Lane, Whitby, Ontario, Canada L1R 2H2

(ꜱᴜʀꜰ) www.umdnj.edu/~kotharne/inxs.html

IRON BUTTERFLY

WHO Vocals/keyboards **Doug Ingle** (b. 9 Sep 1945, Omaha, Nebraska, USA), guitar/vocals **Erik Braunn** (b. 11 Aug 1950, Pekin, Illinois, USA), bass **Lee Dorman** (b. 19 Sep 1941, St Louis, Missouri, USA), drums **Ron Bushy** (b. 23 Dec 1941, Washington, DC, USA),

WHEN 1967–

WHERE San Diego, California, USA

WHAT Proto-Metal Acid Rock

Iron Butterfly's crunching electric Blues was a formative part of Heavy Rock. In 1968, the epic title track (with its coma-inducing drum solo) of *In-A-Gadda-Da-Vida* (US No.4) hit a strange spot in America's psyche and an edited version made US No.30. Its odd name an attempt to pronounce 'In The Garden Of Eden' under the influence of a large quantity of wine, the album spent 140 weeks in the US chart, while *Ball* (1969) bounced to No.3.

Iron Butterfly established a sound that others – Deep Purple, Led Zeppelin, etc – took to long-term success ('In-A-Gadda-Da-Vida' was covered by Slayer) but, after exhaustive gigging, the quartet split in 1971. Having re-formed periodically since 1974, the current Iron Butterfly line-up is Ingle, Bushy and Dorman.

(ʀᴇᴀᴅ) *Iron Butterfly* (1983), Kristin Lynch

(ꜰᴀɴ) Iron Butterfly Info, 9745 Sierra Ave., Fontana, CA 92335, USA

(ꜱᴜʀꜰ) www.ironbutterfly.com/

IRON MAIDEN ☉ ☉ ☉

WHO Vocals **Blaze Bayley** (b. Bayley Cooke, 5 May 1963, Birmingham, England), guitar **Dave 'The Blond Bomber' Murray** (b. 23 Dec 1956, London, England), guitar **Janick Gers** (b. 27 Jan 1957, Hartlepool, Lancashire, England), bass **Steve 'Arry' Harris** (b. 12 Mar 1956, Leytonstone, London), drums **Nicko McBrain** (b. Michael McBrain, 5 Jun 1952)

WHEN 1976–

WHERE East London, England

WHAT Heavy Metal Horror

Though Iron Maiden's most famous face is skeletal band mascot 'Eddie the Head', the real mainstay is softly spoken, bass-playing songwriter Steve Harris. Inspired by British Hard Rock legends UFO, he graduated through fledgling bands Gypsy's Kiss (1973) and Smiler (1974) before assembling Iron Maiden in 1976. The band followed classic Metal guidelines: a ghoulish image, twin lead guitars and labyrinthine line-up changes. The latter yielded

track), platinum US sales and Eddie on innumerable chests. With one further tweak (Burr replaced by charismatic vulgarian Nicko McBrain), Maiden conquered the world with *Piece Of Mind* (1983) and *Powerslave* (1984). The latter occasioned the World Slavery Tour – a characteristic marathon celebrated by *Live After Death* (1985). Smith enjoyed his highest profile on the more melodic *Somewhere In Time* (1986) – the peak of their US success.

Untouched by the Thrash Metal revolution (spearheaded by the transparently Maiden-influenced Metallica), *Seventh Son Of A Seventh Son* (1988) was a Jethro Tull-esque concept affair which topped the UK chart and even gave Maiden-haters something to whistle with 'Can I Play With Madness?'. At their spectacular headliner for 107,000 'rivetheads' at 1988's UK Monsters Of Rock festival, Kiss – who'd given Maiden a support slot in 1980 – were relegated to 'special guests'. It also earned Maiden a place in *The Guinness Book Of Records*, for 'the largest front of house PA' – the sound peaking at 124 dB during their set.

By the 80s' end, however, trouble was brewing. *No Prayer For The Dying* (1990) spawned the UK No.1 'Bring Your Daughter To The Slaughter', but Smith had quit for solo obscurity (replaced by Gers) and Metallica had galloped ahead of the field. Dickinson bowed out with the deservedly chart-topping *Fear Of The Dark* (1992) and another Monsters Of Rock headliner, although Harris bizarrely closed this chapter of Ironography with three 1993 live albums: *A Real Live One*, *A Real Dead One* and *Live At Donington*.

Dickinson's solo career, begun by 1990's *Tattooed Millionaire*, continued with *Balls To Picasso* (1994), *Skunkworks* (1996) and, reunited with Smith, *Accident At Birth* (1997). Maiden recruited Blaze Bayley, formerly of plucky Brit-bashers Wolfsbane, for *The X Factor* (1995) and *Virtual XI* (1998) – which, while not scaling the heights of their heyday, made the UK Top 10. However, Iron Maiden's place in Heavy Metal history – commemorated by *Best Of The Beast* (1996) – had long ceased to rely on chart positions.

read *Run To The Hills* (1998), Mick Wall

Fan Iron Maiden FC, PO Box 10, London SW19 3TW, UK

surf www.ironmaiden.co.uk/maiden

CHRIS ISAAK

WHO b. 6 Jun 1956, Stockton, California, USA

WHAT Heart-throb crooner

His nose broken seven times, Chris Isaak took the hint and quit boxing. Unfortunately, music wasn't much more rewarding: *Silvertone* (1985) and *Chris Isaak* (1987) won critical comparisons to Roy Orbison but overwhelming commercial non-interest.

Heart Shaped World (1989) had already surfaced when movie loon David Lynch put Isaak's 'Wicked Game' in his *Wild At Heart* (1990). The song became a hit, girls went 'oooh' at his Elvis-esque looks and *Heart* was reissued as *Wicked Game* (1991). Isaak returned the favour by starring in Lynch's *Twin Peaks: Fire Walk With Me* (1993), his celluloid CV also boasting *Married To The Mob* (1988), *The Silence Of The Lambs* (1990) and *Little Buddha* (1993).

However, interest waned through *San Francisco Days* (1993), *Forever Blue* (1995) and *Baja Sessions* (1996), to the point where his 1996 *Friends* cameo went unapplauded even by the usually clap-happy studio audience.

surf www.repriserec.com/Reprise_HTML_Pages/chrisisaakfolder/

long-standing guitarist Dave Murray and, in 1978, vocalist Paul Di'Anno. In the intervening years, they ignored prevailing Punk trends, through their brand of Metal (presumed commercially moribund) was enticingly speedier than most 70s sludge.

A rabid fanbase devoured debut EP 'The Soundhouse Tapes' (1979) and UK music paper *Sounds* crowned Maiden heads of the 'New Wave Of British Heavy Metal'. Eleven personnel turnovers endured, *Iron Maiden* (1980) was the work of Harris, Murray, Di'Anno, guitarist Dennis Stratton and drummer Clive Burr. Fuelled by hit anthem 'Running Free' and major-label (EMI) muscle, the album crashed the UK Top 5, establishing a winning streak unmatched in Metal. These giddy heights couldn't prevent more upheaval: out went Stratton and in came Adrian Smith (a frustratingly under-used songwriter, but perfect foil for Murray).

After the disappointing *Killers* (1981), it was 'adios' Di'Anno and 'aloha' Air-Raid Siren, aka former Samson singer Bruce Dickinson (b. 8 Aug 1958, Worksop, Nottinghamshire, England). With the classic *Number Of The Beast* (1982), they became Metal's biggest noise: a UK No.1, two hits ('Run To The Hills' and the title

Island Records

Chris Blackwell began operating an Island company in Jamaica in 1957. He moved to London in 1962 when Island began distributing Jamaican music and produced the 1964 hit 'My Boy Lollipop' by Millie. Significant signings in the late 60s and early 70s resulted in a major roster of British talent featuring Fairport Convention, Cat Stevens, King Crimson, Free, Jethro Tull and Roxy Music, alongside the label's Jamaican superstar Bob Marley. In 1975 Blackwell launched Island Records in America with Joe South and War, and scored further success with Sparks, Stevie Winwood, Frankie Goes To Hollywood (through the ZTT label), U2, Pulp and The Cranberries. Blackwell sold Island to Polygram for $275 million in 1989, but remained Chairman until 1997.

THE ISLEY BROTHERS ✪

WHO Vocals **Ronald Isley** (b. 21 May 1941, Cincinnati, Ohio, USA), vocals

Rudolph Isley (b. 1 Apr 1939, Cincinnati), vocals **O'Kelly Isley** (25 Dec 1937, Cincinnati, d. 31 Mar 1986, Alpine, New Jersey, USA)

WHEN 1958–

WHERE Cincinnati, Ohio, USA

WHAT Enduring Funk Rock Innovators

Who gave Jimi Hendrix an early break? Influenced Prince and Ice Cube? Spearheaded the Rock/Funk fusion? Sounds like a job for the super-hero likes of Sly Stone or George Clinton, but no: it was the mild-mannered Isley Brothers.

After treading the Gospel to Pop path à la Al Green, the Isleys enjoyed mixed fortunes in the 60s. They recorded Doo Wop and Rock 'n' Roll for several labels before narrowly missing the US Top 40 in 1959 with their wild, self-penned classic 'Shout' (on RCA), which became one of Rock's most performed songs.

Their 'Twist And Shout' reached the US Top 20 in 1962, and a year later made the UK chart behind covers by The Beatles and Brian Poole & The Tremeloes. Moved to Motown, they scored a hit and classic with 1965's 'This Old Heart Of Mine (Is Weak For You)', while 'Behind A Painted Smile' was a 1969 UK hit. However, they were not among Motown's chart regulars, and joined the widespread jumping ship from the label in the late 60s.

No longer bound by Motown's sweet straitjacket, they got downright funky on 'It's Your Thing' (1969), the debut of their T-Neck label. The Isleys' evolution was aided by their cousin Chris Jasper on keyboards and brothers Marvin on bass and Ernie on guitar. Ernie was the key: less pyrotechnical than Hendrix, who'd guested with the brothers in his pre-fame days, he wove a space-age spell – notably on 1973's epic restyling of a staid Isleys track from 1964, 'That Lady'. The latter and 'Summer Breeze' made *3+3* (1973) the first of a run of smash albums, notably 1975's US No.1 *The Heat Is On*. From that platinum seller came 'Fight The Power' – nothing to do with Public Enemy's anthem of the same name, but nonetheless one of the angriest songs to scale the US Top 5.

Wah-wahing guitar washes and street-tough lyrics were offset by the tenderest of ballads. *The Heat Is On* had the searing 'Hope You Feel Better Love' against the gorgeous 'For The Love Of You'. *Live It Up* (1974) balanced its burning title track with the exquisite 'Hello It's Me'. Their dual sides can be tasted on 1977's best-of, *Forever Gold*, although interested parties may also check out Prince's debut *For You*, an Isleys album in spirit if not name.

However, despite hits like 'Harvest For The World' (1976) they stumbled in the tailwind of Disco, and only the staunchest fans would defend the likes of 1979's 'It's A Disco Night (Rock Don't Stop)'. *Go All The Way* (1980), *Grand Slam* (1981) and *Between The Sheets* (1983) maintained the Isleys' fortunes on the album chart, but their adventurousness had dissipated, replaced by only intermittently wondrous bedroom balladeering.

They splintered in the mid-80s: Ernie, Marvin and Chris scored a hit as Isley-Jasper-Isley with 'Caravan Of Love' (1985). The other brothers soldiered through O'Kelly's death in 1986, with minor returns. But in the 90s their magic returned. Ronald guested on Rod Stewart's hit remake of 'This Old Heart Of Mine' in 1990 and basked in the shadow of his wife, acclaimed Soulstress Angela Winbush. Like other R&B/Funk pioneers, they provided many a Rap sample, the most poignant example of which was Ice Cube's borrowing of 'Footsteps In The Dark' (from 1977's *Go For Your Guns*) for his deceptively pretty 1993 hit 'It Was A Good Day'.

surf www.his.com/~vincent/isley_brothers/isleys.htm

Isle Of Wight

The first Isle Of Wight Festival, a fund-raiser for the island's Swimming Pool Association, was an all-nighter which took place on 31 August 1968 in a makeshift arena of scaffolding and polythene at Ford Farm, Godshill. Some 10,000 fans enjoyed Pretty Things, Fairport Convention, Tyrannosaurus Rex, The Move and Jefferson Airplane.

A great success, the event returned on a larger scale at Woodside Bay, Wooton, on 29–31 August 1969. The reclusive Bob Dylan headlined the final night, his first British performance since the infamous 'electric' London Albert Hall concert and only his second live appearance since a mysterious motorcycle crash in 1966. An estimated 80,000 witnessed The Nice, Bonzo Dog Doo-Dah Band, Blodwyn Pig, Family, Noel Redding's Fat Mattress, Joe Cocker, The Moody Blues, Richie Havens, Pentangle and headliners The Who and Bob Dylan with The Band. The Who played an acclaimed set, despite suffering a helicopter crash backstage and Keith Moon having broken his foot a week earlier. Dylan was more enigmatic: after a 45-minute set by The Band, he strolled onstage for a 60-minute set with no encore, leaving the audience stunned.

The final festival, again at Woodside Bay, on 27–31 August 1970, had an audience of 50,000 (although local papers estimated 250,000). The line-up included Kris Kristofferson, Supertramp, the Satan-worshipping Black Widow, Rory Gallagher's Taste, Chicago, Procol Harum, Mungo Jerry, Joni Mitchell, Tiny Tim, Miles Davis, Ten Years After, Melanie, Free, Donovan, Joan Baez, Jethro Tull, Leonard Cohen, Sly & The Family Stone and Emerson, Lake & Palmer. The Who played for around four hours, performing <u>Tommy</u> in its entirety. The event will be remembered, however, for two other headliners: the last English concerts of The Doors and Jimi Hendrix. Hendrix died just three weeks after his performance.

JANET JACKSON ⊙✪✪✪✪

WHO b. 16 May 1966, Gary, Indiana, USA

WHAT Sweet Soul sister

Miss Janet: the sister reluctantly recruited to the Jackson family firm, who dallied with bad boy Soul star James DeBarge, united with Minneapolis' musical mafia and went platinum blending lecturing and lust with Hip Hop thunder. Pre-superduperdom, she skidded from one atrocity to another: on stage in Vegas with her siblings, on record with Cliff Richard, on TV in the likes of *Diff'rent Strokes* and *Fame*. The early albums *Janet Jackson* (1982) and *Dream Street* (1984) are of strictly archival interest.

As a last-ditch career kickstart, A&M teamed her with Jam & Lewis, Prince protégés turned platinum producers. They gave Janet cuts rejected by Atlantic Starr's Sharon Bryant, of which the gutsy 'What Have You Done For Me Lately?' hit big and began her reign as one of the most successful female artists of all time.

Control (1986), *Rhythm Nation 1814* (1989) and *janet.* (1993) broke records for sales and hits and, musically, kept ahead of the New Jill Swing acts in her wake. Satisfied parties included Paula Abdul, who graduated from *Control* choreographer to a career that briefly eclipsed her mentor, and Virgin, to whom Janet defected from A&M for a record-breaking (again) $50 million.

She duetted with Luther Vandross ('The Best Things In Life Are Free' made the UK Top 10 in 1992 *and* 1995), Herb Alpert ('Diamonds', 1987) and brother Michael – 'Scream' (1995) was the first single to enter the US chart inside the Top 5. The hit-packed *Design Of A Decade* (1995) confirmed her pre-eminence. A return to acting – *Poetic Justice* (1993), with Tupac Shakur – was acclaimed but commercially negligible,

sending her back to what she does best. The result was *The Velvet Rope* (1997), another jewel in her crown.

READ *Out Of The Madness: The Strictly Unauthorized Biography Of Janet Jackson* (1994), Bart Andrews

FAN Janet Jackson Fan Club, 14755 Ventura Boulevard 1-710, Sherman Oaks, California 91403, USA

SURF friendsofjanet.com

JOE JACKSON

WHO b. 11 Aug 1954, Burton upon Trent, England

WHAT Jerky jazzy Pop

A graduate of London's Royal College of Music, Jackson was a member of Johnny Dankworth's National Youth Jazz Orchestra and countless club bands before forming his first group, Arms & Legs, in the mid-70s. Moving to London in 1978, he signed to A&M and was swept along with New Wave. *Look Sharp* and *I'm The Man* (both 1979) fused his Jazz roots with fashionably jerky Pop, of which the lovelorn 'It's Different For Girls' was a highlight.

Thereafter, he flirted with Reggae (1980's *Beat Crazy*), 40s Swing (1981's *Joe Jackson's Jumpin' Jive*) and minimalist Jazz Funk influenced by relocation to New York (1982's *Night And Day*, featuring his biggest hit, 'Stepping Out'). *Big World* (1986) was entirely live, while *Body And Soul* (1984), *Will Power* (1987) and *Blaze Of Glory* (1989) united the diverse elements of earlier releases. *Laughter And Lust* (1991) returned to conventional Pop, but with *Night Music* (1994) and *Heaven And Hell* (1997), his retirement from the mainstream seemed permanent.

SURF www.joejackson.com

MICHAEL JACKSON
⊙⊙⊙⊙⊙⊙✪✪✪✪✪

WHO b. 29 Aug 1958, Gary, Indiana, USA

WHAT The ultimate Pop Star

A dancer of precocious ability and an exciting and dynamic (if squeaky) vocalist, Michael was, at 11, the obvious star of his older brothers' band The Jackson 5, who signed to Motown in 1969. The label saw the boy's solo potential and, by 1971, he was a chart name in his own right. What nobody could have foreseen was that 'little Michael' would mature into a superstar to compare to Elvis Presley, enjoy sales to rival The Beatles, and provide a scandal-hungry media with more headlines than even Frank Sinatra. In short he became, by the end of the 80s, probably the most famous person on the planet. For all his phenomenal talents, he could also seem the unhappiest. He was certainly the most enigmatic and controversial – which, at times, has succeeded in overshadowing his music.

Back in 1971, however, his debut hit outside The Jackson 5, 'Got To Be There', revealed him as a plaintive young balladeer, an impression confirmed by 1972's cover of Bill Withers' song 'Ain't No Sunshine'. While the same year's 'Rockin' Robin' was a shrill echo of The Jackson 5's uptempo style, the No.1 'Ben' displayed Michael's deepening sensitivity, despite the song's unlikely

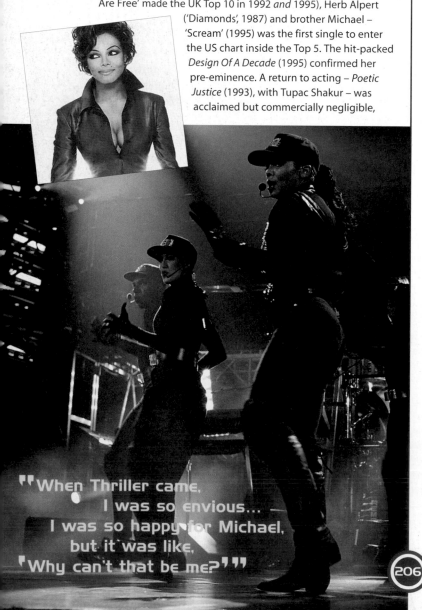

"When Thriller came, I was so envious... I was so happy for Michael, but it was like, Why can't that be me?"

origins in the movie story of a pet rat. A string of Motown solo albums – including *Got To Be There* (1972) and *Ben* (1972) – helped build his independent profile, but subsequent efforts, like *Music And Me* (1973) and *Forever Michael* (1974), suggested the formula was running its course. There was, as yet, no real indication he could outshine his family band.

But, in May 1975, he signed a solo deal with Epic and commenced a career that would outshine every artist in the world. Under the wing of long-time sponsor Diana Ross, Michael took part in the 1977 movie musical *The Wiz*, beginning the key partnership of his career, with legendary arranger/producer Quincy Jones. The self-penned 'Don't Stop 'Til You Get Enough' (1979) brought the now-adult Michael back into the charts and previewed his hugely successful comeback *Off The Wall*, destined to surpass 10 million sales and spawn a string of hits. Jones and Jackson had cannily absorbed the lessons of Disco: *Off The Wall* was unmistakably a dancefloor record. But it was also an album of *songs*, with outstanding compositions by Rod Temperton (such as the title track and 'Rock With You'), Stevie Wonder, Paul McCartney and others. And Michael himself emerged as the songwriter Motown had never allowed him to be.

If *Off The Wall* had been a triumph, then its successor, *Thriller* (1982), was a phenomenon. Selling over 48 million worldwide, it became the most successful album ever – for years it seemed Jackson himself was the only act with any chance of matching it. Musically, he and his producer perfected the approach they had developed on *Off The Wall*, constructing an album that straddled genres of mass appeal. Among a stellar cast of elite session players, Metal guitarist Eddie Van Halen was drafted in to play on Jackson's own song, 'Beat It'. Paul McCartney duetted on the co-written 'The Girl Is Mine' and Rod Temperton was again on hand, supplying the title track and two others.

Michael hit his songwriting peak in 'Beat It', 'Wanna Be Startin' Somethin'' and 'Billie Jean' – all international hits; the latter, in particular, obliged the newly powerful medium of MTV to accommodate black music in its mainstream scheduling. 'Billie Jean' epitomized *Thriller*'s magic – its infectious rhythm gave Jackson full reign to display his dancing, its production was a state-of-the-art update of R&B, Rock and Pop. A guest spot on Motown's 25th anniversary TV special sealed Michael's new status: an electrifying performance of 'Billie Jean' came complete with his trademark dance The Moonwalk. Extravagant videos, such as the 14-minute mock horror film for 'Thriller', directed by Jon Landis, became another crucial ingredient in the marketing mix. Jackson's golden touch was emphasized by an extra hit that year, 'Muscles', written for Diana Ross.

Paul McCartney took his friendship with Jackson a step further by co-writing 'Say Say Say', a hit from the ex-Beatle's 1983 *Pipes Of Peace*. Michael put his global status to lucrative use, signing a sponsorship deal with Pepsi, who were keen to enlist the superstar in their ongoing rivalry with Coca-Cola. In January 1984, he suffered burns when his hair was accidentally set on fire while filming a Pepsi commercial. Meanwhile, he was distracted from solo work by a commitment to The Jacksons, joining his brothers for 1984's *Victory* album and tour. More extra-curricular work came his way in 1985 when he wrote (with

> **"Michael Jackson is never given enough credit for being the biggest thing in the world"**
> Eddie Murphy

> **"Do not judge a man until you've walked two moons in his moccasins. I cry very often because it hurts. I must endure for the world, for the children"**

Lionel Richie) the 'We Are The World' anthem, sung for the Ethiopian famine appeal by celebrity line-up USA For Africa.

But the year also saw an abrupt cooling of his relationship with McCartney, after Michael outbid both him and John Lennon's widow Yoko Ono for ownership of The Beatles' song catalogue. Financial shrewdness and, paradoxically, a childlike simplicity, were becoming seen as key attributes of an increasingly remote, eccentric man. Romantically unattached, growing estranged from his family, and seemingly close only to his private menagerie of animals (particularly Bubbles the chimp), Hollywood child stars and a coterie of jet-set confidantes including Elizabeth Taylor and Jacqueline Onassis, Jackson cut a puzzling figure. Public appearances, often in a surgical face-mask, found Jackson unwilling to communicate much beyond statements of universal love, and his compassion for children. Confusion about his identity was compounded by Jackson's apparent taste for cosmetic surgery.

As the media – who now referred to him as 'Wacko Jacko' – filed bizarre tales of Jackson's strange behaviour, he made a long-awaited return to music with *Bad* (1987), premiered by 'I Just Can't Stop Loving You', a duet with Siedah Garrett. While it was impossible to eclipse *Thriller*, Jackson's new material was bold and contemporary, and *Bad* became another No.1 (outselling *Thriller* in Britain). Written mostly by Jackson himself, *Bad* lacked its predecessor's quota of memorable songs, but showed a commanding grasp of styles, from the soaring, Gospel-flavoured drama of 'Man In The Mirror' to the easy Swing of 'The Way You Make Me Feel', to the edgy aggression of the title track. An ambitious world tour was marked by spectacular effects, costume changes and intricate choreography. With his global popularity at its height, he wrote his autobiography, *Moonwalk*, and ended 1988 with the movie *Moonwalker*. The book revealed more about Michael's childhood isolation than his adult life, while the movie was a gaudy fantasia of lavish set pieces, with no serious acting on Jackson's part.

For all the other-worldly, Peter Pan qualities of Jackson's public image, he remained keenly aware of street-level trends. *Dangerous* (1991) was even more sumptuous than *Bad*, but kept abreast of current Rock, R&B and Hip Hop. Without Quincy Jones, Jackson stepped up his policy of hiring guests with credibility in their own fields to update his sound and broaden its appeal: hence cameos from Guns N' Roses guitarist Slash and co-production and writing credits for Teddy Riley, the inventor of New Jack Swing and hippest figure of the moment, including the title track and another hit, 'Remember The Time', promoted by a video starring Eddie Murphy and the model Iman.

The album's first single, however, was 'Black Or White', whose anti-racist message typified Jackson's move from dancefloor escapism towards messages of social concern. The trend was underlined by 1992's hit 'Heal The World'. Yet the sincerity of Jackson's songs was increasingly called into question. Despite his denials, there was a widespread belief he had altered his features and lightened his skin to change his racial appearance, and his calls for global peace were attacked for their pomposity, especially as Jackson's representatives were persuading the world to refer to him as 'The King of Pop'.

Matters took a turn for the worse in August 1993, when it emerged Jackson was under investigation by the Los Angeles Police Department following allegations of sexual encounters with children. Rumours and media speculation grew dramatically. In November, Pepsi announced they would not be renewing their endorsement deal. Complaining of intolerable pressure and the side effects of pain-killing drugs, Jackson cancelled several shows on his new world tour. The central accusations, concerning a 13-year-old boy named Jordan Chandler, were eventually settled out of court for an estimated $20 million, and it was time for Jackson to restore what he could of his reputation. In the face of general scepticism, he announced his engagement to Lisa Marie Presley, daughter of the late Elvis and heiress to a Rock 'n' Roll fortune. The couple married in May 1994, fiercely denying the romance was a PR exercise on Jackson's part. However, they were separated within 18 months. It was also reported that he had fallen out with his brothers, his father Joe, and sister La Toya.

THE JACKSONS

WHO	Vocals **Michael** (b. 29 Aug 1958, Gary, Indiana, USA), vocals **Jackie** (b. Sigmund Jackson, 4 May 1951, Gary), vocals **Marlon** (b. 12 Mar 1957, Gary), vocals/guitar **Tito** (b. Toriano Jackson, 15 Oct 1953, Gary), vocals/bass **Jermaine** (b. 11 Dec 1954, Gary)
WHEN	1964–
WHERE	Gary, Indiana, USA
WHAT	Super Soul wiz-kids

JACKSON 5:EARL MILLER/LFI

Battling against public opinion, the self-styled King of Pop embarked upon a new world tour, promoting *HIStory* (1995), which combined a 'greatest hits' CD with one of new material. The latter included Jackson's anthem of ecological awareness, 'Earth Song' (which, in Britain, beat The Beatles' 'Free As A Bird' to Christmas No.1). Other songs struck a harsh, defensive note, as Jackson hit back at his detractors in 'They Don't Care About Us', 'Scream' and 'Stranger In Moscow'. Guest stars now included Janet Jackson, R. Kelly and The Notorious BIG. But a live appearance at the televised BRIT awards in London 1996 was marred by a stage invasion by Pulp singer Jarvis Cocker, whose satire of the messianic overtones of 'Earth Song' was applauded by British commentators. In 1996 Michael married again, this time to Debbie Rowe, a nurse, and the following year saw the birth of their first child, Prince Michael Jr. Meanwhile Jackson continued to tour, supported by a loyal fanbase, and returned to No.1 with a remix album, *Blood On The Dance Floor* (1997), whose title track was another hit. He also brought the Jackson dynasty full circle by helping launch 3T, featuring three of his nephews.

READ *Moonwalk* (1988), Michael Jackson

FAN The Michael Jackson International Fan Club, 5443 Beethoven Street, Los Angeles, CA 90066, USA

SURF www.music.sony.com/Music/ArtistInfo/Michael Jackson

Spurred to stardom by despotic dad Joe, sons Tito, Jermaine and Jackie played as The Jackson Family, adding Michael and Marlon in 1964. After gigs with The Vancouvers and Gladys Knight, talk of the Jacksons' amazing act reached Motown boss Berry Gordy. Their Temptations-esque sound and Michael's moves won over Gordy's staff and the group signed in 1969. The family relocated to California, followed by the rest of the Motown empire.

Courtesy of crack writing team The Corporation (Deke Richards, Freddie Perren, Fonce Mizell and Gordy) and US TV showcases, 1969's celestially effervescent 'I Want You Back' conquered the US chart. With the classics 'ABC', 'The Love You Save' and 'I'll Be There', they became the first group to have their first four singles top the US chart – all were also UK Top 10 hits.

The queen of Motown endorsed her protégés on *Diana Ross Presents The Jackson 5* (1970) and they starred in their own cartoon series. A production line of patchy albums ensued: 1970's *ABC* and *Christmas Album*, 1971's *Third Album, Goin' Back To Indiana* (released as 1974's *Stand!* in the UK) and *Maybe Tomorrow*, 1972's *Greatest Hits* and *Lookin' Through The Windows* and 1973's *Skywriter* and *Get It Together*.

Their creativity stifled, The Jackson 5 left Motown after *Dancing Machine* (1974) and *Moving Violation* (1975). When they signed to Epic (without Jermaine, who, married to Gordy's daughter Hazel, remained for a solo career highlighted by 1980's

Let's Get Serious), Motown took revenge with out-takes collection *Joyful Jukebox Music* (1975) and endless compilations. Recruiting youngest brother Randy (b. Steven Randall Jackson, 29 Oct 1962, Gary), they became The Jacksons (Motown retained rights to the '5' moniker), often joined by sisters Janet, La Toya and Rebbie.

After 1976's modest-selling *The Jacksons* and 1977's *Goin' Places* and hit 'Show You The Way To Go', the brothers were reborn as globe-conquering megastars. The self-penned *Destiny* (1978) launched Disco roof-raisers 'Blame It On The Boogie' and 'Shake Your Body (Down To The Ground)', then *Triumph* (1980) tore it up with the rapturous 'Can You Feel It'. With Michael spotlighted thanks to solo sensation *Off The Wall* (1979), a massive tour followed. *Live* (1981), dominated by *Off The Wall* cuts, confirmed Michael's eclipse of his siblings, who did little of note while he conquered the world with *Thriller* (1983).

A strained reunion with Michael and Jermaine yielded the patchy *Victory* (1984), but a controversy-dogged tour was the last straw. Jermaine, Jackie, Tito and Randy's attempt to rekindle the flames on *2300 Jackson Street* (1989) was eclipsed by Michael and Janet's galactic superiority. Jackie, however, watched with pride as offspring Tito, Taryll and Tariano revived Jacksonmania in the 90s as 3T. In 1998, *Billboard* reported that The Jackson 5 (yes, with Michael), plus Randy, reunited for the tentatively titled *J5*.

ReaD *Michael Jackson & The Jackson Family* (1996), Geoff Brown

SURF members.aol.com/mikeljaxn/jacksons/jfive.htm

THE JAM ◉

WHO Guitar/vocals **Paul Weller** (b. 25 May 1958, Woking, Surrey, England), bass/vocals **Bruce Foxton** (b. 1 Sep 1955, Woking), drums **Rick Buckler** (b. 6 Dec 1955, Woking)

WHEN 1976–1982

WHERE Woking, Surrey, England

WHAT Punk-based Mods

The Jam, and Paul Weller's long career, began with four former schoolmates playing Who/Small Faces-style R&B around their hometown Woking. Guitarist Steve Brookes soon departed but, as Punk became the main event in British music, the remaining trio signed to Polydor.

In May 1977, they hit the UK Top 40 with the title track of *In The City*, well received by fans and critics alike. But the follow-up, *This Is The Modern World,* disappointed and might have proved fatal had it not been for two factors. Most important was a rush of inspiration which led Weller to craft 'Down In The Tube Station At Midnight' – a racial murder tale which leaped into the UK Top 20 – and *All Mod Cons* (1978), showing a broadening of lyrical vision and musical style. Second was a revival of the 60s British Mod movement, via bands like Secret Affair and The Merton Parkas. The Jam looked the part, admitted appropriate influences and were eagerly embraced.

Although too British to be an international success, their star kept rising at home. *Setting Sons* (1979) saw Weller's writing grow more polemic, notably on 'The Eton Rifles', the band's first Top 3 hit. 'Going Underground'/'Dreams Of Children' became their first UK No.1 in March 1980, and the Beatles-steal 'Start!' followed it to No.1 in August the same year. *Sound Affects* (1980) expanded their range further, moving towards Soul on songs like 'Boy About Town'. An album-less year, 1981 was filled by 'Funeral Pyre' and 'Absolute Beginners', both peaking at UK No.4.

They returned to centre stage in February 1982, when 'A Town Called Malice'/'Precious' – the former a bass-led tirade, the latter an outright Funk opus – notched a third UK No.1. However, *The Gift* (1982) was a mostly disappointing (though chart-topping) affair – Soul became more prominent and Weller's words switched from social commentary to ill-focused idealism.

In June 1982, Weller told his bandmates he was leaving – adding resonance, for Foxton and Buckler, to 'The Bitterest Pill (I Ever Had To Swallow)', which hit the charts months later. Yet The Jam went out with a flourish, with an extensive farewell tour and final No.1, 'Beat Surrender'.

Contractual obligations forced 1983's release of the live *Dig The New Breed* and best-of *Snap!*. The greatest tribute to The Jam's impact came with a January 1983 chart in which they held 13 spots, Polydor having marked their split by reissuing their singles (they later cashed in on Weller's solo success with 1991's *Greatest Hits* and 1997's box set *Direction Reaction Creation*).

Weller promptly reappeared with The Style Council, while his ex-colleagues rapidly faded from view. Foxton's solo career made no lasting impact and he later joined Stiff Little Fingers. Buckler briefly joined Time UK before retiring from music.

ReaD *A Beat Concerto* (1996), Paolo Hewitt

SURF www.skynet.co.uk/~kefansu/the_jam.frames.html

JAMES ◉

WHO Vocals **Tim Booth** (b. 4 Feb 1960), guitar **Larry Gott** (b. 24 Jul 1957), guitar/violin **Saul Davies** (b. 28 Jun 1965), bass **Jim Glennie** (b. 10 Oct 1963), drums **Dave Baynton-Power** (b. 29 Jan 1961), keyboards **Mark Hunter** (b. 5 Nov 1968)

WHEN 1983–

WHERE Manchester, England

WHAT Fretful Pop

Signed by Manchester Indie Factory and championed by Smiths groaner Morrissey, James' early folky Pop – captured on the excellent 'Jimone' (1983), 'James II' and 'Hymn From A Village' (both 1985) – won them a Factory-infuriating contract with Sire in 1985. Stifled by under-funding, the group recorded their peculiar debut *Stutter* (1986) with Lenny Kaye (of Patti Smith Group fame), but a frustrating delay – during which they took part in hospital drug trials to support themselves – preceded 1988's more accessible *Strip Mine*.

Their Sire ordeal over, James financed 1989's live album *One Man Clapping* with help from Rough Trade, who also released their breakthrough singles 'Sit Down' and 'Come Home' – the anthemic end of the 'Baggy' revolution. Both were reissued when a remodelled James – gone was original drummer Gavan Whelan, in were Baynton-Power, Davies, Hunter and temporary trumpeter Andy Diagram – signed to Fontana for 1990's epochal *Gold Mother* (1990). 'Sit Down' became a hit, a crowd-pleaser and an albatross round their necks.

Seven (1992) approached Simple Minds-esque stadium territory in sound and sales, but 1993's Brian Eno-produced wonder, *Laid* (and ambient 1994 sequel *Wah Wah*), masked more woe: Gott (a member since 1985 when he replaced founder Paul Gilbertson) quit to go to art college and they were crippled by debts. Booth recorded 1996's *Booth And The Bad Angel* (with

Twin Peaks piano-prodder Angelo Badalamenti) and Baynton-Power masterminded 1997's life-saving *Whiplash*. Trailed by the excellent 'She's A Star', it introduced Gott's replacement Adrian Oxaal. *The Best Of James* (1998) included newies 'Run Aground' and the Spice-Girls-spiking 'Destiny Calling'.

Fan Change of Scenery, 1 Thackeray Road, Aylesford, ME20 6TH, UK

surf james.wattyco.com/

RICK JAMES

WHO b. James Johnson, 1 Feb 1948, Buffalo, New York, USA

WHAT Dandy funkateer

Escaping from the US Navy (which he'd joined aged 15), James fled to Canada. There he shared an apartment and formed The Mynah Birds with a then unknown Neil Young and Bruce Palmer (soon to found Buffalo Springfield) and Goldy McJohn (later of Steppenwolf). They were, wrote the label's chronicler Nelson George, "one of several white Rock bands Motown would sign to no avail." However, James spent much of the 70s as writer and producer at Motown, working with The Detroit Spinners and The Marvelettes among others.

After transforming into a garish George Clinton-ish funkateer for his hit breakthrough *Come And Get It* (1978), he mellowed on *Garden Of Love* (1981) before once more unleashing the Funk with *Street Songs* (1981), source of 'Super Freak' – later the basis of MC Hammer's 'U Can't Touch This'.

Thereafter, James kept the Motown flag flying with hits like 1983's 'Cold Blooded', but was eclipsed by the similarly raunchy R&Bster Prince. His protégés The Mary Jane Girls and Eddie Murphy and his own *Glow* (1985) were successful, but James became better known for his extracurricular activities, including a five-year jail sentence for assault. He returned in 1998 with *Urban Rapsody*, featuring Snoop Doggy Dogg.

surf home.dti.net/warr/rjames.html

JAMIROQUAI ⊙

WHO Vocals **Jason Kay** (b. 30 Dec 1969, Manchester, England), guitar **Simon Katz** (b. 16 May 1971, Nottingham, England), bass **Stuart Zender** (b. 18 Mar 1974, Philadelphia, Pennsylvania, USA), drums **Derrick McKenzie** (b. 27 Mar 1962, London, England), keyboards **Toby Smith** (b. 29 Oct 1970, London), didgeridoo **Wallis Buchannan** (b. 27 Nov 1965, London)

WHEN 1992–

WHERE Ealing, London, England

WHAT Funk, fur hats and fast cars

Jamiroquai lit their fire with 1992's 'When You Gonna Learn?'. Opinion was divided between fans who considered them fresh and funky, and critics who thought furry-hatted frontman Jay Kay was a Stevie Wonder wannabe whose mega-deal with Sony was hype gone mad. Neither opinion abated when *Emergency On Planet Earth* (1993) smashed in at the top of the UK chart, but acclaimed live shows and the marginally less derivative *Return Of The Space Cowboy* (1994) renewed their credibility. Kay came (almost) clean about his influences with the Japanese compilation *Jay's Selection* (1996), featuring The Isley Brothers, The O'Jays and Earth Wind & Fire.

Travelling Without Moving (1996) matched these illustrious influences; hits like 'Do You Know Where You're Coming From?' (with mainstream Drum 'n' Bassists M-Beat), 'Virtual Insanity' and 'Cosmic Girl' blended radio-friendly melodies with well-crafted and witty lyrics. The resulting multi-million sales, Red Hot Chili Pepper remixes and MTV awards banished cat-in-the-hat/flash-in-the-pan carping, and kept Jay Kay in the flashy fast car-transported lifestyle to which he had become accustomed.

Fan Jamiroquai, Chalk Farm Parade, Adelaide Road, London, NW3 2BN, UK

Surf www.xsite.net/~kara/archive/

JANE'S ADDICTION

WHO Vocals **Perry Farrell** (b. Perry Bernstein, 29 Mar 1959, Queens, New York, USA), guitar **David Navarro** (b. 6 Jun 1967, Santa Monica, California, USA), bass **Eric Avery** (b. 6 Jun 1967, Los Angeles, California), drums **Stephen Perkins** (b. 13 Sep 1967, Los Angeles)

WHEN 1986-1992

WHERE Los Angeles, California, USA

WHAT Ultra-decadent Rock

After the disintegration of his first band Psi-Com in 1985, former nightclub dancer Perry Farrell (a pun on 'peripheral') formed Jane's Addiction, named after a prostitute who introduced him to bassist Avery and guitarist Navarro. Adding drummer Perkins,

the band slogged around LA clubs with a confrontational and hedonistic live show, including transsexuals, dancers, porn films and Farrell's dreadlocked, girdled form. Their sound, captured on their live debut *Jane's Addiction* (1987) on Indie label Triple X, flitted between acoustic melancholy and throbbing Rock. The skull-crushingly Zeppish *Nothing's Shocking* (1988) saw the band join Warner Bros, creating a storm of controversy over the cover (naked siamese twins on fire).

The resultant high profile made Jane's *the* alternative band *du jour*. "Get bigger than Sonic Youth, but you couldn't get as big as Jane's Addiction," mused Courtney Love. "Those were the rules."

Ritual De Lo Habitual (1991) was their chart breakthrough (thanks partly to the irresistible hit 'Been Caught Stealing') but artistic swan song; after drug-related bust-ups on 1991's Farrell-conceived Lollapalooza tour, the group split. Farrell and Perkins formed the remarkably similar Porno For Pyros. Navarro enrolled in a rehab clinic and Red Hot Chili Peppers. However, 1997's *Kettle Whistle* and accompanying tour saw Jane's Addiction (with Chili Peppers bassist Flea replacing Avery) temporarily reform.

Read *Perry Farrell – The Saga Of A Hypester* (1996), Dave Thompson

Surf members.xoom.com/piginzen/jaballs.html

JAPAN

WHO Vocals/guitar **David Sylvian** (b. David Batt, 23 Feb 1958, London, England), bass/saxophone **Mick Karn** (b. Anthony Michaelides, 24 Jul 1958, London), drums **Steve Jansen** (b. Steve Batt, 1 Dec 1959, London), keyboards **Richard Barbieri** (b. 30 Nov 1958)

WHEN 1974–1983

WHERE London, England

WHAT Brooding New Romantics

Groomed for stardom by future Wham! manager Simon Napier-Bell, Japan won a deal with German label Ariola-Hansa in a talent contest. In 1978, *Adolescent Sex* and *Obscure Alternatives* were a clash of Glam Rock and – at the insistence of Hansa (whose biggest stars were Boney M) – Disco. Success in Japan kept the group afloat (and financed the Giorgio Moroder collaboration 'Life In Tokyo') until 1979's synth-laden *Quiet Life* spearheaded the British New Romantic movement.

Gentlemen Take Polaroids (1980) built on their new-found fashionability. Following a move to Virgin and guitarist Rob Dean's departure, Japan made the UK chart with *Tin Drum* (1981) and its hits 'Visions Of China', 'Ghosts' and 'The Art Of Parties', then a cover of Smokey Robinson's 'I Second That Emotion' (1982) and a rash of Hansa re-releases.

However, their brooding experimentalism failed to transfer to the USA and, after a 1982 farewell tour (recorded for 1983's *Oil On Canvas*), the group split for solo indulgences. Sylvian fared best with solo albums (notably 1984's *Brilliant Trees*) and hook-ups with Ryuichi Sakamoto (notably 1983's 'Forbidden Colours'), ex-Can member Holger Czukay (1988's *Plight & Premonition* and 1989's *Flux + Mutability*) and Robert Fripp (1993's *The First Day*).

An unexpected 1991 reunion as Rain Tree Crow (for an album of the same name) was wrecked by old enmities, but later years brought reconciliation (if not re-formation) with the founding of the group's Medium label.

Fan Medium Information, 74 St Lawrence Road, Upminster, Essex, RM14 2UW, UK

Surf freespace.virgin.net/paul.rymer/homepage.htm

JEAN-MICHEL JARRE

WHO b. 24 Aug 1948, Lyon, France

WHAT Laser-guided melodies

Son of film composer Maurice, Jean-Michel was distracted from Classical music by Rock 'n' Roll, forming his first band, Mystère IV, in 1964. After studying at the Paris Conservatoire, he joined experimental musicians The Music Research Group, followed by early 70s work in film, theatre, TV and ballet.

Jarre first ventured into electronic music on *Deserted Palace* (1973), but 1976's *Oxygène* – a sprawling quasi-Classical 'suite' – defined his super-selling Synth Rock. *Equinoxe* (1978) and *Magnetic Fields* (1981) scaled similar heights, while 1982's *The Concerts In China* commemorated historical performances in Shanghai and Beijing – the first in China by a Western Pop artist.

After 1983's *Music For Supermarkets* (of which only one copy was made and sold at auction) and 1984's experimental *Zoolook*, Jarre became best known for marrying actress Charlotte Rampling and for lavish, laser 'n' light concerts, twice making *The Guinness Book Of Records* for audiences of over a million in Paris (1979) and Houston (1986). *In Concert Lyon/Houston* (1987) and *Jarre Live* (1989) confirm his status as a popular performer.

Revolutions (1988) and giant 'Destination Docklands' concerts in London saw Jarre stray into New Age, continued on *Waiting For Cousteau* (1990) and 1993's *Chronologie* (backed by a more conventional stadium tour). *Tubular Bells II*-esque *Oxygène 7-13* (1996) and *Odyssey To 02* (1998) returned the winning formula.

Fan Conductor Of The Masses, 296 Newton Road, Rushden, Northamptonshire, NN10 0SY, UK

Surf www.free-spirit.demon.co.uk/urlguide/

JEFFERSON AIRPLANE/STARSHIP ✪

WHO Vocals **Grace Slick** (b. Grace Wing, 30 Oct 1939, Chicago, Illinois, USA), vocals **Marty Balin** (b. Martyn Jerel Buchwald, 30 Jan 1942, Cincinnati, Ohio, USA), guitar/vocals **Paul Kantner** (b. 12 Mar 1941, San Francisco, California, USA), guitar **Jorma Kaukonen** (b. 23 Dec 1940, Washington, DC, USA), bass **Jack Casady** (b. 13 Apr 1944, Washington, DC), drums **Spencer Dryden** (b. 7 Apr 1943, New York City, New York, USA)

WHEN 1965–

WHERE San Francisco, California, USA

WHAT Psychedelic pioneers

Inspired by The Byrds, Marty Balin assembled Jefferson Airplane to play Folk Rock at his Matrix Club in San Francisco. With Jorma Kaukonen on lead guitar, Jack Casady on bass, future Moby Grape guitarist Skip Spence on drums, and Signe Toly Anderson sharing vocals with Balin and rhythm guitarist Paul Kantner, the group were signed to RCA for the (then) princely sum of $25,000. *Jefferson Airplane Takes Off* (1966) was their lightweight debut.

When Slick left The Great Society to replace Anderson, their sound crystallized and they became a cornerstone of the hippie scene in San Francisco's Haight-Ashbury district. Unlike most of their Acid Rock contemporaries, they appealed to a mainstream audience without diluting their sound. The more confident *Surrealistic Pillow* (1967, US No.3) brought them their first US hits with Slick's 'Somebody To Love' (No.5) and 'White Rabbit' (No.8).

Artistic and narcotic over-indulgence marred *After Bathing At Baxter's* (1967) but, despite tireless partying, 1968's *Crown Of Creation* (US No.6) was a sterling return to form. After the live *Bless Its Pointed Little Head* (1969), the political tenor of the times was reflected in the rabble-rousing *Volunteers* (1969), particularly the title track and 'We Can Be Together', with its legendary battle-cry "Up against the wall, motherfuckers!".

Their rebelliousness took a knock when Balin, chastising out-of-control Hell's Angels at The Rolling Stones' Altamont disaster, was beaten unconscious by a biker. In May 1971, the alcoholic Slick crashed her Mercedes into a wall on the Golden Gate Bridge Approach whilst racing Kaukonen home from a studio.

The group's formation of its own label, Grunt, led to Airplane's crash. As its members focused on solo projects – most successful being Kantner's sci-fi flavoured *Blows Against The Empire* (1970) – the band's *Bark* (1971) and *Long John Silver* (1972) grew tedious and, after personnel changes, the Airplane split. Kaukonen and Casady made their spin-off Blues combo Hot Tuna full-time in 1972, while Slick and Kantner, joined later by Balin, launched a new line-up as Jefferson Starship in 1974. Buoyed by Balin's US No.3 'Miracles', *Red Octopus* (1975) was their only No.1 album, though million-sellers like *Spitfire* (1976) and *Earth* (1978) came close and sustained them into the 80s, when they were forced to truncate their name to Starship following Kantner's departure.

The new band bore scant resemblance to Acid-era Airplane. Fronted by Slick and new singer Mickey Thomas, Starship moved to the heart of poppy AOR, garnering hits with No.1 anthems like 'We Built This City' (1985), 'Sara' (1986) and 'Nothing's Gonna Stop Us Now' (1987), and the albums *Knee Deep In The Hoopla* (1985) and *No Protection* (1987). Their original idiosyncrasy was all but gone and, when Slick quit in 1988, it ground to a halt.

Through the 90s, various original members periodically re-formed but, as the poor showing of reunion album *Jefferson Airplane* (1989) demonstrated, barely anyone was still listening.

READ *Grace Slick: The Biography* (1980), Barbara Rowers

SURF grove.ufl.edu/~number6/Jefferson.Airplane/airplane.html

THE JESUS & MARY CHAIN

WHO Vocals/guitar **Jim Reid** (b. 29 Dec 1961, Glasgow, Scotland), guitar/vocals **William Reid** (b. 28 Oct 1958, Glasgow)

WHEN 1984–

WHERE East Kilbride, Scotland

WHAT Feedback funsters

Gleefully inept, the brothers Reid, drummer Murray Dalglish and bass player Douglas Hart's Velvet Underground-meets-Jan & Dean sound attracted little interest from Scottish gig promoters. Instead, they sent demos to labels like Creation, whose boss Alan McGee moved the group to London and became their manager.

With part-time drummer Bobby Gillespie (also vocalist with the soon-to-be-stellar Primal Scream), the group set about a legendary series of gigs/riots which ensured a cult following when their debut 'Upside Down' was released in 1984. Moving to Blanco Y Negro, the Mary Chain's first album *Psychocandy* (1985) proved their commercial breakthrough, tempering the noise with classic songwriting, as on the UK hit 'Some Candy Talking'.

'April Skies' and 'Happy When It Rains' from *Darklands* (1987) furthered their Pop fortunes, but 1989's weak *Automatic* lagged behind the UK's 'Baggy' revolution, despite a nod to danceability – a direction followed more fruitfully on 1992's *Honey's Dead*.

By 1993's 'mature' *Stoned And Dethroned* (featuring William's girlfriend, Mazzy Star singer Hope Sandoval), the Reids' sonic violence had been bettered by Nirvana and 1995's 'I Hate Rock 'N' Roll' EP slipped out to universal indifference. The grumpy old men returned to Creation for William Reid's solo debut 'Tired Of Fucking' and the Mary Chain comeback *Munki* (both 1998).

READ *The Jesus And Mary Chain* (1990), John Robertson

SURF www.zip.com.au/~toivo/

JESUS JONES ☉

WHO Vocals/guitar **Mike Edwards** (b. 22 Jun 1964, London, England), guitar **Jerry De Borg** (b. 30 Oct 1963, London), bass **Al Jaworski** (b. 31 Jan 1966, Plymouth, England), drums **Gen** (b. Simon Matthews, 23 Apr 1964, Devizes, England), keyboards **Iain Baker** (b. 29 Sep 1965, Carshalton, Surrey, England)

WHEN 1988–

WHERE London, England

WHAT Zappy, sample-laden Rock

'Info Freako' and *Liquidizer* (1989) briefly convinced the world that Jesus Jones' zappy, sample-laden Rock was the future.

Doubt (1990) made good on this promise, storming to platinum status on both sides of the Atlantic, trailed by 'Right Here, Right Now' (adopted by Bill Clinton as a campaign theme and later a Gulf War anthem), 'International Bright Young Thing' and 'Real, Real, Real'. However, by 1993's *Perverse*, the novelty had worn thin and *Already* (1997) slipped out unnoticed.

surf www.jesusjones.com

JETHRO TULL ⊙✪✪

WHO Vocals/flute/guitar/mandolin **Ian Anderson** (b. 10 Aug 1947, Edinburgh, Scotland), guitar **Martin Barre** (b. 17 Nov 1946, Birmingham, England), bass **Glenn Cornick** (b. 24 Apr 1947, Barrow-in-Furness, England), drums/glockenspiel **Clive Bunker** (b. 12 Dec 1946, Blackpool, England)

WHEN 1967–

WHERE Luton, England

WHAT Folk Prog oddities

Blackpool soulsters The John Evan Smash included three men – John Evans, Jeffrey Hammond-Hammond, Barriemore Barlow – who trickled into Jethro Tull. The first line-up, however, featured Anderson, Cornick, Bunker and guitarist Mick Abrahams. By 1968, they'd named themselves Jethro Tull, after an 18th-century agriculturalist who invented the seed drill. With Anderson's Fagin-esque persona and Abrahams' guitar heroics, they made a breakthrough appearance at August's Sunbury Jazz And Blues Festival. Their debut *This Was* (1968) rose to UK No.10.

Abrahams left to form Blodwyn Pig. Black Sabbath's Tony Iommi stepped in long enough to mime with Tull on The Rolling Stones' *Rock And Roll Circus* film before Barre – with Anderson, the only regular since – joined.Their first UK hit, 'Love Story' (1969), made No.29 and 'Sweet Dream', 'Living In The Past' (a US No.11) and 'The Witch's Promise' were all UK Top 10s. *Top Of The Pops* appearances implanted Anderson's facial hair, tartan tail-coat, one-legged flauting and air of lunacy on a generation.

Transatlantic tours, a UK No.1 for *Stand Up* and a No.2 placing behind The Beatles in *Melody Maker*'s poll made 1969 a triumph. *Benefit* (1970), *Aqualung* (1971), *Thick As A Brick* (1972, the mother of all concept albums) and the lavishly packaged *Living In The Past* (1972) reached the UK Top 10 and remain their key works. They enjoyed another US hit with 1974's 'Bungle In The Jungle'. By the 70s' end, Tull had settled into a cycle of respectable sellers (notably 1977's *Songs From The Wood* and 1978's *Heavy Horses*), successful tours and critical disparagement.

In the 80s, Tull married their Folk Rock to heavy guitars and synths, notably on 1982's *Broadsword And The Beast*. Their 1987 'comeback', *Crest Of A Knave,* followed a live lull, caused by Anderson's recurring throat problems. Tull became an institution – lauded by Iron Maiden, touring like a band half their age and mixing newies with archive releases. *Roots To Branches* (1995) was their best, and best-selling, album for years. Anderson also found fame for his parallel career as a Laird-like fish farmer.

read *Minstrels In The Gallery* (1998), Dave Rees

fan A New Day, 75 Wren Way, Farnborough, Hants, GU14 8TA, UK

surf www.glci.net/~dcote/

JOAN JETT

WHO b. 22 Sep 1960, Philadelphia, Pennsylvania, USA

WHAT Jet-powered Punkstress

From fox to feminist, Joan Jett first hit in garage gals The Runaways – a Kim Fowley-masterminded finishing school for Rock chicks whose other graduates included Metal queen Lita Ford and Bangle bassist Michael Steele. Jett rose from ridicule to Rock star by recording with Sex Pistols Steve Jones and Paul Cook, producing Punk luminaries The Germs and launching her solo career with *Bad Reputation* (1980).

With The Blackhearts, she secured a niche in history with crunching covers of The Arrows' 'I Love Rock 'N' Roll' (a US No.1 and UK No.4) and Tommy James' 'Crimson And Clover', from the million-selling *I Love Rock 'N' Roll* (1982). *Album* (1983) was another success, but the flop of the fabulous *Glorious Results Of A Misspent Youth* (1984) sent Jett's fortunes into a tailspin.

She rose again with 1988's 'I Hate Myself For Loving You' from another million-seller, *Up Your Alley*. In between, she'd turned to acting, in the 1987 movie *Light Of Day*. The latter's Springsteen-penned theme song appeared on her 1997 best-of, *Fit To Be Tied*, alongside Jett-fuelled revamps of classics by Gary Glitter, Sly Stone and Jonathan Richman, plus her own Runaways anthem 'Cherry Bomb'. Other covers fuelled *The Hit List* (1990), her tribute to inspirations including AC/DC, The Doors, ZZ Top and Hendrix.

Latterly renowned more for attitude than artistry, Jett's status as Queen Riot Grrrl was confirmed by hook-ups with L7, Babes In Toyland and Bikini Kill on *Pure And Simple* (1994). As she said in 1997, "I've always kicked boys' asses".

surf www.lcworkshop.com/users/rjk1/

JEWEL

WHO b. Jewel Kilcher, 23 May 1974, Payson, Utah, USA

WHAT Mega-selling mopestress

Of the late 90s contenders for the 'new Joni Mitchell' crown, few staked as strong a commercial claim as Jewel. In its two years on the US album chart, her *Pieces Of You* (1995) has sold 8 million, leaving even new multi-platinum sensations Fiona Apple (jazzy, glum) and Erykah Badu (soulful, determined) trailing in her wake.

Born in Utah, but raised in Alaska, Jewel had an ambiguous introduction to music: she listened to Pink Floyd's *The Wall* under the impression it was by The Pink Panther. A singer since childhood, she fused influences from Ella Fitzgerald to Madonna, then juggled dead-end jobs with one-off gigs. By the early 90s, she was living in her van, surviving on peanut butter and carrot sticks, with only a guitar for a friend. A live following snared Atlantic, who doubtless had one eye on mega-sellers like Tori Amos and Sarah McLachlan. With Neil Young collaborator Ben Keith at the helm, she recorded her debut and returned to gigs.

Little of this would have been noteworthy had 'Who Will Save Your Soul' and 'You Were Meant For Me' not belatedly adhered to the US charts for months on end and propelled *Pieces* from the album chart's murky depths into the Top 5.

Suddenly, Jewel was inescapable: notching up soundtrack cameos (including 1997's *Batman & Robin*), being erroneously linked to Madonna's ex, Sean Penn, winning MTV awards (her photogenic blonde good looks were no impediment to success), playing Dorothy in a starry 1997 New York production of *The Wizard Of Oz* (also featuring Jackson Browne, Roger Daltrey and Ry Cooder) and providing the highlight ('You Make Loving Fun') of *Legacy: A Tribute To Fleetwood Mac's Rumours* (1998).

Though her melancholy ballads are a world away from Alanis Morissette, Jewel has secured a similar niche in the Rap 'n' Rock-dominated 90s, and never needs to sell another record to prove her worth.

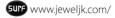 www.jeweljk.com/

BILLY JOEL ✪✪✪✪

WHO b. William Martin Joel, 9 May 1949, Hicksville, Long Island, USA

WHAT Perilous piano man

Jazzed by James Brown, buzzed by The Beatles, Billy Joel was turned on to music in the early 60s. His first bands The Echos, The Lost Souls and The Hassles were uncelebrated bubblegum – hence a last-ditch, Hendrix-inspired leap to Hard Rock.

Tragically, the piano-and-drums power duo Attila flopped even harder with their self-titled 1970 album and – after an attempt at suicide-by-polish ("All I ended up doing was farting furniture polish. I polished all my mother's chairs just sitting there") and a spell in a psychiatric hospital – Joel said 'No!' to stardom and 'Yo!' to songwriting.

Sadly, *Cold Spring Harbor* (1972), intended to showcase this talent, somewhat diminished it with production that made Joel sound "like a chipmunk". Piling mishap on misfortune, he signed away all publishing rights, copyrights and royalties to his producer/manager Artie Ripp.

Ubiquitous talent-spotter Clive Davis took him to Columbia for *Piano Man* (1973), whose title track became Joel's signature tune. Though in tune with worldwide Elton John mania, the album sold only modestly, and when *Streetlife Serenade* (1974) and *Turnstiles* (1976) bombed, Columbia got edgy.

Concern turned to elation when *The Stranger* (1977) became their biggest pre-*Thriller* seller – thanks mainly to 'Just The Way You Are', a soppy ballad that belied Joel's cynicism and self-proclaimed musical range. *52nd Street* (1978) and *Glass Houses* (1980) cemented critical hatred, which seemed to affect the artist more than multi-platinum megastardom and his first US No.1s.

While Columbia cleaned up with the live album *Songs In The Attic* (1981), the credentials of Joel's guardian angel were again called into question when, in 1982, he suffered a serious motorcycle accident, his wife decamped with half his assets and *The Nylon Curtain* (1982) sold a measly 2 million.

Nothing cheers up morose stars quicker than a supermodel, and Joel not only snared Christie Brinkley, but showcased her in the video for 'Uptown Girl' – just one of the jolly gems on 1983's very big-selling *An Innocent Man*. In 1985, the couple married and Columbia celebrated with two volumes of *Greatest Hits*.

However, as we have seen, Billy's world is a perilous place and *The Bridge* (1986) impressed neither fans, critics nor even the artist himself. The less enlightened of Joel's US fans were further disenchanted by Joel's pioneering Russian concerts in Leningrad and Moscow, commemorated on *Kohuept* (1987). Consorting with Communists and selling badly proved just the challenge Joel required and he was soon back on top with *Storm Front* (1989) and *River Of Dreams* (1993), propelled to hugeness by the hits 'We Didn't Start The Fire' and 'River Of Dreams'.

However, Joel reclaimed his crown as Rock's unluckiest star when he was obliged to mount massive tours to recoup millions lost in a lawsuit against his former manager, and Brinkley bid *adios* in 1994. The ensuing silence was broken only by a tour with Elton John (proving that you can never have enough introspective pianists on one bill) and the unremarked *Greatest Hits Volume III* (1997). He mounted another co-headliner with Elton in 1998.

Read *Billy Joel: An Illustrated Biography* (1985), Debbie Geller & Tom Hibbert

Fan Streetlife Serenade, c/o Wells Ink, PO Box 2075, Garden City, NY 11531, USA

Surf www.billyjoel.com/

ELTON JOHN
☉☉☉☉☉☉☉✪✪✪✪✪✪✪

WHO b. Reginald Kenneth Dwight, 25 Mar 1947, Pinner, Middlesex, England

WHAT Unsinkable showman, tunesmith and Pop elder statesman

On 6 September 1997, when Elton John sang a song at the funeral of a friend, he carved out a position in public regard, both British and international, unprecedented in Pop history. The carefully rewritten 'Candle In The Wind', performed at Westminster Abbey in memory of Diana, Princess of Wales, was heard by hundreds of millions around the world.

A Pop song should have been out of its depth in this setting but it was exactly right, as proved in the following months when

the single, styled 'Candle In The Wind 1997', with all profits and royalties dedicated to Diana's favourite causes, sold like no other record has ever done. It became the UK's best-selling single of all time at 5.4 million, overtaking Band Aid's 'Do They Know It's Christmas' (1984). Worldwide it was the same story, taking just 37 days to beat even Bing Crosby's 'White Christmas' (reissued annually since 1942) and going on to sell more than 33 million.

Elton John had always been the misfit who fitted. He was fat, plain, bald, wore glasses, was gay and played the piano. His real name was Reg. As a Pop star, he seemed the ultimate non-starter. The son of an RAF flight lieutenant and amateur trumpeter living on the suburban outskirts of London, his talent for piano was spotted early. At 11, he won a part-time scholarship to London's Royal Academy of Music and proved a fairly able student. Nonetheless, the first record he bought was Jackie Wilson's 'Reet Petite' and his early influences were pianists like Winifred Atwell. By 1961 he had a residency playing pub sing-alongs for £1 a night and had joined his first, local band, Bluesology. The following year, his parents separated and his father Stanley's fierce discipline was replaced by the more relaxed regime of his mother, Sheila, and her new husband. In 1963, Reg Dwight declared his intentions, dropped out of school just before his O-level exams and found an office 'gofer' job at publishing company Mills Music.

Over the next five years – ambitious, yet haunted by his sometimes 200-pound bulk and inevitable nicknames, including 'Fat Reg' and 'Little Bunter' – he served a traditionally ramshackle and arduous apprenticeship in the music business. Bluesology meandered along as pick-up band to visiting Americans like Major Lance and Patti LaBelle. Then British R&B pioneer Long John Baldry took them on long term. Impatient, in 1967 Reg Dwight auditioned for the Liberty label. He failed, but A&R man Ray Williams handed him a sheaf of lyrics by Bernie Taupin (b. 22 May 1950, Sleaford, Lincolnshire, England) to see what he could make of them. Dwight found he could write to

someone else's lyrics at astonishing speed – 15–20 minutes per song, tops. At first, the collaboration proceeded by post. Then Taupin moved in with Dwight at his mother's house in Pinner, Middlesex, England.

At this point, Reg Dwight became Elton John, a change of identity later confirmed by deed poll. He borrowed the name from Bluesology saxophonist Elton Dean (later of Soft Machine) and John Baldry and left the band – who, to his chagrin, were reluctant to let him sing. Signing on, with Taupin, as staff writers at Dick James Music (DJM), a record company and publisher of The Beatles' Northern Songs catalogue, more false starts preyed on the despair lurking beneath the entertainer's ebullience.

In 1968, Elton's first solo single release, 'I've Been Loving You Too Long', on Philips, flopped. So did 'Lady Samantha' the following January. Then, ignominiously, John/Taupin's 'I Can't Go On Living Without You' came last in the Eurovision Song Contest British heat won by 'Boom Bang A Bang' and Elton's debut album, *Empty Sky* (1969), bombed too. He got by on sessions and budget cover-version albums (exhumed in 1994 by an opportunist label as *Elton John: Chartbusters – The Session Years*).

Eventually, in August 1970, his 'Border Song', a UK no-no, reached US No.92. His first American label, Uni, arranged a showcase at the renowned Los Angeles Troubadour and puffed it up to the media as one of *the* Rock events of the year. Elton played the concert of his life to critics who expected "the new English sensation" – and got it. *Rolling Stone* later designated this show one of their "20 Concerts That Changed Rock 'N' Roll History". That October *Elton John* (1970) slowly climbed to US No.4 and UK No.11. Introducing durable John associates Dee Murray (bass) and Nigel Olsson (drums), with string arranger Paul Buckmaster and producer Gus Dudgeon, it delivered the solemn ballads and cheerful rocking which were to characterize his career. The Top 10 hit 'Your Song' confirmed the breakthrough.

The John/Taupin team began an irresistible rampage, in part propelled by a DJM contract demanding two albums a year.

After 1970's *Tumbleweed Connection,* they released *three* in 1971: the *Friends* movie soundtrack, the live *17-11-70* and, with the addition of guitarist Davey Johnstone, the US No.8 *Madman Across The Water*. Elton also met John Reid, then Motown label manager in the UK, and acquired a manager for 28 years.

In 1972, *Honky Chateau* became his first US No.1 (and UK No.2). Touring constantly, his performances, costumes, even his trademark glasses attained legendary levels of extravagance. Album after album rang the bell: *Don't Shoot Me I'm Only The Piano Player* (his first on MCA in America), *Goodbye Yellow Brick Road* (both 1973), *Caribou* and *Elton John's Greatest Hits* (1974) were all UK and US No.1s.

> " **What makes Rock 'n' Roll great** is that somebody like **me** can actually be **a star** "

The John/Taupin musical autobiography *Captain Fantastic And The Brown Dirt Cowboy* (1975) became the first album to enter the US chart at No.1. *Rock Of The Westies* did the same that November. A deluge of smashes carried the albums along: 'Rocket Man', 'Crocodile Rock', 'Daniel', 'Saturday Night's Alright For Fighting', 'Bennie And The Jets' (a US No.1 whose B-side was 'Candle In The Wind', which reached No.11 in the UK). 'Don't Go Breaking My Heart', with Kiki Dee, was his first UK No.1 single.

Meanwhile, he launched his own label, Rocket, and invested heavily in Watford Football Club, the lowly local team he had supported as a boy. Less constructively, he began to immerse himself in alcohol, cocaine and eating disorders. Suddenly, the DJM contract-filling live *Here And There* (1976) hit an unexpected nadir – "I don't regret anything in my professional life except *Here And There*," was Elton's verdict.

He made one more substantial album that year, *Blue Moves* (UK/US No.3), but was entering a period of transition. He fired Murray and Olsson and admitted to *Rolling Stone* that he was "bisexual". For this he was punished by loss of radio play in America and by chanting fans of Watford's opponents in the UK.

In 1977, he announced his retirement from live shows and the flop 'Ego' proved his last Taupin collaboration for several years. In 1978, he promoted *A Single Man* by emerging from 'retirement' to play live with only percussionist Ray Cooper to back him and his virtually instrumental and heartfelt 'Song For Guy' made UK No.4. Despite pioneering tours in Israel and Russia, quality control waned. The John/Taupin reunion *Too Low For Zero* (1983), with its hits 'I Guess That's Why They Call It The Blues' and 'I'm Still Standing', was his only memorable recording for the next ten years, despite re-forming his faithful Olsson/Murray/Johnstone band.

Elton began another durable alliance when he sang 'Don't Let The Sun Go Down On Me' with George Michael at Live Aid (a 1991 version hit UK No.1) and shared a Grammy for his part in AIDS fundraiser 'That's What Friends Are For' (1985) with Dionne Warwick, Gladys Knight and Stevie Wonder. But his commercial and artistic decline continued until *Leather Jackets* (1986) expired at UK No.24 and US No. 91. Hasbeenhood loomed.

He was also assailed by a series of severe personal crises, played out in public. On Valentine's Day 1984, he married studio technician Renate Blauel in Australia although, as he later

accepted, it was fundamentally an attempt to avoid facing his depression and "huge drug addiction".

In 1986, he and Taupin sued his old mentor Dick James for mishandling their early career. They recouped an estimated £5 million, but it cost them a friend. Then, on 25 February 1987, UK tabloid *The Sun*'s front-page headline screamed "Elton In Vice Boy Scandal". Remarkably, this seemed to mark the start of his 'recovery' in personal and career terms. He fought *The Sun* all year, answering every new allegation with a writ.

Finally, its major sources exposed, *The Sun* made an abject apology: a front-page "Sorry Elton" headline and, at the time, a record UK £1-million settlement. Back with MCA in America after a spell on Geffen, his *Live In Australia* (1989) rose steadily to US No.24. The significantly titled *Reg Strikes Back* (1988) went to UK No.18 and US No.16. His long Indian summer was underway.

Another bout of deck-clearing ensued. He auctioned truckloads of possessions and he and Renate announced an "amicable" divorce. Changes in his life were reflected by *Sleeping With The Past* (1989), on which he worked more closely with Taupin than for many years. It took a while to make an impact.

But when the reissued single 'Sacrifice' took off in the summer of 1990 to become his first ever solo UK No.1, the album topped the chart as well. On BBC TV's *The Terry Wogan Show*, he announced that his royalties from 'Sacrifice' and all future British singles would go to AIDS charities (he added US singles royalties in 1992). Then he committed himself to serious treatment for his addictions and eating disorders during a stay at the Parkside Lutheran Hospital, Chicago. It worked. At last, he dropped the vodka martinis, the cocaine, a battalion of unreliable 'friends' and took to a wholesome diet to replace grotesque repasts combining curry, cockles, ice cream and bacon sandwiches.

He consolidated his support for AIDS organizations via the Elton John AIDS Foundation (more than $13 million distributed internationally since December 1992), and sustained a long-term relationship with Canadian film-maker David Furnish, with whom he later attended Diana's funeral. He seemed to have found new stability, respect and self-respect.

Musically, this was reflected by the solid success of *The Very Best Of Elton John* (1990, UK No.1, not released in America), *The One* (1992), *Duets* (1993), *Made In England* (1995) and *The Big Picture* (1997). Affirmation of his revered status came from peer acknowledgments, including the 1991 tribute album *Two Rooms – Celebrating The Songs Of Elton John And Bernie Taupin* (whose highlights included The Who re-forming to storm through 'Saturday Night's Alright For Fighting' and Kate Bush's Reggae-fied 'Rocket Man'), double-headed tours with Billy Joel, an Oscar awarded for 'Can You Feel The Love Tonight', the song he wrote with Tim Rice for Disney's *The Lion King* (1994) and – best of all – a cameo in the Spice Girls' *Spiceworld* (1997). This avalanche of activity made his choice of song on *Legacy: A Tribute To Fleetwood Mac's Rumours* (1998) very appropriate: 'Don't Stop'.

Come September 1997, he had completed his accidental preparation to be the man who, in expressing his personal grief for Diana, could voice the sorrow of millions. As a result, 'Fat Reg' of Pinner, aged 50, became Sir Elton John when knighted by the Queen in 1998.

read *The Many Lives Of Elton John* (1993), Susan Crimp & Patricia Burstein

fan Elton Enquiries, 32 Galena Road, London W6 OLT, UK

surf www.public.usit.net/artboy/ejfan.html

GRACE JONES

WHO b. 19 May 1952, Kingston, Jamaica

WHAT Scary Bond bombshell

Sinister supermodel Jones swapped catwalks for clubs, winning gay disciples with an erotic stage act and an androgynous image masterminded by her boyfriend and Svengali manager Jean Paul Goude. 'I Need A Man' and 'La Vie En Rose' (both 1977) were Disco hits, while The Pretenders cover 'Private Life' took her into the mainstream in 1980. An aggressive reputation – and roles in the James Bond blockbuster *A View To A Kill* (1985) and *Vamp* (1986) – overshadowed her innovative blend of Funk (1981's 'Pull Up To The Bumper'), Reggae (1983's 'My Jamaican Guy') and epic weirdness (1985's 'Slave To The Rhythm').

Warm Leatherette (1980), *Nightclubbing* (1981), *Living My Life* (1982) and *Slave To The Rhythm* (1985) boasted the talents of Trevor Horn and Sly & Robbie, and were filleted for *Island Life* (1986). However, with *Inside Story* (1986), *Bulletproof Heart* (1989) and *Sex Drive* (1993), Jones' appeal became more selective.

HOWARD JONES ⊙

WHO b. 23 Sep 1955, Southampton, England

WHAT Sensitive Synth Pop

After adolescence in Canada, Howard Jones returned to England to study music. Work with Jazz and Funk groups proved fruitless, but switching to Synth Pop secured his fortunes. The UK No.1 *Human's Lib* (1984) evoked an awkward collision of Gary Numan and John Denver, with synth sheen disguising mature lyrics.

Aided by mime artist Jed Hoile, he attracted loyal teens with 1983's hits 'New Song' and 'What Is Love?'. *Dream Into Action* (1985) was similarly successful, notably the hit 'Things Can Only Get Better' and melancholic piano ballad 'No One Is To Blame'.

However, his evolution from Synth Pop to limp Pop proved less popular: *One To One* (1986), *Cross That Line* (1989) and *In The Running* (1992) all undersold. Undeterred, he continued with *Working In The Backroom* (1993), *Live Acoustic America* (1995) and *Angels And Lovers* (1997) – mostly on his own Dtox label.

surf www.howardjones.com/HoJo/home.html

QUINCY JONES

WHO b. 14 Mar 1933, Chicago, Illinois, USA

WHAT Quintessential Soul giant

Quincy Jones paid dues through stints with Lionel Hampton and Ray Charles, rubbed shoulders with Miles Davis, Thelonius Monk and Charlie Parker on New York's Jazz scene, then relocated to Paris. He studied Classical composition, worked as an acclaimed composer/arranger and formed a financially disastrous Jazz orchestra – prompting a return to the USA in 1961.

In New York, he became vice president of Mercury Records (producing, arranging and playing for Lesley Gore, Count Basie and Frank Sinatra), while releasing overlooked solo albums such as 1964's *Golden Boy*. Movie scores proved more rewarding, with *The Pawn Broker* (1965) initiating a train of classics which included *Bob And Carol And Ted And Alice* (1969), Oscar-winner *In The Heat Of The Night* (1967) and *The Italian Job* (1969).

Jones' solo career picked up with *Walking In Space* (1969) and *Smackwater Jack* (1971) and finally hit the US Top 10 with 1974's *Body Heat*. As a producer, he scored with The Brothers Johnson, Rufus, Michael Jackson, George Benson, Donna Summer (notably 1982's 'State Of Independence') and James Ingram, while his solo smash *The Dude* scooped a Grammy and included the hit 'Ai No Corrida'. In 1985, Jones co-produced the movie *The Color Purple* and masterminded USA For Africa's all-star 'We Are The World'.

Back On The Block (1989) boasted cameos by Ray Charles, Barry White, Chaka Khan, Sarah Vaughan, Ice-T, Melle Mel and Big Daddy Kane and was followed by the 1990 biopic *Listen Up: The Lives Of Quincy Jones*. He also headed his own label Qwest (US home of New Order, Tevin Campbell and Keith Washington) and branched out into publishing and television with *Vibe* magazine and the Will Smith sitcom *The Fresh Prince Of Bel Air*. Q's *Jook Joint* (1995) was a *Back On The Block* sequel in all but name.

read *Listen Up: The Lives Of Quincy Jones* (1990), Courtney Ross

surf www.wbr.com/quincyjones/

RICKIE LEE JONES

WHO b. 8 Nov 1954, Chicago, Illinois, USA

WHAT Self-destructive Soft Rock songstress

To any Joni Mitchell fans despairing of their queen's Jazz period, Rickie Lee Jones' cool 1979 hit 'Chuck E's In Love' was a tonic. But the individual artistry of *Rickie Lee Jones* (1979) and *Pirates* (1981) – influenced by Tom Waits, with whom she became romantically entwined –became self-destructive indulgence. "I didn't turn out to be as sweet as I first appeared to be," she declared later. A collection of Jazz revamps, *Girl At Her Volcano* (1983), and *The Magazine* (1984) preceded a five-year hiatus, during which Edie 'What I Am' Brickell appropriated her bohemian style wholesale.

Jones, now sober, returned with *Flying Cowboys* (1989), a straightforward success helmed by Steely Dan-man Walter Becker, then appalled believers with the jazzy *Pop Pop* (1991).

Traffic From Paradise (1993) and *Naked Songs* (1995) provoked few celebrations, and Jones became best known in the 90s as the voice on The Orb's 'Little Fluffy Clouds' (1990). Appropriately, *Ghostyhead* (1997) saw her embrace Trip Hop – a musical if not commercial return to form.

surf www.repriserec.com/RickieLeeJones/

TOM JONES

WHO b. Thomas Jones Woodward, 7 Jun 1940, Pontypridd, Wales

WHAT Earthquake-inducing raunch

From Rock's Mount Olympus, Sex God Tom Jones swaggered down into the Welsh valleys to dispense 'The Voice'. He moved among mortals courtesy of a 1964 deal with Decca. The titanic 'It's Not Unusual' trampled to the top in Britain; in the USA, where DJs thought He was both American and black, it hit No.10. In 1965, *Along Came Jones*, singles 'What's New Pussycat' and 'With These Hands' and Bond movie theme 'Thunderball' paved the way in 1967 for Jones' second UK No.1 (and Wales' unofficial national anthem), 'Green Green Grass Of Home'.

Having set a course for Country-flavoured Greatness, He had no need for 'Release Me' (the song that established Engelbert Humperdinck) and instead forged ahead with 1967's 'Detroit City' and 'Funny Familiar Forgotten Feelings'. In 1968, Jones narrowly missed the UK top spot with the spectacular 'Delilah', although the album of the same name did make No.1.

However, Jones had bigger fish to fry. His TV series, *This Is Tom Jones*, ran from 1969 to 1974 and confirmed Him as all-round entertainer *par excellence*. These shows earned an entry in *The Guinness Book Of Records* – 'largest British TV contract' – with a transatlantic deal worth £9 million. Another record toppled when He set a new figure for attendance at New York's Madison Square Garden in 1970. Legendarily love-drenched performances were showcased on albums including *Live At The Talk Of The Town* (1967), *Tom Jones Live In Las Vegas* (1969) and *Live At Caesar's Palace* (1971).

He outgrew the puny Pop charts in the 70s, preferring to bask in Californian sunshine, but kept His hit hand in with the smashes 'She's A Lady', 'Till' (both 1971), 'The Young New Mexican Puppeteer' (1972) and UK No.1 *20 Greatest Hits* (1975).

Returning to glory in the 80s, He triumphed with 1987's 'A Boy From Nowhere' (from the doomed musical *Matador*) and an unlikely union with Art Of Noise on a hit revamp of Prince's 'Kiss' (1988). He confirmed his grasp on the mainstream with 1994's dance-inflected *The Lead And How To Swing It*, an alien-defying cameo in 1997 movie *Mars Attacks!* and a show-stopping duet with Robbie Williams at 1998's BRIT awards extravaganza.

read *Tom Jones: The Boy From Nowhere* (1988), Colin MacFarlane

fan Tom Jones 'Tom Terrific' Fan Club, c/o Margaret Mariotti, 411 Coram Avenue, Shelton, CT 06484, USA

surf members.aol.com/tjttfc/club1/htm

"I love being a star... more than life itself."

JANIS JOPLIN ✪

WHO b. 19 Jan 1943, Port Arthur, Texas, USA, d. 4 Oct 1970, Hollywood, California, USA

WHAT Full-throttle psychedelic Blues

Breaking the mould for white 60s female singers, Janis Joplin exemplified Rock's hard-livin', hard-lovin' lifestyle, demanding the same recreational opportunities afforded to male stars. Her beaux included Country Joe McDonald, Kris Kristofferson and Leonard Cohen – the latter of whom celebrated their liaison in 'Chelsea Hotel No 2'. But her good-time demeanour disguised the vulnerability which was the source of her vocal talent.

Joplin was captivated by the Blues of Leadbelly, Odetta and Bessie Smith (for whose grave she later purchased a headstone), and left home at 17 to sing in bars in Houston and Austin. In 1963, she moved to San Francisco with her friend Chet Helms, whose Family Dog organization arranged the earliest hippie concerts. Joplin's stay was less fruitful, and she returned to Texas. Helms, however, brought her back to Frisco in 1965 to sing with Family Dog's house band, Big Brother & The Holding Company.

Joplin's raw singing and the band's hit-and-miss Psychedelia were never a perfect fit, but after spending 1966 rehearsing and gigging, they made a splash at 1967's Monterey festival. Bob Dylan's manager, Albert Grossman, signed them to Columbia. *Big Brother & The Holding Company* (1967), a weak album made two years earlier for a small Chicago label, was more hindrance than help, and it was not until *Cheap Thrills* (1968), a live album clad in a classic Robert Crumb cartoon sleeve, that Joplin's potential was realized. Its title shortened, at Columbia's insistence, from *Dope,*

Sex & Cheap Thrills, the album spawned a hit, 'Piece Of My Heart' (1968), but the gulf in ability between Joplin and the band rang out on tracks like 'Ball And Chain' and 'Summertime'.

Its eight-week tenure atop the chart was barely over before Joplin ditched the group. With her own, Soul-influenced outfit Kozmic Blues Band, she made *I Got Dem Ol' Kozmic Blues Again Mama!* (1969) – then disbanded this group too, and formed the smaller, tighter Full Tilt Boogie Band.

Titled after her nickname, and boasting her first No.1 (a take on Kris Kristofferson's 'Me And Bobby McGee') and the a capella 'Mercedes Benz' (used in a car ad 25 years later), *Pearl* (1971) was her masterpiece, topping the chart for nine weeks. Joplin was not around to enjoy her success, having died from a heroin overdose at the Landmark Hotel, Hollywood, before recording could be completed. *Janis Joplin In Concert* (1972) and several compilations have been posthumously released, and in 1979 Bette Midler starred in *The Rose*, a film loosely based on her life.

READ *Buried Alive* (1973), Myra Friedman

SURF www.dartmouth.edu/~modred/janis.html

JOURNEY ✪

WHO Vocals **Steve Perry** (b. 22 Jan 1949, Hanford, California, USA), guitar **Neal Schon** (b. 27 Feb 1954, Midwest City, Oklahoma, USA), bass **Ross Valory** (b. 2 Feb 1949, San Francisco, California), drums **Steve Smith** (b. 21 Aug 1954, Boston, Massachusetts, USA), keyboards **Jonathan Cain** (b. 26 Feb 1950, Chicago, Illinois, USA)

WHEN 1973–

WHERE San Francisco, California, USA

WHAT La crème de la crème of AOR

Few chiming cash registers celebrated ex-Santana members Neal Schon and Gregg Rolie's bid for glory. With Ross Valory and drummer Aynsley Dunbar, *Journey* (1975), *Look Into The Future* (1976) and *Next* (1977) were high on virtuosity, low on sales.

Ordered by CBS to find a frontman, they drafted Steve Perry for the mega-platinum *Infinity* (1978), *Evolution* (1979), *Departure* (1980) and *Captured* (1981). Meanwhile, it was farewell Dunbar and Rolie, hail Smith and Cain. The latter co-wrote *Escape* (1981), which won the hearts of 9 million Americans, including Mariah Carey, who covered 'Open Arms' in 1995. *Frontiers* (1983) kept coffers overflowing, but ego battles prompted solo stabs – Perry's *Street Talk* (1984) selling best. *Raised On Radio* (1986) was their last gasp and *Greatest Hits* (1988) their multi-platinum memorial. Schon and Cain united with John 'Missing You' Waite in the successful but short-lived Bad English ("Grammar is the least of their problems," carped *Musician* magazine).

Journey's retrospective *Time³* (1992) plugged the gap until they reunited for *Trial By Fire* (1996), whose success confirmed AOR's enduring appeal to even post-Grunge America.

READ *Journey* (1984), Robyn Flans

FAN Faithful Ones News, c/o Laura Pike, 214 Dean Road, Depew, NY 14043, USA

SURF journey.simplenet.com/

JOY DIVISION

WHO Vocals/guitar **Ian Curtis** (b. 15 Jul 1956, Macclesfield, Cheshire, England, d. 18 May 1980), guitar/keyboards **Bernard Dicken** (b. Bernard Sumner, 4 Jan 1956, Salford, Manchester, England), bass **Peter Hook** (b. 13 Feb 1956, Manchester), drums **Stephen Morris** (b. 28 Oct 1957, Macclesfield)

WHEN 1977–1980

WHERE Manchester, England

WHAT Sounds of bleakness

Inspired by a Sex Pistols gig at Manchester's Lesser Free Trade Hall in July 1976, Deep Purple fan Peter Hook, scooter boy Bernard Dicken and their friend Terry Mason decided to form a band. Fellow Pistols convert Ian Curtis had the same idea; an obsessive fan of David Bowie, Lou Reed and The Stooges, he worked as a civil servant, but was half-heartedly writing and rehearsing with a guitarist, Iain Gray. By August, he had joined Dicken, Hook and Mason's band, Stiff Kittens, soon renamed Warsaw, an adaptation of 'Warszawa' from Bowie's *Low* (1977).

Warsaw made a first, faltering public appearance alongside local Punk stars Buzzcocks, Penetration, John Cooper Clarke and John The Postman on 29 May 1977, at Manchester's Electric Circus. Mason had by now swapped drums for management. His replacement Tony Tabac lasted only one gig, while ex-Panik drummer Steve Brotherdale was cruelly left by the roadside after getting out of the band's van to investigate a puncture. A permanent drummer arrived in the shape of Stephen Morris, a Can aficionado who answered a notice in a Macclesfield music store. The line-up now stabilized, Warsaw slogged around Manchester, making little impact with their inept rumblings. A demo revealed Warsaw to be not very Punk – or indeed very good.

In early 1978, they were forced to find a new name to avoid confusion with the London band Warsaw Pakt. Joy Division – referring to female prisoners used as prostitutes in Nazi concentration camps and taken from the pulp novel *House Of Dolls* – immediately caused trouble. Their first gig on the last night of The Electric Circus (2 October 1977) was recorded for a commemorative mini-album, *Short Circuit* (1978), which included Curtis' on-stage announcement, "You all forgot about Rudolf Hess" – a shock tactic that backfired, triggering speculation about the band's political sympathies.

The 'Nazi' reputation was not helped by the group's almost military image and first, self-financed EP 'An Ideal For Living', which featured a Hitler Youth drummer and a Nazi stormtrooper on the cover. However, Curtis' lyrics were deeper than the standard Punk flirtation with fascism. Not only were Joy Division concerned with something far darker than their contemporaries, but – with Hook's rumbling basslines, Morris' mechanical rhythms and Dicken's blocks of guitar noise – they were now musically unlike anyone else.

Curtis' pestering of Derek Branwood, an A&R man at RCA, led to recordings in May 1978. However, Branwood's intention of signing the band faltered and relations with the group became acrimonious. New manager Rob Gretton – a DJ at Manchester club Rafters – negotiated them out of the RCA contract, but while the band settled their debts with the company, the already outdated 'An Ideal For Living' was belatedly released in June.

Stuck on the Punk venue circuit, the band began playing at a new Manchester club, The Factory, organized by local TV presenter Tony Wilson and ex-actor Alan Erasmus. Wilson – a champion of Manchester's Punk scene and a friend of Gretton – gave Joy Division their first television exposure: a slot on local news show *Granada Reports*.

In October, they contributed 'Digital' and 'Glass' to the 'A Factory Sample' EP, the first release on Wilson and Erasmus' new label, Factory Records, and the band's first collaboration with producer Martin 'Zero' Hannett, ex-member of Sad Cafe and well-known face around Manchester. Hannett stripped down Joy Division's already skeletal sound, dowsing Morris' pulsing drums and Dicken's guitar in icy reverb, allowing Hook's

"We loved Joy Division. They were an original of the species that became Goth. Never mind..."
Bono

unconventional ringing basslines to lead. The result was something far bleaker than Punk.

Returning from Joy Division's first London gig in December 1978, Curtis suffered a seizure, later diagnosed as epilepsy. He was prescribed barbiturates, which deepened his already introspective character. Soon the seizures were happening at gigs – Curtis would go into his usual trance-like state on stage and fail to return at the end of the song. The band stopped using strobe lighting – making their gigs even more intense – but even Morris' drumming provoked attacks.

The group's busy schedule didn't help: in January 1979, they returned to London to record four songs for BBC DJ John Peel's show and, in April, Tony Wilson financed work on an album. The recordings eventually cost over twice Wilson's budget as Hannett experimented endlessly with expensive effects, but the result – *Unknown Pleasures* (1979) – was a landmark. In an almost featureless black sleeve by Factory designer Peter Saville, *Unknown Pleasures* was colder and deeper than anything they had created before. Sometimes frightening, other times muted, often *silent*, Hannett's production bathed the instruments in ambient crashes and echoes, while Curtis' voice was now a cold, intense baritone. "I always sort of saw Ian Curtis as a kind of Roy Orbison of our generation," said Bono. "I know that sounds pretty vomitty, but even through all that gothic thing, I've always liked people to take themselves painfully seriously."

Absent from the album was Joy Division's first Factory single, the aggressive 'Transmission', released after a legendary show at the Futurama Science Fiction Music Festival in Leeds in September 1979. With *Unknown Pleasures* and 'Transmission', Joy Division achieved the recognition they had strived for and set out on a tour of Britain, supporting Buzzcocks.

Curtis, however, was crumbling: his epilepsy and the drugs he used to treat it exacerbated his depression and the slow disintegration of his marriage was manifested in his lyrics. Some

of these were previewed on 'Earcom 2', a sample EP for the Indie label Fast Records, and their second John Peel session, both recorded at the end of 1979.

Among the new material was the poignant 'Love Will Tear Us Apart', a prophetic story of a doomed relationship. Ashamed of his infidelity, Curtis attempted suicide in January 1980, slashing himself with a knife at his home in Manchester. His wife found him unconscious, but he recovered enough to attend rehearsals the next day as if nothing had happened. Recording in London in March 1980, his condition worsened still. In April he suffered another seizure on stage at London's Rainbow Theatre and, soon after, took an overdose. He survived, but was referred to a psychiatrist and found it increasingly difficult to continue, suffering from black-outs and more seizures on stage, often having to leave after a few songs. After several near riots at cancelled appearances, the band played what was to be their final gig at High Hall, Birmingham, England, on 2 May 1980.

Curtis was now living with his parents, his wife having filed for divorce. On 17 May, two days before the group's first US tour, he went to the house he once shared with her to watch a film – *Stroszek*, about an artist who commits suicide – on TV and hanged himself early the next morning. Deborah Curtis discovered his body hanging in the kitchen.

"The thing we learned with age," said Peter Hook, "is that sometimes people do need looking after, but unfortunately we were all too young at the time to be like that, so we lost him."

The first posthumous releases came a few weeks later. First was a free three-track single of unreleased tracks. Then, in June, came 'Love Will Tear Us Apart' and the second album, *Closer* (1980) – a terrifying companion to *Unknown Pleasures*, contrasting its predecessor's violence with a pervasive sense of resignation and exhaustion. It was easy for critics and fans to perceive confessional pointers towards Curtis' mental state in his lyrics, thus building a legend which remains to this day.

Joy Division's surviving members regrouped as the equally innovative New Order, while Factory released a final single, 'She's Lost Control (version)'/'Atmosphere'.

""She's Lost Control' – that song meant so much to me when I was younger"
Courtney Love

Factory also released a live video, *Here Are The Young Men* (1982) and two sprawling compilations – 1981's *Still* and 1988's *Substance*. London Records (who now own Joy Division and New Order's catalogue following Factory's demise in 1993) compiled *Permanent* (1995) and the box set *Heart And Soul* (1997).

Joy Division's influence – particularly on the 80s Goth genre – can be heard in 1995's *A Means To An End*, a tribute album by artists including Moby and Smashing Pumpkins' Billy Corgan. Nine Inch Nails contributed a version of 'Dead Souls' to the soundtrack of *The Crow* (1994), while Bush reworked 'In A Lonely Place' (Curtis' last song) for *The Crow – City Of Angels* (1996). Paul Young, PJ Proby and Swans have recorded idiosyncratic versions of Joy Division's swan song, 'Love Will Tear Us Apart'.

READ *Touching From A Distance* (1995), Deborah Curtis

surf slashmc.rice.edu/ceremony/ceremony.html

"Heavy Metal is the totality of existence"
Rob Halford

JUDAS PRIEST

WHO Vocals **Rob Halford** (b. 25 Aug 1951, Birmingham, England), guitar **Ken 'KK' Downing** (b. 27 Oct 1951, Birmingham), guitar **Glenn Tipton** (b. 25 Oct 1948, Birmingham), bass **Ian Hill** (b. 20 Jan 1952, Birmingham)

WHEN 1969–

WHERE Wolverhampton, England

WHAT Screaming Metal

Long before singer Rob Halford's 1998 declaration, "I've been a gay man all of my life", Judas Priest broke one of Rock's greatest taboos: admitting to being Heavy Metal. They got off to a good start by sharing geographic origins with Black Sabbath. After stumbling through obligatory personnel upheavals and dues-paying tours, Judas Priest – founded by guitarist KK Downing and bassist Ian Hill – solidified in 1973 with Halford and Glenn Tipton. Drummers came and went, as drummers do.

The drab *Rocka Rolla* (1974) was deservedly ignored, but *Sad Wings Of Destiny* (1976) blueprinted the Judas Priest formula: razor riffing, ludicrous lyrics and vampiric vocals. Halford underlined their 'more Metal than most' image with a leather 'n' studs uniform, a bullwhip to hand, and stage entrances atop a roaring Harley Davidson.

Meanwhile, *Sin After Sin* (1977), *Stained Class* (1978), *Killing Machine* (1979 – aka *Hell Bent For Leather* Stateside) and *Unleashed In The East* (1979) sowed the seeds for the late 70s' New Wave Of British Heavy Metal.

They became huge overseas, too: *British Steel* (1980), *Point Of Entry* (1981), *Screaming For Vengeance* (1982), *Defenders Of The Faith* (1984) and *Turbo* (1986) completed a platinum US run. The onslaught – celebrated on *Priest… Live!* (1987) and *Metal Works 73–93* (1993) – was tempered by chant-worthy choruses, notably 1980 hits 'Living After Midnight' and 'Breakin' The Law'.

This immense popularity rendered them susceptible to the lunatic excesses of the American legal system. Metal has a long tradition – stretching from Led Zeppelin to Marilyn Manson – of being dragged into dysfunctional family disputes, whereby the stubbing of a toe will be blamed on a lyric.

Priest's entanglement in a grim court case – in which the prosecution alleged subliminal messages on *Stained Class* prompted the murder of one suicidal Priest fan by another – overshadowed *Ram It Down* (1988). From an inconclusive judgment ("We were absolved of blame," said Tipton, "but the implication was that there were messages on the album."), they bounced back with 1990's career highlight *Painkiller*.

However, Halford quit to form Fight – an uncelebrated act promptly eclipsed by his cameo in Black Sabbath and 1997 move under the wing of Nine Inch Nails' Trent Reznor for a new band called Two. The latter debuted with *Voyeurs* (1998).

His erstwhile associates floundered before recruiting Tim 'Ripper' Owens from Priest tribute band British Steele for *Jugulator* (1997). "What we'll be looking for in the long term is to be considered legendary, or at least semi-legendary," said Downing, "for being the foremost in what we do: Heavy Metal."

(READ) *Judas Priest – Heavy Duty* (1984), Steve Gett

(SURF) www.lysator.liu.se/~priest/index.html

KC & THE SUNSHINE BAND

WHO Vocals/keyboards **Harry Wayne 'KC' Casey** (b. 31 Jan 1951, Hialeah, Florida, USA), guitar **Jerome Smith** (b. 18 Jun 1953, Hialeah), bass **Richard Finch** (b. 25 Jan 1954, Indianapolis, Indiana, USA), drums **Robert Johnson** (b. 21 March 1953, Miami, Florida)

WHEN 1973–

WHERE Miami, Florida, USA

WHAT Fun-time Disco

Pioneers of Disco, 'KC' and Finch wrote and produced classic transatlantic chart-topper 'Rock Your Baby' for George McCrae in 1974, paving the way for their own 'Get Down Tonight' and 'That's The Way (I Like It)' from 1975's US mega-hit *KC And The Sunshine Band*. Their status as Disco dictators was enshrined with US No.1 'I'm Your Boogie Man' (1977) and their contribution to 1978's *Saturday Night Fever* soundtrack, 'Boogie Shoes'. They even managed to outlive Disco, scoring a US No.1 with 1980's 'Please Don't Go' and 1983's UK No.1 'Give It Up'. In 1997, the KC legend grew with simultaneous smasheroos 'Bamboogie' by Bamboo (which revamped 'Get Down Tonight') and the stupendous Clock's cover of 'That's The Way (I Like It)'.

surf izan.simplenet.com/kc.htm#story

R. KELLY ✪

WHO b. Robert Kelly, 8 Jan 1969, Chicago, Illinois, USA

WHAT Explicit and exquisite R&B craftsman

When R. Kelly burst from R&B renown to Pop superstardom, there was no reason to suppose he would outlast short-lived sensations like Bobby Brown. However, when *Born Into The 90s* (1991) and *12 Play* (1993) sold zillions, his writing and remixing created hits for protégées Aaliyah ('Back And Forth', 1994) and Changing Faces ('Stroke You Up', 1994), and stars like Janet and Michael Jackson. The latter's No.1 'You Are Not Alone' proved Kelly's talent for balladry, although tracks like 'Hump Bounce', from *R. Kelly* (1995), maintained his booty-bumping credentials.

In 1997 he ruled the R&B roost with the epic 'I Believe I Can Fly' and 'Gotham City', and Changing Faces' stark 'G.H.E.T.T.O.U.T.'. In between playing major league basketball with the Atlantic City Seagulls, Kelly found time to record *V.I.P.* (1998) and to produce the soundtrack to the 1998 Eddie Murphy movie *Lifers*.

fan Jive Records, 700 N. Green Street, Chicago, IL 60622, USA

surf www.galactica.it/101/black/arklly.html

CHAKA KHAN

WHO b. Yvette Marie Stevens, 23 Mar 1953, Great Lakes, Illinois, USA

WHAT Sultry Soulstress

While Aretha Franklin and Diana Ross floundered from mid-70s MOR to Disco, Chaka Khan grooved effortlessly to greatness. In 1971, she was plucked from Chicago clubs to front Funk band Rufus, notably on the Stevie Wonder-penned smash 'Tell Me Something Good'. Her solo stardom began with Disco dizbuster 'I'm Every Woman', from *Chaka* (1978). After *Naughty* (1980), *What Cha' Gonna Do For Me* (1981) and *Chaka Khan* (1982), she'd outgrown Rufus, bowing out with the all-time anthem 'Ain't Nobody' from their *Stompin' At The Savoy* (1983).

Echoes Of An Era (1982) – a Khan-fronted collection of Jazz standards – was less heralded, but her take on Prince's 'I Feel For You', featuring Melle Mel's stuttering rap, blew up worldwide. *I Feel For You* (1984), *Destiny* (1986) and *C.K.* (1988) yielded no similar smashes – despite the input of Stevie Wonder and Prince on the excellent *C.K.* – but *Life Is A Dance: The Remix Project* (1989) revitalized 'Ain't Nobody' and 'I'm Every Woman'. Khan also graced Whitney Houston's remake of the latter in 1992.

The Woman I Am (1992), *Epiphany: The Best Of Chaka Khan* (1996) and LL Cool J's UK chart-topping cover of 'Ain't Nobody' ensure she remains revered.

fan Friends Of CK, PO Box 16680, Beverly Hills, CA 90209-5526, USA

surf www.geocities.com/SunsetStrip/Club/1407/chaka.html

KILLING JOKE

WHO Vocals **Jaz Coleman** (b. Jeremy Coleman, 26 Feb 1960, Cheltenham, Gloucestershire, England), guitar **Geordie** (b. K. Walker, 18 Dec 1958 Newcastle upon Tyne, England), bass **Youth** (b. Martin Glover, 27 Dec 1960, Africa), drums **'Big' Paul Ferguson** (b. 31 Mar 1958, High Wycombe, Buckinghamshire, England)

WHEN 1979–

WHERE Notting Hill, London, England

WHAT Post-Punk prophets of doom

Killing Joke burst onto the scene in 1979 with the independently issued EP 'Turn to Red'. EG records signed them for the menacing *Killing Joke* (1980), *What's This For..?* (1981) and *Revelations* (1982). Jaz Coleman, notorious for psychotic live performances, reacted to one unflattering review by throwing maggots at the guilty journalist. The drug-crazed Youth had to be replaced by Paul Raven while an increasingly paranoid Coleman fled to Iceland in 1982, fearing an imminent apocalypse. On his return, the Joke hit a purple patch with the more commercial *Night Time* (1985) and the hit 'Love like Blood'. However, the apocalyptic *Brighter Than A Thousand Suns* (1986) presaged the band's disintegration.

Reunions yielded 1990's *Extremities, Dirt & Various Repressed Emotions* and, with Youth (now a Dance producer), 1994's triumphant *Pandemonium* and 1996's less acclaimed *Democracy*. Coleman is now known for symphonic overhauls of Led Zeppelin and Pink Floyd, a profitable union with arranger Anne Dudley.

(Fan) Killing Joke, 47 Bedford Street, Leamington Spa, CV32 5DA, UK

(Surf) www.zoology.com

B.B. KING

WHO b. Riley B. King, 16 Sep 1925, near Itta Bena, Mississippi, USA

WHAT Supreme six-string R&Being

Balancing integrity and acumen, B.B. King won a white audience while retaining his roots. The son of a sharecropper, he worked in the cotton fields but practised guitar passionately from the age of 12, inspired chiefly by Lonnie Johnson and T-Bone Walker.

In 1946 he moved to Memphis where, a couple of years later, his cousin, Blues legend Bukka White, helped him land his own show on radio station WDIA. They called him 'Blues Boy', abbreviated to 'B.B.'. His debut 'Miss Martha King' (for his first wife) came out in 1949 on Bullet, but the label folded and, via talent scout Ike Turner, Modern soon signed him. King stepped up to the 250-gigs-a-year schedule he sustained into his seventies, usually employing a band of at least a dozen musicians to augment 'Lucille', his ever-present Gibson ES335.

His first hit was the US R&B No.1 'Three O'Clock Blues' (1952), and he reached a wider audience when 'Rock Me Baby' (1964, US No.34) galvanized the post-Beatles wave of white R&B fans and bands. Subsequently, he took every opportunity offered by Rock star reverence, from Keith Richards (King supported the Stones on their 1969 US tour) to U2 (on their 1989 hit duet 'When Love

Comes To Town'). A hippie era festival favourite, he reached a commercial apogee with the US hits 'The Thrill Is Gone' (1969), *Indianola Mississippi Seeds* (1970), featuring Leon Russell, Joe Walsh and Carole King, and *Live In Cook County Jail* (1971).

King maintained quality and respect, winning a Lifetime Achievement Grammy and five for Best Traditional Blues Recording – the last for *Blues Summit* (1993), on which he duetted with peers from Robert Cray to John Lee Hooker. *Deuces Wild* (1997) was a union with stars including, once more, The Rolling Stones – although even more stellar collaborators were The Simpsons, on whose *Sing The Blues* (1991) he appeared.

(Read) *Blues All Around Me: The Autobiography Of B.B. King* (1996), B.B. King & David Ritz

(Surf) www.bbking.mca.com

BEN E. KING

WHO b. Benjamin Earl Nelson, 23 Sep 1938, Henderson, North Carolina, USA

WHAT Light Soul standard bearer

After moving to Harlem, New York, in the mid-50s, Ben E. King sang with various Doo Wop groups, including both The Four Bs and The Five Crowns, before joining The Drifters as lead vocalist. Though only a short-term member, he sang lead on 'There Goes My Baby' and 'Save The Last Dance For Me'. On his departure, he signed with Atlantic as a solo artist and, with producers Leiber and Stoller, spun on a string of classics, including 1961's 'Stand By Me', 'Young Boy Blues' and 'Spanish Harlem'.

The arrival of Motown and Stax in the 60s eclipsed King's type of music, but *Supernatural* (1975) and *Benny And Us* (1977) – a collaboration with The Average White Band – lifted the legend.

In 1986, 'Stand By Me' reached the US Top 10, thanks to the movie of the same name. The following year it topped the UK chart after its use in a Levi's ad. *Stand By Me (The Ultimate Collection)*, featuring King's solo and Drifters gems, reached UK No.14 in 1987 and led to appearances at that year's Glastonbury Festival and The Prince's Trust Rock Gala, and fresh recording for Atlantic. In 1990, 'Stand By Me' was named one of the most performed songs of the previous half-century by the BPI.

CAROLE KING ✪✪✪

WHO b. Carole Klein, 9 Feb 1940, Brooklyn, New York, USA

WHAT Weaver of Pop's rich tapestry

A place in songwriting heaven is assured for Carole King, Queen of Pop. The subject of Neil Sedaka's unrequited love ballad 'Oh! Carol', King worked with her husband Gerry Goffin at 1650 Broadway (around the corner from the Brill Building hit factory) in New York. Together they crafted definitive Pop moments, like The Shirelles' 'Will You Love Me Tomorrow?' (1960), The Drifters' 'Up On The Roof' (1962) and their babysitter Little Eva's 'The Loco-Motion' (1962). King also scored solo with 1962's 'It Might As Well Rain Until September'.

By the close of the 60s, King had divorced Goffin and moved to LA. Ventures like her short-lived label Tomorrow Records and band The City were promptly eclipsed when she transformed the introspective singer/songwriter tradition into a commercial phenomenon with the blockbusting *Tapestry* (1970). Tracks like the US No.1 'It's Too Late' and 'I Feel The Earth Move' kept the album on charts for years and inspired innumerable cover versions. The silver streak continued with US No.1s *Music* (1971) and *Wrap Around Joy* (1974), which sandwiched Top 10 smashes *Rhymes & Reasons* (1972) and *Fantasy* (1973).

By the late 70s she had been upstaged by a new wave of women, including Carly Simon and Linda Ronstadt, but still struck gold with *Thoroughbred* (1976) and *Simple Things* (1977).

In the 90s she moved into acting, appearing on US TV and replacing Petula Clark in the Broadway production of *Blood Brothers*. She also graced Celine Dion's 1997 hit 'The Reason' – Dion having covered King's '(You Make Me Feel Like A) Natural Woman' for tribute album *Tapestry Revisited* (1995), which also starred Bee Gees, Rod Stewart and a uniting of BeBe & CeCe Winans with Aretha Franklin. The 1997 movie *Grace Of My Heart* was loosely based on King's life. Her daughter with Gerry Goffin, Louise Goffin, is now also a singer/songwriter in her own right.

KING CRIMSON

WHO Guitar/keyboards **Robert Fripp** (b. 16 May 1946, Wimborne, Dorset, England), bass/vocals **John Wetton** (b. 12 Jul 1949, Derby, England), drums **Bill Bruford** (b. 17 May 1948, Sevenoaks, Kent, England), drums **Jamie Muir** (b. England), violin/keyboards **David Cross** (b. 1948, Plymouth, England)

WHEN 1969–

WHERE London, England

WHAT The Progfathers

From sleepy English retirement community Bournemouth came guitar whizzkids Robert Fripp and Greg Lake. The latter switched to bass, and they recruited brilliant drummer Michael Giles and keyboard player/saxophonist Ian McDonald, with Pete Sinfield writing lyrics and organizing their light show.

Their debut, *In The Court Of The Crimson King* (1969), is a Prog Rock classic but, following a disastrous US tour, they split while recording a second album. Undeterred, Fripp recruited saxophonist Mel Collins, drummer Ian Wallace and bassist Boz

Burrell for three patchy albums – of which only *Islands* (1971) challenged the quality of their debut. Another US tour preceded what appeared to be a terminal split in early 1972.

However, the classic Crimson line-up (Fripp, Yes' Bill Bruford, Family's John Wetton and, briefly, Jazz muso Jamie Muir) set out to conquer the world with *Larks' Tongues In Aspic* (1973), *Starless And Bible Black* (1974) and *Red* (1974). But in 1974, Fripp, gripped by a loathing of the Art Rock in which he specialized, announced: "King Crimson is over. For ever and ever". The belated live set *The Great Deceiver* (1994) is a fine tribute to this line-up. The band scattered: Fripp to solo weirdness, Wetton to Uriah Heep, Muir to a Tibetan monastery in Scotland and McDonald to Foreigner.

In 1981, Fripp enlisted Bruford, guitar widdler Adrian Belew and bassist Tony Levin in Discipline – renamed, for monetary (or musical, says Fripp) reasons, King Crimson. The rhythmic *Discipline* (1981), the formulaic *Beat* (1982) and the industrial *Three Of A Perfect Pair* (1984) were the results. Bruford returned to Yes, to fund more left-field projects such as the label Earthworks.

Fripp never knew when to let a good thing die. In 1994, the 80s line-up was reconvened, with stick-player Trey Gunn and second drummer Pat Mastelotto to form a 'double trio' – a seemingly meaningless exercise as Bruford was already as skilful as two drummers. The Mini-album *Vrooom* (1994) and *Thrak* (1995) were among the uncelebrated results.

(Fan) We'll Let You Know, 3 Kings Drive, Bradford, BD2 1PX, UK

(surf) www.elephant-talk.com/

THE KINKS

WHO Vocals/guitar **Ray Davies** (b. 21 Jun 1944, London, England), guitar/vocals **Dave Davies** (b. 3 Feb 1947, London), bass **Pete Quaife** (b. 31 Dec 1943, Tavistock, Devon, England), drums **Mick Avory** (b. 15 Feb 1944, London)

WHEN 1963–

WHERE Muswell Hill, London, England

WHAT Kwintessential English karacter studies

More than 30 years after 'You Really Got Me' crashed into the charts, The Kinks' impact is still apparent. Ray Davies has risen to legendary status, his songwriting talent and quintessential Englishness echoed by Blur, Paul Weller and Supergrass.

In 1963, art student Ray joined his brother Dave's band The Ravens. Despite sibling rivalry that dogs them to this day, they signed to Pye as The Kinks. Early singles 'Long Tall Shorty' and 'You Still Want Me' failed to chart but, in August 1964, 'You Really Got Me' and 'All Day And All Of The Night' (among the first Heavy Metal records) thundered into the transatlantic Top 10s. Power chords and chaotic guitar solos littered their R&B-flavoured debut *Kinks* (1964), but Ray's versatile songwriting sent the languid 'Tired Of Waiting For You' to UK No.1 in 1965.

By 1966 he had moved even further from Mod-ish R&B, writing character studies of English society: 'Dedicated Follower Of Fashion' (a tongue-in-cheek anthem for Swinging London), 'Sunny Afternoon' (existential crisis, the calm of the English summer), 'Dead End Street' (proto-Punk working-class fatalism) and the poignant masterpiece 'Waterloo Sunset' (urban alienation). The latter, and Dave Davies' 1967 solo hit 'Death Of A Clown', were from 1967's *Something Else By The Kinks* – an old-

> **"Even though I thought I had something weird to prove, we did it for fun... we celebrated a time, our youth"**
> **Ray Davies**

fashioned contrast to Psychedelia which marked a commercial downturn, particularly in the USA, where legal restrictions temporarily stopped them touring.

Undeterred, Davies plugged away with conceptual efforts like *The Kinks Are The Village Green Preservation Society* (1968) and *Arthur, Or The Decline and Fall Of The British Empire* (1969), by which time long-term session bassist John Dalton had officially replaced Quaife. They finally returned to Rock and the charts with the wry 'Lola' and 'Apeman', from *Lola Versus Powerman And The Moneygoround, Part One* (1970).

The self-destructive Ray spent much of the rest of the 70s on shambolic tours of the USA, interspersed with further non-selling concept albums like *Schoolboys In Disgrace* (1975). In the late 70s, they effected a career turnaround: talent-spotter Clive Davis oversaw the big sellers *Sleepwalker* (1977), *Misfits* (1978) and *Low Budget* (1979), and Van Halen and The Pretenders scored their first hits with Kinks covers ('You Really Got Me' and 'Stop Your Sobbing' respectively). Davies cashed in with more Hard Rock albums and marriage to Pretender Chrissie Hynde.

Fans hankering after the more insightful tunes of yesteryear finally had their wish fulfilled with the nostalgic hit 'Come Dancing' from US No.12 *State Of Confusion* (1983), but glimpses of former greatness were mainly live, as on 1996's *To The Bone*. The 90s brought critical (if not commercial) resurrection, thanks largely to Britpop brat Damon Albarn, who in 1995 duetted with Davies himself on UK TV's *The White Room* (performing 'Waterloo Sunset' and 'Parklife') and to Chrissie Hynde, who covered The Kinks' 'I Go To Sleep' on The Pretenders' *Isle Of View*. Meanwhile, Davies released his 1998 solo album *The Storyteller*.

 READ *X-Ray (The Unauthorised Autobiography)* (1994), Ray Davies

KISS

WHO Vocals/guitar **Paul Stanley** (b. Stanley Eisen, 20 Jan 1952, Queens, New York, USA), vocals/guitar **Ace Frehley** (b. Paul Frehley, 27 Apr 1951, The Bronx, New York), vocals/bass **Gene Simmons** (b. Chiam Witz, 25 Aug 1949, Haifa, Israel), drums **Peter Criss** (b. Peter Criscoula, 20 Dec 1945, Brooklyn, New York)

WHEN 1972–

WHERE New York, USA

WHAT Facepaint and firepower

With the grace of Godzilla, Kiss trampled mid-70s America. The similarly invasive Beatles had influenced Kiss mainstays Gene Simmons and Paul Stanley, whose pre-fame pastimes included busking tunes like 'If I Fell' on street corners. They also dabbled in Jefferson Airplane-esque Psychedelia with their band Wicked Lester, before enlisting Peter Criss and Ace Frehley for brutal Rock 'n' Roll, offset by acoustic guitars and harmony vocals (the latter inspired by The Beatles and Stanley's love of Doo Wop).

The agenda was set on 1974's *Kiss* and *Hotter Than Hell*, though neither attracted as much attention as the band's garish

make-up – 'shock Rock' pioneer Alice Cooper benevolently allowed that, of his imitators, Kiss did it best. The burgeoning 'Kiss Army' agreed, rewarding the band's constant touring with 1975's breakthroughs: the dirty *Dressed To Kill* and shiny *Alive!*.

As their ambition rocketed, *Destroyer* (1976) boasted ballads and orchestras, the shows took spectacle to new heights (blood-spitting, elevating drum-kits, fire-breathing) and the Kiss logo adorned an extraordinary range of merchandise. Their excess was mirrored at the Casablanca label, of which Kiss were the flagship act. Having funded the band's early tours with his credit card, its boss Neil Bogart cashed in on their success – and that of labelmates Donna Summer and The Village People – with legendarily luxurious offices and druggily inconclusive meetings (ironically, Simmons and Stanley are militantly anti-drugs).

The sleazy *Rock And Roll Over* (1976), the self-mocking *Love Gun* (1977) and the gonzoid *Alive II* (1977) continued a platinum run, but ambition bested them in 1978. Within months of the hits set *Double Platinum*, the four members issued simultaneous solo albums. Though Frehley's and Stanley's were as good as anything in the Kiss canon, only Simmons' sold comparably.

They combated market fatigue with the Disco-ish 'I Was Made For Loving You' from *Dynasty* (1979), but began the 80s shakily: Criss was replaced by Eric Carr and the poppy *Unmasked* (1980) was their first album in four years not to go platinum. After *Music From The Elder* (1981) – a commercially disastrous flirtation with Rock Opera, featuring lyrics by Lou Reed – Frehley bailed out for cultdom with Frehley's Comet. Kiss battled on, recruiting Vinnie Vincent for the "Metal 'n' Roll" *Creatures Of The Night* (1982).

Their fortunes improved when they ditched the make-up for *Lick It Up* (1983), but healthy sales for *Animalize* (1984), *Asylum* (1985), *Crazy Nights* (1987), *Smashes, Thrashes And Hits* (1988) and *Hot In The Shade* (1989) were countered by unprofitable tours and chart-clobberings by the blatantly Kiss-inspired Mötley Crüe and Bon Jovi (both of whom supported them live).

Line-up upheavals also took their toll: Vincent was replaced briefly by Mark St John in 1984, then long-term by Bruce Kulick. Carr died of cancer in 1991 and was replaced by Eric Singer.

Despite hits with 'Crazy Crazy Nights', 'Forever' and 'God Gave Rock And Roll To You II', the band were swamped by Grunge – whose leading lights graciously acknowledged Kiss' importance: Stone Temple Pilots aped their make-up, Nirvana covered 'Do You Love Me', Dinosaur Jr covered 'Goin' Blind' and The Melvins issued solo EPs whose covers pastiched Kiss.

The heavier *Revenge* (1992) and *Alive III* (1993) returned them to the US Top 10, but their influence (Garth Brooks being among those roped in for the 1994 tribute album *Kiss My Ass*) continued to outstrip sales. To fans' delight, a tentative reunion with Frehley and Criss for MTV's *Unplugged* (1996) became permanent and the original quartet embarked on the biggest-grossing tour of 1996/1997, complete with the make-up, anthems and blood 'n' fire theatrics that had entranced millions two decades before.

After plugging a release gap with the gratuitous compilations *You Wanted The Best, You Got The Best* (1996), *Greatest Kiss* (1996) and *Greatest Hits* (1997), and the final Bruce Kulick/Eric Singer-era recordings *Carnival Of Souls* (1997), they began recording *Psycho Circus* and planning another worldwide campaign. "We are Kiss, and we're back," Stanley told *USA Today*. "Join us... or go down."

READ *Kiss And Sell* (1997), C K Lendt

FAN Firehouse, #66 7158 138 Street, Surrey, BC V3W 7V7, Canada

SURF kissasylum.com/

KLF

WHO Production/vocals **Bill 'King Boy D' Drummond** (b. William Butterworth, 29 Apr 1953, South Africa), keyboards/production **Jimmy 'Rockman Rock' Cauty** (b. 1954, London, England)

WHEN 1987–1992

WHERE London, England

WHAT Twisted Techno terrorists

Deep in the bowels of the music industry, Bill Drummond (ex-Teardrop Explodes/Echo & The Bunnymen manager) and Jimmy Cauty (then in Brilliant with Killing Joke's Youth) hatched the greatest of Rock 'n' Roll swindles. Hijacking Hip Hop, they unleashed 'All You Need Is Love' as The Justified Ancients Of Mu Mu. In 1987, the album *1987 (What The Fuck Is Going On?)* blew up a storm without even being released: publishers pounced on unauthorized samples from Samantha Fox, Abba, The Sex Pistols and The Fall. Forced to surrender the master tapes, Cauty and Drummond dumped the remaining copies in the North Sea.

After heading for House on 1988's *Who Killed The JAMMs?*, they made a shameless stab at stardom as The Timelords, with the Glitter-rocking *Dr Who* tribute 'Doctorin' The Tardis' – a UK chart-topper in June 1988. Their twisted route to the top is documented in Drummond's 1988 book *The Manual (How To Have A Number One The Easy Way)*.

After the stop-gap compilation *Shag Times* (1989), the duo donned the KLF (Kopyright Liberation Front) alias, fired a blank at the mainstream with 'Kylie Said To Jason' (1989), then got weird. *Chill Out* (1990, "the world's first Ambient House album") and Cauty's collaboration with The Orb's Dr Alex Paterson, *Space*, were masterpieces. KLF went on to conquer the charts with the 'Stadium House' trilogy 'What Time Is Love' (1990), '3 AM Eternal' (a UK No.1 and a US 1991 smash) and 'Last Train To Transcentral' (1991). True to perverse form, Drummond and Cauty poured the profits into the never-finished movie *The White Room*, whose soundtrack (1991) became their only hit album. A chartbusting collaboration with Tammy Wynette ('Justified & Ancient') and the final JAMMs single 'It's Grim Up North' rounded off a bizarre year.

After KLF's climactic hit 'America: What Time Is Love?', Cauty and Drummond tired of their own joke. At a blood-spattered 1992 BRIT ceremony, they exploded '3 AM Eternal' with Hardcore Punks Extreme Noise Terror, fired blanks at the audience and dumped dead sheep outside the venue. "Ladies and gentlemen," they declared, "The KLF have left the music business."

Having ruffled Rock's feathers, they turned their sights on art, under the K Foundation banner: their award for 'worst work' (an attack on 1993's Turner Prize for art) incensed its recipient. In 1994, they took one million pounds – their remaining riches – to a remote Scottish island and filmed its incineration. Sequels were low-key: a version of 'K Sera Sera' postponed until the advent of world peace and a Drum 'n' Bass reworking of the *Magnificent Seven* theme on Bosnia benefit *Help* (1995). In 1997, they resurfaced as 2K and announced their intention to leave the 20th century in chaos with a 23-minute London show, a flop single ('Fuck The Millennium') and the mooted erection of a pyramid.

surf www.mutelibtech.com/mute/2k/2k1.htm

Knebworth

The stately home Knebworth House in Hertfordshire, England, has hosted Rock's elite since 1974, when The Allman Brothers Band attracted 60,000. It has since been the scene of outdoor extravaganzas featuring Pink Floyd (1975, 1990), The Rolling Stones (1976), Genesis (1978, 1992), Frank Zappa (1978), Led Zeppelin (1979), The Beach Boys (1980), Cliff Richard (1983, 1990), Deep Purple (1985), Queen (1986 – their final show), Elton John (1990) and Paul McCartney (1990). In 1996, Kula Shaker, The Charlatans, Manic Street Preachers, Ocean Colour Scene and Prodigy supported Oasis at two shows with a combined audience of over 250,000 – confirming Oasis as Britain's brightest stars and Knebworth owners Lord and Lady Cobbold as England's hippest aristocrats.

GLADYS KNIGHT

WHO b. 28 May 1944, Atlanta, Georgia, USA

WHAT Black satin Soul

At 8 years old, Gladys won a $2,000 first prize for performing 'Too Young' on US TV's *The Ted Mack Amateur Hour*. Her group, The Pips (named after cousin James 'Pip' Woods) – then boasting a sister, brother and two other cousins – debuted with 'Ching Chong' in 1957. They first tasted fame in 1961, when their revival of Johnny Otis' 'Every Beat Of My Heart' topped the R&B chart.

Further Soul stand-outs ensued, but only 1961's 'Letter Full Of Tears' increased their Pop hit tally. However, gems like 'I Heard It Through The Grapevine' (1967), 'Help Me Make It Through The Night' (1972), 'Neither One Of Us' (1973), 'The Way We Were'/'Try To Remember', 'Best Thing That Ever Happened To Me' (all 1975) and 'Midnight Train To Georgia' (1976) returned them to the upper reaches of transatlantic charts.

Legal problems stalled them in the 70s, but hits resumed in the 80s with 'Love Overboard' (1987), giving them a tenth R&B No.1. Thereafter, The Pips (Merald Knight, William Guest and Edward Patten) 'suspended' their career, leaving Knight to star solo on the likes of 1989's Bond theme hit, 'Licence To Kill'.

Over four decades, Knight has sung over 60 US hits, collected six gold albums, won a Lifetime Achievement award from the Rhythm And Blues Foundation and rightfully earned a fistful of Grammys. She was embedded in Rap too, when Wu-Tang Clan hooked their hit 'Can It All Be So Simple' on a Knight sample.

read *Between Each Line Of Pain And Glory – My Life Story* (1997), Gladys Knight

surf www.angelfire.com/tx/savedtoo/gladys.html

KOOL & THE GANG

WHO Vocals **James 'JT' Taylor** (b. 16 Aug 1953, South Carolina, USA), guitar **Claydes Smith** (b. 6 Sep 1948, Jersey City, New Jersey, USA), bass **Robert 'Kool' Bell** (b. 8 Oct 1950, Youngstown, Ohio, USA), tenor saxophone **Ronald Bell** (b. 1 Nov 1951, Youngstown), drums **George 'Funky' Brown** (b. 5 Jan 1949, Jersey City), keyboards **Curtis Williams** (b. 11 Dec 1962, Buffalo, New York, USA)

WHEN 1964–

WHERE Jersey City, New Jersey, USA

WHAT Jungle boogie

One of the most consistently successful R&B groups debuted on the US chart in 1969 with 'Kool And The Gang', a funky Jazz-tinged instrumental that set the pattern for their first releases. In the mid-70s, a new 'party dance' sound was heralded by *Wild And Peaceful* (1974), source of the much sampled smashes (and R&B No.1s) 'Hollywood Swinging' and 'Jungle Boogie'.

The slick title track of 1979's US platinum-seller *Ladies Night*, with new vocalist James 'JT' Taylor, took their magic worldwide. They were the most successful American group in Britain in the early 80s, thanks to gems like 1981's 'Celebration', 1984's 'Joanna' and 'Fresh' and 1985's 'Cherish'. Though better known now for schmaltz, they re-found the Funk with the immortal 'Get Down On It' from *Something Special* (1981) and 'Misled' from *Emergency* (1985), both albums adding to their list of US million-sellers. Sadly, their hits stopped when Taylor went solo in 1988 and even a reunion in 1995 failed to return them to previous heights.

However, Kool covers have become hits for Dance sensations from Kylie Minogue to Lil' Kim, and kudos followed the use of 'Jungle Boogie' in *Pulp Fiction*.

KRAFTWERK

WHO Keyboards/vocals **Ralf Hütter** (b. 20 Aug 1946, Krefeld, Germany) keyboards/vocals **Florian Schneider** (b. 7 Apr 1947, Düsseldorf, Germany), percussion/vocals **Karl Bartos** (b. 31 May 1952, Berchtesgaden, Germany), percussion **Wolfgang Flur** (b. 17 Jul 1947, Frankfurt am Main, Germany)

WHEN 1970–

WHERE Düsseldorf, Germany

WHAT Paranoid androids

Inspired by the industrial sounds of Düsseldorf, Ralf Hütter and Florian Schneider added Robot 'n' Roll to the Rock lexicon. They made their dissonant debut as Organisation on the flop *Tone Float* (1970), then – adding drummers Andreas Hohman and Klaus Dinger – with Kraftwerk (German for 'power plant'). After their eponymous debut (1970), Hohman quit, as did short stayed members Michael Rother (who left with Dinger to form Neu!) and Eberhardt Krahnemann. Even Hütter jumped ship briefly, but returned to their Kling Klang ('ringing sound') studio in Düsseldorf for the friendlier *Kraftwerk 2* (1971).

By 1973, Hütter and Schneider had discarded most conventional instruments: only Schneider's flute and unofficial member Emil Schult's electric violin remained amid the electronics. Schult contributed to the group's increasingly important image, designing artwork for 1973's *Ralf And Florian* and helping brainstorm the groundbreaking *Autobahn* (1974).

With the latter, Kraftwerk went mainstream: Hot Butter's 'Popcorn' (1972) beat them to the charts, but 'Autobahn' (featuring new percussionist Wolfgang Flur and guitarist Klaus Roeder) is electronic Pop's enduring anthem: a 20-minute celebration of German motorways. Its harmonized vocal – a direct descendant from The Beach Boys' 'Fun Fun Fun' – and

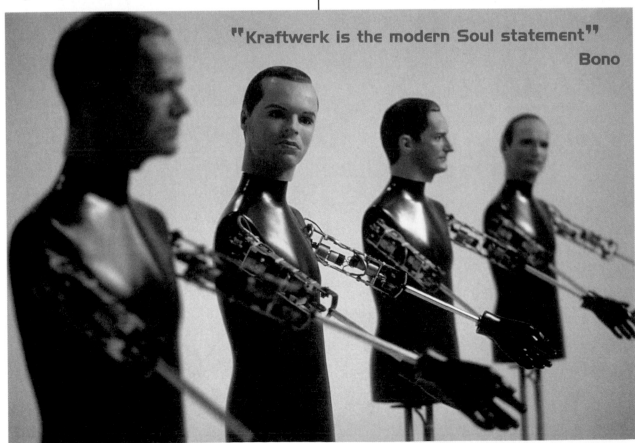

"Kraftwerk is the modern Soul statement"
Bono

Hütter and Schneider's passion for Brian Wilson earned them the nickname 'The Beach Boys from Düsseldorf'. Replacing Roeder with Karl Bartos, they swapped hippie garb for short hair and suits, looking like a bizarre string quartet on their first tour of the USA, where an edited 'Autobahn' became a cult hit.

Radio-Activity (1975), like *Autobahn*, had a unifying concept – radio and atomic energy this time – but its baroque ambient pieces, robotic vocals and synthesized radio noises failed to impress newly-won fans. However, loyal followers included two celebrities name-checked on 1977's *Trans-Europe Express*: "From station to station back to Düsseldorf city/Meet Iggy Pop and David Bowie". Kraftwerk also influenced Disco, notably Donna Summer's classic 'I Feel Love'. Their 'Showroom Dummies' helped to spawn Britain's Synth Pop sound, home of The Human League, Orchestral Maneouvres In The Dark and Depeche Mode. With *The Man Machine* (1978), Kraftwerk confirmed their pre-eminence, making crystalline, electronic Disco and talking about replacing themselves with robots on tour.

By 1981's *Computer World*, they *were* robots. Documenting the impact of computer technology on everyday life, the album's angular basslines and painstakingly constructed bleeps found their way into black American music: first with steals from 'Numbers' (and the earlier 'Trans-Europe Express') on Afrika Bambaataa's pioneering 'Planet Rock', then the work of Techno innovators Juan Atkins and Derrick May. "I was the first DJ that brought 'Trans-Europe Express' to The Bronx," Bambaataa boasted to *Hip Hop Connection*. "I was pumping it like crazy on my system and the blacks and Hispanics just went wild offa this 12-minute groove, man!" Kraftwerk's mooted collaboration with Michael Jackson never happened, but *Thriller* (1982) was full of what its producer Quincy Jones called 'Electro-Funk', a key influence on modern R&B. In 1982, Kraftwerk scored a UK No.1 themselves, with a reissue of *The Man Machine*'s 'The Model'.

After these triumphs, Kraftwerk were stymied by their meticulous standards. With the advent of cheaper technology in the 80s, the world caught up with them and Hütter and Schneider's notorious obsessiveness and secrecy (Kling Klang had no phone or fax) meant a lengthy absence, punctuated only by the excellent 'Tour De France' (1983) and a scrapped album, *Technopop*, which resurfaced as the patchy *Electric Café* (1986). Save for the remix album *The Mix* (1991), Kling Klang fell silent.

Quitting in frustration in the late 80s, Flur formed Yamo while Bartos founded Elektric Music and joined Electronic (The Smiths meets New Order with a soupçon of Kraftwerk). The fun-loving automatons got it together to acknowledge their disciples at 1997 European shows – notably Tribal Gathering – but have otherwise maintained their impenetrable disdain amid now well-worn rumours of a new album. Kraftwerk's absence, however, has only increased their legend.

Ⓡⓔⓐⓓ *Kraftwerk – Man, Machine And Music* (1993), Pascal Bussy

Ⓢⓤⓡⓕ www.kraftwerk.com

LENNY KRAVITZ ⊙

WHO b. 26 May 1964, New York City, New York, USA

WHAT The one-man Funk 'n' Roll jukebox

Lenny Kravitz's stylistic debt to the 60s didn't go unnoticed, but critical carping couldn't halt the impact of his debut *Let Love*

Rule (1989). Among those impressed by his talents – and, doubtless, good looks – were Madonna (for whom he co-wrote and produced 'Justify My Love'), actress Lisa Bonet (to whom he was briefly married) and Guns N' Roses' Slash, star of 'Always On The Run'. The latter heralded *Mama Said* (1991), which flew on the back of 'It Ain't Over Till It's Over'.

Hype translated into arena-filling, platinum-reaping hugeness with the title track of *Are You Gonna Go My Way* (1993): a hard-rockin' hit at the time and DJ favourite ever since. Work on albums with Mick Jagger, French songbird Vanessa Paradis, David Bowie and Aerosmith kept up the celebrity quotient, and he collaborated with his hero Stevie Wonder on 'Deuce' for the Kiss tribute *Kiss My Ass* (1994).

However, interest in his 'retro Rock' waned with *Circus* (1995) and Kravitz headed for Hip Hoppier pastures on 1998's *5*.

Ⓡⓔⓐⓓ *Are You Gonna Go My Way* (1994), Milton Okun

Ⓢⓤⓡⓕ www.virginrecords.com./kravitz/home.html

KULA SHAKER ⊙

WHO Vocals/guitar **Crispian Mills** (b. 18 Jan 1973, London, England), bass **Alonza Bevan** (b. 24 Oct 1970, London), drums **Paul Winterhart** (b. 19 Sep 1971, London), keyboards **Jay Darlington** (b. 3 May 1969, Sidcup, England)

WHEN 1995–

WHERE London, England

WHAT Kool psychedelic karma chameleons

The son of actress Hayley Mills and director Roy Boulting, Crispian Mills met Alonza Bevan at Richmond College in 1988. With a shared passion for Indian mysticism and Arthurian legend, they formed The Objects Of Desire, fronted by Hayley's sometime partner, Marcus Maclaine. Paul Winterhart joined three years later. After a period of stagnation, Mills returned from a visit to India in 1993, determined to break away. With Bevan and Winterhart, he recruited his cousin, singer Saul Dismont, and organist Jay Darlington to form The Kays. Named after both Krishna and King Arthur's brother (Kay), they also failed. On meeting mystic Kula Sekhara, they changed their name again.

Dismont left, Mills took lead vocals, and Kula Shaker were signed by Columbia in 1995. Blending Psychedelia, Hindi lyrics and guitar-powered Pop, they scored UK hits with 1996's 'Tattva', 'Hey Dude' and 'Govinda'. The album *K* reached UK No.1. Keen "to save the world and the whole cosmic manifestation", they supported Oasis at Knebworth and undertook two US club tours.

A 1997 hit with Deep Purple's Joe South-penned 'Hush' was clouded only by ill-judged remarks Mills made about the Nazis. Fellow troublemaker Liam Howlett persuaded Mills to add eastern promise to Prodigy's 'Narayan' on *The Fat Of The Land*.

In 1998, 'Sound Of Drums' (produced by Rick Rubin) was promoted by their Revolution For Fun tour, named in an attempt to take themselves less seriously. Their new album was helmed by Alice Cooper/Pink Floyd producer Bob Ezrin.

Ⓡⓔⓐⓓ *Kula Shaker* (1997), Nigel Cross

Ⓕⓐⓝ Kula Shaker Fan Club, Trinity Street, Alveston Place, Leamington Spa, CV32 4SN, UK

Ⓢⓤⓡⓕ www.kulashaker.co.uk

THE LA'S

WHO Vocals/guitar **Lee Mavers** (b. 2 Aug 1962, Liverpool, England), guitar **Paul Hemmings**, bass/vocals **John Power** (b. 14 Sep 1967), drums **John Timson**

WHEN 1986–

WHERE Liverpool, England

WHAT The Britpop blueprint

While Noel Gallagher was (allegedly) stealing car stereos, there was The La's, whose breezy neo-Merseybeat ensured legendary status when Britpop came to power in the 90s. A local following and the songwriting of near-genius leader Lee Mavers won a contract with Go! Discs, who released the waltzing 'Way Out' (1987) to rave reviews but scant sales – a feat repeated by the classic 'There She Goes' (1988), which saw John Timson replaced by Chris Sharrock, ex-Icicle Works and future Lightning Seed.

When 1989's 'Timeless Melody' appeared, Pete Cammell (guitar) and Lee's brother Neil (drums) had been installed and a long-overdue debut album was underway. The obsessive Mavers, however, seemed hellbent on scuppering the group, insisting on vintage equipment and interminable re-recordings.

By the time the flawed masterpiece *The La's* (1990) limped out, he had disowned it, although 'There She Goes' became a belated UK hit that year and radio perennial ever since.

Power left for Britpop gonks Cast and The La's disappeared amid rumours of Maver's drug problems, reappearing only for low-key gigs and in tributes from Noel Gallagher, Paul Weller and The Bluetones – who owe no small debt to Mavers' songwriting.

In a 1995 *NME* 'Where are they now?' feature, Mavers claimed his latest songs sounded better recorded on a dictaphone.

PATTI LABELLE ✪

WHO b. Patricia Holt, 4 Oct 1944, Philadelphia, Pennsylvania, USA

WHAT Spangly-centred smooth Soul

Raised on Gospel but inspired by girl groups, Patti LaBelle, Cindy Birdsong, Nona Hendryx and Sarah Dash became The Blue Belles. 'I Sold My Heart To The Junkman' (1962) launched a quartet of hits and dynamic live shows, hooking record label Atlantic. However, Atlantic failed to work the magic that they brought to the similarly sensational Aretha Franklin, and Birdsong flew to The Supremes in 1968.

A rethink produced new band LaBelle, who triumphed with 'Lady Marmalade (Voulez-Vous Coucher Avec Moi Ce Soir?)': a 1975 smash and saucy perennial ever since (covered by All Saints in 1997). *Nightbirds* (1975) went gold and LaBelle became a glittery live sensation. When they split in 1977, LaBelle enjoyed a modestly rewarded solo career, whose highlight was *I'm In Love Again* (1983).

Success on the US R&B chart paved her return to the mainstream with hits from the 1985 movie monster *Beverly Hills Cop* ('New Attitude' and 'Stir It Up'), then 1986's US chart-topping Michael McDonald duet 'On My Own' and *Winner In You*. However, *Live* (1992) and a scene-stealing cameo as The Acid Queen at The Who's *Tommy* revivals (1989) confirmed the smooth star could still sail spectacularly over the top.

READ *Don't Block The Blessings* (1996), Patti LaBelle & Laura B. Randolph

FAN Patti LaBelle Fan Club, PO Box 30335, Philadelphia, Pennsylvania 19103, USA

SURF www.pattilabelle.com/map.html

kd lang

WHO b. Kathryn Dawn Lang, 2 Nov 1961, Consort, Alberta, Canada

WHAT Cowpunk/Country crossover

kd lang grew up in rural isolation, listening to Classical and Rock. Her love of Country evolved during her college years and, in 1982, she named her Country backing band The Reclines after legend Patsy Cline. *A Truly Western Experience*, on a small Canadian label in 1983, received little attention. After five years of energetic live performances, dressed in full kitsch Country attire, lang ensnared Sire Records, who signed the band in 1987.

Angel With A Lariat (1987), produced by Dave Edmunds, attracted fans of 'new Country', while alienating US Country radio. lang's zany persona was toned down, with suits replacing fringed cowboy shirts. Her 1987 duet with Roy Orbison, 'Crying', won a Grammy, while *Shadowland* (1988) had an even stronger Country flavour. With appearances by Loretta Lynn, Kitty Wells and Brenda Lee, it proved lang's US Pop chart debut.

Absolute Torch And Twang (1989) spent a year on the US chart and won her another Grammy. In 1992, lang entered the UK chart, as *Ingenue* reached UK No.3. She also made her movie debut in Percy Adlon's *Salmonberries* and became involved in PETA (People for the Ethical Treatment of Animals), contributing to a fund-raising album. Her vegetarian stance and lesbianism endeared her little to her native meat-producing Albertans, and her mother received hate mail. lang's provocative *Vanity Fair* cover picture with model Cindy Crawford created controversy, but she was hailed as an icon of 'lesbian chic' and won another Grammy in 1992, this time for her 'Constant Craving'.

Although her 1993 soundtrack to Gus Van Sant's movie *Even Cowgirls Get The Blues* charted at only UK No.36, the 1995 follow-up, *All You Can Eat*, reached UK No.7. The non-smoking lang raised more eyebrows with *Drag* (1997), which centred on songs about smoking. She also appeared in US TV's *Ellen*, in the

infamous 'coming out' episode. Final proof that this maverick had turned mainstream came in 1997 with her co-writing credit on The Rolling Stones hit 'Has Anybody Seen My Baby' and cameos on the 1997 movie soundtracks *Tomorrow Never Dies* and *Midnight In The Garden Of Good And Evil*.

ReaD *All You Get Is Me* (1994), Victoria Starr

Fan Obvious Gossip, PO Box 33800, Station D, Vancouver, BC, Canada, V6E 5C7

Surf www.wbr.com/kdlang/

CYNDI LAUPER

WHO b. Cynthia Lauper, 22 Jun 1953, New York City, New York, USA

WHAT Kooky Popstress

After dropping out of high school, Cyndi Lauper eventually joined New York Rock band Blue Angel, who split after their eponymous 1980 album. Filing for bankruptcy, she sang in a Japanese restaurant before securing a contract with CBS. Her Grammy-winning debut solo album *She's So Unusual* (1983) yielded the hits 'Girls Just Want To Have Fun', 'All Through The Night', 'She Bop' and 'Time After Time', a song which revealed her serious side, although her Spielberg movie theme 'The Goonies 'R' Good Enough' proved she could still 'do' wacky.

True Colors (1986) was more reflective and less successful, while *A Night To Remember* (1989) and *Hat Full Of Stars* (1993) did little business, despite the former including the hit 'I Drove All Night', later covered by Roy Orbison. A revamped 'Girls Just Want To Have Fun' and compilation *12 Deadly Cyns… And Then Some* (1994, 1995 in the USA) provided a commercial upswing in Europe, where Lauper has always enjoyed a high media profile. She released her sixth album, *Sisters Of Avalon*, in 1997.

Fan Kindred Spirits, PO BOX 752473, Memphis, TN 38175, USA

Surf www.cyndilauper.com

LED ZEPPELIN
◉◉◉◉◉◉◉◉◉☆☆☆☆☆☆

WHO Vocals **Robert Plant** (b. 20 Aug 1948, West Bromwich, Birmingham, England), guitar **Jimmy Page** (b. 9 Jan 1944, Heston, Middlesex, England), bass **John Paul Jones** (b. John Baldwin, 3 Jan 1946, Sidcup, Kent, England), drums **John 'Bonzo' Bonham** (b. 31 May 1948, Redditch, Birmingham, d. 25 Sep 1980, Windsor, England)

WHEN 1968–1980

WHERE London, England

WHAT Satan's little helpers

They came to define Rock, but Led Zeppelin could have been just another weedy Folk band. Guitarist Jimmy Page was partial to Pentangle; singer Robert Plant thought The Incredible String Band were where it was at. Ultimately, the influence of these seminal Folk acts was restricted to Page's acoustic tendencies and Plant's lyrical mysticism. "All their lyrics suck," grumbled Courtney Love. "But the music is so great – it's like Beethoven Rock with really bad, elfin Dungeons and Dragons lyrics."

That 'Beethoven Rock' was crafted by Page and bass player John Paul Jones, 60s session veterans whose credits included The Yardbirds' final album, *Little Games* (1967). By mid-1968, The Yardbirds, swamped by contractual obligations, were somewhat short of members: only Page and bassist Chris Dreja. Their first choice for singer, Procol Harum's Terry Reid, declined, but recommended Plant, then of Birmingham group Hobbstweedle, who brought along former bandmate John Bonham.

With Jones replacing Dreja, they became The New Yardbirds for contract-fulfilling Scandinavian gigs in late 1968, then relaunched as Led Zeppelin – a name derived from Who drummer Keith Moon's prediction that the band would go down like a lead balloon. Indeed they did with aristocrat Eva von Zeppelin, who proclaimed them "shrieking monkeys". In the event, Zeppelin *did* mirror The Hindenburg (pictured on their first album sleeve): taking off, then exploding. They recorded their debut (in two days), then jetted Stateside to support Vanilla Fudge, whose skull-crushing, pseudo-Classical sludge was like an unrefined strand of Zeppelin's sprightly sledgehammering.

Tireless touring established a remarkable chart run (*Led Zeppelin* (1969) was the first of ten US/UK Top 10 smashes) and a reputation for excess that eclipsed even the aforementioned Mr Moon's. To the usual pharmaceutical experimentation and hotel trashing were added Page's reported predilection for sadism, sorcery and Olympic-level groupie-groping. Quick to capitalize on 'Rock God' status, Zeppelin became the toast of LA's teen temptresses ("Said you dug me since you were 13," Plant sneered on 'Sick Again', "Then you giggle as you hurt inside.").

Led Zeppelin II (1969) documented this debauchery, notably on riff monsters 'Heartbreaker' and 'Whole Lotta Love', the latter a Top 5 US hit. Thereafter, they disdainfully shunned the singles market – they didn't release a British single at all until 1997. The media, too, were rarely favoured, especially after *Rolling Stone* led a wave of critical hostility.

Unwilling to expand on their lyrics (Plant's vocals were often mixed incomprehensibly low) or the source of their musical power, they joined an elite whose every nuance was scrutinized for 'significance'. But where the mystique of Pink Floyd and Bob Dylan masked mundane personalities and human frailties, Zep moved in more sinister circles: from Page's fascination with black-magician Aleister Crowley to manager Peter Grant's strong-arm business tactics. Plant played the hard livin' Rock God, Bonham raced motorbikes along hotel corridors and only Jones seemed to keep his feet on the ground. Although Plant later dismissed not only the myths but also most of his own lyrics, Page remained intriguingly cagey, ensuring that rumours of – for example – their pact with Satan outlived the group itself.

Having helped to spawn Heavy Metal, Zeppelin left the genre to the likes of Black Sabbath and Deep Purple. Air guitarists were perplexed by *Led Zeppelin III* (1970), which buried rockers like 'The Immigrant Song' amidst acoustic tunesmithery. They repeated but refined the formula on *Led Zeppelin IV* (1971): pastoral on 'Going To California', seismic on 'When The Levee Breaks', both on 'Stairway To Heaven' (the most-played Rock track on radio). Despite being officially untitled and bearing no identification on the sleeve (the group's names appeared only as cod-mystic symbols), the album outstripped even its multi-platinum predecessors and their legendary status was assured.

Oddly, *Houses Of The Holy* (1973) sounded less like the work of stadium warlords than a playful garage band, with the lightweights 'Dancing Days', 'D'Yer Maker' and James Brown pastiche 'The Crunge'. Meanwhile, the Led legend was bolstered by a record-breakingly successful 1973 tour, commemorated by self-indulgent celluloid spin-off *The Song Remains The Same*, released three years later. True to superstar stereotype, Zeppelin launched – courtesy of the Atlantic label – their own 'vanity' imprint, Swan Song, whose greatest success came with Bad Company. Zep's debut on their own label was *Physical Graffiti* (1975), a hotch-potch of *Holy*

led zeppelin

relics and fresh classics, from which 'Kashmir' was later heralded as their peak by Plant, Page and Jones.

As the group prepared another globe-gobbling tour, Plant and his family were injured in a car crash. Instead of strutting stages, the singer found himself in a wheelchair, his anguish exacerbated by strained relations with the strung-out Page and domineering Grant. Stormy sessions produced the morbid *Presence* (1976), which sold only half as many as *Graffiti*. However, its punchy, Funk-tinged assault makes it their least dated-sounding work. More characteristic was *The Song Remains The Same* (1976), whose belated appearance had allowed for the insertion of stupefyingly indulgent 'fantasy sequences' (Plant as avenging knight, Page as sorcerer, etc). The accompanying soundtrack was an artistic and commercial nadir.

When Plant's son died of a stomach infection in 1977, obliging the cancellation of a US tour, it seemed the 'bad vibes' that surrounded the band had finally swallowed them. Young guns like The Clash took the opportunity to spit on their grave, although it's unlikely that Page – then in a heroin haze – cared. They reconvened in late 1978 at the request of Abba, who wanted a prestigious premiere for their new studio in Stockholm.

Jones seized the reins from Page to create the multi-flavoured *In Through The Out Door* (1979), whose highlights were the Caribbean confection 'Fool In The Rain' and bittersweet ballad 'All My Love'. Preceded by two epochal shows at Knebworth, the album was their last chart-topper. In America, it rejuvenated the record industry, then in post-Disco decline. The rebirth was short-lived: preparing for a US tour in September 1980, Bonham choked to death in an alcohol-induced stupor. The close-knit band announced their dissolution that December and capped their discography with out-takes collection *Coda* (1982) – whose mind-manglingly heavy 'Wearing And Tearing' was one of three classics inexplicably omitted from *In Through The Out Door*.

While Plant embarked on a solo career, Page cleaned up his act, although the artistic results – a soundtrack for *Death Wish II* (1982), a collaboration with Roy Harper (1985's *Whatever Happened To Jugula*), two albums with Paul Rodgers as The Firm and solo effort *Outrider* (1988) – scarcely matched expectations.

Meanwhile, the band's reputation spiralled further into the realms of the fantastic. Reunions in 1985 for Live Aid (with Phil Collins and Chic's Tony Thompson deputizing on drums) and in 1988 for Atlantic's 25th Anniversary (with Bonham's son Jason) were hailed as Second Comings. The sensationalist biography *Hammer Of The Gods* (1985) enshrined many a lewd legend (notably the unusual use of a shark in a groupie encounter), and became a tour bible for Goth goons The Mission, whose aspirations were sealed by John Paul Jones' production of their *Children* (1988). Stateside, Jane's Addiction pursued a similar agenda, while Kingdom Come cleaned up with a 1988 album that barely bothered to disguise its steals. Less reverentially, Dread Zeppelin were an Elvis impersonator-fronted 'tribute' band and Zep samples littered The Beastie Boys' *Licensed To Ill* (1986). The band were in no position to complain, having been found guilty of plagiarizing Blues legend Willie Dixon on 'Whole Lotta Love'. Other victims of the light-fingered Ledders included Robert Johnson and Howlin' Wolf.

Resigned to their legacy, the principals turned Zepwards once more: Plant with the riff-packed *Manic Nirvana* (1990), Page with a remastering programme that yielded 1990's 'hits' set *Remasters* and the multi-platinum box set *Led Zeppelin*. Plant continued to resist the lure of a full-scale reunion, forcing Page into the arms of David Coverdale – whose late 80s incarnation of Whitesnake had been another shameless rip-off. Greeted with contempt by Plant (who instead endorsed Rolf Harris' 1993 hit pastiche of 'Stairway To Heaven') and coolly by consumers, *Coverdale Page* (1993) nonetheless came closer to former glories.

Finally, after the career-mopping *Boxed Set 2* (1993), the duo re-formed for an MTV live set, calling themselves Page & Plant. Released as *No Quarter – Unledded* (1994), it featured distinctly Eastern remodels of classics alongside esoteric newies. Plant later remodelled 'Down On The Seaside', from *Physical Graffiti*, with Tori Amos for 1995's *Enconium – A Tribute To Led Zeppelin*, also featuring Sheryl Crow, Helmet and The Rollins Band.

A following world tour saw Page & Plant mixing Zep classics with oddities like Cure covers (their guitarist Porl Thompson was a former Robert Smith stooge) and cuts from the *Coverdale Page* album. This unsentimental attitude to their heritage presaged a union with former Big Black noisenik Steve Albini (of Nirvana and PJ Harvey production fame) for 1998's *Walking Into Clarksdale* (birthplace of John Lee Hooker and the Blues).

John Paul Jones – excluded from the Page & Plant project – collaborated with arty types Brian Eno, REM (arrangements on *Automatic For The People*) and Diamanda Galas and produced the rocking likes of Heart, Butthole Surfers and Cinderella.

Peter Grant died of a heart attack in November 1995 but, in 1997, Zepmania proved alive and kicking with *BBC Sessions* and a hit reissue of 'Whole Lotta Love' – their first UK single. Years after Zeppelin became the only band to beat The Beatles with eight consecutive *Melody Maker* 'Best Group of the Year' awards, they were confirmed by the Recording Industry Association of America as second only to The Beatles among Rock's all-time best-sellers, having sold 63.8 million records worldwide.

Read *Led Zeppelin – A Celebration* (1995), Dave Lewis

Fan Tight But Loose, 14 Totnes Close, Bedford, MK40 3AX, UK

Surf www.linwood.demon.co.uk/

THE LEMONHEADS

WHO Vocals/guitar **Evan Dando** (b. 4 Mar 1967, Boston, Massachusetts, USA), guitar **John Strohm** (b. 23 Mar 1967), bass **Kenny Lyons** (b. 22 Apr 1956), drums **Patrick Murphy** (b. 21 Dec 1964)

WHEN 1986–

WHERE Boston, Massachusetts, USA

WHAT Bubblegum Grunge

Formed at college, The Lemonheads originally consisted of Evan Dando, Ben Deily, Jesse Peretz and Byron Hoagland. Their debut

'Laughing All The Way To The Cleaners' was released on Taang! Records in 1986, followed by *Hate Your Friends* (1987), *Creator* (1988), *Lick* (1989) and their Atlantic debut *Lovey* (1990).

Their UK chart debut, *It's A Shame About Ray* (1992), fused the Thrash-Punk tendencies of earlier releases with Dando's passion for Gram Parsons and kooky lyrics. In this, their most successful period (courtesy of their cover of Simon And Garfunkel's 'Mrs Robinson'), the line-up stabilized with drummer David Ryan and Australian guitarist Nic Dalton. *Come On Feel The Lemonheads* (1993) was released at the peak of their popularity. Accordingly, it spawned their greatest hit: the soaring 'Into Your Arms'.

In 1994 Dalton left to pursue his Half A Cow record label and Dando became something of an Oasis groupie (a collaboration with Noel Gallagher, 'Purple Parallelogram', was later shelved).

With new members, *Car Button Cloth* (1996) promised a comeback; however, this time around, the singer's spacey lyrics and vague timekeeping (he was bottled off stage at Glastonbury 1995 for delaying Portishead) seemed less endearing. After great singles like 'It's All True' bombed, The Lemonheads parted company from Atlantic in 1998.

Fan The Lemonheads Fan Club, Music Marketing Network, 240 Bridge Ave., Red Bank, NJ 07701, USA

Surf www.home.rica.net/furies/lemonheads.html

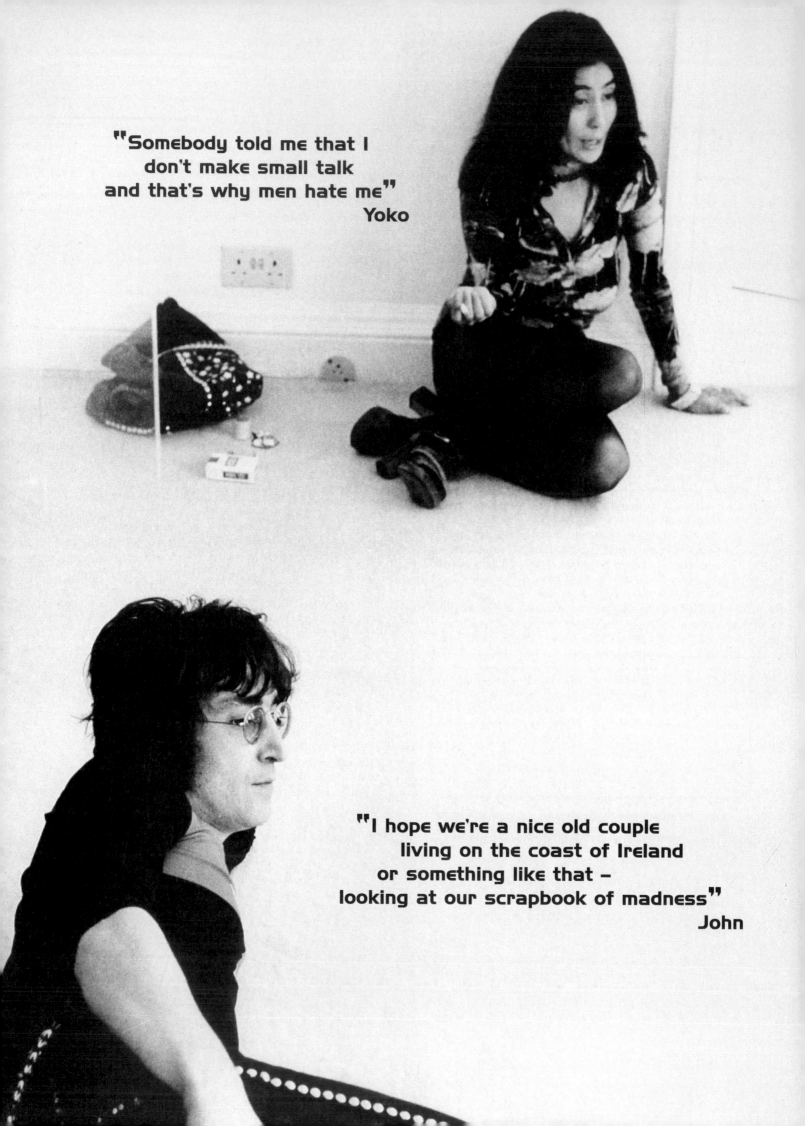

"Somebody told me that I
don't make small talk
and that's why men hate me"
Yoko

"I hope we're a nice old couple
living on the coast of Ireland
or something like that –
looking at our scrapbook of madness"
John

JOHN LENNON ⊙⊙⊙ ✪✪✪

WHO b. 9 Oct 1940, Liverpool, England, d. 8 Dec 1980, New York City, USA

WHAT The outspoken Beatle, peace movement icon & uncomfortable Pop star

The Beatles could not hold John Lennon indefinitely. By 1968, when he fell in love with Japanese avant-garde artist Yoko Ono (b. 18 Feb 1933, Tokyo, Japan), he was eager to find new outlets for his music.

His first extra-curricular works were experimental albums with Yoko: *Unfinished Music No. 1: Two Virgins* (1968), *Unfinished Music No. 2: Life With The Lions* (1969) and *The Wedding Album* (1969). Discordant collages of abstract noise and random speech, they found little favour with the record-buying public.

Increasingly distanced from the Fab Four, and preoccupied by his anti-war campaign, he recorded 'Give Peace A Chance' (1969) at the Montreal 'bed-in' (where John and Yoko invited the media into a hotel room, in which they were staying in bed for peace). The single was credited to the Plastic Ono Band – an ad hoc group whose subsequent personnel would include Eric Clapton. Their stage debut is commemorated on *Live Peace In Toronto* (1969), which previewed Lennon's next non-Beatle single, 'Cold Turkey', a harsh account of heroin addiction.

In February 1970, with The Beatles' split impending, John teamed up with legendary producer Phil Spector for the rousing 'Instant Karma', confirming him as a chart presence in his own right. Assisted by Spector and Ringo Starr, he made his first post-Beatle album, *John Lennon/Plastic Ono Band* (1970). Released simultaneously with Yoko's *Yoko Ono/Plastic Ono Band*, it was a stark affair, documenting his unsettled childhood ('Mother'), alienation from capitalist society ('Working Class Hero') and repudiation of stardom ('God'). His Leftist leanings acquired a more militant edge on the 1971 single 'Power To The People'. In September that year, John decamped with Yoko to New York; he was destined never to see Britain again.

In contrast to Yoko's adventurous *Fly* (1971), Lennon's *Imagine* (1971) was a conscious bid to rejoin the commercial mainstream. It became the biggest success of his solo career: the title track, an idealistic hymn to universal harmony, went high in the US chart and became Lennon's best-loved work. Other formidable cuts were 'Jealous Guy' and a savage satire on Paul McCartney, 'How Do You Sleep?', featuring co-conspirator George Harrison.

An end-of-year single, 'Happy Xmas (War Is Over)', reaffirmed Lennon's talent for the socially conscious sing-along. But his commercial knack soon deserted him. The Lennon/Ono album *Some Time In New York City* (1972) was a poorly received collection of Hard Rock protest songs, made with the New York band Elephant's Memory. The album's subject matter, ranging from the Irish conflict to black power, reflected Lennon's dalliance with the radical chic underground, but only the feminist proclamations 'Woman Is The Nigger Of The World' and Yoko's 'Sisters, O Sisters' were musically persuasive.

Since his arrival in America, Lennon had been threatened with deportation, officially because of a 1968 cannabis conviction in Britain, but fundamentally due to government fears that his fame would make him a figurehead for subversive causes. Sensing the instability of his position, Lennon began to withdraw from political agitation. In August 1972 he played two charity shows in Madison Square Garden, and moved from Greenwich Village to an exclusive uptown address, the Dakota

Building (hence Courtney Love's pro-Yoko cut with Hole, '20 Years In The Dakota').

Mind Games (1973) marked a return to the sweeter, more romantic style of *Imagine*, without that album's power or grace. With the exception of its soaring, mystic title track, *Mind Games* indicated a rather torpid phase in Lennon's life, dramatically curtailed when Yoko requested a trial separation. Moving to LA with his new lover May Pang, Lennon descended into a 15-month 'lost weekend' of heavy drinking. With fellow revellers such as Keith Moon, Ringo Starr and Harry Nilsson, he made unwelcome headlines through sporadic brawls in nightclubs.

With Phil Spector he attempted an album of Rock 'n' Roll oldies, but the chaotic sessions were abandoned. Meanwhile the US authorities continued their efforts to evict him.

Lennon returned to New York to produce Nilsson's *Pussy Cats* (1974), then made his own *Walls And Bridges* (1974). As well as providing his first US No.1 solo single, 'Whatever Gets You Thru The Night', it showed a striking return to form, evidenced by the classic Lennon compositions '#9 Dream' and 'Steel And Glass'. Several songs described the pain of his estrangement from Yoko. But the couple were reunited after Lennon's guest appearance at an Elton John concert (his final stage appearance), and he returned to the Dakota.

He celebrated 1975 with the belated release of his oldies record *Rock 'N' Roll* (salvaged from the Spector sessions) and the hits compilation *Shaved Fish*. Finally out of contract for the first time since The Beatles, he opted to take life easy, prompted by the birth of his child by Yoko, Sean Taro Ono Lennon, born on John's birthday. A court ruling allowed him official US residency, and Lennon began a five-year spell of domesticity, raising the baby while Yoko attended to their business affairs.

Lennon continued to write songs and record home demo tapes, but it was not until 1980, on holiday in Bermuda, that he began to formulate what became *Double Fantasy*. Released on Geffen in November 1980 to a muted welcome, there was some strong material in 'Woman', 'Beautiful Boy (Darling Boy)' and the first single '(Just Like) Starting Over'.

Tragedy struck on the night of 8 December 1980. Returning from recording Yoko's 'Walking On Thin Ice', John was gunned down on the steps of the Dakota. His killer, the unstable fan Mark Chapman, was arrested on the spot. In the aftermath of his murder, various songs became posthumous hits, followed by an album of unfinished material, *Milk And Honey* (1984).

Yoko, meanwhile, continued her musical career with the brilliant but harrowing *Season Of Glass* (1981), *It's Alright* (1983) and *Starpeace* (1985). In 1984, artists including Roberta Flack, Elvis Costello and Harry Nilsson contributed versions of her songs to *Every Man Has A Woman Who Loves Him*, while in 1994, Ono wrote a successful off-Broadway Rock opera, *New York Rock*.

Unreleased Lennon demos from the Dakota period became the basis of the Beatle reunion singles 'Free As A Bird' (1995) and 'Real Love' (1996). Meanwhile, Sean Lennon backed Yoko on 1995's *Rising* and, like his half brother Julian, began his own career with 1998's *Into The Sun*. As 1988's biopic *Imagine* and the tribute album *Working Class Hero* (1995) proved, John Lennon was a songwriter and cultural icon of the first magnitude, cherished for his wit, honesty and social commitment.

Read *We All Shine On: The Solo Songs Of John Lennon* (1997), Paul Du Noyer

Surf bag.home.ml.org/

ANNIE LENNOX ◉ ◉

WHO b. 25 Dec 1954, Aberdeen, Scotland

WHAT Slow-working spell-weaver

After a tenement childhood, Lennox won a Royal Academy Of Music flute scholarship aged 17. She didn't complete it, partly because she met and fell for Dave Stewart, already committed to Rock life. United, they formed The Catch (who stayed unknown), The Tourists (who had some success), then Eurythmics.

When Eurythmics split in 1989, Lennox took time out with her husband Uri Fruchtman. After their daughter, Lola, was born in 1990, Lennox wrote and recorded her solo debut *Diva* (1992) at home, so she could take care of her baby. Although slower and darker than most Eurythmics albums, *Diva* produced six hits, including 'Why', 'Walking On Broken Glass' and 'Little Bird', the latter twinned with the breathtaking 'Love Song For A Vampire' from the 1992 movie *Bram Stoker's Dracula*. Charting for a year, *Diva* sold over 5 million worldwide, earning her Best Album Of The Year at the BRIT awards and the fifth of her six BRITs as Best British Female Artist.

Pausing to have another baby, Lennox then released her second UK No.1 and US No.11 *Medusa* (1995), which comprised versions of her favourite songs, among them Procol Harum's

'Whiter Shade Of Pale', the single to which she had "reappraised boys" when she was 13. Although she covered songs by Bob Marley, Al Green, Paul Simon, Neil Young and The Clash, the obscure The Lover Speaks' 'No More "I Love You's"' proved the biggest hit and took a Grammy for Best Female Pop Vocal.

Live In Central Park, recorded in September 1995, was packaged with limited editions of *Medusa* in some countries, but Lennox played few solo concerts and paused only to pen the movie theme 'Step By Step' for Whitney Houston's *The Preacher's Wife* (1996) before withdrawing to domestic heaven once more.

ᴿᴱᴬᴰ *Annie Lennox* (1991), Lucy O'Brien

ˢᵘʳᶠ www.well.com/user/sunspot/annielennox.htm

LEVEL 42

WHO Vocals/bass **Mark King** (b. 20 Oct 1958, Cowes, Isle of Wight, England), guitar **Boon Gould** (b. Roland Gould, 4 Mar 1955, Shanklin, Isle of Wight), drums **Phil Gould** (b. 28 Feb 1957, Hong Kong), keyboards/vocals **Mike Lindup** (b. 17 Mar 1959, London, England)

WHEN 1980–1994

WHERE London, England

WHAT Bass-driven Funk Popsters

Mark King and the Gould brothers moved to London in the late 70s, enlisted Mike Lindup and formed Level 42 – named after the meaning of life ("42") in Douglas Adams' novel *The Hitch Hiker's Guide To The Galaxy*. Driven by former drummer King's virtuoso thumb-slapped bass, *Level 42* (1981), *The Pursuit Of Accidents* (1982) and *Standing In The Light* (1983) spawned occasional hits, notably 1983's 'The Sun Goes Down (Living It Up)'.

Diluting Funk to Pop, *True Colours* (1984) and *A Physical Presence* (1985) began a commercial upswing which peaked with *World Machine* (1985) and *Running In The Family* (1987). The Goulds exited in 1987, *Staring At The Sun* (1988) and *Guaranteed* (1991) were only fleetingly successful and few tears were shed when *Forever Now* (1994) turned out to be their last gasp.

ˢᵘʳᶠ kumo.swcp.com/synth/level42/

LEVELLERS ◉

WHO Vocals/guitar **Mark Chadwick** (b. 23 Jun 1966, Münster, Germany), guitar **Simon Friend** (b. 17 May 1967, London, England), bass **Jeremy Cunningham** (b. 2 Jun 1965, Cuckfield, West Sussex, England), drums **Charlie Heather** (b. 2 Feb 1964, Beckenham, Kent, England), violin **Jon Sevink** (b. 15 May 1965, Harlow, Essex, England)

WHEN 1988–

WHERE Brighton, East Sussex, England

WHAT Eco Folk Punksters

Named after a 17th-century English republican movement, Levellers' rebel music transcends shifting trends. Initially

ignored by the press, they toured relentlessly and built a following with the righteous energy and anthemic choruses of 1990's *A Weapon Called The Word*. British and European commercial success came in 1991 with *Levelling The Land*, but critical acclaim remained elusive: the band were ridiculed as 'crusties' because of their association with travellers – just one of the radical movements the band have supported.

Whatever the papers said, each album increased the band's following, with 1993's *Levellers* hitting UK No.2 and *Zeitgeist* reaching UK No.1 in 1995. Their lyrics became less polemical and more personal on 1997's *Mouth To Mouth*, but Levellers have always found imaginative new ways to support their causes. In late 1997, they announced plans for the world's first 'carbon neutral' tour, promising to plant enough trees to compensate for the carbon the tour would emit into the atmosphere.

Fan On The Fiddle, PO Box 2600, Brighton, East Sussex, BN 2DX, UK

surf www.levellers.co.uk/

HUEY LEWIS & THE NEWS ✪ ✪

WHO Vocals/harmonica **Huey Lewis** (b. Hugh Cregg III, 5 Jul 1950, New York City, New York, USA), guitar **Chris Hayes** (b. 24 Nov 1957, California, USA), bass **Mario Cipollina** (b. 10 Nov 1954, California), drums **Bill Gibson** (b. 13 Nov 1951, California), keyboards **Sean Hopper** (b. 31 Mar 1953, California), saxophone/guitar **Johnny Colla** (b. 2 Jul 1952, California)

WHEN 1979–

WHERE Marin County, California, USA

WHAT Good-time 80s Pop

Formerly of Clover (the Country Rock protégés of Nick Lowe and Elvis Costello's band on *My Aim Is True*), Huey Lewis and Sean Hopper returned to California from a stint in Britain. With bar-band jammers Cipollina, Colla and Gibson, they became the litigation-baiting American Express who, signed to Chrysalis after adding guitarist Hayes, became Huey Lewis & The News.

Their self-titled 1980 debut raised few roofs, but 1982's *Picture This* was propelled into the US chart by the hit 'Do You Believe In Love'. More smashes – from 1983's 7-million-selling *Sports* – included 'If This Is It' and 'I Want A New Drug'. The latter's uncanny similarity to Ray Parker Jr's 'Ghostbusters' (1984) was not lost on Lewis, who sued and won an out-of-court settlement.

The US chart-topping 'The Power Of Love', from 1985's mega-movie *Back To The Future*, prefaced *Fore!* (1986). Its hits included 'Hip To Be Square' (a sort of anthem for their Yuppie fans) and yet more US No.1s, 'Stuck With You' and 'Jacob's Ladder'.

After *Small World* (1988) and *Hard At Play* (1991), oblivion beckoned, but a live following and the covers album *Four Chords & Several Years Ago* (1994) kept them in credit. They were also immortalized in Bret Easton Ellis' early 90s novel *American Psycho*, whose horrible narrative is broken by bafflingly faithful biographies of the News, Genesis and Whitney Houston.

Read *Huey Lewis And The News* (1987), Andrew Douglas

Fan Newsline II, PO Box 99, Payson, UT 84651, USA

surf www.geocities.com/Hollywood/Set/3884/

JERRY LEE LEWIS ☉

WHO b. 29 Sep 1935, Ferriday, Louisiana, USA

WHAT Archetypal Rock 'n' Roll wildman

Had notoriety not hindered him, Jerry Lee could have rivalled Elvis. Nicknamed 'The Killer' at school, Lewis signed to Sam Phillips' Sun Records in 1956, replacing the recently departed Elvis. Raised on Country but energized by Rock 'n' Roll, he used his prodigious piano skills to innovatory effect: pounding chords with his hands and feet, flipping the stool, jumping, smashing the keyboard and yelping lyrics fuelled by fire and brimstone – a remnant of his religious background (his cousin was disgraced 80s televangelist Jimmy Swaggart).

Local sales translated into national hits when 1957's 'Whole Lotta Shakin' Going On' (US No.3) and 1958's 'Great Balls Of Fire' (US No.2) sold millions. Reeling from Elvis, the Church and media came down particularly hard on Lewis. During his first UK tour in 1958, his third wife Myra was revealed to be not only his cousin but also just 13. He continued to suffer personal problems – two later wives and two sons were killed in accidents, Lewis was arrested outside Elvis' Graceland mansion for possession of firearms, he accidently shot his bassist in 1976 and he has since battled ill health and the IRS.

After the hits – notably 'High School Confidential', 'Break Up' and 'Breathless' (all 1958) – dried up, Lewis lapsed into relative

obscurity until the late 60s, when he began to score US Country No.1s, including 'To Make Love Sweeter For You' (1968) and 'There Must Be More To Love Than This' (1971).

A resurgence of Rock 'n' Roll in the early 70s prompted a comeback. Lewis recorded 1973's *The Session* in London, its all-star cast including Rory Gallagher, Alvin Lee and Peter Frampton. Relentless touring – interrupted by life-or-death surgery for a stomach ulcer – balanced weak sales, but his legendary status was confirmed by *The Survivors* (a 1981 reunion with Sun comrades Johnny Cash, Carl Perkins and Roy Orbison, released in 1982) and *Class Of '55* (1986). His career was the subject of 1988's biopic *Great Balls Of Fire*, starring Dennis Quaid as Jerry Lee, for which he re-recorded many of his hits. 'The Killer' stills records and tours on a regular basis.

read *Killer* (1995), Jerry Lee Lewis & Charles White

fan Fire-Ball Mail, 16 Milton Road, Wimbledon, London, SW19, UK

surf www.student.tdb.uu.se/~m93aum/jerry.html

LIGHTHOUSE FAMILY

WHO Vocals **Tunde Baiyewu** (b. 25 Nov 1968, London, England), keyboards

Paul Tucker (b. 12 Aug 1968, London)

WHEN 1993–

WHERE Newcastle upon Tyne, England

WHAT Soul music for the masses

Songwriter Paul Tucker found singer Tunde Baiyewu when the two were studying in Newcastle and asked him to warble on a demo called 'Ocean Drive'. "We were Soul," he said, "which is the family part and I think a lighthouse is a friendly thing." Polydor liked the demo and reportedly gave them a quarter of a million pounds to record it properly. In 1995, 'Lifted' and 'Ocean Drive' scraped the lower reaches of the UK chart, then disappeared. 'Lifted' (Summery Soul à la Seal) was remixed for 1996 and smashed into the UK Top 10, followed by a reissued 'Ocean Drive'.

All of a sudden, *Ocean Drive* (1995) was glued to the chart and you couldn't turn on the radio or the TV without hearing one of the hits. "Our record is more like British Pop music at the moment than Britpop is," Tucker declared triumphantly. "Britpop isn't Pop at all, it's bloody Rock!" In 1997, they did it again with *Postcards From Heaven* and another inescapable biggie, 'Raincloud'.

surf www.abc.se/~m8877/LHouse/LFamily.html

LIGHTNING SEEDS

WHO Ian Broudie, b. 4 Aug 1958, Liverpool, England

WHEN 1989–

WHERE Liverpool, England

WHAT Perfect Pop purity

Lightning Seeds captured the spirit of the time with the Euro 96 football tournament anthem and UK No.1 'Three Lions', written with comedians Frank Skinner and David Baddiel. The English sound and catchy chorus typify the work of songwriter Ian Broudie, whose career began in 1977 when he joined Liverpool Art Punkers, Big In Japan. Bandmates included Bill Drummond (KLF), Holly Johnson (Frankie Goes To Hollywood), Budgie (Slits and Siouxsie & the Banshees), Pete Burns (Dead Or Alive) and Dave Balfe (The Teardrop Explodes, founder of Food Records).

Throwing himself into work as a producer when two further bands (Original Mirrors and Care) didn't work out, Broudie made his name with Echo & The Bunnymen, The Icicle Works and The Fall, among others. This work brought Broudie to the attention of Ghetto Records, who signed him as a studio-based solo artist, recording as Lightning Seeds (he later moved to Virgin, then Epic). 'Pure', reflecting his 60s Pop and New Order influences, reached UK No.16 in July 1989 and presaged his debut *Cloud Cuckooland* (1990). Applauded for Broudie's ability to craft 'perfect Pop', it was a critical rather than commercial success and initiated on-going collaborations with Ian McNabb (The Icicle Works) and Simon Rogers (The Fall).

Sense (1992) introduced a preoccupation with drum loops and samples and a fruitful union with Terry Hall. Although the single 'Life Of Riley' initially failed to match the success of 'Pure', it was used weekly on BBC TV's *Match Of The Day*.

In between writing his next album, Broudie produced Sleeper, The Wedding Present, The Primitives, Dodgy and Terry Hall. He also co-wrote and produced Alison Moyet's *Essex*.

The double platinum *Jollification* (1994) finally realized Lightning Seeds' commercial potential and 'Lucky You', 'Change', and 'Marvellous' were all hits. Although insecure about his voice, Broudie toured to promote the album, the line-up including Chris Sharrock (The La's) on drums, Paul Hemmings on guitar and Martin Campbell (Rain) on bass.

The touring band reappeared on *Dizzy Heights* (1996). Rawer than before, it featured collaborations with Stephen Jones (Baby Bird) and Nicky Wire (Manic Street Preachers). A best-of collection, *Like You Do*, kept the momentum going in 1997.

 www.penna.demon.co.uk/pureseeds/

LINDISFARNE ◉

WHO Vocals/guitar/piano **Alan Hull** (b. 20 Feb 1945, Newcastle upon Tyne, England, d. 17 Nov 1996, Newcastle upon Tyne), vocals/harmonica/mandolin **Ray Jackson** (b. 12 Dec 1948, Wallsend, England), guitar **Simon Cowe** (b. 1 Apr 1948, Jesmond Dene, England), bass/violin **Rod Clements** (b. 17 Nov 1947, North Shields, England), drums **Ray Laidlaw** (b. 28 May 1948, North Shields)

WHEN 1969–

WHERE Newcastle upon Tyne, England

WHAT Folk Rock perennials

Lindisfarne blended wistful sensitivity, socialist sentiments and boozy revelry. With their roots in Tyneside R&B bands (Alan Hull having recorded with The Chosen Few and as a solo artist), they united when the bluesy Downtown Faction (essentially four-fifths of Lindisfarne) became The Brethren, secured a following in the city of Hull, Yorkshire, and, by 1969, co-opted Hull to join.

Signed to Charisma as Lindisfarne in 1970, their *Nicely Out Of Tune* debut was quirky and refreshing, belatedly charting on the back of two 1972 UK hits ('Meet Me On The Corner' and 'Lady Eleanor') and their definitive second album *Fog On The Tyne* – a UK No.1 and the biggest-selling British LP of 1971. Exhaustive touring enhanced their reputation, but contributed to a split in 1973 after the disappointing *Dingly Dell* (1972).

Two Christmas reunion shows at Newcastle City Hall in 1976 initiated a now annual event, while a fine comeback, *Back And Fourth* (1978), included their last major UK (and only US) hit 'Run For Home'. Later recordings have been patchy or, like the bizarre 1990 UK No.2 revamp of 'Fog On The Tyne' with soccer star Paul Gascoigne, critically suicidal. Nevertheless, Lindisfarne have maintained their impregnable live reputation. When Hull died of heart failure in 1995, it was at the end of the group's busiest year.

Following amicable personnel changes and the renaissance of roots music, Lindisfarne – now based around Clements and Laidlaw – remain an English institution.

READ *Fog On The Tyne* (1998), Dave Hill

FAN Magic In The Air, 14 Victoria Terrace, Whitley Bay, Newcastle upon Tyne, NE26 2QW, UK

LITTLE FEAT

WHO Vocals/guitar/harmonica **Lowell George** (b. 13 Apr 1945, Hollywood, California, d. 29 Jun 1979, Arlington, Virginia, USA), vocals/guitar **Paul Barrère** (b. 3 Jul 1948, Burbank, California, USA), bass **Kenny Gradney** (b. New Orleans, Louisiana, USA), drums **Richie Hayward** (b. Ames, Iowa, USA), keyboards/vocals **Bill Payne** (b. 12 Mar 1949, Waco, Texas, USA), percussion **Sam Clayton** (b. Colfax, Louisiana)

WHEN 1969–

WHERE Los Angeles, California, USA

WHAT Supple polyrhythmic Southern Boogie

Little Feat are a masterpiece of mid-70s America. Lowell George, the band's pivotal figure, established himself as a remarkable instrumentalist by his late teens, when he played oboe and sax on Frank Sinatra sessions. But his passion was slide guitar. From 1965, he meandered through sojourns with flop psychedelic Folksters The Factory, fading hitmakers The Standells and Frank Zappa's Mothers Of Invention (he sang on 1970's *Weasels Ripped My Flesh*). In 1969, he decided to start his own band.

Swiping Mothers' bassist Roy Estrada, he enlisted former Factory drummer Hayward and keyboard player Payne to record *Little Feat* (1970) and *Sailin' Shoes* (1972) for Warner Bros. Their attempts at a feel similar to early material by The Band proved commercially fruitless. Even so, 'Willing', included on both albums, affirmed George's gift for gritty Country, and 'Sailin' Shoes' introduced Little Feat's slippery Southern Boogie.

The flops provoked an upheaval from which the classic Little Feat emerged. Estrada departed to Captain Beefheart's Magic Band. In came Gradney and Clayton from Delaney & Bonnie (both, significantly, from Louisiana), plus guitarist Barrère. Nonetheless, *Dixie Chicken* (1973) stiffed, Warner Bros began to lose interest and it seemed that Feat might break up unfulfilled.

But co-manager Bob Cavallo found a cheap studio, Blue Sea, on a barge near Baltimore, Maryland, whence flowed *Feats Don't Fail Me Now* (1974). Their first chart success, it featured 'Rock And Roll Doctor'. Then *The Last Record Album* (1975) rose to the US and UK Top 40 and was the band's artistic apogee: an ecstatic synthesis of California, New Orleans and Memphis.

Sadly, with George's creativity succumbing to cocaine, steep decline set in, evidenced by *Time Loves A Hero* (1977). Payne and Barrère's Steely Dan imitations didn't help. Surprisingly, the live *Waiting For Columbus* (1978) became their best-seller, peaking at US No.18. But by the following year it was all over.

George released a solo album, *Thanks I'll Eat It Here* (1979) – with few original compositions – and announced he was leaving. The rest finished *Down On The Farm* (1979), then disbanded. Before its release, George died of a heart attack in a hotel room after a gig on his first solo tour.

Hoy-Hoy! (1981), a collection of out-takes, seemed Little Feat's last word until, in 1987, the five remaining members reconvened, augmented by Craig Fuller (vocals), formerly of Pure Prairie League, and guitarist Fred Tackett. They toured and made four decent albums (the latest with Fuller replaced by female singer Shaun Murphy), but Little Feat's swampy voodoo died long ago.

FAN Featprints, PO Box 603, Mt Airy, Maryland 21771-0603, USA

LITTLE RICHARD

WHO b. Richard Wayne Penniman, 5 Dec 1932, Macon, Georgia, USA

WHAT Wild Rock 'n' Roller

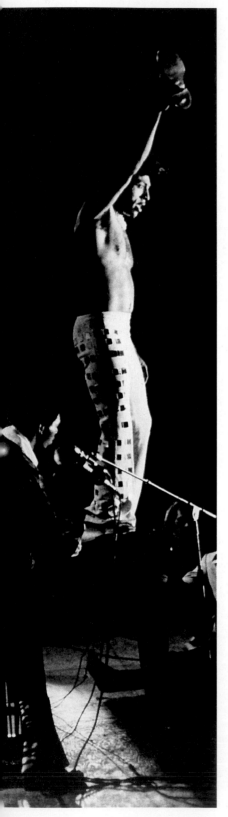

Little Richard is a Rock 'n' Roll legend whose influence can be heard in the work of countless artists, from The Beatles to Bob Dylan to David Bowie. In the late 50s, his no-holds-barred vocal style and untamed stage show shocked the older generation and earned him a fervent teen following.

Raised on Gospel and R&B, Richard won a talent competition in 1951, which led to RCA's Steve Sholes offering him a contract (four years later Sholes signed Elvis Presley). His first tracks were cut in Atlanta under the guidance of R&B artist Billy Wright, who influenced his sound and image. 'Taxi Blues' was the first of four urban Blues singles he released on RCA, none of which sold enough to convince the company to renew his contract.

In 1953 he moved to Houston, Texas, and recorded four sides for Peacock Records. 'Ain't That Good News' created enough interest for the label to cut another handful of tracks with Johnny Otis, one of R&B's top producers. But these proved disappointing and surfaced only after Richard became famous.

After touring the South for the next three years with his band The Upsetters, the turning point came when R&B star Lloyd Price directed him towards his label, Specialty, then "looking for a new sound". Hearing potential in the 20-year-old, they bought his contract from Peacock. Among the dozen tracks producer Robert 'Bumps' Blackwell recorded with him in New Orleans in September 1955 was Rock 'n' Roll classic 'Tutti Frutti'. It rocketed into the R&B Top 5 and entered the US Pop chart the week Elvis recorded his debut hit, 'Heartbreak Hotel'.

'Long Tall Sally' proved even more successful: it topped the R&B chart and was his first US Top 10 hit – despite being covered by clean-cut Pat Boone, who had also successfully recorded 'Tutti Frutti'. Frank Zappa later commented, "Pat Boone singing Little Richard numbers – an absolutely disgusting phenomenon. Can't you just hear his white buck shoes stomping in the distance?!"

Richard's first UK single was 'Rip It Up', in November 1956, which failed to top Bill Haley's earlier released cover version. Nonetheless, his UK follow-up – 'Long Tall Sally'/'Tutti Frutti' – cracked the Top 3, thanks in part to his tearaway treatment of the songs in the movie *Don't Knock The Rock*. This was followed by 'The Girl Can't Help It', 'She's Got It' (both from the movie *The Girl Can't Help It*), 'Lucille', 'Keep A' Knockin'' (both from the movie *Mr. Rock & Roll*) and 'Jenny Jenny' – all major transatlantic hits.

Rumours started circulating about this uninhibited Rocker; that he had died, been put into a mental institution or given up Rock 'n' Roll to enter the church. The latter proved true when, during an Australian tour in October 1957, Richard amazed the Rock 'n' Roll world by announcing he was quitting to enter a theological college. Specialty kept him in the charts by releasing old cuts such as 'Good Golly Miss Molly' and 'Baby Face', his UK chart peak, in 1958, and 'Whole Lotta Shakin' Goin' On' in 1959.

> **"I used to wait outside closed record stores... to be the first in town to get the new Little Richard single. I was just crazy about him'**
>
> **David Bowie**

In late 1962, Richard came out of Rock retirement and made his UK stage debut. Although his trademark pompadour hairstyle had been shorn, the piano pounding Rock 'n' Roller was a top drawing card. Apart from headlining over The Beatles in Liverpool, he was also brought in to top the bill when tickets for a tour which included The Rolling Stones were selling slowly.

After a short second spell at Specialty, Richard recorded for Vee Jay (some tracks featuring band member Jimi Hendrix), Modern, Okeh, Brunswick and Reprise. However, these records sold relatively few and most of his audience only wanted to hear good old Rock 'n' Roll, although by the early 70s he was performing a more camp, glittery Las Vegas version of it.

Richard rejoined the church in 1976, after his brother Tony's death, and spent most of the next ten years preaching. When the Rock And Roll Hall Of Fame was founded in 1986, he was among the first artists inducted. Since then, the 'wild man of Rock' has become a media celebrity, appearing in movies (such as the 1986 box office smash *Down And Out In Beverly Hills*) and videos. He is also a regular awards presenter, TV chat show guest and even helped close the Olympic Games in 1996.

In the 90s, Richard guested with other artists, notably on Jon Bon Jovi's 1990 soundtrack *Young Guns II*. "Little Richard was my *father's* idol," marvelled Bon Jovi, "and here I was introducing Jeff Beck to Little Richard!" Richard also provided the highlight of *A Vision Shared (A Tribute To Woody Guthrie And Leadbelly)* (1988): a crazed rendition of Leadbelly's 'Rock Island Line', featuring Funk Rockers Fishbone and organist Jimmy Stewart.

The man who helped to revolutionize popular music in the 50s was presented with a Lifetime Achievement Grammy in 1993 and a similar award from the R&B Foundation a year later.

Ⓡⓔⓐⓓ *The Life & Times Of Little Richard* (1994), Charles White

Ⓕⓐⓝ Now Dig This, 19 South Hill Road, Bensham, Gateshead, Tyne and Wear, NE8 2XZ, UK

The most ambitious live music spectacle ever staged took place on Saturday, 13 July 1985 – now recognized in the USA as Live Aid Day. For his ambitious telethon, Bob Geldof (aided by promoters Harvey Goldsmith and Bill Graham) drew on legends like Bowie, Dylan, Led Zeppelin and The Who (arm-twisted into re-forming for the occasion) and superstars such as Paul McCartney and Madonna. He even found room for soon-to-be superstars like Bryan Adams and INXS, and for a musical spectrum from Synth Pop (Howard Jones) to Rap (Run DMC). They were watched by 1.5 billion people worldwide.

Geldof resolved to stretch communication technology to its limit to create a 'Global Jukebox'. Satellites fed concurrent shows in London's Wembley Stadium and Philadelphia's JFK Stadium to countries worldwide, who also organized their own shows and fund-raising. For five hours, performances alternated between continents. Mick Jagger and David Bowie had hoped to duet via satellite, but the time-lag proved insurmountable and they submitted a hastily prepared video of 'Dancing In The Street'. The global symbolism was confirmed by Phil Collins, whose Atlantic crossing in Concorde enabled him to play Wembley in the afternoon and JFK that evening.

Live Aid arose from moral outrage triggered in Geldof by 1984 news footage of the horrific Ethiopian famine. 'Do They Know It's Christmas?' – the record he and Midge Ure put together under the self-deprecating name Band Aid – featured chart-topping names and became the biggest-selling UK single to that date, raising millions for famine relief. Geldof and his team of volunteers steered a path through the red tape of the international aid trade, directing funds at the most glaring gaps in the charity patchwork. Live Aid was the next logical step. Geldof popped up on TV between the 15-minute performance slots to badger his worldwide audience into giving money. Moving film of a child crippled by starvation – soundtracked by The Cars' haunting 'Drive' – reminded audiences why it was all happening. The Band Aid trust increased its funds tenfold in a day.

Through pragmatism and fearless confrontation of world leaders, Geldof proved an articulate spokesman. By the sheer force of apolitical arguing, he bent the cast-iron machinery of capitalism to his will. Live Aid was the 80s flipside of Woodstock: all ideology abandoned in the name of practicality. An exhausted Geldof wound up the operation at the end of 1985, handing over subsequent donations to conventional aid agencies. Although Live Aid spawned similar events – including Farm Aid in the USA and Britain's Comic Relief – his amazing spontaneity, inventiveness and determination to work outside established channels have never been replicated.

Wembley

Status Quo (set the stadium bouncing), The Style Council, The Boomtown Rats (big dramatic pause in 'I Don't Like Mondays'), Adam Ant, Ultravox (played 'Vienna', of course), Spandau Ballet (did 'True', of course), Elvis Costello (strummed "old Northern love song" 'All You Need Is Love'), Nik Kershaw, Sade (looked fab), Sting (ditto), Phil Collins, Howard Jones, Bryan Ferry (plugged Boys And Girls), Paul Young (duetted with Alison Moyet), U2 (pulled woman out of audience during 'Bad'), Dire Straits and Sting, Queen (didn't finish writing 'One Vision' in time, did hits instead), Bowie & Jagger (video), David Bowie (made 'Heroes' a global anthem), The Who (re-formed for the occasion, TV coverage broke down, Pete Townshend did the splits and fell down), Elton John (duetted with Kiki Dee and Wham!), Freddie Mercury & Brian May (did 'Is This The World We Created?'), Paul McCartney (didn't realize microphone wasn't working, but crowd carried the lyrics to 'Let It Be'), McCartney/Bowie/Townshend/Moyet/Geldof (had a good old sing-along), The Band-Aid All-Stars ("Feed the wo–ooorld," etc).

JFK

Bernard Watson, Joan Baez, The Hooters, The Four Tops (spangly silver jackets, of course), Billy Ocean, Black Sabbath (did 'Paranoid', of course), Run DMC, Rick Springfield (Springsteen substitute), REO Speedwagon (national grid drains as entire UK switches kettles on), Crosby, Stills & Nash (& Young), Judas Priest, Geldof welcomes USA, Bryan Adams, The Beach Boys, George Thorogood & The Destroyers (with Bo Diddley and Albert Collins), Bowie & Jagger (video), Simple Minds, The Pretenders (rocked), Santana & Pat Metheny, Ashford & Simpson (with Teddy Pendergrass), Madonna, Tom Petty, Kenny Loggins, The Cars, Neil Young, The Power Station, The Thompson Twins (featuring Madonna on tambourine), Eric Clapton (revived his career), Phil Collins (marvelled at the wonders of aviation), Led Zeppelin (clearly lacking match practice), Duran Duran (play then No.1 'View To A Kill'), Patti LaBelle, Hall & Oates (with Eddie Kendricks and David Ruffin), Mick Jagger (pulled Tina Turner's skirt off), Bob Dylan with Keith Richards and Ron Wood (mumbled about aid for farmers), USA For Africa ("We are the world" etc).

AND ELSEWHERE...

INXS (Melbourne), Loudness (Japan), Opus (Vienna), B.B. King (The Hague), Yu Rock Mission (Belgrade), Autograph (Moscow), Udo Lindenberg (Cologne).

WEMBLEY STADIUM

Harvey Goldsmith, Maurice Jones & Bob Geldof present for

BAND AID

LIVE AID

(See Press for details)

TURNSTILES

F

SAT., 13 JULY, 1985

GATES OPEN 10.00 a.m.

No ticket genuine unless it carries the Wembley Lion superimposed on the Towers

7000

Ticket £5 incl. VAT plus £20 donation
All proceeds to BAND AID

TO BE RETAINED | ISSUED SUBJECT TO THE CONDITIONS ON BACK

ROCK L PEDIA

LIVING COLOUR

WHO Vocals **Corey Glover** (b. 6 Nov 1964, Brooklyn, New York, USA), guitar
Vernon Reid (b. 22 Aug 1958, London, England), bass **Muzz Skillings**
(b. Manuel Skillings, 6 Jan 1960, Queens, New York), drums **William Calhoun**
(b. 22 Jul 1964, Brooklyn)

WHEN 1983–1995

WHERE Brooklyn, New York, USA

WHAT Politically aware Metal

Named after an NBC TV introduction ("The following programme is brought to you in living colour"), Living Colour spearheaded 'The Black Rock Coalition' – promoting awareness of African American artists' importance to Rock. They backed Mick Jagger on his *Primitive Cool* (1986) and Vernon Reid guested with Public Enemy. A Jagger-produced demo clinched a deal with Epic and *Vivid* (1988) began a slow climb up the US chart, aided by the hit 'Cult Of Personality'. After more Stonesy shenanigans (support slots, Reid's appearance on Keith Richards' 1988 *Talk Is Cheap*), *Time's Up* (1990) spawned the UK hit 'Love Rears Its Ugly Head'.

However, by 1991's 'Biscuits' EP, Living Colour's Funk Metal was overtaken by Grunge and internal rifts prompted Skillings' replacement with session bassist Doug Wimbish for 1993's swan song, *Stain*. Reid released his solo debut *Mistaken Identity* (1996).

SURF www.geocities.com/Hollywood/Hills/9892/

LL COOL J

WHO b. James Todd Smith, 16 Aug 1968, Queens, New York, USA

WHAT Rap's smooth-talking superstar

Rap's endurance champion, 'Ladies Love Cool James' exploded with classics like 'I Need A Beat' from *Radio* (1985). His good-humoured arrogance and gold chains epitomized pre-Gangsta Rap – hence *Bigger And Deffer* (1987). The latter's hit ballad 'I Need Love' was a first for the genre, but weakened his credibility – a decline accelerated when *Walking With A Panther* (1989) emerged post-Gangsta and LL participated in First Lady Nancy Reagan's anti-drug campaign.

Mama Said Knock You Out (1990) was a spectacular comeback and *14 Shots To The Dome* (1993) became a sixth platinum chart-buster. After false starts in the movies *The Hard Way* (1991) and *Toys* (1992), his acting took off with the US TV series *In The House*.

Mr. Smith (1995) spawned a clutch of hits, of which 'I Shot Ya' launched Rap rude-girl Foxy Brown, who returned the favour by revamping his 'Rock The Bells' on her platinum *Ill Na Na* (1997).

He crowned the resurrection with the hits set *All World* (1996) and UK No.1 'Ain't Nobody'. With Puff Daddy covering his 'Big Ol' Butt' on *In Tha Beginning... There Was Rap* (1997) and upstarts like Method Man and Redman paying respect on the phenomenal *Phenomenon* (1997), 'LL' clearly stands now for 'longer lasting'.

READ *I Make My Own Rules* (1997), LL Cool J & Karen Hunter

SURF www.geocities.com/Hollywood/Hills/1569/allworld.html

Lollapalooza

Inspired by Britain's Reading Festival, Jane's Addiction visionary Perry Farrell created Lollapalooza – the USA's top 'alternative' outdoor extravaganza. Lollapalooza's touring format brings diverse bills to audiences who might never witness conventional tours. Line-ups have included Jane's Addiction, Body Count, Siouxsie & The Banshees, Henry Rollins, Butthole Surfers and Nine Inch Nails (1991), Red Hot Chili Peppers, Ice Cube, Pearl Jam, Lush, The Jesus & Mary Chain, Soundgarden and Ministry (1992), Babes In Toyland, Dinosaur Jr, Arrested Development, Primus and Rage Against The Machine (1993), A Tribe Called Quest, The Breeders, Nick Cave, L7, George Clinton, Green Day, Stereolab, Luscious Jackson, The Beastie Boys and Smashing Pumpkins (1994), Hole, Sonic Youth, Pavement, Beck, Sinead O'Connor and Cypress Hill (1995), Metallica, The Ramones, Rancid, Screaming Trees, Wu-Tang Clan, Devo and Cocteau Twins (1996) and Orbital, Prodigy, Snoop Doggy Dogg, Korn and eels (1997). One dollar of each ticket sale is donated to homeless, environmental, AIDS and education charities.

Lollapalooza's future looked shaky when Farrell declined to headline the 1998 bill with Jane's Addiction, and its thunder was stolen by two other festivals: Sarah McLachlan's Lilith Fair and Ozzy Osbourne's Ozz-Fest. However, the event had already passed into legend when it was immortalized by The Simpsons' spoof 'Homerpalooza', a 1996 show featuring Cypress Hill and Smashing Pumpkins. "Wow, it's like Woodstock," said Lisa Simpson, "only with advertisements and tons of security guards."

LOUISE

WHO b. Louise Elizabeth Nurding, 4 Nov 1974, Lewisham, London, England

WHAT Singer, dancer, glamorous girl-next-door

Pop was rocked twice in July 1995: Robbie Williams left Take That and Louise Nurding exited Eternal. While Robbie played drug-crazed rogue, Louise went wide-eyed innocent – simultaneously whiter-than-white (a factor thought to have inhibited Eternal's R&B credibility in the USA) and red-hot (poll-topping pin-up status quickly ensued). Meanwhile, the Madonna-esque *Naked* (1996) blended ballads like first hit 'Light Of My Life' with the groovy 'In Walked Love' and steamy title tune.

Woman In Me (1997) ignited with 'Arms Around the World' and flamed on with The Average White Band's 'Let's Go Round Again'. Canoodling with footballer Jamie Redknapp, a somewhat premature autobiography and hints of rivalry with Eternal (intriguingly, she performed none of their hits on her first solo tour in 1997) kept the Pop pot bubbling.

ᴿᴱᴬᴰ *Louise – My Story* (1997), Kate Thornton & Jane Preston

ᶠᴬⁿ The Official Louise Fan Club, PO Box 888, High Wycombe, HP11 2NY, UK

ˢᵘʳᶠ www.profound.demon.co.uk/Music/louise/index.htm

LOVE

WHO Vocals/guitar **Arthur Lee** (b. 7 Mar 1944, Memphis, Tennessee, USA), guitar/vocals **Bryan Maclean** (b. 1947, Los Angeles, California, USA), guitar **John Echols** (b. 1944, Memphis), bass **Ken Forssi** (b. 1943, Cleveland, Ohio, USA), drums/keyboards **Alban 'Snoopy' Pfisterer** (b. 1947, Switzerland)

WHEN 1965–1971

WHERE Los Angeles, California, USA

WHAT Acid Rock with Punk attitude

Led by Arthur Lee, Love's groundbreaking, self-titled debut (1966) combined Garage Rock with Folk. Included was 'My Little Red Book', a Bacharach-David song previously performed by Manfred Mann, which became a small American hit for Love.

The more psychedelic *Da Capo* (1967), featuring drummer Michael Stuart and flautist/saxophonist Tjay Cantrelli, included '7&7 Is' – Love's biggest US single, reaching No.33. Pfisterer and Cantrelli left before their masterpiece *Forever Changes* (1968): a dazzling blend of acoustic and electric instruments, exotic strings, Mariachi-style brass, Psychedelia and Latin and Broadway musical influences. Although the music was beautiful and certainly acid-inspired, Love was not a flower-power band, for the songs were mostly dark and unsettling. 'Alone Again Or' – one of two Bryan Maclean-composed tracks – was later covered by The Damned and UFO.

Four Sail (1969) featured a changed line-up, with Lee now accompanied by Jay Donnellan (guitar), Frank Fayad (bass) and George Suranovich

> **"I used to drive my parents crazy, especially on car journeys, because I'd be singing constantly. My dad used to open the windows so the traffic noise would drown me out"**

(drums), but the band's new Hard Rock style alienated critics.

Out Here (1970) and *False Start* (1971) – with Jimi Hendrix on one track – featured further personnel changes, but Lee seemed burnt out. A 1972 solo album, *Vindicator,* was acclaimed only in retrospect. Recording as Love, but with mostly new musicians, Lee released the soulful, R&B-styled *Reel To Real* (1975). Old fans were disappointed, as they were with most of Lee's later work, including a 1978 reunion with Maclean for *Love Live* (1980). Drug abuse and alcoholism seemed to have sapped Lee's talent.

In the 90s, Lee toured with bands like The High Llamas, Baby Lemonade and Shack, posing as Love, but was sentenced to 12 years' imprisonment for illegal possession of a firearm in 1996.

 metro.turnpike.net/~rogers/arthur_lee/

THE LOVIN' SPOONFUL

WHO Vocals/guitar/harmonica/autoharp **John Sebastian** (b. 17 Mar 1944, New York, USA), guitar/vocals **Zal Yanovsky** (b. 19 Dec 1944, Toronto, Canada), bass/piano **Steve Boone** (b. 23 Sep 1943, Camphejeune, North Carolina, USA), drums/vocals **Joe Butler** (b. 19 Jan 1943, Long Island, New York, USA)

WHEN 1965–1968

WHERE New York, USA

WHAT Good-time Rock

Named after a phrase in 'Coffee Blues' by Mississippi John Hurt, a mentor of Sebastian's, the Lovin' Spoonful's sound was flavoured by Rock 'n' Roll, Country, Blues, Folk and Jugband music.

On their most classic albums – *Do You Believe In Magic* (1965), *Daydream* (1966), *Humsì* (1966) and *Everything Playing* (1967), on which the Modern Folk Quartet's Jerry Yester replaced Yanovsky – John Sebastian's glorious songs are written with cleverness, wit, a sense of fun and lyric technique exceptional in Rock. The mainly instrumental soundtracks for Woody Allen's *What's Up, Tiger Lily* (1966) and Francis Ford Coppola's *You're A Big Boy Now* (1966) are mostly inessential to the band's main body of work.

The band had ten US Top 40 hits, with classics including 'Nashville Cats', 'Daydream' and 'Summer In The City' – the latter two their only UK Top 10 successes – but, sensing the magic fading, Sebastian went solo in 1968. Joe Butler assumed control, releasing the undistinguished *Revelation: Revolution '69* (1968).

Sebastian's Woodstock performance (1969), while he was tripping on LSD, became legendary. Rock audiences thereafter appeared more appreciative of his psychedelic, simpleton persona and stoned buffoonery than of his finely honed lyrics. Not surprisingly, his songwriting deteriorated. *John B. Sebastian* (1970), *The Four Of Us* (1971), *Tarzana Kid* (1974) and *Welcome Back* (1976) – whose title track, a TV theme tune, was a US No.1 – were entertaining, but few of the songs ranked with his best.

Subsequently, Sebastian re-formed the Spoonful for the Paul Simon-directed movie *One Trick Pony* (1980), wrote songs for cartoons and movies, and toured. He unexpectedly came back strongly with *Tar Beach* (1993) and *I Want My Roots* (1996).

Since 1991, Butler, Boone and Yester have played the oldies circuit as The Lovin' Spoonful. Yanovsky is now a restaurateur.

 When The Music Mattered (1983), Bruce Pollock

 www.lovinspoonful.com

NICK LOWE

WHO b. 25 Mar 1949, Walton on Thames, England

WHAT Bassist, vocalist, producer and wit

Lowe began as bassist/vocalist with 60s band Kippington Lodge, which became 70s Pub Rock titans Brinsley Schwarz. After they disbanded in 1975, he helped establish the Stiff label, producing acts including The Damned and Elvis Costello, while juggling a solo career with participation in Dave Edmunds' Rockpile.

He scored UK hits with 1978's 'I Love The Sound Of Breaking Glass' and *The Jesus Of Cool* (titled *Pure Pop For Now People* in the USA) and 'Cruel To Be Kind' and *Labour Of Lust* (both 1979), but was more successful as a producer in the 80s. Between *Nick The Knife* (1982) and *Pinker And Prouder Than Previous* (1988), he produced Paul Carrack, John Hiatt, The Men They Couldn't Hang and his wife Carlene Carter, daughter of Johnny Cash.

After 1990's *Party Of One*, Lowe joined Hiatt, Jim Keltner and Ry Cooder in Little Village, before releasing *The Impossible Bird* (1994). Lowe's writing credits include Curtis Stigers' '(What's So Funny 'Bout) Peace, Love And Understanding' (from *The Bodyguard* soundtrack) and Johnny Cash's 'The Beast In Me'.

 www.cnet-sa.or.jp/s/sa013916/nick.htm

LULU

WHO b. Marie McDonald McLaughlin Lawrie, 3 Nov 1948, Glasgow, Scotland

WHAT Scottish Pop belter

Lulu & The Luvvers burst into the charts with 1964's raucous remake of The Isley Brothers' 'Shout' – which, despite over 20 UK and 10 US hits, remains Lulu's most memorable lyric. The singer's infectious enthusiasm propelled her into the public eye and she graced one of the first sessions for BBC DJ John Peel – "Without her Luvvers, sadly," recalled the DJ. "I rather fear they were long gone, like a turkey through the corn." Indeed, The Luvvers became surplus to requirements as Lulu recorded more soulful material, culminating in 'To Sir With Love', the title theme for the movie starring Sidney Poitier and a US chart-topper in 1967. Her two-hits-a-year average continued to the end of the 60s when 'Boom Bang-A-Bang' made No.2, despite its failure as the UK's 1969 Eurovision Song Contest entry. She married Bee Gee Maurice Gibb and hosted her own BBC TV show.

With Soul rather than Pop in mind, she was signed by Atlantic, and Jerry Wexler produced 1970's *New Routes*. Her UK album output never matched her single chart success, although *The Most Of Lulu* (1971) made No.15. 'The Man Who Sold The World' – written by David Bowie and produced by his guitarist Mick Ronson – made No.3, but the UK No.1 remained elusive, despite a high placing for a 1986 Disco reworking of 'Shout'.

Lulu finally made the top spot in 1993, a year which yielded five hits and the album *Independence*. Her rip-roaring cameo on Take That's remake of Dan Hartman's 'Relight My Fire' ended the longest wait by a UK act for a No.1: 29 years and 148 days!

Absolutely Lulu (1997) blended remixes of hits with new cuts. Three decades of recording, modelling and acting (such as TV's *Absolutely Fabulous* and 1997's *Comic Relief,* playing Baby Spice in spoof band The Sugar Lumps) have kept her in the public eye.

LUSH

WHO Vocals/guitar **Miki Berenyi** (b. 18 Mar 1967, London, England), vocals/guitar **Emma Anderson** (b. 10 Jun 1967, London), bass **Philip King** (b. 29 Apr 1960, London), drums **Chris Acland** (b. 7 Sep 1966, Lancaster, England, d. 17 Oct 1996, Kendal, Cumbria, England)

WHEN 1988–

WHERE London, England

WHAT Sweetness and light

Formed by friends Miki, Emma and original singer Meriel Barham (later of The Pale Saints), Lush signed to 4AD after acclaimed live shows and were swept up in 'shoegazing' with their mini-album, *Scar* (1989). Subsequent sparkling EPs 'Mad Love' and 'Sweetness And Light' were collected on 1990's singles set *Gala*. Thereafter, despite *Spooky* (1992), a Lollapalooza tour and *Split* (1994), they became better known for hell-raising than hit-making.

The big-time beckoned again with 1996's *Lovelife* – a cameo by Pulp's Jarvis Cocker and hits 'Single Girl', 'Ladykillers' and '500' (Shake Baby Shake)' – but the suicide of Chris Acland in 1996 led to their eventual demise.

surf www.curve.demon.co.uk/lush/

LYNYRD SKYNYRD

WHO Vocals **Ronnie Van Zant** (b. 15 Jan 1948, Jacksonville, Florida, USA, d. 20 Oct 1977), guitar **Gary Rossington** (b. 4 Dec, 1951, Jacksonville), guitar **Allen Collins** (b. 19 Jul 1952, Jacksonville, d. 23 Jan 1990), guitar **Steve Gaines** (b. 14 Sep 1949, Seneca, Missouri, USA, d. 20 Oct 1977), bass **Leon Wilkeson** (b. 2 Apr 1952, Jacksonville), drums **Artimus Pyle** (b. 15 Jul 1948, Spartanburg, South Carolina, USA), keyboards **Billy Powell** (b. 3 Jun 1952, Jacksonville)

WHEN 1965–

WHERE Jacksonville, Florida, USA

WHAT Southern Rock, neat and raw

The founding fathers of Southern Rock, Lynyrd Skynyrd started out as My Backyard in 1965, featuring Ronnie Van Zant, Gary Rossington, Allen Collins, bassist Larry Jungstrom and drummer Bob Burns. After one single – 1968's 'Need All My Friends', on local label Shade Tree – they became Lynyrd Skynyrd, a twisted tribute to hated gym teacher Leonard Skinner. After their debut single 'I've Been Your Fool' (1971), they rose swiftly.

In 1973, after recruiting Larry Jungstrom's replacement Leon Wilkeson, guitarist Ed King and keyboard player Bill Powell, *Pronounced Leh-Nered Skin-Nerd* featured the classic 'Free Bird'. *Second Helping* (1974) included 'Sweet Home Alabama' – a flag-waving retort to Neil Young's scathing 'Southern Man'. By the end of 1974, Burns had been ditched in favour of Artimus Pyle, and 'Free Bird' had flown into the US Top 20.

Even King's departure failed to halt the progress of *Nuthin' Fancy* (1975) and *Gimme Back My Bullets* (1976), while the addition of guitarist Steve Gaines helped the live *One More From The Road* (1976) to become a transatlantic monster. Skynyrd were poised for major stardom when tragedy struck on 20 October 1977: a plane carrying the band from Greenville, South Carolina, to Baton Rouge, Lousiana, crashed – killing Van Zant, Gaines and his sister, backing vocalist Cassie.

Skynyrd were midway through a US tour promoting *Street Survivors* (1977), whose cover showed them engulfed in flames. The album was withdrawn, and reissued at the end of the year with a more appropriate sleeve. By then, Skynyrd had split.

In 1987, a new Skynyrd rose, with Rossington, Powell, Wilkeson, Pyle and King joined by guitarist Randall Hall and Van Zant's younger brother Johnny on vocals. Hindered by volatile line-ups, Skynyrd have yet to recapture their 70s thunder, but remain a popular live attraction.

fan Lynyrd Skynyrd & Southern Rock Fan Club, c/o Rainbow, Beim Bahnhof 3, 72160 Horb-Altheim, Germany

surf www.skynyrd.com/

M PEOPLE

WHO Vocals **Heather Small** (b. 20 Jan 1965, London, England), vocals/saxophone **Mike Pickering** (b. 21 Feb 1954, Manchester, England), percussion **Shovell** (b. Andrew Lovell, 11 Feb 1969, Jamaica), keyboards/programming **Paul Heard** (b. 5 Oct 1960, London)

WHEN 1991–

WHERE Manchester, England

WHAT Honey-voiced tasteful Dance Soul

M People's driving force (and namesake) Mike Pickering was DJ at New Order's Hacienda Club when he and Paul Heard found former Hot!House singer Heather Small. She had also sung with Orange Juice and Working Week, while Pickering also worked at Factory – he is credited with signing Happy Mondays and James.

Their 1992 debut, *Northern Soul*, earned them a BRIT award for Best Dance Band. Established as powerful live performers, their *Elegant Slumming* reached UK No.2 in 1993 and won the Mercury Music Prize over strong competition from Blur and Pulp. *Bizarre Fruit* (1994) reached UK No.4 and remained on the chart for two and a half years. Their success was boosted by a UK TV ad featuring the hit 'Search For The Hero'.

Bizarre Fruit II (1995) strengthened their arena-filling position, consolidated by the platinum *Fresco* (1997).

 www.m-people.co.uk

PAUL McCARTNEY
◉◉◉◉◉◉☆☆☆☆☆☆

WHO b. James Paul McCartney, 18 Jun 1942, Liverpool, England

WHAT The most successful Rock composer of all time

The keenest Beatle, Paul McCartney was the most frustrated by the band's decline into squabbling. On 10 April 1970, he became the first to break rank, effectively terminating the biggest Pop group in history. Paul's announcement coincided with his solo debut, *McCartney*: a home-made hotch-potch of cheerfully underworked tracks, mostly hymning domestic bliss with wife Linda (b. Linda Louise Eastman, 24 Sep 1942, Scarsdale, New York, USA, d. 17 Apr 1998, near Tucson, Arizona, USA). Only 'Maybe I'm Amazed' attained classic status. His first post-Beatles single, 'Another Day', was even less substantial; critics feared he might miss the abrasive edge of John Lennon (then cutting some of his most brutally confessional music).

Ram (1971), made in New York with a hired band, sported abundant melodies ('Back Seat Of My Car' was a stand-out and 'Uncle Albert – Admiral Halsey' a US No.1) but little stylistic focus or emotional weight. Lennon took some of the lyrics to be an attack on him and Yoko Ono, responding with the vicious 'How Do You Sleep?' on *Imagine*.

McCartney found a long-term sideman in ex-Moody Blues vocalist Denny Laine – who joined him and Linda in a new band, Wings – and ended 1971 with the disappointing *Wild Life*. Nostalgic for his Rock 'n' Roll roots, Paul took Wings on a low-key tour of UK colleges, sometimes turning up without prior notice.

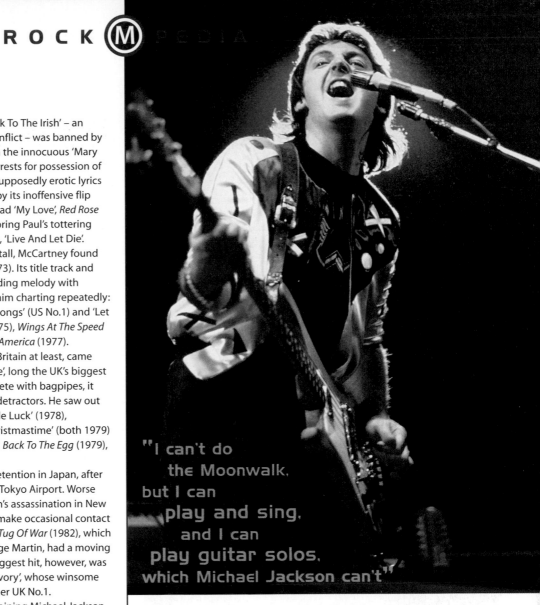

"I can't do
the Moonwalk,
but I can
play and sing,
and I can
play guitar solos,
which Michael Jackson can't"

He won notoriety when 'Give Ireland Back To The Irish' – an angry comment on the Northern Irish conflict – was banned by the BBC and sardonically followed it with the innocuous 'Mary Had A Little Lamb'. There followed two arrests for possession of cannabis and a second BBC ban for the supposedly erotic lyrics of 1972's 'Hi Hi Hi'. The single was saved by its inoffensive flip side 'C Moon'. Thanks to the majestic ballad 'My Love', *Red Rose Speedway* (1973) went some way to restoring Paul's tottering reputation, as did his Bond movie theme, 'Live And Let Die'.

As the other three Beatles began to stall, McCartney found his solo wings with *Band On The Run* (1973). Its title track and 'Jet' recalled McCartney's talent for blending melody with blistering Rock. The next few years saw him charting repeatedly: hits included 'Helen Wheels', 'Silly Love Songs' (US No.1) and 'Let 'Em In'; albums were *Venus And Mars* (1975), *Wings At The Speed Of Sound* (1976) and the live *Wings Over America* (1977).

His greatest commercial triumph, in Britain at least, came with 1977's Christmas hit 'Mull Of Kintyre', long the UK's biggest selling single. A lugubrious waltz, complete with bagpipes, it aroused the deepest ire of McCartney's detractors. He saw out the decade with hits such as 'With A Little Luck' (1978), 'Goodnight Tonight' and 'Wonderful Christmastime' (both 1979) and the albums *London Town* (1978) and *Back To The Egg* (1979), after which he disbanded Wings.

The 80s began with an eight-night detention in Japan, after drugs were discovered in his luggage at Tokyo Airport. Worse followed in December, with John Lennon's assassination in New York; the former partners had begun to make occasional contact for the first time since The Beatles' split. *Tug Of War* (1982), which reunited him with Beatle producer George Martin, had a moving farewell to Lennon in 'Here Today'. His biggest hit, however, was a duet with Stevie Wonder, 'Ebony And Ivory', whose winsome appeal for racial harmony secured another UK No.1.

Another spectacular pairing was his joining Michael Jackson on the co-written 'The Girl Is Mine' on *Thriller*. Michael returned the compliment by duetting on 'Say Say Say' on McCartney's *Pipes Of Peace* (1983). But the friendship soured in 1985, when Jackson outbid both McCartney and Yoko Ono for The Beatles' song publishing rights. Denied control of his own catalogue, Paul ensured his MPL company acquired other important copyrights, from 'Unchained Melody' to the songs of Buddy Holly.

McCartney then turned to movies, concocting 1984's *Give My Regards To Broad Street*, a poorly received fantasia. Its soundtrack was redeemed by the hit 'No More Lonely Nights', a soaring ballad adorned with a superb guitar solo by Pink Floyd's Dave Gilmour. Seldom the critics' darling, McCartney achieved his customary blend of massive sales and derision with 'We All Stand Together', credited to Paul McCartney And The Frog Chorus, from a cartoon starring his childhood hero Rupert the Bear.

McCartney's legendary status was affirmed in 1985 when he headlined the Wembley Live Aid. While 1986's *Press To Play* was, at best, mediocre, the general quality of his solo output was proven by a sturdy compilation of hits, *All The Best!* (1987). In 1989 he reassured the faithful with his strongest album in years, *Flowers In The Dirt*, with several songs co-written by Elvis Costello. More joint efforts appeared on Costello's own records. The album prefaced Paul's first world tour in over a decade; with a new band, he tackled old Beatle numbers and played to sell-out crowds. With a phenomenal audience of 184,000, an April 1990 show in Rio secured him a *Guinness Book Of Records* entry.

Ongoing sales figures confirmed McCartney as Rock's most successful composer of all time, while he was often cited as one of Britain's wealthiest individuals. Yet his work rate still increased. Assisted by Classical composer Carl Davis, he composed a 95-minute work, *The Liverpool Oratorio* (1991). In October 1991, he attended its world premiere at Liverpool Cathedral; the same day he announced plans for a Liverpool Institute For The Performing Arts, to be housed in his old secondary school building, next door to the art college attended by John Lennon. Another new album, *Off The Ground* (1993), prompted a second world tour.

His solo activities were interrupted by a plan, devised with Yoko Ono, to reunite The Beatles by adding tracks to demos from John's last years. With George Harrison, Ringo Starr and producer Jeff Lynne, McCartney took the tapes to his studio in Sussex, emerging with the hits 'Free As A Bird' and 'Real Love'. With George Martin, Paul oversaw The Beatles' *Anthology* series, telling the story of a band he had insisted would never re-form.

In March 1997, he was knighted by the Queen, becoming Sir Paul McCartney. Britpop acts acknowledged him as a pioneering influence and the National Trust bought Paul's boyhood home, a council house in Liverpool, for preservation as a historic site.

Amid this acclaim, he turned out the well-received *Flaming Pie* (1997) and perhaps his most ambitious project to date: a full-length symphony, *Standing Stone* (1997), premiered in London's Royal Albert Hall and New York's Carnegie Hall.

ReaD *Many Years From Now* (1997), Barry Miles

Fan Paul McCartney Fun Club, PO Box 110, Westcliff, Essex, SS0 6NW, UK

MALCOLM McLAREN

WHO b. 22 Jan 1946, London, England

WHAT Punk's merchant of menace

Combining audacity, genius and ineptitude, Malcolm McLaren has navigated between cheap outrage and establishment acceptance. Inspired by the 1968 Paris student riots while at art college in England, he hooked up with fashion designer Vivienne Westwood and opened 50s-themed clothes shop Let It Rock on London's King's Road. There he met visiting Glamsters The New York Dolls and moved to America in 1974 to manage them.

Having remodelled the Dolls as redneck-baiting Maoists (and watched their subsequent disintegration), he returned to London charged with ideas; Let It Rock became the S&M store Sex, five of its clientele became The Sex Pistols and McLaren became an establishment demon, dealing the final blows to Rock's innocence with stage-managed teen revolt.

Following the Pistols' demise, McLaren coasted: New Romantic clothes shop World's End and protégés like Bow Wow Wow – and, briefly, Adam & The Ants and Boy George – were gleefully consumed, but failed to provoke violent uprisings.

With producer Trevor Horn, McLaren assembled the wonderful *Duck Rock* (1983), a grand theft of Folk, African music and Hip Hop, whose highlights ('Soweto', 'Buffalo Gals', 'Double Dutch') stormed the UK chart and singlehandedly added 'rapping', 'scratching' and 'breakdancing' to the English vocabulary, re-establishing him as a post-modern alchemist.

After 1984's remix exercise 'D'Ya Like Scratchin?', *Fans* (1984) fused Hip Hop with opera (yielding the sublime UK hit 'Madame Butterfly'), but *Swamp Thing* (1985) was pure studio indulgence.

Waltz Darling (1989) was epic in scale – its blend of orchestral waltzes with House, Funk and Rock giving nervous breakdowns to six producers and guests Bootsy Collins and Jeff Beck – but moderate in success, hyping 'Vogueing' too late for hipness and too early for mass appeal (Madonna cleaned up a year later).

McLaren dabbled fruitlessly in movies (including a mooted Led Zeppelin biopic starring Jason Donovan as Robert Plant) and romanced Lauren Hutton. He revived his role as Pop's Fagin in 1991's TV special *The Ghosts Of Oxford Street* (a fantasy/history of London's shopping mecca with cameos by Tom Jones, Happy Mondays, The Pogues and Sinéad O'Connor), while the tastefully techno-ish *Paris* (1994) – with McLaren playing Serge Gainsbourg to co-stars like Catherine Deneuve and Françoise Hardy – found praise in Europe, prompting French Prime Minister Jacques Chirac to run for election with a McLaren-composed theme tune.

"I think all kids are anarchists until...

...they get dragged into the system"

DON McLEAN ✪

WHO b. 2 Oct 1945, New Rochelle, New York, USA

WHAT The American pie man

The writer and subject of some of Pop's peaks, Don McLean rose from Folk cultdom to mainstream mythology. His debut *Tapestry* (1970) was forever eclipsed by Carole King's album of the same name, although Perry Como took its 'And I Love You So' into the charts. McLean's breakthrough, *American Pie* (1971), boasted two classics: 'Vincent', inspired by painter Van Gogh, and the epic title track, about Buddy Holly and the demise of the American dream.

Don McLean (1972), the covers collection *Playin' Favorites* (1973), *Homeless Brother* (1974), *Solo* (1976) and *Prime Time* (1977) were less spectacular successes, but – on his own Millennium label – he returned to the upper reaches of the charts with *Chain Lightning* (1980), a UK No.1 cover of Roy Orbison's 'Crying', 'Castles In The Air' (from 1981's *Believers*) and the US hit 'Since I Don't Have You' (an implausible link to Guns N' Roses, who also covered that old Skyliners hit in 1993).

Dominion (1983), *Love Tracks* (1987), *For The Memories Vols. 1 & 2* (1990), *Headroom* (1991) and *The River Of Love* (1995) failed to compete with compilations, live albums and Christmas collections, but McLean is immortalized as the subject of the Roberta Flack/Fugees hit 'Killing Me Softly With His Song'.

surf www.ourline.com/DonMcLean/

MADNESS ◉◉

WHO Vocals **Suggs** (b. Graham McPherson, 13 Jan 1961, Hastings, Kent, England), guitar **Christopher Foreman** (b. 8 Aug 1958, London, England), bass **Mark 'Bedders' Bedford** (b. 24 Aug 1961, London), drums **Daniel 'Woody' Woodgate** (b. 19 Oct 1960, London), keyboards **Mike Barson** (b. 21 Apr 1958, London), trumpet/vocals **Chas Smash** (b. Cathal Smythe, 14 Jan 1959, Rainham, Kent, England), saxophone **Lee Thompson** (b. 5 Oct 1957, London)

WHEN 1979–

WHERE London, England

WHAT The nuttiest sound around

The seeds of Madness were sown in June 1977 when Mike Barson, Lee Thompson and Christopher Foreman formed The Invaders. 'The Prince', released by Ska tubthumpers The Specials' 2 Tone label, catapulted the newly named Madness into the UK Top 20 in September 1979. Stiff Records boss Dave Robinson invited the group to play at his wedding, then signed them.

The title track of *One Step Beyond* (1979) began an exquisite run of 16 UK Top 10 hits, blotted only by 1982's 'Cardiac Arrest' (No.14). They turned the video genre – then more the domain of moody lighting and beautiful babes – into a free-for-all of dancing bees, flying saxophonists, stupid faces, baggy

trousers, parachuting vans and – in a cover of Labi Siffre's 'It Must Be Love' – a cameo by Siffre himself. Rivalled only by Abba and The Human League, they were a singles-band supreme, but *Absolutely* (1980), *Madness 7* (1981) and *The Rise And Fall* (1982) also stuck limpet-like to the album chart. They came unstuck only with the critically slated, celluloid kickabout *Take It Or Leave It* (1981).

The hits set *Complete Madness* (1982) topped the UK chart and hung around for months while 'House Of Fun' became their crowning glory. Across the Atlantic, they made a splash with 1983's 'Our House', then reverted to cultdom. Undeterred by Barson's exit in 1983, they issued *Keep Moving* (1984), whose hit 'Michael Caine' starred the actor himself. Having progressed from their trademark 'nutty' Ska to mainstream Pop, Madness left Stiff to form the Zarjazz label (via Virgin), helping to launch the solo career of Undertones gurgler Feargal Sharkey.

In 1985, the group united with The Specials and UB40 on 'Starvation', in aid of Ethiopian famine relief. However, the mature Madness' popularity dwindled and *Mad Not Mad* (1985) became their first album not to enter the UK Top 10. They announced their split in September 1986, releasing 'Waiting For The Ghost Train' as a farewell. Suggs, Smash, Thompson and Foreman resurfaced briefly and unsuccessfully as The Madness, while Woody and Bedders joined underrated power-popsicles Voice Of The Beehive. Suggs also managed The Farm.

In August 1992, the magnificent seven reunited for 'Madstock', a concert at London's Finsbury Park, accompanied by another hits collection, *Divine Madness* (1992). A series of reunion concerts and a deal with Go! Discs resulted only in the live album *Madstock* (1992). Suggs embarked on a successful solo (and TV) career with *The Lone Ranger* (1995), scoring UK hits with covers of The Beatles' 'I'm Only Sleeping' and Simon & Garfunkel's 'Cecilia'.

In 1998, basking in the adulation of No Doubt and fellow Ska-influenced American stars The Mighty Mighty Bosstones, Madness announced yet another Finsbury Park reunion show.

Fan Nut Inc, 93 St John's Road, Westcliff, SS0 7JY, UK

surf www.madness.co.uk/

MADONNA ⊙⊙⊙⊙✪✪✪

WHO b. Madonna Louise Ciccone, 16 Aug 1958, Bay City, Michigan, USA

WHAT "The woman who pulled herself up by her bra-straps" (Bette Midler)

The architect of her own mythic status, Madonna has made the wildest of dreams come true. She has presented herself so boldly, and in so many guises, that her prominence in the media has barely faded since she bounced to fame with 'Holiday' in 1983. Pop's most confrontational woman, and most famous, Madonna is the queen of MTV, has sold 100 million records worldwide, had nearly 50 hits, and inspired wannabes the world over. "Madonna is the speed boat," said an enthralled Liz Phair (just one of Rock's post-Madonna in-your-face performers). "The rest of us are just The Go-Go's on water skis."

At 20, after quitting a dance scholarship at the University of Michigan, Madonna moved to New York. She tried her luck with dance companies and bands, including the ill-fated Breakfast Club, in which she played drums and sang. After a stint in Europe as singer and dancer for Disco king Patrick Hernandez, she had minor club hits with the dancey 'Everybody' (1982) and rockier 'Burning Up' (1983). *Madonna* (1983) – later reissued as *The First Album* – began the selling not only of Madonna's music, but also the marketing of Madonna herself. Nowhere was this better illustrated than the video for the hit 'Lucky Star', a whirlwind of exhibitionism and dance. Phair again: "She was cool and independent; she had muscles and boobs." The music was mechanical and her voice squeaky, but the power of her body and brazenness redefined the position of women in Pop.

Madonna sold 3 million in its first 18 months, but the real breakthrough came with 1984's *Like A Virgin*. Produced by Nile Rodgers, it spent years in international charts and cemented her celebrity. Two aspects of her image were defined by the videos for 'Material Girl' (a pastiche of Marilyn Monroe's 'Diamonds Are A Girl's Best Friend') and the US chart-topping title track (a Venetian fantasy with Madonna writhing on a gondola).

The media alternately glorified and blasted her materialism and narcissism; the church and censors branded her blasphemous and pornographic. The public, meanwhile, made her a phenomenon whose fame and popularity were rivalled only by Princess Diana. On 1984's Virgin Tour, Madonna played to 355,000 fans in 27 cities (supported by the similarly shy and retiring Beastie Boys). Then – undaunted by a publishing war between *Penthouse* and *Playboy* for pre-fame nude photographs, and the unearthing of her unsalubrious, early 80s movie debut *A Certain Sacrifice* – she played for the world at Live Aid in 1985.

That year, she was rarely out of transatlantic Top 10s; hits from *Like A Virgin* were jostled by reissues of *Madonna*'s 'Holiday' and 'Borderline', and the movie themes 'Crazy For You' from *Vision Quest* and 'Into The Groove' (her first UK No.1) from *Desperately Seeking Susan*. The latter starred Madonna as the titular Susan: an undemanding role that remained the most popular of her celluloid ventures for the next decade. The media frenzy seethed further with her marriage in 1986 to actor Sean Penn, with whom she starred in the hopeless *Shanghai Surprise* (1986). Her relationship with both the press and Penn was highly volatile. She filed for divorce in 1987.

However, she confounded critics with *True Blue* (1986), whose hits – notably the heart-rending 'Papa Don't Preach' and 'Live To Tell' – gave Madonna credibility as a composer and producer (with new creative partner Patrick Leonard joining her long-time collaborator Stephen Bray). 'Papa Don't Preach' documented a father-daughter confrontation: a fight for sexual freedom which mirrored Madonna's own strained relationship with the establishment. The majestic 'Live To Tell' dispelled any lingering doubts that Madonna's musical might was limited to sparkly Dance – although that too was showcased on the explosive 'Open Your Heart'. The Spanish-scented 'La Isla Bonita' made her the first female artist to have four UK No.1s.

Despite a Broadway role in David Mamet's *Speed The Plow* (1988) and another stab at the cinema with *Who's That Girl* (1987), acclaim for her acting proved elusive. However, the latter's soundtrack – boasting four new Madonna hits, including the US/UK charts-topping title track – went platinum and the accompanying tour unveiled her freshly toned physique to the world's stadiums. She rounded the year off with *You Can Dance* (1987), a musically disastrous Hi-NRG remix compilation that nonetheless went platinum – and promoted remix albums from stop-gap schedule-fillers to bona-fide chartbusters.

After spending 1988 in an uncharacteristic low key, Madonna reclaimed her queen-of-controversy title the following year. In a calculated bid for notoriety, she inked a lucrative sponsorship deal with Pepsi – using their TV ads to springboard a new song, 'Like A Prayer'. Its video depicted her as an uncharacteristically pious brunette, but caused uproar with its portrayal of a black Jesus and the use of burning crosses as flattering backlighting.

Typically, the video divided opinion, voted best of the year by MTV viewers and worst by *Rolling Stone* readers. Pepsi's response was unequivocal: when even the Vatican joined a chorus of condemnation, they cancelled the deal. Even these publicity fireworks were no match for the kaleidoscopic *tour de force* of *Like A Prayer* (1989). The influence of fellow 80s icon Prince was evident not only on his cameos ('Love Song', 'Act Of Contrition') but also the eclectic tributes to Sly & The Family Stone ('Keep It Together'), girl-group bubblegum ('Cherish'), Simon & Garfunkel ('Oh Father') and Psychedelia ('Dear Jessie'). Most shocking was 'Till Death Do Us Part', a candid portrait of married life wrapped

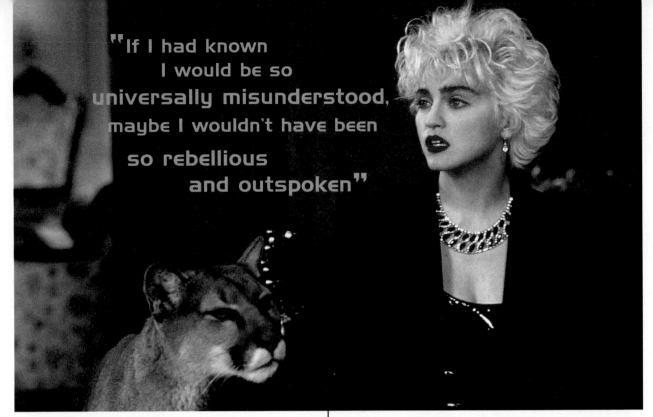

> "If I had known
> I would be so
> universally misunderstood,
> maybe I wouldn't have been
> so rebellious
> and outspoken"

in bubbling House. But although the album topped transatlantic charts, it sold only half as well as *True Blue*, consumers being sidetracked by the uncomplicated charms of Paula Abdul.

However, Madonna's bid for commercial supremacy continued apace in 1990. In another blonde-bubblehead pastiche, she became Breathless Mahoney for the movie *Dick Tracy* (with her then lover Warren Beatty). Its pseudo-soundtrack *I'm Breathless* strayed into show-tune territory, but Madonna's dancefloor credentials were reaffirmed by 'Vogue'. Written for a B-side, the song drew on the gay Disco craze 'vogueing' – stylized poses for an imaginary camera. Complemented by a Hollywood-honouring video, 'Vogue' returned Madonna to the top of international singles charts. Another *Breathless* hit, 'Hanky Panky', trailed 1990's Blonde Ambition world tour, which was dogged by complaints of public lewdness, dubbed an 'offence to good taste' and documented by the 1991 movie *Truth Or Dare*, aka *In Bed With Madonna*.

Her 90s notoriety peaked with 'Justify My Love': a US No.1 and one of two new cuts on the definitive hits set *The Immaculate Collection* (1990). Aggrieved parties included Prince protégée Ingrid Chavez (who co-wrote the song with Lenny Kravitz but was mysteriously uncredited), Public Enemy (who claimed their 'Security Of The First World' had provided its beat) and moral guardians who objected to the video's over-long bedroom scene filmed in Paris' Monceau Hotel. Amid the backlash, Madonna was voted 'Most Boring Personality of 1991' and two dancers from the tour filed suit over the movie. Her turn in *A League Of Their Own* (1992) was less disaster-prone, and spawned the Karen Carpenter-esque 'This Used To Be My Playground'.

The critically slated *Sex* (1992) was a more progressive vehicle for Madonna's fantasies. A metal-covered soft-porn book and the first offering from her multi-media company Maverick, it was ill-judged and badly timed. The viability of Maverick itself was questioned: spurned by Hole,

the label initially scored only with Grunge kids Candlebox, and its seven-year deal with Warner Bros looked like a long time. Neither the book nor its shamefully underrated companion album *Erotica* (1992) did much for her popularity – she had lost her mystery, displaying herself and her fantasies too openly. The text of the book was laughable and sometimes indecipherable, and the photographs coldly blunt.

Her starring role in *Body Of Evidence* (1992) was equally gratuitous: a murderous dominatrix who introduces her lawyer to the joys of S&M. Not surprisingly, this attracted more interest than her role as a trapeze artist in Woody Allen's hand-wringing 1992 movie *Shadows & Fog*. Ironically, *Erotica* was jam-packed with fantastic songs: its hits ranging from the Disco delights 'Fever' and 'Deeper And Deeper' to the epic heartbreakers 'Bad Girl' and 'Rain', its album cuts blending Hip Hop with Jazz. Resolute and confrontational to the last, she rode the *Sex* scandal through to 1994, only to make an argumentative, profanity-strewn appearance on David Letterman's US TV show. The defiant 'Human Nature' – in whose S&M-themed video she played a leather-clad dominatrix – took her critics to task, while the US chart-topping 'Take A Bow' restored her commercial fortunes. Her singing had evolved from formative squeaks to an assertive warmth, and although *Bedtime Stories* (1994) boasted the voguish input of Björk, Babyface and Nellee Hooper, she was most at home on ballads like the hit 'I'll Remember', from the movie *With Honors* (1994). Accordingly, the ballads retrospective *Something To Remember* (1995) was better received, the customary controversy limited to animal rights-antagonizing scenes of bullfighting in the 'You'll See' and 'Take A Bow' videos.

Carrying on regardless, Madonna made a low-key cameo as a singing telegram in Jim Jarmusch's mostly improvised *Blue In The Face* (1995) and as a witch in Alison Anders' contribution to *Four Rooms* (1995). For the much-mooted *Evita* (1996), Madonna fought tooth and nail to play Eva Peron.

In 1988, she had refused to do a screen test, but this time took singing lessons and even filmed while pregnant with daughter Lourdes. Spin-off smashes 'Don't Cry For Me Argentina' and 'You Must Love Me' were polished show songs, but lacked the sparkle of earlier releases.

However, *Ray Of Light* (1998) was a stunning return to form: a collaboration with electronic guru William Orbit, a rejuvenation of her songwriting partnership with Patrick Leonard (which – bar 'I'll Remember' – had lapsed in the 90s) and another redefinition of Madonna. She overhauled her image and broadened her beliefs to encompass New Age motherhood, a reasserted Catholicism, Judaism, Buddhism and Hinduism.

Madonna's chosen confirmation name – Veronica, meaning 'Vera icon', or true image – was uncannily prophetic. She remains a symbol of empowerment, recasting traditional roles in female terms. This was reflected by the escalating fortunes of Maverick: its star Alanis Morissette had a seismic effect on the music industry that paled only alongside Madonna's achievements. The success of fellow Maverick mischief-makers Prodigy, and the explicitly Madonna-inspired Spice Girls, testified to a goddess without whom Pop would be as bereft as life without oxygen.

READ *Madonna – Her Complete Story* (1991), David James

FAN Icon, 8941 Sunset Boulevard #485, West Hollywood, CA 90069-1911, USA

SURF www.mit.edu:8001/people/jwb/Madonna.html

MAGAZINE

WHO Vocals **Howard Devoto** (b. Howard Trafford), guitar/saxophone **John McGeogh**, bass **Barry Adamson** (b. 1 Jun 1958, Manchester, England), drums **Martin Jackson**, keyboards **Dave Formula**

WHEN 1977–1981

WHERE Manchester, England

WHAT Post-Punk paranoia

Quitting seminal Punks The Buzzcocks after 1977's 'Spiral Scratch' EP, weirdie singer Howard Devoto convened Magazine – Art Rockers about town. Their acclaimed debut 'Shot By Both Sides' and *Real Life* (1978) demonstrated Devoto's progress from The Buzzcocks' blast, patenting the post-Punk sound: jagged, bleak soundscapes and those broody Brit lyrical staples – misanthropy and 'urban alienation'. The glacial *Secondhand Daylight* (1979) welcomed drummer John Doyle (Martin Jackson having quit for The Chameleons and, later, Swing Out Sister), but after 1980's *The Correct Use Of Soap*, Magazine fell apart.

Guitarist John McGeogh jumped ship (resurfacing in Visage, Siouxsie & The Banshees and PiL) and, after the weak live album *Play* (1980) and *Magic Murder And The Weather* (1981), they were devoid of Devoto, too. He continued solo with *Jerky Visions Of The Dream* (1983), formed Luxuria for the underbought *Unanswerable Lust* (1988) and *Beast Box* (1990) and penned lyrics for Apollo 440. Bassist Barry Adamson hung with Nick Cave in The Birthday Party and Bad Seeds before becoming fabulous alone with *Moss Side Story* (1990), *Soul Murder* (1992), *The Negro Inside Me* (1993), *A Prayer Mat Of Flesh* (1995), *Oedipus Shmoedipus* (1996) and *As Above, So Below* (1998).

THE MAMAS & THE PAPAS ✪

WHO Vocals/guitar **John Phillips** (b. 30 Aug 1935, Parris Island, South Carolina, USA), vocals **Denny Doherty** (b. 29 Nov 1941, Halifax, Nova Scotia, Canada), vocals **Cass Elliot** (b. Ellen Cohen, 19 Sep 1941, Baltimore, Maryland, USA, d. 29 Jul 1974, London, England), vocals **Michelle Phillips** (b. Holly Michelle Gilliam, 6 Apr 1944, Long Beach, California, USA)

WHEN 1965–

WHERE Virgin Islands, USA

WHAT California dreamers

The Mamas & The Papas' folkish harmonies were the pinnacle of American flower-power Pop. They were helmed by Greenwich Village veteran John Phillips, who enlisted Mugwumps members Denny Doherty and Cass Elliot to join him and his wife, Michelle, in The New Journeymen. Relocating to California, they became The Mamas & The Papas and Phillips wrote some of the finest songs of the 60s. Their first hit, 'California Dreamin', written by Phillips in New York, was inspired by Michelle's homesickness. 'Monday Monday' followed when she returned to LA alone. The third of their nine US Top 40 hits, 1966's 'I Saw Her Again', was inspired by Michelle's affair with Doherty. 'Creeque Alley' (1967) was an autobiography of the increasingly dysfunctional band.

If You Can Believe Your Eyes And Ears (1966) was a US No.1, but Michelle was temporarily replaced by Jill Gibson after flaunting another affair with (ex-Byrd) Gene Clark. *Cass, John, Michelle, Denny* (1966), *Deliver* (1967) and *The Papas And Mamas* (1968) were all hits, but Phillips' inspiration faded and the band fizzled out. *People Like Us* (1971) was a half-hearted reunion.

Cass Elliot had solo hits (notably 1969's 'Make Your Own Kind Of Music') before succumbing to a heart attack; Doherty released nondescript albums; Michelle made *Victim Of Romance* (1977), acted in US TV's *Knot's Landing* and Ken Russell's *Valentino* (1976) and published an autobiography, *California Dreamin'*, in 1986.

Meanwhile, John Phillips released the outstanding *Wolfking Of L.A.* (1970), composed the flop Broadway musical *Man On The Moon* (1975) and, with Stomu Yamashta, soundtracked 1976's *The Man Who Fell To Earth* – to the consternation of its star David Bowie, who had submitted his own score. But Phillips was consumed by heroin addiction; recording work with Mick Jagger and Keith Richards collapsed and, after a 1980 arrest for dealing, he renounced drugs and escaped with a token sentence.

The 80s were awash with complicated Mamas manoeuvres. In 1981, The Mamas & The Papas re-formed with John Phillips, Denny Doherty, Phillips' actress daughter Mackenzie and Elaine McFarlane (ex-Spanky & Our Gang), for *Live In 1982* (1982).

Doherty was replaced by Scott McKenzie (for whom Phillips had written the 1967 hit 'San Francisco'), then returned again, replacing Phillips, who – with McKenzie – wrote The Beach Boys' 1988 US No.1 'Kokomo'. Meanwhile, John and Michelle Phillips' daughter Chynna sold millions with Brian Wilson's daughters Wendy and Carnie as Wilson Phillips.

By 1998, The Mamas & The Papas comprised Scott McKenzie, David Baker, Lisa Brescia and Deb Lyons, but none of its originals.

READ *Papa John* (1986), John Phillips

SURF www.interlog.com/~jman/

MANFRED MANN

WHO Vocals/harmonica **Paul Jones** (b. Paul Pond, 24 Feb 1942, Portsmouth, England), guitar/saxophone **Mike Vickers** (b. 18 Apr 1941, Southampton, England), bass **Tom McGuinness** (b. 2 Dec 1941, London, England), drums **Mike Hugg** (b. 11 Aug 1942, Andover, England), keyboards **Manfred Mann** (b. Michael Lubowitz, 21 Oct 1940, Johannesburg, South Africa)

WHEN 1962–1969

WHERE London, England

WHAT Blues-edged Pop

Alongside the Stones, Manfred Mann introduced R&B to the 60s mainstream. Known as The Mann-Hugg Blues Brothers before adopting their geeky keyboardist's name, they broke through when '5-4-3-2-1' (the theme to UK TV's *Ready Steady Go!*) became a UK Top 5 smash in 1964. Over five years, they made 15 hits, adding Soul and Blues touches to Pop covers – The Exciters' 'Do Wah Diddy Diddy' (1964) and The Shirelles' 'Sha La La' – while pushing Jazz and R&B on albums. *The Five Faces Of Manfred Mann* (1964) included standards like 'Smokestack Lightning'.

When Mike Vickers left in 1965, Tom McGuinness switched to guitar, his hard sound gracing hits like 1966's 'Pretty Flamingo'. Ex-John Mayall bassist Jack Bruce joined before swanning off to Cream. Paul Jones left in 1966 for solo hits (like 1966's 'High Time' and 1967's 'I've Been A Bad Bad Boy') and acting roles (starring opposite model Jean Shrimpton in 1967's *Privilege*).

New singer Mike D'Abo and The Beatles' old pal, bassist Klaus Voorman, added a poppier sound to hits like 'Semi-Detached Suburban Mr. James', yet kept the group's reputation for superb Dylan covers – following Jones-era versions of 'With God On Our Side' and 'If You Gotta Go, Go Now' with 'Just Like A Woman' and their third and final UK No.1, 'Mighty Quinn' – before they split in 1969. McGuinness formed McGuinness Flint and D'Abo went solo. Mann, with Hugg, flopped with the jazzy Manfred Mann Chapter Three , but the prog-rockin' Manfred Mann's Earth Band hit with 'Joybringer' (1973) and a cover of Bruce Springsteen's 'Blinded By The Light' (1976). In the late 70s, Jones (like D'Abo, now a radio presenter) and McGuinness returned with The Blues Band before re-forming Manfred Mann – with Jones and D'Abo on vocals but without Mann himself – in the mid-90s.

READ *Talk To Me Baby: The Story Of The Blues Band* (1994), Roy Bainton

SURF www.escritoire.demon.co.uk/manfredm.htm

MANIC STREET PREACHERS

WHO Vocals/guitar **James Dean Bradfield** (b. 21 Feb 1969, Newport, Gwent, Wales), vocals/guitar **Richey Edwards** (b. 22 Dec 1967, Blackwood, Gwent), bass **Nicky Wire** (b. Nicky Jones, 20 Jan 1969, Tredegar, Gwent), drums **Sean Moore** (b. 30 Jul 1970, Pontypool, Gwent)

WHEN 1988–

WHERE Blackwood, Gwent, Wales

WHAT Majestic melancholy

The Dance revolution might have conquered the British Isles, but it conspicuously missed four angry young men in Wales. Cousins Sean Moore and James Dean Bradfield graduated from bedroom Metal freaks to a garage band Guns N' Roses while bookish friends Nicky Wire and Richey Edwards were at university.

Inspired by Punk's tenth anniversary, Wire, Moore, Bradfield and early guitarist Flicker formed Betty Blue who, by the release of the self-financed 1989 single 'Suicide Alley', had become Manic Street Preachers.

Edwards designed the single's sleeve and found the band early gigs, then – though unable to play a note – replaced Flicker. His flair for angst-ridden soundbites – "We are the suicide of a non-generation," proclaimed the press release for 'Suicide Alley' – was crucial: he and Wire became the group's lyricists while Bradfield and Moore wrote the music.

The slogan-packed 'New Art Riot' EP (1990), on the Indie label Damaged Goods, attracted manager Phillip Hall (who moved the band to London) and the hip label Heavenly, who released 1991's stormers 'Motown Junk' and 'You Love Us'. In the midst of Britain's glum shoegazing scene ("We will always hate Slowdive more than Adolf Hitler," declared Edwards), the Manics were a marvel: their sloganeering backed up by Punk thrash, New York Dolls androgyny and Clash-style sprayed shirts.

The press was polarized, although most ridiculed their plans, especially when the Manics signed to corporate giant Sony and announced their debut album would also be their last: "We wanted to sign to the biggest record label in the world, put out a debut album that would sell 20 million and then break up. Get massive and then just throw it all away." When journalist Steve Lamacq questioned the band's sincerity, Edwards carved '4 REAL' into his own arm with a razor blade.

Generation Terrorists (1992) was a sprawling mess of Metal 'n' manifesto. However, the diamonds in the rough – a revamped 'You Love Us', 'Slash And Burn' and the classic, aching 'Motorcycle Emptiness' – were all UK Top 20 hits, and they graduated to the Top 10 with a rocked-out 'Theme From M.A.S.H. (Suicide Is Painless)' from the *NME* compilation *Ruby Trax* (1992).

Meanwhile, the controversy control jammed in overdrive: Wire injured a security guard when he threw his bass offstage at Reading 1992 and told a London audience he hoped "Michael Stipe goes the same way as Freddie Mercury pretty soon".

By *Gold Against The Soul* (1993), their metallic angst and bluster had been legitimized by Grunge, but the Manics stayed an elegant cut above with the hits 'From Despair To Where', 'La Tristesse Durera', 'Roses In The Hospital' and 'Life Becoming A Landslide'. With typical perversity, they supported Bon Jovi, but the lyrics – particularly Edwards' – were zeroing in on the pain which had driven Joy Division's Ian Curtis to suicide.

The '4 REAL' incident now looked less like a publicity stunt than a cry for help: Edwards confessed to alcoholism, anorexia and self-mutilation. In Thailand, he appeared on stage with blood oozing from wounds in his chest, the result of a fan's gift of knives. In December, their much-loved manager Phillip Hall died of cancer and, in 1994, Edwards was admitted to a psychiatric hospital and, later, a rehab clinic.

His illness could be traced on 1994's desolate masterpiece *The Holy Bible*. From personal despair to genocide, the album was a catalogue of atrocity, but proved their biggest seller, thanks to the hits 'Faster', 'Revol' and 'She Is Suffering'. The press swooped on Edwards' candid descriptions of his condition, but he was well enough to rejoin the band on a European tour with Therapy?

and Suede that ended with an equipment-trashing extravaganza in London. "We'll never be that good again," said Wire.

Having blossomed spectacularly, the band prepared a US tour in February 1995. But on the eve of departure, Edwards fled from his London hotel, leaving a box of books for a friend, and drove home to Wales. Police found his passport, credit cards, Prozac and – two weeks later– his car at a service station near popular suicide spot the Severn Bridge. No body was found and Edwards remained missing, despite unconfirmed sightings in Wales and India.

Manic Street Preachers disappeared, too, until December 1995, when they supported The Stone Roses in London. The military look of recent years was replaced by anonymous leisurewear, the audience-baiting Wire was subdued and their new songs retreated from the horror of the previous year. In April 1996, their first single without Edwards – the glorious 'A Design For Life' – trailed the determinedly hopeful *Everything Must Go* (1996). The title track, 'Kevin Carter' and 'Australia' all smashed the Top 10, broadening their fan base far beyond the 'Cult of Richey' (the distraught disciples who filled *NME*'s letters page for months on end).

Appearances at Oasis' Knebworth show and The Hillsborough Justice Concert preceded their own mega-gigs – including one at Manchester's NYNEX arena, filmed for 1997's *Everything Live* video. Amid the anthems and glory, there were dark moments that still belonged to Richey: 'Kevin Carter' and 'Small Black Flowers That Grow In The Sky', two of *Everything*'s best, were among the songs he had written before his disappearance.

READ *Manic Street Preachers* (1997), Nick Wise & Mick St Michael

Fan Spectators of Suicide, 15 Finnley's Lane, West Cowick, Near Goole, Yorkshire, DN14 9ED, UK

Surf www.manics.co.uk/

BARRY MANILOW ⊙ ✪

WHO b. Barry Alan Pinkus, 17 Jun 1946, Brooklyn, New York, USA

WHAT Adored MOR idol

Though scoffed at by Rock types, Barry Manilow is – to fans the world over – a God. Having graduated from child accordian prodigy to a job in the mailroom at CBS, he wrote the off-Broadway musical *The Drunkard*, moved into TV music (Ed Sullivan, commercials) and became Bette Midler's musical director in the early 70s. Ignored early efforts became smashes in 1975, when the epic 'Mandy' swept to US No.1, dragging parent album *Barry Manilow II* (1973) and his debut *Barry Manilow* (1972) in its wake. Belated Manilow hits besieged the chart that year – 'Could It Be Magic', the US No.1 'I Write The Songs' (actually penned by Beach Boy Bruce Johnston) and the title track of *Tryin' To Get The Feeling* (1975).

As a loving, loyal and predominantly female following lived and breathed Barry, *This One's For You* (1976) and *Barry Manilow Live* (1977) established Manilow as the king of (some might say mawkish) MOR. *Even Now* (1978) yielded chart scorchers 'Can't Smile Without You' and 'Somewhere In The Night/Copacabana (At The Copa)' – the latter a camp classic which spawned a successful musical in the 90s.

Manilow produced Dionne Warwick's comeback *Dionne* (1979) and stormed into the 80s with *One Voice* (1979), *Barry* (1980) and the transatlantic hits 'The Old Songs' and his Four Seasons remake 'Let's Hang On'.

Although later albums failed to reach the Pop peaks of the 70s, the UK No.1 *Barry Live In Britain* (1982) testified to his arena-sized following. Highlights like 1984's *2:00 A.M. Paradise Cafe* (with Jazz legends Sarah Vaughan, Gerry Mulligan and Mel

Tormé), *Swing Street* (1988), the show-tunes set *Showstoppers* (1991), *Singin' With The Big Bands* (1994) and movie soundtracks like *Thumbelina* (1994) and *The Pebble And The Penguin* (1995) demonstrated a talent which stretches beyond schmaltz.

Manilow's refusal to take his adoring fans for granted has allowed him to survive many a critical pasting and change in musical trends. Take That remodelled 'Could It Be Magic' for dancefloor and UK Top 10 action in 1992, but *Summer Of '78* (1996) was a classic Manilow crowd-pleaser.

(READ) *Sweet Life: Adventures On The Way To Paradise* (1987), Barry Manilow

(FAN) Barry Manilow International Fan Club, PO Box 40, Epsom, Surrey KT19 9EP, UK

(SURF) www.manilow.com/

MANSUN ⊙

WHO Vocals/guitar **Paul Draper** (b. 26 Sep 1972, Waretree, Liverpool, England), guitar **Dominic Chad** (b. 5 Jun 1974, Cheltenham, Gloucestershire, England), bass **Stove King** (b. 8 Jan 1975, Ellesmere Port, Merseyside, England), drums **Andie Rathbourne** (b. 8 Sep 1972, Blacon, Chester, England)

WHEN 1995–

WHERE Chester, England

WHAT 90s New Romantics

Originally known as Grey Lantern, then renamed in honour of the Verve song 'Man Called Sun', Mansun sprang forth with 'Take It Easy Chicken'. Released on their own Sci-Fi Hi-Fi label before they'd even played live, it won a deal with Parlophone, who released the UK Top 40 hit 'Egg Shaped Fred' in April 1996.

With a visual image hijacked from early 80s New Romantic and citing U2, Tears For Fears and Duran Duran as influences, Mansun's profile grew through 1996 as 'Stripper Vicar' and 'Wide Open Space' carried the band's dark Pop into the UK Top 20.

MANSUN: TOM SHEEHAN/LFI

Attack Of The Grey Lantern (1997) blended the singles with new songs to tell the tale of 'Mavis' – who turns out to be the aforementioned 'Stripper Vicar'. After entering the UK album chart at No.1, Mansun played their biggest show to date at 1997's Glastonbury mudbath – unfortunately blighted by a power failure. Having huffed off stage, they finished their set later on a different stage. Mansun concluded their triumphant year with the EP 'Closed for Business', which boasted a sleeve painted by the late Beatle Stuart Sutcliffe. They returned in 1998 with *Six*.

(FAN) Manzine Fanzine, 18 Jesmund Street, Liverpool, L15 1EX, UK

(SURF) www.mansun.co.uk/

MARILLION ⊙

WHO Vocals **Steve Hogarth** (b. 14 May 1956, Kendal, Cumbria, England), guitar **Steve Rothery** (b. 25 Nov 1959, Brampton, South Yorkshire, England), bass **Pete Trewavas** (b. 15 Jan 1959, Middlesbrough, England), drums **Ian Mosley** (b. 16 Jun 1953, London, England), keyboards **Mark Kelly** (b. 9 Apr 1961, Dublin, Ireland)

WHEN 1979–

WHERE Aylesbury, England

WHAT Prog Rock's last line of resistance

Long before Phish and Mogwai dragged Progressive Rock into the 90s, another band flew bravely in the face of fashion. While others clung to the coat-tails of Disco and Punk, guitarist Steve Rothery signalled his resolute out-of-stepness by nicking the name of his instrumental combo from fantasy author J.R.R. Tolkien's *The Silmarillion*. With their fortunes secured by the 1981 recruitment of keyboardist Mark Kelly and Scottish poet Derek William 'Fish' Dick providing vocals and visual focus, Marillion became a favourite of disaffected Genesis fans and adventurous headbangers, who sent *Script For A Jester's Tear* (1983), *Fugazi* (1984) and *Real To Reel* (1984) into the UK Top 10.

By 1985, they'd refined their Prog tendencies to include pretty Pop tunes – one of which, 'Kayleigh', became an international hit and made *Misplaced Childhood* their best-seller. The formula broadened further with the beer-stained balladery of *Clutching At Straws* (1987), but its melancholic air proved prophetic: the ambitious, overbearing Fish found himself at odds with the band and quit for a hit (1990's *Vigil In A Wilderness Of Mirrors*) but mostly miss solo career.

Having bid adieu to Fish with 1988's live *The Thieving Magpie*, Marillion enlisted fresh frontman Steve Hogarth and polished their Prog on *Season's End* (1989), *Holidays In Eden* (1991), the post-Fish highlight *Brave* (1994), *Afraid Of Sunlight* (1995), the live *Made Again* (1996), the hits set *Best Of Both Worlds* (1996), *This Strange Engine* (1997) and live releases on their own Racket label.

(READ) *Market Square Heroes* (1987), Mick Wall

(FAN) The Web, PO Box 533, Richmond, Surrey, TW9 2EX, UK

(SURF) www.marillion.com/

"The entire Antichrist Superstar album was about **me** being a **bigger** Rock star than I actually was. But by telling this **massive** lie, I became one"

MARILYN MANSON

WHO Vocals **Reverend Marilyn Manson** (b. Brian Warner, Canton, Ohio, USA), guitar **Zim Zum**, bass **Twiggy Ramirez**, drums **Ginger Fish**, keyboards **Madonna Wayne Gacy**

WHAT 1989–

WHERE Fort Lauderdale, Florida, USA

WHAT Shock Rock stormbringers from the sunshine state

Marilyn Manson are ironic if you get the joke, Satanic if you don't, and pathetic if you think one Alice Cooper is enough. They were spawned by trash-fixated student Brian Warner and guitar geek Scott Putesky – rechristened, in honour of all-American screen icons and serial killers, Marilyn Manson and Daisy Berkowitz. Other exotically monikered cohorts in Marilyn Manson & The Spooky Kids included bassists Olivia Newton-Bundy and Gidget Gein, and keyboard player Zsa Zsa Speck (replaced by Madonna Wayne Gacy).

With the early tapes *Meat Beat Cleaver Beat* and *big black bus*, a Kiss-ish attention to merchandising and image and a blood 'n' guts stage show, they enraptured Nine Inch Nails' Trent Reznor, who took them on tour, signed them to his 'nothing' label and produced *Portrait Of An American Family* (1994). By this time, they'd dropped the Spooky suffix, replaced their drum machine with Sara Lee Lucas, installed bassist Twiggy Ramirez and won a rabid Florida fanbase with the *Grist-O-Line*, *Refrigerator*, *Lunchbox*, *After-School Special* and *Family Jams* tapes.

Another Nine Inch Nails tour made them a national scandal but, while controversy raged, internal relations suffered. After onstage battles, Manson torched Lucas' kit. The drummer, who was behind it at the time, took the hint and quit. Ginger Fish stepped in and Manson joined a 1995 tour with young Industrial bucks Korn and 'Black Metal' survivors Danzig.

With Danzig left in the dust, Manson translated notoriety into sales with the mini-album *Smells Like Children* (1995). Meanwhile, the freaky 'Dope Hat' upheld the tradition of MTV-worrying videos for which Reznor and his associates are renowned. On tour again, Manson found themselves sharing a hotel with the cast of *Sesame Street Live* and the Orlando Magic basketball team, featuring elongated superstar Shaquille O'Neal. "Remember the bar scene from *Star Wars* with all the animals?" said Orlando player Jon Concak. "That's what it looked like last night. It was the Twilight Zone, man. A bunch of basketball players, *Sesame Street* and some guy with green hair dressed like the Grim Reaper, chain-smoking."

Manson got madder in 1996. Recording was blighted by black magic and drugs. More mundanely, Berkowitz was ousted – in what was now a Manson tradition, Marilyn hinted at the split by shoving his guitarist off a stage. MTV put their cover of Eurythmics' 'Sweet Dreams' on heavy rotation – instantly polarizing Manson's followers into 'Spooks' (the hardcore) and 'SweetDreamers' (newcomers). The fanbase united to send *Antichrist Superstar* (1996) straight into the US Top 3. Its mystic trappings were reinforced by fresh-blood guitarist Zim Zum (a name variously defined as "an angel who did God's dirty work" and the blank canvas on which God created the Universe). An avalanche of media fascination confirmed Manson as *the* hype *du jour*. The Dead To The World tour maintained their Alice

Cooperish reputation for onstage outrage, which took a turn for the serious when Interscope – nothing's parent company, already under fire for its association with undesirables like 2Pac and Nine Inch Nails – was accused by shareholders and censorious campaigners of breaking a promise to avoid the "violent or profane" with *Antichrist*'s "filth and crap".

Marilyn maintained his grip on the zeitgeist through 1997: touring with Satanic antecedents Black Sabbath on the Ozzfest, acrimoniously collaborating with the trip-hopping Sneaker Pimps on the *Spawn* soundtrack, planning a collaboration with Snoop Doggy Dogg, penning a scurrilous autobiography, partying with Janet Jackson, covering David Bowie"s 'Golden Years' for the *Dead Man On Campus* soundtrack (1998), and racking up front covers coast to coast. All in all, a hell of a guy…

 READ *The Long Hard Road Out Of Hell* (1998), Marilyn Manson & Neil Strauss

 Fan Marilyn Manson Family, 25935 Detroit Road, Suite #329, Westlake, OH 44145, USA

 surf www.dewn.com/mm/acs1.html

BOB MARLEY ⊙

WHO b. Robert Nesta Marley, 6 Feb 1945, St Ann's, Jamaica, d. 11 May 1981, Miami, Florida, USA

WHAT First international star of Reggae

Bob Marley was just one of hundreds of struggling youths from the ghettos of Kingston, in a freshly independent Jamaica, dreaming of stardom. Working in a welding shop alongside Desmond Dacres, the pair bragged how famous they would become. Dacres got the first break, approaching Ska producer Leslie Kong to begin a long and successful career as Desmond Dekker. Marley followed, and recorded 'Judge Not' and 'One Cup Of Coffee' for Kong in 1963. Both were the standard rocking Ska of the day; neither were hits. However, they set precedents, both for the former's moral lyrics and release by Island in Britain.

In dirt-poor Trench Town, Kingston, Bob formed vocal group The Wailers with Peter Tosh (b. Winston Hubert Peter McIntosh, 19 Oct 1944, Westmoreland, Jamaica, d. 11 Sep 1987, Barbican, Jamaica), Bunny Wailer (b. Neville O'Riley Livingston, 10 Apr 1947, Kingston, Jamaica) and Junior Braithwaite, along with female members Constantine 'Dream' Walker, Cherry Smith and Beverly Kelso. Through the tutelage of Ska star Joe Higgs and drummer Alvin Patterson, they recorded several cuts at Jamaica's legendary Studio One in 1964. The raucous 'Simmer Down' – a warning to local 'rude boys' to calm down – became a hit.

Influenced by Higgs and American acts like The Impressions and The Drifters, The Wailers became Jamaica's most accomplished vocal group of the era. Their Studio One hits included 'Love And Affection', the tender 'I'm Still Waiting' and the Rasta-influenced 'One Love' and 'Put It On'. Marley, Tosh, Wailer and Braithwaite took turns as lead vocalist before the latter left for America in the mid-60s, by which time Studio One had issued *The Wailing Wailers* (1966).

Marley also moved to the USA, where he spent eight months on a Chrysler assembly line in Delaware – an experience that informed 'Night Shift'. Before leaving Jamaica, he married local nurse Rita, who hit with 'Pied Piper' for Studio One in 1966. On

his return in September that year, The Wailers – now a trio with occasional assistance from Rita – launched their own label, variously titled Wail'n'Soul and Wail'n'Soul'm'. Despite several releases, they scored only two hits between late 1966 and 1968: 'Bend Down Low' and 'Hypocrites'/'Nice Time'. Marley wrote an album's worth of material for American R&B singer Johnny Nash, ranging from Rock Steady to Soul, although only singles were released at the time. Nash's hit version of Marley's 'Stir It Up' indicated Marley had potential outside Jamaica.

The Wailers, meanwhile, struggled on with producers Bunny Lee, Ted Pouder, Randys and Leslie Kong – achieving only local hits with 1969's 'Soul Shakedown Party' and 'Caution'. Kong later released *The Best Of The Wailers* (1968), incurring the wrath of the band, who felt they had yet to peak.

An alliance with producer Lee Perry, beginning in 1969, proved more fruitful. Perry's heavier, sparser rhythms and experimentalism spawned the Reggae classics 'Sun Is Shining', 'Small Axe', 'Duppy Conqueror' and 'Soul Rebel' and the albums *Soul Rebels* (1970) and *Soul Revolution* (1971). Instrumental backing tracks from the latter reappeared on *Soul Revolution II* (1972), recorded by Perry's house band, The Upsetters.

Wail'n'Soul was revived for one single by Rita Marley, but the band released their own productions on the Tuff Gong label, named after one of Marley's nicknames. Now committed Rastafarians, The Wailers hit with 'Trench Town Rock' (1972) and attracted Island's Chris Blackwell, then looking for a Reggae band with a rebel image to be marketed like a Rock act. To

Perry's fury, The Wailers stole The Upsetters' ace rhythm section, bassist Aston 'Family Man' Barrett (b. 22 Nov 1946, Kingston) and his drumming brother Carlton 'Carlie' Barrett (b. 17 Dec 1950, Kingston, d. 1987, Kingston). On their Island debut *Catch A Fire* (1973), Rock 'n' Roll licks were added by American guitarist Wayne Perkins. No hits were forthcoming, but 'Baby We've Got A Date (Rock It Baby)' drew favourable reviews in an era when the Rock press regarded Reggae as little more than a joke.

Burnin' (1973) again yielded no hits, but a buzz was building about this group of long-haired Reggae singers with militant lyrics. An appearance on BBC TV's *The Old Grey Whistle Test* spread the word and Eric Clapton covered Marley's 'I Shot The Sheriff' for a UK No.9 in 1974. *Burnin'* also contained Tosh's signature tune 'Get Up, Stand Up' and Bunny Wailer's 'Pass It On', and 'Hallelujah Time'. These were the pair's Wailers swan songs: both quit by the spring of 1974, grumbling about corporate interference, Marley being pushed to the fore and Bunny's reluctance to travel.

Continuing as Bob Marley & The Wailers (a name they increasingly used since the late 60s), the band thrived even without Bob's old partners. With vocal trio The I-Threes (Rita Marley, Judy Mowatt and Marcia Griffiths, all recording artists in their own right), the Barrett brothers, keyboard player Bernard 'Touter' Harvey and guitarist Al Anderson (joined later by Junior Marvin), Marley's star was rising. Packed with classics ('No Woman, No Cry', 'Three O'Clock Roadblock', 'Talkin' Blues'), 1974's *Natty Dread* became a hip purchase across Europe. Bob only needed a hit, which came with the anthemic 'No Woman, No Cry' from *Live!* (1975). Recorded at London's Lyceum and full of good vibes, it was Marley's first single to chart in the UK.

Rastaman Vibration (1976) offered remakes of Studio One single 'Cry To Me' and The Upsetters' 'Man To Man' (retitled 'Who The Cap Fit'), plus militant classics 'Crazy Baldhead' and 'War', the latter's lyric taken from Ethiopian Emperor Haile Selassie's 1968 speech on racial divisions to the United Nations.

The album sold well, particularly in America, but this was of little concern by the end of 1976. In December, Jamaica's political atmosphere became too hot to handle: an election had been called for 16 December, and supporters of the country's major political parties, the PNP and JLP, were fighting in the streets. On 3 December, Marley was at home in the plush embassy area of Kingston when two gunmen burst in. Don Taylor, his manager, was shot five times and a bullet grazed Rita's skull. One bullet scraped Marley's chest, another lodged in his arm. Jamaica's only international star was now a marked man.

Two days later, he made a heroic appearance at the Smile Jamaica festival, and flew to America to convalesce. Recordings in London in February 1977 resulted in the acclaimed *Exodus*,

including the mesmeric, rootsy title track, the classic 'Natural Mystic' and the hits 'Jamming', 'Waiting In Vain', 'Three Little Birds' and 'One Love – People Get Ready'. He was at his peak.

Kaya (1978) was a downbeat, patchy affair, but further hits arrived with 'Satisfy My Soul' and 'Is This Love'. He was locked into the international celebrity tour and party circuit, reflected by the live 'Stadium Reggae' marathon *Babylon By Bus* (1978). But 1978 wasn't all gloom: in April, during a now rare Jamaican appearance, Marley united the heads of the island's two warring political parties, Prime Minister Michael Manley and opposition leader Edward Seaga, a gesture designed to stop the ghetto fighting – although it remained only a gesture.

Returning to Jamaica, Bob planned a three-album suite, the first being 1979's *Survival*, recorded at his newly opened Tuff Gong studio. However, his health was a concern: a toe injury sustained in a football match refused to heal, he looked drained and false rumours that he was into cocaine abounded.

Yet 1980 began well: he and The Wailers played the Zimbabwe Independence Concert in April, 'Could You Be Loved' was his biggest UK hit for two years and there was a lengthy tour to promote *Uprising* (1980). But in September, after stomping shows at New York's Madison Square Garden, he collapsed while

bob marley

jogging in Central Park and was diagnosed with a terminal brain tumour. He played his last gig, in Pittsburgh, Pennsylvania, on 23 September. Further medical reports found cancer, apparently traceable to his injured toe. He died in Miami on 11 May 1981. Marley was buried at Nine Mile, the hamlet in north Jamaica where he was born. There are now museums to him there and at 56 Hope Road, the address of Tuff Gong. The latter became one of the Caribbean's leading music distributors.

Among the many posthumous releases are the final part of his proposed trilogy, *Confrontation* (1983), the UK No.1 *Legend* (1984), the boxed anthology *Songs Of Freedom* (1992) and the hits 'Buffalo Soldier' (1983), 'One Love – People Get Ready' (1984) and 'Iron Lion Zion' (1992). Awarded the Jamaican Order Of Merit, he is officially known as The Honourable Bob Marley.

His influence remains enormous. He proved Reggae could be commercially viable and, without him, there would be no UB40 or Shabba Ranks – or indeed Ziggy Marley. The latter (his son) went platinum in the USA with *Conscious Party* (1988) and united with The Fugees on a 1996 cover of 'No Woman, No Cry'. Marley is a figure Reggae has never replaced, yet his legend lives on.

READ *Catch A Fire* (1984), Timothy White

Fan Distant Drums, c/o Jeremy, 10 The Hamlet, Chippenham, Wiltshire, SN15 1BY, UK

George Martin

Born in 1926, George Martin joined EMI Records in 1950, taking over as head of Parlophone five years later. Among the artists he produced were Cilla Black, Gerry & The Pacemakers and, of course, The Beatles. Martin worked on The Beatles albums from <u>Please Please Me</u> (1963) through <u>Sgt. Pepper</u> (1967) to <u>Abbey Road</u> (1970).

He also became famous for comedy records – notably the Peter Sellers/Sophia Loren duet 'Goodness Gracious Me' (1960) and Sellers' Shakespearian take on 'A Hard Day's Night' (1965). Martin left EMI in 1965 and, with three other EMI producers, set up Associated Independent Recording (AIR) and worked as a freelance producer, enabling him to carry on working with The Beatles. AIR had studios in London, England, and on the island of Montserrat.

Knighted in 1996, Martin retired in 1997, having produced the best-selling single of all time, Elton John's 'Candle In The Wind 97', and an album of Beatles covers <u>In My Life</u> (1998), starring Céline Dion, Sean Connery and Goldie Hawn among others. Often referred to as 'the fifth Beatle', Sir George's story is told in his book <u>All You Need Is Ears</u>.

JOHN MARTYN

WHO b. Iain McGeachy, 11 Sep 1948, Glasgow, Scotland

WHAT Folk Rock cult hero

Donovan was billed as Britain's answer to Bob Dylan but John Martyn's career paralleled the Zimmerman story more closely. The crucial difference was Martyn's relative lack of commercial success. His early albums demonstrated a mastery of Folk guitar and complex timings before *Bless The Weather* (1971) added Jazz elements and the distinctive vocal slur often used as a lead instrument. *Solid Air* (1973) and *One World* (1977) added looping electronic percussion and sustained guitar. The harrowing *Grace And Danger* (1980) was Martyn's *Blood On The Tracks*, chronicling his divorce; the more hopeful *Glorious Fool* (1981) was a determined stab at the MOR market. *Well Kept Secret* (1982) nudged the UK Top 20 before Martyn settled into an inconsistent run of albums which only occasionally hinted at a new direction.

Couldn't Love You More (1992) and *No Little Boy* (1993) saw Martyn and famous names, including Phil Collins, reworking his old songs. More revamps graced *The Church With One Bell* (1998), a covers set ranging from Dead Can Dance to Randy Newman.

surf www.cybercom.nl/'keeslely/martyn.html

MASSIVE ATTACK ⊙

WHO Vocals 3-D (b. Robert Del Naja, 21 Jan 1965, Brighton, England), vocals

Daddy-G (b. Grant Marshall, 18 Dec 1959, Bristol, England), keyboards/

production **Mushroom** (b. Andrew Vowles, 10 Nov 1967, Bristol)

WHEN 1987–

WHERE Bristol, England

WHAT Trip Hop titans

Arising from England's legendary Bristol Hip Hop/graffiti collective The Wild Bunch (associates of Tricky, Goldie and Neneh Cherry), Massive Attack's seismic Dub kickstarted Trip Hop and put Bristol on the musical map.

3-D, Daddy-G, Mushroom and singer Shara Nelson started recording in 1986 and debuted as Massive Attack with 1990's 'Daydreaming', by which time co-founders Milo Johnson and Nellee Hooper had quit – the latter for fame and fortune with Soul II Soul. *Blue Lines* (1991) was a revelation: cameos by Nelson, Tricky and Reggae legend Horace Andy, shimmering Soul, deathly Hip Hop 'n' Dub and two classics in the form of 'Unfinished Sympathy' and 'Safe From Harm'. Barely impeded by a Gulf War-sensitive abbreviation to 'Massive', they scaled the UK charts and secured a BRIT nomination.

Nelson and Tricky were gone by 1994's *Protection*, although the rasping Rapper did pop up on the brooding 'Karmacoma'. Although the epic introductory single 'Sly' was a hit, *Protection*'s highlights came courtesy of Everything But The Girl's Tracey Thorn, who graced the title track and 'Better Things'. Dub master Mad Professor overhauled the entire album for *No Protection* (1994), while Massive reunited with Hooper – now a big-time producer – on their Madonna collaboration 'I Want You', from the 1995 Marvin Gaye tribute *Inner City Blues*.

The disturbing 'Risingson' (1997) preceded the long-awaited *Protection* sequel, *Mezzanine* (1998), which featured Cocteau Twins' warbler Liz Fraser as well as new singer Sara Jay.

Read *Straight Outta Bristol: Massive Attack, Portishead, Tricky And The Roots Of Trip Hop* (1995), Phil Johnson

surf raft.vmg.co.uk/massive/

JOHN MAYALL

WHO b. 29 Nov 1933, Macclesfield, England

WHAT Yes, white men can play the Blues

John Mayall isn't famous for his undoubted musicianship, superb songwriting or even for tabloid-enthralling debauchery. Uniquely, his fame rests with the number and quality of soon-to-be-famous musicians who passed through his band in the 60s.

A childhood love of Blues, inherited from his Jazz musician father, led to Mayall learning the guitar and ukelele while at school. After serving in the Korean War, he played keyboards and harmonica in The Powerhouse Four while studying at Manchester College of Art. Rechristened Bluesbreakers, the group moved south in 1963, spending the next few years gigging across London with an ever-changing line-up and often playing as house band for visiting US bluesmen.

Wider success came in 1966, when *Blues Breakers*, credited to 'John Mayall with Eric Clapton', reached UK No.6. However, by the time of its release, former Yardbird Clapton had already departed for Cream, taking with him bassist Jack Bruce.

Clapton's replacement was the prodigiously talented Peter Green, who in turn left to join Mick Fleetwood, one of Mayall's many drummers, in Fleetwood Mac – soon joined by a third Bluesbreaker, bassist John McVie. Other Mayall protégés included drummers Aynsley Dunbar (Jefferson Airplane, Journey) and Keef Hartley, future Rolling Stones guitarist Mick Taylor, bassist Andy Fraser (Free) and future Colosseum founders Jon Hiseman, Tony Reeves and Dick Heckstall-Smith.

label. His solo career began with a blast: *Curtis* (1970) broke the US Top 20 and 'Move On Up' became his first and biggest UK hit. The latter's effervescence balanced cuts like '(Don't Worry) If There's A Hell Below, We're All Going To Go'; as with Sly and Funkadelic, Mayfield entwined love and life at their best and worst. *Curtis Live!* (1971) is Mayfield at *his* best, blending solo gems and Impressions revamps. *Roots* (1971) presaged patchier later releases, but 1972's movie soundtrack *Superfly* was a deserved US No.1. Its hits 'Freddie's Dead' and 'Superfly' told street stories over edgy Funk – a seam still being mined two decades later by the likes of Ice-T (who collaborated with Mayfield on 1990's *Return Of Superfly*).

Back To The World (1973) furthered the formula to hit effect, but it was exhausted through *Curtis In Chicago* (1973), *Sweet Exorcist* (1974), *Got To Find A Way* (1974) and *There's No Place Like America Today* (1975). He diverted to Disco on *Give, Get, Take And Have* (1976), *Never Say You Can't Survive* (1977), *Short Eyes* (1977), *Do It All Night* (1978) and *Heartbeat* (1978) – all eclipsed by hit productions for Gladys Knight (1974's *Claudine* soundtrack), The Staple Singers (1975's *Let's Do It Again*) and Aretha Franklin (1976's *Sparkle* and 1978's *Almighty Fire*).

In the 80s, he was a cult success: revered by Soul-lovers like Paul Weller and a guaranteed club-filler, but of little concern to chart compilers with *The Right Combination* (1980), *Something To Believe In* (1980), *Love Is The Place* (1981), *Honesty* (1982) or *We Come In Peace With A Message Of Love* (1985). His profile soared in the 90s: *Take It To The Streets* (1990) broke a recording hiatus, Snoop Doggy Dogg and Ice-T sampled the Mayfield magic, En Vogue covered three Mayfield tunes on *Funky Divas* (1992) and Rod Stewart was among the stars on 1993's tribute *People Get Ready*. The originator – despite being paralyzed in a 1990 onstage accident when a lighting rig collapsed – responded with *New World Order* (1996), a star-studded comeback.

surf www.hh.se/stud/d96join/cm/curtis.html

MC5

WHO Vocals **Rob Tyner** (b. Robert Derminer, 12 Dec 1944, Detroit, Michigan, USA, d. 17 Sep 1991), guitar **Fred 'Sonic' Smith** (b. West Virginia, USA, d. 4 Nov 1994, Detroit), guitar **'Brother' Wayne Kramer** (b. 30 Apr 1948, Detroit), bass **Michael Davis**, drums **Dennis 'Machine Gun' Thompson**

WHEN 1964–1972

WHERE Detroit, Michigan, USA

WHAT E=MC5

Fame and acclaim for MC5 came too late: their status as pioneers grew only after their demise. Formed at high school by Rob Tyner, Wayne Kramer and Fred Smith, MC5 (shorthand for Motor City Five – a reference to their home town Detroit) switched from Pop covers to noisy freak-outs in 1965 when Michael Davis and Dennis Thompson replaced the original rhythm section: Pat Burrows and Bob Gaspar. Their high-octane Rock/R&B fusion was patented on their 1966 debut – a cover of the Garage band perennial 'I Can Only Give You Everything' by Van Morrison.

MC5 languished in obscurity until 1967, when radical DJ John Sinclair made them house band of his Love Energies organization – a subversive group linked to the White Panther

---

Despite, or perhaps *because* of, these line-up shenanigans, Mayall managed, remarkably, to place three albums a year in the UK chart for each of the last three years of the 60s. He continually experimented with the band, adding classical instrumentation and recording *The Turning Point* (1970) without a drummer.

A mid-70s move to the USA coincided with a downturn in the quality of his recorded work, but *Wake Up Call* (1993) was a return to form. Again calling on the talents of Mick Taylor and with cameos from Buddy Guy and Albert Collins, it confirmed Mayall's status as a Blues giant.

read *John Mayall: Blues Breaker* (1995), Richard Newman

surf mars.superlink.net/user/wnock/Hist/mayall.html

CURTIS MAYFIELD ✪

WHO b. 3 Jun 1942, Chicago, Illinois, USA

WHAT Superfly Soul guy

Flamboyant Funk 'n' Soul stars like Sly Stone and Isaac Hayes monopolize the 'legend' stakes, but the more bookish Curtis Mayfield was their equal in influence and innovation. The co-founder (at 15) of The Impressions, he led the band through its 60s success, from 1961's 'Gypsy Woman' to social commentary like 'People Get Ready' (1965) and 'We're A Winner' (1968).

Pausing only to recommend his own replacement, Leroy Hutson, Mayfield quit in 1970, although he had a hand in subsequent Impressions material, released on his own Curtom

Party and committed to revolution through free expression. Under the influence of Sinclair's LSD and Free Jazz experimenters Pharoah Saunders and Sun Ra, the group became the antithesis of the hippie scene – confrontational, mighty and angry. Signed to Elektra, their live debut *Kick Out The Jams* (1969) soundtracked late 60s student riots with a censor-baiting shout of "Kick out the jams, motherfuckers!" on the title track, blasts of primal noise and an apocalyptic deconstruction of Sun Ra's 'Starship'.

Dumped by Elektra for advertisements berating a major record store which refused to stock the album, they moved to Atlantic, courted mainstream success with the comparatively weak *Back In The USA* (1970) and *High Time* (1971), then disintegrated. Tyner worked as a songwriter and photographer until his death in 1991, while Kramer tried and failed with Johnny Thunders, Was (Not Was) and his solo album *The Hard Stuff* (1995). Smith formed The Sonic Rendezvous Band, married Punk goddess Patti Smith and worked with her until his death in 1994. Archive releases – including 1983's *Babes In Arms* – testify to MC5's awesome proto-Punk power.

 ourworld.compuserve.com/homepages/rauk/mc-5.htm

MEAT LOAF ◉ ◉ ✪

WHO b. Marvin Lee Aday, 27 Sep 1948, Dallas, Texas, USA

WHAT Rock Opera's Batman of bombast

A ten-year trek to success began when Marvin Lee Aday made the pilgrimage to Rock mecca Los Angeles. Early bands Meat Loaf Soul and Popcorn Blizzard rose only to support status and Mr Loaf (Meat was a childhood nickname) turned to acting, winning roles on stage (*Hair*) and screen (*The Rocky Horror Picture Show*). A 1971 album with fellow *Hair* cast member Stoney set no sales records, and he teamed up instead with New Yorker Jim Steinman (b. 1 Nov 1948). The pair paid dues with the National Lampoon Road Show before unleashing *Bat Out Of Hell* (1977): a no-punches-pulled cocktail of Springsteen, Spector and Wagner that became a near-permanent UK chart fixture, sold millions and, claimed Steinman, earned more for CBS than *Thriller*.

Aboard the post-*Bat* tour treadmill, Loaf, said Steinman, "lost his voice, lost his house and was pretty much losing his mind". He was further distracted by film roles in *Americathon* (1979) and *Roadie* (1980). In 1981, a frustrated Steinman released the intended follow-up as his solo album *Bad For Good*, then promptly pieced together Loaf's *Dead Ringer*. The latter was the first American album to enter at the top of the UK chart and yielded the classic confrontation with Cher, 'Dead Ringer For Love'. However, Loaf became mired in a lawsuit, hitting the bottom in 1983 when he filed for bankruptcy, failed to crack the US Top 200 with *Midnight At The Lost And Found* and watched Steinman's stock soar with hits for Bonnie Tyler and Air Supply.

He spent much of the ensuing decade on the road, doing well in Europe with *Bad Attitude* (1984), *Hits Out Of Hell* (1985) and 1984's 'Modern Girl' (profitably altered from the original 'Modern Duck'). However, the well ran dry with *Blind Before I Stop* (1986), *Live At Wembley* (1987) and a barrel-scraping hits set with Bonnie Tyler, *Heaven And Hell* (1989). Steinman came unstuck with his ambitious act Pandora's Box, whose commercially catastrophic *Original Sin* (1989) ended a platinum production run.

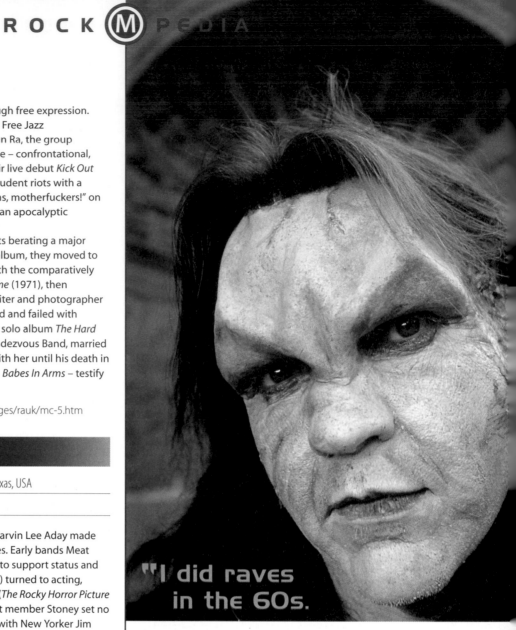

"I did raves in the 60s.

They had those projectors, the funny lighting people take drugs, stay up all night and get someone to play really loud. I did that. I don't want to do it again"

The reunited duo proved the power of branding by rehashing songs from *Bad For Good* and *Original Sin*, adding a handful of new tracks and releasing the result as *Bat Out Of Hell II – Back Into Hell* (1993). Both album and single, 'I'd Do Anything For Love (But I Won't Do That)', were the year's best-sellers, paving the way for marathon tours, cash-in compilations (the most highly recommended of which is 1994's *Meat Loaf And Friends*), an appearance in Disney's 1993 *To Catch A Yeti* (adding to a burgeoning celluloid CV) and the follow-up *Welcome To The Neighborhood* (1995). Though slimmed down from his 70s scale-smashing stature, the Loaf remains larger than life.

READ *Meat Loaf* (1982), Sandy Robertson

Fan Meat Loaf UK Fan Club, PO Box 44, Thirsk, North Yorkshire, YO7 1SG, UK

Surf www.1webplaza.com/meatloaf.html

Even crazier than Phil Spector, but equally inspired, Joe Meek had an eccentric upbringing – his mother dressed him as a girl until the age of 4. Though tone deaf and dyslexic, Meek entered the music industry as an engineer. His first hit was Jazz trumpeter Humphrey Lyttleton's 'Bad Penny Blues' (1956). "The idea of a sound engineer not doing what you tell him… that was a totally new world for me," said Lyttleton. Such disregard for convention established Meek as a maverick and, having been fired from studios all over town, he built his own in North London. With home-made equipment, he became Rock's first independent British producer. His first UK No.1, John Leyton's 'Johnny Remember Me', was a morbid, echo-drenched wail from a dead girlfriend that turned Leyton into a star and attracted a gaggle of later notables – including Rod Stewart, Tom Jones and Ritchie Blackmore – to Meek's studio.

Meek's 45 UK hits gleefully inverted accepted notions of sonic perfection. Best was The Tornados' 1962 smasheroo 'Telstar' – British Rock's first US No.1, the biggest selling British instrumental ever and Margaret Thatcher's favourite record. Success did nothing to calm his legendary temper, manifested in obsessive secrecy (he was sure his ideas and equipment designs were being stolen) and violence. He reportedly destroyed a new tape machine during a disagreement with The Tornados' Clem Cattini, while a pre-Hendrix Mitch Mitchell found a shotgun jammed up his nose when he failed to follow orders. Meek was a musical genius (1960's I Hear A New World Calling predated Brian Wilson's sonic experiments by years) but a business disaster: royalties for 'Telstar' were the subject of a court case and he turned down The Beatles. By the mid-60s, his career was on the slide and his depression was compounded by paranoia about his homosexuality – he was receiving blackmail threats and was under police investigation. On 3 January 1967, having shot dead his landlady during a dispute, he turned the gun on himself. Meek's legend lives on, not only in the producers which followed him – Mickie Most, George Martin and Brian Wilson to name but a few – but also a range of 'Joe Meek' studio equipment, built to his specifications.

MEGADETH

WHO Vocals/guitar **Dave Mustaine** (b. 13 Sep 1963, La Mesa, California, USA), guitar **Marty Friedman** (b. 8 Dec 1962, Washington, DC, USA), bass **David 'Jr' Ellefson** (b. 12 Nov 1964, Minnesota, USA), drums **Nick Menza** (b. 23 Jul 1964, Munich, Germany)

WHEN 1983–

WHERE California, USA

WHAT Thrash Metal is their business… and business is good

Fired from Metallica for obnoxiousness, Dave Mustaine created Megadeth with David Ellefson. *Killing Is My Business… And Business Is Good* (1985), boasting a cover of Nancy Sinatra's 60s smash 'These Boots Were Made For Walking', put them alongside

Anthrax and Slayer in the Thrash Metal vanguard, then *Peace Sells… But Who's Buying* (1986) showcased their best (the skull-splitting 'Wake Up Dead' and wry, political title track) and worst (the Satanic rubbish they had yet to outgrow). Its success didn't stop Mustaine indulging in heroin and high-handedness, hence a reputation for foot-in-mouth interviews (offended parties including the Irish and Iranians) and personnel upheavals.

After *So Far, So Good… So What?* (1988), Nick Menza and Marty Friedman arrived (succeeding drummers Gar Samuelson and Chuck Beehler, and guitarists Chris Poland and Jeff Young, respectively) and Mustaine cleaned up. Now stable, they unleashed the sleek *Rust In Peace* (1990) and began a run of UK hits with the Alice Cooper cover 'No More Mr Nice Guy'. Their popularity peaked with the transatlantic smashes *Countdown To Extinction* (1992) and *Youthanasia* (1994), but the band was again wracked by dissent and Mustaine took time out for MD.45: a collaboration with Lee Ving of seminal Punk act Fear on 1996's *The Craving*. 'Deth disciples were reassured when they returned with 1997's *Cryptic Writings* and a slot on the 1998 Ozzfest bill.

ReaD *Making Music Your Business* (1997), David Ellefson

Fan Megadeth CyberArmy, PO Box 883488, San Francisco, CA 94188, USA

Surf www.megadeth.com/

JOHN MELLENCAMP ✪

WHO b. 7 Oct 1951, Seymour, Indiana, USA

WHAT Hard-fought Rock success story

Of the uncomplicated AOR heroes tarred with the 'Springsteen Lite' brush – including Bryan Adams and Rick Springfield – John Mellencamp got it worst. In his formative, mid-70s years, the tag wasn't undeserved: the management teams behind David Bowie and Rod Stewart attempted to sell him to America as post-*Born To Run* star Johnny Cougar on 1976's *Chestnut Street Incident*.

No one bought the act until *Nothin' Matters And What If It Did?* (1981), a US No.37 credited to John Cougar. Resistance crumbled with *American Fool*, whose hits 'Hurts So Good' and 'Jack And Diane' made it America's biggest album of 1982. Success enabled Mellencamp to broaden his formula to Folk on the smashes *Uh-Huh* (1983), *Scarecrow* (1985), *The Lonesome Jubilee* (1987) and *Big Daddy* (1989) – all credited to John Cougar Mellencamp – and to co-found Farm Aid (highlighting the plight of American farmers) with Willie Nelson and Neil Young.

He entered the 90s minus the 'Cougar' but with a straight platinum average on *Whenever We Wanted* (1991), *Human Wheels* (1993) and *Dance Naked* (1994). The latter spawned the US No.3 'Wild Night', featuring extraordinary female funkateer Me'Shell Ndegeocello. Equally exotically, *Mr Happy Go Lucky* (1996) was produced by New York club king Junior Vasquez. Failing health and sales brought an uncharacteristic lull to the Mellencamp story, broken only by the 1997 hits set *The Best That I Could Do*.

ReaD *American Fool – The Roots And Improbable Rise Of John Cougar Mellencamp* (1986), Martin Torgoff

Fan John Mellencamp Fan Club, PO Box 679, Branford, CT 06405, USA

Surf www.geocities.com/SunsetStrip/Palms/7245/index.html

MEN AT WORK ⊙ ✪

WHO Vocals/guitar **Colin Hay** (b. 29 Jun 1953, Scotland), guitar **Ron Strykert** (b. 18 Aug 1957, Australia), bass **John Rees** (b. Australia), drums **Jerry Speiser** (b. Australia), saxophone/flute/keyboards **Greg Ham** (b. 27 Sep 1953, Australia)

WHEN 1979–

WHERE Melbourne, Australia

WHAT Came, conquered, conked out

Long before Tiffany proved how high one can fly and how far one can fall, Men At Work put their own spin on the here today, gone tomorrow syndrome. Graduating from Australian bar-band status to international megadom a lot quicker than AC/DC or INXS, they scored huge hits with 'Who Can It Be Now?' and the international No.1 'Down Under'. The parent album *Business As Usual* also topped worldwide charts, staying at the US summit for 15 weeks. Astonishingly, they almost did it again with 1983's *Cargo*, source of 'Overkill' and 'It's A Mistake'. Both of these hit titles proved prophetic, as interest plummeted with *Two Hearts* (1985) and, after the inevitable live albums, compilations, squabbles and re-formations, Men At Work were last sighted in a drastically shrunken incarnation, gigging somewhere in Brazil.

 members.aol.com/babsjdonne/menatwrk.htm

MERSEYBEAT

WHAT Early 60s Merseyside-based beat bands put US R&B and early Rock 'n' Roll through a chirpy Pop filter to create Merseybeat – led by hitmakers like The Beatles, Gerry & The Pacemakers, Billy J. Kramer & The Dakotas, The Searchers, Swinging Blue Jeans, The Fourmost and The Merseybeats, but also including lesser-known bands like The Big Three, Faron's Flamingos, Howie Casey & The Seniors and Freddie Starr & The Midnighters. By 1965, the basic Merseybeat sound, which had helped to change the face of Pop music, became unfashionable; groups disassociated themselves from it and the term was mothballed.

WHERE Liverpool/Merseyside, England

WHEN Early 60s

WHO Various This Is Merseybeat (1989), Gerry & The Pacemakers The Very Best Of... (1993), The Beatles Live At The BBC (1994), Swinging Blue Jeans The Best Of The Swinging Blue Jeans 1963–1966 (1995)

METALLICA ⊙ ⊙ ✪ ✪ ✪

WHO Vocals/guitar **James Hetfield** (b. 3 Aug 1963, Los Angeles, California, USA), guitar **Kirk Hammett** (b. 18 Nov 1962, San Francisco, California), bass **Jason Newsted** (b. 4 Mar 1963, Battle Creek, Michigan, USA), drums **Lars Ulrich** (b. 26 Dec 1963, Gentofte, Denmark)

WHEN 1981–

WHERE Los Angeles, California, USA

WHAT Unstoppable Metal monster

Thrash, Glam and Grunge have come and gone, but Metallica remain atop the Hard Rock hierarchy. Having been steered through death and disaster by Lars Ulrich and James Hetfield, whose love of Deep Purple and the punkier likes of Motörhead informed the Metalliracket on early demos, the line-up solidified with Kirk Hammett (replacing soon-to-be Megadeth mainman Dave Mustaine) and Cliff Burton (replacing Hetfield's roommate Ron McGovney). *Kill 'Em All* (1983) hinted at the songwriting strength to come but, commercially, stood out little from the Thrash Metal hordes inspired by fire-and-brimstoners Venom.

With *Ride The Lightning* (1984), Metallica graduated to Thrash template-stampers themselves; soon every act in the genre was mimicking their acoustic intros and bludgeoning riffola. Their escalating fortunes – scraping transatlantic charts, a place on the 1985 Monsters Of Rock festival bill – exploded with 1986's *Master Of Puppets* and a support slot with Ozzy Osbourne. Metallica were heralded as the band who would take the genre into the 90s, a vision stalled only temporarily by Burton's death in a coach crash on 27 September 1986.

New bassist Jason Newsted debuted on 'The $5.98 EP – Garage Days Revisited', a US and UK Top 30 hit in 1987. Its back-to-basics styling was promptly eclipsed by ...*And Justice For All* (1988), an ambitious expansion of the *Puppets* formula, whose best moments – the grinding 'Harvester Of Sorrow' and epic 'One' – were UK hits. Stateside, it became a sensation by rising

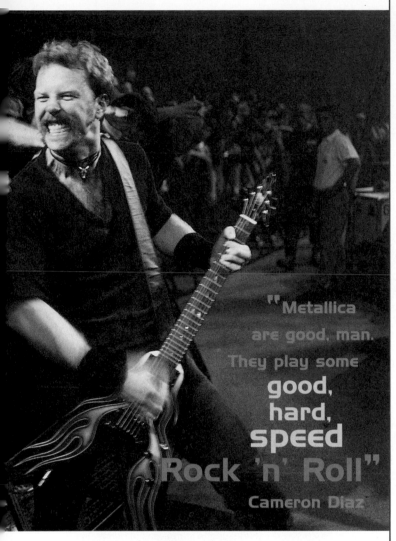

"Metallica are good, man. They play some **good, hard, speed Rock 'n' Roll**"
Cameron Diaz

to No.6 and multi-million sales with no single hits at all. Rivalled only by Guns N' Roses, Metallica entered the 90s as frontrunners: *Metallica* (1991) topped US and UK charts, spawned five UK hits – notably the anthemic 'Enter Sandman' – and spiralled on its way to multi-million sales. Ensuing world tours were celebrated by 1993's video/CD box-set bonanza *Live Shit: Binge And Purge*.

In 1996, they appalled hardcore Metallifans by 'going alternative' with *Load* (1996) and headlining Lollapalooza, but customary No.1 placings and plural-platinum sales suggested ballads and neater haircuts had barely dented their box-office appeal. Going madder in 1997, they unleashed another US chart-topping mega-seller (*Reload*), played London Dance mecca Ministry Of Sound, recruited Marianne Faithfull to "la la la" on the hit 'The Memory Remains', collaborated with DJ Spooky and Orbital for the *Spawn* soundtrack, guested at Neil Young's Bridge Benefit acoustic extravaganzas and generally made a mockery of anyone who dared to suggest Metal is dead.

Read *Metallica Unbound: The Unofficial Biography* (1993), K.J. Doughton

Fan The Metallica Club, PO Box 18327, Knoxville, TN 37928-2327, USA

Surf www.metclub.com/

GEORGE MICHAEL ⦿ ⦿ ⦿ ✪

WHO b. Georgios Kyriacos Panayiotou, 25 Jun 1963, Finchley, London, England

WHAT White Soul wonderkid and funky chartbuster turned morose superstar

Although he came to fame as a teen idol, George Michael has spent many of the ensuing years juggling commercial ambition with a desire for credibility. Michael's long career can be traced to a musical flexibility first evident in his teens. At 16, he busked on acoustic guitar with a friend in the London Underground, singing Queen, Bowie and Elton John songs, to pay for nights as a Soul boy in North London discos. In 1979 he turned to the then stylish Ska music for his first band The Executive, formed with Andrew Ridgeley and school friends, who played gigs in Bushey, Hertfordshire. Accounts of the act do not hint at future success.

When they split in 1980, Ridgeley and Michael continued as Wham! In 1981, Michael left school and – despite creditable exam results – committed to a music career, supporting himself by working as an usher, labourer, shop assistant and DJ. Wham! signed their first record deal in 1982, when Michael was 18. The 'group' was essentially Michael's solo musical project: Ridgeley's role – apart from scattered, early songwriting contributions – was as a promotional prop and companion for Michael.

In 1984, tired of Wham!'s bubbly Pop, but not yet confident to go it alone, Michael kept his options open by announcing that 'Careless Whisper' didn't fit the duo's fun image, hence its credit to him alone (or 'Wham! featuring George Michael' in the USA). Its staggering success – No.1 in 14 countries – established his reputation for life. He raised his profile further in December 1984 with a Ridgeley-less cameo on Band Aid's 'Do They Know It's Christmas?'. The inevitable split came in 1986 and Michael confirmed his solo supremacy with the haunting 'A Different Corner', the UK's first No.1 to be written, produced and recorded by one person alone. He returned to the top of transatlantic charts with 1987's joyful 'I Knew You Were Waiting', a credibility-boosting duet with the Queen Of Soul, Aretha Franklin.

With a eye on the solo superstardom of Madonna and Prince, Michael joined their establishment-rocking ranks with 1987's 'I Want Your Sex'. His protestations of a 'safe sex' message fell on deaf ears and neither the BBC nor MTV were happy with the salacious video. The controversy did sales no harm, but *Faith* (1987) – his greatest commercial triumph – proved he had no need for such tricks. Marred by only a couple of nondescript songs, the album spawned four US No.1s: the rock 'n' rolling Prince rip 'Faith', epic 'Father Figure', elegaic 'One More Try' and scorching 'Monkey'. Most striking was the Jazz-brushed fifth hit 'Kissing A Fool', which rounded off 1988 – the year of his first solo tour. By the end, the tour having taken its mental and physical toll, Michael's unease about fame had grown. His ambivalence had been signalled by *Faith*'s cover: the designer stubble, shades and leather jacket doubled as icons and armour. Now, Michael resolved to make the music, not the man, the centre of attention.

Accordingly, 1990's 'Praying For Time' boasted bleak lyrics and a resolutely un-poppy orchestral accompaniment; neither factor impeded its ascent to the top of the US chart. *Listen Without Prejudice* (1990) continued the downbeat trend, with only 'Freedom 90' recalling the danceable days of old. The latter's video continued the commercial/anti-commercial theme; it didn't feature Michael, but *did* feature hardly unattractive supermodels. However, when the album sold only a fraction of

"Why can't George Michael do what he wants? Why can't he write a ballet if he wants to?"
Prince

OLDER

Faith's millions, Michael blamed not his musical crusade, but on Sony's allegedly lackadaisical promotion. This escalated into a refusal to record any new material for the company, who he claimed resented his switch to a less commercial sound. The ensuing legal attempt to escape his contract lasted three years.

Meanwhile, he seemed happier with other artists' material and the earnest likes of Elton John and Stevie Wonder replaced Prince and Madonna as his role models. At 1988's Wembley Stadium-hosted Nelson Mandela tribute, he performed Wonder's 'If You Were My Woman' to irk beer-swilling fans of bill-toppers Simple Minds. His 1991 Cover To Cover tour honoured the songs he'd enjoyed at late 70s discos and up-to-date Dance sensations like Soul II Soul. Most spectacularly, he returned to the top of transatlantic charts in 1992 with two storming live covers: 'Don't Let The Sun Go Down On Me', a duet with Elton John, and 'Somebody To Love', a scene-stealing contribution to the Freddie Mercury tribute show at Wembley Stadium that sparked slow-to-subside rumours that he would replace Mercury in Queen.

Still at war with Sony, Michael donated three new songs to the AIDS benefit album, *Red Hot + Dance* (1992), of which the hit 'Too Funky' proved a witty Pop star still lurked beneath the serious singer/songwriter veneer. However, the jollity was short-lived: Michael's desire to be treated as an artist rather than a commodity never looked likely to cut ice with a judge and, when the contractual case was pursued to the high court in

1994, he lost to the tune of several million pounds. However, Sony graciously relinquished their grip in exchange for a financial settlement, a percentage of future album profits and the right to issue a dead-cert greatest hits collection.

Fleeing to the arms of Virgin and, in the USA, Dreamworks, Michael hardly sounded celebratory on his next single. Released in January 1996, 'Jesus To A Child' was a candid account of the death of a close friend that nonetheless topped the UK chart and returned him to the US Top 10 for the first time since 1992.

However, events took a depressingly familiar turn: despite a 'Freedom 90'-esque Disco stomper ('Fastlove'), *Older* (1996) was a *Listen*-esque introspective affair that failed to return him to *Faith*-esque bigness, which Michael again blamed on inadequate promotion. This counter-productive stance was rendered more unfortunate by Michael's performance on MTV's *Unplugged* in 1997 and superlative hits like 'Spinning The Wheel' – which proved that however wayward his commercial judgement is, his music-making is as unimpeachable as ever.

READ *Bare* (1990), George Michael & Tony Parsons

SURF www.flipside.simplenet.com/

BETTE MIDLER

WHO b. 1 Dec 1944, Paterson, New Jersey, USA

WHAT Pop flash, showbiz trash

Mixing earthy humour and glitz, Bette Midler straddles showbiz and Pop. Named after the actress Bette Davis, Midler grew up in Hawaii, where she worked in theatre and sang in a Folk trio before leaving for LA, then New York. She played in off-Broadway shows before graduating to female lead in *Fiddler On The Roof* and a Seattle production of The Who's *Tommy*.

Having honed a camp act – a mix of show tunes, Blues, girl-group Pop and comedy – at New York gay club The Continental Baths, she enlisted Barry Manilow as musical director and traded cultdom for a Grammy with *The Divine Miss M* (1972) and a hit cover of The Andrew Sisters' 'Boogie Woogie Bugle Boy'. *Bette Midler* (1973) did equally well, but *Songs For The New Depression* (1976) sank. However, Midler starred in the Janis Joplin-inspired movie *The Rose* (1980), whose platinum-selling soundtrack and title track's US Top 3 placing proved she could Rock.

With the live album *Divine Madness* (1980) and books *A View From A Broad* (1980) and *The Saga Of Baby Divine* (1983), Midler seemed back on top, but the movie flop *Jinxed* (1982) sent her into a tailspin. By the late 80s, however, she was back in demand, thanks to 1986's comedies like *Down And Out In Beverly Hills* and *Ruthless People*. Her role in 1989's weepy *Beaches* also revived her Pop career, with a mega-selling soundtrack and US No.1 with the classic 'Wind Beneath My Wings'. Similarly, 1990's *Some People's Lives* sold truckloads thanks to a transatlantic smash with Nanci Griffiths' 'From A Distance'. More crossover success came with 1991's *For The Boys* soundtrack, since when movies like *The First Wives Club* (1996) have taken precedence over Pop.

READ *Bette: An Intimate Biography* (1996), George Mair

SURF www.nwrain.net/~jstewart/bette.html

MIDNIGHT OIL

WHO Vocals **Peter Garrett** (b. Sydney, Australia), guitar **Jim Moginie** (b. Sydney), guitar **Martin Rotsey** (b. Sydney), bass **Dwayne 'Bones' Hillman** (b. New Zealand), drums/vocals **Rob Hirst** (b. Sydney)

WHEN 1976–

WHERE Sydney, Australia

WHAT Campaigning control freaks of Oz Rock

Originally known as Farm, and around in various forms since 1971, Midnight Oil coagulated in 1976. Founders Jim Moginie, Martin Rotsey, Rob Hirst and original bassist Andrew 'Bear' James (later replaced by Peter Gifford, then 'Bones' Hillman) recruited shaven-headed law student Peter Garrett, and released *Midnight Oil* (1978). By 1979's *Head Injuries*, they were known as troublemakers – their targets including uranium mining, human rights and the unscrupulous music industry.

Oil flowed into the 80s with *Bird Noises* (1980) and *Place Without A Postcard* (1981). *10,9,8,7,6,5,4,3,2,1* (1982) made them domestic stars, spending two years in Australia's Top 40. By *Red Sails In The Sunset* (1984), Garrett's popularity won 200,000 votes when he stood for election to the Australian Senate on a nuclear disarmament ticket. After touring outback towns with Aboriginal group The Warumpi Band, *Diesel And Dust* (1987) sold 5 million worldwide and spawned the international hit 'Beds Are Burning'.

Although *Blue Sky Mining* (1990) fell short of such dizzy heights, Oil's political standing remained high. Garrett was now president of the Australian Conservation Foundation and they played a protest concert in front of oil corporation Exxon's New York offices in 1990. Meanwhile, *Earth, Sun And Moon* (1993) and *Breathe* (1996) were book-ended by 1992's live *Scream In Blue* and *20,000 Watt RSL – The Midnight Oil Collection* (1997).

 pat.nyser.net/oilbase/

ROBERT MILES

WHO b. Roberto Concina, 3 Nov 1969, Fleurier, Switzerland

WHAT 'Dream House' master

Robert Miles earned his first DJ residency at a club near Venice, aged 17. He was also director of programming on an Italian radio station, his shows influenced by Future Sound Of London and Robert Fripp. In 1996, the self-styled 'electronic composer' won worldwide acclaim when 'Children', inspired by the Yugoslavian conflict, sold 13 million, becoming Europe's biggest hit that year. *Dreamland* (1996) sold 8 million and earned him a BRIT for Best Newcomer. *23am* (1997) starred Soulstress Kathy Sledge and furthered his tradition of ambient trance, dubbed 'Dream House'.

 www.deconstruction.co.uk

STEVE MILLER

WHO b. 5 Oct 1943, Milwaukee, Wisconsin, USA

WHAT Blues rockin' Space Cowboy

Steve Miller won a major label deal after a storming set at 1967's Monterey Festival. Five albums for Capitol were accomplished but only mildly successful. *Sailor* (1969), the highlight, combined keyboard experiments, hippie mysticism and straight Blues.

Toured to exhaustion and plagued by ill-health, Miller rested before *The Joker* (1973) broke him on a massive scale, its title track hitting No.1 in the US (hence a tuneless rendition by Homer in a retrospective *Simpsons* episode) and, thanks to a Levi's ad, in the UK in 1990. Lyrically more subtle and musically more straightforward than before, Miller struck platinum with *Fly Like An Eagle* (1976) and *Book Of Dreams* (1977), which blended keyboard washes, Blues roots and accessibly spiritual lyrics. 'Rock N' Me' (1976) hit US No.1 and both albums narrowly missed the top. A tighter, poppier sound took 'Abracadabra' to US No.1 in 1982 and its parent album high in worldwide charts.

After 1988's *Born To Be Blue*, Miller maintained a lower profile and concentrated on a rootsier approach which was critically well received but commercially less so. He has won the kind of professional respect that has earned his skilled, silky guitar-playing session slots on albums by the likes of Paul McCartney.

 www.stevemillerband.com/

MINISTRY

WHO Vocals/guitar **Al Jourgensen** (b. Allen Jourgensen, 9 Oct 1958, Havana, Cuba), bass/keyboards **Paul Barker** (8 Feb 1950, Palo Alto, California, USA)

WHEN 1981–

WHERE Chicago, Illinois, USA

WHAT Erasure go Industrial

Although he claimed to have been inspired by The Ramones, Al Jourgensen's first steps sounded more like Soft Cell. Ministry were wimpy Synth Poppers who, after EPs on Chicago label Wax Trax, signed to Arista for 1983's Howard Jones-esque *With Sympathy* (titled *Work For Love* in Europe), an album Jourgensen bashfully described later as "an abortion". He returned on the Sire label with Paul Barker (the only other Ministry constant) and the Adrian Sherwood co-produced *Twitch* (1986), a wonderfully abrasive mess of Metallic guitars and Industrial electronics.

The re-invention completed with *The Land Of Rape And Honey* (1988), Ministry crashed the mainstream with 1989's *The Mind Is A Terrible Thing To Taste* and Wax Trax side projects Revolting Cocks (whose 1990 *Beers, Steers And Queers* bridged the gulf between Kraftwerk and Hank Williams), Lard (with Jello Biafra), 1000 Homo DJs (with Trent Reznor) and Pigface, an Industrial supergroup starring Paul Barker, Steve Albini, Jello Biafra, Finitribe's Chris Connelly and Skinny Puppy's Dwayne Goettell.

The gonzoid Rockabilly of 1991's 'Jesus Built My Hotrod', with vocals from Butthole Surfers' Gibby Haynes, prefaced Ministry's commercial peak *Psalm 69: The Way To Succeed And The Way To Suck Eggs* (1992). After a chaotic slog through Lollapalooza and nerve-shredding shows of their own, they retreated to a Waco-esque 'compound' in Texas to record 1996's monstrous *Filth Pig*. Lard returned in 1997 with *Pure Chewing Satisfaction*, while Ministry contributed a cover of The Grateful Dead's 'Friend Of The Devil' to Neil Young's *The Bridge School Benefits Vol 1* (1998).

 village.cyberbrain.com/ministry/

KYLIE MINOGUE ◉ ◎ ◎

WHO b. 28 May 1968, Melbourne, Australia

WHAT Multiple-personality Pop princess

From bubble-haired child actress to galactic goddess, Kylie Minogue has trampled all opposition on the well-trodden soap-opera-to-Pop path. She shot to stardom as Charlene Mitchell in Australian TV smash *Neighbours*. Impressed by her cover of 'The Loco-Motion', producer Pete Waterman brought her to England, where she was installed in the Stock Aitken And Waterman 'hit factory'. Her endearingly amateur voice garnished a series of smashes: the UK No.1s 'I Should Be So Lucky', 'Especially For You' (with *Neighbours* sweetheart Jason Donovan, both 1988), 'Hand On Your Heart' (1989), 'Tears On My Pillow', the Waterman-masterminded Band Aid II single 'Do They Know It's Christmas?' (1990), *Kylie* (1988) and *Enjoy Yourself* (1989). 'Got To Be Certain', 'The Loco-Motion' (a US No.3), 'Je Ne Sais Pas Pourquoi', 'Wouldn't Change A Thing' and 'Never Too Late' all narrowly missed the top spot.

Critics were unanimously scathing but, with 'Better The Devil You Know' (from 1990's *Rhythm Of Love*), a frustrated Minogue won control of her visual image from her producers, replacing toothsome grins with smouldering stares. Thus was born what *NME* labelled 'SexKylie'.

Despite new found credibility (Primal Scream's Bobby Gillespie came out as a fan), sales dipped; 1991's *Let's Get To It* demonstrated the inflexibility of the SAW sound amid post-House Pop (although that didn't stop 1992's *Greatest Hits* becoming her third UK chart-topper).

By 1994's *Kylie Minogue* and the hits 'Confide In Me' and 'Put Yourself In My Place', she was in the more sympathetic arms of Deconstruction, who granted her freedom to re-invent herself as a sophisticated dance glamourpuss, courtesy of co-writing and production credits from Brothers In Rhythm.

An implausible 1995 duet with Nick Cave on 'Where The Wild Roses Grow' signalled yet another metamorphosis and she guested live with both Cave and Manic Street Preachers (who wrote 1992's 'Little Baby Nothing' for Kylie, but had to substitute Traci

Lords when the suggestion bounced off the SAW cocoon).

The Manics' James Dean Bradfield contributed to *Kylie Minogue* (1998), which pitched an 'Indie Kylie' persona alongside the familiar Dance Pop entity. Fans who favoured the latter image were spoilt for choice: Kylie's sister Dannii, who had followed in her footsteps, graduated from Pop confection to smooth Housestress around the same time.

surf www.kylie.com/

> "She's so great. You'd love her if you met her. Everyone would. In a way I wish everyone could, to see what a good person she is. She's so sweet and no-bullshit and funny, man, really funny"
>
> **Michael Hutchence**

THE MISSION

WHO Vocals **Wayne Hussey** (b. Jerry Lovelock, 26 May 1958, Bristol, England), guitar **Simon Hinkler**, bass **Craig Adams** (b. 4 Apr 1962, Otley, Yorkshire, England), drums **Mick Brown**

WHEN 1986-

WHERE Leeds, England

WHAT Missing in action Goths

Tired of Andrew Eldritch's despotism, Hussey and Adams quit Goth gods The Sisters Of Mercy and beat their old boss at his own game. First The Sisterhood (until Eldritch made an album under that name), The Mission stormed ahead in the great Goth race with 'Serpent's Kiss' and 'Garden Of Delight', trailing *God's Own Medicine* (1986) and their UK Top 20 debut 'Wasteland'.

The Mission's rockishness was bared on their career peak *Children* (1988), produced by Led Zeppelin's John Paul Jones and boasting the 'Kashmir'-esque epic 'Tower Of Strength'. However, excess aggravated internal rifts (Adams left temporarily after a nervous breakdown) and presumably prompted 1990's remake of Slade's 'Merry Christmas Everybody' under the Glam Rock guise The Metal Gurus. Hinkler quit midway through a tour for *Carved In Sand* (1990) and the band were never the same again.

After *Grains Of Sand* (1990) and a lengthy lay-off, the folky *Masque* (1992) saw the back of Adams (who fled for The Cult), while *Neverland* (1995) and *Blue* (1996) struggled to chart.

 www.geocities.com/sunsetstrip/palms/1566

JONI MITCHELL

WHO b. Roberta Joan Anderson, 7 Nov 1943, Fort Macleod, Alberta, Canada

WHAT Bittersweet lyricist and First Lady of Bohemian Folk Rock

In 1964, a young student tired of art college informed her mother "I'm going to Toronto to be a Folk singer." Thus began the career of one of music's most respected singer/songwriters.

There Roberta Anderson met and married singer Chuck Mitchell, and they took their musical double act to Detroit, where they befriended singer/songwriter Tom Rush. He made Joni's 'The Circle Game' the title track of his next album and persuaded Judy Collins to cover two Mitchell songs – one of which, 'Both Sides Now', gave Collins a major international hit.

When the Mitchells' marriage broke up, Joni moved to New York and met David Crosby, who produced her gentle, romantic 1968 debut *Joni Mitchell/Songs To A Seagull*. *Clouds* (1969) was a more diverse collection, ranging from the exuberant 'Chelsea Morning' to the ominous 'Songs To Ageing Children Come'.

Although Mitchell didn't make it to the Woodstock festival, it inspired one of her most famous songs. 'Woodstock' was a US smash for Crosby, Stills, Nash & Young and UK No.1 for Matthews Southern Comfort. Mitchell's own version appeared on the prettily piercing *Ladies Of The Canyon* (1970), as did the sardonic ecology anthem 'Big Yellow Taxi' – her first and only British hit.

Mitchell took a year off from touring before returning with one of *the* singer/songwriter albums – the stark, deeply personal *Blue* (1971). It contained one of her most upbeat songs ('Carey'), but otherwise evoked a chilling sense of isolation. On *For The Roses* (1972), the arrangements became more elaborate and introspection gave way to third-person observation. Mitchell railed against the music industry on the title track, then found herself in the US singles chart for the first time with 'You Turn Me On, I'm A Radio'. *Court And Spark* (1974) included another US hit in the dramatic 'Help Me', and the album's adventurous rhythms hinted at Mitchell's growing love of Jazz. Her live performances around this time were captured on *Miles Of Aisles* (1974).

The Jazz influence grew on each of Mitchell's mid-70s albums. On *The Hissing Of Summer Lawns* (1975), she coolly studied the lives and attitudes of middle-class America, and engaged in her most extreme rhythmic experiment: Burundi drummers on 'The Jungle Line'. *Hejira* (1976), with its haunting homage to aviatrix Amelia Earhart, and *Don Juan's Reckless Daughter* (1977), boasted Jazz stars like Jaco Pastorius and Larry Carlton. This phase culminated in 1979's *Mingus*, on which Mitchell set lyrics to the legendary Jazz bassist and bandleader Charles Mingus' music. Another live album, *Shadows And Light*, followed in 1980.

Wild Things Run Fast (1982) turned to deceptively accessible Soft Rock, notably 'Chinese Café' and a cover of Leiber & Stoller's 'Baby I Don't Care'. Angered by the ruthlessly competitive 80s, she laced 1985's *Dog Eat Dog* with some of her most polemical lyrics. Thomas Dolby's glossy production was as thoroughly 80s as the situations the songs described. Peter Gabriel, Willie Nelson and Tom Petty were among the guests on 1988's more relaxed *Chalk Mark In A Rain Storm*, then Mitchell returned to the acoustic intimacy that first made her famous on 1991's *Night Ride Home*.

A three-year silence was broken in 1994 with her cameo on 'If I Could' on Seal's second self-titled album. Seal returned the favour on 'How Do You Stop', from her *Turbulent Indigo* (1995), which combined commentary on contemporary issues with a musical style akin to that of *Blue*, and earned Mitchell a Grammy.

'Big Yellow Taxi' was a 1995 smash for Amy Grant, and Janet Jackson's 1997 hit 'Got 'Til It's Gone' sampled Mitchell's original version of the song. Mitchell's spirit infused the confessional/confrontational style of Tori Amos, who covered 'A Case Of You', and Alanis Morissette, who told *Q*, "I've grown to love *Blue*, and I think every song on *Court And Spark* is great." Sheryl Crow also rated *Blue* – "before she slagged me off in the press."

Mitchell's greatest disciple was Prince, who thanked her in *Dirty Mind*'s sleevenotes, titled his protégés The Time's *Ice Cream Castle* after a line in 'Both Sides Now', played 'A Case Of You' live, name-checked her on *Sign O' The Times* and announced that *Summer Lawns* was "the last album I loved all the way through."

Joni Mitchell's induction into the Rock And Roll Hall Of Fame in 1997 belatedly honoured one of Pop's most adventurous artists. The range of her work is encapsulated on 1997's fine *Hits and Misses* – the former featuring Mitchell's best-known tracks, the latter her choice of the songs she felt should be more widely heard. She returned to her first artistic love by devoting creative energies to painting, but the album *Taming The Tiger* appeared in 1998. At the behest of co-headliner Bob Dylan, she embarked on a US tour – her first in more than a decade – in May 1998.

READ *The Complete Poems And Lyrics* (1997), Joni Mitchell

SURF www.JoniMitchell.com/

MOBY

WHO b. Richard Melville Hall, 11 Sep 1965, New York City, New York, USA

WHAT Mighty Morphin' Techno Ranger

Entranced by Techno, Moby – nicknamed after his ancestor, *Moby Dick* author Herman Melville – abandoned a Punk guitarist past (he was a veteran of noisy boys Flipper and, briefly, 4AD darlings Ultra Vivid Scene) and immersed himself in technology.

By 1991, he was a top DJ and the *Twin Peaks*-sampling 'Go' was lodged in the UK Top 10. The eclectic early albums *Instinct Dance* (1991), *Moby* (1992), *Early Underground, The Story So Far* and *Ambient* (all 1993), manic live shows and tempos ('Thousand' exceeded 1000 bpm), and fierce singles such as 'Move' (1993), 'Hymn' and 'Feeling So Real' (both 1994) reflected a complex character. A rarity in Dance circles, Moby was a clean-living Christian and vegan – themes outlined on *Everything Is Wrong* (1995). The critic-confounding *Animal Rights* (1996) was a savage return to Punk and was toured with the decidedly un-wimpy Soundgarden and Red Hot Chili Peppers.

Meanwhile, Moby became gatekeeper of the Rock/Dance crossover with remixes for Aerosmith, Smashing Pumpkins, Metallica, Soundgarden and Blur, and production for Ozzy Osbourne. Collaborations were also mooted with Guns N' Roses and Hole. Movies also proved profitable: 1997's *I Like To Score* compiled soundtrack work including *Scream* ('First Cool Hive'), *Heat* (a cover of Joy Division's 'New Dawn Fades') and a rejected theme for 1997's Bond bonanza *Tomorrow Never Dies*.

surf www.moby.org/

MOBY GRAPE

WHO Guitar/vocals **Peter Lewis** (b. 15 Jul 1945, Los Angeles, California, USA), guitar/vocals **Jerry Miller** (b. 10 Jul 1943, Tacoma, Washington, USA), bass/vocals **Bob Mosley** (b. 4 Dec 1942, Paradise Valley, California), guitar/vocals **Alexander 'Skip' Spence** (b. 18 Apr 1946, Windsor, Ontario, Canada), drums/vocals **Don Stevenson** (b. 15 Oct 1942, Seattle, Washington)

WHEN 1966–1971

WHERE San Francisco, California, USA

WHAT Classic West Coast Rock

What's purple and lives in the ocean? Moby Grape, of course – who, unlike most of their San Franciscan contemporaries, favoured concise songs with great attack and multi-part harmonies. With five singer/songwriters ('Skip' Spence defected from Jefferson Airplane) their unique sound drew on R&B, Rock 'n' Roll, Country and Psychedelia.

Moby Grape (1967) was a classic, sunk by record label hype; *Wow* (1968), *'69* (1969) and *Truly Fine Citizen* (1969) are fine in parts. After *Wow*, Spence was institutionalized, having attacked his colleagues with an axe (in 1969 he released the disturbed, psychedelic *Oar*), and after *'69*, Mosley left to join the US Marines (releasing *Bob Mosley* in 1972) and was replaced by Bob Moore.

The mediocre *20 Granite Creek* (1971) reunited the original line-up. Various members periodically reconvened, under

pseudonyms like Live Grape (for a 1978 album) and The Melvilles aka *The Legendary Grape* (a 1990 cassette). The original name resurfaced for *Moby Grape* (aka *Too Old To Boogie*) in 1983.

Miller released *Now I See* (1993) and *Life Is Like That* (1995); Lewis released *Peter Lewis* (1995). Mosley and Spence, both schizophrenics, tragically spent years as derelicts.

surf www.mobygrape.com/

THE MONKEES ☉ ☉ ✪ ✪ ✪ ✪

WHO Vocals/guitar **Mike Nesmith** (b. 30 Dec 1942, Houston, Texas, USA), vocals/keyboards/bass **Peter Tork** (b. Peter Thorkelson, 13 Feb 1944, Washington, DC, USA), vocals/drums **Mickey Dolenz** (b. 8 Mar 1945, Tarzana, California, USA), vocals **Davy Jones** (b. 30 Dec 1945, Manchester, England)

WHEN 1966–

WHERE California, USA

WHAT Hollywood's prefab Beatles

Following the success of The Beatles' movies, aspiring American directors Bob Rafelson and Bert Schneider decided to produce TV shows based on the same loose idea. An ad in *Variety* brought 437 hopefuls to the auditions, which are now the stuff of legend: mass murderer Charles Manson applied but didn't get close; Stephen Stills almost got Peter Tork's job; and, at one stage, the

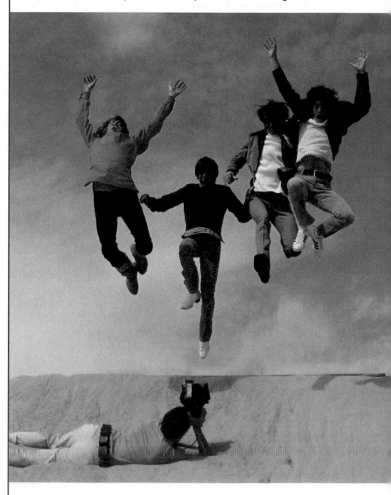

producers considered foregoing auditions and hiring The Lovin' Spoonful. The successful quartet comprised actors Davy Jones and Mickey Dolenz and Folk musicians Tork and Mike Nesmith.

Work started in March 1966 and, on 12 September, the first of 58 shows was screened in the USA. The impact matched the 90s triumph of The Spice Girls: *The Monkees* stayed high in worldwide ratings through two series and two years, supported by a string of Pop classics. Its pastiche sitcom insanity allowed slots to perform songs, often by accomplished writers like Neil Diamond. The presence of Nesmith compositions on the albums suggested The Monkees were a band, a notion supported by skilful direction of the song sequences in the shows and the distinctive vocals of Dolenz and Jones. Live performances were adequate, as belatedly evidenced by *Live 1967* (1985), but fans screamed more than they listened.

The Monkees and *More Of The Monkees* (both 1967) topped UK and US charts. 'Last Train To Clarksville' and 'I'm A Believer' topped the US chart, the latter becoming their only UK No.1. Media attention exposed the secret of their phenomenal work-rate: the band sang but didn't play on their records. Hired hands or not, this point rankled with The Monkees. Casting themselves as victims, they launched a press campaign to win support. Bemused TV and record company executives gave in after a bizarre and acrimonious battle.

The Monkees' 'serious' credentials rested with *Headquarters* (1967), *Pisces, Aquarius, Capricorn And Jones Ltd* (1968), *The Birds, The Bees And The Monkees* (1968) and *Instant Replay* (1969). The opening two hit US No.1, as did the single 'Daydream Believer'. Diminishing returns thereafter owed more to the fickle nature of Pop fame than any lack of musical ability.

The album and movie *Head* (1969) ridiculed their cynical creators with a blinding mixture of savagery and intelligence. The freewheeling narrative took their plastic status to pieces. The movie boasted Victor Mature, boxer Sonny Liston and Frank Zappa; the album boasted Nesmith's surreal psyche-out 'Circle Sky'. Both are now cult items. Tork and Nesmith left in quick succession and the two actors closed the account with the execrable *Changes* (1970). Rock's self importance and Pop's increasing plasticity saw The Monkees' reputation and catalogue dragged through the mill in the 70s.

Dolenz and Jones united with Monkee hit writers Boyce and Hart for a TV special in 1976, by which point Nesmith was a respected solo artist, best known for 'Rio' from 1977's *From A Radio Engine To A Photon Wing*. In the 80s the band, minus Nesmith, raked in dollars on a world tour and recorded new material. The back catalogue was often on radio, and TV re-runs of the shows added younger faces to concert crowds. In 1997, the 'Pre-Fab Four' united for *Justus* (1997) and a world tour. Nesmith had a huge inheritance (his mother invented Liquid Paper!) and his artistic standing to consider, but actually added to his reputation by participating.

Monkees hits are timeless, but debate on the other material is still fierce. The band's standing in this regard isn't helped by the presence of countless hits compilations and the lack of an album featuring the best of their own material. The thorough *Listen To The Band* (1992) collected almost everything of note, but its sheer scale made it inaccessible.

READ *Mutant Monkees Meet the Masters of the Multi-Media Manipulation Machine* (1992), Davy Jones & Alan Green

SURF members.tripod.com/'weeing willowly

Monsters Of Rock

Europe's premier Heavy Rock event, the Castle Donington Monsters Of Rock festival – in Britain's West Midlands – was initiated in 1980, when 35,000 headbangers turned out for a bill headlined by Rainbow. Since then, attendances have grown, with 65,000 enjoying Mötley Crüe, Accept, Y&T, Gary Moore, Ozzy Osbourne, Van Halen and AC/DC in 1984 and an all-time best of 97,900 for Helloween, Guns N' Roses, Megadeth, David Lee Roth, Kiss and Iron Maiden in 1988. Most of Metal's biggest and best have played the Donington stage, including Aerosmith (1994's bill-toppers), Anthrax, Biohazard, Black Crowes, Bon Jovi (1987's headliners), Corrosion Of Conformity, Def Leppard, Dio, Extreme, Headswim, KORN, Machine Head, Motörhead, Pantera, Poison, Queensrÿche, Sepultura, Skid Row, Slash's Snakepit, Slayer, Status Quo (1982's headliners), Terrorvision, Therapy?, Thunder, W.A.S.P., Whitesnake (1983 and 1990's headliners), White Zombie, Wildhearts and ZZ Top (1985's headliners). While AC/DC headlined three times (1981, 1984 and 1991), Metallica made the most awesome ascent – from fourth on the bill in 1985, to third in 1987, second in 1991 and top in 1995. Donington's loudest group was Iron Maiden in 1988. The 'Monsters Of Rock' banner has also graced tours of Europe and South America, headlined by the likes of Ozzy.

Monterey

The Monterey International Pop Festival was one of the 60s' pivotal events – the first time the hippie movement realized just how big it had become. Over one weekend (16-17 June 1967), it presented the cream of the era – Canned Heat, The Grateful Dead, Otis Redding, The Who, Jimi Hendrix, The Byrds, Moby Grape, Simon & Garfunkel, Jefferson Airplane and The Mamas & The Papas.

The preparations were lavish: 100,000 orchids were flown in from Hawaii to ensure there really would be flowers in everyone's hair, and legendary San Francisco LSD chemist Owsley Stanley III brought along a special batch of Monterey Purple acid. Led by the early examples of Simon & Garfunkel and The Mamas & The Papas, all the artists played for free, and much of the festival's profits funded a music instruction programme in Harlem.

Reputations were made at Monterey. The impact of Hendrix's set, climaxing with his celebrated guitar sacrifice, was immense. Before he played, he was unknown in America; afterwards, he was top of the tree, kissing the sky. The same applied for The Who, whose explosive set – the closest the weekend came to violence – was memorably described by Country Joe McDonald as "kind of a combination of wrestling and music". Janis Joplin's appearance with Big Brother & The Holding Company, meanwhile, was so stunning the group was asked to make a second, impromptu appearance on the Sunday. *Monterey International Pop Festival* (1970) featured a side apiece of Otis Redding's and Jimi Hendrix's performances, but 1994's four-CD set gave a more rounded impression of the event. D.A. Pennebaker's film *Monterey Pop*, meanwhile, remains one of the classic 'rockumentaries'.

THE MOODY BLUES ⊙⊙⊙⊙✪✪

WHO Vocals/guitar **Justin Hayward** (b. 14 Oct 1946, Swindon, England), vocals/bass **John Lodge** (b. 20 Jul 1945, Birmingham, England), drums **Graeme Edge** (b. 30 Mar 1941, Roxeter, Staffordshire, England), keyboards/vocals **Mike Pinder** (b. 27 Dec 1941, Birmingham), flute/vocals **Ray Thomas** (b. 29 Dec 1941, Stourport-on-Severn, England)

WHEN 1964–

WHERE Birmingham, England

WHAT Neo-Classical concept Rock

In 1964, guitarist and vocalist Denny Laine, Mike Pinder, Graeme Edge, Ray Thomas and bassist Clint Warwick were The M&B5 – an R&B group with sponsorship from Mitchell & Butler Brewery, playing a residency at Birmingham's Carlton Ballroom. When the sponsorship fell through, the band became The Moody Blues, building a solid fanbase in and around Birmingham and at regular weekly spots at London's Marquee Club.

A cover of Bessie Banks' Soul classic 'Go Now' gave the group a UK No.1 in January 1965 and a US Top 10 hit. Laine (later to join Wings) and Warwick left in 1966 with Rod Clarke replacing Warwick for a European tour. Disbanding three months later, The Moody Blues then re-formed in October with two new recruits who would change the musical style of the band completely.

Justin Hayward and John Lodge ended the group's period of uncertainty with the epic 'Nights In White Satin' in late 1967. Written by Hayward, the song was the blueprint for The Moody Blues' mystical, neo-Classical style, featuring their trademark ethereal Mellotron and flute lines. The album *Days Of Future Passed* (1967) established the group as one of the first English psychedelic groups to enjoy major success in the USA.

Their US fanbase grew with *In Search Of The Lost Chord* (1968). In England, they enjoyed success with *On The Threshold Of A Dream* (1969), registering a massive 73 weeks in the chart. Later that year, they released the first album on their own Threshold label, *To Our Children's Children* (1969). *A Question Of Balance* (1970) and *Every Good Boy Deserves Favour* (1971) continued the hits. Almost five years after their original appearance, 'Nights In White Satin' and *Days Of Future Passed* re-charted in the USA in 1972, both reaching No.1. *Seventh Sojourn* (1972) brought more success, before the group split in 1974 after a long world tour.

After various solo projects, including Hayward's work with Jeff Wayne ('Forever Autumn' on 1978's *War Of The Worlds*) and Lodge (*Bluejays*, 1975), the group re-formed for *Octave* (1978), with ex-Yes keyboard player Patrick Moraz replacing Pinder, who embarked on a solo career. The successful *Long Distance Voyager* (1981) was followed by more albums, including *The Other Side Of Life* (1986), *Sur La Mer* (1988), *Keys Of The Kingdom* (1991) and the live album and video *A Night At Red Rocks* (1992).

In 1993, the group were presented with a cassette of *Days Of Future Passed* and *Seventh Sojourn*, taken into space by NASA astronaut Commander Robert 'Hoot' Gibson. After the five-CD retrospective *Time Traveller* (1994), *The Very Best Of The Moody Blues* (1996) proved the group's popularity was far from waning.

FAN The Official Moody Blues Club, 53 High Street, Cobham, Surrey, KT11 3DP, UK

Robert A. Moog

With degrees in physics, electrical engineering and engineering physics, Robert Moog (pronounced 'Mogue') started building electronic instruments in 1954, unveiling his first synthesizers ten years later. Unwieldy and experimental synthesizers had been around for some time, but Moog's was the first practical design, immediately finding a niche among avant-garde composers. In 1968, 'The Moog' found its way into Pop, via Walter Carlos' <u>Switched On Bach</u>. By the end of the decade, The Byrds, The Beach Boys and The Beatles were all toying with them.

In the 70s, The Moog became a staple of soundtracks and Progressive Rock, courtesy of Jan Hammer, ELP's Keith Emerson and Yes' Rick Wakeman. With the dawn of the more portable Mini-Moog in 1971, Moog became as synonymous with synthesizers as Hoover is with vacuum cleaners. Having helped to inspire the electronification of Disco and Pop, Moog's profile dipped. However, his Big Briar Inc became a big cheese of instrument-building and produced the Theremin, famously used by The Beach Boys and most recently by Portishead. Prodigy named themselves after a Moog and its 'more 70s than thou' sound lives on, courtesy of retro types like Beck and Air.

GARY MOORE

WHO b. 4 Apr 1952, Belfast, Northern Ireland

WHAT Belfast Bluesman

Gary Moore's first band, Skid Row, boasted no less a vocalist than Phil Lynott, who left to form Thin Lizzy. Ironically, it was through later stints with Thin Lizzy that Moore made a name as a guitar-slingin' sideman. Since then, after a long career encompassing Jazz, Celtic Rock, Blues and Metal, Moore has taken the spotlight as a successful solo artist.

Early Skid Row mentor Peter Green of Fleetwood Mac helped the band win a record deal in 1970. After two albums (1970's *Skid* and 1971's *34 Hours*) they disbanded, and Moore launched his solo career with 1973's bluesy *Grinding Stone*. After a 1974 stint with Thin Lizzy and two years of session work, he joined the Jazz Rock outfit Colosseum II for three albums before returning to his solo career with *Back On The Streets* (1979), source of the beautiful ballad 'Parisienne Walkways'.

A brief late 70s reunion with Thin Lizzy – touring with them and playing on 1979's *Night Life* – preceded the solo metallic mastery of *Corridors Of Power* (1982), *Victims Of The Future* (1984), the live *We Want Moore!* (1984), *Run For Cover* (1985), *Rockin' Every Night* (1986) and the hits 'Empty Rooms' (1984) and 'Out In The Fields' (1985) – the latter a duet with old sparring partner Lynott. When Lynott died, Moore recorded the Celtic-flavoured tribute *Wild Frontier* (1988), echoed by *After The War* (1989).

His reinvention as a serious – and successful – Bluesman with *Still Got The Blues* (1990) belatedly brought the critical acclaim that had eluded him. *After Hours* (1992) co-starred legends B.B. King and Albert Collins. On *Blues for Greeny* (1995) – following a brief union with Jack Bruce and Ginger Baker as BBM (*Around The Next Dream*, 1994) – he championed his reclusive idol Peter Green. *Dark Days In Paradise* (1997) saw a reversion to Moore's particularly tough brand of Hard Rock.

ALANIS MORISSETTE ◉ ✪

WHO b. 1 Jun 1974, Ottawa, Ontario, Canada

WHAT Confessional, stadium-therapy Grunge phenomenon

Although Alanis Morissette comes from the Canadian capital Ottawa's middle class, her life was never orthodox. When she was 3, her father got a job at a NATO base in Lahr, Germany, and the family travelled around Europe. Returning to Canada in 1980, she precociously decided on a musical career.

Winning a part in the children's comedy TV show *You Can't Do That On Television* (future *Friends* star Matt LeBlanc played her boyfriend), she had her first brush with Pop via her debut 'Fate Stay With Me' (1987), which she co-wrote and released on her own label, Lamor.

Signed by MCA, *Alanis* (1991) was released only in Canada and aimed squarely at the Tiffany/Debbie Gibson teen market. It sold 200,000 and won her a Juno as Canada's Most Promising Female Artist. However, *Now Is The Time* (1992) proved her first career setback and led to painful self-examination.

Advised by her new manager Scott Welch, she moved to Toronto, then Los Angeles, and sought an artistic identity through collaborations with older male writers. At least ten of these attempted trysts failed until, in February 1994, MCA publishing introduced her to one of their most successful craftsmen, Glen Ballard, best known as composer of Michael Jackson's hit 'Man In The Mirror'. Their premier co-composition arrived within 30 minutes of their first handshake. Morissette credited Ballard with inspiring her to express almost frightening emotional honesty, exemplified by the line "Are you thinking of me when you fuck her?" from her first big hit 'You Oughta Know'.

Musical fulfilment did not prevent an emotional breakdown when she flew back to Canada in December 1994. Yet, thanks to therapy, she recovered. Her new confidence was justified when Madonna's label, Maverick, signed her and released an album featuring about 80% of the original Morissette/Ballard demos.

Subsequently, everything that happened to Morissette was routine hard slog – except that over 18 months *Jagged Little Pill* (1995) grew from a critically lauded 'debut' (outside Canada) to a global gargantuan, selling over 20 million. The blistering 'You Oughta Know' (featuring Red Hot Chili Peppers' David Navarro and Flea) was an attention-snaring trailer. The Hip Hop-flavoured 'Hand In My Pocket' and wryly anthemic 'Ironic' were smash hits, Morissette commanding adoration from young and old, women and men. Among dissenting voices was Courtney Love, whose equally pretty Grunge won less amazing commercial rewards.

Jagged Little Pill topped the US chart in October 1995 and the UK in May the next year. Meanwhile, Morissette graduated from a tour opener at the Electric Ballroom in Tempe, Arizona, in November 1995 to sharing a bill with Bob Dylan, Eric Clapton and The Who in front of 100,000 in Hyde Park, London, in June 1996. That summer she collected four Grammys and five Junos, then withdrew to rest before, again with Ballard, she addressed a prodigious 'follow-that' problem. She unveiled the new songs 'London', 'No Pressure Over Cappucinos' and 'You Gave Me A Wink' at Neil Young's 1997 Bridge benefit show, with a cover of

The Beatles' 'Norwegian Wood', but contributed her first post-*Jagged* release, 'Uninvited', to the soundtrack of *City Of Angels*.

In 1998, she duetted with Aerosmith's Steven Tyler on 'Drift Away', a Dobie Gray cover from Ringo Starr's *Vertical Man*, guested on The Dave Matthews Band's *Before These Crowded Streets* and considered an offer to play God in the movie *Dogma*.

(**Read**) *Alanis Morissette: Jagged* (1997), Paul Cantin

(**Fan**) FYI AM, PO Box 8873, Red Bank, NJ 07701, USA

(**Surf**) www.repriserec.com/Alanis/

MARK MORRISON

WHO b. 3 May 1972, Leicester, England

WHAT Horny, handcuffed Soul star

Mark Morrison was once famous for more than getting arrested and skipping bail. In 1996, he ruled the world: his old-skool Rap 'n' Soul was atop worldwide charts in the form of *Return Of The Mack*'s title track, school-yards resounded to imitations of his Larry 'Cameo' Blackman-derived vocals (the result of teenage years in Florida) and three irresistible hits followed that same year – 'Crazy' (a remix of his 1995 debut), 'Trippin' and 'Horny'.

Tragically, 'The Mack' took global megadom as a licence to return to the law-troubling ways that landed him behind bars in pre-fame years. Bowing out with defiant mini-album *Only God Can Judge Me* (1997), he paused only to discover girl-group sensation Cleopatra before absconding to cop-dodging exile.

(**Surf**) www.wea.co.uk/markmorrison/discmain.html

VAN MORRISON

WHO b. George Ivan Morrison, 31 Aug 1945, Belfast, Northern Ireland

WHAT The Celtic Soul brother

Irish singers have long combined their native music with Gospel and Blues, but Van 'The Man' Morrison did it first. Raised in a working-class household in east Belfast, Van's parents were passionate collectors of American records, and their only son rapidly became immersed in the exotic world of Jazz, Folk and Blues. First featuring in local Skiffle bands, by 1961 he was playing saxophone with local Rock 'n' Rollers The Monarchs, with whom he toured Germany and recorded before they split.

He joined the R&B boom with Belfast band Them, noted for their raucous performances, including Morrison's pile-driving 'Gloria', later hailed as the essence of the no-nonsense 'garage' sound. Second single 'Baby Please Don't Go' charted in Britain and America in 1965 but, a year later, Morrison quit. His first solo single, the classic 'Brown Eyed Girl' (1967), reached US No.10.

His grand reputation was founded on *Astral Weeks* (1968), recorded in New York with a Jazz rhythm section and songs about homesickness and heartache. His stream-of-consciousness lyrics and trance-like wailings earned hippie admiration and cast him as a Celtic seer. In contrast, *Moondance* (1970) was tight and specific, its title track a swinging tribute to Frank Sinatra

In the early 70s, Morrison flitted between San Francisco, New York and Woodstock. The quality of his albums varied, but

Night In San Francisco (1994) and *Days Like This* (1995) sold by the boat-load and a 1994 BRIT award for Outstanding Contribution To British Music was more than well deserved.

Read *Celtic Crossroads* (1997), Brian Hinton

Fan Wavelength, PO Box 80, Winsford, Cheshire, CW7 4ES, UK

Surf www.harbour.sfu.ca/~hayward/van/van.html

MORRISSEY ⊙ ⊙

WHO b. Steven Patrick Morrissey, 22 May 1959, Manchester, England

WHAT Former Smiths singer of bed-sit Pop gone solo

The sudden death of The Smiths in May 1987 shocked nobody more than their singer. By his own admission, Morrissey was "still in a state of shock, still upset and very angry" over Johnny Marr's departure when he recorded his solo debut – hence its title, *Viva Hate* (1988). Nonetheless, his first hit 'Suedehead' outsold any Smiths single in Britain and the album, helmed and co-written by Smiths producer Stephen Street, hit UK No.1 and included the entrancingly miserable 'Everyday Is Like Sunday'. With a guitar sidekick to rival Marr (Durutti Column's Vini Reilly) and his acid wit intact, Morrissey's future looked bright.

However, his creative partnership with Stephen Street fizzled out and sessions with Madness producers Clive Langer and Alan Winstanley failed to yield a second album. The ace singles 'Last Of The Famous International Playboys', 'Interesting Drug', 'Ouija Board, Ouija Board' (all 1989), 'November Spawned A Monster' and 'Piccadilly Palare' (both 1990) plugged the gap and, with their attendant B-sides, formed the excellent *Bona Drag* (1990).

'Our Frank' trailed the long overdue *Kill Uncle* (1991) and a career landslide. Co-written with ex-Fairground Attraction guitarist Mark Nevin, the album was savaged by the press while the singles 'Sing Your Life', 'Pregnant For The Last Time' and 'My Love Life' collapsed outside the Top 10. However, hiring a young Rockabilly band for a successful 1991 tour brought rejuvenation.

Your Arsenal (1992), co-produced by David Bowie's old mate Mick Ronson and mostly co-written with guitarist Alain Whyte, was – if not quite a commercial rebirth – more powerful and urgent than its predecessor. The band were sensational, as 1993's live *Beethoven Was Deaf* proved. Whyte and his fellow guitarist Martin 'Boz' Boorer became Morrissey's most enduring sidemen.

Your Arsenal also established Morrissey in the USA – some consolation for his demolished status as darling of Britain's music press. Criticized for the ambiguous sentiments of songs like 'Bengali In Platforms' and 'The National Front Disco', he provoked outrage by brandishing a Union Jack flag while supporting Madness in 1992 – a year later, the flag was everywhere as Britpop exploded. Guilty of self-involvement rather than racism, Morrissey redeemed himself by endorsing the Smiths-esque Suede and Echobelly. The thoughtful *Vauxhall And I* (1994) earned enthusiastic reviews and became his second UK No.1.

Neither *Southpaw Grammar* (1995) nor *Maladjusted* (1997) won him new fans, but Morrissey remains one of music's most idiosyncratic and intriguing characters as the compilations *World Of Morrissey* (1995) and *Suedehead* (1997) proved.

Read *Big Mouth: Morrissey 1983–1993* (1998), Pat Reid

Surf www.morrissey-solo.com/

1972's *St Dominic's Preview* was a return to spiritual meditation; 'Listen To The Lion' consisted mainly of wordless vocalizings, as Van tried to express his inner thoughts. Three 1974 releases showed various sides of Van: the brass-heavy live album *It's Too Late To Stop Now* (1974) demonstrated his unusual stagecraft, which involved call-and-response vocals and spontaneous revisions of established songs; *Veedon Fleece* self-consciously wove figures of Celtic mythology into his music; and *T.B. Sheets* saw him tear himself apart emotionally in the bleak epic title track with a hard-hitting rawness rare in a white performer.

A period of writer's block was broken after three years by *A Period Of Transition* (1977), but Morrison found himself out of step with current trends. For years, he played to a devoted but relatively small audience, but albums like *Into The Music* (1979) proved his ability to inspire. The relatively sedate *Common One* (1980) covered subjects as diverse as William Blake, the Lake Poets, Zen Buddhism and Arthurian legend, while *Inarticulate Speech Of The Heart* (1983) experimented with synthesizers and paid tribute to the Scientology founder L. Ron Hubbard.

A dramatic career change came with *Irish Heartbeat* (1988), a collection of Folk standards recorded with the Irish traditional act The Chieftains. Meanwhile, 1989's *Avalon Sunset* featured a duet with Cliff Richard on the UK hit 'Whenever God Shines His Light'. His reputation secure – thanks to huge sales of Rod Stewart's version of 'Have I Told You Lately' and the album chart perennial *The Best Of Van Morrison* (1990) – Morrison's 90s output has tended towards the generic. However, *Enlightenment* (1990), *Hymns To The Silence* (1991), *Too Long In Exile* (1993), *A*

MÖTLEY CRÜE ⊛

WHO Vocals **Vince Neil** (b. Vincent Neil Wharton, 8 Feb 1961, Hollywood, California, USA), guitar **Mick Mars** (b. Bob Deal, 3 Apr 1956, Terre Haute, Indiana, USA), bass **Nikki Sixx** (b. Frank Carlton Serafino Ferrano, 11 Dec 1958, San Jose, California), drums **Tommy Lee** (b. Thomas Lee Bass, 3 Oct 1962, Athens, Greece)

WHEN 1981–

WHERE Hollywood, California, USA

WHAT Glam Metal's self-proclaimed sleaze slüts

Gripped by New Wave and AOR, America regarded Glam Metal like discarded chewing gum. Undaunted, Mötley Crüe mixed Kiss-esque spikes and smokebombs, and New York Dollsy Punk. *Too Fast For Love* (1981), released on their own Leathür label before being remixed and reissued by Elektra, spread Mötley's fame from their LA base to Europe. In their first celebrity liaison, Sixx lived with Rock chick Lita Ford. However, heavy touring – including a stint with Kiss – did little for their faltering finances.

Shout At The Devil (1983) turned things around: its Satanism 'n' sleaze blend crashed the US Top 20 on the way to platinum sales. A 1984 tour with Ozzy Osbourne sent them spiralling to new depths; Mötley's excesses could kill lesser mörtals.

Meanwhile, Lee's marriage to model Elaine Bergen (the future Mrs John Mellencamp) lasted a whole month.

Mötley hit Europe at 1984's Monsters Of Rock festival, which proved them leagues above contemporaries like Quiet Riot. But their lifestyle took its toll: Neil crashed his car in December 1984, killing his passenger, Hanoi Rocks' Razzle. The tragedy added pathos to *Theatre Of Pain* (1985), but its hit 'Smokin' In The Boys Room' said more about Mötley's oütlook. Despite snaring Prince protégée Vanity, Sixx spent most of his time in the grip of heroin. More happily, Lee married actress Heather Locklear in 1986.

Girls, Girls, Girls (1987) proved hell-raising hadn't sapped their firepower; denied the US No.1 only by Whitney Houston, it made Mötley arena-filling stars. However, the anti-heroin evangelism of cuts like 'Dancing On Glass' went unheralded by its makers. Even the momentously wasted Guns N' Roses were alarmed when they had to save Sixx from a potentially fatal overdose.

They cleaned up in 1988 and, despite failing to recruit Quincy Jones as producer, topped the US chart with *Dr. Feelgood* (1989). Happiness continued with Sixx's marriage to a *Playboy* playmate in 1990, the hits set *Decade Of Decadence* (1991) and a $25 million renewed record deal. The latter began to look like misplaced confidence by Elektra when Neil was fired in 1992 and replaced by John Corabi. Concern turned to horror when, in the Glam-squashing wake of Grunge, *Mötley Crüe* (1994) bombed, despite its gritty excellence. Overnight, Mötley plummeted from arenas to clubs. Marriages foundered all round.

Lee took solace in Nine Inch Nails (he drummed, uncredited, on their 1994 album *The Downward Spiral*), before falling in love

with Pamela Anderson. Sixx followed suit with *Baywatch*'s Donna D'Erico. These unions fuelled headlines while musical projects like *Personality #9* went ünreleased. In 1996, after years of hostility, Neil was tempted back, his *Exposed* (1993) and *Carved In Stone* (1995) having failed to set the world alight. The reünion album *Generation Swine* (1997) crashed the US Top 5, confirming you can't keep good Glamsters down – though Pamela had a good go when she filed for divorce from Lee *twice*…

(read) *Mötley Crüe: Rüde, Lüde & Crüde* (1994), Sylvie Simmons & Malcolm Dome

(fan) Mötley Crüe, c/o Left Band Organization., 6255 Sunset Boulevard, Suite 1111, Hollywood, CA 90028, USA

(surf) www.motley.com/

MOTÖRHEAD ⊙

WHO Vocals/bass **Lemmy** (b. Ian Fraiser Kilminster, 24 Dec 1945, Stoke-on-Trent, Staffordshire, England), guitar **Phil Campbell** (b. 7 May 1961, Pontypridd, Mid Glamorgan, Wales), drums **Mikkey Dee** (b. 31 Oct 1963, Olundby, Sweden)

WHEN 1975–

WHERE London, England

WHAT The heaviest of Metal veterans

Rock mythology predicts only cockroaches and Keith Richards will survive a nuclear apocalypse. However, it's likely that also scurrying under a stone will be Lemmy: hero of Hell's Angels, roadie for Jimi Hendrix and the voice of Hawkwind's anthem 'Silver Machine'. Dumped from Hawkwind for drugs offences (a bit like getting fired from Hanson for being too young), Lemmy plotted the death of melody with the speed-crazed Bastard – sensitively renamed Motörhead. Guitarist Larry Wallis and drummer Lucas Fox gave way to 'Fast' Eddie Clarke and 'Philthy' Phil Taylor, who followed an eponymous 1977 debut with the classics *Overkill* (1978) and *Bomber* (1979). Loud, fast and rude, Motörhead straddled Punk and Metal – a skull-splitting formula most successfully followed by Metallica. They peaked when 1980's 'The Golden Years EP' and *Ace Of Spades* crashed UK Top 10s, followed by 'The St Valentine's Day Massacre' EP and the chart-topping *No Sleep Till Hammersmith* (1981).

However, *Iron Fist* (1982) was weak and Clarke left in protest at a union with the late Plasmatics bombshell Wendy O. Williams (on a destruction of Tammy Wynette's 'Stand By Your Man'). Thin Lizzy's Brian Robertson deputized on the atypically tuneful *Another Perfect Day* (1983), but their fortunes improved only when a new line-up – riff-mongers Phil Campbell and Michael 'Wurzel' Burston, and drummer Pete Gill – debuted on fresh cuts for the barnstorming best-of *No Remorse* (1984).

After 1986's gloriously grinding *Orgasmatron*, a spate of patchy albums, personnel upheavals and label-hopping rivalled only by The Fall did them no favours, although *1916* (1991) and *March Or Die* (1992) were their strongest for a decade. Motörhead's legacy was celebrated when, at a handful of 1992 US dates, they joined a dream bill of Guns N' Roses, Metallica and Body Count. The latter's Ice-T guested on Motörhead's 1994 hit 'Born To Raise Hell', but contemporary albums were eclipsed by Primal Scream's 1997 cover of their signature tune 'Motorhead', Lemmy's cameo in an insurance ad and the use of 'Ace Of Spades' in a TV ad for Pot Noodles.

(read) *The Illustrated Collector's Guide To Motörhead* (1994), Alan Burridge & Mick Stevenson

(fan) Motörheadbangers, 634 Blandford Road, Poole, BH16 5EQ, UK

(surf) www.ciseg21.demon.co.uk/

Berry Gordy won success as a composer (Jackie Wilson's 'Reet Petite') and performer – charting with 'Money (That's What I Want)' – before launching Motown, the world's greatest black record company in 1960.

Named in honour of Detroit – or 'Motortown' – Motown first scored with Smokey Robinson's 'Shop Around' on the Tamla label. In addition to signing The Marvelettes, The Supremes, The Four Tops, The Temptations, Gladys Knight, Marvin Gaye, Stevie Wonder and The Jackson 5, Gordy convened in-house writer/producers including Smokey, Holland Dozier Holland, Whitfield & Strong and Ashford & Simpson. UK hits on a specially created Tamla Motown label were endorsed by The Beatles, contributing to massive international success for two more decades. The company's fortunes waned in the 80s, despite hits by Rick James, Lionel Richie and Teena Marie. Gordy sold it to MCA in 1988. The 90s saw a rebirth courtesy of Boyz II Men and Motown was acquired by Polygram in 1993.

Motown

MOTT THE HOOPLE

WHO Vocals/guitar **Ian Hunter** (b. Ian Patterson, 3 Jun 1939, Oswestry, Shropshire, England), guitar **Mick Ralphs** (b. 31 May 1944, Hereford, England), bass **Peter Overend Watts** (b. 13 May 1949, Birmingham, England), drums **Terence Dale 'Buffin' Griffin** (b. 24 Oct 1948, Ross-on-Wye, Herefordshire, England), keyboards **Verden Allen** (b. Terence Allen, 26 May 1944, Crynant, Wales)

WHEN 1969–1976

WHERE Hereford, England

WHAT Raucous, riotous, Rock 'n' Roll

While in prison in 1968, producer/manager (and future Clash soundman) Guy Stevens discovered Willard Manus' novel *Mott The Hoople* and vowed to find a band to match the moniker. When The Silence successfully auditioned for Stevens in 1969, they reluctantly agreed to change their name. Original vocalist Stan Tippins was ousted in favour of Ian Hunter, but returned as their road manager. Stevens quickly hustled them into a studio to record their patchy, self-titled debut album (1969) in a week.

Mad Shadow (1970) was a second modest hit, but the band became better known as a raucous live act (a ban on 'Rock acts' resulted after one riotous gig at London's Royal Albert Hall in 1971) and grabbed attention in the USA with constant touring (later chronicled memorably in Hunter's *Diary Of A Rock 'N' Roll Star*). Album sales were still comparatively weak; 1971's *Wildlife* reached UK No.44 while *Brain Capers* failed to chart.

A nadir came in early 1972 when, booked into fourth-rate European venues, they decided to split after a particularly dismal gig in a disused gas holder in Switzerland. Still contracted to tour England, Watts contacted David Bowie, who had offered them *Ziggy Stardust*'s 'Suffragette City'. Bowie donated the ruefully anthemic 'All The Young Dudes', which became a UK No.3 in 1972, although their album of the same name stalled at No.21.

The hard-rocking follow-ups, 1973's *Mott* (UK No.7) and 1974's *The Hoople* (UK No.11), spawned the hits 'Honaloochie Boogie', 'All The Way From Memphis', 'Roll Away The Stone' and 'Golden Age Of Rock 'n' Roll'. However, personnel changes complicated matters when keyboard player Verden Allen was replaced by Morgan Fisher in 1972. Ralphs fled the following year to Bad Company. His replacement was Spooky Tooth's Luther Grosvenor, who was contractually obliged to change his name; singer Lynsey De Paul suggested Ariel Bender. This line-up is celebrated by the compilation *Walkin' With A Mountain* (1990).

In late 1974, Bowie sidekick Mick Ronson (b. 26 May 1946, Hull, England, d. 29 Apr 1993) replaced Bender, who left under a cloud. However, Mott finally disintegrated two months later.

Ronson scored with *Slaughter On Tenth Avenue* (1974) and the superior *Play Don't Worry* (1975), and helped out on Hunter's solo debut *Ian Hunter* (1975). Their erratic partnership was renewed on 1988's *YUI Orta*. Ronson's final album, *Heaven Or Hull*, was posthumously completed by admirers like Def Leppard's Joe Elliot. Meanwhile, the remaining members re-formed briefly as Mott in 1975 and as The British Lions in 1976 with little success.

read *All The Way To Memphis – The Story Of Mott The Hoople* (1997), Philip Cato

THE MOVE

WHO Vocals/guitar **Roy Wood** (b. 8 Nov 1946, Birmingham, England), guitar **Trevor Burton** (b. 9 Mar 1944, Birmingham), bass **Chris 'Ace' Kefford** (b. 10 Dec 1946, Birmingham), drums **Bev Bevan** (b. 25 Nov 1946, Birmingham)

WHEN 1966–1972

WHERE Birmingham, England

WHAT Symphonic Psychedelia

While The Move moved from gangster-clad, psychedelic-tinged Rockers, through cabaret, to studio-based, classically influenced Rock 'n' Roll, one factor remained constant: the songwriting skills of multi-instrumentalist and reluctant frontman Roy Wood.

They were formed after a move (hence the name) to London by members of Birmingham bands determined to make the big time. Shows at The Marquee in London and a revolutionary act (including destruction of TV sets, cars and busts of Hitler) won them a following. Their debut 'Night Of Fear' (1967), built on a guitar riff adapted from Tchaikovsky's '1812 Overture', was, like all their subsequent A-sides, written by Wood. The follow-up 'I Can Hear The Grass Grow' peaked at No.5 and, later in 1967, 'Flowers In The Rain' hit No.2. Featuring an innovative woodwind and string arrangement, it was the first record to be played on BBC Radio 1 in 1967, but a promotional postcard libelling Prime Minister Harold Wilson resulted in court action which the group lost, with all royalties henceforth payable to charity.

They enjoyed another major hit with 'Fire Brigade' (1968), but growing tensions led to Chris Kefford's departure. Trevor Burton took over on bass but, disenchanted with their increasingly commercial drift, left in 1969 to be replaced by Rick Price. The Hendrix-influenced 'Wild Tiger Woman' (1968), their first outright failure, was followed by their only chart-topper, 'Blackberry Way' (1969). Its reliance on mellotron and additional instruments heralded Wood's preoccupation with more Classical sounds and the formation of his new brainchild, the Electric Light Orchestra. To finance the project, they had to keep making hits as The Move; only their eponymous debut album charted (No.15, 1968), but only three out of ten UK hit singles failed to make the Top 7.

After 'Curly' (1969) and a disastrous venture into cabaret, Wayne left, and Jeff Lynne, former leader of Birmingham cult band The Idle Race, joined on condition that he help launch ELO. Wood became frontman and they changed direction with 1970's heavier 'Brontosaurus' (UK No.7). Gradually, live work ceased. Price left and they continued as a trio, existing only on TV and record, and releasing product on EMI's Harvest label under both group names. ELO's eponymous debut was issued at the same time as The Move's last – *Message From The Country* (1971) – which reflected the contrasting future styles of Wood and Lynne.

They bowed out with 1971's excellent 'Tonight' (UK No.11) and 'Chinatown' (UK No.23), and 1972's Jerry Lee Lewis pastiche 'California Man' (UK No.7). Their contract to continue as The Move had three years to run, but was waived by EMI in view of the subsequent success of ELO and Wood's new band Wizzard.

read *Blackberry Way* (1996), Jürgen Wanda

fan Face The Music, PO Box 718, Sidcup, Kent, DA15 7UD, UK

surf www.roywood.com/move.html

ALISON MOYET ⊙ ⊙

WHO b. Genevieve Alison Jane Moyet, 18 Jun 1961, Basildon, Essex, England

WHAT Deep-voiced torch singer

Before flouncing to Erasure, Vince Clarke raised eyebrows by quitting Depeche Mode and recruiting Alison 'Alf' Moyet for Yazoo's biggies 'Only You', 'Don't Go' and *Upstairs At Eric's* (all 1982) and 1983's 'Nobody's Diary' and UK No.1 *You And Me Both*.

Moyet's solo star rose when Yazoo fell: the hits 'Love Resurrection' and 'All Cried Out' made *Alf* (1984) another UK chart-topper – a triumph nearly duplicated by *Raindancing* (1987) and its hits 'Is This Love?' and 'Weak In The Presence Of Beauty'. In between, a cover of the Billie Holiday standard 'That Ole Devil Called Love' (1985) illustrated the Blues roots of Moyet's stentorian style.

Although neither *Hoodoo* (1991) nor *Essex* (1994) were major successes, her hits set *Singles* (1995) became yet another UK No.1. With a session CV boasting James Brown and Ocean Colour Scene, Moyet remains in demand, notably starring on Lightning Seeds' *Jollification* (1994) and Tricky's *Nearly God* (1996).

 www.scu.edu/kscu/webpage/bandpage/alf/

MY BLOODY VALENTINE

WHO Vocals/guitar/keyboards **Kevin Shields** (b. 21 May 1963, Queens, New York, USA), vocals/guitar **Bilinda Butcher** (b. 16 Sep 1961, London, England) bass **Debbie Googe** (b. 24 Oct 1962, Somerset, England), drums/keyboards **Colm O'Ciosoig** (b. 31 Oct 1964, Dublin, Ireland)

WHEN 1983–

WHERE Dublin, Ireland

WHAT Shoegazing slowcoaches

From derivative noise to the sound of God sneezing in slow motion, My Bloody Valentine (named after a trashy horror

movie) gouged a canyon in Indie Rock. Founders Kevin Shields and Colm O'Ciosoig dragged the embryonic Valentines to Berlin for the mini-album *This Is Your Bloody Valentine* (1984), then to London, with new bassist Debbie Googe, for the EPs 'Geek!', 'The New Record By My Bloody Valentine', 'Sunny Sundae Smile', 'Strawberry Wine' and 'Ecstasy' – the latter two compiled on 1987's *Ecstasy And Wine*.

Judged Jesus & Mary Chain copyists by the press, the band pulled a left turn in 1988. Singer Dave Conway and surname-free keyboard player Tina were gone, Bilinda Butcher was in and they signed to Creation. The ecstatic rush of 1988's 'You Made Me Realise' EP paved the way for the epochal *Isn't Anything* (1988) – a glittering collage of bending feedback, backwards melodies and slow-motion drones. Having inadvertently spawned 'shoegazing' (and, Stateside, influenced Smashing Pumpkins and Soundgarden), My Bloody Valentine withdrew to the studio.

After spiralling recording costs and countless broken deadlines, the glorious EPs 'Glider' (1990) and 'Tremelo' (1991) preceded the colossal cosmic storm of *Loveless* (1991).

The group joined Dinosaur Jr and Blur on 1992's Jesus & Mary Chain-led 'Rollercoaster' tour, then disappeared. Creation, nearly bankrupted by *Loveless*, let the band move to Island and Shields resumed his sonic quest. By the mid-90s, only he and Butcher remained and seasoned disciples mocked young fans enquiring about a new album. However, vital signs seemed intact with their contribution to the Wire tribute *Whore* (1996), Butcher's appearance with Collapsed Lung, Shields' pairings with former Spacemen 3 noisenik Sonic Boom and Dinosaur Jr and remixes for Yo La Tengo, Primal Scream and Massive Attack.

 www.triplo.com/mbv/

NAZARETH

WHO Vocals **Dan McCafferty**, guitar **Manny Charlton**, bass **Pete Agnew**, drums **Darrell Sweet**

WHEN 1968–

WHERE Dunfermline, Scotland

WHAT No nonsense, no frills Rock

Evolving from covers band The Shaddettes, Nazareth (from a line in 'The Weight' by The Band) released their eponymous debut in 1971. Commercial breakthrough came after support slots with Deep Purple, whose Roger Glover produced *Razamanaz* (1973), the source of UK hits 'Broken Down Angel' and 'Bad Bad Boy'.

Loud And Proud (1974) broke the band in Europe and the USA, with hard rockin' covers of Joni Mitchell's 'This Flight Tonight' and Bob Dylan's 'The Ballad Of Hollis Brown'. Other successful reworkings were The Everly Brothers' 'Love Hurts' (1974, US No.8) and Tomorrow's psychedelic anthem 'My White Bicycle' (1975).

By *Hair Of The Dog* (1975), however, Nazareth's UK following had all but dried up, though constant touring ensured a measure of success in the USA. Ex-Sensational Alex Harvey Band guitarist Zal Cleminson joined for *No Mean City* (1979), but left soon after. The band was augmented further in 1982 by guitarist Billy Rankin and ex-Spirit keyboard player John Locke, but by 1984 Nazareth was back to its original quartet. Rankin returned for *No Jive* (1991), replacing Charlton who pursued a solo career.

An unlikely tribute came in 1993 when Guns N' Roses covered Nazareth's 'Hair Of The Dog' on *The Spaghetti Incident?*, consolation after they turned down Axl Rose's request for the group to play at his wedding. In 1994, Rankin departed again, but with Jimmy Murrison and keyboard player Ronnie Leahy, Nazareth maintained a live following in Europe and the USA.

(fan) Razamanewz, Headrest, Street End Lane, Heathfield, East Sussex, TN21 8TU, UK

(surf) www.rocksolid-inc.com/nazareth

YOUSSOU N'DOUR

WHO b. 1 Oct 1959, the Medina, Dakar, Senegal

WHAT Afro-Pop visionary

Although Youssou N'Dour gained worldwide exposure in the 80s courtesy of Peter Gabriel, he was already a star in Senegal with his innovative style Mbalax: an electric take on his country's traditional percussive style, named in honour of Senegalese saxophonist Mba. N'Dour had performed since he was 12. In 1976, he joined the Star Band, a long-running Dakar club band influenced by Latin rhythms. Their music also embraced native African folklore and the sound of the 'tama', or talking drum.

Forming his own band, Etoile de Dakar (later Super Etoile) in 1979, he extended Mbalax to include fuzz-guitar solos. After seeing N'Dour perform in 1984, Gabriel invited him to appear on his 1986 album *So*, as did Paul Simon with *Graceland* (1986). In 1988, N'Dour appeared on the Amnesty International Human Rights Now! tour alongside Gabriel, Bruce Springsteen, Sting and Tracy Chapman. He continued to broaden African music

with contributions from Branford Marsalis and Neneh Cherry, who featured on his 1994 album *The Guide* and hit '7 Seconds'. N'Dour collaborated with The Fugees' Wyclef Jean on Wyclef's *The Carnival* (1997) and *Bulworth* soundtrack (1998).

(read) *Hey You!: A Portrait Of Youssou N'Dour* (1989), Jenny Cathcart

RICKY NELSON ✪

WHO b. Eric Hilliard Nelson, 8 May 1940, Teaneck, New Jersey, USA, d. 31 Dec 1985, DeKalb, Texas, USA

WHAT Pop's first TV-assisted teen idol

In the late 50s, Ricky Nelson ranked alongside Elvis and Pat Boone among America's most popular singers. First finding fame as a 9-year-old in his family's successful radio (and later TV) show, *The Adventures Of Ozzie & Harriet*, he started recording at 16 and launched the million-selling debut 'A Teenager's Romance'/'I'm Walking' on the show, making him the first TV-assisted teen idol.

From 1957–1963, Ricky (or Rick as he called himself from 1961) amassed an amazing 26 hit singles and nine hit albums in the USA, and 11 hit singles in Britain, where the show was never seen. Among the biggest were US No.1s 'Poor Little Fool' (1958) and 'Travelin' Man' (1961), gold-sellers 'Be-Bop Baby' (1957), 'Stood Up' (1958) and 'Teen Age Idol' (1962), and transatlantic smashes 'It's Late' (1959), 'Hello Mary Lou' (1961) and 'For You' (1964). Ricky's Elvis-esque voice and first-rate backing band (featuring future Presley sideman James Burton) produced some of Rock's best teen-targeted tracks. He also pioneered Country Rock, notably on 1972's US Top 10 'Garden Party'.

He was inducted into the Rock And Roll Hall Of Fame in 1987, two years after his death in a plane crash en route to a New Year's Eve concert. His sons Gunnar and Matthew had a US No.1 as Nelson – '(Can't Live Without Your) Love And Affection' (1990).

(read) *The Hollywood Hillbilly* (1995), Stafford & Young

(fan) 1046 Northeast Lincoln Street, Roseburg, Oregon 97470, USA

(surf) members.com/~SharonTate/ricky.html

WILLIE NELSON

WHO b. 30 Apr 1933, Abbott, Texas, USA

WHAT Country outlaw, unlucky legend and songwriter supreme

He wrote 'Crazy' for Patsy Cline and 'Always On My Mind' for Elvis, helped to found Farm Aid, recorded four decades' worth of albums and collaborated with U2 and Beck – and yet Willie Nelson is best known for losing everything in the 90s to pay a reported $16.7-million tax bill.

Initially renowned as a songwriter, he moved to Country capital Nashville and scored a US No.1 with Faron Young's 'Hello Walls' (1961). Cline's 'Crazy' (1961) secured his credentials, but Nelson's own albums bombed and the loss of his home in a 1970 fire rounded off a frustrating decade.

Back in Texas, a loyal live following kept him afloat, but albums continued to sink, partly because Nelson's vocals were less polished than those he wrote for – "The voice of imperfect man must now be made manifest," he announced on 1971's

Yesterday's Wine, "and I have been chosen the most likely candidate." After fruitless years of RCA trying to fit him into a spangly Country straitjacket, Nelson found a sympathetic home at Atlantic, whose Soul skills graced his musical breakthrough *Shotgun Willie* (1973). Although premiering his trademark 'outlaw' image, neither that album nor its follow-up, *Phases And Stages* (1974), made his fortune.

Perseverance paid off in 1975. His new label Columbia, initially unconvinced by the bleak concept album *Red Headed Stranger*, relented when its 'Blue Eyes Crying In The Rain' blazed from the Country to Pop charts. Double-platinum album sales and a Country revival ensued. The renaissance continued with 1978's Waylon Jennings collaboration *Waylon & Willie* and the Booker T. Jones-produced 'standards' collection *Stardust*.

Million-sellers and a movie career – notably 1979's *The Electric Horseman* – carried him into the 80s, and he hit his chart peaks with 1982's 4-million-selling *Always On My Mind* and its hit title track – also a smash for Brenda Lee, Pet Shop Boys and Elvis. *Poncho & Lefty* (1983), with Merle Haggard, and 1984's 'To All The Girls I've Loved Before', with Julio Iglesias, brought his platinum run to a close, but Nelson co-founded Farm Aid, formed The Highwaymen (with Johnny Cash, Waylon Jennings and Kris Kristofferson) and remained mind-bogglingly prolific.

However, acclaim for *Across The Borderline* (1993) didn't stop waning sales. He parted company with Columbia, and the tax debt and a pot bust added to his woes. Having paid the IRS with profits from 1992's mockingly titled *Who'll Buy My Memories*, he emerged as a hero. The tribute album *Twisted Willie* (1996) featured Mudhoney, L7, Dinosaur Jr and, notably, members of Alice In Chains, Nirvana and Soundgarden backing Johnny Cash on Nelson's 'Time Of The Preacher'.

In 1997, he appeared in Beck's 'Jackass' video and US TV's redneck-ribbing cartoon *King Of The Hill*, and graced the beautiful U2 B-side 'Slow Dancing'. Nelson's luck might have run out, but his legend remains stronger than ever.

Read *Willie: An Autobiography* (1992), Willie Nelson & Bud Shrake

Surf www.justicerecords.com/~nancy/arp16.html

THE NEVILLE BROTHERS

WHO Vocals **Aaron Neville** (b. 24 Jan 1941, New Orleans, Louisiana, USA), vocals/percussion **Cyril Neville** (b. 10 Jan 1948, New Orleans), vocals/keyboards **Art Neville** (b. 17 Dec 1937, New Orleans), saxophone **Charles Neville** (b. 28 Dec 1938, New Orleans)

WHEN 1977–

WHERE New Orleans, Louisiana, USA

WHAT Family-sized harmonies

The Neville Brothers didn't start performing under that name until 1977, but had been R&B luminaries since 1954, when Art's high-school band The Hawketts recorded the carnival hit 'Mardi Gras Mambo'. Brothers Charles and Aaron joined briefly, Aaron assuming leadership when Art left for the US Navy in 1958. By 1962, Aaron had put his successful solo career on hold to join Art in The Neville Sounds, an eight-piece band which evolved – minus Aaron – into the legendary session group The Meters (cited as an influence by acts from Coolio to Aerosmith).

The brothers reunited (this time with youngest sibling Cyril) in 1975, backing Mardi Gras 'tribe' The Wild Tchoupitoulas. By 1977, they were performing together as The Neville Brothers, although commercial success for their soulful harmonizing proved elusive. Capitol dropped them after the Disco-flavoured flop *The Neville Brothers* (1978), and the acclaimed *Fiyo On The Biyou* (1981) was similarly underbought.

Finally, after years of valiant obscurity, the platinum touch of Daniel Lanois – then producer *du jour* thanks to U2's *The Joshua Tree* and Dylan's *Oh Mercy* – propelled *Yellow Moon* (1989) into the public eye and 1990's *Brother's Keeper* into the US Top 100.

Aaron's parallel solo career flourished with 1989's Grammy-winning duet with Linda Ronstadt, 'Don't Know Much', and the platinum-selling *The Grand Tour* (1993). The Brothers appeared on *The Carnival*, a 1997 solo set by Wyclef Jean of The Fugees.

NEW MODEL ARMY

WHO Vocals/guitar **Justin 'Slade The Leveller' Sullivan** (b. 8 Apr 1956, Jordans, Buckinghamshire, England), bass **Nelson** (b. 22 Sep 1958, Colchester, England), drums **Robert Heaton** (b. 6 Jul 1961, Knutsford, Cheshire, England)

WHEN 1982–

WHERE Bradford, England

WHAT Folk Punk militia

A name from English history is not the only link between New Model Army and Levellers. Like their southern counterparts, the band (named after a 17th-century revolutionary militia) combine Folk's lyricism with Punk's energy. Their impact was heightened by confrontational politics, notably on their debut *Vengeance* (1984), which bluntly advocated "getting the bastards". They shocked their followers by signing to EMI, but broke into the UK chart with 'No Rest' (1985). Constant touring maintained a loyal European following, culminating in the UK chart zenith *Thunder And Consolation* (1989), total album sales of over a million and an eternally unfashionable, uncompromising attitude. *Strange Brotherhood* (1998) was their first studio album in five years.

 NMAFC, PO Box 2168, Burnham-on-Crouch, Essex, CM0 8QZ, UK

www.interlog.com/~cb/

NEW ORDER ⊙⊙

WHO Vocals/guitar/keyboards **Bernard Sumner** (b. 4 Jan 1956, Salford, England), bass/vocals/keyboards **Peter Hook** (b. 13 Feb 1956, Manchester, England), keyboards/guitar/vocals **Gillian Gilbert** (b. 27 Jan 1961, Macclesfield, England), drums/keyboards **Stephen Morris** (b. 28 Oct 1957, Macclesfield)

WHEN 1980–

WHERE Manchester, England

WHAT Agony and Ecstasy

A ray of light in grimy 80s Indie, New Order could be more morose than Morrissey, more Disco than Donna Summer, colder than Kraftwerk, more human than The Human League – often, all at the same time. Their origins date to the demise of their old band, Joy Division, whose Ian Curtis hanged himself in 1980, cutting short the career of Britain's best post-Punk group.

Bernard Sumner, Peter Hook and Stephen Morris decided to continue (they shared vocals on their first demo), but not as Joy Division. After considering 'Stevie & The JDs' and 'Sunshine Valley Dance Band', they settled on 'New Order' – doing little to abate the accusations of fascism levelled at their previous group.

Joy Division's shadow loomed over New Order: their first US tour, in 1980, was booked before Curtis' death, and their debut single's songs – 'Ceremony'/'In A Lonely Place' (1981) – were among the last they wrote with him. With Sumner singing lead, Morris' girlfriend Gillian Gilbert joined on keyboards and guitar and New Order began to earn a 'difficult' reputation: they blew out *Top Of The Pops* because they were not allowed to appear live – this from a band famed for ramshackle performances.

Determined to confound fans and critics, they flirted with Disco on 'Procession'/'Everything's Gone Green', then regressed to gloom on *Movement* (1981). However, having parted with long-time producer Martin Hannett, the self-produced 'Temptation' (1982) plunged into romantic danceability, albeit with a stylishly anonymous sleeve by designer Peter Saville and a record company – Factory – which specialized in perversity.

Most unusual was the 1982 opening of the Manchester club The Hacienda, co-owned by New Order and Factory's directors. It became the focus for Manchester's House scene and, by the late 80s' Acid House boom, was one of Europe's best clubs. But it cost a fortune to keep open, and New Order began paying for it with the 12"-only 'Blue Monday' (1983), a deathly Disco record – created by accident while testing a drum machine – which reached the UK Top 10 after becoming a favourite in holiday resorts around Europe. Remixed in 1988 and 1995 (and even re-recorded for an aborted soft drink ad), it became a monster; when the Quincy Jones-remixed 'Blue Monday '88' fell out of the UK chart, 'Blue Monday' had been in the UK Top 200 for over five years and had become the best-selling 12" of all time.

Power, Corruption & Lies (1983) matched electronic coldness with pristine Pop, but New Order had already moved on. In New York, they collaborated with hip producer Arthur Baker on the Electro-influenced 'Confusion' and the heart-stoppingly lovely 'Thieves Like Us'. Both were hits, but 'The Perfect Kiss'– issued on the same day as its parent album *Low Life* (1985) – ushered in a lean period. In 1986, after minor hits with 'Shellshock' (from the movie soundtrack *Pretty In Pink*) and 'State Of The Nation', the underbought classic 'Bizarre Love Triangle' left little trace. The inept live video *Pumped Full Of Drugs* seemed prophetic.

However, *Brotherhood* (1986) was a rejuvenation – majestic Pop, hard electronics and breezy guitars. Even better were new songs with Pet Shop Boys producer Stephen Hague. 'True Faith' (1987) crashed the UK Top 10 and became their first US hit. *Substance* (1987) compiled their singles – except 'Touched By The Hand Of God', from the 1987 movie soundtrack *Salvation!*.

Meanwhile, House exploded in Britain and the Spanish island of Ibiza, where they recorded the perfect *Technique* (1989). From the weirdie Acid of 'Fine Time' and 'Round And Round' to the delicate 'Run' and 'Love Less', it captured the 'Second Summer Of Love': bright acoustic songs nestling with dancefloor dramas clearly influenced by Ibiza clubs. *Technique* confirmed their amazing evolution from Indie despair to… soccer soundtrackers.

Described by Sumner as "probably… the last straw for Joy Division fans", 'World In Motion' was their theme for England's 1990 World Cup campaign. Written with comedian Keith Allen, it was originally titled 'E For England' – Ecstasy having evidently contributed to *Technique*'s euphoric rush. 'World In Motion' stormed to UK No.1 and soundtracked a glorious summer when England nearly won the World Cup and 'Madchester' reigned.

But New Order were disintegrating. After a miserable 1989 US tour, Sumner moonlighted with Electronic. Hook followed with the rocky Revenge, then Morris and Gilbert, seasoned TV music writers, launched their humorously named The Other Two. Despite highlights – Electronic's 'Getting Away With It' and 'Get The Message', Revenge's '7 Reasons' and 'Pineapple Face' and The Other Two's 'Tasty Fish' – all were diluted New Order, and *Electronic* (1991), *One True Passion* (1990) and *The Other Two And You* (1993) left scant impression on the world.

Factory was in even worse shape, its financial woes exacerbated by the tardiness of New Order and Happy Mondays

> **"God only knows why people think we're cool"**
> Peter Hook

– the only bands which could pull the label back from the brink. When the company crashed, New Order signed to London and *Republic* (1993) hit UK No.1. They broke their 'no lip-syncing' rule to perform 'Regret' on the *Baywatch* set for *Top Of The Pops*, toured and headlined 1993's Reading Festival the same night the excellent documentary *NewOrder Story* premiered on UK TV.

Bigger than ever, but with internal relations at an all-time low, New Order dispersed again, seemingly for good. London picked the bones with 'True Faith '94', 'Nineteen63' (originally a B-side), *(The Best Of) New Order* (1994) and 'Blue Monday '95' – a reworking by German Dance gonks Hardfloor which trailed the inessential remix album *(The Rest Of) New Order* (1995).

Sumner and Johnny Marr reactivated Electronic (augmented by former Kraftwerker Karl Bartos), Hook married (and divorced) comedienne Caroline Aherne, and Revenge mutated into Monaco, who scored with 'What Do You Want From Me?' from *Music For Pleasure* (1997). Gilbert and Morris married in 1995 and continued writing TV music. A 'missing, presumed dead' verdict looked inevitable when The Hacienda closed in 1997 but, amazingly, another retrospective prompted a reunion at 1998's Reading Festival.

Read *From Joy Division To New Order – The Factory Story* (1996), Mick Middles

Surf slashmc.rice-edu/ceremony/neworder/neworder.html

NEW ROMANTIC

WHAT The floppy-fringed, make-up-plastered offspring of Punk and Bowie-esque Glam, New Romantic was invented by the Dame himself and dressed by designer Vivienne Westwood (baggy trousers, tartan, 'the pirate look'). It was copied by kids across Britain and later held up as proof of just how style-less the 80s were. However, it produced some of the decade's best Pop: Duran Duran's 'Planet Earth', Spandau Ballet's 'To Cut A Long Story Short', Visage's 'Fade To Grey'... The movement made its way across the Atlantic but, by the time Duran were filling US stadiums, New Romantic's Art-Rockish origins had given way to the jollier strains of Culture Club and The Thompson Twins. Defying retrospective ridicule, New Romantic enjoyed a renaissance in the 90s thanks to Mansun. Other 'Romo' revivalists like Orlando and Plastic Fantastic fared less spectacularly.

WHERE The Blitz Club, London, England

WHEN 1979–1983

WHO Japan <u>Quiet Life</u> (1979), David Bowie <u>Scary Monsters And Super Creeps</u> (1980), Adam & The Ants <u>Prince Charming</u> (1981), Visage <u>Fade To Grey – The Singles Collection</u> (1983), Arcadia <u>So Red The Rose</u> (1985), Mansun <u>Attack Of The Grey Lantern</u> (1997)

THE NEW YORK DOLLS

WHO Vocals **David Johansen** (b. 9 Jan 1950, Staten Island, New York, USA), guitar **Johnny Thunders** (b. John Genzale, 15 Jul 1952, New York City, New York, d. 23 Apr 1991, New Orleans, Louisiana, USA), guitar **Sylvain Sylvain** (b. Syl Mizrahi), bass **Arthur Kane**, drums **Jerry Nolan** (b. 7 May 1946, New York City, d. 14 Jan 1992, New York City)

WHEN 1971–1976

WHERE New York City, New York, USA

WHAT Glam from the gutter

Rigged-out in glitter, leather and make-up, The New York Dolls seduced Glam kids through gigs at Manhattan's legendary Mercer Arts Center. Their music – a chaotic, Rolling Stones/MC5/ Stooges blast – was overshadowed by Olympic-standard hell-raising. The original drummer Billy Murcia was an early casualty, courtesy of a drug overdose in 1972 – hence Keith Richards' sensitive verdict: "Never heard 'em, but I saw a picture and they looked very pretty. Their drummer died, didn't 'e?"

Their Todd Rundgren-produced debut *New York Dolls* (1973) flopped, despite rave reviews. *Too Much Too Soon* (1974) was produced by George 'Shadow' Morton (The Shangri-Las' Morton-produced 'Give Him A Great Big Kiss' being a Thunders favourite). Despite including the classic 'Human Being', it was another commercial disaster.

As their lifestyle took its toll, the Dolls began to disintegrate, with particular animosity between Thunders and Johansen. Dropped by Mercury, they were pulled from the brink by future

Sex Pistols agitator Malcolm McLaren who, in a vain attempt to surround the Dolls with fresh controversy, transformed them into anti-American demons: dressing them in red and insisting they perform with communist flag backdrops. He succeeded only in drawing attention to a band in its death throes. Thunders and Nolan left to form The Heartbreakers in 1975, while Johansen and Sylvain jettisoned Kane and toured with session players until the band finally fell apart in late 1976.

Former members had mixed fortunes thereafter: Thunders succumbed to a heroin overdose in 1991, while Nolan – long dependent on hard drugs – suffered a fatal stroke in 1992. Johansen, however, resurfaced as spoof lounge-singer Buster Poindexter and appeared in movies including 1988's *Married To The Mob* and *Scrooged*. Unloved during their traumatic life, the Dolls were posthumously embraced by the Punk generation (notably a young Morrissey, who wrote a book about them) and Glam Metal boys Hanoi Rocks and Guns N' Roses, who covered 'Human Being' on 1993's *The Spaghetti Incident?*, bless 'em.

RANDY NEWMAN

WHO b. 28 Nov 1944, New Orleans, Louisiana, USA

WHAT Sardonic singer/songwriter

Never much of a chart star, Randy Newman's ironic observations on American life and his many movie soundtracks have nevertheless given him a solid cult following.

After studying music at university in Los Angeles, Newman released his first single in 1961: the Pat Boone-produced 'Golden Gridiron Boy'. He found greater success as a songwriter when he joined Metric Music, Liberty Records' publishing division, in

1962. He wrote for Cilla Black, Alan Price, Manfred Mann, Gene Pitney, The Walker Brothers and many others before releasing his own debut, *Randy Newman* (1968). One of its tracks, 'I Think It's Going To Rain', was a UK No.6 for UB40 in 1980.

His popularity in the industry grew with his Grammy nomination as an arranger for Peggy Lee in 1969 and Harry Nilsson's 1970 album of Newman covers, *Nilsson Sings Newman*. That year Newman released *12 Songs* (originally a demo), featuring Ry Cooder and Gene Parsons of The Byrds among others. It included 'Mama Told Me Not To Come' (a US No.1 and UK No.3 for Three Dog Night), which was left off Newman's first album because he thought it wasn't good enough. He also contributed 'Gone Dead Train' to the soundtrack of Nicolas Roeg's 1970 movie *Performance*.

Randy Newman Live (1971), recorded at New York's Bitter End club, scraped into the foot of the US chart and the following year's *Sail Away* fared only slightly better. *Good Old Boys* (1974) at last made an impression at US No.36, although it wasn't until 1977 that Newman attracted substantial mainstream attention with *Little Criminals* and its single 'Short People'. A parody on bigoted attitudes, the song incurred the wrath of a group of literal-minded Americans; Newman even received a death threat. The controversy didn't stop the single from reaching US No.2, with the album peaking at US No.9.

The 80s and 90s saw Newman scoring and contributing to movie soundtracks, including *Ragtime* (1981), *The Natural* (1984), 1986's *Three Amigos* (plus the screenplay), *Parenthood* (1989), *Awakenings* (1990), *The Paper* (1994), *Maverick* (1994), *Toy Story* (1995), *Michael* (1996) and *James And The Giant Peach* (1997), garnering seven Oscar nominations in the process.

In between, Newman released the more autobiographical *Land Of Dreams* (1988), produced in part by Mark Knopfler and Jeff Lynne. Lynne had been the butt of a Newman joke in 1979's 'The Story Of A Rock And Roll Band', a send-up of ELO and its theatrics. Newman took a different direction in 1995 with a self-penned book and the premiere of his stage production of *Faust*, which spawned an album featuring James Taylor, Don Henley, Elton John, Linda Ronstadt, Bonnie Raitt and Newman himself.

(surf) www.RepriseRec.com/reprise_html_pages/randyfolder/randynewman

OLIVIA NEWTON-JOHN ✪✪✪

WHO b. 26 Sep 1948, Cambridge, England

WHAT Girl-next-door turned Pop pin-up

Granddaughter of the Nobel prize-winning physicist Max Born, Olivia emigrated to Australia with her family at 5 and began her singing career at 14 with the Sol Four, later becoming a solo act on Australian TV while singing in her brother-in-law's coffee house. Winning a talent competition in 1965, she flew to the UK.

She and her friend Pat Carroll sang together on TV and in clubs. After Olivia's fruitless deal with Decca in 1969, the duo returned to Australia where Carroll married John Farrar (Olivia's future producer and songwriter) and joined the manufactured group Tomorrow, appearing in their eponymous film in 1970.

Olivia's first chart success came with 'If Not For You' (1971). A year later, she was a regular in the UK singles and album charts and appearing on Cliff Richard's BBC TV show. US success began

with 1973's Grammy-winning 'Let Me Be There'. Two more Grammys followed in 1974 for 'I Honestly Love You', as well as fourth place in the Eurovision Song Contest. She also scored two US No.1 albums: *If You Love Me Let Me Know* (1974) and *Have You Never Been Mellow* (1975).

Olivia returned to the UK for more TV work in 1977. After global success alongside John Travolta in 1978 with 'You're The One That I Want' from *Grease*, Olivia was presented with an OBE by the Queen in 1979. Another movie, *Xanadu* (1980), spawned further No.1s, then *Physical* (1981) and its title track topped US charts. After recovering from breast cancer diagnosed in 1992, she split from her husband and resumed recording in 1995, collaborating with Cliff Richard on *Songs From Heathcliff*. A return to concerts, TV and movie work has been accompanied by campaigning in aid of Cancer Relief and the environment.

(fan) Only Olivia, PO Box 388, Ipswich, IP4 2HD, UK

(surf) www.netlink.co.uk/users/ermine/olivia/

THE NICE

WHO Bass/vocals **Lee Jackson** (b. 8 Jan 1943, Newcastle upon Tyne, England), guitar **David O'List** (b. 13 Dec 1948, London, England), drums **Brian 'Blinky' Davidson** (b. 25 May 1942, Leicester, England), keyboards **Keith Emerson** (b. 2 Nov 1944, Todmorden, West Yorkshire, England)

WHEN 1967–1970

WHERE London, England

WHAT Proto-Prog Pop

Formed to back singer P.P. Arnold, The Nice added Classical grandeur to Pop with *The Thoughts Of Emerlist Davjack* (1967), notably on a 1968 hit overhaul of Leonard Bernstein's 'America'. They joined fellow sensations Jimi Hendrix and Pink Floyd on a 1967 package tour, during which Nice guitarist David O'List periodically deputized for unreliable Floyd leader Syd Barrett.

With a stage act that included flag-burning and Keith Emerson assaulting his Hammond organ with knives, they developed a following which put *Nice* (1969), *Five Bridges* (1970) and *Elegy* (1971) into the UK Top 5. However, their eclectic music, covering both Dylan and Bach, cut little ice Stateside. A combination of frustration and Emerson's departure for Emerson, Lake & Palmer tore The Nice apart in 1970.

HARRY NILSSON

WHO b. 15 Jun 1941, Brooklyn, New York, USA, d. 15 Jan 1994, Agoura Hills, California, USA

WHAT Bashful balladeer

Harry Nilsson (who was born Nilsson, not Nelson as has been reported) was influenced by his mother's songwriting and an uncle's singing before combining his California bank job with singing demos and songwriting. During the 60s he worked with Phil Spector, released singles for Mercury and Capitol and sang jingles until RCA signed him in 1967, when he released his debut album *Pandemonium Shadow Show*. The follow-up, *Aerial Ballet* (1969), included Fred Neil's 'Everybody's Talkin'' (1969) which, as the theme to the movie *Midnight Cowboy* (1969), earned Nilsson his first major hit and a Grammy. *Nilsson Sings Newman* (1970) was a Randy Newman tribute album, while *The Point* (1971), an animated TV special, featured songs and stories by Nilsson, narrated by Dustin Hoffman.

Nilsson's definitive version of Badfinger's 'Without You' gave him a transatlantic No.1 and made *Nilsson Schmilsson* (1972) his most successful album. *A Little Touch Of Schmilsson In The Night* (1973), produced by ex-Beatles press officer Derek Taylor, was a tribute to Nilsson's unique vocal style on his treatment of classics such as 'Makin' Whoopee' and 'Lazy Moon'. Despite his success, Nilsson never gave a solo concert, although he occasionally played in a London Mayfair hotel bar. He worried that nobody would come to see him and, when reassured that people would turn up, became anxious about playing in front of an audience.

During their notorious early 70s episode of drinking and drug taking, John Lennon produced Nilsson's *Pussy Cats* (1974), but Nilsson left RCA in 1978. He made one album for Mercury and continued to write during the 80s, contributing songs to the movies *Popeye* (1980) and *The Fisher King* (1991). After Lennon's murder, he lobbied for the control of handguns. Nilsson suffered ill-health throughout the 90s and died at his home in 1994.

NINE INCH NAILS

WHO Vocals/guitar/keyboards/stuff **Trent Reznor** (b. Michael Trent Reznor, 17 May 1965, Mercer, Pennsylvania, USA)

WHEN 1988–

WHERE Cleveland, Ohio, USA

WHAT Aladdin Pain

Kurt Cobain gave Grunge its prettiest star, but the dark heart of the 'alternative' 90s is Trent Reznor. His influence is comparable to that of early 70s David Bowie: his every word hung upon, every lyric scrutinized, every album, performance and video documented. Innumerable websites devoted to his brainchild Nine Inch Nails and protégé Marilyn Manson have made a corner of the information superhighway the 'ninternet'.

Just as Bob Dylan, Boy George and The Cure's Robert Smith had mundane upbringings, giving no hint of their future impact on Pop and culture, so Reznor's childhood was packed with scouts, skateboards, model planes and music-making (a piano teacher compared his playing to Harry Connick Jr). From saxophone and keyboards in high-school Jazz and marching bands, he graduated to local Rock acts, then to a recording engineer career in Cleveland, Ohio.

More minor band engagements ensued, including one with The Problems, rearranging Buddy Holly's 'True Love Ways' for the Michael J. Fox/Joan Jett movie *Light Of Day* (1987). Fed up with synth-prodding for no-hopers, Reznor seized the creative reins for *Pretty Hate Machine* (1989), fusing Industrial influences like Skinny Puppy and Ministry with the poppier likes of Devo and The Human League. The result – a hit with no one – brought only support slots with gloomsters Peter Murphy and The Jesus & Mary Chain. A happier association was with Ministry's Al Jourgenson, who recruited Reznor for the side project Revolting

Cocks. "It was decadence on a new level," marvelled Reznor, "but with a sense of humour." They reunited as 1000 Homo DJs for a devastating demolition of Black Sabbath's 'Supernaut' (1990). Jourgenson later remixed NIN's cover of Queen's 'Get Down Make Love'. Other noteworthy NIN remakes include Soft Cell's 'Memorabilia' and Adam & The Ants' 'Physical'.

Pretty Hate Machine finally took off in 1991 with its screaming hit 'Head Like A Hole' and NIN toured Europe with Guns N' Roses. Reznor: "The first song goes okay. Second song people begin to realize we're not Skid Row... Third song they'd confirmed the fact that they've heard a synthesizer and it's time to attack."

More profitable was hitching aboard the Lollapalooza bandwagon, for which NIN included Jeff Ward from Lard on drums, drummer Chris Vrenna, guitarist Richard Patrick (later of Filter) and keyboard player James Woolley. Thereafter, though Vrenna stuck around awhile, Reznor was the sole constant.

Afterwards, although Reznor waged bitter war with his label TVT, the mini-album *Broken* (1992) – featuring some of their most celebrated cuts – smashed into the US Top 10 and spawned the remixed *Fixed* (1992). 'Happiness In Slavery' became the latest NIN video to cause furrowed brows at MTV: early promos had contented themselves with violent live re-creations and odd hints of S&M and snuff movies. Here they went for the full masochistic monty, as performance artist Bob

Flanagan enjoyed clamps applied in unmentionable places.

Such was the sordid background to *The Downward Spiral* (1994), recorded at the LA house where Charles Manson's 'Family' murdered actress Sharon Tate. Crammed with claustrophobic ballads and crushing drums, it smashed into transatlantic Top 10s. Disaffected youths flocked to the Temple Of Reznor just as glum Brit kids had worshipped Joy Division – a connection cemented when NIN covered the morbid Mancunians' 'Dead Souls' for *The Crow* (1994). They also graced other soundtracks, notably 1996's *The Fan*, which illustrated Robert De Niro's mental decline with NIN songs.

Filmic dabbling culminated in Reznor masterminding music for Oliver Stone's *Natural Born Killers* (1994) – he had long admired the director and sampled dialogue from the Stone-scripted *Midnight Express* in NIN's 'Sanctified'. Reznor took soundtrack artistry to a post-*Pulp Fiction* high, with a gripping blend of diced dialogue, World Music, Rock 'n' Roll, Industrial, Rap and Country. Subsequently, Reznor helmed scores for David Lynch's *Lost Highway* (1997) and the computer game *Quake*.

Amid this multi-media meddling came a graphic reminder of Nine Inch Nail's Rock credentials: a spectacular, mud-splattered headline performance at 1994's Woodstock II. Melancholic musing was trampled beneath a NINcendiary extravaganza – although Reznor was now less inclined to heave thousands of dollars' worth of synthesizers at his bandmates.

Confirmed as a fully-fledged superstar, he proceeded to do appropriately superstarry things: establish his own label ('nothing' – whose roster ranges from Marilyn Manson to Brit Hop pioneers Pop Will Eat Itself), feud with brief belle Courtney Love (having slept with Reznor, she announced "They should be called Three Inch Nails"), hang out with Bowie (Reznor sampled Dame David's 'Time', remixed a couple of Bowie's more NIN-esque cuts and co-headlined a 1995 tour) and get a song parodied by Weird Al Yankovic (who, like upcoming Soul star Maxwell, quoted 'Closer').

While ex-NIN guitarist Robin Finck joined the roundabout of personnel in Guns N' Roses, and Chris Vrenna helped out with Hole (along with Smashing Pumpkin Billy Corgan), Reznor issued the NIN tour video *Closure* (1998) and was reported to have covered 'Personal Jesus' for a Depeche Mode tribute. In between, he readied his next album (reportedly *The Fragile*) with producer Rick Rubin. "The new Nine Inch Nails will be more like a Funk Hip Hop record," he said. "It will piss a lot of people off, and it's going to change the world at the same time, I hope. That's all I can aspire to. That and staying ten steps ahead of Billy Corgan."

READ *Nine Inch Nails: Self-Destruct* (1997), Martin Huxley

SURF news.nin.net/

NIRVANA ⊙⊙✪✪✪✪

WHO Vocals/guitar **Kurt Cobain** (b. 20 Feb 1967, Hoquiam, Washington, USA, d. 5 Apr 1994, Seattle, Washington), bass **Krist Novoselic** (b. Krist Novaselic, 16 May 1965, Compton, California, USA), drums **Dave Grohl** (b. 14 Jan 1969, Warren, Ohio, USA)

WHEN 1987–1994

WHERE Aberdeen, Washington, USA

WHAT Reluctant Grunge superstars

In the 80s, the charts were bloated with blandness, radio waves were clogged with candyfloss and MTV was ruled by mediocre Metal. In Aberdeen, a logging town 100 miles from Seattle, lived Kurt Cobain and Krist Novoselic. Alienated by the local redneck population, depressed by the domination of Van Halen and caught by contrary fondness for Aerosmith, Kiss, Black Sabbath, Led Zeppelin and Butthole Surfers, they met in 1985 through Melvins, an inspirational Hardcore band from nearby Olympia. Cobain dropped out of high school and, with the lanky Novoselic on bass and bit-part singers and guitarists, became the drummer in The Stiff Woodies, Skid Row (not Sebastian Bach's lot) and Fecal Matter. With the addition of drummer Chad Channing, and Cobain's move to vocals and guitar, Nirvana were born.

At college parties and dismal clubs, Nirvana revealed their sludgy thrash of confused Metal/Punk parentage and habitual instrument trashing, which slowly built a following. They joined Seattle Indie label Sub Pop and, in December 1988, released their first single: a sandblasted cover of Shocking Blue's 'Love Buzz'. Monstrously heavy, punkishly inept, it preceded the revelatory *Bleach* (1989), whose recording costs were paid by guitarist (and bubble-haired Metal type) Jason Everman. *Bleach*'s highlights ('School', 'Blew', 'About A Girl') mixed 'n' matched Pixies-esque dynamics, Sabbath-ish riffing, poppy melodies and teen anguish.

College radio endorsement and touring paid off, despite more trashed instruments and one trashed guitarist (Everman departed for Soundgarden and Mindfunk). *Bleach* sold 35,000 copies, sparked a major-label bidding war and elevated Nirvana from happy no-hopers to… a squalid European tour with fellow Sub Pop van-dwellers Tad.

But Nirvana's future looked bright; despite losing Channing, they found producer (and future Garbage leader) Butch Vig. The latter helmed 'Dive', a 1990 double A-side with 'Sliver', whose metallic wonderfulness distinguished them from the sludgier Mudhoney, Dinosaur Jr *et al* (although the former's Dan Peters was their deputizing drummer for the single and one gig). The final pieces fell into place when they poached Dave Grohl from Hardcore band Scream, then were lured from Sub Pop by Geffen offshoot DGC and wrote, among other new songs, a strange, disdainful epic – stolen from Boston's 'More Than A Feeling' – called 'Smells Like Teen Spirit'. With a video full of rioting cheerleaders and splintered guitars, it seduced MTV, then spread to its natural audience – bored teenagers.

Nevermind (1991) – Rock's new rulebook and *the* album of the 90s – toppled Michael Jackson's *Dangerous* from the US No.1 and

"Sometimes it sounded good and sometimes it didn't. But it was always fun"
Dave Grohl

changed the world. Grunge, the virulent strain Nirvana injected into the mainstream, was Metal's mad-cow disease – while *Nevermind* went triple platinum and Sonic Youth, Pearl Jam, Mudhoney, Hole, Soundgarden and Alice In Chains thundered chartward, flies buzzed around 80s Glam gods Poison, Winger, Warrant and Mötley Crüe.

Nirvana's audience expanded to swallow their own targets: the kind of meatheads Cobain railed against on 'In Bloom' were now buying *Nevermind*. They lashed out, treating TV audiences to guitar abuse, cross-dressing, homo-eroticism and pro-feminism. But cracks were beginning to show. A European tour was cancelled, and Cobain's romance with Hole's Courtney Love cast them as Grunge's John & Yoko in the press. Worse was his debilitating lethargy (reported as the sleeping disorder narcolepsy) and a mysterious, agonizing stomach complaint. To relieve the pain, he turned to heroin.

When Cobain and Love married in February 1992, both were addicts. Courtney was also pregnant. Frances Bean Cobain was born healthy in August (Courtney had long since kicked her habit), but Cobain spent the birth in the throes of withdrawal. US magazine *Vanity Fair* reported that Love was using while pregnant, prompting Los Angeles' welfare department to take temporary custody of Frances shortly after her birth, claiming the couple were unfit parents. Meanwhile Nirvana trashed their way through an MTV awards ceremony, grimly aware of their situation: sold out (DGC were cleaning up with rarities sets *Incesticide* and *Hormoaning*), demonized (an American rape support organization was outraged by a new song, 'Rape Me'), paranoid (Cobain and Love threatened the writers of a Nirvana biography) and desperate to shed an audience they hated (*Incesticide*'s sleeve notes pronounced "Don't come to our shows and don't buy our records").

In early 1993, Nirvana recorded their third album – provisionally titled *Verse Chorus Verse* , then *I Hate Myself And I Want To Die* – with former Big Black noisemaker Steve Albini producing. A taste of what was to come was 'Oh, The Guilt' – a ragged single shared with The Jesus Lizard on tiny label Touch & Go – and ''The Priest' They Called Him', a Cobain collaboration with author William S. Burroughs. The controversy continued: DGC reportedly hated the album, Albini disowned it after REM producer Scott Litt was called in to remaster tracks, Cobain returned to heroin (overdosing twice) and Love called police to their home in Seattle when he locked himself in the bathroom, threatening suicide. Accordingly, *In Utero* (1993) was terrifying: disease/bodily functions-obsessed gore, self-loathing, cracked screams, tortured feedback, funereal acoustic interludes – the

sound of a tight band in the throes of chaos. But it was an instant US and UK No.1 and the band set out on tour with former Germs guitarist Pat Smear. The live shows included a crowd-mystifyingly acoustic set, featuring cellist Laurie Goldstein and a ragged cover of Leadbelly's 'Where Did You Sleep Last Night?'.

However, a stripped-down performance on MTV's *Unplugged* – including an apt cover of David Bowie's 'The Man Who Sold The World' – at the end of the year found them in high spirits and reactivated the album, which had slipped down charts soon after its debut. The tour reached Europe in early 1994 (their first performances there for almost two years) and ended abruptly in Rome on 4 March, when Love found Cobain unconscious, overdosed on tranquilizers and champagne – a suicide attempt reported at the time as an accidental overdose.

The band – now known to have effectively split – returned to the USA and Cobain's mental condition deteriorated: the police were called after more suicide threats. Love and Nirvana's management had him taken to an LA rehab clinic in a 'tough love'-style intervention. Within days he escaped, returned to Seattle, persuaded friend Dylan Carlson to buy him a shotgun (he was banned from buying guns after the previous suicide attempt) and bought more heroin.

nirvana

On 8 April, an electrician called at Cobain's mansion to install an alarm system and found his body, which had lain unnoticed for three days. The next day, thousands of fans gathered at a candlelit vigil in the centre of Seattle. A tape played of Love reading extracts from Cobain's suicide note, which included a line from Neil Young's 'Hey Hey, My My (Out Of The Blue, Into The Black)': "It's better to burn out than fade away". "God! You asshole," Courtney replied. Young's response was to drop the song temporarily from his live set and pen the raging title track of *Sleeps With Angels* (1994) in homage.

While offers for film rights and inevitable conspiracy theories began to circulate, sales of *Bleach, Nevermind* and *In Utero* created shortages. *MTV Unplugged In New York* (1994) topped UK and US charts and appeared simultaneously with *Live! Tonight! Sold Out!*, a sometimes hilarious video document of *Nevermind*-era chaos. Subsequently, Love exorcized her demons on a year-long world tour with Hole, Grohl formed Foo Fighters with Pat Smear, Novoselic founded Sweet 75 and, despite Grunge slipping into cliché, the noise-drenched live compilation *From The Muddy Banks Of The Wishkah* (1996) topped the US chart.

In his final weeks, Cobain had been considering an acoustic-based collaboration with REM's Michael Stipe. When these plans were brought to a shocking stop by Cobain's death, the only result was REM's lamentation 'Let Me In' on *Monster*. "If *Murmur* or *Reckoning* had sold 5 million copies, I wouldn't be alive to tell

When the album sank, the group's misery gathered pace: they squabbled with Interscope, Stefani and Kanal's seven-year relationship collapsed, and Stefani's keyboard-playing brother Eric quit to become a cartoonist on *The Simpsons*. Independently produced and raw, *The Beacon Street Collection* (1995) testified to their frayed nerves, but Interscope was persuaded to try again.

The result was *Tragic Kingdom* (1996), which exploded to mega-platinum sales on the back of its colossal hits 'Don't Speak' and 'Just A Girl'. It hurt not at all that Stefani looked like Madonna and that her two anthems cutely evoked the post-Alanis themes *du jour* of heartache and female emancipation. The band hit the road and stayed there for two years, adding extra column inches when Stefani found lurve with Bush bellower Gavin Rossdale.

read *The Story Of No Doubt* (1997), Kalen Rogers

fan ND Friend Club, PO Box 8899, Anaheim, CA 92812, USA

surf www.hallucinet.com/no_doubt/

the tale," Stipe said. However, the link between the two was already well established: more through luck than judgement, their commercial domination had made formerly 'alternative' music – beloved only of college students and music critics – the multi-million-selling mainstream.

read *Come As You Are: The Story Of Nirvana* (1993), Michael Azzerad

surf www.geocities.com/~dperle/ms/

NO DOUBT ✪

WHO Vocals **Gwen Stefani** (b. 3 Oct 1969, Anaheim, California, USA), guitar **Tom Dumont** (b. 11 Jan 1968), bass **Tony Kanal** (b. 27 Aug 1970, England), drums **Adrian Young** (b. 26 Aug 1969)

WHEN 1987–

WHERE Anaheim, California, USA

WHAT Battle-scarred Ska

The much-mooted "Ska revival" repeatedly failed to materialize after the early 80s heyday of Madness and The Specials. However, among aficionados of the Reggae style was Gwen Stefani, fervent fan of Kermit The Frog and funky types Fishbone and Madness. The Muppets' influence ultimately took second place – appropriately enough, given the heartache into which No Doubt promptly plunged. Founder John Spence committed suicide within a year, forcing Gwen into the spotlight. Local gigs landed a deal with Interscope, who failed to sail *No Doubt* (1992) through the choppy post-Grunge waters.

NORTHERN SOUL

WHAT 'Northern' refers both to the part of England where this Soul sub-genre first became popular in the 70s, and to the North American city of Detroit from where the music originally emanated. Clubs in Blackpool, Manchester and Stoke and Wigan's infamous Casino venue gave birth to one of the most exciting scenes witnessed in Britain. The music was fast and furious, as were the amazingly acrobatic dances, performed to a backdrop of obscure (even in America) Motown-influenced tracks. Northern Soul launched many hits in the 70s – including The Tams' 'Hey Girl Don't Bother Me' (1971), The Elgins' 'Heaven Must Have Sent You' (1971) and R. Dean Taylor's 'There's A Ghost In My House' (1974) – and still thrives in Britain.

WHERE Detroit, Michigan, USA; Wigan, England

WHEN 70s–

WHO Various The Wigan Casino Story (1994), Various Dancing 'Til Dawn (1994), Various The Twisted Wheel Story (1995), Various Out On The Floor (1995), Various North Of Watford (1995)

THE NOTORIOUS BIG

WHO b. Christopher Wallace, 21 May 1972, Brooklyn, New York, USA, d. 8 Mar 1997, Los Angeles, California, USA

WHAT From crime to rhyme

"I don't want to be no 30-year-old Rapper," said The Notorious BIG in 1997. Envisioning a relaxed, early retirement, he was instead gunned down on leaving an LA party. It was a brutal end to a story with a tough start: as Biggie Smalls, he had graduated from small-time drug dealing to rhyming alone and with the Brooklyn crew Old Gold Brothers. His reputation rode the Hip Hop grapevine to Sean 'Puffy' Combs, hence Biggie's guest slots with Puffy's production protégés Mary J. Blige and Jodeci. Blige was one of several glamorous gals namechecked on Biggie's early cut 'Dreams' (whose drift can be caught from the rhyming of 'Braxton' with 'action' and 'satisfaction').

Further cameos – including 'Party And Bullshit' on 1993's *Who's The Man* soundtrack – preceded *Ready To Die* (1994), credited to The Notorious BIG. Glossy production and Biggie's seductive malevolence made Gangsta Rap glamorous, and the smooth 'Juicy', 'One More Chance' and 'Big Poppa' were appropriately huge hits on the *Billboard* Pop chart. Hook-ups with R. Kelly and Michael Jackson ensued, and the Biggie/Puffy axis oversaw the debuts of Swing sensations Total and Rap runts Junior MAFIA – the latter featuring Biggie's 'lieutenant', Lil' Kim.

The sordid side to success was a feud with Tupac Shakur, who considered Biggie had appropriated his style (ironic, given the former's stylistic debt to Ice Cube). Friendly rivalry soured – rendering ironic their joint appearance on 'Runnin'', from 1995's *One Million Strong* compilation – and a Biggie cameo was sliced from Shakur's *Thug Life* (1995) set. Darkness descended with Shakur's murder in 1996: killer cuts like 'Notorious Thugs' and 'You're Nobody ('Til Somebody Kills You)' on Biggie's *Life After Death* (1997) were bloody reports from Rap's frontlines. Another acclaimed cameo – on Jaÿ-Z's 'Brooklyn's Finest' – included the casual threats and 'machine gun Funk' Biggie had made his own.

The circle closed just days before *Life*'s release, with Biggie's murder by killers unknown, although the location – Shakur's 'territory' California – inevitably provoked revenge conspiracy theories (Biggie and Shakur having come to represent opposing sides in a feud between Rap's East and West coasts). The attendant publicity, added to his platinum-coated reputation, sent sales spiralling into multi-millions. Worldwide smashes 'Hypnotize' and 'Mo Money Mo Problems' were jostled in the charts by Puffy and Faith Evans' tribute 'I'll Be Missing You' and Lil' Kim's solo hits, including the Biggie-blessed 'Crush On You'.

Meanwhile, chart-busting sales of Shakur's posthumous releases boded well for the fortunes of Biggie's projected final set *Born Again*. The tragedy of the BIG saga is that he seemed keen to slip Gangsta's clutches; the triumph is that he left us with a near unimpeachable body of music.

SURF www.mastaj.com/BiggieSmalls.html

TED NUGENT

WHO b. 13 Dec 1948, Detroit, Michigan, USA

WHAT Heavy Metal hard man

Ted Nugent's legend rests solidly on colourful career moves. His grinding guitar drove The Amboy Dukes into the US charts with 'Journey To The Centre Of The Mind' (1968), defining the garage band era. Under his guidance, the band moved from the centre of the mind to the crotch. A punishing schedule and hardline anti-drug policy gave Nugent the hardest sidemen in the business and, by 1975, the Dukes were dead as Ted signed a lucrative solo deal for *Ted Nugent* (1975) and *Free For All* (1976).

Honing the sound to hard-edged Metal with sharp solos and risqué lyrics, he hit the US chart regularly and pulled massive crowds (often in cahoots with Aerosmith). *Cat Scratch Fever* (1977) set the style that hauled *Weekend Warriors* (1978), *State Of Shock* (1979) and *Scream Dream* (1980) to massive worldwide sales. Brain-bashers like Metallica learned much from Nugent's showmanship and riffing, but also learned something about political correctness. Nugent, by contrast, peppered *Spirit Of The Wild* (1995) with tracks like 'Thighraceous' and 'Kiss My Ass'.

Blatant sexism was only the start. Suicidal volume levels gave rise to the promotional slogan "If it's too loud, you're too old", and legends like the pigeon that disintegrated in mid-flight when hit by the sonic assault emanating from Ted's amps. It's an unlikely story; pigeons generally avoid Nugent gigs and so should squirrels. Ted once bow-and-arrowed 25 to become the 1974 American squirrel-shooting champion.

Inspiration waned through *Nugent* (1982), *Penetrator* (1984), *Little Miss Dangerous* (1986) and *If You Can't Lick 'Em… Lick 'Em!* (1988), and Nugent threw in his lot with AOR supergroup Damn Yankees. The double-platinum *Damn Yankees* (1982) reversed his downward sales curve, thanks to the hit 'High Enough', but did little to mollify fans who, clutching copies of *Double Live Gonzo* (1978), were appalled to see Nugent with former members of Styx and Night Ranger. However, legions of groupies and visitors to his defiantly named Red Meat restaurant can testify to the legendary status of one of the loudest characters in Rock.

READ *The Legendary Ted Nugent* (1982), Robert Holland

SURF www.thewild.com/jngonzo/nuge.html

GARY NUMAN ⊙ ⊙ ⊙

WHO b. Gary Webb, 8 Mar 1958, London, England

WHAT Dark Synth Pop

Joining Punk also-rans The Lasers in 1977, Numan renamed the group Tubeway Army and signed to Beggars Banquet in 1978. During sessions for their first album, Numan discovered synthesizers and considered moving the group away from Punk. The band, except for bassist Paul Gardiner, promptly left him, forming the now forgotten Tubeway Patrol. Numan continued with Gardiner and his uncle, drummer Gerald Lidyard, for his bleak debut *Tubeway Army* (1978).

Synthesizers featured heavily on Numan's dark, paranoid classics 'Are Friends Electric?' and *Replicas* (1979). Never critically acclaimed, Numan was now a household name in England. His brand of sing-along melancholy was halfway between Kraftwerk and Joy Division: a claustrophobic robot-Pop. His seemingly overnight fame was staggering: a 13-date UK tour sold out within days of its announcement and a 'Numanoid' cult grew.

The Pleasure Principle (1979), credited to Numan alone, yielded the hit 'Cars' and continued the popular alienation

themes. On Numan's 1980 world tour, the album became an international hit, and the single his only US chart success. Of the new crop of Synth Pop artists, like The Human League and OMD, Numan was the most accepted by a public that, for the most part, saw the whole genre as unmusical. Suddenly, every schoolkid in Britain wanted a Moog, but made do with a Casio. After a live video, *The Touring Principle* (1980), Numan mounted another UK tour in support of 1980's more conventional *Telekon*.

Moving slowly from the sound that listeners expected from him, Numan knew his days as a major Pop star were numbered. Noted for grandiose concerts, he announced his retirement from live performance at the last of three Wembley Arena shows in London in April 1981. After the boxed compilation *Living Ornaments 1979–1980* (1981), *Dance* (1981) moved further away from synthesized sound, featuring Japan bassist Mick Karn and Queen's Roger Taylor. *I, Assassin* (1982) combined heavy Funk and Rock, a style elaborated on in *Warriors* (1983), with Numan's image converging with the (then) fashionable *Mad Max* look.

Released on his own Numa label, the Industrial *Beserker* (1984) marked a slight return to Numan's electronic past, while *The Fury* (1985) demonstrated a new eclecticism, marrying his familiar themes with danceable, synthesized Funk. 'Change Your Mind', a collaboration with Shakatak's Bill Sharpe, saw Numan return to the higher reaches of the UK chart in 1985.

Strange Charm (1986) suffered the same fate as much of his 80s output: despite a loyal fanbase, public acceptance was elusive and the album's sales stalled soon after release. Closing Numa in 1987, Numan collaborated with English band Radio Heart, before a 'Cars' remix (the 'E-reg' mix, after that year's UK car registration letter) returned him to *Top Of The Pops*. *Metal Rhythm* (1988) and *Skin Mechanic* (1989) continued Numan's commercial misfortune, but he was kept afloat by loyal fans and concentrated on his parallel career as a successful stunt pilot. In 1981, he was held under house arrest in India after an unscheduled landing during a round-the-world airplane voyage.

Now an almost totally self-sufficient artist, Numan explored different facets of his sound on *Outland* (1991), fusing brooding electronics to almost Prince-like Funk. The rockier *Machine + Soul* (1992) continued this powerful style, with Numan covering Prince's 'U Got The Look' and '1999' on the extended CD version. *Sacrifice* (1994), conceived and executed entirely by himself, was a return to the sinister darkness of vintage Numan.

After 'Cars' was used in a 1996 English beer ad, the song was re-released and Numan once again found himself on *Top Of The Pops*. The anthology *The Premier Hits* (1996) proved Numan's influence on electronic Pop, not to mention Techno. With *Exile* (1997), Numan showed himself to be one of the few artists with enough skill to guide his own career, designing his own cover art and Internet site, while running the revived Numa and his fan club with his family. One of the most loyal fanbases in Pop showed its celebrity colours on the tribute albums *Random* (1997) – which featured covers by acts as diverse as St Etienne, The Orb, Republica and Weezer's Matt Sharp with Blur's Damon Albarn – and *Random 2* (1998), on which he was remixed by the likes of Dave Angel. Elsewhere, Foo Fighters and Marilyn Manson separately covered his 'Down In The Park'. Meanwhile, Numan published his autobiography *Praying To The Aliens*.

READ *Praying To The Aliens* (1997), Gary Numan

FAN GNFC, PO Box 14, Staines, Middlesex, TW19 5AU, UK

SURF www.numan.co.uk

NWA:DOROTHY LOW:RETNA

NWA ✪

WHO Vocals/production **Eazy-E** (b. Eric Wright, 7 Sep 1964, Compton, Los Angeles, California, USA, d. 26 Mar 1995, Los Angeles), vocals/production **Dr Dre** (b. Andre Young, 18 Feb 1965, South Central Los Angeles), vocals **Ice Cube** (b. O'Shea Jackson, 15 Jun 1969, Los Angeles), vocals **MC Ren** (b. Lorenzo Patterson, 16 Jun 1966), production **DJ Yella** (b. Antoine Carraby, 11 Dec 1967)

WHEN 1986–1991

WHERE Compton, Los Angeles, California, USA

WHAT Grandpas of Gangsta

Dreaming of dollars, pint-sized entrepreneur Eazy-E swapped drug dealing for music-making, launched Ruthless Records and recruited DJs Dr Dre and Yella, plus vicious verbalist Ice Cube. When the Ruthless crew HBO turned down Cube's 'Boyz N The Hood', Eazy convened Niggaz With Attitude to cut it instead. The track opened *NWA And The Posse* (1987), a showcase set issued by the Malaco label without Eazy's consent. Despite debuting both NWA and cult Rap star The DOC, the album passed largely unremarked. 'Boyz N The Hood', however, became the title of a superb 1991 movie, with a stunning star turn by Ice Cube.

The fireworks started when NWA added MC Ren, Ruthless won a distribution deal with Priority Records (then best-known for TV ad-land's singing fruit The California Raisins) and *Straight Outta Compton* (1988) hit the stores. Unease about the Gangsta Rap of their Cali confederate Ice-T turned the spotlight on NWA, whose very name was shocking – 'Nigger' being a term sparingly used outside 'Blaxploitation' movies. They fuelled the fire with the killer cuts 'Straight Outta Compton', 'Fuck Tha Police' and 'Gangsta Gangsta' – searingly soundtracked, chillingly candid evocations of LA street life. Their notoriety – boosted by an FBI investigation – made for multi-million sales and column inches. Though party-hardy Rap still shifted – hence the empty-headed Vanilla Ice and 2 Live Crew – it was overtaken by Gangsta, whose bitches 'n' ho's, guns 'n' gore, and sex 'n' drugs were, if not invented, certainly popularized by the Compton crew.

Meanwhile, NWA itself fell apart. Irked by the domination of Eazy and their manager Jerry Heller, Cube flounced to solo superiority. The others mined platinum with *Eazy-Duz-It* (1988), the '100 Miles And Runnin'' EP (1990) and the US chart-topping *EFIL4ZAGGIN* (1991). Bereft of Cube's skill, these were notable more for the growing sophistication of Dre's production – a talent further demonstrated by fellow Ruthless acts The DOC (1989's *No One Can Do It Better*) and Michel'le (1990's *Michel'le*).

When Dre quit too, the group was finished. Ruthless Records coasted on platinum-sellers by Ren (1992's *Kizz My Black Azz*) and Eazy, but was eclipsed by the ex-cohorts' feuding – hence the homicidally inclined 'No Vaseline' (banned from the UK release of Cube's *Death Certificate*) and Eazy's *It's On (Dr Dre) 187um Killa* (1993). Although Cube and Dre reunited in the 90s, their hatred for Eazy was abated only by his death from an AIDS-related virus in 1995. Fortunately, Eazy's legacy amounted to more than turning Rap's basest elements into gold: the intricate harmonies of his 90s protégés Bone Thugs-N-Harmony brought a goosebump-raising breeze to Gangsta's chamber of horror. They became US chart-toppers and repaid the favour with a superb cover of NWA's 'Fuck Tha Police' on 1997's tribute to 'Old School' Hip Hop, *In Tha Beginning… There Was Rap.*

surf home4.swipnet.se/~w-40723/eazy2.htm

LAURA NYRO

WHO b. Laura Nigro, 18 Oct 1947, Brooklyn, USA, d. 8 Apr 1997

WHAT Urban Soul Folk

With a Jazz trumpeter father, a three-octave voice and powerful songs, Laura Nyro was ably equipped for the late-60s singer/songwriter boom. An evocative figure, as she sat with her long black hair and long black skirts draped around the piano stool, fans thrilled to her dark city ethos – a relief from the blue-jeaned hippie chicks of the time. Her smokey, ethereal voice, which could suddenly break into a belting howl, graced sophisticated compositions centred on Folk, but bringing in styles as diverse as Jazz and Doo Wop. Her debut *More Than A New Discovery* (1966) included two songs which became hits for others in 1969: 'And When I Die', a No.2 for Blood, Sweat & Tears, and 'Wedding Bell Blues', a No.1 for Fifth Dimension. A performance at Monterey won the admiration of David Geffen, who became her manager and won her a Columbia contract.

Eli And The Thirteenth Confession (1968) again proved more profitable for others: 'Stoned Soul Picnic' (Fifth Dimension again) and 'Eli's Comin'' (Three Dog Night) were both hits, but her own greatest success was 1969's *New York Tendaberry* (with its epic title track), which won acclaim for its streetwise poetry.

The similarly excellent *Christmas And The Beads Of Sweat* (1970) featured a Duane Allman guitar cameo. Retiring to married life after *Gonna Take A Miracle* (1971), she returned with 1975's *Smile*. However her eccentricities – like sporadic performances and refusing to allow radio edits – hindered sales, and *Seasons Of Light* (1977), *Nested* (1978), and *Mother's Spiritual* (1984) were influential but commercial failures.

Five years passed before *Live At The Bottom Line* (1989). Her final studio album, 1993's *Walk The Dog And Light The Light*, appeared before she sadly lost a battle with cancer at 50.

surf www-unix.oit.umass.edu/~glens/nyro.html

OASIS ⊙ ⊙ ⊙

WHO Vocals **Liam Gallagher** (b. William Gallagher, 21 Sep 1972, Manchester, England), guitar/vocals **Noel Gallagher** (b. 29 May 1967, Manchester), guitar **Paul 'Bonehead' Arthurs** (b. 23 Jun 1965, Manchester), bass **Paul 'Guigsy' McGuigan** (b. 9 May 1971, Manchester), drums **Alan White** (b. 26 May 1972, London, England)

WHEN 1991–

WHERE Manchester, England

WHAT Britpop's Beatles

Named after a Beatles B-side, Rain were an unremarkable band formed by bassist Guigsy, guitarist Bonehead and drummer Tony McCarroll in 1991. Having sacked singer Chris Hutton, they gave the job to Liam Gallagher, who bequeathed the name Oasis – the name of a venue he'd seen on an Inspiral Carpets tour poster.

Liam's brother Noel, an Inspirals roadie, had played guitar and written songs since childhood, but never formed a band. He saw Oasis' first gig at The Boardwalk, Manchester, in August 1991, but wasn't impressed, especially when Liam asked him to manage them. Instead, he played them his own songs, offered to join,

oasis

then took over as lead guitarist and sole songwriter. They weren't interested in Indie cultdom: Liam confidently told the unemployment benefit office that if he couldn't be a Rock star, he'd settle for a job as a lumberjack.

Armed with a Lennon & McCartney songbook and a Sex Pistols lifestyle, Oasis set out to conquer. In early 1993, they visited Liverpool, where Noel's friends Tony and Chris Griffiths from The Real People had a studio. Fellow Inspirals roadie Mark Coyle had produced a demo at his home studio, but Oasis were making him deaf. In three months, they recorded 12 tracks at the Griffifths' studio, including 'Digsy's Dinner', about Tony and Chris' cousin Digsy from local band Smaller.

The polished performances on the demo were a far cry from their turbulent gigs. Liam baited the audience and the brothers' constant bickering often continued on stage – an enduring feature of their shows. On 31 May 1993, they intimidated a promoter into letting them play at King Tut's Wah Wah Hut in Glasgow. Creation Records' founder Alan McGee, there to watch his signings 18 Wheeler, had heard of Oasis' yobbishness (and their Union Jack-emblazoned demo) and intended to avoid the band. After two songs, he was ready to sign them. Ex-Smiths

guitarist Johnny Marr also took notice: after being given a tape, he and his manager Marcus Russell saw them in Manchester. Russell promptly took on Oasis' management as well.

They became Rock 'n' Roll stars long before Oasis records were in the shops. By the time the anthemic 'Supersonic' was released in April 1994, they had supported The Milltown Brothers, BMX Bandits, The Verve, Liz Phair, The Real People and Dodgy, garnering more acclaim than all bar The Verve (who they in any case eclipsed by sheer volume of coverage). A first, high-profile London appearance in January sold out in minutes.

The music press took their snarling arrogance to heart, gleefully transcribing rows between Liam and Noel. One such argument – about the band's deportation from Holland after a drunken rampage on a ferry – was even released as the unofficial single 'Wibbling Rivalry'. After 'Shakermaker' sailed them close to the UK Top 10 in June 1994, Oasis were banned from a London hotel when a rock was thrown through the managing director's car window and they smashed a Swedish hotel bar with Creation labelmates Primal Scream. Such antics were far from the navel-gazing activities of Oasis' Britpop contemporaries (a scene ruled by Suede, who rarely indulged in headline-grabbing behaviour). They were further distinguished by 'Live Forever', whose tender balladry was a world away from the entertainingly nonsensical rhymes of 'Supersonic' and 'Shakermaker'.

After a tortuous conception – the original producer David Batchelor was replaced by Owen Morris – *Definitely Maybe* (1994) was unleashed to ecstatic reviews and spectacular sales. It entered the UK chart at No.1 (outselling The Three Tenors) and became one of history's fastest-selling debuts.

They celebrated with riotous gigs in Japan, then began their first American tour in September. Within weeks, they were torn apart by drink and drugs. After a disastrous show in Los Angeles, Noel stormed to San Francisco, hellbent on quitting.

However, he was persuaded to return and the tour resumed in October. Another hit, the drawling 'Cigarettes And Alcohol', summed up their chaotic couldn't-care-less-ness.

Oasis rounded off 1994 with the tootling 'Whatever', their first transparent Beatles steal. More impressively, they transformed 'I Am The Walrus' from a Fabs studio construction to a live monster, which remained in their set longer than some of their own songs. However, more than 100 gigs in a year left the band exhausted. Liam's voice finally cracked in December during a gig in Glasgow, sparking a riot which Noel tried to calm with a solo set. It wasn't the last time they played without their frontman.

More cracks showed in 1995. 'Some Might Say' topped the UK chart but was sandbagged by Tony McCarroll's lousy drumming. Never considered an equal, McCarroll should have got the message when the band dug a grave and buried him in the 'Live

"The funny thing is,
      that mouthing off three years ago about how we were gonna be
the biggest band in the world,
e actually went and done it.

And it was a piece of piss"
Noel

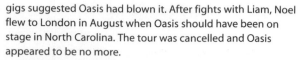

Forever' video. Noel poached his replacement, Alan White (brother of Paul Weller's drummer Steve), from fellow Creation artist Idha. A week later, White was rehearsing for Oasis' second album. During the sessions, Noel quit again after a drunken Liam attacked him. He returned weeks later, but pessimistically predicted in *NME* that Oasis would split after their third album.

After a lacklustre Glastonbury Festival showing in June 1995, Oasis had new material ready to roll – as did Britpop rivals Blur: their 'Country House' was scheduled for 14 August, the same day as Oasis' 'Roll With It'. A showdown was unavoidable, a fact not lost on Britain's frenzied media and the bands themselves. Two days after the release date, it transpired that thousands of copies of 'Roll With It' had been released without the bar code essential for registering sales and that Blur's label EMI had unsportingly rescheduled 'Country House' specifically to clash with 'Roll With It'. When Blur entered the chart at No.1 with Oasis at No.2, Noel and Liam appeared listless on *Top Of The Pops* that week.

Their disappointment didn't last long. In September, Oasis contributed 'Fade Away' to the Bosnian benefit album *Help* (1995) and, with Paul Weller and Paul McCartney, Noel recorded The Beatles' 'Come Together' as The Smokin' Mojo Filters.

(What's The Story) Morning Glory? (1995) was released later that month. Negative reviews did little to hinder sales: the album was a fixture on the UK chart for two years. However, their next tour was postponed until October, with Scott McCleod of Manchester group The Ya Ya's temporarily replacing Guigsy, then ill with exhaustion. When McCleod quit during the tour's US leg, the group appeared on US TV with Bonehead on bass. Against medical advice, Guigsy returned at the end of the month.

After neighbour-worryingly noisy gigs at London's Earls Court in November, Oasis watched 'Wonderwall' climb the charts. Rarely off the radio and TV, Noel's sing-along was also adopted by buskers nationwide – there was even an Easy Listening spoof hit by The Mike Flowers Pops. Though Michael Jackson beat them with 'Earth Song', 'Wonderwall' was, to many, 1995's unofficial UK Christmas No.1. It was also a huge hit Stateside, confirming their ultimate commercial triumph over Blur. At Creation's Christmas party, Alan McGee presented Noel, a non-driver, with a chocolate brown Rolls Royce.

Thereafter, Oasis stopped being just a staggeringly successful Rock band and became a national institution. As earlier singles re-entered the charts again and again, 'Don't Look Back In Anger' took a customary place at the top. Returning from a US tour in March, they played giant British shows, including Manchester's Maine Road – the home of Liam, Noel and Guigsy's beloved Manchester City Football Club – and Scotland's Loch Lomond.

Even these paled beside a record-breaking audience of 210,000 over two nights at Knebworth in August 1996. In two years, they had gone from supporting minor Indie bands to playing a stately home formerly graced by Pink Floyd and Led Zeppelin. They confirmed their ascension to the hierarchy with an appearance on MTV's *Unplugged* – albeit without Liam, who left Noel to sing solo. Oasis seemed unruffled, but the press interpreted his no-show as a sign of impending implosion.

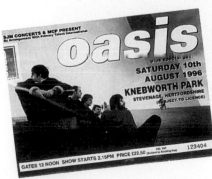

The fire was fuelled when Liam decided buying a house was more important than joining the band on a US tour. He relented days later, but his unruly behaviour at the MTV awards in New York and underwhelming

gigs suggested Oasis had blown it. After fights with Liam, Noel flew to London in August when Oasis should have been on stage in North Carolina. The tour was cancelled and Oasis appeared to be no more.

By October 1996, they were back together, recording a new album at Abbey Road. Cheated of a climax, the press watched closely. When Liam was arrested for possession of drugs, the attention turned to hounding. His relationship with actress Patsy Kensit was never far from the headlines and even his haircut became front page news. Meanwhile, Noel's outspoken defence of drugs in January 1997 prompted calls in the press for his arrest. One of his new songs was called 'My Big Mouth'.

Liam and Patsy shook off reporters long enough to get married in April. Noel's union with Meg Matthews in Las Vegas in June was less problematic, while Guigsy's and Alan White's weddings went almost unnoticed. After support slots with U2 on the US leg of their PopMart tour in June, the brooding 'D'You Know What I Mean' entered at UK No.1 in July. It trailed *Be Here Now* (1997), which inevitably also entered the UK album chart at No.1, selling a record-breaking 696,000 copies in its first week.

By now, much of the excitement that had hallmarked Oasis' early days was gone. Though Noel remained a witty, charismatic media star, and Liam was singing better than ever, their lifestyles had descended into cliché and their songs were formulaic. They barely bothered to disguise the Beatles steals on 'All Around The World' and even recycled their own 'Don't Look Back In Anger' for 'Stand By Me'. Sellout gigs and chart-topping sales meant their fortunes were hardly in jeopardy, but Noel's admission of boredom with the band reflected general disquiet and allowed The Verve and Radiohead to steal their thunder.

Read *Getting High* (1997), Paolo Hewitt

Fan Creation Records, 109x Regents Park Rd, London NW1 8UR, UK

Surf www.oasisnet.com

OCEAN COLOUR SCENE ⊙

WHO Vocals **Simon Fowler** (b. 25 Apr 1965, Birmingham, England), guitar/keyboards **Steve Cradock** (b. 22 Aug 1969, Birmingham), bass **Damon Minchella** (b.1 Jun 1969, Liverpool, England), drums/keyboards **Oscar Harrison** (b.15 Apr 1965, Birmingham)

WHEN 1989–

WHERE Birmingham, England

WHAT Retro rockin' Mods

When the 'Madchester' craze swept Britain in the late 80s, Simon Fowler and Damon Minchella were in Indie band The Fanatics. Inspired by The Stone Roses, they sidestepped obsolescence by poaching Oscar Harrison from Jazz Rock Reggae outfit Echo Base and Steve Cradock from Paul Weller/Jam worshippers The Boys.

With all the ingredients for a timely Indie Dance crossover, the newly named Ocean Colour Scene signed to independent label !Phffft, who released their debut 'Sway' in 1990. But !Phffft was swallowed by Fontana, who found the album they recorded with veteran Rolling Stones' producer Jimmy Miller unacceptably raw and sent them back into the studio with different producers. *Ocean Colour Scene* (1992) emerged with a gloss suited to the

'Shoegazing' trend of the time, but the band were dispirited and wanted out. Three years of legal wrangles ensued, during which time the elf-like Cradock became more famous as Paul Weller's guitarist. When Ocean Colour Scene were finally freed from Fontana, Go! Discs (Weller's label) helped them to build a studio.

A crammed gig schedule – including a tour with Oasis – sprang Ocean Colour Scene from hibernation into the no-frills Mod Rock they'd wanted all along. Rooted in clear pre-Punk harmonies, *Moseley Shoals* (1996) reached UK No.2 and spawned three UK Top 20 hits – 'You've Got It Bad', 'The Day We Caught The Train' and 'The Circle'. The UK No.1 *Marchin' Already* (1997) continued their upward sales curve.

 OCS Music, Suite 17, Jago House, 692 Warwick Road, Solihull, West Midlands, B91 3DA, UK

 www.ammcj.demon.co.uk/OCS/index.htm

PHIL OCHS

WHO b. 19 Dec 1940, El Paso, Texas, USA, d. 9 Apr 1976, Far Rockaway, New York, USA

WHAT Pioneer of political Folk Pop

A journalism student turned Folk singer, Phil Ochs used his lyrics as polemical bulletins. The title of his 1964 debut *All The News That's Fit To Sing* (1964) made his intentions clear, and the title track of 1965's *I Ain't Marching Anymore* became an anthem for US anti-war protesters. *Phil Ochs In Concert* (1966) included two more of his best-known songs: the satirical 'Love Me I'm A Liberal' and 'There But For Fortune', a hit for Joan Baez in 1965.

In a bid to reach a wider audience, Ochs moved towards Rock on *The Pleasures Of The Harbor* (1967), *Rehearsals For Retirement* (1968) and *Gunfight At Carnegie Hall* (1974). On stage, he wore a gold lamé suit and sang Rock 'n' Roll medleys, but the changes won few converts and alienated early supporters.

Ochs' decline was swift and tragic. Attacked during a tour of Africa, he suffered damage to his vocal cords, permanently impairing his singing ability. Ochs found himself unable to write new songs, succumbed to alcoholism and schizophrenia and, in 1976, was found hanged at his sister's home.

 Death Of A Rebel (1979; updated 1995), Marc Eliot

 www.cs.pdx.edu/~trent/ochs/

SINEAD O'CONNOR ☉ ✪

WHO b. 8 Dec 1966, Dublin, Ireland

WHAT The avenging angel of Irish Pop

Within days of the dawning of the 90s, *the* single of the decade had made its mark. Its triumph was anything but predictable: the song was an obscure entry in the Prince canon, its singer was an outspoken, shaven-headed Rap fan who had not charted in two years. But now the whole world knew Sinéad O'Connor's name.

From singing Bob Dylan covers in Dublin pubs, she graduated to fronting Dublin band Ton Ton Macoute in 1985. She co-wrote 'Take My Hand' for Irish band In Tua Nua's first single and sang on 'Heroine' from U2 guitarist The Edge's soundtrack for the movie

Captive (1986). Thereafter, she maintained an erratic relationship with U2; following years of accusing them of dictating the Irish music scene, she unbent enough in 1993 to record Bono's title theme for the movie *In The Name Of The Father*.

Back in 1986, Sinéad was talent-spotted at a Ton Ton Macoute gig by Ensign Records, who signed her alone. After gracing labelmates World Party's *Private Revolution* (1987), she released her extraordinary debut 'Troy'. Inspired by W.B. Yeats' poem 'No Second Troy', it expressed feelings for her mother, Marie, who had died in a car crash two years earlier. Sinéad's singing was full of emotional whoops and ululations. Another trademark – a shaved head – heightened her aggressively honest style. In interviews to promote her debut album *The Lion And The Cobra* (1988) – self-produced while pregnant with her son by drummer John Reynolds – she discussed her history of domestic violence, claiming that she was abused by her mentally unstable mother. A controversial declaration of sympathy with the IRA was later retracted, with Sinéad confessing a certain degree of naivity.

'Mandinka' was a hit in 1988 and the album sold well at home and abroad, but her profile rarely translated into chart placings. A reworking of 'I Want Your (Hands On Me)' with MC Lyte – one of Rap's finest female voices – cemented her loyalty to the genre (she was namechecked on a Public Enemy album after shaving their logo into her head) but did little to boost her fortunes.

Then, January 1990 saw the release of 'Nothing Compares 2 U', originally written by Prince for his under-achieving protégés The Family. Its heart-rending vocal and beautiful orchestration by Soul II Soul matched by a starkly tearful video, the song soon topped both UK and US charts and catapulted Sinéad to fame.

I Do Not Want What I Haven't Got (1990) was also rapturously received: a transatlantic chart-topper, it sold more than 6 million despite its resolutely uncommercial blend of bleak ballads and punky guitars. Her contrariness was confirmed when she refused to play at the Garden State Arts Center, New Jersey, if the venue played (as was traditional) 'The Star Spangled Banner' before the show. Amid the ensuing outcry, Frank Sinatra – who played there the next night – expressed a wish to "kick her ass". Sinéad stayed away from 1991's Grammy and BRIT ceremonies, criticizing the the music industry, and released 'My Special Child', articulating her painful thoughts on an abortion she had experienced.

Even these statements of independence were eclipsed when she appeared on America's *Saturday Night Live* show and tore up a picture of Pope John Paul II, shouting "fight the enemy". Two weeks later, she was booed off stage at a Bob Dylan tribute show at New York's Madison Square Garden on 16 October 1992.

To the bemusement of critics, her next album was a collection of cover versions. *Am I Not Your Girl?* (1992) mixed strident songs like the minor hit 'Success Has Made A Failure Of Our Home' with delicate, Barbra Streisand-ish takes on standards like 'Bewitched, Bothered And Bewildered'. However, she remained in demand, her vocals gracing work by acts ranging from Country legend Willie Nelson to Punk-turned-World-Music-evangelist Jah Wobble. The best of these guest appearances were her wrenching backgrounds on Peter Gabriel's 'Come Talk To Me' and 'Blood Of Eden' on his *Us* (1992).

With the press labelling her paranoid and unhinged, Sinéad's excellent *Universal Mother* (1994) did little to redress the balance. Its musical might went unremarked as critics seized instead on lyrics which ranged from the 'myth' of the Irish potato famine to the stresses of love and fame. But she later appeared more level-headed. She duetted with Shane MacGowan on 1995's superb 'Haunted', and gave birth again in 1996, the motherhood theme informing 1997's 'Gospel Oak' EP. *So Far – The Best Of Sinéad O'Connor* (1997) failed to live up to its title, but celebrated her first recording decade. In 1998, she placed 'Emma's Song' on *The Avengers* soundtrack and co-headlined the US Lilith Fair festival.

(ReaD) *Sinead O'Connor: So Different* (1991), Dermott Hayes

(Surf) www/dowcomputer.com/sinlink.htm

MIKE OLDFIELD ⊙ ⊙ ⊙

WHO b. 15 May 1953, Reading, Berkshire, England

WHAT The young prince of Prog

Despite staggering sales, Mike Oldfield is as enigmatic as the best of his prodigious output. Releasing his own material at the frighteningly young age of 15 – 1968's folky *Sallyangie* – he joined Kevin Ayers' The Whole World as a guitarist. By 19, he was busy crafting an epic: the Stonehenge of Progressive Rock – *Tubular Bells* (1973). It sold 16 million copies (transforming Oldfield's label Virgin from hippie front-room operation to major

league monolith), soundtracked *The Exorcist*, spawned profit-milking orchestral and (wow!) quadrophonic versions and was UK No.1 until dislodged by Oldfield's own *Hergest Ridge* (1974).

The thoughtful *Ommadawn* (1975) is regarded by fans as a masterpiece, but – troubled by Punk's anti-hippie blitzkrieg – he shied away from full-blown pomp with *Incantations* (1978), *Platinum* (1979), *QE 2* (1980) and *Five Miles Out* (1982).

By *Crises* (1983), classic Pop and Folk were on the menu for the hit 'Moonlight Shadow', featuring vocals by Maggie Reilly. Older fans who regarded it as a sellout could take consolation from his excellent soundtrack for 1985's *The Killing Fields*. But as Rock's pendulum swung again, *Islands* (1987) and *Earth Moving* (1989) revisited Oldfield's 70s sounds. *Amarok* (1990) was an album-length suite, whose unfashionability was reflected by now characteristically fleeting chart success.

September 1992 brought the UK No.1 *Tubular Bells II* – not as cynical as one might assume, considering the acclaim Oldfield was receiving from the emerging New Age and Ambient worlds. The Orb proved their allegiance with a remix of his 'Sentinel', while the Arthur C. Clarke-inspired multi-media production *Songs Of Distant Earth* (1994) sounded in touch and sold well. Forever composing and occasionally touring, Oldfield unleashed the first strains of *Tubular Bells III* in 1997 as part of the *XXV* retrospective, celebrating his first quarter century as a solo act.

(ReaD) *A Man And His Music* (1994), Sean Moragham

(Fan) Dark Star, PO Box 2031, Blandford, Dorset, DT11 9YB, UK

(Surf) www.ibmpcug.co.uk/dark star/

THE ORB ⊙

WHO Keyboards **Dr Alex Paterson**, keyboards **Thrash** (b. Kristian Weston)

WHEN 1989–

WHERE London, England

WHAT Dance side of the moon

Having fought the Punk wars (humping equipment for Killing Joke), Dr Alex Paterson (not really a doctor) turned traitor and re-introduced spacey widdling to a generation as The Orb. Inspired by House, Paterson and Jimmy Cauty (also one half of Dance terrorists KLF) became DJs, but spliced Eno-esque Ambient, movie soundtracks, Dub and sound effects with slow-motion beats. Impossible to dance to, this hybrid instead soundtracked post-rave early mornings and became known as Ambient House.

Paterson and Cauty became The Orb for their mind-numbing 1989 debut 'A Huge Ever Growing Pulsating Brain That Rules From The Centre Of The Ultraworld (Loving You)' – a 22-minute voyage into weirdness that, bizarrely, reached the UK Top 50.

Cauty left to concentrate on KLF and Paterson worked with ex-Killing Joke bassist (now respected producer) Youth on the superb 'Little Fluffy Clouds'. Its samples of experimentalist Steve Reich and bohemian songstress Rickie Lee Jones (the use of her space cadet dialogue prompted legal action) made a Dance gem – remixed by Kristian 'Thrash' Weston, Paterson's new partner.

Thrash was the technical foil for Paterson's Prog space fantasies, as proved by 1991's *The Orb's Adventures Beyond The Ultraworld*, which mimicked the sleeve of Pink Floyd's *Animals*, rehabiliated former Gong members Steve Hillage and Miquette

Giraudy (later to find success as the Orb-esque System 7) and spawned remixology *The Aubrey Mixes* (1991). The Orb's zenith, however, was the sprawling UK No.1 *U.F.Orb* (1992) and the UK Top 10 monolith 'Blue Room' – a record-breaking one second under 40 minutes (then the chart limit for the length of a single) of pulsing Dub. However, record company ructions and rifts between Thrash and Paterson scuppered The Orb: 1993's stop-gap *Live 93* prefaced 1994's too-clever-by-half 'Pomme Fritz' EP. With Thrash replaced by Sun Electric's Thomas Fehlmann, *Orbvs Terrarvm* (1995) added little to their legend. However, *Orblivion* (1997) and the UK hit 'Toxygene' (a reworking of a rejected Jean Michel Jarre remix) proved The Orb were back on frazzled form.

 *The Orb* (1992), Margaret Elizabeth Foster

surf www.theorb.com

ROY ORBISON ⊙ ⊙

WHO b. 23 Apr 1936, Vernon, Texas, USA, d. 6 Dec 1988, Nashville, Tennessee, USA

WHAT The sad voice from the Lone Star State

One of Rock 'n' Roll's greatest voices got off to an ignominiously erratic start. Of Roy Orbison's first recordings – 'Trying To Get To You', for Buddy Holly's producer Norman Petty in 1955, then four singles for Sun – only 1956's 'Ooby Dooby' scraped the US chart.

In December 1956, after parting company from his backing band The Teen Kings, he moved to Nashville and signed to RCA. Lack of success prompted another move to Monument, for

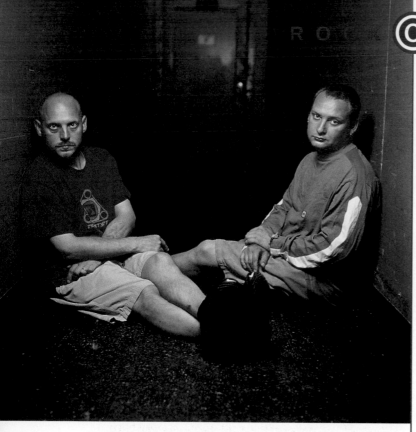

Orbison (1988) anthologized his Monument recordings, then 'You Got It' (written by Orbison, Lynne and Petty) returned him to transatlantic Top 10s for the first time in over two decades.

'You Got It' also graced his million-selling *Mystery Girl* (1989), whose highlight was the heartbreaking 'She's A Mystery To Me' by U2's Bono and The Edge. *King Of Hearts* (1992) yielded a hit cover of the Cyndi Lauper smash 'I Drove All Night' – confirming that charts and hearts will always welcome 'The Big O'.

READ *Dark Star: The Roy Orbison Story* (1990), Ellis Amburn

SURF www.orbison.com

ORBITAL

WHO Keyboards **Phil Hartnoll** (b. 9 Jan 1964, Dartford, Kent, England), keyboards **Paul Hartnoll** (b. 19 May 1968, Dartford)

WHEN 1988–

WHERE Sevenoaks, Kent, England

WHAT Bald, bold and brilliant Techno

Fusing Techno with DIY Punk ethics, Orbital released their debut 'Chime' (1989) on their own Oh Zone label. Recorded in Phil's bedroom at a total cost of 90 pence, it became a big club hit and, following a more widespread release on the ffrr label, entered the UK Top 20 in April 1990.

Further hits 'Satan' and 'Halcyon' followed, as did eponymous albums respectively known as "The Yellow Album" (1991) and "The Brown Album" (1993). However, it was after Orbital's spectacular live appearance at 1994's Glastonbury Festival that the brothers' profile rose. Matching their evolution into one of Britain's most exciting live acts, the critically acclaimed *Snivilisation* (1994) – described by one critic as the "world's first socially aware Techno album" – had a depth and complexity that overshadowed many of the duo's contemporaries.

They spent 1995 touring (including another Glastonbury appearance) and recording their fourth album, from which 'The Box' became their Top 10 debut in March 1996. The majestic *In Sides* (1996) reflected their contributions to movie soundtracks, including *Shopping* (1994) and a reworking of the theme to *The Saint* (1996). They collaborated with Metallica's Kirk Hammett on the *Spawn* soundtrack in 1997 and composer Michael Kamen on *Event Horizon* (1997). 'Satan', a popular track at live shows, hit the UK Top 20 in Prodigy-esque re-jiggled form in 1997.

ORCHESTRAL MANOEUVRES IN THE DARK

WHO Vocals/keyboards/bass **Andy McCluskey** (b. 24 Jun 1959, Heswall, England), keyboards/vocals **Paul Humphries** (b. 27 Feb 1960, London, England)

WHEN 1978–

WHERE Liverpool, England

WHAT Anti-Punk electronic Pop

Orchestral Manoeuvres In The Dark – a name intended to be as 'un-Punk' as possible – were the most melodic group on the late 70s Liverpool scene. Core members Andy McCluskey and Paul

whom his second single, 'Up Town' (1959), made only US No.72. However, The Everly Brothers scored in 1958 with his 'Claudette', which Orbison wrote for his wife and later recorded himself.

'Only The Lonely' (1960) brought the success he had strived for. Originally offered to Elvis, it narrowly missed the US top spot, but became his first UK No.1. His dramatic, wavering tenor was further showcased on 'Blue Angel' (1960), his first US chart-topper 'Running Scared' (1961), 'Crying' (1961) and 'Dream Baby' (1962). He also made the US and UK Top 10s with one of his most popular songs, 'In Dreams', the title track of a 1963 hit album.

On stage, he always wore shades. Having once left his glasses on a plane by accident, he performed in tinted ones, which he retained as his trademark. More chart glory came with 1963's 'Blue Bayou' and 1964's UK No.1s 'It's Over' and 'Oh Pretty Woman'. However, tragedy ensued when his wife was killed in a motorcycle accident in June 1966 and, two years later, his two eldest sons died in a fire at his Nashville home. The personal ballad 'Too Soon To Know' (1966) made the UK Top 3 but barely dented the US chart and paved the way for his hit-free 70s years.

Orbison continued to record – hence *The Big 'O'* (1970), *Hank Williams: The Roy Orbison Way* (1971), *Memphis* (1973) and *Milestones* (1974) – but charted only with best-ofs. Meanwhile, his songs became hits for Linda Ronstadt, Don McLean and Van Halen. *Regeneration* (1977) and *Laminar Flow* (1979) hinted at former glory, but true recognition came only in the mid-80s: the use of 'In Dreams' in David Lynch's 1986 movie *Blue Velvet* prompted another album of the same name, on which Orbison re-recorded – in some cases bettering – 19 of his greatest hits.

In 1987, he was inducted into the Rock And Roll Hall Of Fame, enjoyed the patronage of Bruce Springsteen, Jackson Browne and Bonnie Raitt at a tribute gig later released as *A Black And White Night* (1989), covered Heavy Metaller Glenn Danzig's 'Life Fades Away' on the *Less Than Zero* soundtrack and duetted with kd lang on a Grammy-winning remake of 'Crying'. In 1988, he joined Bob Dylan, Tom Petty, George Harrison and Jeff Lynne in a mock supergroup, The Traveling Wilburys. Sadly, more months later, he died from heart failure in 1988 at his Nashville home.

Inducted into the Songwriters Hall Of Fame in 1989, Orbison was also well served by posthumous releases. *The Legendary Roy*

Humphries had been through several bands – including VCL XI, Hitler's Underpantz and The Id – and were inspired by the synthesizer symphonies of Brian Eno and, in particular, Kraftwerk, whose 'Radio-Activity' they remodelled into their debut 'Electricity', released on the fledgling Factory label in 1979.

Dropping the electronic percussion of their self-titled debut album (1980), they recruited drummer Malcolm Holmes and bassist David Hughes for the breakthrough hit 'Enola Gay' and *Organisation* (1980). *Architecture And Morality* (1981), an acclaimed Synth Pop masterpiece, included the hits 'Souvenir' and 'Joan Of Arc (Maid Of Orleans)', but OMD's ambitions stretched further, with the experimental *Dazzle Ships* (1983) denting their reputation as Pop meisters.

Junk Culture returned them to the charts in 1984, but an obsession with conquering America drowned subsequent albums *Crush* (1985) and *The Pacific Age* (1986) somewhere in the mid-Atlantic. Humphries quit in 1988 to form The Listening Pool. McCluskey continued as OMD for the bland but chart-worthy *Sugar Tax* (1991), *Liberator* (1993) and 1996's partial return to form, *Universal*, which included collaborations with ex-Kraftwerker Karl Bartos.

 www.omdweb.com/~fester

OZZY OSBOURNE

WHO b. John Michael Osbourne, 3 Dec 1948, Birmingham, England

WHAT Beatle-lovin', loony-livin' Metal God

Bad behaviour and bad luck have dogged Ozzy Osbourne since his failed bids at burglary. He toppled off a wall, a stolen TV fell on him, he used fingerless gloves, he got caught. After a three-month jail sentence, Ozzy – inspired by The Beatles – turned to Rock 'n' Roll. However, if he'd hoped to stay out of trouble and emulate the mop-tops' fabness, joining graveyard grinders Black Sabbath wasn't the way to do it.

By 1978, he was a star, but also the bitter enemy of Sabbath's guitarist Tony Iommi, with whom his relationship had been frosty since their shared schooldays. Dragged down by drugs, Ozzy found himself fired. He was rescued by manager – and, soon, his wife – Sharon Arden (daughter of Rock impresario Don Arden), who turned him into Metal's biggest and baddest star.

Despite biting the heads off a live dove (a publicity stunt) and a bat (an on-stage 'accident' – he thought it was rubber), Ozzy's legend was first founded on *Blizzard Of Ozz* (1980) and *Diary Of A Madman* (1981). Both multi-million-sellers, they were sprightlier than Black Sabbath (check out *Blizzard Of Ozz*'s 'Crazy Train'), yet maintained his old band's engagingly evil themes (*Blizzard Of Ozz*'s 'Mr Crowley'). Equally entrancing was his young guitarist Randy Rhoads, who took over from Eddie Van Halen in the bright new string-slinger stakes.

Rhoads' death in a 1982 plane crash was a loss Ozzy bore in strange ways. He rhapsodized about the guitarist for years (hence 1987's *Tribute*), but promptly recruited short-stayed replacement Bernie Tormé for the live *Speak Of The Devil* (1982), recorded apparently to sabotage Black Sabbath's *Live Evil*.

In the aftermath, *Bark At The Moon* (1983) and *The Ultimate Sin* (1986) and their hits ('Bark At The Moon' and 'Shot In The Dark') maintained platinum US sales and, on their respective tours, broke support acts Mötley Crüe and Metallica into the big time.

However, by the end of the 80s, the dangerously fun-loving but hard-living Ozzy was in turmoil once more. The million-selling *No Rest For The Wicked* (1989) and a US smash with Metal queen Lita Ford, 1989's 'Close My Eyes Forever', were countered by alcoholism that eclipsed even his cocaine addiction. At the depths of despair, he tried to strangle Sharon. "He said, 'We've made up our mind, you have to die'," she recalled. "He and his friend, whoever his imaginary friend was, jumped on me."

After years of failed bids at rehabilitation, he was reborn as a fitness freak and put out his biggest-seller, *No More Tears* (1991), whose terrific title track fused 'Strawberry Fields'-ish Beatledom with heart-stopping Hard Rock. An eighteen-month world tour, intended as his farewell (hence the grand 1993 memorial *Live And Loud*), instead reactivated his enthusiasm for the road. After the Retirement Sucks trek in support of another smash, *Ozzmosis* (1995), he and Sharon launched the monstrous Ozzfest, a touring extravaganza that balanced the headliner's antiquity with younger, thrashier upstarts like Pantera.

Defying Metal's rumoured decline, the show grew such that a 1997 reunion with Sabbath looked less like a ticket-boosting gambit than a gesture of goodwill to embattled old friends. *The Ozzman Cometh* (1997) celebrated with a blend of Sabbath and solo hits, and the reunited hell-raisers headlined 1998's Ozzfest.

 Ozzy Osbourne: Diary Of A Madman (1990), Mick Wall

 www.ozzynet.com

THE OSMONDS

WHO Vocals **Marie** (b. 13 Oct 1959, Ogden, Utah, USA), vocals/guitar **Alan** (b. 22 Jun 1949, Ogden), vocals/guitar/bass/saxophone/banjo/drums **Wayne** (b. 28 Aug 1951, Ogden), vocals/bass **Merrill** (b. 30 Apr 1953, Ogden), vocals/drums **Jimmy** (b. 16 Apr 1963, Canoga Park, California, USA), vocals/keyboards **Donny** (b. 9 Dec 1957, Ogden), drums **Jay** (b. 2 Mar 1955, Ogden)

WHEN 1957–1980

WHERE Ogden, Utah, USA

WHAT Teen Pop heaven

Before the Gangsta-related bloodshed which ripped Rap apart, 70s Pop was similarly torn between two powerful American cartels. From Gary, Indiana: The Jacksons – funky and tough. From Ogden, Utah: The Osmonds – cute and toothsome. But they sold 77 million records and excited the lust of girls the world over, so who's laughing? First there were four: Alan, Wayne, Merrill and Jay. Raised as Mormons and trained as a barbershop quartet by their parents, they mounted stardom's stairs with a summer 1962 residency at Disneyland before being snapped up by crooner Andy Williams and becoming US TV's pre-pubescent stars of choice. Tours boosted their audience and, having picked up guitars and transformed themselves into a Rock group, by 1970 The Osmonds were poised for domination.

In 1971, augmented by Donny (the good-looking one), they emerged as hormone-stirring teen sensations: *The Osmonds* and *Homemade* exploded on the back of the Jacksons-esque US No.1 'One Bad Apple'. "Did you know that record was ours at first?" demanded Michael Jackson. "That's why it was mainly like us… They take it and make like they started it. It's like a dog-eat-dog type of situation. I think it's awful." Meanwhile, Donny conquered the charts with 'Sweet And Innocent', the US No.1 'Go Away Little Girl', *The Donny Osmond Album* and *To You With Love, Donny*.

Osmania reached Britain in 1972. *Osmonds Live* and *Crazy Horses* bolted into the UK chart, preceded by 'Crazy Horses' itself – Led Zep-lite for pre-teens. Donny's *Portrait Of Donny* and *Too Young* trailed 'Puppy Love', a UK No.1 which, like The Sex Pistols' 'Anarchy In The UK', provoked inter-generational conflict: kids loved it, grown-ups hated it.

The fire was fuelled by a scream-inducing 1973 UK tour and 'Little' Jimmy Osmond, who kicked off solo superduperdom with the UK No.1 'Long Haired Lover From Liverpool'. There was also *The Plan* (1973), The Osmonds' stab at a concept album – sort of a *Dark Side Of The Mormon*. Trouble brewed only with Wayne's entwining with Cherry 'Daughter of Pat, sister of Debby' Boone. "I'm always surprised how little they know about their own religion," remarked Papa Boone coolly.

Later in 1973, Donny conquered the UK chart pinnacle with 'The Twelfth Of Never' and 'Young Love', Jimmy struck again with 'Tweedle Dee' (1973) and 'I'm Gonna Knock On Your Door' (1974), the brothers hit No.1 with 1974's 'Love Me For A Reason' (covered by Boyzone), and their new weapon, Marie, straddled the Atlantic with 'Paper Roses' (1973) and, with Donny, 'I'm Leaving It (All) Up To You' and 'Morning Side Of The Mountain' (both 1974). But TV was where 'it' was 'at': *The Donny And Marie Show* (later *The Osmond Family Show*) was a veritable Osfest of cutesy comedy, the Mormon Tabernacle Choir and giant ratings.

Though their success survived the onslaught of Disco (those dastardly Jacksons at work again), The Osmonds split in 1980. Marie hit big on Country charts, Donny made periodic comeback bids (notably 1989's *Donny Osmond*), the brothers toured and opened Missouri's Osmond Family Theater and their children constituted The Osmond Boys and Osmonds Second Generation. And, just as Rap's East/West coast conflict cooled after death and disaster, the Osmond and Jackson tribes were reconciled when Little Jimmy became Michael Jackson's business advisor in 1987.

read *Osmonds – A Family Biography* (1983), Marsha Daly

surf www.osmond.com/

ROBERT PALMER

WHO b. Alan Palmer, 19 Jan 1949, Batley, Yorkshire, England

WHAT Sharp-suited Pop

After spending most of his childhood in Malta, Robert Palmer returned to England in his teens and joined The Alan Bown Set in 1969 as vocalist. In 1970, he joined Jazz Rock outfit DaDa, who evolved into the rockier Vinegar Joe. Although acclaimed for their live shows, their albums failed to chart. Retained by Island as a solo artist in 1974, Palmer used musicians from The Meters and Little Feat to record his solo debut *Sneakin' Sally Through The Alley*. His Reggae influences came to the fore on *Pressure Drop* (1975), featuring the Toots & The Maytals title track.

Moving to the Bahamas in 1976, he made his singles chart debut two years later with 'Every Kinda People'. *Secrets* (1979) gave him his second transatlantic hit, 'Bad Case Of Loving You (Doctor Doctor)'. The momentum grew with *Clues* (1980), which spawned 'Johnny And Mary' and 'Looking For Clues' and included Gary Numan and Talking Heads' drummer Chris Frantz.

In 1985, Palmer took a rockier turn with The Power Station, initially a one-album project. Joining Chic's Tony Thompson and Duran Duran's Andy Taylor and John Taylor, their eponymous album gave Palmer his highest chart placings yet. But Palmer's solo career was to peak with 'Addicted To Love' from *Riptide* (1985): a hard-hitting US No.1 later covered by both Tina Turner and Sonic Youth. It also provided one of MTV's most enduring images with the Terence Donovan-directed video: an all-female, mini-skirted and miming backing band (memorably mimicked in the video for Tone Löc's mega-selling Rap gem 'Wild Thing').

Worried about rising crime, Palmer moved to Switzerland in 1987. A stream of hits followed, including 1987's Grammy-winning 'Simply Irresistible' and a collaboration with UB40 on 'I'll Be Your Baby Tonight'. He paid homage to big bands with *Ridin' High* (1992), which he acknowledged as his only concept album. It charted miserably, but his 1995 greatest hits compilation was a safer bet and restored him to the upper reaches of the UK chart.

surf www.fortunecity.com/tattooine/ellison/2/rp.html

PANTERA ✪

WHO Vocals **Philip Anselmo** (b. 30 Jun 1968, New Orleans, Louisiana, USA), guitar **Dimebag Darrell** (b. Darrell Lance Abbott, 20 Aug 1966, Dallas, Texas, USA), bass **Rex Brown** (b. 27 Jul 1964, Graham, Texas), drums **Vinnie Paul** (b. Vincent Paul Abbott, 11 Mar 1964, Dallas)

WHEN 1983–

WHERE Texas, USA

WHAT From mascara to mosh-pits Metal magic

Just as Alanis Morissette would rather forget her bubble-permed Pop debut, so 'power groovers' Pantera are keen to bury their Glam Metal origins under the floorboards. Fuelled by the same tastes in Kiss and mascara that had propelled Mötley Crüe to the top, brothers Darrell and Vincent Abbott christened themselves Diamond and Vince, added bassist Rex 'Rocker' (née Brown) and,

as Pantera, issued *Metal Magic* (1983), *Projects In The Jungle* (1984) and *I Am The Night* (1985) to overwhelming indifference.

In 1986, shouty-voiced Phil Anselmo succeeded Terrence Lee (aka Terry Glaze) and they got scarily heavier through *Power Metal* (1988), *Cowboys From Hell* (1990) and *A Vulgar Display Of Power* (1992). With one boot in Southern Rock and one in Thrash Metal, Anselmo became their skin-headed focus, whose ambiguous views on race and dope sometimes overshadowed the band itself. However, the music got the upper hand when *Far Beyond Driven* (1994) debuted at US No.1 and UK No.3. Its hits – the terrifying '5 Minutes Alone' and a spooky take on Black Sabbath's 'Planet Caravan' – illustrated Pantera's sureness of touch.

Thereafter, they mounted a worldwide campaign against 'alternative music' (which had ensnared fellow brainbashers Metallica) with *The Great Southern Trendkill* (1996) and *Official Live: 101 Proof* (1997) and rivalled the reformed Black Sabbath as the premier attraction on the 1997 Ozzfest. As if these weren't heavy enough, Anselmo – when not annoying liberals and reportedly overdosing on heroin – weighed in with *Nola* (1995), the even harder product of his sideline Down.

In 1998, amid road-hogging touring, Pantera personnel popped up on albums by Anthrax (*Volume 8*) and Alice In Chains guitarist Jerry Cantrell (*Boggy Depot*), while Anselmo pitted his firepower against that of Black Sabbath riffmonster Tony Iommi.

Fan Pantera/MMN, PO Box 7022, Red Bank, NJ 07701, USA

surf www.concretemanagement.com/Pantera.html

Parlophone

The label most famously associated with The Beatles and the 60s Merseybeat boom began life in Germany before the First World War as a Classical label. Launched by Carl Lindstrom, his use of the German letter 'Ŀ' as a logo reputedly led to the label's famous £ trademark.

Parlophone was part of the Columbia Graphophone company before the formation of EMI in 1931, when it took its place alongside the HMV and Columbia labels. American Jazz recordings (including Louis Armstrong's first UK releases), British dance bands and a selection of comedy and novelty records featuring the likes of Charlie Drake and Peter Sellers were the major Parlophone releases until the late 50s, when they were joined by new British talent like Adam Faith, The Temperance Seven and Matt Monro. The signing of The Beatles by label chief and producer George Martin in 1962 led to a roster featuring Cilla Black, Billy J. Kramer and The Hollies. After a dispute with EMI over royalty payments on his Beatles recordings, Martin, who produced over 20 UK No.1s for Parlophone, left in 1966. The label continued under producer/artist Norman 'Hurricane' Smith and issued late 70s/early 80s albums by Lennon and McCartney.

In the 80s, chart-toppers Duran Duran, Dexy's Midnight Runners and Pet Shop Boys appeared on Parlophone, then EMI stalwarts Queen joined Morrissey and Paul McCartney on the label, alongside new, successful 90s acts Blur, Radiohead, Supergrass and Mansun.

GRAM PARSONS

WHO b. Ingram Cecil Connor III, 5 Nov 1946, Winter Haven, Florida, USA, d. 18 Sep 1973, Yucca Valley, California, USA

WHAT Country Rock pioneer

Although Gram Parsons never received the credit he was due, his vision created Country Rock.

Raised on Rock 'n' Roll, Country and R&B, he worked in Folk groups like The Legends and The Shilos. In 1965, he formed The International Submarine Band and made what has been called the first Country Rock album, *Safe At Home,* including his early classic, 'Luxury Liner'. But by its 1968 release, the group had split and Parsons had joined The Byrds.

During his short stay, Parsons revolutionized The Byrds. *Sweetheart Of The Rodeo* (1968), their first move into Country, was his brainchild. He wrote its highlights, like the heart-breaking 'Hickory Wind', and took lead vocals on most tracks. But contractual problems dating from the Submarine Band led to his contributions being cut and, by the time it was released, Parsons graced only three songs. He quit in protest at The Byrds' controversial tour of South Africa.

With ex-Byrd Chris Hillman, Parsons formed The Flying Burrito Brothers, whose *The Gilded Palace Of Sin* (1969) and *Burrito Deluxe* (1970) contained some of his best work – 'Dark End Of The Street', 'Do Right Woman', 'Sin City' and 'Hot Burrito #1'. *Burrito Deluxe* included The Rolling Stones' 'Wild Horses' – which, despite bearing the customary 'Jagger/Richard' credit, arose from the late 60s period when Parsons and Keith Richards were inseparable (including the Muscle Shoals studio sessions that yielded *Let It Bleed* and *Sticky Fingers*).

However, mournful collaborations with Emmylou Harris on *GP* (1973) and *Grievous Angel* (1974) were Parsons' *real* masterpieces. With a band including Elvis Presley's sidemen, Parsons' and Harris' voices blended perfectly, as demonstrated by *GP*'s 'We'll Sweep Out The Ashes' and 'That's All It Took' and *Grievous Angel*'s 'In My Hour Of Darkness'. A 1973 live show was issued as 1982's *Gram Parsons And The Fallen Angels Live*, from which their duet 'Love Hurts' was nominated for a Grammy.

His death in 1973 from an overdose at the Joshua Tree Inn became Rock's most legendary demise. Honouring a pact made before his death, friends stole his coffin during its journey to New Orleans and cremated it at the Joshua Tree Monument in the Mojave Desert. Parsons' legacy can be heard in The Eagles' best and The Lemonheads, whose Evan Dando became a Parsons clone in the 90s.

READ *Hickory Wind, The Life And Times Of Gram Parsons* (1991), Ben Fong-Torres

DOLLY PARTON

WHO b. 19 Jan 1946, Locust Ridge, Sevierville, Tennessee, USA

WHAT Well-loved Country singer and songwriter

Raised in the Great Smoky Mountains, Dolly Parton moved to Nashville in 1964, signing her first record deal with Monument. With Ray Stevens producing, the label aimed her music at the Pop market, but without success. Moving to RCA Records in 1967, her 'Just Because I'm A Woman' reached No.19 on the Country chart and, by the following year, she'd become a regular at the Grand Ole Opry.

> **"I've been guilty of most of the stuff that's been said about me to some degree. And if I ain't done it, I probably will"**

Many of her early albums were recorded with Porter Wagoner, including *Just The Two Of Us* (1969), *Always, Always* (1969) and *Two Of A Kind* (1971). Her first solo album, *Blue Ridge Mountain Boy*, was released in 1969, and her first Country No.1, 'Joshua', came in 1971. She hit the top spot again in 1974 with two self-penned singles: the jealous-girlfriend-themed 'Jolene' and 'I Will Always Love You'. The latter also appeared in the 1982 movie *Best Little Whorehouse In Texas*, in which Parton starred with Burt Reynolds. In 1992, Whitney Houston's cover version made it a worldwide best-seller. Elvis Presley wanted to record it but had to pass when she refused to relinquish his requested half of her publishing rights. "Thank God I didn't," Parton told *Mojo* in 1996, "because that song made me more money than all the others put together."

In 1976 she starred in her own TV show, *Dolly*; the same year, 'Jolene' became a Top 10 UK hit (later covered live by The Sisters Of Mercy). *New Harvest… First Gathering* (1977) moved from Country into Pop, a move further explored in 1979's Disco-influenced hit 'Baby I'm Burnin''. Dolly rounded off the 70s with the gold-selling *The Best Of Dolly Parton* (1978) and *Great Balls Of Fire* (1979), a *Playboy* front cover in a bunny suit (1978) and a Grammy for Best Country Female Vocal Performance (1979).

In the 80s, movie roles, often linked with hit Parton songs, expanded her magnificence. Her debut role in *9 To 5*, with

Jane Fonda and Lily Tomlin, spawned the US No.1 title song and a hit album, *9 To 5 And Odd Jobs* (1981). She soundtracked *Rhinestone* (1984) and co-starred with Sally Field, Daryl Hannah, Shirley MacLaine, Julia Roberts and Olympia Dukakis in her last film of the 80s, *Steel Magnolias*. Other 80s highlights included her US No.1 with Kenny Rogers – 'Islands In The Stream' (1983), written by Bee Gees – and a union with Linda Ronstadt and Emmylou Harris on *Trio* (1987), a success repeated by 1993's *Honky Tonk Angels*, with Loretta Lynn and Tammy Wynette. After years of increasingly poppy albums, she turned back towards Country with *White Limozeen* (1989) – the result, though good, paled beside earlier pearls, notably *Coat Of Many Colors* (1971).

Her 90s career has seen *Eagle When She Flies* (1991), *Slow Dancing With The Moon* (1993), *Something Special* (1995) and *Treasures* (1996), a soundtrack album and star role in the movie *Straight Talk* (1992), numerous TV appearances and the launch of her theme park, Dollywood (1995), attracting thousands of fans every year to her native Tennessee.

READ *My Life And Other Unfinished Business* (1994), Dolly Parton

SURF www.bestware.net/spreng/dolly

PAVEMENT

WHO Vocals/guitar **Stephen Malkmus** (b. 1967, Santa Monica, California, USA), guitar/vocals **Scott Kannberg** (b. 1967, Stockton, California), bass **Mark Ibold** (b. 1967, Cincinnati, Ohio, USA), drums **Bob Nastanovich** (b. 1968, Rochester, New York, USA), drums **Steve West** (b. 1967, Richmond, Virginia, USA)

WHEN 1989–

WHERE Stockton, California, USA

WHAT Lo-fi loons

Little in life escapes the ill-tempered rants of The Fall's Mark E. Smith. In the early 90s, Smith's favourite target was a band whose bendy little songs and near-gibberish lyrics owed much to his own. As the decade continued, The Fall floundered. But Pavement's lo-fi widdling ruled the Indie underworld.

Formed by Stockton schoolmates Stephen Malkmus and Scott Kannberg, Pavement recorded their debut EP 'Slay Tracks: (1933–1969)' in 1989 at local studio Louder Than You Think, owned by Gary Young, a middle-aged alcoholic who also drummed on the EP. Released on their own Treble Kicker label, it garnered underground acclaim from many (including British Indie stalwart John Peel), prompting a move to the more affluent Drag City Records for the EPs 'Demolition Plot J-7' and

'Perfect Sound Forever'. Pavement made their live debut with bassist Mark Ibold and – to mask Young's decidedly elastic timing – second drummer Bob Nastanovich, the line-up on their acclaimed 1992 debut *Slanted And Enchanted*.

However, what the music press saw as endearing experimentalism, the group

recognized as sloppiness. Tired of Young's theatrics (greeting audiences at the door, handstands, drunken blackouts), they replaced him with Steve West after 1992's 'Watery Domestic' EP. Meanwhile, Drag City compiled early material for 1993's *Westing (By Musket And Sextant)*.

Despite a less chaotic sound, Pavement carried on in their own wayward manner. When *Crooked Rain, Crooked Rain* (1994) failed to become the commercial breakthrough critics predicted, Malkmus and Nastanovich assisted Silver Jews on *Starlight Walker* (1994) and returned with the backlash-provoking *Wowee Zowee* (1995).

But salvation was just around the corner. The 'Pacific Trim' EP (1996) was hailed as a sparkling return to form, while *Brighten The Corners* (1997) was helped on its way by the gushing endorsement of formerly anti-American Britpoppers Blur.

Pavement's starry associations expanded when they graced a 1997 edition of The Cartoon Network's *Space Ghost Coast To Coast*, whose superhero host mistook them for The Beatles, then tried to interview Goldie Hawn over the band's noise.

SURF http:/www.slipnet^pavement/

PEARL JAM ✪✪✪

WHO Vocals **Eddie Vedder** (b. Edward Mueller, 23 Dec 1966, Evanston, Illinois, USA), guitar **Stone Gossard** (b. 20 Jun 1966, Seattle, Washington, USA), guitar **Mike McCready** (b. 5 Apr 1965, Seattle), bass **Jeff Ament** (b. 10 Mar 1963, Big Sandy, Montana, USA), drums **Jack Irons** (b. 18 Jul 1962, Los Angeles, California, USA)

WHEN 1990–

WHERE Seattle, Washington, USA

WHAT Arena-sized angst

When Andrew Wood, singer with the fêted Seattle band Mother Love Bone (a descendant of the equally trumpeted Green River) fatally overdosed on heroin, his bandmates Stone Gossard and Jeff Ament enlisted guitarist Mike McCready and Soundgarden's Chris Cornell and Matt Cameron for the tribute album *Temple Of The Dog* (1992). From this platinum-selling springboard, Gossard, Ament and McCready, joined by drummer Dave Kruzen and San Diego surf-bum singer Eddie Vedder, launched Mookie Blaylock – a tribute to the idolized New Jersey Nets basketball player.

Then, after sampling some of Vedder's great-grandma Pearl's psychedelic fruit preserve, they became Pearl Jam – arena-filling angst-mongers with loud guitars.

Replacing Kruzen with the short-stayed Matt Chamberlain (they finally settled on Dave Abruzzese), Pearl Jam toured 1991's *Ten* (Blaylock again – his shirt number) with support slots for Red Hot Chili Peppers, Neil Young and U2 before Nirvana's *Nevermind* opened the floodgates and granted anything from Seattle a first-class ticket to the chart. Packed with unashamedly 70s-style riff-outs and too many tunes for Grunge hipness, *Ten* nonetheless outsold Nirvana on the back of the hits 'Jeremy', 'Evenflow' and 'Alive'. By the time they finished the 1992 Lollapalooza tour, they had far outgrown their early afternoon slot on the bill. The key was Pearl Jam's radio-friendly sound (no noisy feedback pile-ups here) and fashionable angst (courtesy of the twitchy Vedder) which ensured a hero's welcome from the mature Rock press. A self-mocking cameo (as Citizen Dick) in the Seattle-based romantic comedy *Singles* (1991) added to the buzz.

While Nirvana dealt with hugeness by falling apart, Pearl Jam

"I don't like Rock stars,
yet here I am
being turned into one"
Eddie Vedder

survived and grew: 1993's *Vs* sailed to US No.1, despite no singles or videos accompanying its release. The ensuing tour shunned stadiums, favouring college campuses and theatres. They even cancelled a potentially lucrative 1994 summer tour, claiming US ticket agency Ticketmaster was bumping up prices – a battle that ended in defeat when they took the company to court.

Meanwhile, swapping Abruzzese for ex-Red Hot Chili Peppers drummer Jack Irons (who had introduced Vedder to Gossard), they unleashed 1994's *Vitalogy* – an epic marriage of *Ten*'s histrionics to *Vs*' punkish edginess – on vinyl only. Weeks later, it emerged on more popular formats and, again, leapt to US No.1. Embarrassingly rich and uncomfortable with fame, they busied themselves with side projects: Vedder with Hovercraft, Gossard with his funky band Brad and label Loosegroove, McCready with rehab and, with Alice In Chains' Layne Staley, Mad Season.

In 1995, they reconvened as the uncredited backing band on Neil Young's *Mirrorball*, before eschewing Rock convention once more with the harsh *No Code* (1996) – a sales monolith ignored by the chart, owing to its deliberate lack of a bar code. Then, amid reports of internal dissension, they diversified again, although McCready's second album with Brad, *Interiors* (1997), was less well received than their debut, *Shame* (1993).

They returned with the mighty *Yield* (1998), a return to *Ten*'s glory, though its success was offset – as they hit the road again – by the replacement of Irons with Soundgarden's Matt Cameron.

Meanwhile, Robert Plant offered an amused reaction to the resemblance of *Yield*'s uplifting introductory hit 'Given To Fly' to Led Zeppelin's 'Going To California': "It's just one of those amazing coincidences. Do you think that somebody sang it to them in the cradle or something like that and it just came back?"

READ *Pearl Jam* (1994), Mick Wall

FAN PO Box 4570, Seattle, WA 98104, USA

SURF www.fivehorizons.com/band/

PENTANGLE

WHO Vocals **Jacqui McShee** (b. 25 Dec 1943, London, England), guitar/vocals

Bert Jansch (b. 3 Nov 1943, Glasgow, Scotland), guitars/sitar/vocals **John Renbourn** (b. 8 Aug 1944, Kingston, England), double bass **Danny Thompson** (b. 4 Apr 1939, Teignmouth, Devon, England), drums/vocals **Terry Cox** (b. Mar 1936, High Wycombe, Buckinghamshire, England)

WHEN 1967–1995

WHERE London, England

WHAT Folk, Jazz, Blues and Gospel fusion

Basking in critical acclaim and media exposure unprecedented for a Folk-based act from the UK, cult heroes Pentangle enjoyed brief mainstream success from 1969–1970. In 1966, roommates John Renbourn and Bert Jansch (who had recorded the groundbreaking *Bert & John*, 1966) united with Folk Blues singer Jacqui McShee (who had guested on Renbourn's 1966 solo album *Another Monday*). Danny Thompson and Terry Cox, whom Renbourn had met on the TV show *Gadzooks!*, followed.

Initially an experimental band playing in London throughout 1967, Pentangle took their name from an Arthurian symbol of protection from evil, reflecting Renbourn's fascination with medieval esoterica. With press interest aroused, the arrival of New York manager Jo Lustig in early 1968 marked a watershed. A ferocious PR campaign secured the first of many BBC radio and TV appearances, even before their debut *The Pentangle* (1968). A 're-launch' concert in June was recorded for the follow-up *Sweet Child* (1968). The mainstream breakthrough came late in 1969 with *Basket Of Light*, a UK No.5, and minor hit 'Light Flight' – theme to the popular BBC TV drama *Take Three Girls*.

The fourth album, *Cruel Sister* (1970) – followed by a lull in previously relentless touring, including both Isle of Wight festivals – was disappointingly received. Although *Reflection* (1971) and *Solomon's Seal* (1972) were improvements, the group was labelled precious and dull.

With business and personal problems escalating, Pentangle dissolved in March 1973. A Cambridge Folk Festival reunion in 1982 was well received, and the group continued off and on until 1995 with European tours and new albums. While McShee retains the Pentangle name for live work, Jansch, Thompson and Renbourn remain engaged in interweaving solo ventures.

FAN Rosemary Lane, c/o John Higgins, 17 Deerhurst Road, Streatham, London, SW16 2AN, UK

SURF www.demon.co.uk/andys/bjindex.html

CARL PERKINS

WHO b. Carl Perkings, 9 Apr 1932, Ridgely, Tennessee, USA, d. 19 Jan 1998, Jackson, Tennessee

WHAT Rockin' Guitar Man

Carl Perkins, christened the 'Rockin' Guitar Man' by Sam Phillips, recorded some of Rockabilly's finest records and, if for no other reason, will be remembered as the writer of 'Blue Suede Shoes'.

With brothers Clayton and Jay, he was regularly broadcast on Jackson, Tennessee's radio station WTJS, and recorded his first single for Sun Records in December 1954. 'Movie Magg'/'Turnaround', released on Sun's subsidiary, Flip Records, in 1955, became a local hit. Early tours with Johnny Cash formed a friendship that lasted to the end. It was Cash who suggested he write a song based on an incident from Cash's army days when he overhead someone say "don't step on my blue suede shoes". During a show, Perkins spotted a kid in the audience who was paying more attention to his shoes than the girl he was with and subsequently wrote and recorded the classic 'Blue Suede Shoes'. Fate was to deal a bitter blow when, on their way to New York for the Perry Como show, the car they were driving was involved in a horrific accident. Off the road for six months, Carl had to watch while Elvis took his song into the Top 10.

The early 60s were lean times, with spells on Columbia and Decca, although he was still treated as a hero in the UK where The Beatles recorded three of his songs. A regular with Cash's band in 1968, both in the studio and on the road, he still found time to record his own albums. In 1986, he taped a *Rockabilly Session* TV show, featuring tributes from guests like Eric Clapton, Ringo Starr, George Harrison and Rosanne Cash. He died in 1998 from complications resulting from a series of strokes.

READ *Go, Cat Go! The Life And Times Of Carl Perkins* (1997), Carl Perkins & David McGee

PET SHOP BOYS ◉

WHO Vocals **Neil Tennant** (b. 19 Jul 1954, Gosforth, Tyne and Wear, England), keyboards **Chris Lowe** (b. 4 Oct 1959, Blackpool, England)

WHEN 1981–

WHERE London, England

WHAT The odd couple of Synth Pop

Neil Tennant, assistant editor of UK Pop mag *Smash Hits*, spent adolescence avoiding the bearded seriousness of the early 70s (though he later endorsed The Incredible String Band). Chris Lowe played in a showband and studied architecture – anything but join a teenage Rock group. They met in a London hi-fi shop, discovered a shared passion for criminally unfashionable Hi-NRG Disco and became Pet Shop Boys – all electronic elegance, lyrical loucheness and conceptual camp.

Having seen New Order re-invent Disco for the 80s with 'Blue Monday' ("I nearly burst into tears," said an envious Tennant) and flopped with 1984's 'West End Girls' and 1985's 'Opportunities (Let's Make Lots Of Money)', the Boys swept to transatlantic chart tops with a revamped 'West End Girls' in early 1986.

From their lush debut *Please* (1986) came further hits 'Love Comes Quickly', a re-jiggled 'Opportunities' and 'Suburbia'. Their trend-terrorizing views (dissing U2 and standing up for Simple Minds), stated aim to replace themselves with younger stand-ins, a stage act somewhere between Sparks and performance artists Gilbert & George and the unashamed remixology *Disco* (1986) established the Boys' niche: wordy, intelligent, danceable Pop – a trillion miles from 80s Rock's flag-waving pomposity.

Prefaced by the dancefloor tragedy of 'It's A Sin', *Actually* (1987) primed the Pop public for the rehabilitation of the under-valued Dusty Springfield (who duetted with Tennant on the hit 'What Have I Done To Deserve This?'), a grandiose UK No.1 revamp of Elvis' 'Always On My Mind' and a sprawling, more-than-slightly-confusing movie, *It Couldn't Happen Here* (1988).

However, by the masterpiece that was *Introspective* (1988),

House had happened and Pet Shop Boys were recast as pioneers. After more collaborations with Springfield (1989's *Scandal* soundtrack), Manchester supergroup Electronic and gay icon Liza Minnelli (her excellent 1989 album *Results*), their first, long-promised world tour – complete with dancers, theatrics and Liberace-esque costume changes – won the unlikely acclaim of Axl Rose. Meanwhile, they staked their claim as one of the 80s' greatest singles bands with 1988's excellent 'Domino Dancing' and 'Left To My Own Devices' and 1989's cover of Sterling Void's House anthem 'It's Alright'.

For the less calculated *Behaviour* (1990), exuberance was replaced by poignancy on the hits 'So Hard', 'Being Boring' and 'Jealousy', although their caustic wit was unleashed again on 1991's wonderfully arch medley of U2's 'Where The Streets Have No Name' and Boystown Gang's gay Disco classic 'Can't Take My Eyes Off You', which soon had Bono exploring his 'ironic' side.

However, lacking the Pop punch of their predecessors, *Behaviour* and 1991's 'DJ Culture' marked a watershed. No longer arbiters of Dance taste, no longer quite the glittering Pop princes they once were – a story traced by 1991's *Discography* compilation – Pet Shop Boys charted into ever more eccentric territory with the UK No.1 *Very* (1993). Highlights included 'Can You Forgive Her', the angelic 'Liberation' and freebie Dance disc *Relentless* – but ridiculous pointy hats, a storming cover of Village People's 'Go West' and the sit-com/charity tie-in 'Absolutely Fabulous' proved they were bonkers.

After a three-year gap – punctuated by the compilations *Disco 2* (remixes, 1994), *Alternative* (B-sides, 1995) and the David Bowie collaboration 'Hallo Spaceboy' – they returned, rejuvenated, with the excellent *Bilingual* (1996) and a majestic 1997 cover of *West Side Story*'s 'Somewhere'. An acclaimed, stripped-down European tour preceded Tennant's role as coordinator of Noël Coward tribute *20th Century Blues* – featuring Shola Ama, The Divine Comedy, Marianne Faithfull, Bryan Ferry, Elton John, Robbie Williams, Texas, Suede and Sting – and work on Pet Shop Boys' long-promised stage musical.

ⓇⒺⒶⒹ *Literally* (1992), Chris Heath

ⓈⓊⓇⒻ www.unimaas.nl/~mathysen/psb/

TOM PETTY & THE HEARTBREAKERS

WHO Vocals/guitar **Tom Petty** (b. 20 Oct 1950, Gainesville, Florida, USA), guitar **Mike Campbell** (b. 1 Feb 1950, Jacksonville, Florida), bass **Howie Epstein** (b. 21 Jul 1955, Milwaukee, Wisconsin, USA), drums **Stan Lynch** (b. 21 May 1955, Cincinnati, Ohio, USA), keyboards **Benmont Tench** (b. 7 Sep 1953, Gainesville)

WHEN 1976–

WHERE Los Angeles, California, USA

WHAT The jingle-jangle jokers of classic American Rock

In 1961, Elvis Presley met a young Tom Petty. "That," Petty said, "was the end of doing anything other than music with my life."

In school, Petty joined two bands – The Sundowners, then The Epics – before forming Mudcrutch in 1970 with Benmont Tench and Mike Campbell. A demo taped in Tench's living room piqued the interest of several labels and they signed to Shelter Records in 1974, but split before an album was ever completed.

Petty, Tench and Campbell enlisted Stan Lynch and Ron Blair (replaced in 1982 by Howie Epstein) to become Tom Petty & The Heartbreakers. Their self-titled debut (1976) met an apathetic response, but a year of touring pushed 'Breakdown' into the US Top 40 and the album to UK No.24. Its mix of Byrdsy guitars and Dylan-esque vocals – epitomized by the jangly gem 'American Girl' – was honed to gold status by *You're Gonna Get It* (1978).

The Heartbreakers crested with 1979's *Damn The Torpedoes*, whose hard rocking sound perfectly soundtracked Petty's bitter contractual dispute with MCA. It took them into the star league, maintained by 1981's *Hard Promises* and 'Stop Draggin' My Heart Around', a wrenching duet with Stevie Nicks. But *Long After Dark* (1982) showed them running out of steam and they rerouted on *Southern Accents* (1985): an odd blend of their retro sound and the electronic influence of producer Dave Stewart. Thanks to the spookily psychedelic 'Don't Come Around Here No More', they returned to platinum status, but then relegated themselves to Bob Dylan's live backing band. Dylan co-wrote the arresting 'Jammin' Me' from 1987's *Let Me Up (I've Had Enough)* and he and Petty reunited in The Traveling Wilburys (dismissed by Twisted Sister's Dee Snider as "Four superstars and Tom Petty").

The Wilbury-flavoured *Full Moon Fever* (1989), featuring all the Heartbreakers bar Lynch, but credited to Petty alone, became his biggest seller. Infectious hits 'I Won't Back Down', 'Runnin' Down A Dream' and 'Free Fallin'' were MTV and radio staples. *Into The Great Wide Open* (1991) kept sales buoyant. Its hits 'Learning To Fly' and 'Into The Great Wide Open' sealed Petty's MTV revival, the latter's video featuring Faye Dunaway and Johnny Depp. In 1993, it was disclosed Petty had signed a $20-million deal with Warner Bros. The excellent *Greatest Hits* (1993) and box set *Playback* (1995) rounded off his MCA career, while 1994's double-platinum *Wildflowers* – source of the dryly druggy hit 'You Don't Know How It Feels' – gave his Warner career a flying start.

In 1996, the Heartbreakers soundtracked the movie *She's The One* (including a cover of Beck's 'Asshole') and helped out on Johnny Cash's *Unchained*. Meanwhile, Stan Lynch was replaced by session drummers, including Ringo Starr. Future Foo Fighter Dave Grohl nearly joined, but when the Heartbreakers played a historic 20-night stand at San Francisco's Fillmore Auditorium in

1997, Steve Ferrone occupied the drum stool. That year, Petty was awarded his own star on the Hollywood Walk Of Fame.

 **Fan** Makin' Some Noise, 21 Selworthy, Furtzon, Milton Keynes, MK1 4HS, UK

 **Surf** www–personal.ksu.edu/~tomrat/Tom_Petty.html

WILSON PICKETT

WHO b. 18 Mar 1941, Prattville, Alabama, USA

WHAT The wicked star of Soul

Though legendary for raw 'n' raunchy Soul, Wilson Pickett's vocal style was grounded in the church. Moving to Detroit in 1955, he joined the popular Gospel group The Violinaires and, in 1959, R&B act The Falcons, whose 'You're So Fine' had recently been a US hit. He sang lead on several Falcons' tracks, including 1962's Pickett-penned, Gospel-inspired gem, 'I Found A Love', which helped herald 60s Soul and introduced him to a wider audience.

In 1963 he went solo and released two more groundbreaking Soul sides on Lloyd Price's Double-L label: 'It's Too Late' and 'If You Need Me'. Atlantic Records, who'd covered the latter with Solomon Burke, realized Pickett's potential and added him to their roster. When his first Atlantic singles stiffed, they sent him to Stax studios in Memphis with guitarist Steve Cropper. The first hit from this winning combination, 1965's 'In The Midnight Hour' (a Pickett catch-phrase used on earlier releases), headed the R&B chart, made US/UK Top 20s and became an all-time Soul classic.

Hit followed hit for the 'Wicked Pickett', with R&B No.1s '634-5789', 'Land Of 1000 Dances' (both 1966) and 'Funky Broadway' (1967) taking him into the US Top 20. His soulful rendition of 'Hey Jude' (1968), complete with his trademark screams, cracked the equivalent UK chart. Seldom out of the US charts between 1965 and 1973, he had three successive Top 20s with 'Engine Number 9' (1970), 'Don't Let The Green Grass Fool You' (1971) and 'Don't Knock My Love' (1972). After leaving Atlantic in 1973, Pickett recorded for RCA, EMI and Motown, but never achieved the same level of success. In 1991, the seminal Soul superstar, who had amassed a staggering 33 Top 20 R&B entries, was inducted into the Rock And Roll Hall Of Fame and namechecked in Alan Parker's shot-full-of-Soul movie *The Commitments*.

Surf www.cet.ac.il/personnel/yonin/pickett.htm

PINK FLOYD ⊙⊙⊙⊙⊙⊙✦✦✦✦✦

WHO Vocals/bass **Roger Waters** (b. George Roger Waters, 9 Sep 1943, Great Bookham, Surrey, England), guitar/vocals **David Gilmour** (b. 6 Mar 1946, Cambridge, England), drums **Nick Mason** (b. 27 Jan 1945, Birmingham, England), keyboards/vocals **Richard Wright** (b. 28 Jul 1945, London, England)

WHEN 1964–

WHERE Cambridge, England

WHAT Platinum Prog Rock pioneers

"You can only hate Pink Floyd for so long," admitted John Lydon in his autobiography. At his and The Sex Pistols' Punk peak, Pink Floyd were denounced as dinosaurs. Today, their influence is inescapable: from Blur's Syd Barrett fixation to Smashing Pumpkins' Pink-tinged, no-conceit-too-large tendencies. Angst-ridden teenagers who grew up listening to Floyd's *The Wall* (1979) are today's angst-ridden chart-toppers: Trent Reznor, Axl Rose, even Noel Gallagher. Floyd themselves exist in a virtual Rock 'n' Roll world. Having cultivated a corporate identity rather than individual images, they have survived the loss of principal songwriters Syd Barrett and Roger Waters and are rivalled by few in their ability to fill stadiums at whim.

Celebrated for their meticulously conceived mega-sellers, innovative performances and near-mythic status, Floyd's origins are unremarkable. Friends in Cambridge regularly convened at Barrett's home in 1962, playing as Geoff Mott & The Mottoes. The shifting line-up included Waters and Tony Sainty, later bassist in David Gilmour's first professional band, Jokers Wild. Months later, inspired by The Rolling Stones – and distinctly uninspired by the architectural studies he had moved to London to pursue – Waters assembled Sigma 6, aka The Abdabs or Meggadeaths.

The group, including fellow students Rick Wright and Nick Mason, had its future prospects secured by the recruitment of Barrett, who seized the creative reins. Having jettisoned more unpromising names (Leonard's Lodgers and The T-Set) and sundry personnel (including Wright's wife Juliette), The Pink Floyd Sound solidified in 1965 with Barrett, Waters, Mason, Wright and guitarist Bob Klose – their name lifted from American Bluesmen Pink Anderson and Floyd Council.

Streamlined by the loss of Klose – whose R&B leanings were incompatible with the more experimental Barrett – and that extraneous 'Sound', Pink Floyd became leading lights of British Psychedelia. They won a loyal London audience – particularly at the UFO club – but audiences outside the capital reacted with dropped jaws or active antagonism to melodically challenged epics like 'Astronomy Domine' and 'Interstellar Overdrive'.

Nonetheless, the band were signed to EMI and, having scored UK hits with 'Arnold Layne' and 'See Emily Play', began their bid for superstardom. However, no sooner had they completed their debut album *Piper At The Gates Of Dawn* (1967) than the wheels came off the bandwagon. Barrett adapted badly to success, his unreliability exacerbated by LSD. A third single, 'Apples And Oranges', deservedly sank without trace and, after a disastrous American tour, the band began casting about for help.

Envisaging a Brian Wilson-esque role for Barrett as a non-performing writer, Floyd tried to enlist Yardbirds guitarist Jeff Beck. When he turned them down, they recruited Dave Gilmour in January 1968. He brought structure to the crumbling band, which – after struggling through four months as a five-piece – opted to dispense with Barrett altogether. The latter disappeared to cult status, Waters assumed the visionary mantle and Floyd languished in no-management, no-money blues.

Further stabs at the UK singles market with Wright's abysmal 'It Would Be So Nice' and Waters' splendid 'Point Me At The Sky' (1968) flopped horribly, although the latter's B-side – 'Careful With That Axe, Eugene' – became a live favourite and a key track on 1971's "bizarre collection of antiques and curios", *Relics*.

Meanwhile, *A Saucerful Of Secrets* (1968) pointed the way forward: long, spacey jams interrupted by incongruously chirpy interludes. The spacier stuff won them lucrative work with film-makers – notably Michaelangelo Antonioni (*Zabriskie Point*, 1969) and Barbet Schroeder (*More*, 1969). They also developed an enviable live reputation, commemorated by the half-live, half-studio *Ummagumma* (1969). The first success for EMI's

'underground' subsidiary Harvest, the album was a Top 5 UK hit and broke them into the US Top 100. It was also the last time the band worked with producer Norman Smith, who had been bemused by the band since EMI put him in charge of *Piper*. Rejecting the delights of Psychedelia, he became balladeer 'Hurricane' Smith and scored hits with 'Don't Let It Die' (1971) and 'Oh Babe What Would You Say?' (1972).

Floyd mostly remained aloof of prevailing trends, but made their one concession to fashion in the era of the dreaded Classical Rock fusion. However, *Atom Heart Mother* (1970) gave them a first UK No.1 and an unwarranted reputation as musical genii. Though no strangers to self-indulgence, Floyd rarely took it to the virtuoso extremes of their Progressive contemporaries – largely because, Gilmour aside, they were barely above average standards of musical competence. This high-brow reputation was furthered when they scored a ballet by choreographer Roland Petit (1972) and occasionally encored with 'Ave Maria'.

Their musical evolution continued with 1971's *Meddle* and in-concert movie *Live At Pompeii*, after which Waters tired of "the airy-fairy mystical bollocks" that had characterized much Floyd writing. 'Free Four', a throwaway track on *Obscured By Clouds* (soundtrack to Schroeder's 1972 *La Vallée*), contained themes that came to dominate his work: his father's death in World War Two, the stardom treadmill and overwhelming paranoia. A keen advocate of The Concept Album, Waters conceived a song cycle about the pressures of modern life. In its pre-studio incarnation –

toured worldwide in 1972, and briefly known as 'Eclipse' – the piece boasted tapes of speech from British broadcaster Malcolm Muggeridge, dreadful vocal harmonies and a lot of "interminable jamming" that Gilmour had the grace to feel embarrassed about later. In a triumph of studio trickery, this was transformed into *Dark Side Of The Moon* (1973). The album reached US No.1 and rarely left the chart until 1988, bequeathing a US hit with 'Money' and a 70s icon with its striking cover. Popular legend has it that, with the advent of CD, EMI's German pressing plant produced nothing but copies of *Dark Side Of The Moon*, while worldwide sales estimated at 25 million secured it a place in *The Guinness Book Of Records* as the best-selling album by a British group. Quick to cash in on this global success, EMI repackaged *Piper* and *Saucerful* as *A Nice Pair* (1974). In America, the CBS label poached the band from EMI's Stateside subsidiary Capitol.

Dragged around the world for another two years, *Dark Side Of The Moon*'s performances ranged from the merely anticlimactic to the downright shoddy (prime culprits being the Muppet-esque vocals of Waters, Wright and Gilmour). It was laid to rest with a legendarily awful performance at the UK's Knebworth festival in 1975, by which time Floyd had become superstars – albeit of the reluctant, anonymous variety.

Anxiety about their new-found celebrity manifested itself in work on the follow-up. The band laboured fruitlessly for months, first with music played on household objects (elastic bands as bass strings, etc), then with tuneless songs about consumerism: 'Raving And Drooling' and 'Gotta Be Crazy'. The latter pair were even inflicted on audiences at the time before Waters, playing the concept card once again, devised *Wish You Were Here* (1975):

> " We're not ignored by The Guinness Book Of Records, but we've been largely ignored by the media during our lifetime. If you read any article, no mention is ever made of Pink Floyd. We're never included in the same sentences as The Beatles, The Rolling Stones and The Who "
>
> Roger Waters

an elegiac affair inspired by Barrett, and dominated by Gilmour's psychedelic Blues guitar. A true classic and another monster-seller, it was their first album to top both UK and US charts.

Floyd then dispersed to country homes, resurfacing in early 1977 with *Animals*. The songs were *Wish You Were Here* rejects with a fresh lick of paint, topped and tailed with new tracks that likened humans to farm animals. Thus was born a Floydian icon to rival *Dark Side*'s cover prism: the inflatable pig. It graced the *Animals* sleeve, created a media flap by escaping its moorings at the album photo shoot and featured at most subsequent concerts. In contrast to the eye-popping, multi-media shows and carefully woven music of the Floyd, Mason produced *Music For Pleasure* (1978) for Punk upstarts The Damned. The result was a flop, enjoying none of the acclaim that greeted the drummer's earlier production of Robert Wyatt's *Rock Bottom* (1974).

The 1977 In The Flesh tour sounded the death knell for this era of 'Oink' Floyd. Increasingly dissatisfied with playing heartfelt, intricate music to vast audiences, Waters resolved never to do so again, and wrote *The Wall* (1979) as an indictment of stadium Rock. He underlined the point by restricting the album's outings to short, theatrical runs in just four cities: London, New York, Los Angeles and Dortmund. Ironically, demand for the band had rarely been higher, thanks to 'Another Brick In The Wall', a transatlantic chart-topper and Britain's first 80s No.1. The album itself spent 15 weeks atop the US chart.

Despite its grotesque self-indulgence, *The Wall* became the jewel in Waters' crown; hence a 1982 movie version, in which Bob Geldof exposed himself to the merciless microscope of the silver screen. Lambasted by critics, it nonetheless performed well and clearly influenced later movies like *Wall*-director Alan Parker's *Evita* (1996) and Oliver Stone's *Natural Born Killers* (1994).

Once again, EMI cashed in, with the satirically titled compilation *A Collection Of Great Dance Songs* (1981). By this time, Pink Floyd had ceased to function as a group. Mason, who last enjoyed a writing credit in 1973, developed his life-long obsession with cars into a full-time hobby and business.

Wright, at odds with Waters since the band began, was fired in 1979 (making him the only Floyd to profit directly from *The Wall* shows, as he funded none of the staging costs and received a session musician's wage). Gilmour and Waters worked together under sufferance; co-producers Chris Thomas (1973), Bob Ezrin (1979) and Michael Kamen (1983) spent as much time arbitrating as they did producing.

The band's last gasp was *The Final Cut* (1983), billed as 'by Roger Waters, performed by Pink Floyd'. It sold only a fraction of previous releases, and was the first Floyd album in a decade not to be toured – after which, as writer Trevor Dann put it, "As so often during the untidy break-up of a once great band, its constituent parts [fell] over themselves to expose their limitations as solo artists." The warning bells had sounded in 1978, with Wright's anaemic *Wet Dream* and Gilmour's tedious *David Gilmour*. In 1984, consumers' choice was spoiled by Gilmour's *About Face*, Wright's union with Dave Harris of Fashion on *Identity* and Waters' *The Pros And Cons Of Hitch Hiking*. The

ROCK (P) PEDIA

" Jonny made us all watch Pink Floyd Live In Pompeii and said, 'Now this is how we should do videos'. I just remember seeing Dave Gilmour sitting on his arse playing guitar and Roger Waters, with long, greasy hair, sandals and dusty flares, stagger over and pick up this big beater and whack this gong. Ridiculous "

Colin Greenwood (Radiohead)

latter, conceived simultaneously with *The Wall*, had been rejected by the band and came alive only with interjections from Eric Clapton. Waters' and Gilmour's sparsely attended tours, and unspectacular sales, were proof not only of Floyd's anonymity as individuals, but also the mediocrity of their solo endeavours. Not to be outdone, Mason's *Fictitious Sports* (1981) and *Profiles* (1985) sold so poorly that only a handful of listeners are aware how bad they are. Waters rounded off this solo activity with a soundtrack for Raymond Briggs' animated nuclear nightmare *When The Wind Blows* (1986) – a more satisfying affair than *The Body*, his 1970 soundtrack with *Atom Heart Mother* collaborator Ron Geesin.

Having unsuccessfully conspired to resurrect Pink Floyd with Waters, Gilmour and Mason appropriated the name for themselves in 1986, recruiting Wright to make them stronger "legally and musically". Enraged, Waters took them to court in a doomed bid to lay the name to rest. The legal ludicrousness peaked when, to circumvent Waters' copyright on the inflatable pig, Floyd were obliged to add testicles to their porcine pal.

The war raged through 1987: interviews designed to promote Pink Floyd's patchy *A Momentary Lapse Of Reason* and Waters' fine *Radio KAOS* became mired in recriminations, and reviewers gleefully contrasted their respective live extravaganzas. They even squared up in the UK's Christmas singles chart; Waters' 'The Tide Is Turning' reaching one place higher (No.54) than Pink Floyd's 'On The Turning Away'. At the box office, however, Floyd were clear winners, selling out stadiums worldwide, while Waters was forced to cancel arena dates. They capitalized on this good fortune with 1988's live *Delicate Sound Of Thunder* and another tour in 1989, grabbing headlines with a telecast from Venice.

Waters attempted a coup with an all-star charity performance of *The Wall* in Berlin (1990), but shaky musicianship, poor sales of the souvenir album and the media's perception of it as a 'Pink Floyd' show suggested he had again miscalculated. Confirming their supremacy, Pink Floyd returned to Knebworth that summer and erased memories of the 1975 poor showing with a slickly professional performance, headlining over even Paul McCartney.

In the ensuing years, they reverted to type: Mason a motor-racing gentleman, Wright an unconcerned tax exile, the angry Waters toiling at length on *Amused To Death* (1992), Gilmour a guitar-for-hire session player and producer. In demand since the 70s, the latter had notched up over 60 guest appearances and productions, the beneficiaries ranging from Roy Harper to Paul McCartney, from Kate Bush to Grace Jones. Gilmour also found himself sharing the cover of UK music paper *Melody Maker* with The Orb, just one of the Dance acts to cite Floyd as an influence – other fans included Prodigy mainman Liam Howlett, House guru Derrick May and Rap stars EPMD, Public Enemy and Scarface.

After plugging the commercial gap with a self-indulgent soundtrack (*La Carrera Panamericana*, 1991), a retrospective box set (*Shine On*, 1992) and a 20th anniversary reissue of *Dark Side* (1993), Floyd rose again with *The Division Bell* (1994), their best since *The Final Cut*. After years of minor singles success, it was their first album to spawn two UK Top 30 hits: 'Take It Back' and 'High Hopes/Keep Talking', featuring Professor Stephen J.

Hawking's spoken words (as also used on a British Telecom TV ad). Another tour saw them resurrect *Dark Side* – captured on the live *P.U.L.S.E.* (1995) – before they lapsed again into inactivity, broken only by reissues, Wright's Sinéad O'Connor-starring *Broken China* (1996) and their induction (by Smashing Pumpkins' Billy Corgan) into the Rock And Roll Hall Of Fame in 1996.

Having become one of the most discussed acts on the Internet, Floyd sparked two 'Net-nurtured controversies. First, the mystery of Enigma Publius concerned a series of unresolved 'clues' on *The Division Bell* album and tour. Then, in 1997, it transpired that synchronizing *Dark Side* with the Hollywood classic *The Wizard Of Oz* revealed spooky thematic similarities. Floyd reacted to the fun 'n' games with customary silence, as unconcerned with publicity as the need for a new album. However, huge acclaim and sales for Radiohead's Floyd-inspired *OK Computer* in 1997 proved the market for their brand of melancholic musing was as buoyant as ever.

(READ) *Saucerful Of Secrets – The Pink Floyd Odyssey* (1991), Nicholas Schaffner

(FAN) Brain Damage, PO Box 109, Westmont, IL 60559, USA

GENE PITNEY

WHO b. 17 Feb 1941, Hartford, Connecticut, USA

WHAT Enduringly popular 60s balladeer

Gene Pitney's first minor US hits arrived in 1961 with his self-penned '(I Wanna) Love My Life Away', on which he played every instrument, and Goffin & King's 'Every Breath I Take', an early, typically extravagant Phil Spector production. But he was more successful as a songwriter, composing Bobby Vee's 'Rubber Ball', Ricky Nelson's 'Hello Mary Lou' and The Crystals' 'He's A Rebel'.

However, once he began touring extensively, Pitney neglected songwriting and his mid-60s smashes were written by others, such as Bacharach & David's 'Twenty Four Hours From Tulsa' (1963), Jagger/Richards' 'That Girl Belongs To Yesterday' (1964), Mann/Weill's 'I'm Gonna Be Strong' (1964) and Cook/Greenaway's 'Something's Gotten Hold Of My Heart' (1967).

Pitney also recorded Country albums with George Jones, but his classic hits were entertainingly over-the-top, melodramatic ballads, with Pitney struggling manfully with his emotions or conscience – his voice powerful, his diction precise. However, Marianne Faithfull – with whom he toured and had an affair in 1965 – tarred him as a "most pompous, self-satisfied person".

Long after the hits had dried up, he remained a popular live performer. In 1988, he improbably returned to the top of the UK chart, duetting on a remake of 'Something's Gotten Hold Of My Heart' with Marc Almond.

(READ) *Stars In My Eyes* (1980), Spencer Leigh

(SURF) members.tripod.com/~colli/pitney/pitney.html

PIXIES

WHO Vocals/guitar **Black Francis** (b. Charles Michael Kitteridge Thompson IV, 1965, Long Beach, California, USA), guitar **Joey Santiago** (b. 10 Jun 1965, Manila, Philippines), bass **Kim Deal** (b. 10 Jun 1961, Dayton, Ohio, USA), drums **David Lovering** (b. 6 Dec 1961, Boston, Massachusetts, USA)

WHEN 1986–1993

WHERE Boston, Massachusetts, USA

WHAT Brutal but melodic proto-Grunge

Charles Thompson, a student at University of Massachusetts, dropped out while staying in Puerto Rico on a Spanish exchange course in 1986. Instead of his original plan – to fly to New Zealand to see Halley's comet – he went home and persuaded roommate Joey Santiago to form a band with him in Boston.

Renaming himself Black Francis, they chose the name Pixies by flicking through a dictionary, then advertised for a bass player "into Hüsker Dü and Peter, Paul & Mary". "They're bands I've enjoyed," explained Francis. "I'm always interested to hear whether an alien or someone from 1000 years ago would see that much difference between them."

The successful (in fact only) applicant, Kim Deal – then known as Mrs John Murphy – suggested drummer David Lovering and, together, they played chaotic, noisy gigs around Boston.

An eight-track demo sent to British label 4AD became their acclaimed debut *Come On Pilgrim* (1987), also included on the CD release of *Surfer Rosa* (1988). Both were a gloriously violent mess of blood 'n' guts imagery driven by Santiago's brutal guitar and Black Francis' psychotic lyrics. An immediate hit on the Indie scene, Pixies outgrew their niche with *Doolittle* (1988).

With breathtaking start/stop dynamics on tracks like 'Tame', 'Dead' and 'Monkey Gone To Heaven', and Francis' vocal delivery (taught to him by a Thai Rock star who instructed "scream like you hate the bitch!"), the album proved influential on Grunge luminaries Nirvana and Hole. *Doolittle*'s deranged 'Debaser' also found its way into live sets by David Bowie's Tin Machine.

By the time of *Bossanova* (1990), Deal had made the excellent *Pod* (1990) as The Breeders with Throwing Muses' Tanya Donelly and The Perfect Disaster's Josephine Wiggs, and Francis was playing sporadic solo gigs. Pixies now widened their scope, taking in twangy 60s Surf instrumentals and sci-fi lyrical imagery. The intensity returned with a vengeance for their noisiest album *Trompe Le Monde* (1991), conceived almost entirely around space and science themes: 'Alec Eiffel' celebrated the Eiffel Tower architect and "pioneer of aerodynamics", and 'Motorway To Roswell' documented the infamous 1947 New Mexico UFO crash.

After a successful world tour, differences between Francis and Deal culminated in him unexpectedly announcing their split in January 1993. Rechristened Frank Black, he launched an erratic solo career. Deal continued with The Breeders (notably 1993's fabulous 'Cannonball') and, more recently, The Amps. In 1997, 4AD released a live and studio retrospective, *Death To The Pixies*.

surf www.pixies4ad.com/

PLACEBO

WHO Vocals/guitar **Brian Molko** (b. 1972), guitar/bass **Stefan Olsdal**

(b. Sweden), drums **Steven Hewitt** (b. Northwich, Greater Manchester, England)

WHEN 1995–

WHERE London, England

WHAT Androgynous angst-mongers

When Brian Molko was voted alongside Louise as Pop's sexiest stars of 1997, Placebo's blend of post-Grunge thrash and unsettling imagery was confirmed as a mainstream-mangling phenomenon.

Studying in London, Molko and Stefan Olsdal formed Ashtray Heart with drummer Robert Schultzberg. A handful of gigs snared a record deal, support slots with The Sex Pistols and Weezer, and David Bowie's patronage (less credibly, Molko's vocals were likened to those of Rush's Geddy Lee). Now known as Placebo, they powered into the Pop parade with 'Teenage Angst' (1996) before tearing it up with the storming, seedy 'Nancy Boy' from *Placebo* (1996). Molko's mascara'd androgyny made him a favourite with Metalheads and Indie kids alike.

Along the way, they replaced Schultzberg with Steven Hewitt, who had played on Placebo's first demos (his CV also included growing up in Charlatans frontman Tim Burgess' hometown, drumming for The Boo Radleys and K-Klass, and driving a forklift truck). The Bowie connection continued with their appearance in 1998 movie *Velvet Goldmine*, based on one of the Dame's tunes.

 www.levi.demon.co.uk/

ROBERT PLANT

WHEN b. 20 Aug 1948, West Bromwich, West Midlands, England

WHAT Un-ledded solo swinger

Before joining Led Zeppelin and becoming the template for all subsequent Hard Rock frontmen, Robert Plant had had a less than brilliant career. To the chagrin of his parents, he'd quit an accountancy course to front R&B bands (including The Crawling King Snakes, with John Bonham on drums) which went nowhere, the Motown-tinged Listen (boasting Slade's Noddy Holder as roadie), which went nowhere, two 1967 solo singles ('Laughing, Crying, Laughing' and 'Long Time Coming') which went nowhere and the West Coast-influenced Band Of Joy, which at least made it as far as London. One of their regular Marquee shows was seen by Blues singer Terry Reid, who recommended Plant to Jimmy Page for Led Zeppelin.

When Zeppelin split in 1980, Plant resumed his solo career. *Pictures At Eleven* (1982) and *The Principle Of Moments* (1983) were successful hybrids of experimentalism and Zeppelin-esque thunder, the latter producing the sublime hit 'Big Log'. After lightening up with the all-star (Jimmy Page, Jeff Beck, Nile Rodgers) R&B tribute *The Honeydrippers Vol. I* (1984) and *Shaken 'N' Stirred* (1985), Plant returned with a new band of young hotshots for the acclaimed *Now & Zen* (1988) and *Manic Nirvana* (1990) – both hotchpotches of Hip Hop (even Zeppelin ranked among his samples) and Hard Rock.

Fate Of Nations (1993) featured It Bites' guitarist Francis Dunnery, Fairport Convention's Richard Thompson and classical violinist Nigel Kennedy. It led Plant back to Zeppelin's Middle Eastern influences and Zeppelin itself: he reunited with Jimmy Page for the excellent *No Quarter* (1994) and the Steve Albini-produced *Walking Into Clarksdale* (1998). In between, Plant and Page contributed to *Inner Flame* (1997): a tribute album to Blues guitarist/songwriter Rainer Ptacek, executive-produced by Plant.

READ *Robert Plant* (1975), Michael Gross

SURF www.buffnet.net/"sgrab/

POCO

WHO Vocals/guitar **Richie Furay** (b. 9 May 1944, Dayton, Ohio, USA), vocals/guitar **Paul Cotton** (b. 26 Feb 1943, California, USA), steel guitar **Rusty Young** (b. 23 Feb 1946, Long Beach, California), bass/vocals **Timothy B. Schmit** (b. 30 Oct 1947, Sacramento, California), drums/vocals **George Grantham** (b. 20 Nov 1947, Cordell, Oklahoma, USA)

WHEN 1968–

WHERE Los Angeles, California, USA

WHAT Country Rock pioneers

Pogo became Poco in 1969 when legal threats by the powers behind the cartoon strip *Pogo* forced the tiniest name change in

Rock history. Overshadowed by their contemporaries The Eagles and Loggins & Messina, the band debuted with *Poco* (1970) and struggled through numerous personnel changes – including former Buffalo Springfield members Richie Furay and Jim Messina and future Eagles Randy Meisner and Timothy B. Schmit – before hitting the US Top 40 with *Deliverin'* (1970) and *Crazy Eyes* (1973). They struck gold with *Legend* (1979) and its hits 'Crazy Love' and 'Heart Of The Night'.

Five more years of the purest shimmering Country Rock encouraged only modest commercial success before a 1984 split. But re-formation in 1989 for 'Call It Love' returned them to the Top 20. The single and *Legacy* (1989) featured the original line-up of Furay, Messina, Young, Meisner and Grantham, who hadn't played together since their 1969 debut *Pickin' Up The Pieces*. The 90s did not sustain a full-time Poco, but various line-ups re-formed for US tours and benefit concerts.

Fan Poco Legacy, 13 Goose Acre, Chesham, HP5 1YQ, UK

surf www.pond.com/-vanallen/poco/html

THE POGUES

WHO Vocals **Shane MacGowan** (b. 25 Dec 1957, Tunbridge Wells, Kent, England), guitar **Philip Chevron** (b. Philip Ryan, 17 Jun 1957, Dublin, Ireland), banjo **Jem Finer** (b. Jeremy Max Finer, 20 Jul 1955, Stoke-on-Trent, England), tin whistle **Peter 'Spider' Stacy** (b. 14 Dec 1958, Eastbourne, East Sussex, England), mandolin/guitar **Terry Woods** (b. 4 Dec 1947, Dublin), accordian **James Fearnley** (b. 9 Oct 1954, Manchester, England), bass **Cait O'Riordan** (b. 4 Jan 1965, Nigeria), drums **Andrew Ranken** (b. 13 Nov 1953, London, England)

WHEN 1982–1996

WHERE London, England

WHAT Raucous Celtic Punk Folk

"There is drinking in lots of the songs because there is drinking in life. Drinking stimulates the imagination"
Shane MacGowan

While U2 conquered the world with their take on American Rock, their countrymen (and sometime support act) The Pogues raised the roof with a more traditional, but equally thrilling, Irish sound.

The Pogues' prototype was the short-lived New Republicans, which debuted in London in Easter 1981. Its repertoire included Irish ballads and rebel songs such as 'The Bold Fenian Men' (to the displeasure of off-duty British soldiers in attendance). The band disappeared for a year, returning as Pogue Mahone, Gaelic for "kiss my ass" – their agenda now more playful than rebellious.

New singer Shane MacGowan cut his reputation in London's 70s Punk scene, notably with The Nipple Erectors (later amended to The Nips). Although born in England, Shane was raised in the family home in Tipperary, Ireland, and first performed on the family kitchen table aged 6. Back in London, he graced the cover of a music paper even before becoming famous: he was pictured getting his ear chewed half-off at a Sex Pistols gig. The themes of identity and rootlessness became staples of Shane's lyrics.

They debuted with 'Dark Streets Of London' in 1984, the era of flashy videos and designer clothing. The band's ragged style, allied to Shane's dark romanticism, drew a mass of disaffected music fans. The band became The Pogues after complaints from Celtic broadcasters. *Red Roses For Me* (1984) leaned on traditional Folk, but *Rum, Sodomy And The Lash* (1985) showcased Shane's writing, notably the ballad 'A Pair Of Brown Eyes' and dancefloor-filler 'Sally MacLennane'. A union with The Dubliners on 'The Irish Rover' (1987) shot them into the UK Top 10 and their profile rose when they starred in Alex Cox's *Straight To Hell* and contributed 'Haunted' to his *Sid And Nancy*. Cait O'Riordan, who'd married Elvis Costello (producer of *Rum…*), was replaced by Darryl Hunt.

They peaked chartwise with Christmas 1987's wry weepy 'Fairytale Of New York', co-starring Kirsty MacColl. The mighty *If I Should Fall From Grace With God* and the Stonesy stomper 'Yeah Yeah Yeah Yeah Yeah' continued their onslaught into 1988.

The underrated *Peace And Love* (1989) and *Hell's Ditch* (1990) presaged MacGowan's exit. His hell-raising lifestyle and boredom obliged the band to recruit The Clash's Joe Strummer when he refused to tour. Shane finally quit in 1992 after *Best Of The Pogues* (1991). The Pogues scraped a farewell hit with 'Tuesday Morning' from *Waiting For Herb* (1993), then – after a couple of superfluous compilations – retired with a London show on 29 July 1996.

MacGowan, however, recaptured speed-crazed excitement and beer-stained balladry on fine albums with his new band The Popes: *The Snake* (1994) and *The Crock Of Gold* (1997).

read *The Pogues: The Lost Decade* (1988), Ann Scanlon

fan Friends Of Shane, c/o Ingrid Knetsch, Halverscheiderohl 3, 58579, Schalksmüle, Germany

surf www.pogues.com

THE POINTER SISTERS

WHO	Vocals **Ruth** (b. 19 Mar 1946, Oakland, California, USA), vocals **Anita** (b. 23 Jan 1948, Oakland), vocals **Bonnie** (b. 11 Jul 1950, Oakland), vocals **June** (b. 30 Nov 1954, Oakland)
WHEN	1971–
WHERE	Oakland, California, USA
WHAT	Soulful R&B

Preacher's daughters the Pointers paid their dues singing in church and providing backing vocals for Taj Mahal, Elvin Bishop and others. Signed to Blue Thumb in 1973, their eponymous debut album and TV appearances developed their reputation for close-harmony jazzy R&B numbers performed in eye-catching 40s costumes. Extending their range, Anita and Bonnie's self-composed 'Fairytale' won a Grammy for 1974's best Country single. They were also the first black women to appear at Nashville's Grand Ole Opry.

Following legal problems, Bonnie went solo in 1978 and the others signed to Richard Perry's Planet label, adding a highly successful poppy edge to soulful R&B. *Energy* (1979) produced the million-selling Springsteen cover 'Fire' (US No.2), *Black And White* (1981) featured 'Slowhand' (US No.2, UK No.10) and 1984's multi-platinum *Break Out* (US No.8, UK No.9) contained the Top 10 hits 'Jump (For My Love)' and 'Automatic'. They had no later Top 20 albums, apart from *Jump – The Best Of The Pointer Sisters* (1989), but were still touring in the mid-90s.

surf geocites.com/WestHollywood/2107/pointers.html

A Kiss influence even more explicit than Mötley Crüe's, higher hair and madder make-up were Poison's stock-in-trade, honed through countless club gigs after Michaels, Rockett and Dall (then called Paris) arrived in Los Angeles in 1984 and rejected future Guns N' Roses riffer Slash in favour of DeVille.

An entrancingly ludicrous live show (somersaults and smoke bombs) and party-hardy choruses propelled *Look What The Cat Dragged In* (1986) and *Open Up And Say… Ahh!* (1988) to multi-platinum. Unswayed by critical derision, their hit-making evolved from the gutter-level 'Talk Dirty To Me' to the power balladeering US No.1 'Every Rose Has Its Thorn' – as quoted by Bill and Ted in a bid to enter Heaven (*Bill & Ted's Bogus Journey*, 1991).

After final smash *Flesh & Blood* (1990), Poison were knocked sideways by Grunge and DeVille's hell-raising. He was replaced first by Richie Kotzen, then Blues Saracino. The live *Swallow This* (1991) bombed, the bluesy *Native Tongue* (1993) did okay, and the proposed follow-up, *Crack A Smile,* was rejected by Capitol, who issued *Poison's Greatest Hits 1986–1996* instead.

Now, despite DeVille's return, they are best known for Michaels' forays on film, including 1997's *A Letter From Death Row* and a home video of sexploits with former flame Pamela Anderson (another Crüe cönnection), whose release he battled against for two years.

Fan Bret Michaels Fan Club, 23679 Calabasas Road #346, Calabasas, CA 91302, USA

Surf wcafe.com/poison/

POISON

WHO Vocals **Bret Michaels** (b. Bret Michael Sychak, 15 Mar 1963, Harrisburg, Pennsylvania, USA), guitar **C.C. DeVille** (b. Bruce Anthony Johannesson, 14 May 1962, Brooklyn, New York, USA), bass **Bobby Dall** (b. Robert Kuy Kendall, 2 Nov 1965, Miami, Florida, USA), drums **Rikki Rockett** (b. Richard Ream, 8 Aug 1959, Mechanicsburg, Pennsylvania)

WHEN 1983–

WHERE Harrisburg, Pennsylvania, USA

WHAT Bömbast and bubblegüm

THE POLICE ⊙⊙⊙⊙⊙✪

WHO Vocals/bass **Sting** (b. Gordon Sumner, 2 Oct 1951, Wallsend, Tyne and Wear, England), guitar **Andy Summers** (b. 31 Dec 1942, Poulton-le-Fylde, Lancashire, England), drums **Stewart Copeland** (b. 16 Jul 1952, Alexandria, Virginia, USA)

WHEN 1977–1986

WHERE London, England

WHAT From ersatz Punk and white Reggae to perfect Pop

The Police came together through the frustratation of musical craftsmen derailed by Punk. By December 1976, with The Sex Pistols rampaging round England, Stewart Copeland had been with declining Prog Rock act Curved Air for a few years. After playing a pre-Christmas gig at Newcastle Polytechnic, he went to a nearby college and watched Last Exit, Sting's Jazz Rock quartet. Copeland hated the music, but thought the singer was great.

Their backgrounds were polar opposites. Copeland, son of a senior CIA officer, grew up largely in Beirut, Lebanon. Sting, a teacher and the son of a milkman, had always lived on Tyneside. But they talked, rapport was instant and, by early February, Sting had moved to London. With 24-year-old Corsican guitarist Henri Padovani, they recorded The Police's debut 'Fallout', on Copeland's own label, Illegal. However, the raw Punk approach they essayed was scorned by Punk fans and music press alike.

A more credible future dawned on 29 May 1977 in Paris, when Copeland and Sting met Andy Summers – bizarrely, when all three played together in a pick-up band called Strontium 90 at a reunion of hippie doyens Gong. Already 34 and a veteran of

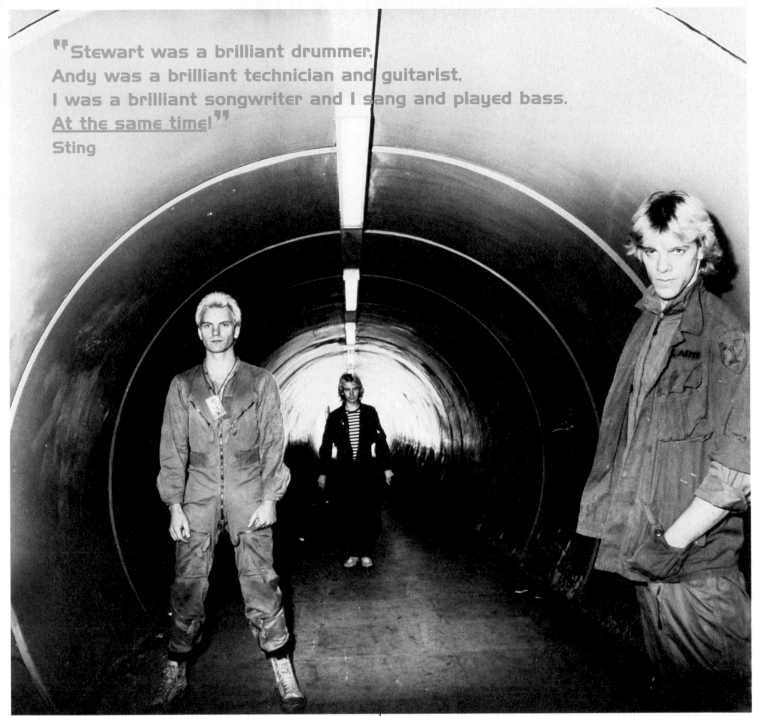

"Stewart was a brilliant drummer,
Andy was a brilliant technician and guitarist,
I was a brilliant songwriter and I sang and played bass.
At the same time!"
Sting

Zoot Money's band, Soft Machine and Eric Burdon's Animals among others, Summers yearned for something new. By August he had joined The Police and Padovani was out.

The 'White Reggae' which became their hallmark was born when Sting came up with 'Roxanne'. Copeland's entrepreneurial brother, Miles, took over management, persuaded A&M to release 'Roxanne' in 1978 and invested in ultra-cheap sessions at untried producer Nigel Gray's own studio.

That autumn, although the release of *Outlandos D'Amour* was barely remarked, Miles' bold strategies began to open doors. Though unknown in America, in October 1978 The Police flew to New York on the cut-price Laker Airlines and played 23 dates.

Even so, when they began recording *Regatta De Blanc* in February 1979, they were still hitless and penniless, surviving on ventures like a TV ad for Wrigleys gum (which gave them the bleach-blond hairdos they decided to keep) and Sting's bit-part movie acting in *Quadrophenia* and *Radio On*.

Then, that April, the re-released 'Roxanne' took off in America and kick-started *Outlandos D'Amour*. Within weeks the same happened in the UK and, in June, 'Can't Stand Losing You' reached UK No.2. By that autumn, astonishingly, The Police had established themselves as the top attraction in Britain with their first UK No.1s: 'Message In A Bottle' and *Regatta De Blanc*.

With 'Walking On The Moon' another UK chart-topper, from January 1980, Miles launched his global campaign with a tour of 19 countries including some, like India and Egypt, previously unexplored by Pop groups. *Zenyatta Mondatta* (1980) and the hits 'Don't Stand So Close To Me' and 'De Do Do Do, De Da Da Da' confirmed their arrival in the world league. Sting's fluent, intelligent songwriting had developed well beyond the original White Reggae formula's limitations, while Copeland and Summers were establishing Pop bench-marks by adapting their sophisticated skills to the pithy demands of 3-minute singles.

Megastardom came with 1982's *Ghost In The Machine* (UK No.1, US No.2) and 1983's *Synchronicity* (UK No.1, US No.1 for 17 weeks), hits including 'Invisible Sun', 'Every Little Thing She Does

THE POLICE: JANETTE BECKMAN/RETNA

Is Magic', 'Every Breath You Take' (the basis of Puff Daddy's mega-seller 'I'll Be Missing You') and 'King Of Pain', plus six Grammys and a BRIT award for Outstanding Contribution To British Music.

The Police recognized their 18 August 1983 show at New York's Shea Stadium, à la The Beatles, as a career apogee. Friction between the strong personalities – Sting-Copeland fist fights were not uncommon – tore them apart and an Amnesty benefit on 11 June 1986 in Atlanta, Georgia, proved their final concert.

The following month they gathered in London to record an album. Instead they blew apart after a bitter row. The outcome was a valedictory compilation, *Every Breath You Take – The Singles* (1986). Only further collections and archive material followed: *Greatest Hits* and the four-CD set *Message In A Box* (both 1992), *Live* (1995) and *The Very Best Of Sting & The Police* (1997).

After the split, all three conducted satisfying solo careers: Sting continuing to record and act, Copeland writing movie and TV scores and, latterly, operas, and Summers playing in instrumental groups and exhibiting his photography.

READ *The Police: L'Historia Bandido* (1981), Hugh Fielder & Phil Sutcliffe

FAN Outlandos Fan Club, Bugle House, 23a Noel Street, London W1, UK

SURF easyweb.easynet.co.uk/~wendavy/outlando.html

BRIAN POOLE & THE TREMELOES

WHO Vocals **Brian Poole** (b. 2 Nov 1941, Barking, Essex, England), guitar **Rick West** (b. Richard Westwood, 7 May 1943, Dagenham, Essex), guitar **Alan Blakley** (b. 1 Apr 1942, Bromley, Kent, England), bass **Alan Howard** (b. 17 Oct 1941, Dagenham), drums **Dave Munden** (b. 12 Dec 1943, Dagenham)

WHEN 1959–1966

WHERE Dagenham, Essex, England

WHAT Two top Pop acts in one

Brian Poole & The Tremeloes were initially cast in the Buddy Holly & The Crickets mould. Decca preferred them to The Beatles, whom they auditioned on the same day. They first charted with a cover of 'Twist And Shout' (1963), which owed much to The Beatles' version, followed by a chart-topping cover of The Contours' US million-seller 'Do You Love Me' the same year.

Before Poole and The Tremeloes went their separate ways in 1966, their renditions of Roy Orbison's B-side, 'Candy Man', and The Crickets' B-side ballad, 'Someone Someone' (both 1964), climbed into the UK Top 10, with the latter peaking at UK No.2 .

Solo, Poole floundered but, after a couple of near misses, the Tremeloes (with Len 'Chip' Hawkes replacing Howard) started an even more successful hit run in 1967 with Cat Stevens' 'Here Comes My Baby' and their No.1 recording of an old Four Seasons' B-side, 'Silence Is Golden'. Both of these singles also cracked the US Top 20 – a feat their records with Poole never achieved. Pop pearls 'Even The Bad Times Are Good' (1967), 'Suddenly You Love Me' (1968) and '(Call Me) Number One' (1969) are also among the nine UK Top 20 entries The Tremeloes totted up without Poole.

In 1996, Poole's daughters Karen and Shellie hit the charts as post-Alanis Popsters Alisha's Attic.

 www.tunes.com/tunes-cgi2/tunes/release/86951/1/4

IGGY POP

WHO b. James Jewel Osterberg, 21 Apr 1947, Ypsilanti, Michigan, USA

WHAT Punk Papa

Having smashed, slashed and gouged his way through the hippie-infested late 60s and Glam-fixated early 70s with The Stooges, Iggy Pop found himself in a quandary in 1974, the year the band breathed its last and the LAPD found him on Sunset Strip, foaming at the mouth, wearing a puke-stained mini-dress. Bruised, battered and hopelessly addicted to heroin, the Igster quit the gutter for a mental home, where his only visitor was David Bowie, himself in the throes of drug-addled paranoia.

Iggy's rehabilitation was slow: on weekend leave in 1975, he recorded demos with former Stooges guitarist James Williamson (later released as 1978's *Kill City*). But after he and Bowie were busted for drugs in New York in 1976, they fled to Berlin. There, they embraced healthy living, went crazy for Krautrock and made some of the best albums of the 70s – including Iggy's 1977 double-whammy *The Idiot* and *Lust For Life*. With The Stooges' 'No Fun' now a fixture of Sex Pistols live sets, he became a Punk hero. Relatively clean, fit and looking fantastic, his 1977 tour (with *Lust For Life* rhythm section brothers Hunt and Tony Sales, former MC5-er Fred 'Sonic' Smith on guitar and Bowie on keyboards) was commemorated on *TV Eye Live* (1978).

Typically, Iggy stumbled: *New Values* (1979) and *Soldier* (1980) died at birth thanks to producers James Williamson and Bowie, while *Party* (1981) was notable only for Patti Smith guitarist Ivan Kral and its sheer awfulness. *Zombie Birdhouse* (1982) proved the final straw: a brave foray into experimentalism, it nonetheless bombed and Iggy found himself label-less. Bowie bailed him out again by turning Iggy's 'China Girl' into an international smash.

After another ego boost with contributions to the Punk-infected *Repo Man* soundtrack (1984), Iggy continued with the Bowie-masterminded *Blah Blah Blah* (1986) – a career-saving slab of mid-80s slickness notable for a cameo by former Sex Pistol Steve Jones ('Cry For Love') and its hit 'Real Wild Child'. Again, he stumbled with the Jones-laden *Instinct* (1988) which, bizarrely, led to a Grammy nomination for 'Best Heavy Metal Performance'.

But, true to form, Iggy dragged himself back: 1990's *Brick By Brick* reconciled his trademark primal pummelling with sales and hipness, courtesy of appearances by Guns N' Roses' Slash and Duff McKagan and, on the hit 'Candy', The B-52's' Kate Pierson.

Meanwhile, 'Well, Did You Evah!', his Cole Porter duet with Deborah Harry, was the highlight of the AIDS benefit album *Red Hot + Blue* (1990). *American Caesar* (1993) and *Naughty Little Doggie* (1996) rocked Stooges-like, but were overshadowed by his dominating presence in the soundtrack – and plotline – of *Trainspotting*, which saw 'Lust For Life' reheated as bait for 1996's *Nude And Rude: The Best Of Iggy Pop*.

Iggy also continued his part-time acting career – highlights: John Waters' *Cry Baby* (1990), Jim Jarmusch's *Dead Man* (1995) and Tim Pope's *The Crow – City Of Angels* (1996); low-points: Alex Cox's *Sid And Nancy* (1986) and *Star Trek: Deep Space Nine* (1997) – and grunted approvingly toward the 1997 tribute album *We Will Fall*, which boasted celebrity back-slaps from Red Hot Chili Peppers, Joan Jett, Joey Ramone and Deborah Harry.

READ *I Need More* (1997), Iggy Pop

SURF virginrecords.com/iggy-pop/

POP WILL EAT ITSELF

WHO Vocals **Clinton Mansell** (b. 7 Nov 1962, Coventry, England), vocals/drums **Graham Crabbe** (b. 10 Oct 1964, Sutton Coldfield, England), guitar **Adam Mole** (b. 8 Apr 1962, Stourbridge, England), bass **Richard March** (b. 4 Mar 1965, York, England), drums **Fuzz** (b. Robert Townsend, 31 Jul 1964, Birmingham, England)

WHEN 1986–1995

WHERE Wolverhampton, England

WHAT Grebo gurus

Pop Will Eat Itself took their name from an *NME* article on Jamie Wednesday (the future Carter The Unstoppable Sex Machine). Their debut EP 'Poppies say GRR!' earned them *NME*'s 'Single Of The Week' and snared DJ John Peel, who offered them a live session. Lumped in with the media-created 'Grebo' movement alongside Crazyhead and Gaye Bykers On Acid, the group's Indie hits included 1987's cover of Sigue Sigue Sputnik's 'Love Missile F1-11' and 'Beaver Patrol', criticized for its sexist connotations.

Box Frenzy (1987) headed for Hip Hop, employing sampling and scratching, and Graham Crabbe swapped drumsticks for a microphone. In 1988, 'There Is No Love Between Us Anymore' and 'Def Con One' dented the UK chart and, although bottled off supporting Public Enemy, they were invited to play the USSR.

Signed to RCA, 'Can U Dig it?' and its parent album *This Is The Day, This Is The Hour, This Is This* (1989) hit the UK Top 40. Bigger hits followed, including 'Touched By The Hand Of Cicciolina' (1990), where the band tried to persuade FIFA to allow Italian porn star and politician La Cicciolina to present the World Cup.

In 1992, the band recruited Fuzz, but were dropped by RCA, ironically just as they scored their first UK Top 10 hit with 'Get The Girl, Kill The Baddies'. Undaunted, they signed to Infectious and *Dos Dedos Mes Amigos* (1994) became their most successful album, entering at UK No.11. But despite signing to Nine Inch Nails' Trent Reznor's nothing label in the USA, the band fizzled out. Richard March found success as half of Bentley Rhythm Ace, charting with 'Bentley's Gonna Sort You Out' in September 1997.

 kzsu.stanford.edu/uwi/pewi.html

PORNO FOR PYROS

WHO Vocals **Perry Farrell** (b. Perry Bernstein, 29 Mar 1959, Queens, New York, USA), guitar **Peter DiStefano** (b. 10 Jul 1965, Los Angeles, California, USA), bass **Martyn Le Noble** (b. 14 Apr 1969, Vlaardingen, Netherlands), drums **Steven Perkins** (b. 13 Sep 1967, Los Angeles)

WHEN 1992–1998

WHERE Los Angeles, California, USA

WHAT Rock 'n' Roll firestarters

Jane's Addiction, arguably the most thrilling band of the late 80s, crashed and burned in heroin-fuelled acrimony. It was a tough act to follow, but mainman Perry Farrell – who'd proved his odds-defying mettle by making the 'alternative' Lollapalooza festival a mainstream sensation – hit back with Porno For Pyros.

Their self-titled debut (1993) was a more straightforward take on Jane's Zeppeliny agenda, of more note for its lyrics – variously inspired by 1992's LA riots (the title track) and the inadequacies of humanity ('Pets') – than its music. Nonetheless, post-Jane's euphoria made it Farrell's highest-charting transatlantic success.

Ensuing years saw Farrell split from his girlfriend and guitarist Peter DiStefano battle against cancer: anguish reflected in 1996's low-key *Good God's Urge*. A cameo by Jane's Addiction/Red Hot Chili Peppers guitarist David Navarro on the cut 'Freeway' trailed a union of Farrell, Perkins, Navarro and Chili Peppers' bassist Flea on 'Hard Charger' for Howard Stern's movie *Private Parts* (1997), which – after months in which Farrell tried to get his Techno-oriented Insect World label and ENIT festival off the ground – turned into a short-lived Jane's reunion for *Kettle Whistle* (1997).

Porno For Pyros fell apart in 1998, Farrell keeping Perkins and DiStefano on board for his new project Gobbelee (bassist Martyn Le Noble had been replaced by Mike Watt for the Pyros' aborted 1997 tour). The Pyros bowed out with a cover of *West Side Story*'s tune 'Tonight' on the 1998 environmental charity album *MOM2*.

 pw1.netcom.com/~murzyn/porno/porno.html

PORTISHEAD

WHO Vocals **Beth Gibbons** (b. 4 Jan 1965, Devon, England), guitar **Adrian Utley** (b. 1958), drums/programming **Geoff Barrow** (b. 9 Dec 1971, Walton In Gordano, Somerset, England), production **Dave McDonald** (b. 1964)

WHEN 1991–

WHERE Bristol, England

WHAT Dark Trip Hop

A tape operator at Bristol's Coach House Studio, Geoff Barrow worked on Massive Attack's *Blue Lines* (1991) among others. He and Gibbons (then moonlighting as a pub singer) met on a government 'Enterprise Allowance Scheme' in February 1991. After nine fruitless months recording at Neneh Cherry's private studio, Barrow and Gibbons tried again with Adrian Utley and Dave McDonald. The result was 'Sour Times', a mix of Utley's Lalo Schifrin/Ennio Morricone/John Barry soundtrack influences, Gibbons' fractured vocals and Barrow's rough Hip Hop beats.

Signed to Go!Beat in 1993, Portishead (named after Barrow's hometown near Bristol) unleashed the Mercury Music Prize-winning *Dummy* (1994). Its bleak, sample-heavy soundscapes placed them with Massive Attack and Tricky at the forefront of the British Trip Hop scene. *To Kill A Dead Man*, a short film based on *Dummy*, was shown at cinemas and projected on the MI5 building in London in May 1995. Meanwhile, their packed appearance was the highlight of 1995's Glastonbury Festival.

In 1997, 'Cowboys' and a New York show broadcast on the Internet heralded *Portishead*. With Gibbons' once luscious vocals ruined by an Eartha Kitt affectation, it dispensed with much of their sampling arsenal and, sadly, much of their greatness.

READ *Straight Outta Bristol: Massive Attack, Portishead, Tricky And The Roots Of Trip Hop* (1995), Phil Johnson

 www.Portishead.co.uk

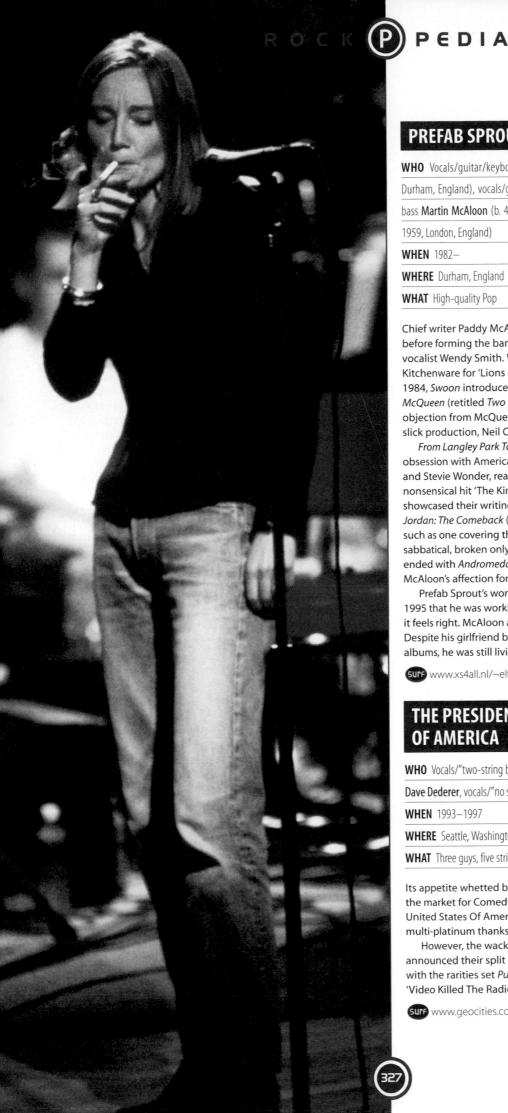

PREFAB SPROUT

WHO Vocals/guitar/keyboards **Paddy McAloon** (b. 7 Jun 1957, Consett, Durham, England), vocals/guitar **Wendy Smith** (b. 31 May 1963, Durham), bass **Martin McAloon** (b. 4 Jan 1962, Durham), drums **Neil Conti** (b. 12 Feb 1959, London, England)

WHEN 1982–

WHERE Durham, England

WHAT High-quality Pop

Chief writer Paddy McAloon invented the name Prefab Sprout before forming the band in 1982 with his brother Martin and vocalist Wendy Smith. Within a year, they'd signed to Indie label Kitchenware for 'Lions In My Own Garden' and 'Don't Sing'. In 1984, *Swoon* introduced their idiosyncratic lyrics. In 1985, *Steve McQueen* (retitled *Two Wheels Good* in the USA owing to an objection from McQueen's family) introduced Thomas Dolby's slick production, Neil Conti on drums and more focused lyrics.

From *Langley Park To Memphis* (1988) – continuing their lyrical obsession with Americana – featured The Who's Pete Townshend and Stevie Wonder, reached UK No.5 and yielded the addictively nonsensical hit 'The King Of Rock 'n' Roll'. *Protest Songs* (1989) showcased their writing strengths through skeletal songs and *Jordan: The Comeback* (1991) split its tracks into themed groups, such as one covering the rise and fall of Elvis Presley. A six-year sabbatical, broken only by the hits set *A Life Of Surprises* (1992), ended with *Andromeda Heights* (1997) – a lush affair expressing McAloon's affection for writers Cole Porter and George Gershwin.

Prefab Sprout's work rate is deceptive – McAloon indicated in 1995 that he was working on five albums – and releases come if it feels right. McAloon also retains some endearing eccentricities. Despite his girlfriend being in the band and royalties from hit albums, he was still living with his parents on his 30th birthday.

surf www.xs4all.nl/~elfasih/muziek/prefabs.html

THE PRESIDENTS OF THE UNITED STATES OF AMERICA

WHO Vocals/"two-string basitar" **Chris Ballew**, vocals/"three string guitbass" **Dave Dederer**, vocals/"no string drums" **Jason Finn**

WHEN 1993–1997

WHERE Seattle, Washington, USA

WHAT Three guys, five strings, united under Grunge

Its appetite whetted by Weird Al Yankovic's 'Smells Like Nirvana', the market for Comedy Grunge lapped up The Presidents Of The United States Of America. Their self-titled debut (1995) went multi-platinum thanks to its irresistible hits 'Lump' and 'Peaches'.

However, the wackiness wore thin with *II* (1996) and they announced their split at the end of 1997, bowing out in 1998 with the rarities set *Pure Frosting* and a cover of The Buggles' 'Video Killed The Radio Star' on *The Wedding Singer* soundtrack.

surf www.geocities.com/Hollywood/Set/7113/

ELVIS PRESLEY

⊙⊙⊙⊙⊙⊙⊙✪✪✪✪✪✪✪✪

WHO b. 8 Jan 1935, East Tupelo, Mississippi, USA, d. 16 Aug 1977, Graceland, Westhaven, Memphis, Tennessee, USA

WHAT *The* Rock 'n' Roll icon of all time

Elvis didn't invent Rock 'n' Roll. But without him, it would never have become the most significant music of the 20th century. The famously lampooned 'Las Vegas' Elvis is a galaxy away from the shy young man who accidentally changed the world.

Elvis Presley was the classic misfit: from childhood in Tupelo, Mississippi, to adolescence in Memphis, Tennessee, music was Presley's comfort. It began with church singing then, after his first public appearance at a talent show when he was 10, the guitar – "I wanted a bicycle," he admitted. Through music, he blossomed from gawky loner to teen rebel. By the time he graduated from high school, he revelled in the ridicule provoked by his long hair, his fascination with Memphis' black area, Beale Street, and his love of R&B and Gospel (The Blackwood Brothers, The Statesmen Quartet). In a town overrun with redneck Country singers, there was little room for one seemingly convinced he was black.

Elvis was a self-conscious singer and never destined to be a great guitarist – he admitted his playing sounded like "someone beating on a bucketlid". When he entered Memphis Recording Service (a studio owned by producer and Sun Records founder Sam Phillips) in 1953, it was only to cut two songs as a present for his mother, Gladys. Horrified by the sound of his own voice, he nonetheless impressed Phillips, whose assistant noted his name and address with the words "Good ballad singer. Hold". They put him to work, disastrously, on Country standards, but when Phillips allowed Elvis to try Gospel and R&B, he found a white singer with the explosive emotion of a black musician – a potential phenomenon in a still segregated America.

Paired with guitarist Scotty Moore and bassist Bill Black, he made history on 5 July 1954. In a break during another fruitless session, they fuel-injected Arthur 'Big Boy' Crudup's pedestrian Blues number 'That's All Right': the bass and guitars locked so tightly that the lack of a drummer went unnoticed and the vocal – joyous, unforced – exploded the barriers between black and white, Country and R&B. Next day, they did the same thing to 'Blue Moon Of Kentucky'.

Though Moore thought their sound too vulgar for Southern radio, Phillips took acetates downtown to Memphis station WHBQ, persuaded DJ Dewey Phillips (no relation) to play 'That's All Right' and watched the switchboard jam with calls for repeat plays. Presley woke the next day a local hero, with a Sun recording contract and a management deal with Scotty Moore. Sun unleashed 'That's All Right'/'Blue Moon Of Kentucky' as a

single and Presley, Moore and Black ('The Blue Moon Boys') played two giant shows at Memphis' Overton Park, where they wiped the floor with Country headliner Slim Whitman.

Outside Memphis, however, their triumph meant little. Having confused Country and R&B radio stations with a single that flouted the rules of both (Sam Phillips recalled "one jockey telling me that Elvis Presley was so Country he shouldn't be played after 5:00 am, and others said he was too black for them"), the trio met a stony response on the ultra-conservative Country radio show *Grand Ole Opry*. However, their lengthy residency on rival show *The Louisiana Hayride* and a new single, 'Good Rockin' Tonight', spread the word across the South and led to Presley singing jingles for the show's sponsors, Southern Made Donuts – the pinnacle of success for a young star.

Within months, he dominated the Southern music scene and was alternately dubbed 'The Hillbilly Cat' or 'The King Of Western Bop'. But bigger things loomed for Presley, as Memphis booking agent 'Colonel' Tom Parker realized. The Colonel – his military rank bestowed by Louisiana governor and Country star Jimmie Davis – was unlike any other figure on the music scene: a crude, cigar-chomping giant, gifted at making a fast buck. Having migrated from Holland, he scraped a living on the carnival circuit before promoting and managing Country artists in the 40s. Moving to Nashville, he controlled every facet of his star charge Eddy Arnold, putting him in movies, TV and Las Vegas.

He prised Presley from Bob Neal (who had succeeded Moore as Presley's manager in 1955) and, assuming managerial duties, sent his boy on tour with Moore, Black and drummer DJ Fontana, Country legend Hank Snow and rising Rock 'n' Roller Bill Haley – every show a blur of knee drops, splits, kicks, leaps and near-riots. Sun released a fourth single, 'Baby Let's Play House' (follow-up to the languid 'Milkcow Blues Boogie'), but Parker pulled the rug from under Sam Phillips' feet, selling his contract with Elvis to RCA. Sun, meanwhile, flourished with Carl Perkins, Johnny Cash and Jerry Lee Lewis.

Presley's RCA debut was 'Heartbreak Hotel' – a smouldering swagger through teen lust and anguish. It was released in January 1956, on the same day as his national TV debut – a blast through Big Joe Turner's 'Shake Rattle And Roll' for the first of six performances on the Jackie Gleason-produced *Stage Show*. "He can't last," Gleason declared. "I tell you flatly: he can't last."

By the end of the year, Elvis Presley had goosed the moral majority with shocking hip-shaking on *The Milton Berle Show*, humiliated the pompous Ed Sullivan (who vowed never to allow Presley on his show – mere weeks before paying $50,000 to do exactly that), made staid audiences blanch with his debut in Las Vegas (the stronghold of mainstream mega-stars), and fractured the US chart with eight No.1s, including Sun sides re-released by RCA – 'Mystery Train', 'Heartbreak Hotel', 'I Want You, I Need You, I Love You', 'Don't Be Cruel', 'Hound Dog', 'Love Me Tender', 'Blue Suede Shoes' and *Elvis Presley* (1956).

When he returned to the state fair where he first performed in public (this time with thousands of fans and hundreds of National Guardsmen), 26 September 1956 was declared Elvis Presley Day in Tupelo. For Elvis Presley and America, 1956 was the year their lives changed forever.

But the cost was compromise. *The Steve Allen Show* had a clearly humiliated 'Elvis The Pelvis' perform 'Hound Dog' in top hat and tails to a basset hound – the first signs of censorship, which culminated in a famously absurd *Ed Sullivan Show*

**"I'm not kidding myself.
My voice alone is just an ordinary voice.
What people come to see is how I use it.
If I stand still while I'm singing, I'm dead.
Man, I might as well go back to driving a truck..."
1956**

Elvis Is Back! (1960) was Presley's first recording after his discharge – having reached the rank of sergeant – from the US Army. But this wasn't the Elvis a generation had waved off in 1957 – the orgasmic demon of 1956 was dead. In his place was a mainstream entertainer, only dimly aware of the power he once held and determined to become a Hollywood idol, despite little aptitude for acting. The sneering rocker 'Elvis Presley' was replaced by the iconic 'Elvis' – a legend rather than a threat. "Elvis died when he went into the army," mourned John Lennon.

After a TV special with Frank Sinatra, he retreated to Graceland – where he built an insular world populated by employees and hangers-on (the 'Memphis Mafia') – and Hollywood, where he sank in a mire of bland movies. The best – *Flaming Star, G.I. Blues* (both 1960), *Blue Hawaii* (1961) and *Viva Las Vegas* (1964) – were far outnumbered by the worst: more than 20 exercises in banal teen exploitation (girls, glamorous locations, predictable plotlines) engineered by Parker. Inevitably, the public lapped it up. The best-selling soundtracks *G.I. Blues* (1960), *Something For Everybody, Blue Hawaii* (both 1961), *Girls! Girls! Girls!* (1962), *Fun In Acapulco, Kissin' Cousins, Roustabout* (all 1964), *Girl Happy, Harum Scarum* (both 1965) yielded scattered classics – 'Can't Help Falling In Love', 'Return To Sender', 'Bossa Nova Baby' – but were mostly indifferently recorded slush.

Rare non-movie recordings sometimes bravely flouted expectations (like the Gospel of 1961's *His Hand In Mine* and 1967's *How Great Thou Art*), but weak material (he was always at the mercy of songwriters) and a desire for mainstream acceptance resulted in adult-pleasers 'It's Now Or Never' and 'Are You Lonesome Tonight'.

Classics came more by accident than design. Written for Elvis' most successful movie, *Blue Hawaii*, 1962's 'Can't Help Falling In Love' fused a Classical melody with confessional lyrics. Three decades later, U2 adopted Elvis' habit of closing shows with the song – less reverentially, Bono covered it for the 1992 movie *Honeymoon In Vegas*, notable for its plane-load of sky-diving Elvis impersonators. Meanwhile, as The Beatles, The Rolling Stones, The Byrds, The Beach Boys and even Herman's Hermits conquered the world.

By 1968, the winning formula was exhausted. Parker's greed, coupled with his client's incredible naivety, had destroyed Elvis' reputation as a Rock 'n' Roller *and* the movie star he desperately wanted to be. Now a husband (to Priscilla Bealieu, the teenage daughter of an army officer he met in Germany), a father (their only child, Lisa Marie, was born in February 1968) and a bored, 33-year-old millionaire, Elvis Presley, it appeared, was finished.

His frustration and hope were poured into a TV special, due for transmission at Christmas 1968. Spurning the Colonel's plans for a bland seasonal pageant, he spent most of that year building a comeback.

On 3 December, the American public (Britain had to wait until New Year's Eve) tuned in to *Elvis* – his first TV appearance in eight years. Elvis Presley stepped into view – on a stage surrounded, like a boxing ring, by a studio audience – in a black leather jumpsuit and a blood red neckerchief. Staring down the camera, he snarled, "If you're looking for trouble, you've come to the right place…" and rebuilt his ailing career in a single stroke. The next hour showcased an Elvis Presley unseen since 1956: slim, impossibly handsome, full of aggression – purposefully, rather than accidentally, threatening. Hunched over a guitar (heartwarmingly played as badly as always) with Scotty Moore, Sun-era drummer DJ Fontana and bassist Charlie Hodge, he tore

appearance where he was filmed only from the waist up. Meanwhile, *The Wall Street Journal* estimated that licensed 'Elvis' memorabilia – hats, jeans, T-shirts, belts, jewellery, magazines, stationery, stuffed hound dogs – had grossed $22 million.

Presley took refuge from the chaos at Graceland, the Memphis mansion he bought for his parents in March 1957. But in December that year he received his draft notice. On 24 March 1958, Elvis Presley was inducted into the US Army as Private 53310761. A day later, the famous hair and sideburns were shorn and he began training in Texas. In August, Gladys Presley died in Memphis, aged 46 – a blow from which Presley never fully recovered. By September, he was stationed in Germany.

In his absence, new artists – Buddy Holly, Ritchie Valens, Jerry Lee Lewis, The Everly Brothers, Little Richard, Peggy Lee – ensured Rock 'n' Roll's big bang continued. Elvis was represented by a rash of stop-gap releases, including the US No.1s 'Too Much', 'All Shook Up', '(Let Me Be Your) Teddy Bear', 'Jailhouse Rock' (all 1957), 'Don't', 'Hard Headed Woman' (both 1958) and 'A Big Hunk O' Love' (1959).

Then there were the movies: having signed a seven-year contract with Paramount Pictures in 1956, Elvis became the first Pop star to conquer Hollywood. Although critically mauled, *Love Me Tender* (1956), *Loving You, Jailhouse Rock* (both 1957) and *King Creole* (1958) rank among Rock 'n' Roll's greatest exploitation movies and kept Elvis in teenagers' hearts. Their soundtracks proved equally successful – *Loving You* (1957) peaked at US No.1 and *King Creole* at No.2, adding to the millions made from *Elvis' Christmas Album* (1957) and *Elvis' Golden Records* (1958).

through old songs with more power than ever. In pre-recorded set pieces with an orchestra, choir and dancers, Presley clung to his Gospel comfort-blanket and, wearing a snow-white suit, overcame years of criminal neglect with a cracked-voice new song 'If I Can Dream'. Released as a single in 1969, it peaked at US No.12 – the closest Presley had been to the US Top 10 in years – while the TV special's soundtrack, *Elvis* (1969), reached US No.8.

Rejuvenated, he spent a month in a Memphis studio – the first fruits of which were the glorious 'In The Ghetto', 'Kentucky Rain', 'Don't Cry Daddy' and 'Suspicious Minds' from 1969's *From Elvis In Memphis* – before starting work on another movie, the aptly-named *Change Of Habit*. On 31 July 1968, he strutted on-stage at the International Hotel in Las Vegas for his first concert in eight years. During a four-week, 57-show engagement, which netted an unprecedented $1.5 million, his rehabilitation continued with a band including Country guitar genius James Burton, Gospel singers The Sweet Inspirations (his long-time vocal backing group The Jordanaires were thankfully absent), an orchestra, karate kicks and a white tassled jumpsuit. After more residencies in Vegas (his spiritual, if not physical, home for the rest of his career), he packed six shows at the Houston Astrodome and announced a 1970 US tour – his first since 1957.

The surprisingly candid 1970 film documentary *Elvis – That's The Way It Is* exposed his self-doubt and indecision. Surrounded by awestruck sidemen, Presley's flamboyant indulgences – wisecracks, pranks, anything but a straight performance – spilled from the rehearsal room to the stage, as if he were scared of his own power.

His marriage on the rocks (he was divorced from Priscilla in 1973), Elvis withdrew into punishing tours, prescription drugs (ironically, President Richard Nixon gave him an honorary Drug Enforcement Administration badge) and binge-eating. But 1972's award-winning *Elvis On Tour* documentary commemorated explosive performances, the best of which were four sellout shows at New York's Madison Square Garden, hence the awesome *Elvis As Recorded At Madison Square Garden* (1972). The year also brought four consecutive Top 10 UK hits, notably a spine-tingling reading of Willie Nelson's 'Always On My Mind' and the majestic 'An American Trilogy'.

In January 1973, he returned to TV with the incredible *Elvis: Aloha From Hawaii*. A live transmission from the Honolulu International Center, watched worldwide by an estimated 1 billion people (more viewers than the moon landings), the show yielded his first US No.1 album since 1964's *Roustabout*. But it masked chaos in Elvis' life: he appointed his father, Vernon, as a financial advisor, and Parker was collecting 50% of his earnings (rather than the customary 10%), courtesy of a complex deal which also sold the rights to Elvis' recordings to RCA for a miniscule flat fee.

With monstrous tax and living bills, Elvis was forced to spend more and more time on tour, despite failing health; he was hospitalized twice with pneumonia. Meanwhile, Parker squeezed more profit with junk like 1974's *Having Fun With Elvis On Stage* (an album not of music, but between-song banter) and turned down Barbra Streisand's offer of a starring role for Elvis in *A Star Is Born* – an appearance (taken by Kris Kristofferson) that could have saved his career.

In December 1976, he played his last Las Vegas show. Within months, tabloid headlines and cameras filming for a TV special hammered home the truth: at 42, Elvis was an obese, incoherent wreck – a picture reinforced by *Elvis: What Happened?*, a

scurrilous exposé by three ex-bodyguards which added drugs and guns revelations. Battered, paranoid, lonely and depressed, Elvis Presley hauled himself on stage in Indianapolis on 26 June 1977. One last time.

Shortly after midnight on 16 August 1977, he returned to Graceland after a late-night visit to the dentist. That day, he was due to fly (aboard his private jet, *The Lisa Marie*) to Portland, Oregon, for a show. He went to bed around 7:00 am. That afternoon, his girlfriend Ginger Alden (the daughter of the officer who inducted him into the army), found him in the bathroom, lying on the floor. He was rushed to Baptist Memorial Hospital in Memphis, but was pronounced dead at 3:30 pm.

Thousands of fans gathered outside Graceland as the news broke around the world. A coroner attributed Presley's death to heart failure, but also revealed arterial decay and an enlarged liver. It was likely his drug intake was a major factor: at the time of his death, his body contained butabarbital, codeine, morphine, pentobarbital, placidyl, quaalude, valium and valmid.

After a funeral at Graceland, where 75,000 fans watched from outside, he was buried, with his mother, in Memphis' Forest Hills cemetery, still wearing his 'TCB' ring – 'Taking Care of Business'. After several break-ins, the grave was moved to Graceland; Vernon, his father, joined them two years later. As tawdry conspiracy theories circulated, bickering over the Presley estate ended in 1983 when Priscilla Presley took control: Parker was ousted and 'Elvis Presley' became a trademark. While his records continue to sell (in excess of 1 billion at the last count), Graceland, opened to the public in 1982, became a poignant monument – Elvis' life, perfectly preserved.

READ *Last Train To Memphis* (1994), Peter Guralnick

FAN The Official Elvis Presley Organisation, PO Box 4048, Milton Keynes, Buckinghamshire, MK8 0JH, UK

SURF www.elvis-presley.com

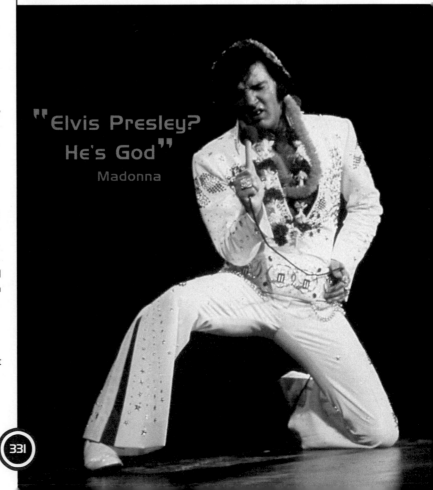

"Elvis Presley? He's God"
Madonna

"When you talk about
music that changed people
you need to talk about
Chrissie Hynde
much more than
Madonna...

...Courtney Love
would not exist without
Chrissie Hynde
Chrissie talked about
hole before Hole"

Tori Amos

SHREWSBURY COLLEGE
LONDON RD LRC

THE PRETENDERS ⊙

WHO Vocals/guitar **Chrissie Hynde** (b. 7 Sep 1951, Akron, Ohio, USA), guitar **James Honeyman-Scott** (b. 4 Nov 1956, Hereford, England, d. 16 Jun 1982, London, England), bass **Pete Farndon** (b. 2 Jun 1952, Hereford, d. 14 Apr 1983, London), drums **Martin Chambers** (b. 4 Sep 1951, Hereford)

WHEN 1978–

WHERE London, England

WHAT Punk-powered Rock 'n' Roll with a voice to die for

From her native Akron, where she'd played in high school band Sat. Sun. Mat. with Devo's Mark Mothersbaugh, Chrissie Hynde joined *NME* in London *circa* 1974. "As a journalist," said Lemmy of Motörhead, "she was singularly bad, so she became a musician instead." Working at Malcolm McLaren's store Sex, she hung out with Johnny Rotten, Sid Vicious and Clash associate Don Letts.

McLaren envisaged her in a group called Masters Of The Backside, including future Damnedster Rat Scabies and designer Vivienne Westwood. When this came to nothing, she wrote with Pistols guitarist Steve Jones, then went on a Clash tour with their bassist Paul Simonon. "Everyone," she said, "had a band but me."

Spurred to get it together by Lemmy, she enlisted bassist Pete Farndon, guitarist James Honeyman-Scott and drummer Gerry Mackeldof and debuted The Pretenders with 1979's Ray Davies cover 'Stop Your Sobbing'. Then, with new drummer and longest-serving sideman Martin Chambers, came 'Kid' and the UK No.1 'Brass In Pocket'. They exploded in 1980: *Pretenders* (1979) sold a million in the US and hit No.1 in the UK. Key to its success were the group's Punk-powered Rock 'n' Roll and Hynde's sultry voice and snappy lyrics. A sexily sneering "Baby, fuck off" on 'Precious' was the first step on the Rock road to Alanis Morissette.

They triumphed again with *Pretenders II* (1981), but Farndon – starstruck with Johnny Thunders and heroin – got himself fired. Two days later, Honeyman-Scott died of a cocaine-induced heart attack. Hynde and Chambers enlisted ex-Average White Band guitarist Robbie McIntosh and came back with their biggest US hit, 'Back On The Chain Gang' (written for Honeyman-Scott). With new bassist Malcolm Foster, a successful US tour and *Learning To Crawl* (1984) made this the most successful Pretenders line-up.

Although Farndon died in 1983, unreconciled with his former bandmates, and Chambers quit in the run-up to *Get Close* (1986), Hynde topped the UK chart with UB40 on a 1985 cover of Sonny & Cher's 'I Got You Babe' and hit with The Pretenders' 'Don't Get Me Wrong' and 'Hymn To Her'. When McIntosh quit after a 1987 tour, a blurred succession of sidemen (including George Clinton's keyboardist Bernie Worrell and Smiths guitarist Johnny Marr) made The Pretenders look increasingly like a vehicle for Hynde alone. By *Packed!* (1990), she seemed more interested in animal rights and environmental issues, then took years off to raise her two daughters, by Ray Davies and Simple Minds' Jim Kerr.

A new line-up solidified with the Honeyman-Scott-ish Adam Seymour (ex-Katydids), bassist Andy Hopson and the returned Martin Chambers. They followed 1994's punchy return to form *Last Of The Independents* (source of the hit 'I'll Stand By You') with 1995's *Unplugged*-ish *The Isle Of View* (with Blur's Damon Albarn). Hynde also guested on US TV series *Friends*.

 www.wbr.com/pretenders/

THE PRETTY THINGS

WHO Vocals **Phil May** (b. 9 Nov 1944, Dartford, Kent, England), guitar **Dick Taylor** (b. 28 Jan 1943, Dartford), guitar **Brian Pendleton** (b. 13 Apr 1944, Wolverhampton, England), bass **John Stax** (b. John Fullegar, 6 Apr 1944, Crayford, Kent), drums **Viv Prince** (b. 9 Aug 1944, Loughborough, England)

WHEN 1962–

WHERE Kent, England

WHAT Gritty 60s British R&B

As The Rolling Stones were harder than The Beatles, so The Pretty Things were harder than the Stones. Phil May and Dick Taylor, old friends of Jagger and Richards, shared a passion for US Blues records. For a time the two bands vied for supremacy of Britain's R&B scene, The Pretty Things (named after a Bo Diddley song) scoring 1964 hits with 'Rosalyn' and 'Don't Bring Me Down', marked by Taylor's stinging guitar and May's vocal snarl. The group's appearance, too, was calculatedly provocative, with May claiming the longest hair in Britain. As the decade wore on, The Pretty Things moved towards Soul, but sales diminished. In 1968, they released a landmark psychedelic album, *SF Sorrow*, and battled on for several years, despite myriad line-up changes.

The 70s saw them signed to Led Zeppelin's label Swan Song, issuing *Silk Torpedo* (1974), but their fortunes faltered. However, May and Taylor kept The Pretty Things alive and, in 1993, recovered royalty payments withheld from them in the 60s.

ALAN PRICE

WHO b. 19 Apr 1942, Fairfield, Durham, England

WHAT Pop Blues organist

Leaving The Animals at their peak because of touring pressures, Price formed The Alan Price Set and was vindicated by the chart success of 'I Put A Spell On You' (1966). Although Price's straight image was unusual in the 60s, distinctive and classy hits ensued, including 1967's 'Simon Smith And His Amazing Dancing Bear' (an early Randy Newman song) and 1968's 'Don't Stop The Carnival', for which he put lyrics to a tune by Jazz legend Sonny Rollins. A union with Georgie Fame produced 1971's hit 'Rosetta'.

Price scored the London Royal Court production of David Storey's play *Home*, and wrote and performed powerful, BAFTA award-winning songs for Lindsay Anderson's extraordinary movie, *O Lucky Man* (1973).

On a creative roll, Price hit with 1974's evocative 'Jarrow Song', which celebrated the women who kept families together during Britain's depression in the 30s. However, a starring role in the film *Alfie Darling* (1975), sequel to *Alfie*, overstretched his talents. "A mistake," he later admitted. "Nevertheless I tried!" 'Just For You' (1977), written for his daughter after his marriage broke up, was classic, but Animals reunions in 1977 and 1983 were unsatisfying.

Thereafter, Price wrote music for movies like *The Plague Dogs* (1982) and *The Whales Of August* (1988), and TV series including *The Further Adventures Of Lucky Jim* (1982) and *Chalkface* (1991), and wrote and appeared in the musical *Andy Capp* (1982). In the 90s he co-helmed the Electric Blues Company with Zoot Money.

MAXI PRIEST

WHO b. Max Alfred Elliott, 10 Jun 1960, London, England

WHAT Reggae's Mr Romance

Until Shabba Ranks came along, Maxi Priest was the boss of Reggae with a Soul groove. While other stars of the UK 80s dancehall explosion were Rappers, Maxi was the vocal sweetening on the country's then leading sound system, Saxon. Signed to Virgin's 10 imprint in 1985, his debut set, *You're Safe*, was a runaway UK Reggae chart success, spawning the hits 'In The Springtime' and 'Strollin'.

Intentions (1986) spread his name further, and his third, *Maxi* (1988), opened his Top 20 account with 'Some Guys Have All The Luck' and 'Wild World'. By now regularly working on R&B rhythms, Maxi's status soared globally through work with Soul II Soul, Jazz guitarist Lee Ritenour and duets with Frankie Paul and Shabba Ranks. Maxi's uncredited voice punctuated the latter's 'Mr Loverman' smash with a keening "Shabba". He scored another smash in 1993 with the sumptuous 'Housecall' and, while his star has slipped somewhat since, he remains the same unaffected South Londoner he has always been.

surf www.virginrecords.com/VR.cgi?ARTIST_NAME=Maxi_Priest

PRIMAL SCREAM

WHO Vocals **Bobby Gillespie** (b. 22 Jun 1964, Scotland), keyboards **Martin Duffy**, guitar **Andrew Innes**, guitar **Throb** (b. Robert Young), bass **Mani** (b. Gary Mounfield, 16 Nov 1962, Crumpsall, Manchester, England)

WHEN 1984—

WHERE Glasgow, Scotland

WHAT Throbbing Dance Rock monsters

From fey Indie Pop to throbbing Dub Rock monsters, Primal Scream's stagger to stardom was fuelled by narcotics and name-dropping. Part-time drummer with The Jesus & Mary Chain, Bobby Gillespie co-founded Primal Scream with Jim Beattie (who left to resurface in Spirea X), joined the Creation label and recruited mainstays Andrew Innes and Throb for the jangly 'All Fall Down' (1985) and 'Crystal Crescent'/'Velocity Girl' (1986).

Dripping with 60s references (Byrds, Stooges, Rolling Stones, MC5), *Sonic Flower Groove* (1987) and *Primal Scream* (1989) confirmed the band as Indie favourites, but Acid House and well, *acid* were the inspirations behind the incalculably great 'Loaded' (1990) – a revamp of 1989's 'I'm Losing More Than I'll Ever Have' by genius DJ Andrew Weatherall. Weatherall (with cameos from

Jah Wobble, vocalist Denise Johnson and The Orb's Dr Alex Paterson) masterminded the majestic *Screamadelica* (1991) which – by seamlessly splicing Rock, Dance and decadence into the likes of 'Movin' On Up', 'Come Together' and 'Higher Than The Sun' – painted the universe strange colours, stormed the UK Top 10 and won the inaugural Mercury Music Prize in 1992.

Transformed from gangly Indie wimps to Rock hell-raisers, Primal Scream toured and settled in Memphis – where, in a cosmic twist of fate, they believed themselves to be The Rolling Stones. Rejecting the technologically assisted Dance magic that made them, they regressed to their classic influences with 1994's *Give Out But Don't Give Up*. It featured cameos from the legendary likes of George Clinton and The Memphis Horns, but – despite the classic 'Jailbird' (later remixed to spectacular effect by The Chemical Brothers) and 'Rocks' – betrayed its Mick 'n' Keef origins too clearly. By Primal Scream's dreadful, drug-addled appearance at 1992's Reading Festival, it seemed their days were numbered.

They fought back with the soccer anthem 'The Scream Team Meets The Barmy Army Uptown', co-penned by Irvine Welsh, and the title track from Welsh's movie *Trainspotting* (1996). Then, augmented by former Stone Roses bassist Mani, they unleashed the amazing *Vanishing Point* (1997). Named after Richard Sarafian's 1971 road movie – the first hit, 'Kowalski', was named after its (anti)hero – *Vanishing Point* trawled through paranoia, darkness, violence and a Motörhead cover, which sprouted a remix of 'If They Move, Kill 'Em' by Kevin Shields of My Bloody Valentine and, courtesy of DJ Adrian Sherwood, a full-blown Dub demolition of the entire album in the form of 1997's *Echo Dek*.

(READ) *Higher Than The Sun* (1997), Grant Fleming

(Fan) c/o Creation Records, 109x Regents Park Road, London, NW1 8UR, UK

(SURF) www.dreamspace.com/astron/primalscream

PRINCE ☧ ⊙⊙⊙⊙⊙⊙✪✪✪

WHO b. Prince Rogers Nelson, 7 Jun 1958, Minneapolis, Minnesota, USA

WHAT Funk-bumpin' modern-day Mozart

Where Sly Stone and George Clinton crashed and burned, Prince triumphed, bringing raw, rude Funk to the masses. It was a meticulously plotted crusade: from high-school covers band Grand Central, through studio work with Champagne and 94 East, on to his solo debut *For You* (1978). Though likened to Stevie Wonder on account of the kid's multi-instrumental flair, two of its songs hinted at the sledgehammer Prince later took to R&B: 'Just As Long As We're Together', a long, electronic dancerama, and 'I'm Yours', a guitar-heavy indulgence often cited as evidence of the otherwise spurious 'new Hendrix' theory.

His first hit, 'Soft And Wet', introduced the Princely penchant for unblushing sexual frankness. The trend continued with 'I Wanna Be Your Lover' ("I wanna be the only one you come for") from *Prince* (1979), his platinum push into the US mainstream.

Prince began the 80s as an acclaimed wonderkid, pitched against 'Punk Funk' king Rick James – whom he supported and promptly eclipsed. Even James – no stranger to saucy rhymes

and squirmy rhythms – was gobsmacked by *Dirty Mind* (1980). A Funk-fest of barely dressed demos whose agenda included oral sex and incest, it secured critical kudos but catastrophic sales.

Undaunted, Prince assembled The Time: the first and best of his protégés. Their success was a mixed blessing: on charts (with 1981's patchy *The Time* and 1982's splendid *What Time Is It?*) and on tour, they threatened to eclipse their mentor. He fought back with *Controversy* (1981), a million-seller despite its tuneless social commentary and dull meditations on sex. Only the effervescent 'Private Joy' (immortalized as Kylie Minogue's favourite Prince song) and 'Do Me, Baby' (the blueprint for a succession of slinky ballads, later superbly covered by Meli'sa Morgan) stand out.

Prince sowed the seeds for global domination with *1999* (1982), dominated by the mechanical beats that characterized the 80s' 'Minneapolis Sound'. The latter was also propagated by producers Jimmy Jam and Terry Lewis, who defected from The Time in 1982 and established a world-conquering production line with The SOS Band and Janet Jackson. Their estranged boss set his sights on Pop immortality with the self-mythologizing but superb *Purple Rain* (1984). Taking its cue from *1999*'s smash title track and 'Little Red Corvette', *Purple Rain* put synthesized sleaze on the backburner in favour of explosive PopRockSoul. Revered by fans for reflective tracks like 'The Beautiful Ones', the album – which spent 24 weeks atop the US chart – made its commercial mark with the punchy hits 'When Doves Cry' and 'Let's Go Crazy'.

For a year, he was inescapable: the box office-busting *Purple Rain* movie and tour, The Time's *Ice Cream Castle*, drummer Sheila E's Prince-produced *The Glamorous Life* and a Senate-level uproar over masturbatorial mindbender 'Darling Nikki' combined to put Prince alongside Springsteen, Jackson and Madonna in Rock's hierarchy. His response was the psychedelic *Around The World In A Day* (1985), of whose trippy tunes the celebrated 'Condition Of The Heart' and 'Raspberry Beret' are sadly buried amid rip-offs of Sly Stone and George Clinton. Undaunted, Prince fostered an image one step removed from sanity, notably an announcement in 1985 that he was giving live work the boot (the traditional cry of stars from Sinatra through Bowie to Elton John) and looking for "the ladder" (as you would if you were as short as he is).

Prince came back to Earth in 1986. Construction began on his Paisley Park studio in Minneapolis and he scored a US No.1 with the gleeful 'Kiss'. The self-indulgent movie *Under The Cherry Moon* was a deserved flop, but its kaleidoscopic soundtrack *Parade* was a triumph and fuelled a sensational return to the stage (although the tour marked the farewell of his band The Revolution). In the last year before work with other acts translated as spreading his talents too thin, he sprinkled stardust on The Bangles (writing the hit 'Manic Monday' under the name Christopher Tracy) and made jolly albums with protégée Jill Jones (*Jill Jones*, 1987) and the Jazz-happy Madhouse (*8*, 1987).

Non-stop recording meant the latter were quickly followed by *Sign 'O' The Times* (1987). Compiled from the unreleased albums *Crystal Ball* and *Dream Factory* and the 'Camille' project, *Sign 'O' The Times* veered from P-Funk to Soul smooch, with nods to idols like Joni Mitchell and Sly Stone, extremes demonstrated by the stark title track and a red hot duet with Sheena Easton, 'U Got The Look'. The proposed follow-up, *The Black Album*, opened promisingly with the pounding 'Le Grind' but bottomed out with 'Dead

I went up to
Prince and said,
'I'm a big fan of your stuff'
and he looked at me
and just walked off...
left me standing
there like a twat.
He's a prat,
but a clever prat

Elton John

On It', an ill-advised dig at Rappers who had stolen Prince's crossover thunder. Fortunately, he shelved the set in favour of *Lovesexy* (1988), an album-length affirmation of God's triumph over Spooky Electric, the demonic muse behind *The Black Album*. The 1988 shows were his best ever, a blur of replica Thunderbird cars, mad medleys and Sheila E's metallic bra. However, they did nothing to revive dwindling domestic sales, which instead relied on a boost from his 1989 movie soundtrack *Batman*. The album and camply wham-bamming 'Batdance' topped the US charts.

As with the *Purple Rain/Under The Cherry Moon* blueprint, Prince's association with celluloid success was followed by an ill-fated venture into similar territory. But lacking the alchemy that yielded *Parade*, *Graffiti Bridge* (1990) was shallow and disjointed, both as a movie and soundtrack. More songs were recycled from earlier, abandoned projects, and Prince unwisely allowed himself to be upstaged by cameos from Mavis Staples, Tevin Campbell and the reunited and better than ever The Time. The latter's vastly superior *Pandemonium* (1990) included material Prince had made for himself and another off-shoot, Mazerati, and cuts like 'Jerk Out' testified to Prince's abilities far better than his own hit 'Thieves In The Temple'. The results were conclusive: though *Graffiti Bridge* was his third consecutive UK No.1, it spent only eight weeks on chart. It was also upstaged, by Sinéad O'Connor's galaxy-gobbling take on his 'Nothing Compares 2 U' (written for The Time's wishy-washy successors The Family in the mid-80s).

Diamonds And Pearls (1991) blatantly attempted to recapture sales commensurate with Prince's fame. It worked too: 'Cream' was a US No.1, the hologram-covered album went double platinum and the smash hit title track became a favourite of Posh Spice Victoria Addams. The resurrection continued with (1992), despite radio programmers' horror at its first hit 'Sexy MF'. The career-compiling *The Hits/The B-Sides* (1993) crowned it off.

Thereafter, his threads unravelled. He declared Prince dead, and proved it with the underwhelming *Come* (1994). Warner Bros, who had made him a well-rewarded board member and indulged the release of the UK No.1 'The Most Beautiful Girl In The World' (1994) on another label, were less amused by his self-reinvention as ♀ or 'The Artist Formerly Known As Prince'. In the ensuing stalemate, he issued *The Black Album* (1994) to fulfil contractural obligations, which were finally jettisoned with the disastrous *Chaos & Disorder* (1996). In between, he flirted with former heights on the glorious *The Gold Experience* (1995) and the splendid Spike Lee movie soundtrack *Girl 6* (1996).

His move to EMI yielded *Emancipation* (1996), a rare example of a stupendous single album lurking in a triple-album guise. Its highlights included sensational covers of The Stylistics' 'Betcha By Golly Wow' and Joan Osborne's 'One Of Us'; its lowlights, the inaudible backing vocals of Kate Bush on 'My Computer' and a load of generic plastic Funk. With sales in free-fall, Prince's lack of quality control seemed terminal – a suspicion strengthened by the archive-dredging, four-CD set *Crystal Ball* (1998), which did, however, find a home for *The Truth* – a set of fine acoustic newies – and long-time fan favourites 'Movie Star' and 'Days Of Wild'.

However, given that Prince has written some of the best songs ever, periodically punctures his own self-importance and is one of the most worthy recipients of the epithet 'genius' in modern music, it would be foolish to write him off.

READ *Prince – A Documentary* (1993), Per Nilsen

FAN Uptown, PO Box 87, SE-590 62 Linghem, Sweden

SURF love4oneanother.com/

PJ PROBY

WHO b. James Marcus Smith, 6 Nov 1938, Houston, Texas, USA

WHAT Enigmatic, controversial crooner and actor

PJ Proby, discovered by TV and stage producer Jack Good, found his greatest fame in England. His hits, including 'Hold Me' (1964) and 'Somewhere' (1965), displayed an affected vocal style which owed much to Elvis. Able to make a simple Pop song deep and dark, he didn't need cheap gimmicks; but when his trousers split onstage in 1965 he adopted the stunt as a regular part of the act. The righteous English press led a backlash and Proby's career – dogged by managerial and money problems – never recovered.

Proby's wayward genius has since been employed in a variety of roles (including inspiring Blur's 'Country Sad Ballad Man'). For every mind-blowing moment, there are five that promise more than they deliver. However, as with Elvis, it is the presence of a talent so blindingly obvious that keeps the faithful coming back. The bizarre 7-minute 'Mary Hopkin Never Had Days Like These' (1968) was a maverick inspiration. The spirited backing on *Three Week Hero* (1969) was provided largely by the then unknown Led Zeppelin. Stints on stage playing the star role in the musical *Elvis* in 1977 and 1995 produced some of his best-ever performances, but resulted in one ignominious sacking when he apparently lost interest in his work.

Manchester label Savoy produced a series of sublime Dance singles using Proby's strong vocal in adaptations of Joy Division's 'Love Will Tear Us Apart', among others. He marched out of hospital, against medical advice, two days after a heart attack in 1991 but, as recently as *The Legend* (1997), still sounded great.

SURF home.wxs.nl/~kilkens/proby.htm

PROCOL HARUM

WHO Vocals/keyboards **Gary Brooker** (b. 29 May 1945, Southend, Essex, England), guitar/vocals **Robin Trower** (b. 9 Mar 1945, Southend), guitar/keyboards **Matthew Fisher** (b. 7 Mar 1946, Croydon, Surrey, England), drums **Barry 'B.J.' Wilson** (b. 18 Mar 1947, Southend), bass **Dave Knights** (b. 18 Jun 1945, Islington, London, England)

WHEN 1967–

WHERE London, England

WHAT English proto-Prog Rock

Procol Harum are celebrated for their 1967 UK No.1 and US No.5 'A Whiter Shade Of Pale', the result of Gary Brooker's work with lyricist Keith Reid. A surreal poem set to a variation on Bach's 'Suite No.3 In D Major', this Pop Prog gem won attention before they had even a live act or an album's worth of material.

Brooker's first solid line-up, The Paramounts, formed at school in 1962. Initial recordings foreshadowed the grandiosity of later material, with poetic lyrics and ponderous melodies similar to contemporaries like The Moody Blues. Cuts like 1967's 'Homburg' kept them on charts while *Procol Harum* (1967), *Shine On Brightly* (1968) and *A Salty Dog* (1969) were experimental and confident. But Trower wanted a harder sound. He found it, as a solo act.

From Trower's exit in 1971, the keyboard-based band, despite lacking the flashiness of Yes or ELP, still pushed barriers. The lavish *In Concert With The Edmonton Symphony Orchestra* (1972) hit US No.5. Procol Harum played the final night of the legendary Rainbow Theatre in London in 1975, gaining their final UK Top 20 hit that year with 'Pandora's Box'. Its parent album, *Procol's Ninth* (1975), saw songwriters Leiber & Stoller producing and writing with the band. By 1977, Procol Harum were playing a 'final' gig in New York and watching *Something Magic* stall at US No.147.

Out of step with the loud late 70s and glossy 80s, Brooker undertook challenging projects, including ballet scores, before contacting Keith Reid about further collaborations. With Brooker, Trower and Fisher, 1991's *The Prodigal Stranger* was a prelude to low-key recording and live work. Meanwhile, of the stories regarding the band name's origin, best is the suggestion that it came from the pedigree certificate of a record producer's pet cat.

 Procul Harum Appreciation Society, 8415 W. 89th St, Overland Park, KS 66212, USA

 www4.cdb.com/xm/cd/rock/910cfb0c.html

PRODIGY ⊙ ⊙ ✪

WHO Keyboards **Liam Howlett** (b. 21 Aug 1971, Essex, England), vocals/dancing **Keith Flint** (b. 17 Sep 1969, Essex), vocals/dancing **Maxim Reality** (b. Keith Palmer, 21 Mar 1967), dancing **Leeroy Thornhill** (b. 7 Oct 1969, Essex)

WHEN 1990–

WHERE Braintree, Essex, England

WHAT Thrashing Hip Hop Techno noise with added arson

In July 1967, The Beatles stormed to the US No.1 with *Sgt. Pepper*. Exactly three decades later, the *Billboard* Top 10 – then stuffed with Pop poppets Hanson, the *Men In Black* and *Batman & Robin* soundtracks and a clutch of Country acts – was crashed by four more blokes from England: Prodigy. Confirming the Anglocentric angle, they knocked another technicolor Brit explosion – Spice Girls – off No.1. "Will this be the harbinger of a trend," wondered *Billboard*, "or simply a singular success?"

Hip Hop devotee Liam Howlett invested wages from a holiday job in turntables and joined local crew Cut 2 Kill as DJ at 16, while still at school. Working for a magazine in London in 1988, Liam played a tape of theirs to the owner, who financed their album. Cut 2 Kill, however, signed to Tam Tam without him. Disillusioned with the elitist British Hip Hop scene, he was converted to Acid House and began DJ-ing at raves around Essex, while recording his own material (mostly re-treads of Meat Beat Manifesto's 'Radio Babylon') on a primitive home studio.

Keith Flint and Leeroy – friends since meeting at The Barn in Essex (scene of Howlett's Acid House epiphany) – drifted into the rave scene. Leeroy, a die-hard Funk fan, was a spectacular dancer, while Keith, a Led Zep enthusiast, had travelled after dead-end jobs and arrived home in Essex in 1989. They met Howlett at an outdoor rave and asked for a tape of his mixing, on which he included four of his own tracks. Impressed, they asked him to record more and – with a female friend, Sharky – named themselves The Prodigy after Howlett's first

Moog synthesizer. Maxim joined as MC at their live debut in late 1990 at The Labyrinth, a club in London's East End.

Howlett signed them to XL Recordings just before Christmas 1990 for their debut, the 'What Evil Lurks' EP, in February 1991. Now a four-piece (Sharky had left at Christmas), the group was gigging constantly when their 'Charly' hit the UK chart in August. 'Charly' fused aggressive beats with mind-bending chords and a ridiculous commentary from a 70s public information film and, sadly, inspired a host of puerile copies such as Urban Hype's 'Trip To Trumpton' and Smart Es' 'Sesame's Treet'.

The Prodigy Experience (1992) proved one of the most successful offerings from a Dance scene yet to yield consistent albums. It sold a million in the UK on the back of frenetic hits like 'Everybody In The Place' and 'Out Of Space'. Their exhausting live show – Liam scurrying behind banks of keyboards, Leeroy loping inconspicuously, Maxim and Keith moshing and menacing – cemented their cartoon psycho personae long before videos like 1996's 'Breathe' etched such images on the mass consciousness.

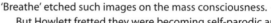

But Howlett fretted they were becoming self-parodic and – to re-establish his street credentials – issued 'One Love' under the pseudonym Earthbound before its official release in October 1993, by which time it had become a massive underground hit.

This rejuvenation trailed his darker, more aggressive marriage of Techno, Industrial and Punk. The result was the UK No.1 *Music For The Jilted Generation* (1994), which veered flawlessly from the metallic 'Their Law' through the ominous Hip Hop of 'Poison' to the climactic Techno trio '3 Kilos', 'Skylined' and 'Claustrophobic Sting' – leaving the hammering 'No Good (Start The Dance)' the sole remnant of their 'happy hardcore' origins. The rest of Britain caught up with what its kids had known for years: that Prodigy (the 'The' got lost along the way) were – despite the impending explosion of Blur and Oasis – the best band in the land. They cemented their Rock 'n' Roll reputation by turning in ever more aggressive performances at festivals and their own concerts, as terrifyingly documented on the video *Electronic Punks* (1995).

But nothing could have prepared the public for 'Firestarter' in March 1996. The lurching and leering Keith Flint – who'd shed his long hair to become a body-pierced Johnny Rotten for the 90s – proved irresistible to MTV-fixated kids, especially when their parents' indignation was heightened by newspaper claims that the track promoted arson. Twelve months before their US triumph, Prodigy had a similar effect in Britain when 'Firestarter' swept teenyboppers Take That from No.1.

Equally pivotal was acclaim from the Rock *and* Dance arenas. They hadn't pioneered the crossover – Run DMC set the wheels in motion a decade before, and even Rage Against The Machine could take some credit – but when the skull-crushing follow-up to 'Firestarter', 'Breathe', was voted Single Of The Year by readers of Metal mag *Kerrang!*, Prodigy could lay reasonable claim to the crossover crown. Howlett proved the point by collaborating with Rage Against The Machine's Tom Morello, and rounding off *The Fat Of The Land* (1997) with a cover of Grunge gals L7's 'Fuel My Fire'. The energetic effervescence of the rest of *Fat* – including an oddly entrancing cameo by Kula Shaker's Crispian Mills – paled only alongside the far more ambitious *Jilted Generation* and shot to No.1 worldwide. On a draining tour, including the Glastonbury and Lollapalooza festivals, Howlett

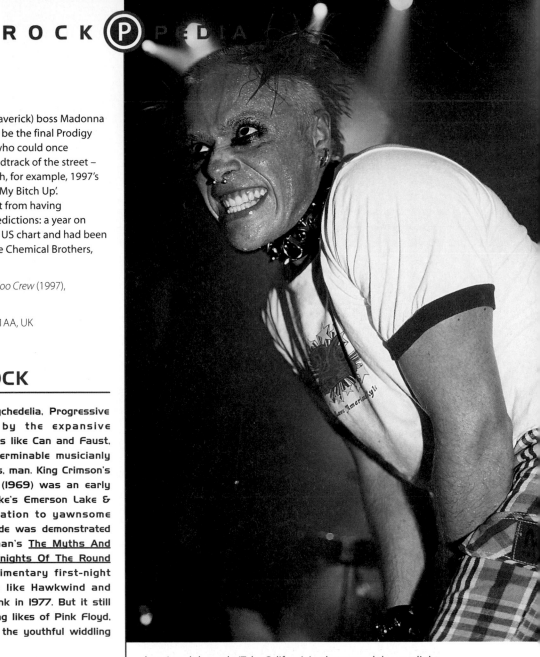

reportedly bad-mouthed his US label (Maverick) boss Madonna and predicted *The Fat Of The Land* would be the final Prodigy album. Most galling was that Prodigy – who could once legitimately claim to have been the soundtrack of the street – now had to *manufacture* controversy with, for example, 1997's sex 'n' drugs video extravaganza 'Smack My Bitch Up'.

However, he could take some comfort from having disproved *Billboard*'s flash-in-the-pan predictions: a year on from their No.1, Prodigy were still on the US chart and had been joined by fellow 'Electronica' acts like The Chemical Brothers, The Crystal Method and Daft Punk.

read *The Prodigy: Adventures With The Voodoo Crew* (1997), Martin James

fan XL, 17-19 Alma Road, London, SW18 1AA, UK

surf www.theprodigy.com

PROGRESSIVE ROCK

WHAT A pompous extension of Psychedelia, Progressive Rock could be characterized by the expansive experimentalism of 'Krautrock' groups like Can and Faust, or by ugly men with long hair, interminable musicianly noodling and 'amaaazing' productions, man. King Crimson's <u>In The Court Of The Crimson King</u> (1969) was an early peak, but Crimson bassist Greg Lake's Emerson Lake & Palmer took instrumental exploration to yawnsome extremes. While Prog's theatrical side was demonstrated brilliantly by Genesis, Rick Wakeman's <u>The Myths And Legends Of King Arthur And The Knights Of The Round Table</u> (1975) provoked few complimentary first-night reviews. Save for stubborn types like Hawkwind and Gong, Prog was taken aback by Punk in 1977. But it still haunts the earth in the stadium-filling likes of Pink Floyd, the wilful misery of Radiohead and the youthful widdling of Mogwai.

WHERE UK

WHEN Late 60s–

WHO Arthur Brown <u>The Crazy World Of...</u> (1968), Brainticket <u>Celestial Ocean</u> (1972), The Enid <u>In The Region Of The Summer Stars</u> (1984), Mogwai <u>Young Team</u> (1997)

PROPELLERHEADS

WHO General racket **Alex Gifford** (b. 29 Dec 1963), drums/sk8ing/additional general racket **Will White** (b. 16 May 1973)

WHEN 1994–

WHERE Bath, England

WHAT Hammond-fuelled Hip Hop and humour

When Prodigy and The Chemical Brothers made it OK for Rock fans to like Dance, the floodgates opened. Bentley Rhythm Ace, Death In Vegas and Daft Punk stopped being white boys with Hip Hop fixations and became the coolest names to drop.

More commercially successful than most, Propellerheads secured a head start when their 1996 debut 'Dive' soundtracked an Adidas ad campaign. However, it was that year's follow up –

the witty club staple 'Take California' – that turned the spotlight on Alex Gifford, a former electronics student whose musical CV included blowing sax with The Stranglers, and Will White, former drummer with obscure Hip Hoppers Junk Waffle.

They hatched their takeover in England's tranquil Bath, where the most Rock 'n' Roll things that happen are Peter Gabriel's World Music hoedowns. "It's the grooviest part of Britain," claimed Gifford. "Beneath that blue-rinsed exterior, you get these seething, putrid excretions of Propellerheads."

Further singles 'Spybreak' and 'Bang On' trailed the chart-busting 'On Her Majesty's Secret Service' – from David Arnold's Bond themes overhaul *Shaken And Stirred* (1997) – and 'History Repeating'. The latter featured Shirley Bassey, reprising a Dance diva role she'd first played on Yello's 1987 hit 'The Rhythm Divine'.

While remaining loyal to groovy UK label Wall Of Sound, the duo signed to Geffen subsidiary DreamWorks (alongside eels) for the USA, remixed Luscious Jackson and 808 State and unleashed their debut *Decksandrumsandrockandroll* (1998). Funkier and fresher than the Chemicals' *Dig Your Own Hole*, it also paid respect to their inspirations with cameos (sadly, on tracks on the US release only) by De La Soul and The Jungle Brothers.

surf www.wallofsound.net/props.htm

PSYCHEDELIA

WHAT A blip in Rock's evolution from early 60s Pop to early 70s singer/songwriting. Psychedelia added weird noises (seagulls on The Beatles' 'Tomorrow Never Knows' and Pink Floyd's 'Set The Controls For The Heart Of The Sun'), Lewis Carroll-esque lyrics (Jefferson Airplane's 'White Rabbit') and the Mellotron (effectively the first sampler, as used on the intro to 'Strawberry Fields Forever') to the bass/guitar/drums formula. It yielded classic singles like the Floyd's 'See Emily Play', but hardly suited albums, as anyone who's sat through The Rolling Stones' <u>Their Satanic Majesties Request</u> will testify. Psychedelia became a quaint curio when it gave way to Progressive Rock, but wove weird and wonderful magic in black music: Jimi Hendrix's trippy tours de forces, The Temptations' fuzzy masterpieces 'Psychedelic Shack' and 'Cloud Nine', George Clinton's acid-fried Funkadelic and Sly Stone's "first fusion of Psychedelia and Rhythm & Blues". From these can be traced a blazing trail to Prince – whose mid-80s madness and explosion–in–a–paint–factory image best exemplified Psychedelia's adventurous legacy.

WHERE UK, USA

WHEN 1966–

WHO The Temptations <u>Psychedelic Shack</u> (1970), Pink Floyd <u>Relics</u> (1971), The Dukes Of Stratosphear (aka XTC) <u>25 O'Clock</u> (1985), Prince & The Revolution <u>Parade</u> (1986), Various <u>Where The Pyramid Meets The Eye – A Tribute To Roky Erickson</u> (1990)

THE PSYCHEDELIC FURS

WHO Vocals **Richard Butler** (b. 5 Jun 1956, Kingston upon Thames, Surrey, England), bass **Tim Butler** (b. 7 Dec 1958, Kingston upon Thames), guitar **John Ashton** (b. 30 Nov 1957), guitar **Roger Morris**, saxophone **Duncan Kilburn**, drums **Vince Ely**

WHEN 1977–1992

WHERE London, England

WHAT Post-Punk prettiness

A session on John Peel's influential BBC Radio 1 show pulled The Psychedelic Furs from the doldrums in early 1980. Despite a CBS/Columbia contract, the band had found it hard to attract any favourable recognition but, after this nationwide exposure, their debut *Psychedelic Furs* (1980) entered the UK Top 20.

This was followed up by more memorable moments, such as 'Dumb Waiters' and 'Pretty in Pink', minor hits from *Talk Talk Talk* (1981). The Todd Rundgren-produced *Forever Now* (1982) was another minor success, but the more Dance-oriented 'Heaven' gave them their first UK Top 40 single.

Relocating to New York, the band scored their biggest hit with a re-recording of 'Pretty In Pink', taken from the soundtrack of the 1986 film of the same name (itself inspired by the original song). However, the band began to disintegrate until only the Butler brothers remained. By 1992, The Psychedelic Furs had ceased to exist. Richard Butler went on to form Love Spit Love.

surf www.geocities.com/SunsetStrip/Palms/3625/furspage.htm

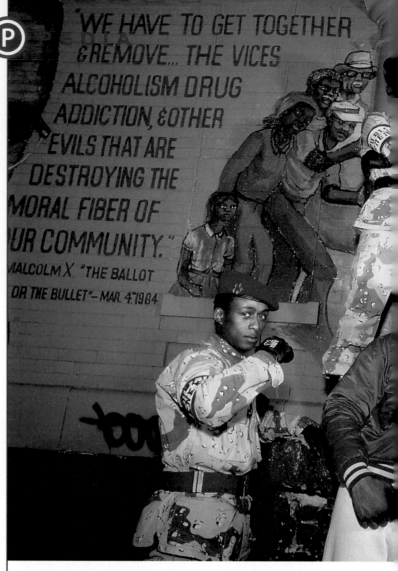

PUBLIC ENEMY

WHO Vocals **Chuck D** (b. Carlton Ridenhour, 1 Aug 1960, Long Island, New York, USA), vocals **Flavor Flav** (b. William Drayton, 16 Mar 1959, Long Island), DJ **Terminator X** (b. Norman Rogers, 25 Aug 1966, New York)

WHEN 1987–

WHERE 'Strong Island', New York, USA

WHAT The Black Panthers of Rap

Public Enemy's Rap revolution began not with a bang but a whimper. "There was no such thing as Public Enemy when I first got involved," Def Jam label boss and producer Rick Rubin told *Rolling Stone*. "There was a tape that Chuck D had made when he was a DJ at the radio station at Adelphi University... I called him every day for close to six months, telling him that we had to make records together. It got to the point where he told his wife that if I called, he wasn't in." Eventually, Chuck convened Public Enemy from a group of Long Island associates: court jester Flavor Flav, DJ Terminator X and 'Minister of Information' Professor Griff.

Yo! Bum Rush The Show (1987) sent shock waves through Rap: party vibes and mic skills were trampled under Black militancy and open threats. The flames were fanned on tour with Run DMC and The Beastie Boys; the openly racist Griff set reporters shivering and the group became indelibly linked with the fake Uzis wielded by their stage dancers Security of the First World.

In 1988, PE unleashed *It Takes A Nation Of Millions To Hold Us Back*, followed by *Fear Of A Black Planet* (1990) and *Apocalypse*

91: *The Enemy Strikes Black* (1991) – all explosive cocktails of lyrical stridency, speaker-shaking Funk and abrasive production. The latter, supervised by 'The Bomb Squad', found keen disciples not only among Rap's movers and shakers (notably Ice Cube) but also Rage Against The Machine, Prodigy and, latterly, The Chemical Brothers – Spike Lee's band of choice having implausibly acquired a vast white audience.

But after three years on top, and having replaced Griff with the equally provocative Sister Souljah, Public Enemy blinked. As they diverted to the Rock arena, touring with U2 and recording with Anthrax, a new sound swept across Rap: Dr Dre's G-Funk. PE's *Greatest Misses* (1992) and *Muse Sick-N-Hour Mess Age* (1994), though intermittently fine, sounded blustery and old-fashioned. The embattled Chuck D, sandbagged by business disputes and Flavor Flav's drug addiction, put Public Enemy on ice in 1995.

The fantastic *Autobiography Of Mistachuck* (1996), blending Curtis Mayfield-esque Soul with scornful lyrics, was the only notable result of his solo endeavours, prompting a resumption of band activities in 1998. Although Chuck mooted a "Pink Floyd meets The Chemical Brothers" style concept album called *Resurrection*, their first new release was the soundtrack to Spike Lee's 1998 movie *He Got Game*.

ReaD *Fight The Power: Rap, Race & Reality* (1997), Chuck D & Yusuf Jah

Surf www.defjam.com/artists/pe/enemy.html

PUBLIC IMAGE LTD

WHO Vocals **John Lydon** (b. 31 Jan 1956, London, England), guitar/keyboards

Keith Levene (b. England), bass **Jah Wobble** (b. John Wardle, England), drums **Jim Walker** (b. Canada)

WHEN 1978–

WHERE London, England

WHAT Johnny Rotten's post-Pistols plaything

More a corporation than a band (hence the business-like name and near-member status for financial advisor Dave Crowe), PiL was the former Johhny Rotten's reaction against the Rock 'n' Roll industry he despised. The original quartet of novice bassist Jah Wobble, ex-early Clash guitarist Keith Levene and former Fureys drummer Jim Walker owed little to the conventional Rock riffing of Lydon's old band The Sex Pistols, but made up for that with sheer originality. PiL emphasized dynamics over melody, as their debut *Public Image* (1978) showed: a messy collage of Krautrock noise with depth-charge Dub basslines by the inspired Wobble. *Metal Box* (1979) – first released as three 12" singles in a metal film can, then reissued conventionally as *Second Edition* (1980) – stretched the sound further, with two new drummers (Richard Dudanski and his replacement Martin Atkins) and a considerably darker mood which pointed the direction later taken by Joy Division on *Closer* (1980). Wobble quit after a riotous gig in New York, while Levene and Lydon were joined by 'visual organizer' Jeanette Lee for 1981's chilling *Flowers Of Romance*. PiL scored its biggest hit with 1983's enchantingly morbid 'This Is Not A Love Song', then Lydon left for New York, assembling a group of session musicians for *Live In Tokyo* (1983) and *This Is What You Want… This Is What You Get* (1984). He took another left-turn in 1985, uniting with Hip Hop god Afrika Bambaataa as Time Zone on the vicious 'World Destruction' (a forerunner of the environmental concerns to which Lydon increasingly devoted himself).

The polished *Album* (1986, also named *Compact Disc* and *Cassette* according to format) sold well, thanks to its Heavy Metal styling (including guitarist Steve Vai and Cream's Ginger Baker) and the hit 'Rise', but 1987's *Happy?* was the beginning of the end. The dull, over-produced *9* (1989) and *That What Is Not* (1992) – despite casts including John McGeogh (ex-Siouxsie & The Banshees), Lu Edmonds (ex-Damned) and Mike Joyce (ex-Smiths) – did little to improve matters. Their final years did, however, yield 1990's impeccable *The Greatest Hits… So Far*, source of the sparkly hit 'Don't Ask Me' and a more fitting home for diamonds like 1987's 'Seattle' and 1989's 'Disappointed' than *Happy?* or *9*.

Having put PiL on hold, Lydon scored his most acclaimed hit in years with 1993's 'Open Up', a partnership with UK Techno warriors Leftfield. However, his 1997 solo debut *Psycho's Path* sold woefully in the wake of The Sex Pistols' 1996 reunion.

ReaD *Rotten: No Irish, No Blacks, No Dogs* (1994), John Lydon with Kent & Keith Zimmerman

Surf home1.gte.net/rottncop/index.html

PUFF DADDY ✪

WHO b. Sean Combs, 1970, Harlem, New York, USA

WHAT *The* Rap performer/producer of the 90s

When Puff Daddy drawled "Puff rule the world" on the Puff and Ma$e hit 'Been Around The World', it sounded less like braggadocio and more like fact. Smashes by The Notorious BIG, Ma$e, Sting, MC Lyte, Faith Evans, The Lox, Mariah Carey and Puff Daddy & The Family made him *the* producer of 1997 and, once the dust has settled, possibly *the* producer of the 90s.

The conquest began when entrepreneurial student Sean 'Puffy' Combs wangled a job at hot 80s R&B label Uptown, where he talent-spotted Swing supremos Jodeci and Mary J. Blige. They made his name as a golden-gloved producer, fusing the shiniest of Soul with the hippest of Hip Hop – hence a Blige remix featuring Puffy's monster signing: The Notorious BIG.

Fired from Uptown when he complained about being passed over for promotion, Puffy launched Bad Boy Entertainment. In 1994, Craig Mack's *Project: Funk Da World* and BIG's *Ready To Die* made Bad Boy the first rival to Death Row's status as a label whose name alone was worth thousands of sales.

Death Row overlord Suge Knight hit back by blasting Puffy's self-promotion, extending an invitation to any Bad Boy acts "sick of their producer being in their videos and on their tracks". As the feud descended into trigger-happy violence, Bad Boy leapt ahead musically with the classy R&B of Faith 'Mrs BIG' Evans, the seductive Swing of Total and the homespun harmonies of 112.

As 1997 dawned, Bad Boy was unstoppable. Tupac Shakur's murder had left the Gangsta market to BIG, whose *Life After Death* had Puffy's prints all over it. The Puffy/Ma$e axis and 112

were conquering US chart peaks with, respectively, 'Can't Nobody Hold Me Down' and 'Cupid'. MC Lyte's Puffy-remodelled 'Cold Rock A Party' was rarely off European Pop radio. The producer's own *Hell Up In Harlem* was in the works.

Then BIG got shot and Puffy was in the world's face with the multi-million-selling tribute 'I'll Be Missing You'. Its sincerity was hotly debated: from the appropriateness of sampling The Police's 'Every Breath You Take' to the speed with which he had translated mourning into music. Even the legendarily nice Janet Jackson wondered, "How much pain is he really in?"

Dissent was drowned out by an awesome commercial onslaught. Puffy and his production partner Stevie J held the US No.1 for the entire summer, with 'I'll Be Missing You', BIG's colossal 'Mo Money Mo Problems' and Mariah Carey's 'Honey'. Puffy's album, grimly retitled *No Way Out*, and Ma$e's *Harlem World* blasted to the top too. Hot 97, the Rap radio station, found they could fill entire shows with his productions, mixes and associates.

The year closed with welcome hints that Puffy – who had long presented a sombre face to the world – was lightening up: a self-mockingly preposterous video for the David Bowie-based 'Been Around The World' ('Let's Dance' with new words), an admission in Ma$e's 'Feel So Good' that much of his success depended on taking "hits from the 80s" and a manic makeover of *No Way Out*'s spine-tingling 'It's All About The Benjamins' by Foo Fighter Dave Grohl. He paid back The Police with a remake of 'Roxanne', featuring Sting, Fugee Pras and a saucy sample of UTFO's Hip Hop classic 'Roxanne, Roxanne'.

Grammy awards followed in 1998, as did a hook-up with Jimmy Page for the *Godzilla* soundtrack and yet more remixes (including his own of The Jackson 5, and Goldie and Trent Reznor's of Puffy's 'Victory'). As Russell Simmons – head of Rap's one-time market-leading label Def Jam – says, "Now the real sound of the street is Puffy."

surf www.csl.mtu.edu/~dlwatenp/puffy/puffy.html

PULP ◉◉

WHO Vocals **Jarvis Cocker** (b. 19 Sep 1963, Sheffield, England), guitar **Russell Senior** (b. 18 May 1961, Sheffield), guitar **Mark Webber** (b. 14 Sep 1970, Chesterfield, Derbyshire, England), bass **Steve Mackey** (b. 10 Nov 1966, Sheffield), drums **Nick Banks** (b. 28 Jul 1965, Rotherham, Yorkshire), keyboards **Candida Doyle** (b. 25 Aug 1963, Belfast, Northern Ireland)

WHEN 1978–

WHERE Sheffield, England

WHAT Barbed, seedy slice-of-life Pop

In 1978, Jarvis Cocker, frontman, lyricist and character of distinction, started a band with schoolmates at Sheffield City Comprehensive. They named themselves Arabacus Pulp – after an obscure coffee commodity listed in the *Financial Times*. And just 17 years later, Pulp's *Different Class* topped the UK chart.

Skinny, clad in ill-assorted charity shop purchases and given to escapist fantasies about space travel, Cocker devoted himself to the band, despite years of line-up changes and a breadline lifestyle. Opportunities arose, then fizzled: in 1981, Pulp's first

"The main thing about Jarvis is his clutter. He is the skip king... I'd come home just wanting to watch the TV and the front room would look like Andy Warhol's Factory"

Steve Mackey

demo led to a session on influential BBC DJ John Peel's show. But the only tangible result was 'What Do You Say?', included on the aptly titled compilation *Your Secret's Safe With Us*. The next year, Pulp released their debut album, *It*, on the independent label Red Rhino (featuring guitarist Simon Hinkler, later of The Mission). Despite promising lyrics, *It* flopped along with Pulp's first two singles, 'My Lighthouse' and 'Everybody's Problem'.

However, in 1983, Cocker gained a long-term ally in business studies graduate Russell Senior – guitarist, violinist, book-keeper and politicizer. Among further upheavals a year later, keyboardist Candida Doyle joined, though she was to quit and return during 1986 after Cocker sacked her brother Magnus (drums) and boyfriend Pete Mansell (bass) for laddish excesses.

With stagnation threatening, London independent label Fire offered them a deal in July 1985. The first fruit was promising: a single, 'Little Girl (With Blue Eyes)'. But then Cocker tried to impress a girl by swinging from a third-floor window ledge and fell, breaking his pelvis. Recovering slowly, he often appeared on stage in a wheelchair. Worse, *Freaks* (1987), subtitled "ten stories about power, claustrophobia, suffocation and holding hands", proved too glum for most tastes.

Despairing, Cocker opted to give education another chance. Pulp – now with Nick Banks on drums – entered a long half-life. In autumn 1987, Cocker left Sheffield to study film-making at St Martin's School of Art, London. There he teamed up with fellow student Steve Mackey, also from Sheffield. Together they made short 'art' films – then shot videos for chart acts, including Tindersticks and The Aphex Twin. In 1988, Mackey joined Pulp on bass, completing a line-up which, at last, proved stable.

However, the band's career continued in desultory fashion. For three years they played only occasional gigs in Sheffield and Fire released *Separations* (1992) two years after it was recorded. Yet, somehow, they were turning the corner. The singles 'My Legendary Girlfriend' (1991) and 1992's 'O.U. (Gone Gone)', together with Cocker's on-stage instinct for cool repartee and wacky shapes, began to attract attention. Suddenly, the long-time losers were hip. In 1993, they bought their way out of the Fire deal to sign with Island and, that November, achieved their chart debut at UK No.50 with 'Lip Gloss'. Its success was promptly exploited by *Pulpintro*, a compilation of tracks from their early 90s excursion with Sheffield's Gift label.

They promoted 1994's 'Do You Remember The First Time?' (UK No.33) with a video in which celebrities described losing their virginity. Their first Island album, *His 'N' Hers*, reached UK No.9 that April (though another former label compilation, *Masters Of The Universe – Pulp On Fire 1985–86*, failed to chart). The album perfected their beguiling blend of nostalgically New Romantic music and lyrical lechery: aside from 'Do You Remember The First Time?' and 'Lip Gloss', the album bore horny highlights like 'Pink Glove' and 'Babies'.

In June 1994, when 'The Sisters EP' brought them a TV debut on *Top Of The Pops*, Cocker flashed the cameras a T-shirt declaring "I Hate Wet Wet Wet" (the group entrenched at No.1 with 'Love Is All Around'). His barbed wit made him an instant media face and *TOTP* even asked him back as guest compère.

Pulp, now including former tour manager Mark Webber on guitar, spent the first half of 1995 recording with veteran producer Chris Thomas (Roxy Music, The Sex Pistols, etc). As always, the band created the music together before Cocker added the lyrics, but this time, while they were still writing, they decided a track called 'Common People' so captured the spirit

of the time that it should be released immediately.

In June it entered the chart at No.2 and, three weeks later, playing the Glastonbury Festival as last-minute replacements for The Stone Roses, they triumphed in front of 50,000. 'Common People' emerged as a youth anthem for the post-Thatcher era. Pulp followed up with UK No.2 double A-side 'Mis-Shapes'/ 'Sorted For E's And Wizz'. The latter landed the band in trouble when a tabloid spotted that the sleeve included a cut-out 'wrap', as used by speed dealers. Unhindered, *Different Class*, released that November, went straight to UK No.1. Further success followed with 'Disco 2000', 'Something Changed' and the retrospective *Countdown 1992–1983* (all Top 10 UK hits).

So Cocker was already a full-blown star domestically when, on 19 February 1996, at the annual BRIT awards, he decided to take on Michael Jackson. As 'The King Of Pop' performed 'Earth Song' surrounded by adoring children, Cocker jumped on stage waving V-signs and wiggling his bottom at the cameras. Falsely accused of injuring a child, he was briefly arrested before being released without charge – unrepentant about his protest at Jackson portraying himself as "a Christ-like figure".

That December, Russell Senior, married with two children, left the band. At the end of a long break, having graced the *Mission Impossible* soundtrack (1996), they contributed 'We Are The Boys' to the *Velvet Goldmine* soundtrack (1998) and 'Like A Friend' to *Great Expectations* (1998). Pulp returned with the dark and gritty UK No.1 *This Is Hardcore* (1998), which was prefaced the previous November by the UK No.8 'Help The Aged'.

READ *Pulp* (1996), Martin Aston

FAN Pulp, c/o PO Box 87, Sheffield S11 8WJ, UK

SURF www.rise.co.uk/pulp

PUNK

WHAT Punk should, by its very nature, be uncategorizable: a volatile, indefinable thing. However, its origins can be traced to America's mid-60s garage bands, who made incompetent but enthusiastic stabs at post-Stones R&B. The Seeds' fuzzy classic 'Pushin' Too Hard' was the benchmark until MC5, The Stooges and The New York Dolls added jaded lyrics to the agenda in the early 70s. From there it was a short step to The Sex Pistols' seething malice and slashing guitar – a DIY destruction of traditional tunesmithery without which Rock would have sunk in musical virtuosity and lyrical vagueness. Stateside, it became New Wave – a catch-all term for acts as diverse as Television, Patti Smith and The Knack, united only by their youthful dissimilarity to The Eagles or any other contemporary mega-seller. Punk's legacy is best measured not by the success of chirpy revivalists like Green Day and Rancid, but the world-shaking impact of The Specials, Joy Division and Metallica – groups who approached Reggae, Rock and Metal in new ways that might have gone ignored had Punk not destroyed so many conventions.

WHERE USA, UK

WHEN 60s (pause) 1976's 'Summer Of Hate'–

WHO The New York Dolls <u>New York Dolls</u> (1973), The Ruts <u>The Crack</u> (1979), Misfits <u>Walk Among Us</u> (1982), Suicidal Tendencies <u>Suicidal Tendencies</u> (1983), Bad Religion <u>The Gray Race</u> (1996), NOFX <u>Heavy Petting Zoo</u> (1996)

SUZI QUATRO

WHO b. Susan Kay Quatrocchio, 3 Jun 1950, Detroit, Michigan, USA

WHAT Leather-clad Glam grrrl

Queen of Britain's Glam Rock boom, Susan Quatro transcended the limited objectives set by her management. Signed by Mickie Most – who had seen her in the Progressive girl group Cradle – she moved to England, shortened her name and hooked up with hit-makers Nicky Chinn and Mike Chapman. In an era of preening male Popsters, Quatro flaunted butch, leather-clad looks, stomping around the stage shaking her thick mane of hair.

This kid sister from Hell was an instant success and 'Can The Can' went to UK No.1 in 1973, the first of a series of gutsy hit Rockers. Eight singles made the UK Top 20, including 1974's No.1 'Devil Gate Drive'. Worldwide success followed, notably in the USA, where Quatro reached No.4 in 1978 with Chris Norman on 'Stumblin' In' from *If You Knew Suzi…* (1979). By the mid-80s, she combined music with motherhood, acting and TV presentation. Her TV career started in 1977 with a notable stint playing singer Leather Tuscadero in US TV's *Happy Days*.

Quatro still records sporadically, staying close to the chunky Rock that established her reputation, but adding a softer edge. Elsewhere, she continues to show a range of talents. A notable success was co-writing her own starring role in the 1991 play *Tallulah Who?*. Pragmatic moves and intelligence have kept Quatro in work. She generally had the ability to stand back from fame. At the height of her career she took pride in passing herself off as teenager and getting half-price cinema tickets!

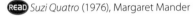
READ *Suzi Quatro* (1976), Margaret Mander

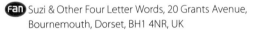
FAN Suzi & Other Four Letter Words, 20 Grants Avenue, Bournemouth, Dorset, BH1 4NR, UK

SURF www.compuserve.co.uk/homepages/sea

FINLEY QUAYE

WHO b. 25 Mar 1974, Edinburgh, Scotland

WHAT The Secret Squirrel of sunny-day Soul

When Finley Quaye won the 1998 BRIT award for Best British Male Solo Artist, he had been famous for less than a year. In 1997, he seemingly emerged from nowhere with a sunny mix of Reggae, Soul and jazzy Funk and claimed the hip Dance Pop throne previously occupied by the likes of Jamiroquai.

The son of Jazz composer Cab Quaye, the brother of noted guitarist Caleb and the uncle of Trip Hop wheezer Tricky, Quaye made his recording debut in 1995 as guest vocalist on A Guy Called Gerald's 'Finley's Rainbow', scored a solo deal with Haiku and, in late 1997, hit the UK Top 20 twice with 'Sunday Shining' and 'Even After All'. His reputation was firmly established by *Maverick A Strike*, an adventurous but accessible album released in September 1997, which sold gold less than three weeks later and led directly to BRIT victory.

However, storm clouds gathered when Tricky – with whom he collaborated on late 1997's 'Please Share My Dappy Umbrella' (also featuring Iggy Pop) – damned him on his 'Can't Freestyle'.

SURF www.finleyquaye.com/

QUEEN ⊙⊙⊙⊙⊙⊙⊙⊙⊙⊙ ✪

WHO Vocals **Freddie Mercury** (b. Faroukh Bulsara, 5 Sep 1946, Zanzibar, d. 24 Nov 1991, London, England), guitar **Brian May** (b. Brian Harold May, 19 Jul 1947, Hampton, London), bass **John Deacon** (b. 19 Aug 1951, Oadby, Leicester, England), drums **Roger Taylor** (b. Roger Meddows-Taylor, 26 Jul 1949, King's Lynn, Norfolk, England)

WHEN 1970–

WHERE London, England

WHAT Pomp Metal Rococo 'n' Roll

With masterly musicianship, a flamboyant frontman who owed as much to Liza Minnelli as Robert Plant, and music that is grandiose, elaborate and totally over the top, Queen is to Rock what the QE2 is to a rubber dinghy. "When Queen do something," as drummer Roger Taylor once put it, "we do it BIG." This philosophy, underlying the band's every move – that if something was worth doing, it was worth *over*doing – made one of the biggest, best-loved Rock bands in the world.

Guitarist Brian May and drummer Roger Taylor put together Smile in college and released one obscure single, 'Earth', in 1970. The band that would be Queen began when Smile vocalist/bassist Tim Staffell quit to join an ex-member of The Bee Gees (in the extraordinarily named Humpy Bong) and his flatmate Freddie Mercury took over. Mercury – then in a band called Wreckage – also shared a fashion clothing stall in Kensington Market with Taylor. Three bass players came and went until, after an exhaustive six months of auditions, they chose John Deacon.

The renamed Queen (Freddie's idea, of course) – instead of playing the usual club circuit – spent a year and a half perfecting their music, letting no one but closest friends hear what they were up to. In 1972, taking up a friend's offer of free studio time, they made a demo with engineers Roy Thomas Baker and John Anthony, which won them a deal with EMI. It was, admitted May, "a kind of studied approach": understandable since they were all, or had recently been, students. Not music students though (even if May made his own first guitar at the age of 16, carving it out of a 19th-century fireplace): the guitarist was actually working on a Ph.D. in astronomy (he chose Queen over an offer to work at the observatory Jodrell Bank), Taylor studied biology, Deacon had just graduated with a first-class honours degree in electronics, and Mercury was at art college, studying graphics and design.

Their self-titled debut album, which appeared in the summer of 1973, successfully blended the styles of the two biggest British Rock acts at the time: the loud, guitar-based Heavy Rock of Led Zeppelin and the melodic, theatrical Glam of David Bowie. Their first single, 'Keep Yourself Alive', failed to chart. But, within months, they were voted *Melody Maker* readers' 'Band Of The Year', having established a reputation as a spectacular live band with headlining shows in the UK and a US tour supporting Mott The Hoople (where, bizarrely, they were then hailed as Britain's answer to The New York Dolls!). Radio 1 sessions recorded in 1973 belatedly emerged as *Queen At The Beeb* (1989).

Queen's second album – Zeppelinly titled *Queen II* (1974) – was an even more splendid and unconventional state-of-the art recording. And a far bigger success: UK Top 5, 29 weeks in the chart, it included their first hit, 'Seven Seas Of Rhye' (UK No.10).

Sheer Heart Attack, released the same year, did even better, hitting UK No.2 during a 42-week chart run. Boasting two memorable hits, 'Killer Queen' and 'Now I'm Here', it was also their first real US hit. Where its predecessor had barely squeezed into the Top 50, *Sheer Heart Attack* just missed the Top 10. Queen were by now a force to be reckoned with. But it was their fourth album, *A Night At The Opera* (1975) – and, more specifically, its immortal first single – that put the band into a class of its own.

'Bohemian Rhapsody' was a mad, elaborate, totally over-the-top 6-minute epic (at a time when radio played 3-minute singles, max) – a masterpiece of May's intricate Metal guitar, Mercury's operatic vocals, layer upon lush layer of harmonies and some of the most peculiar lyrics in Rock ("Bismillah, no! We will not let you go…", etc). The ultimate showcase of Queen's adventurous musicianship and long-time producer Roy Thomas Baker's recording skills, this astonishing and unique single spent nine weeks on top of the UK chart, won the Ivor Novello award for best song of the year and later tied with Procol Harum's 'A Whiter Shade Of Pale' at the BRIT awards for best single of the past 25 years. If that wasn't enough, its innovative video, which stood in for them on *Top Of The Pops* while they were off on tour, has been credited as the first real Rock video as conceptual art form, and the forerunner of MTV.

Meanwhile, *A Night At The Opera*, reputedly one of the most expensive albums ever made, topped the UK chart, reached US No.4 and was a huge hit in Japan, where Queen's tours had established a fanatical audience. *A Day At The Races* (1976) – home of the hits 'Tie Your Mother Down' and 'Somebody To Love' – was as bombastic and compelling as its predecessor, and made Top5 chart positions both sides of the Atlantic.

In the late summer of 1976, Queen played a free concert in London's Hyde Park and a record-breaking 150,000 fans showed up. A large Queen crowd in action was an amazing sight to see: total synchronicity, everyone knowing their words and parts and singing them in perfect time as Freddie strode – or flew – across the stage, raising his arms to heaven. As the band's popularity soared, their critical acclaim sank, and the Rock press loathed them. But their audience adored them, following them along an extravagant and ever-changing musical path that encompassed Heavy Metal, Pomp Rock, Rockabilly, Disco, Sci-Fi soundtracks, opera and Pop.

In 1977 – the year the band became tax exiles – they issued *News Of The World* and the anthemic double A-side 'We Are The Champions'/'We Will Rock You' and embarked upon an even more excessive world tour, with a stage set featuring a massive 5,000-lb crown measuring 54 ft x 26 ft in celebration of the other British Queen, Elizabeth's, Jubilee. The band saw the decade out with the ambitious *Jazz* (1978) – with material ranging from searing Heavy Metal to chart-bound, sing-along ballads – and *Live Killers* (1979), which ably documented Queen's amazingly accomplished, diverse and hit-filled 70s period.

Queen entered the 80s somewhat changed. Their first album of the decade, *The Game* (1980), was more Pop than Rock – the guitars turned way down – and more playful than pompous, its music ranging from Disco ('Another One Bites The Dust') to Rockabilly ('Crazy Little Thing Called Love', penned by Freddie while taking a bath). It was the first record they'd made without producer Roy Thomas Baker (now replaced by engineer Mack). It was also their then biggest seller, logging five weeks at US No.1. Their soundtrack for the daft movie *Flash Gordon* (1980) was another (though less deserved) success. *Hot Space* (1981) –

"Roger is the most extreme in **extravagance** and the Rock 'n' Roll lifestyle...

Freddie is a mystery...

John can be incredibly considerate and inexplicably rude...

I'm the most pig-headed"
Brian May

considered by most fans to be one of Queen's weakest albums – continued Mercury's flirtation with Funk and Disco, although it did bring the UK No.1 'Under Pressure', an elegant duet with David Bowie. *Greatest Hits* (1981) was another UK No.1, and went on to spend a mind-boggling 312 weeks in the charts.

After two years of solid touring, Queen decided to take a year-long sabbatical, and the members set to work on a slew of solo ventures including Taylor's *Fun In Space* (1981) and *Strange Frontier* (1984) and May's *Star Fleet Project* (1983), recorded in Los Angeles with famous friends including guitarist Eddie Van Halen.

The sum was evidently greater than the parts and, in 1984, back they came with the massive hit *The Works* (1984): an engaging mishmash of musical styles, from Synth Pop (the hit 'Radio Ga Ga') to Hard Rock ('Hammer To Fall'), Rock 'n' Roll ('Man On The Prowl') to Pop ('I Want To Break Free': who could forget the infamous cross-dressing video?).

Meanwhile, unbelievably, their shows got bigger and more flamboyant: from Brazil's Rock In Rio festival (where the church accused them of corrupting the nation's youth) to South Africa's Sun City (landing them on the United Nations' cultural blacklist) – and, in July 1985, Live Aid, where their performance was acclaimed by even the sneering British Rock press as the highlight of the event. As organizer Bob Geldof said afterwards,

"It was the perfect stage for Freddie. He could ponce about in front of the whole world!"

And the whole world loved it. Queen's popularity soared to ever greater heights, even as the frequency of group albums diminished as the band continued to dabble in extra-curricular activities. Mercury's solo work was among the most attractive and successful: the album *Mr Bad Guy* (1985) and 'Barcelona', a duet with opera star Montserrat Caballé sung to launch the Spanish city's bid for the Olympic Games. There were more movie soundtracks – some worked on individually, some as a band: 'Love Kills' (1984), for Giorgio Moroder's new soundtrack to Fritz Lang's *Metropolis*, was followed by 1985's 'Foolin' Around' for *Teachers* and 'One Vision' for *Iron Eagle*, and 1986's 'No Turning Back' for *Biggles* and 'A Kind of Magic and 'A Dozen Red Roses For My Darling' for *Highlander*, the last two resulting in 1986's album *A Kind Of Magic*. The latter prompted a colossal stadium tour, climaxing with what turned out to be their final concert, at Knebworth in August 1986. Another fine live album, *Live Magic*, was released at the end of the year.

During another sabbatical, Taylor convened The Cross for the underbought *Shove It* (1988) and *Mad, Bad And Dangerous To Know* (1990). Around this time, rumours were already circulating about the state of Mercury's health. The long wait for a new

348

album didn't help. When *The Miracle* finally appeared in 1989, going straight to UK No.1, its 'party-animal' content seemed to go out of its way to maintain all was well. And Freddie and the band continued to maintain all was well. Only days before his death, two years later, was it confirmed that Mercury had AIDS.

In 1990, after receiving the BPI Award for Outstanding Contribution To British Music, Queen went to Montreux to record a new album. *Innuendo* (1991) – an excellent, grandiose, artistically vital record – was a real return to glory. The title track – a 6-minute epic reminiscent of 'Bohemian Rhapsody' – hit the top of the UK charts in its first week of release; so did the album; so did *Greatest Hits II* (1991). The latter was revamped Stateside as *Classic Queen* (1992) – which, thanks to the use of 'Bohemian Rhapsody' (reissued for a US No.2) in *Wayne's World*, became their biggest US seller. It was a wonderful year for Queen – until, in November, their frontman died of complications from AIDS. Freddie Mercury was buried in a Zoroastrian ceremony – a faith that, aptly, denounces celibacy and declares that it's a man's duty to be happy, a philosophy Mercury firmly embraced in one of his final songs, 'The Show Must Go On'.

The band's statement on their vocalist's death read in part: "We have lost the greatest and most beloved member of our family… As soon as we are able to we would like to celebrate his life in the style to which he was accustomed". Which they did with 1992's 'A Concert For Life'. The massive memorial to Freddie attracted impressive and varied participants – all avowed Queen fans – including Liz Taylor, David Bowie, Guns N' Roses, Bob Geldof, Elton John, Metallica, George Michael, Liza Minnelli and Spinal Tap. Performed in front of an audience of 70,000 and broadcast on worldwide TV, the considerable proceeds of the tribute concert – as with the re-release of 'Bohemian Rhapsody', which again topped the UK chart – went to AIDS charities.

For the rest of the year, nostalgia guaranteed that Queen oldies clogged the charts: *Greatest Hits* (1981) went Top 10 again, as did 1992's *Live At Wembley 86*, with Mercury's 'Barcelona' and *The Freddie Mercury Album* and Brian May's solo *Back To The Light* (all 1992) close behind. Later solo efforts included Taylor's *Happiness?* and May's UK No.20 *Live At The Brixton Academy* (both 1994). Although they have never officially broken up, Queen died with Freddie Mercury. Despite rumours that George Michael might step into his shoes – Michael's performance with Queen at 'A Concert For Life' resulted in a No.1 EP, 'Five Live' (1993) – Freddie Mercury, with his camp, heroic stage presence and unique, magnificent voice, was irreplaceable. So the announcement of a new Queen album four years after his death came as something of a shock. The previously unreleased material

on *Made In Heaven* (1995) – "dedicated to the immortal spirit of Freddie Mercury" – was actually made in Switzerland, during Mercury's final frantic burst of activity during the *Innuendo* sessions. It was worked on and added to by his colleagues, 'Free As A Bird'-style, when they finally felt up to the task.

Though there is nothing on this album quite as magnificent as on *Innuendo*, its overall mood is remarkably cheerful, although its slower, contemplative pieces are terribly poignant in the light of what we now know he was going through. In 'Too Much Love Will Kill You', for example, he sings, "I'm just the shadow of the man I used to be/It seems like there's no way out of this for me". The last song Mercury recorded was 'Mother Love'; the band added, as a coda, part of a song Freddie had recorded and released in 1973 – just before Queen's first single – under the pseudonym Larry Lurex. Its release coincided with a slew of Queen relics: a two-hour video (*We Are The Champions*), two TV specials, a computer game and *The Ultimate Queen Collection*, a limited boxed set of all of Queen's albums in a wall-mounted cabinet with a ghostly hologram of Freddie on the front.

The band rose again in 1997 with heavy hits set *Queen Rocks*, including 'No One But You (Only The Good Die Young)', the first new track recorded by May, Deacon and Taylor since 1991.

(READ) *Queen: As It Began* (1993), Jacky Gunn & Jim Jenkins

(FAN) The Official International Queen Fan Club, The Old Bakehouse, 16a Barnes High Street, London SW13 9LW, UK

(SURF) queen-fip.com/

QUEENSRŸCHE

WHO Vocals **Geoff Tate** (b. 14 Jan 1959, Stuttgart, Germany), guitar **Chris DeGarmo** (b. 14 Jun 1963, Wenatchee, Washington, USA), guitar **Michael Wilton** (b. 23 Feb 1962, San Francisco, California, USA), bass **Eddie Jackson** (b. 29 Jan 1961, Robstown, Texas, USA), drums **Scott Rockenfield** (b. 15 Jun 1963, Seattle, Washington)

WHEN 1981–

WHERE Bellevue, Washington, USA

WHAT Metal's intense intelligentsia

Heavy Metal's Least Promising Start Award goes to Queensrÿche. They came from the Seattle area long before it was voguish to do so, sounded like an operatic Judas Priest and, with *The Warning* (1984), charted for just one week in the UK Top 100 – at No.100.

However, the band (who'd debuted with 1983's EP 'Queen Of The Reich') secured a loyal following with 1985's sophisticated *Rage For Order* and 1988's compellingly conceptual *Operation: Mindcrime* (hence 1991's CD/video package *Operation:livecrime*).

By *Empire* (1990), they'd ditched an ill-advised Glam image and were rewarded with the hit 'Silent Lucidity' and triple-platinum album sales. Regally aloof from prevailing trends, they finally looked like the 'Pink Floyd of Heavy Metal' that reviewers had labelled them from the start – hence platinum sales for *Promised Land* (1994) even after a lengthy lay-off. But after *Hear In The Now Frontier* (1997), the band's first ever line-up change – the exit of guitarist Chris DeGarmo – put their future in question.

(SURF) www.queensryche.com/

HARVEY GOLDSMITH
PROUDLY
PRESENTS

QUEEN

Plus
Special Guests

KNEBWORTH PARK
STEVENAGE, HERTS
SATURDAY
9 AUGUST 1986
GATES OPEN 12 NOON
SHOW ENDS 10.30 p.m.
Subject to Licence

Tickets
V.A.T.
Day
V.A.T.

Do not bring ALCOHOL,
BOTTLES, CANS, VIDEO or
TAPE RECORDERS.

OVERNIGHT CAMPING
Car Parking Available

the park tidy. Put your litter in
ded or take it home. Thank you

R&B

WHAT Once upon a time, R&B was Rhythm 'n' Blues – a descendant of the raunchy elements of Jazz and jauntier bits of Blues. When black musicians diverted into Doo Wop and Soul in the 50s, the genre – exemplified by cuts like Elmore James' 'Dust My Broom' – was appropriated by white acts, notably The Rolling Stones and Peter Green's Fleetwood Mac. Beyond these impeccable imitations, R&B died a slow death... only to resurface as a catch-all term for the early 90s mishmash of Swing, Soul and Hip Hop, whose only connection with Rhythm 'n' Blues is that its principal practitioners are black. But amid the pleasantly poppy work of Babyface and Puff Daddy, a new generation of artists added authenticity to the genre – notably the sultry, jazz-tinged Blues of Erykah Badu.
WHERE USA
WHEN 50s–
WHO Etta James <u>At Last</u> (1961), Howlin' Wolf <u>Aka Chester Burnett</u> (1971), Esther Phillips <u>Black-Eyed Blues</u> (1973), Bobby Bland <u>Dreamer</u> (1974), Loleatta Holloway <u>Queen Of The Night</u> (1978), Ann Peebles <u>Greatest Hits</u> (1988), Erykah Badu <u>Live</u> (1997)

RADIOHEAD ⊙

WHO Vocals/guitar/keyboards **Thom Yorke** (b. 7 Oct 1968, Wellingborough, Northamptonshire, England), guitar/keyboards **Jonny Greenwood** (b. 5 Nov 1971, Oxford, England), guitar **Ed O'Brien** (b. 15 Apr 1968, Oxford), bass **Colin Greenwood** (b. 26 Jun 1969, Oxford), drums **Phil Selway** (b. 23 May 1967, Hemingford Grey, Cambridgeshire, England)

WHEN 1987–

WHERE Oxford, England

WHAT The sublime sulky smog on Pop's sunny day

Oasis and Blur brightened its corners with cheery Britpop, but Radiohead restored Indie-dom to its natural state – epic self-pity. In 1987, frontman Thom Yorke formed On A Friday with school mates Ed O'Brien and Colin Greenwood plus Phil Selway and Colin's brother Jonny – a line-up that has changed only in name.

For the first four years they played little more than occasional gigs during university vacations. But after graduation in summer 1991, they played an Oxford pub packed with A&R scouts – all

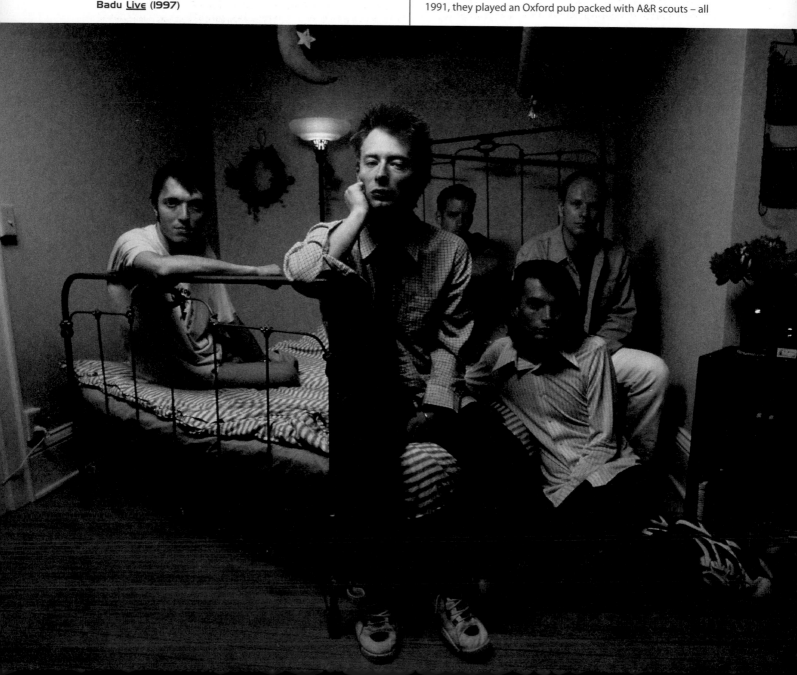

seduced by a demo. By September they'd signed to Parlophone and taken the name Radiohead from a Talking Heads song title.

The grungy 'Drill EP' and 'Creep' (both 1992) had little impact and 1993's weak 'Anyone Can Play Guitar' and *Pablo Honey* made only minor inroads into the UK chart. But they found respite from this indifference in the USA, which flipped for 'Creep' – perfect for self-loathing slackers with just the right amount of anguish and noise (especially the shotgun-like blast in the bridge). Its success carried *Pablo Honey* to a million US sales. When a UK re-release of 'Creep' reached No.7, Radiohead found themselves both lauded and trapped on the American promotional circuit.

Bemused by acclaim for an album even they thought patchy, Radiohead spent 1994 in seclusion – save for a couple of short UK tours and shows at the Glastonbury and Reading festivals. Their only release that year was the searing 'My Iron Lung' EP.

Introduced by the delicate 'High And Dry' (UK No.17), *The Bends* came out in March 1995 to swooning reviews for its blend of Queen-esque power chords, epic balladry and gut-wrenching guitars. A long chart occupancy followed (UK No.6/US No.88), boosted by the UK hits 'Fake Plastic Trees', 'Street Spirit (Fade Out)' and 'Just' (an MTV hit in America thanks to its bewildering video of a man lying on a pavement).

When Radiohead supported REM in July 1995, Yorke became friends with Michael Stipe, one of his heroes. In September, Yorke helped instigate, with Brian Eno, an album, recorded and released within five days to benefit the War Child charity's work in Bosnia. Radiohead's epic 'Lucky' was a highlight of the resultant *Help!*. The band toured through to the following summer, including US support slots with Soul Asylum and Alanis Morissette (who took to covering 'Fake Plastic Trees'). Then, after Yorke and Jonny Greenwood's work on Stipe's Glam Rock movie soundtrack *Velvet Goldmine*, they prepared their next album.

Likened by O'Brien to a "troubled Phil Spector", *OK Computer* (1997) was recorded in an eerie old mansion owned by actress Jane Seymour. One influence on its technological symphonies and bile-packed lyrics was Pink Floyd – confirmed when Yorke (with US Country kickers Sparklehorse) covered Floyd's 'Wish You Were Here' for EMI's centenary set *Come Again* (1997). The album was hailed as a *Dark Side Of The Moon* for the 90s – yet for all its roots in Rock tradition, was distinguished from the similarly retrogressive *Urban Hymns* (The Verve) and *Be Here Now* (Oasis) by inspiration and ambition.

Trailed by the bitter and twisted 'Paranoid Android', *OK Computer* made UK No.1 and US No.21. Though Yorke tested even admirers' patience by becoming the self-obsessed whinger his lyrics suggested, Radiohead scored one victory after another: a breathtakingly brilliant show at the 1996 Glastonbury festival, UK hits with 'Karma Police' and 'No Surprises', most sentient beings' 'Album of the Year', 'Band of the Year' in *Spin* and *Rolling Stone*, No.1 in *Q* readers' 'Best 100 Albums of All Time'.

Yorke used his new-found celebrity to give a leg-up to Indie hopefuls Drugstore (contributing vocals to 'El President', released in 1998), while Radiohead collaborated with Massive Attack, who had long mooted an entire remix of *OK Computer*.

(ʀᴇᴀᴅ) *Radiohead: Coming Up For Air* (1997), Steve Malins

(ꜰᴀɴ) W.A.S.T.E. Correspondence, PO Box 322, Oxford, OX4 1EY, UK

(ꜱᴜʀꜰ) www.radiohead.co.uk

GERRY RAFFERTY ✪

WHO b. 16 Apr 1947, Paisley, Strathclyde, Scotland

WHAT Reclusive Rock legend

Despite his obsessive anonymity, Gerry Rafferty loomed large over 70s Rock. After stints in Scottish combos The Mavericks and The Humblebums (with comedian Billy Connolly), he went solo with *Can I Have My Money Back?* (1971), then joined former Maverick Joe Egan in the folky Stealers Wheel. Their self-titled 1973 debut, helmed by the legendary Leiber & Stoller, included the monster hit 'Stuck In The Middle With You'. But *Ferguslie Park* (1974) and *Right Or Wrong* (1975) were subject to ye olde law of diminishing returns. Management wrangles, bickering and Rafferty's dislike of touring finally saw Stealers Wheel off.

He returned triumphant with 1978's lavish US No.1 *City To City* and 'Baker Street' – official home of Rock's greatest sax break by Raphael Ravenscroft. Despite *City To City*'s US success, Rafferty declined to tour there; a regrettable decision, considering *Night Owl*'s (1979) lowly US No.29 position. *Snakes And Ladders* (1980) and *Sleepwalking* (1982) plummeted similarly, prompting a six-year hiatus, during which he produced The Proclaimers.

With his profile at an all-time low, Rafferty was as surprised as everyone else when 'Stuck In The Middle With You' was included in Quentin Tarantino's *Reservoir Dogs* (1991) and ugly Popsters Undercover's house-ified take on 'Baker Street' made the UK Top 10 in 1992. Adding to Rafferty's transformation from forgotten Folkster into retro cult star, Foo Fighters faithfully covered 'Baker Street' for the EMI centenary album *Come Again* (1997).

(ꜱᴜʀꜰ) www.redstone–tech.cm/gerry/discog.htm

RAGE AGAINST THE MACHINE ✪

WHO Vocals **Zack De La Rocha** (b. 1970, Long Beach, California, USA), guitar **Tom Morello** (b. 1964, New York City, New York, USA), bass **Timmy C** (b. Tim Commerford), drums **Bradley Wilk** (b. 1968, Portland, Oregon, USA)

WHEN 1992–

WHERE Los Angeles, California, USA

WHAT Rap, Rock, REVOLUTION!

As Public Enemy petered out, four Californians with impeccable anti-establishment credentials took over. Tom Morello (son of a Kenyan guerrilla, nephew of Kenyan president Jomo Kenyatta), Zach De La Rocha (son of political artist Beto De La Rocha), Timmy C and Brad Wilk (well, he drummed in a band with Eddie Vedder) became Rage Against The Machine: Rap-flavoured Rock revolutionaries with like, y'know, a political message.

In the post-Grunge climate of loud shouting and seriousness, they flourished; having made waves with an eponymous demo, they signed to the suspiciously corporate Epic. The blisteringly brilliant 'Bullet In The Head', 'Killing In The Name' and 'Bombtrack' trailed giant-selling debut album *Rage Against The Machine* (1993), while their message – which seemed to be the rather vague 'Fuck you I won't do what you tell me' from 'Killing In The Name' – was hammered home by support for causes like FAIR (Fairness and Accuracy In Reporting), Rock For Choice and

Refuse & Resist. On 1993's Lollapalooza, they memorably appeared nude, gagged and silent, as an anti-censorship protest.

Rage's powder-keg tenseness was blamed for the long silence which followed. Amid split rumours, they returned in 1996 with the hit 'Bulls On Parade' and the US No.1 *Evil Empire*. They also busied themselves with more Rock/Rap crossover shenanigans, like an unreleased Snoop Doggy Dogg collaboration, a tour with Wu-Tang Clan, Morello's hook-up with Prodigy for the *Spawn* soundtrack (1997) and with Perry Farrell in Gobbelee and a full-blown Rage effort for the *Godzilla* (1998) soundtrack.

 www.vii.com/~uprising/rage/main.htm

RAINBOW

WHO Guitar **Ritchie Blackmore** (b.14 Apr 1945, Weston-super-Mare, Somerset, England) plus a cast of thousands

WHEN 1975–

WHERE London/Los Angeles

WHAT Dramatic, Classically-influenced Hard Rock

Quitting Deep Purple in 1975, Ritchie Blackmore hired former US support band Elf – led by Ronnie James Dio – to work on songs (like 'Black Sheep Of The Family') that Purple had rejected. Elf (bar unwanted guitarist Martin Birch) soon morphed into Blackmore's Rainbow. Their debut, *Ritchie Blackmore's Rainbow* (1975), was a successful fusion of Blackmore's Classical Metal tendencies and Dio's dramatic delivery. It reached UK No.11, but was not a great album. The second, *Rising* (1976), was. This medieval Metal masterpiece (which also made No.11) featured a new line-up – Dio and Blackmore, joined by Jimmy Bain, Cozy Powell and Tony Carey: the first of a constant shuffling of members that would characterize Rainbow's chequered history.

The perfectionist Blackmore pulled his classic Mark II line-up apart within a year. Bain was replaced by Mark Clarke (ex-Uriah Heep). Then an album was scrapped, Clarke with it – and Carey too, as Blackmore decided to issue *On Stage* (1977) instead. Bob Daisley and David Stone were recruited and the band relocated to the States. But the relationship between Dio and Blackmore – reminiscent of Blackmore and Gillan in Deep Purple – cracked. After 1978's critically and commercially successful *Long Live Rock 'N' Roll*, Dio was out (resurfacing in Black Sabbath) and so was everyone else, Cozy Powell excepted – the legendary drummer lasted until 1980 (when he was succeeded by Bobby Rondinelli) and died in a car crash 18 years later near Bristol, England.

Graham Bonnet, ex-Marbles, was Dio's replacement – for one album, anyway. *Down To Earth* (1979) featured former Deep Purple colleague Roger Glover on bass; Blackmore had also tried, unsuccessfully, to nab Purple vocalist Ian Gillan. Its mainstream sound produced two UK Top 10 hits: a cover of Russ Ballard's 'Since You've Been Gone' and Blackmore/Glover's 'All Night Long'.

By 1980, Brits Bonnet and Powell were out and new members Joe Lynn Turner and Bobby Rondinelli brought an American bias. The commercially oriented *Difficult To Cure* (1981) brought Rainbow's first real US success and a UK hit with another Russ Ballard song, 'I Surrender'. At its populist zenith, if critical low point, Blackmore unveiled a new line-up (Dave Rosenthal replacing Airey) on *Straight Between The Eyes* (1982) – a creative comeback and transatlantic hit. Better still was 1983's *Bent Out Of Shape* with *another* new line-up: Rondinelli out, Chuck Burgi in.

In 1984, Deep Purple reunited, Blackmore along with it, and Rainbow disbanded after a final Japanese show where Ritchie performed Beethoven's *Ninth Symphony* with an orchestra. The posthumous *Finyl Vinyl* (1986) covered Rainbow's extensive line-ups and rarities. But Blackmore's contentment with Purple was not to last. Quitting in 1994, the guitarist made his first attempt to resurrect Rainbow with a patchy comeback album, *Stranger In All Of Us* (1995), featuring new vocalist Dougie White.

ⓇEAD *Rainbow* (1981), Peter Makowski

Ⓢurf www.kuai.se\ hallebro\rainbow\

BONNIE RAITT ✪ ✪

WHO b. 8 Nov 1949, Burbank, California, USA

WHAT Always big-hearted, lately big-time, Blues Rocker

The daughter of 50s Broadway musical star John Raitt, from 1967 Bonnie Raitt was distracted from her African studies by the Blues. Playing the New England coffee-house circuit, she learned from manager Dick Waterman's veteran clients John Hurt, Fred McDowell and Sippie Wallace, developing her heart-felt vocal style and much admired slide guitar skills.

Of her nine albums between 1971 and 1986, 1977's *Sweet Forgiveness* was most successful. Her emphasis shifted from Blues and R&B covers of such artists as Robert Johnson to more mainstream material by the likes of Jackson Browne and Robert Palmer. But, struggling with drink and drug addictions, *Nine Lives* (1986) was a letdown, artistically and commercially.

She recovered with *Nick Of Time* (1989). It made US No.1 and won three Grammys, including Album Of The Year. Raitt picked up a fourth, Best Traditional Blues Recording, for 'I'm In The Mood', a duet with John Lee Hooker from his *The Healer* (1989). "Whew boy, she cooked the cake," Hooker told *Rolling Stone*. "She's so deep into the Blues she'll never get out alive."

The upturn was confirmed by two more blockbusters, 1991's *Luck Of The Draw* (three more Grammys) and 1994's *Longing In Their Hearts* (US No.1, Grammy for Best Pop Album). The latter's 'I Can't Make You Love Me' was covered by Prince (who judged it "Bonnie'samericantreasure") and George Michael. *Fundamental* (1998) included songs by Los Lobos, Willie Dixon and John Hiatt. Raitt's campaigning spirit saw her supporting Musicians United For Safe Energy, Farm Aid and the Rhythm & Blues Foundation.

ⓇEAD *Just In The Nick Of Time* (1996), Mark Bego

RAMONES

WHO Vocals **Joey Ramone** (b. Jeffrey Hyman, 19 May 1951, Forest Hills, New York, USA), guitar **Johnny Ramone** (b. John Cummings, 8 Oct 1951, Long Island, New York), bass **Dee Dee Ramone** (b. Douglas Colvin, 18 Sep 1952, Fort Lee, Virginia, USA), drums **Tommy Ramone** (b. Tom Erdelyi, 29 Jan 1952, Budapest, Hungary)

WHEN 1974–1996

WHERE New York City, New York, USA

WHAT Punk's Rolling Stones

Joey, Johnny, Dee Dee and Tommy left high school in New York's middle-class Forest Hills, adopted the same surname and drifted to New York City, where a scene was forming at a seedy Bowery bar called CBGB. There, they practised their newly learned three chords in front of peers like Patti Smith, Television's Tom Verlaine, The Voidoids' Richard Hell, Blondie and Talking Heads.

After their first gig at a party, the Ramones began a residency at CBGB in 1974 and signed to Sire in 1975. Their trademarks – brevity, speed, rudimentary musicianship and Dee Dee's barking intro of "1-2-3-4!" – were stamped all over *Ramones* (1976). They were hailed as Punk visionaries, though Joey Ramone described their sound as "sick bubblegum music", which continued on *Ramones Leave Home* (1977). Tommy left after *Rocket To Russia* (1977), but became their producer. His replacement, ex-Voidoid Marc Bell, left in 1983 and returned in 1987.

As they tried to pen songs that broke their usual 2¹/₂ minutes, *Road To Ruin* (1978) was their first album to last more than half an hour. While its US chart placing was mediocre, it made UK No.32. They appeared in Roger Corman's 1979 movie *Rock 'N' Roll High School*, their soundtrack cuts remixed by Phil Spector. Spector also produced 1980's *End Of The Century*, but the band regarded it as their worst album. It did, however, yield their biggest UK hit, an endearingly dopey cover of The Ronettes' 'Baby I Love You'.

Relentless touring was punctuated by the return-to-form *Pleasant Dreams* (1981), *Subterranean Jungle* (1983), *Too Tough To Die* (1984), *Animal Boy* (1986), *Halfway To Sanity* (1987), the best-of *Ramonesmania* (1988) and *Brain Drain* (1989). Along the way, self-mocking titles like 'Teenage Lobotomy', 'Pinhead' and 'Cretin Bop' were joined by the acerbically aware 'The KKK Took My Baby Away' and 'Bonzo Goes To Bitburg'. The decade was book-ended by the splendid *It's Alive* (1979) and *Loco Live* (1991), both testaments to their compellingly crazed on-stage onslaught.

Though the drumstool was variously occupied by Ricky Ramone (née The Velveteens' Richard Beau) and former Blondie basher Clem Burke, the front-line remained constant until 1989 when Dee Dee left to flirt disastrously with Rap as Dee Dee King. He was replaced by the considerably younger CJ Ramone (Christopher Joseph Ward), who had just left the US Marines.

Eighteen albums (including 1992's *Mondo Bizarro* and 1993's *Acid Eaters*) and 21 years after their formation, their retirement was announced in 1995 with *Adios Amigos*. A series of farewell tours culminated in 1996's Lollapalooza. Final shows in New York and Hollywood were filmed as a documentary, *We're Outta Here*, which mixed live footage with interviews and early material.

READ *The Ramones: An American Band* (1993), Jim Bessman

SURF radioactive.net:80/radioactive/BANDS/RAMONES/

SHABBA RANKS

WHO b. Rexton Gordon, 17 Jan 1966, St Ann's Parish, Jamaica

WHAT Reggae's Mr Lover Man

Shabba Ranks served the sound-system apprenticeship of all Reggae Rappers before his 1985 debut 'Heat Under Sufferer's Feet', recorded under the name Co Pilot, flopped. However, 1986 brought success as Shabba Ranks with *Original Fresh*. Battling for supremacy in Jamaica, Shabba specialized in 'slackness', the lewd style that culminated in his 1989 anthem, 'Wicked In Bed'.

Hints of broader fame arrived with the singles 'Who She Love' and 'Pirates' Anthem', made with singers Cocoa Tea and Home T4, and 'Mr Loverman', a duet with Deborahe Glasgow.

Shabbamania at a performance in London's Tower Records and a shooting at one of his gigs made it clear he was too big for the Reggae market. He signed to Epic in 1991, scoring high with *As Raw As Ever*'s 'Housecall' (a duet with Maxi Priest), and a revamped 'Mr Loverman', with the beefy Deborahe Glasgow cynically replaced by the more marketable Chevelle Franklin.

Shabba seemed unstoppable. Then he defended the right of rival Buju Banton to attack homosexuals on his 'Boom Bye Bye' single, resulting in an altercation with the presenter of British TV's *The Word*. Shabba's career stalled in the UK. There was also a paternity lawsuit in Jamaica for the man who recorded 'Best Baby Father'. Shabba wisely returned to his roots and, although recently less active, remains a respected talent in Jamaica.

RAP

WHAT "Rap is skillz," says Ice Cube. "Everybody wanna flex they skillz. Everybody wanna say they rhyme to have all the other rappers say, 'Damn, I woulda never thought of that.'" Rap sprang from the political poetry of Gil Scott-Heron and The Last Poets (a tradition continued by KRS-I and Dana Bryant) and the self-aggrandizing DJs at Hip Hop block parties (hence The Sugarhill Gang's ludicrous but pioneering 1979 classic 'Rapper's Delight'). It assumed the form we recognize today in 1982 with Grandmaster Flash & Melle Mel's monumental 'The Message', a lyrical snapshot of America's underbelly with a seductively stark backbeat. Run DMC added arrogance, turned up the drums and set a sonic revolution in motion that led to the nerve-shredding noise of Public Enemy. When Gangsta and G-Funk swept Rap, politics and sonic innovation took a back seat, but the complex wordplay and sparse production of Bone Thugs-N-Harmony, Wu-Tang Clan and Mobb Deep kept Rap's original values alive amid Puff Daddy's poppier onslaught.

WHERE USA

WHEN Late 70s–

WHO The Watts Prophets <u>Rappin' Black In A White Man's World</u> (1971), EPMD <u>Strictly Business</u> (1988), Public Enemy <u>Fear Of A Black Planet</u> (1988), Mobb Deep <u>The Infamous</u> (1995), Missy 'Misdemeanour' Elliot <u>Supa Dupa Fly</u> (1997)

The Radio Corporation of America (RCA) entered the record business in 1929 by purchasing the Victor Talking Machine company, established in 1901 by Emile Berliner, inventor of the gramophone. Using the name RCA Victor, they incorporated the Dog & Trumpet logo, acquired from the British HMV company, before reverting to simply RCA.

The 30s saw RCA at the forefront of Jazz with Fats Waller, Benny Goodman, Glenn Miller and Tommy Dorsey, followed by Pop singers Perry Como, Dinah Shore and Eddie Fisher alongside the famous tenor Mario Lanza. Fortunes floundered in the 50s until the arrival of Elvis Presley, who dominated the label for years. Dolly Parton, Harry Nilsson, Jefferson Airplane, Lou Reed, Hall & Oates and John Denver were added to the roster, followed by British signings The Sweet, David Bowie, Eurythmics and Bucks Fizz before the company's acquisition by the German media company Bertelsmann in 1986.

The 90s saw RCA boasting US signings The Dave Matthews Band, ZZ Top, The Verve Pipe and, via the label's venture with Loud Records, Wu-Tang Clan, alongside the UK's Take That, M People and Gary Barlow.

RCA

CHRIS REA ⊙⊙

WHO b. 4 Mar 1951, Middlesbrough, England

WHAT Gravel-voiced guitar stalwart

In 1973, Rea quit his jobs – one in his family's ice-cream parlour, and the other labouring. Inspired by Joe Walsh and Ry Cooder, he joined Middlesbrough group Magdalene when singer David

Coverdale left to join Deep Purple. They changed their name to The Beautiful Losers, released a one-off single ('So Much Love', 1974) and went on to win *Melody Maker*'s Best Newcomers of 1975. When nothing came of the award however, among an ever-changing line-up, a frustrated Rea left to start a solo career.

He signed to Magnet, guested on *The Hank Marvin Guitar Syndicate* (1977) and issued 'Fool (If You Think It's Over)' in 1978, later covered by Elkie Brooks. His debut *Whatever Happened To Benny Santini?* (1978) refers to Magnet's intention to rechristen the unglamorous Rea. Rea was uncomfortable with that, and the 'Americanization' of his songs by producer Gus Dudgeon. In the post-Punk UK climate, Rea was seen as MOR. He badly needed remarketing, as the difficult early 80s proved. He turned down a US tour to concentrate on building a British following, performed at the Great British Music Festival and recorded *Deltics* (1979). Despite spending the next two years touring, *Tennis* (1980), *Chris Rea* (1982) and *Water Sign* (1983) crashed and burned, and by 1983 Rea was "at rock bottom" and "ready to give up". His label felt the same, but Rea restarted his band "like a family business" and toured tirelessly, establishing a following in Europe, though still stymied by cult status at home. *Wired To The Moon* (1984) was a turning point, reaching the comparative dizzy heights of UK No.35. Similarly, the consistent airplay and consequent success of 'Stainsby Girls', taken from *Shamrock Diaries* (1985), reaffirmed his reputation and boosted album sales. By the release of *On The Beach* (1986), and the laid-back style of the title track (with a 24-week chart run), Rea was a star. The single had a second outing in 1988 when it was remixed and re-released as the ghastly 'On The Beach Summer '88', Rea's first single for WEA.

'Let's Dance' (1987) – later reworked with Middlesbrough football team and, bizarrely, comedian Bob Mortimer – was his biggest hit. It came from *Dancing With Strangers* (1987) – kept from the top spot only by Michael Jackson's *Bad*. The best-of *New Light Through Old Windows* (1988) became a chart mainstay.

However, it was *Road To Hell* (1989), a UK No.1, that really put Rea on the map. Its title track – inspired by the perpetually unfinished M25 motorway – struck a chord with commuters everywhere. Rea then guested on Band Aid II's 'Do They Know It's Christmas' (1989). The grizzly 'Tell Me There's A Heaven' (1990) – about child abuse – was only a momentary lapse in success.

The 90s saw him consistently high in the UK chart: *Auberge* (1991) reached No.1 and 1992's *God's Great Banana Skin*, Elton John's 1993 *Duets* (starring Rea on 'If You Were Me') and *The Best Of Chris Rea* (1994) all made the Top 5. In 1993, Rea raced in the British Touring Car Championship to promote *Espresso Logic*. The album was better than his racing performance, where he was eliminated after the first round. In 1994, dogged by ill health, he lent 'You Can Go Your Own Way' to Ford for their Probe car ad.

His long-term interest in movies led to a soundtrack for *Soft Top, Hard Shoulder* (1993) and a role in Michael Winner's *Parting Shots* (1997) as a terminally ill photographer who sets out to kill his old enemies. His movie credentials were affirmed by 1996's *La Passione*, a musical film project and quasi-soundtrack. And the music keeps coming, as evidenced by 1998's *Blue Cafe* and extracted single 'Square Peg Round Hole'.

SURF www.helsinki.fi/"wikgren/chisrea.html

Reading is the David Bowie of British festivals. Like Bowie, it's flirted with Jazz, R&B, Psychedelia, Punk, Indie and a dodgy Metal phase. It began in 1961 as the First National Jazz Festival in Richmond, Surrey. By 1964, tastes had switched to Blues and R&B, and promoters Harold and Barbara Pendleton responded with The Rolling Stones, The Yardbirds, The Who and The Pretty Things.

As Psychedelia (Cream, Pink Floyd, Arthur Brown) loomed, the festival moved to Windsor (1966, 1967), Kempton (1968) and Plumpton (1969, 1970). Now 'The National Jazz, Blues, Pop And Rock Festival', it found its titular home, Reading, in 1971 – at an old rubbish tip in the town, to be precise. Throughout the 70s, 'Reading Rocks' staged the beardy likes of Family, Traffic, Fleetwood Mac, Lindisfarne, Wishbone Ash, Van Der Graaf Generator, Curved Air, Electric Light Orchestra, The Faces, Genesis, Ten Years After, Yes and many others.

By 1977, few Punks were queuing to play Reading. But in 1978, Patti Smith, Tom Robinson, Penetration, Chelsea and Sham 69 saved it from dinosaurdom and paved the way for 1979 showings by The Cure and The Police.

But festival freaks demanded Rock! So began Reading's Metal years when it became a spiritual home for young men with denim waistcoats: UFO, Iron Maiden, Def Leppard, Black Sabbath (whose Stonehenge stage-set caught fire in 1983), Marillion, Gillan and Thin Lizzy (whose 1983 appearance was their last UK show). A late 80s fallow period (1988's headliners were Starship and Squeeze) ended in 1989, when the event was overhauled as Indie heaven, hosting New Order, Sonic Youth, The Sisters Of Mercy, Iggy Pop, The Wonder Stuff and, in 1991, a little-known band from Seattle called Nirvana.

RED HOT CHILI PEPPERS

WHO Vocals Anthony 'Antoine The Swann' Kiedis (b. 1 Sep 1962, Grand Rapids, Michigan, USA), guitar John Frusciante (b. 5 Mar 1970, New York City, New York, USA), bass Flea (b. Michael Balzary, 16 Oct 1962, Melbourne, Australia), drums Chad Smith (b. 25 Oct 1962, St Paul, Minnesota, USA)

WHEN 1983–

WHERE Los Angeles, California, USA

WHAT FunkPunkSexMagik

In a town and a time where image was everything (on the mid-80s West Coast scene, Glam Metal ruled), Red Hot Chili Peppers exuded a unique cool. Kings of the live-fast, LA skateboard-Metal scene, they were young, bratty, sexy and didn't give a damn. Their blend of Punk and Funk became a successful formula imitated by no end of late 80s/early 90s bands.

Singer Anthony Kiedis, son of actor Blackie Dammett, got his first taste of the limelight playing Sylvester Stallone's son in the movie *F.I.S.T.* He met Flea, a musical prodigy (he had a place in the Junior Philharmonic Orchestra) at Hollywood's Fairfax High School. With classsmates Hillel Slovak on guitar and Jack Irons

"What
part of life
can possibly
be bad for
a Chili
Pepper?
'oh oh! I have so much
money, oh no!'"

Henry Rollins

on drums, they formed the Garage band Anthem, which split when Flea was poached by Punk band Fear, and Slovak and Irons founded What Is This?. But fate had another idea. Club gigs under their new name led to the surprise offer of an EMI deal.

Red Hot Chili Peppers (1984) – produced by Gang Of Four guitarist Andy Gill, and featuring Kiedis and Flea with guitarist Cliff Martinez and drummer Jack Sherman – died a death. Undaunted, the Chili Peppers – with Slovak and Irons back in the fold – built a reputation as a live band. Raucous and outrageous, life on the road was one big party – an attitude they came closer to capturing on *Freaky Styley* (1985), produced by funkmaster George Clinton, and closer still on *The Uplift Mofo Party Plan* (1988) and the EP 'Abbey Road' (1988). The EP's cover parodied The Beatles' zebra-crossing photo – except the Chili Peppers were naked apart from strategically placed sports socks.

But the party turned sour when Slovak died of a heroin overdose on 25 June and Irons left – replaced by John Frusciante and Chad Smith respectively. *Mother's Milk* (1989) gave them their first MTV exposure, with a cover of Stevie Wonder's 'Higher Ground'. It was a troubled time for the band personally – Kiedis, battling drug problems, was arrested for indecent exposure and Flea and Smith were found guilty on charges of battery and sexual harassment – but their career was taking off.

By *Blood Sugar Sex Magik* (1991), it was soaring. Their first album for new label Warners, it was produced by Rick Rubin, best known for Thrash band Slayer, yet featured some of the band's first and finest ballads, like 'Under The Bridge' (reworked by All Saints in 1997). The album sold more than 3 million, but their troubles weren't over. Frusciante departed, as did his successor Arik Marshall. Marshall did, however, last long enough to appear in a 1993 episode of *The Simpsons*, in which the Chilis help to relaunch Krusty The Clown's career and are offered lyrical advice in return – Krusty: "Where you say, 'What I got you gotta get and put it in ya,' how about just, 'What I'd like is I'd like to hug and kiss ya'?". The shortest-stayed guitarist, Jessie Tobias, lasted mere weeks and later resurfaced in Alanis Morissette's live band.

Only the arrival of Dave Navarro, ex-Jane's Addiction, in 1993, brought stability. The band recorded 1995's fine *One Hot Minute* and contributed a thrilling revamp of The Ohio Players' 'Love Rollercoaster' to the *Beavis & Butt-Head Do America* soundtrack. But lengthy inactivity inevitably led to rumours of a split and – after rejoining Jane's Addiction for its 1997 reunion (where Flea kept him company) – Navarro left the Chili Peppers and teamed up with Chad Smith in the band Spread. Smith also continued with the Chilis, who welcomed back John Frusciante in 1998.

(READ) *True Men Don't Kill Coyotes* (1993), Dave Thompson

(SURF) www.unfurled.com/ultimate_artists/red_hot_chili_peppers/index.html

OTIS REDDING ⊙

WHO b. 9 Sep 1941, Dawson, Georgia, USA, d. 10 Dec 1967, Lake Monoma, Wisconsin, USA

WHAT Soul's gritty great

Credited with bringing Stax Soul to a crossover audience, Otis Redding packed an invaluable body of work into five years in the limelight. As a singer he was deeply expressive, despite a limited range; as a performer he was captivating, intense and exuded warmth; as a composer he showed an intuitive genius which carried over into very personal interpretations of other artists' material. Though many consider the last two years of his life to have been spent in artistic decline, Redding's popularity never waned: only six months before his tragic death in a plane crash, he made a triumphant appearance at 1967's Monterey Festival.

Redding began as a singer in 1958, in Macon, Georgia. He first went on the road with Little Richard's former band The Upsetters and, the same year, won a prestigious local weekly talent contest 15 consecutive times. After low-key independent releases, his career took off in 1963: given a slot at the end of a recording session for Memphis label Stax, Redding's 'These Arms of Mine' became a Top 20 R&B hit and dented the US Pop charts. The follow-up, 'That's What My Heart Needs', flopped, but his third Stax single, the ballad 'Pain In My Heart', added Redding's vocal trademark of earthy dynamism to Sam Cooke's Soul blueprint.

'Security', from *Pain In My Heart* (1964), and 'Mr Pitiful' (1965) showcased Redding's feel for upbeat Soul stomps. Backed by Stax house band Booker T & The MG's and horn section The Mar-Keys, Redding did wonders for Stax's profile.

In 1965, *The Great Otis Redding Sings Soul Ballads* was warmly received, but *Otis Blue*, also issued that year, was his masterpiece. Impressive enough were two Sam Cooke covers (Cooke died only months before), including a breathtaking version of 'Shake', plus B.B. King and William Bell songs, and a thumping reworking of The Rolling Stones' 'Satisfaction'. But the album also debuted two Redding classics: 'Respect' (promptly hijacked by Aretha Franklin to become *her* anthem) and his greatest commercial success in his lifetime, 'I've Been Loving You Too Long'.

After this peak, his ad-libs and vocal inflections began to descend into self-parody, yet Redding continued to sell. *The Soul Album* (1966), *Dictionary Of Soul* (1966) and *King And Queen* (with Carla Thomas, 1967) featured gems like 'Try A Little Tenderness', 'Fa-Fa-Fa-Fa-Fa (Sad Song)', and 'Tramp'. Over the same period, he successfully toured Europe, returning to reign at Monterey.

Having undergone throat surgery in late 1967, Redding was singing at his best. Amid frantic recording, he wrote – just days before his death – '(Sittin' On) The Dock Of The Bay'. Issued soon after his death, it hit No.1 in both the US R&B and Pop charts.

Redding's influence lasted into the 80s and 90s with De La Soul sampling the whistling from '(Sittin' On) The Dock Of The Bay' in 1989's 'Eye Know', The Black Crowes' cover of 'Hard To Handle' (1991) and the movie *The Commitments* (1991), in which a cover of 'Try A Little Tenderness' was a highlight.

(READ) *Sweet Soul Music* (1986), Peter Guralnick

(SURF) ourworld.compuserve.com/homepages/luke_the_gr8/otis_redding_main.html

LOU REED

WHO b. Louis Allen Firbank, 2 Mar 1942, Freeport, Long Island, New York, USA

WHAT Walker on the wild side and Rock transformer

By the time Lou Reed left The Velvet Underground in 1970, he'd had enough of the record industry and sought work outside the music world. Strangely, few employers were seeking a worker experienced in singing about heroin and sexual deviancy, so he returned to his old job with the underrated *Lou Reed* (1972).

The lush, R&B-influenced *Transformer* (1972), though more mainstream than Velvets' fans might have expected, fitted the Glam Rock mood of the time (it was produced by David Bowie and his guitarist Mick Ronson). 'Walk On The Wild Side' became a UK Top 10 hit, aided by British radio programmers' obliviousness to its references to transvestism and oral sex.

Reed followed up with one of the most harrowing albums in Rock history, *Berlin* (1973): a relentlessly bleak suite of songs about the abusive and ultimately fatal interaction between a trio of drug-damaged characters. Reed's appearance and public behaviour of the time supported the widely held assumption that *Berlin* was at least partly autobiographical.

The live *Rock 'n' Roll Animal*, the upbeat *Sally Can't Dance* (both 1974) and *Lou Reed Live* (1975) won back fans alienated by *Berlin*. But Reed promptly sent them all away again with the infamous *Metal Machine Music* (1975), a virtually unlistenable double album of feedback and electronic noise – melody making only momentary appearances in an hour of aural torture.

But 1976 brought Reed's gentlest album thus far, *Coney Island Baby* – though 'Kicks' offered a shot of sado-masochistic imagery. *Rock And Roll Heart* (1976) was a thin, tired-sounding effort but, on *Street Hassle* (1978), Reed regained his energy and sardonic humour, the latter on the white liberal-baiting 'I Wanna Be Black'.

After memorably castigating US critics Robert Christgau and John Rockwell on the live *Take No Prisoners* (1978), *The Bells* (1979), *Growing Up In Public* (1980) and especially *The Blue Mask* (1982) displayed more thoughtful, mature writing – although, on *The Blue Mask*, there was a generous measure of anger.

Legendary Hearts (1983), *New Sensations* (1984) and *Mistrial* (1986) were similarly disciplined, yet Reed seemed to be spreading his best ideas too thinly. A long break before *New York* (1989) helped to explain the return to excellence it represents, with Reed exploring his relationship with his home city with stripped-down music and rich, imaginative lyrical imagery.

The death of Andy Warhol, once The Velvet Underground's mentor, in 1987 prompted a collaboration between Reed and the man he had squeezed out of the Velvets two decades previously, John Cale. Their *Songs For 'Drella* (1990) was a moving portrait of the Pop artist as a vulnerable human being.

In interviews, Reed compared *Magic And Loss* (1992) to *Berlin*, and certainly its theme was equally tragic: coming to terms with a year in which he'd watched two close friends die from cancer. The difference was that Reed now engaged with emotions other than anger, and confronted mortality with clear-sighted courage.

After a brief diversion with the Velvet Underground reunion, Reed returned with *Set The Twilight Reeling* (1996). Though less powerful than its immediate predecessors, it was an enjoyable, diverse collection ranging from the cheerfully flirtatious 'Hooky Wooky' to the scathing 'Sex With Your Parents (Motherfucker)'.

In late 1997, the Brooklyn Academy of Music hosted *Time Rocker*, a 'Pop Opera' by Robert Wilson, with music and lyrics by Reed. Meanwhile, the use of 'Perfect Day', a *Transformer* ballad, in the movie *Trainspotting* (1996) inspired its reworking for a BBC promotional film. Stars including Bowie, Bono, Tom Jones and Boyzone sang single lines of the song, Reed himself having the first and last words. Public demand ensured the track's release as a charity single and its subsequent chart-topping status. The film ended on an image of Reed putting a finger to his lips, but his recent releases (including 1998's live *Perfect Night*) show that Lou Reed still has plenty of thought-provoking things left to say.

SURF www.rocknroll.net/loureed/

REGGAE

WHAT Much as 'Rock' covers a multitude of sins, Reggae became a generic name for all Jamaican music. It emerged in 1968 when the slow beat of Rock Steady gave way to the faster, more jagged groove of Reggae. The first record to use the term was The Maytals' 'Do The Reggay' (sic), though the first singles to use the beat were Larry & Alvin's 'Nanny Goat' and Bop & The Belltones' 'No More Heartaches' (both 1968). The word is reputed to be a corruption of 'streggae', Jamaican slang for a woman of easy virtue. Reggae became popular with the UK skinhead movement, which embraced the mad instrumentals of Jamaican producers like Lee 'Scratch' Perry and Harry Johnson, and Trojan's <u>Tighten Up</u> compilations. Reggae changed again in 1970 with the arrival of DJs (talking artists, ie Rappers), the dominance of Rastafarian themes and the arrival of slowed-down skank around 1971. Reggae has since seen periodic amendments like Dub, Lovers Rock, Rockers, Steppers And Flyers, Dancehall, Ragga and New Roots, yet somehow retained its original title.

WHERE Jamaica, then the rest of the world

WHEN 1968–

WHO U Roy <u>Version Galore</u> (1972), Burning Spear <u>Marcus Garvey</u> (1975), Various <u>People Funny Boy</u> (1994), Various <u>Rewind Selacta Lovers Rock Vol. I</u> (1995), Luciano <u>Where There Is Life</u> (1996)

R.E.M. ⊙⊙⊙⊙✪✪

WHO Vocals **Michael Stipe** (b. 4 Jan 1960, Decatur, Georgia, USA), guitar **Peter Buck** (b. 6 Dec 1956, Berkeley, California, USA), bass **Mike Mills** (b. 17 Dec 1958, Orange County, California, USA), drums **Bill Berry** (b. 31 Jul 1958, Duluth, Minnesota, USA)

WHEN 1980–

WHERE Athens, Georgia, USA

WHAT Idiosyncratic For The People

Although they almost single-handedly pulled American Rock into a new age, R.E.M. had modest beginnings: Mike Mills and Bill Berry started a covers band called Shadowfax in Macon, Georgia, USA. Michael Stipe sang with St Louis Punk band Bad Habits and Peter Buck worked at Wuxtry Records, a shop in Athens, Georgia. All four ended up at the University of Georgia in Athens and met on the party circuit through a mutual friend, Kathleen O'Brien.

On 5 April 1980, they debuted live at O'Brien's birthday party in a deconsecrated church where Buck and Stipe lived (fans who make pilgrimages to the church now find only its steeple). They played more gigs around town, notably at student hang-out Tyrone's, and gradually increased their audience. By the end of a triumphant first year they had supported The Police in Atlanta.

Friday to Sunday gigging soon stretched from Thursday to Tuesday. Eventually all four either dropped out of college or were asked to leave. Two events boosted their early development: at Mitch Easter's Drive-In-Studio they recorded their first single for the Hib-Tone label, 'Radio Free Europe', and Jefferson Holt and Bertis Downs took over management of the band from Bill Berry.

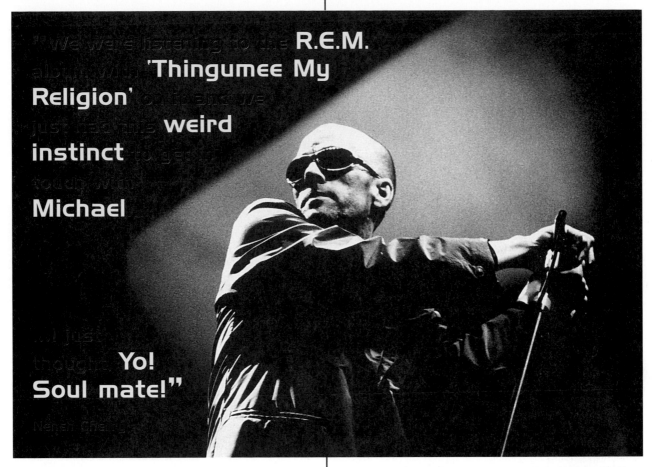

R.E.M.

"We were listening to the R.E.M. album with 'Thingumee My Religion' on it and we just had this weird instinct to get in touch with Michael ...I just thought, Yo! Soul mate!"

Neneh Cherry

In 1982, having turned down RCA, R.E.M. signed to the IRS label, had their set at the Atlanta Arts Festival in May broadcast on radio and released 'Chronic Town', an acclaimed five-track EP. The last quarter of the year was taken up by their longest tour so far: over 20 shows with Peter Holsapple (ex-The db's) as support.

Their first national recognition came in 1983. They appeared on *The David Letterman Show* and again supported The Police in the USA. Their debut album, *Murmur* (produced by Mitch Easter and Don Dixon), was acclaimed; *Rolling Stone* voted it best of the year ahead of *Thriller*. They also toured Europe for the first time.

Reckoning (1984) was less well received, but made US No.27. The band toured for eight months, before moving to England to work with producer Joe Boyd on *Fables Of The Reconstruction* (1985). But the heavy workload, homesickness and miserable London weather created an atmosphere of depression and they came close to splitting. This feeling seeped through to the music, a collection rooted in the storytelling traditions of the American South, and featuring strange and mythical Southern characters. They spent the final seven months of 1985 touring to promote the album, playing more than 120 dates in ten countries.

This intensive touring left R.E.M. in need of a break. The first half of 1986 was spent on their next album with producer Don Gehman, who pushed Stipe's vocals forward in the mix to the point where one could actually hear them. The result, *Life's Rich Pageant* (1986, named after a Peter Sellers quote in 1964 movie *A Shot In The Dark*), almost gave them a first hit with 'Fall On Me'. By now they were playing to thousands rather than hundreds and mainstream rather than cult success began to look inevitable.

Work with producer Scott Litt (who stayed with them for six albums) on material in Athens and Nashville spawned *Document*

(1987). Its 'The One I Love' and 'It's The End Of The World As We Know It (And I Feel Fine)' placed R.E.M. in the chart limelight in the UK and USA, and pushed *Document* into the UK Top 30 and US Top 10. Also released that year was a collection of B-sides and rarities, *Dead Letter Office*, which Buck likened to "browsing through a junk shop". These were their last recordings for IRS. By the end of 1987, *Rolling Stone* had put them on the cover with an accompanying headline, "America's Best Rock And Roll Band".

Having split from IRS, the band signed with Warner Bros and began their next album in Memphis. The result was the excellent *Green* (1988). Released on US election day, it was the band's most outspoken album to date. Videos for 'Stand' and 'Orange Crush' increased the band's coverage on MTV and the excellent 1988 compilation *Eponymous* capitalized on R.E.M.'s growing market.

R.E.M.'s ambitious Green Tour (1989) took in four continents over 11 months with guitarist/keyboardist Peter Holsapple as honorary fifth member. Several dates were filmed for *Tourfilm* (1990) – one of Rock's best documentaries. Augmented by back-projected images, slogans and films, the tour had a strong environmental theme, with Greenpeace stalls at every show.

Afterwards, they took things easy, toying with experimental acoustic pieces that became the classic *Out Of Time* (1991). To the jangly Rock of their earlier work, R.E.M. added a sombre tone, spiced by trilling harmonies, Stipe's unpredictable lyrics and the occasional jolly Pop song. Buck played mainly mandolin instead of guitar and string sections were included along with cameos from Kate Pierson (B-52's) and Rap prophet KRS-1.

Out Of Time went straight to No.1 in both the UK and US, helped in no small part by 'Losing My Religion' (US No.4), 'Shiny Happy People' (US No.9), 'Radio Song' and 'Near Wild Heaven'.

The video for 'Losing My Religion' cleaned up at the MTV awards. For the first time, the band didn't tour, but played a short series of acoustic shows, including MTV's *Unplugged* and two nights at London's tiny Borderline club, under the name Bingo Hand Job.

Following such a groundbreaking album would not be easy. To avoid putting undue pressure on themselves, they travelled across the USA, recording *Automatic For The People* (1992) in Athens, New York, Miami, Seattle and New Orleans. The album (and the hits 'Drive', 'Everybody Hurts', 'The Sidewinder Sleeps Tonight' and 'Man On The Moon') skyrocketed R.E.M. to superstardom, shifting around 10 million copies. Again, they declined to tour and Stipe refused to give interviews, which prompted widespread (but erroneous) rumours about his health.

Rare live appearances at Bill Clinton's inauguration in January 1993 and the MTV Awards in September that year punctuated R.E.M.'s most low-profile year ever. The band held a 'secret' meeting in Acapulco to decide their plan for the next five years.

Requiring a full-throttle Rock album to tour with, they made *Monster* (1994) – a delightful clash of Glam Rock and Grunge. A world tour sold out immediately and much of 1995 was spent on the road, for the first time since 1989. Many fans had never seen the band live, having picked up the trail with *Out Of Time* and *Automatic For The People*. The tour opened to mixed reviews in Australia (the day after Buck's second wedding) and took in the Far East before moving to Europe in February.

In Lausanne, Switzerland, on 1 March 1995, Berry was rushed from the stage complaining of severe headaches. It turned out to be an aneurysm which was successfully treated, but a worrying few weeks followed before the outcome was clear. The tour was cancelled indefinitely, with a San Francisco restart in May. In July, a shorter break was needed when Mike Mills was hospitalized in Germany for a laparatomy operation, and in August Stipe required treatment for a hernia. Several shows from this jinxed tour were filmed and later released as 1996's video *Roadmovie*.

Despite being on the road for a year, the band had managed to write new material and went almost straight to work on the next album. In August 1996, *Roadmovie* was premiered at the Edinburgh Film Festival (it was later released on video) and 'E-Bow, The Letter' (with Patti Smith) was released, followed by *New Adventures In Hi-Fi* (1996) which, despite gushing reviews, failed to sell spectacularly. This must have caused concern at Warner, as they'd just re-signed the band for $80 million. Manager Jefferson Holt was dismissed under mysterious circumstances, leaving Bertis Downs in sole command.

Though officially a 'year off', 1997 saw Stipe producing *Velvet Goldmine*, a movie about a fictional 70s Glam Rock band. Buck was involved with his side projects Tuatara and The Minus Five and also with Mark Eitzel, with whom he toured for a couple of months. Mills undertook the first solo album by a member of the band, scoring the movie *A Cool, Dry Place*. Berry played golf, wrote music and, in October, announced he was leaving. He bowed out with R.E.M.'s Christmas 1997 fan club single 'Live For Today', backed by 'Happy When I'm Crying' by Pearl Jam.

The remaining three reconvened with new producer Pat McCarthy and Screaming Trees drummer Barrett Martin to work on their 11th studio album.

read *It Crawled From The South* (1996), Marcus Gray

fan Rivers Of Suggestion, 19 Cornhill Road, Carlton, Nottingham, NG4 1GE, UK

surf www2.s-gimb.lj.edus.si/peter/rem/rem.html

REO SPEEDWAGON ✪

WHO Vocals **Kevin Cronin** (b. 6 Oct 1951, Evanston, Illinois, USA), guitar **Gary Richrath** (b. 18 Oct 1949, Peoria, Illinois), keyboards **Neal Doughty** (b. 29 Jul 1946, Evanston), bass **Bruce Hall** (b. 3 May 1953, Champaign, Illinois), drums **Alan Gratzer** (b. 9 Nov 1948, Syracuse, New York, USA)

WHEN 1968–

WHERE Champaign, Illinois, USA

WHAT AOR firestoppers

Named after an antique fire engine, REO Speedwagon swapped modest Midwest success for stadium superduperdom in the 80s. Discovered by Eagles mastermind Irving Azoff, REO's 1972 self-titled debut flopped. Original vocalist Terry Luttrell made way for Kevin Cronin, who brought a laid-back feel but negligible commercial benefits. Cronin soon left for a short-lived solo career, his replacement Michael Murphy remaining until 1976, when Cronin rejoined along with new bassist Bruce Hall. Extensive touring yielded their first platinum disc, 1977's live *You Get What You Play For*.

Widespread success came with *Nine Lives* (1979), followed by the US chart-toppers *High Infidelity* (1981) and 'Keep On Lovin' You'. A second US No.1 single, 1985's 'Can't Fight This Feeling', proved their last major hit. By the early 90s, Gary Richrath had left for his own eponymous group and further releases climbed only the lower rungs of the US chart. Inevitably, a new line-up continued to tour as REO Speedwagon, opening a US tour in 1997.

 REO Fans, 3017 Sowers Court, Topeka, Kansas 66604-2666, USA

 www.speedwagon.com/reofans.html

REPUBLICA

WHO Vocals **Saffron** (b. Samantha Sprackling, 3 Jun 1968, Lagos, Nigeria), guitar **Jonny Male** (b. 10 Oct 1963, Windsor, Berkshire), keyboards **Tim Dorney** (b. 30 Mar 1965, Ascot, Berkshire, England)

WHEN 1994–

WHERE London, England

WHAT Spunky smash hitters

As Baggy stragglers Flowered Up disintegrated, keyboard player Tim Dorney approached remixer Andy Todd to form a new band

with former ballerina Saffron (who'd brushed with fame as vocal stooge to Dance nerds N-Joi and The Shamen) and ex-Bow Wow Wow drummer Dave Barbarossa (he and Todd left after the first album). Mixing tasteful Dance widdling, Indie guitars and Saffron's Hazel O'Connor-esque bellowing, Republica followed the Bush template (bigger in the USA than Britain), although 'Out Of This World' and 'Bloke' were club hits at home.

While 1996's 'Ready To Go' became a US MTV fixture and was adopted by the New York Rangers ice hockey team, Republica's success eventually reached Britain in 1997. 'Ready To Go' made UK No.12, 'Drop Dead Gorgeous' peaked at UK No.7, *Republica* (1997) sold millions and Saffron became tough girl Power Pop babe of the month. She confirmed her credentials with backing vocals on Prodigy's *Fat Of The Land* cover of L7's 'Fuel My Fire'.

surf www.republica.com

CLIFF RICHARD ⊙⊙⊙⊙⊙⊙⊙⊙

WHO b. Harry Webb, 14 Oct 1940, Lucknow, India

WHAT The Peter Pan of British Pop

At a studio above the HMV shop in London's Oxford Street in the summer of 1958, a Pop legend began. Cliff Richard, then known as Harry Webb, cut his first demo: 'Breathless' and 'Lawdy Miss Clawdy'. Within months, he and his band The Drifters (renamed The Shadows to avoid muddles with the same-named Soul act), were signed to Columbia.

Changing his name to Cliff Richard, or Richards as spelt on his first record, he entered Abbey Road to record Bobby Helms' hit 'Schoolboy Crush', but it was the original B-side that became Britain's first Rock 'n' Roll record – 'Move It'. Cliff's first toured as support for The Kalin Twins. *Serious Charge*, his movie debut, yielded his first No.1, 'Living Doll' (1959) – the first in a run of hits that included 1959's 'Travellin' Light', 1960's 'Please Don't Tease' and 'Nine Times Out Of Ten' and 1961's 'The Young Ones', which entered the UK chart at No.1 after notching up advance sales of over 500,000.

More movies – 1961's *The Young Ones*, 1962's *Summer Holiday* and 1964's *Wonderful Life* – spawned soundtracks and hits. However, success in America eluded him, despite US tours and recordings in Nashville and New York.

An 1966 appearance with evangelist Billy Graham, in which Cliff performed 'It Is No Secret' and talked about discovering Christianity, fuelled rumours of him giving up show business; instead, he combined the two. Cliff represented Britain in 1968's Eurovision Song Contest with 'Congratulations', coming second to Spain. He came third, five years later, in 1973's contest, with 'Power To All Our Friends'.

He split from The Shadows in 1968 and issued material aimed at a wider audience, failing to achieve the chart success that had once been guaranteed.

His TV series in the early 70s saw him work with Hank Marvin and Olivia Newton-John, but it would be another few years before he would see a return to form.

In 1976, *I'm Nearly Famous* and the hits 'Miss You Nights' and 'Devil Woman', produced by ex-Shadow Bruce Welch, began Cliff's re-emergence as a serious force in Pop music. Hit singles and albums followed and, ten years after their split, Cliff and The Shadows reunited for concerts at London's Palladium, which were recorded and filmed. Another No.1, Alan Tarney's 'We Don't Talk Anymore', followed and, in 1980, Cliff was awarded an OBE.

The 80s found Cliff working with comedians *The Young Ones* on a spoof of 'Living Doll' and appearing in Dave Clark's musical *Time* with Laurence Olivier. *Always Guaranteed* (1987) became his biggest-selling album to date. In June 1989, Cliff held two sellout concerts at Wembley Stadium. Before crowds of 72,000, Cliff reunited with The Shadows and, in his own set, featured the hits 'I Just Don't Have The Heart', produced by Pop-meisters Stock, Aitken & Waterman, and his 100th single 'The Best Of Me'. Cliff fulfilled a lifelong ambition in 1995 when he played lead in the stage musical *Heathcliff*, based on Emily Brontë's *Wuthering Heights*. In 1996, he was knighted for his dedication to charity.

In terms of UK chart success, Cliff is tough to beat, placing a record-breaking 118 singles in the chart, including 13 No.1s.

read *The Ultimate Cliff* (1996), Peter Lewry & Nigel Goodall

fan Dynamite International, Harry de Louw, Postbox 94164, 1090 GD, Amsterdam, Netherlands

surf home.pi.net/~msching/home.html

LIONEL RICHIE ☉☉✪✪

WHO b. 20 Jun 1949, Tuskegee, Alabama, USA

WHAT Ceiling-dancin' Soul superstar

Having helmed The Commodores, Lionel Richie followed writing and producing Kenny Rogers' 'Lady' and 'Share Your Love' with a mega-selling solo career in the 80s. In 1981, his duet with Diana Ross on the movie theme 'Endless Love' became his first US No.1, and *Lionel Richie* (1982) featured the smash 'Truly'. But *Can't Slow Down* (1983) was a chart monolith: the cool carnival atmosphere of 'All Night Long (All Night)' reached US No.2, and the mawkish but timeless 'Hello' topped charts *everywhere*.

In 1985, inspired by Bob Geldof's Band Aid, Richie hooked up with Michael Jackson to write the USA For Africa hit 'We Are The World', another transatlantic chart-topper. In the same year, 'Say You, Say Me' (from the movie *White Nights*) earned him an Oscar.

Dancing On The Ceiling (1986) was another dollop of soulful Pop, whose title track reached UK No.7 and produced two more US Top 10 giants: 'Love Will Conquer All' and 'Ballerina Girl'. Having won five Grammys and sold millions, Richie took time out, waiting until 1992 for his next hits 'Do It To Me' (a US No.1) and 'My Destiny', both from the compilation *Back to Front* (1992).

 Lionel Richie: An Illustrated Biography (1985), David Nathan

JONATHAN RICHMAN

WHO b. 16 May 1951, Boston, Massachusetts, USA

WHAT Childlike Punk troubadour

Though perpetually characterized as a Punk visionary, it would be hard to imagine a character less like Sid Vicious than Jonathan Richman, the eternal wide-eyed innocent.

The label fitted better when Richman began as frontman with glorious Garage Rock act The Modern Lovers in 1970. They wrote brilliant Velvet Underground-infected songs like 'Hospital' and 'Roadrunner', engaged John Cale to produce, then sank without trace – Warners refused to release their debut, *The Modern Lovers*. Downcast, they split in 1973; keyboardist Jerry Harrison surfaced in Talking Heads, drummer Dave Robinson in The Cars.

Richman retained the Lovers' name for his new backing band, pursuing an acoustic, child-like pastiche of 50s/60s Rock 'n' Roll and Doo Wop. US Indie label Beserkley issued *The Modern Lovers* and scored giant UK hits in 1977 with 'Roadrunner' and 'Egyptian Reggae'. Richman was hoisted aloft as godfather of gobbing.

He became increasingly eccentric on *Back In Your Life* (1979), *Jonathan Sings!* (1983), *It's Time For Jonathan Richman And The Modern Lovers* (1986) and *Jonathan Richman* (1989). There was no room for negativity in Richman's world, but plenty for simple, love-struck songs about ice-cream men and flying saucers. He could seem either uniquely uplifting or unbearably twee.

However, *I, Jonathan* (1992) included the excellent 'I Was Dancing In The Lesbian Bar', while 1996's *Surrender To Jonathan* (recorded for Neil Young's Vapor label) augmented Richman's usual starkness with bursts of brass. In the 90s, he seems, at last, to be aiming beyond his ever-faithful cult following.

surf www.base.com/jonathan/jonathan.html

RIDE

WHO Vocals/guitar **Mark Gardener** (b. 6 Dec 1969, Oxford, England), guitar/vocals **Andy Bell** (b. 11 Aug 1970, Cardiff, Wales), bass **Steve Queralt** (b. 4 Feb 1968, Oxford), drums **Laurence Colbert** (b. 27 Jun 1970, Kingston, Surrey, England)

WHEN 1988–1995

WHERE Oxford, England

WHAT Shoegazing central

With their wall of hazy guitars, majestic songs, fey vocals and negligible stage presence, Ride *were* shoegazing. Hailed as Rock's new hope, they scaled Indie's Olympus. And fell off. United by a love of My Bloody Valentine, House Of Love and The Jesus & Mary Chain, Ride joined the Creation label for 1990's acclaimed 'Ride' EP – its highlights the classic 'Drive Blind' and 'Chelsea Girl'.

Later EPs 'Play' and 'Fall' (both 1990) punctured the UK Top 40 and built Ride's peerless reputation on the likes of 'Dreams Burn Down' and 'Taste'. *Nowhere* (1990) confirmed it: blistering noise, heart-wrenching tunes and the excellent 'Vapour Trail' prompted the kind of journalistic excess previously reserved for Cocteau Twins – 'shimmering sonic cathedrals' abounded.

After months of scene-setting silence, they emerged from the depths with the panoramic 'Leave Them All Behind' – an 8-minute nouveau-Prog fanfare that declared "Citizens of Earth. Stop what you are doing. Ride are here". Then the shoddy mess of *Going Blank Again* (1991) trailed a two-year disappearance.

Tired of being the ugly brains behind the handsome Mark Gardener, Ride bickered. Andy Bell helped kickstart the career of his wife (and fellow Creation-ite) Idha, then took centre-stage for Ride's limp 'Birdman'. *Carnival Of Light* (1994) wore the scars of their feuding. Packed with petty individual writing credits and giant debts to 60s Psychedelia, it was resoundingly ignored by Indie kids now steeped in Suede. Whipped by the press, Ride set about a follow-up (posthumously released as 1996's *Tarantula*), only to split in the process. Gardener disappeared to New York muttering about a Dance-oriented sound, while Bell pursued his muse with Creation's Oasis wannabes Hurricane #1.

surf irix.bris.ac.uk/~dm5751/ride/ride.html

THE RIGHTEOUS BROTHERS

WHO Vocals **Bill Medley** (b. 19 Sep 1940, Santa Ana, California, USA), vocals **Bobby Hatfield** (b. 10 Aug, 1940, Beaver Dam, Wisconsin, USA)

WHEN 1962–

WHERE Anaheim, California, USA

WHAT Epic ballad duo

Soon after they united in 1962, Bill Medley and Bobby Hatfield were nicknamed The Righteous Brothers because of their Gospel and R&B-influenced vocals. The name stuck, and the duo scored minor US hits with 'Koko Joe' and 'Little Latin Lupe Lu' in 1963.

Their breakthrough came in 1964, when Phil Spector put their contrasting voices to stunning use on 'You've Lost That

Lovin' Feelin'", a transatlantic No.1. Further hits followed in 1965 with 'Just Once In My Life' and 'Ebb Tide', but 'Hung On You' flopped – until DJs started playing its flipside, 'Unchained Melody'. The 50s ballad then became another international hit.

Having parted company with Spector, they topped the US chart again in 1966 with '(You're My) Soul And Inspiration'; but later releases were less successful, and the duo split in 1968. Medley went solo, while Hatfield and his new partner Jimmy Walker continued to use The Righteous Brothers name. Medley and Hatfield reunited in 1974 and reached the US Top 5 with 'Rock 'n' Roll Heaven', but were unable to sustain their success.

In 1987, Medley scored high with his hit duet with Jennifer Warnes, '(I've Had) The Time Of My Life', from the movie *Dirty Dancing*. Three years later, 'Unchained Melody' became a transatlantic hit all over again, thanks to its inclusion in the soundtrack of *Ghost* , and 'You've Lost That Lovin' Feelin'" subsequently scaled the UK chart too, prompting Medley and Hatfield to record new versions of old classics on *Reunion* (1991).

surf www.righteousbrothers.com/

SMOKEY ROBINSON

WHO b. William Robinson, 19 Feb 1940, Detroit, Michigan, USA

WHAT Smooth-sounding Motown pioneer

Although Bob Dylan never said (as has been endlessly repeated), "Smokey Robinson is America's greatest living poet", the verdict is hardly inappropriate to the genius behind immortals like The Marvelettes' 'The Hunter Gets Captured By The Game' (covered by Massive Attack and Blondie), The Temptations' 'My Girl', Mary Wells' 'My Guy' and The Miracles' 'The Tracks Of My Tears'.

Destiny beckoned when vocal group The Matadors – Smokey, Ronnie White, Bobby Rogers and Pete Moore – failed to impress Jackie Wilson's manager and were adopted instead by Motown founder Berry Gordy. With Claudette Rogers (Bobby's sister and Smokey's future wife), they became The Miracles and gave the fledging Motown its first million-seller with 1961's 'Shop Around'. Gordy returned the favour by making Smokey corporate vice president, and nurturing his considerable songwriting talent. "I wanted to be like Beethoven or Bach or Chopin," he told *Q* magazine, "and write music which lived on forever."

An extraordinary run of 30 hits fulfilled his destiny: from 1963's smoochy 'You've Really Got A Hold On Me', through 1965's dramatic 'The Tracks Of My Tears' (as poetic as anything Dylan or Lennon were doing at the time) and 1966's raunchy 'Going To A Go Go', to 1970's transatlantic No.1 'The Tears Of A Clown'.

Smokey bowed out of The Miracles with the live *1957–1972* (1972). They enlisted William Griffin, hit US No.1 with 'Love Machine' from *City Of Angels* (1975), then disbanded. Smokey had mixed solo success with the patchy *Smokey* (1973), *A Quiet Storm* (1975) and *Deep In My Heart* (1977). He recovered his form and fortune with 1979's spellbinding *Where There's Smoke…*, source of sexy smash 'Cruisin'. The elegantly romantic Soul of *Warm Thoughts* (1980) and *Being With You* (1981) wafted Smokey into the 80s, the latter's title track taking him to the UK top spot.

He returned to the US Top 10 with 'Just To See Her' and the title track from *One Heartbeat* (1987), and enjoyed a UK Top 30 hit with The Four Tops on 1989's 'Indestructible'. His songs having become hits for admirers as diverse as The Rolling Stones, Japan and The (English) Beat, Smokey's influence extended into the 90s with Maxwell, who repaid his obvious debt by covering 'Cruisin'.

read *Smokey: Inside My Life* (1989), Smokey Robinson & David Ritz

surf www.srv.net/"roxtar/robinson-smokey.html

TOM ROBINSON

WHO b. 1 Jul 1950, Cambridge, England

WHAT Polemical singer/songwriter

The Kinks' Ray Davies gave Tom Robinson his first break, signing Café Society – a trio of Robinson, Hereward Kaye and Raphael Doyle – to his Konk label and producing their eponymous 1974 album. But Punk brought Robinson to prominence: with The Tom Robinson Band (guitarist Danny Kustow, keyboard player Mark Ambler and drummer Dolphin Taylor), he wrote songs laden with pointed, if sometimes clumsy, political commentary.

One of Robinson's few apolitical songs, the stomping '2-4-6-8 Motorway' reached the UK Top 5 in 1977. It was followed into the chart by their 1978 album *Power In The Darkness* and the 'Rising Free' EP, which contained the sardonic '(Sing If You're) Glad To Be Gay'. *TRB 2* (1979) was poorly received, critics complaining the polemics overwhelmed the music, and TRB promptly split. Robinson flirted with a new band, Section 27, before going solo.

He hit the UK chart again with 1983's romantic 'War Baby', from *North By Northwest*, and re-formed TRB for a tour and 1990's live *Last Tango*. Now a radio presenter, Robinson continues to record (hence 1996's *Having It Both Ways*) and perform.

fan The Castaway Club, PO Box 3185, London, SW18 3JG, UK

surf www.tomrobinson.com/

ROCK 'N' ROLL

WHAT Though <u>Back To The Future</u> traces its origin to 1955 and Michael J. Fox's proto-Chuck Berry stage antics, the Rock 'n' Roll story is an Old Testament-style epic, which began when African music was transplanted to America in the 18th century by slaves. There, it incorporated elements of European music (harmony, poetic narrative) but retained driving rhythm, call-and-response shouts and scales with dissonant notes, known as 'blue notes'. Having acquired the name 'rocking and reeling', it filtered into American culture, mixing with the Scottish and Irish Folk of European settlers. In the 20th century, black Church singing mutated into Gospel and vocal harmony groups. Rural Bluesmen made it to the cities and discovered electric guitars and Boogie Woogie, while bandleaders like Count Basie added horns, solos and volume – the origins of Jazz. Blues and Jazz fused in the 40s with the rougher 'Jump Blues' style of prototype Rockers like Lionel Hampton's 'Flying Home' (1942). But in a society founded on racial segregation, it inevitably took a white man to turn this experimentation into a commercial phenomenon. DJ Alan Freed played black Doo Wop R&B (or 'Race Music' as it was charmingly known at the time) to mainly white audiences and called it 'Rock 'n' Roll'. He later tried to copyright the term, although The Boswell Sisters had recorded a song called 'Rock 'n' Roll' in 1934 and it had been a Blues euphemism for sex since the 40s. In 1954, The Crew-Cuts whitened up The Chords' 'Sh-boom' and Country bumpkin Bill Haley, having recorded the pioneering 'Rocket 88' in 1951, hit with '(We're Gonna) Rock Around The Clock'. In 1956, Elvis Presley's 'Heartbreak Hotel' smashed the chart and nothing was ever the same again.

WHERE USA

WHEN 50s–

WHO Chuck Berry <u>Chuck Berry</u> (1963), Elvis Presley <u>The Sun Years</u> (1977), Little Richard <u>Little Richard: 18 Greatest Hits</u> (1985), Various <u>From Spirituals To Swing: Carnegie Hall Concerts 1938/39</u> (1987), Fats Domino <u>My Blue Heaven: The Best Of Fats Domino</u> (1990), Various <u>Risqué Rhythms</u> (1991), Gene Vincent <u>The Sun Story</u> (1987), Rocket From The Crypt <u>Scream, Dracula, Scream!</u> (1996)

LARRY BUSACCA:RETNA

Rock And Roll Hall Of Fame

Does Rock 'n' Roll, that most mercurial form of self-expression, belong in a museum? In 1983, a group of successful individuals from the US music industry decided it did. They set up the Rock And Roll Hall Of Fame Foundation to, in their words, "honour the men and women who have made unique contributions to the energy of Rock and Roll." At the same time, they began to gather Rock memorabilia to exhibit in a museum, for which a site in Cleveland, Ohio, was chosen.

A committee of historians and musicologists was commissioned to name the most influential Rock performers of all time, with the stipulation that those performers chosen must have released their first record at least 25 years previously. In 1986, the nominees were voted on by an international group of about 1,000 Rock experts and the chosen few announced: Chuck Berry, James Brown, Ray Charles, Sam Cooke, Fats Domino, The Everly Brothers, Buddy Holly, Jerry Lee Lewis, Elvis Presley and Little Richard. 50s DJ Alan Freed and Sun Records chief Sam Phillips were also admitted in a 'non-performers' category, while a section for 'early influences' from the pre-Rock 'n' Roll era honoured Robert Johnson, Jimmie Rodgers and Jimmy Yancey. Record producer John Hammond was the first winner of a 'lifetime achievement' award.

A list of new inductees has been announced each year since then. Aretha Franklin became the first female Hall Of Fame member in 1987, and The Beatles became the first non-Americans to be admitted in 1988. The museum, housed in a futuristic 150,000-sq-ft building, finally opened to the public in September 1995.

Many have argued that such an institution is contrary to the iconoclastic spirit of much of the best Rock music, but the building undeniably contains exhibits likely to stir the emotions of many mature music-lovers. They include such priceless artifacts as John Lennon's 'Sergeant Pepper' uniform, the black leather outfit Elvis Presley wore for his 1968 'comeback' TV special and the lyrics to 'Purple Haze' as handwritten by Jimi Hendrix.

The Foundation also deserves credit for broadening its definition of 'Rock 'n' Roll' in recent years to allow the induction of innovative artists like Bob Marley, Frank Zappa, Joni Mitchell, David Bowie and The Velvet Underground. Perhaps The Sex Pistols will receive the coveted call from the Hall when they reach the 25-year threshold in 2001.

SURF /www.rockhall.com/

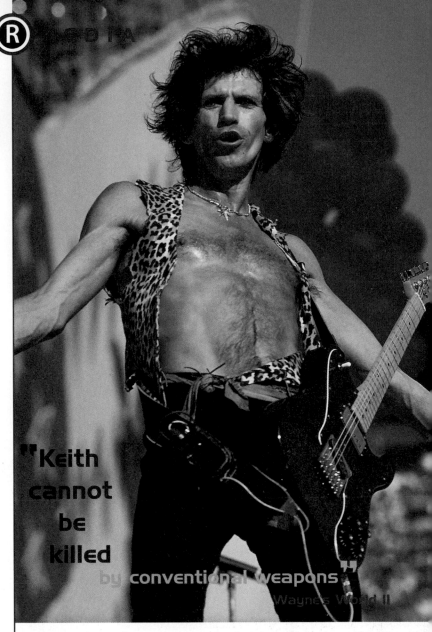

"Keith cannot be killed by conventional weapons"

Wayne's World II

KENNY ROGERS ✪

WHO b. 21 Aug 1938, Houston, Texas, USA

WHAT Boundary-bending Pop/Country Texmix

Kenny Rogers debuted with other high school students in the aptly named Scholars. His first solo single (as Kenneth Rogers), 'That Crazy Feeling', became a hit in Texas in 1958. In ensuing years he played in The Bobby Doyle Trio, sang in The Lively Ones vocal quartet and released overlooked solo singles.

He first tasted fame in 1966 with New Christy Minstrels. A year later Rogers and three colleagues left to form The First Edition, a boundary-bending mix of Pop, Folk, Rock and Country whose 'Just Dropped In (To See What Condition My Condition Was In)' became the first of five US Top 20 hits. Among their other big sellers were the UK Top 10 entries 'Ruby, Don't Take Your Love To Town' (1969) and 'Something's Burning' (1970).

By 1972, their peak had passed and Rogers went solo. He escorted 'Lucille' (1977) into the US Top 5 and to UK No.1. Over the next six years, the white-bearded vocalist notched up hit after hit on Pop and Country charts. Biggest were 'The Gambler' (1978), which launched a string of movies starring Rogers, and 1979's easy-on-the-ear 'She Believes In Me', 'You Decorated My Life' and his second UK No.1, 'Coward Of The County'. Rogers finally topped the US pop chart in 1980 with his eighth Country No.1, 'Lady', written and produced by Lionel Richie.

In 1983, Rogers signed with RCA for a reported $20 million, and recorded that year's biggest US hit, 'Islands In The Stream', with Dolly Parton. However, his period with RCA was otherwise disappointing, although it included another six Country No.1s.

During the 80s, Rogers devoted time to charity work, such as USA For Africa, Hands Across America and Voices That Care. He has kept a high profile in the 90s, thanks to TV and live shows. Having amassed a horde of awards (including a record 18 from the AMA), his recordings have transcended musical barriers and he is still adding to his reported 80 million album sales.

READ *Kenny Rogers* (1987), Jay Pirtle

FAN Kenny Rogers Fan Club, PO Box 769, Hendersonville, TN 37077, USA

SURF www.kennyrogers.nef/

THE ROLLING STONES
⊙⊙⊙⊙⊙⊙⊙⊙⊙⊙⊙⊙⊙✪✪✪✪✪✪✪

WHO Vocals **Mick Jagger** (b. 26 Jul 1943, Dartford, Kent, England), guitar **Keith Richards** (b. 18 Dec 1943, Dartford), drums **Charlie Watts** (b. 2 Jun 1941, Islington, London, England), guitar **Ron Wood** (b. 1 Jun 1947, Hillingdon, London), bass **Bill Wyman** (b. William Perks, 24 Oct 1936, Lewisham, London)

WHEN 1962–

WHERE London, England

WHAT The Greatest Rock 'n' Roll Band In The World

"I want to be like Roy Rogers and play guitar," Keith Richards told Mick Jagger, soon after they met in 1951 at Wentworth Primary School, Dartford. Since opportunities for singing cowboys were hard to come by in London's suburban sprawl, he badgered his mother into buying a guitar which, in due course, he redirected to fanatically rehearsed Chuck Berry riffs – though his love of music also found a rather different outlet via his stint as a boy soprano chorister of sufficient purity to sing, on one occasion, for the Queen at Westminster Abbey.

Not close as children, they drifted apart through their teens, the more academic Jagger securing a university place at the London School Of Economics while Richards went to Sidcup Art School. But, in 1961, they bumped into each other again at Dartford railway station and under Jagger's arm were import albums by Muddy Waters and Chuck Berry. So they got talking.

Jagger asked Richards to join his Little Boy Blue & The Blue Boys, and soon they were denizens of Ealing Jazz Club in West London. Frequented by fresh-faced R&B fans like Eric Clapton, Ron Wood, Dave Davies and Jeff Beck, the venue often featured Alexis Korner's Blues Incorporated with drummer Charlie Watts and guitar guest 'Elmo Lewis', aka Brian Jones (b. Lewis Brian Hopkin-Jones, 28 Feb 1942, Cheltenham, England).

When, in April 1962, Jones was introduced to Jagger and Richards at the club, he spotted kindred spirits and pulled them into his band, unnamed until that June when they started gigging as The Rollin' Stones – taken from Muddy Waters' line "I'm a rollin' stone" in 'Mannish Boy'. The line-up included Ian Stewart on piano and former Blue Boys bassist Dick Taylor, with

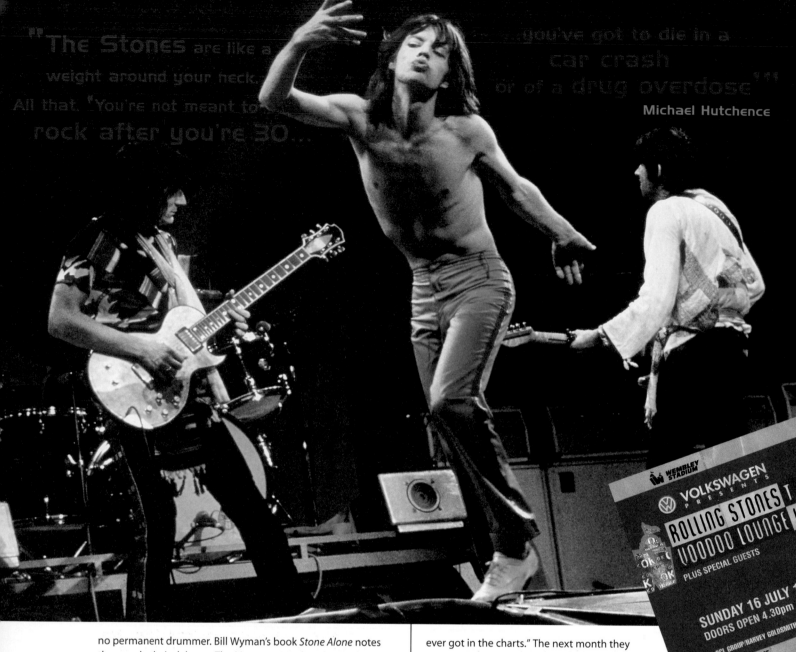

"The Stones are like a ... weight around your neck. All that, "You're not meant to ... rock after you're 30 ...

.... you've got to die in a car crash or of a drug overdose"

Michael Hutchence

VOLKSWAGEN PRESENTS
ROLLING STONES T
VOODOO LOUNGE
PLUS SPECIAL GUESTS

SUNDAY 16 JULY 1
DOORS OPEN 4.30pm
A BCL GROUP/HARVEY GOLDSMITH
SUBJECT TO LICENCE

PRICE (inc V
£25

No. 013759

ENTER BY T

no permanent drummer. Bill Wyman's book *Stone Alone* notes they made their debut at The Marquee, London, on 12 July 1962.

Jagger, Richards and Jones moved into a legendarily squalid flat in the West London neighbourhood of Chelsea. Constant jamming developed the two guitarists' innovative style of seamless lead and rhythm playing. But their first demo of Muddy Waters, Jimmy Reed and Bo Diddley covers produced no takers.

In December 1962, Bill Wyman joined on bass, partly because he had a spare Vox AC30 amplifier (Dick Taylor moved on to The Pretty Things). He dropped into an unusual rhythmic slot: following the beat set down by Richards – which, says Wyman, "is the reason for our sound". The revised line-up first played at Berkshire's Ricky Tick club on 11 January 1963 – six days before The Beatles' first big hit, 'Please Please Me', entered the UK chart.

Then Andrew Loog Oldham entered the scene. A 19-year-old publicist who had worked for designer Mary Quant and Beatles manager Brian Epstein, he saw them play and, in May 1963, took on their management (with his partner Eric Easton). His first gambits included installing himself as producer, replacing the 'g' in Rolling, cutting the 's' off Richards, and pushing 'straight' Ian Stewart into the background (he remained as road manager, occasional pianist and the 'sixth Stone' until his death in 1985).

On 9 May, the Stones signed to Decca. The following day they recorded their first single, a cover of Chuck Berry's 'Come On'. "It really was shit," Jagger moaned to *NME* later. "God knows how it

ever got in the charts." The next month they were at UK No.21 and on TV Pop show *Thank Your Lucky Stars*. The race was on.

Their next hit arose when Oldham brought John Lennon and Paul McCartney to a Stones' rehearsal. On the spot, The Beatles finished writing 'I Wanna Be Your Man' and gave it to their rivals. It went to UK No.12 in December 1963, propelling the Stones to co-headline status with The Ronettes on a UK package tour.

Oldham made most impact by telling them they wouldn't last as a covers band and locking Jagger and Richards in a room until they had a song. While their next hits were Buddy Holly's 'Not Fade Away', Bobby Womack's 'It's All Over Now' (their first UK No.1) and Willie Dixon's 'Little Red Rooster', early Jagger-Richard songs went to Gene Pitney ('That Girl Belongs To Yesterday') and Marianne Faithfull ('As Tears Go By'), soon Jagger's girlfriend.

Their debut album *The Rolling Stones* ousted *With The Beatles* from UK No.1 in May 1964. The following month Oldham took them to America for the first time, after which the album went to US No.11. The trip also included an interlude at Chess studios, Chicago, where they met Muddy Waters – he was painting the ceiling – and recorded 'It's All Over Now'.

Although 1965 began with the Stones arraying themselves at the feet of Howlin' Wolf on US TV's *Shindig!*, it soon produced their first Jagger-Richards UK No.1, 'The Last Time'. They confirmed their writing ability with a drum-roll of immortal hits: '(I Can't Get No) Satisfaction' (their first US No.1), 'Get Off Of My Cloud', '19th Nervous Breakdown' and 'Paint It, Black'.

While the Stones concentrated on hits, their US label London assembled tracks recorded for British EPs to make *12x5* (1964), *The Rolling Stones No.2*, *The Rolling Stones Now*, the US No.1 *Out Of Our Heads* and *December's Children* (all 1965). Buried in a mass of R&B covers were diamonds like the menacingly acoustic 'Play With Fire', the proto-Punk 'She Said Yeah' and the optimistic 'I'm Free' (a 1990 smash for bandwagon-hoppers The Soup Dragons).

Aftermath (1966) was the turning point. "A good album," said Jagger, "and the first one for which we wrote all the songs." Pop's first really long album (52 minutes, of which 11 are 'Goin' Home') cemented Stones lyrical motifs, notably drugs ('Mother's Little Helper') and feminine failings ('Stupid Girl'). In the latter category fell 'Under My Thumb', whose ominous mood and marimbas, coupled with the sitar-driven drama of 'Paint It, Black' (included on the US edition of *Aftermath*) and dulcimer-driven 'Lady Jane' – all the product of Jones' musical ambition – helped to push Rock above its R&B roots (though Dylan's *Blonde On Blonde* and The Beatles' *Revolver*, both also from 1966, nabbed the credit).

Meanwhile, the Stones forged a reputation as the 'bad boy' antithesis of The Beatles. There was rioting at gigs (50 in casualty after a Blackpool gig in July 1964), uproar on staid TV shows (Ed Sullivan warned "They'll never be back" after audience disorder, but later relented) and a legendary garage wall urination (Jagger, Wyman and Jones were fined for "insulting behaviour" in July 1965). During 1965, hard-nosed American manager Allen Klein ousted Easton as their co-manager. The Stones did not appear to be in training for the summer of love; in fact, their most notable shows of 1967 were in court rooms. In February, police raided Richards' country house, Redlands in Sussex, charging him and Jagger with narcotics offences. They were convicted and Richards sentenced to a year in prison, Jagger to three months.

Bailed after a night in jail, they became a *cause célèbre*, most notably for *Times* editor William Rees-Mogg, whose headline quoted Alexander Pope: "Who breaks a butterfly on a wheel?". Richards' conviction was quashed because of a trial irregularity and Jagger's sentence reduced to a conditional discharge.

Jones, depressed at losing control of the band he'd founded to Jagger and Richards and also losing his girlfriend, actress Anita Pallenberg, to Richards, sank into a mire of personal problems. Arrested at his home in May 1967 for possession of drugs, he avoided a prison sentence only because his lawyer pleaded that he was showing "suicidal tendencies". In September 1967 the Stones split with Oldham, signing wholly to Klein.

Musically too, unease prevailed. *Got Live If You Want It!* (1966) was exciting but patchy; *Between The Buttons* (1967) was, said Jagger, "more or less rubbish"; and *Their Satanic Majesties Request* (1967) betrayed the promise of their first, thrilling hop aboard the psychedelic bandwagon, the post-trial hit 'We Love You'.

NME's Poll-winners' Concert, in May 1968 (their first show for more than a year), heralded a recovery. The new single, 'Jumping Jack Flash', exulted in the first of a new generation of Richards power-riffs and a new production partnership with Jimmy Miller. After a last psychedelic pratfall in the ill-conceived *Rock And Roll Circus* film (with The Who and John Lennon) – which the band

refused to release until 1997 – the Stones strutted into their dark prime. *Beggars Banquet* (1968) reflected Richards' having "had the time to fool around and figure out some of those old Blues tunings" – hence much of the album's acoustic earthiness. Its best-known cuts, however, are the Satanic samba 'Sympathy For The Devil' and the ragged rocker 'Street Fighting Man' – later victims of covers by, respectively, Guns N' Roses and Oasis.

The sleazy, magnificent 'Honky Tonk Women' – their last UK and US No.1 – was their keynote single of 1969, the year in which Jones left ("I no longer see eye to eye with the others over the discs we are cutting," he announced), then died in his pool on 3 July (coroner's verdict: "drowned while under the influence of alcohol and drugs"). Two days later, their colossal free gig in Hyde Park, London, turned into a memorial to Jones. It was also the initiation of former John Mayall band guitarist Mick Taylor (b. 17 Jan 1948, Welwyn Garden City, Hertfordshire, England). Days later, after Jagger flew to Australia with Faithfull to film *Ned Kelly*, she took an overdose and lay in a coma for eight days.

The band closed the peace and love decade with Rock's most notorious concert. At California's Altamont speedway track on 6 December, they presided over a day of seething menace. When Meredith Hunter, an 18-year-old standing in front of the stage, pulled a gun, he was stabbed to death by Hell's Angels whom the Stones, on The Grateful Dead's advice, had put in charge of security – an event recorded for the 1972 movie *Gimme Shelter*.

The film took its title from the lead cut on *Let It Bleed* (1969). That album and *Sticky Fingers* (1971) – recorded around the same time – alternately dressed their sex, death 'n' drugs themes in monolithic Rock ('Gimme Shelter', 'Sway'), wiry R&B ('Live With Me', 'Bitch') or scary Blues ('Midnight Rambler', 'Moonlight Mile'). In between, the live *Get Yer Ya's Out* (1970) documented a 1969 return to the road that ushered in the band's mega-touring.

Their lyrics and lifestyles now the epitome of 70s decadence, the Stones sailed into high finance and high society. In July 1970, they severed ties with Klein, placed their affairs with financial adviser (and minor Austrian royal) Prince Rupert Loewenstein and launched suits against both Klein and Oldham-Easton. Klein doggedly held the rights to the 60s material for the next three decades. The band quit Decca with the unreleasable 'Cocksucker Blues' and launched their Rolling Stones Records label, complete with a now immortal, Andy Warhol-designed tongue logo.

Jagger's movie career took its first steps in 1970 with the dire *Ned Kelly* and controversial *Performance,* the latter co-starring Anita Pallenberg and yielding the scabrous solo single 'Memo From Turner'. Jagger grabbed more of the limelight on 12 May 1971 by marrying Nicaraguan model Bianca Moreno de Macias.

As they moved among the glitteratti, Richards plunged into heroin addiction, but drove the Stones' music to its ecstatic peak. At his home in Nellcôte, France, where they'd decamped for tax purposes, he charged the Stones £250 a week each for room and board and bridled every time Jagger slunk to Paris to see gang-outcast Bianca. Nonetheless, the resulting *Exile On Main Street* (1972) alchemized its sprawling blend of spooky Gospel, blitzed Blues and fuel-injected Rock 'n' Roll into a gripping whole.

After *Exile*, Richards confessed, "It tailed off a little bit… that was not so much to do with being the 70s rich-jet-set-superstar-Rock 'n' Roll-whatever, but more to do with the fact that, in order to keep the band together, we'd had to leave England." However, the sloppy *Goat's Head Soup* (1973) spawned the weepy US No.1 'Angie', *It's Only Rock 'N' Roll* (1974) was self-mocking but strong and *Black And Blue* (1976) was a tragically

were arrested in Toronto and charged with possession of heroin and cocaine. The media focused even more on the band when Canadian Prime Minister Pierre Trudeau's wife Margaret joined the Stones' entourage. Amid the outraged decency and outlaw glamour surrounding the "world's most elegantly wasted human being", Richards began to haul himself back from the brink.

The case hanging over him for more than a year threatened his own liberty and his band's ability to travel the world. Richards – who re-adopted his terminal 's' following constant repetition of his proper name in court reports – sought out Dr Meg Paterson, whose 'Black Box' method of applying low-voltage electric current had helped to cure Eric Clapton. A first try failed: he used heroin while recording *Some Girls* (1978). But with Jagger and his new girlfriend Jerry Hall in attendance while the album was mixed in New York, he put himself through a personal variant on the Paterson process, which embraced cocaine and alcohol as an alternative to heroin. Astonishingly, it seemed to work.

The Stones were buoyed by the frazzled *Love You Live* (1977), although that was eclipsed by 1978's quadruple-platinum *Some Girls* (1978). Though its biggest hits were the Disco-ish US No.1 'Miss You' and witty 'Beast Of Burden', the best cut was Richards' autobiographical but cheerful 'Before They Make Me Run'.

Appropriately, when he finally stood trial in October 1978, he received only a suspended sentence and an order to play a gig to benefit the Canadian National Institute For The Blind. The life-style transition was completed when, in July 1980 (shortly before Jagger and Bianca's divorce), he parted from Pallenberg to set up house with his future wife, American model Patti Hansen.

The Stones crashed the new decade with *Emotional Rescue* (1980) which, reported author Nicholas Schaffner, "sparked a running debate in *The Village Voice* over whether its contents are magnificently contrived junk or just plain unredeemed junk."

There was less debate about *Tattoo You* (1981). Ranging from the riffmasterly throwback 'Start Me Up' to the sun-drenched 'Waiting On A Friend', it heralded the most lucrative concert tour ever (a record the Stones broke again in the 80s and 90s) – hence 1982's *Still Life (American Concert 1981)*. They rounded off the resurgence with *Undercover* (1983) – source of the Funk-fuelled, plasma-splattered hits 'Undercover Of The Night' and 'Too Much Blood'. Their gory videos (and the raunchy one for 'She Was Hot') went out of their way to court controversy in the wake of belated establishment recognition – they'd won a 1982 Silver Clef award for Outstanding Contribution To British Music.

But by then they were drifting apart. Wyman – who'd scored minor hits with *Satanic Majesties*' 'In Another Land' (credited to him alone), *Monkey Grip* (1974) and *Stone Alone* (1976), hit big with '(Si Si) Je Suis Un Rock Star' from *Bill Wyman* (1981). Wood took to painting and Watts practised his passion for Jazz with his Big Band. The Stones' shaky state made 1984's excellent *Rewind (1971-1984)* look like an epitaph, an impression strengthened when they played separately at Live Aid (Jagger with Hall & Oates and Tina Turner, Richards and Wood with Dylan).

Most damaging to the band's future was Jagger's solo career. Having duetted with The Jacksons on 'State Of Shock' (1984), he stepped out alone with *She's The Boss* (1985), which coincided with an attempted Stones revival. But the sessions were riddled with rows: Richards felt Jagger was committing the cardinal sin of not putting the Stones first; Jagger reasonably pointed out that everyone else had done solo projects, so why shouldn't he?

They squeezed out the underrated *Dirty Work* (1986), but its only hit was a cover of Soul duo Bob & Earl's 'Harlem Shuffle'.

underrated immersion in Funk and Reggae (trailed by *It's Only Rock 'N' Roll*'s 'Fingerprint File' and 'Luxury') that also boasted two of their greatest ballads, 'Fool To Cry' and 'Memory Motel'. All three topped the US chart.

With Richards consumed by heroin, Jagger took over the motivator role: "Mick had to cover for me. He did exactly what a friend should do." He kept the money-making machine running, especially on the US stadium circuit, with spectacular shows and effects, such as 1975's giant, unfolding lotus-shaped stage and 20-ft inflatable penis. But chaos kept veering towards collapse. Richards was repeatedly busted for drugs, driving and even weapons offences and, in 1976, his son Tara died at 10 weeks. Mick Taylor, who had contributed hugely, succumbed to heroin and, in December 1974, had to quit and "move on to something new" – a modest career of occasional sessions and solo ventures.

His successor, The Faces' Ron Wood, was the man the Stones always wanted, despite auditioning other players on *Black And Blue*. Their long jamming friendship convinced Richards that he would prove the true substitute for Brian Jones, bonding lead and rhythm where the Taylor-Richards tandem had found it necessary to divide them. "Me and Woody don't know who played the last lick. It's as close as that," Richards once observed.

The Stones' redemption – a peculiar concept – began amid their worst crisis. On 28 February 1977, Richards and Pallenberg

Their own 'One Hit (To The Body)' – with uncredited lead guitar by Jimmy Page – was the first Stones single not to chart in the UK. Irking Richards even more, Jagger refused to tour, arguing that the band – still dogged by drink and drugs – "couldn't walk across the Champs Èlysées, much less go on the road".

The split looked even more serious when Jagger made 1987's *Primitive Cool* (1987). Even Richards went solo: he (with Wood) guested on Aretha Franklin's cover of 'Jumpin' Jack Flash' (theme to the 1986 movie of the same name), then helmed 1987's Chuck Berry tribute movie *Hail! Hail! Rock'n'Roll* – Richards had inducted Berry into the Rock And Roll Hall Of Fame in 1986, admitting "I lifted every lick he ever played". Finally, he let loose the fantastic solo album *Talk Is Cheap* (1988), a return to *Exile*-ish Rock 'n' Roll.

When the Stones gathered for a meeting at the Savoy Hotel, London, on 18 May 1988, it was the first time they had been in a room together for two years. The following January, Jagger and Richards reconvened in Barbados and, after a spirited shouting match, clicked back into writing like old times. A few days later, aptly, they were inducted into the Rock And Roll Hall Of Fame.

Steel Wheels (1989), including US No.5 'Mixed Emotions', was their biggest seller since *Tattoo You* and proved the platform for their middle-aged glory days of colossal, cleverly paced tours, surpassing all previous profits. *Rolling Stone* magazine's readers rewarded them with Best Artist, Best Band, Best Tour and Best Comeback of the year awards (as well as Worst Album Cover).

Their stately tread through the 90s was marked by 1991's live *Flashpoint*, 1994's patchy *Voodoo Lounge* (the first Stones album without Wyman, who retired in March 1992 and was replaced by Darryl Jones), 1995's live *Stripped* (including a cover of Dylan's 'Like A Rolling Stone') and 1997's *Bridges To Babylon* (including the hit 'Anybody Seen My Baby', whose inadvertent resemblance to 'Constant Craving' won kd lang a co-credit). Meanwhile, finally reconciled to the idea of solo albums, Richards made the tedious *Main Offender* (1992) and Jagger weighed in with the more ambitious but equally unmemorable *Wandering Spirit* (1993).

To purist chagrin, they also explored more tangential sources of income: making $2.8 million when Klein allowed Snickers to use '(Can't Get No) Satisfaction' in a 1991 TV ad, launching a Rolling Stones credit card for the *Voodoo Lounge* tour, and selling 'Start Me Up' for $5 million to advertise Microsoft's Windows 95.

With Jagger a grandfather and elected Honorary President of his LSE *alma mater* ahead of both Mother Theresa and Carlos The Jackal, the Stones have passed beyond criticism and censure into the realm of myth. The approaching millennium found them on a year-long *Bridges To Babylon* tour, with Richards and Wood solo albums on the stocks and reviews for Jagger's role as a drag queen in a Nazi concentration camp in the movie *Bent* (1998) suggesting he might have a future as an actor after all.

(READ) *The Rolling Stones Complete Recording Sessions* (1990), Martin Elliott

(FAN) Shattered! International, PO Box 3723, London, SE15 1HW, UK

(SURF) www.the–rolling–stones.com

HENRY ROLLINS

WHO b. Henry Garfield, 13 Feb 1961, Washington DC, USA

WHAT Testosterone Punk angst

Tattooed, crop-headed, muscular Henry Rollins might not look like most people's image of a renaissance man, but that is what he's become since his former band, Black Flag, split in 1986. Rollins tells the story of the seminal Punk band he fronted in his book *Get In The Van: On The Road With Black Flag*, the audio version of which won a Grammy.

A prolific author and, via his 2.13.61 imprint, the publisher of his own and others' work, including that of Nick Cave and Iggy Pop, he is also an actor (90s movie credits appear on *Johnny Mnemonic, Heat* and *Lost Highway*), spoken-word performer, record producer and label boss. The teetotal, drug-free lifestyle Rollins advocates has doubtless helped him to do all this while leading The Rollins Band, formed in 1987 with guitarist Chris Haskett, drummer Sim Cain and bassist Andrew Weiss. Applying Blues and Jazz influences to ferocious Metallic Rock, they're acclaimed for their compelling live shows and for Rollins' intensely personal, confrontational lyrics.

The Rollins Band debuted with *Hot Animal Machine* (1986), won acclaim for *The End Of Silence* (1991) and finally charted with the celebrated *Weight* (1994), by which time Melvin Gibbs had replaced Weiss. In 1997, sound engineer Theo Van Rock graduated to member status for *Come In And Burn*, while Rollins hooked up with Goldie for the *Spawn* soundtrack.

(READ) *The Portable Henry Rollins* (1997), Henry Rollins

(SURF) www.two1361.com/rband/rollins.html

LINDA RONSTADT ✪✪✪

WHO b. 15 Jul 1946, Tucson, Arizona, USA

WHAT Crystalline Country to OTT Opera

In a career spanning nearly 30 years, Linda Ronstadt has tackled Country, Rock, Light Opera, Mariachi and Big Band music.

Moving to LA at 18, she formed The Stone Poneys, who made three albums of Country Folk. By the third, 1967's *Stone Poneys And Friends Vol. III*, Linda had stepped out alone and scored a US hit with her version of Michael Nesmith's 'Different Drum'. Her first solo album, *Hand Sown Home Grown* (1969), was a step in the direction that would bring her success. *Silk Purse* (1970) and *Linda Ronstadt* (1972) contained material by Gene Clark, Neil Young and Jackson Browne. *Don't Cry Now* (1973) went gold and preceded the quality albums *Heart Like A Wheel* (1974), *Prisoner In Disguise* (1975) and *Hasten Down The Wind* (1976).

The 80s found Ronstadt tackling Opera (*La Bohème* and *The Pirates Of Penzance*), Spanish-influenced music (1987's *Canciones De Mi Padre* and 1991's *Mas Canciones*) and standards (1983's *What's New* and 1984's *Lush Life*). In recent years she has returned to her 'mainstream' career, recording with Aaron Neville on 1989's *Cry Like A Rainstorm (Howl Like The Wind)* and an album that paid tribute to some of the great female vocalists of the past – *Winterlight* (1993) – featuring material originally recorded by Etta James, Dusty Springfield and Dionne Warwick.

Her first UK chart entry was in 1976 with 'Tracks Of My Tears' and two singles later hit the UK Top 10: 'Somewhere Out There' (a duet with James Ingram from the 1987 movie *An American Tail*) and, with Aaron Neville, 'Don't Know Much' (1989). She rose to even greater heights in a 1992 edition of *The Simpsons*, advertising the virtues of barfly Barney's snow plow business.

READ *It's So Easy* (1990), Mark Bego

SURF www.WCO.com:80/~sashlock

ROSE ROYCE ☉

WHO Vocals **Gwen Dickey**, guitar **Kenji Chiba Brown**, bass **Lequeint 'Juke' Jobe**, drums **Henry 'Hammer' Garner**, percussion **Terral Santiel**, keyboards **Mike Nash**, trumpet **Kenny Copeland**, trumpet **Freddie Dunn**, saxophone **Michael Moore**

WHEN 1976–

WHERE Los Angeles, California, USA

WHAT Disco diamonds

Enlisted by Motown producer Norman Whitfield, the future members of Rose Royce – bar Gwen Dickey – backed Edwin Starr (as Total Concept Limited), Yvonne Fair (as Magic Wand), Undisputed Truth and The Temptations. Centre stage beckoned when they recruited Dickey and became Disco diamonds with the platinum-selling, Grammy-winning soundtrack of *Car Wash* (1976) and the hits 'Car Wash' (a US No.1), 'I Wanna Get Next To You' and 'I'm Going Down' (both 1977).

They made a splash in Europe, too, with 'It Makes You Feel Like Dancing', 'Ooh Boy' and the sublime 'Wishing On A Star'

from *In Full Bloom* (1977) and 'Love Don't Live Here Anymore' from 1979's *Rainbow Connection*. However, after the latter's splendid 'Is It Love You're After' and UK No.1 *Greatest Hits* (1980), they sank into the usual morass of personnel changes and minor sellers that customarily affect legends of yesteryear. Though they continue gigging and recording, their legacy is best represented by S'Express' sampling of 'Is It Love You're After' for 1988 Acid House monster 'Theme From S'Express' and covers of their classics, from Madonna's 1984 take on 'Love Don't Live Here Anymore' to Mary J. Blige's 1994 revamp of 'I'm Going Down'. Rap respect led to Ice Cube's inclusion of 'I Wanna Get Next To You' in his *Friday* (1996) soundtrack and Jaÿ-Z's 1997 resurrection of 'Wishing On A Star', co-starring Rose queen Gwen Dickey.

> **Roskilde** is a festival, held in Denmark, that makes Glastonbury look like a few tramps drinking in the park. From inauspicious beginnings in 1971 (10,000 gathered for headliners Joe Cocker and Skin Alley), Roskilde audiences have steadily grown. In 1988, the festival became a three-day event, with 62,100 attending for a bill headlined by Sting, Bryan Adams, Toto and Leonard Cohen. Other 80s notables were U2, Lou Reed, The Clash, Metallica, Eric Clapton, Pixies and Iggy Pop. By 1990, the festival had grown to four days and 90s headliners included Björk, Bob Dylan, Paul Simon, Nirvana, Neil Young, REM, Bowie, Black Sabbath, Marilyn Manson, Garbage and The Beastie Boys. Roskilde is organized almost entirely by volunteers, with profits going to a charity that works with Denmark's government to support humanitarian and cultural work for children and young people.

Roskilde

DIANA ROSS ☉ ✪

WHO b. Diane Ross, 26 Mar 1944, Detroit, Michigan, USA

WHAT Elegantly electrifying Soul empress

Diana Ross had two of 1997's greatest hits, despite releasing no new records: her 'I'm Coming Out' was the basis of The Notorious BIG's 'Mo Money Mo Problems' and 'Upside Down' was remodelled as MC Lyte's 'Cold Rock A Party'. Both were masterminded by producer Puff Daddy, whose use of further Ross samples on his *No Way Out* (1997) confirmed her place in his heart and her royal Soul status.

She sprang to superstardom from the wondrous Supremes. Not a 'great' singer in an Aretha Franklin sense, Ross nonetheless boasted an effortless elegance – showcased on her first major hit, the heart-stopping 'Ain't No Mountain High Enough'. Other Nicholas Ashford and Valerie Simpson-penned and produced hits, including 'Reach Out I'll Be There', graced her solo debut *Diana Ross* (1970). The album also premiered her penchant for confusing titles: 'Diana', 'Ross' and 'Diana Ross' graced later releases which have nothing bar the singer in common.

Success continued with the UK No.1 'I'm Still Waiting', from 1970's *Everything Is Everything* (or *I'm Still Waiting* in the UK). After 1971's live *Diana!* and flop *Surrender*, Ross won grudging critical acclaim for her blazing portrayal of Billie Holiday in the biopic *Lady Sings The Blues* (1972), whose soundtrack reached US No.1. She clung to the top with the title track of *Touch Me In*

The Morning (1973) and sent Soul fans' spines a-shivering with *Diana And Marvin* (1973), a fine collection of Marvin Gaye duets, including the hit 'You Are Everything'.

Last Time I Saw Him (1973) and *Live At Caesar's Palace* (1974) went unremarked, but *Diana Ross* (1976) boasted two US No.1s: the smoochy 'Theme From Mahogany (Do You Know Where You're Going To)' and the heavenly 'Love Hangover', which married a dreamy intro to an ahead-of-its-time Disco symphony.

Inspiration and sales waned through *Greatest Hits* (1976), *An Evening With Diana Ross* (1977), *Baby It's Me* (1977) and *Ross* (1978), and her involvement in Motown's musical *The Wiz* (1978) hardly turned things around. She emerged from the doldrums with *The Boss* (1979), whose funky defiance coloured 'I Ain't Been Licked', 'It's My House' and the title track. However, this was but a trailer for the effervescent platinum-reaper *Diana* (1980). Helmed by Chic's Nile Rodgers and Bernard Edwards, it spawned 'I'm Coming Out', 'My Old Piano' and the US No.1 'Upside Down'.

The revival continued with two movie themes: 1980's 'It's My Turn' (also included on 1981's cuddly collection *To Love Again*) and 1981's universal weepy 'Endless Love', with Lionel Richie. She also joined one of Rock's least plausible romances, her beau at the time being Heavy Metal monster Gene Simmons of Kiss.

Coincidentally, among the smashes from *Why Do Fools Fall In Love* (1981) was the metallic 'Mirror, Mirror', although the album is most celebrated for its title track – a sparkling remake of a Frankie Lymon hit from 1956. Michael Jackson, whom Ross had championed since his early Motown days, returned the favour by penning the slinky 'Muscles' for *Silk Electric* (1982). The

delicate 'Missing You' similarly sustained *Swept Away* (1984), but 1983's intervening *Ross* was more indicative of the hit-free turn her career took. The explosive, Bee Gee-penned UK No.1 'Chain Reaction' made *Eaten Alive* (1985) a minor success, but nothing could save *Red Hot Rhythm & Blues* (1986) or *Workin' Overtime* (1989) from the dumper – even, in the latter's case, a return to Nile Rodgers and Motown after seven years on RCA.

However, while her US chart fortunes never fully recovered, Ross conquered the UK again with *The Force Behind The Power* (1991) and its hits 'When You Tell Me That You Love Me', 'One Shining Moment' and 'If We Hold On Together' – the latter originally from Steven Spielberg's 1988 dino-movie *The Land Before Time*. Fans were spoilt for choice in 1993: a fine, live return to her Billie Holi-days with *Stolen Moments (The Lady Sings… Jazz And Blues)*, the four-CD retrospective *Forever Diana*, the UK chart-topping collection *One Woman* and, with Placido Domingo and José Carreras, *Christmas In Vienna*.

A further festive collection, 1994's *A Very Special Season*, preceded the triumphant *Take Me Higher* (1995), which pitched the hearty, housey title track against the breathtakingly beautiful 'Gone'. Most commercially successful, however, was its cover of 'I Will Survive' – a redundant declaration from a woman whose effervescent excellence needs no further reinforcement.

read *Secrets Of A Sparrow* (1993), Diana Ross

fan International Diana Ross Fan Club, PO Box 32152, Detroit, MI 48232-0152, USA

surf dianaross.com/

Wow!

fabulous

Toni Braxton

More than any other Indie label, Rough Trade embodied DIY Punk ethics. Founded by Geoff Travis in 1976 as a London record shop – it became <u>the</u> place for hip US and Reggae imports, independent releases and fanzines. Travis founded Rough Trade Records in 1978. Launched with industrialists Metal Urbain, its diverse roster boasted Reggae artist Augustus Pablo alongside Stiff Little Fingers and prickly electronic types Cabaret Voltaire. Rough Trade's best – The Pop Group, Aztec Camera, The Go-Betweens, The Fall, Scritti Politti, Jonathan Richman, Pere Ubu – bravely bent Pop's rules. The success of The Smiths bankrolled such indulgences and led to Travis' joint label with Warner Music UK, Blanco Y Negro – home to Dinosaur Jr, Catatonia, Everything But The Girl and The Jesus & Mary Chain. However, when The Smiths defected to EMI and bright hopes The Sundays failed to conquer the universe, Rough Trade hit a rough patch. Its distribution network collapsed in 1991, but the label – and an international chain of shops – thrives to this day.

ROXETTE

WHO Vocals **Marie Fredriksson** (b. 30 May 1958, Östra Ljungby, Sweden), guitar/vocals **Per Gessle** (b. 12 Jan 1959, Halmstad, Sweden)

WHEN 1986–

WHERE Sweden

WHAT Light Rock, heavy sales

Having soared with the platinum-plated Abba, Sweden coasted with Roxette – party Poppers bereft of their forerunners' sparkle, but with almost as much selling power. Per Gessle (formerly of domestic stars Gyllene Tider) and singer Marie Fredriksson stormed the US Top 10 with *Look Sharp!* (1988), the US No.1 'The Look' and US No.2 'Listen To Your Heart'. More US chart-toppers came with the *Pretty Woman* soundtrack cut 'It Must Have Been Love' (1990) and the title track of *Joyride* (1991).

Tourism (1992) sank Stateside, but Europe was crazy for Roxette and sent 1994's *Crash! Boom! Bang!* to UK No.3 and rushed to buy 1995's best-of *Don't Bore Us… Get To The Chorus!*.

But after 1996's Spanish set *Baladas En Español*, Roxette fell silent, and their Pop position was hijacked by Savage Garden.

(READ) *Roxette – Tourism* (1995), Milton Okun

(SURF) www.roxette.nl/

ROXY MUSIC ⊙ ⊙ ⊙ ⊙

WHO Vocals/keyboards **Bryan Ferry** (b. 26 Sep 1945, Washington, Tyne and Wear, England), guitar **Phil Manzanera** (b. Philip Targett-Adams, 31 Jan 1951, London, England), saxophone **Andy Mackay** (b. 23 Jul 1946, Lostwithiel, England), keyboards **Brian Eno** (b. 15 May 1948, Woodbridge, England)

WHEN 1970–1982

WHERE London, England

WHAT Art Rock to AOR

The Roxy story began when Bryan Ferry and bassist Graham Simpson left Newcastle R&B band Gasboard. Ferry had made his stage debut at a Sunderland working men's club in 1964 with The Banshees. Years later, another band called (Siouxsie &) The Banshees would be formed after meeting at a Roxy Music show.

Ferry and Simpson moved to London and hooked up with Eno, Andy Mackay, drummer Dexter Lloyd and ex-Nice guitarist David O'List. The latter two were replaced by Paul Thompson and Phil Manzanera before the making of *Roxy Music* (1972).

Roxy Music was feverishly imaginative, mixing 50s Rock 'n' Roll guitars, honking sax and tinkling Jazz piano with Brian Eno's weird electronic sounds. Hovering above it all was Ferry's heavily mannered voice, his lyrics sardonically toying with the traditional romantic vocabulary of Pop. Roxy hit the UK Top 10 with their first singles, 'Virginia Plain' (1972) and 'Pyjamarama' (1973), and startled TV viewers with their extravagant visual image: a bizarre hybrid of 50s Teddy Boy style and Glam Rock androgyny.

Simpson was replaced by Rik Kenton, but he quit before *For Your Pleasure* (1973) and Roxy used session bassists thereafter. The album, even more diverse than its predecessor, ranged from the camp stomp of 'Do The Strand' to the eerie 'In Every Dream Home A Heartache', a neurotic love song to an inflatable sex doll.

A series of clashes with Ferry prompted Eno's departure, and

Eddie Jobson took his place in time for *Stranded* (1973). Its 'Street Life' provided another UK hit, and the album's lyrics consolidated Ferry's adopted persona as a tormented lounge lizard. *Country Life* (1974), another powerful set, included the upbeat 'All I Want Is You' and adventurous 'Triptych', but attracted attention mainly for its cover (two women in transparent underwear). 'Love Is The Drug', from *Siren* (1975), was Roxy's first transatlantic hit, but the album was generally seen as disappointing. A four-year silence followed, broken only by solo releases and 1976's live *Viva!*

Roxy regrouped in 1979 as a trio comprising Ferry, Manzanera and Mackay. They enjoyed considerable success with *Manifesto* (1979), *Flesh And Blood* (1980) and *Avalon* (1981), and topped the British singles chart with a cover of John Lennon's 'Jealous Guy', recorded as a tribute following his murder.

However, by then, style seemed to have overwhelmed content. The three late-period albums contained moments of languid loveliness like 'Dance Away' and *Avalon*'s title track, but lacked the edge and experimentation of the Eno era.

The band continued touring after *Avalon*, releasing 1983's live *Musique/The High Road*. Another live recording, from 1982, was belatedly released as *Heart Still Beating* in 1990, but there has been no new material since the early 80s. However, many of the New Romantic bands who emerged during that time displayed a huge Roxy influence; Japan's David Sylvian, in particular, had clearly studied Ferry's vocal technique with great care.

In a 1997 interview, Mackay hinted at a Roxy Music reunion, perhaps even including Eno. The fact that Ferry's *Mamouna* (1994) was his first album of original material for seven years suggests that fans would be well advised not to hold their breath but, then again, Roxy Music have surprised us before.

Fan Bryan Ferry & Roxy Music Information Service, PO Box 829, Dumbarton G82 1BG, UK

surf www.cco.caltech.edu/~bryan/roxy/

RUN D.M.C.

WHO Vocals **Run** (b. Joseph Simmons, 14 Nov 1964, Hollis, Queens, New York, USA), vocals **DMC** (b. Darryl McDaniels, 31 May 1964, Hollis), DJ **Jam Master Jay** (b. Jason Mizell, 21 Jan 1965, Hollis)

WHEN 1982–

WHERE Hollis, Queens, New York, USA

WHAT Hell-raisin', way-walkin' Rap demigods

They stopped The Spice Girls! They topped *Titanic*! They are the great, the grumpy Run DMC – whose Jason Nevins-revamped 'It's Like That' ruled European charts from late 1997, keeping both the Girl Power posse and Céline Dion from the UK top spot. Back in 1983, the original single impacted only on hardcore Hip Hop heads, whose collections were otherwise likely to have been dominated by the party-hardy likes of Whodini and Kurtis Blow.

Run was DJing for Kurtis at the time, seizing every chance to grab the mic himself. This grandstanding fuelled the single's cataclysmic flipside 'Sucker MCs' – a sneering put-down of rival DJs that, like the A-side's social commentary, shaped Rap's lyrical evolution. Their authenticity was bolstered by a black-clad, sneaker-shod image: a stark contrast to the futuristic Funk outfits of their predecessors like Grandmaster Flash & The Furious Five.

Most important was their addition of guitar to the Hip Hop formula of bragging over beats. The single 'Rock Box' pointed the way, and helped *Run DMC* (1984) to secure a year-long tenancy on the US chart. Ironically, they'd blueprinted a style that, thanks mainly to The Beastie Boys, made millions for the Def Jam label – co-founded by Run's brother Russell Simmons – yet remained bound to Profile, with whom they'd signed in 1983.

King Of Rock (1985) was Rap's first platinum album and they added a street cachet to Artists Against Apartheid's 'Sun City' smash and the back-slapping star-fest Live Aid. Russell Simmons – their producer, despite his Def Jam ties – cashed in with *Krush Groove* (1985), a loosely autobiographical movie also featuring Kurtis Blow, the Beasties and The Fat Boys. Having conquered Rap, Run DMC were now set to take on the world.

But global conquest arose from an afterthought rather than a masterplan. Rick Rubin, a Rock fan who'd founded Def Jam with Simmons and joined him in Run's production booth, suggested they embellish a reworking of Aerosmith's 'Walk This Way' with Steven Tyler and Joe Perry. The duo were enticed by an $8,000 fee to a session where confusion reigned. Run, who "used to rap over 'Walk This Way' when I was 12", thought they were called Toys In The Attic, the title of the Aerosmith album on which the song first appeared. Meanwhile, Tyler and Perry – noting the trio "huddled in a corner, really intent on something" – assumed they were "probably smoking crack". It turned out, said Tyler, "They'd been eating lunch from McDonald's."

The song crashed US and UK charts, spurring *Raising Hell* (1986) to multi-million sales. It sent shockwaves through Rap and Rock: a crossover so natural today was then a headline-grabbing sensation. Adidas returned the plaudits paid on their cut 'My Adidas' by marketing a Run DMC model sneaker and renowned bandwagon-hopper Michael Jackson called for a collaboration.

The truculent trio, however, instead set off on tours with the Beasties and Public Enemy – the latter a bottom-of-the-bill act who took Run's street styling to paramilitary proportions and ripped them off wholesale on their Rubin-produced debut *Yo! Bum Rush The Show*. From these humble origins, Public Enemy vaulted to the top of the Rap tree, leaving their predecessors looking, all of a sudden, leaden and old-fashioned. It didn't help that, within months of unleashing 1987's B-Boy bruisers like 'It's Tricky', they were dropping dross like 'Christmas In Hollis'.

Despite its hit soundtrack, their self-mocking movie *Tougher Than Leather* (1988) flopped. At war with Profile, their credibility was crippled by 1989's *Ghostbusters II* theme and the flop *Back From Hell* (1990), listeners remaining unmoved by their sampling of The Stone Roses' 'Fool's Gold' for the flop 'What's It All About'.

They returned triumphant with 1993's *Down With The King*. However, its success – returning them to the US Top 10 – wasn't enough to stop reformed alcoholic Run pursuing his new-found Christian beliefs to a career in the pulpit. Contractual quibbling and the odd gig here and there filled the years before Hip Hop nerd Nevins rejigged 'It's Like That'… and that's the way it is.

Meanwhile, Wu-Tang Clan bowed down with an ace cover of 'Sucker MCs' on 1997's tribute *In Tha Beginning… There Was Rap*. The cut's message was confirmed with DMC's 1998 declaration: "Hip Hop isn't about gangs, being a B-boy isn't about packing heat… It's about dropping the baddest rhymes over the dopest beats and saying to the next crew, 'Beat that, suckas'".

(ReaD) *Tougher Than Leather* (1987), Bill Adler

(surf) www.users.interport.net/~tjbeat/code/rdmain.html

TODD RUNDGREN

WHO b. 22 Jun 1948, Upper Darby, Pennsylvania

WHAT Progressive Art Rocker

After three albums and a couple of minor hits leading the Garage Pop band Nazz, Todd Rundgren built a cult reputation as an all-round eccentric Anglophile Pop genius in 1970 with 'We Gotta Get You A Woman' (US No.20) and *Runt* – a nickname given him by Patti Smith – and *The Ballad Of Todd Rundgren* (1971).

Signed to Albert Grossman's Bearsville company as solo artist and house producer for acts such as The Band (whose *Stage Fright* he engineered), Rundgren's breakthrough came with 1972's sprawling *Something/Anything?*, on which he played virtually everything himself. The album furnished the US hits – 'I Saw The Light' and 'Hello It's Me' – followed by the grandiose diversity of *A Wizard, A True Star* (1973) and *Todd* (1974). Having mucked up the first New York Dolls album, he thereafter lived a triple life as solo artist; producer of acts as disparate as Meat Loaf (the immense *Bat Out Of Hell*), Hall & Oates, Grand Funk Railroad and Patti Smith; and guitarist/leader of Prog Rock band Utopia.

His own albums ranged from the pseudo-mysticism of 1975's *Initiation* to the Pop exercises of 1976's *Faithful*, which featured note-perfect covers of songs like 'Good Vibrations', 'Strawberry Fields Forever', 'If Six Was Nine' and 'Most Likely You Go Your Way And I'll Go Mine' (as if that might make him equal to The Beach Boys, Beatles, Hendrix and Dylan). Utopia's indulgent albums likewise swung between 1977's Egyptologically-inclined *Ra* (UK No. 27), the more Pop-oriented *Oops! Wrong Planet* (1977) and the Beatles pastiches of *Deface The Music* (1980).

Rundgren remained, however, a master of both audio and video studio techniques, releasing a self-produced video special to accompany *The Ever Popular Tortured Artist Effect* (1983) and using only treated samples of his own voice to make *A Cappella* (1985) – although, ironically, a promotional tour required an 11-piece band. He continued to expand into other media: a musical production of Joe Orton's script *Up Against It* (originally intended as the sequel to *Help!*), for which he wrote the score, enjoyed a run at New York's Public Theatre in August 1989 and, in the early 90s, he increasingly concentrated on computer software, developing the Flowflazer psychedelic-graphics package and the NuTek Video Toaster "mini-TV studio".

In 1994 he became TR-I (Todd Rundgren Interactive), issuing the interactive CD *No World Order* (1993) and playing gigs which afforded the audience control over the show's music. A further multi-media CD-Plus album, *The Individualist*, arrived in 1995.

RUNRIG

WHO Vocals/bass **Rory MacDonald** (b. 27 Jul 1949, Dornoch, Western Isles, Scotland), vocals/guitar **Donnie Monro** (b. 2 Aug 1953, Uig, Isle of Skye, Scotland), vocals/drums **Calum MacDonald** (b. 12 Nov 1953, Lochmaddy, North Uist, Scotland), guitar/pipes **Malcolm Jones**, keyboards **Peter Wishart**

WHEN 1973–

WHERE Glasgow, Scotland

WHAT Gaelic Heritage writ – and sung – large

The part-time covers-playing Run Rig Dance Band (Run Rig refers to ridges left by a plough, which gave their name to an old form of communal farming) was formed by brothers Rory and Calum MacDonald and accordionist Blair Douglas. In 1974, Donnie Munro joined and Robert MacDonald (no relation) replaced Blair.

After touring more widely, including successful forays south of Hadrian's Wall, 1977's folky *Play Gaelic* – released on Scottish label Lismor – comprised original material, sung largely in Gaelic. The band set up its own label, Ridge Records, for the more Rock-based *Highland Connection* (1979) as the band became full-time professionals and Malcolm Jones replaced Robert MacDonald (who died in 1986). *Recovery* (1981), with drummer Iain Bayne, was a concept album about the social history of the Scottish Gael, clearly indicating the band's roots and political inclination.

Despite an abortive liaison with a London record company, *Heartland* (1985) appeared with the addition of English keyboard player Richard Cherns. When he left for a career in theatre, another Scot, Peter Wishart, formerly of Big Country, stepped in.

Relative stability followed with musicianship maturing and audiences growing. After *The Cutter And The Clan* (1987), they signed to a major label, Chrysalis, who immediately re-released the album and issued subsequent work, including *An Uhbal As Airde* (1995), the first Gaelic single to make the UK Top 20.

In 1997, despite the band's continuing success and the release of *Recovery*, Munro announced his intention to leave and stand as a Labour candidate in the UK General Election in his home constituency. He came a respectable second, failing to become Rock's first Member of Parliament. Their winter 1997 tour was Munro's formal farewell, although he stated his intention to return for one-off concerts on special occasions.

ⓇEAD *Going Home – The Story* (1991), Tom Morton

Ⓕan Runrig Official Fanclub, 1 York Street, Aberdeen AB11 5DL, UK

Ⓢurf www.runrig.co.uk/

RUSH

WHO Vocals/bass **Geddy Lee** (b. Gary Lee Weinrib, 29 Jul 1953, Toronto, Ontario, Canada), guitar **Alex 'Lerxst' Lifeson** (b. Alex Zivojinovic, 27 Aug 1953, Fernie, British Columbia, Canada), drums **Neil Peart** (b. 12 Sep 1952, Hamilton, Ontario)

WHEN 1968–

WHERE Toronto, Ontario, Canada

WHAT Pomp Rock Professors

Basement band buddies Alex Lifeson and Geddy Lee secured their long-term prospects by replacing drummer John Rutsey (featured on their eponymous 1974 debut) with learned lyricist and percussionist Neil Peart in 1974. Ditching Zeppish powerhousing for Yes-esque pomp, they dashed off *Fly By Night* (1975) and *Caress Of Steel* (1976), unswayed by chart placings that began poorly and got worse. Tours zig-zagged across the USA, governed by wherever and whomever would have them. Disdainful of show-bizzy Hard Rock contemporaries, Rush made their mark musically: *2112* (1976) was an instant classic that mitigated the 20-minute title track's conceptual silliness with jolly riffing and a sideful of actual songs.

Despite charting low in the USA and not at all overseas, they acquired a loyal following. Accordingly, *A Farewell To Kings* (1977) made the Top 40 on both sides of the Atlantic and initiated a string of sellout tours and classy albums: *Hemispheres* (1978), *Permanent Waves* (1980), fans' favourite *Moving Pictures* (1981) and *Signals* (1982). But class turned to cliché, and *Grace Under Pressure* (1984), *Power Windows* (1985), *Hold Your Fire* (1987) and *Presto* (1989) sounded less like bold steps forward than variations on a theme – the band having jettisoned its Prog Rock roots in favour of radio-friendly AOR. They plumbed the depths with *A Show Of Hands* (1989), their third and least interesting live album (after 1976's *All The World's A Stage* and 1981's *Exit... Stage Left*).

However, a label change (from Mercury to Atlantic), the turn of the decade and breathing space provided by the *Chronicles* collection (1990) combined to add zest to the Rush formula. Pounding rather than ponderous, *Roll The Bones* (1991) and *Counterparts* (1993) sold well amid the onslaught of Grunge. Further vindication came when *Test For Echo* (1996) matched its predecessors' high-flying success on the US charts. In between, Peart masterminded *Burning For Buddy: A Tribute To The Music Of Buddy Rich* (1994 – a second volume followed in 1997) and Lifeson issued solo album *Victor* (1996).

Nearly two decades after Canada's government hailed them the country's Ambassadors of Music, Rush were named, in 1997, officers of the Order of Canada (a title acknowledging 'significant achievement in important fields of human endeavor', bestowed before on Bryan Adams, kd lang and Neil Young). Lee said "I'm going to wear it all the time and see if it gets me better tables at restaurants". Meanwhile, fans, who prize skills over showmanship, remain as committed as detractors remain hostile.

ⓇEAD *Rush – Visions: The Official Biography* (1988), Bill Banasiewicz

Ⓕan A Show of Fans, c/o Steve Streeter, PO Box 292, Canton, CT 06019, USA

Ⓢurf syrinx.umd.edu/rush.html

SADE ◉ ✪

WHO b. Helen Folasade Adu, 16 Jan 1959, Ibadan, Nigeria

WHAT Cool, classy queen of 80s Yuppie Soul Jazz

Before signing solo to CBS/Epic in 1984, Sade fronted Arriva (with whom she first performed 'Smooth Operator'), Pride, and Sade – the group. After low-key gigs at Ronnie Scott's, and an investment from manager Lee Barrett, her Epic deal meant band members Andrew Hale, Paul Denman and Stewart Matthewman signed in turn to her. 'Your Love Is King' and 'Smooth Operator' made the UK Top 20 and *Diamond Life* (1984) was a 99-week chart mainstay – one of the most successful female debuts of all time. A soundtrack for yuppiedom, with MOR appeal and huge sales, *Promise* (1986) topped US and UK charts.

Sade was flavour-of-the-80s – a fact amplified by a Live Aid appearance, a Best New Artist Grammy, the cover of *Time* and a part as a torch singer in the 1987 movie *Absolute Beginners*. In 1988, *Stronger Than Pride* reached UK No.3, and a sellout world tour showcased Sade's restrained, sultry delivery.

She resurfaced after a four-year absence with 'No Ordinary Love' (featured on 1993's *Indecent Proposal* soundtrack) and *Love Deluxe* (1992). Awarded Best Artist at the first Black Music Awards, Sade toured the USA in 1993, but began to slip from view and 'Cherish The Day' languished outside the Top 50. Despite another Grammy in 1994, former drummer Paul Cook issued a writ against Sony and Sade for royalties in 1995 and interest dwindled as Sade's work rate reduced.

read *Sade* (1986), Mark Bego

surf www.epix.net/'awarner/sade

SAINT ETIENNE

WHO Vocals **Sarah Cracknell** (b. 12 Apr 1967, Chelmsford, Essex, England), keyboards/programming **Bob Stanley** (b. 25 Dec 1965, Horsham, Sussex, England), keyboards/programming **Pete Wiggs** (b. 15 May 1966, Reigate, Surrey, England)

WHEN 1990–

WHERE London, England

WHAT Glossy, elegant Dance Pop

Saint Etienne say it loud: they're synthetic and they're proud. In their world, style is all and 'Rock' is an offensive four-letter word.

After 1990's singles with guest singers ('Kiss And Make Up' and an as-good-as-the-original cover of Neil Young's 1970 hit 'Only Love Can Break Your Heart'), golden-voiced Sarah Cracknell joined for their first hit, 'Nothing Can Stop Us', from the in-jokey but excellent *Foxbase Alpha* (1991). *So Tough* – a breathtaking set of graceful dancefloor Pop – glided into the UK Top 10 in 1993 and the year was book-ended by the fine singles 'You're In A Bad Way' and, with The Charlatan's vocalist Tim Burgess, 'I Was Born On Christmas Day'. Between those was a majestic cover of Candlewick Green's 1974 hit 'Who Do You Think You Are'. In 1994, Saint Etienne toured with Oasis as their support act, but dipped in profile with the disappointing *Tiger Bay* and rumours of a split.

However, 1995's *Reserection*, a union with French star Etienne Daho, yielded their biggest hit, 'He's On The Phone'. Accordingly, they rounded off 1995 with *Too Young To Die – The Singles*, whose bonus disc of remixes (including fab manglings by Aphex Twin and The Chemical Brothers) reappeared as *Casino Classics* (1996).

While Bob Stanley and Pete Wiggs launched their Emidisc label – whose biggest stars are punky Pop outfit Kenickie – Sarah Cracknell stepped out solo with 1996's near-miss 'Anymore'. Saint Etienne resurfaced in 1998 with the hit 'Sylvie' from *Good Humor*.

fan Lovers Unite, c/o Emidisc, 47 Brewer St, London, W1R 3FD, UK

surf saint.etienne.net/

SALT-N-PEPA

WHO Vocals **Salt** (b. Cheryl James, 8 Mar 1964, Brooklyn, New York, USA), vocals **Pepa** (b. Sandra Denton, 9 Nov 1961, Kingston, Jamaica), vocals **Spinderella** (b. Deirdre Roper, b. 3 Aug 1971, New York City, New York)

WHEN 1985–

WHERE Queens, New York, USA

WHAT Rap's finest flavas

Two new acts exploded after playing 1988's Wembley Stadium Nelson Mandela tribute gig. One was earnest singer/songwriter Tracy Chapman. The other, Salt-N-Pepa. Their ribald 'Push It' was as refreshing as Chapman's cool 'Fast Car'. That they parlayed this success into a decade-plus career was a triumph for female Rap – then otherwise characterized by one-offs like Roxanne Shanté.

Although they climbed to the head of the pack, Cheryl James and Sandi Denton began as mere mouthpieces for producer Hurby 'Luv Bug' Azor. As Super Nature, they fronted his 'Showstoppa' (1985) – a response to Doug E. Fresh's Hip Hop classic 'The Show' – then transformed into Salt-N-Pepa. With Hurby at the helm, they scored with cuts like 'Tramp', an update of Otis Redding's 1967 duelling duet with Carla Thomas. Platinum sales beckoned when the remixed 'Push It' – 'Tramp"s B-side – reached the US Top 20, sending *Hot, Cool & Vicious* (1986) into the chart too.

With DJ Latoya Hanson replaced by 'Dee Dee' Roper (who inherited her predecessor's pseudonym Spinderella), they scored again with the funky *A Salt With A Deadly Pepa* (1988) and *Black's Magic* (1990). Salt challenged Hurby as the band's brains, advancing her case with 1990's platinum US hit 'Expression'. Confirmation of their maturity came when 1991's 'Let's Talk About Sex' replaced 'Push It' as their anthem and highest charting single (hence 1991's *A Blitz Of Salt-N-Pepa Hits*).

By 1993, they'd ditched Hurby entirely. *Very Necessary* (1993) vindicated the slimmed-down crew – it sold millions, scooped saucy hits like 'Shoop' and 'Whatta Man' (an all-time classic with En Vogue) and gave a feminine sheen to Rap, then overrun by boys with guns. It also confirmed Salt as one of Rap's most dextrous, yet underrated, lyricists and producers. They coasted with oddities (Terrorvision backing a 1995 *Top Of The Pops* performance of the corrosive 'Ain't None Of Your Business' and their revamping of 'Gee, Officer Krupke' for a 1996 reworking of *The Songs Of West Side Story*) until the eclectic excellence of *Brand New* (1997). Including a Sheryl Crow cameo, it was belied by its empty-headed trailer 'RU Ready', but gold sales confirmed S-N-P as the spice girls with staying power.

Fan Jireh Records, Inc., PO Box 6206, McLean, VA 22106-6206, USA

Surf www.execpc.com/~mwildt/snp.html

> "You're always gonna get hit with **bricks** in this business. People are **coming at you** from different directions.
> And if that core is **not tight** – if there's **no love** in the group – **you can't stay together**"
> **Cheryl 'Salt' James**

SANTANA ✪✪

WHO Guitar/vocals **Carlos Santana** (b. 20 Jul 1947, Autlán de Navarro, Mexico), bass **David Brown** (b. 15 Feb 1947, New York City, New York, USA), drums **Mike Shrieve** (b. 6 Jul 1949, San Francisco, California, USA), keyboards/vocals **Greg Rolie** (b. 17 Jun 1947, Seattle, Washington, USA), percussion **José Chepito Areas** (b. 25 Jul 1946, Léon, Nicaragua)

WHEN 1966–

WHERE San Francisco, California, USA

WHAT Latin Rock rulers

With jamming partners David Brown, Greg Rolie, Rod Harper (drums) and Tom Frazer (guitar), Carlos Santana founded the Santana Blues Band, a cooperative in all but name (a musician's union rule made them designate a leader). Its ever-shifting line-up experimented with diverse cultural elements and sounds: Blues, Acid Rock, Latin and African. Their 1968 debut as Santana at San Francisco's Fillmore West won a standing ovation, but after a mesmerizing set at Woodstock (of which Shrieve's drum solo during 'Soul Sacrifice' was a highlight), the band signed to Columbia. Their revelatory debut *Santana* (1969), led by the US Top 10 hit 'Evil Ways', hit US No.4.

Abraxas (1970) stretched their multicultural space jams to US No.1 and 4 million copies, with storming versions of Tito Puento's 'Oye Como Va' and Peter Green's 'Black Magic Woman'. *Santana III* (1971) showcased Neal Schon, a 16-year-old guitarist whose Santana-like playing festooned the likes of 'Batuka' and the hits 'No One To Depend On' and 'Everybody's Everything' and who took Rolie with him when he left to form Journey.

Carlos launched himself into collaborative noodling in 1972 with the massive-selling *Carlos Santana And Buddy Miles Live*. While *Caravanserai* (1972) notched another US and UK Top 10 hit, his brother Jorge conceived his own band with a remarkably similar version of the Santana sound – 1994's *Brothers* project eventually combined the pair's skills.

In 1973, an intensified interest in religion prompted Carlos to add the prefix 'Devadip' to his name and record *Love, Devotion, Surrender* (1973) with Mahavishnu Orchestra members John McLaughlin and Billy Cobham and keyboard player Jan Hammer. But Santana was starting to stagnate by the mid-70s: dizzying line-up changes didn't help *Welcome* (1973). However, *Amigos* (1976) featured the hit 'Dance Sister Dance' and live/studio mix *Moonflower* (1977) returned them to the UK Top 10 with a funky cover of The Zombie's 'She's Not There'.

After success with *Zebop!* (1981) and *Shangó* (1983), Santana (now essentially Carlos and dozens of occasional members) continued into the 80s with *Havana Moon* (1983), *Beyond Appearances* (1985), Live Aid, a 20th anniversary show with all the band's previous members in 1986, 1987's Grammy-winning *Blues For Salvador* and the box set *Viva Santana!* (1988). Santana was also hailed as an influence by Prince and, as 90s releases like *Milagro* (1992) show, he remains innovative. In 1998, he was inducted into The Rock And Roll Hall Of Fame by Blues Traveler's John Popper: "You listen to 'Oye Como Va' and you see God."

Read *Summer Of Love* (1994), Joel Schin

Surf www.santana.com

ROCK ⓢ PEDIA

THE SCORPIONS

WHO Vocals **Klaus Meine** (b. 25 May 1948, Hanover, Germany), guitar **Rudy Schenker** (b. 31 Aug 1948, Hildesheim, Germany), guitar **Matthias Jabs** (b. 25 Oct 1955, Hanover), bass **Francis Buchholz** (b. 19 Jan 1950, Germany), drums **Herman 'Ze German' Rarebell** (b. 18 Nov 1949, Lubeck, Germany)

WHEN 1971–

WHERE Hanover, Germany

WHAT Metal mongers with a melodic sting

With enough over-the-top anthems and silly album covers to embarrass even Def Leppard, The Scorpions are Germany's biggest Metal export. After early incarnations fizzled in the late 60s, The Scorpions solidified in 1971 around mainstays Rudolf Schenker, his younger brother Michael (guitar) and Klaus Meine.

After 1972's ignored *Lonesome Crow*, UFO poached Michael in 1973. With his Hendrixy replacement Uli Jon Roth, they balanced Stateside failure with European success, courtesy of *Fly To The Rainbow* (1974), *In Trance* (1975), *Virgin Killer* (1976) and *Taken By Force* (1977). The live album *The Tokyo Tapes* (1978) proved Roth's swan song: he left to form Electric Sun (who peaked with 1981's *Firewind*). Michael Schenker guested on the melodic Metal classic, *Lovedrive* (1979), then Matthias Jabs, who'd deputized on Michael's off-days, was promoted to full-time status.

Animal Magnetism (1980) and the US million-seller *Blackout* (1982) thrust the band to superstardom, particularly with the latter's hit 'No One Like You'. But 1984's *Love At First Sting* was the killer, securing double-platinum status in the USA and yielding the anthemic 'Rock You Like A Hurricane'. Live, they reached Van Halen-esque heights of frenzy, as 1985's *World Wide Live* proved.

After *Savage Amusement* (1988), the trans-European smash 'Wind Of Change' made *Crazy World* (1990) The Scorps' biggest seller. Thereafter, they followed their own formula with gently diminishing returns on *Face The Heat* (1993), *Live Bites* (1995), *Pure Instinct* (1996) and a bewildering variety of compilations.

 scorpweb.simplenet.com/

SCRITTI POLITTI

WHO Vocals/guitar/keyboards **Green Gartside** (b. 22 Jun 1956, Cardiff, Wales)

WHEN 1977–

WHERE Leeds, Yorkshire, England

WHAT Sugar-coated Soul

In the pollution-choked 80s, Scritti Politti's mainman Green Gartside thoughtfully planned to preserve the world's vinyl resources by releasing a new album only every five or ten years. So far, the plan has worked spectacularly. And although its side effect was relative obscurity, Scritti Politti will be remembered for concocting some of the decade's finest Pop.

Befitting a former Young Communist, Gartside conceived Scritti Politti (Italian for 'political writing') as a vehicle for political rants. With three fellow art students, he moved to London, recorded their debut 'Skank Bloc Bologna' (1978) and

supported post-Punk heroes Joy Division and Gang Of Four. However, progress was halted in 1980 by Gartside's ill-health.

When they returned with 1981's *Songs To Remember* and its hit 'The Sweetest Girl' (later covered by Madness for a 1986 hit, and Robert Wyatt), bassist Nial Jinks had been lost to obscurity, keyboardist Matthew Kay had become their manager and Scritti's sound was worlds away from Punk: dreamy Pop, dollops of Soul, Jazz and Reggae and Gartside's breathy vocals.

Following drummer Tom Morley's departure, Green relocated to New York with engineer David Gamson, recruited drummer Fred Maher and spent an eternity crafting what he described as a "very super, hyper, syncopated, ping-ponged bif pow zip thing" – the sublime *Cupid And Psyche 85* (1985) and its hits 'Wood Beez (Pray Like Aretha Franklin)', 'Absolute', 'The Word Girl' and their sole US smash, 'Perfect Way'.

Having penned songs for Chaka Khan and Al Jarreau and graced the soundtrack to Madonna's movie *Who's That Girl* (1987), Green again retreated, emerging in 1988 with the excellent 'Oh Patti (Don't Feel Sorry For Loverboy)' – featuring Miles Davis – and *Provision* before ill-health prompted another lengthy absence. Since then, Green has broken cover only in 1991: he appeared on Heaven 17 spin-off BEF's *Music Of Quality And Distinction Volume 2* (1991) and, as Scritti Politti, with Reggae stars Shabba Ranks and Sweetie Irie on covers of The Beatles' 'She's A Woman' and Gladys Knight & The Pips' 'Take Me In Your Arms And Love Me' respectively. Fans holding their breath in anticipation of a new album are advised to refrain.

 www.brainlink.com/~taliesin/AREAS/sp/spFRAME.html

THE SEAHORSES

WHO Guitar **John Squire** (b. 24 Nov 1962, Broadheath, Greater Manchester, England), vocals **Chris Helme** (b. 22 Jul 1971, York, England), bass **Stuart Fletcher** (b. 16 Jan 1976, York, England)

WHEN 1996–

WHERE York, England

WHAT Guitar-helmed Indie Rock

The 28th of March 1996 began with John Squire announcing his departure from The Stone Roses and ended with the birth of The Seahorses in a York pub. First he spotted bassist Stuart Fletcher guesting with the pub band. Then, as he was leaving, he struck his head on a huge decorative fibre-glass seahorse.

The band name sorted, he turned his attention to finding a singer. Discovered busking on the streets of York, Chris Helme contributed songs ('premiered' by him outside Woolworth's) on The Seahorses' debut *Do It Yourself* (1997). Drummer Andy Watt completed the line-up for the Tony Visconti-produced recordings in Hollywood.

Do It Yourself became a platinum chart mainstay, having peaked at UK No.2 and spawned three hits: 'Love Is The Law', 'Blinded By The Sun' and the Squire/Liam Gallagher co-written 'Love Me And Leave Me'. Sellout tours, showcasing the familiar Squire guitar heroics and the swaggering stage presence of Helme, confirmed a confident start for a band who ended 1997 without Andy Watt but with a new hit, 'You Can Talk To Me'.

Fan The Seahorses, PO Box 319, Manchester, M3 3FT, UK

SEAL ◉ ◉

WHO b. Sealhenry Samuel, 19 Feb 1963, London, England

WHAT Golden-voiced dramatic Soul

Escaping a traumatic childhood at 15, Seal survived on odd jobs while performing with the ill-fated Stay Brave. He designed clothes, sang on beer ads and was an electrical engineer before contracting the skin disease lupus at 23, which left him with facial scarring. In 1987, he travelled in India after a production deal fell through, and performed with Funk band Push in Japan.

Fame came a-knocking in 1990: 'Killer', a collaboration with Adamski, reached UK No.1, and his own 'Crazy' reached UK and US Top 10s, paving the way for *Seal* (1991). Produced by Trevor Horn, it boasted Prince protégées Wendy & Lisa and orchestral arrangements by Anne Dudley. Its tracks 'Future Love' and 'The Beginning' were hits, as was 'Killer', revamped as a solo effort.

In 1992, he sang 'Who Wants To Live Forever' with Queen at the Freddie Mercury tribute show, and contributed to Jeff Beck's 'Manic Depression' on *Stone Free* (1993), a Jimi Hendrix tribute.

After 'Violet' (1992) struggled just inside the Top 40, 1994's grizzly 'Prayer For The Dying' (re-released with 'Don't Cry' the following year) reached UK No.14. After a disastrous two years (Seal witnessed a shooting, suffered a car crash and contracted double pneumonia and post-viral fatigue), his next album – also titled *Seal* (1994) – starred Jeff Beck and Joni Mitchell (on whose 1994 single 'How Do You Stop' he sang) and reached UK No.1.

Reissued on 1995's *Batman Forever* soundtrack, the album's magnificent 'Kiss From A Rose' made US No.1 and relaunched his career. He supported The Rolling Stones at massive shows in the USA and, in 1996, sang 'What's Going On' with Annie Lennox as a tribute to Marvin Gaye. In 1997, Seal moved from the ZTT label to Warner and split, acrimoniously, from Trevor Horn.

surf www.ultim.demon.co.uk/seal/

THE SEARCHERS

WHO Vocals/guitar **Mike Pender** (b. Michael Prendergast, 3 Mar 1942, Liverpool, England), vocals/bass **Tony Jackson** (b. 16 Jul 1940, Liverpool), guitar **John McNally** (b. 30 Aug 1941, Liverpool), drums **Chris Curtis** (b. Christopher Crummy, 26 Aug 1941, Oldham, Greater Manchester, England)

WHEN 1963–

WHERE Liverpool, England

WHAT Jingle jangle Merseybeat

The Searchers, who took their name from the 1956 John Wayne Western, were one of the few Liverpool groups not managed by Brian Epstein. A regular attraction at the city's Iron Door club, their jangly guitar, enthusiastic harmony and R&B background produced early hits like 1963's 'Sweets For My Sweet' (the first of three UK chart-toppers), 'Sweet Nothins' and 'Sugar And Spice'.

Replacing Tony Jackson's vocals with Pender's softer voice and twelve-string lead guitar for their second No.1, 'Needles And Pins' (co-written by Sonny Bono), led to the equally mellow 'Don't Throw Your Love Away' (the third No.1), 'When You Walk In The Room' and the anti-nuclear protest, 'What Have They Done To The Rain' – whose close harmonies over electric guitars were a major influence on Folk Rock. Their 1963 debut album version of 'Where Have All The Flowers Gone?' was also one of the earliest Folk Rock recordings.

Line-up changes began in 1964 and, by the end of 1966, the hits had dried up. A revival on Sire Records in 1979 with 'Hearts In Her Eyes' just missed the charts. Pender formed Mike Pender's Searchers in 1985 and both groups now play the club circuit.

NEIL SEDAKA

WHO b. 13 Mar 1939, Brooklyn, New York, USA

WHAT Teen-love hit writer

Neil Sedaka, a piano student at 9, started composing in 1952 with schoolfriend Howard Greenfield. Their first composition was 'My Life's Devotion', their first hit Connie Francis' 'Stupid Cupid' (1958). Sedaka's own 'The Diary' (1959) reached US No.14 and he made his UK chart debut that year with 'I Go Ape'. In 1959, he played piano on Bobby Darin's 'Dream Lover', scored his own hit with 'Oh! Carol' (dedicated to Carole Klein, a girlfriend from his schooldays, who became better known as Carole King) and issued his debut album *Rock With Sedaka*, which failed to chart.

However, he scored with 1961's 'Calendar Girl' and 'Little Devil', and 1962's 'Happy Birthday Sweet Sixteen', 'Breaking Up Is Hard To Do' (his first US chart-topper and million-seller) and 'Next Door To An Angel'. By 1963, he had enough material for *Neil Sedaka Sings His Greatest Hits*.

He gave up recording and touring in 1966 to concentrate on songwriting, and returned to form with *Emergence* (1972) and 'I'm A Song, Sing Me' (1972), 'That's Where The Music Takes Me' (1973) and 'Laughter In The Rain' (1974). A re-recorded slow version of his 1962 hit 'Breaking Up Is Hard To Do' (1975) reached the US Top 10 and, in 1980, the US Top 20 enjoyed 'Should've Never Let You Go', a duet with his daughter Dara. In 1983, he was inducted into the Songwriters Hall Of Fame. *Timeless* (1991), a collection of his hits, some re-recorded, reached UK No.10.

surf members.aol/com/sedaka1/index.html

BOB SEGER ✪

WHO b. 6 May 1945, Ann Arbor, Michigan, USA

WHAT Arena-rocking Springsteen substitute

Bob Seger fronted several local Michigan bands during the 60s and early 70s, touring and recording albums that sold poorly. A national breakthrough came in 1976, fuelled by the energetic in-concert *Live Bullet* and subsequent studio set *Night Moves*, with its haunting, introspective title track. Both albums credited his long-standing backing outfit, The Silver Bullet Band, for the first time. UK success came initially through cover versions of his songs: Dave Edmunds and Eddie & The Hot Rods recorded 'Get Out Of Denver' and Thin Lizzy had a hit with 'Rosalie' (1978).

He cracked the UK charts with *Stranger In Town* (1978) and its hits 'Hollywood Nights' and the much-covered 'We've Got Tonite' (live versions and reissues corrected the spelling to 'Tonight'). *Against The Wind* (1980), a US No.1, was his biggest seller yet. As a long-time friend of The Eagles, several members guested on his albums and he returned the compliment by co-writing the group's US No.1 'Heartache Tonight' (1979). In 1987, he topped the US singles chart himself with 'Shakedown', from the movie *Beverly Hills Cop II*, originally offered to The Eagles' Glenn Frey, who had to turn it down owing to laryngitis.

Less prolific in the 90s, he squeezed out *The Fire Inside* (1991) and *It's A Mystery* (1996). But his status as a radio AOR favourite continued on both sides of the Atlantic, particularly in the UK where *Greatest Hits* (1995) became his first Top 10 album and a reissue of 'We've Got Tonight' finally made the Top 30.

surf walden.mo.net/~rhall/seger1.html

SEPULTURA

WHO Vocals/guitar **Max 'Possessed' Cavalera** (b. Massimiliano A. Cavalera, 4 Aug 1969, Belo Horizonte, Brazil), guitar **Andreas Kisser** (b. 24 Aug 1968, Sao Bernado Do Campo, Brazil), bass **Paulo 'Destructor' Jr** (b. Paulo Xisto Pinto Jr, 30 Apr 1969, Belo Horizonte), drums **Igor 'Skullcrusher' Cavalera** (b. 4 Sep 1970, Belo Horizonte)

WHEN 1984–

WHERE Belo Horizonte, Brazil

WHAT Thrash crash Brazilian bangers

Sepultura's evolution from Thrash Metal wannabes to leaders of the genre owes much to producer Scott Burns, who fashioned a controlled blend of their rough-hewn riffs and snarling vocals.

Morbid Visions (1986) and *Schizophrenia* (1988) were less compelling than competent, but *Beneath The Remains* (1989) – with Max Cavalera roaring politically-powered lyrics over fearsome riffing and his brother's drumming – suggested more depth than the competition. "Time to take Sepultura seriously," enthused UK Metal magazine *Kerrang!*.

Arise (1991) continued the upswing, confirmed when *Chaos AD* (1993) crashed into the UK Top 20 and US Top 40 with no mainstream media support whatsoever. Their live reputation rose with prestigious gigs, including the UK's Monsters Of Rock.

Sepultura's scope widened further with *Roots* (1996), which took in Brazil's cultural heritage and used local guest musicians alongside the relentless thrash assault. The results included two UK hits: the ferocious 'Roots Bloody Roots' and the drumbusting 'Ratamahatta' (the latter boasting a gripping claymation video).

With everything to gain, the band splintered in 1997 when their manager Gloria – wife of Max Cavalera – took time out to mourn the death of her son. Max resisted pressure from the rest to get back to work and the split began to look ominous. To the horror of fans, Cavalera quit; to their delight, he resurfaced with a new band, Soulfly, whose fortunes were secured by poaching a guitarist from modern Metal sensations Machine Head.

Meanwhile, Sepultura recruited ex-Alpha Jerk singer Derrick Greene for a new album, tentatively titled *Aggressive*.

surf www.sepultribe.com/

THE SEX PISTOLS ⊙

WHO Vocals **Johnny Rotten** (b. John Lydon, 31 Jan 1956, London, England), guitar **Steve Jones** (b. 3 Sep 1955, London), bass **Glen Matlock** (b. 27 Aug 1956, London), drums **Paul Cook** (b. 20 Jul 1956, London)

WHEN 1975–1978

WHERE London, England

WHAT Spunk Rock

When the bloated, geriatric Sex Pistols were hoisted on stage in London in 1996, it might have been the first time the band had played to a crowd not intent on killing them. No one liked them and they didn't care.

The Sex Pistols were formed to sell clothes for a shop run by a failed Rock manager. But in the process, they released a handful of brilliant singles, made one of the best albums ever, frightened everyone over 18, ruined the careers of countless bands, inspired countless more and destroyed themselves.

In 1975, Malcolm McLaren returned to London from the USA, where he had mismanaged the ailing New York Dolls. Before that, he and his partner Vivienne Westwood ran Let It Rock, a 50s-themed London boutique. On his return, he and Westwood renamed the store Sex and sold kinky clothing to perverts and bored teenagers, including Steve Jones and Paul Cook. Friends since school, Jones and Cook had stolen enough instruments to start a band. With guitarist Wally Nightingale and bassist Del Noone, they became The Strand – a mess of Faces covers and weak originals who played just one gig.

Plotting to use the band to publicize Westwood's clothes, McLaren adopted and renamed them. 'The Sex Pistols' was guaranteed to annoy and sell plenty of Westwood's porno T-shirts and bondage gear. Jones switched from vocals to guitar, Cook remained on drums, Nightingale and Noone were ousted and Glen Matlock, a sales assistant at Sex, was installed on bass.

Inspired by New York's proto-Punk scene, McLaren tried (and failed) to recruit former Television figurehead Richard Hell. Then John Lydon, an antagonistic urchin from a north London slum, appeared. He was *horrible*: an anti-fashion car-crash of second-hand clothes held together with safety pins, green cropped hair (which had lost him a teaching job), rotting teeth, a constant, piercing stare (courtesy of childhood meningitis) and a customized Pink Floyd T-shirt embellished with "I HATE".

Jones and Cook *hated* him. When he auditioned, miming to Alice Cooper's 'Eighteen' on the Sex jukebox, it became clear he couldn't sing a note. A gleeful McLaren made him a Sex Pistol –

rechristened, thanks to his teeth – and Jones, whose best defence against Lydon's sarcasm was the feeble 'You're fuckin' rotten, you are" – Johnny Rotten.

After false starts (they stood Rotten up the first time), the Pistols started rehearsing. Jones and Cook wanted some kind of Faces/Bay City Rollers hybrid. Rotten didn't care, as long as it wasn't cute and nice like those awful Beatles. Matlock wanted them to *be* The Beatles. In a moment of clarity, the Pistols found their inspiration: they hated Glen Matlock. "He was such a good boy," sneered Jones. "He had this pompous face you just wanted to slap."

By their first gig at London's St Martin's College Of Art in November 1975, the Pistols had found other things they hated: students, hippies, most of Rock's recent history – especially the bloated indulgences of bands like Pink Floyd, Yes and Emerson, Lake & Palmer. Aside from a few mutilated covers – including The Who's 'Substitute', The Small Faces' 'Whatcha Gonna Do About It', The Stooges' 'No Fun' and Jonathan Richman's 'Roadrunner' – their set was little more than a chaotic blast, topped by Rotten's audience-baiting and screams.

Gigs around London through 1975 and 1976 ended in spitting, violence, bans – complete chaos. Outside London, the overwhelming reaction was shock: "Complete silence after kicking up a filthy racket on stage," recalled Lydon. "It can be the loudest sound on God's earth. Nothing. Not even chit-chat at the bar. Dead stone-cold silence."

But their reputation grew. Led by the 'Bromley contingent' (fans from South London suburbs including Billy Idol and Siouxsie Sioux), Pistols gigs became rallying points for disillusioned teenagers, freaks and fakes. Early witnesses included Joe Strummer, who ditched Pub Rock act The 101'ers to form The Clash. When they played Manchester in 1976, they inspired Buzzcocks, Joy Division and The Smiths. The music press scrambled to cover the emerging scene. In the process, it acquired a name: Punk.

Punk exploded in September 1976 when The Sex Pistols, The Clash, The Damned and Buzzcocks headlined a Punk festival at London's 100 Club. It was here that the Pistols' most ardent fan, Sid Vicious (b. John Simon Ritchie, aka John Beverly, 10 May 1957, London), became notorious. A friend of Lydon's (who'd nicknamed him after his hamster and Pink Floyd's founder Syd Barrett), Sid drummed with The Flowers Of Romance (a makeshift group that evolved into Siouxsie & The Banshees) and smashed a glass against a wall, reportedly half-blinding a girl in the 100 Club audience. A gangly fool who'd bought the Punk image wholesale, Sid once attacked *NME* writer Nick Kent (who jammed with Matlock, Jones and Cook in their Strand days) with a bicycle chain just for fun. Sid's unpopular girlfriend, Nancy Spungen, was even worse. She'd followed former New York Doll Johnny Thunders over from New York, latched on to the naive Sid and introduced him to heroin.

Sid faithfully followed the Pistols, but they were to be ripped from their cultish following. In October 1976, they signed to EMI and unleashed 'Anarchy In The UK'. While Britain lived in fear of riots and terrorist bombings, the Pistols glorified them with a song that sounded like petrol bombs crashing against the Houses of Parliament. Its outrageous content went unnoticed at first, but in December the Pistols (and some of the Bromley contingent, including Siouxsie) appeared on the early evening, live UK TV show *Today* in place of EMI labelmates Queen.

Arriving drunk, the Pistols endeared themselves little to the host, Bill Grundy – seemingly as uninhibited as his guests – who decided to take these ingrates down a peg. Expletives flew. Britain choked on its tea. Then Grundy hit on Siouxsie…

Jones: "You dirty sod! You dirty old man!"

Grundy: "Go on! You've got another five seconds, say something outrageous!"

Jones: "You dirty bastard!"

Grundy: "Go on, again."

Jones: "You dirty f*er!"**

Grundy: "What a clever boy."

Jones: "What a f*ing rotter!"**

The next day, thanks to front-page headlines on every British newspaper, *everyone* knew who The Sex Pistols were. EMI, meanwhile, had second thoughts. On tour with The Clash, The Damned and Johnny Thunders' Heartbreakers, the band played only three shows – most were cancelled by terrifed promoters or picketed by irate locals. Meanwhile, 'Anarchy In The UK' was dropped by distributors and banned from most stores. Then EMI dropped the Pistols. They – or, more precisely, McLaren – waltzed away with the label's £40,000 advance.

Meanwhile, tensions with Glen Matlock peaked. His claim that the fantastic 'Pretty Vacant' (which, like other Pistols gems, he wrote) was inspired by Abba proved the final straw for Jones, Rotten and Cook. McLaren – capitalizing on the Pistols' 'can't play' reputation – replaced Matlock (who resurfaced with The Rich Kids) with someone who definitely couldn't play: Sid.

In March 1977, the Pistols joined A&M who, to plug the forthcoming 'God Save The Queen', arranged a contract-signing ceremony outside Buckingham Palace. A week later, gripped by the same jitters that afflicted EMI (and under pressure from one of their biggest earners, Rick Wakeman), A&M sacked the band with another £40,000 kiss-off.

They settled with the Virgin label – dominion of hippie king Richard Branson, home of Mike Oldfield and *Tubular Bells*. "Never trust a hippie," McLaren had always maintained. But Virgin dared to release 'God Save The Queen', the monarchy-bashing anthem A&M had baulked at. In fact, they scheduled it for May, on Jubilee Day – a national holiday commemorating the 25th anniversary of the Queen's coronation.

Launched with a police-raided Jubilee boat party on the River Thames, 'God Save The Queen' fell foul of moralistic TV and radio programmers and, despite selling enough for a UK No.1, stalled at No.2 – allegedly thanks to music industry foul play. In the aftermath, Cook and Rotten were assaulted by angry royalists and the follow-ups 'Pretty Vacant' and 'Holidays In The Sun' were boycotted by record stores. Meanwhile, the problem of finding gigs continued and they resorted to pseudonyms including 'SPOTS' (Sex Pistols On Tour Secretly), 'Acne Rabble' and 'Tax Exiles'.

Then their long-awaited debut album appeared. Twice. First came the raw bootleg *Spunk* (aka *No Future UK*), then the polished *Never Mind The Bollocks – Here's The Sex Pistols* (1977) – enjoyed at wall-shaking volume 20 years later by Noel Gallagher's neighbours. Controversy-fuelling title aside, its lyrics attacked sex ('Bodies'), McLaren ('New York') and their former labels ('EMI'). Despite charitable writing credits, Sid was incapacitated by heroin and Nancy Spungen. Jones and a temporarily reinstated Matlock filled in on bass. Rotten tried to wean his friend off drugs, but was already isolated from Sid, Jones, Cook and, in particular, McLaren, who was hatching a Sex Pistols movie with smut-meister Russ Meyer.

Relations had all but disintegrated when they began their first US tour in January 1978. As they zig-zagged across the South, the cracks widened: redneck crowds threw bottles, Sid (in cold turkey since leaving Nancy behind in London) carved 'GIMME A FIX' into his chest and smashed his bass into what/whoever was within range, Jones and Cook huddled closer to McLaren, while Rotten plotted his escape.

He ended the final Pistols show, in San Francisco, with the words "Ha ha, ever get the feeling you've been cheated?" and quit. Cook and Jones flew to Rio, where they recorded the awful 'No One Is Innocent' (aka 'Cosh The Driver') with fugitive train robber Ronnie Biggs. Sid, reunited with Nancy (and heroin), recorded parodic covers of 'My Way' and Eddie Cochran's 'C'mon Everybody', then moved to New York, where the couple lived a squalid existence as Sid tried to kickstart a solo career. Then, on 12 October 1978, Nancy was found stabbed to death in their Chelsea Hotel room. Sid was charged with her murder.

Awaiting trial in New York, he followed Nancy on 2 February 1979, courtesy of a heroin overdose. In London, the urn carrying his ashes smashed, making his final resting place the air conditioning system of Heathrow Airport. Alex Cox's widely savaged 1986 movie *Sid And Nancy – Love Kills* (whose soundtrack was supervised by Steve Jones) attempted to document their horrific decline and even included a cameo from the (then) Spungen-obsessed Courtney Love.

Better was *The Great Rock 'N' Roll Swindle* (1979) – the rambling documentary (eventually directed by Julien Temple) that McLaren had spent so much time and (other people's) money making. Post-Rotten hits abounded: Ronnie Biggs' 'No One Is Innocent' backed with Sid's 'My Way' (1978), and 1979's 'Something Else'/'Friggin' In The Riggin', 'Silly Thing'/'Who Killed Bambi' and Sid's appalling *Sid Sings*. Cook and Jones became The Professionals, who made an ignored debut album (1981's *I Didn't See It Coming*) and were immortalized in the cult US Punk movie *Ladies And Gentlemen, The Fabulous Stains* (1982).

Johnny Rotten, now plain John Lydon, formed the sporadically brilliant PiL, moved to the USA, appeared in the movie *Order Of Death* (1983) with Harvey Keitel, published his compelling autobiography, *Rotten: No Irish, No Blacks, No Dogs* and fronted the US radio show *Rotten Day*. Matlock wrote his

own autobiography, *I Was A Teenage Sex Pistol* (1990), but otherwise joined Jones and Cook in solo obscurity.

While Cook became a session drummer (notably for Edwyn Collins), Jones decamped to LA, kicked heroin and joined under-performing supergroups Chequered Past (with Blondie's Clem Burke and Nigel Harrison, and ex-Silverhead and Power Station singer Michael Des Barres) and Neurotic Boy Outsiders (with Guns N' Roses' Duff McKagan and Matt Sorum and Duran Duran's John Taylor). His solo albums *Mercy* (1987) and *Fire And Gasoline* (1989) remain lost to obscurity, but his 'Black Leather' was covered by Guns N' Roses on *The Spaghetti Incident?* (1993).

The post-Pistols fall-out continued with *The Great Rock 'N' Roll Swindle* soundtrack (1979), and compilations like 1979's *Some Product – Carri On Sex Pistols* and 1980's *Flogging A Dead Horse*. Even EMI (who, ironically, bought Virgin in the 90s and released 1992's *Kiss This* collection) cashed in with *Original Pistols Live* (1985). However, in 1986, when Cook, Jones, Lydon and Vicious' estate won damages and control over Pistols' product from McLaren (a court battle which had raged for eight years), the sordid story seemed to have closed. Then, in 1996, the unthinkable occurred: it was announced that Pistols Lydon, Jones, Cook and, shockingly, Matlock had re-formed. "The Pistols never ended properly," said Lydon. "It just kind of

the sex pistols

fizzled. So many people have copied, imitated and fucked up what was pure and perfect that it's about time that that was readdressed. I don't give a shit if no one in the world turns up – quite frankly it'd be to my benefit – but it's just for us as a band to say goodbye to each other properly."

They said goodbye with the globe-trotting Filthy Lucre tour (and 1996's *Filthy Lucre Live* album), of which a highlight was their homecoming performance in Finsbury Park – Rotten's old London home.

The prospect of the Pistols choking on their own hypocrisy attracted the morbid, but the band began with 'Bodies' – the most vicious and horrific song in the Punk canon.

Old, bloated and irrelevant they may have been, but their cynical contrariness was a fitting end to their career-long mockery of music biz convention. Younger fans were thrilled by a fiery performance; veterans took comfort from the fact that the tour collapsed in classic Pistols style: booing audiences, cancelled shows, violence and acrimony. No one liked them and they still didn't care.

(read) *Rotten: No Irish, No Blacks, No Dogs* (1994), John Lydon with Kent & Keith Zimmerman

(surf) www.users.wineasy.se/ludde/

THE SHADOWS ⊙⊙⊙⊙

WHO Guitar **Hank Marvin** (b. Brian Rankin, 28 Oct 1941, Newcastle, England), guitar **Bruce Welch** (b. Bruce Cripps, 2 Nov 1941, Bognor Regis, Sussex, England), drums **Brian Bennett** (b. 9 Feb 1940, London, England)

WHEN 1958–

WHERE London, England

WHAT Twangy instrumental/vocal group and Cliff Richard's backing band

Opportunity knocked for Hank Marvin when Cliff Richard's manager, seeking a guitarist for Cliff's touring band, spotted his band The Drifters at London's 2i's Coffee Bar. Marvin agreed to join if he could bring his friend Bruce Welch along. With bassist Jet Harris and drummer Tony Meehan, their 'Feelin' Fine', a vocal number, clinched a deal with Columbia. Their first instrumental, 'Chinchilla', was featured on the soundtrack EP 'Serious Charge'.

When US vocal group The Drifters objected to the use of their name, Harris suggested the name Shadows; the renamed group scored their first No.1 with 'Apache' – featuring Cliff on Chinese drum. A run of more than 20 hits included four more UK No.1s: 'Kon-Tiki' (1961), 'Wonderful Land' (1962), 'Dance On!' (1962) and 'Foot Tapper' (1963). They had two UK chart-topping albums – *The Shadows* (1961) and *Out Of The Shadows* (1962) – and appeared in several of Cliff's movies and soundtracks.

Meehan and Harris left to score UK hits of their own: 1963's instrumentals 'Diamonds', 'Scarlett O'Hara' and 'Applejack'. In came Brian Bennett and Brian 'Liquorice' Locking. Welch almost left in August 1963, but changed his mind. Two months later, Locking, who had become a Jehovah's Witness, *did* quit – to be replaced by John Rostill, although John Paul Jones (later of Led Zeppelin) was also considered.

The Shadows starred in the short film *Rhythm & Greens* (1964) and as puppets in the Gerry Anderson movie *Thunderbirds Are Go* (1966), but – after celebrating ten years in the business – split amid bad feeling and lack of success. A meeting with Australian guitarist and singer/songwriter John Farrar gave rise to Marvin, Welch and Farrar, who hit with 1971's self-titled debut and *Second Opinion*. But Welch quit when his relationship with Olivia Newton-John dissolved in 1972. Then tragedy struck when Rostill was fatally electrocuted at his home studio in 1973.

Asked to represent the UK in 1975's Eurovision Song Contest, The Shadows re-formed for the vocal number 'Let Me Be The One', but came second to the Dutch entry 'Ding-A-Dong'. This track, plus other possible contest contenders and new material, was released on *Specs Appeal* (1975). Farrar moved to the USA to work with Olivia in 1976 but, with the UK No.1 *20 Golden Greats* (1977), The Shadows were back on top.

In 1978, they worked with Cliff again to celebrate 20 years in show business. Solo projects abounded: Marvin issued *The Hank Marvin Guitar Syndicate* (1977) and *Words And Music* (1982), while Bennett composed theme music for British TV's *The Ruth Rendell Mysteries* and released *Rock Dreams* (1977) and *Voyage* (1978).

Cover versions filled *String Of Hits* (1979), *Another String Of Hits* (1980) and *Hits Right Up Your Street* (1981). Marvin continued a successful solo career with *Hank Plays Cliff* (1995) and *Hank Plays Holly* (1996) and toured with Bennett.

Read *The Story Of The Shadows* (1983), Mike Read

Fan Shadsfax, 48 Oak Tree Lane, Haxby, York, YO3 3YL, UK

Surf www.muse.com.au/org/scofa

SHAKESPEAR'S SISTER

WHO Vocals **Siobhan Fahey** (b. 10 Sep 1957, London, England), vocals/guitar **Marcella Detroit** (b. Marcella Levy, 21 Jun 1959, Detroit, Michigan, USA)

WHEN 1989–

WHERE Los Angeles, California, USA

WHAT Sophisticated Goth Pop

When Siobhan Fahey left Bananarama in 1987, she distanced herself from their disposable Pop by adopting (and misspelling) the title of a Smiths song for her new project – to which Marcella Detroit (whose biggest claim to fame had been co-writing 'Lay Down Sally' with Eric Clapton) made a crucial contribution.

Fahey's white-painted face filled the cover of their self-titled debut (1989), but Detroit's multi-octave voice was prominently featured on the breakthrough hit 'You're History', which reached UK No.3. Detroit's dramatic vocals played an equally crucial role on the song for which the duo are likely to be best remembered: 'Stay' (1992) topped the UK chart for eight weeks and hit the US Top 5. Its parent album, *Hormonally Yours*, reached UK No.3.

However, later singles sold less spectacularly, and Detroit quit in 1993 to launch a moderately successful solo career. Fahey, still billed as Shakespear's Sister, returned in 1996 with 'I Can Drive'. An album recorded at the same time remains unreleased. Fahey reunited with Bananarama in 1998 for a TV poll-winning version of Abba's 'Waterloo', featured on the *A Song For Eurotrash* album.

Surf www.netmatters.co.uk/users/neilg/

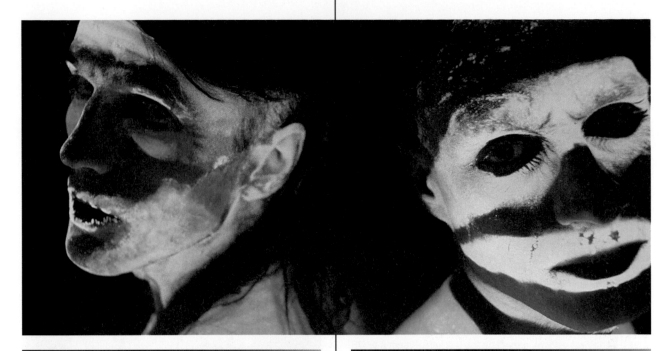

SHALAMAR

WHO Vocals **Jody Watley** (b. 30 Jan 1959, Chicago, Illinois, USA), vocals

Howard Hewett (b. 1 Oct 1955, Akron, Ohio, USA), vocals **Jeffrey Daniels**

(b. 24 Aug 1957, Los Angeles, California, USA)

WHEN 1978–

WHERE New York City, New York, USA

WHAT Glorious good-time R&B

Sweating through club gigs is one route to stardom. The other is to hitch aboard a bandwagon – or, in this case, a train. Shalamar was originally a Disco-driven vehicle for US TV's *Soul Train* booking agent Dick Griffey. Their first hit was the 1977 Motown medley 'Uptown Festival', whose success inspired Griffey to replace his sessioneers with Jody Watley, Jeffrey Daniels and Howard Hewett (the latter replacing short-time member Gerald Brown) in 1978.

Their silver streak peaked Stateside with 1979's 'The Second Time Around' and in the UK with 1982's 'I Can Make You Feel Good', 'A Night To Remember' and 'There It Is'. Their good-time R&B took a knock when Watley and Daniels left in 1983 but, with Delisa Davis and Micki Free, Shalamar returned to the US Top 20 with 'Dancing In The Sheets' from *Footloose* (1984) and won a Grammy for 'Don't Get Stopped in Beverly Hills' from *Beverly Hills Cop* (1985). However, when Hewett left in 1986 to be replaced by Sydney Justin, the band dropped into the 'Do you recognize these people?' cabaret circuit.

Most successful of the classic trio was Watley, who – with former Prince sidekick André Cymone – made classy solo albums and hit with gems like 1987's 'Looking For A New Love', 1989's 'Friends' and 1994's 'When A Man Loves A Woman'. She reunited with Hewett and Daniels, plus LL Cool J, on Babyface's irresistable 1996 hit 'For The Lover In You' – a revamp of a song from Shalamar's *Three For Love* (1981), one of three gold US albums they scored in their heyday.

THE SHAMEN

WHO Vocals **Mr C** (b. Richard West, 1964, London, England), vocals/guitar/

keyboards **Colin Angus** (b. 24 Aug 1961, Aberdeen, Scotland)

WHEN 1985–

WHERE Aberdeen, Scotland

WHAT Transcendental Techno Rock

Taking their name from South American Indians, The Shamen were among the first to fuse Techno and Rock. Their 1987 debut album *Drop* ploughed the same psychedelic furrow as their previous incarnation, Alone Again Or. However, with the addition of bassist/keyboard player Will Sinnott (b. 23 Dec 1960, Glasgow, Scotland, d. 23 May 1991, Gomera, Tenerife), they sweetened their political manifesto with Hip Hop beats and samples.

After the acclaimed *In Gorbachev We Trust* (1988), founders Peter Stephenson and Keith McKenzie departed and Colin Angus and Sinnott relocated to London. There they conceived the Acid House-inspired Synergy club nights and dented the UK chart with 'Omega Amigo', 'Pro-Gen', 'Make It Mine' and *En-Tact* (1990).

Tragedy struck The Shamen (now augmented by Rapper Mr C) as they approached their zenith: Sinnott drowned in Tenerife while filming a video for a revamped 'Pro-Gen'. Re-titled 'Move Any Mountain', it peaked at UK No.4 in 1991 and thrust The Shamen into the mainstream. The mega-selling *Boss Drum* (1992) was some compensation for their loss. But it also sowed the seeds of their decline: the controversial Ecstasy anthem 'Ebeneezer Goode' topped the UK chart, but decimated their credibility. It relegated the band to novelty status and the belated *Axis Mutatis* (1995) and *Hempton Manor* (1996) to bargain bins. Long-time label One Little Indian kissed them goodbye with the 1996 retrospectives *Collection* and *Stars On 25*. However, their hipness quotient upped by C's London club The End, they pressed on with 1998's *Ultimate Voyage*.

surf www.nemeton.com/

THE SHANGRI-LAS

WHO Vocals **Marge Ganser** (d. 1976), vocals **Mary Ann Ganser** (d. 1971, New York, USA), vocals **Mary Weiss**, vocals **Liz 'Betty' Weiss**

WHEN 1963–1969

WHERE Queens, New York, USA

WHAT Myrmidons of melodrama

Cooler than The Crystals, rougher than The Ronettes, The Shangri-Las were the 60s girl group supreme. As teenagers, they recorded two singles before being adopted by producer/writer George 'Shadow' Morton. With a demo of 'Remember (Walking In The Sand)', he persuaded top Brill Building writers Ellie Greenwich and Jeff Barry to produce the single for The Shangri-Las. Its melodramatic piano, finger snaps and seaside sound effects made it a US No.5 hit in 1964 – and a haunting perennial.

Their chart peak came with 1965's Morton/Barry/Greenwich-penned 'death song' 'Leader Of The Pack'. Tragic lyrics, motorbike sound effects and impassioned lead vocals by Mary Weiss – who broke down in tears on the last verse – sent it to US No.1. In the UK, although banned on first release, it visited the Top 10 three times. Throughout this time the group often performed as a trio, with either Mary or Betty Weiss absent.

The formula of tear-jerking themes and cinematic effects (thunder, kisses, train whistles, footstomps, bells, spoken intros) fuelled 'Give Us Your Blessings', 'Out In The Streets', 'Past Present And Future' and 'I Can Never Go Home Anymore', but wore thin. They split in 1969, periodically re-forming for nostalgia tours.

Their songs have been covered by admirers from The Grateful Dead to Bette Midler and from Twisted Sister to Tracey Ullman. Aerosmith's Steven Tyler – who'd fulfilled an adolescent fantasy by copping a peek at Mary Weiss in a backstage bathroom – had a minor hit with his band's 1979 'Remember (Walking In The Sand)' revamp, while Johnny Thunders made the fantastic 'Give Him A Great Big Kiss' a staple of The New York Dolls and solo sets. However, The Shangri-Las' legacy is best celebrated by 1995's anthology *Myrmidons Of Melodrama*.

READ *Will You Still Love Me Tomorrow* (1989), Charlotte Greig

SURF home.ica.net/~phil/thegirls/shangri.html

DEL SHANNON

WHO b. Charles Westover, 30 Dec 1934, Coopersville, Missouri, USA, d. 8 Feb 1990, Santa Clarita Valley, California, USA

WHAT Rock 'n' Roll runaway

A star of forces radio in his US Army days, Del Shannon began his civilian life as a carpet salesman and ended it as a Rock 'n' Roll legend. In 1960, he won a deal with Big Top Records and, with bar-band keyboardist Max Crook (responsible for Shannon's signature 'musitron' organ sound), wrote the classic US and UK No.1, 'Runaway' (1961); hence the line "Me and Del were singing, 'little Runaway'" in Tom Petty's 1989 hit 'Runnin' Down A Dream'.

Their majestic Rock 'n' Roll formula yielded further hits with 'Hats Off To Larry' (1961), 'So Long Baby', 'Hey! Little Girl', 'The

Swiss Maid' (all 1962) and 'Little Town Flirt' (1963). In 1963, *Hats Off To Del Shannon* and *Little Town Flirt* hit the UK Top 10.

Meanwhile, he introduced The Beatles to the US chart, via a 1963 cover of Lennon & McCartney's 'From Me To You', formed his own label – Berlee Records – and churned out hits into the mid-60s, the peaks of which were the US Top 10 and UK Top 3 'Keep Searchin' (We'll Follow The Sun)', (US, 1964 and UK, 1965) and Peter & Gordon's cover of his 'I Go To Pieces' (1965). But an aborted collaboration (*Home And Away*) with The Rolling Stones' manager Andrew Loog Oldham and legal problems sidelined Shannon for years.

Meanwhile, he became a producer/arranger (for Smith – an LA band who hit US No.3 with a 1969 cover of The Shirelles' 'Baby It's You' – and for Brian Hyland) and, in the early 70s, went to the UK to record fruitless sessions with Dave Edmunds and ELO's Jeff Lynne. However, a union with Tom Petty & The Heartbreakers in the early 80s yielded the Petty-produced *Drop Down And Get Me* (1981) and US hit 'Sea Of Love'.

In 1990, Shannon was working on a comeback with Lynne and mooted as a replacement for Roy Orbison in The Traveling Wilburys. But depression – exacerbated, his wife claimed, by side effects from anti-depressants – prompted his tragic suicide.

 www.bugmusic.com/delfan.html

SANDIE SHAW

WHO b. Sandra Goodrich, 26 Feb 1947, Dagenham, Essex, England

WHAT Barefoot 60s songbird

Sandie Shaw became one of the first British female teenage Pop stars when her second single, the Bacharach & David-penned '(There's) Always Something There to Remind Me' (1964), topped the UK chart. Brilliantly distinguished by her distinctive soprano and mature vocal delivery, which belied her 17 years, the song remained in the charts for 11 weeks. Shaw became as influential for her style, particularly her preference for going barefoot, as for her string of 60s hits with songwriter/producer Chris Andrews, but her most famous, 1967 Eurovision winner 'Puppet On A String', was penned by Bill Martin and Phil Coulter. Her biggest US hit was 1965's 'Girl Don't Come'.

Married to fashion designer Jeff Banks, Shaw spent most of the 70s in semi-retirement. But she was lured back into music by Heaven 17 (guesting on their side project BEF's *Music Of Quality And Distinction*, 1983) and Shaw-worshipping Smiths groaner Morrissey and hit the UK chart with a revamp of The Smiths' 'Hand In Glove' (1984). Following a near-hit with the Lloyd Cole-penned 'Are You Ready To Be Heartbroken?' (1986), *Hello Angel* (1988) was a veritable festival of fey Indie, with songwriting contributions from The Jesus & Mary Chain and Morrissey, who wrote the single 'Please Help The Cause Against Loneliness'.

However, *Reviewing The Situation* (1991) was overshadowed sales-wise by compilations like *Nothing Less Than Brilliant: The Best Of Sandie Shaw* (1994). Shaw united with Indie also-runs Cud on a 1993 cover of The Rolling Stone's 'Gimme Shelter'. Meanwhile, she also graduated from university, trained as a counsellor and helped to set up The Arts Clinic in 1997.

 The World At My Feet (1991), Sandie Shaw

 www.castleus.com/courtyard/palisades/album/s1017.html

THE SHIRELLES

WHO Vocals **Shirley Owens Alston** (b. 10 Jun 1941, Passaic, New Jersey, USA), vocals **Addie 'Micki' Harris** (b. 22 Jan 1940, Passaic, d. 10 Jun 1982, Los Angeles, California, USA), vocals **Doris Coley Kenner** (b. 2 Aug 1941, Passaic), vocals **Beverly Lee** (b. 3 Aug 1941, Passaic)

WHEN 1958–

WHERE Passaic, New Jersey, USA

WHAT Proto-girl-group Pop

The Shangri-Las and The Supremes perfected girl group Pop, but The Shirelles did it first and, along the way, delivered some of Pop's greatest moments. They were discovered by a school classmate (whose mother, Florence Goldberg, became their manager and label boss) singing their own 'I Met Him On A Sunday (Ronde-Ronde)'. The song became a radio hit then, when Decca bought it, a US No.49 in 1958.

The follow-up 'Dedicated To The One I Love' – a cover of The 5 Royales' 1958 R&B hit, later covered by The Mamas & The Papas – flopped but, with help from producer/arranger Luther Dixon and writers of the calibre of Gerry Goffin & Carole King, Burt Bacharach & Hal David and Van McCoy, they hit a Pop chart purple patch. The classics 'Will You Love Me Tomorrow?' (1960), 'Mama Said' (1961), 'Baby It's You' (1962), 'Soldier Boy' (1962), 'Foolish Little Girl' (1963) and a reissued 'Dedicated To The One I Love' (1971) were all works of genius, as The Beatles (who reverentially covered 'Baby It's You' and 'Boys' on their debut album) could testify.

The hits dried up when they parted company with Dixon, but The Shirelles continued to record and tour until their demise in the late 60s, although reunions during the 70s and 80s inevitably included various permutations of original members and flirted with more modern R&B. The 90s saw the three surviving original Shirelles performing together again.

MICHELLE SHOCKED

WHO b. Karen Michelle Johnston, 24 Feb 1962, Gilmer, Texas, USA

WHAT The cowgirl with a conscience

Having outgrown adolescent passion for Kiss, Michelle immersed in the San Francisco Punk scene, then her political protesting led to time in psychiatric hospitals and jails. Returning to Texas from Amsterdam in May 1986, her performance at the Kerrville Folk Festival in Texas was recorded on a Walkman by producer Pete Lawrence for *The Texas Campfire Tapes* (1986).

She peaked with *Short Sharp Shocked* (1988), an alternately witty, sexy and acerbic set that yielded the hardy hit 'Anchorage'.

After the brilliantly bluesy *Captain Swing* (1989), Michelle recorded *Arkansas Traveller* (1992) in several American cities with musicians including The Band's Levon Helm, Taj Mahal and Hothouse Flowers. Leaving the Mercury label in 1994 in frustration at her lack of creative control, *Kind Hearted Woman* was sold at gigs until its release by Private Music in 1996.

 www.shellshock.com/

SIMON & GARFUNKEL ⊙⊙✪✪✪

WHO Vocals/guitar **Paul Simon** (b. 13 Oct 1941, Newark, New Jersey, USA),

vocals **Art Garfunkel** (b. 5 Nov 1941, Queens, New York, USA)

WHEN 1955–1981

WHERE New York City, New York, USA

WHAT Pristine-harmonied Folk Rock duo

Influenced by the harmonies of The Everly Brothers and the Folk Protest of Bob Dylan, Simon & Garfunkel became the most successful duo of the 60s with literate, melodic records aimed at the collegiate baby-boom audience. Their first success, however, was less intellectual: as Tom & Jerry, they scored a minor US hit with 1957's 'Hey Schoolgirl'. Less successful solo singles followed, recorded under pseudonyms True Taylor, Jerry Landis, Tico & The Triumphs (all Simon) and Artie Garr (Garfunkel).

They reunited in 1964 as Simon & Garfunkel, recording a Folk album, *Wednesday Morning 3 A.M.* (1964). When that bombed, Simon went to England and recorded *The Paul Simon Songbook* (1965). Producer Tom Wilson – inspired by the new Folk Rock of his main client Bob Dylan on that year's *Bringing It All Back Home* – added electric backing to 'The Sound Of Silence', a track from *Wednesday Morning 3 A.M.*, which became a US No.1 and belatedly kick-started the duo's career.

In 1966, *Sounds Of Silence* included 'Homeward Bound' and 'I Am A Rock', and *Parsley, Sage, Rosemary & Thyme* debuted the ambitious, eclectic arrangements which marked later releases.

'A Hazy Shade Of Winter' (1966), 'At The Zoo', 'Fakin' It' (both 1967) and 'Scarborough Fair/Canticle' (1968) brought moderate success, but the duo's involvement with Mike Nichols' movie *The Graduate* was more rewarding. Its 1968 soundtrack, comprising mainly old material and the catchy new 'Mrs Robinson', was a smash. But the duo's *Bookends* (1968), with a side of hits backed by an extended suite on ageing – from childhood ('Save The Life Of My Child') through youthful maturity ('America') to old age ('Old Friends/Bookends') – remains their masterpiece.

They released only one record – 'The Boxer' – in 1969, but the following year Simon & Garfunkel reached their commercial peak with 'Bridge Over Troubled Water' and the album of the same name, which spent a total of 41 weeks atop the UK chart. Inspired by Gospel outfit The Swan Silvertones' recording of 'Oh Mary Don't You Weep', the title track became a standard, since covered by more than 200 artists. Other hits from the album in 1970, such as the bouncy 'Cecilia' and Andean-flavoured 'El Condor Pasa', prefigured Simon's later interest in blending ethnic music with Pop – but another track, 'So Long, Frank Lloyd Wright' (a veiled reference to the former architecture student Garfunkel) proved more immediately prescient, as musical differences and Garfunkel's acting commitments (in *Catch-22*, *Carnal Knowledge* and *Bad Timing*) forced the duo to separate.

Garfunkel's Easy Listening *Angel Clare* (1973), *Breakaway* (1975) and *Watermark* (1978) culminated in two UK No.1s: 'I Only Have Eyes For You' (1975) and the *Watership Down* movie theme 'Bright Eyes' (1979), while Simon became a solo star.

In December 1981, the duo re-formed for a one-off free concert, released as *The Concert In Central Park* (1982).

read *Bookends – The Simon & Garfunkel Story* (1982), Patrick Humphries

surf www3.mistral.co.uk/rkent

CARLY SIMON ✪

WHO b. 25 Jun 1945, New York City, New York, USA

WHAT Sultry singer of standards and self-penned sagas

Carly Simon became a household name only after several false starts. From a wealthy New York family, she gravitated to the Folk clubs of Greenwich Village as a teenager. With her sister Lucy, she made two albums as The Simon Sisters in 1964 and 1965. A solo bid, nurtured by Bob Dylan's manager Albert Grossman, yielded only demos and ended in disarray.

She recovered with 1970's *Carly Simon*, whose hit 'That's The Way I've Always Heard It Should Be' was a candid questioning of marriage. 'You're So Vain' (US No.1/UK No.3) from the US No.1 *No Secrets* (1972) took such confession even further with its exposé of an ex-lover – reportedly either Mick Jagger (who sings backing vocals on the song) or actor Warren Beatty.

Another partner, James Taylor, joined her on 'Mockingbird', a hit from *Hotcakes* (1974), and Simon became a sort of sultry version of fellow domestic angst documenter Joni Mitchell. Amid albums like her best-seller *Boys In The Trees* (1978), Simon also hit with 1977's Bond theme 'Nobody Does it Better', from *The Spy Who Loved Me*.

In the 80s, she did best with one-offs like 1982's hypnotically funky, Chic-produced 'Why?' and uncredited backing vocals on Will Powers' 'Kissing With Confidence' (1983). She returned to the mainstream with 1986's platinum-coated *Coming Round Again*, which boasted a Stevie Wonder-graced take on *Casablanca*'s 'As Time Goes By' and scored its biggest hit with the title track, also the theme to the 1986 movie *Heartburn*. Movies proved fruitful again when she won an Oscar for 'Let The River Run' from 1989's *Working Girl*. She has since recorded and performed sporadically, and achieved an odd entrance into Rap when A Tribe Called Quest sampled 'Why' on their 1989 hit 'Bonita Applebum'.

surf www.ziva.com/carly/

PAUL SIMON ⊙ ⊙ ⊙ ✪

WHO b. 13 Oct 1941, Newark, New Jersey, USA

WHAT From rhymin' Simon to rhythm 'n' saints

Bar a one-off hit with Art Garfunkel as Tom & Jerry, Paul Simon pursued an unsuccessful solo career under various pseudonyms – True Taylor, Tico & The Triumphs and Jerry Landis – while financing himself through college (studying English and Law) by cutting demos for music publishers. After graduation, playing the Folk circuit, he visited England twice from 1964–1965. There he famously wrote 'Homeward Bound' on Widnes railway station and recorded *The Paul Simon Songbook* in one hour in May 1965 in a studio in London. It had passionately sung acoustic versions of future favourites 'I Am A Rock', 'Kathy's Song' and 'Leaves That Are Green', yet Simon had the album deleted in 1979.

Following Simon & Garfunkel's split in 1970, his *Paul Simon* (1972) and *There Goes Rhymin' Simon* (1973) were two of the 70s' most literate albums, consolidating Simon's reputation as a fine singer/songwriter. Both albums also displayed Simon's interest in World Music, featuring Reggae ('Mother And Child Reunion'), Hispanic Calypso ('Me And Julio Down By The Schoolyard') and New Orleans Jazz ('Take Me To The Mardi-Gras'). The Dixie Hummingbirds provided Gospel back-up on 'Loves Me Like A Rock' and Simon toured with Peruvian group Urubamba in 1973, catching the results on 1974's *Paul Simon In Concert/Live Rhymin'*. 'Mother And Child Reunion' and 'Kodachrome'/'Take Me To The Mardi-Gras' were Top 10 hits on both sides of the Atlantic.

The mid-70s to mid-80s were difficult for Simon. The jazzy *Still Crazy After All These Years* (1975) topped the US chart, but many of the songs alluded to his troubled personal life and divorce from his first wife. Remorse hung over the title track and others like '50 Ways To Leave Your Lover' (his only US No.1 single) and 'Slip Slidin' Away', the chart single from 1977's *Greatest Hits, Etc.*

Simon guested on US TV's *Saturday Night Live*, made cameos in The Rutles spoof-Beatles movie *All You Need Is Cash* (1978) and Woody Allen's *Annie Hall* (1978), and wrote and starred in *One Trick Pony* (1980), a movie about the decline of a Rock star which, despite its Salsa-style hit 'Late In The Evening', was a flop.

Hearts And Bones (1983), based on his delicate relationship with actress Carrie Fisher, was intended as a new Simon & Garfunkel album. They had happily reunited for one track – 'My Little Town' on *Still Crazy After All These Years* – and a brief 1981 tour was showcased on *The Concert In Central Park* (1982), but old enmities resurfaced in the studio and the idea was abandoned.

Simon was trying to express the concerns of his generation,

but *Hearts And Bones*' lack of success convinced him he had nothing to lose when a bootleg tape introduced him to Soweto's township jives and African rhythms. He was soon in South Africa recording with The Boyoyo Boys, General M.D. Shiranda and Ladysmith Black Mambazo for 1986's self-produced masterpiece, *Graceland* which, in his words, "spoke to the world in the musical language of Black South Africa". Even the more 'American' tracks captured an African feel, such as the penny whistle on the hit 'You Can Call Me Al', whose video starred Chevy Chase. The Everly Brothers and Linda Ronstadt also sang on the album.

Simon was temporarily black-listed by the UN and ANC, and had concerts picketed, for breaking a boycott on recording in South Africa. But the multi-award-winning *Graceland* is now recognized as a major force and Simon as probably one of the biggest influences in legitimizing World Music.

Instead of writing music to fit lyrics, he'd worked "backwards" on *Graceland*, starting with percussion and adding layers to the backing track so the music itself eventually created the melody. He used the same method on *The Rhythm Of The Saints* (1990), based on the polyrhythmic drumming of Brazil. He recorded one group, Oludun, just as he found them – playing drums in the streets. The album evoked a dreamy South American mañana mood, with lyrics often selected for sound rather than meaning.

After 1988's best-of, *Negotiations And Love Songs 1971–1986*, and 1991's live *Paul Simon's Concert In The Park*, he appeared on Annie Lennox's cover of 'Something So Right' (1994) and spent much of the 90s working on a musical, *The Capeman*. Mixing Doo Wop and Latin rhythms, and co-written with Nobel Prize-winning poet Derek Walcott about a regular Simon theme of the possibilities of redemption, it tells the story of a 16-year-old Puerto Rican who murdered two white teenagers in 1959. Simon's *Songs From The Capeman* emerged to mixed reviews in 1997 and the musical opened on Broadway in early 1998.

read *The Paul Simon Companion* (1997), ed. Stacey Luftig

SIMPLE MINDS ⊙⊙⊙⊙⊙

WHO Vocals **Jim Kerr** (b. 9 Jul 1959, Glasgow, Scotland), guitar **Charlie Burchill** (b. 27 Nov 1959, Glasgow), bass **Derek Forbes** (b. 22 Jun 1956, Glasgow), drums **Mel Gaynor** (b. 29 May 1959, Glasgow)

WHEN 1978–

WHERE Glasgow, Scotland

WHAT Stadium Rock stallions

"We must have been the only band who said 'Yeah, I like Pink Floyd – my second concert was Genesis'"

As Punk – and their band Johnny & The Self Abusers – ran out of steam, Jim Kerr, Charlie Burchill and drummer Brian McGee (later replaced by Mel Gaynor) reverted to their Bowie/Roxy roots as the art-rockin' Simple Minds. Recruiting short-stayed guitarist Duncan Barnwell, bassist Derek Forbes ("the joker of the band", according to UK Pop magazine *Smash Hits*) and keyboard player Mick McNeil, Simple Minds joined Indie label Zoom, whose boss Bruce Findlay became their manager.

Following the mediocre *Life In A Day* (1979) – which the band disowned – *Real To Real Cacophony* (1979) and *Empires And Dance* (1980) flirted magically with Electronic ambience. The latter's 'I Travel' became a New Romantic dancefloor favourite and outdid The Human League in the futuristic stakes.

Acclaim paved the way for cult classics 'The American', 'Love Song' and 1981's Virgin-released *Sons And Fascination/Sister Feelings Call* double album, which scraped the UK Top 10. But their breakthrough came with 1982's excellent *New Gold Dream 81, 82, 83, 84* – an epic of synthesized grandeur and air-punching anthems like the hits 'Promised You A Miracle', 'Glittering Prize' and 'Someone Somewhere In Summertime'.

As their success skyrocketed, Simple Minds targeted the USA and adopted the bombast of fellow bright new hopes U2. 'Waterfront' (1983) replaced arty experimentalism with crashing chords and Bono-esque vocals. *Sparkle In The Rain* (1984) became the first of four Simple Minds albums to top the UK chart and US obscurity abated with 1985's No.1 'Don't You Forget About Me' (from the 'Brat Pack' coming-of-age movie *The Breakfast Club*). *Once Upon A Time* (1985) was packed with great Pop, like the transatlantic biggies 'Alive And Kicking', 'Sanctify Yourself' and 'All The Things She Said'. But while Forbes' and McNeil's swan song *Live In The City Of Light* (1987) reflected Simple Minds' ascent to stadia, it rivals *Frampton Comes Alive* as a dated artifact of a bygone age.

Critical savaging only strengthened their fanbase. Easily the biggest stars of 1988's Nelson Mandela tribute show in London, Simple Minds hit UK No.1 with the moving 'Belfast Child'. Its political edge was elaborated on 1989's *Street Fighting Years*, whose 'Mandela Day' and a haunting version of Peter Gabriel's 'Biko' tackled troubles in South Africa. But while the album topped the UK chart, it was sunk by its seriousness in the USA. Back home, loyalty was tested by 1989's 'Amsterdam' EP, which included a misguided version of Prince's 'Sign O' The Times'.

While 1990's singles box sets *Themes* kept sales ticking over, Kerr, Burchill and Gaynor re-invented themselves for the post-House 90s. They returned with 1991's dancey 'Let There Be Love' and just missed the UK No.1 with *Real Life*. However, with Simple Minds now about as fashionable as mullet haircuts, Kerr became more famous for his marriages to The Pretenders' Chrissie Hynde and actress Patsy Kensit (who flounced off with Liam Gallagher).

Although the best-of collection *Glittering Prize* (1992) topped the chart, the 'proper' album, *Good News From The Next World* (1995) – despite its fine hits 'She's A River' and 'Hypnotised' – didn't. Their comeback appearance at the 1995 Glastonbury festival, although performed with typical aplomb, was critically murdered. Meanwhile, Gaynor played on Drum 'n' Bass pioneer Goldie's *Timeless* (1995) and returned, with Forbes, for Simple Minds' overnight chart guest *Neapolis* (1998).

Read *Simple Minds: A Visual Documentary* (1991), Mike Wren

Fan Shadowlands, PO Box 276, Northampton, NN1 4AX, UK

Surf www.simple-minds.demon.co.uk/

SIMPLY RED ⊙ ⊙ ⊙ ○ ○ ⊙

WHO Vocals **Mick Hucknall** (b. 8 Jun 1960, Manchester, England)

WHEN 1984–

WHERE Manchester, England

WHAT CD Soul

Named after their redhead singer, Simply Red have never had a stable line-up, members being hired and fired by kingpin Mick Hucknall. "This is a solo career," he said in 1991, "and it always has been, but it's taken me five years to realize it. I just don't like the name Mick Hucknall very much." An art student, he formed his first band, The Frantic Elevators, in 1979. As anarchic as their name suggested, their punkish style belied Hucknall's tastes: Reggae, Soul and 60s Pop. He grew impatient – a development suggested by the plangent ballad 'Holding Back The Years', which he co-wrote and released while with the band.

Still known as 'Red', Hucknall ditched the Elevators in 1984 and started Simply Red. The acclaimed debut album *Picture Book* (1985) – a UK and US Top 10 hit – boasted covers of Talking Heads' 'Heaven' and The Valentine Brothers' 'Money's Too Tight (To Mention)', but it was a revamped 'Holding Back The Years' which stole the show and hit US No.1. Quibbles about Simply Red's 'authenticity' dogged him, yet there was general agreement that Hucknall possessed a genuinely fine voice.

Caught up in the rush of success, he concocted 1987's *Men And Women* but was dissatisfied by the result. Although its sales matched those of its predecessor, his increasing fame masked a decline in Stateside popularity, which he's struggled to recover. Covers and co-writers abounded, including Bunny Wailer's 'Love Fire', Sly Stone's 'Let Me Have It All' and Cole Porter's 'Ev'ry Time We Say Goodbye' and collaborations with legendary Soul writer Lamont Dozier (credited to 'Hucknall/Dozier/Hucknall' in dubious homage to writing team Holland/Dozier/Holland). Yet the best was Hucknall's own Funk Pop effort 'The Right Thing'.

A second US No.1 came with a cover of Harold Melvin & The Blue Notes' 'If You Don't Know Me By Now', the centrepiece of *A New Flame* (1989). Giant worldwide sales confirmed Hucknall's key contribution to 80s Pop: the glossy Anglo-Soul style shared with CD staples Sade, Culture Club and Alison Moyet.

Though US interest again faltered, *Stars* (1991) had five UK hits ('Something Got Me Started', 'Stars', 'For Your Babies', 'Thrill Me' and 'Your Mirror') and world sales of more than 9 million. Progressing from old school Soul to glossy House, Hucknell's first album of originals helped overcome the 'cover band' stigma.

Life (1995) confirmed his club culture affinity, its highlight the slick 'Fairground'. Meanwhile, in spite of his left-wing sympathies, he became more noted for a glamorous bachelor lifestyle: good food, football and a succession of models and celebrity friends like tennis star Steffi Graf. In 1996, he earned a reported £150,000 performing for the rulers of Dubai and achieved a football fan's ambition by writing 'We're In This Together', official theme for the Euro 96 soccer tournament. *Greatest Hits* (1996) featured a cover of Aretha Franklin's 'Angel', a collaboration with The Fugees. A year later he was back with a cover of Gregory Isaacs' Reggae classic, 'Night Nurse', with Sly & Robbie.

Hucknall founded the Blood & Fire label to rescue his beloved vintage Reggae from obscurity. Simply Red rose again with *Blue* (1998), trailed by the beautiful hit 'Say You Love Me'.

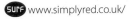

READ *Simply Mick* (1994), Robin & Rob McGibbon

FAN So What Ltd, PO Box 334, Manchester, M60 1JD, UK

SURF www.simplyred.co.uk/

SIOUXSIE & THE BANSHEES

WHO Vocals **Siouxsie Sioux** (b. Susan Dallion, 27 May 1957, Bromley, Kent, England), bass **Steve Severin** (b. 25 Sep 1955, London, England), drums **Budgie** (b. Peter Clarke, 21 Aug 1957, St Helens, Merseyside, England)

WHEN 1976–1996

WHERE London, England

WHAT Punk protégés turned Goth mainstays

A hastily convened fledgling Banshees debuted at the 100 Club's Punk Festival in 1976 with a now legendary 20-minute version of 'The Lord's Prayer'. With waitress Siouxsie on vocals, future Sex Pistol Sid Vicious on drums, Steve Havoc (later Steve Severin) on bass and Marco Pirroni (later of Adam & The Ants) on guitar, they were shambolic. Although the band split immediately, it was enough to inspire the formation of a permanent outfit.

After a graffiti campaign by fans, a debut TV performance of 'Make Up To Break Up' and a 1977 Radio 1 session with guitarist John McKay (who replaced Pete Fenton), Severin and drummer Kenny Morris, the Banshees signed to Polydor. In 1978, they appeared in Don Lett's *Punk Rock Movie*, but were cut from Derek Jarman's *Jubilee*. 'Hong Kong Garden' and *The Scream* were UK hits, the latter including a revamp of The Beatles' 'Helter Skelter' – the cutting edge of post-Punk. Siouxsie's image (sometimes with breasts exposed, or in Nazi regalia) and a debut UK tour (supported by The Human League) prompted a media frenzy.

After 1979's slated *Join Hands* (boasting a new 'Lord's Prayer'), McKay and Morris quit on the second date of a UK tour. With their replacements Budgie and Robert Smith (hijacked from The Cure), then ex-Magazine guitarist John McGeogh, *Kaleidoscope* (1980) premiered a psychedelic sound. The hugely influential *Ju Ju* (1981) continued their vision of dysfunctional suburbia and prompted the singles set *Once Upon A Time* (1981). Siouxsie and future husband Budgie also began a side project, The Creatures.

After *A Kiss In The Dreamhouse* (1982) – their finest hour – McGeogh was replaced by Smith for the Royal Albert Hall show that became *Nocturne* (1983), as 'Dear Prudence' (1982) reached UK No.3. In 1983, Severin and Smith formed The Glove, whose *Blue Sunshine* appeared on the Banshees' own Wonderland label.

The Banshees' *Hyena* (1984) was critically slated, though a US success; *Tinderbox* (1986) enjoyed slightly better reviews, as John Carruthers (ex-Clock DVA) replaced Smith. *Through The Looking Glass* (1987) – consisting entirely of covers, including Iggy Pop's 'The Passenger' – was similarly panned.

With cellist and keyboardist Martin McCarrick, and Carruthers' replacement Jon Klein (ex-Specimen), the Banshees were back on form with 1988's bombastic *Peep Show*, 1991's *Superstition*, 1992's superb singles set *Twice Upon A Time* and 1995's John Cale-produced *The Rapture* – their most accessible work to date, despite its 14-minute title track. But the Banshees split in 1996 – in part, a disgusted response to the reunion of The Sex Pistols.

In 1998, Siouxsie collaborated with Marc Almond and David Bowie. The Creatures contributed, with Juno Reactor, to the *Lost In Space* soundtrack and released *Mount Venus*. Severin contributed to the soundtrack for the banned *Visions Of Ecstasy*.

Another band to lay claim to the 'best in the world' title, the Banshees remained paradoxical. They played charity concerts for MENCAP in 1979 (where they were charged £2,000 for the damage they caused) and the Disabled Children's International Games in 1981. In 1983, they played for the Italian Communist Party. Siouxsie herself also remains contradictory – from bored teenager (as part of the Bromley contingent) to 80s icon; from riotous Punk subversion to contributing 'Face To Face' to 1991's *Batman Returns*; from a swastika-clad vamp to the winner of a libel suit against the *Mirror* newspaper (who said she'd had a nose job) – but has become an Alternative Rock mainstay.

READ *Entranced: The Siouxsie & The Banshees Story* (1989), Brian Johns

SURF www.vamp.org/Siouxsie/

"I hate Genesis. I despise them...
I think they should be torched.
And Abba"

SISTER SLEDGE

WHO Vocals **Debra** (b. 1955), vocals **Joni** (b. 1957), vocals **Kim** (b.1958), vocals **Kathie** (b. 1959)

WHEN 1971–

WHERE Philadelphia, Pennsylvania, USA

WHAT The sleek, chic sound of sisterly Soul

Long before Spice Girls translated sisterhood into glittery Pop, Sister Sledge did it with 1979's 'We Are Family'. It vindicated the sisters, whose only previous glimpse of mainstream chart action had been their 1975 UK hit 'Mama Never Told Me', despite recording since 1971 and touring the world, sometimes supporting Funk legends Rick James and George Clinton.

They were plucked from relative obscurity by Nile Rodgers and Bernard Edwards, whose elegant Disco was being honed with Chic. The platinum *We Are Family* (1979) – with its anthemic title track, 'He's The Greatest Dancer' and 'Lost In Music' – was as key to establishing the Chic sound as that band's own records.

After *Love Somebody Today* (1980) and a 1982 hit with Mary Wells' 'My Guy', their US profile slid again, but Europe faithfully bought remixes and best-ofs and sent 1985's jaunty 'Frankie' (from *When The Boys Meet The Girls*) to UK No.1. Thereafter, despite Kathie's solo stab *Heart* (1992) and ongoing touring, they hit the news only in 1998, when Will Smith reworked 'He's The Greatest Dancer' as the US No.1 'Gettin' Jiggy Wit It' and Spice Girls took to encoring with, appropriately enough, 'We Are Family'. Their anthem was also adopted by another bunch of noisy gals: Babes In Toyland included it on 1995's *Nemesisters*.

SURF www.onlinetalent.com/sledge_homepage.html

THE SISTERS OF MERCY

WHO Vocals/general dictatorship **Andrew Eldritch** (b. Andrew Taylor, 15 May 1959, Ely, Cambridgeshire, England)

WHEN 1980–

WHERE Leeds, Yorkshire, England

WHAT Synth-rockin' Goth spooks

Years before bright graduate Brian Warner mutated into Marilyn Manson, a student in England tried the same trick. Plucking the name Eldritch from a dictionary ("unearthly, weird"), Andrew Taylor – a "very bad drummer" – and singing guitarist Gary Marx debuted with 1980's self-confessedly awful 'The Damage Done'.

Resolving to "start again, properly", Eldritch took the mic in 1981. Marx stuck to guitar, Craig Adams joined on bass and Doktor Avalanche, a drum machine, took care of the rest. Live, they ruined songs by Leonard Cohen (from whose repertoire they'd taken their name) and The Velvet Underground. A version of the Velvets' 'Sister Ray' pricked the ears of Generation X's Tony James, who fruitlessly invited Eldritch to form a new band.

With successive guitarists Ben Gunn and Wayne Hussey (the latter formerly of Dead Or Alive), the Sisters became Indie idols with 1982's 'Body Electric' and 'Alice', and 1983's 'Reptile House' EP and 'Temple Of Love'. They brushed the UK Top 40 with

1984's 'Body And Soul' and 'Walk Away', and 1985's 'No Time To Cry', but rifts and Eldritch's health were worsened by drugs. Marx quit and, within months of their battle-scarred *First And Last And Always* (1985), Eldritch announced their farewell.

Adams and Hussey's resurrection was scuppered by Eldritch's rush-released single ('Giving Ground') and album (*Gift*) under their planned name The Sisterhood. As The Mission – a name he traced to the working title of the Sisters' second album, *Left On Mission Of Revenge* – they mopped up mourning fans, while Eldritch's profile was maintained by Syd Barrett-esque music press sightings.

He returned triumphant with the Jim Steinman-produced 'This Corrosion'. Building on *Gift*'s groundwork, it married OTT opera to sinister synths, premiering 1987's fabulous *Floodland*. His ambition finally matched by epic writing and production, Eldritch conquered the charts with a new partner, Goth goddess Patricia Morrison (formerly of rocky New Wavers The Gun Club).

By 1990, she had departed in a litigious flurry. Tony James, who'd followed Generation X with the credibility-crippling Sigue Sigue Sputnik, completed a new line-up for *Vision Thing* (1990), which put rocking guitars before spooky synths. Now arena-fillers, the Sisters toured through 1991, but gigs with Rap gods Public Enemy ground to a halt and James quit. Undaunted, Eldritch celebrated the Sisters' legacy with 1992's 'early stuff' set *Some Girls Wander By Mistake* and 1993's best-of *A Slight Case Of Overbombing*. The latter yielded new hits in the slow-burning 'Under The Gun', with Berlin's Terri Nunn, and a titanic 'Temple Of Love' revamp with Yemeni superstar Ofra Haza.

Thereafter, Eldritch waged war with his label, WEA off-shoot East West, offering a mock-ambient album by side project SSV ('Screw Shareholders' Value') to fulfil his contract. Resurfacing for gigs in 1997 and 1998, the Sisters failed to recapture previous peaks, but the wily Eldritch has proved he can never be safely written off.

fan Glasperlenspiel, The C Foundation, PO Box 23, Manchester, M13 9BN, UK

surf www.cm.cf.ac.uk/Sisters.Of.Mercy/

RONI SIZE

WHO b. Ryan Williams, 29 Oct 1969, Bristol, England

WHAT Award-winning Drum 'n' Bass pioneer

Roni Size went straight from school into Bristol's Dance scene, learning his trade as DJ, programmer and producer. The 1992 release on the London-based V label of 'It's A Jazz Thing' elevated him to the Drum 'n' Bass hall of fame, and established a yardstick for his aim of bringing the form in from the cold. Often teaming with fellow Bristolians DJ Krust (with whom he started the Full Cycle label) and DJ Die, the prolific Size continued his alchemical mixtures of sample-heavy rhythmic trickery and subsonic bass with Ragga, Jazz and Soul, as showcased on seminal cuts like 1993's 'Music Box' and 1994's 'Timestretch'.

A rapprochement with conventional music-making came a step closer when Size, Krust and Die teamed up with DJ Suv, MC Dynamite and vocalist Onalee as the live Drum 'n' Bass outfit Reprazent. With Portishead drummer Clive Deamer and bassist Fi Johns on board, they released the excellent 'Brown Paper Bag' and *New Forms* (1997) for the Talkin' Loud imprint.

The major label collaboration paid off when, against long odds, Reprazent netted the 1997 Mercury Music Prize.

surf www.fullcycle.co.uk

SKA

WHAT A resilient style of Reggae. Ska emerged in the late 50s in Jamaica when sound-system bosses – discovering that the American sources of the locally popular jump R&B records had dried up – took to recording their own. Early releases featured local Jazz musicians like trombonist Don Drummond, pianist Cluett 'Clue J' Johnson, and saxman Roland Alphonso. They honed a hard-edged, exciting music with a choppy "ska, ska" beat that gave the music its onomatopoeic name. In Britain, the music was called Blue Beat – after the label most associated with releasing it – and Prince Buster ('Al Capone'), Millie ('My Boy Lollipop') and The Skatalites ('Guns Of Navarone') all hit with it. The style was picked up by UK acts like Georgie Fame. By 1968, Ska had been replaced by the more sinuous Rock Steady in Jamaica. But it enjoyed a worldwide revival from 1979 onwards with the arrival of the 2 Tone label – which saw The Specials, Madness and The Beat return it to the charts – and in late 90s America and Japan, where acts like Jump With Joey and The Ska Flames have relaunched the original Jamaican sound.

WHERE Jamaica

WHEN 1959–1966

WHO The Skatalites Ska Authentic (1965), Prince Buster Fabulous Greatest Hits (1968), The Specials The Specials (1979), Various Ska Island (1998)

SKID ROW ✪

WHO Vocals **Sebastian Bach** (b. Sebastian Bierk, 3 Apr 1968, Bahamas), guitar **Dave 'The Snake' Sabo** (b. 16 Sep 1962), guitar **Scotti Hill** (b. 31 May 1964), bass **Rachel Bolan** (b. 9 Feb 1964), drums **Rob Affuso** (b. 1 Mar 1963)

WHEN 1986–1998

WHERE New Jersey, USA

WHAT Heavy Metal's youth gone wild

The missing link between Rock gods Bon Jovi and Indie stars The Breeders is the hyperactive Sebastian Bach, who started out in Jon Bon Jovi's pet project Skid Row and wound up in The Last Hard Men alongside ex-Breeder (and sister of Pixies/Breeders bassist Kim) Kelley Deal. The Skids themselves began as a partnership of Dave Sabo and Rachel Bolan. Sabo had grown up with Jon Bon Jovi, who made good on a pact that whoever became famous first would help the other out – hence the Skids' Bon Jovi-endorsed leap to the big-time in 1989. Their secret weapon was the Bahamas-born, Canada-raised Bach, for whom their first hit, 'Youth Gone Wild', became a motto for life. He walked and talked BIG AND LOUD and was as convincing on snarling Metal as on ballads. Accordingly, the tough-but-tender '18 & Life' and 'I Remember You' crashed the US Top 10, shoving the hook-packed *Skid Row* (1989) to the multi-platinum plateau.

Having squabbled with Bon Jovi (over money) and upstaged Mötley Crüe and Aerosmith live, they slammed back with 1991's vicious *Slave To The Grind*, a million-selling US No.1. Their new-found heaviosity fuelled gigs with Guns N' Roses, a place on the 1992 Monsters Of Rock UK bill and an 18-month tour with soon-to-be Metal kings Pantera in support. However, despite its chilling hit 'Breakin' Down', the even heavier *Subhuman Race* (1995) was a comparative failure and, by mid-1996, Bach found himself out of the band, who refused to re-form even for support slots with their beloved Kiss.

Bach graced tributes to Ace Frehley (1996's *Spacewalk*), Rush (1996's *Working Man*) and Led Zeppelin (1997's *Stairway To Heaven*), then teamed with Kelley Deal, Frogs' keyboardist Jimmy Flemion and ex-Smashing Pumpkins drummer Jimmy Chamberlin in The Last Hard Men, who debuted with a cover of Alice Cooper's 'School's Out' on 1997's *Scream* soundtrack. They also revamped 'Tonight's The Night', with Smashing Pumpkins' D'Arcy Wretzky, for a Rod Stewart tribute. But when Atlantic ummed and ahhed over a Last Hard Men album, Bach went solo in 1997.

Skids bassist Rachel Bolan – apparently the principal opponent to a group reunion – pursued glory with the implausibly monikered Prunella Scales, named after the *Fawlty Towers* actress. In 1998, he, Sabo, Hill and Affuso resurfaced with singer Shawn McCabe as the poppier Ozone Monday. Their Metal legacy was celebrated by 1998's *Forty Seasons: The Best Of Skid Row*.

 www.ifu.net/~bachoff/

SKUNK ANANSIE

WHO Vocals **Skin** (b. Deborah Anne Dyer, 3 Aug 1967, London, England), guitar **Ace** (b. Martin Ivor Kent, 30 Mar 1967, Cheltenham, Gloucestershire, England), bass **Cass Lewis** (b. Richard Keith Lewis, 1 Sep 1960, London), drums **Mark Richardson** (b. 28 May 1970, Leeds, England)

WHEN 1994–

WHERE London, England

WHAT Prejudice-pounding Punk Metal

Grunge's breaking down of the division between Rock and Indie in the early 90s created ideal conditions for Skunk Anansie to flourish. Their music is hard and fast enough to appeal to Metal fans, but has enough melody and thoughtful, polemical lyrics to win over Indie kids in search of a guaranteed adrenalin buzz.

They won early attention thanks to striking, shaven-headed singer Skin. Black and openly bisexual, her very presence at the front of a loud guitar band challenged Rock convention. In July 1994, five months after Skunk's formation, Indie label One Little Indian signed them. Their debut album *Paranoid And Sunburnt* (1995) went gold in Britain and yielded four UK hits – notably the

Top 20 'Weak' (covered by Rod Stewart in 1998) and 'Charity', which demonstrated their range and subtlety.

Stoosh (1996) included the radio-friendly hits 'Hedonism (Just Because You Feel Good)' and 'Brazen (Weep)', which further broadened the band's fanbase, but other songs, like 'Yes It's Fucking Political' and 'We Love Your Apathy', removed any fears that success might mellow Skunk Anansie. In 1997, the band's broad appeal was illustrated by Prodigy sampling their high-octane 'Selling Jesus' on *The Fat Of The Land*'s 'Serial Thrilla', and a Kiss support slot.

 www.indian.co.uk/skunk/

SLADE ⊙⊙⊙⊙

WHO Vocals/guitar **Noddy Holder** (b. Neville Holder, 15 Jun 1946, Walsall, England), guitar **Dave Hill** (b. 4 Apr 1952, Fleet Castle, Devon, England), bass/keyboards/violin **Jim Lea** (b. 14 Jun 1952, Wolverhampton, England), drums **Don Powell** (b. 10 Sep 1950, Bilston, West Midlands, England)

WHEN 1966–

WHERE Wolverhampton, England

WHAT Self-styled Glam Rock yobs

While David Bowie was taking Glam Rock to arty heights, Slade were stomping the ground and storming the charts with an irresistible Pop riot. Hailing from Britain's grimy West Midlands, Noddy Holder and Jim Lea joined The N'Betweens in 1966. They evolved through styles and name changes – including a 'boots 'n' braces' skinhead phase – before being adopted by former Jimi Hendrix manager (and Animals bassist) Chas Chandler.

Emerging as Slade in 1971, they hit with a raucous cover of Little Richard's 'Get Down And Get With It', ushering in a period of staggering success when they became a UK chart fixture.

Slade's sound was a good-natured bludgeoning: Holder's roar and jokey wordplay, Hill's grinding guitar, Powell's no-nonsense tub-thumping and Lea's skilful melodic touch. This classic teamwork sent 1971's 'Coz I Luv You', 1972's 'Take Me Back 'Ome', 'Mama Weer All Crazee Now' and *Slayed?*, 1973's 'Cum On Feel The Noize', 'Skweeze Me Pleeze Me', 'Merry Xmas Everybody' and *Sladest*, and 1974's *Old, New, Borrowed And Blue* to UK No.1.

Visually, they were stunning: not built for Bowie/Bolan-esque skinny elegance, they were nonetheless fully glammed up. Hill, in particular, struck an incredible figure with shimmering stage suits, a guitar body which spelled out the word 'YOB' and the weirdest hair *ever*. He once headed out for a TV appearance telling songwriters Holder and Lea, "You write 'em, I'll sell 'em".

Changing fashions and fruitless attempts to crack America claimed Slade's crown. Despite a riotous stage act (a confessed influence on Kiss), Slade's working-class/cartoon-glam image and the word games of their biggest hits made little sense to US audiences. After a two-year stint in which they lived in New York and, said Chandler, "did 200 shows a year", they gave up in 1977. Europe, Australia and Japan were more generous but, by the end of the 70s, it looked like Slade's luck had run out.

Yet, with the riff-heavy genius of the Holder/Lea songwriting partnership intact, they reversed their fortunes with scattered

UK hits like 1983's 'My Oh My' and 1991's 'Radio Wall Of Sound'. Belated Stateside recognition came via Quiet Riot's 1983 Top 5 cover of 'Cum On Feel The Noize', followed in 1984 with Slade's own 'Run Run Away' and *Keep Your Hands Off My Power Supply*.

However, from 1988, Slade were a part-time band and, in the 90s, Hill and Powell were Slade II, a floor-shaking hits review. Holder became a TV/radio presenter and Lea a psychotherapist. But the ghost of Slade will always haunt British Pop: the million-selling 'Merry Xmas Everybody' visits the chart each year like an irritating but loved relative; comedians Reeves & Mortimer aped them in their 'Slade In Residence' sketches; their underrated, semi-autobiographical movie *Flame* (1974) has become a cult item and numerous hits sets sell steadily. But their legacy is an anarchic attitude which ran through Punks like The Damned and 80s faves The Wonder Stuff to 90s giants Oasis, whose cover of 'Cum On Feel The Noize' fitted seamlessly with their own songs.

 Slade and Slade II Fan Club, PO Box 4YD, London, WIA 4YD, UK

 www.mrscsi.com/slade/home.htm

SLAYER

WHO Vocals/bass **Tom Araya** (b. 6 Jun 1961, Chile), guitar **Kerry King** (b. 3 Jun 1964, Huntington Beach, California, USA), guitar **Jeff Hanneman** (b. 31 Jan 1964, Los Angeles, California), drums **Dave Lombardo** (b. 16 Feb 1965)

WHEN 1982–

WHERE Huntington Beach, California, USA

WHAT Brutal, satanic, Speed Metal

First heard on the *Metal Massacre III* compilation (1983), Slayer's terrifying take on Thrash compelled Metal Blade to sign them for an EP, 'Haunting The Chapel' (1984) and two albums, *Show No Mercy* (1984) and *Hell Awaits* (1985). Their grinding, sonic maelstrom ("I don't like melody too much," said Tom Araya) and diabolic imagery (inverted crosses, blood, six-inch-nail studded wristbands) proclaimed them the heaviest band around. But it was their Rick Rubin-produced third album, *Reign In Blood* (1986) – brutal Satanic Speed Metal – that established them, alongside fellow Southern Californians Metallica, as kings of Thrash. This status meant a certain caginess about Kerry King's riff-supplying role on the Beastie Boys' 'No Sleep Till Brooklyn' (1986).

South Of Heaven (1988) refined the sound while cutting down the speed. *Seasons In The Abyss* (1990) was a superb synthesis of the previous two albums (and, allegedly, the music of choice for US troops in the Gulf War). After 1991's live *Decade of Aggression*, Lombardo was replaced with Paul Bostaph, ex-Forbidden, who sounded very like his predecessor on 1994's *Divine Intervention*. Lombardo resurfaced in 1998 with Faith No More's Mike Patton.

Bostaph was replaced in 1996 by ex-Testament drummer John Dette for their long-discussed Punk covers set *Undisputed Attitude*. *Diabolus In Musica* (1998) continued the attack. If Slayer had even noticed Grunge, they weren't letting on.

 Thrash Metal (1989), Malcolm Dome

 Slayer Fan Club, Statonic Wehrmacht, Dept. SL-01, PO Box 884564, San Francisco, CA 94188, USA

 www.slaytonic.com/abyss.html

PERCY SLEDGE

WHO b. 25 Nov 1940, Leighton, Alabama, USA

WHAT One-off Soul legend

Moonlighting from a hospital orderly job with R&B covers band the Esquires Combo, Percy Sledge shot to stardom in 1966 when his mournful solo 'When A Man Loves A Woman' hit US No.1.

Sledge recorded for three years at Atlantic's famous Muscle Shoals studios but – despite US R&B chart smashes with 'Warm And Tender Love', 'It Tears Me Up' (both 1966), 'Out Of Left Field' (1967), 'Sudden Stop', 'Take Time To Know Her' (both 1968), and 'Any Day Now' (1969) – never repeated his mainstream success.

Unusually, he also recorded Country songs – 1967's 'Love Me Tender' and 'The Dark End Of The Street'. Save for scattered 70s R&B hits (1973's 'Sunshine' and 1974's 'I'll Be Your Everything'), Sledge was absent from the chart until 'When A Man Loves A Woman', featured in Oliver Stone's *Platoon* and a Levi's ad, hit UK No.2 in 1987. In 1991, Michael Bolton gave the song his unique treatment and followed its writer to the US chart summit.

SLEEPER

WHO Vocals/guitar **Louise Wener** (b. 30 Jul 1968, Ilford, Essex, England), guitar **Jon Stewart** (b. 12 Sep 1967, Sheffield, England), bass **Kenediid 'Diid' Osman** (b. 10 Apr 1968, Mogadishu, Somalia), drums **Andy McClure** (b. 4 Jul 1970, Manchester, England)

WHEN 1992–

WHERE London, England

WHAT The Indie 'It' girl

Having slogged through college bands like Surrender Dorothy, Louise Wener and Jon Stewart graduated from Manchester University in 1992 with a band, Sleeper. They moved to London, advertised "Bassist, drummer wanted. Pixies, Partridge Family. Serious applicants" and enlisted Andy McClure and Diid Osman.

Signing to Indolent in 1993, 'Alice In Vain' (1993) and 'Bucket and Spade' (1993) were kitchen-sink dramas for the middle classes – with teenage romance, suburban anguish and Wener playing a self-appointed feisty heroine. 'Delicious' (1994) and 'Inbetweener' (1995) put Sleeper in Britpop's heyday. Wener courted the press: serious and ambitious in fashion favourite *Elle*; coquettish in lad's monthly *Loaded*; ironic in the music press with her T-shirt slogan 'just another female-fronted band'.

Smart (1995) was catchy and made UK No.5. 'Vegas' followed close behind. But Wener's honeymoon with the press was near its end. She slated feminists and vegetarians, and supported pornography and racists' right to free speech.

'What Do I Do Now? (1995)', 'Sale Of The Century' and *The It Girl* (1996) showcased Wener's role as Sleeper's primary writer – citing Blondie and Madonna as influences. The 1996 singles 'Nice Guy Eddie' and 'Statuesque' made the Top 20. In 1997, Osman was fired and *Pleased To Meet You* was written by Wener alone.

 www.2.bitstream.net/"sleeper/sleepstart.htm

THE SLITS

WHO Vocals **Ari Up** (b. Arianna Foster, 1962 ,Germany), guitar **Viv Albertine** (b. Viviane Albertine, 1955, France), bass **Tessa Pollitt** (b. 1959, England), drums **Palmolive** (b. Paloma Romero, 1955, Spain)

WHEN 1976–1981

WHERE London, England

WHAT Punky Reggae

Younger readers may find this incredible, but not all that long ago few women played instruments in bands. Today's healthier climate owes much to Punk pioneers like The Slits.

The first line-up featured guitarist Kate Korus and bassist Suzi Gutzy. They were replaced by Viv Albertine and Tessa Pollitt well before *Cut* (1979) – an intoxicating mixture of Reggae rhythms, scratchy guitars, anger and mischief. Palmolive left during the sessions, partly because she disliked the others' sleeve concept: the group wearing only loincloths and mud. Peter 'Budgie' Clarke played drums on *Cut* before being replaced by Bruce Smith. The Slits' finest moment, post-*Cut*, was their spirited cover of John Holt's 'Man Next Door' (1980). *Bootleg Retrospective* (1980) was a scrapbook of studio doodles. *Return Of The Giant Slits* (1981) was confused and disappointing, after which they soon disbanded.

Ari Up moved to Jamaica and has been active in the Reggae scene, but her Punk connection continues: her mother Nora married John Lydon. Palmolive, a born-again Christian, plays in covers band Hi-Fi, whose repertoire includes The Slits' 'FM'.

 www.comnet.ca/~rina/slits.html

SLY & ROBBIE

WHO Bass **Robbie 'Basspeare' Shakespeare** (b. 27 Sep 1953, Kingston, Jamaica), drums **Sly 'Drumbar' Dunbar** (b. Lowell Charles Dunbar, 10 May 1952, Kingston)

WHEN 1975–

WHERE Kingston, Jamaica

WHAT Mighty Reggae Soul Funk performer/producers

Both Sly & Robbie had been Kingston studio sessioneers for the best part of five years before they united as the backbone of Reggae band The Revolutionaries in 1975, backing everyone from Dennis Brown to Dillinger. Riding on Sly's fierce, metronomic rhythms and Robbie's no-frills basslines, they became Jamaica's ace rhythm section. They formed their own label, Taxi, in 1979, initially recording stars Gregory Isaacs and Junior Delgado. A liaison as rhythm section/producers to vocal group Black Uhuru took their fame worldwide and, known as the Riddim Twins, they spent much of the 80s backing the likes of Bob Dylan, Ian Dury and Grace Jones. They also scored a worldwide Dance hit with 'Boops (Here To Go)' in 1987.

Instead of suffering when Reggae went electronic in the mid-80s, they embraced new technology and Taxi remained at the genre's pinnacle. In the 90s, their production on Chaka Demus & Pliers gave the duo six worldwide hits and, on a more 'rootsy' tip, they helped make young star Luciano Reggae's most-likely-to.

SLY & THE FAMILY STONE ✪

WHO Vocals/keyboards/guitar **Sly Stone** (b. Sylvester Stewart, 15 Mar 1944, Dallas, Texas, USA), guitar **Freddie Stone** (b. 5 Jun 1946, Dallas), trumpet **Cynthia Robinson** (b. 12 Jan 1946, Sacramento, California, USA), saxophone **Jerry Martini** (b. 1 Oct 1943, Colorado, USA), vocals/piano **Rosemary Stone** (b. 21 Mar 1945, Vallejo, California), bass **Larry Graham** (b. 14 Aug 1946, Beaumont, Texas), drums **Greg Errico** (b. 1 Sep 1946, San Francisco, California)

WHEN 1967–

WHERE San Francisco, California, USA

WHAT Stoned and stratospheric Funk deities

Bar The Beatles, few people could claim to have influenced Brian Eno, Prince, The Verve *and* Janet Jackson. But Sly Stone wasn't any old musician: he was a superman sent from the planet Funk.

His extraterrestrial excellence first shone when, at 4, he was recorded singing Gospel. Later he was a Doo Wop singer, a music theory student, a DJ in Oakland, California, and a producer of US hits for The Beau Brummels and Bobby Freeman in 1965.

Based close to San Francisco, cradle of the hippie hordes, he formed his own band with family members and white musicians Greg Errico and Jerry Martini. Suddenly, Funk king James Brown had a madcap, psychedelic pretender to his throne: an explosive riot of rubbery bass, rolling drums, and vocals and guitars that were silent one moment, all over the place the next. The final twist was that – in contrast to the well-drilled sound that James had made his own – Sly appeared to have the shortest attention span in music; hence his songs that suddenly speed up midway.

A jaw-droppingly kaleidoscopic run of hits from 1968–1969 etched him into legend: 'Dance To The Music', 'Life', 'M'Lady', 'Everyday People', 'Sing A Simple Song', 'Stand', 'I Want To Take You Higher' and 'Hot Fun In The Summertime' made albums like *Stand!* (1969) essential purchases. Sly & The Family Stone's 1970 *Greatest Hits* made every other album with that title look silly.

They were triumphant at Woodstock in 1969, then perfectly mirrored the decade's descent into violence and paranoia. Once they'd preached unity ('Everyday People') and dressed political commentary in deceptively dancey disguise ('Hot Fun In The

Summertime'. Now they were cynical (1970's US No.1 'Thank You (Falettinme Be Mice Elf Agin)'), sulky and stoned (1971's US No.1 'Family Affair'). As the band disintegrated (Larry Graham jumped ship to launch a glittering career first as Graham Central Station, then solo), Sly carved out a graveyard groove, later plundered by Tricky, on the US No.1 *There's A Riot Goin' On* (1971) and *Fresh* (1973), the latter acclaimed by Brian Eno as "one of the most important records in the history of Rock music".

Small Talk (1974) was the Family Stone's last hit, with only the cognoscenti applauding Sly's solo *High On You* (1975), *Heard Ya Missed Me, Well I'm Back* (1976), *Ten Years Too Soon* (1979) and *Back On The Right Track* (1979). He nearly came back with *Ain't But The One Way* (1982), a 1986 duet with The Time's Jesse Johnson ('Crazay') and a production credit on Funkadelic's *The Electric Spanking Of War Babies* (1981), but his legacy was better celebrated by Red Hot Chili Peppers' George Clinton-produced cover of 'If You Want Me To Stay' (1985), Janet Jackson building her *Riot*-esque 'Rhythm Nation' (1989) on a sample of 'Thank You (Falettinme Be Mice Elf Agin)', Ice-T and Jane's Addiction playing 'Don't Call Me Nigger, Whitey' on 1991's Lollapalooza, Arrested Development remodelling 'Everyday People' as 'People Everyday' (1992) and Shabba Ranks funking up 'Family Affair' (1993). Asked by *Q* to name "the greatest Funk record", Prince's band The New Power Generation nominated: "Any Sly & The Family Stone track", "*Fresh*", "Graham Central Station's first record" and "'Thank You (Falettinme Be Mice Elf Agin)'". Prince proved the point by taking Graham out on a successful US tour in 1997. And there was even respect from The Verve's frontman Richard Ashcroft, long christened 'Mad Richard': "When I first went onstage," he told *Q*, "my heroes were Sly & The Family Stone and I used to think, if they're calling me mad in the press, what would they say if Sly & The Family Stone came onstage?"

 'Sly Stone – The Myth Of Stagger Lee' in *Mystery Train* (1975), Greil Marcus

Surf www.cc.columbia.edu/~jhd10/funkpub/familynews.html

THE SMALL FACES ⊙

WHO Vocals/guitar **Steve Marriott** (b. 30 Jan 1947, London, England, d. 20 Apr 1991, Arkesden, Essex, England), bass **Ronnie Lane** (b. 1 Apr 1946, London, d. 4 Jun 1997, Colorado, USA), keyboards **Ian McLagan** (b. 12 May 1945, Middlesex, England), drums **Kenney Jones** (b. 16 Sep 1948, London)

WHEN 1965–1969

WHERE London, England

WHAT Mod, Psychedelia and prototype Britpop

Steve Marriott, Ronnie Lane, Kenney Jones and keyboard player Jimmy Winston formed The Small Faces, their name reflecting their status (Mods were 'faces') and stature (none were tall). Their 1965 debut, 'Whatcha Gonna Do About It?', was spiky, belligerent and a UK hit. But in its troubled aftermath, Winston quit to be replaced by Ian McLagan and the follow-up, 'I Got Mine', flopped.

However, 'Sha La La La Lee' (1966), written for them by hit-makers Kenny Lynch and Mort Shuman, restored their chart fortunes. The march of these Mods continued through to 1967,

with *Small Faces* spending almost half of 1966 on the chart. In 1966, 'Hey Girl' proved Marriott and Lane could write commercial Pop songs of their own, and 'All Or Nothing', a return to their R&B roots, was a UK No.1. In 1967, 'Here Comes The Nice' paid blatant tribute to the Mod drug of choice – amphetamine – but radio programmers didn't seem to mind; 'Itchycoo Park' was a classic slice of English Psychedelia; and the soulful 'Tin Soldier' boasted P.P. Arnold providing vocal support.

In 1968, 'Itchycoo Park' became a US hit and they produced one of the few concept albums that remain listenable today: the chart-topping *Ogden's Nut Gone Flake*, a kind of Cockney *Sgt. Pepper*. In common with The Beatles' masterpiece, it had an innovative (circular) sleeve, segues between songs and nods to English popular music tradition. Comedian Stanley Unwin gave a surreal narration in his unique garbled English and 'Lazy Sunday' was modern Music Hall; as a single, it made UK No.2.

But business naivety cost the band dearly, adding to internal tensions. Between the hits 'The Universal' (1968) and 'Afterglow Of Your Love' (1969), Marriott quit for Humble Pie. In 1969, Lane, McLagan and Jones relaunched the band as The Faces, enlisting Rod Stewart as their new frontman.

'Itchycoo Park' and 'Lazy Sunday' were reissued in 1975 and 1976, prompting a reunion. Lane, ill with multiple sclerosis, joined only briefly, but the other three recruited bassist Rick Wills and continued for some undistinguished albums.

A worthier continuation of The Small Faces' 60s legacy came from Britpop bands – notably Blur, whose *Parklife* (1994) might have been subtitled 'Albarn's Nut Gone Flake'. In 1996, Primal Scream, Ocean Colour Scene and Paul Weller were among those who acknowledged The Small Faces' influence by covering their songs for a tribute album, *Long Ago And Worlds Apart*.

ReaD *Small Faces: The Young Mods' Forgotten Story* (1996), Paolo Hewitt

Surf ourworld.compuserve.com/homepages/Martin_Payne/

SMASHING PUMPKINS

WHO Vocals/guitar **Billy Corgan** (b. 17 Mar 1967, Chicago, Illinois, USA), guitar **James Iha** (b. 26 Mar 1968, Elk Grove, Illinois), bass **D'Arcy Wretzky** (b. 1 May 1968, South Haven, Michigan, USA), drums **Jimmy Chamberlin** (b. 10 Jun 1964, Joliet, Illinois)

WHEN 1988–

WHERE Chicago, Illinois, USA

WHAT Screams, strings and sadness

"Billy doesn't have blood," observed Bono of chief Pumpkin Billy Corgan. "He has oil. We call him The Terminator." Corgan's steely demeanour protected him against one disaster after another. His early attempt to carve a niche with The Marked failed miserably, so he enlisted Indie kids James Iha and D'Arcy Wretzky and, after tentative gigs, replaced their drum machine with talented Jazz drummer Jimmy Chamberlain. "I was trying," Corgan told *Mojo*, "to blend Black Sabbath power and Led Zeppelin dynamics with Pink Floyd Psychedelia." However, although 'I Am One' (1989), 'Tristessa' (1990) and the Butch Vig-produced *Gish* (1991) united Indie and Metal fans, they were thoroughly eclipsed by Nirvana.

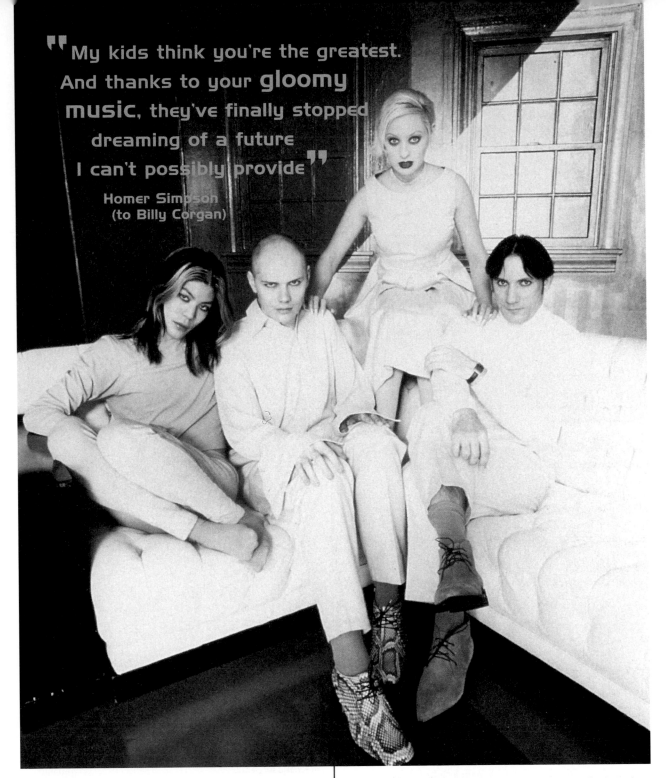

" My kids think you're the greatest.
And thanks to your **gloomy
music**, they've finally stopped
dreaming of a future
I can't possibly provide **"**

Homer Simpson
(to Billy Corgan)

But the buzz was enough to net a Virgin deal and unleash the full force of Corgan's megalomania. With his obsessiveness at an all-time high and inter-band relations at an all-time low (Wretzky and Iha's romance came to a rancorous end), Corgan played Wretzky's and Iha's parts for *Siamese Dream* (1993), perfectionism which paid off when it went triple platinum and reached the US Top 10 and UK Top 5, thanks to hits like the triumphant 'Today'.

On tour, Wretsky and Iha polished their act to their dictator's standards and – Corgan recalled – "three months after that we could play it even better, so…". With their release schedule plugged with rarities set *Pisces Iscariot* (1994), Corgan embarked on conquering the universe. The result was *Mellon Collie And The Infinite Sadness* (1995), a two-hour sledgehammer symphony, whose conceptual ambition can be gauged from its two discs being subtitled 'Dawn To Dusk' and 'Twilight To Starlight'. But bar isolated pretty moments like 'Tonight Tonight', the title track, the delicate 'Cupid De Locke' and Joy Division-y hit '1979', the album

was full of Rock and rage: hence its brain-mangling first smash 'Bullet With Butterfly Wings'. Another colossal tour made it Rock's best-selling double CD, and it was joined on many a Smashing shelf by *The Aeroplane Flies High* (1996), a lovingly packaged collection of *Mellon Collie*'s singles and other assorted goodies.

But just when it looked like the dark days were over, on-tour keyboard player Jonathan Melvoin died from a heroin overdose on the eve of a show at New York's Madison Square Garden in July 1996, turning the spotlight on Chamberlin's long-time drug problems. Within weeks, Chamberlin was out of the band and the Pumpkins were back on the road with Matt Walker, of Filter, on drums. In 1998, Iha stepped out solo with the resolutely un-rockish *Let It Come Down* and, mere seconds later, Corgan, Iha, Wretzky and hired hands were back with the Pumpkins for *Adore*.

read *Smashing Pumpkins* (1996), Jim Stapleton

surf www.smashing-pumpkins.net

wrote a novel, *The Coral Sea* (1996), dedicated to him. Richard Sohl died in June 1990 and Patti's grief was compounded by her husband's death in March 1994 and her brother's in December 1994. Throwing herself into live work, she toured with one-time hero Bob Dylan in 1995 and recorded a new album, *Gone Again* (1996). Dedicated to Fred Smith, it combined raw guitar Rock with Dylanesque ballads, exploring issues of pain, loss and separation. Other recent activities have included duetting with fan Michael Stipe on REM's 1996 hit 'E-Bow The Letter' and bad-mouthing Bono at *Q* magazine's 1998 awards ceremony.

READ *Patti Smith: A Biography* (1997), Nick Johnstone

SURF www.oceanstar.com/patti/

WILL SMITH

WHO b. Willard C. Smith II, 25 Sep 1968, Philadelphia, Pennsylvania, USA

WHAT From Hip Hop to Hollywood

Few stars could more creditably protect the earth from the scum of the universe than one who survived a near-novelty Rap career to become a multimedia demi-god. Having won the name 'Prince' in honour of his smooth-talking style, he added 'Fresh' (a ye olde Hip Hop prefix à la 'Def' and 'MC') and associate Jeff Townes to become DJ Jazzy Jeff & The Fresh Prince. They debuted with *Rock The House* (1987), then scored with *He's The DJ, I'm The Rapper* (1988), thanks to the cartoony hit 'Parents Just Don't Understand'. This irreverent take on Rap, a world away from the urban angst of acts like Public Enemy and NWA, continued with cuts like 'I Think I Could Beat Mike Tyson' from *And In This Corner…* (1989), then took a soulful turn with the graceful 'Summertime' from *Homebase* (1991). The UK No.1 'Boom! Shake The Room', from 1993's *Code Red*, rounded off their career, which had sunk Stateside.

This decline was odd; not only was the music increasingly great, but Smith had become a TV megastar thanks to *The Fresh Prince Of Bel Air*, a sly sitcom based on the real-life experience of Warner Bros executive Benny Medina, born poor in LA but raised in a rich Beverly Hills household (Smith himself was middle class from birth). During *Fresh Prince*'s six-year reign from 1990, its star kicked off a movie career which scored its first blockbuster with 1995's *Bad Boys*. Scene-stealing star roles in *Independence Day* (1996) and *Men In Black* (1997) proved him the natural heir to Eddie Murphy: a star based in black culture whose appeal transcended racial lines.

Men In Black's irresistible title theme reintroduced Smith to the world of chart-topping Rap – hence the self-mocking "I ain't never seen the Wu dancing with no alien" in the intro to his 'comeback' *Big Willie Style* (1997). Platinum sales and the US No.1 'Gettin' Jiggy Wit It' confirmed him back in the game, while anyone wondering what became of Jazzy Jeff (who wrote The Simpsons' 1991 hit 'Deep Deep Trouble') could take comfort from his credit on Smith's album alongside voguish producers like Trackmasters. Their legacy was celebrated on *Greatest Hits* (1998), which mixed the duo's diamonds with solo Smith gems.

READ *Will Power! A Biography Of Will Smith* (1997), Jan Berenson

FAN Will Smith, 330 Bob Hope Drive, Burbank, CA 91523, USA

SURF www.geocities.com/~tonyorth/willm.html

PATTI SMITH

WHO b. 31 Dec 1946, Chicago, Illinois, USA

WHAT Uncompromising poet and Punk innovator

Influenced by author William Burroughs, French poet Arthur Rimbaud and French novelist Jean Genet, Patti Smith established her own reputation as a poet on the New York circuit before her groundbreaking debut, *Horses*, was released in 1975. Produced by John Cale and featuring contributions from Blue Öyster Cult's Allen Lanier (with whom Patti lived for five years) and Television's Tom Verlaine, *Horses* presaged Punk with its raw energy, fusing Rock 'n' Roll with Smith's poetic lyrics and intense vocal delivery.

The album also celebrated the improvisational approach typical of Smith's poetry performances, accompanied by Lenny Kaye on guitar and Richard 'DNV' Sohl on piano. As a trio, they'd released one of the first Indie 7" singles – 'Hey Joe'/'Piss Factory' – in 1974. Becoming known as The Patti Smith Group, they signed to Arista in 1975 after Ivan Kral joined on bass and Jay Dee Daugherty on drums. Unusually, the deal gave her total artistic control, which extended to her album cover shots. Those taken by Patti's close friend Robert Mapplethorpe show her, for the time, as shockingly androgynous.

As uncompromising in her writing as in her appearance, Smith's albums explored issues of sex and death, gender orientation and religion. *Horses* covered male rape and lesbian suicide, while her next album, *Radio Ethiopia* (1976), dealt with her conflict with God and her concern with the artist as outsider, an issue recalled in 'Rock 'n' Roll Nigger' from *Easter* (1978).

Easter signalled Smith's rejuvenation after a 1977 neck injury, received falling off a stage, had put her out of action for a year. It gave Smith her first hit, the UK No.5 'Because The Night', co-written with Bruce Springsteen and addressed to her lover, MC5 guitarist Fred 'Sonic' Smith. Patti released the more conventional *Wave* (1979) before marrying Fred in 1980 and retiring to Detroit to raise their two children and continue writing poetry.

Her anticlimatic 1988 comeback, *Dream Of Life*, featured Fred on guitar. Deeply affected by Mapplethorpe's death in 1989, Patti

THE SMITHS – MIKE JOYCE, JOHNNY MARR, MORRISSEY & ANDY ROURKE/PAUL SLATTERY/RETNA

THE SMITHS ⊙⊙

WHO Vocals **Morrissey** (b. Steven Patrick Morrissey, 22 May 1959, Manchester, England), guitar **Johnny Marr** (b. John Maher, 31 Oct 1963, Ardwick, Manchester), bass **Andy Rourke** (b. 17 Jan 1963, Manchester), drums **Mike Joyce** (b. 1 Jun 1963, Manchester)

WHEN 1982–1987

WHERE Manchester, England

WHAT Britain's most important band of the 80s

Steven Morrissey spent his first 20 years on the fringes. After an unhappy education, he drifted between work and idleness, crippled by social inadequacy. Movies, poetry and Pop were his escape: Sandie Shaw, Dusty Springfield, David Bowie, Marc Bolan, The New York Dolls (he managed their UK fan club and wrote Dolls and James Dean biographies) and Patti Smith. Fired by Punk, he joined also-rans Ed Banger & The Nosebleeds (with The Cult's Billy Duffy) and wrote bitter letters to *NME*.

Johnny Marr was the exact opposite: a happy-go-lucky kid obsessed with clothes, hair and guitars. Fascinated by Morrissey, he started writing songs with him and enlisted friends Mike Joyce and Andy Rourke. Appalled by Synth Pop, they became the deliberately drab Smiths (a rebuttal to Orchestral Maneouvres In The Dark and A Flock Of Seagulls), lost themselves in Pop history – 50s rockers like Johnny Ray (to whom Morrissey's hearing aid was a tribute) and Billy Fury, The Byrds, pre-army Elvis, Leiber & Stoller – and played their first gig in Manchester in 1982.

The bitter 'Hand In Glove' (1983), their debut on Indie label Rough Trade, turned The Smiths into cult sensations. Six months later, they hit the UK Top 30 with 'This Charming Man', appeared on *Top Of The Pops* and rewrote Pop's rules. Pop was not supposed to wail foppishly about ambiguous relationships with men. Pop was not supposed to be *anything* like Morrissey, whose nerdy spectacles, 50s rocker hair, hearing aid and flowers entranced Britain's pale Indie kids. Others, like the teenage Noel Gallagher, just wanted to be Johnny Marr – the first and best guitar hero of the 80s. "God help us," thought grown-ups.

They were baited further by *The Smiths* (1984), whose thorny themes of abused innocence yielded the classic 'Suffer Little Children'. It chillingly documented Manchester child murderers Ian Brady and Myra Hindley and, misinterpreted by the press, cast Morrissey as a sicko. Nonetheless, *The Smiths* made UK No.2 and regenerated an Indie scene which had coasted since Punk.

They cast the same spell with 1984's radio sessions/B-sides set *Hatful Of Hollow*: an album *packed* with happy, sad, angry and hilarious classics like 'William It Was Really Nothing', 'How Soon Is Now?', 'What Difference Does It Make?' and 'Please Please Please Let Me Get What I Want' – all from a band just two years old.

The bleak UK No.1 *Meat Is Murder* (1985) focused on violence, emotional and physical, from humiliation at school ('The Headmaster Ritual'), through domestic violence ('Barbarism Begins At Home'), to the slaughter of animals (the title track).

No sooner had The Smiths become an Indie institution than they began to disintegrate. Overworked to near exhaustion,

they were derailed by Rourke's heroin problem, wrangles with his temporary replacement Craig Gannon and Marr's car crash, making hellish the recording of *The Queen Is Dead* (1986). But its chaotic conception only heightened its thrilling rollercoaster of Music Hall romp ('Frankly, Mr. Shankly'), pitch-black despair ('I Know It's Over'), spiteful anti-royalist comedy and metallic riffing ('The Queen Is Dead') and joyous anthems ('The Boy With The Thorn In His Side' and 'There Is A Light That Never Goes Out').

They weren't finished yet: 1987 began with two of their best singles – the inflammatory 'Shoplifters Of The World Unite' and the sweet 'Sheila Take A Bow' – and two blistering retrospectives, *The World Won't Listen* and *Louder Than Bombs*. The band signed to EMI and began *another* album. But by the time *Strangeways Here We Come* (1987) was released, The Smiths were no more.

Burned out, Marr quit – a rift which might have healed were it not for, as Morrissey claimed, the press exacerbating the divide. The Smiths' death was quick: after a (very) brief period as a trio, Morrissey starred solo in *Strangeways'* videos. The album was a flawed epitaph. Though self-parodically gloomy, it sparkled on 'Paint A Vulgar Picture', a scathing attack on the music biz, and the fabulous 'Stop Me If You Think You've Heard This One Before'.

While Marr toyed with Talking Heads, The The, The Pretenders and, more permanently, Electronic, 1988's live *Rank* was the first in a torrent of posthumous compilations. Rourke resurfaced with former Happy Monday Gaz Whelan in the unlamented Delicious, Joyce fulfilled a teenage ambition by joining the Buzzcocks, while both (and, say rumours, Marr) made cameos in Morrissey's solo career. But Joyce's greatest triumph was in the High Court in 1996, when he successfully sued Morrissey and Marr for a 25% share of The Smiths' earnings – a sad postscript to one of the most inspired bands of the 80s.

ⓡⓔⓐⓓ *Morrissey & Marr: The Severed Alliance* (1993), Johnny Rogan

ⓢⓤⓡⓕ www.shocking.com/~despair/smiths.htm

SNEAKER PIMPS

WHO Vocals **Kelli Dayton**, guitar **Chris Corner**, keyboards **Liam Howe**

WHEN 1992–

WHERE Birmingham, England

WHAT Trip Hop meets Folk meets Marilyn Manson

Though mere children in Pop's scheme of things, Sneaker Pimps' CV is already crammed with celebrity associations. Named after a Beastie Boys employee whose sole task was to purchase antique trainers, they've covered a Stevie Winwood tune, graced star-studded soundtracks and collaborated with Marilyn Manson.

United by their fondness for Kraftwerk, Liam Howe and Chris Corner created the Techno act Line Of Flight. With singer Kelli Dayton, they became Sneaker Pimps and trip-hopped aboard the blunted beats bandwagon. In 1996, it looked like they were racing fellow Brit trio Morcheeba to see who could rip Tricky off most successfully. Despite being outed as closet Folkies by *Mojo* magazine ("Punk and Folk resonate together", Howe announced), the Pimps pulled ahead with the hit '6 Underground' from 1996's *Becoming X*. When it wound up on the soundtrack to *The Saint* (1997), they were lumped in with the US 'Electronica' boom.

In 1997, with Armand Van Helden's remix of 'Spin Spin Sugar' enabling them to rule Dance charts without lifting a finger, the Pimps dallied with Marilyn Manson on the *Spawn* soundtrack, but declared disappointment with his final mix of 'Long Road Out Of Hell'. "I wouldn't waste my time having hard feelings," quoth Mr Manson. "I've already forgotten their names."

ⓢⓤⓡⓕ www.virginrecords.com/sneaker_pimps/index.html

SNOOP DOGGY DOGG ✪ ✪

WHO b. Calvin Broadus, 20 Oct 1972, Long Beach, California, USA

WHAT Bad-to-the-bone Rap star

Though nicknamed after a comic-strip character and one of Rap's politest people, Snoop Doggy Dogg has had a whole lotta trouble. He spent his adolescence rappin' 'n' rhymin' with Warren G and Domino, but was seduced by the dark side and wound up in jail for dealing cocaine. His break came courtesy of Warren, who gave a Snoop demo to his half-brother Dr Dre, then casting for frontmen after quitting NWA. Their first cut was the title track to the *Deep Cover* soundtrack (1992), a perfect premiere to their partnership: Dre's ominous 'G-Funk' topped by Snoop's sing-song psychosis.

From there they bounded to Dre's *The Chronic* (1992). Mostly co-written and fronted by Snoop, the album re-routed Rap, replacing the political noise of Public Enemy and Ice Cube with bouncy-bottomed homages to sex, drugs and guns. When the cut 'Nuthin' But a "G" Thang' hit too, they became the face of MTV-generation Gangsta. Snoop's profile suffered not at all from his being charged in connection with the murder of an LA gang member – in a *Natural Born Killers*-esque media/reality interface, Snoop waited until he'd presented an MTV award to En Vogue before turning himself in.

At the height of his notoriety, Snoop's Dre-helmed *Doggystyle* (1993) slammed to the top of the US chart. For a year, everything went doggystyle: Warren G's *Regulate… G Funk Era* (1994) and the Snoop-starring soundtracks *Above The Rim* (1994) and *Murder Was The Case* (1995) went platinum. Even the Dogg's old chum Domino got in on the act with 1994's smooth-sailing 'Getto Jam'. The momentum pushed Tha Dogg Pound – who'd debuted on *Doggystyle* – to platinum too with *Dogg Food* (1995), but Snoop himself was

sidetracked. After a trial at which he was represented by O.J. Simpson's lawyer, he was cleared of the 1993 murder charge, but then joined the East/West coast affray between his label Death Row and Puff Daddy's Bad Boy. The video for his 1996 duet with fellow Death Row figurehead Tupac Shakur, '2 Of Amerika's Most Wanted', unflatteringly caricatured Puffy and The Notorious BIG.

This squabbling turned serious when Shakur was murdered, and Snoop seemed more sober on *Tha Doggfather* (1996). But the inspiration had gone too: minus Dre, who'd flown the Death Row roost, the album had none of *Doggystyle*'s flair. Its trailing hit, a Snoopified take on The Gap Band's 'Oops Upside Your Head', was a transparent echo of his debut's anthem 'Who Am I (What's My Name)?'. With only one solid cut to its name (the hit 'Vapors'), the album plummeted from the US No.1 within weeks.

In the fall-out, US Rap mega-seller Master P announced his No Limit label would unleash Snoop's 1998 album *Da Game Is To Be Sold, Not To Be Told*. Death Row indignantly announced he was still contracted to them. Meanwhile, Snoop played 1997's Lollapalooza and collaborated with Rage Against the Machine for a mooted EP called 'Doggumentary' and Jodeci refugees K-Ci and JoJo on their hit 'You Lift Me Up'. He contributed to 1997's *Men In Black* soundtrack and notched up movie cameos himself, in 1995's *The Show* and 1998's *Half-Baked*, *Ride* and *Caught Up*. In the last, he plays Kool Kat, though it would be overly optimistic to take this as proof of a bright end to the dark days of Dogg.

 www.mit.edu:8001/people/madmike/snoop.html

SOFT CELL

WHO Vocals **Marc Almond** (b. Peter Marc Almond, 9 Jul 1957, Southport, Merseyside, England), multi-instrumentalist **Dave Ball** (b. 3 May 1959, Salford, Greater Manchester, England)

WHEN 1979–1984

WHERE Leeds, Yorkshire, England

WHAT Sinful Synth Pop

Formed to relieve Dave Ball and Marc Almond's "post-degree depression", Soft Cell inflicted horrible things (leather, whips, chains, etc) on the previously innocent world of Synth Pop. Following the self-financed 'Mutant Moments' (1980), they joined The The and Depeche Mode on Some Bizarre, plaything label of eccentric entrepreneur Stevo. 'The Girl With The Patent Leather Face' and 'Memorabilia' were cult hits, then their creepy cover of Gloria Jones' Soul classic 'Tainted Love' hit UK No.1, became the biggest-selling UK single of 1981 and the tenth-biggest seller ever in the USA. *Non Stop Erotic Cabaret* (1981) mixed heartbreakers like 'Say Hello, Wave Goodbye' with unashamed naughtiness like 'Sex Dwarf', taught adolescent Pop fans more than a lifetime of school sex education classes and was followed by remix counterpart *Non Stop Ecstatic Dancing*.

But critical disdain and the fatalistic *The Art Of Falling Apart* (1983) presaged their demise. Having dallied solo and briefly gone into retirement, Almond was coaxed into making 1984's industrial-ish *This Last Night In Sodom* before Soft Cell split.

Almond became a solo star, while Ball made *In Strict Tempo* (1983), worked with Cabaret Voltaire and Psychic TV and formed Dance meisters The Grid, whose 'Swamp Thing' was a hit in 1994.

SOFT MACHINE

WHO Vocals/drums **Robert Wyatt** (b. Robert Ellidge, 28 Jan 1945, Bristol, England), bass/vocals **Kevin Ayers** (b. 16 Aug 1944, Herne Bay, Kent, England), keyboards **Mike Ratledge** (b. 1943, Canterbury, Kent)

WHEN 1966–1976

WHERE Canterbury, Kent, England

WHAT Crazy Jazz Rock freak-outs

When early 60s Canterbury became the unlikely base for new directions in English Rock, Soft Machine were at its epicentre. Their earliest incarnation featured the core of Wyatt, Ayers and Ratledge alongside guitarists Daevid Allen and Larry Nolan and, while Nolan's stay was brief, the Australian Allen, several years his colleagues' senior, left an indelible mark. Well acquainted with the Beats in bohemian Paris, he sought William Burroughs' permission before naming the group after the writer's novel.

Earlier, several of Soft Machine's future players, including Wyatt and Ayers in addition to the founding members of Caravan, had assembled in The Wilde Flowers, a now legendary, under-recorded Canterbury combo. As that group splintered, Soft Machine evolved, gigging regularly at underground London haunts like UFO and The Roundhouse.

Their Ayers-penned debut, 'Love Makes Sweet Music', was released by Polydor in 1966, but flopped. Then, en route to Edinburgh after a French date, Daevid Allen was mysteriously deported and his involvement in the band ended. On returning to Paris, he formed Gong.

The classic Soft Machine three-piece, briefly augmented by future Police guitarist Andy Summers, embarked on an exhausting six-month US tour with The Jimi Hendrix Experience, and cut *Soft Machine* for the American label Probe in 1968. This delightfully eccentric set favourably threw together Ratledge's Jazz-influenced keyboards, Ayers' skewed Pop sensibility and Wyatt's singular, heartfelt vocal. Although solely released in the States, imports to the UK generated such interest that Soft Machine, having dispersed, were forced to re-form. This they did without Ayers (who moved to Ibiza and went solo), and Hugh Hopper – already on the fringes of the group as a co-writer – was installed on bass.

Soft Machine Volume Two (1969), a contractual obligation to Probe, showed the group leaving behind English Psychedelia and formulating their own brand of Jazz Rock. With the introduction of brass spearheaded by Elton Dean on sax, the CBS double set *Third* (1970) presented four extended pieces, highlighting Wyatt's increasing alienation from the rest of the group, who hated his contribution, 'Moon In June'.

Their most inventive days were now arguably behind them. After recording his solo *The End Of An Ear*, Wyatt's creative, humorist influence was notably absent from 1971's *Fourth*, and he was fired soon after. The 70s Rock emphasis on technical prowess engulfed Soft Machine, who recorded *Fifth* (1972), *Six And Seven* (1973), *Bundles* (1975) and *Softs* (1976) with various transitory personnel. Hugh Hopper left in May 1973 and, by the time the last founder Mike Ratledge departed in 1976, the group name had long become a byword for English fusion seriousness.

surf www.sonnet.co.uk/musart/watrat/

SONIC YOUTH

WHO Guitar/vocals **Thurston Moore** (b. 25 Jul 1958, Coral Gables, Florida, USA), guitar/vocals **Lee Ranaldo** (b. 3 Feb 1956, Glen Cove, New York, USA), bass/vocals **Kim Gordon** (b. 28 Apr 1953, Rochester, New York), drums **Steve Shelley** (b. 23 Jun 1962, Midland, Michigan, USA)

WHEN 1981–

WHERE New York City, New York, USA

WHAT Art Rock architects

Sonic Youth are the biggest band never to make it. Formed in 1981 by Kim Gordon, Lee Ranaldo, Thurston Moore and Josh Baer, the band debuted at the Noise Festival – a showcase of No Wave acts which they set up and staged themselves. Their early line-up included Ann DeMarinis (keyboards) and Richard Edson (drums), their name being an amalgamation of Moore's favourite bands: Sonic Rendezvous and Big Youth. Their sound – dissonant, saturated in feedback, sludgy and distorted – was achieved live with dozens of down-tuned guitars with objects such as screwdrivers stuck between the strings. In pioneering new sounds, Sonic Youth have become legendary.

Their self-titled debut EP (1982) – featuring a power-drill – was released on avant-garde guitarist Glenn Branca's Neutral label (Moore and Ranaldo had recently played on Branca's *Symphony No.3*). The US Indie label Ecstatic Peace issued *Sonic Death: Sonic Youth Live* (1984), showcasing their discordant live set. In 1983, drummer Jim Sclavunos (ex-Teenage Jesus & The Jerks) was replaced by Bob Bert for a European tour, *Confusion Is Sex* and *Kill Yr. Idols*. British fan Paul Smith was so impressed with the band that he left his day job, became their manager and, after little interest from record companies, set up the Blast First label for them, issuing the menacing *Bad Moon Rising* in 1985. Back home, they graduated from Neutral, through Homestead, to SST, with whom they later fell out.

Playing that year at London's ICA, they issued the 'Death Valley '69' EP (a collaboration with Punk's Mae West Lydia Lunch), whose theme was the Charles Manson murders. When Bert quit, they recruited drummer Steve Shelley, completing their most enduring line-up. *Evol* (1986), its spin-off 'Starpower' EP (1986), *Sister* (1987) and *Master Dik* (1988) were brooding and industrial, similarly concerned with the downside of popular culture.

Evol's 'Expressway To Yr Skull' (described by Neil Young as "the best guitar song ever") had two alternative titles: 'Madonna, Sean and Me', and 'The Crucifixion of Sean Penn'. Accordingly, *The Whitey Album* (1988), under the (Madonna-derived) alias Ciccone Youth (including Minutemen's Mike Watt), featured bizarre versions of Madonna's 'Into The Groove(y)' and 'Burnin' Up', and a DIY video/karaoke cover of Robert Palmer's 'Addicted to Love'.

Daydream Nation (1988) expanded themes set out in *Evol* and *Sister*, and included the cacaphonous 'Teenage Riot'. The

"I'm surprised that our records have been consistently well-reviewed"

Kim Gordon

score for the arthouse film *Made In USA* (1986) was in keeping with their long-term interest in Pop culture and contemporary art. The soundtrack was released in 1995.

Snapped up by DGC, they released the more accessible *Goo* (1990), 'Kool Thing' (featuring Public Enemy's Chuck D) and 'Dirty Boots', with its teenage 'boy meets girl' video. As Moore was instrumental in Nirvana's signing to Geffen, and Gordon in the creation of Hole, Sonic Youth were hailed as godfathers of Grunge. The connection was commemorated by 1993's video *The Year That Punk Broke*, a Sonic Youth-dominated affair spiced by tracks from Nirvana and Dinosaur Jr. Meanwhile, Sonic Youth opened for fan Neil Young on his *Ragged Glory* tour (to the bemusement of his fans) and became Lollapalooza mainstays.

The more conventional *Dirty* (1992), co-produced by Butch Vig (who'd produced *Nevermind*), was released into a mass of guitar-heavy Alternative Rock influenced by Sonic Youth. Further boosted by the band's first UK hit – the very groovy '100%' – *Dirty* stomped into the UK Top 10.

It was followed there by 1994's *Experimental Jet Set, Trash And No Star*, again co-produced with Vig. Released a month after Kurt Cobain's suicide, it reached a comparatively high US No.34, affording them – finally – commercial success (although this breakthrough cut little ice with Homer Simpson, who lumped them in with Nine Inch Nails as one of the "no-name bands" who had relegated the far superior likes of Styx to the bargain bins).

Sonic Youth's contribution to 1994's tribute album *If I Were A Carpenter* gave The Carpenters a new cool – 'Superstar' was released as a single backed with Redd Kross's 'Yesterday Once More', though Gordon's suggestion that "Karen Carpenter died for our sins" was met with stony incomprehension by Karen's brother Richard.

In 1995, Moore released the solo *Psychic Hearts* (featuring Shelley). Meanwhile, his wife Kim released *Call Now* (1992), *Nice Ass* (1995) and *Sentimental Education* (1997) as Free Kitten with Pussy Galore's Julie Cafritz, gave birth to their daughter Coco, starred in a Gap advert, then launched a range of clothing, 'X-Girl' (an off-shoot of Beastie Boy Mike Diamond's Grand Royal empire). Ranaldo continued to work on solo projects, amid rumours of his departure, including 1995's 'Power To The People' with Minus Five (featured on the John Lennon tribute *Peace*) and the solo *East Jesus* (1996).

Amid these solo projects, *Washing Machine* (1995), including 'Little Trouble Girl', a collaboration with The Breeders' Kim Deal, surfaced. In 1998, they released three 12"s on their own label before *A Thousand Leaves* – with a more stripped-down sound, it featured a collaboration with Art Rock scenester Jim O'Rourke.

READ *Confusion Is Next* (1995), Alec Foego

FAN Sonic Death Fan Club, PO Box 1599, Hoboken, NJ 07030, USA

SURF www.techline.com/"loser/sonichi/html

SOUL

WHAT Although the term 'Soul' has gathered dust since the catch-all 'R&B' rose to power, the music remains sweet relief from the hard noise of Rock and Dance. From the rapturous roots of Gospel, it assumed a recognizable form in the mid-50s when James Brown and Ray Charles added the earthy lust Church music lacked. Soul historian Peter Guralnick pinpoints its blossoming to "the 1961 success of Solomon Burke's 'Just Out Of Reach'" – a pioneering smash for Soul's flagship label Atlantic. Wilson Pickett, Percy Sledge, Otis Redding and Aretha Franklin followed Burke's lead, while rival label Motown (whose founder Berry Gordy copyrighted the word 'Soul' for a mooted Gospel label) added poppier elements. In the late 60s, mavericks like Sly Stone and Motown producer Norman Whitfield added Rock to the mix and by the end of the 70s – despite the success of Marvin Gaye, Stevie Wonder and producers Gamble & Huff's 'Philly Sound' – Soul had split into Funk and Disco. However, it lives on in the sweet harmonies of acts like Brownstone, Sounds Of Blackness and Kirk Franklin.

WHERE USA

WHEN 50s–

WHO Otis Redding & Carla Thomas <u>King And Queen</u> (1967), Millie Jackson <u>Caught Up</u> (1974), Various <u>Atlantic Soul Classics</u> (1987), Sounds Of Blackness <u>Africa To America: The Journey Of The Drum</u> (1994), Kirk Franklin <u>Nu Nation God's Property</u> (1997), Various <u>Love Train: The Ultimate Sound Of Philadelphia</u> (1998)

SOUL ASYLUM

WHO Vocals/guitar **Dave Pirner** (b. 16 Apr 1964, Green Bay, Wisconsin, USA), guitar **Dan Murphy** (b. 12 Jul 1962, Duluth, Minnesota, USA), bass **Karl Mueller** (b. 27 Jul 1962, Minneapolis, Minnesota), drums **Grant Young** (b. 5 Jan 1964, Iowa City, Iowa, USA)

WHEN 1981–

WHERE Minneapolis, Minnesota, USA

WHAT Country Punk Cinderellas

It took a mere decade for Soul Asylum to evolve from Punk caterpillars to Rock butterflies. The runts of Minneapolis' early 80s Punk litter (eclipsed by Hüsker Dü and The Replacements), they began with the Bob Mould-produced *Say What You Will… Everything Can Happen* (1984), a manic pile-up of Punk, Folk and Country, revamped in 1986 as *Say What You Will, Clarence… Karl Sold The Van*. Mould also produced *Made To Be Broken* (1986), which still failed to elevate the band above their Indie ghetto.

Soul Asylum took the hard route, touring constantly to promote 1986's *While You Were Out*, 1988's *Clam Dip And Other Delights* and *Hangtime*, and 1990's *Soul Asylum And The Horse They Rode In On*. But indifference from record buyers sent the band back to their day jobs and Dave Pirner to psychiatric care.

While in limbo, the band constructed their breakthrough: 1992's *Grave Dancer's Union*. Heavy on melancholy and acoustic guitars (because Pirner thought he was going deaf), it spawned the US No.1 'Runaway Train'. Pirner cheered up a little, making a fleeting cameo in the 1994 movie *Reality Bites* and dating its star, Winona Ryder. Meanwhile, Soul Asylum replaced Grant Young with Sterling Campbell for *Let Your Dim Light Shine* (1995) and Dan Murphy continued with his side project Golden Smog. Soul Asylum took another bite with 1998's *Candy From A Stranger*.

surf home.sprynet.com/sprynet/cagedrat/sanews.htm

SOUL II SOUL ⊙⊙

WHO Visionary **Jazzie B** (b. Beresford Romeo, 16 Jan 1963, London, England)

WHEN 1982–

WHERE London, England

WHAT Ace of bass-heavy beats

British Soul blossomed fabulously with Soul II Soul. Founded by Jazzie B and Philip 'Daddae' Harvey and named after a Stax LP, they began as a sound system collective, fusing Reggae, Soul, Rap and Two-step at club nights and warehouse parties and on London pirate radio.

By 1988, Soul II Soul had settled around Jazzie and Massive Attack affiliate Nellee Hooper. They scored a giant hit with 1989's wonderful 'Keep On Movin'', a showcase for the angelic vocals of Caron Wheeler and Jazzie and Nellee's rough but smooth production. In America, they were seen as returning Soul to its roots; at home, they were hailed as innovatory.

They scored again with 'Back To Life (However Do You Want Me)' and the epic *Club Classics Vol. 1* (1989), launched a fashion label and shops and became hip remixers/arrangers for Sinéad O'Connor and The Family Stand. Wheeler's absence weakened *Vol. II 1990 – A New Decade* (1990); she returned for *Vol. III – Just Right* (1993), but Hooper had quit to become one of the 90s' best producers. Their future looked bleak with 1995's underwhelming *Vol. V – Believe*, but 1997's *Time For A Change* confirmed Jazzie's status as Britain's black music bossman and his "A happy face, a thumpin' and lovin' bass for a thumpin' and lovin' race" credo.

SOUNDGARDEN ✪

WHO Vocals/guitar **Chris Cornell** (b. 20 Jul 1964, Seattle, Washington, USA), guitar **Kim Thayil** (b. 4 Sep 1960, Seattle), bass **Ben Shepherd** (b. Hunter Shepherd, 20 Sep 1968, Okinawa, Japan), drums **Matt Cameron** (b. 28 Nov 1962, San Diego, California, USA)

WHEN 1984–1997

WHERE Washington, USA

WHAT The heavy, heavy sound of Seattle

The cheers that met Nirvana's explosive sales doubtless drowned out gnashing teeth *chez* Soundgarden. While Kurt Cobain was still dipping a toe in Rock's waters, fellow Seattleites Chris Cornell, Kim Thayil, Hiro Yamamoto and Matt Cameron plunged in with the 'Screaming Life' (1987) and 'FOPP' (1988) EPs on Nirvana's alma mater Sub Pop, then *Ultra Mega OK* (1989) on SST.

But neither a deal with A&M nor the replacement of bassist Yamamoto with Nirvana's Jason Everman propelled Soundgarden closer to stardom. Despite the excellence of their debut album and *Louder Than Love* (1989), their sound owed too much to the Heavy hierarchy (Black Sabbath, Led Zeppelin) to find favour with either their punkier Seattle contemporaries or the prevailing Glam winds of late-80s Metal. They did, however, find a home in support slots with the more traditional Metallica and Guns N' Roses – exposure which, combined with the post-*Nevermind* spotlight on anything from Seattle, pushed *Badmotorfinger* (1991) to platinum.

The 1992 hit 'Jesus Christ Pose' (whose Sabbath-covering B-side 'Into The Void' made their ancestry explicit) and a Lollapalooza slot paved the way for *Superunknown* (1994): a US No.1 and source of the brooding classic 'Black Hole Sun'. Ben Shepherd was now in on bass, but more crucial was Cornell's evolution from bare-chested, long-haired screecher into a smouldering, smartly cropped crooner. With less to distract from their lyrics, Soundgarden enjoyed acclaim beyond Metal's hinterlands (Johnny Cash covered *Badmotorfinger*'s 'Rusty Cage'), though Thayil's piercing guitar kept those roots alive.

For a while, it seemed they would laugh last. Alice In Chains and Pearl Jam stumbled, Nirvana collapsed, yet Soundgarden flew with *Down On The Upside* (1996) and motored along melody's yellow brick road with the hit 'Burden In My Hand'. But despite headlining Lollapalooza 1996 with Metallica, they split – allegedly amicably – in April 1997, leaving the hits set *A-Sides* (1997) as their flawless epitaph.

Cornell's outside career – which had taken in the platinum *Temple Of The Dog* (a 1991 tribute to Andrew Wood, deceased singer with Metal's great lost hopes Mother Love Bone), shrieking on Alice In Chains' *Sap* (1991) and a solo cut on the *Singles* soundtrack (1992) – resumed on 1997's *A Very Special*

Christmas (that old heavy hymn 'Ave Maria') and 1998's *Great Expectations* soundtrack ('Sunshower').

read *Soundgarden – New Metal Crown* (1995), Chris Nickson
fan Soundgarden Fan Club, PO Box 61275, Seattle, WA 98121, USA
surf imusic.com/soundgarden/

SPACE

WHO Vocals **Tommy Scott**, guitar **Jamie Murphy**, bass **Dave 'Yorkie' Palmer**, drums **Leon Caffrey**, keyboards **Franny Griffiths**

WHEN 1993–

WHERE Liverpool, England

WHAT Indie Pop laced with dark humour

There has long been a special place in British Pop for witty social commentators. The Kinks and Madness have worthy successors today in Pulp and Space.

Formed by Tommy Scott, Jamie Murphy, Franny Griffiths and drummer Andy Parle, Space's breakthrough came in 1996 with 'Female Of The Species', a parody of 50s crooners that Scott wrote to please his father. Bassist Dave Palmer joined after playing on *Spiders* (1996), which yielded three more UK hits – notably the Specials-like 'Neighbourhood', a surreal cartoon view of inner-city life.

During 1997, the stress of success took a severe toll. Nervous illness put Murphy in hospital, while Scott temporarily lost his voice and Parle was replaced by Leon Caffrey in January 1998.

Mercifully, happier times followed as Space hit the UK Top 5 with 'The Ballad Of Tom Jones', a hilarious duet between Scott and Catatonia's Cerys Matthews. *Tin Planet* followed to great acclaim in March 1998, its wry words proving Scott's sense of humour had survived the previous year's traumas.

fan PO Box 274, Liverpool, L69 3TN, UK
surf www.geocities.com/SoHo/Lofts/1899.space.htm

SPANDAU BALLET ⊙

WHO Vocals **Tony Hadley** (b. 2 Jun 1960, London, England), guitar/keyboards

Gary Kemp (b. 16 Oct 1959, London), bass **Martin Kemp** (b. 10 Oct 1961, London), drums **John Keeble** (b. 6 Jul 1959, London), saxophone/percussion

Steve Norman (b. 25 Mar 1960, London)

WHEN 1979–

WHERE London, England

WHAT New Romantic fops turned pseudo-Soul smoothies

From London's New Romantic hotbed the Blitz club, Spandau Ballet minced to Duran Duran-rivalling massiveness, clad in kilts and highlighted hairdos.

They set up their own Reformation label with manager Steve Dagger and smashed into the UK Top 10 with their debut 'To Cut A Long Story Short' in 1980. *Journeys To Glory* (1981) notched up more hits, but *Diamond* (1982) produced only one smash, the funky mardi-gras of 'Instinction'.

Amid accusations of style over content, they swapped kilts for sharp suits and Synth Funk for slick Soul on 1983's UK No.1 *True*, source of the transatlantic hits 'True' and 'Gold'.

But by 1984's *Parade*, the kids were mad for Wham!, Frankie Goes To Hollywood and Prince and cared little for Spandau's maturing sound. Meanwhile, ructions with Chrysalis (to whom they licensed their recordings) prompted a lengthy sabbatical.

Resurfacing on CBS, they courted Rock on 1986's *Through The Barricades* – and hit the Top 10 with its title track – but 1989's swan song, *Heart Like A Sky*, drowned in a market flooded with House. Hadley embarked on a barely successful solo career with *Lost In Your Love* (1992) and *Tony Hadley* (1997), while Spandau revisited higher chart echelons with PM Dawn's 1991 'True'-sampling 'Set Adrift On Memory Bliss'. Gary Kemp released the solo album *Little Bruises* (1995) and appeared in the movies *The Krays* (with his brother Martin, 1990) and *The Bodyguard* (1992).

surf www.geocities.com/SunsetStrip/Palladium/7994/

SPARKS

WHO Vocals **Russell Mael** (b. 5 Oct 1955, Santa Monica, California, USA), keyboards **Ron Mael** (b. 12 Aug 1950, Culver City, California)

WHEN 1972–

WHERE Los Angeles, California, USA

WHAT The Morecambe & Wise of Synth Pop

Former child models Ron and Russell Mael started out in 1970 with college friends Earle Mankey (guitar), Jim Mankey (bass) and Harley Feinstein (drums) in the splendidly named Halfnelson, whose self-titled, Todd Rundgren-produced debut (1971, reissued as *Sparks* in 1972) flopped.

Changing their name to Sparks, they released the similarly doomed *A Woofer In Tweeter's Clothing* (1972) before the brothers Mael decamped to England. There they assembled a new group – bassist Martin Gordon, guitarist Adrian Fisher and drummer Norman 'Dinky' Diamond – for the phenomenally successful *Kimono My House* (1974) and the operatic epic 'This Town Ain't Big Enough For Both Of Us'. Nobody who saw Sparks on *Top Of The Pops* could forget them: Russell, a young, androgynous dandy; Ron a shifty-looking nerd with a Hitler moustache. Quite what they were no one knew, but further hits with 'Amateur Hour', 'Never Turn Your Back On Mother Earth' and *Propaganda* (1974) continued the Sparks craze in Britain and Europe. *Indiscreet* (1975), however, proved their commercial undoing: lacking the satirical bite of previous efforts, it set the trend for the flops *Big Beat* (1976) and *Introducing* (1977).

In 1979, however, they emerged from sessions with Donna Summer's producer Giorgio Moroder clutching the brilliant *No.1 In Heaven*, a synth-heavy Disco masterpiece which yielded the hits 'Number One Song In Heaven' and 'Beat The Clock' and provided a blueprint for subsequent Synth Poppers like Erasure and Pet Shop Boys. But the follow-up, *Terminal Jive* (1980), proved Sparks were far from back with a vengeance and *Whomp That Sucker* (1981), *Angst In My Pants* (1982), *Sparks In Outer Space* (1983), *Pulling Rabbits Out Of A Hat* (1984) and *Music That You Can Dance To* (1986) languished in obscurity.

Sparks have since concentrated on a more Dance-oriented sound, as on *Interior Design* (1988), *Gratuitous Sax And Senseless Violins* (1994) and live shows in Europe. These prompted a critical reappraisal in the mid-90s, helped by the patronage of Blur and ex-Suede guitarist Bernard Butler. *Plagiarism* (1997) was a collection of reworked Sparks classics, befitting a group whose favourite music is MOR covers of their own material.

surf www.doremi.co.uk/sparks/

THE SPECIALS

WHO Vocals **Terry Hall** (b. 19 Mar 1959, Coventry, England), vocals/percussion **Neville Staples** (b. 11 Apr 1956, Christiana, Jamaica), guitar **Lynval Golding** (b. 24 Jul 1951, St Catherines, Jamaica), guitar **Roddy Radiation** (b. Rodney Byers), bass **Sir Horace Gentleman** (b. Horace Panter), drums **John Bradbury**, trombone **Rico Rodrigues** (b. 17 Oct 1934, Jamaica), keyboards **Jerry Dammers** (b. Gerald Dankin, 22 May 1954, India)

WHEN 1977–

WHERE Coventry, England

WHAT Socially conscious Ska

Having failed with Punk/Reggae fusion, Jerry Dammers, Horace Gentleman and Lynval Golding enlisted Roddy Radiation, Terry Hall, Neville Staples and drummer 'Silverton' and shifted to Ska. As The Coventry Automatics, they suffered a fruitless spell in London under Clash manager Bernie Rhodes.

With new drummer John Bradbury, they released 'Gangsters' (1979) as The Special AKA on their own 2 Tone label (inspired by their multiracial line-up). 2 Tone became Chrysalis' Ska imprint with Madness, The Beat, The Bodysnatchers and The Selecter. Meanwhile, 'Gangsters', credited to The Specials, was a UK hit.

The Elvis Costello-produced *Specials* (1979) mixed stomping Ska with bleak social commentary, as did 'Too Much Too Young' from 1980's 'The Special AKA Live' EP – a rare UK No.1 about teen pregnancy and contraception. With England gripped by Ska-mania, The Specials moved beyond it with *More Specials* (1980) – whose classic tale of urban decay 'Ghost Town' topped the UK chart in 1981 during a week of inner-city riots across Britain. But the group fragmented as Hall, Golding and Staples left for Fun Boy Three. Radiation disappeared with Roddy Radiation & The Tearjerkers, while Gentleman resurfaced in General Public.

Dammers continued as The Special AKA and hit with *In The Studio*'s 1984 anti-Apartheid anthem 'Nelson Mandela'. In 1986, Dammers founded Artists Against Apartheid, staging two Nelson Mandela tribute shows in 1988 and 1990 at Wembley Stadium.

Meanwhile, Staples and Gentleman formed Special Beat. By 1991's *The Specials Singles*, Dammers had retired the group, but Golding, Staples, Gentleman and Radiation convened as The Specials for *Today's Specials* (1996), *Concrete Jungle* and *Guilty 'Til Proved Innocent* (both 1998). Celebrated by modern Ska stars like No Doubt, The Specials were also remembered by Prodigy – who dumped a cover of 'Ghost Town' from *The Fat Of The Land* (1997) when versions by Mercury Rev and Tricky beat them to it.

 pw2.netcom.com/~miles.1/thespecials.html

JON SPENCER BLUES EXPLOSION

WHO Vocals/guitar/Theremin **Jon Spencer**, guitar **Judah Bauer**, drums **Russell Simins**

WHEN 1991–

WHERE New York, USA

WHAT Fire 'n' brimstone Blues

Phil Spector

Producer and songwriter Phil Spector (b. 25 Dec 1940, New York, USA) turned teen traumas into Pop triumphs. In the process, he almost lost his mind. After early success with The Teddy Bears' 1958 US No.1 'To Know Him Is To Love Him', he worked with legendary hitmakers Jerry Leiber and Mike Stoller on Ben E. King's 'Spanish Harlem' (1961), joined Atlantic as an A&R man and produced hits for Gene Pitney, Curtis Lee and The Paris Sisters. By 21, Spector was the best producer in the USA. His productions stretched Rock 'n' Roll to classical dimensions – "little symphonies for the kids," he called them.

The secret was Spector's 'Wall of Sound' – orchestras, guitars, pianos, drums, bells, echo – which reached its zenith on hits for The Crystals ('Da Doo Ron Ron', 'Then He Kissed Me'), The Ronettes ('Be My Baby', 'Baby, I Love You', 'Walking In The Rain'), Darlene Love ('Wait 'Til My Bobby Gets Home'), Bob B Soxx & The Blue Jeans' 'Zip-A-Dee-Do-Da' and The Righteous Brothers' 'You've Lost That Lovin' Feelin''. When The Rolling Stones and The Beach Boys conquered the USA, they did so with productions clearly influenced by Spector (as did Bruce Springsteen and Meat Loaf producer Jim Steinman in the next decade).

However, his teen symphonies fell from fashion and, when Ike & Tina Turner's 'River Deep, Mountain High' (1966) flopped in the States, he went into bitter retirement. While his legend grew, he allegedly mistreated his wife Ronnie (a former Ronette) and grew obsessed with guns. Legend has it that he employed bodyguards to protect others from his outbursts. His triumphs since the 60s include The Beatles' Let It Be (1970), George Harrison's All Things Must Pass (1970), John Lennon's Imagine (1971), Leonard Cohen's Death Of A Ladies Man (1977), Ramones' End Of The Century (1980) and Yoko Ono's Season Of Glass (1981). His own A Christmas Gift (1963), featuring The Crystals' 'Santa Claus Is Coming To Town', is re-released almost every year. His legacy is best celebrated by the 1991 box set Back To Mono.

Having done the anti-Rock thing in the late 80s as leader of Pussy Galore (which also spawned the rockin' Royal Trux), Jon Spencer went all post-modern with the Blues Explosion: a scuzzy, zealous deconstruction of Blues and Rockabilly which became New York's hippest export in the early 90s. With drummer Russell Simins, guitarist Judah Bauer, no bass (too 'Rawk', presumably) and inspired use of a Theremin, the trio's gloriously horrible noise seduced critics with 1992's self-titled debut which, like everything else in the Blues Explosion canon, walked a tightrope between gleeful anarchy and smug posturing.

By *Extra Width* (1993), proper songs were the norm – tight structures, funky beats (a by-product of their bonding with the Beastie Boys), chunky riffs and new clarity in Spencer's Elvis-ish drawl. While Simins formed Crunt with Babes In Toyland's Kat Bjelland, Spencer moonlighted with his wife (and former Pussy Galore gal) Cristina Martinez's Boss Hog. His own *Orange* (1994) courted controversy by being listenable (countered by 1995's *Experimental Remixes*). *Now I Got Worry* (1996) was plain brilliant and even boasted a telephone cameo by Spencer's golf pal Beck.

surf www.megalink.net/~jbean/jsbe/blues.html

SPICE GIRLS ◉ ◉ ⊛

WHO Vocals **Geri Estelle Halliwell** aka Trixie Firecracker (b. 7 Aug 1972, Watford, England), vocals **Mel C** aka Katrina Highkick (b. Melanie Jayne Chisholm, 12 Jan 1976, Liverpool, England), vocals **Emma Lee Bunton** aka Kung Fu Candy (b. 21 Jan 1976, London, England), vocals **Victoria Addams** aka Midnight Miss Suki (b. 7 Apr 1975, Cuffley, England), vocals **Mel B** aka Blazin' Bad Zula (b. Melanie Janine Brown, 29 May 1975, Leeds, England)

WHEN 1993–

WHERE Maidenhead, Berkshire, England

WHAT The high priestesses of superfunkycalifragisexy girl-powered Pop

To conquer Pop, a good slogan can only help, as transatlantic tides of 'FRANKIE SAY' shirts testified back in 1984. Spice Girls came up with four: "Girl Power", "…what I really, really want", "Too much emotions" and the immortal "Zig ah zig aah!".

When 'Wannabe' went to the top worldwide, it burned all four phrases into the collective consciousness, which swiftly found room too for the five banner-carriers: Geri, Mel C, Emma, Victoria and Mel B. That they were the fastest-selling new act since The Beatles meant little; more important was that Spice Girls were the first act since The Beatles whose members could be identified by *everyone*.

Back in 1993, however, they languished in obscurity. United in spirit by failure in big-league auditions – like one for the lead role in the *Tank Girl* movie – they were united in fact by an ad in the theatre journal *The Stage*: "R.U. 18–23 with the ability to sing/dance? R.U. streetwise, outgoing, ambitious and

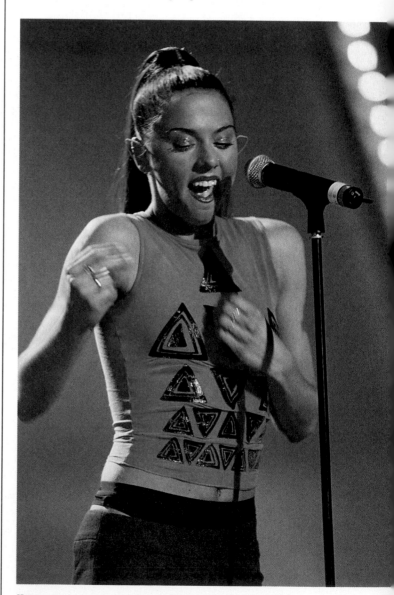

"I really like the black girl. Her name's Mel B, isn't it? There's something about the way she shook her, erm, boobs in the 'Wannabe' video that really turned me on!"

Jon Bon Jovi

"That's the Spice Girls philosophy: to have a good time – and we do! Having said that, Mel C's always going to bed early!"

Geri

dedicated?" Living together in Maidenhead, England – and still known as Touch when last-to-join Emma hopped aboard – they conjured 'Wannabe', '2 Become 1' and the name soon on the world's lips. "We were in an exercise class, Melanie C and I," says Geri, "and we said, What about Spice?"

Groomed for the big-time by Annie Lennox's manager Simon Fuller, they signed to Virgin and stormed to the top in July 1996. Their ascension to Pop's royalty came mere months after the fall of Take That, whose Gary Barlow they knocked from the UK No.1 slot. After aeons in the grip of boy bands, the chart was ruled by women: Les Spices, Fugee femme Lauryn Hill, Alanis Morissette.

Though Morissette was signed to Madonna's label, it was the Spices who owed Madonna the biggest debt: she'd made Geri realize that looks and talent were less crucial than ambition, and was the woman Mel C wanted to be. Even the title 'Wannabe' could be traced to Madonna's *Like A Virgin*-era lookalike fans.

Mel B added Neneh Cherry funkiness to the mix and the result was a refreshing world away from the earnest boys with guitars left looking gormless in their wake. A running war with Oasis, including exchanged threats between Liam Gallagher and Mel C at a BRIT award ceremony, peaked when Noel Gallagher fancifully claimed to be 'bigger than God'. "If Oasis are bigger than God, what does that make us?" challenged Mel C. "Bigger than Buddha? Because we are a darn sight bigger than Oasis." This antagonism notwithstanding, Liam Gallagher and Geri both nominated C.S. Lewis' *The Lion, The Witch & The Wardrobe* as their favourite book on World Book Day, 23 April 1998.

By the end of 1996, they had three hits gracing European charts: 'Wannabe', the sparklingly funky 'Say You'll Be There' (whose superb video cast 'Trixie Firecracker' *et al* as sci-fi vixens) and the seductive stunner '2 Become 1'. Then the sensational *Spice* (1996) – a dancey delight peppered with nods to TLC,

"I always think Posh looks the coolest. She looks like she doesn't spend as much time getting ready as everyone else"

Madonna

"Can I have more than one? The blonde, what's her name? Emma? Yeah, I'll take Emma"
Ice-T

Madonna and Hip Hop – exploded. With the girls woven into the fabric of life – magazine covers, billboards, teenage bedrooms, school playgrounds, office coffee breaks, construction sites – it followed the hits to the top and multi-million sales. More than that, it was an event: with generational, gender and racial divides trampled, everyone liked, loved or hated Spice Girls. "I try not to think about the Spice Girls too much," Foo Fighters mainman Dave Grohl warned *Select* magazine, "and if you ask me who my favourite one is, I'm gonna hang up!"

America fell in 1997: 'Wannabe' became the most successful debut single by any act. Key to the conquest was their becoming globally famous faces. Names invented by the UK's *Top Of The Pops* magazine assumed international recognition: Geri was 'Ginger Spice', Mel C 'Sporty Spice', Emma 'Baby Spice', Victoria 'Posh Spice' and Mel B 'Scary Spice'. "They've got a lot of different spices for different moods," marvelled Will Smith. "You could

"Geri is near retirement age now, but there's life in the old girl yet"

Mel C

have five different spice moods – one for each day of the week. I'd have any of them that would have me!" It didn't hurt that they were happy to toy with Britain's sleazy tabloid press and reacted with cheerful nonchalance even to the unearthing of nude photos that Geri had starred in pre-stardom. "I thought, why not?" she recalled. "I didn't have to go to drama school for this."

Back home, they set a UK record with the double A-side 'Mama'/'Who Do You Think You Are', becoming the first act to make No.1 with their first four singles. Such achievements sometimes eclipsed the splendour of the music: 'Mama' was the gentlest of Trip Hop, 'Who Do You Think You Are' the most seismic of Disco floor-shakers.

They unveiled a harder edge on the Rap-happy 'Step To Me', the theme to a 1997 Pepsi campaign. The Pepsi association was among the first of many that made them Pop's most successful endorsees ever. "We wanna be the biggest superstars in the world," announced Mel C. To the media and envious co-stars in the musical galaxy, this in-your-face commercialism did nothing to validate 'Girl Power', a hazy manifesto summed up as being "about spreading a positive vibe, kickin' it for the girls… and having a laugh." Girl Power stood for something that detractors had conveniently forgotten: that Pop should be inspirational, not educational.

Their positivity was affirmed in late 1997 with the Latin-lit 'Spice Up Your Life'. Their light was dimmed neither by their ubiquity nor the secrecy-shrouded dumping of their manager Simon Fuller, and *Spiceworld* (1997) was another worldwide mega-seller. Though packed with pastiche – of themselves, The Jackson 5 and, of course, Madonna – it spawned yet another UK No.1: their second smoochy Christmas chart-topper, 'Too Much'. The frenzy flowed into 1998 with *Spiceworld: The Movie*, a star-studded send-up of their ludicrous lives – *A Hard Day's Night* meets The Monkees.

Although Geri quit in May 1998 and a run of UK No.1s ended when 'Stop' failed to become their seventh, Spiceadelica had long outgrown mere chart statistics or lone personalities. As if a spectacular world tour wasn't proof enough of their global goddessness, they earned the respect of Madonna herself, who voted Victoria her favourite and responded to Geri's concern that she would either "love or hate us" with the supremely cool "Honey, I don't hate anything except cowboy boots".

(READ) *Girl Power* (1997), Spice Girls

(FAN) Spice Girls, Freepost, PO Box 859, London SW11 4BR, UK

(SURF) www.kig.co.uk/spice/index.html

SPIRITUALIZED

WHO Vocals/guitar **Jason Pierce** (b. 19 Nov 1965, Rugby, England), bass/harmonica **Sean Cook** (b. 16 Apr 1969), drums **Damon Reece** (b. 16 Feb 1967), keyboards **Kate Radley** (b. 19 Feb 1965)

WHEN 1990–

WHERE Rugby, England

WHAT The strung-out sound of sadness

The bootleg *Taking Drugs To Make Music To Take Drugs To* described Spacemen 3's sound perfectly – only space itself was

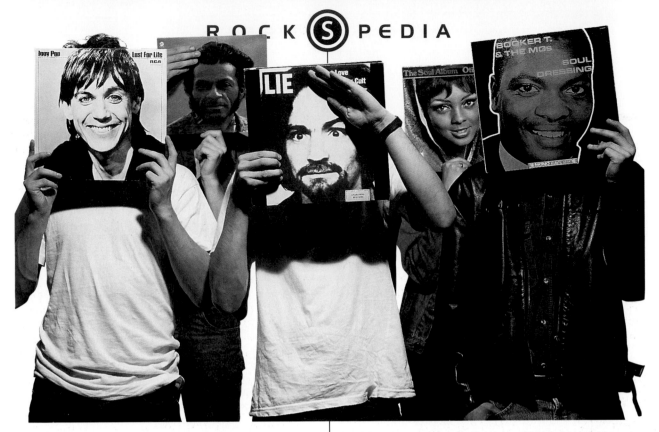

spacier. And despite repeated moans to music journalists, former Spaceman Jason Pierce can't seem to shake off the 'drug' tag – not surprising, really, considering the languid majesty of his band Spiritualized.

Founded with bassist Willie B. Carruthers, drummer Jon Mattock and guitarist Mark Refoy (and soon, keyboardist Kate Radley), Spiritualized mangled the Spacemen's trance Rock blueprint on their debut 'Anyway That You Want Me' (1991), then drew a new one with *Lazer Guided Melodies* (1992) – a mesmeric whirlwind of Velvets-style drones, lysergic Blues and strung-out sadness.

Cook replaced Carruthers before 1993's limited edition live album *Fucked Up Inside*, while both Refoy and Mattock were gone when the wonderful *Pure Phase* (credited to Spiritualized Electric Mainline) thundered into view in 1995. Not that anyone cared: on a UK Indie scene swamped with Britpop, an album whose tracks were linked by the same, omnipresent drone was considered junkie Rock noise – hence Pierce's constant denials and protests that Spiritualized were "Soul music". Of course, it didn't help that *Phase*'s lead track was called 'Medication'.

However, by *Ladies And Gentlemen We Are Floating In Space* (1997), the world was theirs. A frazzled, broken-hearted masterpiece (Pierce had lost his girlfriend Radley to The Verve's Richard Ashcroft), it boasted cameos from Blues legend Dr John, junglists Spring Heel Jack, strings, gospel choirs and – replacing the minimalist drones and noise of old – songs like the majestic 'Electricity', 'I Think I'm In Love' and 'Come Together'. Massive sales, a world tour and acclaimed concerts at London's Royal Albert Hall and Toronto's CN Tower followed. The latter set a record as 'the highest gig in the world', but all this drug talk has nothing to do with the music, alright?

surf www.no-fi.com/spiritualized/

DUSTY SPRINGFIELD

WHO b. Mary O'Brien, 16 Apr 1939, London, England

WHAT Husky-voiced soulful singer

Mary O'Brien was 16 when she cast aside her convent-girl past and started along the path that would lead to her becoming one of Britain's top singers. After a brief period with vocal trio The Lana Sisters, she teamed with her brother Tom Springfield (b. Dion O'Brien) and Tim Field in 1961 to form The Springfields.

The Folk-based trio's intricate harmonies and international flavour brought them five UK Top 40 hits – of which 1962's 'Island Of Dreams' and 1963's 'Say I Won't Be There' were the biggest – but Dusty, hankering for more R&B, left the group in 1963 to go solo. Her first offering, 'I Only Want To Be With You', hit UK No.4 in 1963 and reflected her love of the burgeoning Motown sound. It was also the first record to be played on BBC TV's *Top Of The Pops*.

A regular on UK TV's *Ready Steady Go!*, Dusty was dubbed 'Queen of the Mods' with her beehive hair, mascara'd panda eyes and R&B tastes. In South Africa in 1964, she stipulated she would play non-segregated venues only. After one performance before a multiracial crowd, she was served with a deportation order.

A stream of hits characterized her 60s career, including 'I Just Don't Know What To Do With Myself' (1964), 'You Don't Have To Say You Love Me' (1966), her only UK No.1, and 'I Close My Eyes And Count To Ten' (1968). She went to Memphis in 1969 to record her best album, *Dusty In Memphis*. Produced by Jerry Wexler, Arif Marden and Tom Dowd, it was her first not to chart in Britain, despite yielding the UK No.9 'Son Of A Preacher Man' (prominently featured in 1994's *Pulp Fiction*).

Springfield lived in California for most of the 70s, and rarely troubled charts. Her relocation to Britain in 1987 marked a comeback when she joined Pet Shop Boys for the UK No.2 'What Have I Done To Deserve This?', 'Nothing Has Been Proved' (from the movie soundtrack of 1988's *Scandal*) and *Reputation* (1990).

A Very Fine Love (1995), recorded in Nashville where The Springfields had recorded their second album back in 1963, took her full circle.

read *Dusty* (1989), Lucy O'Brien

fan Dusty Springfield Bulletin, 88 Rosebank, Holyport Road, London SW6 6LJ, UK

surf www.isd.net/mbayly/

BRUCE SPRINGSTEEN ⊙ ⊙ ⊙ ⊙ ✪ ✪ ✪ ✪

WHO b. Frederick Joseph Springsteen, 23 Sep 1949, Freehold, New Jersey, USA

WHAT The blue-collar superstar

Downtrodden by a Catholic upbringing and authoritarian father, Bruce Springsteen – fired up by Elvis and Chuck Berry – was blown away by Motown Soul and the Beatles-led British Invasion.

The awed teenager scraped $18 together, bought a second-hand guitar and found himself a place in local band The Rogues. This was the first of a string of groups performing covers and his own early songs. One such act, The Castiles, entered the studio in May 1966 to record two of his tunes – a small step in songwriting standards, a major leap for Springsteen.

Next, he emulated Cream's power-trio format in Earth. Their lengthy Blues jams lacked musical muscle, so he started a new group, Child, with organist 'Phantom' Dan Federici, drummer Vini 'Mad Dog' Lopez and bassist Vini Roslin. When Springsteen met guitarist 'Miami' Steve Van Zandt (so-called because he hated the cold), the pair began a long partnership. Van Zandt replaced Roslin on bass and the name changed to Steel Mill. This "Humble Pie-type band" became the nucleus of the E Street Band.

In early 1969, Springsteen followed his family to California. It proved a fruitful journey: within months of landing on Pacific shores, Steel Mill landed dates at venues such as The Matrix in San Francisco. Powerful promoter-mogul Bill Graham took note and offered him a recording contract. Springsteen declined, returned to his New Jersey stronghold Asbury Park, disbanded Steel Mill at the height of its $3,000-per-night success and created Doctor Zoom & His Sonic Boom. The latter opened for The Allman Brothers, but broke up to give way to the variously monikered Bruce Springsteen & The Friendly Enemies and The Bruce Springsteen Blues Band. This line-up featured Garry 'W' Tallent (bass), Lopez (drums), Van Zandt (guitar), David Sancious (keyboards), Harvey Cherlin (trumpet) and vocal trio Barbara Kinkins, Francine Daniels and Delores Holmes. Even manager Tinker West was allowed to slap out time on congas.

The ensemble splintered when fame and fortune eluded them. Springsteen teamed with managers Mike Appel and Jim Cretecos and met Columbia Records mentor John Hammond, who'd signed Bob Dylan. Hammond later suffered a heart attack at a Springsteen show, attributed to excessive enthusiasm.

Signed in 1972, Springsteen recalled Lopez, Sancious, Federici, Tallent and Van Zandt, and added saxophonist and on-stage foil Clarence 'Big Man' Clemons. His *Greetings From Asbury Park, N.J.* (1973) emerged on the same day as the debut of another bunch of young hopefuls. As the latter's manager David Krebs recalled, "For every dollar Columbia put into Aerosmith, they put $100 into Springsteen." Despite this support, the album failed to set charts alight, owing partly to its emphasis on Springsteen the solo artist. "It wasn't what he did best," said Van Zandt. However, its cut 'Blinded By The Light' became a 1977 US No.1 for Manfred Mann, and David Bowie covered 'Growin' Up'.

The Wild, The Innocent & The E Street Shuffle (1974) had more of a band feel, but no more impact on charts. However, Springsteen met *Rolling Stone's* Jon Landau, who – having predicted "I have seen Rock 'n' Roll's future and his name is Bruce Springsteen" – replaced Appel as manager and guided his charge to become 'The Boss'. The new team also included keyboardist 'Professor' Roy Bittan and drummer 'The Mighty' Max Weinberg.

> **"The one album that led me to write was Born To Run... That was when the boring, small town of my 13/14-year-old New Jersey became a romantic mythologized scene of neon light, fast cars and the shore bars.**
> **It gave me a reason to dream...**
>
> **Thanks, Bruce"**
>
> Jon Bon Jovi

In August 1975, Springsteen unleashed the classic *Born To Run*, became a press darling and appeared simultaneously on the covers of the prestigious US journals *Newsweek* and *Time*. The title track became his first anthem and the album went to US No.3, selling 500,000 in its first week. Not impressed, however, were Elvis Presley's security guards – who escorted a blushing Boss from Graceland when he jumped the fence in April 1976.

Springsteen's career was stalled by litigation with Appel, but reignited when the latter accepted a million-dollar cash settlement and the much-delayed *Darkness On The Edge Of Town* (1978) went platinum. Displaying none of the melancholy that informed the album's lyrics, he embarked on a 118-date US tour.

Among his shows of the period was a 1979 'MUSE' (Musicians United for Safe Energy) show in New York – aka 'No Nukes' – with The Doobie Brothers, Crosby Stills & Nash and Jackson Browne. Browne later wrote 'For A Rocker' (*Lawyers In Love*, 1983) for The Boss, with whom he periodically shared a stage – notably at a second 'No Nukes' show at the Hollywood Bowl in 1981, and the 1982 'Peace Walk' rally in Central Park. Meanwhile, The Pointer Sisters had a 1979 smash with Springsteen's 'Fire', and his magic touch gave Patti Smith her only hit, 'Because The Night' (1978).

The River (1980) – its working title *The Ties That Bind* – yielded his first Top 10 hit, 'Hungry Heart' (written for the Ramones but sensibly kept for himself) and returned Springsteen to the premier league. In April 1980, a New Jersey State assemblyman moved to make 'Born To Run' the official state song. A year later, the newly opened Meadowlands Brendan Byrne Arena was baptized by The Boss: "When we got onstage," he marvelled, "I couldn't hear the band. We felt like The Beatles."

Springsteen used his celebrity status to pay a debt to Gary 'US' Bonds, 60s Rock 'n' Roller and pivotal influence; he and Van Zandt co-produced Bonds' 1981 comeback, *Dedication*.

Frustrated by attempts to craft a follow-up to *The River* with the E Street Band, Springsteen was persuaded by Landau to issue his demos in 1982. The result, *Nebraska* – or, as one critic sniped, *Born To Crawl* – sold more on Springsteen's reputation than on its stripped-down, acoustic laments. But the whole world embraced 1984's blasting *Born In The USA*. The synth-powered 'Dancing In The Dark' and five other hits spurred the album to transatlantic top spots and 25 million sales. President Ronald Reagan and car manufacturers Chrysler separately attempted to adopt the title track for promotional purposes, oblivious to its cynical lyric.

By the end of the accompanying tour – for which Nils Lofgren replaced Van Zandt – more than 5 million fans had witnessed the extravaganza. Appropriately, it was followed by *Live 1975–85*, the first multi-disc live set to enter the US chart at No.1. Spin-off hits included thrilling takes on 'Born To Run' and Edwin Starr's 'War'. This hoopla masked the dissolution of the E Street Band, each member receiving a $2 million bonus, a hug and walking papers.

The Country-fied *Tunnel Of Love* surfaced in 1987. A stunning reflection on the dissolution of Springsteen's May 1985 marriage to model Julianne Phillips, it again soared to chart peaks, but marked the start of a graceful exit from the mainstream.

His early ambitions met, Springsteen could afford to widen his interests, one being the worldwide Human Rights Now! tour for Amnesty International in 1988 with Peter Gabriel, Sting, Tracy Chapman and Youssou N'Dour. In ensuing years, Springsteen concentrated on raising a family with his ex-backing singer, and new wife, Patti Scialfa (he co-produced her 1993 set *Rumble Doll*).

The silence was broken by the simultaneous release of 1992's US No.3 *Lucky Town* and US No.2 *Human Touch,* which quickly plummeted down charts, selling platinum instead of the usual multi-platinum. Cheerfully unconcerned, Springsteen toured the world again and demonstrated his antipathy for traditional career paths with a resolutely electric set on MTV's *Unplugged* (released in the UK in 1993 and the USA in 1995 as *Plugged*).

He returned to the spotlight with 'Streets of Philadelphia', the Oscar-winning theme to the 1993 movie *Philadelphia*. This soft-spoken stormer trailed a long overdue *Greatest Hits* (1995), which traced the singer from his early obsessions – parodied by Prefab Sprout on their 'Cars And Girls' – to a latter-day concern with relationships. The album also served as a postscript to the E Street Band, who reunited for a couple of tracks.

With *The Ghost Of Tom Joad* (1995), Springsteen appeared to put a final nail in his commercial coffin. Even more subdued than *Nebraska*, it sold only to aficionados – circumstances with which Springsteen seemed entirely comfortable: "I don't need my records at this point to be No.1." His first solo tour, swapping stadiums for theatres, attracted rapturous reviews and Rage Against The Machine covered *Tom Joad*'s title track. There was more soundtrack work, his sedate contributions to the movies *Dead Man Walking* (1995) and *Jerry Maguire* (1997) contrasting starkly with the earlier, fiery *Light Of Day* (1984) soundtrack. In 1998, he recorded six songs for a tribute album for Folk legend Pete Seeger, *Where Have All The Flowers Gone*.

Though his commercial fortunes have waned, Springsteen remains a creative and crucial mouthpiece for America's heartland. In his depictions of the forlorn, the transient or the street dweller seeking respite from the storm, he has few equals.

Read *Born To Run – The Bruce Springsteen Story* (1979), Dave Marsh

Fan Backstreets, PO Box 51225, Seattle, WA 98115, USA

Surf members.aol.com/joeroberts/

SQUEEZE

WHO Vocals/guitar **Glenn Tilbrook** (b. 31 Aug 1957, London, England), guitar/vocal **Chris Difford** (b. 11 Apr 1954, London), piano **Jools Holland** (b. Julian Holland, 24 Jan 1958, London), drums **Gilson Lavis** (b. 27 Jun 1951, Bedford, England)

WHEN 1974–

WHERE London, England

WHAT Snappy soap-opera songwriter survivors of New Wave

Squeeze came to fame as part of Britain's New Wave in the late 70s. Like Elvis Costello, XTC and Joe Jackson, they were more melodic and literate than Punk. Founders Chris Difford and Glenn Tilbrook's tuneful flair and observations of English life put Squeeze in a tradition of writing that stretches from The Kinks to Blur. It was even common to hear Difford and Tilbrook called 'the new Lennon and McCartney'.

The pair met when Tilbrook answered Difford's ad in a shop window, promising a non-existent tour and record contract. Recruiting new members as they went along (including Glenn's friend, pianist Jools Holland), they debuted in 1977 with the independently released 'Packet Of Three' EP, moving on to A&M.

By 1979 they had scored three of their most memorable Top 20 hits: 'Take Me I'm Yours', 'Cool For Cats' and 'Up The Junction', each a witty narrative inside an irresistible arrangement. Most were sung by Tilbrook (who wrote the music), though 'Cool For Cats' was an exception, bearing the gruffer vocals of wordsmith Difford. Squeeze's albums (1978's *Squeeze*, 1979's *Cool For Cats*,

1980's *Argybargy*, 1981's *East Side Story* and 1982's *Sweets From A Stranger*) made only a moderate chart impact, but the group won acclaim for their singles, further hits including 1980's 'Another Nail In My Heart' and 'Pulling Mussels (From The Shell)' and 1981's 'Tempted'. Significantly, their only Top 10 album was 1982's compilation *Singles 45's And Under*. Labouring to break America, and maintain their initial success, the strain was telling. Holland left to pursue his own music and a TV career and, in late 1982, the entire group split – a decision they later regretted.

Difford and Tilbrook collaborated on a musical, *Labelled With Love*, and released their own album before re-forming Squeeze in 1985. Holland and drummer Gilson Lavis returned briefly, but the line-up underwent frequent changes. Difford and Tilbrook aside, only new bassist Keith Wilkinson became anything like a regular fixture. As much to their amazement as everyone else's, Squeeze suddenly became a Stateside sensation with 1987's 'Hourglass' and *Babylon And On*, but 1989's *Frank*, 1990's live *A Round And A Bout*, 1991's *Play*, 1993's *Some Fantastic Place* and 1995's *Ridiculous* won diminishing returns.

By 1997 they were without a label, although A&M compiled the box set *Six Of One*, after 1996's rarities set *Excess Moderation*. They remain popular live, however, thanks to a much-loved hits catalogue. Tilbrook often plays solo dates, while Jools Holland became the public face of British music TV in the 90s.

 Squeeze, PO Box 12695, London, SE10 92J, UK

 www.squeezefan.com/

LISA STANSFIELD

WHO b. 11 Apr 1966, Rochdale, Lancashire, England

WHAT Shimmery Soul

Leaving behind children's Pop programme *Razzmatazz* and local talent shows (in one of which she beat Shaun 'Black Grape' Ryder's dad into second place), Lisa Stansfield formed Blue Zone in 1986 with schoolmates Andy Morris and Ian Devaney. Signing to Arista, their 1987 debut *Big Thing* (and three singles) bombed.

Success arrived in 1989, when she sang on Coldcut's 'People Hold On'. Her debut solo hit 'This Is The Right Time' – penned by Morris and Devaney – paved the way for the transatlantic smash 'All Around The World' (1989), which she later revamped with her idol Barry White, and *Affection* (1989) – a UK No.2 and US million-seller. Domestic success continued with *Real Love* (1991) and *So Natural* (1993), from which the smoochy 'All Woman' and 'In All The Right Places' were the most cherished hits. She also scored in 1993 with 'Someday (I'm Coming Back)' from *The Bodyguard*.

She contributed 'Friday's Child' to the 1994 Van Morrison tribute *No Prima Donna*, 'Dream Away' – a duet with Babyface – to 1995's movie soundtrack *The Pagemaster* and 'Just To Keep You Satisfied' to 1995's Marvin Gaye tribute *Inner City Blues*. She also sang on George Michael's UK No.1 'Five Live EP'.

However, *Lisa Stansfield* (1997) was upstaged by Puff Daddy's 'Been Around The World', which quoted 'All Around The World', and a remix of 'People Hold On' that hijacked the backing of the Tori Amos hit 'Professional Widow'. But Stansfield maintained her newsworthiness by punching ex-Pogue Shane McGowan in a dispute about poetry and embarking on her movie debut *Swing*.

 www.aristarec.com/aristaweb/LisaStansfield/

EDWIN STARR

WHO b. Charles Hatcher, 21 Jan 1942, Nashville, Tennessee, USA

WHAT Soul commander

While other Soul legends swooned and crooned their way to immortality, Edwin Starr shouted. Having spent most of the 60s on Motown competitor Ric Tic – with whom he hit US charts with 1965's 'Agent Double-O-Soul' and 1966's 'Stop Her On Sight (also a UK hit) – Starr hit the big-time when Motown bought the label. Rubbing shoulders with Berry Gordy's finest inspired him and he penned 1969's classic hits 'Twenty-Five Miles' and 'I'm Still A Strugglin' Man'. But it was a pairing with producer Norman Whitfield that lodged Starr in legend, with 1970's storming 'War' (a rejected Temptations cut) and 'Stop The War Now'. However, after 1971's 'Funky Music Sho Nuff Turns Me On', he holidayed from the charts until 1979, when 'H.A.P.P.Y. Radio' and 'Contact' reached the UK Top 10. Starr's legendary status on Britain's Northern Soul scene prompted his migration there in the 80s. Meanwhile, the anthemic 'War' lived on courtesy of covers by Frankie Goes To Hollywood and Bruce Springsteen.

RINGO STARR

WHO b. Richard Starkey, 7 Jul 1940, Liverpool, England

WHAT Beatlebum

Never the safest bet for solo success, Beatles drummer Ringo Starr unleashed a double-whammy debut in 1970. *Sentimental Journey* and *Beaucoups Of Blues* saw him tackle old-style ballads (to please his mum, he said) and Country songs, followed by the hits 'It Don't Come Easy' (1971) and 'Back Off Boogaloo' (1972). Having starred in *Candy* (1967) and *The Magic Christian* (1969) while still a Beatle, *That'll Be The Day* (1970) and a director's credit on Marc Bolan's *Born To Boogie* (1973) added to his celluloid CV.

Ringo (1973) and *Goodnight Vienna* (1974) employed lavish production and a celebrity horde (including his former Fab Four colleagues) for the UK No.1s 'Photograph' and 'You're Sixteen' (from *Ringo*) and the hits 'Oh My My', 'Only You' and 'No No Song'. Although commercial decline set in with his *Rotogravure* (1976), Ringo remained in demand, hence cameos on George Harrison's *The Concert For Bangla Desh* (1971), Peter Frampton's *Wind Of Change* (1972) and The Band's *The Last Waltz* movie (1978).

Lifestyle problems scuppered him and the flops *Stop And Smell The Roses* (1981) and *Old Wave* (1983) preceded his legal action to block the release of 1987 recordings. But narrating kids' TV show *Thomas The Tank Engine* (known Stateside as *Shining Time Station*) kept his profile up while he assembled various permutations of an All-Starr Band, which has included Joe Walsh, Dr John and Todd Rundgren, and released *Ringo Starr And His All-Starr Band* (1990) and *Time Takes Time* (1992). *Vertical Man* (1998) featured appearances from Stone Temple Pilots' Scott Weiland, Ozzy Osbourne, Alanis Morissette and Aerosmith's Steven Tyler. But his immortalization on canvas at the hand of *The Simpsons'* Marge must rank as Ringo's proudest solo moment.

surf web2airmail.net.cshultz

STATUS QUO ⊙⊙⊙⊙

WHO Vocals/guitar **Francis Rossi** (b. 29 May 1949, London, England), vocals/guitar **Rick Parfitt** (b. Richard Harrison, 12 Oct 1948, Woking, England), bass **John 'Rhino' Edwards** (b. 9 May 1953, London), keyboards **Andy Bown** (b. 27 Mar 1947, London), drums **Jeff Rich** (b. 8 Jun 1953, London)

WHEN 1962–

WHERE Beckenham, Kent, England

WHAT Boogie, ballads and blue denims

Two decades after Status Quo scored their only No.1 single with 'Down Down', Oasis took an identical blend of cheerfully mindless lyrics and headbanging boogie into the charts in the shape of 'Roll With It'. In the intervening years, Quo had become the subject of critical derision, but their colossal popularity still translates into arena-filling bigness as the next century looms.

Having met in a school band, Alan Lancaster and Francis Rossi switched from brass to guitars after hearing The Shadows. From 1962–1967, they evolved from The Spectres to Traffic Jam to, in 1967, Status Quo, leaving behind a holiday camp residency and three flop singles. Dallying with Psychedelia gave them hits with 1968's 'Pictures of Matchstick Men' and 'Ice In The Sun', but they were never destined to follow Pink Floyd's path from that scene, and switched to chugging Blues (elements of which could be traced to The Doors) and buzz-saw riffing. Having honed the sound through *Spare Parts* (1969), *Ma Kelly's Greasy Spoon* (1970) and *Dog Of Two Heads* (1970), they broke through with *Piledriver* (1973), source of the hit 'Paper Plane'.

Ignoring charges of repetition, Quo swelled their fanbase with 1973's *Hello* (UK No.1 and the source of fan faves 'Caroline' and '4500 Times'), 1974's *Quo*, 1975's *On The Level* (No.1 and home to 'Down Down') and 1976's *Blue For You* (*another* No.1, whose gentle title track proved it wasn't all Rock *chez* Quo). In 1976, they signed a pioneering sponsorship deal with Levi's.

Undaunted by the advent of Punk, Quo added more classics to their canon in 1977 with the storming *Live* and *Rockin' All Over The World*. The latter's title track, a minor hit for its writer John Fogerty (of Creedence Clearwater Revival) in 1975, became one of their most enduring anthems. They coasted with *If You Can't Stand The Heat* (1978), but hit another high with *Whatever You Want* (1979), whose classics were its slashing title track and the unrecognizably soft-rocking 'Living On An Island'.

They entered the next decade triumphant with 1980's hits set *12 Gold Bars* and the excellent *Just Supposin'*. Bar the sway-along ballad 'Rock 'n' Roll', the latter was packed with vicious cuts like 'Run To Mummy' and, thanks to a resurgence of Metal in Britain, Quo suddenly found themselves back in fashion. After 1981's indifferent *Never Too Late*, they celebrated their 20th anniversary in 1982 in style: having replaced grumpy drummer John Coghlan with Pete Kircher, they topped the UK chart with *1+9+8+2*, headlined the UK's Monsters Of Rock, played a televised show attended by Prince Charles and, with the lavish *From The Makers Of…*, made one of the few box sets to enter the UK Top 5.

But then the juggernaut stalled. Older fans were appalled by the wimpy hit 'Marguerita Time' from *Back To Back* (1983), Quo played what was billed as their final show in 1984 and mainstay Alan Lancaster quit acrimoniously, returning only to help them open Live Aid in 1985 with 'Rockin' All Over The World'. In 1986, however, frontmen Francis Rossi and Rick Parfitt reunited, with bassist John Edwards, drummer Jeff Rich and long-serving keyboard player Andy Bown (whose CV also boasted The Herd and Pink Floyd). They shared stadium bills with Queen and hit with *In The Army Now* (1986) and its mournful title track.

The late 80s were harder: mostly minor hits, and their worst-charting albums since the early days in *Ain't Complaining* (1988) and *Perfect Remedy* (1989). But their fortunes flew again with the mega-selling hits set *Rocking All Over The Years* (1990), the fiery return-to-form *Rock 'Til You Drop* (1991), *Live Alive Quo* (1992) and *Thirsty Work* (1994). In 1991, they made it into *The Guinness Book Of Records* by playing four venues in 12 hours.

Radio 1 claimed they were too old, declining to play 1996's Beach Boys-backed 'Fun, Fun, Fun', but *Don't Stop* (1996), though hardly breaking sweat creatively, proved the loyalty of the 'Quo Army' by charting at UK No.2. With a total of eight years in the UK singles charts and nine years in the album charts, they are a national institution.

read *Just For The Record* (1993), Francis Rossi and Rick Parfitt

fan From The Makers Of…, Official Quo Fan Club, PO Box 153, Stanmore, Middlesex HA7 2HF, UK

surf www.statusquo.co.uk/

Jim Stewart, a graduate from Memphis State University, launched the hugely influential black record label Stax in 1961 when he renamed his original Satellite Records following a claim on the name by a rival record company.

Stewart combined the first two letters of his surname with the first two letters of his sister Estelle Axton's surname to create Stax, whose first successes were Rufus Thomas and his daughter Carla. A distribution deal with Atlantic Records put Stax on the map and led to hits for The Markeys (who became Booker T & The MG's), William Bell, Isaac Hayes, Eddie Floyd, The Staple Singers, Sam & Dave and international best-seller Otis Redding.

After Redding's death in 1967, Stax ended its association with Atlantic, who retained ownership of all past recordings, and sold the company to Gulf & Western. In 1970, Stewart and partner Al Bell bought the company back but, amid accusations of financial irregularities and departure of its major artists, Stax ceased operating in 1976. Its assets were bought at auction by Fantasy Records, who continue to distribute the Stax catalogue.

STEEL PULSE

WHO Vocals/guitar **David Hinds** (b. 15 Jun 1956, Birmingham, England), guitar/vocals **Basil Gabbidon**, bass **Ronnie McQueen**, keyboards/vocals **Selwyn 'Bumbo' Brown** (b. 4 Jun 1958, London, England), drums **Stephen 'Grizzly' Nisbett** (b. 15 Mar 1948, Nevis, West Indies), drums/percussion/vocals **Fonson**, vocals **Michael Riley**

WHEN 1975–

WHERE Handsworth, Birmingham, England

WHAT Reggae rabble-rousers

Roots Reggae group Steel Pulse emerged in the mid-70s with an uncompromising stance in songs like 'Ku Klux Klan' and 'Prodigal Son'. Striking a chord with Punk fans, their message echoed the Rock Against Racism movement of the time.

Signed to UK Reggae label Island after two singles, 1978's *Handsworth Revolution* went Top 10, becoming one of the few British Reggae albums to be found in many 70s Rock collections.

But all was not well within the band and, in the first of many line-up shifts, vocalist Michael Riley quit, eventually forming The Reggae Philharmonic Orchestra. Steel Pulse ploughed on through two further Island albums, *Tribute To The Martyrs* (1979) and *Caught You* (1980), both less successful, before signing with Elektra in 1982 for *True Democracy* on the strength of widespread US tour success, then MCA for *State Of Emergency* (1988).

A genuinely globe-trotting outfit, they were the first Reggae act to appear on Johnny Carson's US TV show *Tonight*, and when leader David Hinds sued the New York Taxi and Limousine Commission in 1992, claiming cab drivers discriminated against black people, he drew approval from many African-American groups. Whether Steel Pulse ever achieve the record sales their reputation demands, however, remains to be seen.

surf www.mcarecords.com/library/bios/bio.steel.html

STEELEYE SPAN

WHO Vocals **Maddy Prior** (b. 14 Aug 1947, Blackpool, England), guitar/vocals **Tim Hart** (b. 9 Jan 1948, Lincoln, England), guitar/vocals **Bob Johnson** (b. 17 Mar 1944, Enfield, England), bass **Rick Kemp** (b. 15 Nov 1941, Little Hanford, Dorset, England), violin **Peter Knight** (b. 27 May 1947, London, England)

WHEN 1970–

WHERE St Albans, Hertfordshire, England

WHAT Prolific architects of British Folk Rock

Electric Folk came to life when Ashley Hutchings quit Fairport Convention to continue his collision of traditional balladry and electric stylings. His new band Steeleye Span comprised two duos from the Irish and English Folk scenes: Terry and Gay Woods, and Tim Hart and Maddy Prior.

Recording *Hark! The Village Wait* (1970), tensions between the couples prompted the Woods' exit. Hutchings' replacements were inspired: established songwriter Martin Carthy, who'd just 'gone electric', and Peter Knight, a Classical violinist led astray by Irish fiddle-playing. They hit the college circuit and, in 1971, made two distinctly different albums: the harsh, experimental *Please To See The King* and the fluid Folk of *Ten Man Mop*.

Uncomfortable with *Mop*'s easy-going Irishness, Hutchings left to start The Albion Band. Carthy resumed his solo career and was succeeded by Bob Johnson, another formidable songwriter. With a Rock rhythm section – bassist Rick Kemp and drummer Nigel Pegrum – Steeleye Span developed into a powerful live act. Their albums drew on a widening Folk spectrum and yielded two UK hits: 'Gaudete' (1972) and 'All Around My Hat' (1975).

After the ill-received *Rocket Cottage* (1976), Span started to disintegrate, but contractual commitments brought Carthy back in, with concertinist John Kirkpatrick, to replace Johnson and Knight, who'd jumped ship. Ironically, the 'obligation' albums – *Storm Force Ten* (1977) and *Live At Last!* (1978) – proved their most all-encompassing, stretching from Country dances to sonically intense epics.

The band reunited two years later for an album and tour, a process they've sporadically repeated. But despite Gay Woods' 1996 homecoming, the head-count of original members has steadily waned, including mainstay Prior's departure in 1997.

surf rzdspc77.informatik.uni-hamburg.de/~zierke/steeleye.span/

STEELY DAN

WHO Vocals/keyboards **Donald Fagen** (b. 10 Jan 1948, Passaic, New Jersey, USA), bass/guitar/vocals **Walter Becker** (b. 20 Feb 1950, Queens, New York, USA)

WHEN 1971–

WHERE New York City, New York, USA

WHAT Sophisticated, sardonic Jazz Pop

Steely Dan brought sophistication to Rock music, welding Jazz and Rock into an alloy so smooth and shiny it was hard to tell

"**They're one of those bands that you** couldn't be heard **saying you like.** For years you would have been **strung up by the nuts** for even **admitting to having heard one of their albums. But whenever** I heard **Steely Dan, I'd always really** like the sound of the guy's voice... **They're a very good band and now I don't care if that's cool or not**"

Bob Geldof

where one ended and the other began. Though they broke up in 1981, their meticulous, polished albums were pinnacles of studio art and continued to sell through the 80s as CDs replaced vinyl.

Donald Fagen met Walter Becker at Bard College in New York in 1967. Both were fans of Jazz and hip comedy, elements which remained an integral part of their work. When Fagen graduated, the pair relocated to New York City to become songwriters, though their subject matter was deemed uncommercial by the Brill Building publishers to whom they played the songs.

The duo briefly joined Demian, a band founded by guitarist Denny Dias, before becoming sidemen for Jay & The Americans. Through JATA's Kenny Vance, who became their first manager, they were commissioned to do the soundtrack for a low-budget movie, an unauthorized album of which was issued when they became successful (1976's *You've Got To Walk It Like You Talk It*), along with demos recorded for Vance (1984's *Becker & Fagen: The Early Years*, 1985's *Berry Town*, etc). Vance put them in touch with production partners Richard Perry and Gary Katz, who proved crucial in their career: Perry used the duo's 'I Mean To Shine' on Barbra Streisand's album *Barbra Joan Streisand* (1971) and Katz, when offered an A&R position at ABC Records in LA, accepted on condition that Becker and Fagen be hired as staff songwriters.

The three New Yorkers formed a group, with guitarist Denny Dias, singer David Palmer, drummer Jim Hodder and ex-Ultimate Spinach guitarist Jeff 'Skunk' Baxter from the East Coast. Named after a dildo in William Burroughs' book *The Naked Lunch*, Steely Dan issued their debut 'Dallas' (1972), with Hodder singing. It wasn't a hit, but the slinky mambo rhythms and electric sitar of 1973's 'Do It Again' (US No.6) helped hoist their enigmatic debut *Can't Buy A Thrill* (1975) into the charts. 'Reelin' In The Years' (1973), was also successful. Since both hits featured Fagen's vocals, Palmer was deemed surplus to requirements, and left.

Countdown To Ecstasy (1973), widely considered their best, profited greatly from months spent honing new material on the road. Where their debut album had seemed like a prefabricated Pop marvel, this one presented Steely Dan as a great live band, bursting with energy. But touring pressures meant Becker and Fagen had to rely on old material like 'Parker's Band', 'Barrytown' and 'Charlie Freak' for *Pretzel Logic* (1974). A harbinger of future working methods, it featured extensive use of session musicians like Rick Derringer, the subject of their biggest hit, 'Rikki Don't Lose That Number' (1974). Following Fagen's throat illness, they retired from performing for several years, concentrating on ever-more-perfectionist studio works like *Katy Lied* (1975) and *The Royal Scam* (1976). With no live work, Hodder, Dias and Baxter drifted away, the latter joining The Doobie Brothers in 1974.

In 1977, Steely Dan achieved its biggest UK hits with 'Haitian Divorce' and the jazzy *Aja*. The album took months to complete, with Becker & Fagen's perfectionist approach driving sessionmen to the brink of tears. In 1978, 'Peg', 'Deacon Blues' and 'Josie' were all moderate hits, as was their theme to the movie *FM*, 'FM (No Static At All)'. But *Gaucho* (1981) was delayed by calamities including a broken leg Becker sustained when hit by a car, his drug problems, and his girlfriend's suicide, for which he was sued by her mother. Though 1981's 'Hey Nineteen' was their biggest hit since 'Rikki…', the experience left them drained and 'Time Out Of Mind' (1981) was their last hit before they split.

However, Becker overcame his drug addiction and produced the likes of China Crisis and Rickie Lee Jones before recording his solo debut *11 Tracks Of Whack* (1994). Fagen recorded the acclaimed concept album *The Nightfly* (1982), contributed to more soundtracks and briefly became music editor of movie magazine *Premiere* before – alongside Boz Scaggs and Phoebe Snow – becoming a prime mover in The New York Rock And Soul Revue, recording *Live At The Beacon* (1992).

Making Fagen's second solo album, *Kamakiriad* (US No.10/UK No.5, 1993) with Becker as producer, the pair decided to reunite as Steely Dan in 1994. The live *Alive In America* (1995) was the first fruit of their new union. Meanwhile, Steely Dan had become a source of samples for Hip Hop acts, from De La Soul's 'Eye Know' (1989) to All Saints' 'I Know Where It's At' (1997).

(READ) *Steely Dan – Reelin' In the Years* (1994), Brian Sweet

(SURF) www.mcarecords.com/amp14/f.steely.html

STEPPENWOLF

WHO Vocals/guitar **John Kay** (b. Joachim Krauledat, 12 Apr 1944, Tilsit, Germany), guitar **Larry Byrom** (b. 27 Dec 1948, USA), bass **Nick St Nicholas** (b. Klaus Kassbaum, 28 Sep 1943, Plön, Germany), keyboards **Goldy McJohn** (b. John Goadsby, 2 May 1945), drums **Jerry Edmonton** (b. Jerry McCrohan, 24 Oct 1946, Canada, d. 28 Nov 1993, nr. Santa Ynez, California, USA)

WHEN 1966–

WHERE Los Angeles, California, USA

WHAT Heavy, driving Rock

Infamous for coining the phrase 'Heavy Metal' in their biggest (and only UK) hit 'Born To Be Wild', Steppenwolf were formerly Sparrow, the band John Kay and Jerry Edmonton had formed in New York before relocating to California in 1966. Kay's tale of hardship, prior to making it as a Rock star, began when he escaped from East to West Germany as a legally blind 4-year-old.

Producer Gabriel Mekler suggested their new name, taken from a Herman Hesse novel. Their debut single, 'Sookie Sookie', flopped, but its follow-up, 'Born To Be Wild', rose to US No.2, propelling *Steppenwolf* (1968) into the US Top 10. 'Magic Carpet Ride', released in November 1968, narrowly missed the top of the US chart, as did *Steppenwolf The Second* (1968). Five months later, *At Your Birthday Party* (1969) also entered the US Top 10.

This busy schedule was accompanied by live appearances, notably at festivals alongside the likes of The Grateful Dead and Jimi Hendrix. After the concept album *Monster* (1970), the band began to decline, eventually splitting in 1978. However, Kay began touring with a new line-up of Steppenwolf and, despite long-serving drummer Edmonton's tragic death in a car accident in 1993, the band are still a popular attraction in the 90s.

Read *John Kay: Magic Carpet Ride* (1998), John Kay & John Einarson

Fan The Wolfpack, PO Box 271495, Nashville, TN 37227-1495, USA

Surf www.steppenwolf.com/

STEREO MC's

WHO Vocals **Rob B** (b. Robert Birch, 11 Jun 1961, Nottingham, England), DJ/producer **The Head** (b. Nick Hallam, 11 Jun 1960, Nottingham), vocals **Cath Coffey** (b. Catherine Muthomi Coffey, 1965, Kenya), drums **Owen If** (b. Ian Frederick Rossiter, 20 Mar 1959, Newport, Wales)

WHEN 1987–

WHERE London, England

WHAT The big boys of British Rap

While many US Rap stars mask poverty with ostentatious status symbols, Stereo MC's are a model of level-headed frugality. Nick Hallam and Rob Birch founded their Gee Street studio and label with money they were given to leave their London flat and, instead of using a backing band, travelled to early gigs on buses with bags of tapes.

When Gee Street caught the eye of the 4th & Broadway label, they recorded the debut Stereo MC's album *33–45–78* (1989) on a shoestring budget with DJ Cesare, drummer Owen If and backing singer Cath Coffey. In 1990, the Stereos' 'Elevate My Mind' was the first British Rap record to reach the US R&B chart. Back home, the emergent Indie Dance scene (they supported Happy Mondays in the USA) and a hook-up with The Jungle Brothers ensured ultimate hipness for *Supernatural* (1990) and remixes for the likes of U2, PM Dawn, Queen Latifah, Disposable Heroes Of Hiphoprisy, Monie Love and Electronic.

Acclaimed live shows – they assembled a furious live band (including singers Andrea Bedassie and Verona Davis) and were one of the (then) few Rap outfits to play Rock festivals – paved the way for 1992's breakthrough *Connected*, a UK No.2 which spawned the smashes 'Connected', 'Step It Up', 'Creation' and 'Ground Level' and won them BRITs for Best Group and Best Album. While Hallam and Birch set up music publisher Spirit Songs (who signed Finley Quaye), the Stereos confirmed their Rock star status by taking an eternity to record *Connected*'s follow-up. "They are," a spokesperson told *Q* magazine in 1997, "very keen not to repeat themselves." However, remixes for Madonna ('Frozen') and The Jungle Brothers ('Jungle Brother') in 1998 confirmed that the Stereos were at least still alive.

Surf www.stereomcs.co.uk

STEREOLAB

WHO Vocals/keyboards **Laetitia Sadier** (b. 6 May 1968), vocals/guitar keyboards **Mary Hansen**, guitar/keyboards **Tim Gane** (b. 12 Jul 1964), bass **Richard Harrison**, drums **Andy Ramsay**, keyboards **Morgane Lhote**

WHEN 1990–

WHERE London, England

WHAT Space-age bachelor pad music

Obscure Krautrock, Samba, Bossanova, movie soundtracks, the avant-garde, Marxism, Moogs, Farfisa organs and complicated electronic gadgetry are just some of the contents of Stereolab's workshop – tools for their experimental space-age Pop.

Built around a nucleus of Tim Gane (formerly of Indie boys McCarthy), Laetitia Sadier (his girlfriend, also an ex-McCarthyist), Mary Hansen and Andy Ramsay, Stereolab emerged in 1991 with the splendid 'Super 45' on their own Duophonic Ultra High Frequency Disks label. Early, hard-to-find releases were compiled on 1992's *Switched On*, issued simultaneously with debut album *Peng!*.

Thrown in the 'Shoegazing' bin with Lush, Chapterhouse and Ride (though not quite in their league commercially), Stereolab built a cult following through their 'Lab Report' concerts. With help from Microdisney/High Llamas guitarist Sean O'Hagan (with whom Ramsay and Gane collaborated on 1997's *Turn On*), they blossomed in 1993 with *The Groop Played Space Age Batchelor Pad Music, Transient Random Noise Bursts With Announcements* and the near-hit 'French Disko' – also their first US releases, courtesy of a deal with Elektra. Meanwhile, Sadier contributed Jane Birkin-esque French mumbling to Blur's 'To The End' (1994) and Stereolab continued their blitz of mini-releases (there are far too many to mention here) with the 'Music For The Amorphous Body Study Centre' EP (a soundtrack for an interactive art exhibit by Charles Long), and released the patchy *Mars Audiac Quintet* (1995) – an overlong foray into poppier territory .

Having compiled more of their complex history on 1995's *Refried Ectoplasm*, Stereolab returned triumphant with help from Tortoise's John McEntire on the excellent *Emperor Tomato Ketchup* (1996), 'Flourescences' EP and the Drum 'n' Bass-influenced *Dots And Loops* (1997).

(fan) Duophonic Ultra High Frequency Disks, PO Box 3787, London, SE22 9DZ, UK

(surf) www.elektra.com/alternative_club/sterolab.stereolab.html

STEREOPHONICS

WHO Vocals/guitar **Kelly Jones** (b. 3 Jun 1974, Aberdare, Wales), bass **Richard Jones** (b. 23 May 1974, Aberdare), drums **Richard Cable** (b. 19 May 1970, Aberdare)

WHEN 1996–

WHERE Cwmaman, Mid-Glamorgan, Wales

WHAT Indie Rock eloquence

If you've heard their music, it's no surprise to discover that Stereophonics come from a small town. Their sturdy Indie Rock is distinguished by lyrics telling of the tensions common to any place where everyone knows everyone else. Two of Kelly Jones' evocative word-portraits of outsiders featured on their debut 'Looks Like Chaplin'/'More Life In A Tramp's Vest' (1996), which – reissued in May 1997 – became Stereophonics' first Top 40 hit.

The hits continued in 1997 with 'Traffic', 'A Thousand Trees' and a 1998 reissue of their second single, 'Local Boy In The Photograph'. Extensive touring helped Stereophonics prove the truth of their album's title, *Word Gets Around*. Entering the UK chart at No.6, it went silver by Christmas 1997. Stereophonics' swift success was recognized in the 1998 BRIT awards when they were named Best Newcomer.

(fan) Stereophonics, PO Box 5594, Newbury RG18 9YH, UK

(surf) vzone.virgin.net/nigel.sachdev/phonics.html

CAT STEVENS ✪

WHO b. Steven Demetri Georgiou, 21 Jul 1947, London, England

WHAT Confessional singer/songwriter

Cat Stevens was discovered by producer and ex-Springfield Mike Hurst. His early, idiosyncratic hits included 'I Love My Dog' (1966) and 1967's 'Matthew And Son' and he appeared on one of the last of the great Pop package tours with Engelbert Humperdinck, The Walker Brothers and Jimi Hendrix. Taken out of circulation by tuberculosis in 1968, he returned with a more thoughtful style.

His first three albums – 1970's *Mona Bone Jakon* and *Tea For The Tillerman* (featuring his best song, 'Father And Son') and 1971's *Teaser And The Firecat* – form the heart of his best work: fragile tunes about dashed hopes and dreams of better times.

These albums produced the hits 'Lady D'Arbanville', 'Moon Shadow' and his version of the traditional hymn, 'Morning Has Broken', and launched Stevens in America. Other artists have covered his songs with arrangements that, surprisingly, often improved on the originals: The Tremeloes' 'Here Comes My Baby', Jimmy Cliff's 'Wild World', Rod Stewart and PP Arnold's 'The First Cut Is The Deepest' and Boyzone's 'Father And Son'.

His best-sellers – 1972's US No.1 *Catch Bull At Four*, 1973's *Foreigner* and 1974's *Buddha And The Chocolate Box* – hinted at disillusionment with the Pop life. In 1977, he embraced Islam, took the name Yusuf Islam and retired to run a Muslim school.

He agreed to appear at Live Aid with a specially written a cappella song, 'The End', but Elton John over-ran and squeezed him out. A trip to Iraq to save British Muslim hostages just before the Gulf War, a religious album, *The Lifes Of The Last Prophet* (1995), charity concerts in Bosnia (1997) and a new song, 'The Little Ones', on Muslim peace album *I Have No Cannons That Roar* (1998) have since signalled his dedication to the cause.

(read) *Cat Stevens* (1985), Chris Charlesworth

(surf) catstevens.com

SHAKIN' STEVENS ◎

WHO b. Michael Barratt, 4 Mar 1948, Ely, Cardiff, Wales

WHAT Most successful 80s UK singles chart performer

Before signing solo with Epic Records worldwide in 1978, Shaky had successfully toured for years with his band The Sunsets, and starred in Jack Good's multi-award-winning musical *Elvis*, which ran for 19 months in London's West End. His 1980 hits, 'Hot Dog' and 'Marie, Marie', kicked off a run of 31 smashes in that decade, making him the most successful UK singles chart star of the 80s. Included in this run were four No.1s – 1981's 'This Ole House' and 'Green Door', 1982's 'Oh Julie' and 1985's 'Merry Christmas Everyone' – and the album *Shaky* (1981) also topped the chart.

Shaky's vocal capabilities have enabled him to cover various musical styles, from Country, Rock, Cajun and R&B to straight-forward Rock 'n' Roll. He has collaborated with Bonnie Tyler, Hank Marvin, Roger Taylor and Albert Lee and his work has been covered by artists including Eddie Raven ('A Letter To You') and Sylvia ('Cry Just A Little Bit'), both Nashville No.1s. In 1982, Barry Manilow had a US hit with the Shaky-penned classic 'Oh Julie'.

Hit albums and singles continued well into the 90s, confirming his enduring popularity as a chart star and as an exceptional live performer worldwide.

(fan) Shaky's News Club, 15 Campie House, Colney Hatch Lane, Muswell Hill, London N10 1AR, UK

(surf) www3.mistral.co.uk/steve.m/

AL STEWART

WHO b. 5 Sep 1945, Glasgow, Scotland

WHAT Underrated Folk troubadour

Always the bridesmaid, never the bride, Al Stewart is overlooked and underbought, despite his excellent output. Stewart started out playing in The Sabres with future radio star Tony Blackburn then – having flipped for Bob Dylan – moved to London where residencies at hip clubs Bunjies and Les Cousins established him as an important part of mid-60s Folk. He was distinguished by his radical material: honest accounts of relationships and angry rants at society which spilled from *Bedsitter Images* (1967) and *Love Chronicles* (1969). The latter's 18-minute title track (starring Led Zeppelin's Jimmy Page) typified Stewart's passionate and unflinchingly frank songwriting, but was avoided by radio owing to its 'shocking' use of the word 'fuck'.

Unlike his contemporaries Cat Stevens, Sandy Denny and Paul Simon (with whom Al briefly lived and almost bought 'I Am A Rock', 'Homeward Bound' and 'Sound Of Silence' from), Stewart's critical acclaim failed to translate into major sales. *Zero She Flies* (1970) was his first album to chart, but *Orange* (1972) and *Past, Present And Future* (1974) were crashing flops.

Then, amazingly, Stewart came through with 1975's US hit *Modern Times* and 1977's unashamedly Pop *Year Of The Cat* which, led by its Top 10 title track, took Stewart into the US Top 5 and platinum sales. *Time Passages* (1978) also went US Top 10. In LA, Stewart was reportedly one of the many victims of an unstable Phil Spector, whose bodyguards stepped in to protect poor Al. But his brush with Pop superstardom was brief: though *24 Carrots* (1980), *Indian Summer Live* (1981), *Russians And Americans* (1984), *Last Days Of The Century* (1988), *Rhymes In Rooms* (1992), *Famous Last Words* (1994) and *Between The Wars* (1995) were US successes, they were overshadowed in Britain by compilations like *Chronicles – The Best Of Al Stewart* (1991).

Fan The Chronicles, 1 Whitenap Close, Romsey, S051 8RT, UK

Surf www.fish.com/music/al_stewart/

ROD STEWART ⊙⊙⊙⊙⊙⊙⊙⊙⊙☆☆

WHO b. Roderick David Stewart, 10 Jan 1945, London, England

WHAT Gravelly-voiced Rock crooner

Having attended North London's William Grimshaw school with Kinks brothers Ray and Dave Davies, Rod Stewart had trials for Brentford Football Club in 1961 and also joined local band The Raiders. At an audition, producer Joe Meek was extremely dismissive of the 16-year-old's singing abilities. Soon afterwards, Stewart busked around Europe with Folk singer Wizz Jones. Their adventures, later immortalized in 'Every Picture Tells A Story', ended with the pair being deported from Spain for vagrancy.

Now a bit of a Beatnik – playing Folk music at anti-nuclear rallies – Stewart worked as a gravedigger and undertaker before joining R&B outfits Jimmy Powell & The Five Dimensions in 1963 (on harmonica and vocals), then The Hoochie Coochie Men in 1964. He released his first solo single, 'Good Morning Little Schoolgirl', in October 1964, then united with Long John Baldry

in the R&B act Steampacket, performing covers of Otis Redding, Wilson Pickett and his lifelong hero Sam Cooke.

In 1966 he spent a few months with singer Beryl Marsden and future Fleetwood Mac musos Mick Fleetwood and Peter Green in Shotgun Express, failed to replace Paul Jones in Manfred Mann, then ended up alongside future Face Ron Wood in The Jeff Beck Group from 1967–1969. Their seminal *Truth* (1968) influenced Heavy Metal generally and Led Zeppelin in particular, as well as containing Stewart's excellent ballad 'I've Been Drinking'.

Originally so prone to stage fright that he had to be coaxed from behind the speakers, all the ingredients of Stewart's success – the stage presence, the vulnerable, gravelly voice and the cockatoo hairstyle – were in place by the time he and Wood left to help form The Faces in 1969, with Stewart also planning a solo career. He released *An Old Raincoat Won't Ever Let You Down* (1969), featuring 'Handbags And Gladrags', and *Gasoline Alley* (1970) before *Every Picture Tells A Story* (1971) – the first of six consecutive UK No.1 albums – made him an international star.

The early 70s albums, with their mix of ballads, Dylan and Motown covers and the odd Rocker, were Stewart's most creative work – pulling together the influences of his earlier career in Soul, R&B and especially Folk. He also demonstrated his skill at writing sensitive, if sentimental, lyrics – most apparently on 'Mandolin Wind' (a tale of romantic love in the freezing Mid-west, actually written in Muswell Hill), the gloriously nostalgic 'You Wear It Well' from 1972's *Never A Dull Moment* and 'Farewell' from 1974's *Smiler*. Musically, the upbeat, folky feel of much of the songs on these albums was a big nod towards mid-60s Dylan. In acknowledgement of his other big influence, Sam Cooke, the under-rated *Smiler* also contained the superb medley 'Bring It On Home to Me'/'You Send Me'.

The year 1975 was a watershed for Stewart. He moved to LA, started a relationship with Britt Ekland, left The Faces and made the patchy *Atlantic Crossing*, with its ubiquitous hit, 'Sailing'. Bar *A Night On The Town* (1976) and its poignant account of a New York gay murder, 'The Killing of Georgie (Parts 1&2)', the next ten years were a mixture of gossip-column lifestyle, leggy blondes and bland music. Disappointing albums like *Footloose And Fancy Free* (1977) and *Blondes Have More Fun* (1978) – plus Stewart's kitsch persona during these butt-waggling, leopard-skin-trousered years – lead critics to accuse him of wasting his talent.

Married to Hollywood socialite Alana Hamilton, he frequently put his social life before his music from 1979–1984. Although *Foolish Behaviour* (1980), *Tonight I'm Yours* (1981), *Body Wishes* (1983) and *Camouflage* (1984) were disappointing, most were hits. The double A-side 'I Don't Want To Talk About It'/'The First Cut Is The Deepest' kept The Sex Pistols' 'God Save The Queen' off the UK No.1 in 1977, while 1978's Disco anthem 'Da Ya Think I'm Sexy' and 1983's 'Baby Jane' were both UK chart-toppers.

After *Every Beat Of My Heart* (1986), Stewart rehabilitated his image with the box set *Storyteller – The Complete Anthology 1964–1990*, and his most successful UK album since 1976, 1991's *Vagabond Heart* (also US No.1), including the hits 'Downtown Train' and 'It Takes Two', a duet with Tina Turner. Live, Stewart often dedicated the album's cover of Van Morrison's 'Have I Told You Lately' to his second wife, model Rachel Hunter, whom he'd married in December 1990 after five years with Kelly Emberg.

In the mid-90s, Stewart emerged as a family man, watching his adopted Scotland football team, recording their Euro 96 team 'anthem' 'Purple Heather' and playing the game himself. A well-received acoustic album with Ron Wood – 1993's *Unplugged*…

And Seated – helpfully compiled the highlights of his incredibly successful career. *A Spanner In The Works* was released in 1995, and *When We Were The New Boys* (1998) boasted songs by Oasis, Primal Scream, Nick Lowe, Graham Parker and Ron Sexsmith.

READ *Rod Stewart – Vagabond Heart* (1993), Geoffrey Guiliano

FAN Smiler, PO Box 475, Morden, Surrey SM4 6AT, UK

SURF members.aol.com/smilerfrg/rod/sminfo.htm

Stiff

Founded in 1976 by Dave Robinson and Jake Riviera, Stiff became the beer-soaked home of Pub Rock legends like Dr Feelgood, Nick Lowe, Dave Edmunds and Ian Dury and New Wave prophets The Damned, Wreckless Eric and Elvis Costello. As the UK's leading Indie label, few argued with their T-shirt slogan "If It Ain't Stiff It Ain't Worth A Fuck" – especially as the Stiff gang were a renowned gang of hell-raising fruitcakes as their chaotic 1977 Stiffs Greatest Hits – Live! package tour proved. The label's biggest 70s successes were Ian Dury's New Boots And Panties!! (1979) and Elvis Costello's My Aim Is True (1978), but after Riviera's departure to form Radar, Robinson added hitmakers like Lene Lovich, Jona Lewie, Madness and Graham Parker. Stiff's sad demise came when it was incorporated into Island in 1984, but its legend lives on as a much-loved loony bin of a label.

STEPHEN STILLS

WHO b. 3 Jan 1945, Dallas, Texas, USA

WHAT Workaholic, guitarist, singer/songwriter

Childhood in the southern states of America and adolescence in Panama and Costa Rica grounded Stephen Stills in Blues, Latin and Country music. In 1966, after a year with New York band The Au Go-Go Singers and an audition for The Monkees (his friend Peter Tork got the job instead), he and Neil Young formed Buffalo Springfield. When they split in 1968, he attained superstardom with Crosby, Stills, Nash & Young. A flourishing solo career began with *Stephen Stills* (1970). Jamming partners Jimi Hendrix and Eric Clapton guested on the album, which peaked at US No.3 and included the much-covered hit 'Love The One You're With'.

The less inspiring *Stephen Stills 2* (1971) preceded Stills' most ambitious project, Manassas – another supergroup (named after a town steeped in American Civil War history), with Dallas Taylor, Chris Hillman, Al Perkins, Paul Harris, Calvin Samuels and Joe Lala. *Manassas* (1972) explored a variety of styles and made US No.4, though *Down The Road* (1973) signalled the band's demise.

Stills' best writing seemed reserved for CSN but *Stills* (1975), *Illegal Stills* (1976) and, with old sparring partner Neil Young, *Long May You Run* (1976) had their moments. *Thoroughfare Gap* (1978) and *Right By You* (1984) made doomed bids for hipness, but an acoustic return to basics characterized *Stills Alone* (1991).

In 1997, Stills became the first to be inducted into The Rock And Roll Hall Of Fame twice, for his work with Buffalo Springfield and CSN. He made an implausible entrance into Rap in 1998 by revamping Springfield's 'For What It's Worth' with Public Enemy.

FAN 2 Mill Lane, North Kelsey, Market Rasen, LN7 6ED, UK

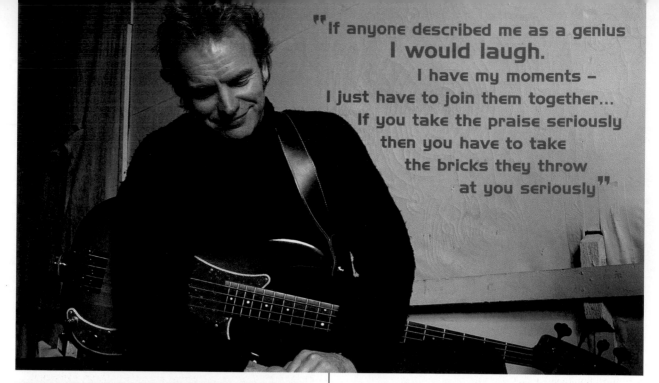

"If anyone described me as a genius I would laugh. I have my moments – I just have to join them together... If you take the praise seriously then you have to take the bricks they throw at you seriously"

STING ◉ ◉

WHO b. Gordon Sumner, 2 Oct 1951, Wallsend, Tyne and Wear, England

WHAT Adult Pop Adonis

The Police had yet to split when Sting began his first solo album in early 1985. Their management were adamant the band was still together; Sting was guarded: "In my mind I'd already left The Police… and I never intended to go back." He'd tested the waters with 1982's 'Spread A Little Happiness', recorded for the TV film *Brimstone And Treacle* – one of his early acting ventures. Now he recruited top-flight musicians, including saxophonist Branford Marsalis – a return to his pre-Police roots in Newcastle's jazzy Last Exit. *The Dream Of The Blue Turtles* (1985) spawned the hits 'If You Love Somebody Set Them Free', 'Russians' and 'Fortress Around Your Heart'. Sting's social concern was evident in 'Russians', which addressed the threat of nuclear annihilation, 'Children's Crusade', which united the poppies commemorating casualties of war with the opium trade and heroin and 'We Work The Black Seam', drawing on Sting's upbringing in England's industrial north-east.

A tour led to 1986's live *Bring On The Night*. Two other 1985 events raised Sting's profile: his Live Aid show and his plaintive intro ("I want my MTV") to Dire Straits' 'Money For Nothing'.

In June 1986, The Police reunited for a show in Atlanta in support of Amnesty International, then attempted to follow up 1983's *Synchronicity*. The plan, to reinterpret Police favourites, was abandoned when the sessions collapsed in what Sting described as "a nightmare of ego and recrimination and fighting". The affair confirmed Sting was now a solo artist.

…*Nothing Like The Sun* (1987) sealed his pre-eminence among adult-oriented stars, topping the UK chart, entering the US Top 10 and being voted Best British Album at the BRIT awards. Its title taken from a Shakespeare sonnet, …*Nothing Like The Sun* reaffirmed his idealistic streak, exemplified by the tender 'They Dance Alone', which honoured victims of repression in Chile. Critics found him preachy and pretentious, but as a Pop craftsman he retained the common touch; among the album's best-loved tracks is 'Englishman In New York', written for flamboyant eccentric Quentin Crisp.

In 1986, Sting played the Artists Against Apartheid concert in London, and joined the Conspiracy Of Hope tour for Amnesty International with Bryan Adams, Bob Dylan and U2. He played a 1988 Wembley concert to mark the 70th birthday of Nelson Mandela, then – after another tour for Amnesty in 1988 (with Bruce Springsteen and Peter Gabriel) – was drawn to the plight of Brazilian Indians and the destruction of their rainforest habitat. He helped found The Rainforest Foundation, and visits to tribal villages became a feature of his image, leading him to wonder if his celebrity helped or hindered the campaign: "You're pointing at the moon, but people are looking at your finger".

After a lead role in *Stormy Monday* (1988), nothing – including *The Adventures Of Baron Munchausen* (1989) and *The Grotesque* (1995) – matched earlier acting roles such as *Quadrophenia* (1979) and *Dune* (1984). A stint in a 1989 production of Brecht/Weill's *The Threepenny Opera* in Washington, DC, received mixed reviews. Meanwhile, in 1988 he launched the Pangaea label, to showcase artists from outside the Rock mainstream.

He returned with 1991's *The Soul Cages*, a sombre work arising from the death of his father (his mother's death influenced …*Nothing Like The Sun*). Despite the jaunty hit 'All This Time', it remains his least approachable album, but he considers it his favourite. Another UK No.1, its sales of around 6 million matched most of his releases. Nevertheless, he adopted a lighter style for *Ten Summoner's Tales* (1993), its title a Chaucer-inspired pun on Sting's real name Gordon Sumner. Thanks to the hits 'If I Ever Lose My Faith In You' and 'Fields Of Gold', the album reached No.2 on both sides of the Atlantic and restored his reputation for tuneful sophistication.

Fields Of Gold: The Best Of Sting 1984–1994 (1994) contained two new hits: 'When We Dance' and 'This Cowboy Song'. He had even greater success with 'All For Love', from the movie *The Three Musketeers* (1993) and sang with Bryan Adams and Rod Stewart. *Mercury Falling* (1996) revisited *Ten Summoners' Tales*' thoughtful Pop with jazzy tendencies.

In 1995, it transpired that his accountant had cheated him of £6 million. But Sting's strong back catalogue alleviated worries for his solvency. More wealth was assured by Puff Daddy's 1997 hit 'I'll Be Missing You', a reworking of The Police's 'Every Breath You Take'. Citing a Country influence on recent cuts like 'This Cowboy Song', he duetted with singer Toby Keith at the Country Music Association's awards ceremony in Nashville in 1997. In 1998, he duetted with Aswad on a cut for *The X-Files* soundtrack.

🎵 **Fan** Sting, Bugle House, 21A Noel Street, London W1V 3PD, UK

🌐 **Surf** www.teleport.com/~aceface/Police.html

424

THE STONE ROSES

WHO Vocals **Ian Brown** (b. 20 Feb 1963, Ancoats, Greater Manchester, England), guitar **John Squire** (b. 24 Nov 1962, Broadheath, Greater Manchester), bass **Mani** (b. Gary Mountfield, 16 Nov 1962, Crumpsall, Greater Manchester), drums/vocals **Reni** (b. Alan Wren, 10 Apr 1964, Manchester)

WHEN 1984–1996

WHERE Manchester, England

WHAT The Rise And Fall Of Baggy Stardust

The Stone Roses changed British Rock forever. Fusing classic guitar Pop to Acid House attitude, they spearheaded the Manchester-centric 'Baggy' movement and laid the foundations for Britpop. But for years, The Stone Roses were Manchester's best-kept secret. Formed by schoolfriends Ian Brown and John Squire with Reni (replacement for the short-stayed Simon Wolstencroft, later of The Fall), Andy Couzens (bass) and Pete Garner (guitar), they cut the unremarkable 'So Young' (1985) and languished in obscurity. By 1987's much better 'Sally Cinnamon' on local label FM Revolver, Couzens and Garner were gone (the former to The High) and old friend Mani was on bass. But still the Roses struggled, despite a vast local following, legendary impromptu rave-like warehouse gigs and a cross-town graffiti campaign.

The band broke through in 1988. Signed to Silvertone Records, they released the stunning 'Elephant Stone' – a spine-tingling mix of Hendrixy wah-wah, Byrds-like jangle, hypnotic drums and deceptively cute vocals masking cynical lyrics. Produced by New Order's Peter Hook and dressed in one of John Squire's Pollock-esque paint-spattered sleeves, 'Elephant Stone' was a turning point for The Stone Roses and Britain's Indie scene.

Then *The Stone Roses* (1989) appeared. From the arrogant rumbles of 'I Wanna Be Adored', the sparkling 'She Bangs The Drums', the dreamy 'Waterfall' and its backwards counterpart 'Don't Stop', the bitter 'Elizabeth My Dear' ('Scarborough Fair' with anti-royalist lyrics), through the languid 'Sugar Spun Sister' and 'Shoot You Down', to the epic 'I Am The Resurrection', whose coda exploded with a breathtaking surge of guitars, it was a masterpiece of inspiration and overwhelming confidence.

But despite gushing reviews and cult sales ('She Bangs The Drums' dented the UK Top 40), the Roses failed to kill the monarchy, topple the government, legalize drugs or save the universe. Until 'What The World Is Waiting For'/'Fool's Gold' hit the UK Top 10, that is. Released late in 1989, 'Fool's Gold' was

another landmark: its sampled breaks, unashamedly funky wah-wah guitar and ten-ton bassline taught spotty Indie kids to dance overnight. It charted the same week in November as fellow Mancunians Happy Mondays' pivotal 'Madchester Rave On' EP (they both appeared on an electrifying edition of *Top Of The Pops*) and made Manchester the centre of the Dance/Rock crossover 'Baggy' (aka the Mondays-christened 'Madchester').

Lesser mortals like Inspiral Carpets and The Charlatans swept to power, paint-spattered 'Reni' Kangol hats and long-sleeve T-shirts became *de rigueur*, Mancunian slang like 'In the area' and 'Dish, nish, clish' became conversational fixtures and the unthinkable happened: flares came back in fashion.

Meanwhile, the Roses set their sights on legend. In 1990, avenging FM Revolver's unauthorized reissue of 'Sally Cinnamon', Brown, Squire, Reni and Mani gatecrashed their offices, splashed paint over desks, cars and staff and ended up in court amid fan pandemonium reminiscent of Mick Jagger and Keith Richards' 60s drug busts and T-shirts proclaiming "Ian Brown Is Innocent". These antics trailed their mega-concert on 27 May 1990 at Spike Island, a patch of waste ground between Manchester and Liverpool. The 30,000-strong crowd looked far bigger than it was and the organization, sound and performance were appalling, but it was the Roses' greatest moment. As fireworks during 'I Am The Resurrection' brought the

[circular graphic with text: second coming · MADCHESTER · SPIKE ISLAND · ELEPHANT STONE · seahorses · GOLD · FOOL'S GOLD · i wanna be adored · I AM THE RESURRECTION · BAGGY · the stone roses]

day to a climax, The Stone Roses became legends.

The triumph was short-lived. Mere weeks after Spike Island, 'One Love' hit the UK Top 10 but was clearly a weak 'Fool's Gold' re-tread. And, when they could have been conquering the USA, the Roses were in court again, battling out of their Silvertone contract. Freed from the label in early 1991, they signed to Geffen a year later for a reported £20 million. Then they disappeared. Years passed, punctuated only by press rumours of frivolous spending and drug abuse. Meanwhile, Silvertone cashed in with the rarities compilation *Turn Into Stone* (1992), the first in a series of retrospectives that also included *The Complete Stone Roses* (1995) and *Garage Flower* (1996).

By 1994, their sloth had exhausted the patience of all but the most devoted. But this was nothing compared to the crushing disappointment of the 'Voodoo Chile'-ish 'Love Spreads' and its Zep-heavy parent *Second Coming* (1994). Dominated by Squire's rockist widdling and tune-free songs, its highlights were few – the *Apocalypse Now*-ish opening of 'Breaking Into Heaven', the anthemic 'Ten Storey Love Song', Brown's 'Straight To The Man' and the ambitiously electronic 'Begging You'.

Although the album made UK No.4, a backlash began. It was exacerbated by Reni's mysterious departure on the eve of a tour (he was replaced by sessioneer Robbie Maddix) and a cancelled

appearance at Glastonbury 1995 (owing to Squire's broken collarbone), and reached a crescendo when Squire quit in spring 1996 to form The Seahorses.

Meanwhile, as speculative obituaries circulated in the press, Brown and Mani continued with Maddix, recently recruited keyboard player Nigel Ipinson and guitarist Aziz Ibrahim. But vultures gathered for their woeful Reading festival headliner, which was ruined by Brown's injured cat-like howl. Within weeks, Mani jumped ship for Primal Scream (he graced their 1997 return-to-form *Vanishing Point*) and Brown announced The Stone Roses were no more. He returned solo (with help from Reni, Mani, Ipinson and Ibrahim) in 1998 with the splendid *Unfinished Monkey Business* and a rash of anti-Squire outbursts in the press.

Despite their messy demise, the Roses still bloom in the hearts of many, as proved when their debut finished second only to The Beatles' *Sgt. Pepper's Lonely Hearts Club Band* in a 1998 poll of the British public's favourite albums.

 The Stone Roses (And The Resurrection Of British Pop) (1997), John Robb

 www.freestyle.com/roses/

STONE TEMPLE PILOTS ✪

WHO Vocals **Scott Weiland** (b. 27 Oct 1967, Santa Cruz, California, USA), guitar **Dean DeLeo** (b. 23 Aug 1961, New Jersey, USA), bass **Robert DeLeo** (b. 2 Feb 1966, New Jersey), drums **Eric Kretz** (b. 7 Jun 1966, Santa Cruz)

WHEN 1987–

WHERE San Diego, California, USA

WHAT The grandchildren of Grunge

No sooner had Grunge crushed the 80s' Glam Metal hordes than it spawned its own copycats. Alice In Chains and Soundgarden could reasonably claim that they were punkifying Black Sabbath riffs long before Nirvana came along, but Stone Temple Pilots had fewer defences: they emerged in the wake of Pearl Jam, hired Pearl Jam's producer and, oddly enough, sounded exactly like Pearl Jam.

Their origins were much more interesting: singer Scott Weiland and bassist Robert DeLeo met at a Black Flag gig and realized they were dating the same woman; DeLeo's guitar-playing brother Dean was enlisted out of desperation. With drummer Eric Kretz, they debuted live as Mighty Joe Young in 1990, before – to avoid the legal wrath of a bluesman who shared their Mighty moniker – changing their name to the meaningless Stone Temple Pilots.

Helmed by Pearl Jam producer Brendan O'Brien, and boasting the hits 'Sex Type Thing' and 'Plush', *Core* (1992) sold millions and paved the way for 1994's credibility-confirming US No.1 *Purple*. Even critics had to applaud the poppy hit 'Interstate Love Song' and the Pilots appeared on 1995's Led Zeppelin tribute *Enconium*. But success set Weiland on the Kurt Cobain path to immortality: he befriended Courtney Love, appeared on the Love-masterminded *Tank Girl* movie soundtrack (1995) and was subsumed by heroin.

Critical opinion finally matched public acclaim on the platinum-selling *Tiny Music... Songs From The Vatican Giftshop* (1996) and the Pilots were invited to support their heroes Kiss.

But Weiland's addiction made it impossible for them to continue; the remaining trio flopped dismally with a 1997 album as Talk Show, while their former frontman (ironically) flourished in 1998 with his solo album *12 Bar Blues* and cuts on the *Great Expectations* soundtrack.

 Stone Temple Pilots (1995), Mick Wall & Malcolm Dome

 www.stonetemplepilots.com/

THE STOOGES

WHO Vocals **Iggy Pop** (b. James Jewel Osterberg, 21 Apr 1947, Ypsilanti, Michigan, USA), guitar **Ron Asheton** (b. 17 Jul 1948, Washington, DC, USA), bass **Dave Alexander** (b. 3 Jun 1947, Ann Arbor, Michigan, d. 10 Feb 1975, Detroit, Michigan), drums **Scott Asheton** (b. 16 Aug 1949, Washington, DC)

WHEN 1967–1974

WHERE Detroit, Michigan, USA

WHAT Proto-Punk Garage Rockers

Iggy (a nickname from his first band The Iguanas) Osterberg returned to his native Michigan after leaving Chicago band the Prime Movers to form the MC5-inspired Psychedelic Stooges with Dave Alexander and brothers Ron and Scott Asheton. They debuted in Ann Arbor on Halloween 1967, scaring the hippie audience with raw Rock while Iggy screamed, stage-dived and gouged himself with broken glass. Critical opinion was divided, although most despised them.

In 1969, signed to Elektra and streamlined to The Stooges, their menacing, self-titled debut album was recorded in four days by Velvet Underground bassist John Cale and included their definitive statement, the delightfully primitive and aggressive 'I Wanna Be Your Dog'. *Fun House* (1970), described as "Osterberg's fifth symphony", saw the addition of saxophonist Steve Mackay and Iggy's permanent surname 'Pop', while the unreliable Alexander was replaced first by Zeke Zettner, then Jimmy Reca. Short-stayed second guitarist Bill Cheatham was replaced by James Williamson before the group imploded in 1971, reportedly nursing heroin habits.

After a year mowing lawns and improving his golf – yes, *golf* – in Florida, Iggy started again in 1972 in the care of David Bowie's manager Tony DeFries. The revived Iggy & The Stooges (Iggy, the Asheton brothers and Williamson) joined CBS, and recorded *Raw Power* (1973) in London. Back in the USA, internal bickering and a chaotic six-month tour spelled the end, with Iggy back on drugs and a bewildering procession of new personnel, including keyboardists Robert Sheff and Scott Thurston and future Blondie bassist Nigel Harrison.

By the time Iggy entered a mental hospital in 1974, it was all over. Alexander died in 1975. Ron Asheton formed The New Order (not the UK group), then Destroy All Monsters with several ex-MC5ers and collaborated with US Indie journeymen Thurston Moore and Steve Shelley (Sonic Youth), Mark Arm (Mudhoney), Don Fleming (Gumball), Mike Watt and Jim Dunbar as The Wylde Rattz for two cuts on 1998's *Velvet Goldmine* soundtrack (the Glam Rock movie produced by REM's Michael Stipe). Meanwhile, the solo Iggy was hailed as a Punk hero. The posthumous *Metallic KO* (1976) was The Stooges' last record.

THE STRANGLERS

WHO Vocals/guitar **Hugh Cornwell** (b. 28 Aug 1948, London, England), keyboards **Dave Greenfield** (b. 29 Mar 1949, Brighton, Sussex), bass **Jean Jacques Burnel** (b. 21 Feb 1952, London), drums **Jet Black** (b. Brian Duffy, 26 Aug 1938, Ilford, Essex, England)

WHEN 1974–

WHERE Guildford, Surrey, England

WHAT Punk's pensionable meninblack

Jet Black was a successful businessman in the early 70s – running an ice-cream business, a liquor store and a domestic equipment company – when he answered a *Melody Maker* ad for a drummer for Wanderlust, headed by research biochemist-turned-guitarist Hugh Cornwell. Formed in Sweden where Cornwell was doing a Ph.D., Wanderlust moved into Black's liquor store in Guildford.

Black, Cornwell, guitarist Hans Wärmling and Jean Jacques Burnel played under various names before registering The Stranglers in 1974. Wärmling exited in 1975 and Dave Greenfield joined, answering their ad for a "Soft Rock band" keyboardist.

Sexist (seemingly), psychedelic (in a Doorsy sort of way) and clearly older than The Clash (hence their self-mocking moniker for secret gigs, The Old Codgers), they were utterly unsuited to Punk. But they graduated from support slots with Ramones and Patti Smith in 1976 to spectacular success in 1977: scoring UK Top 10 hits with 'Peaches', 'Something Better Change', 'No More Heroes', *Stranglers IV (Rattus Norvegicus)* and *No More Heroes*.

Despite a well-earned reputation for trouble – rioting at gigs, Burnel bashing critics and Cornwell being jailed for drugs – the band's success continued unabated with 1978's *Black And White* and 1979's *Live (X Cert)* and 3D-sleeved *The Raven*. But *The Gospel According To The Meninblack* (1981) spent only five weeks on the chart – a disaster after months-long residencies by earlier efforts. "Unanimous slagging," Burnel remembered in UK music magazine *Select*. "Even the fans said it was fucking horrible."

They were saved by 'Golden Brown', a weirdly waltzing smash from *La Folie* (1981). Its harpsichord-powered music eclipsed its drug-fuelled lyric, making it a favourite for radio programmers ever since. While their Punk contemporaries stumbled and fell, The Stranglers coasted comfortably through the 80s with *Aural Sculpture* (1984), *Dreamtime* (1986), *All Live And All Of The Night* (1988) and *10* (1990). But Cornwell – who'd charted alone in 1988 with *Wolf* – left for a low-key solo career in 1990 and *Greatest Hits 1977-1990* became a hugely successful epitaph to their heyday.

With singer Paul Roberts, ex-Vibrators guitarist John Ellis and new drummer Tikake Tobe, The Stranglers continued to tour – they celebrated the 21st anniversary of their record deal with a 1997 show at London's Royal Albert Hall – and even scraped the chart with *Stranglers In The Night* (1992) and *About Time* (1995). However, they achieved their highest latter-day profile when Elastica pilfered 'No More Heroes' for their 1995 hit 'Waking Up'. The band's most recent studio album was 1997's *Written In Red*.

read *No Mercy: The Authorised And Uncensored Biography Of The Stranglers* (1997), David Buckley

Fan PO Box 50, Houghton-le-Spring, Tyne and Wear, DH5 5YP, UK

surf sky.wwdc.com/~adrian/stranglers/

THE STRAY CATS

WHO Vocals/guitar **Brian Setzer** (b. 10 Apr 1959, Long Island, New York, USA), bass **Lee Rocker** (b. Lee Drucker, 1961), drums **Slim Jim Phantom** (b. Jim McDonnell, 20 Mar 1961)

WHEN 1979–1983

WHERE Massapequa, New York, USA

WHAT Rockabilly revisionists

When Punk swept away the indulgence of Prog and returned Rock to its roots, some people took it all too far. The Stray Cats – three young men from suburban America – inexplicably regressed to previous lives: those of 50s Rock 'n' Rollers. Moving to London (presumably because you could still get frothy coffee there) in 1980, they signed to Arista and jumped 'n' jived all over the UK hit parade with 'Runaway Boys' (1980), 'Rock This Town' (1981), 'Stray Cat Strut' (1981) and *Stray Cats* (1981).

Gonna Ball (1982) failed to scale such heights while, Stateside, *Rant 'n' Rave* (1983) yielded the bouncing babies 'Sexy+17' and 'I Won't Stand In Your Way' before expiring at a lowly No.14. Then they split. Phantom (momentarily famous for marrying Britt Ekland) and Rocker joined ex-Bowie sidekick Earl Slick in Phantom, Rocker & Slick. Setzer made ignored solo albums *The Knife Feels Like Justice* (1986) and *Live Nude Guitars* (1988), played Eddie Cochran brilliantly in 1987's Richie Valens biopic *La Bamba* and helmed the swinging Brian Setzer Orchestra. However, the Cats reunions *Rock Therapy* (1986), *Blast Off* (1989), *Let's Go Faster* (1991) and *Choo Choo Hot Fish* (1992) proved uneventful.

BARBRA STREISAND
◉ ◎ ◉ ☆ ☆ ☆ ☆ ☆ ☆ ☆ ☆

WHO b. Barbara Joan Streisand, 24 Apr 1942, Brooklyn, New York, USA

WHAT One-woman army of singer, actress and entrepreneuse

Although Barbra Streisand's concert career was halted from 1967–1994 by stage fright (afflicting her after she forgot a lyric when singing to 135,000 in Central Park, New York) she became the highest-selling female recording artist ever. When *Higher Ground* (1997) topped the US chart 33 years after *People* (1964), she broke The Beatles' record time-span between No.1 albums.

Streisand was discovered via Broadway musicals, especially *Funny Girl* (1964). She had clear comic talent ('Second Hand Rose', 1966; *What's Up Doc?*, 1972), but won superstardom via US No.1s like 1973's 'The Way We Were', 1977's 'Evergreen (Love Theme From *A Star Is Born*)', 1979's 'No More Tears (Enough Is Enough)' (with Donna Summer), 1980's 'Woman In Love' (by Barry Gibb) and 1997's 'Tell Him' (with Celine Dion), and movies like 1968's *Funny Girl* and 1973's *The Way We Were*. She has constantly established 'firsts' for female artists – notably with *Yentl* (1983): she was the first woman to produce, direct, write and star in the same movie.

Fan All About Barbra, c/o Lynn Pounder, 17 Adrian Place, Peterlee, County Durham SR8 5SR, UK

surf www.barbra-streisand.com

With *Our Favourite Shop* (1985) stretching Weller's musical vocabulary, the group appeared at Live Aid and were involved with the ill-fated Red Wedge – a 1986 tour to raise awareness of England's Labour party among young voters. Negative press reaction dissuaded Weller from any further political involvement.

After 1986's live *Home And Abroad*, 1987's *The Cost Of Loving* continued the group's success, but began Weller's fall from grace with the music press, who condemned its earnest themes. The wilfully obscure short film *JerUSalem* (1987) drew a blank with press and fans, 1988's Muzak-like *Confessions Of A Pop Group* was eclipsed by 1989's hits set *The Singular Adventures Of The Style Council*, then their label Polydor took exception to their latest direction – slick Chicago House – and refused to release *Decades Of Modernism* (1989). The Council were dropped and soon split.

Weller continued solo, with White on drums, while Talbot has contributed to albums by Galliano and The Young Disciples, and made two albums with White. After leaving Weller, Lee resumed her solo career. Polydor released the retrospective *Here's Some That Got Away* (1993) and *The Style Council Collection* (1996).

(surf) ourworld.compuserve.com/homepages/wholepoint

THE STYLISTICS ⊙ ⊙

WHO Vocals **Russell Thompkins Jr** (b. 21 Mar 1951, Philadelphia, Pennsylvania, USA), vocals **Airrin Love** (b. 8 Aug 1949, Philadelphia), vocals **James Smith** (b. 16 Jun 1950, New York City, New York, USA), vocals **Herbie Murrell** (b. 27 Apr 1949, Lane, South Carolina, USA), vocals **James Dunn** (b. 4 Feb 1950, Philadelphia)

WHEN 1968–

WHERE Philadelphia, Pennsylvania, USA

WHAT Silky 70s Soul

If you were Prince in the early 70s, you probably wanted to be Sly Stone, but you were also movin' 'n' groovin' to the slinky sound of The Stylistics. Their lead singer Russell Thompkins Jr was an arresting figure: a lanky veteran of Philly club and theatre stages, he was tipped to become a basketball player before his astonishing falsetto voice took him into music. More important, however, was the patronage of Soul supremo Thom Bell, who'd perfected his sophisticated smooch with hits for The Delfonics – 'La-La Means I Love You' and '(Didn't I) Blow Your Mind This Time'.

The Stylistics' first hit was 1971's 'You're A Big Girl Now', but – thanks to Bell and co-writer Linda Creed – they carved a niche in Soul history with 'You Are Everything' and 'Betcha By Golly, Wow' from the fabulous *The Stylistics* (1971) and 'Break Up To Make Up' and 'I'm Stone In Love With You' from *Round 2* (1972). After their US peak, 'You Make Me Feel Brand New', Hugo Perretti and Luigi Creatore – who'd been producers in the 50s – replaced Bell.

Their domestic success plummeted, but The Stylistics had an astonishing nine consecutive Top 10 smashes in the UK, notably 1975's No.1 'Can't Give You Anything (But My Love)'. That year's *The Best Of The Stylistics* topped the UK chart too. After 1977, they gracefully gave way to Disco, and – after moving fruitlessly from label to label – hopped aboard the cabaret circuit. In 1996, Prince called 'Betcha By Golly, Wow' "the prettiest melody ever written" (adding "manyacherryburst…") and returned it to the UK chart.

THE STYLE COUNCIL ⊙

WHO Vocals/guitar **Paul Weller** (b. 25 May 1958, Woking, Surrey, England), keyboards **Mick Talbot** (b. 11 Sep 1958, London, England), drums **Steve White** (b. 31 May 1965, London), vocals **D.C. Lee** (b. 6 Jun 1961, London)

WHEN 1983–1989

WHERE London, England

WHAT The Soul spread in Paul Weller's success sandwich

Having split The Jam, Paul Weller binned rage and Rickenbackers and formed The Style Council with Mick Talbot, from London Mod band The Merton Parkas, and Steve White. Returning to the Soul and Jazz Weller had visited in The Jam's final days, The Style Council's upbeat debut 'Speak Like A Child' (1983) married social commentary to brassy R&B. The dreamy 'Long Hot Summer' from 1993's 'Paris Match' EP and 1984's Jazz-tinged *Cafe Bleu* (issued in a slightly different form as *My Ever Changing Moods* in the USA) underlined Weller's rejection of his Beatles/Small Faces roots, with keyboards and harmonies replacing the trademark bluster.

The Council's debut gig was at 1983's May Day Show For Jobs And Peace in Liverpool. In 1984, they played with Wham! singer D.C. Lee (now a Style Councillor and Weller's wife) at a striking miners' benefit in London. Weller sang with Band Aid and the band made 'Soul Deep' as Council Collective in aid of the miners.

Sub Pop

The only label brave enough to sign the elephantine Tad, Sub Pop developed Grunge from a quiet sidestreet to a super highway. Formed in 1986 by Bruce Pavitt (editor of a fanzine called <u>Subterranean Pop</u>) and promoter Jonathon Poneman, Sub Pop took its identity from Motown, its business acumen (and neat line in slogans) from Malcolm McLaren and its raw material from the rain-soaked city of Seattle. For years, Seattle had cultivated a bizarre and (in an industry where New York and LA ruled) ignored scene: Grunge. Sub Pop signed its brightest – Green River (who spawned Mudhoney and Pearl Jam), Tad, Dwarves, Soundgarden, L7 and, of course, Nirvana – and started a major-label goldrush. With their much-loved singles club, they released limited-edition gems like Nirvana's ultra-rare 'Love Buzz'. But Grunge's explosion in 1991 nearly killed the label: Nirvana had already decamped to DGC for the platinum-plated <u>Nevermind</u>, while L7, Soundgarden, Mudhoney and even perennial under-achievers Tad also swelled the coffers of other labels. However, the excellence of Sebadoh, Sunny Day Real Estate, Combustible Edison and Mark Lanegan kept Sub Pop afloat through the 90s.

SUEDE ◉

WHO Vocals **Brett Anderson** (b. 27 Sep 1967, Haywards Heath, Sussex, England), guitar **Richard Oakes** (b. 10 Oct 1976, Perivale, Middlesex, England), bass **Mat Osman** (b. 9 Oct 1967, Haywards Heath, Sussex), drums **Simon Gilbert** (b. 23 May 1965, Stratford-on-Avon, Warwickshire, England), keyboards **Neil Codling** (b. Stratford-on-Avon)

WHEN 1990–

WHERE London, England

WHAT Britpop's unstoppable fops

Before Oasis galloped to gargantuanness, Suede ruled Britpop. Their blend of David Bowie and The Smiths was an elegantly British riposte to Nirvana's global domination, making Suede the first group since Frankie Goes To Hollywood to become cover stars before they'd released more than ten minutes' music.

Divining that chart conquests would remain elusive if they continued as Jeff (their first, mid-80s band name), singer Brett Anderson and bassist Mat Osman left to study in London. They conceived the short-lived Suave & Elegant before recruiting guitarist (and Anderson's chief co-writer) Bernard Butler in 1989.

Named Suede after Morrissey's hit 'Suedehead', their ranks were bolstered by Anderson's girlfriend Justine Frischmann on guitar and ex-Smiths drummer Mike Joyce. Joyce played on 'Be My God'/'Art', the band's aborted debut for Indie label RML in 1990. When a dispute with RML led to the single being scrapped, Suede retreated to rehearsal rooms. By the time they signed to Nude in 1992, Simon Gilbert had replaced Joyce and Frischmann had quit to mastermind Elastica. Her subsequent entwining with Blur's Damon Albarn added an intriguing note of soap opera to the traditionally uneventful Indie scene.

Fuelled by a *Melody Maker* cover story declaring Suede the

'Best New Band In Britain' and the endorsement of Morrissey, they scored hits with 1992's 'The Drowners' and 'Metal Mickey'. The Bowie connection was cemented by Anderson's ambiguous declaration of bisexuality – a claim even less plausible, but just as headline-worthy, as Bowie's similar, early 70s declaration.

'Animal Nitrate' and *Suede* (1993) justified the hype. Anderson confirmed his talent for lascivious lyrics and anthemic choruses, and Butler took Smiths string-slinger Johnny Marr's floppy-fringed guitar-hero crown. But domestic acclaim – including winning the Mercury Music Prize for Best Album – meant little in the USA, where they were embarrassingly eclipsed by support act The Cranberries, and legal grumbling by a singer called Suede obliged them to be billed as The London Suede.

These strains contributed to disintegrating relations between Butler and his bandmates, and *Dog Man Star* (1994) coincided with the announcement that Butler had quit. When sales proved inconsequential, gleeful cynics derided the album's ambitiously orchestrated sound. However, while few tracks approached the breathtaking beauty of 'Stay Together' – a one-off hit in early 1994, omitted from the album – *Dog Man Star* remains a refreshing alternative to the parochial Britpop that rose in Suede's shadow. Most galling was the success of Blur and Elastica. Albarn's arch-enemy Noel Gallagher joined the fray by hailing Anderson as a lyricist *par excellence*.

While Butler sped through short-lived collaborations with All About Eve songstress Julianne Regan and vampy vocalist David McAlmont, Suede enlisted young guitarist Richard Oakes and, on keyboards, the pretty Neil Codling. While their underwhelming 'New Generation' (1995) was no match for McAlmont & Butler's explosive 'Yes', the stunning *Coming Up* (1996) rewarded the audiences who'd faithfully turned out while Oakes and Codling were road-tested. The introductory 'Trash' was their hardest hit to date, and smashes like 'The Beautiful Ones' struck a balance between the immediacy of *Suede* and ambition of *Dog Man Star*.

As the band returned to headlining and Top 10 status, relations thawed with Justine Frischmann (she guested with them at the Reading festival in 1997, playing an old Suede tune, 'Implement Yeah!') and Bernard Butler. The latter, who'd joined The Verve for about five seconds, scored with 'Stay' and 'Not Alone' from his solo debut *People Move On* (1998). Meanwhile, Suede gathered their B-sides for *Sci-Fi Lullabies* (1997) and an odd tribute came from Professor Charlemagne Nkobo of the University of Durban, who named a newly discovered species of lizard after Neil Codling!

READ *Suede: The Illustrated Biography* (1996), York Membery

SURF www.geocities.com/SunsetStrip/Palms/2560/index.htm

"We'd all be lying sick and feverish in our beds if we released a record we weren't happy with"

Brett Anderson

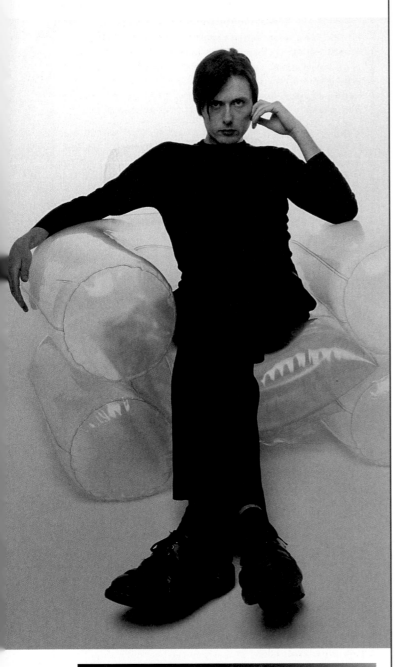

his home city, Reykjavik. It raised enough money for him to set up a multi-media arts organization, Bad Taste, and finance their debut, 'Birthday', by its Pop division, The Sugarcubes (née Kukl).

Erlingsson soon left but, thanks to 'Birthday' (1987) and *Life's Too Good* (1988), they acquired an international following. Gigs highlighted their distinctive mix of Dance, Rap and Indie Rock, and showcased the dynamic pairing of Björk and Einar Örn.

Here Today, Tomorrow, Next Week (1989) was widely regarded as over elaborate, and they waited until 1991 before releasing *Stick Around For Joy*. This, with the aptly titled 'Hit', restored their success, which continued with the remix album *It's It* (1992) and a guest spot on U2's 1992 American dates.

Björk's unique voice ensured she always received the most attention, and it was no surprise when she finally opted for solo stardom. But The Sugarcubes' collective talent is apparent on the 1998 retrospective, *The Great Crossover Potential*.

surf www.saga.is/badtaste/

SUICIDE

WHO Vocals **Alan Vega** (b. 1948), keyboards **Martin Rev**

WHEN 1970–1980

WHERE New York City, New York, USA

WHAT Electronic enemy-makers

Nobody liked Suicide. At least not when they were around. Years after their demise, Suicide – the first Synth Pop duo – joined the 'underrated US proto-Punk groups' club: the alternative Rock And Roll Hall Of Fame founded by fellow underachievers The Velvet Underground, MC5, The New York Dolls and The Stooges. A sculptor and free-Jazz musician respectively, Alan Vega and Martin Rev's earliest performances at New York's legendary Mercer Arts Center attracted few fans – not least because Vega liked swinging a motorcycle chain at anyone within range while Rev made weird noises on a primitive synthesizer.

In 1977, with New York's Punk scene exploding around them, they emerged from hibernation with the slightly more commercial sound of *Suicide* (1977). However, if machines were made to measure such shifts, their lights would barely flicker: Rev's repertoire expanded to two-note drones, while Vega's echo-drenched, Elvis-esque croon told lurid low-life tales. But still nobody liked them: their UK shows with The Clash and Elvis Costello were characterized by hails of bottles and even by Vega having his nose broken by one irate stage-invader – which at least saved him having to do it himself. A Belgian gig erupted into a full-scale riot, commemorated by the live album *24 Minutes Over Brussels* (1980).

Not even endorsement from Bruce Springsteen and The Cars' Ric Ocasek (he produced 1980's acclaimed Martin Rev/Alan Vega album *Suicide*) helped sales figures, which fluttered around zilch. They split soon after, both making ignored solo albums – though Vega mysteriously had a Top 5 French hit with 'Juke Box Babe'.

By their reunion for the weak *A Way Of Life* in 1988, however, they were lauded as visionaries; devotees included nasty industrial types like Throbbing Gristle and Ministry and Popsters like Depeche Mode and Primal Scream. Another re-formation in London in 1998 added Spiritualized and Pulp to the long list of fans queuing to lavish praise on this most under-loved of groups.

THE SUGARCUBES

WHO Vocals **Björk Gudmundsdottir** (b. 21 Nov 1965, Reykjavik, Iceland), vocals **Einar Örn** (b. 29 Oct 1962, Copenhagen, Denmark), guitar **Thor Eldon** (b. 2 Jun 1962, Reykjavik), bass **Bragi Olaffson** (b. 12 Aug 1962, Reykjavik), drums **Sigtryggur 'Siggi' Baldursson** (b. 2 Oct 1962, Stavanger, Norway), keyboards **Margrét 'Magga' Örnólfsdottir** (b. 21 Nov 1967, Reykjavik)

WHEN 1986–1992

WHERE Reykjavik, Iceland

WHAT Indie, Dance, Rap – and Björk

In 1986, guitarist Fririk Erlingsson designed and sold a postcard commemorating Presidents Reagan and Gorbachev meeting in

DONNA SUMMER ✪✪✪

WHO b. Adrian Donna Gaines, 31 Dec 1948, Boston, Massachusetts, USA

WHAT The Queen of Disco

The Crow were a forgotten US Rock band, starring young Donna Gaines. When they split, she fled to Europe – hence an appearance in a 1968 German production of *Hair*. Amid other roles in musicals, she made her solo debut with 1971's 'Sally Go 'Round The Roses'.

However, the real story begins in 1974. Now known as Donna Summer, and with uncredited backing vocals on Three Dog Night's *Hard Labor* (1974) on her CV, she united with producers/writers Giorgio Moroder and Pete Bellotte for her first European hit, 'The Hostage' (1973). Her debut album, *Lady Of The Night* (issued on the delightfully named Groovy label in 1974), fell into history's bargain bin, although its 'Full Of Emptiness' reappeared on *Love To Love You Baby* (1975). But more important was the latter's hit title track: its marriage of the producers' orchestrated electronica and Summer's orgasmic breathlessness tapped the same mega-selling naughty nerve as Serge Gainsbourg's 'Je T'Aime (Moi Non Plus)' – a debt they acknowledged by covering that song for 1978's *Thank God It's Friday* movie.

The new Queen of Disco raised roofs with 1976's *A Love Trilogy* and *Four Seasons Of Love* and 1977's *I Remember Yesterday* and *Once Upon A Time*. Along the way, Moroder and Bellotte's backing began to sound less like Barry White and more like Kraftwerk: hence 1977's hypnotically ahead-of-its-time 'I Feel Love'. Summer also sang and co-wrote John Barry's theme for the 1977 movie *The Deep*, guested on Casablanca labelmate Gene Simmons' solo album (one of four solo albums by Kiss band members in 1978) and topped US charts with *Live And More* (1978) and its reading of Jimmy Webb's 'MacArthur Park'.

Bad Girls (1979) – her biggest-seller, thanks to the US No.1s 'Hot Stuff' and 'Bad Girls', and US No.2 'Dim All The Lights' – proved Disco could produce great albums as well as inspirational singles: only Summer has had three consecutive chart-topping double albums. One of its best cuts, the trancey 'Sunset People', was co-written by Harold Faltermeyer, who conquered the world in 1985 with 'Axel F'. Meanwhile, Summer's hits collection *On The Radio* (1979) was her third US No.1 album, and housed another landmark: the genre-busting and, of course, US chart-topping 'No More Tears (Enough Is Enough)', with Barbra Streisand.

In the 80s, she dumped Disco for the Pop Rock Soul delights *The Wanderer* (1980), *Donna Summer* (1982), *She Works Hard For The Money* (1983), *Cats Without Claws* (1984) and *All Systems Go* (1987). Hits included 1983's 'Unconditional Love' (with Reggae kids Musical Youth), 1987's 'Dinner With Gershwin' (whose writer, Brenda Russell, had a hit with 1988's 'Piano In The Dark') and 1982's revamp of Jon & Vangelis' 'State Of Independence' – "one of the all-time great pieces of music" (Brian Eno).

After 1989's Stock, Aitken & Waterman-helmed *Another Place And Time*, revamps of 'I Feel Love' and 'State Of Independence', 1994's C+C Factory-made 'Melody Of Love (Wanna Be Loved)' and *The Full Monty*'s 'Hot Stuff' revival did more than *Mistaken Identity* (1990) and *Christmas Spirit* (1994) to keep her star aloft, while she readied an autobiographical musical, *Ordinary Girl*.

ⓇⒺⒶⒹ *Donna Summer: Unauthorized* (1983), Jim Haskins & J.M. Stifle

ⓈⓊⓇⒻ members.aol.com/CHawk25619/tribute.html

In 1952, two years after opening his Memphis Recording Service, former DJ Sam Phillips launched Sun Records as a home for local black artists, including Rufus Thomas (whose 'Bear Cat' – a play on Mama Thornton's original hit 'Hound Dog' – was the label's first success), Little Milton and The Prisonaires, a vocal group made up of ex-prisoners.

Sun's most famous artist, Elvis Presley, first visited the studios in 1954 to make a private recording and released his debut, 'That's All Right Mama', the same year. Presley made four more singles for Sun before Phillips sold his contract to RCA in late 1956. Phillips added Rock 'n' Roll artists Carl Perkins, Johnny Cash and Jerry Lee Lewis to the roster and made early recordings with Charlie Rich and Roy Orbison, but the departure of these performers to other companies brought Sun's golden years to an end. Mickey Gilley, Sonny Burgess and Bill Justis were signed in the 60s, but Sun was unable to compete with the emerging major record companies and Phillips sold the label to music publisher and producer Shelby Singleton in 1969. Original Sun recordings are still reissued in America by the SSS label and through Charly Records in the UK.

Although the Sun studio is now principally a museum, U2 made a pilgrimage there to record 'Angel Of Harlem', 'Love Rescue Me' (with Bob Dylan) and 'When Love Comes To Town' (with B.B. King) for the 1988 album <u>Rattle And Hum</u>.

SUPER FURRY ANIMALS

WHO Vocals **Gruff Rhys** (b. 18 Jul 1970, Haverfordwest, Wales), guitar **Huw 'Bunf' Bunford** (b. 15 Sep 1967, Cardiff, Wales), bass **Guto Pryce** (b. 4 Sep 1972, Cardiff), drums **Dafydd Ieuan** (b. 1 Mar 1969, Bangor, Wales), keyboards **Cian Ciaran** (b. 16 Jun 1976, Bangor)

WHEN 1993–

WHERE Cardiff, Wales

WHAT Idiosyncratic Indie and demented Dance

Super Furry Animals' career to date has been brief but highly colourful. Their exploits include touring Britain's Rock festivals in a tank (from which they fired Dance music) and hitting the UK chart with a song ('The Man Don't Give A Fuck') which required the insertion of 50 bleeps for radio play. They've also made two fine albums of Techno-influenced psychedelic Indie Rock.

Super Furry Animals recorded two EPs for Cardiff-based label Ankst before signing to Creation. *Fuzzy Logic* (1996) included their first Top 20 hit, 'Something 4 The Weekend'.

After extensive international touring, they returned to the UK chart with 'Hermann Loves Pauline', a song about Albert Einstein and Marie Curie. *Radiator* followed in August 1997, darker than *Fuzzy Logic*, but equally distinctive and fascinating. One track, 'Demons', opened with the quintessential Super Furry sentiment: "Clarity just confuses me". 'Smokin', the lead track on their 1998 'Ice Hockey Hair' EP, suggested another cause for their confusion in its joyous chorus: "No one told us we could get so high".

ⓈⓊⓇⒻ www.creation.co.uk/superfurry/

SUPERGRASS ⊙

WHO Vocals/guitar **Gareth 'Gaz' Coombes** (b. 8 Mar 1976, Oxford, England), bass/vocals **Micky Quinn** (b. 17 Dec 1969, Oxford), drums **Danny Goffey** (b. 7 Feb 1974, Oxford), keyboards **Bob Coombes** (b. 27 Apr 1972, Oxford)

WHEN 1992–

WHERE Oxford, England

WHAT Pogo-ing Britpop princes

Gaz Coombes, Danny Goffey, his brother Nick and bassist Andy Davies formed The Jennifers while Coombes was still at school. In 1992, they signed a one-single deal with Nude, and released 'Just Got Back Today'. With Davies at university, Gaz met Micky Quinn at a restaurant and, by 1994, they were known as Theodore Supergrass.

That year they signed to Parlophone and distributed 'Caught By The Fuzz' – as Supergrass – on local label Backbeat, to sell at gigs. Later re-jigged for release by Parlophone, it became their debut single (released in the USA with a photograph of Hugh Grant in police custody on the cover – a court battle ensued).

In 1995, their spunky follow-up 'Mansize Rooster' reached the UK Top 20 and they supported The Bluetones on tour.

'Lose It' (1995), released on Sub Pop, was superseded by *I Should Coco* (1995) – a phenomenal debut at UK No.1, as Britpop was at its height. The album also marked Gaz's brother Bob Coombes' debut on keyboards and he became a regular touring member thereafter.

'Lenny' (1995) hailed the beginning of the summer of Supergrass – 'Alright' (with 'Time'), a UK No.2, gushed with teenage abandon. Their live appearances were explosive, thanks to Goffey's Keith Moon-style drumming.

Swamped with offers – Coombes rejected a Calvin Klein underwear campaign, having already graced Italian *Vogue* and the group turned down a Spielberg-directed, Monkees-style TV series – they continued with 1996's majestic 'Going Out' and full-throttle Punk-out 'Richard III'.

In It For The Money (1997) was critically lauded, reached UK No. 2, and proved that Britpop had yielded a group of lasting appeal. In 1997 they released 'Sun Hits The Sky' and 'Late In The Day', and graced Dr John's comeback *Anutha Zone* (1998).

READ *Supergrass: The Illustrated Story* (1996), Everett True

FAN Supergrass Info Service, PO Box 2212, Reading RG1 4YH, UK

SURF www.homepages.enterprise.net/bsm/Supergrass

SUPERGRASS•MARTYN GOODACRE•IN

SUPERTRAMP ✪

WHO Vocals/keyboards **Richard Davies** (b. 22 Jul 1944, Swindon, England), guitar **Roger Hodgson** (b. 21 Mar 1950, London, England), saxophone **John Helliwell** (b. 15 Feb 1945, Todmorden, Lancashire, England), bass **Dougie Thomson** (b. 24 Mar 1951, Glasgow, Scotland), drums **Bob C. Benberg** (b. Robert Siebenberg)

WHEN 1969–

WHERE London, England

WHAT Radio-friendly Prog Rock

Financial patronage from Dutch millionaire Stanley August Miesegaes enabled Richard Davies to form Supertramp in 1969. With a *Melody Maker* ad, Davies recruited Roger Hodgson (bass), Richard Palmer (guitar), Dave Winthrop (sax) and Bob Miller (drums). In 1970, the band signed to A&M and released their debut *Supertramp*. A meandering mix of self-indulgent solos and Progressive Rock, the album promptly sank without trace. Palmer and Miller quit to be replaced by Frank Farrell and Kevin Currie, while Hodgson switched to guitar. *Indelibly Stamped* (1971) proved equally unspectacular and, by 1972, Farrell, Currie, Winthrop and their millionaire benefactor had all jumped ship. Only songwriters Davies and Hodgson remained.

The band's change of fortune came in 1974 when, with new recruits John Helliwell, Dougie Thomson and Bob C. Benberg, they released their third album, *Crime Of The Century*. The first in a series of million-sellers, it moderated their Prog leanings with a poppier sound, themes of madness and melancholy and searingly infectious hooks. Davies' falsetto vocals and stabbing electric piano powered the distinctive sound. It also provided their UK Top 20 hit 'Dreamer' and US Top 40 'Bloody Well Right'.

> **"We've had entire Pop movements come and go between our albums and we haven't even noticed"**
>
> Richard Davies

Crisis? What Crisis? (1976) and *Even In The Quietest Moments* (1977), though lacking *Crime Of The Century*'s consistency, consolidated the band's success, with the latter providing the US hit 'Give A Little Bit'. The band undertook a 150-date US tour and 1979's *Breakfast In America* shot them to superstardom. It spent six weeks at US No.1, reached UK No.3 and sold 18 million copies. 'The Logical Song', 'Take The Long Way Home', 'Goodbye Stranger' and the title track became transatlantic hits. Supertramp's lush, melodic sound was ideal FM radio fodder.

After the live *Paris*, they released the bluesier *Famous Last Words* (1985), which made US and UK Top 10s. Hodgson quit soon afterwards, but the band continued as a quartet, releasing the proggy *Brother Where You Bound* (1985), a UK No.20 album. But *Free As A Bird* (1987) failed to dent the US Top 100.

After the disappointing *Live '88* (1988), Supertramp dissolved. Re-forming in 1997 with a new line-up, including ex-Crowded House Mark Hart, they released their first studio album for a decade, *Some Things Never Change,* and returned to the road.

THE SUPREMES ⊙⊙⊙ ✪✪✪

WHO Vocals **Florence Ballard** (b. 30 Jan 1943, Detroit, Michigan, USA, d. 22 Feb 1976), vocals **Diana Ross** (b. Diane Ross, 26 Mar 1944, Detroit), vocals **Mary Wilson** (b. 6 Mar 1944, Greenville, Mississippi, USA)

WHEN 1959–1977

WHERE Detroit, Michigan, USA

WHAT Archangels of Motown Soul

"The Beatles were there," Madonna told *Q* about her early tastes, "but I was more eager about The Supremes." She wasn't the only one: the band were one of the 60s' most successful hitmakers, have been covered by everyone from psychedelic behemoths Vanilla Fudge to peroxide popstress Kim Wilde (taking in Booker T & The MG's, Rod Stewart, Tom Jones and Ann Peebles along the way) and – despite Bananarama's claim to the crown – were the biggest girl group in history until les Spices came along.

Although they are most famously associated with Diana Ross, The Supremes' lynchpin was Florence Ballard. Discovered singing Doo Wop by Eddie Kendricks and Paul Williams, she recruited Mary Wilson, Barbara Martin and Betty Travis for The Primettes, a sister act to Kendricks and Williams' vocal quartet The Primes.

Travis was replaced by Diane Ross, who made up in ambition what she lacked in vocal power. She persuaded her neighbour, Smokey Robinson, to let them audition for the Motown label, who told them to come back when they had more experience.

The Primettes met a better reception at the Lupine label: they sang back-up for soon-to-be Soul stars Eddie Floyd and Wilson Pickett and got to release two flop singles of their own. But when The Primes – shortly to become The Temptations – were signed by Motown, their 'sisters' took to hanging around Motown too, and were signed in January 1961. Ballard suggested their new name The Supremes – "At least I get credit for something," she quipped years later, after Ross had stolen the limelight.

They debuted with 1961's 'I Want A Guy', then became almost an in-house joke at Motown when early singles either flopped or climbed into only the lower reaches of the chart. But they began to shine when they were teamed with hit writers Holland-Dozier-Holland; 'When The Lovelight Starts Shining Through His Eyes' (1963) made US No.23. Nonetheless, The Supremes envied what they considered the superior songs that H-D-H were writing for Martha Reeves & The Vandellas, and only reluctantly recorded 'Where Did Our Love Go?'. Their scepticism proved unfounded when it became the first of an amazing five US No.1s from 1964-1965, with 'Baby Love', 'Come See About Me', 'Stop! In The Name Of Love' and 'Back In My Arms Again'. All were spectacular songs with a fair helping of sonic innovation ('Where Did Our Love Go?' began with the novel percussive effect of two boards being bashed together), but owed much of their success to Motown's decision to spotlight Ross' crystal-clear vocals (which, to achieve a special echo, were sometimes recorded in the Motown toilets).

Their run of hits – which had by now crossed into the UK – included yet more US No.1s: 1965's 'I Hear A Symphony', 1966's 'You Can't Hurry Love' and 'You Keep Me Hangin' On' and 1967's 'Love Is Here And Now You're Gone' and 'The Happening'.

In 1967, Ballard – now, to her displeasure, eclipsed by Ross – was replaced by Cindy Birdsong (b. 15 Dec 1939, Camden, New Jersey). Her band forged ahead as Diana Ross & The Supremes.

Ross, now being groomed as a solo singer, sometimes even appeared on the group's hits without the others' participation, as on 1968's 'Forever Came Today' and the US No.1 'Love Child'. When The Supremes' success began to dry up – five hits in 1969 fell outside the Top 20 – destiny beckoned. After a final flourish – the US No.1 'Someday We'll Be Together', Ross left in early 1970.

With Jean Terrell, the group enjoyed more hits from 1970–1972, notably 'Up The Ladder To The Roof', 'Stoned Love', 'River Deep, Mountain High' (with The Four Tops), 'Nathan Jones' and 'Floy Joy'. *Right On* (1970) was their final US chart album (1977's *20 Golden Greats* was a UK No.1), but its No.25 placing looked puny besides the chart-topping success of 1966's *The Supremes A' Go-Go*, 1967's *Greatest Hits* and 1969's *TCB* (the latter a reunion with The Temptations, with whom The Supremes scored the hits 'I'm Gonna Make You Love Me' and 'I'll Try Something New').

After further personnel changes, The Supremes played their final show in 1977. Their shine was tarnished by Ballard's death in 1976, wrangling between Ross and Wilson, and cabaret acts with no original members, but their star can never be dimmed.

READ *Where Did Our Love Go?* (1985), Nelson George

SURF members.tripod.com/~Supremes/

SWEET

WHO Vocals **Brian Connolly** (b. Brian McManus, 5 Oct 1945, Hamilton, Scotland, d. 9 Feb 1997, Slough, Berkshire, England), guitar **Andy Scott** (b. 30 Jun 1951, Wrexham, Wales), bass **Steve Priest** (b. 23 Feb 1950, Hayes, Middlesex, England), drums **Mick Tucker** (b. 17 Jul 1949, London, England)

WHEN 1968–1981

WHERE London, England

WHAT Teeny Pop to Glam Metal

When Ian Gillan left covers band Wainwright's Gentlemen (later to join Deep Purple) in 1965, Brian Connolly stepped in. Then he and Mick Tucker formed Sweetshop with Steve Priest and Frank Torpy. As Sweet – after several flops and replacing Torpy with Andy Scott – success began when they teamed with writers Nicky Chinn and Mike Chapman in 1971. 'Funny Funny' was the first of several bubblegummy hits, but the band's self-penned Rock songs on the singles' B-sides revealed their real ambitions.

Chinn and Chapman began to write harder-edged songs and the innuendo-laden 'Little Willy' began a series of glorious hits which the band performed in increasingly outrageous costumes. 'Blockbuster' was a UK No.1 in 1973. 'Hell Raiser', 'Ballroom Blitz' (both 1973) and 'Teenage Rampage' (1974) all made UK No.2.

Splitting from Chinn and Chapman, Sweet rocked out on the self-penned *Sweet Fanny Adams* (1974). *Desolation Boulevard* (1975) included another hit – 'Fox On The Run' – and they finally found success in America. But the hits dried up after 1976's 'Love Is Like Oxygen'; Connolly quit in 1978 and the band split in 1981.

Various incarnations re-formed: *Live At The Marquee* (1989) was recorded by Scott, Priest, Tucker and singer Paul Mario Day. In the 90s, Connolly and Scott toured with rival bands billed as BC Sweet and Andy Scott's Sweet, but Connolly's health steadily declined due to a muscular condition and he died in 1997.

SURF www.thesweet.u-net.com/home/htm

SWING

WHAT When superproducers Jimmy Jam and Terry Lewis abandoned the sumptuous Soul of The SOS Band for the harder beats of Janet Jackson, two new teams followed their lead. LA & Babyface scored with their smooth Sunset Sound, epitomized by Karyn White. But New York producer Teddy Riley hit harder, popularizing New Jack Swing with smashes like Keith Sweat's 1987 hit 'I Want Her' and his own group Guy. It blew up with Bobby Brown's **Don't Be Cruel** (featuring Riley and LA & Babyface), making the style the first challenger to super-sellers Heavy Metal and Country. When Michael Jackson hired Riley to toughen up **Dangerous** (1991), every Pop act in the world took notice, hence Take That's loping 'Sure' (1994). Even Jam & Lewis got in on the act, with Janet Jackson's swinging **janet** (1993). Along the way, New Jack Swing – poppy, radio-friendly Funk – evolved into Swingbeat, now known as Swing if you don't want to sound like a geriatric. Though it encompasses moist-eyed ballads and dirty dealings of the carnal variety, Swing's key element is its head-nodding tempo – a beat perfectly suited to the laid-back Rap of the 90s. A platinum-certified phenomenon, the crossover is characterized by the work of Riley's new supergroup BLACKstreet with Rap stars like Dr Dre ('No Diggity') and Foxy Brown ('Get Me Home').

WHERE New York City, New York, USA

WHEN 1987–

WHO Bobby Brown **Don't Be Cruel** (1988), Guy **Guy** (1988), SWV **It's About Time** (1993), Jodeci **Diary Of A Mad Band** (1993), Various **New Jack Swing Mastercuts Vol. 3** (1994), Levert, Sweat, Gill **LSG** (1997)

T. REX ☉☉☉

WHO Vocals/guitar **Marc Bolan** (b. Mark Feld, 30 Sep 1947, London, England, d. 16 Sep 1977, Barnes Common, London)

WHEN 1969–1977

WHERE London, England

WHAT The God of Glam Rock

In his head, Mark Feld was already a Pop star by the time he became Marc Bolan in 1965. As a teenager, he became immersed in the fashion-conscious Mod movement. But in the mid-60s, he flipped for Folk, especially Bob Dylan – the dominant influence on his first demo (under the pseudonym Toby Tyler) in 1964.

A year later, he released the remarkably Donovan-esque single, 'The Wizard'. A promotional campaign revealed his flair for self-mythology: he claimed he'd spent "18 months at a wizard's chateau in France", which bore little relation to an actual trip to Paris. After two more flops (1966's 'The Third Degree' and 'Hippy Gumbo'), manager Simon Napier-Bell placed Marc with another of his charges, John's Children. Bolan augmented their frenetic live act, whipping his guitar with a chain while the band sought to match the notoriety of The Who and The Creation. He also wrote their 1967 single 'Desdemona' – banned for its allusions to witchcraft. But after a disastrous tour with The Who, John's Children disintegrated.

By summer 1967, Bolan had teamed up with percussionist Steve Peregrine Took, started wearing cloaks and plunged into Psychedelia. As Tyrannosaurus Rex, they were whimsically acoustic, inspired by Syd Barrett's Pink Floyd and Eastern artists like Ravi Shankar. Bolan's interest in fantasy (Tolkien and C.S. Lewis were counter-culture staples) littered his new lyrics.

Hippie festival favourites, Tyrannosaurus Rex edged into the mainstream with their 1968 hit 'Deborah'. In 1969, exploiting his 'woodland pixie' reputation to the full, Bolan (or rather, he claimed, the Celtic bard he was in a past life) produced a book of poetry, *The Warlock Of Love*. Meanwhile, *My People Were Fair And Had Sky In Their Hair, But Now They're Content To Wear Stars On Their Brow* and *Prophets, Seers And Sages, The Angels Of The Ages* (both 1968) and *Unicorn* (1969) trod a tightrope between mysticism and utter nonsense. The first two topped the UK chart in 1972 in the wake of Bolan's later success.

Retaining only the elfin lyrics, he ditched Took (who played with Pink Fairies, bid for solo stardom but died, penniless, in 1980) for bongo slapper Mickey Finn, amended the name to T. Rex and traded rambling Folk for riffy Rock 'n' Roll. In 1970, the fuzzily fab 'Ride A White Swan' peaked at UK No.2, *T. Rex* hit the Top 20 and 'Hot Love' stormed to No.1. In a puff of fairy dust, Marc Bolan emerged, clad in feather boas, satin, lurex and women's tap shoes – the shiniest star of the Glitter age. "I wanted to boogie," he said. So he did. 'T. Rextasy', the closest Britain had come to teen mania since The Beatles, began.

With drummer Bill Legend and bassist Steve Currie, T. Rex delivered 1971's UK No.1 *Electric Warrior*, source of the glorious 'Get It On' (another UK No.1) and 'Jeepster'. In America, 'Get It On', renamed 'Bang A Gong' (Get It On)', made No.10. Back home, the gold rush continued with 1972's compilation *Bolan Boogie*. With Bowie and Slade also scrambling teen minds, Glam Rock – Rock 'n' Roll for the year 2000 – was a reality. Bolan's "I drive a Rolls Royce/'cos it's good for my voice" on 'Children Of The Revolution' now seemed less like rhyming rubbish than the word of God.

Sadly, Bolan fell for his own hype. Claiming superiority over John Lennon and Pete Townshend, he scored again with *The Slider* (1972), source of the UK No.1s 'Metal Guru' and 'Telegram Sam'. But David Bowie's *Ziggy Stardust* claimed the Glam crown and Bolan's US success evaporated. As a backlash gathered pace, the Ringo Starr-directed movie *Born To Boogie* (1972) documented his acute complacency and megalomania.

Incapable of Bowie's transformations, T. Rex went down with the Glam Rock ship: Legend left in 1973, Finn endured 1973's *Tanx*, 1974's *Zinc Alloy And The Hidden Riders Of Tomorrow* and 1975's *Bolan's Zip Gun* (released as *Light Of Love* in the USA) then quit, after Currie had left. Bolan got fat, went cocaine crazy and moved to America with his girlfriend Gloria 'Tainted Love' Jones (mother of Bolan's son Rolan) in a fruitless bid to crack the States again. Despite minor UK hits like 1975's 'New York City' and 'Dreamy Lady', neither *Futuristic Dragon* (1976) nor *Dandy In The Underworld* (1977) troubled the chart for long.

Amazingly, a comeback beckoned with *Marc*, Bolan's UK TV show. Guests like The Damned, The Jam and Generation X did wonders for his credibility and when Bowie dropped in for a jam, a return to glory seemed imminent. But the Bowie show was Bolan's

last – he was killed when Gloria Jones' car hit a tree by the road at Barnes Common, London. The tree is now a shrine and – courtesy of covers, tributes and rip-offs by Guns N' Roses, Oasis, The Power Station, Frankie Goes To Hollywood, Morrissey and Placebo – Marc Bolan is still a Pop star.

ReaD *Twentieth Century Boy: The Marc Bolan Story* (1992), Mark Paytress

Fan T.Rextasy, 8 Moriarity Close, London N7 OEF, UK

SurF t.rex.connections.tm/tomb/tomb.html

TAKE THAT ⊙⊙⊙

WHO Vocals/keyboards **Gary Barlow** (b. 20 Jan 1971, Frodsham, Cheshire, England), vocals **Robbie Williams** (b. 13 Feb 1974, Stoke-on-Trent, England), vocals **Mark Owen** (b. 27 Jan 1974, Oldham, England), vocals **Jason Orange** (b. 10 Jul 1970, Manchester), vocals **Howard Donald** (b. 27 Apr 1970, Droylsden, Manchester)

WHEN 1991–1996

WHERE Manchester, England

WHAT Archetypal boy band for the 90s

Noting the huge success of US boy band New Kids On The Block, manager Nigel Martin-Smith enlisted five young singer/dancers and launched them to an indifferent reception in July 1991. They built a small following in youth discos and gay clubs, but only one journalist turned up at the London press launch of one of the 90s' biggest British success stories. Their first single 'Do What U Want' – co-written by Gary Barlow and issued on their own Dance UK label – missed the UK Top 75. But a gig at London's Limelight Club – later described by the group as their worst ever, owing to their having to dodge bottle missiles – seized industry attention. After minor hits with 1991's 'Promises' and 'Once You've Tasted Love', the breakthrough came with 1992's cover of Tavares' 'It Only Takes A Minute' and *Take That And Party*. Their second UK Top 10 hit, 'A Million Love Songs', which they described as a "grown-up ballad", was written by Barlow when he was just 16. By July 1993, when the joyful 'Pray' entered at UK No.1, Take That were Britain's brightest Pop sensations. No.1s flowed with 'Relight My Fire' (an explosive duet with Lulu), 1993's *Everything Changes* and 'Babe', and 1994's 'Everything Changes'. *Nobody Else*, the first album to be written entirely by Barlow (bar 'Sure', co-penned by Robbie Williams and Mark Owen) hit UK No.1 in 1995 and yielded three more chart-toppers: 'Sure', 'Never Forget' and 'Back For Good' (their first US smash).

But in July 1995, Williams – tired of Boy Band bounciness – quit. The remaining quartet enjoyed a triumphant tour and a US No.69 placing for *Nobody Else*, but didn't relish paying Williams a fifth of their earnings (his entitlement as a Take That board member). Keen to kickstart a solo career free from the theatrics to which he was clearly unsuited, Barlow dissolved the band in February 1996. Having sold 9 million albums and 10 million singles worldwide, they bowed out with a Bee Gees cover, 'How Deep Is Your Love' – like *Greatest Hits* (1996), another UK No.1.

Helplines run by the Childline and Samaritans charities were reportedly deluged with calls from grieving fans, who could take consolation from the five's solo careers. Barlow and Williams fared best, while Owen bravely flopped with *Green Man* (1997). Howard Donald busied himself with Pop hopeful Kavana and Jason Orange went into acting. Then along came Spice Girls…

ReaD *Take That: Our Greatest Hits* (1996), Take That

SurF www.geocities.com/Broadway/3005/takethat.html

TALK TALK

WHO Vocals/guitar/keyboards **Mark Hollis** (b. 1955, Tottenham, London, England), bass **Paul Webb** (b. 16 Jan 1962), drums **Lee Harris**

WHEN 1981–1991

WHERE London, England

WHAT Meticulous monuments to misery

Few noticed, but occasionally in the 80s, *just occasionally*, Talk Talk emerged from hibernation, muttered bitterly about their discomfort with the limelight and disappeared again. Even fewer noticed that they left some of the 80s' most indescribably brilliant music. Founded by Mark Hollis, they joined EMI, who moulded them into New Romantic popsters à la Duran Duran.

When their synth-heavy debut *The Party's Over* (1982) died – despite the hits 'Talk Talk' and 'Today' – they ditched keyboard player Simon Brenner and returned with 1984's beautifully bleak, predominantly Hollis-penned *It's My Life*. Stalling at UK No.35, its excellent title track was a hit only when reissued in 1990.

Talk Talk shrugged and disappeared again, then released the majestically mournful *Colour Of Spring* (1986), their only UK Top 10 hit. Its highlights – the hits 'Life's What You Make It' and 'Living In Another World', 'Give It Up', the jazzy 'Chameleon Day' and a lush production from long-time collaborator Tim Freise-Greene – confirmed their disconnection from the mainstream. EMI, keen to recoup enormous recording costs, made a last-ditch effort to make them play the Pop game. But aside from touring, Talk Talk's impenetrable disdain prevailed; stylists, video directors and publicists wept.

Nonetheless, they were given an unlimited budget for their next album. But by 1988's critically acclaimed *Spirit Of Eden*, EMI's patience had evaporated; Talk Talk could have existed in another dimension for all the commercial impact *Eden* made. Amid its melancholic ebb and flow – a collision of Peter Green, John Coltrane, Miles Davis and The Velvet Underground – there were no highlights: it was *all* great. But EMI disagreed and, following a rancorous courtroom divorce, cleaned up with the surprisingly successful compilation *Natural History* (1990) and the unauthorized remixology *History Revisited* (1991) – the latter the subject of another band vs. label legal battle.

Talk Talk flounced to Jazz label Verve for 1991's abstract masterpiece *Laughing Stock* – an album without one nod to commercialism – then disintegrated. Webb and Harris worked with the Talk Talk-esque Bark Psychosis and formed the Dance-flavoured O'Rang, while Hollis issued his splendid, self-titled solo debut (one of the quietest albums ever made) in 1998. EMI promptly followed with the retrospective *Asides Besides* and DJ Shadow, himself no stranger to meticulous monuments to misery, voted *Laughing Stock* among his favourites.

SurF home.earthlink.net/~landrvr/

TALKING HEADS

WHO Vocals/guitar **David Byrne** (b. 14 May 1952, Dumbarton, Scotland), bass/keyboards **Tina Weymouth** (b. 22 Nov 1950, Coronado, California, USA), drums **Chris Frantz** (b. 8 May 1951, Fort Campbell, Kentucky, USA), keyboards/guitar **Jerry Harrison** (b. 21 Feb 1949, Milwaukee, Wisconsin, USA)

WHEN 1975–1991

WHERE New York City, New York, USA

WHAT White Funk Punk weirdos

What were Talking Heads? White nerds who accidentally turned black music and Pop into a unique hybrid? Art-school students with a rare sense of humour? Abstract experimentalists who still sold millions? Whatever they were, they weren't saying.

David Byrne, Chris Frantz (members of bubblegum covers band The Artistics, aka The Autistics) and Tina Weymouth (Frantz's girlfriend) met at art college in the early 70s. In 1974, they moved to New York, where they rehearsed as The Portable Crushers, Vague Dots and, after an accidental discovery in a *TV Guide*, Talking Heads – TV terminology for a newsreader-style head-and-shoulders shot.

By 1975, having debuted live supporting the Ramones, Talking Heads were installed on the New York Punk scene, whose centre was the legendary CBGB club. But there was little to link them with the Ramones' thrash, Blondie's girl group glossiness or Television's guitar odysseys. Talking Heads were a weird hotchpotch of deadpan 1910 Fruitgum Company covers and jerky, paranoid Funk – of which 'Psycho Killer', Byrne's brilliant steal from Otis Redding's 'Fa Fa Fa Fa Fa (Sad Song)', was a perfect example.

With former Jonathan Richman sideman Jerry Harrison, they signed to Sire for 1977's acclaimed *Talking Heads '77* – boasting the aforementioned 'Psycho Killer', 'Don't Worry About The Government', Frantz and Weymouth's elastic rhythms and Byrne's blank stories. A jarringly strange album, it was eclipsed by *More Songs About Buildings And Food* (1978) – their first tryst with producer Brian Eno and African rhythms – and its incongruous hit cover of Al Green's 'Take Me To The River'. *Fear of Music* (1979) was funky enough for them to be dubbed "the new Parliament" (P-Funkateer Bernie Worrell joined on keyboards), experimental enough for arty hipness (its opener 'I Zimbra' was inspired by Dadaist Hugo Ball) and accessible enough to sell.

Their partnership with Eno blossomed with 1980's *Remain In Light*, including stunt guitarist Adrian Belew. It yielded the beyond brilliant 'Once In A Lifetime' (whose innovative video cast Byrne as a puppet-like televangelist) and became their biggest US hit yet. But this was nothing compared to the wonder of Eno and Byrne's collaboration, *My Life In The Bush Of Ghosts* (1981). Meanwhile, Weymouth and Frantz sparkled with their sideline band Tom Tom Club.

Though none of the latter's albums (1981's *Tom Tom Club*, 1983's *Close To The Bone* and 1988's *Boom Boom Chi Boom Boom*) demand close investigation, the 1981 hits

'Wordy Rappinghood' and 'Genius Of Love' proved Weymouth and Frantz could be just as quirkily inventive and funky as Byrne. Accordingly, 'Genius Of Love' was reworked into both the fantastic 'It's Nasty' by Rap god Grandmaster Flash and the fabulous 'Fantasy' by Mariah Carey.

The big Heads were commemorated by the live *The Name Of This Band Is Talking Heads* (1982), and 1983's *Speaking In Tongues* – the Eno association now over – spawned their biggest US hit, the synth-funking 'Burning Down The House'. On another tour (their last, as it turned out), they filmed the compelling *Stop Making Sense* (1984) with director Jonathan Demme.

Little Creatures (1985), by the once again shrunken Heads, turned to deceptively simple Pop, including the fab 'Road To Nowhere' (whose video was shamelessly cannibalized for Peter Gabriel's 'groundbreaking' 'Sledghammer'). Their biggest album sales duly ensued. By now, Byrne's ideas dominated and the other Heads were pressed into service for his movie *True Stories* (1986). This surreal sojourn through America's psyche yielded two soundtracks – an album of Heads originals (one of whose songs gave Radiohead their name) and another of awful versions by the cast (including *Roseanne*'s John Goodman).

Byrne led Talking Heads to Paris where – with an all-star cast including ex-Smith Johnny Marr, Mory Kante, Wally Badarou and the ubiquitous Kirsty MacColl – they constructed *Naked* (1988). Its joyful juggle of Funk, Pop and African and Latin influences made for a wonderful album, but did nothing to soothe tensions in the band, who'd tired of Byrne's control.

While Byrne went solo, Harrison continued with The Casual Gods but reaped greater rewards producing Crash Test Dummies (whose *God Shuffled His Feet* namechecks Byrne). Frantz and Weymouth produced Happy Mondays' underrated *…Yes Please!* (1992) and, with Harrison, formed The Heads – an all-star poke in

Byrne's eye – whose *No Talking, Just Heads* (1996) featured cameos from the likes of Shaun Ryder, Maria McKee and Deborah Harry. After years of hopeful murmurings from band and fans alike, Byrne announced the end of Talking Heads in 1991. They formally bowed out with the retrospective *Popular Favorites 1976–1992: Sand In The Vaseline* (1992), which was filleted for the bite-size best-of *Once In A Lifetime*.

READ *Talking Heads* (1993), Alan Bennett

SURF www.talking-heads.net/

TANGERINE DREAM

WHO Keyboards/guitar **Edgar Froese** (b. 6 Jun 1944, Tilsit, Germany), keyboards **Christopher Franke** (b. 6 Apr 1953, Berlin, Germany)

WHEN 1967–

WHERE Berlin, Germany

WHAT Perpetual Prog synth-prodders

In Tangerine Dream's labyrinthine history (a free line-up change with every album!), Edgar Froese is the only constant. Inspired by Dada and Surrealism (particularly Salvador Dali, with whom he hung out in Spain), Froese – with synth noodler Klaus Schulze and flautist Conrad Schnitzler – conceived Tangerine Dream as a crazy free Rock psychedelic freak out. And they *did* freak out on their debut *Electronic Meditation* (1970) – a Krautrock classic of ebb and flow, echoes and electronics.

But Schulze and Schnitzler promptly trotted off to be wonderful with Ash Ra Tempel and Cluster respectively; both also carved solo niches as ambient types. Froese replaced them with Christopher Franke and, after the short-stayed Steve Schroeder, keyboard player Peter Baumann: Tangerine's most stable line-up and the team behind the Moog-laden wig-outs *Alpha Centauri* (1971), *Zeit* (1972) and their commercial breakthrough *Atem* (1973).

Tangerine Dream cleaned up with trancey hippie faves *Phaedra* (1973) and *Rubycon* (1975). Progressive Rock milestones or atrocious spacey widdling? It depends whether you think their fondness for playing cathedrals (commemorated on 1975's *Ricochet*) was the last word in Rock 'n' Roll. But lofty artiness was left behind on 1976's *Stratosfear*, which embraced traditional Rock instrumentation. By 1978's Baumann-free *Cyclone,* they'd added singer Steve Jolliffe and drummer Klaus Krieger and gone completely Rock. But few were listening – thanks to Punk, 'the Tangs' were about as fashionable as the Black Death.

By 1980's *Tangram*, Tangerine Dream's nucleus was Froese, Franke and keyboard player Johannes Schmoelling. Unveiled at a concert in East Berlin, the new line-up busied themselves with successful movie soundtracks including *Risky Business, The Keep, Flashpoint, Firestarter* and

Legend. Meanwhile, 'proper' albums *Exit* (1981), *Hyperborea* (1983), *Poland – The Warsaw Concert* (1984) and *Le Parc* (1985) continued in typically experimental style. But *Tyger* (1987) saw the back of Franke (Schmoelling left before *Le Parc*), who jetted back to Hollywood for soundtrack successes, including the theme to US TV's *Star Trek* surrogate *Babylon 5*.

Since then, Tangerine Dream have slimmed down to a core of Froese and his son Jerome, earning a Grammy nomination (their seventh) for *Rockoon* (1992) and flirting with Dance on the likes of 1995's *Tyranny Of Beauty* and *The Dream Mixes*.

SURF www.netstore.de/tadream/

JAMES TAYLOR

WHO b. 12 Mar 1948, Boston, Massachusetts, USA

WHAT Tinker, Taylor, singer, songwriter

After spells in psychiatric care (where he wrote his first songs), New York group The Flying Machine and an English rehab clinic (he picked up a heroin problem), James Taylor debuted on The Beatles' Apple label. But, despite cameos from Fabsters Paul McCartney and George Harrison, *James Taylor* (1966) made little impact at first. He returned to the USA, joined Warner Bros and picked up the pieces of an already ragged career.

A motorcycle accident scuppered a planned appearance at Woodstock, but Taylor hooked up with Carole King (who penned his 1971 US No.1 'You've Got A Friend') for *Sweet Baby James* (1970), whose highlights included 'Fire And Rain' (US No.3) and the Blues parody 'Steamroller', later covered by Elvis.

Mud Slide Slim And The Blue Horizon (1971) featured girlfriend Joni Mitchell, but Taylor married Carly Simon in 1972. Mitchell's heartbreak was a main theme of her 1972 album, *For The Roses*. Joni wasn't the only female struck by the Taylor phenomenon: dark and handsome, with country-boy charm, he was the prototype of the artistic and sensitive 70s heartthrob. He even hit the movies, co-starring with Beach Boy Dennis Wilson in *Two Lane Blacktop* (1971). With co-sex symbol singer/songwriter Carly, the Taylors were a star couple of the time, and duetted on the hit 'Mockingbird' in 1974, famously pastiched in 1995's juvenile jape movie *Dumb And Dumber*.

The sensitive singer/songwriter stereotype continued for *One Man Dog* (1972) and *Walking Man* (1974), while *Gorilla* (1975) saw him return to touring (he'd last appeared, endorsing presidential candidate George McGovern, in 1972) and hit with a cover of Marvin Gaye's 'How Sweet It Is (To Be Loved By You)'.

In The Pocket (1976) failed to equal earlier successes, a side-effect of Taylor's prodigious drug intake. "James sounds awake," said critic Robert Christgau of *J.T.* (1977). "Worth a headline in itself." Nonetheless, *J.T.* made US No.4, confirming his supremacy among America's troubled souls.

Both *Flag* (1979) and *Dad Loves His Work* (1981) peaked at US No.10, but a five-year absence reduced the audience for *That's Why I'm Here* (1985). *Never Die Young* (1988) and *New Moon Shine* (1991) punctured the US Top 40, but it was as a live performer that Taylor shone, hence 1993's *Live*. In 1994, Taylor was the hero of the hour in *The Simpsons*, saving civilian astronaut Homer Simpson from marauding space shuttle ants with a custom-built vacuum device co-designed by Art Garfunkel.

SURF www.jamestaylor.com

THE TEARDROP EXPLODES

WHO Vocals/bass **Julian Cope** (b. 21 Oct 1957, Deri, Mid Glamorgan, Wales)
guitar **Mick Finkler**, keyboards **Paul Simpson**, drums **Gary Dwyer**

WHEN 1978–1983

WHERE Liverpool, England

WHAT Eccentric, psychedelic Punk

When The Crucial Three (including soon-to-be Bunnyman Ian McCulloch and Liverpool scenester Pete Wylie) dissolved, Julian Cope joined Mystery Girls, Nova Mob, then – with guitarist Mick Finkler and keyboard player Paul Simpson – Shallow Madness.

As The Teardrop Explodes (a name taken from Marvel comic *Daredevil*), with new drummer Gary Dwyer, their reputation grew with 1979's trippy 'Sleeping Gas' EP (on the Zoo label owned by manager Bill Drummond, who later masterminded The KLF) and 'Bouncing Babies' (1979). By the new decade, Simpson had been replaced by Dave Balfe, and the Teardrops entered the UK charts with 1980's 'When I Dream' and *Kilimanjaro* (produced by cult band The Chameleons). In 1981, they scored their biggest hit with the brassy 'Reward', followed by 'Treason' (co-written with McCulloch, and for which Alan Gill replaced Finkler), 'Passionate Friend' (on Zoo), and 'Colours Fly Away'. But Duran Duran soon claimed their crown and their *Wilder* (1981) sold unspectacularly.

'Tiny Children' (1982) appeared amid line-up changes and ego clashes, which threatened the future of the band. As the EP 'You Disappear From View' (1983) charted, they abandoned a third album and split. Cope had a successful solo career, fuelling the demand for retrospectives *Everybody Wants To Shag the Teardrop Explodes* (1990), *Piano* (1990) and *Live In Concert* (1993). Meanwhile, Balfe, who waged a long war of words with Cope, founded Blur's Food label.

 Head On, Memories Of The Liverpool Punk Scene And The Story Of The Teardrop Explodes 1976–82 (1994), Julian Cope

SURF trouserpress.com/bandpages/THE_TEARDROP_EXPLODES.html

TEARS FOR FEARS ◉ ◉ ✪

WHO Vocals/guitar/keyboards **Roland Orzabal** (b. Roland Orzabal de la Quintana, 22 Aug 1961, Portsmouth, England), vocals/bass **Curt Smith** (b. 24 Jun 1961, Bath, England)

WHEN 1981–

WHERE Bath, England

WHAT Seriously anthemic worry warriors

In school bands together at 13, Roland Orzabal and Curt Smith first recorded with white Ska band Graduate (1980's *Acting My Age*). Then they became a duo, dubbed Tears For Fears in homage to primal scream therapist Arthur Janov's book *Prisoners Of Pain*. They broke through with 'Mad World' (1982) and 'Change' (1983). Then *The Hurting* (1983), written entirely by Orzabal, hit UK No.1, staying on the chart for 65 weeks.

Two globe-bestriding years ensued, triggered by the anthemic US No.1s 'Shout' and 'Everybody Wants To Rule The World'. *Songs From The Big Chair* (1985) – inspired by *Sybil*, a TV drama-documentary about multiple personalities – swept to US No.1/ UK No.2. After a debilitating world tour and a 1986 revamp of their greatest hit as 'Everybody Wants To Run The World' to raise funds for African famine relief, they took a lengthy recess. It proved their undoing.

Torn between longing for spontaneity and obsession with detail, they spent more than two years on 1989's *The Seeds Of Love* (UK No.1, but only US No.8). The Beatle-esque 'Sowing The Seeds Of Love' and soulful 'Woman in Chains' (featuring Oleta Adams, the singer/pianist they had spotted playing a Kansas City hotel bar) were hits, but their time had passed.

In 1991, Smith quit. Subsequently, 1992's hits set *Tears Roll Down* did well, but Orzabal, still trading as Tears For Fears, saw his fortunes wane through *Elemental* (1993) and *Raoul And The Kings Of Spain* (1995). The 1995 album appeared on Epic after a dispute with Mercury – who parted with Smith, too, after *Soul On Board* failed in 1993. Smith eventually released a follow-up on his own label, Zerodisc, under the guise of *Mayfield* (1998), the name a product of the ghastly pun, "Curt is Mayfield".

READ *Tears For Fears* (1986), Ann Green

SURF www.epiccenter.com

TECHNO

WHAT In 1981, when Kraftwerk rebuilt Pop with a mechanical heart and electronic brain, the effect was seismic. Europe fell to Synth Pop. In the USA, Derrick May, Kevin 'Inner City' Saunderson and Juan 'Cybotron'/'Model 500' Atkins heard it and saw a future where the bleeps and blurps of synthesizers replaced the primitive guitar. A future called Techno! With junk store equipment, they DJed around Detroit producing their own mechanized Dance music. Ignored at home (except by Carl Craig and Richie Hawtin aka Plastikman/Fuse), their influence crossed to England, where Nightmares On Wax, The Black Dog, A Guy Called Gerald, Aphex Twin, David Holmes, LFO, Orbital, 808 State, Dave Angel, Underworld, The Chemical Brothers and Prodigy mangled the clean lines of the original blueprint. Elsewhere, Belgium's R&S label became Techno heaven, releasing the Detroit masters' tunes and inspiring England's ultra-adventurous Warp label. While Saunderson's Inner City hit the UK chart, Techno mutated into speed-crazed Hardcore (springboard for Drum 'n' Bass and the nose-bleedingly stupid Gabba). German-led Trance (tree-huggers' Techno epitomized by Sven Väth, Banco De Gaia et al), Techno Popsters (2 Unlimited and Technotronic) and Electronica (a Beatles/Stones-esque US invasion by The Chemical Brothers and Prodigy).

WHERE Detroit, USA, Europe

WHEN 80s–

WHO Kraftwerk <u>Computer World</u> (1981), Derrick May <u>Strings Of Life</u> (1987), Inner City <u>Paradise</u> (1989), Fuse <u>Dimension Intrusion</u> (1993), Orbital <u>Snivilisation</u> (1994), Carl Craig <u>Landcruising</u> (1995), Model 500 <u>Classics</u> (1995), Dave Clarke <u>Archive I</u> (1996), LFO <u>Advance</u> (1996), The Chemical Brothers <u>Dig Your Own Hole</u> (1997), The Crystal Method <u>Vegas</u> (1997), Björk <u>Homogenic</u> (1997)

TEENAGE FANCLUB

WHO Vocals/guitar **Norman Blake** (b. 20 Oct 1965, Glasgow, Scotland), guitar/vocals **Raymond McGinley** (b. 3 Jan 1964, Glasgow), bass/vocals **Gerard Love** (b. 31 Aug 1967, Motherwell, Scotland), drums **Brendan O'Hare** (b. 16 Jan 1970, Motherwell)

WHEN 1989–

WHERE Glasgow, Scotland

WHAT Near-perfect Pop

If medals were awarded for career-crunching contrariness, then Teenage Fanclub would have won more metal than Patton. But despite mixing brilliance with rubbish, TFC remain, according to Liam Gallagher, "The second best band in the world".

Rising from the unlamented remains of The Boy Hairdressers and BMX Bandits, Teenage Fanclub debuted with 1990's wonderful *A Catholic Education*, a good-natured ramble through grungey swamplands à la Dinosaur Jr, but with a golden Pop sheen inherited from The Byrds' Gene Clark and cult US Power-poppers Big Star. Its highlight was the heartbreakingly brilliant 'Everything Flows'. A beacon of tenderness in the (then) Baggy-obsessed Indie scene, critics fell for them. So did Alan McGee, who poached the band from little-league label Fire/Paperhouse and installed them as his new best friends at Creation.

Armed with Creation's 'hipper-than-thou' cool, stacks of McGee's money and the promise of a breakthrough, TFC followed their acclaimed debut with the irritating in-joke *The King* (1991) – a collection of their favourite instrumentals including an abysmal trawl through Pink Floyd's 'Interstellar Overdrive'. Then, just as everyone began to lose interest, they released their *real* second album. It was all a joke! Ha!

Thankfully, *Bandwagonesque* (1991) was a masterpiece: the best bits of Neil Young, The Beach Boys, Dinosaur Jr, Big Star and Sonic Youth distilled into inspired songs of love, confusion and Status Quo. By the end of the year, having notched up Indie hits with the *Bandwagonesque* cuts 'The Concept' and 'What You Do

To Me' and signed to Geffen in the USA, Teenage Fanclub were poised for greatness.

But, as ever, the Fannies plucked defeat from the jaws of victory. Despite some magical moments, the self-produced flop *Thirteen* (1993) was long overdue and mediocre. Consequently, 1995's *Grand Prix* was met with resounding indifference, despite its greatness. In the two years between albums, TFC swapped drummer Brendan O'Hare (who hopped off to Telstar Ponies and Mogwai) for former Soup Dragon Paul Quinn, dropped their often annoying penchant for irony and rapidly rebuilt their reputation, ensuring that 1997's 'more-of-the-same' *Songs From Northern Britain* scaled heights similar to *Bandwagonesque*.

(Fan) Teenage Fanclub Info Service, c/o Trinity Street, 3 Aliston Place, Off Oxford Street, Leamington Spa, CV32 4FN, UK

(surf) www.teenagefanclub.com/

TELEVISION

WHO Guitar/vocals **Tom Verlaine** (b. Thomas Miller, 13 Dec 1949, Mount Morris, New Jersey, USA), guitar/vocals **Richard Lloyd**, bass **Fred Smith** (b. 10 Apr 1948, New York City, New York, USA), drums **Billy Ficca**

WHEN 1973–1978

WHERE New York City, New York, USA

WHAT New Wave visionaries

The guitar solo reigned supreme in the 70s. Before Punk, Peter Frampton's widdling was perfectly acceptable. After Punk arrived, it was not. Strange then that Television, the greatest US Punk band *ever*, were built on *very* long guitar solos. Their story began when school friends Thomas Miller and Richard Meyer (b. 2 Oct 1949, Lexington, Kentucky) moved to New York City in the late 60s. Arty Jazz addict Miller fell for The Velvet Underground and became Tom Verlaine, while Meyer became self-styled nihilistic poet and junkie Richard Hell.

With Hell on bass and Verlaine on guitar, they formed The Neon Boys with drummer Billy Ficca in 1972. In 1973, they recruited Richard Lloyd, renamed themselves Television and began a series of gigs (mostly at the legendary CBGB) which kick-started the Punk scene.

In spirit, Television belonged to Richard Hell – the prototype Punk who wandered around New York with a "KILL ME" T-shirt and penned angst-ridden early classics like '(I Belong To The) Blank Generation'. But his scrappy bass playing irked the perfectionist Verlaine, who ousted him soon after they recorded a demo for Island with Art Rock egghead Brian Eno. Hell formed The Heartbreakers with doomed former New York Doll Johnny Thunders, then went solo with The Voidoids on the excellent *Blank Generation* (1977). He was replaced by ex-Blondie bassist Fred Smith in time for Television's acclaimed debut 'Little Johnny Jewel' (1975). Released on the tiny Ork label, it revealed their poetic bent and innovative guitar hijinks and was covered by Siouxsie & The Banshees on *Through The Looking Glass* (1987). But it prompted the first of many tiffs 'twixt Verlaine and Lloyd, who flounced out and refused to come back for a little while.

In 1977, Television released their masterpiece: the incredibly un-Punk (in the pogoing/thrashing/shouting/puking sense) *Marquee Moon*. Dominated by Verlaine and Lloyd's clanging,

"I'm just warming up for that 50-year-old age where I can sing at Holiday Inn..."

Tom Verlaine

crackling, duelling guitars, it was… *brilliant* – Rock re-invented as romantic melodrama in eight songs. Its peak was the title track: a 9-minute symphony overflowing with abstract guitar solos that were never less than electrifying. It was covered by The Kronos Quartet on the *Rubaiyat* compilation (1990). Little more than a cult classic in the USA, *Marquee Moon* reached the UK Top 40 (as did 'Marquee Moon' and 'Prove It') and Television toured the UK with Blondie.

But the majesty of their debut all but exhausted Television. By 1978, relations between Lloyd and Verlaine were at breaking point and that year's *Adventure,* despite highlights like the hit 'Foxhole' and 'Glory', could never match *Marquee Moon's* power. Television knew it too: after the *Adventure* tour, they split.

Ficca joined the wonderful Waitresses (a sort of Art Rock version of Blondie, best remembered for 'Christmas Wrapping'). Verlaine and Lloyd launched acclaimed but cult-sized solo careers. The highlight of the former's was 1979's *Tom Verlaine*, whose 'Kingdom Come' was covered by David Bowie on *Scary Monsters* (1980). Verlaine followed up with *Dreamtime* (1981), *Words From The Front* (1982), *Cover* (1984), *Flash Light* (1987), *The Wonder* (1990), *Warm And Cool* (1992) and the anthology *The Miller's Tale* (1996). Lloyd weighed in with *Alchemy* (1979), *Field Of Fire* (1985) and the live *Real Time* (1987). Television's live legacy was celebrated by the 1982 collection *The Blow Up*.

In 1992, having become some of the most influential musicians ever (Echo & The Bunnymen, REM, Lloyd Cole, the whole of Punk Rock), Verlaine and Lloyd reunited with Ficca and Smith for *Television,* more arguments and another split.

Verlaine's most recent claim to fame was collaborating with Jeff Buckley on work which appears on Buckley's posthumous 1998 set *Sketches (For My Sweetheart The Drunk)*.

SURF www.slip.net/~rivethed/tvsite.htm

THE TEMPTATIONS ⊙ ✪

WHO Vocals **Melvin Franklin** (b. David English, 12 Oct 1942, Montgomery, Alabama, USA, d. 23 Feb 1995, Los Angeles, California, USA), vocals **David Ruffin** (b. Davis Eli Ruffin, 18 Jan 1941, Whynot, Mississippi, USA, d. 1 Jun 1991, Philadelphia, Pennsylvania, USA), vocals **Eddie Kendricks** (b. 17 Dec 1939, Union Springs, Alabama, d. 5 Oct 1992, Birmingham, Alabama), vocals **Otis Williams** (b. Otis Miles, 30 Oct 1939, Texarkana, Texas, USA), vocals **Paul Williams** (b. 2 Jul 1939, Birmingham, d. 17 Aug 1973, Detroit, Michigan, USA)

WHEN 1960–

WHERE Detroit, Michigan, USA

WHAT Emperors of Soul

Best known for the cheerful 'My Girl' – a transatlantic smash from 1965 – The Temptations rarely win the sort of acclaim afforded to fellow Motown innovators like Stevie Wonder and Marvin Gaye. Yet they fronted some of the greatest music of all time and were, said *Billboard*, "recognized as America's favorite Soul group".

Formed from amateur acts The Primes and The Distants, and first known as The Elgins, they joined Motown subsidiary Miracle in 1961. Success arrived only after they ditched founder member Eldridge Bryant and hooked up with choreographer Cholly Atkins and, in 1964, writer/producer Smokey Robinson.

They hit big with Smokey's 'My Girl', fronted by Bryant's successor David Ruffin. The first No.1 by a male Motown group, it kicked off a decade of US hit albums including 1965's *The Temptations Sing Smokey*, 1965's *Temptin' Temptations* and 1966's *Gettin' Ready* – which yielded the near-title track 'Get Ready', the second most celebrated track of their early years.

The real story begins with the funky 'Ain't Too Proud To Beg' in 1966. Writer/producer Norman Whitfield replaced Smokey and turned The Temptations from princes of Pop into Emperors of Soul, who peaked again with 1968's 'I Wish It Would Rain Down'.

They still did typically Motown-ish stuff, notably *TCB*: a 1969 US No.1 with their old singing partners The Supremes. But when Ruffin – whose heartbreaking lead vocal dominated the group – was ousted in 1968, Whitfield took the opportunity to push them into psychedelic Soul. Inspired by Sly Stone, the producer stirred a bubbling brew of Funk and Soul on a hit run whose excellence and innovation are rivalled only by Sly himself – to whom 1971's hit 'Superstar (Remember How You Got Where You Are)' was addressed – and James Brown: from 1968's 'Cloud Nine', through 1970's 'Psychedelic Shack' and 'Ball Of Confusion', to 1972's US No.1 'Papa Was A Rolling Stone'. But they could be tender as well as fiery, illustrated by the US No.1s 'I Can't Get Next To You' (1969) and 1971's 'Just My Imagination (Runnin' Away With Me)'.

They also aided the crusade led by Stevie Wonder and Marvin Gaye: making albums rather than just collections of hits, notably *Sky's The Limit* (1971), *All Directions* (1973) and *Masterpiece* (1973). But the latter and its title track marked the end of their US Top 10 supremacy. By 1974, Kendricks had quit to go solo, Paul Williams had committed suicide and Whitfield – whose protégés included Edwin Starr (hence Starr's Temptations-esque *Involved* in 1971) and The Undisputed Truth – quit to mastermind Rose Royce.

When The Temptations sank in a hitless mire of personnel and label changes, fans found more to admire in the solo work of David Ruffin and Eddie Kendricks, who scored smashes of their own with, respectively, 1975's 'Walk Away From Love' and 1973's 'Keep On Truckin' (Part 1)'. Ruffin and Kendricks guested on The Temps' *Reunion* (1982), though Dennis Edwards took most of the leads and the biggest influence was Motown's then-biggest star, Rick James. Later, while the band scored a one-off UK hit with 1984's 'Treat Her Like A Lady', Ruffin and Kendricks contributed to the anti-apartheid anthem 'Sun City', united with Hall & Oates for the excellent *Live At The Apollo* (1985), played at Live Aid and made a fine album of their own, *Ruffin & Kendricks* (1988).

The Temptations were tarnished in the 90s: Ruffin died of an overdose in 1991; cancer claimed Kendricks in 1992; the band were reduced to backing Rod Stewart on 1991's hit 'The Motown Song' and scored their highest charting UK hit with a reissue of 'My Girl' from the same-titled 1992 movie. But their legacy – as collected on 1994's plush box set *Emperors Of Soul* – lives forever.

Read *Temptations* (1989), Otis Williams & Patricia Romanowski

10cc

WHO Guitar/vocals **Eric Stewart** (b. 20 Jan 1945, Manchester, England), guitar/vocals **Lol Creme** (b. Lawrence Creme, 19 Sep 1947, Manchester), bass/vocals **Graham Gouldman** (b. 10 May 1946, Manchester), drums/vocals **Kevin Godley** (b. 7 Oct 1945, Manchester)

WHEN 1972–

WHERE Manchester, England

WHAT Pop Art

Grounded in the 60s Beat boom Pop of ex-Mindbender Eric Stewart and hit songwriter (for such acts as The Yardbirds, Herman's Hermits and The Hollies) Graham Gouldman, 10cc devised some of the wittiest Pop music of the 70s.

The four first united at Stewart and Gouldman's Strawberry Studios in Manchester to work on material for the Kasenatz-Katz bubblegum Pop outfit. As Hotlegs, they hit with 1970's UK No.2 'Neanderthal Man', but failed to evolve their career further. Two years later, Stewart's friend, Pop entrepreneur Jonathan King, signed them to his UK label on the strength of a demo of 'Donna'

(UK No.2, 1972), allegedly renaming them after a double-sized dose of the average human ejaculate (5cc). This single, and other early releases like the UK No.1 'Rubber Bullets' and 'The Dean And I' – collected on their debut album *10cc* (1973) – presented the band as able pasticheurs of 50s Pop, but their reputation blossomed with 1974's ambitious *Sheet Music*, an eclectic set of clever modern Pop that included the hit 'Wall Street Shuffle'.

Signed to Phonogram for a reported £1 million, *The Original Soundtrack* (1975) found them delving deeper into sophisticated studio techniques, particularly on the UK No.1/US No.2 'I'm Not In Love', whose lush, ethereal harmonies were the product of countless vocal overdubs. A confessed influence on REM's 'Star Me Kitten', 'I'm Not In Love' was also covered by Fun Lovin' Criminals. Following *How Dare You?* (1976) and its hits 'Art For Art's Sake' and 'I'm Mandy Fly Me', Godley and Creme left the band, ostensibly to develop a new guitar effect, the Gizmo.

At first, Stewart and Gouldman's 10cc (now with drummer Paul Burgess) were more successful, scoring UK Top 3 albums – *Deceptive Bends* (1977) and *Bloody Tourists* (1978) – thanks to the 1977 hits 'The Things We Do For Love' and 'Good Morning Judge' and 1978's UK No.1 Reggae pastiche 'Dreadlock Holiday'. Godley & Creme's albums, notably 1977's triple set *Consequences*, made little impression. But following the success of 1981's 'Under Your Thumb' (1981), Godley & Creme proved to have the more reliable grasp of modern Pop mores, scoring further hits with 'Wedding Bells' (1981), 'Cry' (1985) and *Ismism* (1981), while developing a profitable career as video directors for early 80s New Romantics like Visage, Toyah and Duran Duran, then Michael Jackson.

Trevor Horn remixed 10cc and Godley & Creme tracks on *The History Mix* (1985), but both parties' subsequent albums failed to chart. Godley & Creme did, however, branch into feature films with *Howling At The Moon* (1988), a direction Creme continued with *The Lunatic* (1992), while Godley helped found the environmental organization ARK, for which he produced the album and TV special *One World One Voice* (1990).

ⓇⒺⒶⒹ *10cc Story* (1976), George Tremlett

Ⓕⓐⓝ Phil Loffus, The Official 10cc Fanclub, 45 Windsor Road, Droylsden, Manchester, M23 6WB, UK

Ⓢⓤⓡⓕ www.pacifier.com/"mikes/10cc.html

10,000 MANIACS

WHO Vocals **Natalie Merchant** (b. 26 Oct 1963, Jamestown, New York, USA), guitar **Robert Buck** (b. 3 Aug 1958, Jamestown), guitar **John Lombardo** (b. 30 Sep 1952, Jamestown), keyboards **Dennis Drew** (b. 8 Aug 1957, Buffalo, New York), bass **Steven Gustafson** (b. 10 Apr 1957, Madrid, Spain), drums **Jerry Agustyniak** (b. 2 Sep 1958, Lackawanna, New York)

WHEN 1981–

WHERE Jamestown, New York, USA

WHAT Thoughtful Folk Rock

10,000 Maniacs took their name exaggerated for comic effect – from the 1964 horror movie *2,000 Maniacs*, in which the dead citizens of Pleasant Valley return to life on the centenary of their slaughter during the American Civil War. They established their

Folk Rock credentials – often subtly incorporating World Music influences – with the 'Human Conflict Number Five' EP (1982), *Secrets Of The I-Ching* (1983) and the Joe Boyd-produced *The Wishing Chair* (1985). But they found their voice and big success with 1987's million-seller *In My Tribe*, with melodic arrangements and Natalie Merchant's articulate lyrics about illiteracy ('Cherry Tree'), child abuse ('What's The Matter Here') and the nature of manhood ('Gun Shy'). Taking a moral attitude to fame, they played at American Earth Day eco-charity concerts and deleted their cover of Cat Steven's 'Peace Train' from *In My Tribe* after his alleged support for the *fatwa* against writer Salman Rushdie.

After *Blind Man's Zoo* (1989) and *Our Time In Eden* (1992), they scored another hit with the acoustic *Unplugged* (1993) and its cover of Springsteen's 'Because The Night'. Merchant then left to enjoy spectacular sales with *Tigerlily* (1995) and *Ophelia* (1998). The Maniacs, whose founder John Lombardo rejoined after a nine-year absence, promoted backing singer Mary Ramsey to the front and struggled on with *Love Among The Ruins* (1997).

Ⓕⓐⓝ 362 Rhode Island Street, Buffalo, NY 14213-2238, USA

Ⓢⓤⓡⓕ www.maniacs.com

TEN YEARS AFTER

WHO Vocals/guitar **Alvin Lee** (b.19 Dec 1944, Nottingham, England), bass **Leo Lyons** (b. 30 Nov 1943, Bedford, England), keyboards **Chick Churchill** (b. 2 Jan 1949, Flint, Wales), drums **Ric Lee** (b. 20 Oct 1945, Cannock, Staffordshire, England)

WHEN 1967–

WHERE Nottingham, England

WHAT Hard-rocking Blues

If John Mayall was the patron saint of mid-60s British Blues Rock and Eric Clapton its god, Alvin Lee was its fast, flashy superstar. Lee, a guitar player since 13, teamed up with Leo Lyons, who'd performed publicly since 15, in 1964. Their skills honed on the Hamburg club circuit, they formed Ten Years After (named after the supposed tenth anniversary of the birth of Rock 'n' Roll) with Chick Churchill and Ric Lee (no relation) in 1967.

Their live reputation – notable for Alvin's speedy fretwork – grew on both sides of the Atlantic, with residencies at London's Marquee and New York's The Scene (where they jammed with Hendrix and Janis Joplin). Their self-titled 1967 debut flopped, but *Stonedhenge* (1968) and the live *Undead* (1968) sold well.

The big break came in 1969 when they played Woodstock – Alvin's 11-minute guitar showcase on 'Goin' Home' was hailed as a highlight – and America adopted them as its own. *SSSSH* (1969) was a transatlantic hit, followed by 1970's *Cricklewood Green* (source of their first hit single, the UK No.4 'Love Like A Man') and *Watt*, 1971's *A Space In Time* and 1973's *Recorded Live*.

In 1974 – after discontentment within the band, much of it to do with Alvin being singled out as the star, hence Lee and Churchill's solo albums – Alvin dissolved the band and formed the underachieving Ten Years Later in 1978, which split in 1980.

Ten Years After re-formed in 1989 for *About Time*. Critically acclaimed but commercially unpopular, it made only US No.122.

Ⓢⓤⓡⓕ www.bekkoeame.or.jp./-tadatk/music/tenyrsaftr.htm/

TERRORVISION

WHO Vocals **Tony 'Tone' Wright** (b. 6 May 1968), guitar **Mark 'Sark' Yates** (b. 4 Apr 1968), bass **Leigh 'Flare' Marklew** (b. 10 Aug 1968), drums **Shutty** (b. David Shuttleworth, 20 Mar 1967, Keighley, Yorkshire, England)

WHEN 1989–

WHERE Bradford, England

WHAT Mirthful Metal muthas

It's easy to forget in the Radiohead-racked 90s that there's more to life than introspective whining. Thankfully, mixing party Metal and Pop, Terrorvision have widened the emotional palette to include, as one review noted, "A laugh, a joke and a crate of ale".

Mark Yates and childhood friends Shutty and Leigh Marklew laboured desperately as Spoilt Bratz before recruiting Tony Wright and redubbing themselves Terrorvision after a 60s sci-fi movie. Signed to EMI in 1991, they supported Ramones and debuted with *Formaldehyde* (1992), from which the cheery 'My House' reached the UK Top 40 and laid bare Terrorvision's special features: unashamed mainstream Pop, unafraid to Rock.

Their breakthrough was confirmed by 1994's chart-bustin' 'Oblivion', 'Pretend Best Friend', 'Alice, What's The Matter' and *How To Make Friends And Influence People*. Pausing only to delight the Metal masses with trillions of festival shows, Terrorvision's onslaught continued with the Bond-themed *Regular Urban Survivors* (1996), the joyous hits 'Bad Actress', 'Perseverance' and 'Easy' and a cover of David Bowie's 'Moonage Daydream' on the all-star benefit album *Long Live Tibet* (1997).

surf www.brunel.ac.uk/^me95jjc/terror/

THE THE

WHO Vocals/guitar **Matt Johnson** (b. 15 Aug 1961, London, England)

WHEN 1979–

WHERE London, England

WHAT Slow-motion misanthropy

Though others sometimes drop by to cheer him up, The The is but one man – Matt Johnson – a lone avenger against the horrors of late 20th-century existence who could challenge Kate Bush with his snail-like release rate.

Inspired by Punk (but more fond of Bluesmen like Muddy Waters and Howlin' Wolf), Johnson cut a demo with Wire's Bruce Gilbert and Graham Lewis and joined 4AD for his debut, 1979's 'Controversial Subject', and 1981's arty experimental collage *Burning Blue Soul*. As The The, he was adopted by Some Bizarre's fun lovin' scenester Stevo, who secured a deal with Epic (signed on the lion statues in London's Trafalgar Square).

Having scrapped an entire album (the presumably cheery *The Pornography Of Despair*), The The unleashed *Soul Mining* (1983), a shadowy mix of African, traditional American and soulful Pop which became a cult classic. Its achievement was overshadowed by the big-budget *Infected* (1986) which, aside from its crafted songs and hi-tech sound, was accompanied by a book and a feature-length video of every track.

But Johnson switched direction with the grimly excellent *Mind Bomb* (1989), assembling a band which featured former Smith Johnny Marr (whose influence took The The closer to Indie Pop) and setting out on a world tour.

Marr stayed for their best-seller *Dusk* (1993), whose obsession with seedy 'n' swampy Americana was surpassed only by *Hanky Panky* (1995). This misguided collection of Hank Williams covers, originally intended to feature guest vocalists like Leonard Cohen and Michael Stipe, ended up a typical The The construction: Johnson did all the work himself.

surf www.tezcat.com/~juanyen/mick/thethe.htm

THERAPY?

WHO Vocals/guitar **Andy Cairns** (b. 22 Sep 1965, Antrim, Northern Ireland), guitar/cello **Martin McCarrick** (b. 29 Jul 1962, Luton, England), bass **Michael McKeegan** (b. 25 Mar 1971, Antrim), drums **Graham Hopkins** (b. 20 Dec 1975, Dublin, Ireland)

WHEN 1989–

WHERE Belfast, Northern Ireland

WHAT Sabre-toothed Metal tigers

Having cut their teeth with local gigs and support slots with The Stone Roses, Therapy? debuted with the self-financed 'Meat Abstract', then let loose the mini-albums *Babyteeth* (1991) and *Pleasure Death* (1992). The latter, caught on the post-*Nevermind* Grunge breeze, elevated Therapy? to cultdom for their acclaimed *Nurse* (1992) and the hits 'Teethgrinder', 'Accelerator' and, from 1993's 'Shortsharpshock' EP, the particularly nasty 'Screamager'.

TEXAS ⊙

WHO Vocals **Sharleen Spiteri** (b. 7 Nov 1967, Glasgow, Scotland), guitar **Ally McErlaine** (b. 31 Oct 1968, Glasgow), bass **John McElhone** (b. 21 Apr 1963, Glasgow), drums **Richard Hynd** (b. 17 Jun 1965, Aberdeen, Scotland), keyboards **Eddie Campbell** (b. 6 Jul 1965)

WHEN 1986–

WHERE Glasgow, Scotland

WHAT Bluesy Rock with a Pop Sh(arl)een

Having dipped a toe in Pop with Altered Images and Hipsway, John McElhone enlisted Sharleen Spiteri, Ally McErlaine and original members Craig Armstrong (keyboards) and Stuart Kerr (drums) and set off in search of U2-esque Rock majesty as Texas.

Named after Wim Wenders' *Paris, Texas*, they summoned the spirit of Ry Cooder's mournful slide guitar on debut hit 'I Don't Want A Lover' (1989) and *Southside* (1989), but slowly sank with 1991's soulful *Mother's Heaven* and 1993's *Rick's Road*, despite a sizeable fanbase and a hit with Al Green's 'Tired Of Being Alone'.

However, their wilderness years ended with 1997's UK No.1 *White On Blonde*. While the rest of the band faded into almost Sleeper-esque anonymity, Spiteri emerged as primary writer and Pop pin. They reached a pinnacle with 'Say What You Want', 'Halo', 'Put Your Arms Around Me' and 'Black Eyed Boy', which all soared into the UK Top 10 – a feat marred slightly by their dire reworking of 'Say What You Want' with Wu-Tang Clan's Method Man and RZA.

surf ourworld.compuserve.com/homepages/texasfan/texashp.htm

Troublegum (1994) proved Therapy?'s zenith, uniting Indie, Pop and Metal and selling truckloads, but a cover of Joy Division's 'Isolation' in their live set proved Therapy?'s dark heart was still beating. Their ascent continued with 1995's refined *Infernal Love* (their last with original drummer Fyfe Ewing), whose sparse cover of Hüsker Dü's 'Diane' was dominated by new recruit Martin McCarrick's cello. Years of heavy-duty touring took its toll, particularly on Andy Cairns, prompting a lengthy wait for the noisy return-to-form *Semi-Detached* (1998).

 PO Box 28, Blackrock, Co Dublin, Ireland

surf www.therapyquestionmark.co.uk

THIN LIZZY

WHO Vocals/bass **Phil Lynott** (b. 20 Aug 1949, West Bromwich, England, d. 4 Jan 1986, Salisbury, Wiltshire, England), guitar **Scott Gorham** (b. 17 Mar 1951, Santa Monica, California, USA), guitar **Brian Robertson** (b. 12 Sep 1956, Glasgow, Scotland), drums **Brian Downey** (b. 27 Jan 1951, Dublin, Ireland)

WHEN 1969–1983

WHERE Dublin, Ireland

WHAT Evergreen Rock from the Emerald Isle

Stadium stomper Jon Bon Jovi and Hardcore heavy Henry Rollins doubtless agree on very little, but both publicly salute Thin Lizzy's Phil Lynott. He embodied the sex, drugs 'n' Rock 'n' Roll life, but was a writer *par excellence* and a bright diamond in Hard Rock's rough.

Raised by his grandmother in Crumlin, a working-class estate in Dublin (his expatriate Irish mother struggled as a single parent in England), Lynott accentuated his striking looks with an Afro hairdo and rakish moustache à la his hero Jimi Hendrix. Singing in amateur R&B band The Black Eagles, he united with drummer Brian Downey, a neighbour of Phil's and ally for most of his career thereafter.

From another act (Orphanage), Lynott and Downey united with Eric Bell, a Belfast guitarist who had played in covers groups on the showband circuit. Bell also brought in short-stayed keyboard player Eric Wrixon. Thin Lizzy debuted in Dublin in spring 1970 and issued their first single, 'The Farmer', in July. Blending Rock and Folk, *Thin Lizzy* (1971), *Shades Of A Blue Orphanage* (1972) and *Vagabonds Of The Western World* (1973) boasted remarkable lyrics that evoked heroes of Irish mythology. Accordingly, they scored a 1973 hit with an updated take on the Folk song 'Whisky In The Jar', in whose hit-less aftermath Bell was replaced by the short-stayed Gary Moore.

The classic Lizzy line-up came together in 1974. Guitarists Scott Gorham and Brian Robertson alternated a soft-edged US style with aggressive Celtic Blues: a twin-guitar tapestry honed

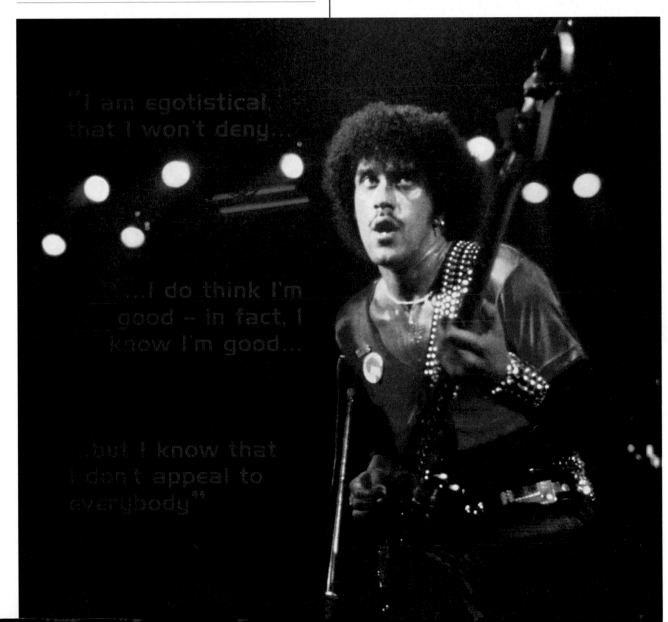

"I am egotistical, that I won't deny...

...I do think I'm good – in fact, I know I'm good...

...but I know that I don't appeal to everybody"

over *Nightlife* (1974) and *Fighting* (1975), then commercially realized on *Jailbreak* (1976). The latter's slow-burning title track and good-time anthem 'The Boys Are Back In Town' became hits and enduring classics.

Though plagued by indulgence – Moore had to deputize for Robertson – Lizzy bore more classics with 1976's *Johnny The Fox*, 1977's *Bad Reputation* and 1979's *Black Rose (A Rock Legend)*, which respectively hit with 'Don't Believe A Word', 'Dancin' In The Moonlight' (covered by Smashing Pumpkins on their 1994 'Disarm' single) and 'Waiting For An Alibi'. They also made one of *the* great live albums, *Live And Dangerous* (1978).

Temporarily enlisting future Ultravox saviour Midge Ure and then Snowy White, formerly Dave Gilmour's deputy in Pink Floyd, Lizzy shot into the new decade with *Chinatown* and Lynott's *Solo In Soho* (both 1980). But their stock fell with 1982's *Renegade* and White went solo for the 1983 hit 'Bird Of Paradise'.

Revived by guitarist John Sykes (who later hot-wired Whitesnake too) and keyboard player Darren Wharton, *Thunder And Lightning* (1983) was a brilliant blend of Metal and poetic balladry (extremes illustrated by the hits 'Cold Sweat' and 'The Sun Goes Down'). But Lynott and Scott Gorham's addictions stalled the recovery, and Thin Lizzy played their last gig in Nuremberg, Germany, on 4 September 1983. Lynott formed the underachieving Grand Slam in 1984, scored a hit with 1985's Gary Moore duet 'Out In The Fields' and was toying with a Lizzy revival when he died in 1986. His legacy is celebrated by hits sets and regular tribute shows starring Lizzy's other members.

READ *The Ballad Of The Thin Man: The Authorised Biography Of Phil Lynott And Thin Lizzy* (1997), Stuart Bailie

FAN Black Rose, 7 Rockfield Rise, Maynooth, Co Kildare, Ireland

SURF dspace.dial.pipex.com/thinlizzy/

RICHARD THOMPSON

WHO b. 3 Apr 1949, London, England

WHAT Underrated guitar hero

After leaving Fairport Convention in 1971, Richard Thompson became one of those artists whose critical plaudits didn't translate into sales.

After immersing himself in session work, Thompson was working with Fairport alumni in 1972 in The Bunch, which included session singer and future wife and musical partner Linda Peters. His first solo effort, *Henry The Human Fly* (1972), got slated and was the lowest selling album of any division of Warner Bros. After hiding in the comparative safety of Folk clubs for two years, the newly married Thompsons released the classic-in-hindsight *I Want To See The Bright Lights Tonight* (1974), which had lain in Island Records' vault for nearly a year.

A conversion to the Sufi branch of Islam followed, as did the uncharacteristically cheerful *Hokey Pokey* (in contrast, a later fan club cassette was cheekily but accurately titled *Doom & Gloom From the Tomb*) and the Sufi-influenced *Pour Down Like Silver* (both 1975). Little was heard for the next three years, which included a period in a Suffolk commune. In 1980, Gerry Rafferty produced *Shoot Out The Lights* in an attempt to crack the American market. Thompson thought the production too polished and, after some salvaging, released it in 1982.

Receiving rave American reviews, it prompted the Thompsons to tour the USA. It swiftly became the tour from hell, as Richard had fallen in love with American promoter Nancy Covey and separated from Linda.

Solo again, Thompson finally crept in to the lower reaches of the UK chart with *Across A Crowded Room* (1985), *Daring Adventures* (1986) and *Amnesia* (1988). Then 1991's *Rumour And Sigh* cracked the Top 40, 1994's *Mirror Blue* reached No.23 and 1996's *You? Me? Us?* made No.32. A three-CD box set, *Watching The Dark* (1993), contained rare and unreleased material, including some of the aborted Rafferty sessions, while the tribute album *Beat The Retreat* (1994) had the likes of David Byrne, Dinosaur Jr, Shawn Colvin, Bonnie Raitt, Bob Mould and REM offering their interpretations of Thompson songs.

READ *Richard Thompson – Strange Affair* (1996), Patrick Humphries

THOMPSON TWINS ⊙

WHO Vocals/keyboards **Tom Bailey** (b. 18 Jun 1957, Halifax, West Yorkshire, England), vocals/saxophone **Alannah Currie** (b. 20 Sep 1959, Auckland, New Zealand), vocals/percussion **Joe Leeway** (b. 15 Nov 1957, London, England)

WHEN 1977–

WHERE Sheffield, England

WHAT Agit-Pop then Synth Pop

The first two Thompson Twins albums, *A Product Of…* (1981) and *Set* (1982), came from a septet who combined Funk, African rhythms and polemical lyrics. Neither album sold well, but one atypically commercial track from *Set*, 'In The Name Of Love', became an American dancefloor hit. That convinced Tom Bailey, Alannah Currie and Joe Leeway that their future lay in glossy electronic Pop. The other four Twins disagreed, and quit.

The new Twins trio – critically despised but commercially successful – scored nine UK hits from 1983–1984, the biggest – 'You Take Me Up' – reaching No.2. *Quick Step And Side Kick* (1983) and *Into The Gap* (1984) were internationally popular, the latter topping the British chart, but the major hits dried up in 1985. Leeway quit in 1986, but Bailey and Currie persisted, dropping the reviled Thompson Twins name in 1992 to become Babble.

SURF www.interlog.com/~ditko37/ttwins.html

THREE DOG NIGHT

WHO Vocals **Danny Hutton** (b. 10 Sep 1942, Buncrana, Ireland), vocals **Chuck Negron** (b. 8 Jun 1942, The Bronx, New York), vocals **Cory Wells** (b. 5 Feb 1942, Buffalo, New York), guitar **Mike Allsup** (b. 8 Mar 1947, Modesto, California), bass **Joe Schermie** (b. 12 Feb 1945, Madison, Wisconsin), drums **Floyd Sneed** (b. 22 Nov 1943, Calgary, Alberta, Canada), keyboards **Jimmy Greenspoon** (b. 7 Feb 1948, Los Angeles, California)

WHEN 1967–1977

WHERE Los Angeles, California

WHAT Soul-flavoured Pop Rock

Although their albums never charted in Britain, Three Dog Night were one of the biggest-selling bands in the USA in the late 60s and early 70s, with 18 consecutive US Top 20 hits. Despite their dependence on cover versions, they championed unknown writers and chose, arranged and co-produced their songs.

After auditioning unsuccessfully for The Monkees in 1965, Danny Hutton envisaged three lead vocalists with a backing band. Their debut *Three Dog Night* (1968) reached US No.11 and the final single released from it was their first big hit, a cover of Harry Nilsson's 'One' (US No.5). Their 1969 follow-up, *Suitable For Framing*, provided more hits, courtesy of new songwriter Laura Nyro ('Eli's Coming') and 'Easy To Be Hard' from the musical *Hair*.

Their UK chart debut was 1970's version of Randy Newman's 'Mama Told Me (Not To Come)' – UK No.3/US No.1. Their second and final transatlantic hit, Hoyt Axton's 'Joy To The World' (UK No.24), was a US No.1 in 1971. They disbanded in 1977, but have re-formed sporadically thereafter.

 Three Dog Night Fan Club, c/o Madonna Nuckolls, PO Box 1975, Rowlett, TX 75030, USA

 www.threedognight.com/

THROWING MUSES

WHO Vocals/guitar **Kristin Hersh** (b. 7 Aug 1966, Atlanta, Georgia, USA), guitar/vocals **Tanya Donelly** (b. 14 Jul 1966, Newport, Rhode Island, USA), bass **Leslie Langston** (b. 1 Apr 1964, Newport), drums **David Narcizo** (b. 6 May 1966, Newport)

WHEN 1980–1997

WHERE Newport, Rhode Island, USA

WHAT Spooky and the banshees

Formed by Kristin Hersh, her stepsister Tanya Donelly (both 14) and Elaine Adamedes, Throwing Muses were to be an all-girl band, were it not for the fact that the only drummer they knew was David Narcizo. As Leslie Langston replaced Adamedes, they moved to Boston, were the first US band signed to 4AD, and let loose the mighty *Throwing Muses* (1986) and 1987's 'Chains Changed' and 'The Fat Skier' EPs.

The glorious *House Tornado* (1988) showcased their songwriting strengths and *Hunkpapa* (1989) aimed squarely at the mainstream. The music had evolved from quavery Folk Punk to an REM-ish Country thrash, though still distinguished by the wailing vocals and obscure lyrics of Hersh, who – driven by mental disorder – had long fought to separate her songs and hallucinations, both auditory and visual. This tended to eclipse her sister's songwriting, which found more rewarding outlets with The Breeders' *Pod* (1990), alongside Pixies' Kim Deal, then Belly (who scored with 1993's *Star* and 1995's *King*). Donelly's Muses swan song was 1990's crunching *The Real Ramona*, on which Fred Abong deputized for Langston.

After 1992's rockier *Red Heaven* (boasting a Bob Mould cameo), Langston again ducked out, as Hersh went solo for the resplendent *Hips And Makers* (1994). This beautiful acoustic set, boasting a duet with REM's Michael Stipe on the hit 'Your Ghost', outsold the Muses and, although Hersh and Narcizo enlisted bassist Bernard Georges for 1995's underwhelming *University* and 1997's *Limbo*, the end was nigh. The band split in dire financial straits, fans finding consolation in Donelly's Belly-less *Songs For Underdogs* (1997) and Hersh's *Strange Angels* (1998).

 www.throwingmusic.com/

TINDERSTICKS

WHO Vocals/guitar **Stuart Staples** (b. 14 Nov 1965, Nottingham, England), guitar **Neil Fraser** (b. 22 Nov 1962, London, England), violin/guitar **Dickon Hinchcliffe** (b. 9 Jul 1967, Nottingham), bass **Mark Colwill** (b. 15 May 1967, Nottingham), drums **Al Macaulay** (b. 2 Aug 1965, Nottingham), keyboards **David Boulter** (b. 27 Feb 1965, Nottingham)

WHEN 1992–

WHERE Nottingham, England

WHAT Sumptuous sombre soundscapes

Stuart Staples, Dave Boulter and Dickon Hinchcliffe first made melancholy music together in Asphalt Ribbons, releasing numerous singles and one mini-album, *Old Horse* (1991), before evolving into the hugely acclaimed Tindersticks in 1992.

Tindersticks (1993) revealed a band with a unique style and vision. The 21-song album was an epic examination of the darker areas of life and love, with deeply personal lyrics set to subtle, sombre and frequently beautiful music. Staples' mournful vocals, sometimes murmured rather than sung, enhanced the sense of intimacy.

Tindersticks have explored similar shadowy territory on their subsequent studio albums, *The Second Tindersticks Album* (1995) and *Curtains* (1997), and on two live recordings, *Amsterdam 1994* and *The Bloomsbury Theatre 12.3.95*. They've also ventured into film music, recording the soundtrack for Claire Denis' movie *Nenette Et Boni* (1996). Their reputation and audience have grown with each new release.

surf huizen.dds.nl/~totos/tinder.htm

TINDERSTICKS:FRANK COURTES:RETNA

TLC

WHO Vocals **T-Boz** (b. Tionne Watkins, 26 Apr 1970, Des Moines, Iowa, USA), vocals **Left-Eye** (b. Lisa Lopes, 27 May 1971, Philadelphia, Pennsylvania, USA), vocals **Chilli** (b. Rozonda Thomas, 27 Feb 1971)

WHEN 1991–

WHERE Atlanta, Georgia, USA

WHAT Sultry sirens of Swing

Swingbeat was a sweaty thing in the 80s, ruled by bare-chested boys. A much-needed note of feminine elegance was added by Pebbles, who hit with 'Girlfriend' and 'Mercedes Boy' in 1988. When her success tailed off in the 90s, Pebbles (married to L.A. Reid, half of the hit-making duo LA & Babyface) masterminded TLC, who joined the 'New Jill Swing' wave alongside En Vogue and SWV.

With rock-solid connections (remixed by Swing supremo Teddy Riley, released on LA & Babyface's label), *Oooooooohh… On The TLC Tip* (1992) went double platinum on the back of the very rude indeed 'Ain't 2 Proud 2 Beg' (nothing to do with the similarly titled Temptations tune), 'Baby-Baby-Baby' and 'What About Your Friends'.

With the Prince-penned 'Get It Up', TLC graced the soundtrack of *Poetic Justice* (a 1993 movie with Janet Jackson and Tupac Shakur), then hit back in 1994. Out were the zany image and squeaky vocals, in were combat boots and almost jazzy grooves.

They were further distinguished by the charismatically unhinged Left-Eye, who swore at awards ceremonies and torched her boyfriend's home. Meanwhile, 'Creep' shot to US No.1, taking *CrazySexyCool* to double platinum too, and the whole world fell in love with 'Waterfalls' (aided by its video, in which TLC were reborn as *Terminator 2*-esque animatrons, and which featured Wu-Tang wonderkid Shyheim).

But the trio were dogged by financial hassles and a split loomed when T-Boz put out 1997's 'Touch Myself'. They could take some consolation from the success of All Saints, whose R&B, rudeness and Bart Simpson-esque rapping owed a whole lot to the TLC template.

PETER TOSH

WHO b. Winston Hubert Peter McIntosh, 19 Oct 1944, Westmoreland, Jamaica, d. 11 Sep 1987, Barbican, St Andrew, Jamaica

WHAT Reggae outlaw

Having grown up in the Kingston ghetto of Trenchtown in the 50s, Peter Tosh hooked up with Bob Marley and Bunny Livingstone to form The Wailers, who joined the Studio One label in 1964. He fronted The Wailers on rude boy anthems 'I'm The Toughest' and 'Maga Dog', released as Peter Touch and The Wailers (Touch is how 'Tosh' sounds in the Kingston dialect) and continued recording with Livingstone as The Wailers during Marley's 1966 stay in America.

After a brief stay in prison, circa 1967, on marijuana charges (in 1978 he smoked a joint on stage in front of the Jamaican prime minister as a protest to legalize marijuana), Tosh also launched a parallel solo career which blossomed when he quit The Wailers in 1973. Running his own label, Intel-Diplo HIM (Intelligent Diplomat for His Imperial Majesty) in Jamaica, he signed to Virgin for the classic dope-smoker's album *Legalize It* (1976) and *Equal Rights* (1977). *Bush Doctor* (1978) found Tosh on Rolling Stones Records, skimming transatlantic charts with a cover of The Temptations' '(You Got To Walk And) Don't Look Back' (1978) – a duet with Mick Jagger on a track he'd previously recorded in 1967.

Tosh signed to EMI for *Mama Africa* (1983), but 1987's *No Nuclear War* proved his final album: he died later that year, shot during a robbery at his home. He left an uncompromising and feisty musical legacy, best illustrated on 1993's video *Stepping Razor – The Red X Tapes*.

TOTO

WHO Vocals **Bobby Kimball** (b. Robert Toteaux, 29 Mar 1947, Vinton, Louisiana, USA), guitar **Steve Lukather** (b. 21 Oct 1957, Los Angeles, California, USA), bass **David Hungate**, drums **Jeff Porcaro** (b. 1 Apr 1954, Hartford, Connecticut, USA, d. 5 Aug 1992, Holden Hills, California), keyboards **David Paich** (b. 25 Jun 1954, Los Angeles), keyboards **Steve Porcaro** (b. 2 Sep 1957, Hartford)

WHEN 1977–

WHERE Los Angeles, California, USA

WHAT Airbrushed AOR

They made AOR more adult and less Rock than ever! Their drummer died, Spinal Tap-style, in a bizarre gardening accident! Session aces all (their collective CV boasts Pink Floyd, Steely Dan, Earth Wind & Fire, Boz Scaggs and Cheap Trick), Toto took their name from Bobby Kimball's real surname, the dog in *The Wizard Of Oz* and, possibly, a well-known Japanese toilet manufacturer. They lurched into action with 1979's US hit 'Hold The Line', which sent *Toto* (1978) skyward. The oily *Hydra* (1979) and *Turn Back* (1981) sold only moderately, but the Grammy-winning *Toto IV* (1982) menaced charts worldwide, thanks to airbrushed hits 'Africa' and 'Rosanna' – a gift from the love-struck Steve Porcaro to actress Rosanna Arquette. She dumped him.

Also swift to jump ship were Kimball and Hungate, but with new singer Dennis 'Fergie' Frederiksen and bassist Mike Porcaro, Toto ploughed on – as backing band on USA For Africa's 'We Are The World', as soundtrackers (David Lynch's 1984 *Dune*) and as spectacular failures (1984's *Isolation* and 1986's *Fahrenheit* and *The Seventh One*, with Frederiksen's replacement Joseph Williams). Undaunted, they installed new warbler Jean-Michel Byron and continued with presumably brief hits set *Past To Present 1977–1990* (1990) and *Kingdom Of Desire* (1993).

Cementing their post-Arquette luckless streak, Jeff Porcaro's allegedly cocaine-linked death was ludicrously reported as an allergic reaction to garden pesticides.

surf www.sony.com/music/artistinfo/toto

TRAFFIC

WHO Vocals/keyboards/guitar/bass **Steve 'Stevie' Winwood** (b. Stephen Philip Winwood, 12 May 1948, Birmingham, England), vocals/guitar **Dave Mason** (b. 10 May 1945, Worcester, England), flute/saxophone **Chris Wood** (b. 24 Jun 1944, Birmingham, d. 12 Jul 1983, London, England), drums/vocals **Jim Capaldi** (b. 24 Aug 1944, Evesham, England)

WHEN 1967–

WHERE Aston Tirrold, Berkshire, England

WHAT Psychedelic Folk Jazz Blues Rock

Traffic's diverse and inventive music epitomized the questing spirit of British progressive music in the late 60s, and at its best

TLC/JEFFREY SCALES/CORBIS

still manages to sound fresh and distinctive several decades later, a measure of both the group's abilities and the authentic mulch of influences in which it was rooted.

Traffic was formed by teenage R&B prodigy Stevie Winwood when he quit The Spencer Davis Group, for whose mid-60s hits he had provided searing Soul vocals. With drummer and lyricist Jim Capaldi, flautist Chris Wood and fellow multi-instrumentalist Dave Mason, he initiated the hippie practice of retreating to a country cottage (celebrated in their debut album's 'Berkshire Poppies') to 'get an album together'. The first fruits of their labours – 1967's sitar-strewn 'Paper Sun' and fairy-tale fantasy 'Hole In My Shoe' – were immediate hits. Further success with 'Here We Go Round The Mulberry Bush' (1967), recorded for the movie of the same name, kept them in the public eye until their acclaimed debut album, the eclectic *Mr. Fantasy* (1967).

Shortly after contributing the popular 'You Can All Join In' and 'Feelin' Alright' to the equally impressive follow-up *Traffic* (1969), Mason left to pursue a solo career whose highlight was *Alone Together* (1970). The remaining members soldiered on with the patchy, partly live *Last Exit* (1969) before Winwood was tempted away to form the short-lived supergroup Blind Faith with Eric Clapton, Ginger Baker and Ric Grech. When that project collapsed ignominiously, he regrouped with Wood and Capaldi to make the Folk Jazz landmark *John Barleycorn Must Die* (1970) which, at No.5, was to be their biggest US hit.

After this, Traffic took on a less focused, more open-ended 'jamming' sound with the addition of bass player Grech, drummer Jim Gordon and Ghanaian percussionist Reebop Kwaku Baah. Mason returned briefly for the live *Welcome To The Canteen* (1971), but had gone again by the time of *The Low Spark Of High Heeled Boys* (1972).

Winwood's complications from appendicitis then rendered Traffic inactive for most of 1972, but later that year a new line-up, with Winwood, Capaldi, Wood and Kwaku Baah, augmented by the celebrated Muscle Shoals rhythm section of bassist David Hood and drummer Roger Hawkins, made *Shoot-Out At The Fantasy Factory* (1973) and remained for the live double *On The Road* (1973). A final album, *When The Eagle Flies* (1974), was recorded by the central trio and bassist Rosko Gee, before Traffic split up for good. Winwood, Mason and Capaldi all enjoyed successful solo careers, but Wood suffered a lengthy illness and died of liver failure in 1983. A lacklustre reunion album, *Far From Home* (1994), featured a nucleus of Winwood and Capaldi.

THE TRAVELING WILBURYS

WHO Vocals/keyboards/guitar **Otis/Clayton Wilbury** (b. Jeff Lynne, 30 Dec 1947, Birmingham, England), vocals/guitar **Nelson/Spike Wilbury** (b. George Harrison, 24 Feb 1943, Liverpool, England), vocals/guitar **Charlie T. Junior/Muddy Wilbury** (b. Tom Petty, 20 Oct 1952, Gainesville, Florida, USA), vocals/guitar **Lefty Wilbury** (b. Roy Orbison, 23 Apr 1936, Vernon, Texas, USA, d. 6 Dec 1988, Nashville, Tennesse, USA), vocals/guitar **Lucky/Boo Wilbury** (b. Robert Zimmerman, 24 May 1941, Duluth, Minnesota, USA)

WHEN 1988–1990

WHERE California, USA

WHAT A(gglomerating) O(ld) R(ockers)

Where did old Rock stars go when the sparkle dimmed? Why, to The Traveling Wilburys, of course. Dreamt up as a superstar get-together at Dave Stewart's house and rehearsed in Bob Dylan's garage, *The Traveling Wilburys Volume 1* (1988) proved a commercial godsend for Dylan, George Harrison, Jeff Lynne and Tom Petty. Even Roy Orbison – who died shortly after their first hit, 'Handle With Care' – had his biggest solo hit for decades with 1989's Wilbury-ish 'You Got It'. The video for the Wilburys' 'End Of The Line' poignantly focused on an empty chair during Orbison's verse.

Their laid-back humour was maintained by an updating of their fictitious identities on 1990's Orbison-less *The Traveling Wilburys Volume 3*, but this time the joke was thinner and the commercial rewards fewer.

 cvrc.med.upenn.edu/~greenberg/al-twl-l.html

TRICKY

WHO b. Adrian Thawes, 27 Jan 1968, Bristol, England

WHAT Trip Hop's twisted twin

After an unsettled childhood (his mother died when he was 4 and he was raised by his grandmother in Bristol's tough Knowle West area), Tricky graduated from petty crime to Hip Hop collective The Wild Bunch – the seeds of Massive Attack. Having graced Massive's *Blue Lines* (1991) and *Protection* (1994), he jumped ship, recruiting angel-voiced teenager Martina Topley-Bird (a lovely contrast to his own asthmatic wheeze) for his debut 'Aftermath' (1994).

Fame came with 1995's bewitching *Maxinquaye*. A mischievous doppelgänger to Trip Hop rivals Massive Attack and Portishead, it sampled Smashing Pumpkins ('Pumpkin'), savaged Rage Against The Machine ('Brand New You're Retro') and steamrolled Public Enemy ('Black Steel'). By the end of the year, he'd collaborated with Björk, Luscious Jackson and – on the 'The Hell EP' – Wu-Tang Clan's RZA. He also issued 'I Be The Prophet' as Starving Souls and made *Nearly God* (1996) – a queasily claustrophobic collection of duets with Martina, Terry Hall, Björk, Alison Moyet and Neneh Cherry.

By 1996's 'Grass Roots' EP and *Pre-Millenium Tension*, Tricky was holed up in New York, overseeing Rap protégés Drunkenstein and sprinkling magic misery dust on remixes for Elvis Costello, Garbage, Yoko Ono and Bush. More remixes (The Notorious BIG, Black Grape), a role in *The Fifth Element* (1997), and the one-offs 'Divine Comedy' and 'Can't Freestyle' (which respectively rubbished Polygram and his uncle Finlay Quaye), filled time before the release of *Angels With Dirty Faces* (1998), trailed by a collaboration with Polly Harvey, 'Broken Homes'.

 www.primenet.com/~aboo/tricky/index.html

"I'm actually very very very normal. Cheese sandwich normal"

TRIP HOP

WHAT Just as no one would voluntarily describe themselves as 'Goth', so the banner-carriers for Trip Hop would rather bury the term. "Anyone here like Trip Hop?" enquired Tricky of one audience. "Well, fuck off, then." However, Tricky was just as much to blame for the phenomenon, given his links with England's Wild Bunch posse. When they evolved into Massive Attack and made stoned Soul a critical and commercial sensation, the stage was set for Portishead and Tricky to score too with scratchy samples, jazzy ambience and drawled vocals. When wannabes like Morcheeba and Sneaker Pimps stepped in, Trip Hop promptly seemed more like a marketing than musical term.

WHERE Bristol, UK

WHEN Early 90s–

WHO John Barry The Ipcress File (1965), Massive Attack Protection (1994), Tricky Maxinquaye (1994), Portishead Dummy (1994), Various Headz (1995), DJ Shadow Endtroducing (1996), Howie B Music For Babies (1996), Morcheeba Big Calm (1998)

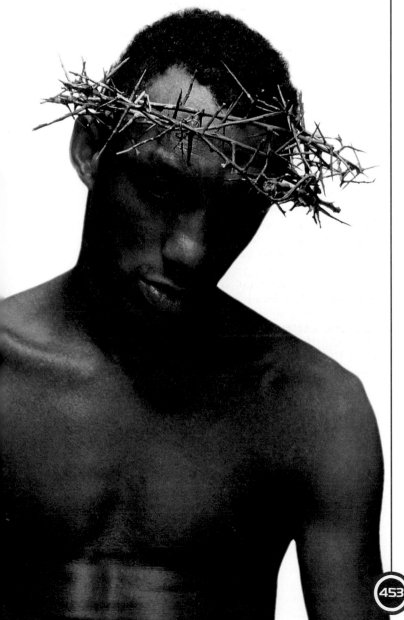

THE TROGGS

WHO Vocals **Reg Presley** (b. Reginald Ball, 12 Jun 1941, Andover, Hampshire, England), guitar **Chris Britton** (b. 21 Jan 1944, Watford, Hertfordshire, England), bass **Pete Staples** (b. 3 May 1944, Andover), drums **Ronnie Bond** (b. Ronald Bullis, 4 May 1943, Andover, d. 13 Nov 1992, Winchester)

WHEN 1964–

WHERE Andover, Hampshire, England

WHAT Stone Age Pop

This missing link between Wet Wet Wet and REM was a hybrid of Andover groups The Troglodytes (Reg Presley and Ronnie Bond) and Ten Feet Five (Chris Britton and Pete Staples). The Troggs laboured as Kinks copyists before apprentice bricklayer Presley swapped bass for vocals and their primitive power Pop hit UK No.2 with 1966's 'Wild Thing'. Originally a cult US hit for Jordan Christopher And The Wild Ones, it boasted a three-chord trick straight from 'Louie Louie', marvellously dumb lyrics and a Presley ocarina solo. The Troggs reasserted Pop's instant gratification at a time when most British groups were churning out maudlin Dylan replicas. Subtlety was alien to them and Presley, on the evidence of the raunchy 'I Can't Control Myself', was an untamed sex beast. As Psychedelia loomed, their stock-in-trade simplicity looked outmoded but, while Hendrix stole their thunder with his monstrous 'Wild Thing' remake, they courted the Summer Of Love with 'Maybe The Madman' – a comical acid trip without the acid, shot through with country bumpkin charm – and the excellent 'Love Is All Around'.

Though declining fortunes prompted the departure of Staples (1969, replaced by Tony Murray) and Britton (1972, replaced by Richard Moore), they found a new audience with the unwitting comedy of *The Troggs Tapes* (1976). This bootleg of Presley's foul-mouthed squabble with Bond, as they tried to concoct another hit, proved a major influence on Spinal Tap.

But The Troggs refused to quit. Either bravery or lunacy prompted 1975 covers of The Beach Boys' 'Good Vibrations' and The Rolling Stones' 'Satisfaction', but their wonderfully heavy-handed style was celebrated by the growing Punk scene. In 1976, they (plus new guitarist Colin Fletcher) played with The Damned and The Flamin' Groovies, but it was the USA which held them most dear, ensuring a cult following through the 80s.

The 90s brought reappraisal: REM's Peter Buck graced 1991's acclaimed *Athens Andover* and, though Bond's death marred the occasion, Presley and Britton (who returned in 1979) were vindicated when Wet Wet Wet's 1994 cover of 'Love Is All Around' topped the UK chart for 15 weeks. Presley spent his royalties researching UFOs and crop circles, presumably concluding that if The Troggs can get to No.1, anything can happen.

TINA TURNER ◉ ◉

WHO b. Anna Mae Bullock, 26 Nov 1939, Nutbush, Tennessee, USA

WHAT Sired in Soul, resurrected in Rock

Precociously jumping on stage with Ike Turner's Kings of Rhythm at 17, Anna Mae Bullock became first Ike's singer, then his lover. Her first recording, as Ike & Tina Turner, was 'A Fool In Love' (1960) – stepping in for a session singer who didn't show up. Later billed as the Ike & Tina Turner Revue, they recorded the fantastic 'River Deep, Mountain High' (1966), 'Proud Mary' (1971) and 'Nutbush City Limits' (1973). They were one of the most explosive and influential acts of the 60s. Money, fame and a part for Tina in *Tommy* (1973) followed but, amid Ike's infidelities and drug addiction, he beat and imprisoned Tina.

Ditching Ike in 1976 – and leaving with only 36 cents – Tina struck out on her own. Converted to Buddhism, heavily in debt, and struggling to kick off Ike's reputation, she played low-key gigs (including a McDonald's sales convention in 1984). New manager Roger Davies arrived as a ray of light.

In 1981, she supported The Rolling Stones and Rod Stewart, and undertook an unlikely collaboration with Heaven 17 on *Music Of Quality And Distinction* (1982). Still, a record deal was elusive until David Bowie touted her to Capitol as "his favourite singer". 'Let's Stay Together' (1983) marked Turner's rebirth. The stomping US No.1 'What's Love Got To Do With It?' and 'Better Be Good To Me' saw Tina eclipse Ike, and *Private Dancer* (1984) made the Top 3 both sides of the Atlantic.

By the mid-80s she was one of the few women included in the Rock aristocracy. In a Live Aid duet, she out-strutted Mick Jagger. In 1985, 'We Don't Need Another Hero (Thunderdome)' – from the movie *Mad Max: Beyond Thunderdome* – reached UK No.3/US No.2. To this she also contributed an expertly played Aunt Entity – having allegedly turned down a role in Steven Spielberg's *The Color Purple*.

In 1996 she appeared at the Prince's Trust concert with Eric Clapton, Elton John and Bryan Adams (with whom she had duetted on 'It's Only Love' the previous year), and was awarded a star on Hollywood's Walk Of Fame. A No.1 album still eluded her, though 'Typical Male' and *Break Every Rule* (1986) boasted production work by Mark Knopfler and Adams.

She toured the world in 1987 – hence 1988's *Live In Europe* – and even her ad for corporate sponsors Pepsi was a recording of a live performance. Continuing into 1988, she made *The Guinness Book Of Records* with a performance in Rio to 182,000. *Foreign Affair* (1989) spawned 'The Best' – an omnipresent Rock standard whose enormity swamped even high-charting releases like 1989's 'I Don't Wanna Lose You' and 'Steamy Windows', and 1990's 'Look Me In The Heart' and 'Be Tender With Me Baby'. A reworking of Marvin Gaye and Tammi Terrell's 'It Takes Two' with Rod Stewart for Pepsi, and the hits set *Simply The Best* (1991), became chart mainstays. In 1991, she and Ike were inducted into The Rock And Roll Hall Of Fame, as Ike languished in prison.

Her contributions to 1991's *Music Of Quality And Distinction Vol. 2* ('A Change Is Gonna Come') and 1992's *Two Rooms*; a tribute to Elton John and Bernie Taupin ('The Bitch Is Back'); a rainforest benefit concert with Bryan Adams, Herb Alpert, Tom Jones, George Michael and Sting; and a $50,000 donation to a child abuse centre were all low-key. For the Trammps cover 'Disco Inferno', though, she was again gloriously ostentatious.

She achieved further recognition for her aptly-titled 'I Don't Wanna Fight' (1993), co-written with Lulu, 1993's biopic *What's Love Got To Do With It?* and its No.1 soundtrack, and a three-decade-spanning anthology, *The Collected Recordings* (1995).

Her legendary status was confirmed with 'Goldeneye' – the title track to 1995's Bond movie. *Wildest Dreams* (1996), boasting duets with Sting and Antonio Banderas, preceded another sellout world tour. In 1998, she helped open the new wing of The Rock And Roll Hall Of Fame and won the ultimate accolade – topping the 1997 Sexy Legs Survey alongside Jean Claude Van Damme, beating Cindy Crawford and Mel Gibson hands down.

reaD *I Tina* (1986), Tina Turner & Kurt Loder

surf www.wallofsound.com/artists/tinaturner/index.html

THE TURTLES

WHO Vocals/saxophone **Howard Kaylan** (b. Howard Kaplan, 22 Jun 1947, New York City, USA), vocals/saxophone/violin **Mark Volman** (b. 19 Apr 1947, Los Angeles, California, USA), guitar/piano/vocals **Al Nichol** (b. 31 Mar 1946, Winston Salem, North Carolina, USA), bass **Jim Pons** (b. 14 Mar 1943, Santa Monica, California), drums **John Barbata** (b. 1 Apr 1946, New Jersey, USA)

WHEN 1963–

WHERE Westchester, Los Angeles, California, USA

WHAT Close-harmony Pop

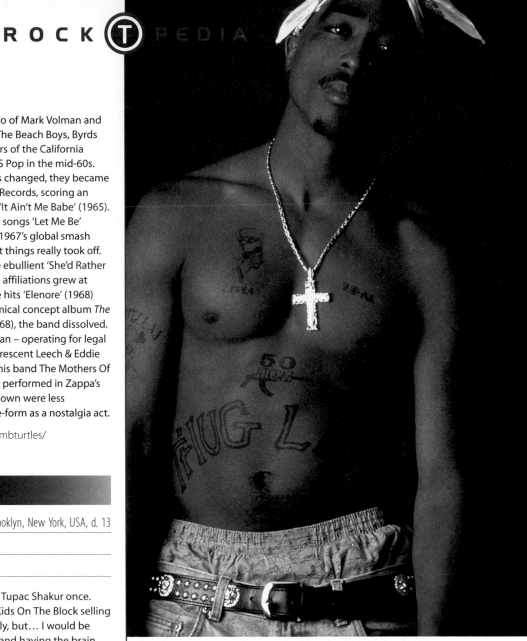

Fronted by the engaging, portly vocal duo of Mark Volman and Howard Kaylan, The Turtles were – with The Beach Boys, Byrds and The Mamas & The Papa – practitioners of the California harmony sound that dominated white US Pop in the mid-60s. Switching from Surf to Folk Rock as times changed, they became The Turtles after signing to White Whale Records, scoring an instant hit with a strong cover of Dylan's 'It Ain't Me Babe' (1965).

Despite further hits with the P.F. Sloan songs 'Let Me Be' (1965) and 'You Baby' (1966), it was with 1967's global smash 'Happy Together' (US No.1/UK No.12) that things really took off. They consolidated their position with the ebullient 'She'd Rather Be With Me' (1967), but the band's hippie affiliations grew at odds with their clean-cut music. After the hits 'Elenore' (1968) and 'You Showed Me' (1969), and the comical concept album *The Turtles Present The Battle Of The Bands* (1968), the band dissolved.

Frank Zappa drafted Volman and Kaylan – operating for legal reasons under the pseudonyms The Phlorescent Leech & Eddie (aka Flo & Eddie) – along with Pons, into his band The Mothers Of Invention, with whom they recorded and performed in Zappa's movie *200 Motels* (1971). Albums of their own were less successful, and the 80s saw The Turtles re-form as a nostalgia act.

 www.bymgroup.com/smwebpage/smbturtles/
turtlecrossing.html

2PAC ✪ ✪ ✪

WHO b. Tupac Amaru Shakur, 16 Jun 1971, Brooklyn, New York, USA, d. 13 Sep 1996, Las Vegas, Nevada, USA

WHAT The Kurt Cobain of Rap

"I look over at what's successful," mused Tupac Shakur once. "Marky Mark, Hammer, Vanilla Ice, New Kids On The Block selling 22 million copies, and I want that so badly, but… I would be wrong to do that, knowing what I know and having the brain that I have. For me to even go and write some simple shit would be wrong even though I would get paid and I would get more people's money. I would rather leave something so that when people pick up *2Pacalypse Now* or any of my other albums in 1999, they'll go, 'Damn! Brothers had it hard back in the day, but brothers were working it out.'"

But Tupac is less likely to be remembered for early socio-political sermons than for soaring too close to the sun in his final years. His music was superb from start to finish, but his death betrayed his early promise: the son of a freedom-fighting Black Panther (his mother, Afeni Shakur) died a misguided martyr to sex and cash.

Battle-hardened by an upbringing that saw his mother addicted to crack, his father absconded and his stepfather wanted by the FBI, Tupac shone early on at The Baltimore School For Performing Arts. His first fame, however, came with California's Digital Underground, an act as pivotal to Rap's evolution as Dr Dre (both updated George Clinton's P-Funk for the 90s). From dancing with the Underground, Tupac graduated to rapping, such as on the Gangsta-ish 'It's A Good Thing That We're Rappin'. The latter was a bitter end to the good-natured *Sons Of The P* (1991): a mix of rolling Funk and street poetry honed on Tupac's debut *2Pacalypse Now* (1991). Though celebrated for the balladic 'Brenda's Got A Baby', it might have gone the underappreciated way of very similar solo sets by Public Enemy's nutty Professor Griff had it not been for a fiery cauldron of controversy.

Among other legally troubling activities, he was involved in a shoot-out with police, and *2Pacalypse Now* was denounced by Vice-President Dan Quayle. Tupac's crazed credentials were secured by his alarmingly convincing role as a psycho in the 1992 movie *Juice*, hence the suggestion that he *became* his character. Accordingly, *Strictly 4 My N.I.G.G.A.Z.* (1993) sounded livid: bar the Underground-helmed hit 'I Get Around', hectoring vocals and distorted basslines reigned – an obvious debt to Ice Cube, who guested on the album's 'Last Wordz' with Ice-T.

The anger abated temporarily in 1993 while Tupac starred in the movies *Poetic Justice*, with Janet Jackson, and *Above The Rim*. Two cuts he contributed to the latter's soundtrack illustrated his retreat from jagged-edge Rap to bittersweet G-Funk: the melancholic 'Pour Out A Little Liquor' and the spine-tingling 'Pain' (his best ever song, ignominiously tacked onto a Warren G single from the film). These trailed 1994's *Volume 1* by Thug Life (effectively Tupac and friends) – a fine album sadly eclipsed by the events that followed.

First Tupac went on trial for the sexual assault of a fan, then he was shot in New York. Though logic suggested his assailants were the others implicated in the assault, he blamed Puff Daddy and The Notorious BIG: prime movers of an East Coast Rap scene that threatened the domination of Tupac's adopted West Coast

(home to stars like Ice Cube, Dr Dre and Snoop Doggy Dogg).

In December, Shakur was acquitted of the assault itself, but convicted of a role in it. A harsh sentence – four and a half years in prison – rendered the title of *Me Against The World* (1995) bitterly appropriate. It shot to the top of the US chart, its multi-million sales aided by the beautiful 'Dear Mama' – which, like 1991's 'Brenda's Got A Baby' and 1993's 'Keep Ya Head Up', sounded a note of empathy with women amid Gangsta Rap's notorious sexism.

Eight months into his sentence, Tupac was bailed out by Suge Knight, the terrifying CEO of Dr Dre's Death Row label. At his new corporate home, Tupac was lavished in riches – a lifestyle reflected by *All Eyez On Me* (1996), which *Rolling Stone* dubbed "a Cali thug-life version of Pink Floyd's *The Wall* – pure gangsta ego run amok over two CDs". Demand for the Dr Dre-helmed trailer 'California Love' was so strong that Death Row withheld its release as a single, obliging consumers to buy the album instead. Multi-platinum sales ensued.

Meanwhile, Death Row's feud with Puff Daddy escalated: Tupac fuelled by arrogance and paranoia, Knight by professional loathing (exacerbated by the murder of his best friend at a party where the two camps clashed). The results included Tupac's 'Hit 'Em Up': a bile-filled attack on Puffy and his associates, which immortalized Tupac's claim to have slept with The Notorious BIG's wife, Faith Evans. BIG also got a preview of Tupac's next album: "I didn't know who it was. It was 9:30 in the morning. Then I recognized his voice and I said 'Yo 'Pac, stop acting crazy'… he just flipped: 'Nah, nigga, Tupac is dead. Long live Makaveli!' He started singing his whole album!"

The Don Killuminati/The 7 Day Theory (1996) – indeed credited to Makaveli, a persona Tupac had conceived in jail – aimed venom too at Dr Dre, who'd decamped from Death Row when the conflict got out of hand: "Quick to jump ship, punk trick, what a dumb move – cross Death Row, now who you gon' run to?" This lyrical blood-letting stained a superb album, and later rang hollow: on 13 September 1996, Tupac died of bullet wounds, sustained as he and Knight left a Mike Tyson fight in Las Vegas on 7 September.

Issued after Tupac's death, the Makaveli album was his third US No.1. Its singles jostled more hits from *All Eyez On Me*, including the mellow 'I Ain't Mad At Cha', whose video visualized Tupac's ascent to Heaven. Other posthumous releases included 'Wanted Dead Or Alive', a duet with Snoop Doggy Dogg from the soundtrack of one of Tupac's final movies, *Gridlock'd* (1997). His star turns in that and *Gang Related* (1998), to whose soundtrack he also contributed, and a mooted cameo in *Terminator III*, confirmed his death was a tragic loss to both Hip Hop and Hollywood.

He was also kept alive by conspiracy theories, notably those of Public Enemy's Chuck D, whose claim that Tupac had faked his own death prompted *NME* to suggest Chuck had faked his own sanity. A more fitting memorial was the first in a planned series of out-takes sets: 1997's *R U Still Down (Remember Me)*, another multi-million seller. The legend – whose star's good looks, great music, enduring sales and senseless death make him the Kurt Cobain of Rap – lives on.

(read) *Rebel For The Hell Of It: The Life Of Tupac Shakur* (1997), Armond White

(fan) 2PAC Fan Club, PO Box 2694, Decatur, GA 30031, USA

(surf) stallion.jsums.edu/~awil0997/tupac.htm

2 UNLIMITED ⊙ ⊙

WHO Vocals **Ray Slijngaard** (b. 28 Jun 1971, Amsterdam, Netherlands), vocals **Anita Dels** (b. 28 Dec 1971, Amsterdam)

WHEN 1990–1996

WHERE Amsterdam, Netherlands

WHAT Technotechnotechnotechno!

Euro Pop is littered with shooting stars – Technotronic, Culture Beat, Milli Vanilli, Boney M – but none as spectacular as 2 Unlimited. The brainchild of studio eggheads Phil Wilde and Jean-Paul DeCoster, 2 Unlimited's pretty public side was singer Anita Dels and Rapper Ray Slijngaard, whose rhymes were cruelly cut from most of their UK hits. Fusing the toughest of Techno with the plinky-plonkiest of Pop, they stormed charts with 1991's atomic 'Get Ready For This' and *Get Ready* (1992), source of super smashes 'Twilight Zone', 'Workaholic' and 'The Magic Friend'.

But these were nothing compared to 1993's *No Limits*, whose 'No Limit' – "No no/No-no no-no/No-no No-no/No-no/THERE'S NO LIMIT!' barked Dels – simulated the sound giant dinosaurs might make stomping on cities. As if its chant-worthy chorus weren't enough, the 2 spoiled us with Ray's immortal insert "Technotechnotechnotechno!" – their manifesto in a nutshell. More dancefloor workouts – 'Tribal Dance', 'Faces', 'Maximum Overdrive' and 'Let The Beat Control Your Body' – ravaged charts and minds across the globe.

However, US success proved elusive and though *Real Things* (1994) topped the UK chart, 'The Real Thing', 'No One' and 'Here I Go' lacked sparkle. Admirably, they knew when to quit, releasing the neat retrospective *Hits Unlimited* (1995) before disappearing. Dels and Slijngaard formed production companies, had solo hits back home in Holland, and linger forever in the hearts of true music lovers.

(surf) www.geocities.com/SunsetStrip/Palms/1837/2Unlimited.htm

UB40 ⊙⊙

WHO Vocals **Astro** (b. Terence Wilson, 24 Jun 1957, Birmingham, England), vocals/guitar **Ali Campbell** (b. 15 Feb 1959, Birmingham), guitar/vocals **Robin Campbell** (b. 25 Dec 1954, Birmingham), bass **Earl Falconer** (b. 23 Jan 1959, Birmingham), keyboards **Mickey Virtue** (b. 19 Jan 1957, Birmingham), sax **Brian Travers** (b. 7 Feb 1959, Birmingham), drums **Jim Brown** (b. 20 Nov 1957, Birmingham), percussion **Norman Hassan** (b. 26 Jan 1957, Birmingham)

WHEN 1978–

WHERE Birmingham, England

WHAT White Reggae chart klingons

Taking their name from a UK unemployment welfare form, UB40 were spotted by Chrissie Hynde and supported The Pretenders on their first UK tour. Blending doom-laden Reggae with socialist themes, UB40 hit with their 1980 debut 'King', inspired by Martin Luther King – thanks to its fab flipside 'Food For Thought'. *Signing Off* (1980) and *Present Arms* (1981) both reached UK No.2, the latter the first on their own DEP International label. Their political passion reached fever pitch on 1981's 'One In Ten', and they played benefit gigs for inner-city riot victims.

Present Arms In Dub (1981) was the first Dub album to chart in Britain and 1982's *UB44* sported an innovative hologram cover. *Labour Of Love* (1983) – a set of reggaefied covers – was their first UK No.1, trailed by a chart-topping take on Neil Diamond's 'Red Red Wine' (also their US chart debut). The hit was revived in America when a Phoenix radio station rediscovered it in 1988, giving UB40 a US No.1 for the single and a US No.14 for the album – which also spawned a successful sequel, *Labour Of Love II* (1989). Hits flowed with two Chrissie Hynde duets – a cover of Sonny & Cher's 'I Got You Babe' (1985),

then 'Breakfast In Bed' (1988) – and their own *Geffrey Morgan* (1984), *Baggaraddim* (1985), *Rat In The Kitchen* (1985) and *UB40* (1988). Tragedy struck in 1987 when Earl Falconer's car went out of control, killing his brother, who was their sound engineer. Falconer was jailed for drunk driving before their 1988 tour. They hit headlines again in 1990: deported from the Seychelles for alleged drug possession.

'(I Can't Help) Falling In Love With You' took them to the top of transatlantic charts in 1993; *Promises And Lies* was another UK No.1. Ali Campbell scored solo with *Big Love* (1995) and UB40 made a big screen debut in 1996, playing themselves in *Speed II*.

Guns In the Ghetto (1997) returned them to their Reggae roots, hence a DJ/dancehall version in 1998, featuring Jamaican DJs recording their own lyrics over UB40's original songs.

(Read) *UB40 – Portraits* (1984), Isiak Pere

(Fan) UB40 Info, PO BOX 117, Birmingham, B5 5RJ, UK

(Surf) www.ub40-dep.com

ULTRAVOX

WHO Vocals/guitar **Midge Ure** (b. James Ure, 10 Oct 1953, Gambusland, Scotland), keyboards/violin **Billy Currie** (b. 1 Apr 1952, Huddersfield, England), bass/keyboards **Chris Cross** (b. Christopher St. John, 14 Jul 1952, London, England), drums **Warren Cann** (b. 20 May 1952, Victoria, B.C., Canada)

WHEN 1976–

WHERE London, England

WHAT The popes of po-faced Synth Rock

When they were good, they were very very good, but when they were bad, they were po-faced Synth Rockers. In 1976, the Roxy

Music-inspired Tiger Lily (Chris Cross, singer John Foxx, Warren Cann, Billy Currie and guitarist Steve Shears) became Ultravox! for the underbought classics *Ultravox!* (1977), *Ha! Ha! Ha!* (1977) and *Systems Of Romance* (1978). The Island label dropped them; Foxx went solo (notably for 1980's *Metamatic*) and ex-Slik/Rich Kids/Thin Lizzy journeyman Midge Ure stepped in.

Binning the Art Rock widdlings of earlier albums, *Vienna* (1980) was all silly moustaches, sucked-in cheeks, electronic gloss and New Romantic glamour. Its sombre title track – a synthetic 'Stairway To Heaven' – was held off the UK No.1 in 1981 by wacky pretend Italian Joe Dolce's 'Shaddap You Face'.

Ultravox brushed this indignity aside and scored with *Rage In Eden* (1981), *Quartet* (1982), *Monument – The Soundtrack* (1983), *Lament* (1984) and a stream of increasingly rocky hits including 'All Stood Still', 'The Thin Wall', 'The Voice' (all 1981), 'Reap The Wild Wind' (1982), 'One Small Day', 'Dancing With Tears In My Eyes' and 'Love's Great Adventure' (all 1984).

But with Ure distracted by Band Aid, TV show *Max Headroom* (with Cross) and a briefly bright solo career (the UK No.1 'If I Was' from 1985's *The Gift*), Ultravox went into hibernation. Returning in 1986, minus Cann, as the abbreviated U-Vox, they soon split again. Ure and Currie resumed solo careers, but the success of *If I Was – The Very Best Of Ultravox And Midge Ure* (1993) prompted a partial reunion, Tony Feneller replacing Ure.

  Fan Extreme Voice, 19 Salisbury St, St George, Bristol, BS5 8EE, UK

surf www.ultravox.org.uk/

THE UNDERTONES

WHO Vocals **Feargal Sharkey** (b. 13 Aug 1958, Londonderry, Northern Ireland), guitar **John** (later **Sean**) **O'Neill** (b. 26 Aug 1957, Londonderry), guitar **Damian O'Neill** (b. 15 Jan 1961, Belfast, Northern Ireland), bass **Michael Bradley**(b. 13 Aug 1959, Londonderry), drums **Billy Doherty**

WHEN 1978–1983

WHERE Londonderry, Northern Ireland

WHAT Tremulous Punk Pop

Whenever veteran UK Radio DJ John Peel is asked to name his favourite song from the innumerable records he's heard in his time, the answer is invariably The Undertones' 'Teenage Kicks' – the title track of an EP that started five years of fame for a quintet of unlikely lads from Londonderry.

The group's early music was comparable to that of Buzzcocks: raucous Punk guitaring atop melodic songs of teenage torment. 'Jimmy Jimmy' took them into the UK Top 20 in spring 1979. That year they released their self-titled debut album: a set of simple but sparkling songs, with Feargal Sharkey's distinctive, tremulous vocals perfectly suited to the romantic vulnerability of the lyrics.

Their most commercially successful album, *Hypnotised* (1980) displayed growing sophistication. It contained their biggest hit in the witty 'My Perfect Cousin', which namechecked The Human League as they became The Undertones' UK chart rivals.

Positive Touch (1980) included some tracks melodic and yearning enough to satisfy early fans, one of which – 'It's Going To Happen' – provided a return to the UK singles chart. However, other tracks like 'Crisis Of Mine' and 'You're Welcome' had a considerably darker atmosphere. The more mature Undertones received a mixed reception, and the group disbanded in 1983 after the Soul-influenced *The Sin Of Pride* sold disappointingly.

The O'Neill brothers went on to form That Petrol Emotion, whose lengthy career was attended by more critical acclaim than record sales. Sharkey briefly formed The Assembly with Vince Clarke, previously of Depeche Mode and Yazoo and later of Erasure, and hit the UK Top 5 with 'Never Never' (1983). He then began a solo career, whose main highlight was 1985's cover of Maria McKee's 'A Good Heart' – an international hit.

After a final UK hit with 'I've Got News For You' (1991), Sharkey retired from performance and became an A&R man.

UNDERWORLD

WHO Vocals/guitar **Karl Hyde** (b. 10 May 1957, Worcester, England), keyboards **Rick Smith** (b. 25 May 1959, Ammanford, Wales), keyboards **Darren Emerson** (b. 30 Apr 1971, Hornchurch, Essex, England)

WHEN 1991–

WHERE London, England

WHAT Electronica eccentrics

Though Underworld doubtless describe themselves as 'altered-pre-love-restricted-phone-smell-man-begging-for-it-reverend-Al-Green-shouting-lager-lager-lager-lager' (or something equally weird), they're two old men and a young DJ. They're also super Techno experimentalists, plotting a crazy course between full-on, head-bangin' Dance freak outs, Dub and weirdie Rock, embellished with Karl Hyde's stream-of-consciousness lyrics.

Their origins lie in Hyde and Rick Smith's Freur – silly-wigged Synth Rockers with even sillier songs – who scored one minor UK hit, 'Doot Doot' (1983), before disintegrating. In 1987, the duo resurfaced (Hyde having played with Debbie Harry and Prince) as Underworld. But this Underworld was a seven-piece Funk troupe. After *Underneath The Radar* (1988), *Stand Up* (1989) and *Change The Weather* (1989), salvation came with a road-to-Damascus conversion to Techno, thanks to new member and top DJ Darren Emerson, in 1992.

The trio signed to hip Dance label Junior Boys Own and, as Lemon Interrupt, unleashed 1992's wondrous 'Dirty/Minneapolis' and 'Bigmouth/Eclipse'. They reverted to the Underworld banner in 1993 for the excellent 'Rez', 'Mmm… Skyscraper I Love You', 'Spikee/Dogman Go' and 'Dark And Long', then the epochal *Dubnobasswithmyheadman* – the point at which Techno began to sell to Rock fans (they even became favourites of Elton John).

While crafting their next album, they remixed the likes of William Orbit and Front 242 and built a reputation in hip media circles with their design/advertising collective Tomato. Then, in 1996, 'Born Slippy' – an underbought epic from 1995 – featured on the *Trainspotting* soundtrack, installed itself at UK No.2 and shot *Second Toughest In The Infants* (1996) into the chart. More credibility-boosting remixes (Depeche Mode, Björk, Simply Red, Orbital, Leftfield, Chemical Brothers) confirmed their miraculous metamorphosis: rubbish old Rockers to shadowy Techno art terrorists in a mere decade. Mere seconds later, they joined Pop's bright new hopes on 1997's *Batman & Robin* soundtrack.

surf www.fas.harvard.edu/~ tremblay/news.html

Napier gave way to Nigel Olsson by their debut *Very 'Eavy, Very 'Umble* (1970), which established the Heep trademarks: grandiose melodies and multi-layered vocals on cuts like 'Gypsy'.

Keith Baker replaced Olsson for 1971's altogether bolder *Salisbury*, then *his* replacement, Ian Clarke, gave way to Lee Kerslake. Newton was replaced by Mark Clarke before Gary Thain took up the four-string duties, completing the classic line-up.

Finally finding their stride, *Look At Yourself* (1971) was their first UK chart album, and they established themselves among the most musically fluent of all British Hard Rock bands. *Demons And Wizards* (1972) was the first of five successive US Top 40 albums, the others being *The Magician's Birthday* (1972), *Uriah Heep Live* (1973), *Sweet Freedom* (1973) and *Wonderworld* (1974).

Thain was asked to leave because of his erratic behaviour and ex-King Crimson bassist John Wetton joined for *Return To Fantasy* (1975). Ironically, this was their biggest UK album (No.7), but marked the start of their commercial decline Stateside.

Hensley quit after the patchy *High And Mighty* in 1976. Then Byron and Wetton were out, singer John Lawton and (ex-Spider From Mars) Trevor Bolder were in, and it was hello again to Ken Hensley. Vocalist John Sloman was brought in to try to halt the slide for 1980's *Conquest*, but without success. Hensley left for good, and Box reinvented the band, bringing in keyboard player John Sinclair, bassist Bob Daisley, and new singer Pete Goalby.

The result was 1982's *Abominog* which, with its more contemporary style, saw Heep enjoy their biggest UK chart success since *High And Mighty*. But the revival was short-lived. After 1983's *Head First*, Heep signed to Portrait for 1984's *Equator* (now with Bolder again), but their liaison with the label proved brief and unsatisfactory.

Since 1987 – when Bernie Shaw and Phil Lanzon replaced Goalby and Sinclair respectively – Heep have concentrated primarily on touring constantly and occasionally releasing musically consistent, if unfashionable, albums.

Fan The Uriah Heep Appreciation Society, PO Box 268, Telford, Shropshire, TF2 6XA, UK

Surf www.uriah_heep.com/

URIAH HEEP

WHO Vocals **David Byron** (b. 29 Jan 1947, Epping, Essex, England, d. 28 Feb 1985), guitar **Mick Box** (b. 8 Jun 1947, Walthamstow, London, England), keyboards **Ken Hensley** (b. 24 Aug 1945, London), bass **Paul Newton** (b. 1946, Andover, Hampshire, England), bass **Gary Thain** (b. 15 May 1948, Wellington, New Zealand, d. 19 Mar 1976), drums **Lee Kerslake** (b. 16 Apr 1947, London)

WHEN 1969–

WHERE London, England

WHAT Seminal melodic Rock

The world got Girl Power, but it could have got *Grrr* Power, a sort of lumpy Rock equivalent – for when David Byron and Mick Box first united, Britian's least fashionable band were called Spice. They became Uriah Heep in 1970, the line-up being completed by Ken Hensley, Paul Newton and drummer Alex Napier.

USHER

WHO b. Usher Raymond, 14 Oct 1979, Chattanooga, Tennessee, USA

WHAT Pecs, sex 'n' Swing

Xeroxed Beatles? No thanks, daddio! Oasis' 'All Around The World' was toppled from the UK top spot by a slinky little number called 'You Make Me Wanna'. Penned by Jermaine Dupri (the Puff Daddy of Swing) and issued on Babyface's LaFace label, it was fronted by Usher Raymond, a teen hunk from Chattanooga.

His self-titled debut (1994), co-helmed by Puff Daddy, hit with 'Think of You'. But Puffy re-routed to Rap and Dupri took over for *My Way* (1997), which boasts input by Babyface and Teddy Riley, and cameos by rude rapstress Lil' Kim and Swing songbirds Monica and Shanice Wilson. In between, Usher guested on the 1995 smash 'U Will Know' by Swing supergroup Black Men United.

Fan Usher Fan Club, PO Box 500338, Atlanta, GA 31150-998, USA

Surf www.galaxyrecords.com/InDaMix/van-helden.html

U2 ⊙⊙⊙⊙⊙⊙⊙⊙⊙ ✪✪✪✪✪

WHO Vocals **Bono** (b. Paul Hewson, 10 May 1960, Ballymun, Dublin, Ireland), guitar **The Edge** (b. Dave Evans, 8 Aug 1961, Barking, London, England), bass **Adam Clayton** (b. 13 Mar 1960, Chinnor, Oxfordshire, England), drums **Larry Mullen Jr** (b. 31 Oct 1961, Artane, Dublin)

WHEN 1978–

WHERE Dublin, Ireland

WHAT Planet-sized PopMartyrs

One of the most perplexing, iconoclastic and *biggest* bands on earth, U2 are also one of the most despised. Detractors cite pomposity, pretension, earnestness and egotism; the flag-waving bluster of their 80s peak; the studied ironic posturing of their 90s guise; their terminally uncool Christianity; the *bigness* of it all. But one thing is often forgotten: U2 have twisted into ever more inspired shapes, made consistently brilliant albums and, despite Bono's on-stage sermons, made soulless stadium shows into multi-media meetings of grand passion, pizzazz and power.

Their origins were banal: a notice-board appeal for musicians posted by 15-year-old Larry Mullen at his school, Mount Temple, in Dublin. He found Dave Evans and his brother Dick, Adam Clayton and Paul Hewson, a chess champion who, with his friend Fionan Hanvey, joined a school 'clan' called Lypton Village. Part of the Lypton Village ritual was taking a new name – Hanvey was Gavin Friday, non-villager Dave Evans was The Edge, and Hewson was rechristened Bono Vox after a local hearing-aid store.

So bad was Bono's guitar playing that he was relegated to the unwanted vocalist role. They struggled through covers like Peter Frampton's 'Show Me The Way', but sheer confidence turned limitations into strengths, especially for The Edge, who – unable to play bluesy lead licks – settled on a chiming sound which, anchored by Mullen's militaristic beat, became their cornerstone.

As Feedback, then The Hype, they made waves in Ireland's stale sea of showbands and, when Dick Evans left to form The Virgin Prunes with Gavin Friday in 1978, became U2 – a pun on 'you two' (they considered the audience part of the band) and a reference to a US spy plane. As Punk hit Ireland, they drew inspiration from the similarly spiky Television, Talking Heads and Joy Division, whose intensity matched their own, innocent zeal.

Triumph in a 1978 talent contest attracted manager Paul McGuinness and led to a brief deal with CBS, who released their Irish-only debut, 1979's 'U23' EP. An Irish No.1, it was followed in 1980 by another chart-topper, 'Another Day'. But, despite winning five awards in Irish paper *Hot Press*' annual poll, success outside the Irish Indie scene seemed unthinkable: their London debut in 1979 (as the mis-billed 'V2') drew a crowd of nine.

Rescue came from Island, who paired U2 with hip producer Martin Hannett for the Joy Division-esque '11 O'Clock Tick Tock' (1980). Having seduced the music press with 'A Day Without Me' (dedicated to the recently deceased Ian Curtis) and 'I Will Follow', they slowly moved to the mainstream with 1980's wide-eyed and innocent *Boy* (1980) – a belated and minor UK and US hit in 1981.

A devoted fanbase grew ('Fire' became their first UK hit in 1981), but critical disdain welled for U2's tendency towards sermonizing, especially when Bono's lyrical preaching took the darker *October* (1981) dangerously near Christian Rock.

But 1983's excellent, troubled *War* silenced doubters. Trailed by the icy 'New Year's Day' (their debut US hit), it was helped to multi-million sales by shows at the mammoth 'US' festival and Colorado's Red Rocks Festival. The latter's televised highlight was a flag-waving reading of one of *War*'s best – 'Sunday Bloody Sunday', a plea for peace in Ireland. Its impact meant 1983's live *Under A Blood Red Sky* – filleted from Red Rocks and shows in Boston and Germany – swiftly followed *War* to the top spot.

All this might never have happened, since U2's committed Christians – Bono, Edge and Mullen – had begun to question whether Rock was the best way to serve the Lord. But instead of splitting, they abandoned personal themes for the specifics of songs like 'Sunday Bloody Sunday' – a policy which proved just as repellent to critics, who now ludicrously accused them of taking sides in the Irish conflict.

The attention heaped on their manifesto obscured the fact that, in three years, U2 had evolved from scratchy post-Punk wannabes into an inventive, dynamic Rock band. Jaded by the lengthy *War* tour, they set about creating a new U2. They'd found new ways of galvanizing their weaknesses into strengths; Edge, in particular, had created a revolutionary guitar sound through initial ineptitude, imagination and digital delay.

With Brian Eno and his associate Daniel Lanois producing, the band – in Eno's words – built four or five new U2s on 1984's *The Unforgettable Fire*. Bathed in watery soundscapes, its sonic sweep matched its weighty themes: the anthemic 'Pride (In The Name Of Love)' – "The only successful Pop song we've ever written," said Edge – and 'MLK' eulogized Martin Luther King; 'Bad', echoing The Velvet Underground, dealt with Dublin's desperate heroin problem; 'Promenade' and 'Elvis Presley And America' were collages of Bono's poetry and Edge's echoing guitars.

Mournful, angular and sonically oblique, it was far from the mainstream product Island expected. But it raced to UK No.1, yielded the hits 'Pride' and 'The Unforgettable Fire' and elevated the band to arenas and stadiums – a fitting backdrop for their new, expansive sound, as show-stealing appearances at Live Aid (1985) and 1986's Amnesty International's Conspiracy Of Hope tour and the beautiful live *Wide Awake In America* (1985) proved.

Rolling Stone proclaimed U2 "the band of the 80s", a title they fulfilled with 1987's *The Joshua Tree*, which transformed them from a hugely successful band into a household name. Another collaboration with Eno and Lanois, it replaced the European sound of *The Unforgettable Fire* with wide-screen Americana. From its title (the Joshua Tree was the scene of Country Rock legend Gram Parsons' cremation), through its dusty desert sleeve shot, to Bono's evangelical lyrics, America was *everywhere*.

There were themes if you wanted them: redemption, God, politics, war, injustice. But for all its worth as a Rock milestone, *The Joshua Tree*'s strength was its *songs*: from the anthemic ('Where The Streets Have No Name', 'In God's Country'), through the joyful ('I Still Haven't Found What I'm Looking For', 'Trip Through Your Wires') and heartbreaking ('With Or Without You', 'Red Hill Mining Town') to the sinister ('Bullet The Blue Sky', 'Exit'). It sold 15 million and *Time* magazine put U2 on its cover, uniting them with the likes of The Beatles and Bruce Springsteen.

The band whose ambition had never acknowledged cultural boundaries no longer sounded Irish, or even European. But having assimilated American music so successfully, they *imitated* on *Rattle And Hum* (1988) – an album and movie documenting their 1987 US tour. Envisaged as a tour film and homage to

American music, it was crippled by ambition. When Larry Mullen claimed the film was "a musical journey", not even the rest of the band could take him seriously. There were electrifying scenes – notably Bono's scream of "Fuck the revolution!" in a 'Sunday Bloody Sunday' taped after the IRA bombed a Remembrance Day service in Enniskillen, Northern Ireland. But Bono's sermons reached new heights of pomposity and the awe with which they regarded American legends (Elvis, Graceland, Sun studios, B.B. King, Dylan's 'All Along The Watchtower') was excruciating. *Rattle And Hum* was savaged by critics and, later, U2 themselves. However, its soundtrack yielded a handful of diamonds: the B.B. King duet 'When Love Comes To Town', the wonderful 'Angel Of Harlem', 'All I Want Is You' and their first UK No.1 single, 'Desire'.

But times had changed. Dance seeped into Rock while U2 dressed like Quakers and murdered Dylan songs. Their crusade wound down with a 1989 New Year's Eve show in Dublin. How – or even *if* – U2 would adapt to the 90s was anyone's guess.

As they painfully re-invented themselves, U2 moved to Berlin, where David Bowie had made his *Low/Heroes/Lodger* classics with Brian Eno. While Pet Shop Boys lampooned them

"If I had more money than he did, I would try and pay him to shut up. ono, I will give you a million dollars a day not to play"
Henry Rollins

with a big Disco production of 'Where The Streets Have No Name', early clues to their new incarnation came with an electronic version of Cole Porter's 'Night And Day' on the AIDS benefit album *Red Hot + Blue* (1990) and The Edge's score for a stage version of Anthony Burgess' *A Clockwork Orange*, but when 'The Fly' emerged in 1991, almost all traces of the old U2 were gone. Where once Bono frowned, now he leered. Except this wasn't Bono – it was 'The Fly', an alter ego who personified the decadent Rock stars U2 were too afraid to be.

Achtung Baby (1991) was a shock: colour instead of black and white; confusion instead of certainty; Industrial noise and dirty beats instead of stadium bombast. The earnest rootsiness of *Rattle And Hum* crumbled under sampler-mashed blast and irony. As if this didn't desecrate their past enough, the cover montage featured a naked Adam Clayton. Fuss over the album's sound eclipsed the strength of its songs, any of which could have been hits. Five were: 'The Fly', 'Even Better Than The Real Thing', 'Mysterious Ways', 'One' and 'Who's Gonna Ride Your Wild Horses'.

The big lyrical themes were still present, but they were interpersonal rather than international. Drawing on the same vein as Bono and Edge's heartbreaking song for Roy Orbison, 'She's A Mystery To Me', *Achtung Baby* was coloured by distress and, in Edge's case, divorce. But it wasn't all misery – 'One' in particular translated individual anguish into anthemic optimism.

No longer ashamed of their bigness, they lavished millions of what Bono called "fuck off money" on the spectacular stadium tours Zoo TV and its European Zooropa counterpart – which mixed live TV (on hundreds of screens), giant slogans (notably "EVERYTHING YOU KNOW IS WRONG"), satellite link-ups and prank phone calls. Highlights included Bono ordering pizzas for the audience, calling world leaders and duetting 'Satellite Of Love' with a giant TV image of Lou Reed.

They even managed to make another album, 1993's *Zooropa*. Recorded with Eno at soundchecks and overnight visits to their Windmill Lane studio in Dublin, it distilled the chaos of the tour into a blistering riot of electronics, savage noise, soundbites and samples. But there were moments of calm: the Wim Wenders movie theme 'Stay

"It's only cos we're white and we're Rock that we get asked about what it all means. The simple answer is, we couldn't take that seriousness any further"

Bono

(Faraway So Close!)' (a UK hit whose flipside was Bono's duet with Frank Sinatra, 'I've Got You Under My Skin') and 'The Wanderer', a synthesized Country fable sung by Johnny Cash. Other highlights were the robotic 'Numb', a mock fascist sermon by The Edge, and 'Lemon' – U2's first truly successful foray into Dance, courtesy of remixes by then hip House DJ Paul Oakenfold.

Their cultural crossover continued on *Original Soundtracks 1* (1995), a highbrow collaboration with Eno, Trip Hopper Howie B, Opera bloke Luciano Pavarotti and Japanese singer Holi under the name Passengers. Publicized as the new U2 album (then an Eno album when it flopped), it yielded the heavenly hit 'Miss Sarajevo' and not much else. Still, it proved U2 couldn't be pigeonholed (as did their 1995 hit 'Hold Me Thrill Me Kiss Me Kill Me' for the movie *Batman Forever*).

After the grand gesture of Zoo TV and Zooropa, it seemed U2 could only scale down. But *Pop* (1997) was, if not re-invention, then refinement. Their first studio album without Eno since *War*, it was coloured by Howie B's beats, partly because Mullen was out of action owing to a back operation. Although they posed as The Village People in the 'Discotheque' video, *Pop* was that most *un*-ironic of things – a Rock album. A semi-successful Rock album at that: 'Mofo', 'Staring At The Sun', 'If God Will Send His Angels' and 'If You Wear That Velvet Dress' soared, the rest coasted.

With help from support act Oasis, the colossal PopMart tour lurched into action with a technically disastrous show in Las Vegas. PopMart's extravagance was breathtaking: the band emerged from inside a giant lemon, played beneath a giant yellow arch and were backed by a *giant* video screen.

The tickets sold almost as slowly as *Pop*, but U2's status as political evangelists remained intact: PopMart took them to South Africa and, for the first time, Sarajevo. When the Irish peace process began in earnest, it was *Pop*'s 'Please' – a muted companion to 'Sunday Bloody Sunday' – which soundtracked it.

Their endorsement of Homer Simpson's bid to become Springfield sanitation commissioner suggested U2's concerns had diminished in scale, but the band cannot be relegated from the list of the world's most powerful cultural icons. As Bono remarked to MTV in 1998: "People like you have reduced us to cartoons before we ever got involved in *The Simpsons*".

read *U2 At The End Of The World* (1996), Bill Flanagan

fan Propaganda, PO Box 18, Wellingborough, NN8 1HE, UK

surf www.u2popmart.com

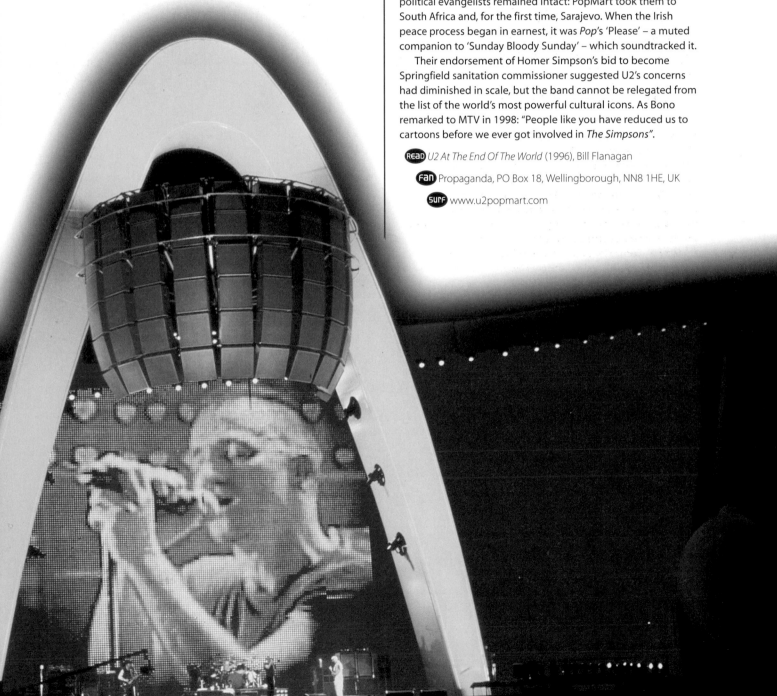

VAN HALEN ✪✪✪

WHO Vocals **David Lee Roth** (b. 10 Oct 1953, Bloomington, Indiana, USA), guitar/keyboards **Edward Van Halen** (b. 26 Jan 1955, Nijmegen, Netherlands), drums **Alex Van Halen** (b. 8 May 1953, Nijmegen), bass **Michael Anthony** (b. Michael Sobolewski, 20 Jun 1954, Chicago, Illinois, USA)

WHEN 1974–

WHERE Pasadena, California, USA

WHAT Platinum Flash Metal

Mid-70s Metal was given a shot in the arm by Van Halen. Party-hardy cartoons of Led Zeppelin, their apprenticeship in clubs and bars (as Rat Salade and Mammoth) bred a *bonhomie* that lasted well into their own football field-filling career. Chief merry-maker 'Diamond' David Lee Roth's flamboyance was matched only by Eddie Van Halen's six-string pyrotechnics. The heady mix exploded on *Van Halen I* (1977) and a scene-stealing support slot in 1978 with stumbling megastars Black Sabbath.

With the hard-partying *Van Halen II* (1979), *Women And Children First* (1980), *Fair Warning* (1981) and *Diver Down* (1982), they evolved from imitators to influencers, their descendants including Mötley Crüe, Bon Jovi, Extreme and Poison. Even before the all-time anthem 'Jump' boosted their stardom beyond American shores, their reputation was assured by a $1.5-million-earning headliner at the 1983 'US' festival and Eddie's cameo on Michael Jackson's 'Beat It' (1982).

'Jump' (1984) and its parent album *1984* were the final fruits of VH Mark I. Strained relations snapped and Roth departed for a shooting-star solo career. *Eat 'Em And Smile* (1986), *Skyscraper* (1988), *A Little Ain't Enough* (1991) and *Your Filthy Little Mouth* (1994), though more colourful than contemporary VH efforts, nonetheless paled against the latter's sales.

Roth's replacement was Sammy Hagar (b. 13 Oct 1947, Monterey, California, USA), formerly of another 'Son-of-Zeppelin' outfit, Montrose, and latterly a solo star. *5150* (1986) confirmed their platinum-plastered longevity, aided by the smash hit 'Why Can't This Be Love'. *OU812* (1988), *For Unlawful Carnal Knowledge* (1991), *Live: Right Here, Right Now* (1993) and *Balance* (1995) all flouted Metal's flagging fortunes Stateside.

However, after a decade of 'Van Hagar', the singer slot fell vacant once more. Fans' hopes were raised by the return of Roth for new cuts on *Best Of – Volume 1* (1996), but – despite Diamond Dave's support for a long-term reunion – the job went to former Extreme mic-man Gary Cherone. As the new line-up's *Van Halen III* (1998) prepared to set sail, Roth launched a pre-emptive strike with the simultaneous US release of *The Best* (1997) and autobiography-cum-manifesto *Crazy From The Heat*.

Read *Crazy From The Heat* (1997), David Lee Roth

Fan The Inside, 1739 East Broadway Road, Suite 105, Tempe, Arizona 85282, USA

Surf www.van-halen.com/

ARMAND VAN HELDEN

WHO b. 1972, Boston, Massachusetts, USA

WHAT House-hopper turned hip overhauler du jour

In a role call of DJs in ads for 1995's remix set *The Rest Of New Order*, Armand Van Helden's name was omitted – quite deservedly, so awful was his mix of New Order's 'Bizarre Love Triangle'. But within two years, he'd conquered the world with a storming 'star trunk funkin'' remix of Tori Amos' 'Professional Widow' and a 'dark garage' revamp of Sneaker Pimps' 'Spin Spin Sugar' – both staples of 1997's charts.

Previously, he'd risen from Boston's X-Mix remix service, through credibility-crippling production work with Euro Pop acts like The Real McCoy and Rednex to stormers like CJ Bolland's 'Sugar Is Sweeter' and Daft Punk's 'Da Funk'. A parallel solo career opened with 'Witch Doktor' (1993), let loose a monster with 'The Funk Phenomena' (1995) and led to 1997's atypically hip hoppy *Sample Slaya (Enter The Meat Market)*. His CV now stars the Stones, Puff Daddy and Janet Jackson.

Surf www.galaxyrecords.com/InDaMix/van-helden.html

LUTHER VANDROSS ⊙

WHO b. 20 Apr 1951, New York City, New York, USA

WHAT Swoonsome Soulster

Luther Vandross' comfortable stardom suits his comfortable Soul style. Learning piano at 3, he joined theatre project Listen My Brother in his teens, performing with them at the Harlem Apollo.

His big Pop break came in 1974 when David Bowie's musical director Carlos Alomar recommended him to his boss. Vandross arranged and sang back-up on Bowie's *Young Americans* (1975), which also included his own 'Fascination'. By the end of the 70s, he'd backed Chic, Bette Midler, Barbra Streisand and The Average White Band, sung anonymous leads with the band Change and won three awards for advertising jingles.

His first two 1976 solo albums (as 'Luther') sank without trace, but 1981's *Never Too Much* and its title track topped the US R&B chart. Thereafter, his smooth Soul crooning guaranteed R&B No.1s for the likes of *Forever, For Always, For Love* (1982), *The Night I Fell In Love* (1985) and *Give Me The Reason* (1986), whose 'Stop To Love' proved his mainstream chart breakthrough.

As a producer, he sprinkled stardust on Aretha Franklin, Teddy Pendergrass and Dionne Warwick. His own mega-sellers were *Any Love* (1988), 'Here And Now' (from 1989's *The Best Of Luther Vandross… The Best Of Love*), 1991's *Power Of Love* and the 1994 UK No.1 *Songs,* from which the Mariah Carey duet 'Endless Love' was a transatlantic smash. Another hit hook-up came with Janet Jackson on the breezy 'The Best Things In Life Are Free' (1992), while the platinum-plated *This Is Christmas* (1996) and *Your Secret Love* (1997) proved there's life in the old smoothie yet.

VANGELIS ✪

WHO b. Evanghelos Papathanassiou, 29 Mar 1943, Vólos, Greece

WHAT Celestial synthesizer symphonies

Though Jean Michel Jarre, Kitaro and Yanni stole his quasi-Classical crown, Vangelis was *the* 70s synth supremo. Having hit with Demis Roussos in Progsters Aphrodite's Child (notably on 1968's 'Rain And Tears'), he began his sonic quest with *Dragon* (1971) and movie soundtrack *L'Apocalypse Des Animaux* (1973), then moved to England. Considered too wild to replace Rick Wakeman in Yes, he hit his synthetic stride with the soundtrack to Carl Sagan's *Cosmos* (1974), *Heaven And Hell* (1975), *Albedo 0.39* (1976) and hits with Yes-man Jon Anderson as Jon & Vangelis – including 'I Hear You Now' and 'I'll Find My Way Home', 1980's *Short Stories* and 1981's *The Friends Of Mr. Cairo*.

Best were his movie scores: the title track of 1981's Oscar-winner *Chariots Of Fire* hit US No.1, while other highlights were 1982's *Blade Runner* (a neo-Techno classic revamped in 1994), *The Bounty* (1984), *1492 – The Conquest Of Paradise* (1992) and *Bitter Moon* (1994). He also scored Euripides' *Electra* at Greece's Epidauros amphitheatre and ballet versions of *Frankenstein* and *Beauty And The Beast*. Meanwhile, he continued majestically with 1995's *Voices* and 1996's *Oceanic*.

READ *Vangelis: The Unknown Man* (1994), Mark J.T. Griffin

SURF www.il.fontys.nl/~lodewks/elsewher.htm

STEVIE RAY VAUGHAN

WHO b. 3 Oct 1954, Dallas, Texas, USA, d. 27 Aug 1990, East Troy, Wisconsin, USA

WHAT Blues guitar-slinger

The 80s Blues revival launched no brighter star than Stevie Ray Vaughan, whose fiery style closed the gap between Blues and Rock. Inspired by big brother Jimmie (guitarist with The Fabulous Thunderbirds), Vaughan dropped out of school at 17 and flirted with Austin bar bands. One of them, Triple Threat, became Blues trio Double Trouble when he took over vocals.

Local acclaim paid off when Jackson Browne bankrolled early recordings and David Bowie collared Vaughan for *Let's Dance* (1983). With Vaughan hailed as a guitar genius, Double Trouble's *Texas Flood* (1983), *Couldn't Stand The Weather* (1984), *Soul To Soul* (1985) and *Live Alive* (1986) sold truckloads. Their progress slowed only by Vaughan's excessive lifestyle, Double Trouble ploughed on with 1989's Grammy winner *In Step*.

His profile at an all-time high, Vaughan was joined by legends Eric Clapton, Buddy Guy and Robert Cray on stage in Wisconsin in August 1990. But it proved his last show: he was killed when a helicopter taking him to Chicago crashed. Posthumous releases include 1990's *Family Style* (a duel with brother Jimmie), *The Sky Is Crying* (1991), *In The Beginning* (1992) and *Greatest Hits* (1995).

READ *Stevie Ray Vaughan: Caught In The Crossfire* (1993), Joe Nick Patoski & Bill Crawford

SUZANNE VEGA

WHO b. 11 Jul 1959, Santa Monica, California, USA

WHAT The cool princess of Folk Pop

Suzanne Vega spent her teen years as a student at New York's High School For The Performing Arts, immortalized in the 80s TV show *Fame*. But instead of dancing on cars, she crafted introspective Folk songs and impressed Patti Smith mainman Lenny Kaye. He produced her self-titled 1985 debut, a delightful mix of Leonard Cohen-esque bleakness and delicate tunesmithery which seduced angsty teens (hence her 'Left Of Center' on *Pretty In Pink*'s soundtrack) and yielded the hit 'Marlene On The Wall'. *Solitude Standing* (1987) was another delicate Folk Pop flower, especially the transatlantic hit 'Luka' – a tale of child abuse with a deceptively pretty tune.

Though 1990's *Days Of Open Hand* coasted, 'Tom's Diner', an a capella *Solitude* cut, became an unlikely hit thanks to a remix by Dance dweebs DNA. It also prompted 1991's *Tom's Album* – a collection of covers of 'Tom's Diner', starring REM among others.

Accordingly, 1992's *99.9°F* was jam-packed with electronic beats and weird samples, especially on the near-hits 'Blood Makes Noise' and '99.9°F'. Refining her sound on *Nine Objects Of Desire* (1996), its superb songs sadly failed to reach the dizzying commercial heights attained by fellow electronic angst-mongers like Garbage and Alanis Morissette.

SURF www.vega.net/

THE VELVET UNDERGROUND

WHO Vocals/guitar **Lou Reed** (b. Louis Firbank, 2 Mar 1942, Freeport, Long Island, New York, USA), vocals **Nico** (b. Christa Päffgen, 16 Oct 1938, Cologne, Germany, d. 18 Jul 1988, Ibiza, Spain), viola/keyboards/bass **John Cale** (b. 9 Mar 1942, Crynant, West Glamorgan, Wales), guitar **Sterling Morrison** (b. 29 Aug 1942, East Meadow, Long Island, d. 30 Aug 1995), drums **Maureen Tucker** (b. 1944, Queens, New York)

WHEN 1965–1973

WHERE New York City, New York, USA

WHAT Art Rock audio violent experimentalists

There's a little bit of The Velvet Underground in almost every Rock group since the 60s. Never has a band so ignored in its lifetime exerted such an enduring influence. From Krautrock, through David Bowie to Punk and all directions since, their legacy looms large. In 60s New York, they conjured seedy street life in violent musical settings – the flipside of hippiedom.

Lou Reed was a hack songwriter when he formed The Primitives with Sterling Morrison and the classically-trained John Cale. Adding drummer Angus MacLise, they became The Velvet Underground, named after a sensationalist S&M novel.

Under Pop Art guru Andy Warhol's management, German actress and model Nico was installed as singer, despite strong resistance from the band. MacLise was replaced by the androgynous Maureen Tucker on drums. Ensconced in Warhol's multi-media Exploding Plastic Inevitable 'happenings', the Velvets assaulted audiences with sheer volume, and the material performed at these shows formed the basis of 1967's extraordinary *The Velvet Underground And Nico*. Reed's lyrics – about hard drugs, sado-masochism and death – ensured that radio reaction was cold.

Although Reed assumed a leading role, Nico's dark, ghostly solo spots were as memorable as anything on the album, and characteristic of its diversity. The feedback-soaked guitar duel 'European Son' was as brutal as 'Sunday Morning' was plaintive, and the classic 'Venus In Furs' captured Cale's viola in its greatest performance. Even Tucker's unadorned rhythmic simplicity has proved inestimably influential. But by the time the album was released, Nico had left. Warhol, who claimed a dubious production credit but whose peeling banana sleeve image has become as iconic as the album, had also parted company with the band.

White Light/White Heat may not have compared to its predecessor but, in 1968, was as loud and frighteningly intense as any Rock record yet heard. The 17-minute 'Sister Ray', a tale of sailors, drag queens and heroin, culminated in a distorted crescendo of organ and guitar.

When constant ego struggles became too much, Cale was squeezed out of the group by Reed, who brought in the more conventional bass player Doug Yule. Many songs from this 1968/1969 transition wouldn't surface until *VU* (1985) and *Another View* (1986), and indeed it wasn't until spring 1969 that a self-titled third album emerged. As strong a collection as any Reed has put his name to, with such gems as 'Pale Blue Eyes', 'What Goes On' and 'Candy Says', it was nonetheless straighter and more melodic, leaving no doubt as to who led the group.

In 1970, with the release by Atlantic of the mainstream *Loaded*, the Velvets finally achieved commercial success but, by the time it appeared, Reed had already quit, leaving Yule in charge. Reed later complained that the album was completed with its two strongest songs, 'Sweet Jane' and 'New Age', edited to their detriment. Morrison and Tucker left in 1971, and Yule's *Squeeze* (1972) was a Velvet Underground record in name only. Two live albums, the bootleg-quality *Live At Max's Kansas City* (1972) and the superior double *1969* (1974), dated from the Reed/Yule line-up and were the last Velvet Underground product until the retrospectives which appeared in the mid-80s .

Having buried the hatchet on the Warhol tribute *Songs For Drella* (1990), Reed and Cale joined Morrison and Tucker in Paris in 1990 for a live version of 'Heroin' and, in 1993, set out on a financially motivated European tour and released *Live MCMXCIII*. They eventually played the USA (and supported U2), but friction between Reed and his bandmates – and Morrison's death in 1995 – ended their renaissance. The retrospective *Peel Slowly And See* (1995) preceded their 1996 induction into the Rock And Roll Hall Of Fame.

READ *Uptight* (1983), Victor Bockris & Gerard Malanga

SURF www.angelfire.com/ny/vu1/

THE VERVE ⊙

WHO Vocals/guitar **Richard Ashcroft** (b. 11 Sep 1971, Wigan, England), guitar **Nick McCabe** (b. 14 Jul 1971), bass **Simon Jones** (b. 29 Jul 1972), guitar/keyboards **Simon Tong**, drums **Peter Salisbury** (b. 24 Sep1971)

WHEN 1990–

WHERE Wigan, Lancashire, England

WHAT Band of mope and glory

"History has a place for us," declared Richard Ashcroft in 1993. "It may take us three albums, but we will be there." At the time, the statement sounded ludicrously arrogant – they didn't call him 'Mad Richard' for nothing. Now it seems prophetic.

Shrouded in mystique from the beginning, Ashcroft, Nick McCabe, Simon Jones and Peter Salisbury's first singles as Verve – 'All In The Mind', 'Gravity Grave' and 'She's A Superstar' – trailed *A Storm In Heaven* (1993), a dark sonic whirlwind of 60s Psychedelia, 90s shoegazing and wide-eyed druggy mysticism. Reviews were gushing; sales were moderate.

In 1994, legal action by Jazz label Verve forced them to add a 'The'. Ashcroft quipped that they'd have preferred to become 'Verv', so they could claim to have "dropped an 'E' for America."

The joke soon turned sour. Work on a new album began well, but – as Jones recalled – ended with the band "in each others' faces, coming down off whatever drugs we'd been doing for that three weeks, and all very intense and paranoid. People got a little mad…" Ashcroft, in fact, got so mad that he briefly quit. But, in 1995, 'On Your Own' became their first UK Top 30 hit, and the emotive *A Northern Soul* won yet more praise. However, in August, Ashcroft quit again: a split described as "irrevocable", making the brilliant 'History' their final single and Oasis' 'Cast No Shadow' the only tribute to mad Richard's ambition in a world where chirpy Britpop ruled.

But by February 1996, Ashcroft, Jones and Salisbury were back together. Simon Tong joined on guitar and – having tried Suede's Bernard Butler – Ashcroft persuaded McCabe to return.

The Verve's return from the wilderness was stunning: in June 1997, they unleashed 'Bitter Sweet Symphony', on which Ashcroft summarized the mysteries and miseries of human existence over a majestic string sample from an orchestral version of The Rolling Stones' 'The Last Time'. Its UK No.2 peak vindicated The Verve at last – even if all their royalties went to The Rolling Stones' former manager Allen Klein.

The equally epic 'The Drugs Don't Work' followed its predecessor to instant classic status, entering at UK No.1. It struck a sad chord with a generation of reformed ravers who'd realized that being loved up was no real substitute for being loved. Then again, the fact that it had 'drugs' in the title might have helped. More smouldering stuff appeared on the UK chart-topping *Urban Hymns* (1997) – an impossibly *big* album (in both sound and sales) which earned a clutch of 1998 BRIT awards and placed The Verve alongside Radiohead as masters of glossy angst. Somehow, 'mad' old Richard's prophecy had come true: their Wigan homecoming show in May 1998 sold out, attracted 30,000 people and BBC coverage and set the seal on the most remarkable story of triumph over adversity in recent Pop history.

surf raft.vmg.co.uk//theverve/

VILLAGE PEOPLE

WHO Vocals/cop **Victor Willis**, vocals/Sioux Indian **Felipe Rose** (b. 12 Jan 1954), vocals/G.I. **Alexander Briley** (b. 12 Apr 1951), vocals/construction worker **David 'Scar' Hodo** (b. 7 Jul 1947), vocals/cowboy **Randy Jones**, vocals/leather man **Glenn M. Hughes** (b. 18 Jul 1950, Bronx, New York, USA)

WHEN 1977–

WHERE New York City, New York, USA

WHAT Non-stop ecstatic dancing

Fresh from US hits with The Ritchie Family, music masterminds Henri Belolo and Jacques Morali were entranced by Philly Soul, Disco and gay culture. With belting Soul singer Victor Willis, they unleashed the gay-and-proud late 70s club anthems 'San Francisco (You Got Me)', 'Macho Man' and 'Fire Island' as Village People – a tribute to New York's Greenwich Village gay district.

But Morali and Belolo's vision went beyond cult hits: they wanted "to put together a very special group, very American and very happy". Their six happy guys (of whom only 'Sioux Indian' Felipe Rose was gay) dressed as macho stereotypes and conquered the world with the classics 'Y.M.C.A.', 'In The Navy' (both 1978) and 'Go West' (1979) – the latter two with Willis' replacement Ray Simpson. The gay scene elevated them to icon status, the whole world loved the 'Y.M.C.A.' 'letter dance' (hence its use in *Friends* and the movie *Wayne's World II*), while the US Navy loaned them a battleship for the video of 'In The Navy' and even considered using the song for a recruitment drive – until they discovered what it was really about.

But after the title track from their atrocious movie *Can't Stop The Music* (1980), the hits dried up. Adrift in a sea of flops, they flirted with New Romantic and Frankie Goes To Hollywood-style seediness with disastrous results. They continued on the cabaret circuit even after Morali's AIDS-related death in 1991.

Meanwhile, the joyous 'Go West' (a celebration of San Francisco's gay scene), became a soccer crowd anthem and 1993 hit for Pet Shop Boys. Even the sober U2 weakly lampooned them in the video for their 'Discotheque'.

 www.geocities.com/TheTropics/4210/

GENE VINCENT

WHO b. Eugene Vincent Craddock, 11 Feb 1935, Norfolk, Virginia, USA, d. 12 Oct 1971, Newhall, California, USA

WHAT *The* Rock 'n' Roll bad boy

Though 'Be-Bop-A-Lula' (1956) was his only major hit, Gene Vincent is assured a place in history as the original Rock 'n' Roll bad boy: a limping, leather-clad greaser who lived fast and died young – a kind of rockin' Richard III.

Vincent began singing in the US Navy, but a motorcycle accident left him with a leg brace and a discharge in 1955. He became a minor Country star in Virginia and, with 'Be-Bop-A-Lula', the song he penned with 'Sheriff' Tex Davis in 1956, was snapped up by Capitol. Backed by the brilliant Blue Caps and a reverb-drenched, Sam Phillips-style production, he was launched as an Elvis clone. But while Presley was threatening by accident, Gene Vincent was threatening by intent, right down to his much-copied limp.

In fact, with 'Be-Bop-A-Lula', Vincent outdid Elvis. At turns raunchy (its flipside, 'Woman Love' was widely banned for suggestive lyrics), aggressive and gentle, it soared to US No.7 and UK No.16. Equally dark and dramatic was his follow-up, 'Race With The Devil' (1956). But Vincent's second (and final) US Top 20 hit was 1957's 'Lotta Lovin', despite a fabulous cameo

alongside Fats Domino and Little Richard in the best Rock 'n' Roll movie of all time – *The Girl Can't Help It* (1956).

But in England he was worshipped as a greaser God. 'Blue Jean Bop' (1956), 'Wild Cat', 'My Heart', 'Pistol Packin' Mama' (all 1960) and 1961's 'She She Little Sheila' and 'I'm Going Home' were all hits and an inspiration to everyone from Alex Harvey to John Lennon. While on tour there in April 1960, he and Eddie Cochran were in a car crash. Vincent survived; his friend died.

The accident seemed to put a full stop on Vincent's career: despite sporadic activity throughout the 60s, he never recaptured the wonder – or sales – of his debut. Heavy drinking, crippling leg pain and marital problems (he was married and divorced four times) conspired to prevent a comeback, despite a loyal first-generation Rocker following in his new home, the UK. Not even Lennon's endorsement (he played on the same bill as Vincent at the 1969 Toronto Peace Festival) could save the Kim Fowley-produced *I'm Back And I'm Proud* (1970). Despondent, he returned to the USA in 1971, where he died that year from a ruptured stomach ulcer – his career in tatters, his legend intact.

READ *Gene Vincent: A Discography* (1998), Derek Henderson

SURF www.athenet.net/~genevinc/index2.html

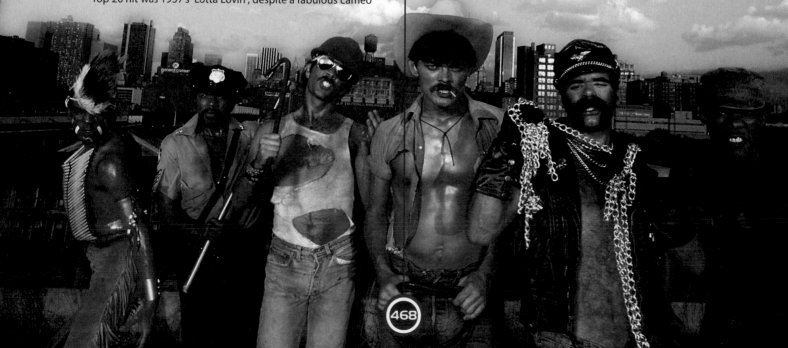

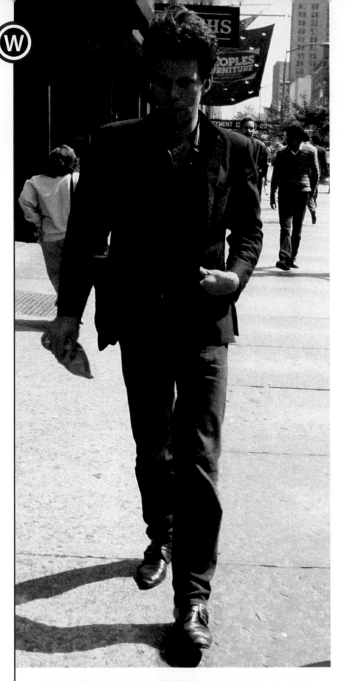

TOM WAITS

WHO b. 7 Dec 1949, Pomona, California, USA

WHAT Gravel-voiced eclecticism

Early albums such as *Closing Time* (1973), *The Heart Of Saturday Night* (1974) and the live double *Nighthawks At The Diner* (1975) developed Tom Waits' reputation as an idiosyncratic singer/ songwriter, inspired by Beat writers like Jack Kerouac and Charles Bukowski and Realist painters like Edward Hopper. Although his influences continued to be drawn primarily from American outsider culture, its applications became more widespread as his career progressed, taking in theatre and movie work, as both a composer and actor. While early songs like 1973's 'Martha' and 'Ol' 55' were generic enough to be covered by Tim Buckley and The Eagles, Waits' work grew more jazzy and personal on *Small Change* (1976), *Foreign Affairs* (1977) and *Blue Valentine* (1978), whose sleeve depicted the singer with his then lover Rickie Lee Jones. His live performances at the time were low-key, intimate affairs whose stage sets featured small pieces of furniture and standard lamps. The more R&B-flavoured *Heartattack And Vine* (1980) also included the beautiful 'Jersey Girl', later covered by Bruce Springsteen.

His collaboration with Country singer Crystal Gayle on the soundtrack to Francis Ford Coppola's *One From The Heart* (1982) remains Waits' most sentimental work, profiting greatly from the contrast between Gayle's crystalline voice and his gravelly tones. A cameo in the movie led to further roles in *Rumble Fish* (1983), *The Cotton Club* (1984), *Down By Law* (1986), *Ironweed* (1987), *Bram Stoker's Dracula* (1992) and *Short Cuts* (1993).

Moving from Asylum to Island brought the acclaimed *Swordfishtrombones* (1983). Waits adapted the ideas of 30s composer Harry Partch, whose innovative works were performed on bizarre, sculptural instruments he built from bell jars, lightbulbs and chunks of polished wood and scrap metal. This influence transformed Waits' songs into clanking, honking, growling junkyard demons, along with his usual poetic renderings of life's underbelly. *Rain Dogs* (1985) added elements of Folk forms like tangos, polkas and nursery rhymes. The result was as complete an evocation of multi-ethnic American culture as exists in Rock music, yet 'Downtown Train' was direct enough to be taken to the charts by Rod Stewart.

With his playwright wife Kathleen Brennan, Waits expanded a short character-study from *Swordfishtrombones* into a musical, *Frank's Wild Years* (1987), which enjoyed short runs in Chicago and New York. Always on the verge of poverty, his situation improved drastically in 1990 when he was awarded $2.5 million damages in a lawsuit against American snack food company Frito-Lay, who had used an impersonation of his distinctive voice in an advert. A similar 1995 case following the use of Screamin' Jay Hawkins' version of 'Heartattack And Vine' in a Levi's advert also swelled Waits' coffers. These afforded Waits the financial security to pursue his musical vision with impunity for *Bone Machine* (1992) and *Black Rider* (1993), the latter a collaboration with dramatist Robert Wilson and writer William Burroughs, which had a two-week theatrical run at the Brooklyn Academy in New York.

(READ) *The Underwear Of Strangers* (1998), Duncan Webster

(SURF) www.gameverse.com/music/waits/

SCOTT WALKER/WALKER BROTHERS ⊙

WHO Vocals/guitar/bass/keyboards **Scott Walker** (b. Noel Scott Engel, 9 Jan 1944, Hamilton, Ohio, USA), guitar/vocals **John Maus** (b. 12 Nov 1943, New York City, New York, USA), drums/vocals **Gary Leeds** (b. 3 Sep 1944, Glendale, California, USA)

WHEN 1964–1967

WHERE London, England

WHAT Bleak, brilliant and baffling

Scott Walker had already made the US charts (playing bass) with The Routers' instrumental US hit 'Let's Go' when he joined John Maus and former PJ Proby drummer Gary Leeds in 1964. In 1965, with the Vietnam draft looming, they migrated to England, hooked up with impresario Jack Good (who christened them The Walker Brothers) and scored a UK hit with a cover of The Everly Brothers' 'Love Her'.

Its sweeping strings, reverb-drenched, Phil Spector-style production and Walker's aching baritone introduced their majestic melancholia and a run of immaculate hits including 1965's UK No.1 'Make It Easy On Yourself' and 'My Ship Is Coming In', 1966's 'The Sun Ain't Gonna Shine Anymore' (another chart-topper), and the albums *Take It Easy* (1965), *Portrait* (1966) and *Images* (1966). But the stress of their teen sensation status sent Walker into depression – he'd already attempted suicide and sought refuge in a monastery by the time his enmity with Maus split the band in 1967.

While Maus and Leeds shone briefly as solo artists, Walker veered between MOR Pop crooner and tortured artist: his version of Jacques Brel's 'Jackie' (1967) was banned for raunchy lyrics; his second single, 'Joanna' (1968), was a romantic ballad by TV composers Tony Hatch and Jackie Trent. Walker also hosted his own TV series. *Scott 1* (1967), *Scott 2* (1968) and *Scott 3* (1969) blended melodrama (including more Brel covers), existential pondering ('Plastic Palace People' on *Scott 2*) and Easy Listening classics by the likes of Bacharach & David.

Finally exorcising The Walker Brothers' teen appeal with 1969's *Scott 4*, he revealed just how bleak he could be; with no covers and its opening tribute to Ingmar Bergman's darker-than-dark movie *The Seventh Seal*, it hinted at the mournful direction he was to take. Though 1969's *Songs From His TV Series*, a friendly collection of MOR standards, reached UK No.7, *Scott 4* effectively signalled the end of Walker's Pop charting days.

He flirted fruitlessly with the mainstream on the underbought *'Til The Band Comes In* (1970), *The Moviegoer* (1972), *Any Day Now* (1973) and *We Had It All* (1974). Then, in 1975, The Walker Brothers reconvened for the UK hit 'No Regrets', more MOR covers – *No Regrets* (1975) and *Lines* (1976) – and 1978's excellent *Nite Flights*, source of Walker's legendary 'Nite Flights' and 'The Electrician' (the former later covered by Walker's great admirer David Bowie).

Warner

Asked why REM signed to Warner Bros in 1988, Michael Stipe replied "Bugs Bunny". The US film company entered the music biz disastrously in 1930 with the purchase of Brunswick Records, but bounced back in 1958 with the launch of Warner Bros Records. The label's first major success was The Everly Brothers (who reached US and UK No.1 with 'Cathy's Clown'), followed by comedian Bob Newhart and Folk trio Peter, Paul & Mary. In 1963, Warner expanded with the acquisition of Frank Sinatra's Reprise label. Artists at the forefront of a new wave of 70s American music such as The Grateful Dead, Alice Cooper, Randy Newman, James Taylor, Ry Cooder, The Doobie Brothers and Van Morrison signed to Warner Bros while Joni Mitchell and Neil Young joined Reprise. In 1970, Warner joined forces with Elektra/Asylum and Atlantic as WEA, adding Led Zeppelin, The Rolling Stones, Yes, Crosby, Stills, Nash & Young, Bad Company, Aretha Franklin and Roberta Flack. Further success came from Fleetwood Mac, Van Halen, ZZ Top, Paul Simon, Rod Stewart, Elvis Costello, Eric Clapton and a-ha. WB subsidiary Sire signed Talking Heads and Madonna (a decade later her Maverick label, a Warner Bros affiliate, signed Alanis Morissette, Prodigy and Cleopatra). In the 90s, kd lang, Red Hot Chili Peppers and Reprise's Green Day were added, alongside million-selling soundtrack albums from the Batman movies, Evita and Space Jam.

Warp

"We Are Reasonable People," argue Rob Mitchell and Steve Beckett, masterminds behind Warp. Considering the demonic noise of their protégé Aphex Twin's 'Come To Daddy' (1997), their sincerity seems doubtful. Founded in 1989, the Warp label eschewed fey indie jangling and became synonymous with cold, experimental Techno. Mitchell and Beckett started with Sheffield's FON record store, which – hijacked by House and Techno DJs – became the centre of a local Dance explosion. They issued Forgemaster's 'Track With No Name' with little expectation. When it sold 10,000, they became Warp and hit the UK Top 40 in 1990 with wondrous UK Techno pioneers Nightmares On Wax, Tricky Disco and LFO. But Warp's speciality was not the wide-eyed silliness of Hardcore, nor the dullness of Handbag House. With their excellent Artificial Intelligence compilations (the first came in 1992), they showcased a growing wave of DIY Techno terrorists – Aphex Twin, Autechre, The Black Dog, B12, Richie Hawtin (as FUSE) and Mike Paradinas' µ-Ziq (as Jake Slazenger) – who bled Dance's experimental potential dry with mind-bogglingly weird collages of electronics and noise. Other classics came courtesy of DJ Andrew Weatherall's Sabres Of Paradise and Two Lone Swordsmen, Plaid, Broadcast, Jimi Tenor, Squarepusher and US legends Drexciya. Even an old-timer like Cabaret Voltaire's Richard H. Kirk found comfort in Warp's bosom. And anyone can join in: Warp releases carry the message "If you think on the same wavelength, contact/send tapes to…" Warp: the greatest record label in the world ever.

Walker disappeared but became a legend thanks to gushing praise from Ian McCulloch, Marc Almond and Julian Cope, who compiled 1981's *Fire Escape In The Sky: The Godlike Genius Of Scott Walker*. He re-emerged in 1984 with another brilliant flop, *Climate Of Hunter*, then retreated again. Silent for more than a decade, he collaborated with Brian Eno on an unfinished, unreleased album and studied Fine Arts in London while 1990's *Boy Child* (a solo retrospective) and 1992's *No Regrets* (Walker Brothers hits) circulated. Then, in 1995, he re-appeared with *Tilt* – a bleak, oblique mix of sonic violence, near silent ambient atmospheres and political lyrics which left critics struggling for words to describe its excellence.

READ *Scott Walker: A Deep Shade Of Blue* (1994), Mike Watkinson & Pete Anderson

SURF www.crl.com/~tsimon/walker.htm

DIONNE WARWICK

WHO b. Marie Dionne Warrick, 12 Dec 1940, East Orange, New Jersey, USA

WHAT The soulful voice of 60s Pop

Long before Whitney Houston conquered Soul, Dionne Warwick laid claim to it. Having performed with Gospel groups The Drinkard Singers (managed by her mother) and The Gospelaires (with her sister Dee Dee, cousin Cissy Houston and friend Doris Troy), Warwick became an in-demand session singer. At a session for The Drifters, she was spotted by legendary songwriter Burt Bacharach who, with his partner Hal David, guided her to the Pop queen throne. The US hit 'Don't Make Me Over' (1962) initiated a run of Burt & Hal-penned masterpieces, graced by Warwick's delicate voice and immaculate phrasing. 'Anyone Who Had A Heart' (1963), 1964's 'Walk On By', 1965's 'Are You There (With Another Girl)', 1966's 'I Just Don't Know What To Do With Myself', 1967's 'Alfie', '(Theme From) Valley Of The Dolls' (her only non-Bacharach & David song of the period) and 'I Say A Little Prayer', 1968's 'Do You Know The Way To San Jose' and 1969's 'This Girl's In Love With You' and 'I'll Never Fall In Love Again' were just some of Warwick's transatlantic mega-hits. Her interpretations also became blueprints for British hits by Dusty Springfield (1964's 'I Just Don't Know What To Do With Myself') and Cilla Black (1966's 'Alfie').

After leaving Bacharach & David in 1971, Warwick's career nose-dived. Adding a final 'e' to her surname on the advice of a numerologist didn't help, but a duet with The Detroit Spinners, 'Then Came You' (1974), became her first US chart-topper. Her renaissance continued with 1977's live album with Isaac Hayes, *A Man And A Woman*, but a full-blown comeback came courtesy of Barry Manilow – he produced the US smash *Dionne* (1979) – while 1982's Barry Gibb-masterminded *Heartbreaker* revitalized her UK profile. Her biggest 80s hit was 1985's AIDS charity single, 'That's What Friends Are For'; a Grammy-winning US No.1 with Elton John, Stevie Wonder and Gladys Knight which transcended its earnest subject with a brilliant tune.

Love Songs (1990) peaked at UK No.6 and *Friends Can Be Lovers* (1993) featured a reunion with Bacharach & David and a duet with cousin Whitney Houston – the daughter of Dionne's old Gospelaires partner Cissy. *Dionne Sings Dionne* (1998) starred a Hip Hop revamp of 'What The World Needs Now Is Love'. Meanwhile, the secret of her superhuman skills was revealed in 1997's movie *Men In Black*: Dionne Warwick is a benign alien.

SURF www2.netdoor.com/~lmorgan/dionne_links.html

WAS (NOT WAS)

WHO Bass **Don Was** (b. Donald Fagenson, 13 Sep 1952, Detroit, Michigan, USA), saxophone/flute/vocals **David Was** (b. David Weiss, 26 Oct 1952, Detroit), vocals **Sweet Pea Atkinson** (b. 20 Sep 1945, Oberlin, Ohio, USA), vocals **'Sir' Harry Bowens** (b. 8 Oct 1949, Detroit), vocals **Donald Ray Mitchell** (b. 12 Apr 1957, Detroit)

WHEN 1980–1993

WHERE Detroit, Michigan, USA

WHAT Funny funkateers

The 'Was brothers', Don Fagenson and David Weiss, hooked up despite Weiss moving to LA in the 70s. They began a long-distance collaboration and, with R&B singers Sweet Pea Atkinson, 'Sir' Harry Bowens and Donald Ray Mitchell, embellished their frazzled Funk Pop with unusual guests like Mel Torme, Leonard Cohen and Iggy Pop. They also made a point of featuring their first hit, 1982's 'Out Come The Freaks', on

their self-titled 1981 debut and the two subsequent albums.

Having built a cult following with 1983's *Born To Laugh At Tornados*, their breakthrough came with 1987's 'Walk The Dinosaur', a funky warning against nuclear annihilation also featured on *What Up, Dog?* (1988). They updated The Temptations' 'Papa Was A Rollin' Stone' in 1990 with Rapper G Love E. One of their more bizarre collaborations was 1992's UK No.4 'Shake Your Head', featuring an uncredited Ozzy Osbourne and Kim Basinger – the latter replacing Madonna, who declined to reprise her pre-fame role on the original demo.

Meanwhile, Don Was reaped rewards in his parallel career as a producer, twiddling knobs for The Rolling Stones, Bonnie Raitt, Iggy Pop, Brian Wilson, Carly Simon, Bob Seger, Neil Diamond, Roy Orbison, David Crosby, Ringo Starr, Willie Nelson, Randy Newman, Michelle Shocked and The B-52's. After Was (Not Was) split in 1993, he released his solo debut, the cinematic *Forever's A Long Long Time* (1997), as Orquestra Was.

W.A.S.P.

WHO Vocals/bass **Blackie Lawless** (b. Steve Duren, 4 Sep 1954, Florida, USA), guitar **Chris Holmes** (b. 23 Jun 1961, USA), guitar **Randy Piper** (b. USA), drums **Tony Richards** (b. USA)

WHEN 1983–

WHERE Los Angeles, California, USA

WHAT Shock Rock 'n' stings

Wild, outrageous, over-the-top – everything US Heavy Metal had ceased to be when they came along – W.A.S.P. (We Are Sexual Perverts) was spawned by ex-New York Doll Blackie Lawless from an earlier LA act, Sister, which featured Chris Holmes (plus Nikki Sixx, who left for Mötley Crüe). Sister hung dummies on meat-hooks and ate worms onstage; W.A.S.P looked like a Hell's Angels basketball team: bottomless leathers and buzz-saw codpieces (Blackie's spurted fire – it backfired once, painfully). They threw raw meat at audiences and whipped near-naked girls on torture racks. Their Alice Cooper-esque blood-and-pyrotechnics shows – "psychodrama", said Lawless – and their accessible anthems guaranteed a teenage following. When US senator's wife Tipper Gore heard her adolescent son playing their 1984 single 'Animal (Fuck Like A Beast)' – released independently when their label, Capitol, wouldn't touch it – she formed the censorship committee PMRC (Parents' Musical Resource Committee), making Lawless an unlikely spokesman for free speech.

After 1984's thrillingly tacky *W.A.S.P.*, 1985's ambitious *The Last Command*, 1986's patchy *Inside The Electric Circus* and 1987's *Live In The Raw*, their biggest hit was 1989's double-platinum *The Headless Children*, featuring a splendid cover of The Who's 'The Real Me'. Blackie began the 90s minus most of his band and with the conceptual *The Crimson Idol* (1992). Interest waned through 1995's *Still Not Black Enough*, a reunion with Holmes (drummer Stet Howland and bass player Mike Duda completed the line-up) on 1997's *W.A.S.P – K.F.D* ('Kill, fuck, die') and 1998's *Double Live Assassins*, but Marilyn Manson proved they hadn't lived in vain.

Fan W.A.S.P. Nation, 4872 Topanga Canyon Boulevard, Suite 322, Woodland Hills, CA 91364, USA

Surf www.geocities.com/SunsetStrip/Towers/9611/index.html

THE WATERBOYS

WHO Vocals/guitar **Mike Scott** (b. 14 Dec 1958, Edinburgh, Scotland)

WHEN 1981–1993

WHERE London, England

WHAT The Mr Big of mystic music

Half mystic seer, half space cadet, Mike Scott led The Waterboys from 'Big Music' (and big success) through Celtic Folk to, sadly, commercial obscurity. Having made little impact on Punk's fringes, Scott conceived The Waterboys (from a line in Lou Reed's 'The Kids') to, like Van Morrison, bring Celtic roots to Rock. He enlisted multi-instumentalist Anthony Thistlethwaite and drummer Kevin Wilkinson for *The Waterboys* (1983) and added keyboard player Karl Wallinger and trumpeter Roddy Lorimer for 1984's *A Pagan Place*. But those albums' sweeping spiritualism proved a mere rehearsal for 1985's *This Is The Sea*: a thrilling, majestic rush which made their stadium Rock peers seem flat-footed. It included the hit 'The Whole Of The Moon', a shining example of the sound Scott conceptualized on *A Pagan Place*: 'The Big Music' – lyrical mysticism, musical might.

But after *This Is the Sea*, Wallinger walked, forming the mildly psychedelic World Party, who hit with *Private Revolution* (1987), *Goodbye Jumbo* (1990), *Bang!* (1993) and *Egyptology* (1997). Scott and Thistlethwaite moved to Ireland and returned with a gaggle of traditional Irish musicians for the none-more-Celtic *Fisherman's Blues* (1988), whose heart-rending title track notched up another UK hit. They stumbled with 1990's *Room To Roam* – an unfocused 'raggle taggle' ramble through Irish Folk, which saw the band swell to include the likes of accordionist Sharon Shannon. It gave The Waterboys their first UK Top 10 album, but the rocked-out accompanying tour alienated new fans and failed to sway disenchanted older ones. Scott moved to New York and courted Rock on 1993's *Dream Harder*, then returned to his native Scotland and dropped the Waterboys name for the folky *Bring 'Em All In* (1995) and his return to 'Big', *Still Burning* (1997).

Surf www.vgernet.net/nmoreau/water.scott/

MUDDY WATERS

WHO b. McKinley Morganfield, 4 Apr 1915, Rolling Fork, Missouri, USA, d. 30 Apr 1983, Chicago, Illinois, USA

WHAT The emperor of electric Blues

While The Beatles, The Rolling Stones and Led Zeppelin were still in diapers, Muddy Waters was pioneering the music that shaped their destinies. Plantation worker McKinley Morganfield (his stage name arose from a childhood fondness for playing in a muddy creek) was raised in Mississippi on Blues legends Son House and Robert Johnson. He moved to Chicago in 1943, rewiring rural Blues standards into electric monsters with a guitar bought with wages from a paper mill job.

Waters joined Blues label Aristocrat (which became Chess) and made his reputation with raw classics like 1948's 'I Can't Be Satisfied' and 'I Feel Like Going Home', and 1950's 'Rollin' Stone' (yes, that's where they got their name from). In the 50s, he

scored 13 US R&B hits – including 1952's 'She Moves Me', 1954's 'I'm Your Hoochie Coochie Man', 'I Just Want To Make Love To You', 'I'm Ready' and 'Got My Mojo Working', and the sinister 'Mannish Boy', a 1955 reply to Bo Diddley's 'I'm A Man'. Some of Chicago's finest passed through his backing band, including Otis Spann, Little Walker, Jimmie Rodgers, Junior Wells and Buddy Guy. He even proved instrumental in the success of fellow legends Howlin' Wolf and Chuck Berry.

As Rock 'n' Roll steamrollered Blues, Waters' sales declined. But a fanatical following among hipsters like The Rolling Stones ensured sold-out gigs and seminal 60s albums like *Muddy Waters At Newport* (1960). Such fan worship spawned super-jams like 1969's *Fathers And Sons* (featuring Blues Rock masters Paul Butterfield and Mike Bloomfield), an ecstatically received cameo at The Band's 1976 'Last Waltz' concert and some of his biggest-selling albums: the Johnny Winter-helmed *Hard Again* (1977), *I'm Ready* (1978) and *King Bee* (1981).

Waters' last show was with Eric Clapton in 1982. He died from a heart attack in 1983, but his legend was confirmed when he was one of the first inductees to the Rock And Roll Hall Of Fame in 1987. His first UK hit came a year later, when 'Mannish Boy' was used in a Levi's jeans commercial.

(READ) *Muddy Waters: The Mojo Man* (1997), Sandra Tooze

(SURF) www.deltablues.com/muddy.htm

WEATHER REPORT

WHO Keyboards **Joe Zawinul** (b. 7 Jul 1932, Vienna, Austria), saxophones **Wayne Shorter** (b. 25 Aug 1933, Newark, New Jersey, USA), percussion **Pete Erskine** (b. 5 May 1954, Somers Point, New Jersey), bass **Jaco Pastorius** (b. 1 Dec 1951, Norristown, Pennsylvania, d. 21 Sep 1987, Fort Lauderdale, Florida)

WHEN 1971–1986

WHERE New York City, New York, USA

WHAT Virtuoso Jazz Rock fusion

Having helped Miles Davis invent Fusion, Wayne Shorter and Joe Zawinul left in 1971 to form Weather Report with percussionist Airto Moreira and bassist Miroslav Vitous. Early albums like *I Sing The Body Electric* (1972) differed little from Miles' style but, with *Sweetnighter* (1973), *Mysterious Traveler* (1974), *Tale Spinnin'* (1975) and *Black Market* (1976), they developed Jazz Rock which swung and dawdled by turns, but was always original: Zawinul was one of the first Jazz players to use synthesizers, while Shorter dabbled with the lyricon, a weird wind synthesizer. Moreira was replaced by Dom Um Romao, and Vitous by a series of bassists, notably the virtuoso Jaco Pastorius, who also worked with Joni Mitchell and pursued a solo career before drink and drugs led to his violent death outside a Florida nightclub. The drum seat was occupied by such rhythmic genii as Chester Thompson, Omar Hakim, Steve Gadd and Tony Williams.

Heavy Weather (1977) was their biggest-seller – a US No.30 peak after which Weather Report grew more diffuse. Zawinul and Shorter wound the band up after 1986's *This Is This*, but a Weather Report sample graced Portishead's *Dummy* (1994).

(SURF) members.harborcom.net/"jmayer/jorcki/weather.html

THE WEDDING PRESENT

WHO Vocals/guitar **David Gedge** (b. 23 Apr 1960, Leeds, England), guitar **Peter Salowka** (b. Manchester, England), bass **Keith Gregory** (b. 2 Jan 1963, Darlington, County Durham, England), drums **Simon Smith** (b. 3 May 1965, Lincolnshire, England)

WHEN 1985–

WHERE Leeds, England

WHAT The archetypal Indie band

As Indie as they come, The Wedding Present proudly displayed all its 80s hallmarks: an 'ironically' banal name; fast, scratchy guitars; a singer who could only sort-of sing; drooling adoration from guru-like Indie DJ John Peel; and fair-to-middling record

PAUL WELLER ⊙

WHO b. John Weller, 25 May 1958, Woking, Surrey, England

WHAT The grumpy elder statesman of Britpop

As The Style Council dribbled to an ignominious end in 1989, few could recall Paul Weller as the fiery Mod Rocker who'd begun the 80s as leader of The Jam. The whimsy and tepid Jazz-isms of his recent work had alienated the loyal following he once commanded, and his label had lost interest too. The task he faced was to reinvent himself for the 90s. And, defying all expectations, he did – first with a low-key tour with a new, Mod-ish band (The Paul Weller Movement); then, in 1991, a small hit with the self-financed 'Into Tomorrow'. He signed to Go! Discs for his solo debut, *Paul Weller* (1992), and its Top 20 hit, the excellent 'Uh Huh Oh Yeh'.

His return from the commercial wilderness was confirmed by 1993's masterful *Wild Wood* and its hit 'Sunflower'. Weller's rediscovery of the guitar gave the music new dynamism, recapturing some of his old intensity, while his musical scope extended to the heavy 70s sounds of Traffic and Humble Pie, showcased on 1993's 'The Weaver' EP and 1994's *Live Wood*.

These were brought to fruition on *Stanley Road* (1995), whose hit highlights included 'Broken Stones', 'You Do Something To Me' and 'The Changingman'. Its cover designed by *Sgt. Pepper* Pop artist Peter Blake, *Stanley Road*'s title was a reference to Weller's childhood home in Woking. Perhaps his most introspective album, it was also the most successful, reaching UK No.1 in May 1995. After the collapse of Go! Discs, Weller transferred to Island for 1997's *Heavy Soul*, a UK No.2 that continued the critically condemned retro style of its predecessor. Musicians included drummer Steve White (a fixture *chez* Weller since the Style Council days) and guitarist Steve Cradock of Ocean Colour Scene, two of a legion of Weller disciples which also included Noel Gallagher. Indeed, the reverence afforded him by the Britpop bunch took Weller's reputation to its highest point since The Jam's glory days. The angry young man had become a grumpy elder statesman.

Read *Paul Weller: My Ever Changing Moods* (1996), John Reed

Surf www.columbia.edu/"als3/splinter.html

WET WET WET ⊙⊙⊙⊙

WHO Vocals **Marti Pellow** (b. Mark McLoughlin, 23 Mar 1966, Clydebank, Scotland), guitar **Graeme Duffin**, bass **Graeme Clark** (b. 15 Apr 1966, Glasgow, Scotland), drums **Tom Cunningham** (b. 22 Jun 1963, Drumchapel, Glasgow), keyboards **Neil Mitchell** (b. 8 Jun 1967, Helensburgh, Scotland)

WHEN 1982–

WHERE Glasgow, Scotland

WHAT Popped In, Souled Out

The unacknowledged standard-bearers for Scottish Pop, Wet Wet Wet quietly became massive without the acclaim lavished on countrymen Runrig and Deacon Blue. Their 1987 debut, 'Wishing I Was Lucky' – a bitter depiction of unemployment

sales. They established these features with their 1985 debut 'Go Out And Get 'Em Boy!' on their own Reception label. Carried on the tide of the shambling 'C86' scene, they seduced critics with *George Best* (1987), scraped the UK Top 40 with 1988's 'Nobody's Twisting Your Arm' and 'Why Are You Being So Reasonable Now?', then made a credibility-busting move to 'big' label RCA.

Their reputation soared with *Ukrainski Vistupi V Johna Peela* (1989) – a collection of Ukranian folk songs – and the harsh *Bizarro* (1989), source of the hits 'Kennedy' and 'Brassneck'.

This was enough to impress Indie high priest Steve Albini who, after producing their whimsical cover of Steve Harley's 'Make Me Smile (Come Up And See Me)', helmed the noisy *Seamonsters* (1991), whose grungey tendencies attracted US fans. With Salowka gone to The Ukranians, 1992 saw the Weddoes release a new single every month, scoring a record-breaking 12 UK hits. These (and their flipsides, which included covers of Isaac Hayes' 'Theme From Shaft', The Monkees' 'Pleasant Valley Sunday' and Bow Wow Wow's 'Wild In The Country') were collected on 1992's twin *Hit Parade* compilations. However, adrift from RCA since 1993, the Weddoes coasted with *Watusi* (1994) and *Saturnalia* (1996).

Read *Thank Yer, Very Glad* (1990), Mark Hodkinson

Fan PO Box HP25, Leeds, LS6 1RU, UK

Surf www.westnet.com/weddoes/front.html

married to punchy Pop Soul – punctured the UK Top 10 and, aided by the toothsome grin of Marti Pellow, established the Wets as teen favourites. The summer anthem 'Sweet Little Mystery' and the dreamy ballad 'Angel Eyes' were also hits from the UK No.1 *Popped In Souled Out* (1987).

In 1988, they scored a BRIT award for Best Newcomer and a UK No.1 with a cover of The Beatles' 'With A Little Help From My Friends' from children's charity album *Sgt. Pepper Knew My Father*. But critical wounds and discomfort with their Pop persona prompted them to force the release of *The Memphis Sessions* (1988) – a collaboration with veteran producer Willie Mitchell which pre-dated *Popped In*, but had been withheld by their label, Phonogram. Its raw and authentic Soul sound presaged the direction of *Holding Back The River* (1989), and a commercial dive.

With 1992's UK No.1 'Goodnight Girl', the Wets returned to the limelight. *High On The Happy Side* (1992) came with covers album *Cloak And Dagger* and recast the band as arena-sized adult sophisticates – hence monster sales for 1993's *Live At The Albert Hall* and *End Of Part One (Their Greatest Hits)*.

Even this paled beside a fifteen-week sit-in at UK No.1 by their 1994 cover of The Troggs' 'Love Is All Around'. From the hit movie *Four Weddings And A Funeral*, its mind-boggling residency ended only when the band ordered its deletion, one week shy of Bryan Adams' 1991 chart run record.

Picture This (1994) topped the UK chart and spawned the hits 'Julia Says', 'Don't Want To Forgive Me Now', 'Somewhere, Somehow' and 'She's All On My Mind'. The platinum *Wet Wet Wet 10* (1997) marked their decade in the charts, but proved enough for drummer Tom Cunningham, who left in December that year.

fan Splash, 1 Park Gate, Glasgow, G3 6D2, UK

surf www.wetwetwet.co.uk/

WHAM! ⊙⊙✪

WHO Vocals **George Michael** (b. Georgios Panayiotou, 25 Jun 1963, London, England), guitar/vocals **Andrew Ridgeley** (b. 26 Jan 1963, Surrey, England)

WHEN 1981–1986

WHERE Hertfordshire, England

WHAT All-conquering Pop princes

George Michael (bespectacled and shy) met Andrew Ridgeley (outgoing) at Bushey Meads school, Hertfordshire, in 1975 and dabbled with teen Ska band The Executive. Then, in 1981, they became Wham! and conquered the entire Pop universe.

Their 1982 debut – the tub-thumping 'Wham Rap' – flopped, but the fresh and funky 'Young Guns (Go For It)' sped to UK No.3, propelled by their good looks and raunchy gyrations with backing singers Shirlie Holliman and D.C. Lee, later replaced by Pepsi. Teenzines flipped and 1983's hits (a reissued 'Wham Rap', 'Bad Boys' and the super 'Club Tropicana') trailed *Fantastic* (1983).

Their assault reached frenzied heights with 1984's UK chart-toppers 'Wake Me Up Before You Go Go' and 'Freedom' and the smash-packed transatlantic No.1 *Make It Big*. However, that year – with Ridgeley long shunted to the sidelines – Michael made his first bid for solo stardom with the Ridgeley co-penned 'Careless Whisper' – a smouldering, sax-driven lament which, naturally, topped the UK chart. Wham! returned in December

with *another* classic, 'Last Christmas'/'Everything She Wants' and a 1985 tour, including pioneering shows in China.

Late in 1985, they returned to the top with 'I'm Your Man', but the end was nigh: 'Careless Whisper' had already weakened Ridgeley's relevance to Wham!'s music, and Michael's second solo No.1, 'A Different Corner' (1986), confirmed suspicions. They topped the chart again with the storming 'Edge Of Heaven' EP, then – after a triumphant farewell at Wembley Stadium (commemorated on 1986's *The Final*) – split. Michael and Ridgeley's fortunes diverged thereafter: one became a megastar, the other dabbled disastrously in motor racing and Rock with *Son Of Albert* (1988). However, their collective legacy was revisited on 1997's *The Best Of Wham!: If You Were There*.

surf www.geocities.com/SunsetStrip/Palms/9988/

BARRY WHITE ✪

WHO b. 12 Sep 1944, Galveston, Texas, USA

WHAT The Walrus of lurve

Although Satan is the symbol on which Rock hangs, an equally potent icon is The Walrus. Its first sighting was in John Lennon's 1967 invocation 'I Am The Walrus' from their *Magical Mystery Tour*. A year later, Lennon claimed (on *The Beatles*' 'Glass Onion') that "The Walrus was Paul". But, make no mistake: Barry White *is* The Walrus – The Walrus of lurve.

The Walrus is a man whose house-shaking bass drawl and raunchy lyrics have become synonymous with sex. At 16, White was a serious criminal. He took the classic escape route, putting his choir boy past to good use in LA soulsters The Upfronts, arranging Bob & Earl's 1963 classic 'The Harlem Shuffle' and joining Mustang Records as A&R man. There, he adopted the vocal trio Love Unlimited and married their Glodean James.

White produced their 1972 hit 'Walking In The Rain With The One I Love', then put them into action on his 1973 solo debut. *I've Got So Much To Give* and its hit 'I'm Gonna Love You Just A Little Bit More Baby' established the White style: long titles, spoken intros, lush strings, solid rhythms and unparalleled raunch.

A string of transatlantic smashes followed, including 1973's 'Never, Never, Gonna Give You Up' and 'I've Got So Much To Give', 1974's US chart-topper 'Can't Get Enough Of Your Love, Babe' and UK No.1 'You're The First, The Last, My Everything' and 1977's 'It's Ecstasy When You Lay Down Next To Me'. Meanwhile, *Can't Get Enough* (1974), *Just Another Way To Say I Love You* (1975), *Barry White Sings For Someone You Love* (1977), Love Unlimited's 'Under The Influence' and Disco side-project Love Unlimited Orchestra's 'Love's Theme' (1973) and *Rhapsody In White* (1974) brought us closer to The Planet Of The Walrus.

But as the 70s wore on, so White's appeal wore thin. He continued as an acclaimed producer (he was mooted to helm Marvin Gaye's sequel to *Midnight Love*), then re-emerged, rampant, with the hit 'Sho' You Right' from 1987's *The Right Night & Barry White*. He guested on Quincy Jones' *Back On The Block* (1989) and *Q's Jook Joint* (1995), Rap demi-god Big Daddy Kane's 1991 hit 'All Of Me' and Tina Turner's *Wildest Dreams* (1996).

Having struck back with harder grooves, a new-found Rap influence and plenty of the old tricks, White won 'Album Of The Year' at the Soul Train Music Awards for 1994's *The Icon Is Love*.

surf www.globacs.nl/home/p/pklein/bw.html

WHITESNAKE

WHO Vocals **David Coverdale** (b. 22 Sep 1951, Saltburn-by-the-Sea, North Yorkshire, England)

WHEN 1977–

WHERE London, England

WHAT Metal's mouth and trousers

When Deep Purple broke up in 1976, David Coverdale recorded *Whitesnake* (1977) and *Northwinds* (1978) to the utter indifference of the burgeoning Punk era, before forming the band dubbed with his own phallic nickname. A torrential early output established their European standing: 1978's *Trouble*, 1979's *Lovehunter* (its notorious sleeve picturing a naked woman astride a monstrous serpent), 1980's *Ready An' Willing* (home of the hit 'Fool For Your Loving') and *Live… In The Heart Of The City* (source of an anthemic cover of Bobby Bland's 'Ain't No Love In The Heart Of The City') and 1981's UK No.2 *Come An' Get It*.

A constantly shifting line-up – including Purple veterans Jon Lord (keyboards) and Ian Paice (drums) – took a toll on their creativity and *Saints 'N' Sinners* (1982) sounded hollow. Still, they played the UK's Monsters Of Rock festival in 1981, headlined it in 1983 and made a splendid comeback with 1984's *Slide It In*.

But Coverdale was frustrated by fruitless bids to crack the USA and his career was stalled by throat problems. Then it took two completely different bands to get through the next album. The first producer, Mike Stone, constructively dismissed himself by suggesting a new singer was called for. The musicians went too, before Keith Olsen took over production of an all-new line-up, introducing Coverdale's most faithful collaborator, guitarist Adrian Vandenburg. However, the painful process paid off when *1987* became a worldwide multi-million-seller, thanks to shiny hits like 'Here I Go Again' and 'Is This Love' (the latter originally penned for Tina Turner). With a mostly young, MTV-compatible band, Coverdale finally escaped the ignominy of supporting Mötley Crüe and found massive Stateside success.

Metal guitar hero Steve Vai twinned Vandenburg for 1989's entertainingly ludicrous *Slip Of The Tongue* and another world tour, culminating with Whitesnake's third Monsters Of Rock show. But Coverdale grew tired of superstardom, divorced his second wife, American actress Tawny Kittaen (who'd starred in the steamy *1987* videos), and put the band on hold.

A short-lived partnership with Led Zeppelin's Jimmy Page produced 1993's spirited *Coverdale/Page* – a great source of amusement to Page's Zep pal Robert Plant, who'd long accused Coverdale of ripping him off (see Whitesnake's 1987 hit 'Still Of The Night' for irrevocable proof).

Whitesnake made a brief comeback to promote *Greatest Hits* (1994), until Coverdale bade a 'final' farewell with *Restless Heart* (1997). Solo again, he vowed to pursue a lifelong passion for R&B, which had often been concealed by commercial ambition.

surf www.st.rim.or.jp/"kino1989/Coverdale/

> **"I think I'm actually starting to get a little tired of standing out there screaming my lungs out…"**
> **David Coverdale**

THE WHO ⊙

THE WHO Vocals **Roger Daltrey** (b. 1 Mar 1944, Hammersmith, London, England), guitar/vocals **Pete Townshend** (b. 19 May 1945, Chiswick, London), bass/vocals **John Entwhistle** (b. 9 Oct 1944, Chiswick), drums **Keith Moon** (b. 23 Aug 1947, Wembley, London, d. 7 Sep 1978, London)

THE WHEN 1964–

THE WHERE London, England

THE WHAT Mod gods bring the noise

Choppy riffs, searing vocals, explosive drums, trashed gear, anthems about adolescent anxiety and gnawing unease about the monster they'd spawned: The Who were the proto-Nirvana.

Beginning as the Roger Daltrey-led The Detours in 1961, they progressed from Pop covers to American R&B, ditched singer Colin Dawson and, in 1964, became The Who. Drummer Doug Sandom was ousted by Keith Moon, Daltrey switched from guitar to vocals, John Entwhistle stayed on bass and Pete Townshend played guitar – when he wasn't busy smashing it, that is. Having accidentally broken his guitar neck on a low ceiling during a show, he made this vandalism their trademark, egged on by the legendarily destructive Moon. Every Rock star who ever rams a guitar into an amplifier, upturns a drum kit or wrecks a hotel room does so in the spirit of The Who.

In 1964, manager Pete Meaden transformed them into The High Numbers, a house band for his beloved Mod movement – obsessed with style, fixated with R&B and fuelled by speed. Although their sole single – the Meaden-penned 'I'm The Face'/'Zoot Suit' (1964) – flopped, The High Numbers were taken over by managers Kit Lambert and Chris Stamp. Renamed The Who, a residency at London's Marquee Club secured their reputation as masters of 'Maximum R&B'.

After the aggressive Daltrey was threatened with expulsion from the band he'd created, he let Townshend lead the band. The latter often wrote to fit Daltrey's tough-guy image, hence their first hits: 1965's 'I Can't Explain', 'Anyway Anyhow Anywhere' and 'My Generation', and 1966's 'Substitute'. Though not the first to battle The Beatles with razor-sharp riffing – The Kinks and The Rolling Stones were already in the ring – The Who matched musical might with lyrical angst, notably "Hope I die before I get old" ('My Generation') and "I was born with a plastic spoon in my mouth" ('Substitute'). The fire was fuelled by Townshend's claim that, like The Sex Pistols and Faith No More in later years, the band members hated each other.

My Generation (1965) scaled the UK Top 5, but equally indicative of The Who's ambition was *A Quick One* (1966). Its centrepiece was 'A Quick One While He's Away' – a 'mini Rock opera' of the type that, in engorged forms, would later blight The Who and Rock in general. Entwhistle's droll 'Whiskey Man' and 'Boris The Spider', also on that album, premiered his knack of balancing the prevailing pomposity.

The Who scored Stateside in 1967 with hit 'n' run gigs in New York and the incongruously chirpy 'Happy Jack', then stole the show at the Monterey Pop Festival. But the restless Townshend, already fretting about Rock's destiny, was wounded by what he saw as the failure of 1967's 'I Can See For Miles'. Though it gave The Who their only US Top 10 hit and brilliantly showcased

Moon's pyrotechnical drumming, it didn't follow 'Happy Jack' and 'Pictures Of Lily' into the UK Top 5. This apparent disappointment was compounded when the ambitious *The Who Sell Out* (1967) stalled outside the UK Top 10 and US Top 40, and 'Dogs' and 'Magic Bus' made only minor impact.

Townshend sought consolation in the wisdom of Indian mystic Meher Baba. "One minute I was freaked out on acid," he said, "the next minute I was into Baba." Envisaging Rock as a spiritual rather than primal thing (though thankfully abstaining from a George Harrison-esque overhaul of the actual music), Townshend came up with *Tommy* (1969), a conceptual affair whose deaf, dumb and blind hero connects with the outside world only through the unlikely medium of pinball.

It charted on the back of the irresistible 'Pinball Wizard', which briefly reversed their downward hit trend. "In fact," Daltrey told *Q* magazine, "*Tommy* was not a particularly big success… It was only after us flogging it on the road for three years, doing Woodstock and things like that, that it got back in the charts. Then it stayed there for a year and took on a life of its own."

Manager Kit Lambert, who'd encouraged Townshend to pursue the Rock Opera angle, played on it by staging *Tommy* in worldwide opera houses. It spawned a 1972 musical version (starring, among others, Rod Stewart), a 1974 movie (directed by Ken Russell and starring Tina Turner) and, in the 90s, a highly successful Broadway incarnation. These productions got increasingly further from the true spirit of The Who, which was caught on *Live At Leeds* (1970). Meanwhile, Townshend devised a fitting follow-up to *Tommy*, the sci-fi extravaganza *Lifehouse*. When it proved incomprehensible to everyone bar its creator, the project was filleted to create *Who's Next* (1971), the band's only No.1 and their undisputed peak. Book-ended by the synth-driven anthems 'Baba O'Riley' and 'Won't Get Fooled Again', it also boasts 'Behind Blue Eyes', a stunning marriage of slashing riffs and lyrical unease.

Such a classic again created the problem of a follow-up. From abandoned sequels came one-off hits like 1972's 'Join Together' and 'Relay'. Solo projects abounded: Entwhistle's *Smash Your Head Against The Wall* (1971), *Whistle Rhymes* (1971), *Rigor Mortis Sets In* (1973) and *Mad Dog* (1975); Moon's Surf tribute *Two Sides Of The Moon* (1975); Daltrey's *Daltrey* (1973) and *Ride A Rock Horse* (1975).

Amid the chaos – exacerbated by a band/management rift – the new Who megawork emerged: *Quadrophenia* (1973). This story of a Mod's spiritual journey to self-awareness housed powerhouses like 'Love Reign O'er Me' and '5:15', but its ambitious production led to Townshend and Daltrey punching each other in a dispute over the mix, and proved problematic to re-create on stage. Adding to their woes, Moon's appetite for destruction increasingly took its toll. His role in a now legendary San Francisco show ended a few songs into the set with – as detailed in the biography *Moon The Loon* – "a nosedive into one of his floor-standing tom-toms". As a backstage investigation revealed the drummer's bloodstream was swimming in tranquillizers of the sort "designed to put down huge gorillas", the band continued with a volunteer from the audience.

Townshend too was in terrible shape. Chronically tired and at war with Daltrey, his disillusionment surfaced in the bitter *The Who By Numbers* (1975). But hits were few and gigs – including a record-breakingly loud show in 1974 at the UK's Charlton Athletic football ground – endlessly (if successfully) recycled past glories. Stop-gap compilations (1971's *Meaty Beaty Big And Bouncy* and 1974's *Odds And Sods*) and solo albums (1977's *One Of The Boys* by Daltrey, 1972's *Who Came First* and 1977's *Rough Mix* by Townshend) confirmed the impression of a band adrift.

They stopped touring in 1976, split from Lambert and Stamp in 1977 and watched The Sex Pistols create the sort of furore in which they used to specialize. After a drunken encounter with Pistols Paul Cook and Steve Jones, Townshend wrote the vicious 'Who Are You', title track of the 1978 album that proved Moon's swan song; he died of an accidental overdose of sleeping pills on 7 September 1978. At the time, Townshend suggested the drummer's death might allow the band to explore new styles and prosper again. Buoyed by the hit soundtrack of 1978's autobiographical movie *The Kids Are Alright*, they capitalized on a British Mod resurgence with a superb movie of *Quadrophenia* starring Phil Daniels (who reappeared on Blur's Mod tribute 'Parklife'). They returned to the stage in 1979 with ex-Small Faces thumper Kenney Jones, a resurrection marred by 11 fans being trampled to death at a Cincinnati gig in December.

Their mixed fortunes flowed into the 80s. In 1980, Townshend's excellent *Empty Glass* yielded the sparkly hit 'Let My Love Open The Door' and Daltrey scored with 'Free Me' from *McVicar*, soundtrack to the movie in which he starred. In 1981, few bought Entwhistle's *Too Late The Hero*, but a million parted with cash for The Who's *Face Dances*, thanks to its self-mocking hit 'You Better You Bet'.

Ironically, Townshend – after years of keeping a healthy distance from on-the-road madness – plunged, via alcohol and cocaine, into a heroin hell. He cleaned up after a near-fatal overdose, but had lost interest in The Who and conceded Kenney Jones' accusation that he was keeping his best songs for his solo career (1982's *All The Best Cowboys Have Chinese Eyes*). After 1982's gloomy *It's Hard*, a tour (documented on 1984's live *Who's Last*) so riven with bitterness that Townshend stayed in a different hotel to his bandmates and a failed attempt at a final album, they officially split on 16 December 1983.

Solo albums ensued, notably Townshend's *White City* (1985) and, with Pink Floyd's Dave Gilmour, *Deep End Live!* (1987), and Daltrey's *Under A Raging Moon* (1985), whose title track was a tribute to Keith Moon. Best were Townshend's sets of demos and unreleased songs, *Scoop* (1983) and *Another Scoop* (1987).

Who reunions at Live Aid in 1985 and the 1988 BRIT awards left fans wishing they hadn't bothered, and solo tours by Daltrey and Entwhistle (which respectively played in venues as big as Madison Square Garden and the average living room) were no one's idea of an adequate substitute. Finally, Townshend agreed to a Who tour, motivated (he confessed) by money and the chance to publicize his latest solo venture, a musical version of Ted Hughes' children's book *The Iron Man* (1989) – the conclusion of a publishing career he'd nurtured throughout the 80s.

With a twelve-piece band, Daltrey, Townshend and Entwhistle (Kenney Jones had been replaced, at Daltrey's insistence, by the brilliant Simon Phillips) triumphed in US stadiums. There were also full-length revivals of *Tommy*, starring Billy Idol, Patti Labelle, Elton John, Phil Collins and Stevie Winwood, although neither these gala events nor the tour's mix of *Tommy* titbits and songs ranging from 1967's 'Mary Anne With The Shaky Hand' to 1982's 'Eminence Front' are well served by 1990's live *Join Together*.

Despite pressure from Daltrey, Townshend refused to make the reunion permanent, diverting his energies instead into the *Tommy* musical, which premiered in 1993, and *Psychoderelict* (1993). Daltrey staged a tribute to Townshend at New York's Carnegie Hall in 1994, then toured the States with Entwhistle, Townshend's brother Simon on guitar and Ringo Starr's son Zac Starkey on drums. Purists were pacified by 1994's *30 Years Of*

Maximum R&B box set and a loving programme of remastered albums, complete with bonus tracks.

In 1996, The Who rose again to take *Quadrophenia* on the road, beginning with a star-studded show in London's Hyde Park (where they narrowly avoided being eclipsed by support act Alanis Morissette). Even cynical reviewers conceded the shows were good, but The Who's relentless trading on past success looked threadbare compared to their prolific contemporaries The Rolling Stones. However, their legacy is enshrined in cover versions, from David Bowie's 'I Can't Explain' and 'Anyway Anyhow Anywhere', through The Sex Pistols' 'Substitute' and W.A.S.P.'s Townshend-approved 'The Real Me', to Sugar's 'Armenia City In The Sky' and Blur's 'Substitute'. But few could match The Who's originals, whose competitiveness and confusion inspired every angsty star from Paul Weller to Eddie Vedder and every musical misfit from Johnny Rotten to Kurt Cobain.

(READ) *The Who – Maximum R&B* (1996), Richard Barnes

(FAN) Generations, 1 Egbert Road, Wirral, Merseyside L47 5AH, UK

(SURF) www.thewho.net/

THE WILDHEARTS

WHO Vocals/guitar **Ginger** (b. David Walls, 17 Dec 1964, South Shields, Tyne and Wear, England), bass/vocals **Danny McCormack** (b. 28 Feb 1972, South Shields), guitar **Jef Streatfield** (b. 8 Jun 1971, Southampton, England), drums **Richard 'Ritch' Battersby** (b. 29 Jun 1968, Birmingham, England)

WHEN 1989–

WHERE London, England

WHAT Metal, Punk, Pop and chaos

Thrown out of semi-successful pseudo-Stones The Quireboys, guitarist Ginger flirted with The Throbs before helming The Wildhearts. A volatile Punk Pop Metal cocktail, they won acclaim with early releases like 1992's 'Mondo-Akimbo-A-Go-Go' EP and *Don't Be Happy… Just Worry* mini-album. They also settled into a tiresomely complex rut of line-up changes, due mainly to their leader's volatile methods. They seemed to stabilize at last with guitarist Chris 'CJ' Jagdhar, bassist Danny McCormack, drummer Andrew 'Stidi' Stoddolph and 1993's *Earth Vs. The Wildhearts*, a showcase for Ginger's sardonic songs. But having crashed the UK chart with 1994's 'Caffeine Bomb', the fan club-only dinky-disc *Fishing For Luckies* found CJ gone (to the ill-fated Honeycrack) and Stidi replaced by Ritch Battersby.

After more ker-razy antics – trashing disrespectful journalists and guitarists Mark Keds and Devin Townsend, threatening to split, then deciding not to, then changing their minds, etc – they recruited guitarist Jef Streatfield and unleashed the hard-as-nails *P.H.U.Q.* (1995). While 1996's 'Sick Of Drugs' became their biggest UK hit, they whinged about old label East West's cash-in release of *Luckies* and promised to split up for good, honest.

They *hadn't* split by the vicious *Endless, Nameless* (1997), but Ginger cancelled its tour, claiming certain Wildhearts were in no fit state to play.

(FAN) Wildhearts Mailing List, PO Box 4226, London, SW6 2XG, UK

(SURF) www.zen.co.uk/home/page/peter.s/wild/

ROBBIE WILLIAMS ◉

WHO b. 13 Feb 1974, Stoke-on-Trent, Staffordshire, England

WHAT Hard-and-soft-rockin' heart-throb

Strange things were afoot in Pop, mid-1995. Outhere Brothers were No.1 in Britain. Hootie & The Blowfish ruled the roost Stateside. And Robbie Williams – mutinous instincts fuelled by hanging out with Oasis – stopped straining at the choreographed leash of Take That and quit the fab five altogether. In the process, he triggered their demise and the Girl Power coup, but that's another story.

Sandbagged by legal hassles and a diet that would have made even Ozzy Osbourne blanch, Williams debuted solo in August 1996 – a year after his Take That swan-song 'Never Forget' – with a cover of George Michael's 'Freedom' (Noel Gallagher wrote a song called 'Freedom' *for* Williams, who forgot to record it). But 'Freedom 96' failed to displace Spice Girls from the UK No.1 and Williams seemed to be sinking in the wake of fellow Take That graduate Gary Barlow.

His recovery began in 1997 with a trio of hits: the Oasis-ish 'Old Before I Die', the see-sawing 'South Of The Border' and the superbly psychedelic 'Lazy Days'. But *Life Thru A Lens* (1997) barely troubled chart compilers and it looked like Williams would go the way of his underbought old bandmate Mark Owen.

Then 'Angels' – a Bon Jovi-esque ballad – clung to the UK Top 10 for months. Williams attributed this success to its use at "hatches, matches and despatches" – births, weddings and funerals. New fans just reckoned it was a great song and, further fired by the riotous 'Let Me Entertain You' and its Kiss-mimicking video, sent *Life Thru A Lens* to UK No.1. Suddenly the cheeky chap was everywhere – crooning Cole Porter's 'Ev'ry Time We Say Goodbye' on the 1997 EMI centenary set *Come Again*, souping up 'Bad Times Are Just Around The Corner' on the 1998 Noel Coward tribute *Twentieth Century Blues*, duetting with Tom

Jones at 1998's BRIT awards and selling to people who wouldn't have been seen dead with a Take That record.

READ *Take That: After The Break-Up In Their Own Words* (1998), Michael Heatley

FAN The Official Robbie Williams Fan Club, PO Box 479, Newcastle, ST5 1BT, UK

SURF www.robbiewilliams.co.uk/

JACKIE WILSON

WHO b. 9 Jun 1934, Detroit, Michigan, USA, d. 21 Jan 1984, Mount Holly, New Jersey, USA

WHAT A shiny diamond of 60s Soul

A boxing champion in the 40s, Jackie Wilson swapped pugilism for Pop, issuing 'Danny Boy' under his fighting name Sonny Wilson and replacing lead singer Clyde McPhatter in Billy Ward & His Dominoes in 1951. With a vocal style to match his onstage athletics, he shone on Dominoes hits like 'Rags To Riches' (1953) and 'St. Therese Of The Roses' (1956).

Leaving the Dominoes in 1956, he hired cousin Billy Davis (alias Tyrone Carlo) and Berry Gordy as writers. Their 'Reet Petite' (1957) was a classic: Wilson's voice soared above Gordy's Big Band brass, crashing the UK chart. In 1957, he scored a US smash with 'Lonely Teardrops', the first of a chart run which included 1959's 'That's Why (I Love You So)' and 'I'll Be Satisfied', and 1960's 'Doggin' Around', '(You Were Made For) All My Love', 'A Woman, A Lover, A Friend' and 'Night'. The latter – a revamp of Saint-Saëns' 'My Heart At Thy Sweet Voice' – was a Pop/Classical mix which inspired Elvis' 'It's Now Or Never' (1960) and continued with 'Alone At Last' (1960) and 'My Empty Arms' (1961).

After splitting from Gordy, Wilson coasted through the mid-60s, save for 1963's funky 'Baby Workout'. With producer Carl

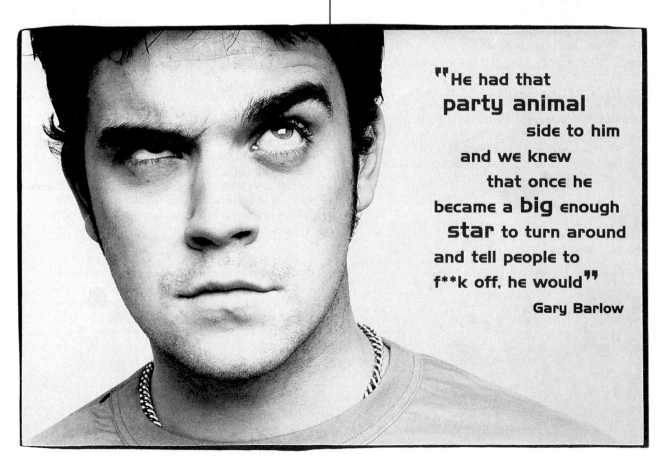

"He had that **party animal** side to him and we knew that once he became a **big** enough **star** to turn around and tell people to f**k off, he would"

Gary Barlow

Davis, he stormed back with 1966's 'Whispers (Gettin' Louder)', and 1967's '(Your Love Keeps Lifting Me) Higher And Higher'.

But this renaissance was brief: by the mid-70s Wilson was playing the club circuit. He suffered a heart attack on stage at the Latin Casino, New Jersey – reportedly having just sung the line "My heart is crying" from 'Lonely Teardrops' – and spent his final years in hospital care. A wave of UK Wilson mania in the 80s sent 'Reet Petite' to No.1 in 1986, followed by hits in 1987 (the year he was inducted into The Rock And Roll Hall Of Fame) with '(Your Love Keeps Lifting Me) Higher And Higher' and the superb 'I Get The Sweetest Feeling', his final US hit from 1968. In an unrelated tribute, Dexy's Midnight Runners scored a 1982 hit with 'Jackie Wilson Said (I'm In Heaven When You Smile)'.

 Lonely Teardrops – The Jackie Wilson Story (1997), Tony Douglas

STEVE WINWOOD ✪

WHO b. 12 May 1948, Birmingham, England

WHAT Traffic-stopping R&B smoothie

Steve Winwood had plenty of time to get used to Pop stardom – 17 when he topped the UK chart with The Spencer Davis Group's 'Keep On Running' (1965); 19 when he formed the stupendously successful Traffic with Dave Mason, Jim Capaldi and Chris Wood; 21 when he joined Eric Clapton and Ginger Baker in Blind Faith.

His solo career – discounting Traffic's *John Barleycorn Must Die* (1970), a Winwood album in all but name – began with 1977's *Steve Winwood*. Defiantly old-school in the face of Punk, it reached UK No.12 and US No.22. But a three-year wait followed for the acclaimed *Arc Of A Diver* (1980) – a moderate UK success, but a million-seller in the US.

Talking Back To The Night (1982) was patchy, but Winwood returned victorious with *Back In The High Life* (1986), which boasted Joe Walsh, James Taylor, Nile Rodgers and Chaka Khan and spawned the transatlantic hit 'Higher Love'. Its success meant 1988's *Roll With It* was a sure-fire US No.1, but *Refugees Of The Heart* (1990) sold weakly. He reunited with Jim Capaldi as Traffic in 1994, then returned with 1997's *Junction Seven*.

 www.stevewinwood.com/

WIRE

WHO Vocals/guitar **Colin Newman** (b. 16 Sep 1954, Salisbury, England), guitar **Bruce Gilbert** (b. 18 May 1946, Watford, England), bass **Graham Lewis** (b. 22 Feb 1953, Grantham, England), drums **Robert Gotobed** (b. Mark Field, 1951, Leicester, England)

WHEN 1976–1992

WHERE London, England

WHAT The spikiest of spiky Punk

Though too old and middle class (they'd been to university, an absolute no-no), Wire found their niche in Punk, whose economy, brevity and affection for strange spellings ('kutz', 'vox', etc) perfectly suited their sharp 'n' spiky Pop deconstructions. In fact, it's possible the word 'spiky' might never have been used in

Rock writing before Wire. Eschewing Punk credibility, they signed to EMI Prog label Harvest (home to Pink Floyd). But far from crafting 20-minute space odysseys, Wire crammed 21 songs onto *Pink Flag* (1977) – a masterpiece of jerky, noisy, experimental Art Punk which included their debut single, 'Mannequin'. Leaping ahead with 1978's more complex *Chairs Missing* and 1979's denser *154*, they released the classic 'Map Ref 41N93W' (1979) as their progress gathered pace, supported Roxy Music, splurged remaining energy into the 15-minute 'Crazy About Love' for a BBC Radio 1 session and neatly "ceased trading" in 1980 – leaving a chaotic but exhilarating legacy of sharp Pop and disturbing noisescapes.

Newman made *A–Z* (1980) and *Provisionally Titled The Singing Fish* (1981); Gilbert and Lewis went bonkers as Dome, Duet Emmo, Cupol, P'O, He Said and Gilbert & Lewis; then, in 1986, Wire "commenced trading" again, this time with Mute Records. Heralded by 1986's 'Snakedrill' EP, they simply picked up where they'd left off with 1987's *The Ideal Copy*, 1989's *A Bell Is A Cup… Until It Is Struck* and *Its Beginning To & Back Again* and 1990's *Manscape*. Meanwhile, REM covered *Pink Flag*'s 'Strange' on *Document* (1987) and its writers nearly hit the chart with 1989's excellent 'Eardrum Buzz'. But, alarmed by Newman, Gilbert and Lewis' love of drum machines, Gotobed quit following 1991's 'The Drill' EP. Charmingly, they abbreviated themselves to 'Wir' for 1991's *The First Letter* and "ceased trading", seemingly for good.

While its members busied themselves alone (Newman with ambient label Swim, Gotobed with farming, Gilbert as DJ Beekeeper and Lewis as Halo), Wire haunted Pop – either in the the angular Indie Pop of Blur, the 'difficult' Techno of Aphex Twin or in direct steals. Elastica pilfered the Wire classics 'I Am The Fly' and 'Three Girl Rhumba' for their own 'Line Up' and 'Connection' and even posed Wire-like on the cover of *Elastica* (1995), while Britpop also-rans Menswear recycled typically Wire-y riffs for their 'Daydreamer' (1995).

 Everybody Loves A History (1996), Kevin S. Eden

www.contrib.andrew.cmu.edu/~qwerty/wire/

BILL WITHERS

WHO b. 4 Jul 1938, Slab Fork, West Virginia, USA

WHAT Folk, Funk, Gospel and Soul alchemist

A master of understatement, Bill Withers blended Folk, Funk, Gospel and Soul into pristine Pop. But until he was nearly 32, making aeroplane toilet seats was more profitable. His demos rejected by record labels, Withers' salvation came in the form of Booker T. Jones, who won him a deal and produced 1971's delicate *Just As I Am*. Backed by Stephen Stills and MG's Al Jackson and Duck Dunn, its highlight was the lovely Grammy-winner 'Ain't No Sunshine', a US No.3.

The funkier *Still Bill* (1972) boasted members of the Watts 103rd St. Rhythm Band, the wonderfully paranoid 'Who Is He And What Is He To You' (a Funk classic via a cover by Creative Source), the hits 'Use Me' and 'Kissing My Love' and the classic US No.1 'Lean On Me'. Its success ensured the album's US Top 5 placing, but +*Justments* (1974), *Making Music* (1975) and *Naked And Warm* (1976) lacked sparkle. It returned in bucketloads on the sweeping 'Lovely Day' from *Menagerie* (1978).

Withers sightings grew more sporadic: 1980's cameos on The Crusaders' *Rhapsody & Blues* and Grover Washington Jr's *Winelight* (for which he co-wrote the hit 'Just The Two Of Us') preceded 1985's *Watching You Watching Me* and semi-retirement. However, Withers' legend was kept intact by a UK hit revamp of 'Lovely Day' in 1988, a sinisterly funked-out 1996 cover of 'Who Is He And What Is He To You' by Me'Shell Ndegéocello and cameos on Bobby Womack's *Soul Of Bobby Womack* (1996) and the soundtrack to Quentin Tarantino's *Jackie Brown* (1998).

JAH WOBBLE

WHO b. John Wordle, 1962, London, England

WHAT Transcendental Dub bass genius

A reformed thug from The Sex Pistols' London gang, Jah Wobble learned on Sid Vicious' bass and joined the first – and best – incarnation of ex-Pistols singer John Lydon's PiL in 1978. After two albums dominated by his seismic basslines, he left after his debut solo album *The Legend Lives On...* in 1980.

Albums with ex-Can men Jaki Leibezeit and Holger Czukay – 1982's *Full Circle* and 1983's *Snakecharmer* – pointed to his later direction, but first Wobble went through a mid-80s wilderness, sporadically issuing singles and working for London Transport.

After collaborations with ex-PiL guitarist Keith Levene, Gary Clail and Andrew Weatherall, his Jah Wobble's Invaders Of The Heart debuted with the acclaimed *Rising Above Bedlam* (1991), featuring the UK hit 'Visions Of You' with Sinéad O'Connor. *Take Me To God* (1994) boasted walk-ons from Gavin Friday and The Cranberries' Dolores O'Riordan, while Wobble's dubby bass graced albums by Primal Scream and The Orb. *Spinner* – a 1995 collaboration with Brian Eno – proved Wobble could noodle with the best of them, while the self-produced *Heaven And Earth* (1995) and *The Inspiration Of William Blake* (1996) were collages of spoken word and World Music-influenced Funk. Establishing his own 30Hz label in 1997, he continued with *Jah Wobble Presents The Light Programme* and *Requiem*.

 www.30hertzrecords.com/

BOBBY WOMACK

WHO b. 4 Mar 1944, Cleveland, Ohio, USA

WHAT The Last Soul Man

It is apt that 'Across 110th Street' accompanies Pam Grier walking to work in the opening credits of Quentin Tarantino's *Jackie Brown* (1998). After all, the song's writer, Bobby Womack, was described by *Q* magazine as "the history of Soul on two legs". Having learned on his father's guitar as a child, Womack spent the late 50s on the Gospel circuit with siblings Cecil, Curtis, Harris and Friendly Jr as The Womack Brothers.

After Bobby moonlighted as Sam Cooke's guitarist, they signed to Cooke's Sar label and became The Valentinos. They scored US hits with his 'Lookin' For A Love' (1962), 'I'll Make It Alright' (1963) and 'It's All Over Now' (1964). Within months, The Rolling Stones turned the latter into a transatlantic smash, but The Valentinos split, victims of Sar's collapse in the wake of Cooke's death. Womack married Cooke's widow, Barbara

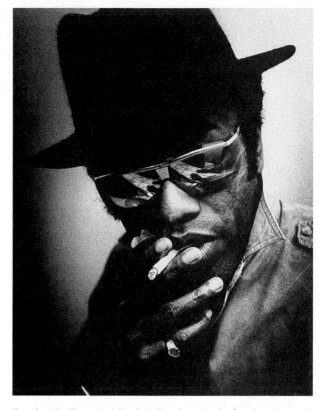

(brother Cecil married Cooke's daughter Linda, forming Womack & Womack in the process), and threw himself into session work, backing the likes of Ray Charles, Joe Tex, Aretha Franklin, Janis Joplin and Wilson Pickett, for whom he also wrote 17 singles, including 'I'm In Love' (1967) and 'I'm A Midnight Mover' (1968).

Despite flops *Fly Me To The Moon* (1968) and *The Womack 'Live'* (1971), Womack's solo career started brightly in 1968 with hit covers of 'Fly Me To The Moon' and 'California Dreamin'', 'How I Miss You Baby' (1969) and 'More Than I Can Stand (1970).

Pausing only to play on Sly & The Family Stone's *There's A Riot Going On* (1971), he released the unspeakably excellent *Communication* (1971) and *Understanding* (1972) and the hits 'That's The Way I Feel About Cha' (1971), 'Woman's Gotta Have It' and 'Harry The Hippie' (both 1972).

His decline was as rapid as his rise: 1973's movie soundtrack *Across 110th Street* was the only diamond among 1973's *Facts Of Life*, 1974's *Lookin' For A Love Again* (which saw him reprise the Valentinos hit), 1975's *I Don't Know What The World Is Coming To*, 1976's *BW Goes C&W*, *Safety Zone*, *Home Is Where The Heart Is* and *Pieces* and 1979's *Roads Of Life*. After his brother Harry (the subject of 'Harry The Hippie') was murdered, Womack disappeared, only to resurface on Wilton Felders' *Inherit The Wind* (1980), the excellent *The Poet* (1981) and *The Poet II* (1984). The latter yielded a sublime US R&B smash with Patti Labelle, 'Love Has Finally Come At Last'.

Continuing with 1985's *So Many Rivers* and 1986's *Womagic* (repackaged as 1987's *The Last Soul Man*), he used his new flush of fame to help old friends: he failed to coax Sly Stone back to work, but acted as conciliator on The Rolling Stones' troubled *Dirty Work* (1986) and was reunited with his brothers for 1989's *Save The Children*. Another fallow period ended with *Resurrection* (1994), a triumphant comeback on Rolling Stone Ron Wood's Slide Music label featuring Wood, fellow Stones Keith Richards and Charlie Watts, Queen's Brian May and Stevie Wonder.

STEVIE WONDER ✪✪✪

WHO b. Steveland Morris, 21 May 1950, Saginaw, Michigan, USA

WHAT From wonder kid to wonder man

Noel Gallagher and Coolio probably wouldn't have much to chat about, but if they were ever forced to make polite conversation, one fruitful topic could be Stevie Wonder. Why, Noel could ask, did I have to pull a song off *(What's The Story) Morning Glory?* just because it nicked a title and tune from Stevie's 1966 hit 'Uptight (Everything's Alright)', yet you could turn his 1976 cut 'Pastime Paradise' into 1995's biggest smash 'Gangsta's Paradise'? Hmm…

Given too much oxygen in an incubator, Steveland Morris lost his sight soon after birth. Though raised poor by a single parent, his musical ability flourished. As a toddler, he beat spoons on furniture and boxes until he was given a drum. Later, he took up the harmonica and piano and sang in a local Gospel choir. At 10, his talent ensnared Roland White, singer with Motown act The Miracles. White took Stevie to meet Motown boss Berry Gordy who – amazed at Stevie's ability to play any instrument he chose – signed him and launched him as Little Stevie Wonder.

Stevie became part of the family on transatlantic tours: fitted out in suits, given a weekly wage, his songs and career path largely chosen for him. Early singles flopped, but shows with the Motown revue were a big success. Accordingly, 1963's live *The 12 Year Old Genius* and its 'Fingertips Pt 2' became US No.1s.

When his voice broke in 1964, he lost the 'Little' but, minus his initial cuteness, Motown were now unsure how to market him. Hits proved elusive and there were whispers that Motown would drop him. Then the bold 'n' brassy 'Uptight (Everything's Alright)' turned his fortunes around in 1964, convincing Gordy to release Stevie's version of Bob Dylan's 'Blowin' In The Wind', showing his early trait for recording songs with a social message.

The 'Uptight' songwriting team established a formula over the next three years: Sylvia Moy writing the lyrics, Wonder the tunes and Henry Cosby arranging and producing. They made six hits together, the most outstanding being 'I Was Made To Love Her' (1967) and 'My Cherie Amour' (1969). But having completed school lessons he was obliged to attend alongside his career, Wonder found more time for music, hence his writing credits on Smokey Robinson & The Miracles' 'The Tears Of A Clown' and The Spinners' 'It's A Shame' (both transatlantic hits in 1970).

When Wonder reached 21 in 1971 and his Motown contract ran out, he negotiated a new agreement that gave him freedom to make albums as complete artistic statements rather than sets of singles. Each had at least one song highlighting social ills: drugs, drink driving, poverty, apartheid and genocide.

The sprawling *Where I'm Coming From* (1971) and *Music Of My Mind* (1972), on which Wonder played most of the instruments, lacked strong commercial appeal. Many of the lyrics were co-written with his new wife Syreeta Wright. Both used synthesizers, which usurped the harmonica as his trademark instrument.

Wonder's fortunes flourished with *Talking Book* (1972), thanks to the US No.1s 'Superstition' and 'You Are The Sunshine Of My Life'. Their upbeat feel was swamped by cynicism on *Innervisions* (1973), made in the wake of his split from Syreeta but arguably his finest achievement. Its driving 'Higher Ground' was covered by Red Hot Chili Peppers, and 'Livin' For The City' – his angriest cut yet – was voted by Tori Amos the song she wished she'd written. Its rage flowed on into Rap with the likes of NWA.

Shortly before *Innervisions'* release, a car crash left Wonder in a coma for four days. The accident made him re-evaluate his life and, in 1974, it was rumoured he would give up touring to work for children's charities in Africa. Wonder, who'd once recorded for 48 hours non-stop, became less workaholic, and *Fulfillingness' Last Finale* (1974) was more subdued. Its supremely glum 'They Won't Go When I Go' was covered by George Michael when he wanted to prove just how serious he could be. However, its hits – the terse US No.1 'You Haven't Done Nothin'' and the bubbly 'Boogie On Reggae Woman' – proved his spark still flickered. He also masterminded Minnie Riperton's classic 'Loving You' and new partner Yolanda Simmons gave birth to his first child.

Revitalized, Wonder began a new work. Recording stretched so long that a September 1975 release date became September 1976, making it one of the 70s' most eagerly awaited albums. Wonder signed a new $13-million contract with Motown, at the time the largest ever in the music business. But *Songs In The Key Of Life* (1976) was a work of genius. It made UK No.2 and stayed at the US top spot for 14 weeks. Among the highlights were 'Isn't She Lovely', 'Pastime Paradise', 'Village Ghetto Land', the US No.1s 'I Wish' and 'Sir Duke', and his most polemic song yet, 'Black Man'.

Journey Through The Secret Life Of Plants (1979), recorded for a botanical documentary, was full of instrumentals and stuff about flowers, leaving fans appalled and confused. But he jumped back with his most commercial album, *Hotter Than July* (1980). Nearly all the tracks sounded like hits and four *were*: the US No.1 'Masterblaster (Jammin')' (honouring Bob Marley), 'I Ain't Gonna Stand For It', 'Lately' (later covered by Swing supremos Jodeci) and 'Happy Birthday'. The latter celebrated black leader Martin Luther King – Wonder succeeded in making the US government institute a national holiday on the great man's birthday.

After the classic-packed hits set *Original Musiquarium I* (1982), Wonder's credibility was dealt deadly blows by 1982's schmaltzy, transatlantic No.1 'Ebony And Ivory', a duet with Paul McCartney,

STEVIE WONDER/ROCKOPEDIA

and the equally soppy but successful 'I Just Called To Say I Love You'. The latter came from his soundtrack to *The Woman In Red* (1984), the first of three consecutive US million-sellers. *In Square Circle* (1985) was patchy but yielded the hit 'Part-Time Lover', and *Characters* (1987) was almost a return to his old form, notably on the sinister 'Skeletons'. He also graced Chaka Khan's cover of his 1970 hit 'Signed, Sealed, Delivered I'm Yours' (on her *CK*, 1989).

Amid these credibility-restoring efforts came the gloriously gloopy US No.1 'That's What Friends Are For' (1985), with famous friends Dionne Warwick, Elton John and Gladys Knight.

Wonder returned with the soundtrack to Spike Lee's *Jungle Fever* (1991), sped Top 10-wards with *Conversation Peace* (1995) and made *Natural Wonder* (1995), his first live album since *Talk Of The Town* (1970). He remains one of *the* artists of Pop and Soul.

READ *Stevie Wonder* (1977), Constanze Elsner

SURF www.xmission.com/-matthew/wonder/stevie.html

THE WONDER STUFF

WHO Vocals/guitar **Miles Hunt** (b. 29 Jul 1966, Birmingham, England), guitar/vocals **Malcolm Treece**, bass **Paul Clifford** (b. 23 Apr 1968, Birmingham), violin/mandolin **Martin 'Fiddly' Bell**, drums **Martin Gilks**

WHEN 1986–1994

WHERE Stourbridge, West Midlands, England

WHAT The eight-legged groove machine

Though London, Manchester and Liverpool have all ruled Pop's waves, the quiet town of Stourbridge briefly shone as a beacon for Indiedom with home-grown 'Grebo' heroes Pop Will Eat Itself, Ned's Atomic Dustbin and, biggest of them all, The Wonder Stuff.

Having slummed with Pop Will Eat Itself's Clint Mansell in From Eden, Miles Hunt and Malcolm Treece recruited ex-Mighty Lemon Drop Martin Gilks, invoked the spirit of Slade and became The Wonder Stuff, a name courtesy of Hunt's father's friend John Lennon, who declared of the infant Miles "Your boy sure has the wonder stuff". The gambling winnings of last-minute recruit Rob 'The Bass Thing' Jones financed their 1987 debut, 'Wonderful Day'. *The Eight Legged Groove Machine* (1988) was an exhilarating blast of stomping Pop and Hunt's lyrical bile, of which their UK chart debut 'It's Yer Money I'm After Baby' was but one highlight.

The spunky *Hup* (1989) introduced violinist 'Fiddly' Bell and did even better, but saw off The Bass Thing (who, after 1990's Dance-ified 'Circlesquare', moved to the USA and died in 1993). With new bassist Paul Clifford, the Stuffies joined the mainstream in 1991 with the stompin' booze anthem 'Size Of A Cow', a UK No.1 cover of Tommy Roe's 'Dizzy' (with comedian Vic Reeves) and their finest moment: the masterful *Never Loved Elvis*.

But the more earnest *Construction For The Modern Idiot* (1993) failed to win over the Grunge hordes, notably in the USA, where the band fell flat. Disillusioned, the Stuffies bid farewell at 1994's Phoenix Festival. Hunt became an MTV VJ and formed the short-lived Vent 414, while Treece, Bell, Gilks and Clifford joined ex-Eat singer Ange Dolittle in the equally brief Weknowwhereyoulive.

READ *The Eight Legged Atomic Dustbin Will Eat Itself* (1992), Martin Roach

SURF www.enteract.com/~shabadoo/Stuff.html

Declared "a state of emergency" by one US governor, described by The Grateful Dead's Jerry Garcia as a scene of "biblical proportions", visited by the National Guard and awash with enough rain to stop seven hours of music, The Woodstock Music & Arts Fair might have sunk into muddy oblivion. Yet the "Three Days Of Peace And Music" (Friday to Sunday, 15-17 August 1969) joined man's first step on the moon (the preceding month) in history.

It started life as an improbable joint venture between 'straight' businessmen John Roberts and Joel Rosenman and rich hippies Artie Kornfield and Michael Lang – their optimism dampened only when the site had to be switched from Woodstock to Max Yasgur's farm in nearby Bethel. A stage was hastily assembled but, before turnstiles and fences were completed, flower children from across the USA began arriving, contributing to what turned out to be an audience of up to 500,000 – ten times the expected attendance. Not even a 25-mile jam on the New York State Freeway could stop the invasion. Kornfield, Lang, Roberts and Rosenman had little choice but to declare Woodstock a free festival. Meanwhile, Yasgur, residents of Bethel and nearby White Lake and the National Guard helped with emergency food and medical supplies. Soon Woodstock became a little world in itself: a baby was born there on the first day.

While the site was declared a disaster zone, the bands lounged around a pool at the nearest Holiday Inn and helicoptered to the site. Richie Havens opened the largely acoustic first day, followed by John Sebastian, Arlo Guthrie, Joan Baez, Tim Hardin, Melanie, Sweetwater and Ravi Shankar. Saturday starred Quill, Keef Hartley, Santana (giving the performance of their lives), Mountain, Canned Heat, The Incredible String Band, Creedence Clearwater Revival, The Grateful Dead, Janis Joplin, Sly & The Family Stone, The Who and Jefferson Airplane.

Joe Cocker and Country Joe & The Fish began the Sunday line-up before torrential rain stopped the show. With the schedule in tatters, Ten Years After, The Band, Blood Sweat & Tears, Paul Butterfield, Johnny Winter, Crosby, Stills, Nash & Young and Sha Na Na preceded headliner Jimi Hendrix, who didn't walk onstage until Monday morning – by which time the audience had dwindled to a few thousand. But his demonic performance of 'The Star Spangled Banner' became the Woodstock moment. It was stunningly captured (alongside highlights including The Who, Richie Havens, Sly & The Family Stone and CSN&Y) by Michael Wadleigh in Woodstock (1970) – a movie whose soundtrack made US No.1 in 1970, followed a year later by Woodstock Two.

In 1994, Woodstock II, a 25th anniversary festival (actually at Woodstock this time) starred Nine Inch Nails, Aerosmith, Metallica, Sheryl Crow, Cypress Hill, Green Day and Salt-N-Pepa with Crosby, Stills & Nash and Joe Cocker from the original event. Apart from these stalwarts, any similarity to the musical event that shook the world ended at the size of the crowd and the mud.

READ Woodstock: The Oral History (1989), Joel Makower

WU-TANG CLAN ⊙ ✪

WU'S WHO Producer **The RZA** aka Bobby Steels aka Rakeem Allah aka The Rzarector aka Chief Abbot aka Prince Rakeem (b. Robert F. Diggs), **Method Man** aka Johnny Blaze aka Meth Tical aka Shakwon aka The MZA aka Ticallion Stallion (b. Clifford Smith, 1 Apr 1971), **Ol' Dirty Bastard** aka Osirus aka Unique Ason aka Dirt McGirt/Joe Bananas aka Big Baby Jesus (b. Russell Jones, 15 Nov 1968), **Ghostface Killah** aka Ironman aka Tony Starks aka Sun God (b. Dennis Coles, 9 May 1970), **The GZA** aka Genius aka Maximillion aka Justice (b. Gary Grice), **Raekwon The Chef** aka Shallah Raekwon aka Lex Diamonds (Louis Rich Diamonds) (b. Corey Woods), **Inspectah Deck** aka Rebel INS aka Rollie Fingers (b. Jason Hunter), **U God** aka Baby-U aka Golden Arms aka 4-Bar Killer aka Lucky Hands (b. Lamont Hawkins), **Masta Killa** aka Noodles (b. Elgin Turner)

WU'S WHEN 1990–

WU'S WHERE Staten Island, New York, USA

WU'S WHAT The Spice Girls of Rap

"KA-BOOM! GUESS WHO STEPPED IN THE ROOM? THE CLAN! COMIN' FROM THE SHAOLIN ISLE!"

wu-tang clan

This cheery hello is from SWV's 'Anything': the most swaggeringly superb Rap 'n' Swing cut *ever* and an example of the phenomenon whereby no 90s Hip Hop record is complete without a link to the wacky world of the Wu-Tang Clan.

In the decade before the Wu landed on Earth, Rap had become as much about image as music (not that pre-1983 pioneers like Grandmaster Flash & The Furious Five *didn't* have an image, but you wouldn't find many Hip Hop fans wearing glittery shoulder pads and cowboy boots with the jeans tucked into the tops). From Run DMC through NWA and Public Enemy to Snoop Doggy Dogg, the biggest Hip Hop stars were those who not only made great records, but also offered the opportunity to buy into a visual image, a lyrical philosophy and a warped world view.

The Wu offer all that and more. For a start, there are nine core members, out-numbering even Public Enemy's massed military ranks. There are so many solo albums, affiliated acts and cameos with other artists that even determined discographers give up in despair. There's a barely believable belief system. Most tellingly, there's a ubiquitous Batman-esque "W" logo that adorns all their records and the grossly overpriced Wu Wear line of clothing *and* their branded cosmetics. Blimey, they're the Spice Girls of Rap!

Their myth-making has been so meticulous that it's almost a shame to admit the Wu came about because solo efforts by Clan mainstays Genius (1991's *Words From The Genius*) and his cousin RZA (1992's 'Ooh We Love You Rakeem', as Prince Rakeem) had mounted no threat to Rap's then biggest noise, Ice Cube. "I'm still proud of it, though," Genius told *Select* magazine of his album. "The beats ain't all that but, lyrically, shit was bangin'. So it wasn't all peaches an' cream, but I was determined to break through."

With Ol' Dirty Bastard, they conceived Wu-Tang Clan, drawing inspiration from martial arts movies. The *original* Wu-Tang were rebels from China's Shaolin temple, skilled in the art of 'Wu-Tang Sword', whereby victims are despatched via blows to any one of 36 death points on the body. The *new* Clan were Staten Island (or 'Shaolin' as it became in WuWorld) low-lifes: RZA had been tried for attempted murder and, as *Select* reported, "Inspectah Deck and Dirty have done time, while Raekwon, Method Man and RZA have all either dealt or spent time ingesting a chemical panopoly that includes crack, weed, angel dust and mescaline."

The Clan debuted on their own Wu-Tang Records label with 1992's 'Protect Ya Neck' single. Its flip, 'Method Man', showcased their secret weapon: the six-foot-plus Clifford Smith, aka Method Man. Although Ol' Dirty Bastard – a manic mix of Public Enemy's court jester Flavor Flav and a rottweiler – is the Wu's obvious focal point, Meth is their star. While his bandmates hector, the raspy, laconic Meth is the cool voice of authority.

The other key element was RZA's production. Rap was then graduating from the multi-layered cacophony of Public Enemy to the G-Funk of Dr Dre. But RZA stripped the Wu's backing to starkly minimal beats, punctuated by scratchy snatches of violin and piano – the cinematic flavour of which grew into the 'horrorcore' of his sideline Gravediggaz' *Niggamortis* (1994) and *The Pick, The Sickle And The Shovel* (1997). Having created a buzz on the Rap underground, the Wu were signed by Loud Records for 1993's *Enter The Wu-Tang (36 Chambers)*, its title a reference to the levels, or 'chambers', of attainment in Wu-Tang Sword. As students progressed through the 36 chambers, they replaced their teeth with gold incisors, then platinum at the final chamber, adding authenticity to RZA and Dirty's decorative dentistry.

36 Chambers had everything: the ear-catching cuts 'Protect Ya Neck' and 'Method Man', the soon-to-be anthems 'C.R.E.A.M.' (or 'Cash Rules Everything Around Me') and 'Bring Da Ruckus', the myth-making 'Wu-Tang: 7th Chamber' and 'Da Mystery Of Chess-boxin'. But, crucially, it also had 'Can It Be All So Simple', whose mournful title phrase was sampled from Gladys Knight's 1975 hit 'The Way We Were'. The beautiful result was an unlikely radio hit and sped the album to platinum sales. Suddenly, there was an alternative for Hip Hop heads who viewed with distaste the MTV-ization of Rap by the likes of Snoop Doggy Dogg.

WU-TANG CLAN – OL' DIRTY BASTARD∙GAVIN EVANS∙RETNA

The trend continued with the Wu's Loud labelmates Mobb Deep, whose amazingly gloomy *The Infamous* (1995) featured a cameo by Clan member Raekwon The Chef on 'Your Beef Is Mine'.

Having bounded from low-life to legend, RZA hatched his plan to make millions by holding the world to ransom: a grandiose way of describing the Wu signing to Loud but its stars securing solo deals with other labels (with RZA overseeing the production side of things). Meth joined Def Jam, who were then in something of a post-Public Enemy slump. His *Tical* (1994) shot the Wu into the mainstream, thanks to Def Jam mainman Russell Simmons bribing Meth to recut the album's 'All I Need', replacing the Clan's backing vocals with those of Mary J. Blige, the Queen of Hip Hop Soul. The result was the spine-tingling, transatlantic smash 'I'll Be There For You/You're All I Need To Get By', hooked on the 1968 Marvin Gaye/Tammi Terrell hit 'You're All I Need To Get By'. Equally spectacular were revamps of *Tical*'s 'Bring The Pain' and 'Release Yo'delf' by The Chemical Brothers and Prodigy.

The onslaught continued in 1995 thanks to Dirty. His *Return To The 36 Chambers (The Dirty Version)* was no one's idea of a Wu classic, but it went gold and spawned the splendidly deranged 'Brooklyn Zoo'. Bigger waves, however, rippled from his cameo on a Puff Daddy revamp of the clean-cut Mariah Carey's US No.1 'Fantasy'. "Me an' Mariah go back like babies an' pacifiers," Dirty bragged amusingly. The golden gal herself gushed: "He just tore it up." The Carey connection continued in 1997 when Raekwon guested on her protégées Allure's album cut 'Give It All I Got'.

Of more interest to Clan fans was Raekwon's *Only Built 4 Cuban Linx* (1995). Hailed as the best Wu album – although non-partisan listeners might find it hard going – the album devised mafioso guises for his guesting compadres (the 'Wu Gambinos') and its chiming classic 'Criminology' namechecked Julio Iglesias.

Raekwon's chief collaborator was Ghostface Killah, who weighed in with his own *Ironman* (1996). Its highlight was the heartbreaking 'All That I Got Is You', which sampled The Jackson 5's 1971 US hit 'Maybe Tomorrow' and returned Mary J. Blige's soothing tones to WuWorld.

In between, Genius stepped out with the classic *Liquid Swords* (1995), the only Wu album to stray near Trip Hop. Its most acclaimed cuts, however, were the Rap gems 'Shadowboxin'' (a showcase for the guesting Meth) and 'Labels', widely interpreted as an attack on the companies who had let him down before the Wu rose but essentially an excuse to weave loads of label names into lyrically dextrous rhymes.

All these efforts, however, were eclipsed by Meth's duet with Rap star Redman. 'How High', from Def Jam's soundtrack *The Show*, was *the* summer jam of 1995 and one of *the* Hip Hop anthems of recent years

(Wu watcher Tim Burgess nicked the title for his band The Charlatans' own hit 'How High'). It also spotlighted Meth's alter ego Johnny Blaze, which some interpret as a reference to lighting up the marijuana cigarettes that young people enjoy (also the meaning of Wu words 'Metical', 'Tical' and 'Method' itself). Meth also popped up on hoop-shooter-turned-Rapper Shaquille O'Neal's *Shaq Fu – Da Return* (1994), the *Batman Forever* soundtrack (1995) and Foxy Brown's *Ill Na Na* (1996).

When Rap was rent by Gangsta's civil war, the Wu kept a foot in each camp: RZA produced a cut on East Coast emperor The Notorious BIG's *Life After Death* (1997) and Meth guested on West Coast wildchild 2Pac's *All Eyez On Me* (1996). Meth had previously duetted on BIG's wonderfully weird 'The What' (1994).

In 1996, the Clan contributed the scary 'America' to the *America Is Dying Slowly (AIDS)* album and Raekwon graced Dirty associate 12 O'Clock's cut 'Nasty Immigrants' on the *The Nutty Professor* soundtrack. While the world impatiently awaited a new Clan album, RZA and Raekwon squared up to Reggae nut Bounty Killer on 'Ask Fi War' (1997) and Wu off-shoots sprouted left, right and centre. Longest standing was cool kid Shyheim, whose *The Rugged Child* (1994) and *The Lost Generation* (1996) were not bad at all. Also on the plate were Sunz Of Man, whose driving force was Wu lieutenant Killah Priest. The eccentric Mr Priest made a fine solo stab with 1998's *HeavyMental*, whose great 'One Step' attempted to document the entire history of the black struggle *and* his concerns about religion. "It all relates," he said earnestly.

But when the new Wu did appear, its No.1 placings and multi-million sales clearly owed more to its makers' reputations than its actual worth. Varying the notion that most double albums would make great single albums, *Wu-Tang Forever* (1997) was a double album that would make a great *single*. Conspicuously, it featured new Clan recruit Cappadonna more than Meth and Dirty. True to tradition, Cappadonna made a much better solo album, 1998's *The Pillage* – whose black and yellow styling continued the Wu's long-held lyrical analogy: killer bees.

Meanwhile, 1997 also brought the titanic team of Meth, DMX, Redman, Canibus and Master P on LL Cool J's '4, 3, 2, 1', and a characteristically crazed cameo by Dirty (now changing his name on a biannual basis, *noms des plumes* including Osirus and Big Baby Jesus) on BLACKstreet's hit 'Fix'. There were more off-shoots too, though Killarmy's *Silent Weapons For Quiet Wars* (1997) proved the formula was wearing thin. Even worse was Meth 'n' RZA's revamp of Texas' 'Say What You Want', the worst crossover work they've done. Sticking to Rap, Dirty (dis)graced 'Ghetto Superstar' on Fugee Wyclef Jean's 1998 *Bulworth* soundtrack, and – with Sunz Of Man – Wyclef's reworking of Earth Wind & Fire's 'Shining Star' (featuring spacey Soulsters EWF themselves). Clan member Masta Killa stepped out to guest on Public Enemy's 'Resurrection' (1998). Even a Spice hook-up isn't completely unthinkable. "I don't know those girls, but I love all music," Dirty told *Select*. "Are the Spice Girls sexy? Yes? Well, I love them even more."

 www.thedsc.com/

ROBERT WYATT

WHO b. 28 Jan 1945, Bristol, England

WHAT Stark Rock and Jazz-influenced melodies

In early 1971, singer/drummer Robert Wyatt left Soft Machine, the band he'd formed in Canterbury five years earlier with Kevin Ayers and Mike Ratledge. His first solo step was in the shape of *The End Of An Ear*, revisiting the Jazz Rock avenues Soft Machine had pioneered. This was followed by Matching Mole, a band whose name was a phonetic pun on the French for Soft Machine. In 1972, *Matching Mole* and *Matching Mole's Little Red Record* again leaned towards avant-Jazz, but featured political content at a time when polemics were deeply unfashionable in Rock.

Wyatt's return to solo work in 1973 was interrupted when a fall from a window left him paralyzed from the waist down. His old psychedelic pals Pink Floyd played two benefit gigs and Floyd's Nick Mason produced Wyatt's classic *Rock Bottom* (1974). Now playing keyboards and percussion, Wyatt sang peculiar, haunting ballads in instantly recognizable, high-pitched tones. "It's one of the things I'm most proud of doing in 30 years of music," Mason told *Mojo*. "I still find it very moving to listen to."

Next came *Ruth Is Stranger Than Richard* (1975), an odd aggregation of avant-garde nursery rhymes and a cover of The Monkees' 'I'm A Believer', which became a surprise hit.

Subsequent silence ended in the early 80s when the Rough Trade label unleashed a typically idiosyncratic batch of Wyatt singles. These songs – covers of Chic, Billie Holiday and Ivor Cutler, plus several traditional Folk anthems – were compiled as 1982's *Nothing Can Stop Us*, alongside 'Shipbuilding', another chart entry for Wyatt, written for him by Elvis Costello.

His work became overtly political (he'd joined the Communist Party in the late 70s) and his soundtrack to *The Animals Film* – a documentary about animal exploitation – and numerous artistic collaborations continued to highlight struggle and injustice.

After further minimalist albums – 1985's *Old Rottenhat* and 1991's *Dondestan* – 1997's *Shleep* was his first collection for six

years. Employing Brian Eno, Paul Weller and others, it was a brighter, more optimistic Wyatt than had been heard in ages. "I want to get lost and diffused in the world…", he announced. "That's my idea of freedom and happiness."

READ *Wrong Movements: A Robert Wyatt History* (1994), Michael King

TAMMY WYNETTE

WHO b. Virginia Wynette Pugh, 5 May 1942, Itawamba County, Mississippi, USA, d. 6 Apr 1998

WHAT The First Lady of Country

When Tammy Wynette's autobiography *Stand By Your Man* (1979) became a TV biopic, it proved the events of Wynette's life were more tumultuous than most. Fully embodying Country's themes – tragedy and hardship – she became its First Lady.

Raised by her grandparents (her musician father died when she was 8), she worked in the cotton fields to pay for her musical education. But her dreams of singing stardom ended when she married at 17. By 20, she was a divorced mother of three in Birmingham, Alabama, paying for one of her children's medical bills by working as a beautician and part-time singer.

In 1966, having worked her way on to local TV shows (including that of Country legend Porter Waggoner), she moved her family to Nashville. A year later, she met producer Billy Sherrill, signed to Epic and, as Tammy Wynette, hit No.3 on the US Country chart with her second single, 'Your Good Girl's Gonna Go Bad' (1967). Her third, 'My Elusive Dreams' (a duet with David Houston), was the first of 20 Country No.1s, while her fourth, 'I Don't Wanna Play House', was Wynette's first Grammy winner.

In 1968, her classics 'Stand By Your Man' and 'D.I.V.O.R.C.E.' topped Country charts, and the former leapt into the Pop Top 20. 'Stand By Your Man' hit UK No.1 in 1975 – the first single by a female Country singer to top that chart. In 1969, she married Country star George Jones and, in the 70s, they made hit duets including the Country No.1s 'We're Gonna Hold On' (1973), 'Near You' and 'Golden Ring' (both 1976). The pair continued charting together long after the marriage ended in D.I.V.O.R.C.E. in 1975.

By the 80s, Wynette's hits were drying up. But despite losing her Country crown, she remained in the spotlight, mainly through press headlines: her fourth marriage lasted less than two months, she romanced actor Burt Reynolds, married again, had serious health problems, was kidnapped, spent time in the Betty Ford Clinic and lost millions when a bank crashed.

But in 1991, she reclaimed her rightful place in international charts, courtesy of a bizarre hook-up with dancefloor terrorists The KLF on 'Justified And Ancient'. A year later, she graced the chart-topping *Sleepless In Seattle* soundtrack. Other 90s highlights included *One* (a 1995 reunion with George Jones), having a highway named after her, winning the prestigious AMA Award of Merit and a public apology from another First Lady, Hillary Clinton, who defended her husband Bill's alleged infidelity claiming "I'm not sitting here like some little woman, standing by my man like Tammy Wynette".

Despite the ill health which plagued her career, she was planning another UK tour for 1998 – making doubly tragic her death (caused by a blood clot) in April.

READ *Stand By Your Man* (1979), Tammy Wynette

X-RAY SPEX

WHO Vocals **Poly Styrene** (b. Marion Elliot), guitar **Jak Airport** (b. Jack Stafford), bass **Paul Dean**, drums **Chris Chrysler** (b. B.P. Hurding), saxophone **Lora Logic** (b. Susan Whitby)

WHEN 1977–1979

WHERE London, England

WHAT Day-Glo plastic Pop Punks

One of the best things about Punk was its transforming of ugly ducklings into glittering stars. Witness Johnny Rotten (once plain John Lydon), Joe Strummer (who fronted dreadful Pub Rockers The 101ers in his pre-Clash days), even Adam Ant (once boring Stuart Goddard). Best by far was the transformation of Marion Elliot – a plain teenager of English/Somali descent – into Poly Styrene, the eccentrically clothed, brace-flaunting frontwoman of England's finest Punk Popsters X-Ray Spex.

Styrene released the Disco-ish 'Silly Billy' under her real name before witnessing The Sex Pistols in 1976. She set up a Punk clothes stall in London, became a face on the scene and assembled X-Ray Spex in 1977. Their limited musicianship (Lora Logic could barely coax a note from her sax) was balanced by attitude: the words "Some people think little girls should be seen and not heard/OH BONDAGE, UP YOOOOUUUURRRRSSSS!" heralded their debut 'Oh Bondage, Up Yours!' (1977).

Joining EMI, they swapped Logic (who formed Essential Logic) for the more skilled Rudi Thompson (and, later, Glyn Johns) and hit the UK Top 30 in 1978 with 'The Day The World Turned Day-Glo' and the bitter 'Identity'. But by the time 1978's *Germ Free Adolescents* – an excellent attack on consumerism and Punk – emerged, Styrene had had enough: she had a nervous breakdown (reportedly after a UFO sighting), converted to Krishna and split the Spex in 1979. Her solo album *Translucence* (1980) and EP 'Gods And Goddesses' (1986) became cult classics.

X-Ray Spex reconvened for 90s nostalgia tours and *Conscious Consumer* in 1995, a mere 17 years after its predecessor.

 www.terrapin.co.uk/xrayspex/

XTC

WHO Vocals/guitar **Andy Partridge** (b. 11 Nov 1953, Valletta, Malta), vocals/bass **Colin Moulding** (b. 17 Aug 1955, Swindon, Wiltshire, England), guitar **Dave Gregory** (b. 21 Sep 1952, Swindon)

WHEN 1975–

WHERE Swindon, Wiltshire, England

WHAT Olde English post-Punk Pop

The West of England is usually associated with Bristol-centric Trip Hop, thanks to Massive Attack, Tricky and Portishead. But maybe, one day, old men will exclaim to their grandchildren, "It were all intelligent post-Punk Pop round here when I was a lad!" – for the nearby town of Swindon yielded an altogether different Pop sensation with the critically revered XTC.

Their labyrinthine history began in Glam-rocking 1973, when

Andy Partridge joined bassist Colin Moulding, drummer Terry Chambers and guitarist Dave Cartner in The Helium Kidz. They became XTC in 1975 with a fluid line-up, including vocalist Steve Hutchins and keyboard player Jon Perkins. A shake-up in 1976 settled XTC around Partridge, Moulding, Chambers and ex-King Crimson keyboardist Barry Andrews, who joined after a drunken night out with the band, despite the image-conscious Partridge's misgivings about Andrews being both a Londoner and bald.

Steeped in Pop tradition, Moulding and Partridge proved masterful writers with 1978's New Wave classics *White Music* and *Go 2* but, despite seducing critics with their off-kilter songs, the charts remained locked to XTC. That is, until 1979's Andrews-less (he joined Robert Fripp's League Of Gentlemen, then Shriekback and was replaced by Dave Gregory) *Drums And Wires* yielded the excellent 'Making Plans For Nigel' – a wry ticket to the UK Top 20.

Black Sea (1980) and *English Settlement* (1982) were packed with hits – 'Generals And Majors', 'Sgt. Rock (Is Going To Help Me)', 'Towers Of London' and their biggest smash, 'Senses Working Overtime'. But their moment of glory was scuppered by Partridge's nervous breakdown (which ended their touring days) and Chambers' departure. Thereafter, XTC drifted with session drummers, becoming increasingly studio-bound.

Thus *Mummer* (1983), despite the beguiling 'Love On A Farm Boy's Wages', was strangled by studio indecision. The same fate befell *The Big Express* (1984), but dwindling commercial fortunes were reversed by side project The Dukes Of Stratosphear, whose *25 O'Clock* (1985) and *Psonic Psunspot* (1987) were inspired pastiches of 60s Psychedelia.

The former's success re-energized the band, who enlisted Todd Rundgren to produce *Skylarking* (1986) then, after bitter rows, regretted it. They needn't have worried – a rich tapestry of Pop, it yielded the US smash 'Dear God' and sold truckloads.

XTC's renaissance continued with 1989's 'Mayor Of Simpleton' and the brilliant *Oranges & Lemons*, its success unhindered by gushing praise from REM and a tour of US college radio stations. Another assured work of genius, *Nonsuch* (1992) was recorded in typically tortuous XTC fashion with Elton John producer Gus Dudgeon and yielded the hit 'The Disappointed'. But their disdain for touring exhausted their label Virgin's patience who dropped them in 1996, despite reverential namechecks from Britpoppers like Blur. Dave Gregory popped up on ex-Take That poppet Mark Owen's *Green Man* (1996) – another implausible entry on a CV that already included Peter Gabriel and Jason Donovan – but quit in 1998. In honouring his obligations to XTC, he missed joining the Blondie reunion by one day.

Partridge followed 1980's experimental solo albums *Lure Of Salvage* and *Take Away* with 1994 collaborations with Harold Budd (*Through The Hill*) and Martin Newell (*The Greatest Living Englishman*). He has also sung with The Residents, guitared with Ryuichi Sakamoto and Joan Armatrading, drummed and blown harmonica with Thomas Dolby, and produced The Wallflowers.

Covered by acts from Primus (Funk Metal) to Spacehog (Goth Rock), Partridge and Moulding continue to fly the XTC flag.

READ *XTC: Chalkhills And Children* (1992), Chris Twomey

FAN The Little Express, Box 1072, Barrie, ON, Canada, L4M 5E1

SURF reality.sgi.com/relph/chalkhills

THE YARDBIRDS

WHO Vocals/harmonica **Keith Relf** (b. 22 Mar 1943, Richmond, Surrey, England, d. 14 May 1976, England), guitar **Eric Clapton** (b. 30 Mar 1945, Ripley, Surrey), guitar **Chris Dreja** (b. 11 Nov 1945, Surbiton, Surrey), bass **Paul Samwell-Smith** (b. 8 May 1943, Richmond), drums **Jim McCarty** (b. 25 Jul 1943, Liverpool, England)

WHEN 1963–

WHERE Richmond, Surrey, England

WHAT Proto-Metal psychedelic Blues blasters

The Yardbirds were *the* link from Blues to Heavy Metal. Aside from spawning Led Zeppelin and being Alice Cooper's favourite band, they excelled at spaced-out Psychedelia when Pink Floyd were still struggling with Blues covers and – in springboarding Jimmy Page, Jeff Beck and Eric Clapton to superduperdom – were one of the most pivotal bands in Rock.

They were formed in 1963, when Keith Relf and Paul Samwell-Smith from The Metropolitan Blues Quartet merged with Chris Dreja, Jim McCarty and guitarist Andrew 'Top' Topham from Surbiton R&B. Six months later, they replaced Topham with Eric Clapton, inherited the Stones' 'house band' gig at Richmond's Crawdaddy Blues club and won a residency at London's Marquee as The Most Blueswailin' Yardbirds.

Initially reliant on Blues standards – by the likes of Jimmy Reed, Elmore James and Bo Diddley – they diversified when the poppier 'Good Morning Little Schoolgirl' (1964) hit the UK chart. But after *Five Live Yardbirds* (1964) and *The Yardbirds With Sonny Boy Williamson* (1965), they scored their first original hit with 'For Your Love' (a Pop gem by 10cc's Graham Gouldman) and Clapton – disgusted at what he saw as creeping commercialism – picked up his guitar and walked into the arms of John Mayall.

But there were plenty more brilliant plank-spankers around. Less purist than his predecessor, the flashy Jeff Beck eagerly experimented with Eastern music, Classical and off-the-wall studio techniques. The Yardbirds entered their most successful phase, notching up UK hits with 1965's 'Heart Full Of Soul' and 'Evil Hearted You'/'Still I'm Sad' and 1966's 'Shapes Of Things' (covered by David Bowie on 1973's *Pin-Ups*) and 'Over Under Sideways Down' – pre-psychedelic masterpieces of fuzzed guitars and trippy weirdness.

But more personnel troubles loomed. Eight months after Beck's arrival, Samwell-Smith, who produced *The Yardbirds* (1966), took flight. Then fortune delivered another guitar genius: Beck's schoolfriend and session whiz Jimmy Page. Originally recruited to play bass, Page switched to rhythm guitar then, when Beck was taken ill, to lead. On Beck's return, he and Page played joint lead while Dreja took over on bass. But aside from standing in for The Who in Michelangelo Antonioni's swinging London movie *Blow Up* (1966) and making the groundbreakingly psychedelic 'Happening Ten Years Time Ago', this supercharged Yardbirds was short-lived: by the end of 1966, Beck's ill health prompted his departure.

Page took control on stage, producer Mickie Most ruled the studio and The Yardbirds became increasingly schizophrenic. Live, they dazzled with embryonic versions of Page's 'Dazed And Confused' and 'White Summer'; on vinyl, they were trapped in a Pop straitjacket. Desperation, surely, prompted their US-only cover of Manfred Mann's 'Ha Ha Said The Clown' (1967). The Yardbirds finally gave up after a college gig in July 1968.

Relf and McCarty formed Folk duo Together who became Renaissance. But there were still contractual obligations to fulfil – a Scandinavian tour. Page and manager Peter Grant recruited Robert Plant, John Bonham and John Paul Jones. When they returned to London, they were Led Zeppelin.

As Clapton, Beck and Page became millionaire guitar legends, a Yardbirds reunion looked highly unlikely – certainly after Relf's death from electrocution in May 1976. But, in 1983, Dreja, Samwell-Smith and McCarty hooked up with Beck for two gigs and the Beck-less band Box Of Frogs. Twelve years on, a more permanent regrouping saw The Yardbirds hit the nostalgia circuit.

fan Yardbirds Experience, 1600 South Gardens Street, Suite 1031, South Arlington, VA 2202, USA

surf www.idsonline.com/yardbirds/

YES ⊙ ⊙

WHO	Vocals **Jon Anderson** (b. 25 Oct 1944, Accrington, Lancashire, England), guitar **Steve Howe** (b. 8 Apr 1947, London, England), bass **Chris Squire** (b. 4 Mar 1948, London), drums **Alan White** (b. 14 Jun 1949, Pelton, Durham, England), keyboards **Rick Wakeman** (b. 18 May 1949, London)
WHEN	1968–
WHERE	London, England
WHAT	The Prince Regents of Prog

Yes' ambition, musical wizardry and sheer indulgence will never be topped – unless cloaks become fashionable again. Yet unlike their contemporaries (Pink Floyd, ELP, Genesis), Yes wear their Prog medals with pride, safe in the knowledge that no one could ever out-Yes Yes, despite legions of imitators.

Founded by Jon Anderson and Chris Squire with drummer Bill Bruford, guitarist Pete Banks and keyboard player Tony Kaye, Yes opened for Cream at their final show and issued the psychedelic Simon & Garfunkel-ish *Yes* (1969) and *Time And A Word* (1970).

By 1971's *The Yes Album*, Banks had been replaced by former Tomorrow widdler Steve Howe and the journey into hyperspace had begun. 'Yours Is No Disgrace' and 'Starship Trooper' perfected their blend of virtuoso Rock and Classical. It sold well too, giving hope to music lovers not enthralled by The Osmonds.

When Kaye left, Yes recruited former Strawbs keyboardist Rick Wakeman, who had an arsenal of synthesizers. And wore cloaks. His noodlings dominated *Fragile* (1971) – their first to bear one of Roger Dean's intricately ornate sleeve designs – which smashed transatlantic charts and even yielded a US hit in the chuggingly wonderful 'Roundabout'.

Could they get more Prog? Why, of course. *Close To The Edge* (1972) moved from gothic keyboard solos to quasi-Zeppelin riffing, topped with Anderson's lyrics-as-music (a polite way of describing vaguely religious gibberish, from which only the most die-hard fans attempt to infer meaning). Oddly enough, it was great and, accordingly, transported them to transatlantic Top 5s.

Now a top-flight stadium stegosaurus, Yes took Bruford's exit (to King Crimson) in their stride, installing former Plastic Ono Band drummer Alan White and issuing the live extravaganza *Yessongs* (1973). But so ponderous and self-indulgent was the conceptual double album *Tales From Topographic Oceans* (1973) that even Wakeman – later to stage the unbelievable *The Myths & Legends Of King Arthur* (*on ice*, remember) – quit in bemusement.

Their chart glory was unabated: *Topographic Oceans* topped the UK chart and 1974's tuneless *Relayer* – with Patrick Moraz on keyboards – also made US and UK Top 5s. Musically, both paled beside 1977's superb *Going For The One*, for which Wakeman returned. Another UK No.1, it refined their musical flights of fancy into real songs, of which 'Wonderous Stories' was a UK hit. *Tormato* (1978) was a paler imitation but another big-seller, though that wasn't enough to stop Wakeman fleeing once more – this time accompanied by Anderson.

Despite rumours that Squire and White would join Jimmy Page in a post-Zeppelin power trio called XYZ, Yes ploughed on with – to widespread astonishment – former Buggles members Geoff Downes and Trevor

Horn on keyboards and vocals. Their *Drama* (1980) sold well, but Yes without Anderson seemed a lost cause and, in 1981, they split – their epitaph the excellent live album *Yesshows* (1980).

Squire recruited whiz-kid guitarist Trevor Rabin for a new band called Cinema, who – under pressure from the Atlantic label – transmogrified into a re-formed Yes with Anderson, Kaye and White. The Trevor Horn-produced *90125* (1983) was their best since *Going For The One*, packed with sing-along songs and soulful harmonies, like the irresistible hits 'Owner Of A Lonely Heart' and 'Leave It'. Sadly, they undid this good work with the jaw-droppingly indulgent *9012Live* (1985), a live album of – believe it or not – solos. *Big Generator* (1987) trod an uneasy path between inspiration and rubbish, and the resurfacing of old enmities threw YesWorld into turmoil. For years, a ridiculous war raged between two claimants to the Yes crown: the band itself, led by Squire, and the legally monikered Anderson, Bruford, Wakeman and Howe. The latter got the upper hand with a well-received tour and self-titled 1989 album, but were sandbagged without Squire's thunderous bass and, of course, the Yes name.

The war ended when – to the glee of critics – the two factions united as an eight-piece for 1991's *Union* and a world tour. By 1994's *Talk*, however, they had slimmed to their 1983 line-up, with the mainly live *Keys To Ascension* appearing in 1996. In late 1997, Anderson, Howe, Squire and White, with Billy Sherwood on keyboards and guitar, released *Open Your Eyes*, a new studio album that strayed little from the proven formula.

read *Yesstories* (1996), Tim Morse

fan Yes Magazine, 12 Chelsea Place, Dix Hills, NY 11746, USA

surf www.yesworld.com

NEIL YOUNG ⊙ ✪

WHO	b. 12 Nov 1945, Toronto, Ontario, Canada
WHAT	The world-weary whine of Don Grungeone

"I keep getting younger," Neil Young said on 1989's *Freedom*. "My life's been funny that way." It's true: while his hippie colleagues rusted and seized up, Neil Young – folky poet, Country balladeer, Godfather of Grunge, wise hippie, thrashing Punk, obstinate old bugger – kept moving. When his 60s band Buffalo Springfield became a phenomenon, he quit. When he won acclaim as a solo artist, he joined Crosby, Stills & Nash. When the Woodstock generation hailed him as a hippie icon, he played with noise – only to return with an acoustic guitar and a battered straw hat to re-invent Country Rock. While Punk repelled his dinosaur peers, Young embraced it and gave it a soundtrack – 1979's *Rust Never Sleeps*. While his contemporaries spent the 80s mired in mid-life crises and bad albums, Young dabbled in experimental music and movies (OK, and maybe *some* bad albums) and celebrated turning 50 by making an album with Pearl Jam.

Born in Toronto, Young moved to Winnipeg with his mother after she and his sports journalist father, Scott Young, divorced. High-school bands like The Jades (twangy Ventures-style instrumentals) and The Classics (Duane Eddy covers) mutated into Neil Young & The Squires – at first a Beatles/Shadows hybrid, then a Folk Rock band. Young also became a regular at local Folk club 4-D, where he met Joni Mitchell (who wrote 'The Circle Game' about him) and Stephen Stills.

In 1966, the penniless Young joined future funkateer Rick James' Mynah Birds. When James was arrested for deserting the US army, Young and bassist Bruce Palmer packed up Young's hearse and headed for California. Meeting up again with Stills, they formed Buffalo Springfield, who were both influential and critically acclaimed. But, two years, three albums and countless arguments with Stills later, Young went solo – securing Joni Mitchell's manager Elliot Roberts and a record deal with Reprise.

His plaintive, folky, self-titled first album appeared to minimal interest in January 1969 – but Young had already moved on. He'd been jamming with Danny Whitten, Ralph Molina and Billy Talbot of LA band The Rockets, and invited them to his house in Laurel Canyon to play 'Down By The River', 'Cinnamon Girl' and 'Cowgirl In The Sand'. The try-out turned into 1969's excellent *Everybody Knows This Is Nowhere* and The Rockets, mourned in 'Running Dry (Requiem For The Rockets)', became Crazy Horse – his longest-lasting sparring partners. Just four months from his debut, this was a completely different Young: raw, emotional, with fuzzy guitars and feedback. The album went gold. So Young put aside his solo career and joined Crosby, Stills & Nash…

CS&N became CSN&Y in the summer of 1969 with a show at the Fillmore East – the first of a series of mega-events that included Woodstock and Altamont. But even though their debut, 1970's *Déjà Vu*, was that year's biggest-selling US album, Young had no intention of abandoning Crazy Horse. Dividing his time between the two acts, he released a third solo album, 1970's immaculate *After The Goldrush*. Packed with classics – the mournful 'Birds' and 'I Believe In You', the misty-eyed 'Tell Me Why' and 'Only Love Can Break Your Heart', the joyful 'When You Dance I Can Really Love' and the savage 'Southern Man' – it mixed the acoustic tranquillity of *Neil Young* with the noisy freakouts of *Nowhere* and scored Young another gold album.

But *Harvest* (1972) made him a fully-fledged Pop star. While Crazy Horse made their 1971 self-titled debut, Young assembled a countrified backing band, The Stray Gators, and recorded in Nashville. A glittering mix of delicate Country Rock and orchestral epics (the tear-jerking 'A Man Needs A Maid' was about actress girlfriend Carrie Snodgress), *Harvest* was propelled by the US No.1 'Heart Of Gold'. But as its sales reached millions, Young stamped on the brakes.

"'Heart Of Gold' put me in the middle of the road." he wrote in 1977's liner notes to *Decade*. "Travelling there became a bore so I headed for the ditch." *Journey Through The Past* (1972) was the soundtrack to an autobiographical movie which might have been a work of genius had anyone understood it. Both were mauled by critics expecting a *Harvest* sequel. What they *didn't* expect was 1973's chaotic *Time Fades Away* – recorded live on a stressful US tour that saw the death of Young's friend and roadie Bruce Berry. It was the second drugs death to hit Young in a year – Crazy Horse guitarist Danny Whitten (whose 'I Don't Want To Talk About It' was a hit for Rod Stewart and Everything But The Girl) had overdosed on heroin the previous November. The album's prevailing mood of raw desperation permeated Young's sound for the next two years.

On The Beach (1974) was so dark and nihilistic that Young still allegedly refuses to sanction its release on CD. It appeared instead of the harrowing *Tonight's The Night* – a beautiful wake for Whitten and Berry recorded with Crazy Horse, belatedly released in 1975 in place of the shelved *Homegrown*.

By the time *Tonight's The Night* appeared, the darkness had lifted. *Zuma* (1975) returned to the muscular riff-mongering of *Nowhere*, its highlights including the epic 'Cortez The Killer', the heartbreaking 'Dangerbird' and a one-track reunion with Crosby, Stills & Nash, 'Through My Sails', another episode in the love/hate relationship with his sometime colleagues. Having joined them for a multi-million-dollar tour, Young had gone straight back to Crazy Horse (now with guitarist Frank 'Poncho' Sampedro). Yet he teamed up with Stills for 1976's uninspiring *Long May You Run*.

The years to the decade's end were typically varied. While the giant retrospective *Decade* (1977) charted the strange story so far and *American Stars 'N' Bars* (1977) was saved only by the awesome 'Like A Hurricane', the nearly brilliant *Comes A Time* (1978) seemed a way of soothing *Harvest* fans dismayed by Punk.

What they didn't know was that Young had written a tribute to Sex Pistol Johnny Rotten for *Rust Never Sleeps* (1979) – his best since *Zuma*. Half delicately acoustic ('Pocahontas', 'Thrasher'), half monstrously electric ('Powderfinger', 'Sedan Delivery'), *Rust* was book-ended by 'My My, Hey Hey (Out Of The Blue)' and 'Hey Hey, My My (Into The Black)': mirror images of a song which shed Young's past with "The king is gone but he's not forgotten/This is the story of Johnny Rotten" and "It's better to burn out/than fade away". Years later, Kurt Cobain quoted the latter in his suicide note. Meanwhile, the theatrical *Rust* tour, complete with giant Fender amps, 'Road Eyes' and 'Rust-O-Specs' (given to the crowd so they could see the 'rust' falling off his guitar in the older songs) was immortalized in the live movie *Rust Never Sleeps* and album *Live Rust* (both 1979).

Having ended his Reprise contract with 1980's *Hawks And Doves* and 1981's *Re-Act-Or*, Young signed to Geffen – a marriage which turned sour almost as soon as he delivered 1982's *Trans*. Desperate to stave off boredom or, worse still, rust, he toyed with synthesizers on half its cuts and disguised his voice with a vocoder. Geffen, critics and fans were united in their hatred, but *Trans* is one of Young's best: its electronics reflected the paranoia of the computer age and Young's efforts to communicate with his son Ben, born with cerebral palsy.

However, his subsequent genre-hopping, despite isolated flashes of excellence, exasperated his audience and Geffen alike. He toyed with bands, identities and styles: pseudo-Rockabilly as Neil Young & The Shocking Pinks (1983's *Everybody's Rockin'*), straight Country (1985's *Old Ways*), more electronic Rock (1986's *Landing On Water*) and pedestrian Crazy Horse (1987's *Life*). Geffen, bewildered by Young's waywardness and diminishing sales, took him to court, ludicrously claiming his music was 'unrepresentative' – although they later cashed in with 1992's *Lucky Thirteen*, the best moments from his Geffen career.

His other activities were no less strange: endorsing (then) presidential candidate Ronald Reagan; soundtracking the Hunter S. Thompson biopic *Where The Buffalo Roam* (1980); making the anti-nuclear movie *Human Highway* (1982) with Devo; playing Live Aid; co-founding Farm Aid; instigating the annual Bridge Concert benefit for his son's school; and reuniting with Crosby, Stills & Nash for the disappointing *American Dream* (1988).

Geffen got a poke in the eye when Young returned to Reprise and reversed his commercial fortunes, first with 1988's bluesy *This Note's For You* (whose title cut satirized corporate sponsorhip of Rock) and 'Eldorado' EP, then 1989's fully-fledged return-to-form *Freedom*. Like *Rust Never Sleeps*, *Freedom* mixed folkiness with noise ('Eldorado') and social commentary ('Crime In The City') and, like *Rust*, was sandwiched by acoustic and metallic versions of the same song – 'Rockin' In The Free World'.

Coinciding with the 1989 tribute album *The Bridge* (starring covers by Pixies, Sonic Youth, Dinosaur Jr, Nick Cave, Flaming Lips and Soul Asylum), *Freedom* was Neil Young reborn as a fiery, guitar-abusing Grunge God. *Don Grungeone*, if you will.

The Don indulged his fondness for feedback with Crazy Horse on 1990's excellent *Ragged Glory* and a noise-drenched tour with Sonic Youth and Social Distortion, captured on the raucous *Weld* (1991). Early editions also included *Arc*, a 35-minute feedback symphony edited together from *Weld*'s lengthy noise interludes.

After three years with the volume cranked up to 11, Young's ears were shot. Thus *Harvest Moon* (1992) was the gentle, all-acoustic *Harvest* sequel older fans (not to mention Reprise) had waited 20 years for and his biggest US hit since *Live Rust*. It was followed by 1993's intimate *Unplugged* and a grunged-out globe-trotting tour with Pearl Jam and, oddly, Booker T & The MG's. He also wrote the moving title song to *Philadelphia* (1993) and shone at Bob Dylan's otherwise dull 50th birthday show.

Troubled by Kurt Cobain's death (and quote from 'My My, Hey Hey' in his suicide note), Young joined Crazy Horse again for the rumbling *Sleeps With Angels* (1994) and, after his induction into The Rock And Roll Hall Of Fame, collaborated with an uncredited Pearl Jam on *Mirror Ball* (1995).

Fittingly for someone so concerned with environmental issues, Neil Young's late 90s output has turned into a relentless process of recycling: two of *Sleeps With Angels'* tracks were reprises, while 1996's Jim Jarmusch movie soundtrack *Dead Man* and Crazy Horse hook-ups *Broken Arrow* and live *The Year Of The Horse* (which was accompanied by a Jarmusch-directed tour movie) were ever more formulaic rewrites of *Rust Never Sleeps* and *Ragged Glory*. But it's little more than a phase – just Neil Young burning his past for fuel as he heads into the future.

Read *Neil Young – The Rolling Stones Files* (1994), Eds. *Rolling Stone*

Fan Neil Young Appreciation Society, 2A Llynfi Street, Bridgend, Mid Glamorgan, CF31 1SY, UK

Surf www.wallofsound.com/artists/neilyoung/index.html

PAUL YOUNG ⊙ ⊙ ⊙

WHO b. 17 Jan 1956, Luton, Bedfordshire, England

WHAT Cuddly teddy bear of Soul

Soul? From Luton? Impossible, surely! Well, Paul Young smashed that common myth with a string of sultry hits in the 80s. But he didn't get it right first time. First, he was a member of Streetband, lightweight funkers who blighted the UK chart with the quirky novelty hit 'Toast' in 1978. Then Streetband mutated into the eight-piece Q-Tips – his first step toward serious Soul.

In 1980, after Q-Tips' eponymous debut flopped, Young went solo and, with a UK No.1 cover of Marvin Gaye's 'Wherever I Lay My Hat', became a top tasteful Soul smoothie. Backed by his Royal Family band and backing singers The Fabulous Wealthy Tarts, he struck further chart gold with 'Come Back And Stay', 'Love Of The Common People', a cover of Ann Peebles' 'I'm Gonna Tear Your Playhouse Down' and the UK No.1 *No Parlez* (1983) – a rulebook of slick Soul, from its pin-up cover shot to its improbable reworking of Joy Division's 'Love Will Tear Us Apart'.

As the Tarts left to pursue a (presumably bleak) solo career, Young unleashed 1985's *The Secret Of Association* – another UK No.1 – and the mature smashes 'Everything Must Change' and the tear-jerking 'Every Time You Go Away'. But, uncomfortable with being a Pop heart-throb, Young took control for 1986's *Between Two Fires* and suffered his first flop. *Other Voices* (1990) boasted Nile Rodgers, Chaka Khan, Stevie Wonder and Dave Gilmour but, apart from a US Top 10 hit with a cover of The Chi-Lites' 'Oh Girl', was quickly forgotten.

A 1991 duet with Italian pretend Bluesman Zucchero, 'Senza Una Donna (Without A Woman)' returned Young to the UK Top 10 and made *From Time To Time – The Singles Collection* (1991) his third UK No.1. His singles have since made a comfortable home outside the Top 40, while neither *The Crossing* (1993) nor *Reflections* (1994) troubled charts long.

FRANK ZAPPA

WHO b. 21 Dec 1940, Baltimore, Maryland, USA, d. 4 Dec 1993, Los Angeles, California, USA

WHAT The maddest music you never heard in your life

More than any other act in this book, Frank Zappa makes a mockery of the 'Rock' banner. From album to album, from song to song, *from verse to chorus*, he'd veer from Metal to Jazz to Doo Wop. Zappa came to prominence in his late 20s, with a broken marriage and prison sentence behind him. But he hadn't been wasting time: he'd been involved with music most of his life. His father, a government scientist, moved the family around the USA, settling in Lancaster, California, when Frank was 10.

The young Zappa became obsessed with R&B, Doo Wop and Classical composers like Edgard Varèse, Anton Von Webern and Igor Stravinsky. Despite a flair for chemistry (especially explosives – he blew up his school's toilets), he persuaded his parents to buy him a drum kit and formed high-school bands The Ramblers and The Black-Outs, the latter with his friend Don Van Vliet aka Captain Beefheart. In 1959, a year after he first picked up a guitar, Zappa moved to Hollywood and studied music theory.

There he met his wife and, having dropped out of school within six months, scraped a living playing the cocktail lounge circuit, scoring B-movie soundtracks and selling encyclopedias. In 1962, Zappa met producer Paul Buff, who owned a studio in Cucamonga, California. They wrote songs together, while Zappa played on singles by bands passing through the studio and formed The Soots, a short-lived band with Captain Beefheart.

One of the scores, *Run Home Slow*, yielded royalties in 1963. While Zappa divorced his wife, he bought Buff's studio, christened it Studio Z and moved in. But the studio was shut down in 1964 when the vice squad set him up: they asked him to soundtrack a porno film, then jailed him for ten days on obscenity charges. On his release, Zappa moved to Los Angeles and joined Soul Giant. After a spell as Captain Glasspack & The Magic Mufflers, they became The Mothers on Mothers Day 1964.

By 1965, they were The Mothers Of Invention, freak scene favourites with a residency at LA's Whisky-A-Go-Go club and a deal with MGM's Jazz label Verve. They made their mark with *Freak Out!* (1966) – a frazzled collision of satire, cynicism, social commentary, Classical and insane experimental Rock which Paul McCartney cited as an influence on The Beatles' *Sgt. Pepper*. The Mothers expanded to include two saxophonists for *Absolutely Free* (1967) and a 50-piece orchestra for *Lumpy Gravy* (1967), a Zappa brainchild of cut-up composition.

They moved to New York's Greenwich Village and debuted their Pigs And Repugnant show – an art Rock 'happening' with rotten vegetables and a whipped cream-spurting giraffe. Zappa was on a roll, exorcising his musical demons on 1967's Doo Wop tribute *Cruising With Ruben & The Jets*, 1968's *We're Only In It For The Money* (a cynical, anti-hippie rant sleeved in a pastiche of *Sgt. Pepper*) and 1969's fusion monster *Uncle Meat*. Then he returned to LA, remarried (a union which produced the kids Moon Unit, Diva, Dweezil and Ahmet Rodan), signed to Warner Bros, and got two subsidiary labels to play with – Straight and Bizarre.

Zappa gleefully recorded his favourites – including comedian Lenny Bruce, drooling maniac Wild Man Fischer and Captain Beefheart's seminal *Trout Mask Replica* (1969) – while working on

1970's *Burnt Weeny Sandwich* and *Weasels Ripped My Flesh*, with The Mothers now augmented by doomed future Little Feat leader Lowell George. But Zappa ditched the band for 1969's *Hot Rats* – his only UK Top 10 hit – which had cameos by Beefheart and Jazz violinists Jean-Luc Ponty and Don 'Sugarcane' Harris.

The 70s saw Zappa recording and touring with a series of Mothers line-ups (including singers Flo and Eddie aka ex-Turtles Mark Volman and Howard Kaylan, drummer Aynsley Dunbar and multi-instrumentalist George Duke) on the deranged *Fillmore East June 1971* (1971), the hated-even-by-fans *Just Another Band From LA* (1972), *The Grand Wazoo* (1972), *Over-Nite Sensation* (1973), *Roxy & Elsewhere* (1974) and *One Size Fits All* (1975). The latter – the last to bear the Mothers Of Invention credit – is regarded by fans as his best, as is its opening track 'Inca Roads'.

Zappa's solo *Chunga's Revenge* (1970), *Waka/Jawaka* (1972), *Apostrophe (')* (1974, his US commercial peak), *Bongo Fury* (1975, with Beefheart), *Zoot Allures* (1976) and live *In New York* (1978) seduced fans and critics, but it wasn't all roses: he was left wheelchair-bound for nine months after being knocked off stage by an angry fan at London's Rainbow Theatre in 1971,

mere days after a Mothers show in Montreux, Switzerland, went up in flames, chronicled in Deep Purple's 'Smoke On The Water'.

He also acrimoniously split with Warner Bros (who refused to release a four-disc set called *Läther* and issued 1978's *Studio Tan* and 1979's *Sleep Dirt* and *Orchestral Favorites* instead) and manager Herb Cohen, moving to Mercury for 1979's excellent *Sheik Yerbouti* and enormous Rock opera *Joe's Garage, Acts I, II & III*. He continued his tradition of showcasing virtuoso musicians: guitarists Steve Vai, Adrian Belew and Warren Cuccurullo and drummer Terry Bozzio passed through the ranks.

The decade was book-ended with forays into movies: 1971's *200 Motels* delved into the debauched Rock lifestyle with cameos by Ringo Starr and Keith Moon; 1979's *Baby Snakes* was a slapstick-laden rockumentary interspersed with claymation.

The 80s brought Zappa's only hit single: 'Valley Girl', from *Ship Arriving Too Late To Save A Drowning Witch* (1982), on which his daughter Moon Unit lampooned airhead Californian teens to a crunching Metal backing. After 1981's *Tinseltown Rebellion*, *You Are What You Is* and the live *Shut Up 'N Play Yer Guitar*, Zappa indulged a love of modern Classical music, producing concerts of Varèse and Webern in 1981 and 1983 while wrangling with Mercury (he left and set up his own Barking Pumpkin label) and America's moral guardians (chronicled on 1985's *Frank Zappa Meets The Mothers Of Prevention*).

While Zappa unleashed 1983's *The Man From Utopia*, 1984's extreme *Them Or Us* and *Thing Fish* (an aborted Broadway musical) and 1986's live *Does Humor Belong In Music?*, and won a Grammy for the hi-tech *Jazz From Hell* (1987), he also exhumed his past with the autobiography *The Real Frank Zappa* (1989) and six-volume live set *You Can't Do That On Stage Anymore* (1988-1992). The orchestral albums *Boulez Conducts Zappa/The Perfect Stranger* (1984) and *LSO Vols. 1 & 2* (1983, 1987) reflected his 'serious composer' acclaim.

His growing political concerns extended in the 90s, as Czech president, playwright and Zappa fan Vaclav Havel appointed him an emissary for trade and culture in 1990. Lithuania honoured him with a statue in its capital city Vilnius.

He was even considering running for the US presidency – the theme of his final tour, promoting 1988's politically-charged *Broadway The Hard Way*. But, in 1991, he was diagnosed with cancer. A bewildering output of albums continued with 1991's live *Make A Jazz Noise Here* and *The Best Band You Never Heard In Your Life* and 1993's *The Yellow Shark* (an album of his work by Classical group Ensemble Modern), until his death in 1993. His final work – the inpenetrable *Lumpy Gravy* sequel *Civilization Phaze III* (1995) – appeared posthumously, as did *Läther* (1996), the 'best-of' *Strictly Commercial* (1995), a Zappa-compiled set of his least radio-friendly anthems called *Have I Offended Someone?* (1997) and the orchestral taster album, *Strictly Genteel* (1997).

Zappa left a huge body of work, a devoted following and an inspirational approach to music. He gave Alice Cooper an early deal and inspired future musical mavericks like the funky freaks Fishbone and Primus. Dweezil's music has shown a command of guitar pyrotechnics and humour similar to his father. But neither he – nor, indeed, anyone else – is ever likely to come close to the exciting/frustrating, acute/crude, virtuoso/simplistic whirlwind of Frank Zappa himself.

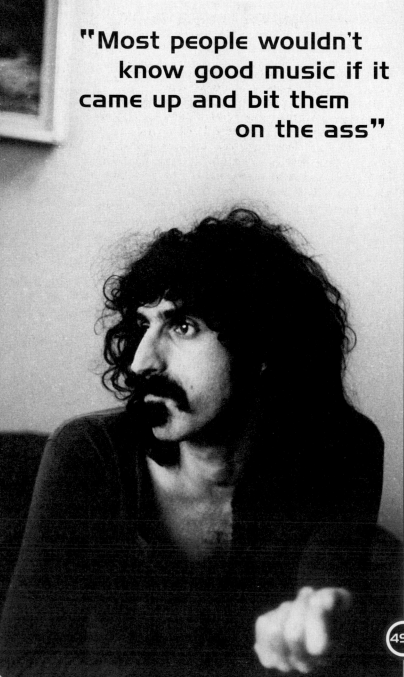

"Most people wouldn't know good music if it came up and bit them on the ass"

ⓡⓔⓐⓓ *Zappa – Electric Don Quixote* (1997), Neil Slaven

ⓕⓐⓝ T'Mershi Duween, PO Box 249, Chesterfield, S40 4DZ, UK

ⓢⓤⓡⓕ www.zappa.com/

THE ZOMBIES

WHO Vocals **Colin Blunstone** (b. 24 Jun 1945, Hatfield, England), keyboards

Rod Argent (b. 14 Jun 1945, St Albans, England), guitar **Paul Atkinson** (b. 19 Mar 1946, Cuffley, England), bass **Chris White** (b. 7 Mar 1943, Barnet, England), drums **Hugh Grundy** (b. 6 Mar 1945, Winchester, England)

WHEN 1963–1967

WHERE St Albans, Hertfordshire, England

WHAT Melancholic 60s Beat group

Whose most famous song became a hit for Santana and UK Subs? The Zombies, that's who. After replacing co-founder Paul Arnold with Chris White, they won a 1964 talent contest, which led to a Decca record contract and their debut, 1964's million-selling 'She's Not There' (US No.2/UK No.12). This melancholic tale of romantic betrayal, with Blunstone's tenor vocals and Argent's jazzy keyboard solo, was typical of their output.

They issued their 1965 debut album, *The Zombies* (*Begin Here* in the UK), and performed in the 1966 movie *Bunny Lake Is Missing* but, after a mixed reception for 1965's 'Tell Her No' (US No.6/UK No.42) and US success, they had no further UK hits.

Victims of financial rip-offs and lack of proper promotion, they split in December 1967 after recording the unsuccessful and misspelt *Odessey And Oracle* (1968) for CBS, now a classic. Its 'Time Of The Season' hit US No.3 in 1969, but they refused to re-form. Songwriters Rod Argent and Chris White started Argent, Blunstone went solo ('She's Not There' remade under the name of Neil MacArthur, 'What Became Of The Broken-Hearted' with Dave Stewart) and Atkinson and Grundy became A&R men. In 1991, Blunstone, White and Grundy re-formed for the one-off *New World* and the retrospective set *Zombie Heaven* appeared.

read *Call Up The Groups* (1985), Alan Clayson

surf www.arrowfm.com/artists/zombies/zombies.shtml

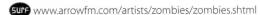

ZZ TOP

WHO Guitar/vocals **Billy Gibbons** (b. 16 Dec 1949, Houston, Texas, USA), bass/vocals **Dusty Hill** (b. 19 May 1949, Dallas, Texas), drums **Frank Beard** (b. 11 Jun 1949, Frankston, Texas)

WHEN 1969–

WHERE Texas, USA

WHAT Technologically-assisted boogie men

Despite augmenting their guitars with new-fangled synthesizers, ZZ Top have remained almost exactly the same since 1970. When their commercial peak came and went in the 80s, the only perceptible change was a touch of grey in the luxuriant face fungi of Billy Gibbons and Dusty Hill.

Gibbons won the acclaim of Jimi Hendrix as guitarist in Garage Rock act The Moving Sidewalks. Hill and Frank Beard (yes, that's his real name and no, he hasn't got a beard) were members of the less revered American Blues. Named ZZ Top in honour of Texan bluesman ZZ Hill (thus ensuring 'last entry'

"It's important not to appear too pompous"
Billy Gibbons

status in Rock encyclopedias), they unleashed their crunching boogie on 1970's no-nonsense *ZZ Top's First Album*.

The studio wasn't their favourite place. For seven years they toured ceaselessly, earning support slots with The Rolling Stones and a 100,000-strong audience for their ZZ Top's First Annual Texas Size Rompin' Stompin' Barndance Bar-B-Q festival in 1972. Sales grew through *Rio Grande Mud* (1972), *Tres Hombres* (1973), *Fandango!* (1975), *Tejas* (1976) and the US hits 'Francene' (1971), 'La Grange' (1974), 'Tush' (1975) and 'It's Only Love' (1976).

The Worldwide Texas Tour in 1976 – with snakes, sand, cattle, cacti and Texas-shaped stage – sent ZZ Top global. After a break, they returned with the 'weird beards' and 1979's monstrous *Deguello*, on which they backed themselves as 'The Wolf Horns'.

Like some crazy Rock freight train with no brakes, they were unstoppable. They hit with the ballad 'Leila' and bonkers parent album *El Loco* (1981), then – thanks to some of the best videos ever – 'Gimme All Your Lovin', 'Sharp Dressed Man', 'Legs' and 'TV Dinners', from 1983's *Eliminator*, stormed international charts.

Amazingly, they topped this success with *Afterburner* (1985) – which dosed the stew with more electronics and weirdness than ever and yielded the hits 'Sleeping Bag', 'Rough Boy', 'Velcro Fly' (whose video was choreographed by Paula Abdul) and 'Stages'. In 1987, they announced their booking as 'house band' on the Space Shuttle, while their tireless campaigning helped to found a Delta Blues museum in Clarksdale, Mississippi.

With 1990's less-than-brilliant *Recycler* and 1994's *Antenna*, it looked like ZZ Top had exhausted the electr(on)ic Blues that had served them so well, despite a hit cover of Elvis' 'Viva Las Vegas' (1992), so they restarted with 1996's earthily bluesy *Rhythmeen*. Confirming their grasp on the ghoulish, two of the album's cuts – 'Vincent Price Blues' and 'She's Just Killing Me' – first appeared on the soundtrack to Quentin Tarantino's *From Dusk Till Dawn*.

read *Elimination: The ZZ Top Story* (1986), Dave Thomas

surf www.geocites.com/SunsetStrip/towers/5680/zyggyz.htm

Where it's at

A&M RECORDS ABBA ABBEY ROAD STUDIOS ABC PAULA ABDUL AC/DC ACE OF BASE ACID HOUSE ACID JAZZ ADAM & THE ANTS BR
ADAMS AEROSMITH A-HA ALICE IN CHAINS ALL SAINTS THE ALLMAN BROTHERS BAND MARC ALMOND HERB ALPERT AMBIENT TORI AM
LAURIE ANDERSON THE ANIMALS PAUL ANKA ANTHRAX APHEX TWIN APPLE ARGENT JOAN ARMATRADING ARRESTED DEVELOPMENT ART
NOISE ASH ASIA ASWAD ATLANTIC RECORDS THE AVERAGE WHITE BAND KEVIN AYERS AZTEC CAMERA BABYFACE BURT BACHAR
BACHMAN-TURNER OVERDRIVE BAD COMPANY JOAN BAEZ BANANARAMA THE BAND THE BANGLES BARCLAY JAMES HARVEST GARY BARL
SYD BARRETT BAUHAUS THE BAY CITY ROLLERS THE BEACH BOYS BEASTIE BOYS THE BEATLES THE BEAUTIFUL SOUTH BECK JEFF BECK
GEES BEGGARS BANQUET PAT BENATAR GEORGE BENSON CHUCK BERRY THE B-52'S BIG BLACK BIG COUNTRY BJÖRK THE BLACK CROV
BLACK FLAG BLACK GRAPE BLACK SABBATH MARY J BLIGE BLONDIE BLOOD SWEAT & TEARS THE BLUE NILE BLUE ÖYSTER CULT BLUES
BLUES BROTHERS THE BLUETONES BLUR MICHAEL BOLTON BON JOVI BONEY M BOO RADLEYS BOOKER T & THE MG'S THE BOOMTOWN R
BOSTON DAVID BOWIE BOY BANDS BOYZ II MEN BOYZONE BILLY BRAGG THE BRAND NEW HEAVIES TONI BRAXTON BREAD BRITPOP BRON
BEAT ELKIE BROOKS GARTH BROOKS BOBBY BROWN JAMES BROWN JACKSON BROWNE JEFF BUCKLEY TIM BUCKLEY BUFFALO SPRINGFI
BUSH KATE BUSH BUTTHOLE SURFERS BUZZCOCKS THE BYRDS DAVID BYRNE C+C MUSIC FACTORY J.J. CALE JOHN CALE GLEN CAMPB
CAN CANNED HEAT CAPITOL RECORDS CAPTAIN BEEFHEART MARIAH CAREY BELINDA CARLISLE MARY-CHAPIN CARPENTER THE CARPENT
THE CARS CARTER THE UNSTOPPABLE SEX MACHINE JOHNNY CASH DAVID CASSIDY CAST CATATONIA NICK CAVE & THE BAD SEEDS TR
CHAPMAN THE CHARLATANS RAY CHARLES CHEAP TRICK CHUBBY CHECKER THE CHEMICAL BROTHERS CHER NENEH CHERRY CHESS C
CHICAGO CHRYSALIS CLANNAD ERIC CLAPTON THE DAVE CLARK FIVE THE CLASH PATSY CLINE GEORGE CLINTON EDDIE COCHRAN JOE COC
COCTEAU TWINS LEONARD COHEN LLOYD COLE & THE COMMOTIONS PHIL COLLINS COLUMBIA/CBS THE COMMODORES THE COMMUNARDS
COODER NORMAN COOK SAM COOKE COOLIO ALICE COOPER JULIAN COPE ELVIS COSTELLO COUNTING CROWS COUNTRY JOE & THE F
COUNTRY ROCK THE CRANBERRIES CRASH TEST DUMMIES RANDY CRAWFORD ROBERT CRAY CREAM CREATION CREEDENCE CLEARWAT
REVIVAL CROSBY STILLS NASH & YOUNG SHERYL CROW CROWDED HOUSE THE CULT CULTURE CLUB THE CURE CYPRESS HILL DAFT PUNK
DAMNED TERENCE TRENT D'ARBY MILES DAVIS THE SPENCER DAVIS GROUP CHRIS DE BURGH DE LA SOUL DEACON BLUE DEAD KENNE
DEATH ROW DECCA DEEP PURPLE DEF JAM DEF LEPPARD DEFTONES DESMOND DEKKER DEL AMITRI JOHN DENVER DEPECHE MO
DES'REE DEVO DEXY'S MIDNIGHT RUNNERS NEIL DIAMOND BO DIDDLEY DINOSAUR JR CÉLINE DION DIRE STRAITS DISCO DISC JOCKEYS
SHADOW DODGY FATS DOMINO LONNIE DONEGAN JASON DONOVAN THE DOOBIE BROTHERS THE DOORS DR DRE DR FEELGOOD
JOHN NICK DRAKE THE DRIFTERS DRUM 'N' BASS DUB DUBSTAR DURAN DURAN IAN DURY BOB DYLAN THE EAGLES EARTH WIND & F
EAST 17 ECHO & THE BUNNYMEN ECHOBELLY DUANE EDDY DAVE EDMUNDS EELS 808 STATE EINSTÜRZENDE NEUBAUTEN ELASTICA ELECT
LIGHT ORCHESTRA ELECTRONIC ELEKTRA/ASYLUM EMERSON LAKE & PALMER EMF EMI EN VOGUE BRIAN ENO ENYA BRIAN EPST
ERASURE GLORIA ESTEFAN ETERNAL EUROVISION SONG CONTEST EURYTHMICS THE EVERLY BROTHERS EVERYTHING BUT THE G
EXTREME THE FACES FACTORY FAIRPORT CONVENTION ADAM FAITH FAITH NO MORE MARIANNE FAITHFULL THE FALL FAMILY THE FA
FAUST JOSÉ FELICIANO BRYAN FERRY FINE YOUNG CANNIBALS ROBERTA FLACK FLEETWOOD MAC THE FLYING BURRITO BROTHERS FOO
FOLK ROCK FOO FIGHTERS FOREIGNER 4AD THE FOUR SEASONS THE FOUR TOPS KIM FOWLEY PETER FRAMPTON FRANKIE GOES
HOLLYWOOD ARETHA FRANKLIN FREE ALAN FREED ROBERT FRIPP THE FUGEES FUN LOVIN' CRIMINALS FUNK BILLY FURY FUSION PET
GABRIEL GABRIELLE GALLAGHER & LYLE RORY GALLAGHER GANGSTA RAP GARBAGE MARVIN GAYE GLORIA GAYNOR GEFFEN THE J GE
BAND GENERATION X GENESIS GERRY & THE PACEMAKERS GLAM ROCK GLASTONBURY GARY GLITTER THE GO-GO'S GOLDEN EARRI
GOLDIE BERRY GORDY GOTH BILL GRAHAM THE GRATEFUL DEAD AL GREEN GREEN DAY GRUNGE GUNS N' ROSES ARLO GUTHRIE WOO
GUTHRIE HAIRCUT 100 BILL HALEY HALL & OATES HAMMER HANOI ROCKS HAPPY MONDAYS STEVE HARLEY & COCKNEY REBEL ROY HARF
EMMYLOU HARRIS GEORGE HARRISON ALEX HARVEY PJ HARVEY HAWKWIND ISAAC HAYES HEART HEAVEN 17 HEAVY METAL JIMI HEND
DON HENLEY HERMAN'S HERMITS STEVE HILLAGE SYSTEM 7 HIP HOP ROBYN HITCHCOCK HOLE HOLLAND-DOZIER-HOLLAND THE HOLL
BUDDY HOLLY JOHN LEE HOOKER HOOTIE & THE BLOWFISH HOT CHOCOLATE HOTHOUSE FLOWERS HOUSE THE HOUSEMARTINS WHITN
HOUSTON THE HUMAN LEAGUE HUMBLE PIE HÜSKER DÜ JANIS IAN ICE CUBE ICE-T THE ICICLE WORKS BILLY IDOL THE INCREDIBLE STR
BAND INDIE INDUSTRIAL INSPIRAL CARPETS INXS IRON BUTTERFLY IRON MAIDEN CHRIS ISAAK ISLAND RECORDS ISLE OF WIGHT THE IS
BROTHERS JANET JACKSON JOE JACKSON MICHAEL JACKSON THE JACKSONS THE JAM JAMES RICK JAMES JAMIROQUAI JANE'S ADDICT
JAPAN JEAN-MICHEL JARRE JEFFERSON AIRPLANE/STARSHIP THE JESUS & MARY CHAIN JESUS JONES JETHRO TULL JOAN JETT JEW
BILLY JOEL ELTON JOHN GRACE JONES HOWARD JONES QUINCY JONES RICKIE LEE JONES TOM JONES JANIS JOPLIN JOURNEY JOY DIVISI
JUDAS PRIEST KC & THE SUNSHINE BAND R. KELLY CHAKA KHAN KILLING JOKE B.B. KING BEN E. KING CAROLE KING KING CRIMSON T
KINKS KISS KLF KNEBWORTH GLADYS KNIGHT KOOL & THE GANG KRAFTWERK LENNY KRAVITZ KULA SHAKER THE LA'S PATTI LABELLE K
LANG CYNDI LAUPER LED ZEPPELIN LEIBER & STOLLER THE LEMONHEADS JOHN LENNON ANNIE LENNOX LEVEL 42 LEVELLERS HUEY LEV
& THE NEWS JERRY LEE LEWIS LIGHTHOUSE FAMILY LIGHTNING SEEDS LINDISFARNE LITTLE FEAT LITTLE RICHARD LIVE AID LIVING COLO
LL COOL J NILS LOFGREN LOLLAPALOOZA LOUISE LOVE THE LOVIN' SPOONFUL NICK LOWE LULU LUSH LYNYRD SKYNYRD M PEOPLE PA
MCCARTNEY MALCOLM MCLAREN DON MCLEAN MADNESS MADONNA MAGAZINE THE MAMAS & THE PAPAS MANFRED MANN MANIC STRE
PREACHERS BARRY MANILOW MANSUN MARILLION MARILYN MANSON BOB MARLEY GEORGE MARTIN JOHN MARTYN MASSIVE ATTACK JO
MAYALL CURTIS MAYFIELD MC5 MEAT LOAF JOE MEEK MEGADETH JOHN MELLENCAMP MEN AT WORK MERSEYBEAT METALLICA GEOR
MICHAEL BETTE MIDLER MIDNIGHT OIL ROBERT MILES STEVE MILLER MINISTRY KYLIE MINOGUE THE MISSION JONI MITCHELL MOBY MO
GRAPE THE MONKEES MONSTERS OF ROCK MONTEREY THE MOODY BLUES ROBERT A. MOOG GARY MOORE ALANIS MORISSETTE MA
MORRISON VAN MORRISON MORRISSEY MÖTLEY CRÜE MOTÖRHEAD MOTOWN MOTT THE HOOPLE THE MOVE ALISON MOYET MUTE
BLOODY VALENTINE NAZARETH YOUSSOU N'DOUR RICKY NELSON WILLIE NELSON THE NEVILLE BROTHERS NEW MODEL ARMY NEW ORD
NEW ROMANTIC THE NEW YORK DOLLS RANDY NEWMAN OLIVIA NEWTON-JOHN THE NICE HARRY NILSSON NINE INCH NAILS NIRVANA
DOUBT NORTHERN SOUL THE NOTORIOUS BIG TED NUGENT GARY NUMAN NWA LAURA NYRO OASIS OCEAN COLOUR SCENE PHIL OC
SINÉAD O'CONNOR MIKE OLDFIELD THE ORB ROY ORBISON ORBITAL ORCHESTRAL MANOEUVRES IN THE DARK OZZY OSBOURNE T
OSMONDS ROBERT PALMER PANTERA PARLOPHONE GRAM PARSONS DOLLY PARTON PAVEMENT PEARL JAM PENTANGLE CARL PERKINS P
SHOP BOYS TOM PETTY & THE HEARTBREAKERS WILSON PICKETT PINK FLOYD GENE PITNEY PIXIES PLACEBO ROBERT PLANT POCO T
POGUES THE POINTER SISTERS POISON THE POLICE BRIAN POOLE & THE TREMELOES IGGY POP POP WILL EAT ITSELF PORNO FOR PYR
PORTISHEAD PREFAB SPROUT THE PRESIDENTS OF THE UNITED STATES OF AMERICA ELVIS PRESLEY THE PRETENDERS THE PRET
THINGS ALAN PRICE MAXI PRIEST PRIMAL SCREAM PRINCE P.J. PROBY PROCOL HARUM PRODIGY PROGRESSIVE ROCK PROPELLERHEA
PSYCHEDELIA THE PSYCHEDELIC FURS PUBLIC ENEMY PUBLIC IMAGE LTD PUFF DADDY PULP PUNK SUZI QUATRO FINLEY QUAYE QUE
QUEENSRŸCHE R&B RADIOHEAD GERRY RAFFERTY RAGE AGAINST THE MACHINE RAINBOW BONNIE RAITT RAMONES SHABBA RANKS R
RCA CHRIS REA READING RED HOT CHILI PEPPERS OTIS REDDING LOU REED REGGAE REM REO SPEEDWAGON REPUBLICA CLIFF RICHA
LIONEL RICHIE JONATHAN RICHMAN RIDE THE RIGHTEOUS BROTHERS SMOKEY ROBINSON TOM ROBINSON ROCK 'N' ROLL ROCK AND RC
HALL OF FAME KENNY ROGERS THE ROLLING STONES HENRY ROLLINS LINDA RONSTADT ROSE ROYCE ROSKILDE DIANA ROSS ROUGH TRA
ROXETTE ROXY MUSIC RUN D.M.C. TODD RUNDGREN RUNRIG RUSH SADE SAINT ETIENNE SALT-N-PEPA SANTANA THE SCORPIONS SCRIT
POLITTI THE SEAHORSES SEAL THE SEARCHERS NEIL SEDAKA BOB SEGER SEPULTURA THE SEX PISTOLS THE SHADOWS SHAKESPEAR
SISTER SHALAMAR THE SHAMEN THE SHANGRI-LAS DEL SHANNON SANDIE SHAW THE SHIRELLES MICHELLE SHOCKED SIMON & GARFUNK
CARLY SIMON PAUL SIMON SIMPLE MINDS SIMPLY RED SIOUXSIE & THE BANSHEES SISTER SLEDGE THE SISTERS OF MERCY RONI SIZE S
SKID ROW SKUNK ANANSIE SLADE SLAYER PERCY SLEDGE SLEEPER THE SLITS SLY & ROBBIE SLY & THE FAMILY STONE THE SMALL FAC
SMASHING PUMPKINS PATTI SMITH WILL SMITH

SHREWSBURY COLLEGE
LONDON RD. LRC

YOUTH SOUL SOUL ASYLUM SOUL II SOUL SOUNDGARDEN SPACE SPANDAU BALLET SPARKS THE SPECIALS PHIL SPECTOR JON SPENC
BLUES EXPLOSION SPICE GIRLS SPIRITUALIZED DUSTY SPRINGFIELD BRUCE SPRINGSTEEN SQUEEZE LISA STANSFIELD EDWIN STA
RINGO STARR STATUS QUO STAX STEEL PULSE STEELEYE SPAN STEELY DAN STEPPENWOLF STEREO MC'S STEREOLAB STEREOPHONICS C
STEVENS SHAKIN' STEVENS AL STEWART ROD STEWART STIFF STEPHEN STILLS STING THE STONE ROSES STONE TEMPLE PILOTS T
STOOGES THE STRANGLERS THE STRAY CATS BARBRA STREISAND THE STYLE COUNCIL THE STYLISTICS SUB POP SUEDE THE SUGARCUBE
SUICIDE DONNA SUMMER SUN RECORDS SUPER FURRY ANIMALS SUPERGRASS SUPERTRAMP THE SUPREMES SWEET SWING T. REX TAL
THAT TALK TALK TALKING HEADS TANGERINE DREAM JAMES TAYLOR THE TEARDROP EXPLODES TEARS FOR FEARS TECHNO TEENA
FANCLUB TELEVISION THE TEMPTATIONS 10CC 10,000 MANIACS TEN YEARS AFTER TERRORVISION TEXAS THE THE THERAPY? THIN LIZ
RICHARD THOMPSON THOMPSON TWINS THREE DOG NIGHT THROWING MUSES TINDERSTICKS TLC PETER TOSH TOTO TRAFFIC TR
TRAVELING WILBURYS TRICKY TRIP HOP THE TROGGS TINA TURNER THE TURTLES 2PAC 2 UNLIMITED UB40 ULTRAVOX THE UNDERTON
UNDERWORLD URIAH HEEP USHER U2 VAN HALEN ARMAND VAN HELDEN LUTHER VANDROSS VANGELIS STEVIE RAY VAUGHAN SUZAN
VEGA THE VELVET UNDERGROUND THE VERVE VILLAGE PEOPLE GENE VINCENT VIRGIN TOM WAITS SCOTT WALKER THE WALKER BROTHER
WARNER WARP DIONNE WARWICK WAS (NOT WAS) W.A.S.P. THE WATERBOYS MUDDY WATERS WEATHER REPORT THE WEDDING PRESE
PAUL WELLER WET WET WET WHAM! BARRY WHITE WHITESNAKE THE WHO THE WILDHEARTS ROBBIE WILLIAMS JACKIE WILSON STEV
WINWOOD WIRE BILL WITHERS JAH WOBBLE BOBBY WOMACK STEVIE WONDER THE WONDER STUFF WOODSTOCK WU-TANG CLAN ROBER
WYATT TAMMY WYNETTE X-RAY SPEX XTC THE YARDBIRDS YES NEIL YOUNG PAUL YOUNG FRANK ZAPPA THE ZOMBIES ZZ TO